Social **P**SYCHOLOGY

ABOUT THE AUTHOR

Charles G. Lord received his B. A. in psychology in 1976 from the University of Rhode Island and his Ph.D. in 1980 from Stanford University, on a fellowship from the National Science Foundation. At URI, he studied with Wayne Velicer and Al Lott. At Stanford, he studied with Daryl Bem, Mark Lepper, and Lee Ross. Lord's first academic position was at Princeton University, where he served as an Assistant Professor from 1980 through 1987. In 1987, he moved to Texas Christian University, where he served as department chair for four years from 1990 through 1994. Lord previously served on the editorial board of the *Journal of Personality and Social Psychology* (JPSP) and is now an Associate Editor of *Social Cognition*. His research is on attitudes and attitude change. His published articles include "Biased assimilation and attitude polarization: The effects of prior theories on subsequently considered evidence" (1979), "Attitude prototypes as determinants of attitude–behavior consistency" (1984), "Effects of structured contact on attitude prototypes and attitude change" (1991), and "Typicality effects in attitudes toward social policies: An attitude concept map approach" (1994), all published in JPSP. At TCU, Lord teaches courses on general psychology, social psychology, personality psychology, attitudes, social cognition, and the self.

Social Psychology

CHARLES G. LORD
Texas Christian University

HARCOURT BRACE COLLEGE PUBLISHERS

FORT WORTH PHILADELPHIA SAN DIEGO NEW YORK ORLANDO AUSTIN SAN ANTONIO
TORONTO MONTREAL LONDON SYDNEY TOKYO

DEDICATION

for Sandy and Warren

Publisher	CHRISTOPHER P. KLEIN
Executive Editor	EARL MCPEEK
Developmental Editor	NANCY CROCHIERE
Senior Project Editor	LAURA J. HANNA
Senior Production Manager	KATHLEEN FERGUSON
Art Director	CAROL KINCAID
Picture and Rights Editor	SANDRA LORD
Photo Researcher	ELSA PETERSON LTD.
Senior Product Manager	SUSAN KINDEL

PREFACE

I remember when, in elementary school, I first learned about the poet Homer, who traveled throughout ancient Greece telling the tales of the Trojan War. "What a noble profession," I remember thinking, "to be a storyteller!"

Many years later, I became a storyteller of sorts—a university professor. Instead of having to travel from town to town to tell my tales, I have the luxury of staying in one place and having students come to me. My students will tell you that I love to tell stories about the studies conducted in social psychology. In my experience, you do not need to be as skillful a storyteller as Homer to keep your audience interested, as long as you have stories that are intrinsically fascinating.

When Harcourt Brace approached me about writing a social psychology text, the editors wanted to know how my version of social psychology would be different from previous textbooks. I told them that I wanted to write the **story** of social psychology—a connected narrative about how people influence each other's thoughts, feelings, and actions. Because the studies conducted by social psychologists make such a fascinating story, I told the publishers, I would try to get out of the way and let the stories tell themselves.

Along the way, I had to make some strategic decisions that greatly influenced the final manuscript. To understand why the book is written the way it is, I want to tell you about those key decisions and why I chose to present the material as I did.

THEMES FOR CONSTANCY AND COHERENCE

First, I felt that a good story ought to have some underlying themes that are woven into the tale and provide a sense of constancy and coherence. One way to present social psychology is as 14 (or more) separate short stories, having very little relevance to each other. In such a "disconnected" approach, the author surveys the literature on each topic–person perception, attitudes, helping, aggression, etc.–separately and describes the significant principles and discoveries within each topic with little or no indication to the audience that these seemingly disconnected findings might be related to each other. The "disconnected" approach leaves students wondering why social psychologists see themselves as having anything in common. Instead of calling themselves social psychologists, why don't they call themselves "person perception psychologists," "attitude psychologists," "helping psychologists," "aggression psychologists," and so on?

That's not how I see social psychology. To me, the social psychologists who conduct research on at least 14 different topics are united not only by what they all study–how people influence each other's thoughts, feelings, and actions–but also by common themes that recur in many seemingly disparate areas of inquiry. I identified three themes that recur across all these areas and use those themes throughout the text to provide students with a sense of why we all call ourselves social psychologists.

SPONTANEOUS VS. DELIBERATIVE REACTIONS

The first theme involves spontaneous versus deliberative reactions. Researchers in almost all areas of social psychology have been discovering that people's thoughts, feelings, and actions are different depending on whether they react quickly and spontaneously or instead react after a delay and some deliberation. The spontaneous versus deliberative reaction theme has emerged independently in research laboratories that study social cognition, person perception, attribution, the self, attitudes, attitude change, prejudice, attraction, close relationships, social influence, helping, aggression, power, and groups. It makes sense, when you think about it, that human beings might have two separate "systems" for coping with their social worlds–one system that deals effectively with situations that require a speedy response and a second system that takes many factors into account before making a commitment. When students begin to recognize the spontaneous versus deliberative theme as it occurs throughout the text, they develop a sense that many social psychology studies, though they might appear on the surface to be about unrelated topics, are informed by an underlying, unifying concept.

PERSONAL IDENTITY VS. SOCIAL IDENTITY

The second theme involves two identities that affect people's social behavior: a personal identity versus a social identity. When people emphasize a personal identity, their thoughts, feelings, and actions reflect a concern with themselves as individuals who are distinct from other individuals. They "look out for number one," for instance, but they also take personal responsibility for what they think, feel, and do. When people emphasize a social identity, in contrast, their thoughts, feelings, and actions reflect a concern with themselves as part of a larger social "unit," whether that unit is a spouse with whom they have been "joined together" or a larger group so important to them that they celebrate the group's victories and mourn its defeats. The personal versus social identity theme reflects a more general tendency of human beings to practice either discrimination (in which they sharpen perceived differences) or assimilation (in which they emphasize similarities and blur distinctions). This theme informs many social psychology studies that at first glance appear to examine entirely different topics such as person perception, prejudice, close relationships, social influence, helping, and many more.

BEING RIGHT VS. BEING LIKABLE

The third theme woven into the fabric of the story involves two goals: being right versus being likable. If you ask *why* people use both spontaneous and deliberative reactions and *why* they emphasize both personal and social identities, the answer is that these ways of coping with the social environment operate in the service of at least two important goals. It is important for people to be correct in their perception of others, the conclusions they reach, the attitudes they hold toward others and themselves, and other aspects of everyday social thoughts, feelings, and actions. It is obviously beneficial to see social reality for what it is, rather than falling prey to unwanted errors and biases. When dealing with other people, however, it is also important to be likable. Other people can provide both rewards for those who appear likable and punishments for those who appear unlikable. It seems logical, then, that people want to be both right and likable, whenever they can, in their dealings with fellow human beings. As the text explains, however, some situations demand a choice between being right and being likable. In those situations, people behave differently depending on which of the two goals they choose to pursue.

As with the other two themes, the choice between being right and being likable recurs across studies that are on the surface concerned with many disparate topics. Once students recognize these underlying themes, social psychology begins to seem like one connected story.

LAW

HEALTH

BUSINESS

EDUCATION

MULTICULTURAL

ENVIRONMENT

PRACTICAL APPLICATIONS

A second decision involved how to emphasize social psychology's many practical, everyday applications. Students should know that social psychologists have much to offer applied disciplines such as law, health, business, education, cross-cultural understanding, and environmental studies. Uninformed legislators, government officials, and organizational executives may pursue non-optimal strategies because they have never had a course in social psychology and do not understand the underlying principles that social psychologists have worked to discover. In telling the story of social psychology, I wanted to make a salient part of that story the many studies that have *applied* the abstract principles of social thoughts, feelings, and actions to such disciplines. To write separate chapters on "social psychology and law," "social psychology and health," or "social psychology and business" might give students the erroneous impression that these different types of applications stand as separate entities that have little to do with each other or with the more abstract principles that were discussed in separate "non-applied" chapters.

Instead, I chose to emphasize each applied study in the process of describing the abstract principles behind that application. When a theoretical principle or abstract process such as the theory of reasoned action in attitude change has many different applications, for instance, I explain the theory and then describe studies that applied that theory to a variety of different practical concerns. In this way, the applications become a part of the ongoing narrative. To assist students in recognizing practical applications when they appear in the text, I inserted icons in the margins next to the relevant study. These icons include a pillar for the law, a cross for health, a stock chart for business, a book for education, a globe for multicultural studies, and a leaf for applications to the environment. The margin icons in each chapter alert students to social psychology's many contributions (and potential contributions) to improving everyday life.

CLASSIC AND CURRENT STUDIES

A third strategic decision was to include a mix of both classic and very recent studies. It would be easy to write a textbook that concentrated almost exclusively on the classic, tried-and-true stories. Students are reliably enthralled by the Milgram obedience studies, Asch's conformity studies, the Zimbardo prison experiment, the delightful, engaging studies that Darley and Latané used to flesh out their decision tree model of helping, and many other "oldies but goodies" that social psychology storytellers have used for generations. To concentrate exclusively on the classic studies, however, would keep students from knowing about the avalanche of new studies that are emerging every day in the major social psychology journals. Some of these new studies merely fill in the gaps in previous knowledge. Many others, however, make brilliant, innovative contributions, taking the story of social psychology in directions that no one could have anticipated even five years ago. To incorporate these new, exciting ideas into the text, I wrote to over 500 leading social psychologists around the world and asked them to send me preprints of any papers that they had "in press," that readers of the leading journals would be reading about during the next year. To put it mildly, the response to my request was greater than anticipated. I built a "wall" of preprints that reached all the way to the ceiling of my office and the department secretaries refused to carry my mail from the university post office!

I read every word of every preprint that these currently active researchers sent to me. I was not able to incorporate them all into the story of social psychology, but I found that many, many of these yet-to-be-published articles helped me to reorganize and reconceptualize the details of the story that I was trying to tell. The primary result of soliciting all these new articles, however, was that the text balances classic with new studies and gives the student a sense of how currently active is the field. I sincerely believe that the text contains more new, exciting research discoveries than are usually presented in an overview of an academic discipline, which is as it should be when the story of social psychology is advancing at such a rapid pace that we all have difficulty keeping up with the latest developments.

TELLING THE STORY

I chose to tell the story of social psychology by asking questions. The introductory chapter, for instance, asks "What is social psychology?" "How do we study social psychology?" and "What are some problems in studying social psychology?" These are all questions that I thought a student might want to know when starting to learn about the discipline. For each topic after the introductory chapter, I read all the relevant literature and then tried to discover what questions researchers in the area were trying to answer. In the huge and rapidly increasing literature on the self, for instance, I concluded that researchers wanted to know how people know the self, how they present the self to others, and how they protect a threatened sense of self. These three fundamental research questions, each addressed in many different ways by many different researchers, provided the basic organization of the self chapter into three parts that tell a cumulative story. Once we know how people decide who they are, we are set to discover how they try to project that identity to others. Once we know how they project a desired identity, we are set to discover what they do when the identity is called into question. The flow of ideas is presented as a set of three questions that follow logically from one to the next—a flow of ideas that emerges from an understanding of what modern researchers want to know.

At the same time, the text provides more than the usual historical background and cross-cultural emphasis. The historical background is evident in extended discussion of how the questions of interest have evolved not just in social psychology, but in art, literature, philosophy and other related disciplines. Chapter 5 on The Self, for instance, surveys the goals, problems, and consequences of how people in different historical eras arrived at self-knowledge. The chapter uses this history to introduce the concerns and discoveries of current researchers. The cross-cultural emphasis is apparent in many studies, scattered throughout the text, in which universal principles of human social behavior underlie and yet are affected by different local norms and socialization practices.

INTERIM SUMMARIES

I also believe that it is appropriate in telling a story to pause from time to time and remind the audience of what we know up to that point, to get them ready for new questions to be asked and new answers to be added. For this reason, I provide brief summaries at the end of each major chapter section. If the three summaries within each chapter were to be abstracted from the text and laid end-to-end, so to speak, I believe that they would follow one from the next and provide the framework or glue that holds the story together.

OVERALL ORGANIZATION

I have also tried to arrange the chapters in such a way that if all the part summaries were abstracted from the text and laid end-to-end, the overall story would have a beginning, a middle, and an end, with unifying themes and a genuine plot. It makes sense to ask questions about social thinking first, move from there to social feelings, and finally to social actions. Also, within each of the three major sections of the textbook, there is a progression. Within the section on social thinking, for instance, the story first addresses the basic cognitive processes and then focuses in turn on how those processes are used in forming impressions of others, drawing attributions about them, and applying the processes to oneself.

SUPPORT MATERIALS

The text is also accompanied by helpful ancillary materials that are available from the publisher:

The INSTRUCTOR'S MANUAL was written by Susan Beers of Sweet Briar College, a master teacher who is very skilled at presenting information in the most interesting way. The manual includes, for each chapter, an outline and summary of the chapter; learning objectives; class lecture topics; discussion topics; class exercises; and recommended films. It will also include a chapter of general information and teaching tips, and one on helping students to improve their study skills.

The TEST BANK was constructed by Charles Bond of Texas Christian University, an eminent teacher and researcher who has been writing effective test questions as a faculty member for the past 16 years. Professor Bond's test bank includes 75 questions per chapter and contains both multiple choice and essay questions. A combination of analytical and recall questions is included, and all questions are page referenced to the text. A COMPUTERIZED version of the TEST BANK is also available for IBM and Macintosh computers.

A STUDENT STUDY GUIDE was written by Susan Kirkendol of Pfeiffer College, an experienced professor who loves good teaching. The study guide contains, for each chapter, an outline of the chapter; learning objectives; chapter review questions in multiple choice, true/false, fill-in-the-blank, matching, and short answer formats. The answer key provides not only a complete explanation of the answer, but also the appropriate page reference in the text.

ACKNOWLEDGMENTS

Finally, I had considerable help in telling my part of the story. I could never have produced a final draft without the wise counsel, excellent suggestions, and good-natured prodding of my developmental editor Nancy Crochiere. In addition, the editorial, marketing, and production team at Harcourt Brace, including Earl McPeek, Susan Kindel, Laura Hanna, Kathy Ferguson, Carol Kincaid, Elsa Peterson, and Sandy Lord, deserve credit for knowing how to assemble a textbook properly. I am very deeply indebted also to the many active researchers who took time out from their busy schedules to send me their in-press articles and to the following talented teachers of social psychology who so generously helped me with constructive comments and suggestions on earlier drafts of the manuscript.

Jeffrey Adams	St. Michael's College
Judith Allen	Drake University
Jean Alvers	Johnson County Community College
Galen Bodenhausen	Michigan State University
Charles F. Bond, Jr.	Texas Christian University
Nyla R. Branscombe	University of Kansas
Kyle Ann Campos	Des Moines Area Community College
Catherine Cozzarelli	Kansas State University
Eric Cooley	Western Oregon State College
Linda Foley	University of North Florida
Marita Inglehart	University of Michigan
Donn L. Kaiser	Southwest Missouri State University
Mary Kite	Ball State University
Scott Madey	University of Toledo
Linda Musante	University of Tampa
Virginia A. Norris	South Dakota State University
Bernadette Park	University of Colorado
Brett Pelham	University of California, Los Angeles
Marilyn A. Pugh	Texas Wesleyan University
Mark Schaller	University of Montana
Laura Sidorowicz	Nassau Community College
Steve Slane	Cleveland State University
Janice M. Steil	Adelphi University
Stephan Vodanovich	University of Florida
Katherina Vorwerk	University of Massachusetts
Ann L. Weber	University of North Carolina, Asheville
Patrick S. Williams	University of Houston

Homer probably had to make his own travel arrangements and edit his own manuscripts, but I have had the luxury of having a world-class team at my side every inch of the way.

Social **P**SYCHOLOGY

CHARLES G. LORD

A NARRATIVE STYLE ▲

Throughout the book, I've deliberately used a narrative style to tell the *story* of social psychology. I believe that you will find this connected narrative style more enjoyable than the traditional textbook approach that sometimes reads like an encyclopedia of disconnected facts. A good narrative has plots and subplots, times when the author reminds you of what you have learned so far, central themes that recur as the story unfolds, and some puzzling or surprising aspects that get the reader personally involved. In my story of social psychology, the plots and subplots are the questions that social psychologists are trying to answer, reminders of what you know come in section summaries, the central themes unite story elements across chapters, and the puzzles are questions that accompany illustrations.

I've written this Student Preface to help you get the most benefit from the textbook. The following pages highlight key features of the book that will make your learning more enjoyable and successful. I suggest that you read these pages before you begin reading the book.

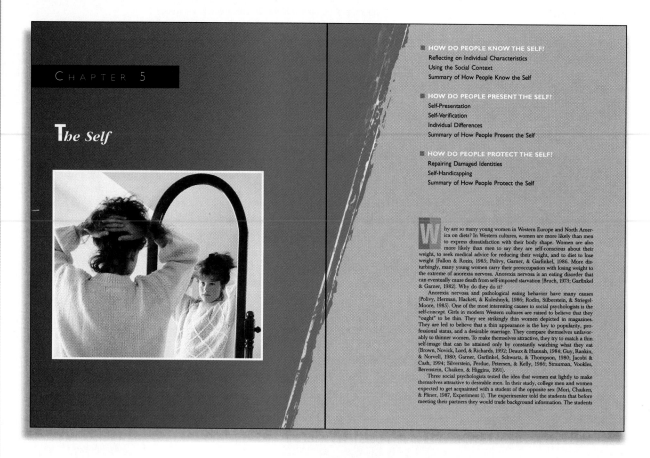

CHAPTER 5

The Self

W hy are so many young women in Western Europe and North America on diets? In Western cultures, women are more likely than men to express dissatisfaction with their body shape. Women are also more likely than men to say they are self-conscious about their weight, to seek medical advice for reducing their weight, and to diet to lose weight (Fallon & Rozin, 1985; Polivy, Garner, & Garfinkel, 1986. More disturbingly, many young women carry their preoccupation with losing weight to the extreme of anorexia nervosa. Anorexia nervosa is an eating disorder that can eventually cause death from self-imposed starvation (Bruch, 1973; Garfinkel & Garner, 1982). Why do they do it?

Anorexia nervosa and pathological eating behavior have many causes (Polivy, Herman, Hackett, & Kuleshnyk, 1986; Rodin, Silberstein, & Striegel-Moore, 1985). One of the most interesting causes to social psychologists is the self-concept. Girls in modern Western cultures are raised to believe that they "ought" to be thin. They see strikingly thin women depicted in magazines. They are led to believe that a thin appearance is the key to popularity, professional status, and a desirable marriage. They compare themselves unfavorably to thinner women. To make themselves attractive, they try to match a thin self-image that can be attained only by constantly watching what they eat (Brown, Novick, Lord, & Richards, 1992; Deaux & Hannah, 1984; Guy, Rankin, & Norvell, 1980; Garner, Garfinkel, Schwartz, & Thompson, 1980; Jacobi & Cash, 1994; Silverstein, Perdue, Petersen, & Kelly, 1986; Strauman, Vookles, Berenstein, Chaiken, & Higgins, 1991).

Three social psychologists tested the idea that women eat lightly to make themselves attractive to desirable men. In their study, college men and women expected to get acquainted with a student of the opposite sex (Mori, Chaiken, & Pliner, 1987, Experiment 1). The experimenter told the students that before meeting their partners they would trade background information. The students

CHAPTER OPENING QUESTIONS ▲

At the beginning of each chapter, three major questions are presented to help you see what will be covered in the chapter, or the chapter's "plot." Use these questions as a reference point or framework for what you will be learning. When you finish reading each chapter, you should know the answer to the three major questions, and to other more detailed questions about human social behavior as well.

INTERIM SUMMARIES ▶

Brief summaries are presented at the end of each major section within a chapter. These summaries are designed to remind you of what has been covered so far and to set the stage for the story elements that are going to be covered next. If you read a chapter's summaries, you will see that they have a beginning, a middle, and an end— just like a story.

SUMMARY OF HOW PEOPLE KNOW THE SELF

P eople who lived in early European cultures did not have to worry about who they were. A person's self was defined and accepted by society from birth to death. In modern times, however, people have many choices about who they are and who they will become. As a result, they may find it hard to define a self-concept, to understand and fulfill their potential, and to relate to society.

Modern people define themselves in part by constructing a self-schema or set of beliefs about how they typically deal with life events. The self-schema can be relatively simple or complex. It includes beliefs about people's past and possible future actions. It also includes beliefs about what people wish they were, what they think they are obligated to be, what other people wish they would be, and what other people think they are obligated to be. Problems arise when people's beliefs about their actual selves are discrepant from what they or other people wish they were or from what they or other people think they ought to be.

People also define themselves by comparing themselves to others. We define self-esteem and personal fulfillment by how well we are doing compared to others. Comparing ourselves upward to others who are doing better can help plans for improvement, but it can also remind us of our shortcomings. Comparing ourselves downward to others who are doing worse can make us feel better, but it can also be discouraging. The modern sense of self is not fixed but is instead extremely malleable. Different aspects of the self become more important from one moment to the next, depending on whether the person is distinctive or stands out in the immediate social context.

HOW DO PEOPLE PRESENT THE SELF?

The first section of this chapter examined the question "How do people know themselves?" The answer might be summarized as "Many people in twentieth-century Western cultures do not know themselves confidently." They have so many present and future selves that it is difficult to keep all the possible selves in balance. They have large discrepancies between what they are, what they want to be, what they think they ought to be, and what other people think about them. They are subjected to changing social contexts that make a stable self-concept very difficult. The best they can do is to construct a tentatively held theory about a person called "myself." If the self is a theory that we have about the type of person we are and about the type of person we think we might become, then the theory is constantly evolving and being reinvented (Epstein, 1973; Gergen, 1982). The most important reason why a self-concept must be reinvented from day to day and from one social context to the next is that a self-concept must be validated by other people (Cooley, 1902; Mead,

THREE THEMES ▶

One of the difficulties facing students of social psychology is the vast array of seemingly unrelated material covered in a traditional course. To help you unify the various topics of social psychology and see the big picture, I've identified three major themes that underlie many different components of how people think about, feel about, and act toward each other. These themes are defined in Chapter 1. Throughout the rest of the chapters, I draw your attention to the major themes again and again, so that you will come to recognize them for yourself and see how social psychologists who appear to be studying entirely different topics are discovering and using the same underlying principles.

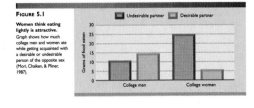

TABLE 1.2	Examples of the Three Themes As They Occur in Chapters of This Book		
	SPONTANEOUS VS. DELIBERATIVE REACTIONS	PERSONAL VS. SOCIAL IDENTITIES	BEING RIGHT VS. BEING LIKABLE GOALS
Social Cognition	Jurors who are busy thinking about something else cannot ignore inadmissible evidence (Gilbert, Tafarodi, & Malone, 1993)	When two people see themselves as a couple, they overestimate their similarity to each other (Pelham & Wachsmuth, 1995)	
Person Perception	First impressions, which rely on stereotypes of such social categories as sex and race, "stand" unless people are both motivated and able to perceive another person as an individual (Brewer, 1988; Fiske & Neuberg, 1990)	People in collectivistic cultures inhibit displaying their emotions to others (Scherer & Wallbott, 1994)	Chronically depressed people form more careful impressions of other people, because they want to perceive the world accurately (Weary & Edwards, 1994b)
Attribution	When people are busy thinking about something else, they tend to explain another person's actions by that person's traits rather than by situational pressures (Gilbert, 1991)	People in China tend to explain murders by something about the situation; people in the U.S. tend to explain murders by something about the murderer (Morris & Peng, 1994)	Trying too hard to be liked can distract people from noticing the situational pressures that caused another person's behavior (Gilbert & Malone, 1995)
The Self	Self-schemas for a trait let people evaluate themselves and others on that trait more quickly (Markus, Smith, & Moreland, 1985; Klein & Loftus, 1993)	Health problems can be caused by discrepancies between personal and social identities (Higgins, in press)	People with low self-esteem would rather be viewed accurately than in flattering but inaccurate ways (Swann & Schroeder, 1995)
Attitudes	Attitudes that come to mind easily are more likely to guide behavior than are attitudes that are not as "accessible" (Fazio, 1990, 1995)	Attitude importance is related to both social identities and personal self-interest (Krosnick, et al., 1993)	Some attitudes are held because they express inner convictions; other attitudes are held because they reap social rewards (Snyder, 1993)
Attitude Change	Unless they are motivated and able to deliberate, people are not as much influenced by a message's central arguments as by characteristics "peripheral" to the arguments (Cacioppo, Petty, & Criss, 1994)	Product ads are more effective in Korea when they emphasize communal goals of ownership, but more effective in the U.S. when they emphasize individualistic goals (Han & Shavitt, 1994)	People think about persuasive communications in greater depth when they have a high need for "cognitive closure" (Kruglanski, in press)

QUESTIONS WITH THE ILLUSTRATIONS ▶

Current learning theory suggests that you are more likely to retain information if you are able to think critically about the new material. To encourage you to practice your critical thinking skills, each photograph within a chapter is captioned with a "puzzler" or question designed to elicit a personal response. Some of the questions have an easy, commonsense answer. Other answers may surprise you when you read the relevant material in the text. Either way, by trying to answer the questions that accompany the illustrations, you are likely to remember the text better and be well on your way to the type of critical thinking that might get you an A in the course.

How might the pictures in fashion magazines make people ill?

read a description of their partners' hobbies, interests, and career goals. Although the student did not realize it, the partner was an experimental confederate who completed the questionnaire to look either desirable or undesirable. To look desirable, the partner wrote about being interested in travel, photography, athletics, reading, planning to attend law school, and being currently unattached. To look undesirable, the partner wrote about being currently attached, having no interests or hobbies other than watching television, parties, reading *National Lampoon*, and no career goals other than making money. The experimenter then left the student to hold a 20-minute conversation with the partner who had supposedly written the desirable or undesirable answers. On the way out of the room, seemingly accidentally, the experimenter paused in front of a cabinet, grabbed two bowls that contained a mixture of M&Ms and peanuts, and handed them to the students. The experimenter added that "these were left over from a lab party. Feel free to eat as much as you like."

As you may have guessed, the experimenters were interested not in what the student said during the conversation, but in how much the student ate. They weighed the M&Ms and peanuts before and after the conversation. Also, the confederate always ate the same amount. As Figure 5.1 shows, college men ate approximately the same amount whether the woman they were talking to was desirable or undesirable. If anything, they ate a little more when she was desirable. College women, in contrast, ate approximately one-quarter as much when the man was desirable than when he was undesirable. Because they were socialized to believe that eating lightly is attractive, they altered how much they ate depending on their male partner's desirability (Chaiken & Pliner, 1987).

In a follow-up study, college women held a getting-acquainted conversation with an attractive male confederate. Because of a staged mix-up of personality test results, the confederate saw the woman's scores (Mori et al., 1987, Experiment 2). The women thought the man had seen scores saying that they (the women) were very feminine or very unfeminine. During the conversation, women who thought the desirable man expected them to be unfeminine ate less than half the amount eaten by women who thought the desirable man expected them to be feminine. They seemed to say, "So, you think I'm not feminine, do you? I'll show you how feminine I can be. Even though I'm hungry, I wouldn't touch those M&Ms if it killed me!" Their self-concepts had been questioned. They responded by reaffirming their identity as "feminine" light eaters (Strauman et al., 1991). Preoccupation with protecting a thin self-image alters how much women in Western cultures eat.

FIGURE 5.1

Women think eating lightly is attractive. Graph shows how much college men and women ate while getting acquainted with a desirable or undesirable person of the opposite sex (Mori, Chaiken, & Pliner, 1987).

Undesirable partner ▪   Desirable partner ▪

(Bar graph — Grams of food eaten, axis 0 to 30; categories: College men, College women)

APPLICATIONS ▶

Why should you study the principles of social psychology? One good reason is that it can help you better understand the world around you. To show you how the theories and principles of the discipline operate in the everyday world, I provide numerous examples from law, health, business, education, environmental studies, and different cultures. You'll find, for instance, that some principles of social psychology apply equally across world cultures, whereas others are applied differently in different cultures. To help you identify these important applications, I've inserted icons in the page margins opposite where the application is described in the text.

HEALTH

BUSINESS

ENVIRONMENT

LAW

MULTICULTURAL   EDUCATION

I hope you enjoy your study of social psychology and that you find this textbook a useful tool. Please feel free to send me any comments or suggestions you may have regarding the book.

Warm Regards,

Charles G. Lord

CHARLES G. LORD
DEPARTMENT OF PSYCHOLOGY
TEXAS CHRISTIAN UNIVERSITY
FORT WORTH, TX 76129

◀ COVERAGE OF CLASSICAL AND CONTEMPORARY RESEARCH

Social psychologists have a strong history of exciting and valuable theories. For you to truly understand social psychology, it is important that you become familiar with the classic research studies conducted by noted social psychologists such as Stanley Millgram and Solomon Asch. To help you in knowing these famous studies, I describe them in such detail that you can imagine what it might have been like to have been one of the original participants. I also want you to share the excitement of the latest developments in social psychology, which are occurring so rapidly that it is difficult for any one person to know everything that is happening at the "cutting edge" of research. Many of the references you'll see in the following chapters refer to studies that have only just recently been completed. I knew about the results in advance of the studies being published in social psychology journals because today's researchers use the Internet and other means to tell each other about their discoveries faster than the printed media allow. The most current studies have dates that say "1996" or "in press."

To assist you in your study, a student study guide has been prepared specifically for this text. This guide contains an outline of each chapter, learning objectives, chapter review questions in multiple choice, true/false, fill-in-the-blank, matching, and short answer formats. The answer key provides not only a complete explanation of the answer, but also the appropriate page reference in the text. Contact your local bookstore to purchase the study guide (ISBN 0-03-019108-4).

BRIEF TABLE OF CONTENTS

CONTENTS

CONTENTS

CONTENTS

CONTENTS

CONTENTS

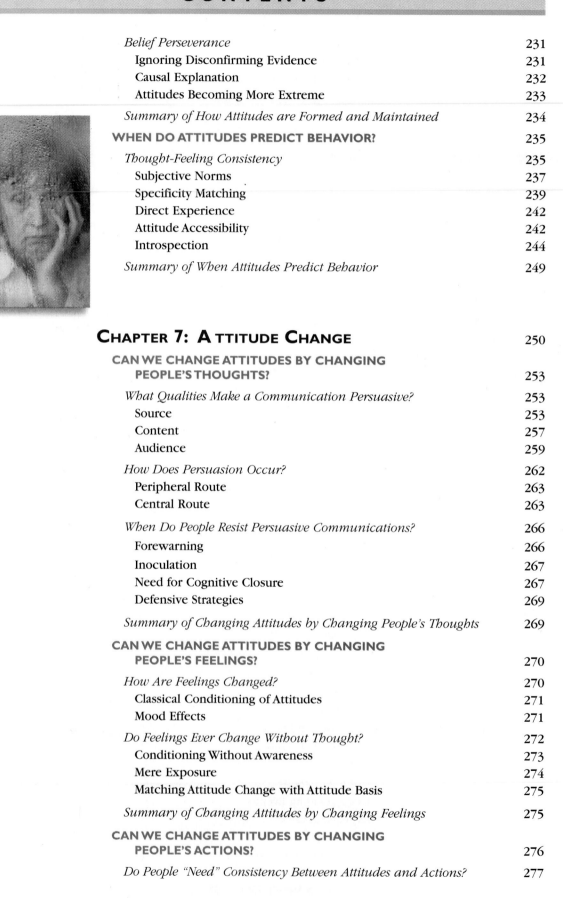

CONTENTS

CHAPTER 8: STEREOTYPING, PREJUDICE, AND DISCRIMINATION

CONTENTS

CONTENTS

CONTENTS

CONTENTS

CHAPTER 13: AGGRESSION

CONTENTS

CONTENTS

Introduction to Social Psychology

Imagine walking across a bridge that is 230 feet above rocks and shallow rapids. The bridge consists of nothing but ropes, wires, and wooden slats. You step carefully from one slat to the next, watching your feet but trying not to look down at the rushing water. You feel your heart beating wildly. As you near the center of the bridge, you see walking toward you an incredibly gorgeous member of the opposite sex, who stops to speak to you. Will you feel attracted to this person? Might your attraction have anything to do with the arousal that you feel because of being on a scary bridge? Does preexisting arousal magnify the allure of a physically attractive man or woman?

To answer questions about the relationship between preexisting arousal and romantic attraction, two social psychologists at the University of British Columbia conducted an interesting study (Dutton & Aron, 1974). They manipulated arousal by means of two bridges that crossed the Capilano River. The scary bridge consisted of little more than 5-foot-wide planks attached to wire cables. It was a suspension bridge that "tended to tilt, sway, and wobble, creating the impression that one is about to fall over the side . . . a 230-foot drop to rocks and shallow rapids below" (p. 511). The safe bridge, farther up-river, wider, and firmer, "was only 10 feet above a small, shallow rivulet" and did not tilt or sway. People who crossed these two bridges said that they felt much more afraid and aroused when crossing the scary bridge than when crossing the safe one.

In the study, an attractive female experimenter waited until she saw a man crossing one of these bridges alone. The experimenter met the man on the bridge and asked him to fill out a brief questionnaire. Almost all the men agreed. The questionnaire involved making up a story to describe what was happening in an ambiguous picture. The picture showed a woman who was covering her face with one hand and reaching for something with her other hand. As predicted, men on the scary bridge were more likely than were men on the safe bridge to invent stories about love, kissing, and sexual intercourse (Dutton & Aron, 1974, Experiment 1).

The researchers also wondered whether men who met the woman on the scary bridge would *do* anything to indicate their romantic interest, such as call her on the telephone. The experimenter wrote her name and telephone number on a piece of paper in case the man had questions about the study. Figure 1.1 shows how many men called a male or a female experimenter whom they met on either a safe or a scary bridge. As you can see on the left side of the bar graph, very few men (1 or 2) were curious enough about the details of the study to telephone a male experimenter, regardless of where they met him. As you can see on the right side of the bar graph, the results were very different when the experimenter was female. When they met her on the safe bridge, the men were no more curious about the study than were men who met a male experimenter. Only two of them called. When they met her on the scary bridge, in contrast, nine men called the attractive woman later "to talk about the study." The investigators concluded that arousal *might* magnify romantic attraction.

We used the word "might" in the last sentence *because no one experiment can prove beyond doubt that an idea is either correct or incorrect.* As described in Chapter 9, on Interpersonal Attraction, many other studies support the idea that arousal magnifies romantic attraction. The scary bridge study is merely a good example of what social psychologists do. We will examine other examples

Are people who meet each other in a scary place more likely to fall in love?

FIGURE 1.1

Arousal magnifies romantic attraction. Graph shows number of men who telephoned a male or female experimenter that they met on a safe or scary bridge (Dutton & Aron, 1974).

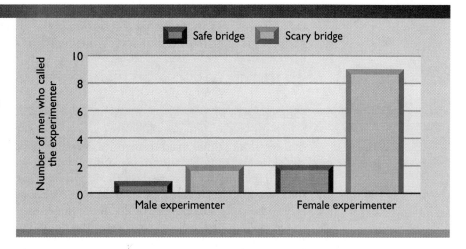

throughout the three sections of this chapter. The first section of the chapter describes the many and varied types of questions that social psychologists try to answer. It also explains three major themes that recur in many areas of social psychology. The second section of the chapter describes methods that social psychologists use to answer their questions, with a research example for each method. The third section discusses problems that social psychologists face when they try to answer their questions. One goal of the chapter is to convince you that questions about social psychology are *worth* answering, regardless of how many problems we have to solve.

WHAT IS SOCIAL PSYCHOLOGY?

Social psychology is the scientific study of the way in which people's thoughts, feelings, and behaviors are influenced by the real or imagined presence of other people (Allport, 1985).

Think about how the definition of social psychology applies to the scary bridge study. The researchers tried to study all three—*thoughts, feelings,* and *behaviors.* To measure the men's *thoughts* and *feelings,* they asked the men to tell fantasy stories. The researchers believed, based on other research, that the fantasy stories people invent reflect what is on their minds and in their hearts. People who are hungry invent stories about food; people who are romantically inclined invent stories about hugs, kisses, and sex. To measure the men's *behaviors,* the researchers recorded whether the men called the woman on the telephone. When a man calls a woman who gave him her telephone number, even if he has the excuse of being curious about a study, one interpretation is that he is romantically interested.

The researchers also measured the effects of both the experimenter's *real* presence and her *imagined* presence. The men invented fantasy stories while the experimenter was physically present, standing next to them on the bridge. When the men called the woman on the telephone, in contrast, she was not physically present, but they presumably remembered how aroused they felt when they met her. Finally, the *scientific study* part of the definition refers to how we answer social psychology questions. Poets and philosophers answer questions about thoughts, feelings, and behaviors through intuition or logic, but social psychologists collect physical evidence. To be convinced that they have discovered believable answers to their questions, they collect evidence using methods that they and other scientists agree are valid. We examine some commonly used methods in the second section of the chapter. Before we get to the methods, though, we need to survey the questions of interest.

QUESTIONS OF INTEREST

Can we be more specific about what social psychologists study? Although we might use many different organizing schemes, this book divides the questions of interest into three major categories: thinking about the self and others, evaluating persons and relationships, and interacting with others. Table 1.1 shows these three major categories, with examples of four or five types of questions that fit within each category. The 14 types of questions correspond with the other 14 chapters of this book. The three major categories correspond roughly to the *thoughts, feelings,* and *behaviors* in the definition of social psychology. The three-part organization, however, is merely a convenient way to present the material. In reality, questions from one part of social psychology overlap with and have complicated implications for questions from other parts.

■ THINKING ABOUT THE SELF AND OTHERS

At first glance, the four types of questions shown in the first major category of Table 1.1 seem very diverse. They include questions about jury decisions, lying, AIDS victims, and body image. On closer inspection, however, you will

TABLE 1.1	Questions of Interest in Social Psychology, with Specific Examples
TYPE OF QUESTION	**SPECIFIC EXAMPLE**
Thinking About the Self and Others	
Social Cognition	How do juries decide guilt or innocence?
Person Perception	How do we know when someone is lying?
Attribution	Why do some people blame AIDS victims for their illness?
The Self	When does a thin body image promote eating disorders?
Evaluating People and Relationships	
Attitudes	Why do people who say they favor term limits reelect their members of congress?
Attitude Change	How can we instill in young children a positive attitude toward school?
Prejudice	How can society reduce stereotyping and discrimination?
Interpersonal Attraction	Why do many people marry the "boy or girl next door"?
Close Relationships	Why do so many happy marriages end in bitter divorce?
Interacting with Others	
Social Influence	Why can't people cooperate to conserve natural resources?
Helping	How can we convince more people to help the poor, sick, elderly, and homeless?
Aggression	Do media violence and pornography encourage rape and other violent crimes?
Interpersonal Power	Why do individual citizens follow the immoral orders of authoritarian dictators?
Groups	Why do groups of smart military leaders sometimes make dumb decisions?

notice that all four types of questions involve people's *thoughts*. Psychologists who study social cognition, person perception, attribution, and the self want to crawl inside people's heads and discover what they are thinking.

Social cognition is the most basic of these four fields of study, because it is about thought processes in general, rather than about specific kinds of thinking. As long as the thought processes involve the real or imagined presence of others, psychologists who study social cognition want to know how they work. They want to know, for instance, what thought processes go into a jury decision that a defendant is guilty or innocent.

Psychologists who study person perception, in contrast, investigate one specific type of thinking. They study the thought processes that occur when we form impressions of other people. They want to discover, for instance, what cues we use to tell whether another person is lying to us or telling the truth.

Psychologists who study attribution also investigate one specific type of thinking. They study the thought processes that occur when we decide what caused another person's behavior. They want to discover, for instance, what goes on in the heads of individuals who blame AIDS victims for causing their own illness.

Finally, psychologists who study the self investigate how people think about themselves, including how they perceive themselves and how they make causal attributions about their own behavior. One such line of inquiry involves the mental images that people have of their own physical bodies. Some research suggests that distorted body images may lead to eating disorders such as anorexia nervosa.

■ EVALUATING PERSONS AND RELATIONSHIPS

The middle part of Table 1.1 shows five questions that also seem very diverse. They include questions about voting issues, children's love of learning, racial stereotyping, next-door romance, and divorce. When you look more closely at these questions, however, you will discover that they all involve people's *feelings*. Psychologists who study attitudes, attitude change, prejudice, interpersonal attraction, and close relationships want to understand gut-level, emotional responses to the real or imagined presence of others.

Attitudes is the most basic of these five fields of study, because it is about feelings in general, rather than about specific kinds of feelings. Psychologists know that people's feelings influence and are influenced by their thoughts and behaviors, but many researchers believe that feelings lie at the core of positive and negative attitudes. One intriguing question about attitudes is how thoughts, feelings, and behavior relate to each other. Psychologists who study attitudes, for instance, wonder why people sometimes feel one way about a social issue such as term limits and yet behave in exactly the opposite way.

Psychologists who study attitude change want to know when and why people alter their attitudes over time. They believe, for instance, that people of different races might get along with each other better if we could discover the best ways to change negative attitudes. They also believe that children might benefit more from education if we knew how to impart a positive attitude toward school and a love of learning.

The study of prejudice, stereotyping, and discrimination involves trying to understand both how prejudicial attitudes toward groups are formed and how best to change negative feelings for the better. Psychologists who study prejudice believe, for instance, that their discoveries might help society find ways to reduce or eliminate the negative biases that have hindered the advancement of women and minority groups.

Psychologists who study interpersonal attraction also want to learn about feelings, but primarily the feelings of attraction that we have for other people.

They want to know, for instance, whether most people have a "need to belong" that prompts them to form romantic attachments, what men and women do to attract potential mates, and why we fall in love with some people but not with others.

Finally, psychologists who study close relationships investigate how our romantic feelings toward significant others change over time. They want to know, for instance, why some people stay married for their entire lives, whereas other seemingly just as happy marriages end quickly in bitter divorce. They hope that their research will help couples understand how to nurture and extend positive feelings toward each other.

■ INTERACTING WITH OTHERS

The bottom part of Table 1.1 shows five questions that are very diverse, if only because human beings interact through many different *behaviors*. The category includes questions about conservation, volunteering to help the disadvantaged, violence in the media, blind obedience, and military blunders. Psychologists who study social influence, helping, aggression, interpersonal power, and groups investigate a wide range of real and imagined social interactions.

Social influence is the most basic of these five fields of study, because it is about how one person's behavior influences another person's behavior in general and not about any specific kind of behavior. Some research suggests, for instance, that we behave differently in many ways when other people are present than when we are alone, even if the other people do not *do* anything. Psychologists who study social influence start from such simple interactions as another person's mere presence and try to understand more complex interactions, such as cooperation to conserve natural resources.

One complex interaction is *helping*. Psychologists who study helping want to know what makes people help each other and what goes wrong when people fail to help victims in emergency situations. Their research has obvious implications for increasing the rate at which citizens volunteer to help the poor, sick, elderly, and homeless. These psychologists would like to increase the bright side of social interaction.

Psychologists who study *aggression* would like to overcome the dark side of social interaction. They want to know why people assault, maim, rape, and kill each other. One important question that they study is whether media violence and pornography encourage rape.

Psychologists who study *interpersonal power* also investigate the dark side of social interaction. They ask such disturbing questions as why ordinary citizens sometimes follow immoral orders to engage in torture, ethnic cleansing, or genocide. They believe that the principles of interpersonal power can explain both what makes a good leader and what makes people follow bad leaders.

Finally, the most complex form of behavior occurs when people interact in *groups*. Psychologists who study groups want to know whether people behave differently when they are in groups than when they are alone and whether groups do things better or worse than individuals. Their research has implications for business productivity, military decision making, and other important everyday applications.

THREE THEMES IN SOCIAL PSYCHOLOGY

Now that we have defined social psychology and identified some questions of interest, you can gain a better understanding by considering three themes that guide the research. Although they are not the only themes that inform research in social psychology, they are themes that receive considerable attention. If you know the three themes that run through this textbook, you will have a better idea of what to look for as you read the individual chapters. You might also understand why, even though social psychologists study questions that seem very different from each other, they all consider themselves to be part of the same scientific enterprise (Vallacher & Nowak, 1994).

■ SPONTANEOUS VERSUS DELIBERATIVE REACTIONS

The first theme that occurs in many chapters of the book is that people have both spontaneous and deliberative reactions (Bargh, 1994; Beike & Sherman, 1994; Epstein, Lipson, Holstein, & Huh, 1992; Gilbert, 1989; Martin, Seta, & Crelia, 1990; Martin & Stoner, in press; Smith, 1994). To show why knowing about the two reactions is important, imagine that you had a friend named Juan García who was on trial for assault. Suppose you believed that jury members had negative stereotypes about Hispanic males being violent. Would you advise Juan's lawyer to tell a few jokes because jury members would be less likely to take out their negative stereotypes on the defendant if they were in a good mood? You might, if you did not know about the difference between spontaneous and deliberative reactions.

Most of the time, people think in very simple, ways (Smith, 1994). They go with their initial, spontaneous reactions and assume that their first impressions are valid (Brewer, 1988; Carlston & Skowronski, 1994; Fiske & Neuberg, 1990). They assume that other people do what they do because "that's the kind of person he is" (Gilbert, 1991). They base their actions on whatever attitudes come readily to mind, use stereotypes, and like the people they date merely because "we have a good time together" (Devine, 1989; Fazio, 1990; Macrae, Milne, & Bodenhausen, 1994; Wilson, Dunn, Bybee, Hyman, & Rotondo, 1984). They believe whatever an expert tells them and assume that the people who belong to groups other than theirs are all alike (Chaiken, Liberman, & Eagly, 1989; Hamilton & Sherman, 1994). They strike back without thinking when they are attacked and fall into old habits when they are under stress (Berkowitz, 1989; Zajonc, 1965). They blindly assume that the majority must

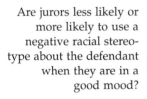

Are jurors less likely or more likely to use a negative racial stereotype about the defendant when they are in a good mood?

PEANUTS reprinted by permission of United Feature Syndicate, Inc.

be right (Moscovici, 1985). When they rely on spontaneous reactions, people can respond rapidly as events unfold, without invoking time-consuming, effortful deliberation.

At other times, people react in a more deliberative, "controlled" way (Tesser, Martin, & Mendolia, 1994). Although it takes time and energy, people sometimes think things through instead of reacting off the top of the head. They correct or adjust their first impressions by taking account of additional information (Gilbert, 1991). They realize that the circumstances might have conspired to make other people do what they did (Gilbert & Malone, 1995). They consider carefully before they act on whatever attitudes happen to be salient (Fazio, 1990). They feel guilty about entertaining negative stereotypes and consider carefully their reasons for liking the person they are dating (Devine & Monteith, 1993; Wilson, et al., 1984). They look beyond a communicator's expertise to see whether her arguments are valid and notice ways in which members of groups other than theirs are not always alike (Cacioppo, Petty, & Crites, 1994; Chaiken, et al., 1989; Hamilton & Sherman, 1994). They consider the other person's perspective before striking back and overcome old habits (Berkowitz, 1989; Zajonc, 1965). They consider the minority's point of view (Moscovici, 1985). When they rely on deliberative reactions, people sacrifice spontaneity so that they can exercise greater control.

Greater control, by the way, is not always better (Wilson & Brekke, 1994). First impressions are sometimes superior to carefully thought-out decisions. Participants in one study evaluated several different brands of strawberry jam, based only on their first impressions. They rated the jams closer to the way experts rated them than did people who thought in depth about their evaluations (Wilson & Schooler, 1991). People who make snap decisions sometimes regret those decisions less than do people who go through an extended analysis before they act (Wilson, Lisle, Schooler, Hodges, Klaaren, & LaFleur, 1993). People who seriously analyze their reasons for liking a dating partner sometimes decide that they do not like him or her much after all (Wilson, Dunn, Kraft, & Lisle, 1989). Sometimes spontaneous reactions work better; sometimes deliberative reactions work better (Wilson & Brekke, 1994). Also, people do not use one type of reaction to the exclusion of the other, but one or the other usually predominates.

Two factors that determine whether people use predominantly spontaneous reactions or deliberative reactions are motivation and ability (Fiske & Neuberg, 1990; Fazio, 1990; Gilbert, 1991; Macrae, Hewstone, & Griffiths, 1993; Pendry & Macrae, 1994; Wegener & Petty, in press). When people are not motivated or when they are busy doing something else, they rely on spontaneous reactions. When they care enough, have time enough, and do not have to worry about other matters, they rely more on deliberative reactions. Interestingly, a person's mood affects whether he or she relies predominantly on spontaneous or deliberative reactions. When people are in a good mood, they are very likely to rely on spontaneous reactions such as stereotypes. They are unwilling to do much deliberative thinking, because deliberative thinking might ruin their good mood (Esses, Haddock, & Zanna, 1994; Hamilton & Mackie, 1993; Mackie, Queller, Stroessner, & Hamilton, in press). Now that you know how a good mood affects spontaneous versus deliberative reactions, how would you advise Juan García's lawyer? Some social psychologists conducted the appropriate study (Bodenhausen, Kramer, & Süsser, 1994). They found that jurors who are in a happy mood are *more,* not less, likely to take out their negative stereotypes on a Hispanic defendant. You will find many other research findings in the other chapters of this textbook that make more sense if you know about the difference between spontaneous and deliberative reactions. A few of the relevant results are listed in Table 1.2.

■ PERSONAL VERSUS SOCIAL IDENTITY

The second theme that occurs in many chapters of the book is that people have both a personal identity and a social identity (Abrams, 1992; Brewer, 1991; Cousins, 1989; Crocker, Luhtanen, Blaine, & Broadnax, 1994; Deaux, 1993; Ethier & Deaux, 1994; Markus & Kitayama, 1994; Miller & Prentice, 1994; Oyserman, 1993; Trafimow, Triandis, & Goto, 1991; Turner, Oakes, Haslam, & McGarty, 1994). To show why knowing about the two identities is important, imagine that you work for an advertising agency. The agency is planning an expensive ad campaign to sell telephone answering machines to consumers in Korea. Would you advise the company president to use phrases such as "Be the first to adopt new technology," "Make yourself a leader among leaders," and "Make your way through the crowd" in the ads? You might, if you did not know about the difference between personal and social identities.

Sometimes people think about themselves as individuals. They have a personal identity, in which they see themselves as a collection of unique, individual characteristics (Markus & Kitayama, 1994). They think about the kind of person they might become in the future (Markus & Nurius, 1986). They think

Are people in Asian cultures impressed by ads that promise a product will make them "leader of the pack"?

TABLE 1.2	Examples of the Three Themes As They Occur in Chapters of This Book		
	SPONTANEOUS VS. DELIBERATIVE REACTIONS	**PERSONAL VS. SOCIAL IDENTITIES**	**BEING RIGHT VS. BEING LIKABLE GOALS**
Social Cognition	Jurors who are busy thinking about something else cannot ignore inadmissible evidence (Gilbert, Tafarodi, & Malone, 1993)	When two people see themselves as a couple, they overestimate their similarity to each other (Pelham & Wachsmuth, 1995)	
Person Perception	First impressions, which rely on stereotypes of such social categories as sex and race, "stand" unless people are both motivated and able to perceive another person as an individual (Brewer, 1988; Fiske & Neuberg, 1990)	People in collectivistic cultures inhibit displaying their emotions to others (Scherer & Wallbott, 1994)	Chronically depressed people form more careful impressions of other people, because they want to perceive the world accurately (Weary & Edwards, 1994b)
Attribution	When people are busy thinking about something else, they tend to explain another person's actions by that person's traits rather than by situational pressures (Gilbert, 1991)	People in China tend to explain murders by something about the situation; people in the U.S. tend to explain murders by something about the murderer (Morris & Peng, 1994)	Trying too hard to be liked can distract people from noticing the situational pressures that caused another person's behavior (Gilbert & Malone, 1995)
The Self	Self-schemas for a trait let people evaluate themselves and others on that trait more quickly (Markus, Smith, & Moreland, 1985; Klein & Loftus, 1993)	Health problems can be caused by discrepancies between personal and social identities (Higgins, in press)	People with low self-esteem would rather be viewed accurately than in flattering but inaccurate ways (Swann & Schroeder, 1995)
Attitudes	Attitudes that come to mind easily are more likely to guide behavior than are attitudes that are not as "accessible" (Fazio, 1990, 1995)	Attitude importance is related to both social identities and personal self-interest (Krosnick, et al., 1993)	Some attitudes are held because they express inner convictions; other attitudes are held because they reap social rewards (Snyder, 1993)
Attitude Change	Unless they are motivated and able to deliberate, people are not as much influenced by a message's central arguments as by characteristics "peripheral" to the arguments (Cacioppo, Petty, & Crites, 1994)	Product ads are more effective in Korea when they emphasize communal goals of ownership, but more effective in the U.S. when they emphasize individualistic goals (Han & Shavitt, 1994)	People think about persuasive communications in greater depth when they have a high need for "cognitive closure" (Kruglanski, in press)

Prejudice	People are more likely to apply negative stereotypes when they are in a happy mood, because they want to avoid thinking in depth (Bodenhausen, Kramer, & Süsser, 1994)	Differences between groups seem larger to people who belong to one of the groups (Mackie, 1986; Tajfel & Turner, 1986)	Even the oppressed sometimes justify an unequal system because they believe in a "just world" (Jost & Banaji, 1994)
Interpersonal Attraction	People have a spontaneous "repulsion" for strangers, which gives way to liking when the objects become more familiar (Rosenbaum, 1986; Zajonc, 1980)		People who want to be right would rather love someone they cannot trust than someone about whom they are not sure (Sorrentino, Holmes, Hanna, & Sharp, 1995)
Close Relationships	Some false beliefs about relationships come to mind spontaneously, especially when the individual is under stress (Fletcher, Rosanowski, & Fitness, 1994)	Some relationships are communal, in which two people regard themselves as a unit; others are exchange, in which the two people retain separate identities (Clark, Mills, & Powell, 1986; Buunk & Van Yperen, 1991)	
Social Influence	People fall back on overlearned habits when other people are watching (Zajonc, 1965)	People loaf when they are part of a group, because they cannot be personally identified (Geen, 1991; Karau & Williams, 1993; Paulus, 1983)	Expectations are self-fulfilling when the perceiver wants to be right and the target wants to be likable (Snyder, 1992)
Helping	People are less likely to help when they are distracted or in a hurry (Darley & Batson, 1973; Latane & Darley, 1970)	Reasons for helping are different in collectivistic versus individualistic cultures (Triandis, 1994)	Praise increases helping, but only when people care about being likable (Deutsch & Lamberti, 1986)
Aggression	People "lash out" in anger, without considering mitigating circumstances, when they have been attacked or annoyed (Anderson, 1989; Berkowitz, 1989)	People are more aggressive as part of a group than as individuals (Diener, 1980; Zimbardo, 1970)	
Interpersonal Power	When a minority disagrees, majority group members are motivated to give the topic deeper thought (Nemeth, 1986)	Draftees follow orders because they adopt the military unit's identity (Turner, Hogg, Oakes, Reicher, & Wetherell, 1987)	The majority "gives in" when it wants to be right; the minority "gives in" when it wants to be likable (Moscovici, 1985)
Groups	Restrictive leaders prevent groups from thinking about a group decision in depth (Janis, 1982)	People make more extreme decisions as members of a group than they would as individuals (Myers & Lamm, 1976)	Groups make extreme decisions because members want to be right and they want to be likable (Kaplan & Miller, 1987)

Calvin and Hobbes   by Bill Watterson

about who they are now, the type of person they would like to be, and the type of person they think they ought to be (Higgins, Vookles, & Tykocinski, 1992). They stand on their own two feet and accept personal responsibility for their actions (Alicke, 1992). People can also think about themselves as individuals within relationships. When they do, they view their romantic relationships as a partnership, in which partners share equally in costs and benefits (Clark, Mills, & Powell, 1986). They help other people because they get something out of it (Dovidio, Piliavin, Gaertner, Schroeder, & Clark, 1991). If they belong to a group that succeeds, they expect to be rewarded according to how much they contributed (Triandis, 1989b). They make their own decisions, independent of other people.

At other times, people think about themselves as indistinguishable from a group. They have a "collective" or social identity (Tajfel, 1981; Turner, 1991). They feel as happy when their family, school, or business succeeds as they would have felt had they succeeded as individuals, because in some sense they *are* the family, school, or business (Cialdini & De Nicholas, 1989; Crocker & Luhtanen, 1990). They think of themselves as matching or falling short of the person other people want or expect them to be (Higgins, 1989). They lose themselves in group efforts and view their romantic relationship as one unit, not two separate individuals (Clark, et al., 1986; Diener, 1980; Karau & Williams, 1993). They help people who are close to them because empathy makes them one with the other person (Batson, 1987, 1991). They do not count how much they contributed and how much they received when their group succeeds, because the group is a unit in itself, not a collection of individuals (Triandis, 1989a). They are so interdependent with other group members that their fate becomes the group's fate.

Interestingly, cultures differ in whether they emphasize the personal identity or the social identity. Individualistic cultures such as the United States, Canada, Great Britain, the Netherlands, Australia, and New Zealand emphasize the personal identity. Collectivistic cultures such as China, Japan, Korea, Pakistan, Jamaica, and countries in West Africa emphasize the social identity (Hofstede, 1983). People treat each other very differently in individualistic cultures than they do in collectivistic cultures (Triandis, Bontempo, Villareal, Asai, & Lucca, 1988). People swear at each other more in individualistic cultures than in collectivistic cultures, for example (Semin & Rubini, 1990). Nonetheless, one type of culture is not better than another, but merely different (Triandis, 1994). People who live in individualistic cultures typically live in a rich, complex society. They belong to many different groups but owe no group their absolute allegiance. They also take great pride and satisfaction from their unique accomplishments and make new friends easily. People who live in collectivistic cultures, in contrast, typically make enduring commitments to their friends and relatives. They enjoy very low rates of crime, divorce, child abuse, suicide, and mental illness (Triandis, McCusker, & Hui, 1990). Also, no person or culture is entirely one way or the other. Sometimes the personal identity is salient and at other times the social identity is salient (Brewer, 1993).

People in collectivistic cultures where the social identity is salient, however, might respond to different appeals than would people in individualistic cultures where the personal identity is salient. Now that you know that people in the United States tend to emphasize their personal identity, whereas people in Korea tend to emphasize their social identity, how would you advise the president of the advertising agency about ads for answering machines? Some social psychologists conducted the appropriate study. They found that ads that emphasize personal identity with phases such as "A leader among leaders" are more persuasive in the United States. In Korea, however, ads that emphasize social identity with phrases such as "We have a way of bringing people together" are more persuasive (Morris & Peng, 1994). You will find many other research findings in the other chapters of this book that make more sense if you know about the difference between personal and social identities. A few of the relevant results are listed in Table 1.2.

■ WANTING TO BE RIGHT VERSUS WANTING TO BE LIKABLE

The third theme that occurs in many chapters of the book is that people have at least two fundamental goals: to be right, and to be likable (Baumeister & Leary, 1995; Snyder, 1993, 1994; Swann, 1987, 1990). To show why knowing about the two goals is important, imagine that you knew a woman with very low self-esteem who had just flunked a big exam. Would you advise her to talk to her dating partner about failing the exam, because you were confident that he would reassure her and bolster her damaged ego? You might, if you did not know about the difference between wanting to be right and wanting to be likable.

Do people always want their friends and lovers to soothe their bruised egos?

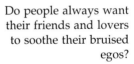

Sometime people are very concerned about being right–having a correct, objectively valid view of themselves, other people, and relationships (Kenny, 1991; Mischel & Shoda, 1995). When people are chronically depressed, for example, they take great pains to form careful impressions of other people, perhaps as a way of restoring the personal control that they feel slipping away from them (Weary & Edwards, 1994b). People who have very low self-esteem want other people to be brutally honest with them, rather than engaging in what they perceive as insincere flattery (Swann, Stein-Seroussi, & Geisler, 1992). When they are concerned about being right, people hold attitudes that express their inner convictions, regardless of whether their opinions are popular or not (Snyder, 1993). They distort what they see other people do, so that their expectations are fulfilled (Jones, 1990b; Snyder, 1992). They also have a driving need to have an answer–any answer–just so that they can avoid uncertainty and ambiguity (Kruglanski, in press). Similarly, when members of a group are too concerned with being right, they can make ill-advised decisions, because they are afraid to take even reasonable chances (Kaplan & Miller, 1987).

At other times, people are more concerned about being likable–feeling good about themselves and making a good impression on others. Cancer patients and other sufferers, for instance, may compare themselves with people who are worse off, so that they can feel better about themselves (Taylor & Brown, 1988, 1994). People who have high self-esteem may delude themselves into thinking that they have those characteristics which predict a happy, successful future (Dunning & Story, 1991; Kunda, 1987). People who have high self-esteem may also choose to associate with others who give them compliments (Swann, Hixon, & de La Ronde, in press). Furthermore, people who are too concerned with being likable hold attitudes merely because the attitudes happen to be politically correct (Snyder, 1993). Even people who are themselves oppressed may praise the very system that oppresses them. By doing so, they can continue to believe that the world is "just" and that they are being treated as well as they deserve (Jost & Banaji, 1994). Similarly, people some-

THE FAMILY CIRCUS®   **By Bil Keane**

© 1995 Bil Keane, Inc.
Dist. by Cowles Synd., Inc.

"I need somebody."

Reprinted with special permission of King Features Syndicate.

times alter their behavior to match the expectations of someone they want to like them and help more if they think they are going to be praised for doing so (Deutsch & Lamberti, 1986; Snyder, 1993). Finally, when members of a group are too concerned with being likable, they can make ill-advised decisions rather than jeopardize group harmony (Kaplan & Miller, 1987).

Being right is neither a better nor worse goal than being likable. The two goals are merely different. It is obviously adaptive to see things as they really are, rather than to live in a fantasy world where everything is for the best. Recognizing your shortcomings would seem to be a necessary first step on the road to improvement (Weary & Edwards, 1994b). It is also adaptive to take an optimistic rather than a pessimistic outlook on your role in the world and to try to get along with other people (Taylor & Loebel, 1989). The world would be a dreadful place if people did not feel a need to belong with at least one other human being—if they did not care what other people thought of them (Baumeister & Leary, 1995). Also, no one pursues one of these goals to the exclusion of the other. Sometimes the need to be right predominates; sometimes the need to be likable predominates. At other times, the two goals conflict. When they face a majority who are clearly incorrect, for instance, people have to decide whether the topic is important enough to them to tell it like it is, even if others do not approve (Turner, 1991).

Now that you know that some people who have low self-esteem would rather hear the truth about themselves than be told that they are wonderful, how would you advise the woman who failed the big exam? Some social psychologists conducted the appropriate studies. They found that men and women who have very low self-esteem often chose romantic partners who tell them what they already believe about themselves, which is that they are unworthy (Swann, et al., 1995). Worse yet, when such a person fails an exam, the dating partner does exactly the opposite of bolstering the person's ego. Instead, the dating partner tells it like it is, which is what the person prefers to hear (Swann & Predmore, 1985). For such people, talking to their romantic partner is not likely to reassure them about failing the exam. You will find many research findings in the other chapters of this book that make more sense if you know about the difference between wanting to be right and wanting to be likable. A few of the relevant results are listed in Table 1.2.

SUMMARY OF WHAT SOCIAL PSYCHOLOGY IS

Social psychology is the scientific study of the way in which people's thoughts, feelings, and behaviors are influenced by the real or imagined presence of other people. The three parts of this textbook describe the three major categories of questions that social psychologists address. The three major categories are thinking about the self and others, evaluating persons and relationships, and interacting with other people. Thinking about the self and others involves social cognition, person perception, attribution, and the self. Evaluating persons and relationships involves attitudes, attitude change, prejudice, interpersonal attraction, and close relationships. Interacting with others involves social influence, helping, aggression, interpersonal power, and groups.

(*Continued on page 16*)

Three themes pervade research in social psychology: spontaneous versus deliberative reactions, personal versus social identity, and wanting to be right versus wanting to be likable. Studies in several chapters of the book suggest that people have both immediate, spontaneous reactions and more controlled, deliberative reactions to people and events. The spontaneous reactions are often dramatically different from the deliberative reactions, but not necessarily better or worse. Studies in several chapters of the book also suggest that people have a personal identity, in which they regard themselves as an individual. People also have a social or collective identity, in which they regard themselves as part of a group. Cross-cultural and other research shows that people respond very differently to the same event, depending on whether the personal identity or the social identity is salient. Finally, studies in several chapters of the book suggest that people pursue at least two goals that are sometimes incompatible. They want to be right, but they also want to be likable.

HOW DO WE STUDY SOCIAL PSYCHOLOGY?

The first section of the chapter identified and discussed some of the major questions of interest in social psychology. This second section addresses the related issue of *how* we study social psychology—how we answer the questions. Recall that social psychology is the *scientific* study of the way in which people's thoughts, feelings, and behaviors are influenced by the real or imagined presence of other people. To qualify as scientific, a research project has to use what other scientists regard as a valid method. Poets and philosophers settle for intuition and logic. Scientists do not.

To answer their questions, social psychologists use three major research methods: laboratory experiments, field studies, and correlational studies. These three are not the only methods that social psychologists use, but they represent most of the research. Also, the three methods are not as distinct from each other as the neat labels imply. Studies that use one method sometimes have characteristics that are usually found in the other methods. Nonetheless, the three parts of this section discuss the three major research methods in turn, providing for each method both a description and a concrete example. Because we have used the relationship between fear and attraction as an example research topic so far in the chapter, we illustrate each method with a study that also addressed this relationship.

LABORATORY EXPERIMENTS

Suppose you thought that the scary bridge results were just one aspect of a more general tendency that human beings have: to be drawn to others when they are afraid. You might believe that people find the presence of others reassuring. You might believe that people seek strength in numbers when they are threatened. You might also believe that people look to others to figure out whether it is appropriate to be afraid. For all these reasons, you might predict that fear promotes affiliation—that people who are afraid want to be with other

How would you prove that people seek each other's company when they are anxious and afraid?

people, even when the other people are complete strangers, not romantic partners.

How would you find out whether your speculations were correct? How would you do it so that other social psychologists would accept your results as having demonstrated an important characteristic of people's thoughts, feelings, and behaviors? If you chose the method used by most of the researchers whose work is described in this textbook, you would conduct a laboratory experiment. An **experiment** is a procedure used to test whether one event (which is manipulated) causes a second event (which is not manipulated, but merely measured). Laboratory experiments attempt to model or imitate real-world events in a highly controlled setting (the experimental laboratory). In such a setting, experimenters can manipulate a single factor and measure the effect that the manipulation has on participants' thoughts, feelings, and behavior *when all else is held constant*. Social psychologists use the laboratory experiment frequently, because it is the only research method in which it is possible to control or hold constant every characteristic of the setting except the one that the investigator wants to manipulate.

■ A LABORATORY EXPERIMENT ON FEAR AND AFFILIATION

In a classic laboratory experiment on fear and affiliation, the researcher wanted to make some participants, but not others, anxious and afraid. The researcher then wanted to measure whether anxious participants were more likely than nonanxious participants to seek the company of others (Schachter, 1959). The first step in conducting the experiment was to recruit participants. Because women in the 1950s were less likely than men to claim a macho lack of fear, the investigator recruited only college women, who received extra points on a final examination for participating. The second step in conducting the experiment was to create an artificial situation that the investigator hoped would make the women anxious and afraid. It seemed at least plausible that the women would become anxious if they anticipated receiving very painful electric shocks.

When the women arrived at the laboratory, they found themselves in a room with several other participants, none of whom knew each other before the experiment. To keep the women from talking to each other and getting to know each other, the experimenter had them complete a questionnaire while they were waiting. The experimenter was trying to show that even *strangers* want to be with other people when they are anxious and afraid. When all the women had arrived, the experimenter instructed them in one of two ways that represented the experimental manipulation. For some groups of women, the experimenter wore a white laboratory coat and had a stethoscope dangling from his pocket. He introduced himself in a very serious way as "Dr. Gregor Zilstein," a professor of neurology who was investigating the effects of electric shocks. Waving at a large array of threatening-looking electrical equipment, Dr. Zilstein explained his experiment. He said that he would be giving the women intense and very painful electric shocks while taking their pulse rate, blood pressure, and other physiological measures. He told the women: "I do want to be honest with you and tell you that these shocks will be quite painful but, of course, they will do no permanent damage" (Schachter, 1959, p. 13). For the other groups of women, Dr. Zilstein was relaxed and friendly. He told the women that they would be receiving very mild electric shocks—"more a tickle or a tingle than anything unpleasant" (p. 14).

The two speeches were two levels of the independent variable. The **independent variable** in an experiment is the aspect of the participant's experience that the investigator (or someone else) manipulates. It is called a variable because it varies (is at different levels) from one participant to the next. In the Dr. Zilstein experiment, the investigator manipulated whether each participant received the painful shock instructions or the mild shock instructions. By using these two kinds of instructions, the experimenter was trying to manipulate the participant's fear and anxiety. The experimenter was also trying to hold every aspect of the situation except the independent variable constant, to control as many as possible of the extraneous variables. **Extraneous variables** are aspects of the experimental situation that might vary of their own accord, if the experimenter did not control them. When the experimenter in the Dr. Zilstein experiment would not allow the women to speak to each other before the experiment began, for instance, he was trying to control a possible extraneous variable. He did not want participants in the two conditions to differ in how well acquainted they were.

After delivering one of the two speeches, Dr. Zilstein asked the women to rate on a five-point scale how much they liked versus disliked the idea of being shocked. The five-point scale was a **manipulation check,** a test of whether the experimental manipulation had the intended effect. The intended effect in the Dr. Zilstein experiment was to make one group of women more anxious than the other group about the anticipated shocks. The manipulation check indicated that the manipulation worked. Women who anticipated receiving painful shocks disliked the idea more than did women who anticipated receiving mild shocks. (In later similar studies, the experimenter asked participants directly about how anxious they were feeling, with similar support for the effectiveness of the painful-versus-mild shock manipulation.)

With anxiety effectively manipulated, the investigator was ready to measure possible differences in affiliation between women in the painful and mild shock conditions. One way to measure preferences for affiliation would have been simply to ask the women how much they wanted to be in each other's company. Such a measure, however, would have been almost useless for discovering whether anxiety promotes affiliation. As we shall see later in this chapter, people often say that they would behave in one way and then behave in an exactly opposite way. The goal of social psychology is not to study what people *say* they would do. Instead, the goal is to study what people actually *do* when they are not aware that their behavior is being observed, measured, and studied. To test the predicted relationship between fear and affiliation, therefore, the researcher gave the women a chance to act on their need to affiliate, but without the women realizing what the investigator was studying.

Dr. Zilstein explained, in exactly the same way whether he was talking to women who expected painful shocks or to women who expected mild shocks, that there would be a ten-minute delay while he prepared the electrical equipment. Because it would be difficult to prepare the equipment with so many people in the room, the women would have to wait elsewhere. To accommodate individual preferences, he said he had arranged individual waiting rooms. These rooms, which were more than spacious enough for one person, contained armchairs, books, and magazines. He had also reserved a larger room where women who wanted to be with the others could wait as a group. Dr. Zilstein asked each woman to check the preferred alternative on a sheet of paper that listed "I prefer being alone," "I prefer being with others," and "I really don't care."

The women's choices were the dependent variable. The **dependent variable** in an experiment is the aspect of the participant's behavior that the experimenter measures. The investigator predicts that the dependent variable will be different for participants who received different levels of the independent variable. In the Dr. Zilstein experiment, the investigator predicted that participants who received different levels of the independent variable (painful versus mild shock instructions) would choose different ways to wait (in a group versus alone). One helpful memory clue is that differences in the independent variable do not depend on what the participant chooses to do, whereas differences in the dependent variable do depend on what the participant chooses to do.

Figure 1.2 displays the results of the Dr. Zilstein experiment. As the figure shows, very few women chose to wait in a room by themselves regardless of the type of electric shocks they were expecting to receive. The important differences were between the "said they did not care" and "chose to wait with other women" alternatives. As predicted, women who thought they were going to receive intense, painful electric shocks were more than twice as likely to choose the company of other women than not to care about how they waited. Women who thought they were going to receive only mild "tickles" made exactly opposite choices: almost twice as many of them did not care as chose company.

The Dr. Zilstein experiment showed that people who are anxious seek the company of others. The experiment did not discriminate, however, among explanations for the result. Women who felt anxious and afraid might have wanted to be with other women because the mere presence of others was reassuring, because they sought strength in numbers, or because they wanted to find out how afraid other people were. To distinguish among these alternative explanations, the researcher conducted a second laboratory experiment, in which the procedure was the same as just described, except that there were two painful shock conditions (Schachter, 1959). In one of the painful shock conditions, the women had a choice of waiting alone or waiting with other women who were going to be shocked. In the other painful shock condition, the women had a choice of waiting alone or waiting with other women who were *not* in the experiment, but only waiting to talk to their advisers. As predicted, 60 percent of women chose to wait with other women who were also going to be shocked, but *not one woman* chose to wait with other women who were not waiting to be shocked. Simply being with others was not enough if the women could not learn from others how afraid it was appropriate for them to feel. As the investigator aptly described these laboratory experiments on affiliation, "Misery doesn't love just any kind of company, it loves only miserable company" (p. 24).

■ ADVANTAGES AND DISADVANTAGES

As a method of answering the questions of social psychology, laboratory experiments have both advantages and disadvantages. The most important advantage of this research method is that the investigator is able to *control* and to hold constant all other aspects of the experience except for manipulation of

FIGURE 1.2

Fear and anxiety increase affiliation.

Graph shows the percentage of women who chose different ways to wait for an experiment in which they expected to receive mild or painful electric shocks (Schachter, 1959).

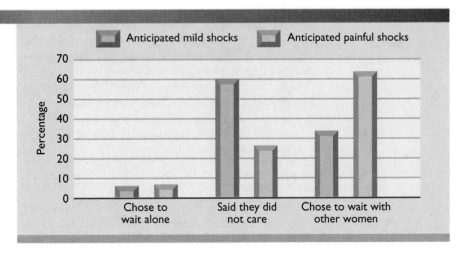

the independent variable. All participants are treated identically, except for the *one* event that the investigator believes will alter their thoughts, feelings, or behavior. As a result, the investigator can unambiguously attribute differences in how participants in the groups react to the independent variable and not to extraneous variables.

The only ambiguity might arise if participants in the different conditions differed *before* the manipulation. If Dr. Zilstein had given the mild shocks speech to women who volunteered for a morning session and the painful shocks speech to women who volunteered for an evening session, for instance, the experiment would have been invalid. Night people might like more company than do day people, even without any manipulation. To protect against such unwanted systematic differences, experimenters routinely use random assignment. **Random assignment** involves assigning participants to conditions randomly rather than systematically, so that possible extraneous variables occur equally across conditions. With random assignment, night people and day people, introverts and extroverts, Democrats and Republicans, and so on, are equally likely to be assigned to and represented in each condition of a laboratory experiment.

The most important disadvantage of laboratory experiments is also part of their strength. The setting is so tightly controlled that participants may perceive it as artificial and irrelevant to the way they behave outside the laboratory. If participants perceive the experimental setting and events as artificial, then they may be playacting rather than reacting as they normally would. Investigators who use the laboratory experiment are thus careful to construct experimental scenarios that are high in experimental realism. **Experimental realism** occurs when participants become so caught up in the experimental scenario that they react as they would to important, involving events outside the laboratory (Aronson, Brewer, & Carlsmith, 1985). If the investigator in the Dr. Zilstein experiment successfully convinced women that they were going to receive electric shocks, he might (cautiously) generalize the results to such anxiety-provoking real-world events as fire alarms, automobile accidents, and terrorist attacks. Experimental realism is more important than mere **mundane realism,** which is the extent to which the laboratory setting is superficially–as opposed to psychologically–similar to the real world (Aronson, Brewer, & Carlsmith, 1985).

FIELD STUDIES

The Dr. Zilstein laboratory experiment had much experimental realism. The women in the painful shock condition seemed convinced that they were going to receive painful electric shocks. They acted nervous and afraid. If you had conducted the Dr. Zilstein experiment and its follow-up, however, you might still want to demonstrate a relationship between fear and affiliation outside the psychology laboratory, in a naturally occurring environment. You might want to conduct a field study that addressed the same basic questions as the Dr. Zilstein laboratory experiment. Field studies get their name because they are typically conducted in "the field," which means "not in a psychology laboratory." They are called studies rather than experiments because the researcher typically does not exercise complete control over the independent variable or extraneous variables.

■ A FIELD STUDY OF FEAR AND APPROACH

We have already seen an example of a field study in the scary bridge results that we discussed at the start of the chapter (Dutton & Aron, 1974). Instead of making people afraid in a laboratory setting, the researchers chose to go out into the field. They chose to measure thoughts, feelings, and behaviors that occur in a natural setting, with as little intrusion on their part as possible. To manipulate fear and arousal, the researchers found two naturally occurring settings that they thought would make people feel either calm or anxious and afraid. To be sure that they were not merely projecting their own fears onto the setting, they asked people who crossed the different bridges to rate how anxious and afraid they felt. As the researchers predicted, people who crossed on the suspension bridge said they felt much more anxious and afraid than did people who crossed on the safer bridge. When this manipulation check showed that the two bridges differed in their effects, the researchers then let the environment do part of their work for them.

The researchers in the scary bridge study intervened only as much as they had to if they wanted to measure the dependent variables of interest. First, they wanted to see whether men who were on the scary bridge had more romantic thoughts and feelings than did men who were on the safe bridge. They especially wanted to know whether an attractive woman would be more likely to trigger spontaneous thoughts about love, kissing, and sexual intercourse in men who were on the scary as opposed to the safe bridge. They were interested not in a general tendency to affiliate, as was the Dr. Zilstein researcher, but rather in a specific tendency to seek romantic attachment. The researchers did not want to rely on the men's retrospective reports of what thoughts they were having when they met an attractive woman on the bridge. The men might not have remembered what they were thinking. The men might also have been embarrassed to tell an experimenter some of their thoughts. Now you see why the researchers chose to have the men invent fantasy stories about a picture of a woman who was covering her face. The researchers thought that men would let slip what they were really thinking and how they really felt about the woman in the kinds of stories that they invented. As described earlier, the researchers' assumptions were correct. Men who met the woman on the scary bridge invented more romantic and sexier stories than did men who met her on the safe bridge.

For the other dependent variable, the researchers wanted to measure actual behavior. They were not content to show that men had more romantic thoughts and feelings when they met the woman on the scary rather than the safe bridge. They also wanted to show that men who met the woman in the different settings would *behave* differently, in a way that the researchers could reasonably interpret as expressing romantic interest. The researchers correctly reasoned that very few men would ask the woman for a date on either bridge when the woman was interviewing them rather than meeting them in a casual way. Also, they could not allow the woman to express any romantic interest in the man. If they did, they would be measuring his reaction to her overtures, rather than actions that he took simply because of meeting her. To measure behavior, they had to give the men an opportunity to approach the woman, and yet have a good excuse for doing so. As described earlier, the researchers cleverly scripted a scenario in which the woman gave the man her telephone number in case he wanted more information about the study. The researchers' ingenuity was rewarded when many more men called the woman after meeting her on the scary bridge than on the safe bridge.

■ ADVANTAGES AND DISADVANTAGES

This more detailed description of the scary bridge study allows us to examine the differences between a laboratory experiment and a field study. First, as we noted previously, a field study occurs outside the psychology laboratory. Second, the investigator does not have as tight control over the independent and extraneous variables in a field study as in a laboratory experiment. The scary bridge study is a good example. The independent variable was the level of anxiety the different bridges were thought to arouse, not something that the experimenter manipulated directly. Third, field studies typically do not entail random assignment to conditions. Students in the scary bridge study assigned themselves to conditions by choosing to cross the river on either the suspension bridge or the lower, wider bridge. Because they had the choice of walking along the river to cross on the other bridge, men who chose to cross on the scary bridge might have had more risk-taking personalities. More of them might have fancied themselves as Don Juans who frequently called women for dates, regardless of where they met them. The results might have been caused by the different personalities of men who assigned themselves to the scary bridge versus the safe bridge conditions, and not by a relationship between fear and romantic attraction.

One way of summarizing the difference between field studies and laboratory experiments, other than merely the setting, is that field studies typically do not control all the extraneous variables. The air temperature might have been different 230 feet above a river than 10 feet above it. The men who chose the scary bridge might have had different personalities from the men who chose the safe bridge. The woman experimenter, no matter how carefully she was trained to behave exactly the same in the two conditions, might have acted more helpless and afraid when she was on the scary bridge than when she was on the safe bridge. As Chapter 3 of this book describes, people are often unaware of subtle nonverbal cues that reveal their emotions, such as fidgeting or tightening their facial muscles. If we included all possible differences in atmospheric conditions and body movements as extraneous variables, we could list hundreds of ways in which the scary bridge condition was different from the safe bridge condition, other than arousing different levels of fear and anxiety.

From a field study alone, the researchers who conducted the scary bridge study could not be sure, as they could from a more tightly controlled laboratory experiment, that they had demonstrated a causal relationship between fear and romantic attachment. As a result, they conducted a follow-up laboratory experiment, which is described in greater detail in Chapter 9. In the follow-up study, they manipulated fear by telling men that they were going to receive either painful or mild electric shocks (Dutton & Aron, 1974, Experiment 3). While they were waiting, the men completed a questionnaire that asked, among other questions, how much they would like to date and kiss the other subject, who was an attractive female confederate. As predicted, men who expected to receive painful shocks said they wanted to date and kiss her more than did men who expected to receive mild shocks. Field studies and laboratory experiments, then, complement each other.

Laboratory experiments sacrifice the opportunity to investigate ongoing real-world events for tight control over the situation, so that only the independent variable could possibly be responsible for changes in the dependent variable. Field studies sacrifice control over the extraneous variables for the opportunity to see what happens in nonartificial settings that are more natural and involving for participants. The best research approach is to use both methods, as the researchers who conducted the scary bridge study did. Better yet, a proposed relationship can be investigated by all three methods: laboratory experiments, field studies, and correlational studies.

CORRELATIONAL STUDIES

To understand correlational studies, you need to understand the term correlation as psychologists use it. A simple **correlation** is the degree of relationship between two variables. In a correlational study, psychologists call them both merely variables and do not use terms such as independent and dependent. Some pairs of variables have no relationship to each other. People might vary in how many social psychologists they know and in how many times they have been to the movies, but we have no reason to suspect that the two variables of knowing social psychologists and going to movies would be correlated. Other pairs of variables have either a positive or a negative relationship to each other. If one variable is how many people you invite to a party and the other variable is how much food you need to provide, you might expect a positive relationship between the two variables. The more people who attend, the more food they will consume. When one variable goes up as the other goes up, we have a positive correlation. If one variable is how much food you consume and the other variable is how much weight you lose, in contrast, we might expect a negative relationship between the two variables. The more you eat, the less weight you lose; the less you eat, the more weight you lose. When one variable goes down as the other goes up, we have a negative correlation.

■ A CORRELATIONAL STUDY OF FEAR AND SEEKING SUPPORT

Now that you know what a correlation is, consider how we might use correlations to examine the relationship between fear and approaching other people. We might, for instance, rate women on how afraid they act as they cross a scary bridge. The women would presumably vary all the way from whistling and being totally unconcerned to clutching the side and praying fervently. Degree of acting afraid would be one variable. We might also arrange to have each woman's dating partner waiting at the end of the bridge. We could rate each woman on how close she gets to her dating partner. The women would presumably vary all the way from standing 10 feet away to throwing their arms around the dating partner. Proximity to the partner would be the second variable. If the two variables were positively related, women who acted least afraid would stand farthest from their dating partners and women who acted most afraid would embrace them warmly. If the two variables were negatively related, women who acted least afraid would embrace them warmly and women who acted most afraid would stand 10 feet away.

It might be difficult, however, to arrange for women's dating partners to be standing at the far side of a scary bridge, much less to explain why. Instead, three social psychologists conducted a correlational study of the relationship between how afraid women acted and how much support they sought from their dating partners (Simpson, Rholes, & Nelligan, 1992). To understand what they did and what they discovered, you need one more piece of information—about romantic attachment styles. As discussed more at length in Chapter 9 (on Interpersonal Attraction), people have different romantic "attachment styles," different ways of attaching themselves to a loved one. Some psychologists believe that we develop our adult romantic attachment styles from the relationships that we had with our mothers when we were infants (Bowlby, 1979; Hazan & Shaver, 1987). Although there are three styles, the relevant two are the "secure" attachment style and the "avoidant" attachment style. People who have a *secure* attachment style say that "I find it relatively easy to get close to others and am comfortable depending on them and having them depend on me. I don't often worry about being abandoned or about someone getting too close to me." People who have an *avoidant* attachment style, in contrast, say "I am somewhat uncomfortable being close to others. I find it difficult to trust them completely, difficult to allow myself to depend on them. I am nervous when anyone gets too close, and often, love partners want me to be more intimate than I feel comfortable being."

Do you think that the relationship between fear and approaching a romantic partner might be different for people who have different attachment styles? The participants in the correlational study of acting afraid and seeking support were college women who had a current dating relationship (Simpson et al., 1992). Through a previous questionnaire, the researchers knew each participant's characteristic attachment type—whether she had a secure or avoidant romantic attachment style. To conduct their study, the researchers arranged that the dating couple "happened" to be sitting in the same room, while supposedly waiting to participate in two separate psychology experiments. The woman, but not the man, expected to participate in a study that, she was told, "arouses considerable anxiety and distress in most people." Before coming to the waiting room, the experimenter had let her peek inside a dark, windowless isolation chamber that contained intimidating electrical equipment. Although the couple did not know it, they were videotaped while they sat in the waiting room. After five minutes, the experimenter returned, explained the true purpose of the study, and requested permission to keep and score the videotape. All couples gave their permission. From the videotape, the investigators rated how anxious and afraid the woman acted (the first variable) and how much comfort and support she sought from her partner (the second variable).

Figure 1.3 shows the results of this correlational study. The results for secure women are represented on the upwardly sloping line with triangles. The results for avoidant women are represented on the downwardly sloping line with squares. As you can see, the relationship between acting afraid and seeking support was positive for secure women. The more anxious and afraid they acted, the more they sought comfort and support from their dating partner. The relationship between acting afraid and seeking support for avoidant women, in contrast, was negative. The more anxious and afraid they acted, the *less* they sought his comfort and support. This correlational study, then, provided valuable information about how women interact with their dating partners when they think that the two of them are alone and cannot be observed. Specifically, the study showed that secure women approach their romantic partner more when they are more anxious and afraid, whereas avoidant women do exactly the opposite. You can imagine how useful this kind of information is to marriage counselors, who are trying to understand why a relationship is on the rocks.

■ ADVANTAGES AND DISADVANTAGES

One advantage of the correlational method is that psychologists can use it to investigate events long after they have occurred, as long as someone kept records or "archives" of what happened. When correlations are applied to old records, the technique is called an "archival study." A good example is a study that tried to examine the relationship between frustration and aggression. The researchers reasoned that when people were economically deprived, they would take out their frustrations on convenient scapegoats such as minority groups. To conduct their study, the researchers collected yearly records of cotton prices from 1882 to 1930 in 14 states of the southern United States (Hovland & Sears, 1940). When the price of cotton was down, White farmers in the region were in economic hard times and were presumably very frustrated. The researchers also got records of the number of lynchings in the same region, for the same years. In the vast majority of such lynchings, White men hanged a Black man without benefit of a trial. The two variables, then, were the price of cotton in each year and the number of lynchings in each year. When they correlated the two variables, the investigators discovered a negative relationship. In years when the price of cotton decreased, lynching increased. When the price of cotton increased, lynching decreased. If the price

FIGURE 1.3

Attachment styles affect reactions to fear. Graph shows how much comfort and support secure and avoidant women who displayed low or high fear sought from their romantic partners (Simpson, Rholes, & Nelligan, 1992).

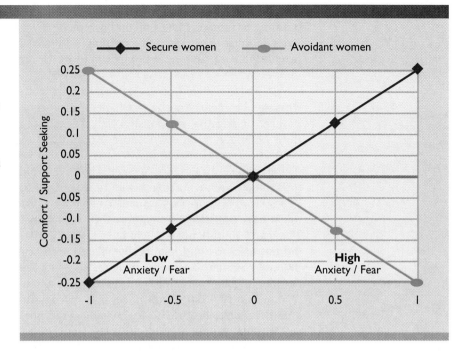

of cotton was an indicator of frustration, then this correlational study established that frustration and aggression, as described more at length in Chapter 13, are highly related (Hepworth & West, 1988).

Another advantage of the correlational method is that it can be applied in cases where it would be unethical to manipulate or *create* one of the variables. The investigators in the study of dating couples created conditions in which women were free to act afraid or not afraid. They did not, however, make any one woman act afraid or act unafraid, nor did they make any one woman approach or avoid her partner. Their study had some potential ethical pitfalls that the investigators were careful to avoid, but it did not create problems just so that someone could study them. This distinction becomes more apparent when you think about the study of lynchings. Even if they could, no ethical researchers would ever force cotton prices down so that people lost their farms, or stand idly by making observations in a notebook while people were being lynched. Similarly, if we wanted to discover whether people are more afraid the closer they live to a disaster like a nuclear meltdown, we would never consider sabotaging a nuclear energy plant. Nonetheless, records exist of lynchings, public reactions to nuclear and other disasters, and thousands of other variables that might be conceptually related. We may be sorry that the events occurred, but researchers did not create them and can glean very useful information from them by using the correlational method.

The correlational method, however, also has a serious disadvantage. Correlation is not the same as causation. When two variables have a positive or negative relationship, we know *only* that they are related. We do not know that one caused the other. Consider the avoidant women in the study of dating couples. The more afraid they were, the more they stayed away from their dating partners. Did being afraid *cause* them to avoid their partners? It might have, but we can never know for sure when we use the correlational method. For all we know, sitting far from their partners caused avoidant women to fidget more and display other behavioral signs of fear and anxiety. Instead of the first variable (having an avoidant attachment style) causing the second variable (avoiding the partner when afraid), the second variable may have caused the first.

From a correlational study, we can never know. Similarly, a high incidence of lynching in southern states might have made investors leery of investing their funds in what they regarded as a politically unstable region. The number of lynchings might have caused fluctuations in the local economy, including cotton prices.

To make matters worse, the correlational method is plagued by the "third variable" problem. The two variables that were measured might have had a positive or negative relationship only because they were both affected by a third variable that we did not measure. In that case, there would be no causal connection at all between the two variables that we measured. In the study of dating couples, for instance, women who have avoidant attachment styles might tend to date men who become angry when they participate in psychology experiments. The more they wanted to avoid an argument, the more these women might have fidgeted and the more they might have sat far from their partners. The men's short tempers might have been a third variable that the researchers did not measure, and might have caused both acting afraid and avoiding the partners. Similarly, extreme heat in the 14 southern states during certain decades might have both ruined cotton crops and made people aggressive. The relationship between cotton prices and lynchings might have been caused by a third variable—heat—that the researchers did not include in their study.

Fortunately, we know from other studies that these relationships discovered by the correlational method are probably causal and that the direction of causality is just what the researchers thought it was. Fear and anxiety probably do cause avoidant women to avoid their romantic partners. Economic and other forms of frustration probably do cause aggression against convenient scapegoats. The causal relationships had to be verified through methods other than the correlational method, but they do exist. Some of the most interesting relationships in social psychology cannot ethically be investigated with any method other than a correlational study. Also, many of the most interesting causal relationships were first suggested by correlational studies. As suggested in the section on field studies, the best research approach is to seek convergent evidence for a proposed relationship by using all three methods: laboratory experiments, field studies, and correlational studies. Table 1.3 lists some

TABLE 1.3	Some Advantages and Disadvantages of Three Methods That Social Psychologists Use		
METHOD	**ADVANTAGES**		**DISADVANTAGES**
Laboratory experiment	tight control over independent and extraneous variables		situation may be perceived as artificial
	participants randomly assigned to conditions		dangerous to generalize to important real-world situations
Field study	situation usually perceived as natural		no tight control over independent and extraneous variables
	easy to generalize to important real-world situations		participants not randomly assigned to conditions
Correlational study	can use any existing data, even archival data		dangerous to infer causal relationship
	can use when manipulation would be unethical		unmeasured third variable might be the real cause

advantages and disadvantages of each method. In the table, you can see that each method's disadvantages are offset by advantages of another method. When we obtain converging results from all three methods, as researchers have for the relationship between fear and affiliation, we cannot explain the results merely by pointing to a disadvantage of any one method.

SUMMARY OF HOW WE STUDY SOCIAL PSYCHOLOGY

The methods used to answer the questions of social psychology may be classified into three types: laboratory experiments, field studies, and correlational studies. In laboratory experiments, the investigator manipulates one factor (the independent variable) and measures the manipulation's effect on a second factor (the dependent variable). An important advantage of laboratory experiments is that the investigator can control and hold constant all aspects of the participants' experience except the independent variable. A major drawback is that the results may not generalize to behavior outside the laboratory if participants perceive the laboratory setting as artificial. In field studies, the investigator typically uses a naturally occurring event or setting to manipulate the independent variable indirectly. A field study involves a relatively spontaneous ongoing event that more readily generalizes to important real-world issues than usually occurs with a laboratory setting. Field studies, however, entail little or no control over extraneous variables that might have caused the result. In correlational studies, the investigator predicts that two variables are related to each other, such that when one of the variables is at high (or low) levels, so is the other. The correlational method is ideal for investigating factors that cannot ethically be manipulated or that were recorded in the past. Investigators cannot, however, infer from a relationship that changes in one of the variables *caused* changes in the other variable.

WHAT ARE SOME PROBLEMS IN STUDYING SOCIAL PSYCHOLOGY?

We have seen in the first two sections of this chapter that the reasons for studying social thoughts, feelings, and behavior are compelling. We also know that investigators have at their disposal several effective research methods. It would be a serious mistake to conclude from the availability of diverse research methods, however, that social psychology is easy. In reality, social psychology is one of the most difficult of all research topics. This section of the chapter explains two problematic aspects of conducting research in social psychology and then examines some ethical considerations.

PROBLEMS IN CONDUCTING STUDIES

One problem in studying social thoughts, feelings, and behavior alluded to earlier in the chapter is that it is often useless or misleading to rely on simply asking people why they behave as they do. Surprisingly, in all too many circumstances of interest to social psychologists, people think that they know why they behave as they do, but they are wrong. They *lack awareness* of factors that affect their behavior. A second, equally frustrating problem is that, unless they follow very careful procedures, investigators may inadvertently create an *experimental demand*. Lack of awareness and experimental demand can bias the results of even the most cleverly conceived studies.

■ LACK OF AWARENESS

In the scary bridge field study, the Dr. Zilstein laboratory experiment, and the correlational study of secure-versus-avoidant women, the investigators were very careful to disguise their true purpose. In the scary bridge field study, the researchers did not tell the men that "we want to know whether people are more susceptible to romantic attraction when they are afraid and anxious." Instead, they misled the men into thinking that they were participating in nothing more than an ordinary survey. Dr. Zilstein did not tell the women that "we want to know whether being afraid and anxious causes people to seek each other's company." Instead, he deliberately misled participants into believing that the study concerned the physiological effects of electric shock. In the correlational study of secure and avoidant women, the researchers did not tell the women that they were being videotaped to see whether they sought support more when they acted more afraid.

Why, you might ask, did the investigators in these research projects not simply ask people how they would react? Why not ask women whether they would be more likely to seek company if they were anxious or afraid. Why not ask men whether they would be more likely to have romantic thoughts if they met a woman in a scary place. Why not ask women whether they would sit farther from their dating partners when they were afraid? For some of these questions, the answer is obvious: People are unlikely to admit to thoughts, feelings, and behaviors that make them look bad. Women might think that avoiding the company of other women is antisocial. Men might not want to admit lusting after a female experimenter. Women might not want to admit that they avoided their romantic partners when they were under stress. One reason for not simply asking people what social psychologists want to know, then, is that people, unlike the physical objects studied by chemists, physicists, and other nonpsychologists, want to make a favorable impression on the investigators.

The other reason for not simply asking people what social psychologists want to know is less obvious, but it presents every bit as thorny a research problem. Suppose that people did not misrepresent their thoughts, feelings, and behaviors to make a favorable impression. Suppose that participants in social psychology research projects wanted to tell the whole truth and nothing but the truth. It might still be futile to ask them how they would behave given this or that circumstance, because in many cases *they do not know!* An extensive program of research has shown that people are unaware of having been influenced by factors that actually affect their behavior. Also, people think they would be affected by factors that in fact have no impact.

Two social psychologists conducted a field study to test whether people are always aware of the true causes of their behavior. They staged a "consumer

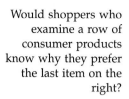

Would shoppers who examine a row of consumer products know why they prefer the last item on the right?

survey" in department stores and other commercial establishments (Nisbett & Wilson, 1977). When shoppers passed by, an investigator asked them to examine and evaluate some items of clothing (either four nightgowns or four pairs of nylon stockings). As is customary in carefully conducted studies, the investigators varied which nightgown or which pair of stockings was in the first, second, third, and fourth position from the left in their display. Nonetheless, shoppers preferred by a wide margin whichever item the investigators placed at the extreme right, perhaps because most people examine items from left to right.

The investigators proved, beyond any reasonable doubt, that item position influenced the shoppers' evaluations. But were the shoppers themselves aware that an item's position affected their evaluations? No, they were not. The investigators asked the shoppers to explain why they preferred one item of clothing. The shoppers typically cited various advantages of one item over another, even though the items were actually identical. Not one shopper ever mentioned the position of the items. When the investigators asked specifically about the possible influence of item position, shoppers denied that they had been influenced. They also started to worry about the investigator's sanity. They usually looked at the investigator with a worried glance, "suggesting that they felt either that they had misunderstood the question or were dealing with a madman" (Nisbett & Wilson, 1977, p. 244).

In everyday life, the order in which people examine alternatives affects their preferences. Used car dealers and real estate agents, for instance, may show unsuspecting buyers a couple of duds before they take them to the one vehicle or house that they really have in mind. The old salesperson's trick would not work unless their customers did not realize that they might be swayed by order effects. In many research studies as well, the investigators asked participants directly about factors that the investigators knew had an effect. The participants, however, were unaware of factors that actually influenced their behavior. These factors were as diverse as the investigator's attitude toward participants, social pressure on participants to misrepresent their attitudes, taking pills that had an unexpected effect, and the presence versus absence of other people (Bem & McConnell, 1970; Latané & Darley, 1970; Storms & Nisbett, 1970; Zimbardo, Cohen, Weisenberg, Dworkin, & Firestone, 1969).

Would it spoil your enjoyment of a movie if someone was using a loud power saw that could be heard plainly inside the theater?

Besides being unaware of many factors that influence their behavior, research participants often falsely believe they *were* influenced by factors that had no effect on their behavior. In a representative experiment, introductory psychology students watched a documentary movie on the plight of the Jewish poor in large cities (Nisbett & Wilson, 1977). Some of the students got to watch the movie without distractions. For other students a "workman" operated a loud power saw just outside the room in the hallway. After they watched the film, the investigators asked both groups of students how interesting the movie had been, how much they thought other people would be moved by it, and how much sympathy they had for the main character.

After the students made these ratings, the investigator apologized for the loud noise in the hallway. The investigator also asked students in the noise condition whether they would have found the movie more interesting, more moving, and more sympathy-arousing had the power saw, with its high-pitched metallic whine, not been operating. Fifty-seven percent of the noise students said that the irritating noise had kept them from enjoying the movie as much as they would have had the power saw not been distracting them. They claimed that their ratings had been affected and that they would have rated the movie higher on all three questions had they not been subjected to the power saw noise. When investigators compared the noise students' ratings to ratings by students who watched the movie without distraction, however, there were no differences. Students in the noise condition claimed to have been influenced by a factor that actually had no impact on their evaluations.

Many investigators have discovered that, when they are asked why they behaved as they did, participants in social psychology experiments provide plausible reasons. In some experiments, the participants' reasons are plausible and valid. Participants know whether they were influenced, and by what factors. In all too many other experiments, however, the plausible or common-sense reasons are incorrect. Even though participants confidently provide plausible reasons for their behavior, they are often mistaken about the true influences (Wilson & Brekke, 1994). Investigators can never be certain before they conduct a study whether the effect is one for which participants are capable of providing accurate reasons for their behavior. They also cannot be sure that participants know how they would have behaved had the situation been different. As a result, social psychologists cannot rely on introspective reports of the factors that do and do not influence people's thoughts, feelings, and behaviors.

■ EXPERIMENTAL DEMAND

Besides the problem of participants lacking awareness, social psychologists have to cope with the even thornier problem of experimental demand. **Experimental demand** occurs when the experiment or study is constructed in such a way that the experimenter or the procedure virtually demands that participants behave in the predicted way (Orne, 1962). To understand experimental demand, consider the case of Clever Hans (Pfungst, 1911). In the early 1900s, a Mr. von Osten, who taught mathematics in Germany, tried to teach mathematics to his horse, whose name was Hans. After working with the horse for a while, von Osten discovered that he had an exceptionally smart horse. Hans quickly developed the ability to add, subtract, multiply, and divide even difficult sets of numbers by tapping his front foot a certain number of times, until he reached the correct answer. When asked to find the square root of 25, for example, Hans would tap his foot precisely five times and then stop, looking at van Osten for the expected reward.

Mr. van Osten was amazed that he had been so successful in teaching mathematics to a horse. He contacted professors at the local university. The professors said, "Yes, yes, animals can be trained to perform parlor tricks, but can Hans still answer mathematics questions when you, Mr. van Osten, are out of the room?" Van Osten left the room, the professors posed a few mathematics problems, and Hans answered them all perfectly!

The professors soon discovered, however, that Hans was not so clever at mathematics after all. When Hans could not see the person who was asking,

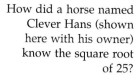

How did a horse named Clever Hans (shown here with his owner) know the square root of 25?

Hans could not answer even questions as simple as "What is two plus two?" Hans also could not answer questions for which the questioner did not know the answer. In reality, Hans was not so clever at mathematics, but he was extremely clever at "reading" the body language of his questioners. When people asked Hans a question, they typically leaned forward slightly to watch his foot. When the number of foot taps got near the correct answer, the questioner would start to straighten up. When the correct answer had been reached, the questioner would look up at the horse. Hans stopped tapping his foot and got the expected reward. Even when the questioner was careful to stand perfectly still, Hans would stop when he saw a slight lift of the questioner's head, a twitch of the questioner's eyebrows, or even a slight dilation of the questioner's nostrils. Hans had many ways of arriving at the correct answer, as long as the questioner knew the answer and expected Hans to produce that answer.

The implications of the Clever Hans episode for the scientific study of social psychology are frightening. Suppose that investigators were to tipoff the participants in their studies about what they (the investigators) believed was going to happen. Suppose the investigators unintentionally conveyed their expectancies to participants, even when the investigators were not trying to bias the results. Suppose Dr. Zilstein treated the women differently not only when he led them to believe that they were going to get painful as opposed to mild shocks (the independent variable), but also when he asked them whether they wanted to wait alone or in company (the dependent variable). Suppose, to push the problem to an extreme, Dr. Zilstein asked women in the painful shock condition, "You'd rather wait with other people than alone, wouldn't you?" Suppose also that the woman experimenter in the scary bridge study came on blatantly to the men she met on the scary bridge, but glared coldly at the men she met on the safe bridge. These examples are outrageous, but suppose people are as clever as horses at detecting minute nonverbal cues. A science of social psychology would be impossible if participants in research efforts acted like Clever Hans. It would be impossible if participants simply did and said what the investigator expected or subtly demanded.

Do we have any evidence that experimental demand might pose a significant threat to the integrity of social psychology research? Yes, we do. In one study of experimental demand, the primary investigator cut photographs from a weekly news magazine and mounted the photographs on index cards (Rosenthal, 1966). The primary investigator had students rate the photographs on how much success they thought the person in each photograph had been experiencing. From the photographs, the primary investigator selected ten that were consistently rated as neither successful-looking nor unsuccessful-looking. The primary investigator next gave these ten photographs to seven undergraduate psychology majors and three psychology graduate students, all of whom knew nothing about the earlier ratings. The investigator asked each participant to conduct interviews in which they got other students to rate the photographs on how successful or unsuccessful the person looked. Five of the student investigators were told that they were merely replicating a "well-established" finding that the people in the photographs looked moderately successful. The other five student investigators were given exactly the same photographs, except they were told that they were replicating the "well-established" finding that the people in the photographs looked moderately *un*successful. The primary investigator cautioned all student investigators to do nothing but read the written instructions to the people that they interviewed and to say nothing else except "hello" and "goodbye." Each student investigator interviewed from 18 to 24 other students.

Every student investigator who expected to get relatively successful ratings got higher (more successful) ratings from interviewees than did any of the student investigators who expected to get relatively unsuccessful ratings. In other words, the student investigators' expectations about what they would find produced significant differences in the results that they obtained, even though all student investigators were working with exactly the same photographs. Subsequent studies replicated this result. These studies showed that the effect did not occur because the student investigators were reporting interviewees' responses inaccurately (Rosenthal, 1966). The students tried their utmost to play the part of dispassionate and objective scientists. Nonetheless, the people that they interviewed, like Clever Hans, gave them the answers that the student investigators expected to hear.

Similar evidence for experimental demand emerged from a study of animal learning (Rosenthal & Fode, 1963). The primary investigator told the student investigators that they were merely replicating a well-established finding that "maze-bright" rats learn to negotiate a maze faster than do "maze-dull" rats. The primary investigator explained to the students that he had bred separate strains of rats to be smart or stupid when it came to learning to negotiate a maze. Although the students did not realize it, the investigator told half of them that they were working with maze-bright rats. He told the other half that they were working with maze-dull rats. In reality, they were all working with rats randomly selected from litters that were as genetically equivalent as possible.

Each student investigator had to place rats at the start of a runway that had a turn to the left and a turn to the right. According to a prearranged schedule, the student investigator varied the hue of the paths that led to the left and to the right. Sometimes the left path was dark and the right path light; sometimes the hues were reversed. The students always rewarded rats for going down the dark path, regardless of whether the dark path was placed to the left or to the right. Figure 1.4 shows how well the "maze-bright" and "maze-dull" rats learned the maze. The figure displays the average number of trials on which student investigators' rats chose the correct path on five consecutive days of training. As the figure shows, maze-bright rats did better than maze-dull rats on the first and every other day. Maze-bright rats also improved more than did maze-dull rats across time.

The student investigators who conducted the maze-learning study, like the student investigators who conducted the "successful photographs" study, did not realize that they treated their subjects differently, but they did. The professors eventually discovered Clever Hans' trick not by watching the horse, but

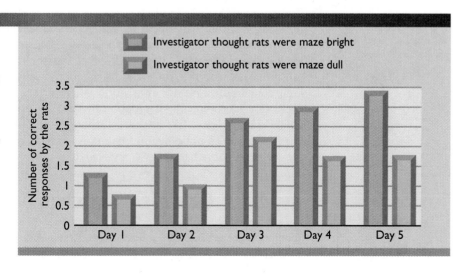

FIGURE 1.4

Investigators' expectancies influenced learning by albino rats.
Graph shows mean number of correct responses by rats the investigators erroneously believed were "maze bright" and "maze dull" (Rosenthal, 1966).

by watching the questioners. Similarly, researchers eventually discovered how participants confirm investigators' expectations not by watching the participants, but by watching the investigators. Investigators, whether students or experienced professionals, may not mean to, but they unwittingly act more friendly toward participants who behave in the expected way. They also handle "bright" rats more affectionately than they handle "dull" rats.

Novice investigators and research participants are no different from anyone else. They frequently behave according to other people's expectations. College women are more animated when they are talking to men who expect them to be animated (Snyder, Tanke, & Berscheid, 1977). Job applicants behave more competently when their interviewer expects them to be sharp (Word, Zanna, & Cooper, 1974). Schoolchildren learn more when their teachers expect them to be bright (Rosenthal & Jacobsen, 1968). When the participants in social psychology studies behave according to the investigators' expectations, however, the validity of the results and important practical applications may be called into question.

Social psychologists know about these problems with participants altering their behavior to make a favorable impression and doing what they think the experimenter wants them to do (Sigall, Aronson, & Van Hoose, 1970). As a result, they employ very strict safeguards against getting misleading results. One of the safeguards is to keep individual experimenters "blind" to the experimental hypothesis. In a representative study, the researchers tried to show that participants who were made to feel insecure would have lower self-esteem than would participants who were made to feel secure (Swann & Predmore, 1985). The primary investigators had one experimenter deliver the independent variable manipulation by making participants feel secure or insecure. Then they sent participants to a second room, where a second experimenter recorded the dependent variable–answers on a self-esteem scale. The second experimenter did not know which manipulation the participant had received. The second experimenter, therefore, could not possibly, even without meaning to, influence the participant to behave in line with the primary investigators' predictions.

The other major weapon against invalid results is to keep the participants themselves blind to the experimental hypothesis. We know that horses can use such subtle cues as eyebrow twitches and nostril dilation to detect what they are expected to do. Human beings who know what is being studied might, either consciously or unconsciously, perform as they think they are *expected* to perform. Even if the experiment involves several stages, each conducted by an experimenter who is blind both to what happens in the other stages and to the primary investigator's predictions, bias can occur. Student participants who figure out the primary investigator's predictions are very likely to fulfill those predictions rather than to behave spontaneously (Carlsmith, Ellsworth, & Aronson, 1976; Rosenthal, 1966). If they do, neither the investigator nor policymakers who rely on social psychology results will have a valid basis for their conclusions. We live in a world where errors in person perception or in predicting the behavior of groups can have disastrous interpersonal or even global consequences. We cannot afford to act on the results of studies in which participants were not behaving naturally, but rather doing what they thought they were supposed to do.

ETHICAL CONSIDERATIONS

If social psychologists must keep research participants in the dark during the experimental procedure, however, then they must also cope with serious ethical considerations. Does the knowledge we might gain from the research justify the procedures that we have to use? Do the procedures place participants at any risk of physical or psychological harm? If knowledge is withheld from research participants, how can we adequately safeguard the participants' rights?

One safeguard against unethical research is that the people who participate in research must do so with informed consent. The principle of **informed consent** is that research participants must be told in advance as much as possible of what will happen to them. The investigator must tell them, for instance, that they are free to withdraw their participation at any time without penalty. The investigator must also tell them that their participation is voluntary. The investigator must assure them that their responses will be confidential and known only to the experimenters. The investigator must also assure them that any records of their participation will be kept confidential—in a secure place, available only to the experimenters, with names removed and code numbers substituted. The investigator must assure them that no individual names will ever be used in any published report. The investigator must also provide participants with the researchers' names and phone numbers, as well as the names and phone numbers of other responsible authorities to contact for answers to their questions.

Also, investigators must keep participants *fully* informed once the experiment has ended. Investigators who are forced by concerns for scientific validity to deceive participants about the true purpose of the procedure have an ethical obligation to justify their actions. Deception is unethical unless the benefits to be gained from deception outweigh the costs. We all sometimes refrain from telling the truth when doing so would hurt another person's feelings. Keeping research participants in the dark just long enough to record their reactions is not an unusual violation of the ordinary rules of social interaction. Justifiable deception is often more moral than telling the truth.

But to whom must investigators justify their keeping participants in the dark or deliberately misleading them? To whom must the investigators in the scary bridge study, the Dr. Zilstein laboratory experiment on the relationship between anxiety and affiliation, the correlational study about secure and avoidant women, and other social psychology studies justify their procedures? One answer is that investigators must justify their procedures to other investigators and review committees that oversee the ethics of research conducted on both human beings and animals (Rosnow, Rotheram-Borus, Ceci, Blanck, & Koocher, 1993). Far more important, however, is that investigators in social psychology must justify their procedures to the *participants*.

To justify their actions to participants, investigators end their experiments with a thorough debriefing. A properly conducted **debriefing** consists of explaining to participants both the actual hypothesis and the reason, if scientifically necessary, for withholding or misstating the purpose of the procedure. In a properly conducted debriefing, the investigator has a responsibility to convince participants that they were deceived for compelling reasons. The investigator must convince participants that the research hypothesis had important implications. The investigator must also convince them that there was no other way short of deception to obtain accurate information about people's thoughts, feelings, and behavior. A responsible investigator would not say, for example, "We tricked you. We made you think that you were going to receive painful electric shocks because we thought that if you were afraid and anxious, you would be more likely to want company. There are no shocks. Thanks for participating."

Instead, a responsible investigator might say, "It's vitally important for understanding social relationships to know the conditions under which people want to be with each other and the conditions under which they want to be alone. We thought that being anxious or afraid might make people seek each other's company. How would you test that hypothesis? At first, you might think that you could simply ask people, but suppose they are motivated to give you a socially acceptable answer or the answer that they think you want to hear? Merely asking them wouldn't prove anything. Another possibility might be to have people pretend that they are going to experience pain, but pretending isn't the same as actually becoming anxious. If you had serious questions about people's preference for company versus solitude when they are anxious, the only way you could get meaningful answers would be to convince people that they actually *were* going to have a frightening experience, such as receiving electric shocks. If you wanted to get answers that would address the human condition, answers that would genuinely enhance our understanding of inter-personal relationships, you would be forced, however reluctantly, to misstate the facts. You would be forced to put participants in a *temporary* state of anxi-ety. That's what we had to do in order to conduct our study. We hope you agree that we had no recourse. We had to tell you that there would be electric shocks even though we knew that, of course, no one would receive any shocks. We had to choose between this temporary deception and letting an important question about people's thoughts, feelings, and behavior go unanswered. Do you understand the necessity for telling you that you would receive shocks? We want to be sure, before you leave, that you understand why we had to mis-state the facts. We want to be sure that you leave the experiment feeling no more anxious (and perhaps more knowledgeable) than when you arrived." The usual debriefing is more thorough than this brief summary, but the summary conveys some of the important aspects of the experimental experience that the investigator must address in an ethical debriefing.

Responsible experimenters, including the investigators whose work is dis-cussed throughout the textbook, are ethical people. They deceive participants only when the questions to be answered are important and when they have considered and found scientifically invalid every procedure that does not in-volve deception. Responsible experimenters also try to make participating in social psychology experiments an educational experience that leaves the par-ticipant psychologically and emotionally richer rather than poorer. Researchers who study the impact of erroneous information on participants' self-esteem, for instance, explain very thoroughly during debriefing the thought processes that might contribute to temporarily lowered self-esteem (Ross, Lepper, & Hub-bard, 1975). Researchers who study the effects of positive and negative moods take care to provide participants in the negative mood condition with an up-lifting experience before they leave (Clark & Isen, 1982). Researchers who study men's reactions to pornography are careful to explain how pornography creates erroneous impressions of women (Donnerstein & Berkowitz, 1981). Such care is routine in studies that involve every important aspect of social thoughts, feelings, and behavior. The goal of social psychology is to treat research par-ticipants with such respect and consideration that we enhance recruitment and collect scientific evidence that is important and meaningful (Blanck, Bellack, Rosnow, Rotheram-Borus, & Schooler, 1992).

It is impossible in describing every study in the textbook to explain in de-tail the scientific necessity for withholding or misstating information. It is im-possible to describe the precise debriefing procedures that the investigators fol-lowed to ensure that participants left the study better off, or at least no worse off, than when they entered. Nonetheless, you may be sure that studies of so-cial psychology involve serious consideration of alternatives to deception. Also, where it is impossible to obtain scientifically valid results without deception, studies of social psychology include a detailed and ethically responsible de-briefing.

Researchers in social psychology tend to be very aware of these ethical considerations and very cautious in protecting the rights and interests of participants. As a group, they are ingenious in addressing important questions (such as those shown in Tables 1.1 and 1.2) in ethically responsible ways. As the other chapters of this book describe, social psychologists continue to make important discoveries. These discoveries can help society to cope with pressing problems in business, law, health, the family, the environment, and other extremely important everyday concerns.

SUMMARY OF PROBLEMS IN STUDYING SOCIAL PSYCHOLOGY

Social psychologists cannot get valid answers to important research questions simply by asking people how they might behave in various circumstances. Even in cases where people are not trying to look good by giving false answers, they often do not know which factors affect their behavior and which do not. When asked why they behave as they do, people provide plausible answers, but plausible or commonsense answers are all too often inaccurate.

Social psychologists must also beware of letting their assumptions and expectations influence the behavior of research participants. Not only do investigators give away their expectations through subtle cues of which they are themselves unaware, but participants "read" those cues and then do whatever they think they are expected to do.

One safeguard against the dangers of experimental demand is for the investigator who measures the dependent variable to be kept unaware of either the manipulation that each participant received or the hypothesis. Another safeguard against participants guessing the hypothesis and behaving as they think they are expected to behave is to withhold or misstate the facts of the experimental procedure.

When investigators must deceive participants to maintain the scientific integrity of their research, however, they have an ethical obligation to convince participants that the gains of deception outweigh the costs. Ethical investigators also take care that participants leave the experimental setting better off, or at least no worse off, than when they entered.

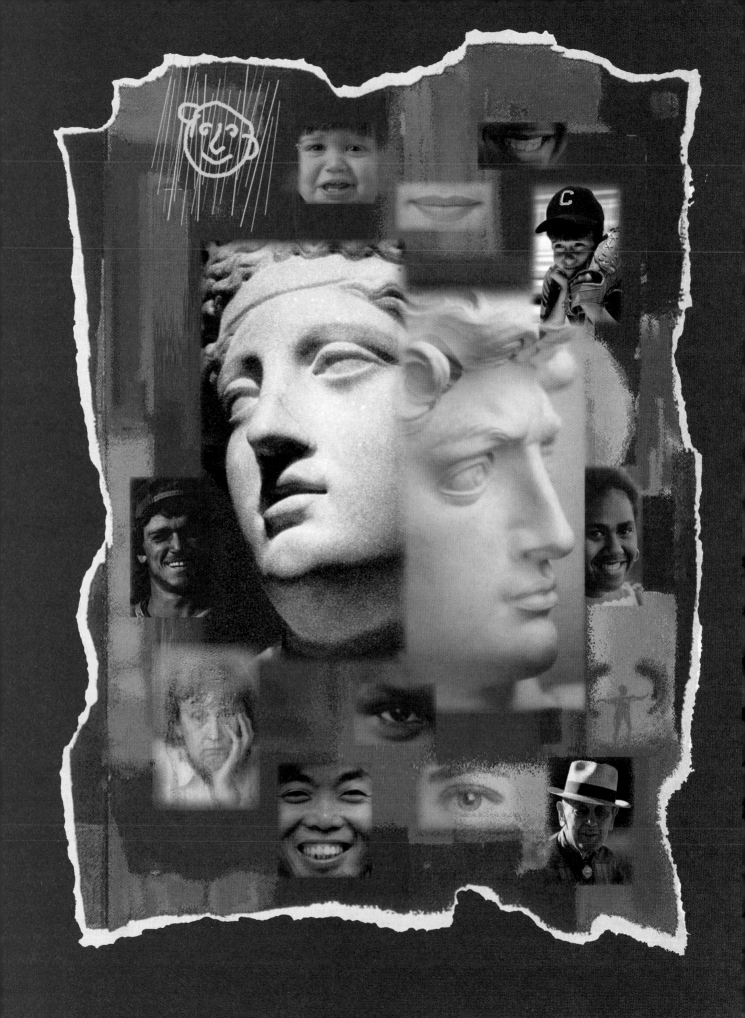

PART I

Thinking About the Self and Others

CHAPTER 2

Social Cognition

Imagine being a juror in a rape trial where attorneys present the following evidence. Sally, a 20-year-old college student, was walking to her car at approximately 8:00 P.M. As she entered the parking lot, she noticed a stranger sitting on a motorcycle. The stranger looked up at her as she passed and said, "Would you like to go for a ride on my motorcycle?" Sally politely declined his offer and continued walking toward her car. The stranger got off his motorcycle, grabbed her by the arm, and started pushing her toward a dark alley. As she was being shoved into the alley, Sally swore at the man and screamed, "Let me go. How dare you? Who do you think you are!" When the man tried to push her to the ground, Sally lashed out and kicked him in the groin. She continued to swear at him and to struggle violently, but he raped her.

Assume that the prosecution presented such conclusive evidence that Sally's attacker were found guilty of rape. How severe a sentence should he get? Does it help or hurt the prosecution's case that Sally swore, kicked, and fought so violently? Most people believe that the more a rape victim resists, the more clearly the attacker's action is defined as rape and the more severely the attacker will be punished. That "most people believe" a proposition, however, is not proof. To discover the actual relationship between a rape victim's resistance and her attacker's assumed guilt and punishment, two social psychologists had college students read one of four different trial transcripts (Branscombe & Weir, 1992). In some of the transcripts, Sally's *verbal* resistance was low. She said only "Please let me go" and "Please don't hurt me." In other transcripts, Sally's *verbal* resistance was high. She cursed and screamed at her attacker. Within each of these conditions, some students learned that Sally's *physical* resistance was low. She went limp. Other students learned that, as described, Sally's *physical* resistance was high. She kicked and struggled. Except for the sentences about Sally's verbal and physical resistance, the four transcripts were otherwise identical.

Would a woman kick this man in the groin if he tried to rape her?

Figure 2.1 shows how severely student "jurors" in each of the four conditions wanted to punish Sally's attacker. As the graph shows, students who learned that Sally offered very little verbal or physical resistance did not want to punish her attacker as severely as did students who learned that she offered a medium amount of resistance, either by cursing and yelling while going limp or by saying little while punching and kicking. Surprisingly, students who learned that Sally offered *both* high verbal resistance and high physical resistance wanted to punish her attacker *less* than did students who learned that she offered a medium amount of resistance. They were also less convinced that Sally's attacker was guilty.

The results are disturbing. Apparently, if women who are attacked want their attackers to be found guilty and to be punished, they have to walk a very fine line between resisting too little and resisting too much! How could students who served as mock jurors in the study have reached such an unfair conclusion? "What's wrong with them?" many people who read about the study ask. "What could they possibly be thinking?"

This chapter describes what people "could possibly be thinking" when they think about other people. Dictionaries define "cognition" as "the process by which knowledge is acquired." Although the topic of "social cognition" covers such a broad range of research that no short definition is adequate (Ostrom, 1994), in this chapter we use the terms "social cognition" and "social thinking" interchangeably to mean the process by which people acquire and use knowledge about each other. Technically speaking, social cognition includes thoughts about both other people and oneself, as well as social and linguistic influences on those thoughts (Hardin & Banaji, 1993; Ickes & Gonzalez, 1994; Lavine, Borgida, & Rudman, 1994). Most of the research on self-relevant thoughts is described in Chapter 5.

A "social cognition" interpretation of the results in Figure 2.1 holds that the student jurors had set ideas about how women are supposed to act and the amount of resistance that the victim offers in a "typical" rape (Branscombe & Weir, 1992). When Sally swore and fought, she violated those expectations. In trying to form impressions of Sally and her attacker, student jurors had to reconcile Sally's actions with what they expected. In doing so, the student jurors constructed imaginary scenarios in which, had she not resisted so violently, Sally's attacker might not have continued with the rape. Women students who

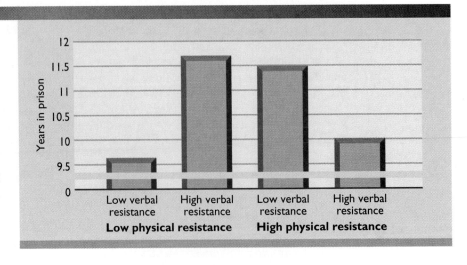

FIGURE 2.1

Juries give less severe sentences to rapists when victims violate expectations.

Graph shows number of years in prison student jurors gave to a rapist whose victim offered high or low verbal and physical resistance (Branscombe & Weir, 1992).

participated in the study said they thought that Sally's forceful verbal and physical resistance might have "turned the man on" and got him all the more excited. Male participants, in contrast, believed that the rapist was most excited when Sally offered little resistance, when she said only "Please don't hurt me" and went limp. Both male and female participants agreed, however, that when Sally acted in what they termed an "exciting" way, she was partially responsible for her own rape! If Sally's behavior excited the attacker, then jurors thought he was less guilty and deserved less punishment.

The rest of the chapter will help you to understand the social cognition interpretation of these and other results more in depth. The chapter has three sections. The first section describes how social thinking works, which is usually very well. The second section suggests that the very strengths of social thinking may, in certain circumstances, render social thinking less than accurate. The third section asks what success people have in controlling their own thoughts.

HOW DOES SOCIAL THINKING WORK?

Social thinking usually works very well. People pay attention to the most rather than to the least important aspects of their environment, think about other people in an organized way, and integrate seemingly inconsistent facts appropriately. They remember what they need to remember, draw accurate conclusions, and make reasonable and adaptive behavioral decisions. This first section of the chapter describes a "recipe" for how social thinking operates. It also describes two important aspects of the recipe–the use of heuristics and mental models.

A "RECIPE" FOR SOCIAL THINKING

One of the major themes in social psychology, described in Chapter 1, is that people have both spontaneous and deliberative reactions (Brewer, 1988; Fazio, 1990; Fiske & Neuberg, 1990; Gilbert & Malone, 1995; Smith, 1994). Sometimes they react to people and events spontaneously or "off the top of the head." They assume, for instance, that experts *must* be right or that exotic foods *must* taste bad, without taking the time or making the effort to gather additional information. At other times, they react to people and events more deliberatively, refusing to fall back on old habits or top-of-the-head assumptions, but instead engaging in a more elaborate, in-depth analysis. These two types of reaction are especially noticeable in social thinking, which occurs in *two stages*. The spontaneous stage of social thinking involves greater *automaticity* than does the deliberative stage. Also, certain *operating principles* predispose social thinking toward spontaneous rather than deliberative reactions.

■ TWO STAGES

A "process" is a continuing development that involves many steps, operations, and changes. Baking a cake, for example, is a process. You assemble the ingredients, use them according to the directions, and then serve them as a finished product. The finished product may not resemble any of the individual ingredients, because you "processed" those ingredients. Similarly, social cognition involves a process. You take the pieces of information that you learn about a person or social event and use those pieces of information to produce an impression, conclusion, decision, or intention. Your impression, conclusion, decision, or intention may not resemble any of the individual pieces of information, because you "processed" those pieces of information. Models of social thinking are called "information processing models" because they describe the types of "ingredients" and the steps or operations by which people acquire and use information and knowledge about each other. Psychologists who study social cognition want to develop a workable model or "recipe" that describes the steps and operations that people use to get from the individual pieces of information to their impressions, conclusions, decisions, and intentions.

Most recipes for information processing involve two stages that correspond roughly with spontaneous and deliberative reactions. Table 2.1 lists the components of each stage (Wyer & Srull, 1986). A good way to understand the components is to consider how jurors in the rape case at the beginning of this chapter might have processed information, facts, and evidence to arrive at their decision.

SPONTANEOUS STAGE During the spontaneous stage of information processing, as shown in Table 2.1, people take in pieces of information or *raw sensations* such as sights, sounds, words, and sentences. Jurors in the rape trial, for instance, read sentences such as "Sally was walking to her car," "A stranger offered her a ride on his motorcycle," "Sally refused," "He pushed her in an alley," and "Sally kicked him in the groin." The words and sentences were the raw sensations with which jurors started to process information about Sally and her attacker. People who speak English have an immediate, spontaneous *initial comprehension* of such words. They know, without giving the matter much

TABLE 2.1	A "Recipe" for Information Processing in Social Thinking (Abstracted from Wyer & Srull, 1986)
SPONTANEOUS STAGE	
TAKE	raw sensations (pieces of information)
ADD	initial comprehension
ORGANIZE	by whatever categories are handy
INTEGRATE	with whatever you happened to be thinking about at the time
GENERATE	original thoughts, which are organized and integrated with the initial pieces of information

Do all these operations as quickly and "automatically" as possible.
If you are willing and able, proceed to the deliberative stage.
If not, serve immediately as your final impression, conclusion, decision, or intention.

DELIBERATIVE STAGE	
USING	your current goals
APPLY	general world knowledge
APPLY	goal knowledge
APPLY	person, group, and event knowledge

Spend as much time as you want and can afford on each of these operations.
Serve the finished product as your final impression, conclusion, decision, or intention.

thought, what the words mean. They also spontaneously *organize* and categorize the people and events involved. They "know" without conscious deliberation that Sally was probably female, that the stranger on the motorcycle was probably a man, and that the situation was probably dangerous for Sally. As the "recipe" in Table 2.1 shows, they also spontaneously *integrate* the organized information with whatever they happened to be thinking about at the time. The spontaneous stage, that is, might be different if a juror had recently been thinking about Batman rather than about Charles Manson. Finally, people spontaneously *generate* new thoughts of their own and mix those thoughts with the pieces of information. A juror, for instance, might spontaneously wonder, "What if Sally hadn't kicked him?" and treat the self-generated answer to this question as an additional piece of information to be organized and integrated with the rest.

As the "recipe" in Table 2.1 also shows, the spontaneous stage of information processing occurs very quickly and "automatically." Furthermore, information processing sometimes stops after the spontaneous stage. People sometimes add, organize, integrate, and generate in a split second to reach a quick, easy impression, conclusion, decision, or intention. If the topic is not important to them—for instance, if they do not know Sally and have what they consider more pressing concerns to think about—they do not continue. They are content to rely on their initial, spontaneous reactions, which are usually just as valid (and sometimes more valid) than the reactions they would have if they spent more time and effort to deliberate (Wilson & Brekke, 1994). Because the spontaneous stage of information processing is usually sufficient, people go on to the deliberative stage only when they are both willing and able to do so. If Sally was their best friend, for instance, they would not settle for an impression, conclusion, decision, or intention that they had reached merely in the spontaneous stage. Instead, they would enter the deliberative stage.

DELIBERATIVE STAGE   During the deliberative stage, people pursue their *current goals*. Suppose, for instance, that jurors had the goal of trying to understand why the man pushed Sally or why she kicked him. They would pursue their goal by applying three types of existing knowledge to their initial reaction from the spontaneous stage. *General world knowledge* is what you already know about how the world works. You probably did not need to read far into the story at the start of this chapter before you realized that Sally was in a dangerous situation. Once you learned that a stranger offered Sally a ride on his motorcycle when she was alone at night, you probably recognized that Sally was in danger. No one had to say so explicitly. *Goal knowledge* is what you already know about the goals that people have and what they typically do to pursue those goals. You probably knew what the strange man's goal was when he started pushing Sally toward a dark alley. You know what potential robbers do, what potential rapists do, and some subtle ways in which the two goals differ. *Person, group, and event knowledge* is what you already know about a specific person, a group of people, or typical events. You may already know that Sally is very aggressive, which would help you to understand why she kicked the man in the groin. You may already know (or think you know) that men who ride motorcycles tend to treat women like sex objects. You may already know (or think you know) that the victim in a typical rape does not hurl swear words at her attacker or kick him in the groin. In the deliberative stage of information processing, as the "recipe" in Table 2.1 shows, you apply these three types of existing knowledge in an in-depth analysis of the topic.

Sometimes the in-depth analysis merely confirms the initial impression, conclusion, decision, or intention that you had reached spontaneously. At other

Calvin and Hobbes

by Bill Watterson

times, the in-depth analysis requires that you "adjust" or alter your initial impression, conclusion, decision, or intention. Jurors, for instance, are often told to disregard inadmissible evidence. The judge instructs them to use the deliberative stage of information processing to pursue the current goal of applying general world knowledge about when evidence "does not count." The jurors are supposed to use the deliberative stage to adjust whatever conclusions they may have reached during the spontaneous stage when they first heard the evidence. As the two-stage "recipe" suggests, however, they cannot make the adjustment. Because they are distracted, they cannot use the deliberative stage of social thinking.

In a relevant study, college women read descriptions of two crimes (Gilbert, Tafarodi, & Malone, 1993). One crime was that Kevin robbed a convenience store. The other was that Tom robbed a stranger who gave him a ride. The crime descriptions appeared on a computer screen in black letters. Interspersed between the sentences in black were other sentences in red. The women were told, much as jurors are told to ignore inadmissible evidence, that the sentences in red were *false* and should be ignored. Had the sentences in red been true, they would have provided additional evidence in favor of one defendant and additional evidence against the other defendant. The investigators gave some of the women an additional task. The women had to count the number of times that the digit "5" appeared in various locations on the screen while they were trying to read the case descriptions. This task made it difficult for the women to use the deliberative stage of information processing. The investigators told other women to ignore the digits. These women *could* use the deliberative stage.

After reading both crime descriptions, the women recommended how many years in prison each defendant should receive. As predicted, women who were not distracted gave the defendants approximately equal prison terms regardless of what the admittedly false statements said. Women who had to count 5's did not. They gave longer prison terms to a defendant when admittedly false statements *added* to his guilt than when admittedly false statements *subtracted* from his guilt. They could not ignore admittedly false statements, even though their task was easier than that faced by jurors in actual trials. Such jurors are not *warned in advance* that some statements will be false.

The outcome of information processing, then, may be different depending on whether it was based predominantly on the spontaneous stage or predominantly on the deliberative stage. The spontaneous stage, however, has an advantage because it occurs more "automatically" than the deliberative stage.

■ AUTOMATICITY

The components of information processing or social thinking are usually not entirely spontaneous (automatic) or entirely deliberative (Berkowitz & Devine, 1995). Instead, they are either more automatic or less automatic, depending on four criteria (Bargh, 1994). To be completely spontaneous and automatic, thinking must be efficient and must occur without intention, control, or awareness.

■ **EFFICIENCY** One way to tell whether a thinking process is "automatic" is to measure how efficient it is–how much it makes thinking easier. Automatic thinking is efficient. Some ways of organizing information become automatic and occur spontaneously because they allow thinking to occur rapidly, without time-consuming deliberation. People process chronically accessible trait constructs (ones they think about all the time), for instance, even when the information comes so fast that they ignore other trait constructs. People who are chronically depressed, for example, notice traits like "sad" and "gloomy" just as fast when they are simultaneously distracted by deliberating about an unrelated topic as when they are not (Bargh & Thien, 1985). Chronically depressed people have so much practice at processing ideas related to depression that they can do it effortlessly, using very few cognitive resources. The advantage is that they can think about depressing topics quickly and easily, regardless of what else is happening. The disadvantage, of course, is that they think about depressing topics almost all the time.

■ **INTENTION** A second way to tell whether a thinking process is "automatic" is to discover whether people do it even when they do not intend to. Automatic thinking occurs unintentionally. We *have* to pay attention to some types of information whether we want to or not. In one study of automatic evaluation, the investigators flashed a word on a screen for such a short time that it was nothing but a raw sensation. The participants did not even know the word was there, much less comprehend it. Nonetheless, they could still tell whether the word was positive or negative (Bargh, Litt, Pratto, & Spielman, 1989). They could not possibly have *intended* to evaluate the word, because they did not know it existed. However, they automatically "registered" at least one aspect of the word's meaning–whether it was "good" or "bad" (Pratto & John, 1991).

Another instance in which social thinking occurs without intention is in spontaneous trait inferences. As described in greater detail in Chapter 3, when people get such information as "Sally swore at the man" or "Sally kicked the man in the groin," they draw inferences about Sally's traits ("Sally is aggressive"). They draw such inferences without conscious intention (Newman, 1991; Newman & Uleman, 1989; Winter & Uleman, 1984; Winter, Uleman, & Cunniff, 1985).

■ **CONTROL** A third way to tell whether a thinking process is "automatic" is to discover whether people can control it. Automatic thinking is difficult to control. When people are strongly motivated to do so, they can *sometimes* bring under control thought processes that usually occur without intention (Sedikides, 1990; Thompson, Roman, Moskowitz, Chaiken, & Bargh, 1994). When they have been deprived of control over previous activities, for example, social thinkers sometimes "fight back" by taking control of otherwise spontaneous thoughts (Pittman & D'Agostino, 1989).

People who do not want to be biased by negative stereotypes (such as stereotypes of men who ride motorcycles) can sometimes control their thought processes. They recognize that they might be prejudiced. Instead, they lean over backwards to be fair (Devine, 1989). Their "control," however, may lack precision and be too much of a good thing. In trying to be fair, they may lean too much in the opposite direction, which is itself a form of prejudice (Bargh, 1994; Martin, Seta, & Crelia, 1990; Strack, 1992). Similarly, people who know that they will be rewarded for accuracy or held accountable for their impressions can, by trying hard enough, bring under conscious control some of the thinking processes that are normally automatic (Fiske & Neuberg, 1990; Fiske & Von Hendy, 1992; Tetlock & Kim, 1987). Nonetheless, as we shall see in the third section of this chapter, control over otherwise "automatic" thoughts is difficult to practice and can produce problems.

AWARENESS A fourth way to tell whether a thinking process is "automatic" is to discover whether people are unaware of doing it. Automatic thinking occurs even when people are not aware that they are doing it. Social thinking can be influenced without the thinker being consciously aware. In one study of how people can be influenced without awareness, the investigators showed college men a photograph of another man. They flashed the photograph on a screen so fast, however, that it was impossible to detect consciously (Bornstein, Leone, & Galley, 1987). (Think of the photograph as a piece of information that got only as far as "raw sensations" and was never comprehended.) Next, the students tried to decide, in groups of three, whether poetry excerpts had been written by men or by women. The other two "group members" were experimental confederates who frequently disagreed. The actual student participant had to break the tie. Unknown to the students, one of the other men was the person whose photograph they had previously "seen." According to research that is discussed in greater detail in Chapter 9, we like familiar people more than we like complete strangers. As predicted, the students took the side of the man they had "seen" more often than the other man, even though they were completely unaware of having "seen" either man before.

A social thinker might also be aware of the information but unaware of its impact. In a relevant study, waitresses in a restaurant touched some customers and not others. They touched some customers lightly on the palm or shoulder while returning change. They also interacted with other patrons just as pleasantly, but without touching them (Crusco & Wetzel, 1984). The patrons were probably aware of being touched, but they were probably not aware that it influenced their decision about how much of a tip to leave. They gave the waitress a larger tip when she touched them. Had they been asked why, they would probably have given a plausible reason such as good service (Schwarz, 1990; Schwarz & Clore, 1983).

Table 2.2 summarizes the four criteria for determining whether social thinking is automatic or not. Efficiency, lack of intention, lack of control, and lack of awareness all operate more in some situations and less in others. A specific social thinking process can meet one, two, three, or all four criteria, each to a different degree. It is difficult, then, to separate the "automatic" or spontaneous stage of social thinking from the deliberative stage. We can only conclude that any specific process occurs in a *relatively* automatic, spontaneous way or in a *relatively* deliberative way.

OPERATING PRINCIPLES

When social thinkers use the "recipe" in Table 2.1, they follow some interesting "operating principles" (Wyer & Srull, 1986). These operating principles include the "cognitive miser" principle, recency, and self-generation.

COGNITIVE MISER Social thinkers follow the "cognitive miser" principle (Fiske & Taylor, 1991). People are said to be cognitive misers because they use only as many of their cognitive resources as they need, and no more.

TABLE 2.2	Four Criteria for Determining Whether Social Thinking Occurs Automatically (Bargh, 1994)

CRITERION	A MEASURE
Efficiency	Can you think about it even when you are distracted by thinking about something else? yes = automatic no = not automatic
Intention	Do you think about it even when you do not intend to? yes = automatic no = not automatic
Control	Can you bring the thought under conscious control? yes = not automatic no = automatic
Awareness	Do you know when you are thinking about it? yes = not automatic no = automatic

We have already seen that new information can quickly and easily be comprehended, organized, and integrated with currently active and self-generated thoughts in the spontaneous stage. People have to be both willing and able to spend precious time and effort before they go on to the deliberative stage and apply their existing knowledge. If we used the deliberative stage for every fleeting sensation that came to our attention, we would never get anything done. We would find ourselves lost in thought. The vast majority of what goes on around us never gets beyond the spontaneous stage, because it would be wasteful to think about it in depth (Smith, 1994).

One consequence of the cognitive miser principle is that some types of knowledge become so "automatic" that they become incorporated into the initial "organizing" activity (Wyer & Srull, 1986). Initial organizing and categorizing can occur without conscious deliberation. If a man rides a motorcycle, he might be classified as "one of those" instantly when information about him becomes available. Immediate classification is very adaptive. It is important to know immediately whether an image of black-and-yellow stripes on the retina represents a pattern of shadows or a voracious tiger. The cognitive miser principle puts considerable categorization "up front" in the system, where it can occur rapidly, without the additional "expense" of deliberation.

■ **RECENCY** A second important principle in the information-processing recipe involves "recency." The more recently people have used a category or a piece of existing knowledge, the more likely they are to use it again (Wyer & Srull, 1986). Only a few thoughts, for example, can be entertained at the same time. When a new thought occurs, you may not "lose" your most recently active thoughts, but you might forget topics that you had been thinking about five or ten minutes ago. Similarly, the most recently used ways of organizing information are most likely to be used again. Sally might be categorized differently depending on whether the juror has most recently been thinking about women or about rape victims. We also apply the three types of existing knowledge (see the deliberative stage of Table 2.1) according to how recently we have been thinking about them.

When it is combined with the cognitive miser principle, the recency principle means that people stop when they find a "good enough" piece of existing knowledge to satisfy their current goals. If they remember a recently publicized rape trial that seems similar enough to Sally's story, they use that trial as a standard of comparison by which to judge Sally's attacker. Had they continued to search their memories, they might have remembered an even more appropriate trial, but instead they stopped when they found one that was close enough. When people reuse their most recent thoughts in processing new information, they usually process the new information efficiently and effectively. Unfortunately, as we shall see in the second and third sections of the chapter, the cognitive efficiency gained by following the recency principle is purchased at the cost of occasional unwanted consequences (Wilson & Brekke, 1994).

SELF-GENERATION A third important operating principle is self-generation. The "generate" part of the spontaneous stage does not depend on raw sensations or new pieces of information (Wyer & Srull, 1986). We generate our own thoughts even when we are sitting alone in a darkened room. We have no raw sensations and nothing to comprehend. Nonetheless, information processing "runs along on its own." It fills our minds with self-generated thoughts that move from one topic to another, sometimes seemingly at random (Martin & Tesser, in press). As we shall see in subsequent sections of the chapter, however, the thoughts that flit in and out of our conscious awareness are not entirely random. They can be biased toward significant topics that have been used recently or that have become "chronic" ways of organizing and integrating.

Another consequence of self-generation is that we might generate scenarios that are mere figments of our imagination. We might imagine that Sally would not have been raped had she resisted less forcefully. We can "picture" the imaginary scene, in which Sally's attacker is deterred by her medium resistance, so vividly that it almost seems real. Such scenarios might be imaginary, but they might also serve as biased standards of comparison. We might, for instance, blame Sally for kicking and cursing at her assailant, even though the "comparison" scenario, in which Sally fought less viciously and avoided rape, is one that we only imagined.

We cannot always distinguish between self-generated thoughts and the information that comes from raw sensations (Johnson, Hashtroudi, & Lindsay, 1993). We cannot always remember whether we locked the door before getting into bed or whether we only imagined doing so. Similarly, we cannot always distinguish between self-generated scenarios or interpretations and the actual content of incoming information. People may be aware of what conclusions they reached, but they are not usually aware of the precise process by which a conclusion or decision was reached. They do not say to themselves: "I first remembered all the relevant facts that I knew about Sally, then I tried to remember the details of other rape trials for comparison, then I imagined ways in which Sally might have avoided being raped, then I gave the most importance to Sally's characteristics, the next most importance to the rape trial . . ." and so on. Except in very unusual circumstances, people have no need to remember details of the social thinking process, only the outcome.

Table 2.3 summarizes the three operating principles by which people process social information. Even though they sometimes introduce some seemingly unusual "quirks" in the process, these three operating principles help social thinking to be both spontaneous and effective. So do certain heuristics and mental models.

TABLE 2.3	Three Principles People Use to Process Social Information (Fiske & Taylor, 1991; Wyer & Srull, 1986).
PRINCIPLE	**"OPERATING INSTRUCTIONS"**
Cognitive Miser	Use only as much cognitive effort as you need to produce a satisfactory result
Recency	Use whatever you have been thinking about recently as an aid in comprehending, organizing, and integrating new information
Self-Generation	"Flesh out" the information that you are given with original thoughts of your own, even if you sometimes forget which is which

HEURISTICS AND MENTAL MODELS

We use some organizing procedures and some parts of our existing knowledge so frequently that they become part of the way new information is spontaneously comprehended and organized. Two such over-learned and relatively automatic aspects of the information processing "recipe" involve heuristics and mental models.

■ HEURISTICS

Heuristics are "rules of thumb" that simplify thinking. These rules of thumb make judgments and inferences easier by stripping away the complexity from persons, objects, and events so that we can quickly understand and act on them. When we have been in a particular type of situation or interacted with a particular type of person often enough, we abstract from these diverse instances a heuristic for dealing with similar situations and persons. We know from experience what we are expected to do at a funeral and that used car dealers exaggerate a car's good points.

By applying an overlearned heuristic to a situation or person, we avoid the difficult and time-consuming process of "starting from scratch." As cognitive misers, we do not have to figure out how to act, as though we had no previous experience. The only risk we take by using heuristics to categorize and interpret a situation or person is that the specific situation or person might differ from the one that the heuristic addresses. An inappropriately applied heuristic might elicit too simple judgments and inappropriate actions. In this section, we discuss four heuristics that are used extensively in social thinking: anchoring and adjustment, availability, representativeness, and simulation.

▒ **ANCHORING AND ADJUSTMENT** The **anchoring and adjustment heuristic** (Kahneman & Tversky, 1973) implies that when making a judgment, people start from an initial "anchor point" and make mental adjustments. The population of Cleveland, Ohio, is approximately 550,000. If we ask one person whether Cleveland's population is more than 100,000 and ask another person whether Cleveland's population is less than 1,000,000, they will both likely say "Yes." When we ask both to estimate Cleveland's population, the person who "starts" from 100,000 might guess 450,000, whereas the person who "starts" from 1,000,000 might guess 650,000. They both rely too much on the "anchor" point and adjust toward the correct answer, but insufficiently.

The anchoring and adjustment heuristic affects conclusions about such important issues as protecting the environment. In a relevant study, some students ranked six environmental issues—air-pollution, garbage disposal, toxic substances in food, energy conservation, the quality of drinking water, and presevation of wildlife—from most to least important. Other students ranked the same six issues, but from least to most important (Schwarz & Wyer, 1985). Later, all students rated the importance of these six and four other environmental issues: noise, mass transit, nuclear waste, and recycling of bottles. Students who had earlier started their rankings from the most important issue deemed all ten environmental issues to be more important than did students who had earlier started their rankings from the least important issue. The starting point, then, can affect people's overall level of concern with issues that are vitally important to our planet.

The anchoring and adjustment heuristic can even affect how likely people judge a nuclear war. In one survey, the investigators asked some respondents whether nuclear war had more than a 1% chance of occurring soon (Plous, 1989). They asked other respondents whether nuclear war had less than a 90% chance of occurring soon. Finally, they asked all respondents to estimate the likelihood of nuclear war occurring soon. Respondents who "started" from the 1 percent "anchor" thought that we had about 1 chance in 10, whereas respondents who "started" from the 90% anchor thought we had about 1 chance in 4 of nuclear war.

Even when people realize that they might have been influenced by an anchor, they do not know how much they ought to adjust. The researchers in one study asked students to estimate how many of 20 anagrams they could solve correctly (Cervone & Peake, 1986). Before they made their estimates, one group of students answered the question "Will you get more than 4 correct?" A second group of students answered the question "Will you get fewer than 18 correct?" The students clearly understood that the numbers 4 and 18 were chosen at random, yet students who "started" from 4 estimated their success as less likely than did students who "started" from 18. They also gave up earlier on trying to complete the anagrams. The anchoring and adjustment heuristic has serious implications for social judgment and action.

AVAILABILITY To illustrate another important heuristic, please read the names in Table 2.4. Return to this place in the text only after you have read all the names in the table.

TABLE 2.4	Famous Names		

Read the following names carefully. Then return to the text for instructions.

Elizabeth Taylor	Alvin Barclay	Queen Elizabeth II	Hillary Clinton
Jackson Pollock	Edward Teller	Agatha Christie	Philip K. Dick
Julia Child	Madonna	Richard Rogers	Barbara Bush
Warren Burger	Margaret Thatcher	Joan of Arc	Richard Helms
Mother Teresa	Daryll Waltrip	Troy Donahue	Paul Simon
Raymond Chandler	Meryl Streep	Millard Fillmore	Nancy Reagan
James Buchanan	Sandra Day O'Connor	Richard Darman	Thurgood Marshall
Jane Fonda	Winnie Mandela	Edmund Hillary	

Now, without looking back at the table, try to recall the list of names and decide whether there were more males or more females. When you have made your best guess, count the male and female names. The answer may surprise you.

The **availability heuristic** suggests that people judge the frequency of an event by how easy it is to bring to mind (Tversky & Kahneman, 1973, 1974). Normally, this heuristic works very well. Events that we have experienced more frequently are easier to imagine than events that we have experienced less frequently. Most people can imagine going to a fast-food restaurant more easily than they can imagine being on a jury, for instance, because most people have been to a fast-food restaurant more times than they have been on jury duty. The easier it is to call a person, object, or event to mind, the more frequently we have come across it and the more frequently it actually occurs in our everyday world. In the list of famous names, most people find it easy to recall names such as Queen Elizabeth II, Agatha Christie, Madonna, Joan of Arc, Mother Teresa, Nancy Reagan, Barbara Bush, Elizabeth Taylor, and Hillary Clinton. As a result, they guess that there are more (or at least as many) women's names. The men, who include two United States presidents and one vice-president, a renowned mystery writer, an actor, two eminent Supreme Court justices, the conqueror of Mount Everest, and the inventor of the H-bomb, are less famous. People find it harder to bring these men's names to mind, so they falsely believe that the list contained fewer men's than women's names.

Because of the "recency" principle in information processing, people can be misled about why events are easy to bring to mind. The recency principle holds that recently active thoughts are relatively easy to bring to mind. Thus the media, by publicizing some types of events more than others, can increase the perceived ease of bringing an event to mind and induce erroneous estimates of frequency. To illustrate, the availability heuristic affects estimates of how frequently people die from various causes. Some forms of death receive more publicity. They are thus easier to call to mind. Respondents in one study guessed that more people die from firearm accidents than from asthma, cancer than from stroke, accidents than from emphysema, and homicides than from floods (Slovic, Fischhoff, & Lichtenstein, 1976). These estimates are all *backwards,* some by as much as 270–1. Similarly, media coverage can convince citizens that drug use in the United States is increasing even at times when it is actually decreasing (Eisenman, 1993). In these examples, the availability heuristic can mislead policymakers into misguided decisions. They might, for instance, spend public funds on research and prevention of problems that are actually infrequent, while they shortchange research and prevention of problems that affect millions.

REPRESENTATIVENESS   Another heuristic that is used frequently in everyday decisions is representativeness (Kahneman & Tversky, 1973; Tversky & Kahneman, 1982). The **representativeness heuristic** suggests that people judge a person, object, or event by how similar it is to what they imagine as the typical representative of its category. They apply the seemingly reasonable rule: "If it looks like a duck, walks like a duck, and quacks like a duck, then it probably *is* a duck." Student jurors in the study that began this chapter, for example, might have reached their sentence recommendations through the representativeness heuristic by comparing Sally's rape to what they perceived as a "typical" rape scenario. When the two scenarios were similar, Sally's rape seemed representative. When the two scenarios were dissimilar, Sally's rape seemed less representative, which introduced doubt about whether it was "really rape" or whether Sally contributed by exciting her attacker.

The representativeness heuristic works well in almost every circumstance, but, like the other heuristics discussed in this section, it can sometimes be misleading (Nisbett & Ross, 1980; Triplet, 1992). Jurors may have distorted ideas about what constitutes a "typical" rape or other crime. Many prospective jurors falsely believe, for example, that the victim of a typical robbery receives physical injury. They may hold such a belief because the media report so many violent muggings. They may also find sensational crime stories easier to remember than robberies in which no physical violence occurred (Stalans, 1993). Many jurors also erroneously believe that the "prototypical" kidnap victim is a child who is held for ransom (Smith, 1991). The legal definition of kidnapping says only that a person must be confined against his or her will. It requires neither a child victim nor a ransom demand. In one study, the investigators asked student jurors to consider court cases in which the evidence was equivalent, except that the crime was either "representative" or not. The "representative" crimes included what the students erroneously believed were typical elements, such as a child victim and a ransom note for a kidnap case (Smith, 1991). The student jurors were more likely to convict the defendant when the crime story contained representative elements than when it did not. Jurors may let the representativeness heuristic influence their decisions in ways that are not supposed to be part of the legal system.

 SIMULATION   According to the **simulation heuristic** (Kahneman & Tversky, 1982), people invent "mental simulations" or scenarios of past, future, and alternative "realities" against which to judge the information that they receive. Because people cannot always distinguish their own original thoughts from reality, these mental simulations take on a life of their own. Imagining an event makes it seem more vivid and more likely, because to imagine an event the individual temporarily assumes that it is true (Koehler, 1991).

In a relevant study, physicians were asked how often they had imagined a scenario in which they contracted AIDS from a patient (Heath, Acklin, & Wiley, 1991). Many had. Some physicians said they had frequent imaginary scenarios in which they were diagnosed as HIV-positive and had to cope with the possibility of agonizing illness and death. The researchers later asked physicians to estimate the level of risk that they ran in treating patients with AIDS. Those who had frequently imagined contracting and suffering from the disease considered themselves more at risk than did physicians who had not imagined such scenarios. Interestingly, some of the physicians had treated many AIDS patients. Others hardly ever saw an AIDS patient. Objective exposure to AIDS patients, however, had very little to do with perceived risk of contracting the disease. Perceived risk was much more highly related to the self-generation of imaginary scenarios.

Lawyers, of course, try to help juries to simulate the crime scenarios that they prefer. They know that jurors try to invent a "story" that makes sense of the evidence presented at a trial. According to the **story model of juror decision making,** "jurors impose a narrative story organization on trial information, in which causal and intentional relations between events are central" (Pennington & Hastie, 1992, p. 189). Good story structure involves a causal chain in which one event leads logically to a goal that causes an action, which in turn causes the next event. Acceptable stories incorporate the bulk of evidence presented at the trial, contain no internal contradictions, have no parts missing, and seem consistent with the juror's existing knowledge. It is an advantage, then, for an attorney to present the evidence on his or her side in as close to "story order" as possible. In one study that tested this prediction, student jurors were more likely to consider a defendant guilty (or innocent) when the prosecution (or defense) presented the evidence in story order than in issue order (Pennington & Hastie, 1992). In story order, each witness gave testimony that added to a compelling story about the accused murderer's motives, opportunity, character, and relationship with the victim. In issue order, witnesses provided exactly the same evidence, except that it was categorized into separate topics, with no narrative link.

"Good" stories also contain concrete details. Concrete details are easier to visualize than abstract references. When jurors get concrete details, they find it relatively easy to simulate a plausible scenario. In one study, the researchers asked why jurors believe some crime scene eyewitnesses more than others. Student "jurors" read a summary of a criminal court case in which a man tried to hold up a small grocery store (Bell & Loftus, 1989). When the clerk hesitated about handing over money from the cash drawer, the man shot and killed the clerk and drove away. The police later stopped a car that matched the descriptions of eyewitnesses. One eyewitness identified the driver from a lineup. Although the eyewitness testified at the trial that she was positive about the defendant's identity, an eyewitness for the defense testified just as confidently that the police had arrested the wrong man.

The investigators used four different case summaries. The summaries varied only in one sentence in which either the prosecution's eyewitness, the defense's eyewitness, both, or neither provided concrete details of what happened. When no concrete details were provided, the witness said that before the holdup, "The man went and got a few store items." When concrete details were provided, the witness said, "The man went and got a box of Milk Duds and a can of Diet Pepsi." Figure 2.2 shows what percentage of student jurors found the defendant guilty in each of the four conditions. As shown in the figure, a few seemingly trivial details made a large difference in the verdict. When the prosecution's eyewitness did not provide details and the defense's eyewitness did, few jurors were willing to convict. In the other three conditions, however, when either the prosecution's eyewitness provided details or the defense's eyewitness failed to provide details, approximately one-third of the student jurors voted to convict. Concrete details enhance the plausibility of eyewitness testimony and contribute to what jurors consider an acceptable story.

Table 2.5 summarizes the four heuristics that, despite their infrequent weird results, almost always help people to think about each other efficiently and effectively. The four heuristics function as well as they do because people supplement them with several types of mental models.

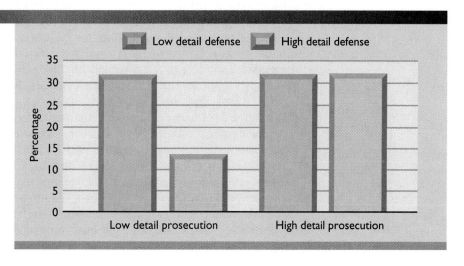

FIGURE 2.2

Stories with more details are easier to simulate and thus more believable.

Graph shows percentage of guilty verdicts when prosecution witness and/or defense witness provided details (Bell & Loftus, 1989).

TABLE 2.5	Four Heuristics or "Rules of Thumb" That Help Make Social Thinking Efficient
HEURISTIC	**HOW TO APPLY THE "RULE OF THUMB"**
Anchoring and Adjustment	Start from a recently thought-about "anchor point" and make what you believe is an appropriate adjustment to arrive at a final judgment
Availability	Judge how frequently an event occurs by how easy it is to bring to mind
Representativeness	Judge people, objects, and events by how similar they are to the "typical" representative of a category
Simulation	Use imaginary scenarios of alternative past and future events as standards against which to judge the information you are given

■ MENTAL MODELS

Social thinking depends on both heuristics and mental models. Heuristics, as described, are rules of thumb such as "if it's easy to imagine, it must occur frequently." Mental models, in contrast, are what people imagine to be "typical" persons and social events, such as the typical person with AIDS or the typical rape scenario. Three types of mental models have received extensive research attention: schemas (or "schemata"), scripts, and prototypes.

■ **SCHEMAS Schemas** are mental maps or blueprints for how familiar people, objects, and events usually function. Like a table of contents, they provide an organizing framework that helps us to understand relationships among various topics and subtopics. Schemas also help us to remember information that is either consistent with or strikingly inconsistent with expectations (Hastie, 1981; Rojahn & Pettigrew, 1992). Some people have schemas for understanding football games. A football fan would easily understand a sentence such as "When the reverse play didn't work, the quarterback tried a Hail Mary pass." Medical patients have schemas for understanding and reacting to their illness (Leventhal, Diefenbach, & Leventhal, 1992). People who often listen to heavy metal lyrics have morbid schemas about death, sex, and suicide (Hansen & Hansen, 1991). For any specialized activity, experienced "insiders" have a shorthand way of encapsulating information in terms of procedures and relationships that an "outsider" does not even know exist (Brewer & Nakamura, 1984; Fiske & Linville, 1980; Hastie, 1981; Taylor & Crocker, 1981).

Many social schemas are shared by almost all members of a culture. One frequent type of social schema is what might be called a "role schema," because we use it to understand a person's actions by knowing the person's role in life. We all have at least a rudimentary "burglar schema," for example, in that we know what a burglar might be interested in and what a burglar does.

In one study of social schemas, students read a story about two boys who were truants from school at one of the boys' homes (Anderson & Pichert, 1978). The house had a large front yard, some new siding and plumbing, a damp basement, some expensive cut glass and china, jewelry, an expensive color TV, a back door that was usually left unlocked, and so on. Some of the students read the story from the perspective of a burglar; others read the same story from the perspective of a home buyer.

Later, all students tried to recall as many details as possible from the story. Those who took a burglar perspective remembered the unlocked door and the items that could easily be stolen. Those who took a home buyer perspective remembered features that would make the house an attractive or unattractive purchase. Some students used a "burglar schema" to comprehend the information; others used a "home buyer schema." Schemas involve the assumptions, expectations, and general world knowledge that we bring to bear in comprehending a person, an object, an event, or a type of relationship (Baldwin, 1992; Fiske & Taylor, 1991; Zadny & Gerard, 1974).

SCRIPTS   Scripts are "event schemas" (Abelson, 1981). A **script** is a "stereotyped sequence of actions that defines a well-known situation" (Schank & Abelson, 1977, p. 41). To say that a person has a script for a particular type of event (such as a "typical" rape) is to say that the person knows what to expect in situations of that type. We all know what to expect when we enter a restaurant, for example, because we have been in many restaurants and they all seem to operate in much the same way. Suppose you learned that

> Donald entered the restaurant. He told the hostess that he wanted a table for one. The hostess led him to the table and gave him a menu. When the waiter came, Donald ordered fried shrimp and hot tea. Although the delay was unusually long, the waiter eventually brought Donald's dinner. When the check came, Donald paid with a credit card and left the minimum tip.

You would not be surprised at anything that happened. Everything occurred in precisely the order that you have come to expect in restaurants. All the people in the restaurant played their prescribed roles. All the necessary props were on hand, such as a menu and a dinner check.

Scripts have a compelling power to restructure anomalies. When people read a restaurant story in which parts of the script appear out of sequence, they later misremember the events as having occurred in the order prescribed by the script (Black, Galambos, & Read, 1984). If they read about paying the check before getting a menu, for instance, they "remember" the opposite order. If props such as a menu are omitted, students "fill them in" from memory. They are convinced that the props were mentioned. Even if researchers warn them to provide verbatim recall of a sequence, students frequently make the assumptions indicated by the script. Without looking back, can you remember what Donald *ate* in the restaurant? If you said "fried shrimp," look back at the story. We never said that Donald ate anything. "But he must have," you say. "He paid the check, didn't he?" Paying without eating is not part of the script. A script is a set of expectations and assumptions that helps us understand an event by filling in details that were not mentioned. People who share a common culture do not have to mention those details explicitly. One person can communicate to another only the unusual events that occurred at a restaurant, knowing that the listener will fill in the usual details from a "restaurant script."

Scripts can be very helpful. They tell us what to expect in a situation like a first date. In one study of contemporary first-date scripts, the researchers

Would an NFL team draft a new quarterback who came from the same hometown as Super Bowl winner Steve Young?

asked men and women college students to describe what happens on a typical first date (Rose & Frieze, 1993). Both men and women agreed that in the "typical" first date, the man worries about his appearance; picks up his date; meets her parents or roommates; takes her someplace where they can talk, joke, and laugh; takes her to eat; takes her home; and kisses her goodnight. They also agreed that the woman grooms and dresses, is nervous, gets picked up, makes introductions, gets to know and evaluate her date, accepts or rejects his "moves," gets taken home, and kisses him goodnight.

Scripts can also bias judgments and decision processes (Abelson, 1976). The "first date" script is obviously biased. In the script, men take the more active role and women take the more passive role. In one study of how scripts bias judgments, sports writers for leading newspapers were asked to select from college records the players most likely to succeed in professional football if drafted. Even these *experts* were influenced by irrelevant factors like hometown. They rated a player who came from the same hometown as the famous quarterback Joe Montana higher than if he had the same record of football performance but came from a different hometown (Gilovich, 1981). When scripts and other mental models fire the imagination, they develop a momentum of their own.

■ **PROTOTYPES** Prototypes are mental models that "stand for" or symbolize a category. Specifically, a **prototype** is the category member that a person imagines to best represent the category (Smith, 1988). If you are asked to think of a professor, you may think of the one who is teaching the course for which this textbook was assigned. Alternatively, you may think of an idealized portrait of a professor. The portrait may not match any one professor you have ever taken a course from. Instead it may be a composite of all the professors you have ever known (Posner & Keele, 1968, Medin, 1989; Linville, Fischer, & Salovey, 1989; Smith & Zarate, 1990.) The same principle applies to imagining the "typical" AIDS victim, the "typical" homosexual, the "typical" Nobel Prize winner, and so on. In every case, the category member that springs to mind as the "best" concrete example is your prototype for that category.

Prototypes can affect important everyday behaviors. The investigators in one study asked adults who wanted to quit smoking to describe the typical smoker (Gibbons et al., 1991). Over time, as the former smokers continued to refrain from smoking, their descriptions of the typical smoker became less admirable and increasingly different from themselves. The prototype thus served an important purpose. Reformed smokers could take satisfaction from comparing themselves favorably to the prototype. As expected, those ex-smokers who did *not* describe progressively more negative prototypes of the typical smoker also relapsed and started smoking again.

Prototypes of racial groups can also affect jury decisions, especially when jurors are not willing or able to engage in the deliberation necessary to adjust for their initial, spontaneous, prototype-based reactions (Bodenhausen, 1993). An all too common prototype of the "typical" Hispanic man, for instance, is someone prone to violence. In one study, some participants (but not others) were asked to recall a life event that made them feel very happy (Bodenhausen, Kramer, & Süsser, 1994). The purpose was to put some participants in a good mood, because people who are in a good mood are either unwilling or unable to engage in in-depth deliberation. They rely instead on spontaneous reactions (Forgas, 1994b; Hirt, McDonald, & Melton, in press; Mackie & Worth, 1991; Schwarz, Bless, & Bohner, 1991).

After the mood manipulation, all participants read a case description that was supposedly under consideration by a peer disciplinary review board. In

FIGURE 2.3

People in happy moods fall back on "easy" prototypes.

Graph shows how guilty of assault students in two different moods rated a defendant with Hispanic or non-Hispanic name (Bodenhausen, Kramer, & Susser, 1994).

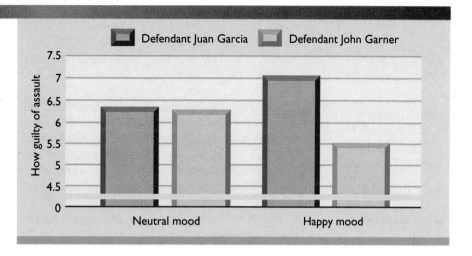

the case, a student named either Juan García or John Garner was accused of assault because of beating up his roommate. The participants estimated how likely it was that the accused was guilty of assault. As Figure 2.3 shows, participants who had no mood instructions were *not* more likely to think that the accused was guilty of assault when his name was Juan García than when his name was John Garner. Participants who were in a happy mood, in contrast, were more likely to think that the accused was guilty of assault when he had a Hispanic as opposed to a non-Hispanic name. Participants who were in a happy mood relied on the spontaneous, initial categorization and their prototype of Hispanic males. Participants who were in a neutral mood, in contrast, expended the cognitive effort necessary to deliberate on the details of the case, which were the same regardless of the defendant's name.

Table 2.6 summarizes the three types of mental models that people use to think efficiently and effectively about each other. These three types of mental models, like the four heuristics that we discussed earlier, *help* social thinking in almost every instance. Only on rare occasions do they lead us astray. Social psychologists focus their research on precisely those occasions, because biased judgments afford the most convincing proof that people are using heuristics and mental models.

TABLE 2.6	Three Types of Mental Models That People Use to Make Their Social Thinking More Efficient and Effective
TYPE OF MENTAL MODEL	**EXPLANATION**
Schema	Mental map or blueprint for how familiar people, objects, and events usually work
Script	Schema for how a familiar event usually unfolds
Prototype	The category member that a person imagines to represent a category

SUMMARY OF HOW SOCIAL THINKING WORKS

We typically think about people in two stages. One stage is more spontaneous. The other stage is more deliberative. In the spontaneous stage of social thinking, we "automatically" comprehend new information about a person in terms of currently salient goals and categories. In the deliberative stage, we adjust our initial comprehension through a more in-depth analysis. Thinking is said to be automatic or spontaneous when it is efficient and occurs without intention, control, or awareness. We often rely on spontaneous rather than deliberative social thinking because we are cognitive misers who find it easier to use recently thought-about goals and categories than to spend time and effort trying to adjust our initial comprehension. Furthermore, we cannot always distinguish our self-generated thoughts, which are heavily biased toward "chronic" ways of organizing new information, from reality.

These chronic ways of organizing new information include heuristics and the use of mental models. Some frequently used heuristics include anchoring and adjustment, availability, representativeness, and simulation. Anchoring and adjustment involve relying too much on an initially salient piece of information instead of making an appropriate adjustment. Availability involves assuming that easy-to-imagine events are objectively frequent. Representativeness involves judging members of a category by how many of the "typical" member's characteristics they have. Simulation involves inventing alternative scenarios for past and future reality. Mental models include schemas, scripts, and prototypes. A schema is a mental map or blueprint for how the world usually works, such as a "burglar schema" for what burglars usually do. A script is a specialized schema for how an event, such as going on a date, usually happens. A prototype is an imaginary "best" representative of a category, such as Queen Elizabeth II for the category "monarchs."

HOW ACCURATE IS SOCIAL THINKING?

The first section of the chapter described the way that social thinking normally works. As described, research evidence suggests that social thinking sometimes has unwanted consequences. Practice at dealing with familiar persons, objects, and events renders certain aspects of the information-processing system relatively automatic, but at what cost? The second section of the chapter examines how accurate social thinking is by concentrating on three areas in which unwanted biases and errors sometimes occur. The three areas of interest involve the accessibility of thoughts, the ways in which information is integrated and remembered, and mental simulations. It is important to realize, however, that biases and errors occur precisely because certain ways of social thinking are effective almost all the time (Einhorn & Hogarth, 1981; Nisbett & Ross, 1980). The correct answer to the question "How accurate is social thinking?" is "Social thinking is usually very accurate."

ACCESSIBILITY

One consequence of two-stage information processing, as we have seen, is that initial reactions are sometimes influenced without our being aware of the influence. Recently "activated" thoughts influence the way new information is organized, which in turn biases the way we organize and interpret subsequent information. When we construct an impression from raw sensations and initial comprehension, the resulting "construct" can be biased in one direction or another without our realizing it. The bias can occur because one type of mental construct is more accessible than another. Thoughts of a particular type can be "primed" in the same way that a pump is primed with water to get it going. Depending on how motivated people are to adjust the initial impression, priming can result in either "assimilation" or "contrast."

■ CONSTRUCT ACCESSIBILITY

Once you get a person thinking about certain trait constructs, those constructs become more accessible or "easier to come by" (Bargh, 1994; Bargh & Pietromonaco, 1982; Herr, 1986; Srull & Wyer, 1979). In one demonstration

Would you describe this man as "adventurous" or would you call him "reckless?"

of construct accessibility, students first participated in a "perception" experiment, in which they memorized a list of words (Higgins, Rholes, & Jones, 1977). Some of the students memorized words like "adventurous," "self-confident," "independent," and "persistent." Other students memorized instead words like "reckless," "conceited," "aloof," and "stubborn." The two sets of words represented positive and negative trait constructs. Adventurous is the "good" side of being reckless, conceited is the "bad" side of being self-confident, and so on. All students then participated in a "reading comprehension" experiment that was supposedly unrelated to the perception experiment. In the reading comprehension experiment, they read about the exploits of a person named Donald.

> Donald claims that he likes excitement. Last year, he climbed Mt. McKinley, shot the Colorado rapids in a kayak, and drove in a demolition derby. By the way he acts, one can tell that Donald is well aware of his own ability to perform a variety of tasks well. He feels that he does not need to rely on other people and he seldom changes his mind when he has decided exactly how he wants to proceed.

After reading a similar passage, students characterized Donald's actions and rated how much they liked him. Consistent with the experimental predictions, trait constructs involved in the earlier "perception" task primed related constructs in the "reading comprehension" task. Students who had been primed with words like adventurous, self-confident, independent, and persistent used those constructs to interpret Donald's actions. When he shot the rapids, he was being adventurous, not reckless. As a result, they liked Donald. Students who had been primed with words like reckless, conceited, aloof, and stubborn used very different connotations to interpret Donald's actions. When he shot the rapids, they saw him as reckless, not adventurous. As a result, they did not like Donald. Students in the two conditions of the study interpreted the same behavior differently, depending on which traits were more accessible for them.

Another demonstration of construct accessibility concentrated on the trait construct hostility (Srull & Wyer, 1979). The investigators wanted to show that social thinkers are more likely to interpret ambiguous behavior when they have recently been thinking about hostile actions. In a "word comprehension" experiment, some students formed sentences from jumbled words that could be rearranged to convey hostility, such as "legs break arms and his." Other students formed sentences from jumbled words that had nothing to do with hostility. Later, in an "unrelated experiment," all students read a paragraph similar to the following:

> When I was at Donald's apartment, a salesman knocked but Donald told him to go away. The landlord called about back rent, but Donald said he was refusing to pay until the place was painted. We left Donald's car at a garage, where Donald told the manager that he had to have the car back by the next day or he would take his business elsewhere. I then took Donald to a hardware store where he demanded his money back for a gadget he bought the previous week that did not work.

As predicted, students who had formed sentences having to do with hostility in the earlier "unrelated" experiment were more likely than their counterparts to interpret Donald's actions as signs of hostility rather than mere assertiveness. They were also more likely to dislike Donald. Some people "see" hostility everywhere. Even people who are not chronically sensitive to hostil-

FIGURE 2.4

Accessibility is different from availability.
Graph shows how women rated their own assertiveness after they tried to recall either 6 or 12 times when they had behaved either assertively or unassertively (Schwarz et al., 1991).

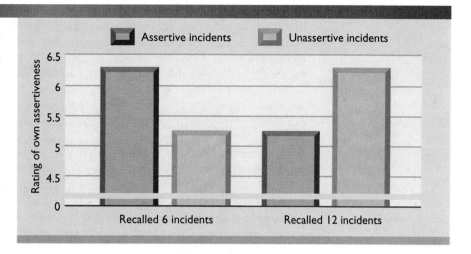

ity, though, can unwittingly become very aggressive merely because they have recently processed hostility-relevant information (Bargh, 1994; Bargh & Pietromonaco, 1982; Herr, 1986).

Accessibility is not the same as availability. Availability has to do with the *amount* of information. Accessibility has to do with how easy it seems to be to remember the information. A library might have many books available on a particular topic, but the books might all be hidden in dark alcoves, where they are inaccessible. In one study that examined the difference between availability and accessibility, some female students at a German university had to recall six incidents when they had behaved very assertively (Schwarz, Bless, Strack, Klumpp, Rittenauer-Schatka, & Simons, 1991). Other women had to recall six incidents when they had behaved very unassertively. Women in these two conditions found it easy to recall six such incidents. In two other conditions, however, the women had to recall either 12 incidents when they had behaved very assertively or 12 incidents when they had behaved very unassertively. Women in these two conditions found the task difficult. Then the experimenter asked all the women to rate their own assertiveness on a scale from 1 to 10.

As shown in Figure 2.4, women who recalled six assertive incidents rated themselves as more assertive than did women who recalled six unassertive incidents. "If it was that easy to think of the incidents," they told themselves, "then I must *be* that type of person." Women who had to recall 12 incidents displayed an opposite bias. As the figure shows, women who recalled 12 assertive incidents rated themselves as *less* assertive than did women who recalled 12 unassertive incidents. "If it was that difficult to think of the incidents," they told themselves, "then I must *not* be that type of person." Information about their assertiveness or unassertiveness was equally *available* to women in the four different conditions. The information, however, seemed less *accessible* to women who had to recall 12 incidents than to women who had to recall six incidents. The determining factor in how the women rated themselves was not availability. The six-incident women could have generated 12 incidents if they were required to do so. The important factor was accessibility.

■ PRIMING

Not just trait constructs, but thoughts of many different types can be "primed." People who frequently watch television, for example, are more likely than

Do devout Roman Catholics feel more guilty about their transgressions after they catch a brief glimpse of the Pope?

ple who seldom watch television to believe (and to act as though they believe) that the world is a dangerous place, because crime-related constructs are more accessible for them (Shrum & O'Guinn, 1993). College students who watch many rock music videos are more apt than students who watch few rock music videos to believe that men directly control their own fate. They also believe that women exercise control only indirectly, by manipulating men's sexual needs (Hansen & Hansen, 1988). Students who frequently think about the possibility of pregnancy say that they have sex less frequently than do students who have fewer thoughts about possible pregnancy (Norris & Devine, 1992). Priming has important effects on everyday social behavior.

Priming occurs when people are aware of the prime, as students who participated in the "Donald" studies were aware of having memorized or rearranged words. Priming also occurs when people cannot possibly be aware of the prime. In one study of priming without awareness, college students were asked to view Chinese ideographs and to give "snap judgments" of how much they liked or disliked each ideograph (Murphy & Zajonc, 1993). A photograph of a smiling or scowling face was shown briefly before each ideograph appeared on the screen—so briefly that it was impossible to see anything but the ideograph. When students "saw" a smiling face immediately before viewing an ideograph, they liked the image quite a bit. When they "saw" a scowling face immediately before viewing an ideograph, they did not like it at all.

In another study of priming without awareness, Roman Catholic women read about another woman's sexual dream (Baldwin, Carrell, & Lopez, 1990). Although they did not realize it, the women were selected because they described themselves as devout practitioners of their religion, so reading the "sex dream" passage presumably made them feel guilty. Next, the women looked at "five brief flashes of light" projected on a screen. Unknown to them, the experimenters inserted within the light flashes either pictures of a blank white card, a stranger, or Pope John Paul II. Finally, the women rated themselves on competence, morality, and freedom from anxiety. Although they were unaware that any pictures had been shown in the light flashes, the women were "primed" to evaluate themselves differently. Women who had just finished reading a sexual dream and who were "primed" with pictures of the Pope said they felt less competent, less moral, and less free from anxiety than did women who were "primed" with either blank pictures or pictures of a stranger. For a devoutly religious person, it is hard to feel moral when you have been reading about sex and the Pope is "watching from the back of your mind."

■ ASSIMILATION AND CONTRAST

In many studies of construct accessibility and priming, subsequent thoughts became more similar to (were "assimilated" with) previously active thoughts. Subsequent interpretations of Donald's behavior, for example, were assimilated with thoughts about hostility. The two-stage nature of social thinking suggests, however, that assimilation is not the only possible outcome of priming. Assimilation is the likely outcome when people are unaware that their initial reactions have been influenced or when the primes are moderately similar to the new information. At other times people might realize that they have been "primed." The new information might also be drastically different from the prime. When people are reminded about the prime, they display contrast rather than assimilation (Strack, Schwarz, Bless, Kübler, & Wänke, 1993). They *over*-adjust away from their initial reaction, so they make judgments that are exactly opposite to or "in contrast to" the prime.

In one study of contrast effects, some students had to find names like Dracula, Charles Manson, and Adolph Hitler embedded in a matrix of letters (Herr, 1986). Other students had to find names like Shirley Temple, Peter Pan, and Santa Claus. In a subsequent "unrelated" experiment, all students read the paragraph about Donald turning away salesmen, not paying the landlord, and so on. Students who had recently been thinking about Manson and Hitler found Donald *less* (not more) hostile than did students who had recently been thinking about Shirley Temple and Santa Claus. By comparison to the anchor point of Hitler's behavior, Donald must have seemed positively benign! When circumstances prime an extreme version of the trait construct, the result is a "rebound" or contrast effect. People interpret subsequent ambiguous behavior as different from, not similar to, the primed trait construct.

According to the **set-reset hypothesis** (Martin, 1986), exposure to a trait construct sets an anchor point from which social thinkers adjust by resetting the "anchor." When people realize that their interpretations of ambiguous behaviors may have been biased by recent thoughts, they *reset* the anchor point, but they overadjust in an opposite direction. In a relevant study, the researchers either interrupted students or allowed them to complete an initial task that involved trait constructs like "reckless and conceited" or "adventurous and self-confident" (Martin, 1986). All students then read the passage about Donald shooting the rapids, driving in demolition derbies, and trusting only himself. Students who had completed the task did not dwell on it while reading about Donald. As a result, they displayed the usual priming effect. They viewed Donald in a way consistent with the primed constructs. Exactly the opposite result occurred for students who were not allowed to complete the task but were led to believe that they would do so later. These students were presumably still aware of the priming procedure while reading the passage, so they made allowances for its possible effect on their interpretations. They reset their anchor points and found Donald to be *opposite* to the primed constructs. They displayed contrast effects instead of the usual assimilation, because they reset their anchor points opposite to the initial reaction.

Similar effects on priming and contrast occur when social thinkers try to process another person's behaviors while they are cognitively busy (Martin, Seta, & Crelia, 1990). Presumably, it takes cognitive effort to reset an anchor point. People who try to perform some other distracting task at the same time, such as trying to count the number of digits being recited by someone in the next room, are unable to do the extra work. They do not make allowances for having been primed. The set-reset hypothesis thus explains why priming has a greater effect when a long delay occurs between learning about the ambiguous behavior and evaluating it (Wyer & Srull, 1980; Wyer & Srull, 1981). In that case, the social thinker has presumably forgotten about and no longer makes adjustments for having had certain traits primed. After a long enough delay, only the overall impression remains, not memory for the priming that created that impression (Carlston, 1980).

INTEGRATING AND REMEMBERING SOCIAL INFORMATION

Another area where the information-processing system has interesting consequences is in integrating and remembering social information, topics that are discussed in the next two sections. The section on integrating describes what happens when people receive and must reconcile conflicting pieces of social information. The section on remembering describes the goals and processes that influence what we remember about other people.

■ INTEGRATING

The "integrating" part of the social information-processing "recipe" in Table 2.1 represents attempts to combine disparate pieces of information. Sometimes the pieces of information enter our currently active thoughts one after another. At other times, the pieces of information come from both currently active thoughts and existing knowledge (Hastie & Park, 1986). We might be trying to integrate what we are hearing about Sally, for example, with what we already know about her. Integrating separate pieces of information to form an overall impression involves two "competitions." The first competition is between information that is congruent versus incongruent with expectations. The second competition is between information that is positive versus negative.

■ **INCONGRUENCY EFFECTS** The competition between congruent and incongruent information determines which counts more heavily in the final impression. Suppose a jury member who expects females to be dainty learns that Sally told her attacker "Please don't hurt me." Such a statement would constitute congruent information. Suppose the same jury member learns that she simultaneously kicked the man in the groin, which would be incongruent information. Which piece of information is more likely to capture the juror's attention and to influence the juror's judgment? Dozens of studies have asked this question by having people read both congruent and incongruent information and later asking them to remember what they read. Across studies, incongruent information is more memorable, so presumably it was more actively involved in the "integrating" process (Stangor & McMillan, 1992).

In a specific study, students were first led to believe that a person had a particular trait, for example, that "Donald is very friendly" (Sherman & Hamilton, 1994). Then the students read both congruent and incongruent trait-implying sentences, such as "Donald belongs to several social groups" (congruent) and "Donald crossed the street to avoid having to talk to a classmate" (incongruent). As they read the new information about Donald, the students were interrupted from time to time and asked to remember whether a sentence had been presented previously. The interruption occurred immediately after a sentence that was either congruent, incongruent, or irrelevant. Suppose students who got incongruent information tried to make sense of it by calling back to mind information that they had previously incorporated into their existing knowledge. If they did, then more of the previous information about Donald should have been currently active (and accessible) immediately after a new incongruent sentence than immediately after a new congruent sentence. Consistent with this logic, students were quicker to recognize a previously presented sentence when they had just learned something incongruent about a person than when they had just learned something congruent or irrelevant.

Incongruency effects occur more often when the initial expectancies are weak than when they are strong (Stangor & McMillan, 1992). They also occur more often when people are trying to form an accurate impression than when they are trying to maintain their existing beliefs (Driscoll, Hamilton, & Sorrentino, 1991). Incongruency effects occur as strongly in everyday life as they do in the psychologist's carefully controlled laboratory environment. Students in one study, for instance, kept diaries of events that involved themselves and their friends. They later remembered times when friends behaved in ways that violated their expectancies better than they remembered times when friends behaved predictably (Skowronski, Betz, Thompson, & Shannon, 1991).

■ **POSITIVE-NEGATIVE ASYMMETRY** A second "competition" in information integration is between positive and negative information. For most social judgments, people integrate what they learn in a relatively straightforward way. They assign each piece of information an "importance weight" and then combine the pieces of information algebraically to form a final impression (Anderson, 1981). For some types of social thinking, however, negative information seems to carry more weight than positive information–a positive-negative asymmetry (Forgas, 1992; Ikegami, 1993; Isen, 1993). Suppose we learn that "Donald paid back money to an acquaintance who had forgotten about the loan," which is positive information. We also learn that "Donald caused an accident and then ran away," which is negative information. We do not conclude that "one positive plus one negative equals a neutral impression" (Skowronski & Carlston, 1987; Wojciszke, Brycz, & Borkenau, 1993). Instead, especially if we happen to be in a negative mood at the time, we give greater weight to the negative information and conclude that Donald is dishonest (Mayer & Hanson, 1995; Mayer, McCormick, & Strong, 1995).

One reason why negative information gets greater weight than positive information is because it is adaptive to notice negative information first. Negative information might "have undesirable consequences for the perceiver's well-being" (Pratto & John, 1991, p. 380). Suppose that Jeff offers a woman a ride on his motorcycle. She is less likely to pay attention to "Jeff collects toys for tots at Christmastime" than to "Jeff was convicted of raping Sally." Negative information about a person's morality seems to be "flagged" with a "PAY ATTENTION" label.

Negative information also gets greater weight than positive information in evaluating a person's *morality* because the negative information is more meaningful (Reeder & Brewer, 1979; Reeder & Coovert, 1986; Skowronski & Carlston, 1987). It tells us more about Donald's character to know that he ran away from an accident than that he repaid a forgotten loan, because we believe that running away from accidents is more "exceptional" than repaying forgotten loans. Following this logic, the "negativity bias" in integrating information about morality is reversed and becomes a "positivity bias" when people integrate information about *competence* (Skowronski & Carlston, 1987). Suppose we learn that "Donald can't remember to tie his shoelaces," which is negative information. We also learn that "Donald invented a device to control industrial pollution," which is positive information. We do not form a neutral impression of Donald (Skowronski & Carlston, 1987). Instead, we place greater emphasis on the positive information than on the negative information and conclude that Donald is very intelligent. If what people remember is any indication of what they initially notice, social thinkers have a negativity bias for information about morality and a positivity bias for information about competence.

■ REMEMBERING

Memory for social information is an important clue to the processes that occur during initial organization, categorization, and integration. Memory is also affected by the objectives that occur in the "current goals" part of the information-processing "recipe" shown in Table 2.1. The topic of "person memory" is large enough to require a book of its own (e.g., Hastie, Ostrom, Ebbesen, Wyer, Hamilton, & Carlston, 1980). Because space is limited, however, we concentrate in this section on the way that initial categorization affects how we remember people (the "recapitulation hypothesis") and on the way that current goals affect social memory ("processing goals").

RECAPITULATION HYPOTHESIS How do we remember our acquaintances? The **recapitulation hypothesis** holds that we remember people by their social categories before we remember them by their personality traits (Bond & Brockett, 1987). We remember people as psychology majors, professors, and motorcyclists before we remember them as introverts, gloomy people, and nervous people (Andersen, Klatzky, & Murray, 1990). According to the recapitulation hypothesis, memory for acquaintances *recapitulates* the process by which we originally formed our impressions. As described more extensively in Chapter 3, impressions are formed through a process of anchoring and adjustment. When we first meet a person, we spontaneously categorize the person as, for instance, "female," "elderly," "Chinese," or "artist" (Brewer, 1988; Fiske & Neuberg, 1990). The initial categorization carries with it assumptions about the person's characteristics, such as "artists are flamboyant and impulsive." We use these initial assumptions as an anchor that tells us how we expect the person to behave. As we get to know the person better, we make adjustments away from the anchor-point assumptions, but the category assumptions come first and the adjustments occur later (Woodworth, 1938).

According to the recapitulation hypothesis, categories also precede traits in trying to remember acquaintances. If we try to list all our acquaintances, we first list all the psychology majors, then all the professors, and so on. Within each of these categories, we then remember the introverted ones, the gloomy ones, and so on. In one study, some students were asked to name an acquaintance who belonged to a social category and then told that it had to be someone with a particular personality trait (Bond & Brockett, 1987). Other students were asked to name an acquaintance who had a personality trait and then told that it had to be someone who belonged to a particular category. As predicted, students took longer (found it harder) to recall an acquaintance when they got the trait first than when they got the category first. Personality traits are subcategories that we remember inside social categories (Bond & Sedikides, 1988).

███ **PROCESSING GOALS** The "current goals" part of the social cognition "recipe" represents another important aspect of social memory. Processing goals affect the way that information is integrated and the conclusions that become part of our existing knowledge. Suppose Brian and Bob meet several strangers at a college "mixer." Brian tries to memorize each stranger's major, hometown, pet peeve, dorm, favorite game, and favorite performer. "Leslie is a business major from Three Forks, Minnesota, who doesn't like gossip. She lives in Stanton Hall, likes to play charades, and enjoys listening to Poison." Bob, in contrast, does not try to memorize anything. He simply tries to form personality impressions of the people he meets. Although it may seem counterintuitive, Bob will remember more of the personal details than will Brian (Hamilton, Katz, & Leirer, 1980; Srull & Brand, 1983).

Trying to form an impression of someone forces us to note more of the connections between items of information than does merely trying to memorize a list of unconnected details (Klein & Kihlstom, 1986). "Because she is from a small town, Leslie dislikes gossip." "People from cold climates stay indoors during the winter and get good at charades." Because he is trying to make sense of the *relationships* among these details, Bob thinks about what Leslie tells him more deeply and elaborately than does Brian, who is merely memorizing a list. Later, when Bob recalls that Leslie is from a small town, that one detail will remind him that she is from a cold place where they play charades, and so on. In contrast, when Brian recalls that Leslie is from a small town, he has recalled one item on his mental list. That one item, however, is unlikely to elicit connections with any of the other details.

The memory benefits of mental connections are especially noticeable when we meet people with whom we may have to interact (Hoffman, Mischel, &

Mazze, 1981). In a relevant study, students learned five items of information (favorite game, a personality trait, hobby, dorm, part-time job) about each of five strangers (Devine, Sedikides, & Fuhrman, 1989). The students had 6 seconds to study each item. The investigators led some students to believe that one of the five strangers would be their partner for a subsequent problem-solving task. They asked the other students to concentrate on that same person and to form an overall personality impression of her. These students, however, did not anticipate interacting with her. Yet other students were asked to concentrate on the same person and to memorize all the details about her. Later, all students tried to recall the 25 items and to say which item went with which one of the five strangers.

As predicted, anticipated interaction and impression formation instructions elicited better recall for items of information about the specific target person than did explicit instructions to memorize her details. Also, anticipated interaction and impression formation students were more likely than memorization students to list related items in order, as though they had thought about the connections. Finally, anticipated interaction seemed to increase motivation to form a coherent impression, which helped memory.

MENTAL SIMULATIONS

Social thinking is sometimes inaccurate because of the way information is organized and integrated. Social thinking is also sometimes inaccurate because thinkers "construct their own realities," inventing imaginary scenarios and letting those imaginary scenarios influence judgments and decisions. We described mental simulations in general terms when we discussed the simulation heuristic. This section describes in greater detail two specific types of mental simulations: overconfident estimates and counterfactual thinking.

■ OVERCONFIDENT ESTIMATES

Mental simulations make us overconfident that we can estimate both past and future events. Overconfident estimation of past events is a bias of hindsight. Overconfident estimation of future events is a bias of foresight.

■ **HINDSIGHT**   Did you ever notice that in retrospect previous events seem to have a compelling logic about them, as though they "just had to hap-

Calvin and Hobbes   by Bill Watterson

pen that way"? Did you ever believe that you "knew all along" how a football game, an election, or a marriage was going to turn out? According to the **hindsight bias** (Fischhoff, 1982), also known as the "knew it all along effect," people who know an outcome erroneously believe that they knew the outcome or would have known the outcome in advance. They are influenced by knowing the outcome, but they do not realize that they have been influenced (Hawkins & Hastie, 1990). After a presidential election, for instance, many voters erroneously believe that they knew the outcome very confidently before it ever happened (Powell, 1988).

The hindsight bias occurs because people selectively remember the relevant evidence. They emphasize evidence congruent rather than incongruent with the known outcome. They also integrate the evidence in a biased way to construct a plausible "story" that has the known outcome as its ending (Harvey & Martin, 1995; Hawkins & Hastie, 1990). People use whatever information they have about a past event, including the outcome if they know it, to "rewrite the story." In their new stories, they supply the missing causal connections that make sense of the outcome. They do not realize that they might have constructed a different mental simulation had they been given a different outcome (Wasserman, Lempert, & Hastie, 1991).

People display less hindsight bias when the events affect them personally. In one study of self-relevance and hindsight, the investigators surveyed people who lived near a large factory (Mark & Mellor, 1991). The factory had unexpectedly laid off many workers. Community members who did not work at the factory and were not themselves affected by the layoffs claimed to have "seen the signs" long before the event occurred. People who worked at the factory but did not lose their jobs were less likely to claim hindsight. Finally, people who were laid off claimed that "there was no way to know" the layoffs were coming. These differences in hindsight may reflect differences in processing goals, because laid-off workers (and those who survived but might lose their jobs later) were motivated to avoid blaming themselves. "If I could see it coming, why didn't I change jobs or work harder so that I would not be laid off?" The differences in hindsight may also have occurred because the laid-off workers could vividly remember the actual sequence of events. They did not have to rely on an imaginary scenario that made the layoffs seem inevitable.

To explore the role of hindsight bias in legal decisions, the investigators in one study had student jurors read a case summary (Casper, Benedict, & Kelly, 1988). Mr. James Duncan requested $50,000 in damages. He claimed that the police department and two of its detectives had violated his civil rights. On the night in question, the two detectives received a tip that a big drug sale was scheduled to occur in an apartment building at 103 W. Ninth Street. They did not know which apartment was involved. The drug dealer was said to be a slim, tall man in his late thirties. When the detectives entered the building, they knocked on the first of four apartment doors. The door was opened by Mr. Duncan, who was of average height and build, but seemed to be in his thirties. When the detectives identified themselves and requested entrance, Mr. Duncan said "Leave me alone, man" and tried to close the door. The detectives shoved the door open, knocking Mr. Duncan backwards. In falling, he cut his head on the corner of a table. The detectives frisked Mr. Duncan, handcuffed him to a radiator, and searched the apartment.

Some student jurors learned that the police found 340 bags of heroin in the apartment. Others learned that the police found no drugs. Student jurors who knew that drugs were found constructed scenarios in which the detectives "knew it all along," so they gave the plaintiff a relatively low damage award. Student jurors who knew that drugs were *not* found, in contrast, constructed alternative scenarios in which the detectives violated an innocent man's civil

Are police more justified when they break into an apartment without a warrant and find drugs than when they do the same thing but find nothing?

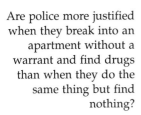

rights, so they gave the plaintiff a relatively high damage award. Subsequent research shows that this hindsight bias in juror decision making occurs even when the judge *explicitly instructs* jurors that a civil rights decision must be independent of the plaintiff's guilt (Casper, Benedict, & Perry, 1989).

■ **FORESIGHT** Mental simulations also produce overconfident estimates of future events. In several studies, people who imagined future events convinced themselves that the events they imagined were very likely to occur (Gregory, Cialdini, & Carpenter, 1982). Student participants in one study, for example, read a detailed clinical case history of a man named George. George was a former mental patient. He left home early in life over disagreements with his father. After leaving home, George lived as a hobo for several years, served in the military, and started several unsuccessful small businesses. Finally, he returned home to care for his dying mother (Ross, Lepper, Strack, & Steinmetz, 1977). The investigators asked some of the students to explain why George might run for a seat on the city council. They asked others to explain why George might be the driver in a hypothetical hit-and-run accident. When they later estimated the likelihood that either hypothetical event would actually occur, both groups of students assigned higher likelihood to whichever event they had explained.

Events that we explain may seem more likely because the hypothetical "story" that we construct seems plausible and accessible. In one study, the experimenters had some students draw cartoon strips in which they donated blood and had other students draw cartoon strips in which they refused to donate blood (Anderson, 1983b). The investigators later asked students to estimate their likelihood of donating to a campus blood drive. Students who had constructed scenes of themselves agreeing thought it more likely than did students who had constructed scenes of themselves refusing. In a follow-up study, some students drew one cartoon strip depicting the future event, whereas other students drew several such imaginary scenarios. The more frequently they drew the scene, the easier they said the scene was to imagine and the more likely they thought it was to occur (Anderson & Godfrey, 1987). Subjective accessibility of an imagined scene made the imaginary future event seem more likely.

People are also overconfident that mentally simulated future events will occur, because they fail to realize that circumstances might change (Dunning, Griffin, Milojkovic, & Ross, 1990; Ross, 1987, 1989; Ross & Nisbett, 1991; Vallone, Griffin, Lin, & Ross, 1990). In one study, students estimated how much time and money they would spend in various situations, such as answering a telephone survey (Griffin, Dunning, & Ross, 1990). Later, the same students made the same predictions a second time, but with four different sets of instructions. One group of students merely answered the questions a second time. They did not change how much confidence they expressed in their predictions. A second group of students wrote about what the specific circumstances might be. They described, for instance, how busy they imagined being when the telephone rang, what the survey questions were about, and whether the survey-taker was male or female. After they had explained their own (sometimes highly idiosyncratic) mental simulations of the potential situation, they made their predictions, which also did not change from the first time they had answered.

A third group of students first wrote about how they imagined the situation, and then made their predictions contingent on the circumstances being *exactly* as they had described in every detail. These students also did not change their original predictions! Their mental simulations were so compelling that they failed to realize that future circumstances are often quite different from those that we imagine. The fourth group of students were explicitly instructed to invent scenarios that were *different* from what they had originally imagined. "Suppose my date were waiting impatiently outside?" Only these students, deliberately instructed to invent alternative scenarios, lowered their confidence levels to be more in line with what previous research had suggested might be accurate (Griffin et al., 1990).

Unfortunately, people who are chronically depressed suffer from overconfidence in predicting negative events. They are very confident that bad things are going to happen to them, because they can imagine negative consequences so easily (Dunning & Story, 1991). People who are chronically depressed appear to have a relatively "automatic" future event schema in which everything goes wrong (Andersen, Spielman, & Bargh, 1992). They are the victims of their own mental simulations.

■ COUNTERFACTUAL THINKING

Besides simulating past and future events, people can simulate events that never happened but that "might have been." **Counterfactual thinking** involves imagining ways in which events might have occurred differently (Miller, Turnbull, & McFarland, 1990). It happens whenever we say to ourselves: "If only I hadn't bought that car that turned out to be a lemon" or "What if the professor had picked different questions for the final exam?" We construct a mental simulation in which we compare reality to "what might have been" (Dunning & Madey, in press). Much of counterfactual thinking involves either mentally "taking back" actions or "undoing" outcomes.

■ **"TAKING BACK" ACTIONS** We "take back" an action mentally when we imagine having done things differently, usually because what we did led to an unwanted outcome. In everyday life, many people have thoughts about what might have happened had they continued their education, not married early, or in various other ways acted differently (Landman & Manis, 1992). Sally, in the rape story that began this chapter, might also have engaged in counterfactual thinking. She might have added an action ("If only I had screamed at the top of my lungs so someone would hear"). She might also have subtracted an action ("If only I hadn't cursed him").

Counterfactual thinking is more likely when the outcome arouses strong emotions (Kahneman & Miller, 1986; Miller & Taylor, in press). People who lose thousands of dollars because they bought the wrong stock are more likely to speculate on "What if I had acted differently" scenarios than are people who lose 50 cents in a soft-drink machine. Also, more extreme emotions are likely to be elicited by a negative outcome when the action that led to that outcome was abnormal rather than "routine" (Gavanski & Wells, 1989; Kahneman & Tversky, 1982).

In a relevant study, student jurors learned that a woman named Lucy requested damages from an Indian restaurant that had served her a dish of curry (Macrae, 1992). On arriving home from the restaurant, Lucy had become violently ill and consulted a doctor, who diagnosed food poisoning. The illness was traced to the curry. Some student jurors learned that Lucy ate at the restaurant frequently. Others learned that Lucy "felt like a change." Instead of going to her usual Indian restaurant just down the street, she went to a restaurant in the center of town that she had not previously visited. Legally, it should not matter to the verdict whether Lucy took routine or nonroutine actions. The only relevant issues are the restaurant's culpability and the extent of Lucy's suffering, which were the same in both trial summaries. Nonetheless, student jurors gave much higher compensation and negligence awards to Lucy when she was poisoned in a nonroutine restaurant than in a routine restaurant. It is easier to imagine a counterfactual scenario in which Lucy followed her usual routine than to imagine a counterfactual scenario in which she broke with her routine. Jurors felt greater sympathy for Lucy when they could mentally "take back" her nonroutine action.

Another factor that alters the likelihood of "taking back" an action in imagination is whether the action that led to the emotionally charged outcome was something the individual *did* or something the individual *failed to do*. Donald canceled a reservation for transatlantic Flight 747 and took a seat on Flight 395. Bob bought a ticket on Flight 395 and stayed with that flight. Who do you think is more likely to "take back" his actions mentally as Flight 395 goes down into the ocean? Most people believe that Donald is more likely than Bob to engage in counterfactual thinking (Kahneman & Tversky, 1982), even though, strictly speaking, their reasoning is odd. Statistically, Donald and Bob had the same likelihood of dying in an airplane crash. Donald's chance of avoiding the crash had he not switched flights was exactly equal to Bob's chance of avoiding the crash had he switched flights. One traveler, though, did something that produced his death. The other traveler merely failed to take action. People who suffer unwanted outcomes through taking the wrong action experience stronger emotions immediately after the event than do people who suffer the same fate through failing to act (Gleicher, Kost, Baker, Strathman, Richman, & Sherman, 1990; Landman, 1988). Interestingly, this difference may be reversed in the long term, when we may regret more the actions (such as completing an education) that we did *not* take (Gilovich & Medvec, 1994).

Finally, the likelihood of mentally "taking back" an action depends importantly on whether the action is perceived as having been constrained versus taken freely (Wells & Gavanski, 1989). Suppose that Bethany chose one of 20 empty parking spaces in a shopping mall parking lot. When she finished shopping, she backed out of the parking space and collided with a truck driver who was looking the other way. Tiffiny went to a different shopping mall on the same day. There was only one empty parking space, so she took it. When she was leaving, she backed out and collided with a truck driver who was looking the other way. After the accident, Bethany is more likely than Tiffiny to entertain counterfactual thoughts. She is more likely to say to herself, "If only I hadn't parked in that particular space." She is also more likely to blame herself for the accident, as though one parking space was more "accident-prone" than another (Miller et al., 1990). When people perceive that they might have been able to control an outcome and that a close alternative outcome would have been preferable, they tend to imagine better "possible worlds" (Markman, Gavanski, Sherman, & McMullen, 1995).

■ **"UNDOING" OUTCOMES** Another way of altering an unwanted event in imagination, different from "taking back" actions, is to imagine that the outcome itself was different. People "undo" outcomes in two ways: by inventing an "upward" or better imaginary ending and by inventing a "downward" or worse imaginary ending. The rape victim Sally, for instance, might have imagined an alternative reality. She might have imagined that her attacker gave up and ran away (an upward counterfactual thought). She might also have imagined that she was seriously injured or even killed (a downward counterfactual thought). Both upward and downward counterfactual thoughts are more likely to occur when the actual outcome aroused strong emotions and when it came about in an abnormal way (Roese, 1994).

Consider Mel and David, two travelers who both missed airline flights that were scheduled to leave at 8:00 A.M. Mel and David both arrived at the airport at 8:30 A.M. Mel learned that his flight had left on time. David learned that his flight was delayed, but departed the gate at 8:28 A.M. Students who read this scenario in a relevant study believed that David would be more up-

Would you feel worse if you missed a plane by two minutes than if you missed it by half an hour? If you would, then why?

set about missing his flight than Mel. They believed that David would be more likely to "undo" the outcome through imaginary scenarios in which he just made it to the gate on time and caught his flight. In other words, David would be more upset and more likely to engage in counterfactual thinking (Kahneman & Tversky, 1982). But why? The most likely reason is that it is easier to imagine a 2-minute deviation from what actually happened than a 30-minute deviation from what actually happened. The 2-minute deviation seems "normal." It seems well within the general knowledge that we have about one lane moving faster than another in a traffic jam and cars just catching versus just missing a particular stoplight. The 30-minute deviation, in contrast, seems highly abnormal and more divorced from reality (Miller et al., 1990).

When we say that "undoing" outcomes in imagination is more likely when an alternative outcome is easy to imagine because it seems so normal, we mean "normal" as defined by the thinker. We do not mean "normal" as defined by objective reality. In one study, for instance, the experimenters staged a lottery in which they randomly assigned 500 numbered tickets to participants (Turnbull, 1981). Suppose that the winning number were 333. Most of the other 499 participants reported very little disappointment that they did not win, because they knew all along that the chance of winning was only 1 in 500. A more intense and emotional sense of disappointment was reported, however, by the two people who held tickets 332 and 334. "I came so close" was their reaction, even though in reality they came no closer to winning than did people who held the tickets numbered 001 and 499. The mental model involved does not have to be a rational one to elicit feverish counterfactual thinking. The social thinker need only *believe* that the outcome might have been altered by a "normal" scenario that seems like only a minor deviation from what actually happened.

Interestingly, counterfactual scenarios seem less a deviation from reality when they involve altering an event that occurred later rather than earlier in a sequence (Miller & Gunasegaram, 1990). To understand this difference in how easy it seems to change one outcome as opposed to another, consider the case in which Paul and Luther each toss a coin. If the two coins match, they get $1,000. Paul's toss is a head. Luther tosses second and gets a tail, so they lose. Who will blame himself more, Paul or Luther? If you said "Luther," you might be reasoning that "Paul's toss was an established fact. It was all up to Luther whether they won or not." Had Paul and Luther tossed their coins simultaneously, of course, it would be obvious that, in reality, they were equally to blame for the mismatch.

Juror decisions are also influenced by counterfactual thinking. Jurors in one study, for example, gave sentences to two burglars. One burglar had robbed a home one day before the homeowner's return from a three-month vacation. The other had robbed the same home during the middle of the homeowner's vacation (Macrae, Milne, & Griffiths, 1993). The jurors found it easier to imagine a counterfactual scenario in which the homeowner returned one day earlier than to imagine a counterfactual scenario in which the homeowner returned 45 days early. They got more emotionally involved and felt greater sympathy for the homeowner who might not have been robbed "if only . . ." As a result, they sentenced the "day before return" burglar more severely than the "middle of the vacation" burglar.

As for whether people prefer to construct upward or downward counterfactual thoughts, it depends on their goals. People use downward counterfactual thoughts to make themselves feel better. They remind themselves how things could have been worse. In contrast, they use upward counterfactual thoughts to prepare for the future. They remind themselves how things could have been better (Markman, Gavanski, Sherman, & McMullen, 1993; Roese, 1994). Counterfactual thoughts, like other mental simulations, serve functions that are usually very adaptive (Roese & Olson, 1993). They are maladaptive only when they lead to inaccurate conclusions, cause people unnecessary anguish ("worrying over spilt milk"), and cause unnecessary changes in behavior (Sherman & McConnell, in press).

SUMMARY OF ACCURACY IN SOCIAL THINKING

Although social thinking usually works well, it is sometimes inaccurate. Accessible constructs can be primed because they were recently active. When the primes are similar to new information or when social thinkers do not realize that they have been primed, judgments are biased toward similarity with the prime. When the primes are very dissimilar from new information or blatant, social thinkers overadjust. Their judgments are biased away from the prime.

When social thinkers try to integrate separate pieces of information, their judgments can be biased by incongruency effects and by positive-negative asymmetry. Information incongruent with expectations carries greater weight than does congruent information. Negative information carries greater weight than does positive information when judging another person's morality, because the negative information seems more useful. For the same reason, positive information carries greater weight than does negative information when judging another person's competence.

When social thinkers try to remember their acquaintances, they recapitulate the process by which they originally formed impressions. First, they remember acquaintances according to their social categories. Within each social category, they remember category members who differ in their personality traits. Social thinkers also remember more details about other people when they try to form personality impressions than when they try to memorize details. Coherent personality impressions, especially about people with whom we expect to interact, require generating causal connections between the separate pieces of information. These causal connections improve memory.

Social thinkers let their own mental simulations influence their judgment, often without realizing the influence. In hindsight, people construct causal scenarios that make a known outcome seem inevitable. In foresight, people are overconfident that mentally simulated future events will occur, because they fail to realize that future circumstances might be different from their imagined scenarios. Finally, judgments are influenced by counterfactual scenarios in which social thinkers mentally "take back" actions or "undo" outcomes. Counterfactual thinking is more likely when the action that led to the outcome was unusual and when the outcome aroused strong emotions.

CAN WE CONTROL SOCIAL THINKING?

In the third and final section of the chapter, we discuss times when people try to control their social thinking. As the first section of the chapter described, much of social thinking occurs spontaneously or automatically. One of the criteria for automaticity is that the thought cannot be controlled. Even so, people are sometimes very motivated to think about something else. What happens when they try to intervene in their own thought processes and exert greater control than they usually have? The empirical evidence suggests that attempts at thought control often have both ironic effects and unwanted health consequences.

IRONIC EFFECTS OF THOUGHT CONTROL

Recall the self-generation principle discussed in the first section of this chapter. Even when no new information occurs, the information-processing system "runs along on its own," generating one thought after another. What happens when we try to control the types of thoughts that become currently active? Have you ever tried to stop thinking about food when you were on a diet? Have you ever had an emotionally charged argument with someone and later, when you were trying to sleep, you could not stop yourself from thinking, "When he said that, I should have said *this*?" As you may have discovered, *not* thinking about something is not as easy as it sounds (Wegner, 1989; Wegner & Wenzlaff, in press). Attempts to control mental processes sometimes succeed, but at other times, ironically, they produce exactly the opposite of the desired result (Wegner, 1994).

Suppose that an individual has the goal of avoiding thoughts about food. The goal directs the deliberative stage of information processing, which does two things (Wegner, 1994). First, it tries to concentrate on a different topic, for example, counting the number of red cars that pass. Second, it sends a "signal" to the organizing operation, saying, "When you find thoughts about food, displace them from your current thoughts before they get to the deliberative stage." The problem is that the organizing operation is "on the lookout" for exactly the wrong types of thoughts. If a passing car has a red color similar to that of ketchup, for instance, the organizing operation gives that thought special attention. It sends a signal to the deliberative stage that says "Do not deliberate on this, because it might remind you of FOOD!" With exceptional motivation and cognitive resources, the deliberative stage can do its job by generating alternative thoughts. When motivation and resources are low, setting the organizing operation to watch for thoughts that might be relevant to food can be counterproductive. The irony is that suddenly *everything* seems related to the very thought that the individual has been trying to avoid. When the deliberative stage loses its concentration on alternative topics, currently active thoughts are suddenly flooded with thoughts about food.

In one study of how attempts at mental control might have ironic effects, the researchers left college students alone for five minutes in a room with a tape recorder (Wegner, Schneider, Carter, & White, 1987). They asked the students to say everything that came to mind. They asked some students to think about a white bear as often as they could during the 5 minutes. They asked other students to "try *not* to think of a white bear." They also told students in both groups to ring a bell every time they thought about a white bear, even

FIGURE 2.5

Thought suppression has ironic effects.
Graph shows number of times students thought about a white bear when they tried to suppress the thought in either the first or the second session (Wegner, Schneider, Carter, & White, 1987).

Think about, then suppress   Suppress, then think about

Frequency of occurrence

8
7
6
5
4
0

Bell rings
First session

Bell rings
Second session

though they had not mentioned it aloud. The left side of Figure 2.5 shows what happened during this first session. Students who tried to suppress thinking about a white bear rang the bell almost as many times as did students who *wanted* to think about a white bear. Students in one group kept talking about polar bears standing on icecaps, what black noses they have, and so on. Students in the other group talked about unrelated topics. Nonetheless, trying not to think about a specific topic had no immediate effect in squelching the unwanted thought (Wegner et al., 1987).

Does temporarily suppressing an unwanted thought have a "rebound effect"? When the thought occurs later, does it unleash many unwanted associations? After students in the study had completed their first sessions, the researchers asked them to switch roles. In the second 5-minute session, those who had formerly tried to think about a white bear tried to suppress such

Will you still be thinking about this white bear even after you close the book?

thoughts. Conversely, those who had formerly tried to avoid thinking of a white bear now tried to think about one. The right side of Figure 2.5 shows what happened in the second session. Students who had formerly tried to think about white bears were unsuccessful in suppressing the unwanted topic. They could avoid talking about it, but they could not avoid thinking about it as often as they had in the first session. The more interesting result, however, was that students who had formerly suppressed thoughts of a white bear were *full* of such thoughts once the prohibition had been lifted. They rang the bell frequently, even when they were not verbalizing their white bear thoughts, perhaps because they were disturbed by having failed to squelch thoughts about the white bear in the first session (Martin, Tesser, & McIntosh, 1993).

How effective is the strategy of thinking about something else? Students who were trying to suppress thoughts in a follow-up study were told that, to avoid thinking about a white bear, they should concentrate instead on thinking about a red Volkswagen. Unfortunately for them, the strategy was not successful. Red Volkswagen students thought about a white bear as much as did students who had no strategy. The strategy helped, however, in overcoming the rebound effect. When they were released from thought suppression in the second session, students who had distracted themselves with the red Volkswagen did *not* experience a flood of previously suppressed thoughts (Wegner et al., 1987).

Paradoxically, it might not be such a wise strategy for people who have disturbing thoughts to try suppressing them, especially when the thoughts are more important than thinking about white bears. A defining characteristic of depression, for instance, is that people who are chronically depressed ruminate excessively about negative topics. They contemplate their guilt about previous failures to achieve even minor goals, their pessimism about future life chances, and their doubts about their own worth. For some unfortunate individuals, depressing thoughts are maximally accessible and intrusive. In a study of the strategies that depressed people use to suppress unwanted thoughts, the investigators asked depressed and normal students to picture themselves as the main character in either a happy story or a sad story (Wenzlaff, Wegner, & Roper, 1988). In the happy story, they found a missing baby. In the sad story, they sped through an intersection on the yellow light, hit another car broadside, and saw the other driver emerge from the wreckage crying, with her dead baby in her arms.

After they had imagined either the happy story or the sad story, the investigators asked all participants to write whatever thoughts came to them during the next 9 minutes. They also told the participants to make a check mark on the page whenever they happened to think about the story. Some students received no other instructions. Others were asked to "*not* think about the story that you just read." Despite these instructions, the depressed students were no more successful at suppressing thoughts of the sad story than students had been in the previous research where the unwanted thought was of a white bear. In keeping with the rebound effect found in the earlier research, depressed students kept thoughts of the sad story under partial control for the first 6 minutes of writing their thoughts. During the last 3 minutes, however, they had many intrusive thoughts about the story.

When the investigators analyzed what depressed and normal students had written, they discovered that depressed students were just as likely as normal students to try distracting themselves by thinking about a different topic. The depressed students, unfortunately, used other *negative* topics. "I can't think about killing that woman's baby, so instead I'll think about the history exam that I failed." Thinking about other negative topics may lead to further negative thoughts. Interestingly, depressed students *knew* that negative topics are not as effective as positive topics when you are trying to distract yourself from an unwanted negative thought. They recognized the appropriate strategy, but they failed to use it, because, for them, positive topics were not as accessible as negative topics (Wenzlaff et al., 1988).

In a follow-up study, the investigators listed for students some positive and negative topics that they might think about to distract themselves. Both normal students and depressed students chose positive topics over negative topics to distract themselves from thinking about a sad story. As long as positive topics are made easily accessible, people who are depressed will use them. Chronically depressed people, however, are unlikely to hit upon positive topics by themselves when they are seeking an alternative topic (Wenzlaff et al., 1988). To make matters worse, the intrusion of thoughts that arouse the autonomic nervous system can occur even 30 minutes after an attempt to suppress them. When they do occur, they are especially arousing because they are unexpected (Wegner, Shortt, Blake, & Page, 1990). Research on thought suppression suggests that it may be better in the long run to let the negative thoughts happen, or even to dwell on them deliberately, as though trying to induce a bad mood (Wegner, 1989).

When people try to control their moods, they sometimes produce unintended ironic effects. The deliberative stage of social thinking can usually compensate for the organizing operation's increased attention to undesirable thoughts. When the deliberative stage is otherwise occupied, however, the organizing operation's increased vigilance for unwanted thoughts gains control. In one study of two-stage processing as it applies to attempts at mood control, the investigators asked students to remember either a very happy event in their lives or a very sad event in their lives (Wegner, Erber, & Zanakos, 1993). Regardless of which type of event they remembered, some of the students were asked to make themselves feel happy. If they remembered a happy event they were told to "feel the happiness." If they remembered a sad event they were told, "Don't let yourself feel sad." Likewise, the investigators asked other students to make themselves feel sad, either by "feeling the sadness" of a sad event or by resisting the happiness of a happy event. A third group of students received no mood control instructions. Within each of the three groups, the investigators told some of the students, but not others, to hold in memory a 9-digit number. This additional task was intended to "overload" conscious deliberation.

Students wrote their thoughts during the next 7 minutes. Compared to the no instruction group, students who did not have to remember the 9-digit number successfully generated more positive thoughts when they were trying to feel happy than when they were trying to feel sad. Students who had to remember the 9-digit number, in contrast, were unable to control their thoughts. They generated the same number of positive thoughts regardless of mood instructions. When the 7 minutes had ended, the experimenter asked all students to rate their own current moods. As shown in Figure 2.6, attempts at mood control were successful when students were not simultaneously trying to remember a 9-digit number, but had ironic effects when students were cognitively "overloaded." Compared to students who were given no mood instructions, overloaded students felt *worse* when they were trying to make themselves feel happy and *better* when they were trying to make themselves feel sad. Extrapolating beyond the experiment, "the negative mood itself could become a mental load of sorts" (Wegner et al., 1993), which might precipitate a cycle of ever more serious ironic effects.

FIGURE 2.6

People who are cognitively overloaded produce ironic effects when they try to control their moods.

Graph shows rated happiness of students who had or did not have to remember a number while trying to control their moods (Wegner et al., 1993).

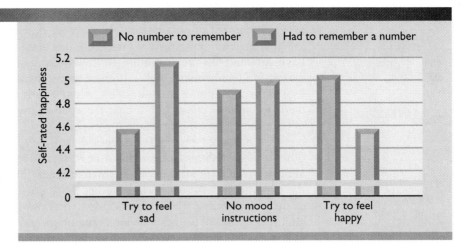

HEALTH CONSEQUENCES

If attempts at mental control have ironic effects, then refusing to think or talk about traumatic events might be unhealthy. Women who were raped, children who were physically or sexually abused, former soldiers who saw their best friends killed, and holocaust survivors who saw their parents gassed or beaten to death may inhibit thinking or talking about such traumatic experiences, but at what cost? Would it be better for trauma victims' peace of mind and physical health to confront such experiences openly? Does it make a difference whether they relate the experience in a matter-of-fact way or confess their innermost feelings? These and other questions about inhibiting versus expressing traumatic experiences have been addressed in a remarkable set of studies. To begin with, the researchers noted that the unexpected death of a spouse is an especially traumatic experience that affects different people differently. Some people talk it through with trusted friends or family members; others keep it bottled up inside them, neither confiding in anyone else nor even allowing themselves to think through their own abused emotions. These two kinds of people differ dramatically in their general physical health. Those who confided the traumatic event to others, for example, reported fewer health problems one year after their spouse died by suicide or automobile accident (Pennebaker & O'Heeron, 1984).

Correlational evidence, then, supports the theoretical notion that retelling traumatic experiences is good for a person's health. The effort of inhibiting or suppressing traumatic thoughts may put extra stress on the body. The cumulative effect of such extra stress may be a breakdown of the body's natural defenses (Lazarus & Folkman, 1984; Selye, 1976; Silver & Wortman, 1980; Tomaka, Blascovich, Kelsey, & Leitten, 1993). The problem with correlational evidence, though, is that it cannot distinguish between two alternative explanations of the relationship between confiding traumatic experiences and better health. From correlational evidence alone, it is possible that inhibiting such thoughts creates stress-related health problems. It is equally possible that people who are in poor health get around less and have fewer friends in whom to confide. The only way to settle such issues is to perform an experiment. In the experiment, we would ask individuals, randomly selected from people in reasonably good health, to describe what they consider the most traumatic events in their lives. We would ask other individuals, also randomly selected, to spend an equal amount of time talking about trivial everyday events.

Just such an experimental procedure has been used in several studies that have enriched our understanding of trauma inhibition as compared to trauma expression (Pennebaker, 1989). In these experiments, the investigators left college students alone in a comfortable, almost-dark room. They asked the students to write or speak into a tape recorder anonymously an honest account of "the most upsetting or traumatic experience of your entire life, preferably one you have not previously discussed with anyone." The investigators left other college students alone in the same room and asked them to write or speak about a trivial topic such as "what you plan to do this afternoon after you leave the experiment." Across several studies that used the "talk about a traumatic event" instructions, students responded with powerful portrayals. They told about the deaths of friends and family members, painful romantic failures, beatings, suicide attempts, overwhelming guilt, drug problems, rape, and even incest. Their voices cracked and many of them broke down and cried. In one study, more than 60 percent of them said that they had never previously discussed the topic with anyone. They also said that reexperiencing these traumatic events made them feel terrible (Pennebaker, 1989). The short-term effects are definitely aversive, but what of the long-term health effects of expressing versus inhibiting traumatic thoughts?

One experiment examined both the long-term health consequences and the precise nature of disclosure that might have an impact on physiological well-being (Pennebaker & Beall, 1986; see also Pennebaker, Colder, & Sharp, 1990). In the study, college students were randomly divided into four groups. The researchers asked some of them to write about trivial events. They asked others to write about traumatic events. Of those who wrote about traumatic events, one-third were told to describe their feelings, another third were told to describe the facts without reference to how the incident made them feel, and the other third were told to describe both the facts and their feelings.

Students who described either trivial events or the bare facts of traumatic events had approximately the same number of illnesses per month after as before the experiment. Students who described either their feelings about a traumatic event or both facts and feelings experienced fewer illnesses, as though the act of thinking through the previously inhibited traumatic event relieved stress. These conclusions were supported also by university records of how many times each student visited the health center per month before and after the experiment. The only significant decrease in visits was by students who described both the facts and their feelings. Other experiments have produced similar results for many different measures of physiological stress (Pennebaker, Hughes, & O'Heeron, 1987; Pennebaker & Susman, 1988). Just as people who try to think only happy thoughts sometimes make themselves sad, people who avoid telling traumatic experiences sometimes make themselves sick (Pennebaker, 1989).

SUMMARY OF TRYING TO CONTROL SOCIAL THINKING

Social thinking is often difficult to control. Worse, attempts to control social thinking can have ironic effects and undesirable health consequences. When people try *not* to think about something, they find it difficult to refrain. Furthermore, their suppressed thoughts often redouble when they relax their vigilance. Chronically depressed people are especially prone to the ill effects of thought suppression, because they try to distract themselves from one negative topic by thinking about other negative topics. Finally, suppressing thoughts about traumatic events can be detrimental to physical health. People who get the opportunity to describe the feelings involved in previously suppressed traumatic experiences have fewer subsequent health problems than do people who are not so fortunate.

CHAPTER 3

Person Perception

ow well do you know your friends and lovers? How confident are you that you perceive them accurately? Do you feel confident enough to bet your life?

In a study of unsafe sex on college campuses, seven social psychologists formed students into four-to-eight–person discussion groups (Williams, Kimble, Covell, Weiss, Newton, Fisher, & Fisher, 1992). The investigators asked the students to discuss the types of sexual relationships they had experienced, what methods of protection they used, and whether they thought that AIDS was a concern. Because the investigators believed that students might discuss their sexual experiences more openly in same-sex groups, the students in each group were either all men or all women. The experimenter in charge of each group was also of the same sex as the students, who knew that the discussion was being audiotaped. The investigators believed that the students would have sexual experiences to report, because they had earlier surveyed other students at the same college. The vast majority were sexually active. A majority had two or more sexual partners during the previous year.

The investigators later analyzed the audiotaped discussions by identifying themes that arose consistently in both all-male and all-female groups. The most consistent theme to emerge was that these college men and women used condoms primarily at the start of a relationship, when they felt that they did not know their partner well. Once they got to know their partner, they believed that they did not need to worry about HIV infection. A representative participant said: "When you get to know a person . . . as soon as you begin trusting the person . . . you don't really have to use a condom." Another said: "I knew

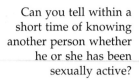

Can you tell within a
short time of knowing
another person whether
he or she has been
sexually active?

my partner really well before we had sex, so I didn't really have to worry about her sexual history" (Williams et al., 1992, p. 926).

Unfortunately, the men and women had little or no direct information about their partner's sexual history or HIV status. Instead, they relied on inferences. They believed that they could tell when to use a condom from such indirect clues as whether the person dressed provocatively, met them in a bar, was older than most college students, or was from a large city. Certain behaviors also raised danger signals. One man said: "You don't want to trust someone who just went on the pill" (Williams et al., 1992, p. 926). The men and women assumed that from knowing one piece of information about another person you can accurately infer other characteristics (Schneider, 1973).

How reasonable is such an assumption? Are people's inferences about each other so accurate that men and women are justified in taking great risks that are based only on their impressions? The part of social psychology that deals with how we form impressions of other people is called "person perception." Person perception begins at the split second when we first become aware of another person and continues throughout a relationship (Brewer, 1988; Fiske & Neuberg, 1990; Harvey & Barnes, 1994; Zebrowitz, 1990). The topic encompasses such diverse questions as how we get from the raw information about other people to confidently held impressions, whether inferences are accurate, and whether some people, perhaps because they disguise their true selves, might be more difficult to "read" than others (Jones, 1990). In this chapter we describe three aspects of person perception: how it works, to what extent it is accurate, and when it is most challenging.

HOW DO WE PERCEIVE OTHER PEOPLE?

Person perception is about how we form impressions of other people. Obviously, impression formation is a process that never stops. It continues from the first glimpse of a person through a continuous updating of the overall impression that we have of that person. Some of your best friends may be people you did not think you would like when you first met them. Conversely, you may have learned to your sorrow that people whom you previously admired were not to be trusted. We begin the discussion, therefore, with a model of how impression formation works and then move to describing two types of information on which impressions are based: verbal information and nonverbal information.

A MODEL OF PERSON PERCEPTION

The process of person perception illustrates one of the three major themes that occur in chapters throughout this text–the "two-stage" idea that people have spontaneous initial reactions, followed by deliberative "adjustments" (Bargh, 1994; Beike & Sherman, 1994; Brewer, 1988; Epstein, et al., 1992; Gilbert, 1989; Martin, et al., 1990; Smith, 1994). The two stages are analogous to the anchoring and adjustment heuristic described in Chapter 2. Whether the topic is social thinking, attribution, attitudes, stereotypes, the self, social influence, or other aspects of social psychology, some of people's reactions are relatively "automatic" and spontaneous; others are more deliberative. Person perception is no exception. Person perception involves a relatively automatic, spontaneous initial reaction to a person, which acts as an anchor point or "first impression." It also sometimes involves a deliberative adjustment to that first impression (Brewer, 1988; Fiske & Neuberg, 1990).

In all, person perception involves four steps: categorization, inferences, gathering more information, and recategorization. Categorization and inference are part of the spontaneous stage. Perceivers spontaneously notice social categories such as sex or race and draw preliminary inferences from the person's category membership. Gathering more information and recategorization are part of the deliberative stage. Perceivers sometimes seek additional information about the other person and reevaluate which social category is most useful for forming an accurate impression. Categorization and inference occur whenever we learn information about a person. Gathering more information and recategorization occur only when we are willing and able to exert greater effort to perceive the person accurately. To understand these important distinctions, you should examine Table 3.1, which lists the four steps and gives an example of each. We next discuss two important aspects of the model: the way that people use initial categories in the spontaneous stage and the way they gather additional information in the deliberative stage.

■ INITIAL CATEGORIES

Merely seeing a male or a female elicits a spontaneous initial categorization. Other obvious distinctions such as Black versus White or old versus young also occur spontaneously (Andersen, Klatzky, & Murray, 1990; Cohen, 1983; Fried & Holyoak, 1984; Gaertner & McLaughlin, 1983; Klatzky, Martin, & Kane, 1982; Krueger & Rothbart, 1988; Rasinski, Crocker, & Hastie, 1985; Tajfel, Sheikh, & Gardner, 1964). Evidence for spontaneous use of social categories comes from studies of sorting and from studies of memory confusions.

Participants in one study sorted photographs of target persons who varied in age and sex (Brewer, Dull, & Lui, 1981). They spontaneously arranged the photographs into categories and subcategories of young men, old men, young women, and old women. In addition, they spontaneously recategorized elderly women into such subcategories as "grandmotherly types" and "senior citizens." The more they knew about the category (for instance, if they were themselves

TABLE 3.1	A Two-Stage, Four-Step Model of Person Perception (Based Loosely on Brewer, 1988, and Fiske and Neuberg, 1990)
STEP	**DESCRIPTION**
Spontaneous Stage	
Categorize	"automatically" notice the person's sex, race, age, etc.
Infer	spontaneously assume the person has whatever characteristics you think are typical of that social category
Deliberative Stage	
Gather More Information	add new information, preferably information that confirms the initial, spontaneous, category-based impression
Recategorize	if new information disconfirms the initial impression, find either a subcategory or a different category that fits both the initial impression and the additional information

Note: Person perception ends at the spontaneous stage unless the perceiver is both willing and able to enter the deliberative stage.

elderly and thus familiar with many older people), the finer were the subcategory distinctions that they drew (Brewer & Lui, 1985; Mackie & Worth, 1989). Person perception relies heavily on perceivers spontaneously fitting people into neat categories and subcategories (Devine, 1989; Weber & Crocker, 1983). The categories that we use for significant others may be richer, more distinctive, and easier to call to mind than the categories that we use for strangers, but they are still categories (Andersen & Cole, 1990; Andersen & Glassman, in press).

Another way of identifying the major categories that people use in initial categorization is through memory confusions (Arcuri, 1982; Beauvais & Spence, 1987; Fiske, Haslam, & Fiske, 1991; Frable & Bem, 1985; Jackson & Hymes, 1985; Miller, 1986; Taylor & Falcone, 1982; Taylor, Fiske, Etcoff, & Ruderman, 1978). If you confuse what one person said with what another person said, you may have mixed them up because, to you, they belong to the same social category and are "all the same." In one study of memory confusions, students read statements that other students had made about their ambitions and career plans (Stangor, Lynch, Duan, & Glass, 1992, Experiment 2). Each statement was accompanied by a photograph. The photographs showed a White man, a White woman, a Black man, or a Black woman. Later, the students were unexpectedly asked to remember which person had made which statement.

Figure 3.1 shows the number of times that students confused two people of the same sex and race, the same sex but a different race, the same race but

FIGURE 3.1

Memory confusions reveal perceivers' initial categories.

Graph shows number of times students confused statements made by people who were similar or dissimilar to each other in sex and race (Stangor, Lynch, Duan, & Glass, 1992).

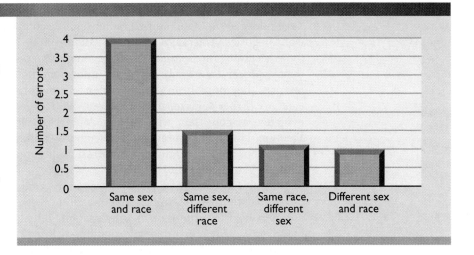

a different sex, and different race and sex. As the figure shows, students most often confused statements made by people of the same sex and race. Because the memory test was unexpected, the experimenters concluded that, without intending to, students spontaneously labeled the statements as having been made by a White man, a Black man, a White woman, or a Black woman. With so many statements and photographs to remember, the students unwittingly revealed through their memory confusions that they were using these categories and subcategories as initial anchor points for person perception.

Perceivers use categories and subcategories when they start forming an impression because doing so provides useful information. If you know nothing about a person, many perceivers believe that the most useful piece of information you could get is his or her gender (Stangor et al., 1992). When you hear that someone had a baby, for instance, most people immediately ask "What was it?" Race is another social category that many perceivers consider relevant. In several studies, highly prejudiced perceivers were more likely to confuse people of the same race than were relatively unprejudiced perceivers (Frable & Bem, 1985; Stangor et al., 1992, Experiment 3). Prejudiced perceivers may be more likely than unprejudiced perceivers to believe that they can learn valuable information merely from knowing another person's race.

Finally, initial categorization by race and sex occurs without conscious intent or deliberation, which, as described in Chapter 2, is a hallmark of "automatic" thinking (Bargh, 1994; Stangor et al., 1992). Even when perceivers are instructed to pay attention to race, for instance, their subsequent memory confusions reveal that they automatically categorize people by sex. Category confusions for sex and race also occur regardless of how similar the members of each category are to each other. Such confusions do not occur for relatively noninformative characteristics such as two people wearing similar clothing.

■ ADDITIONAL INFORMATION

Perceivers spontaneously use categories. Perceivers also slant their deliberative gathering of additional information to confirm category expectations (Bodenhausen, 1988; Cohen, 1981; Hastie, 1981; Park, DeKay, & Kraus, 1994; Rothbart, Evans, & Fulero, 1979; Stangor & Ruble, 1989; Wyer & Martin, 1986). When perceivers believe that two other people are lovers, for instance, they remember behaviors consistent with a romantic relationship such as holding hands better than they remember behaviors inconsistent with it such as asking for separate checks (Frey & Smith, 1993). Perceivers are also more likely to believe information that confirms rather than disconfirms their stereotypes of social categories (Macrae, Shepard, & Milne, 1992). Although a conscious effort to be accurate (for example, during an employment interview) reduces this tendency, perceivers usually probe for information consistent with whatever inferences they drew from the target person's membership in a particular social category (Erber & Fiske, 1984; Neuberg, 1989). They also interpret even mixed evidence as consistent with preconceptions (Darley & Gross, 1983; Darley, Fleming, Hilton, & Swann, 1988; Kreuger & Rothbart, 1988). Category-based impressions are easy; individual impressions are more difficult (Ruscher, Fiske, Miki, & VanManen, 1991).

Finally, the model of person perception applies equally to verbal and to nonverbal information. Initial categorization can be based on verbal labels that are conveyed in writing or in conversation. Initial categorization can also be based on salient nonverbal information such as a person's sex, race, or age (Brewer, 1988; Fiske & Neuberg, 1990). The information that is added and used to "adjust" the initial impression in the deliberative stage can also come in either verbal or nonverbal form (Patterson, 1994). The next two sections, therefore, discuss person perception research that has concentrated on either verbal or nonverbal information.

VERBAL INFORMATION

Much of the research on two-stage processing in person perception has provided participants with an initial category and then given them access to additional verbal information, conveyed either in speech or in writing. One important line of research on verbal information addresses the factors that affect whether impressions depend more on the initial category or on additional, individuating information. Another important line of research addresses the possibility that perceivers draw spontaneous trait inferences merely from learning about the way that another person has behaved.

■ CATEGORIZATION VERSUS INDIVIDUATION

In one study of how perceivers rely on category-based versus individuating information, college students learned that they would be working in partnership with "Frank" to design creative games out of colorful wind-up toys (Neuberg & Fiske, 1987). Before they met Frank, the students learned that he had recently been released from St. Mary's Memorial Hospital, where he was treated for schizophrenia. According to the two-stage model of person perception, this information triggered immediate initial categorization of Frank as "one of those schizo mental patients." Other students at the college said that schizophrenics are nervous, edgy, suspicious, withdrawn, and inflexible, so students who participated in the study probably expected Frank to have these characteristics (Desforges et al., 1991).

Before they met Frank in person, the students received some background information about his hobbies, interests, and goals. This information made Frank appear to be outgoing, determined, adaptive, and likable—exactly opposite to what would be expected from the category label "schizophrenic." The researchers wanted to know how much attention the students would pay to the category label (in which case they would not like Frank) as opposed to the individuating information (in which case they would like him). The researchers suspected that the determining factor would be how motivated students were to exert the extra effort necessary to gather additional individuating information about what a likable person Frank was. To manipulate motivation and effort, the experimenters told half of the subjects that they would receive a $20 prize if they and Frank, working as a team, produced the most creative games. Because these students could win the prize only by working well with Frank, they were motivated to learn everything they could about him. The other half of the students were told that they would win the $20 prize if they, as individuals, invented more creative games than students who were working in other student-patient pairs. Because these students could succeed without Frank's help, they were not as motivated to learn about his unique personal characteristics and could safely continue to regard him as "one of those schizos."

With a hidden stopwatch, the experimenter timed how long students in these two conditions spent reading the individuating information about Frank's hobbies, interests, and goals. As predicted, students who thought they needed Frank to win the prize spent more time reading about Frank than did students who thought they could win without him. The experimenter then asked the students to complete "one more form before you meet Frank in person." The first question was "How generally likable does this person seem?" Students who needed Frank considered him more likable than did students who did not need him. Motivated students, one could argue, were more likely to decide that more effort was warranted. They went beyond spontaneous categorization and inference. By using the deliberative stage of person perception, they arrived at a more individual than category-based impression of Frank.

Other studies showed that it takes greater cognitive effort to arrive at individual than category-based impressions. Social perceivers are motivated to exert the extra effort when the other person has personal significance for them or when they are taking special pains to be accurate (Brewer & Lui, 1985; Erber & Fiske, 1984; Fiske, Neuberg, Beattie, & Millberg, 1987; Kruglanski & Freund, 1983; Pavelchak, 1989). In some circumstances, they allow additional information to "dilute" category-based assumptions, but the information must seem to be broadly applicable, diagnostic, and worth the effort (Hilton & Fein, 1989; Krull, 1993). Chronically depressed people exert the extra effort to form individual rather than category-based impressions even in circumstances where nondepressed people are satisfied to use the category. Chronically depressed people may be especially motivated to understand, predict, and control their social environment (Edwards & Weary, 1993). In everyday person perception, however, even when individuating information is potentially available, many perceivers are satisfied to form category-based impressions and to regard an easily categorized person as "just one of those."

■ SPONTANEOUS TRAIT INFERENCES

Perceivers do not rely on initial categorization merely because they are lazy (Fiske & Taylor, 1984). They also draw **spontaneous trait inferences,** which are relatively "automatic" inferences from another person's behavior to that person's likely personality traits (Newman & Uleman, 1989; Smith & Zarate, 1990; Uleman & Moskowitz, 1994; Winter & Uleman, 1984). In one study of spontaneous trait inferences, students viewed head-and-shoulders photographs of other students (Carlston & Skowronski, 1994, Study 1). Beneath each photograph was a statement that the other student had supposedly made. Beneath one man's photograph, for instance, was the statement "I hate animals. Today I was walking to the pool hall and I saw this puppy. So I kicked it out of my way." No one ever said that the man was cruel, but the investigators predicted that students would draw such an inference spontaneously, whether they meant to or not. The investigators tested this prediction by later showing the photographs again without the statements, but with trait words such as "stupid" or "cruel" attached. Then they asked the students to recall which words had been paired with which photographs. The students remembered the paired words better when the word was a trait that had been implied by the photographed person's statement than when it was a different trait. For the man who said he had kicked the puppy, for instance, students found it easier to remember when his photograph was paired with the word "cruel" than when it was paired with the word "stupid." They must have already connected his face with "cruel" even before anyone mentioned the word.

More important, the students remembered the implied trait better than other traits whether they were deliberately *trying* to draw trait inferences from the statements or merely looking at the photographs and statements with no particular goal in mind. In other words, they drew trait inferences from behavior "automatically" and spontaneously. In follow-up studies, the investigators also showed that memory for spontaneous trait inferences occurs as much as one week after seeing the original photographs. It also occurs even when students can no longer recall which photographs and self-statements were originally presented (Carlston & Skowronski, 1994). Spontaneous trait inferences are relatively "unavoidable," at least for people who rely on such inferences frequently in their daily lives (Newman, 1991, 1993).

Not everyone, however, relies to the same degree on trait inferences. Recall that people who confused "who said what" within race and sex were the same people who were most likely to *use* such perceptually salient categories in forming impressions (Stangor et al., 1992). Initial category-based and behavior-based assumptions also become "automatic" and spontaneous when the perceiver finds them useful and gets frequent practice using them (Bassili, 1993; Moskowitz, 1993; Smith, Stewart, & Buttram, 1992). Children younger than fifth grade do not make spontaneous trait inferences, presumably because they have not yet developed the idea that a person's past behaviors predict the person's future behavior (Newman, 1991). Also, students who take a "collectivist" perspective (discussed in Chapter 1) are not as likely as are students who take an "individualist" perspective to draw trait inferences from verbal descriptions of behavior. People who take a collectivist perspective predict an individual's future behavior from the *group's* tendencies and not from the individual's tendencies (Newman, 1993). For verbal information, at least, trait inferences become spontaneous only when they are useful.

NONVERBAL INFORMATION

Both the initial categorization and the "gathering additional information" steps in the model of person perception can be either verbal or nonverbal (Brewer, 1988; Fiske & Neuberg, 1990). This section of the chapter concentrates on information that perceivers glean from nonverbal sources, such as another person's face, voice, and movements (Tickle-Degnan, Hall, & Rosenthal, 1994).

■ FACE CUES

The face provides important nonverbal information. Some faces, for example of George Washington or Abraham Lincoln, seem so dominant or powerful that they command respect. Other faces, for example of fashion models and movie stars, are so beautiful that they are keys to fame, fortune, or at least preferential treatment. In the two-stage model of person perception, people who are blessed with certain types of faces may have an advantage on favorable first impressions from the very start of the spontaneous stage—an edge that continues through the deliberative stage in the form of biased gathering and interpretation of additional information.

People infer from facial photographs and portrait paintings, for example, whether another person is dominant or submissive. One sign of dominance is having a visually prominent face. Faces that take up nearly all of a frame,

Why do White faces take up a larger percentage of the frame than do Black faces on United States postage stamps?

whether in a photograph, a painting, or other visual image, seem powerful. Faces that look tiny inside a large frame seem puny and insignificant. Two social psychologists wondered whether White artists might inadvertently reveal their racism by depicting White faces as taking up a larger percentage of the frame than Black faces (Zuckerman & Kieffer, 1994). The psychologists called this very subtle form of racism "face-ism." To test their hypothesis, the investigators examined facial photographs and portraits in current U.S. and European magazines, U.S. paintings (by White artists) in the nineteenth and twentieth centuries, and U.S. commemorative stamps done by White artists.

Figure 3.2 shows the face-ism scores (percentage of the frame taken up by the face) for portraits of Whites and Blacks in each of the four sources. As the figure shows, White photographers, White artists, and even the U.S. Postal Service chose to display White people with more prominent faces than Black people. As in previous studies of face-ism, men were also depicted with more prominent faces than were women, and American Indians were depicted with especially tiny, nonprominent faces (Archer, Iritani, Kimes, & Barrios, 1983; Copeland, 1989; Trimble, 1988; Zuckerman, 1986). The photographers, artists, and postal authorities probably did not intend to be racist, but their choices of how to depict Whites and Blacks betrayed their assumptions about the relative dominance of different races. Portraits by Black artists, for example, did *not* depict the faces of Whites more prominently than the faces of Blacks (Zuckerman & Kieffer, 1994).

Faces can also bias impressions by being attractive or unattractive. What does it mean, though, to have an attractive face? In one study of facial attractiveness in women, the experimenter took careful measurements of eye, chin, and nose size, cheekbone width, cheek width, eyebrow height, pupil width, smile width, and other physical characteristics in photographs of women from around the world (Cunningham, 1986, Experiment 1). College men from the United States then rated the photographed women on attractiveness. The men found most attractive women who had the "baby" features of big eyes, small nose, and small chin, combined with the "mature" features of wide cheekbones and narrow chin, plus the "expressive" features of high eyebrows, wide pupils, and wide smiles. Men preferred these features in women of all races, as though certain facial features were universally attractive.

In one follow-up study, the experimenter discovered that men perceive women who have these attractive facial features as especially bright, sociable,

FIGURE 3.2

"Face-ism" may be a subtle form of racism.

Graph shows percentage of the frame subsumed by the face in portraits of Whites and Blacks from four sources (Zuckerman & Kieffer, 1994).

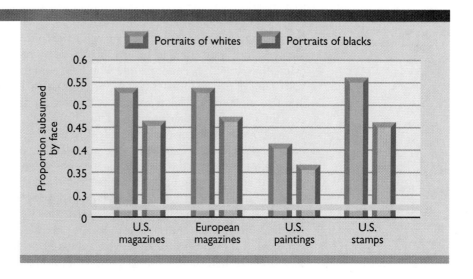

in good health, and fertile (Cunningham, 1986, Experiment 2). The men recognized that women with such attractive features might be more likely than their peers to have extramarital affairs. Nonetheless, they said they preferred to date them, preferred them for sex, and preferred them for raising children. For women who had "baby" features, men said that they would be more likely to save them from drowning by swimming one-half mile from shore, rescue them from the second story of a burning building, and shield them by jumping on a terrorist hand grenade. In a second follow-up study, women rated the attractiveness of photographed men (Cunningham, Barbee, & Pike, 1990). Both White and Black women preferred men who had some "baby" features like large eyes and small nose, but also mature features such as prominent cheekbones and a "strong" chin, plus "status" symbols such as a dark suit, light shirt, and tie. The experimenters speculated that women have "mixed motives" regarding which men they find attractive. The "ideal man conveyed both cuteness and ruggedness and may have elicited female responses of both nurturant affection and respect" (Cunningham et al., 1990, p. 65).

■ VOICE CUES

Another important piece of nonverbal information is a person's voice—not *what* the person says, but *how* he or she says it. Voices, like faces, differ in how attractive they seem to other people (Berry, 1990). An attractive voice is resonant, articulate and has a good range; it is not shrill, high-pitched, or monotonous (Zuckerman & Miyake, 1993). Perceivers who listen to people reciting the alphabet agree with each other about which voices are attractive and which are unattractive, even though they cannot see the person who is speaking (Berry, 1992).

Perceivers also attribute different personalities to people who have attractive versus unattractive voices. When speakers have attractive voices, they seem both strong and interpersonally warm (Berry, 1992). People whose voices differ also view themselves in the same way as do perceivers. Men who have "weak" high-pitched voices, for example, describe themselves as relatively unassertive (Berry, 1991a). Women who have "weak," hesitant, "immature" voices describe themselves as socially submissive. Similarly, women who have voices that other people regard as "warm" describe themselves as having many close relationships (Berry, 1991a).

These correspondences between people's voices, the way others see them, and the way they see themselves may occur for two reasons. First, we may treat people as though their voice qualities were valid signs of their internal dispositions (Snyder, Tanke, & Berscheid, 1977). After years of other people treating him like a doormat, a man who was born with a thin, reedy, high-pitched voice may come to believe that he is by nature weak and unassertive (McArthur, 1982). Second, people who lack confidence may speak in "weak" voices full of pauses and hesitations (Scherer, 1986). When women talk to their intimate male friends, they use voices that sound more approachable and sincere than when the same women talk to casual male acquaintances (Montepare & Vega, 1988). Both males and females are easier to understand when they are talking about females than when they are talking about males (Rieder & Rosenthal, 1994). Patients who are talking to a physician who sounds anxious start using an anxious tone of voice themselves (Hall, Roter, & Rand, 1981). Perhaps without realizing that they are doing so, people may use voice quality to show how they are feeling in interpersonal situations.

In an interesting study of voice quality in interpersonal situations, participants rated the voices of people who appeared on television, either in television dramas or in talk shows (Hall & Braunwald, 1981). Because they rated only brief segments, the raters did not know whether the speaker was addressing a man or a woman. The investigators discovered that the male characters in television dramas speak in a more "macho" way (dominant, condescending, unpleasant, and businesslike) than do men who appear on talk shows. Presumably, the actors who portray men in dramas alter their voices subtly to reflect an exaggerated stereotype of how "real men" are supposed to talk, a vocal style that they do not use on talk shows when they are "being themselves." Also, the raters were correct in guessing that men used a more "dominant" tone of voice when they were addressing other men, but were incorrect in their assumptions about female speakers, at least on television. The raters mistakenly believed that women who used a more "dominant" tone of voice were talking to other women and not to men. In reality, both male and female television actors used more dominant voices when they were addressing men than when they were addressing women. Contrary to a commonly held stereotype, women do *not* use a weak, submissive voice when they talk to men.

■ MOVEMENT CUES

Is this child happy or sad?

A third type of nonverbal information involves movement. Just as perceivers draw confident inferences about people they can hear but not see, perceivers also draw confident inferences about people when all they have to go on is how the person moves. The researchers in one study put pieces of reflective tape on the wrists, elbows, knees, hips, and shoulders of people who walked across a stage wearing dark clothing (Montepare & Zebrowitz-McArthur, 1988). The researchers videotaped the walkers, who were either 5–7 years old, 13–14 years old, 26–28 years old, or 65–70 years old, against a black background. Later, the researchers showed college students the videotapes, in which the perceiver could see only moving points of light. This unusual technique eliminates all other nonverbal information except movement, yet viewers quickly recognize that the points of light are made by a person who is walking (Johannson, 1973).

The student perceivers tried to guess each walker's age. They also rated each walker's power, happiness, warmth, and sexiness. Merely from moving points of light, perceivers could tell that children were the youngest, then adolescents, then young adults, then older adults. Perceivers agreed as well that people who walk with a "youthful gait" sway their hips, bend their knees, pick up their feet, take more steps per second, and have a large arm swing, loose joints, and a bouncy rhythm. These differences in gait also created different impressions. People who walked with a youthful gait seemed happier and more powerful. Regardless of the walker's sex, children and older walkers seemed less sexy than did adolescents and young adults.

One explanation of these results is that body movements convey both universal and culture-specific information (Montepare & Zebrowitz-McArthur, 1988). Children aged 5–7 and older adults are either too young or too old to have children, so they move in less sexually attractive ways than do adolescents and young adults. Such a relationship should be universal for the human species. Perceptions of power, however, might be specific to cultures. Older people might have little power in the United States, where the "moving points of light" study was initially conducted, but older people retain considerable power and respect in Asian cultures (Bond & Hwang, 1986). Researchers, therefore, asked college students in Korea to view the moving light displays of U.S. walkers (Montepare & Zebrowitz, 1993). They found that Korean perceivers, like U.S. perceivers, attributed less sexiness to the gaits of children and older adults than to the gaits of adolescents and young adults. Korean perceivers, in contrast, did *not* attribute less power to the gaits of older walkers.

Calvin and Hobbes

by Bill Watterson

MOM, CAN I GET A BIG TATTOO? I WANT A WINGED SERPENT COILING AROUND ONE ARM, CLUTCHING A SHIP ON MY CHEST, WITH...

.. UM... I MEAN... ... WELL...

.. SIGHHHH..

DID YOU KNOW MOM CAN COMMUNICATE TELEPATHICALLY?

Gait is one of many body movements that contribute to person perception. Gestures sometimes supplement verbal expression and at other times speak for themselves (Kendon, 1989; Krauss, Morrel-Samuels, & Colasante, 1991). Different postures also convey information about individuals and their relationships. People who are getting along well with each other, for example, adopt postures that are synchronous with or mirror images of each other (Bernieri, Reznick, & Rosenthal, 1988). Similarly, waiters and waitresses who squat rather than stand next to their customers, thus matching the customer's posture, receive larger tips (Lynn & Mynier, 1993).

One intimate and revealing type of body movement involves physically touching another person (Burgoon, 1991). Touch is an important aspect of interpersonal relationships. Mothers comfort newborn children with touch as much as with words (Maurer & Maurer, 1988). Healing may be enhanced when the physician touches a patient (Borelli & Heidt, 1988). People who touch and get touched by others experience less tension and anxiety in their everyday lives than do those who seldom touch (Andersen, Andersen, & Lustig, 1987). Perceivers also form spontaneous first impressions and gather additional nonverbal information about other people from observing how often and how intimately they touch. Romantically involved couples, for instance, increase their touching as the relationship becomes warmer and more intimate (Hall & Veccia, 1990; Heslin & Alper, 1983). The first physical touch is usually hand to hand, followed (in order) by arm to shoulder, arm to waist, mouth to mouth, hand to head, hand to body, mouth to breast, hand to genitals, and genitals to genitals.

Also, men and women differ in how frequently they initiate touch. In one United States study, communication majors unobtrusively observed couples who were waiting in line at movie theaters and at the zoo. They recorded how many times the couple touched and who initiated the touching (Guerrero & Andersen, 1994). The experimenters later asked whether the couples were casual daters, serious daters, or married. Figure 3.3 shows how often the man and the woman initiated touching in each type of relationship. As shown in the figure, men were more likely to take the initiative on casual dates. Men and women initiated touching almost equally when the relationship became more serious. Wives initiated touching more often than did their husbands. No study has yet established whether this male-female difference in initiating touch is universal or culture-specific.

FIGURE 3.3

Men and women differ in who initiates touching at each stage of a relationship.
Graph shows percentage of times men and women initiated touch between couples in public places (Guerrero & Andersen, 1994).

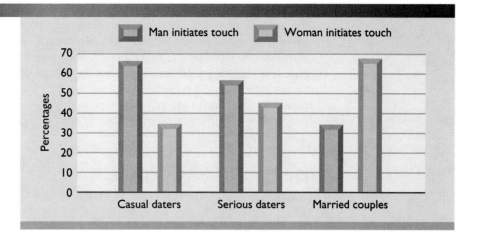

SUMMARY OF HOW PERSON PERCEPTION WORKS

When we perceive other people, we start with salient categories such as sex, race, or age. We use the category to make initial assumptions about the person. If we are willing and able to do so, we also gather additional verbal or nonverbal information. We often interpret the new information as consistent with our first impression. If the new information seems inconsistent enough, we sometimes recategorize the person or come to regard the person as an individual. Person perception, however, is slanted toward perceiving people as merely instances of a category rather than as individuals. Additional verbal information can sometimes undo category-based assumptions, but only when the perceiver is highly motivated to form an individual impression. Some types of verbal information, such as knowing how the individual behaves, are as likely as physically salient categories to generate spontaneous trait inferences. Nonverbal information also offers many cues to forming an impression. We draw different inferences about people depending on how dominant and attractive their face appears, how high-pitched their voices seem, how youthfully they walk, and how often and intimately they touch each other.

HOW ACCURATE IS PERSON PERCEPTION?

Now that we know something about the way that person perception works, it is time to address its accuracy. How likely are people who meet at a college mixer to form accurate impressions of each other? How likely are they, should their relationship continue and eventually become more intimate, to know each other well enough to base important life decisions on their accuracy? Do people get to know each other's personality traits better as the relationship continues? Do they develop the ability to detect each other's emotions so that they would know whether the other person is feeling love, hate, guilt, or indifference? To examine such issues, this section of the chapter first defines and discusses what social psychologists mean by "accuracy." Next, the section addresses some quirks in inferring traits that sometimes lead to inaccurate perception. Finally, it tackles the issue of how accurately we can tell what emotions another person is experiencing.

DEFINING "ACCURACY"

Table 3.2 lists three ways that social psychologists define and measure accuracy in person perception. As the table shows, we say that perceivers are accurate when they form an impression that agrees with what the target person says about himself or herself, when they agree with each other about what a target person is like, and when their impression predicts the target person's future behavior. Each of these three ways of defining and measuring accuracy has its advantages and disadvantages (Ickes, 1993; Kenny, 1991).

Agreeing with self-reports, for instance, might be essential to continued friendship. If two roommates disagree about how honest or sincere one of them is, they may not stay roommates for long. Unfortunately, though, accuracy defined by self-reports can change over time. When two roommates agree today and disagree next month about the same trait, who is to say whether the perceiver was more "accurate" the first time or the second? In a relevant study,

TABLE 3.2	Three Ways of Measuring Accuracy in Person Perception, with Advantages and Disadvantages of Each Measure (Kenny, 1991)
MEASURE	**QUESTION**
Agreeing with Self-Reports	Does the perceiver's impression agree with what the target person believes about himself or herself? Advantage: good indicator of whether two people will get along Disadvantage: people sometimes disagree more as they get to know each other better
Agreeing with Others	Does the perceiver's impression agree with other people's impressions of the target person? Advantage: a good "reality check" for perceivers who do not realize they are biased Disadvantage: people often assign different meanings to the same behavior
Predicting Future Behavior	Does the perceiver's impression allow the perceiver to predict what the target person will do? Advantage: tells whether impressions are useful Disadvantage: perceivers predict behavior toward people in general better than they predict behavior toward themselves

college roommates who lived together for a long time got more "accurate" (agreed with each other more) about who was outgoing versus reserved and who was irritable versus good-natured, but they got less accurate (agreed with each other less) over time about who was independent versus conforming (Bernieri, Zuckerman, Koestner, & Rosenthal, 1994). Any measure on which the same perceivers are more accurate over time on some traits and less accurate over time on other traits has serious disadvantages.

Agreement with others may seem like an objective way to measure "reality," but this type of accuracy also has some disadvantages. It is affected by whether two perceivers use the same initial categories, gather the same amount of information, observe the same behaviors, assign the same meaning to those behaviors, and communicate with each other. It is also affected by whether one perceiver happens to be in an especially good or bad mood (Keltner, Ellsworth, & Edwards, 1993; Kenny, 1991; Kenny & Albright, 1987; Kenny & La Voie, 1984; Malloy, Sugarman, Montvilo, & Ben-Zeev, 1995). Two perceivers can also agree more about some traits and target persons than others. Finally, they can agree with each other even when neither agrees with what the target person says about himself or herself (Albright, Kenny, & Malloy, 1988; Funder & Colvin, 1988; Funder & Dobroth, 1987; Kenny, Albright, Malloy & Kashy, 1994; Kenny & Kashy, 1994).

Finally, we can measure accuracy by how well the perceiver's impression predicts the target person's future behavior (Kruglanski, 1989). Perceivers, however, can sometimes predict a target's behavior toward people in general, even when they cannot predict how the target will behave toward *them*. In a relevant study, college women who had talked to each other for five minutes tried to predict each other's behavior during later one-on-one conversations with them and with other women (Levesque & Kenny, 1993). They tried to predict, for instance, how much the other woman would talk, gesture, and lean forward. They were "accurate" in predicting the total talking, gestures, and leaning the other woman would display across several different conversations, but inaccurate about how much of each she would do when she talked to them. Predicting future behavior, then, has disadvantages as serious as the other ways of defining and measuring accuracy. Keep these advantages and disadvantages in mind as we discuss the relationship between accuracy and acquaintance, as well as whether some traits are more "accurate" or easily diagnosed than others.

■ ACCURACY AND ACQUAINTANCE

Returning to the study with which we began this chapter, college students of both sexes said that they practiced safe sex only until they "got to know the person." They seemed to assume that accuracy improves with acquaintance. Surprisingly, this commonsense idea appears to be contradicted by the results of several studies. Regardless of how we measure "accuracy," research evidence suggests that people do *not* become more accurate over time in perceiving each other, unless they choose to continue living together and the measure of accuracy is agreement with self-reports (Bernieri et al., 1994; Kenny, 1991; Paulhus & Bruce, 1992; Park & Judd, 1989).

In a relevant study, four students who had never met each other sat in a room together for a few minutes (Kenny, Horner, Kashy, & Chu, 1992, Study 2). They could look at each other, but they were not allowed to speak. Next, the students rated each other on various personality traits. After the students made these ratings, the investigators arranged separate one-on-one "getting acquainted" conversations. Each student held an 8-minute conversation with each of the other three. Then all students rated each other again. The measure of accuracy was agreeing with others.

On this measure of accuracy, perceivers were much more accurate when they knew nothing about each other than after they held one-on-one conversations! When they were merely strangers who sat in a room and looked at each other, the students all tended to notice the same things about each other. They drew personality trait inferences from how often a particular student smiled, how she dressed, how tense or relaxed she was, and so on. For any one student "target," the three student perceivers all observed the same nonverbal behavior, so their personality trait inferences tended to agree. When they held separate one-on-one conversations, however, the students got additional information that varied from one perceiver to the next. A woman who smiled frequently in the initial meeting, when talking was not allowed, might later "talk a blue streak" when she met with one of the other students with whom she shared a common interest, but "clam up" when she met with a different student whom she did not like. The two perceivers might have initially agreed, based only on their observation of smiling, that the target student was sociable. After their separate one-on-one conversations, however, they would disagree on how sociable she was.

The study's results support the principle, discussed in Chapter 1, that two-stage reactions do not always become more accurate in the second, more deliberative stage than they were during the first, more spontaneous stage (Wilson & Brekke, 1994). Deliberative thinking sometimes results in too large or too small an adjustment. The students may have placed too much weight on the one-on-one conversation, because they did not realize that they may themselves have caused the target person to behave differently from how she normally behaved (Gilbert & Jones, 1986). When students held group conversations instead of separate one-on-one conversations, for instance, perceivers were just as accurate after as before the interaction (Kenny et al., 1992, Study 3). In group conversations, no one perceiver could dramatically alter the target person's normal behavior, nor could different perceivers observe entirely different behaviors. They all had similar spontaneous reactions and they all had the same additional information on which to form deliberative reactions.

■ ACCURACY FOR DIFFERENT TRAITS

One interesting hypothesis is that perceivers are more accurate on some traits than on others because some traits are more likely than others to have adaptive significance (Gangestad, Simpson, DiGeronimo, & Biek, 1992; Levesque & Kenny, 1993). One of the most accurately diagnosed traits, for instance, is extroversion. Across several studies, perceivers display greater accuracy in telling whether another person is extroverted versus introverted than in judging other personality traits. From an evolutionary standpoint, it would have been very adaptive for early human beings to recognize who was extroverted and who was introverted, because extroversion is correlated with leadership (Lord, De Vader, & Alliger, 1986). "When groups of hunters found themselves in smaller groups, knowing who to follow and from whom to take orders was essential" (Levesque & Kenny, 1993, p. 1179). Group members who could recognize the active, outgoing, adventurous types may have lived longer than their less perceptive peers. As a result, they may have been more likely to have children, who would also recognize extroversion when they saw it (Brewer & Caporael, 1990).

Fortunately for college students who believe that extended acquaintance is insurance against AIDS, another "accurate" personality trait is "socio-sexuality" (Simpson & Gangestad, 1991). People who score high on socio-sexuality report that they have had many different sexual partners and "one-night stands," foresee having many different sexual partners in the future, fantasize about having sex with someone other than their current dating partner, and think that "casual" sex without love is acceptable and desirable. In one study of perceiving socio-sexuality, students at one university watched 20-minute videotaped interviews with strangers from a different university (Gangestad et al., 1992). From the videotapes (which were shown without sound), the perceivers estimated each target person's socio-sexuality and several other personality traits.

To make the ratings, perceivers used nonverbal cues like eye contact, forward body lean, an "open" posture, flirtatious glances, and eyebrow flashes. Perceivers were more accurate for socio-sexuality than for the other traits, especially when male perceivers were rating female targets. The results make sense if it is evolutionarily advantageous for human beings to choose a mate who is willing to invest heavily in offspring rather than "sleeping around" (Gangestad et al., 1992). In other words, people are most accurate in perceiving traits in others that are of vital importance to their own reproductive success. Nonetheless, it is wise to remember that agreement with the target is not the best or only measure of accuracy. Also, accuracy is at best moderate even for evolutionarily significant traits like extroversion and socio-sexuality (Kenny, 1991; Kenny et al., 1994).

INFERRING TRAITS

If perceivers are only moderately accurate in forming impressions of others, where do they go wrong? One bias in inferring traits from verbal information comes from primacy effects. Another comes from implicit personality theories.

■ PRIMACY EFFECTS

Primacy effects in person perception occur when perceivers place greater weight on initial information than on later information in forming an impression. Suppose you were trying to gather information about a woman named Susan that you met at a college mixer. One of your friends tells you that Susan is *intelligent*. A little later, a different friend tells you that Susan is *industrious*. Then someone else says that Susan is *impulsive*. The next day, a student who had a course with her remarks that Susan is *critical*. After that, you are in a group in which someone says that Susan is *stubborn* and another person adds that she is also *envious*. What kind of person do you expect Susan to be? Try to imagine ways in which one person could be intelligent, industrious, impulsive, critical, stubborn, and envious. You may have decided that Susan is a smart, hard-working type who sometimes lets her emotions run away with her. Because she's so smart, she tends to be critical of shoddy performance and stubbornly stands up for what she knows to be right when other less talented and less hard-working people are wrong. The only reason she's envious occasionally is that she has such high aspirations. Susan is a likable character.

Suppose instead that the first piece of information you got about Susan was when one of your friends remarked that she is *envious*. Not only that, but you later learned that Susan is *stubborn,* so she probably holds a grudge. Next you learned how *critical* Susan is, which may be her way of putting down other people whose accomplishments make her *envious*. In addition, you discover that she's *impulsive,* which means that she might fly off the handle in one of her envious rages. Worse yet, you hear that Susan is *industrious* and *intelligent,* so she probably works hard in her sly and crafty way to take her jealousy out on other people. Susan is one dangerous person!

As you may have noticed, Susan had exactly the same six attributes in each of these two scenarios. Only the order was changed, yet the order made a significant difference in the final impression. In a classic social psychology study, students formed more positive impressions of someone who had the six traits starting with intelligent and ending with envious than of a person who had the identical traits but presented in reverse order, with envious first and intelligent last (Asch, 1946). The first pieces of information that we gather have a greater effect on the eventual impression than later pieces of information (Jones, Rock, Shaver, Goethals, & Ward, 1968; Luchins, 1957).

Why do primacy effects play such a large part in impression formation? The model of person perception presented earlier in the chapter suggests one reason: Social perceivers may not be as motivated to pay attention later in the process as they are earlier. When they average the likability of all six traits, they give greater weight to the ones that came first. This is the "averaging model" of primacy effects (Anderson, 1974). The first piece of information that we get about a person seems important because at that point it is all that we know. The second piece of information adds something to the portrait, but each succeeding piece of information seems a little less important. Students who learn about a person in the order that starts with intelligent are apt to consider the first few traits important and give them considerable weight in the overall impression. By the time the more negative traits come along, the "extra" traits hardly seem worth the effort to think about very deeply. Envious and stubborn almost "go in one ear and out the other." If you know only one fact about a person, the next piece of evidence matters a lot; if you already know a hundred facts about a person, fact number 101 doesn't make much of an impact.

Although this "greater weight to the first pieces of information" argument makes sense, you probably noticed that the Susan example involved more than mere differential weighting of traits. During the impression-formation process, some of the traits took on different meanings as a result of what came before them. Besides differential weighting, primacy effects may also occur because of a **change of meaning,** in which initial information about a target person changes the meaning of subsequent information (Zanna & Hamilton, 1977). The trait "stubborn," for example, takes on a different connotation when it applies to an intelligent, industrious person than when it applies to an envious person. The intelligent person's stubbornness is admirable persistence. The envious person's stubbornness is pigheadedness. The "change of meaning" phenomenon suggests an additional reason for believing that category-based impressions predominate over individualized impressions. Even if a perceiver is motivated to expend the effort necessary to gather additional information (see Table 3.1), the decision about whether this new information fits the category assumptions is likely to be biased. The new information is not interpreted fairly. It is twisted and turned until it "makes sense" and fits expectations. The new information is often made to tell a coherent story even when it is inconsistent with category-based assumptions.

Person perceivers are adept at interpreting even inconsistent information in a way that makes sense, thus resolving potential impression-formation discrepancies. When two traits are said to belong to the same person, they ought to make sense as a unit, as part of the same person's character (Allport, 1961; Asch, 1946; Funder, 1991). If social perceivers routinely reconcile seemingly contradictory traits as belonging to the same person, then they have probably established some systematic ways of resolving discrepancies. Students in a study of how perceivers resolve trait discrepancies were asked to imagine a person who had a pair of seemingly contradictory traits. They were asked, for example, to explain how the same person could be both brilliant and foolish, lonely and sociable, dependent and hostile, cheerful and gloomy, or kind and strict

TABLE 3.3	Five Commonly Used Strategies Person Perceivers Use to Reconcile Another's Seemingly Inconsistent Personality Traits (Asch & Zukier, 1984)	
STRATEGY	**RECONCILIATION**	**EXAMPLE**
Differentiate by roles or situations	target person displays the two traits in different roles or situations	some *brilliant* professors are so *foolish* they couldn't change a lightbulb
Attribute to different "selves"	target person displays one trait "on the surface" and the other "deep down"	some *sociable* people are *lonely* because they have many acquaintances but few deep friendships
Invent causal connections	target person displays one trait as a result of having the other trait	some children become *hostile* when their parents force them to be *dependent*
Discover a common source	both traits are logical consequences of having a third, previously unmentioned trait	some people are both *cheerful* and *gloomy* because they are moody
View one trait as the means to accomplish the other	target person displays one trait only because it creates the conditions necessary to display the other trait	some parents are *kind* to their children by being *strict* about rules

(Asch & Zukier, 1984). According to our model of person perception, this is exactly what happens when initial categorization implies a trait, for example that the person is very smart, and subsequent information reveals a seemingly inconsistent trait, for example that the person is also foolish.

Students who participated in this study found it easy to resolve the apparent inconsistencies in a way that retained the target person's unity. In doing so, they relied on five commonly used and well-practiced strategies. The five strategies for reconciling seemingly inconsistent personality traits are listed in Table 3.3, along with a description of how each strategy works. Briefly, the five strategies involve claiming that the person acts in different ways in different situations, the person has an inner self that is different from the outer self, one trait causes the other, a third trait causes both of the traits in question, and one trait is a means to the end of displaying the other. Students in the study used all five of these strategies. They found explaining two inconsistent traits such as smart and foolish no more difficult than explaining two consistent traits such as smart and witty.

It is easy to see, then, how person perceivers who spontaneously infer personality traits from a target person's appearance or nonverbal behavior can gather seemingly contradictory new information in the deliberative stage and yet convince themselves that the new information "fits" with their initial category-based assumptions. Some traits, however, are more potent than others in generating implicit assumptions and inferences.

■ IMPLICIT PERSONALITY THEORY

Recall that students in the "safe sex" study at the start of this chapter said they could tell a lot about a potential partner's sexual history and risk from knowing such facts as whether the person was from a big city or a small town. They appeared to assume that people from big cities are more "dangerous" than people from small towns. Person perceivers routinely rely on assumptions about "what goes with what" in traits and behaviors. They have **implicit personality theories.** They believe that some trait pairs are more likely than others to belong to the same person. They also believe that knowing one piece of information about a person allows confident inferences about other traits of the person (Schneider, 1973). When they gather more information about someone, therefore, initial information can have a "ripple effect" in suggesting many likely trait and behavior associates.

The ripple effect is more likely for some traits than for others. Some personality traits, called **central traits,** carry an unusually wide range of inferences about other traits and behaviors. Extrovert and introvert or warm and cold, for instance, play a more central, influential role in impression formation than do "lesser" traits, such as polite and blunt, that have fewer associations. In a classic study, some students tried to form impressions of someone who was intelligent, skillful, industrious, warm, determined, practical, and cautious. Other students tried to form impressions of someone who had all the same traits but with "warm" changed to "cold." The two groups of students formed dramatically different impressions. They regarded the warm person as more generous, better-natured, and happier than the cold person (Asch, 1946). Substitute polite versus blunt for warm versus cold in these lists and the impressions are not very different from each other. Polite and blunt are not as "central" as warm and cold. They have fewer implications for other traits. They are less likely to change the meaning or connotation of words like "intelligent" or "determined."

The centrality of the traits warm and cold was demonstrated in a study of impressions that college students formed of a guest lecturer (Kelley, 1950; see also Widmeyer & Loy, 1988). Students in a course were told that they would have a guest lecture by a visiting educator. The experimenter described the educator as having a wide variety of characteristics, one of which was "warm" for half of the students, but "cold" for the other half. The single word "warm" or "cold" was only a small part of the background material that students received. The guest lecturer also delivered exactly the same 20-minute talk to all students. Changing one central trait, however, led to far different final impressions. Students who expected a cold person regarded the lecturer as more formal, irritable, lacking in humor, self-centered, and ruthless than did students who expected a warm person.

Another central trait is introversion versus extroversion (Eysenck, 1973). We all know both introverts and extroverts and we all know that they are different types of people who can be depended on to engage in different types of behavior. Our implicit personality theories tell us that introverts are more likely to be meditative, soft-spoken, unsociable, keep their feelings to themselves, and look away when other people talk to them. Extroverts, in contrast, are more likely to be dominating, ambitious, bold, show their enthusiasm openly, and throw water balloons off the dorm balcony. The characteristics normally attached to each of these central traits—introversion and extroversion—are semantically associated. "Dominating," "ambitious," and "bold," for instance, are practically synonyms. They are not as closely associated with each other in the English language, however, as they seem when they are all attributed to the same target person.

One study tested whether extroverted traits and behaviors imply each other more strongly when they belong to an extroverted person than when they are considered separately. Students rated the likelihood that a person known to have one extroverted attribute would also have another. They estimated, for instance, "How likely is it that someone who is ambitious would also dance the hustle for hours at a party with another guest?" (Schneider & Blankmeyer, 1983). Half of the students received just these instructions; the other half learned

Do you think this person
is an introvert or an
extrovert?

that the person in question was an extrovert. As predicted, students who knew they were rating an extrovert thought the extroverted traits and behaviors implied each other more strongly than did students who merely considered the two traits separately. This study's results offer one more reason to believe that, once perceivers use an initial category in the spontaneous stage, they interpret additional trait information as consistent with category-based expectations. The results imply that category-based final impressions are more common than individualized final impressions.

DECODING EMOTIONS

Biases such as primacy effects and implicit personality theories make it difficult to be accurate in inferring another person's traits from verbal information. It is also difficult to be accurate in inferring another person's emotions from nonverbal information. Although we would like to know whether another person is feeling happy, sad, fearful, angry, or disgusted about being with us, other people are often difficult to "read." The difficulty comes from the subtlety of decoding cues and the necessity for experience.

■ SUBTLETY OF CUES

Researchers disagree on what are the "basic" human emotions. They disagree even about how to answer such a question. Some theorists believe there are six primary human emotions, whereas others believe that there are either more or fewer than six (Buck, 1984; Clore, Ortony, & Foss, 1987; Ekman et al., 1987; Russell, Lewicka, & Niit, 1989; Schwartz & Shaver, 1987). Most researchers agree, however, that people express their emotions nonverbally, through their faces, voices, and body movements. Instead of relying on what people say, perceivers who get mixed signals about emotions rely primarily on the nonverbal rather than the verbal cues. Many of these nonverbal cues are very subtle (Aronoff, Woike, & Hyman, 1992; DePaulo, Rosenthal, Eisenstat, Rogers, & Finkelstein, 1978; Ekman, Friesen, & Ellsworth, 1982; Kleck & Mendolia, 1990; Mehrabian, 1972; Mehrabian & Wiener, 1967; Rosenberg & Ekman, 1994; Wagner, MacDonald, & Manstead, 1986).

People often display their genuine emotions in microexpressions. **Microexpressions** are fleeting facial expressions that last only a brief fraction of a second and that might give away a person's actual emotion before he or she can rearrange facial muscles to disguise it (Ekman, 1985). Investigators detect microexpressions by freezing frames of a videotape. Perceivers, though, would have to be watching very closely to detect them during everyday social interaction. Microexpressions are especially difficult to detect when people are trying to "keep a straight face" or faking a smile. The facial muscles used in smiling are only slightly different in a real smile versus a fake smile (Ekman, Friesen, & O'Sullivan, 1988). Genuine emotions show on people's faces when they do not think they are being watched, but not when they know that their faces are appearing on closed circuit television (Malatesta, Izard, Culver, & Nicolich, 1987; Wagner et al., 1986). We also let our faces reveal more of our emotions when we are with friends than with strangers (Buck, Losow, Murphy, & Costanzo, 1992). Nonetheless, people are better at controlling their faces and disguising their emotions than they think they are (Barr & Kleck, 1995).

Some emotional expressions involve movements of facial muscles so tiny that they *are* imperceptible. In some studies, microelectrodes on students' faces detected systematic differences in how the facial muscles immediately under the eyebrow move when the students are experiencing different emotions. These minute changes, much smaller than those involved in microexpressions, are undetectable by the human eye. An operator who is monitoring the electrical recording equipment, however, can tell whether the student is watching a pleasant or unpleasant videotape scene, even when the student is only *imagining* the scene (Cacioppo, Martzke, Petty, & Tassinary, 1988; Cacioppo, Petty, Losch, & Kim, 1986; Fridlund, 1990). Adults, of course, are better at quickly disguising their microexpressions than are children (Ekman, 1985).

Investigators have not linked any specific vocal qualities to specific emotions. Both children and adult perceivers, across different cultures, can sometimes distinguish from voice qualities alone whether a speaker is experiencing positive or negative emotions (Burns & Beier, 1973; Fenster, Blake, & Goldstein, 1977; Van Bezooijen et al., 1983). Much of the information necessary to recognize a specific emotion, however, may be conveyed in the subtle cue of voice *changes* rather than in specific voice characteristics (Frick, 1985; Scherer, 1986). Interestingly, though no one is sure exactly why, negative emotions like fear and anger are easier to recognize from voice qualities than are positive emotions. Positive emotions like happiness, in contrast, are easier to recognize from facial expressions than are negative emotions (Fenster et al., 1977; Van Bezooijen et al., 1983).

Body movements may also convey emotions, but not if the target person is "putting on a show." Stage and screen actors study for years to convey emotions to an audience through such body cues as posture and gait. Perceivers can recognize these "posed" emotions, even across cultures (Sogon & Izard, 1987). Target persons have also been asked to imagine various scenarios while walking (Montepare, Goldstein, & Clausen, 1987). To elicit a sad walk, for instance, they imagine themselves walking down a hospital corridor on the way to visit a close friend who is dying of cancer. To elicit an angry walk, they imagine themselves stomping in to confront someone who slandered their reputation. People also walk with a different gait and posture when they are experiencing different kinds of emotions (Montepare et al., 1987). Unless they try to disguise what they feel, people who are angry walk with long, heavy-footed strides. People who are sad walk slowly and keep their arms at their sides. People who are happy walk briskly (Montepare & Zebrowitz-McArthur, 1988). Such subtle cues to emotion may be difficult to "decode," especially for perceivers who have little experience with local customs.

■ NECESSITY FOR EXPERIENCE

Emotions are not displayed in the same way across cultures. Certain ethnic groups, for instance Italians, are widely regarded as letting their emotions show more readily than do other ethnic groups, for instance the British with their "stiff upper lip." In the United States, also, women are allowed to express certain emotions, such as grief, more openly than men, but just the reverse is true for other emotions, such as anger. Each culture has its own "display rules" that dictate the appropriate and acceptable displays of emotion in that culture. These display rules sometimes differ for males and females (Ekman & Friesen, 1969).

Newborn infants the world over turn the corners of their mouths up in a smile when mother approaches and put on the same "disgusted" face as an adult when they taste bitter fruit. Newborn infants can also tell the difference between happy and angry adult faces or voices and prefer the happy ones (Caron, Caron, & MacLean, 1988; Nelson, 1987; Schwartz, Izard, & Ansul, 1985). The adults in each society also model for children the "acceptable" ways to express each emotion. Adults reward or punish children for exhibiting what that particular society considers too much or too little of each emotion. In pre-literate tribes in New Guinea, for instance, even adults cannot distinguish between surprise and fear (Ekman & Friesen, 1971), because the display of surprise is not considered useful in their particular way of life. Outward emotional displays, then, may be either inhibited or exaggerated in different cultures, either for emotions, in general, or for specific emotions.

One interesting discovery about one emotion predominating over others is that, at least in the United States, people recognize facial anger faster than they recognize other emotions. The **face-in-the-crowd effect** illustrates that one angry face in a crowd of neutral or happy faces is easier to "spot" than one happy face in a crowd of neutral or angry faces. Students in one study inspected several photographs, each of which depicted a "crowd" of five women and four men. The students were asked to decide quickly whether all the individuals in a photograph were displaying the same emotion or not (Hansen & Hansen, 1988). In some of the photographs, all the individuals were looking happy, all were looking angry, or all had a neutral expression. In other photographs, there was one happy face in a crowd of angry or neutral expressions. In a third set of photographs, there was one angry face in a crowd of happy or neutral faces.

The students noticed one angry face in a crowd faster than they noticed one happy face in a crowd. The one angry face stood out. The face-in-the-crowd effect could occur for at least two reasons. First, local display rules in the United States might make it more useful for perceivers to recognize anger than to recognize happiness. Angry faces occur so infrequently in U.S. culture that they attract attention. Second, it might be evolutionarily adaptive for human beings to recognize anger more quickly than happiness. To support the evolutionary view, the researchers conducted a second study in which they varied the size of the "crowds" from four faces to nine. Crowd size affected how quickly students could detect the happy face in an angry or neutral crowd. It had no effect, however, on how quickly students could detect the angry face in a happy or neutral crowd. The result suggests that people recognize an angry face "automatically," without conscious effort. The angry face "pops out" from any size crowd, as it would if it served as an evolutionarily adaptive danger signal. The face-in-the-crowd effect thus seems more likely to be universal than a local display rule, but complete confidence in this conclusion awaits cross-cultural research.

People who live in the same culture for many years improve in both sending and decoding nonverbal messages as they gain experience and familiarity

(Patterson, 1994b). Between the ages of four and 12, children improve dramatically at sending and interpreting emotions through face and voice cues (Bullock & Russell, 1984; DePaulo & Rosenthal, 1982; Morency & Krauss, 1982). The largest improvement at these ages is in correctly recognizing fear. Fear is the one emotion that young children communicate better than adults. It is also the emotion that children are worst at identifying in other people (Fenster et al., 1977). This discrepancy makes sense from an evolutionary perspective. Fear is the most important emotion for infants to be able to convey nonverbally, but they do not have to recognize it in others, because they are too young to provide assistance. Practice at recognizing emotions, however, usually improves accuracy, as does familiarity with the person being judged. Spouses, for instance, usually judge each other's emotions more accurately than do strangers (Sabatelli, Buck, & Dreyer, 1980, 1982).

Experience with local display rules is necessary for developing expertise in accurately recognizing emotions. Both the perceiver's and the target person's experiences matter. Japanese perceivers, for instance, recognize positive emotions in other Japanese more accurately than they recognize negative emotions. In Japan, local display rules inhibit expressing negative emotions (Shimoda, Argyle, & Ricci-Bitti, 1978). Japanese perceivers get very little experience in reading negative emotions, so they are not very good at it. Also, U.S. Blacks are better than U.S. Whites at correctly recognizing the inner emotions of both Blacks and Whites. The "oppression hypothesis" is that society members who have relatively low power protect themselves in part by learning to "read" other people's moods and intentions (Gitter, Black, & Mostofsky, 1972).

Cross-cultural differences in display rules emerge also in how people from different cultures interpret smiles. Japanese children, more than children in the United States, are taught to control their emotions. Being able to remain stoic and serious despite one's true inner feelings is a sign of maturity, whether the emotions are positive or negative. Children in the United States, in contrast, are taught to disguise their negative more than their positive emotions. Smiles thus have different meanings in Japanese culture than in U.S. culture. In a cross-cultural study, the experimenters showed U.S. and Japanese college students photographs of Japanese and U.S. people who were either smiling or maintaining a neutral expression (Matsumoto & Kudoh, 1993). Perceivers from both cultures rated smiling people as more attractive than people who were not smiling. U.S. perceivers were more likely than Japanese to rate smiling people as more sociable. Only U.S. perceivers, not Japanese, rated smiling people as more intelligent. These differences in interpreting smiles may hinder, for example, international trade agreements, if U.S. representatives attribute negative characteristics to Japanese representatives who seldom smile.

Other cross-cultural studies suggest that people in different cultures display, interpret, and even *experience* emotions differently (Scherer & Wallbott, 1994). Individuals who, because of local display rules or their personal experiences, spend their lives inhibiting one type of emotion and expressing others may "set" their faces in a permanently furrowed brow. Perceivers might then see the person as experiencing a specific emotion, for example, being sad, whether the person actually feels that way at the time or not (Malatesta, Fiore, & Messina, 1987). Also, individuals who are themselves frequently happy, sad, or angry tend to "see" the corresponding emotion in other people more frequently than it actually occurs. They may be so familiar with the emotion that they overuse it in interpreting the emotions of others (Toner & Gates, 1985).

Finally, although the cues for detecting emotion are subtle, women seem to be more accurate than men at both communicating and interpreting emotions. Women who are trying to communicate emotions nonverbally are more successful than men at getting a perceiver to interpret the posed expression in the intended way. Women also score higher than men on tests of individual and group differences in nonverbal sensitivity (Hall, 1984). In the United States, gender differences in expressing emotions may be attributed to local display rules. Because boys are discouraged and girls are encouraged to display their emotions openly, girls get better at communicating their emotions throughout childhood, whereas boys get worse (Buck, 1977; Zuckerman & Przewuzman, 1979). United States perceivers appear to acknowledge these gender differences in expressing emotions implicitly. For instance, they "expect" more female than male targets to communicate whatever emotion the context suggests, such as being sad at a funeral (Wallbott, 1988).

SUMMARY OF ACCURACY IN PERSON PERCEPTION

Accuracy in person perception can be defined as agreement between the perceiver and the target of perception, agreement between two or more perceivers, or whether the perceiver's impression predicts the target person's future behavior. By any measure, perceivers are more likely to be accurate about evolutionarily significant traits than about other traits. Contrary to popular belief, accuracy does not improve with length of acquaintance.

Person perception from verbal information is subject to several biases. When perceivers learn about a target person's traits in a specific order, for example, the initial traits affect the final impression more than do subsequent traits. Initial traits also change the meaning of subsequent traits, because perceivers use several effective strategies to interpret seemingly inconsistent information in a way that "fits" the initial impression. Perceivers are also biased by implicit personality theories. They believe that knowing one fact about a person, especially the person's standing on a "central trait," allows confident inferences about many other facets of the person's character.

Perceiving people's emotions from nonverbal information is also difficult. Despite some universals in how people display their emotions, different cultures have different "display rules." Knowledge of local display rules is necessary for successful "decoding" of a target person's emotions. Also, people are good at faking facial expressions and other nonverbal cues when they want to mislead perceivers. Women are better than men at "reading" the valid cues to emotion.

WHEN IS PERSON PERCEPTION MOST CHALLENGING?

Person perception is the foundation of all social interaction. Initial categorization, subsequent impressions, and their accuracy influence such diverse situations as doctor-patient relationships, romantic attachments, politics, job interviews, television commercials, legal decisions, rape outcomes, and international diplomacy (Bond, 1993; Brownlow & Zebrowitz, 1990; Guerrero & Andersen, 1994; Jacobs, Kulik, & Fichman, 1993; Kowalski, 1992; Lassiter, Slaw, Briggs, & Scanlan, 1992; Schwarz & Bless, 1992; Shapiro & McDonald, 1992; Wyer, Budesheim, Shavitt, Riggle, Melton, & Kuhlinski, 1991). For the most part, person perception is very accurate and adaptive. It works well. Some types of person perception, however, pose serious challenges to the perceiver. For lack of space, this final section of the chapter focuses on just two instances when person perceivers must overcome serious obstacles if they are to perceive other people accurately. The two instances involve times when the target person has a baby face and times when the target person may be lying. Both topics incorporate basic principles that were described in the first two sections of the chapter.

PERCEIVING PEOPLE WHO HAVE BABY FACES

One of the most intriguing challenges to person perceivers is to apply the same rules to forming impressions of people who have an unusual characteristic, such as an obvious physical handicap or speech impediment, as they would to anyone else. It is often difficult to be completely objective in forming impressions of people who have unusual physical characteristics. Human beings, for example, may be "prepared" by their evolutionary history to treat baby-faced adults the same way they treat children. The young of many species are able to fend for themselves within weeks, or even days, of being born. Human infants, in contrast, remain almost entirely helpless and dependent for years. For the human species to survive, adults need to protect young children. Just as ripe fruit "calls out" to be eaten, something about young children calls out to be protected. One theory is that the characteristic in question is a baby face (Berry & McArthur, 1986).

When adults see another human being who has a baby face, they initially assume that the person is weak and innocent—that the person needs to be protected. Considerable evidence suggests that people may generalize this initial assumption of weakness and innocence, which is appropriate and adaptive, to adults as well as to children. Adults may assume that other adults who have baby faces also have childlike traits. These assumptions about baby-faced adults are stable across age groups and across cultures. The assumptions also have important positive and negative consequences for people who have baby faces.

Why should you want to nurture and protect this person?

■ STABILITY OF FACIAL FEATURES

One study tested whether adult perceivers can discriminate baby-faced from mature-faced persons in each of six age groups: infants, preschoolers, fifth graders, eighth graders, young adults, and older adults (Zebrowitz & Montepare, 1992). The adult perceivers rated facial photographs of many persons in each age group. As predicted, the adult perceivers agreed almost perfectly on which were the more baby-faced persons and which were the more mature-faced persons in each age group. They could tell a baby face when they saw one. A baby face has large eyes, a round face, small chin, thin eyebrows, and a small nose (Berry & McArthur, 1986; Zebrowitz-McArthur & Montepare, 1989). Also, regardless of the age group that the adult perceivers rated, they said that the more baby-faced individuals within that age group were more likely than their peers to be physically weak, interpersonally warm, honest, naive, and dependent on others. Finally, having a baby face was independent of attractiveness. Perceivers draw strong inferences about ways in which physically attractive persons differ from the physically unattractive (Eagly, Ashmore, Makhijani, & Longo, 1991). These inferences, however, are *not* the same inferences that perceivers draw about baby-faced versus mature-faced individuals (Berry, 1991b; Zebrowitz & Montepare, 1992).

People who have baby faces also tend to keep their immature facial features as they move from one age group to the next. In a study of physical appearance across the life span, adult perceivers rated photographs that had been taken of the same person when he or she was a child, at puberty (approximately 13 for girls, 14 for boys), at high school graduation age, in his or her thirties, and in his or her fifties (Zebrowitz, Olson, & Hoffman, 1993). According to the adult perceivers' ratings, both males and females who had a baby face as children were also likely to have a baby face at puberty, although the relationship was stronger for girls than for boys. In both sexes, those who had baby faces at puberty were very likely to have baby faces when they graduated from high school. Interestingly, men who had baby faces on graduating from high school also had baby faces when they were in their thirties. Women were less likely to retain their baby faces from high school to their thirties. For both sexes, having a baby face at age 30 did not predict having a baby face at age 50.

Because people retain baby faces from childhood through at least adolescence, people who have baby faces may also develop stable personality characteristics (Berry & Brownlow, 1989). Throughout their early years, adults may treat baby-faced individuals as though they are weak and incompetent. Eventually, in what is known as a "self-fulfilling prophecy" (discussed in Chapter 11), baby-faced individuals may come to believe that they "must" have the personality traits that others assume they have. Such beliefs may constrain the way that baby-faced individuals interact with their peers in situations that require strength. The investigators in one study asked college women if they would be the one who pushed a stalled car or lifted the heavy objects in an apartment move (Berry & Brownlow, 1989). As predicted, women who were seen by both strangers and themselves as having baby faces were less likely than their mature-faced peers to say they would be involved in tasks that required strength. In other words, they had learned to play a role in the "theater of life" that required little physical competence. As we shall see, such roles have both advantages and disadvantages.

The assumptions that other people make about baby-faced individuals are also remarkably stable across cultures (McArthur & Berry, 1987). In one cross-cultural study, White U.S. college students, Black U.S. college students, and Korean college students rated photographs of male faces from the three different racial groups (Zebrowitz, Montepare, & Lee, 1993). Raters of all three races agreed on which were the baby faces, regardless of whether they were rating individuals from their own race or from one of the other two races. Raters of all three races also used the same characteristics to identify baby-faced individuals: a round face, large eyes, and thin eyebrows. Finally, raters of all three races ascribed the same traits to baby-faced individuals, regardless of the photographed person's race. Whether they were rating their own or another race, these perceivers called baby-faced individuals submissive, naive, and physically weak, but also warm and honest. Interracial and cross-cultural agreement is exactly what we should expect if such traits are attributed to baby-faced individuals because of their childlike appearance. Children of all races and cultures have rounder faces, larger eyes, and thinner eyebrows than do adults.

■ POSITIVE AND NEGATIVE CONSEQUENCES

Evidence for cross-cultural stability combines with evidence for cross-age stability to suggest that people who have baby faces might incur both positive and negative consequences because of their physical appearance. Some of the consequences include the way that baby-faced individuals are educated, how well they succeed when they try to persuade other people, the types of jobs for which they are likely to be hired, and their prospects for being convicted if they are accused of a crime.

Did you ever notice that adults speak differently when they are talking to young children than when they are talking to other adults? When talking to children, adults take pains to make what they are saying perfectly clear. They use short, simple words. They use the child's name or endearments to hold attention. They speak slowly. They use a singsong voice with high pitch and exaggerated up-and-down intonation, just as they do when talking to people who are mentally retarded (DePaulo & Coleman, 1986). Adults talk "baby talk" to people who might not otherwise understand.

If adult teachers assume that baby-faced children are less competent than mature-faced children, they might alter their teaching to match the pupil's assumed intellectual competence. One study tested whether adults are more likely to use baby talk when teaching children who have baby faces than when teaching children who have relatively mature faces (Zebrowitz, Brownlow, & Olson, 1992). College students taught two complicated tasks to a preschool child over the telephone. Because the child was not physically present, the experimenter was able to mislead the students about the child's physical appearance. The experimenter provided each student teacher with a photograph that was supposedly of the pupil. Some of the college students thought they were teaching a child who had a baby face. Others thought they were teaching a child of the same age who had a more mature face. The children who were taught bore no systematic relationship to these photographs, nor were they aware that their teacher was looking at a photograph while speaking to them on the telephone.

The telephone conversations were recorded so that the experimenters could later determine the extent to which student teachers clarified, simplified, tried to get and hold attention, spoke slowly, and used a singsong voice. Figure 3.4 shows how extensively student teachers used each of the five types of speech when teaching preschoolers that they thought had either baby faces or more mature faces. As the figure shows, adult teachers were more apt to use

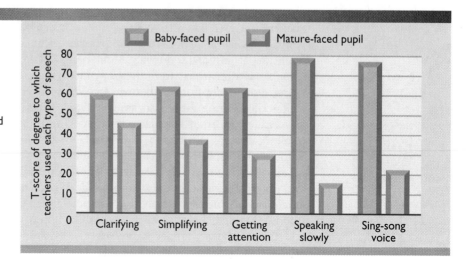

FIGURE 3.4

Adults assume the baby-faced are intellectually weak.

Graph shows the extent to which student teachers used five different indicators of "baby talk" when teaching baby-faced versus mature-faced preschoolers (Zebrowitz, Brownlow, & Olson, 1992).

baby talk when talking to the baby-faced. Interestingly, preschoolers who were subjected to baby talk learned the tasks neither better nor worse. The negative self-inference that went with being treated like a baby may have been offset by having the task explained more clearly (Zebrowitz et al., 1992).

Adults may assume that baby-faced individuals are more honest but less intellectually competent than their more mature-faced peers. Childlike innocence has both advantages and disadvantages when you are trying to persuade other people. The advantage is that they may trust you. The disadvantage is that they may regard you as incompetent. In one study of how having a baby face might affect persuasion, adults viewed videotapes of 150 television commercials that were taken from morning, afternoon, and evening time slots (Brownlow & Zebrowitz, 1990). These were all commercials in which one or more actors, either male or female but not celebrities, had speaking parts. As predicted, actors who had baby faces were cast primarily in commercials that emphasized trust. They said, for instance, that they had used the product before and were going to use it again. Actors who had mature faces were cast primarily in commercials that emphasized expertise. They cited statistics, scientific information, and medical reports. Television commercial producers realize intuitively that baby-faced individuals are ascribed childlike qualities, a fact of which they take full advantage.

Another important consequence of having a baby face occurs when people apply for jobs. Baby-faced applicants may be at a disadvantage compared to their mature-faced peers when they apply for certain types of jobs, most notably higher-status jobs that require leadership. In a study of how facial characteristics might influence occupational hiring, college students examined résumés that included age, employment experience, high school and college class ranks, and college grades (Zebrowitz, Tenenbaum, & Goldstein, 1991). The experimenters attached to each résumé a photograph of a person who had either a baby face or a mature face. The baby-faced applicant and the mature-faced applicant were equally attractive. Across participants, each photograph was attached an equal number of times to each résumé. Any differences in preferring one job applicant over the other had to come from the applicant's facial qualities and not from the applicant's credentials.

The students made hiring decisions about two jobs at a children's day care center: teacher and director. The experimenter provided job descriptions. The teacher should be warm enough to provide emotional support to the children and submissive enough to submit to the director's decisions. The director should be shrewd about finances and dominant enough to decide promotions and firing. As predicted, women applicants were more likely to be hired for the teacher job and male applicants for the director job. Regardless of sex, however, baby-faced applicants were more likely to be hired for the teacher job, whereas mature-faced applicants were more likely to be hired for the director job. People who have baby faces have an advantage when it comes to seeking lower-status positions where they are expected to be warm and docile. They have a disadvantage trying to convince employers that they would make strong, effective leaders. Baby-faced individuals of both sexes may be discriminated against in ways that are legally prohibited for race and sex.

Would this woman make a better nurse or hospital administrator?

Finally, baby-faced individuals may be held to a "double standard" of justice in the legal system. Across hundreds of cases in small claims courts, for example, baby-faced defendants who are accused of causing intentional harm get convicted less often, but baby-faced defendants who are accused of causing negligent harm get convicted more often (Zebrowitz & McDonald, 1991). In one laboratory demonstration of the double standard, college students pretended to be jurors for a trial in which the defendant was accused of committing a crime intentionally or through negligence (Berry & Zebrowitz-McArthur,

1988). The defendant, for instance, was accused of underreporting income from a summer job as a waiter, either because he wanted to avoid taxes (intention) or because he failed to keep adequate records (negligence). As in the previously described study of job applicants, the experimenters varied facial maturity by attaching to a folder of "intake information" a photograph of either a baby-faced person or a mature-faced person. Because the photographs were rotated among defendants, all relevant information other than facial maturity was equivalent.

Figure 3.5 shows how willing student jurors were to convict baby-faced and mature-faced defendants for each type of crime. As the figure shows, defendants with baby faces were less likely to be convicted of intentional crimes, but they were more likely than their mature-faced counterparts to be convicted of negligent crimes. Jurors found it relatively difficult to believe that someone who looked as innocent as a child might have violated the law intentionally. They found it easy, though, to believe that someone who looked as naive as a child might have violated the law out of sheer incompetence. This jury study, like the other studies described, suggests that adaptive protectiveness toward children has serious consequences when it is generalized to adults who happen to look like children (Berry & McArthur, 1986).

DETECTING LIES

People who have either baby faces or attractive faces look honest (Berry & McArthur, 1986; DePaulo, 1992). Looking honest is clearly an advantage in many situations. The success or failure of business deals, romantic attachments, international trade agreements, and murder trials, for instance, depend importantly on whether perceivers believe that another person is telling the truth. An important challenge to accurate person perception, then, involves detecting lies. This section of the chapter describes research on why people lie, on the cues that perceivers use to detect lies, and on the ability to detect lies.

■ WHY PEOPLE LIE

People lie because it is adaptive to do so (Bond & Robinson, 1988). Lies are worth the effort, because when they succeed, the liar benefits. For this reason, plants and animals deceive each other frequently. So do human beings.

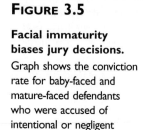

FIGURE 3.5

Facial immaturity biases jury decisions.
Graph shows the conviction rate for baby-faced and mature-faced defendants who were accused of intentional or negligent crimes (Berry & Zebrowitz-McArthur, 1988).

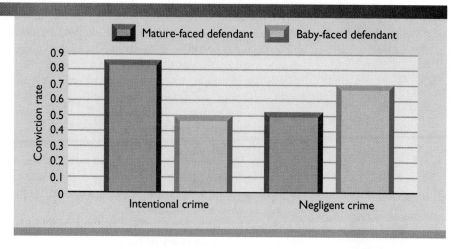

■ **MANY SPECIES BENEFIT FROM DECEPTION**   Many species employ camouflage and imitation to their selective advantage (Hyman, 1989). Moths that are the same color as tree trunks are less likely than moths of a different color to be eaten, because the camouflage fools birds (Kettlewell, 1973). Birds, in turn, sometimes make the fatal mistake of landing on the backs of crocodiles that resemble weed-covered driftwood. The orchid *Ophrys speculum* has a thick set of hairs very similar to the hairs on a female wasp's abdomen. Male wasps are thus deceived into "copulating" with the orchid's lip, then spreading the pollen on their bodies to other orchids, which through this trick reap the benefits of cross-pollination (Trivers, 1985). Similarly, male fireflies imitate the flash of certain insects that female fireflies eat. When the female firefly gets close enough to this deceptive flash, the male firefly pounces on her for his own sexual gratification (Lloyd, 1986).

Some birds feign a broken wing to lure predators away from their vulnerable nests (Dennett, 1978). Hungry young baboons have been observed to scream in pain, for no apparent reason, when standing next to an older baboon that was eating. When their mothers chased away the "offending" older baboon, the young baboons calmly ate the food that the older baboons had dropped (DeWall, 1986). Male chimpanzees avoid showing their teeth when bluffing other males about their willingness to fight, because for a chimpanzee to show its teeth is a sign of fear. The male chimpanzees turn their backs and manually rearrange their faces before turning back to face the potential adversary (DeWall, 1986). Similarly, gorillas that have been taught sign language use the signs to blame their own misdeeds on other gorillas or even on their human trainers (Patterson & Linden, 1981). Deceptive communication, then, is common in species other than human beings.

■ **HUMAN BEINGS BENEFIT FROM DECEPTION**   Of all organisms, however, perhaps the most skilled deceiver is the human being. In love, in war, in the courtroom, and in all the "little white lies" of everyday social interaction, human beings are the acknowledged masters of deceit. Human beings, like the members of other species, lie because they benefit from deception. Some individuals are better at it than others, because they look more honest (Berry & McArthur, 1986; McArthur & Berry, 1987; Zuckerman, De-Frank, Hall, Larrance, & Rosenthal, 1979). Other individuals are not blessed with an honest demeanor. People suspect them of lying even when they are telling the truth. Interestingly, even people who look dishonest do not avoid situations where they might have to lie. If anything, they are more willing than their honest-looking peers to engage in deception. They may have concluded that "If people act as though I'm dishonest even when I'm telling the truth, why not lie?" (Bond, Berry, & Omar, 1994). For the average person, though, lies are more likely to succeed than to fail (Bond, Kahler, & Paolicelli, 1985).

One reason why lying succeeds more often than it fails is that perceivers have a "truthfulness bias" (Zuckerman, DePaulo, & Rosenthal, 1981). Perceivers tend to believe that other people are telling the truth. To do otherwise is impolite and likely to impede the smooth flow of social interaction (Goffman, 1959; Schlenker, 1980). Another reason why lies succeed is that most behavior is accepted uncritically at face value, as meaning exactly what it appears to mean (Gilbert, 1991; Ross, 1977). Whether right or wrong, people assume that all nurses have kindly dispositions and that all professional boxers have hostile dispositions (Jones, 1979). Finally, to doubt a target person's sincerity often runs the risk of hurting the perceiver's own feelings. Not many perceivers would want to conclude that "She doesn't really have a previous engagement. She just doesn't want to go out with me" or "He doesn't really like my new hairstyle. He's just saying so to be polite" (Jones, 1990).

For all these reasons, deceivers get the benefit of any doubt (Zuckerman et al., 1981; Schlenker & Leary, 1982). Because perceivers assume honesty unless their suspicions are aroused, lies succeed most of the time (Bond et al., 1985). This is not to say that perceivers never know whether they are receiving true or false verbal and nonverbal communications, however. Perceivers who are deliberately trying to detect deceit can sometimes do so (DePaulo, Zuckerman, & Rosenthal, 1980; Kraut, 1980). How do they do it?

■ CUES TO DECEPTION

Social psychologists have studied extensively the cues associated with deception—what people do differently when they are lying. They have also asked perceivers what cues they believe are useful in trying to detect deception. Interestingly, the two sets of cues do not match very well. When lies succeed, it is often because perceivers rely on invalid cues and ignore valid ones. When lies fail, it is because motivation impairs the ability to control nonverbal cues and because some types of cues violate the perceiver's expectancies.

VALID AND INVALID CUES Table 3.4 lists some cues that betray deception and some cues that perceivers say they look for when they are trying to detect deception. The cues in Table 3.4 are divided into four types: verbal, vocal, visual, and miscellaneous.

As the table shows, the verbal category (what people say) offers several valid cues that perceivers ignore: negative statements, irrelevant statements, generalizing, and distancing. Imagine a husband who tells his wife that he will be having dinner with an important client. At the last minute, the client cancels and the husband uses his "free night" to take his attractive female secretary out for dinner and dancing. When he arrives home, his wife asks how the meeting went. The husband's verbal statements might reflect subtle differences between a person who is telling the truth and a person who is telling lies. The lying husband might be more negative in what he says ("I'm not wasting any more time on that deadbeat"). He might throw in irrelevant statements that change the subject ("His company has as poor a credit record as your brother Ralph's company"). He might make broad generalizations ("People don't pay their bills on time"). He might use sentence structures that are less immediate and more distancing ("One wonders [not "*I* wonder"] how Ralph is going to avoid a jail term"). These verbal differences occur regularly in the verbatim transcripts of people who are lying. When perceivers say what they look for to detect lies, however, they mention none of them. Perceivers assume, and rightly so, that actions speak louder than words. Some people might put others down, switch topics, speak in generalities, and use distancing sentence structures all the time, whether they are lying or telling the truth. Also, motivated liars may take the time to get their stories straight and avoid these revealing verbal cues (DePaulo Stone, & Lassiter, 1985a).

Perceivers are more attuned to valid cues in the vocal than in the verbal category. They recognize intuitively that liars hesitate more, speak in a higher-pitched voice, make more speech errors, and speak more slowly (Stiff, Miller, Sleight, Mongeau, Garlick, & Rogon, 1989). As shown in Table 3.4, perceivers err on only two of the vocal cues. Although they believe that liars take longer to answer questions, careful research has failed to establish any such difference. Also, although people give shorter answers when they are lying, this is one cue that perceivers fail to mention. The higher-pitched voice, by the way, occurs because most people are emotionally aroused when they are deliberately telling lies. Arousal heightens voice pitch (Zuckerman et al., 1981).

One problem with using pitch, hesitations, and speech errors as cues to deception is that these valid indicators can sometimes produce an Othello er-

TABLE 3.4	Cues Perceivers Say They Look for to Detect Lies and Whether Cues Are Valid (Abstracted from DePaulo, Stone, & Lassiter, 1985a, and Ekman, 1985).	
	DO PERCEIVERS SAY THEY LOOK FOR IT?	**IS IT A VALID CUE?**
Verbal Cues		
Negative statements	no	yes
Irrelevant statements	no	yes
Generalizing	no	yes
Distancing	no	yes
Vocal Cues		
Hesitation	yes	yes
Higher pitch	yes	yes
Speech errors	yes	yes
Delay before speaking	yes	no
Speaking slowly	yes	yes
Length of speaking	no	yes
Visual Cues		
Dilated pupils	no	yes
Adaptor behaviors	no	yes
Blinks	no	yes
Shrugs	no	yes
Avoiding eye contact	yes	no
Posture shifts	yes	no
Not smiling	yes	yes
Emblems	no	yes
Illustrators	no	yes
Manipulators	yes	no
Miscellaneous		
Discrepancies	no	yes
Planning time	no	yes
Seem rehearsed	no	yes

ror. The **Othello error** consists of misinterpreting a truthful person's emotional response to being accused of lying as evidence that the person *is* lying. It is named for the Shakespeare character who accused his wife of infidelity and mistook her anxiety about not being believed as an indication of guilt (Ekman, 1985). When people know that they are suspected of lying, they get emotional. Their voices rise even if they are telling the truth. Unfortunately, people who vehemently deny any wrongdoing are seen as "protesting too much," which makes them look even more guilty (Holtgraves & Grayer, 1994).

Perceivers rely heavily on visual cues, the next category in Table 3.4 (Stiff et al., 1989), but they often rely on the wrong ones (Ekman, 1985). Perceivers spontaneously mention only one valid deception cue. Perceivers are correct when they say that liars smile less than do truth tellers. They are not correct, however, when they say that people cannot look you in the eye when lying or that liars give themselves away by constantly fidgeting and shifting their posture. People who are trying to deceive know perfectly well that perceivers look for this cue, so they concentrate on sitting still and looking the other person right in the eye (DePaulo et al., 1985).

More interesting in the category of visual cues are four reliable cues that perceivers do not use: shrugs, blinks, adaptor behaviors, and dilated pupils (DePaulo et al., 1985a). When they are lying, people shrug and blink a lot. They also engage in what are called "adaptor behaviors," which occur when one action is used to disguise another action that "slips out" involuntarily. When a liar feels a hand start to shake, for instance, he or she tries to disguise the shaking by grasping a coffee cup or some other object. Also, if perceivers only knew it, the pupils of the eye dilate when people are experiencing heightened emotions. Unfortunately for perceivers, it is considered impolite to stare into other people's eyes while they are speaking to you.

Also interesting in the category of visual cues are three body movements called "emblems," "illustrators," and "manipulators" (Ekman, 1985). Two of these body movements are valid cues to deception but are not mentioned by perceivers. The other one is not a valid cue but is believed to be. Without their being aware of it, people's bodies sometimes automatically emit "emblems." Emblems are body movements that are used in normal conversation to "stand for" a specific communication. Emblems include a shrug to indicate "I don't know," thumb and index finger in a circle to indicate "OK," head nods to indicate agreement, and head wags to indicate disagreement.

In one study of emblems, a professor deliberately subjected clinical psychology graduate students to a stressful interview (Ekman, 1985). If they said they wanted to do research, he accused them of shirking their responsibility to help people who suffer from mental illness. If they said they wanted to work in a clinic, he berated them for wanting to make money from mental illness instead of finding cures. He constantly interrupted and insulted them, but they could not defend themselves, because of the power that a professor has to end a graduate student's career. The first graduate student who was interviewed accepted this abuse stoically. However, she sat with her hand in her lap, pointed directly at the professor, with only the middle finger raised! When told about her nonverbal behavior after the interview, the student refused to believe that she had made such a powerful emblem to the professor until she saw it for herself on a videotape. Emblems like giving someone the finger may be construed as "slips of the body" analogous to "slips of the tongue." Although emblematic slips are rare, when they occur they are very reliable cues to deception (Ekman, 1985).

A second type of body movement that gives away deception is an "illustrator." Illustrators are gestures that draw a picture of what is being said. People sometimes make a jabbing motion for emphasis, a zigzag motion to describe a mountain road's tight turns, or curving motions to describe an attractive woman's body. Illustrators are valid cues to lying when they do *not* occur. Illustrators normally accompany words to make the ideas clearer. Liars usually do not want what they say to be inspected all that closely. Liars are on uncertain ground when making up their stories, so they illustrate less. Illustrators, however, are valid cues only when they decrease. The perceiver must be aware of the target person's normal level of illustrators. Some people are naturally less expressive with their hands than other people, even when they are not lying.

Certain other body movement cues, although they are commonly thought to indicate lying, do not. Most people believe that liars fidget, squirm, scratch themselves, push back their hair, rub, massage and pick at their bodies compulsively while lying. These movements are called "manipulators." Unfortunately for those who would detect lies, even an increase in this type of activity is not a reliable sign of lying (Ekman, 1985). Manipulators occur not only when people are anxious, but also when they are completely relaxed and at ease. We all do them more with family than we do with strangers. Also, everyone knows about manipulators, so liars are likely to inhibit them consciously, especially if the stakes are high.

Finally, at the bottom of Table 3.4 are three reliable miscellaneous cues to deception that perceivers seldom mention. Liars, especially those who tell relatively inconsequential lies, sometimes have discrepancies in their stories. The couple trying to leave a boring party may tell the hostess that their baby-sitter cannot stay past 10:00 PM, forgetting that the hostess may have recently used the same baby-sitter. People who are given all the time they need to prepare also spend more time planning their remarks when they will be lying instead of telling the truth. Finally, people who are lying sometimes give too "perfect" a performance and seem somewhat stilted and rehearsed. The three miscellaneous cues, however, are difficult to spot unless you know the person very well.

Lies are often detected by intimates because the liar exhibits one of three characteristics that do not appear in Table 3.4: fear of being caught, guilt, or "duping delight" (Ekman, 1985). When people fear being caught in their deceptions, their emotions are heightened. Then they give themselves away through inadvertent nonverbal cues such as blinking a lot, speaking in a higher-pitched voice, shrugging, and sweating profusely. In a key scene of the movie *Total Recall,* Arnold Schwarzenegger is about to trust a doctor who is lying to him, until he notices a bead of sweat running down the doctor's otherwise perfectly composed face. Schwarzenegger takes the bead of sweat to mean that the doctor is lying, so he blasts the doctor into oblivion.

When people experience pangs of guilt and shame, their emotions rise and their lies become easier to detect. This is the premise behind the polygraph or lie detection machine that measures a person's physiological responses to incriminating questions. Unfortunately for the criminal justice system, psychopathic killers often fool the polygraph, because they genuinely experience no guilt about their misdeeds. They display no physiological signs of heightened emotion (Lykken, 1974). Finally, when people enjoy getting away with their lies, their unusually cheerful demeanor often tips off the other person that something is wrong. They give themselves away because they regard deception as an accomplishment that brings them "duping delight" (Ekman, 1985).

If there is an overall message to be gleaned from inspecting Table 3.4, it is that the best cues to deception are external signs that betray internal emotion and that are not part of the cultural stereotype. Because liars know the cultural stereotype of "valid" cues as well as do perceivers, skilled liars can stay "one jump ahead" of perceivers by monitoring their own nonverbal displays. The only problem they have is that in emotional situations, words are easier to control than actions. It is easier to form sentences that indicate that you are not feeling guilty or aroused than to stop your hand from shaking or your voice from cracking. Verbal behavior is normally under conscious control, but many "give-away" nonverbal behaviors are emitted automatically and require conscious vigilance if they are to be inhibited (Ekman, 1982; Ekman & Friesen, 1969). As a result, some cues become more reliable and some cues become less reliable as the liar becomes more motivated to succeed.

Do people sweat more when they are lying?

■ **MOTIVATIONAL IMPAIRMENT**   Some deceivers have more at stake than do others. International spies and unfaithful spouses, for instance, are more motivated to succeed in their deceptions than are party guests who "have to leave because of the baby-sitter" or depressed people who answer "Fine" when asked "How are you?" An interesting question, then, is whether deceivers are

Calvin and Hobbes

by Bill Watterson

more successful when they are more motivated to succeed. The answer is "yes and no." On the one hand, highly motivated deceivers take greater care than do less motivated deceivers to "get their stories straight." Their lies are likely to be better planned and more believable. On the other hand, because they have more to lose if detected, they experience more extreme emotions than do liars who have less to lose. Heightened emotions exaggerate such nonverbal behaviors as hesitations, dilated pupils, and high-pitched voice, that might give deceivers away.

Highly motivated deceivers might be more successful than less motivated deceivers when person perceivers pay attention only to their words. They might be less successful, though, when person perceivers pay attention to vocal and visual cues. With the **motivational impairment effect,** the more motivated a liar is to avoid detection, the more emotional the liar becomes and the easier it is for perceivers to detect deception by paying attention to nonverbal cues. In a relevant study, college students were videotaped while making true and untrue statements (DePaulo, Kirkendol, Tang, & O'Brien, 1988; DePaulo, Lanier, & Davis, 1983). To instill high motivation, the investigators told some of the students that deception is an important ability that is linked to professional success and that they should consider themselves to be "on trial." To instill low motivation, they told other students that the task was only a trivial intellectual game. Later, another group of students viewed the videotape and tried to detect whether the videotaped statements were true or false. Some of these "lie detector" students were allowed to scrutinize only the verbal content (a verbatim typed transcript). Others had access to vocal and visual information about the target person's nonverbal behavior.

As Figure 3.6 shows, perceivers were better at detecting deception from the verbal statements than from the nonverbal behavior of students who thought it was all a game. The relatively unmotivated students were too complacent and did not take pains to get their stories straight. The reverse was true for liars who thought they had a lot at stake. They cared too much. Their heightened emotions "leaked." This leakage through nonverbal channels is especially likely for highly motivated liars who expect to be caught in their lies, an expectation that police detectives and other professionals encourage (DePaulo, LeMay, Epstein, 1991).

EXPECTANCY VIOLATION One of the most frequently used cues to deception is inconsistency between verbal and nonverbal information (Roten-

FIGURE 3.6

When liars are highly motivated, their deception success is impaired.

Graph shows perceiver accuracy in detecting lies told by high and low motivation liars when perceivers had four types of information (DePaulo, Lanier, & Davis, 1983).

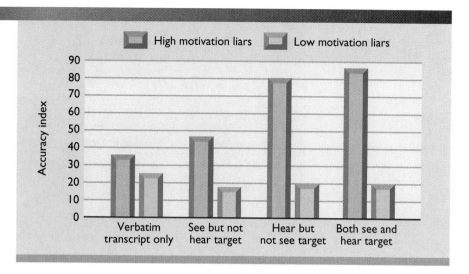

berg, Simourd, & Moore, 1989). We do not expect people to smile when offering their condolences, to frown when offering congratulations, or to tremble when they claim to be fearless. Verbal–nonverbal inconsistency, however, may be a special case of a more general rule: Perceivers suspect lying when a target person violates situational expectancies. Expectancies, of course, can vary from one situation to the next. It is reasonable and expected for a student to sit in class with his arm pointed at the ceiling if he is trying to ask the professor a question. It would be very unexpected for him to sit in an intimate restaurant with his arm pointed at the ceiling while telling his date how attractive he finds her.

In a study of expectancy violation as it pertains to lie detection, college students watched videotapes of other students who described four acquaintances: two whom they honestly liked and two whom they honestly disliked (Bond, Omar, Pitre, Lashley, Skaggs, & Kirk, 1992, Experiment 1). Although videotaped students were telling the truth, the experimenter led perceivers to suspect that some of the descriptions might be lies. The experimenters predicted that students would think the target person was lying whenever he or she exhibited behaviors that were unexpected. They deliberately chose weird behaviors that no perceiver has ever suggested as a deception cue. Throughout their truthful descriptions, some of the videotaped students kept their eyes closed. Some stared at the camera. Some held their arms pointed toward the ceiling. Some held their arms pointed toward the camera. Some kept one or the other shoulder raised.

Perceivers attributed dishonesty to targets who violated expectancies by behaving in any of these weird ways. Additional research established that expectancy violations elicit only attributions of dishonesty, not attributions of unrelated negative traits like selfishness. Also, dishonesty is attributed only when the target person behaves weirdly, not when other weird events occur, such as the camera being tilted 90 degrees (Bond et al., 1992, Experiment 2). Furthermore, people who are telling the truth do not arouse suspicion when they simultaneously engage in weird behaviors that the perceiver cannot see. They do not appear to be lying, for instance, when they hold one foot with the toe raised in the air and the other with the heel raised, but off camera (Bond et al., 1992, Experiment 3). When perceivers can see the weird behavior, however, they can be misled into thinking that a person is lying when he or she is telling the truth.

Is this person lying or
telling the truth?

■ ABILITY TO DETECT LIES

Because perceivers rely on cues that are often invalid, lies are difficult to detect. Nonetheless, some perceivers are better or more "expert" than others at detecting lies. This section of the chapter examines research on lie detection expertise, gender differences, and cross-cultural differences.

■ **EXPERTISE** Just as trying harder does not guarantee success at lying, trying harder does not guarantee success at detecting lies. If interviewers are warned in advance that interviewees will deliberately lie on some questions and tell the truth on others, they detect many more lies than if they had not been warned. Unfortunately, many of the lies they think they detect are actually truths (Toris & DePaulo, 1984). Merely trying harder to detect lies makes perceivers more suspicious of everyone, but not necessarily more accurate. To become more accurate at detecting lies, perceivers must be warned that they might be deceived. They must also ignore the target person's words and concentrate instead on the valid voice and body cues in Table 3.4. They must concentrate on the "leaky" nonverbal cues that liars do not usually monitor, because those cues are not part of the cultural stereotype (DePaulo, Lassiter, & Stone, 1982; Vrij, 1994). Lie detection is also easier, of course, when perceivers are very familiar with the liar's normal demeanor and know how that person usually acts when telling the truth (Brandt, Miller, & Hocking, 1980).

Although familiarity with the target person helps in detecting lies, practice at detecting lies is not necessarily beneficial. You might believe, for instance, that law enforcement officers and customs inspectors get so much practice in being lied to that they develop uncanny ability to tell who is lying. This is not the case. When college students, law enforcement officials, robbery investigators, judges, and court psychiatrists compete at trying to detect lies in a laboratory situation, the students perform every bit as well as the professionals (De-Paulo & Pfeifer, 1986; Ekman & O'Sullivan, 1991).

In one study, airline travelers tried to smuggle small pouches of white powder past experienced customs inspectors (Kraut & Poe, 1980). The travelers' nonverbal behaviors were videotaped and rated by observers on categories such as posture shifts, smiling, looking away, speech errors, evasiveness, and general nervousness. The travelers who were carrying the white powder behaved no differently on these measures than did other travelers who had nothing to hide. The observers and the experienced customs inspectors agreed on who the smugglers were and who were innocent travelers, but they were both wrong! This is not to say that experienced police and customs officials do not detect actual criminals and smugglers more frequently than would inexperienced personnel. They do, but they rely on characteristics, such as suspicious documents, that are not a part of nonverbal communications.

SEX DIFFERENCES   Successful deception is more difficult the more the deceiver cares. Heightened emotions elicit nonverbal behaviors like trembling hands, blinking eyes, and high-pitched voice that betray deceivers. It follows, therefore, that there might be sex differences in getting away with lies. Women typically care more about social approval than do men (Crowne & Marlow, 1964). As a result, women get more emotionally upset by lying about some topics than do men. Women might "get their stories straight" and be convincing in what they say, but their heightened emotions might give them away by, for instance, raising the pitch of their voices when they are lying.

In a study designed to test these predictions about sex differences in deception success, male and female college students tried to make a good impression on another person by falsely claiming that their opinions were the same as the other person's (DePaulo, Stone, & Lassiter, 1985b). The other person was hidden behind a one-way mirror. Some of the students thought the other person was of their own sex. Some thought the other person was of the opposite sex. The investigators predicted that students would be more anxious to make a good impression and thus more motivated to lie successfully when the other person was of the opposite rather than the same sex.

Lies told to a target person of the same sex were virtually undetectable. Lies told to a target person of the opposite sex were much more detectable, primarily through the nonverbal cues. Also as predicted, lying was especially unsuccessful for female deceivers. The women presumably cared more than did male deceivers about social approval. They felt they had more to lose if they were caught, so they let their emotions show in unusual nonverbal behavior. Finally, deceivers were least successful when they believed they were talking to an extremely attractive person of the opposite sex, when the stakes were presumably raised to their interpersonal limit. These results combined to suggest that women may be less successful than men at getting away with interpersonal lies, because they care more and become motivationally impaired.

CROSS-CULTURAL DIFFERENCES   Besides sex differences in deception and detection, there are cross-cultural differences. Recall that local display rules govern how emotions are displayed. People in all cultures may feel guilty and aroused when they lie, but local display rules may dictate the acceptable ways to display such emotions. There may also be important differences in the specific face, voice, and body cues that suspicious perceivers look for in different cultures and thus differences in which parts of their own performance liars concentrate on and ignore. If there were universal cues to deception, all human beings would have learned them by now and lying would have gone out of style millions of years ago (Kraut, 1980).

In an interesting study of lie detection across cultures, the researchers videotaped college students in the United States and in Jordan (Bond, Omar, Mahmoud, & Bonser, 1990). The students told truths about some of their acquaintances. They said they liked people they actually liked and said they disliked people they actually disliked. The students also told some lies. They claimed

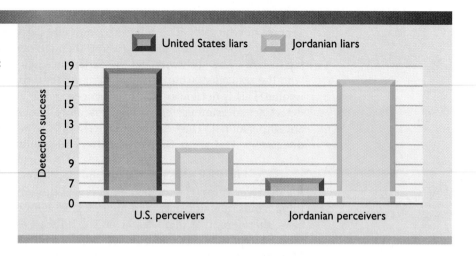

FIGURE 3.7

Lie detection is difficult across cultures.

Graph shows detection success when targets from the perceiver's own or another culture were trying to conceal or reveal their lies (Bond, Omar, Mahmoud, & Bonser, 1990).

to like people they actually disliked and claimed to dislike people they actually liked. The researchers showed the videotape, without sound, to other United States and Jordanian students who tried to tell the difference between lies and truths. The study showed that display rules in nonverbal communication differ across cultures and make it difficult to tell when a person from a different culture is lying. As Figure 3.7 shows, U.S. perceivers detected U.S. lies better than they detected Jordanian lies. Jordanian perceivers, in contrast, detected Jordanian lies better than they detected U.S. lies.

Although some of the U.S. and Jordanian liars deliberately tried to reveal that they were lying by "hamming it up," their antics did not help perceivers from a different culture to be more accurate. Jordanian perceivers could not tell when U.S. students were lying, even when the U.S. students went out of their way to reveal their deceit. Also, U.S. perceivers could not tell when Jordanian students were lying, even when the Jordanians deliberately behaved in ways that they thought any perceiver could see through. There were some differences in the cues that perceivers looked for. U.S. perceivers, for instance, relied more than Jordanian perceivers on a lack of head movements and hand gestures. Perceivers from both cultures, however, tended to suspect speakers who avoided eye contact, paused in the middle of speaking, and touched themselves frequently. Jordanian and U.S. perceivers thus agreed on who looked like a liar and who did not, whether that person was a citizen of Jordan or of the United States. They could not tell from these characteristics, however, whether a person from another culture was lying.

Subsequent research suggests that perceivers from many cultures rely on violations of what local display rules lead them to expect, even though expectancy violations are often invalid cues to deception (Bond et al., 1992). Even within a single country, people of different races have different display rules that other races interpret as expectancy violations. In one study, White police officers in Europe suspected citizens of lying whenever the citizen used "Black" nonverbal behavior (moving the hands and arms frequently), regardless of the citizen's skin color (Vrij & Winkel, 1992). Perceiver accuracy in detecting deception depends importantly on knowing the target person's display rules well enough to know when those display rules have been violated.

SUMMARY OF HOW PERSON PERCEPTION IS APPLIED

Because babies need protection, perceivers assume that adults who have baby faces also have childlike traits. Baby faces are easy to identify across cultures and across the life span. People who have baby faces are treated as though they are warm and approachable, but also as though they are weak and incompetent. Perceivers trust baby-faced actors in television commercials to be honest, hire baby-faced applicants for jobs that require interpersonal warmth, and treat baby-faced defendants leniently when they are charged with causing intentional harm. Conversely, perceivers "talk down" to baby-faced pupils, avoid choosing baby-faced workers for leadership positions, and consider baby-faced defendants likely to have caused negligent harm.

People lie because they benefit from doing so. Ironically, the more liars have to gain from lying, the easier they are to detect. Lie detection, however, is far from accurate. Perceivers rely on cues that are not helpful and ignore cues that would be helpful. One frequently used cue is an "honest face." Another is expectancy violation. Because expectancies differ from one culture to the next, lie detection across cultures is very difficult. Within a culture, some people are better than others at telling and detecting lies.

CHAPTER 4

Attribution

magine that you are at a busy city hospital when ambulances bring two new patients to the emergency room. Both are men in their early fifties who have liver failure. They are both in desperate need of a liver transplant operation, but you know that vital organs are hard to obtain for such operations. For this reason, medical personnel are forced to set priorities, selecting as organ recipients only those patients most likely to benefit. You overhear the men's friends and relatives talking about each of the two new patients. You learn that one of the men, Frank Fitness, has led a very healthy life and avoids drinking alcohol, but liver disease runs in his family. The other man, Tom Tippler, is the same age but has led an entirely different type of life. Tom has been an alcoholic for years. His liver has most likely been damaged by his frequent alcoholic binges. Which man do you regard as most responsible for bringing on his own health problems? If he gets an organ transplant, which man is most likely to follow the doctor's orders and take care of his body in the future? Which man do you think might prove to be a burden to the nurses and other hospital staff? The hospital's budget and resources are stretched to the limit. If it becomes necessary to cut back on services and the quality of care for some patients, would you have the hospital staff give slightly less priority to Frank Fitness or to Tom Tippler?

Questions about priorities are increasingly important as health care facilities struggle with rising costs and increased demand for their services. Is every sick person entitled to the same quality of care? When liver donors are rare, for instance, does it make more sense to give a liver transplant to a patient who "lives right" but has a family history of liver disease or to an alcoholic whose excessive drinking has brought on alcoholic cirrhosis? Social psychologists want to discover whether people make such difficult, life-or-death decisions at least in part by deciding what *caused* the illness. Four social psychologists conducted a relevant study (Madey, DePalma, Bahrt, & Beirne, 1993). They had college students read brief case histories of patients whose health problems had different likely causes. The students read descriptions of two liver disease patients similar to Frank and Tom. The descriptions used in the study, of course, did not contain potentially biasing names such as Frank Fitness and Tom Tippler. The names are used in this chapter only because these names make it easier for you to remember which patient drank and which patient did not. The students also read about a heavy smoker and a nonsmoker who both had lung disease, an out-of-shape couch potato and a physically active person who both had heart attacks, and two men who contracted AIDS. One got it from sharing a dirty needle with other drug addicts. The other got it from a blood transfusion.

After reading these brief case histories, the students estimated how conscientiously each patient would follow the doctor's orders. They also estimated how long each patient would be in the hospital, how likely it was that the patient would have a recurrence of the health problem after treatment, and what quality of medical care should be provided. For all four medical problems, both male and female students blamed one of the patients more than the other. They thought that the patient who caused his own illness would be less likely to follow his doctor's orders. They also thought that the patient who caused his own illness would be more likely to have the illness recur. As Figure 4.1 shows, however, men and women differed in the quality of care that they would assign. For all four types of illness, male students thought that patients who caused their own illness should receive a lower quality of care than patients who did not cause their own illness. Female students, in contrast, thought that all patients should receive the highest quality of care, regardless of whether the patient caused the illness or not.

Medical problems are not the only topic for which people care about the cause (Weiner, Perry, & Magnusson, 1988). We care, for instance, about the causes of fires, explosions, and other disasters. We care about the causes of unusual sports and academic achievements. When such events occur, we do not merely accept that they happened. Instead, we want to know *why*. This chapter is about how we answer the "why" question for other people's behavior

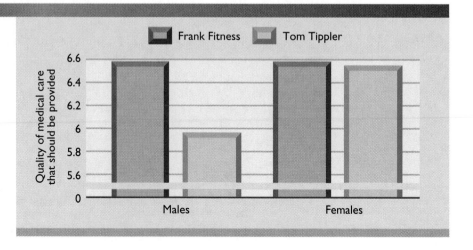

FIGURE 4.1

Males say that patients responsible for their illness deserve lower quality medical care.

Graph shows quality of care males and females assigned to two liver patients (Madey, DePalma, Bahrt, & Beirne, 1993).

Calvin and Hobbes   by Bill Watterson

and for our own–how we make *causal attributions*. One definition of an "attribution" is "regarded as having been caused by someone or something." When people wonder why an event occurred and reach a conclusion about its cause, they are making a causal attribution. The attribution might be about what caused a patient's liver to fail, why a student failed an exam, why the universe is expanding, or any other event that requires explanation. The first section of the chapter describes the process of making causal attributions. The second section examines the accuracy of causal attributions. The third section describes some consequences of causal attribution.

HOW DO WE ATTRIBUTE THE CAUSES OF SOCIAL EVENTS?

A central theme that runs through several of the chapters in this book is the two-stage model that attributes to people both spontaneous initial reactions and subsequent deliberative reactions. Causal attribution is a good example of a process that involves two stages (Gilbert, 1989; Gilbert, Pelham, & Krull, 1988; Jones & Davis, 1965; Kelley, 1976; Trope, 1986). Attributers use an initial identification stage, which provides an "anchor," plus a subsequent interpretation stage, which consists of "adjustments" away from that anchor (Gilbert & Hixon, 1991; Quattrone, 1982). Thus causal attribution follows the "anchoring and adjustment" heuristic described in Chapter 2. It follows a two-stage process similar to the processes that underlie social cognition, person perception, and other social psychological processes discussed throughout the text (Anderson, Krull, & Weiner, in press). Table 4.1 shows the two stages of the attribution process, with examples of each component of the two stages. You might want to refer to Table 4.1 frequently as you read the following descriptions.

SPONTANEOUS IDENTIFICATION AND CATEGORIZATION

The two-stage model of causal attribution begins with initial information about an event. The initial information might be, for example, that a *person* (a man named Tom) engaged in a *behavior* (drank heavily) in a particular context or

TABLE 4.1	A Two-Stage Model of Causal Attribution with Examples (Adapted from Gilbert, 1989; Jones & Davis, 1965; Kelley, 1967; Trope, 1986)

SPONTANEOUS IDENTIFICATION AND CATEGORIZATION STAGE

	Information	*What Caused the Event?*
Identify & categorize behavior	A person has many alcoholic drinks	People who drink too much are weak and foolish
Identify & categorize situation	After work	Work might have been stressful
Identify & categorize person	It's Tom	Tom may be weak and foolish

DELIBERATIVE ADJUSTMENT STAGE

Variance of the behavior	Tom drinks frequently, even when others abstain, at work and at home	Tom is weak and foolish
Effects of the behavior	Tom's doctor warned him about his liver	Tom is very weak and foolish
Constraints on the behavior	Tom had to borrow money to buy drinks	Tom is extremely weak and foolish
Emotional impact of the behavior	Tom is my spouse	Tom is *extremely* weak and foolish!

Note: Attribution ends at the spontaneous stage unless the perceiver is both willing and able to enter the deliberative stage.

situation (after work). In the first stage of the model, the initial information elicits an immediate, spontaneous reaction in which the three elements (person, behavior, and situation) are identified or categorized. A man named Tom might be identified either as an individual or as belonging to a particular category. We might know, for instance, that Tom sells used cars. From his occupational category, we might assume that he has various characteristics such as "gregarious." We might identify a behavior such as drinking heavily as "a weak, foolish thing to do." We might identify a situation such as "after work" as "at the end of a stressful day." When spontaneous identifications and categorizations are ambiguous, we try to resolve the ambiguity to arrive at either a dispositional or a situational attribution.

■ RESOLVING AMBIGUITIES

Identifications can be either ambiguous or unambiguous. You might know who Tom is unambiguously, for instance, but the term "after work" might remain ambiguous. You might not know whether "after work" meant Tom was drinking in a bar, surrounded by other people, or alone in his office after everyone else had gone. Identification of one component can influence how people identify the other components (Trope, 1986). If you are very familiar with the person and have definite expectations for how that person (or that type of person) is likely to behave, the way you identify the person influences how you identify an ambiguous behavior (Trope & Cohen, 1989). If you knew that Tom was very gregarious, you might assume (unless told otherwise) that he was drinking with other people rather than alone.

In an illustrative study, some students saw a videotape of a child playing near a wealthy home. Other students saw a videotape of the same child playing near a ghetto home (Darley & Gross, 1983). The two groups of students presumably identified and categorized the child differently. Both groups of students also watched the child taking an achievement test. The child's behavior on the test was ambiguous. She missed some easy problems, but she also got some difficult problems right. Students who had categorized her as from a wealthy home identified her ambiguous behavior as *above* average for her grade level. Students who had categorized her as from a ghetto home identified the same ambiguous behavior as *below* average for her grade level. Both groups identified the ambiguous behavior in line with what their identification of the person led them to expect.

Similarly, an unambiguous behavior such as kicking a puppy might identify a stranger as "a cruel person" regardless of the situation (Carlston & Skowronski, 1994). Also, an unambiguous situation which featured an enraged grizzly bear might identify a moving person's behavior as "running for his life" rather than "jogging," regardless of who it was (Trope, 1986). When attributers are certain about only one of the three elements (person, situation, or behavior), the element about which they are certain biases how they identify and categorize the other two.

When all else is equal, however, behavior may be a more important factor in causal attributions than either the person or the situation. An unambiguous behavior such as kicking a puppy is likely to be identified as exactly what it seems (Baron & Misovich, 1993). It is taken at face value (Gilbert & Malone, 1995). It defines the person "automatically," because behaviors and persons seem to "belong together" (Heider, 1958; Newman & Uleman, 1993). Also, unambiguous behaviors such as kicking puppies or getting drunk grab our attention, are well remembered, and cry out for explanation (Bassili, 1989; Zimbardo, Andersen, & Kabat, 1981). Of person, behavior, and situation, therefore, behavior is most likely to be unambiguous. It often dominates the identification and categorization process and defines both the person's likely disposition and the situation.

■ DISPOSITIONAL VERSUS SITUATIONAL ATTRIBUTIONS

The two most likely "causes" of an event, then, are the person's disposition and the situation. In a **dispositional attribution** the event was caused by the person's temperament, tendency, or inclination—by something internal to the person. An attributer might see Tom drinking heavily, for instance, and attribute Tom's behavior to his having a weak, foolish disposition. In a **situational attribution** the event was caused by some pressure exerted by the situation or circumstances—by something external to the person. A different attributer might see Tom drinking heavily and attribute Tom's behavior to the stressful situation he was under during his work hours.

One interesting aspect of causal attribution is the extent to which people make dispositional rather than situational attributions (Jones, 1990). Attributers seem to connect a behavior with the person's disposition more spontaneously than they connect the same behavior with compelling aspects of the situation (Fletcher, Reeder, & Bull, 1990; Gilbert et al., 1988; Pittman &

D'Agostino, 1985). Unless some aspect of the situation is a very obvious cause, they more readily make dispositional than situational attributions. Attributers more readily attribute Tom Tippler's drinking, for instance, to his traits and inclinations than to the pressure that his sales job puts on him.

This tendency to draw dispositional rather than situational attributions has important consequences. The males in the study described at the start of this chapter, for instance, made the dispositional attribution that Tom Tippler (and others like him) caused his own health problems. This dispositional attribution led them to conclude that Tom was a weak, foolish person who did not have the will power necessary to follow his doctor's orders. If he did not follow his doctor's orders, of course, he would not take care of his liver, which made him a poor candidate for a transplant operation. When a behavior elicits dispositional rather than situational attributions, attributers make an initial identification and categorization that biases all subsequent considerations. Not surprisingly, then, much of the research on attribution concentrates on the factors that bias initial attributions either toward the dispositional side or toward the situational side even before attributers enter the deliberative stage.

DELIBERATIVE ADJUSTMENTS

When attributers are willing and able to enter the deliberative stage, they do exactly what the name implies. They *deliberate* on the cause of an event. They go beyond the dispositional or situational attribution implied by spontaneous identification and categorization. They adjust their first impression of the cause either more to the dispositional side or more to the situational side. A complete stranger might learn about Tom in the emergency waiting room, draw a dispositional or situational attribution, and give the matter no further thought. Tom's friends and relatives, however, would presumably care enough to deliberate on why he drank. They might start from the assumptions implicit in their initial, spontaneous reactions, but they would also take additional factors into consideration (Jones & McGillis, 1976; Trope, 1986; Weisz & Jones, 1993). When they make deliberative adjustments to their initial attributions, people use four types of additional information: the variance of the behavior, the effects of the behavior, constraints on the behavior, and the emotional impact of the behavior.

■ VARIANCE OF THE BEHAVIOR

One important factor in making deliberative adjustments is how much the behavior *varies*. Does Tom drink every day after work or just this once? Is he one of many or the only one drinking? Does he drink only after work or in many different settings? The three ways in which behavior might vary are in its consistency, consensus, and distinctiveness (Kelley, 1967).

To understand consistency, consensus, and distinctiveness, examine Table 4.2. First, you might learn that a behavior had high or low consistency. **Consistency** accounts for whether the person always behaves the same way when faced with the same situation. If the initial information was that Tom drank heavily after work, you might learn, for instance, either that he frequently drank after work (high consistency) or drank only once (low consistency). High consistency, which indicates that the behavior did not vary from one time to the next, implies a dispositional attribution. Low consistency, which indicates that the behavior varied from one time to the next, implies a situational attribution. In the eight entries of Table 4.2, all the entries on the left side reflect high consistency (Tom drank often). All the entries on the right side reflect low consistency (Tom drank once). In the deliberative adjustment stage, high consistency

TABLE 4.2	An Example of How Attributers Might Deliberate on the Cause of an Event by Analyzing Information about the Behavior's Variance across Time (Consistency), Person (Consensus), and Situation (Distinctiveness) (Abstracted from Kelley, 1967)

	HIGH CONSISTENCY		LOW CONSISTENCY	
	Low Consensus	*High Consensus*	*Low Consensus*	*High Consensus*
Low Distinctiveness	Tom drank often (D)	Tom drank often (D)	Tom drank once (S)	Tom drank once (S)
	No colleagues drank (D)	All colleagues drank (S)	No colleagues drank (D)	All colleagues drank (S)
	Tom drank in many settings (D)	Tom drank in many settings (D)	Tom drank in many settings (D)	Tom drank in many settings (D)
High Distinctiveness	Tom drank often (D)	Tom drank often (D)	Tom drank once (S)	Tom drank once (S)
	No colleagues drank (D)	All colleagues drank (S)	No colleagues drank (D)	All colleagues drank (S)
	Tom drank only after work (S)	Tom drank only after work (S)	Tom drank only after work (S)	Tom drank only after work (S)

Note: D means that the information suggests a dispositional cause. S means that the information suggests a situational cause.

often "strengthens" an initial dispositional attribution. If you think that drinking heavily once was weak and foolish, then doing it several times makes the person all the more weak and foolish.

Second, you might learn that a behavior had high or low consensus. **Consensus** accounts for whether other people behave the same as the person when they are faced with the identical situation. You might learn, for instance, that Tom was or was not the only salesperson from his used car lot who drank heavily after work that day (low consensus) or that all the salespeople drank (high consensus). High consensus, which indicates that the behavior did not vary from one person to the next, implies a situational attribution. Low consensus, which indicates that the behavior varied from one person to the next, implies a dispositional attribution. In the eight entries of Table 4.2, those in the first and third columns reflect low consensus (no colleagues drank). Those in the second and fourth columns reflect high consensus (all colleagues drank). In the deliberative adjustment stage, low consensus often "strengthens" an initial dispositional attribution. If you think that drinking to excess in the company of other drinkers was weak and foolish, then doing it when no one else was drinking makes the person all the more weak and foolish.

Finally, you might learn that a behavior had high or low distinctiveness. **Distinctiveness** accounts for whether the person behaves this way only in this specific situation and not in other seemingly similar situations. If the initial information indicated that Tom drank heavily after work, you might learn, for instance, either that he drank heavily only after work (high distinctiveness) or that he drank heavily at the beach, after golf tournaments, and in many other types of situations (low distinctiveness). High distinctiveness, which means that the behavior varied from one situation to the next, implies a situational attribution. Low distinctiveness, which means that the behavior did not vary from one situation to the next, implies a dispositional attribution. In the eight entries of Table 4.2, all the entries on the bottom row reflect high distinctiveness (Tom drank only after work). All the entries on the top row reflect low distinctiveness (Tom drank in many settings). In the deliberative adjustment stage, low distinctiveness often "strengthens" an initial dispositional attribution. If you think that drinking after work is weak and foolish, then doing it in many different situations makes the person all the more weak and foolish.

If they are willing and able to engage in further thinking after the initial categorization or identification, people use information about consistency, consensus, and distinctiveness to modify or "adjust" their initial reactions (McArthur, 1972). Suppose you learned, for instance, that Tom frequently drank too much (high consistency), that he was the only sales associate who got drunk that day (low consensus), and that "after work" was not the only situation in which he became inebriated (low distinctiveness). You might make an even more dispositional attribution than was indicated by your initial identification. Suppose instead you learned that Tom did it only once (low consistency), that many of his associates did it (high consensus), and that he only did it after work (high distinctiveness). You might "adjust" away from a dispositional attribution and toward a situational attribution. "It wasn't his fault, because it might have happened to anyone."

One way of characterizing consistency, consensus, and distinctiveness is to say that they draw our attention to abnormal conditions (Hilton & Slugoski, 1986). In the example of Tom and his drinking, attributers make dispositional attributions when the person stands out or is "abnormal" compared to other persons (low consensus). They make situational attributions when the situation stands out or is "abnormal" compared to other situations (high distinctiveness). When consensus is high and distinctiveness is low, the attribution depends on whether the combination of consensus and distinctiveness seems abnormal or not. If Tom and his associates were all drinking at an evening stag party, you might consider the information meaningless for making attributions either to Tom or to the day he had at work, because Tom's behavior followed an expected "script" (Abelson, 1981; Hilton & Slugoski, 1986). You might blame the situation ("That's what guys do at stag parties") rather than any individual.

In other words, attributers use the available information about consistency, consensus, and distinctiveness to construct a plausible explanation for the behavior, based on previous knowledge of how the world usually works. They use assumptions about which causes have to be present for an unlikely event to occur. They also use counterfactual reasoning (explained in Chapter 2) about what might have happened had the cause not been present (Hamilton, Grubb, Acorn, Trolier, & Carpenter, 1990; Jaspers, Hewstone, & Fincham, 1983; Lipe, 1991; Pennington & Hastie, 1992; Sherman, Lim, Seidel, Sinai, & Newman, 1995). They tend to attribute "rare" or unusual behaviors to "rare" or unusual dispositions (Johnson, Boyd, & Magnani, 1994; Medcof, 1990).

■ EFFECTS OF THE BEHAVIOR

Besides information about how the behavior varies from one time, person, and situation to the next, attributers also sometimes have information about the effects that the behavior produced. These effects strengthen or weaken dispositional attributions because they tell us something about what the person intended by his or her actions (Jones & Davis, 1965). Attributers adjust their initial impressions by deciding whether another person's internal traits *correspond with* that person's words or deeds. If an attributer knew that Tom drank heavily after work, for instance, the attributer would try to decide whether Tom had a weak, foolish disposition that corresponded with his behavior. Knowing the effects of the behavior allows us not only to decide between a situational and a dispositional explanation, but also to decide *which one* of several dispositions the person is most likely to have. By knowing the effects of the behavior, we can draw specific dispositional attributions even when we have no information about whether the event varies across time, persons, or situations.

If a person chooses one of two possible behaviors, as Tom might have in deciding whether to go to a bar after work, we make attributions about the person's internal dispositions by thinking about the likely outcomes of the two different courses of action (Jones, 1990; Jones & Davis, 1965; Jones & McGillis, 1976). Suppose Tom thought that stopping for a drink and going home to his wife and family had exactly the same effects, except that if he went home he would not get to talk with the other sales associates. We might not only make a dispositional attribution for Tom's behavior, but also attribute the cause of Tom's behavior to a specific disposition—namely, that he is gregarious. In contrast, suppose Tom thought that he could call his friends on the telephone, but that if he went home his wife would want him to do some household chores. Then we might also make a dispositional attribution for his behavior, but the disposition would be to a different trait—to laziness rather than to gregariousness.

Multiple effects detract from confident dispositional attributions. Suppose Tom thought that stopping for a drink would *both* let him talk to his friends *and* get him out of household chores. In that case, we could not be sure which effect he wanted most to create, because no one effect was distinctive. Because stopping for a drink produced two effects that could not be produced by going home, we could not be sure that Tom had either of the corresponding dispositions (Jones & Davis, 1965).

■ CONSTRAINTS ON THE BEHAVIOR

Another important factor that attributers consider in the deliberative stage is how situational constraints might have affected the behavior. A situational constraint is pressure that the situation brings to bear. Depending on what they learn about such constraints, people adjust their initial attributions through discounting or augmentation. **Discounting** involves making a weaker dispositional attribution when situational constraints might have facilitated the behavior. Sometimes the context that surrounds a behavior seems so powerful that attributers "make allowances." If we believe that "given the circumstances, anyone would have reacted that way," we adjust or weaken our initial dispositional attributions by discounting during the deliberative stage (Kelley, 1972). If you believed that Tom's day at work was horrendous, even if you lacked consensus information, you might regard the situational constraints as so powerful that they were bound to affect Tom's behavior. If the situation offered other plausible explanations for drinking heavily, you might weaken your initial reaction that "Tom is a weak, foolish person." Discounting is an adjustment away from a dispositional attribution.

The opposite of discounting is augmentation (Kelley, 1972). **Augmentation** involves making a stronger dispositional attribution when the behavior was performed in spite of powerful constraints. Sometimes the situation exerts powerful pressure *against* performing a behavior. If we believe that, given the circumstances, almost no one would have reacted that way, we strengthen or augment initial dispositional attributions during the deliberative stage (Kelley, 1972). If you believed that Tom had to borrow money to buy drinks after work, then you might conclude that most people would have gone home instead of going to a bar. If you thought that Tom had to overcome situational constraints or obstacles to behave the way he did, then you might augment your initial reaction that "Tom is weak and foolish." You might adjust it to "Tom is extremely weak and foolish." Augmentation is an adjustment toward an even more dispositional attribution.

In one study that demonstrated the effects of discounting and augmentation, college students listened to a tape-recorded job interview (Jones, Davis, & Gergen, 1961). Half of the students were led to believe that the applicant was being interviewed for a job as an astronaut. The job required an "inner-directed" personality, because astronauts have to spend long hours in isolation. The job candidate answered all interview questions as though he were an introverted, inner-directed person. When asked what other occupations he would consider, for example, he replied, "I would like to be a forest ranger." The other half of the students were led to believe that the applicant was being interviewed for a job as a submariner. The job required an "outer-directed" personality to get along well with peers in cramped quarters. The submariner applicant answered all interview questions as would an extremely extroverted, gregarious, outer-directed person. When asked about other occupations, for example, he replied, "I would like to be a door-to-door salesman."

The investigators asked students how introverted versus extroverted each candidate *really* was. Even though the applicant depicted himself as extremely inner-directed for the astronaut job and extremely outer-directed for the submariner job, the students expressed only moderate confidence that the applicant had the personality his words indicated. They discounted his behavior because of the powerful situational constraints. The applicant *had* to answer as he did if he wanted to get the job. Given the constraints, his behavior might have been caused by factors other than his true personality or disposition, as every personnel manager knows.

Augmentation occurred when, for another group of students, the experimenters switched the interview tapes. These students heard the applicant for

If astronaut applicants knew that NASA was looking for an "inner-directed" person who could endure lengthy isolation in space, what would you think of an applicant who admitted wanting to meet many people?

the astronaut job describe himself as very outer-directed even though he knew that the job, which he presumably wanted, required an inner-directed personality. Other students in this second group heard the applicant for the submariner job describe himself as very inner-directed even though he knew that the job required an outer-directed personality. These students made very confident, extreme dispositional attributions. They said, "He must be very introverted [or extroverted] if even during an important job interview he could not bring himself to emphasize those moments when he behaved in an outgoing [or introspective] way." Thus attributions can be weakened or strengthened when the surrounding circumstances appear to facilitate or to impede another person's words or deeds.

Interestingly, powerful situational constraints can have opposite effects on the spontaneous identification stage of attribution than they have on the subsequent deliberative stage, where discounting and augmentation occur (Trope, 1986; Trope & Liberman, 1993). If you knew that Tom had a horrendous day at work, for instance, you might initially identify his stopping for drinks on the way home as "trying to drown his troubles," which might imply that Tom was weak and foolish. You might be less likely to identify Tom's behavior as "trying to drown his troubles" if you knew that he had a normal day at work. At the initial identification stage, then, a powerful situational constraint prompts behavior identifications that encourage dispositional attributions. At the subsequent deliberative stage, in contrast, powerful situational constraints discourage situational attributions, because of discounting (Read & Miller, 1993).

Discounting also differs from one type of behavior to another (Reeder, 1993). For behaviors that concern morality, for instance, it is easier to make allowances for situational constraints on the "moral" side than on the "immoral" side (Coovert & Reeder, 1990). If you learned that a gangster gave money to charity, for instance, it might be easy to imagine situational constraints that would argue against drawing the dispositional inference that he was generous. The gangster might have been trying to get rid of illegally obtained money before he was audited by the IRS (Shoda & Mischel, 1993). If you learned that a minister got roaring drunk, in contrast, it would be difficult to "make allowances."

Similarly, for behaviors that concern ability it is easier to make allowances for situational constraints on the "poor performance" side than on the "outstanding performance" side. In one study, for instance, students said that a boy who drew an outstanding portrait was artistically gifted regardless of whether the teacher asked him to draw well or poorly. In contrast, they said that a boy who drew a poor portrait might or might not lack artistic talent, depending on what the teacher asked him to do (Reeder & Fulks, 1980). To fully understand discounting and augmentation, then, we need to know not only the person and the situation, but also the type of disposition that is involved (Reeder, Pryor, & Wojciszke, 1992).

■ EMOTIONAL IMPACT OF THE BEHAVIOR

The final factor that attributers consider during the deliberative stage is the emotional impact the behavior has for them. Some behaviors, like kicking a puppy, make us cringe. They carry such a large emotional impact that we make stronger dispositional attributions than we might have without the emotional component. Behavior that carries a large emotional impact elicits extreme dispositional attributions. In one study, for instance, students learned that a parked car rolled away from the curb and down a steep hill, destroying an old jalopy (Walster, 1966). They attributed much less blame to the car's owner than did other students who were given the same scenario, except that the car hit a school bus and injured children. Even though the car owner's actions (setting the brake but forgetting to turn the wheels in toward the curb) were identical in the two scenarios, the one that elicited greater emotion also elicited more extreme dispositional attributions.

Perhaps the ultimate emotional impact occurs when another person's actions affect *us* (Jones & Davis, 1965). In a relevant study, students in a low emotional impact condition learned that an interviewer had evaluated four previous candidates either positively or negatively. The interviewer then evaluated a fifth candidate negatively (Enzle, Harvey, & Wright, 1980). Students took the variance of behavior into account. They made more dispositional attributions for the interviewer's evaluations when he evaluated all five candidates negatively (low distinctiveness) than when he evaluated only the fifth candidate negatively (high distinctiveness).

A second group of students, however, experienced high emotional impact. *They were themselves the negatively evaluated fifth candidate.* These students did not take distinctiveness into account at all. They made dispositional attributions to the interviewer ("He has an overcritical personality," for example) whether he had evaluated the preceding four candidates positively or negatively. Their attributions were as personalized as those of Yossarian, the hero in Joseph Heller's novel *Catch-22,* who kept telling his wartime aviator colleagues that enemy gunners were trying to kill him. When one of his colleagues explained that "No one's trying to kill you," Yossarian asked, "Then why are they shooting at me?" "They're shooting at everyone" was the reply. "And what difference does that make?" said Yossarian. Yossarian and other attributers make more extreme attributions about another person's actions when they are themselves affected by those actions.

SUMMARY OF HOW CAUSAL ATTRIBUTION WORKS

When people try to attribute an event's cause, they first identify or categorize the person, the behavior, and the situation. At this identification and categorization stage, the behavior is central. Its implications affect how the person and the situation are identified, especially when the person and the situation are ambiguous. If further thinking does not occur, the attributer uses initial identification and categorization to make a situational attribution (the situation caused the event) or a dispositional attribution (the person's internal disposition caused the event). If further thinking does occur, the attributer deliberates on four additional factors. One factor is how much the behavior varied across time, persons, and situations. The second factor is what effects the behavior was likely to have. The third factor is whether the behavior was facilitated or impeded by situational constraints. The fourth factor is how much emotional impact the event had. Emotionally moving behavior that was performed despite powerful constraints is likely to elicit intense dispositional attributions.

HOW ACCURATE IS CAUSAL ATTRIBUTION?

The attribution process described in the first section of this chapter must work well or people would not use it. The two-stage process shown in Table 4.1 is a way of collapsing a huge amount of information into a manageable few factors that usually allow us to predict what other people might do. We can make very shrewd estimates of a person's character and likely behavior from an initial identification and categorization and from knowing the variance of the behavior, the effects of the behavior, the constraints on the behavior, and the emotional impact of the behavior. The process that most people use for making causal attributions is an efficient and effective one that allows us to learn from experience what to expect of other people. The attribution process, however, has built into it certain tendencies that sometimes render conclusions less than optimal (Nisbett & Ross, 1980). Because they illustrate how efficiency is sometimes purchased at the expense of accuracy, we describe in this section of the chapter three well-researched attribution biases: the correspondence bias, actor-observer differences, and self-serving biases.

CORRESPONDENCE BIAS

The **correspondence bias** is a tendency to assume that a person's words and deeds correspond with that person's underlying traits, attitudes, and intentions, even when the words or deeds were facilitated by situational constraints. Because of the correspondence bias, attributers often do not discount appropriately for constraints that might have caused a person to behave as he or she did.

In the study that first demonstrated the correspondence bias, college students were assigned to give speeches in praise of Fidel Castro (Jones & Harris, 1967). None of the students had a high opinion of Fidel Castro, but they delivered speeches claiming that they respected and admired him. Other students watched these speeches on videotape and were told that the speakers had been assigned by a debate coach to take a pro-Castro position. The experimenters asked the students to estimate the speaker's own true attitude toward Fidel Castro. If the students discounted for situational constraints, they should have concluded that someone who was assigned to write a speech on a particular side of an issue does not necessarily believe it. With no other information available, the safest guess would have been that the student who gave the speech had the average student's opinion, which was against Fidel Castro. Nonetheless, the students who watched these videotapes displayed a correspondence bias. They knew that the person on the videotape had been assigned to take a pro-Castro position and had no choice. Nonetheless, they concluded that someone who spoke in favor of Castro must lean at least a little in that direction. Similarly, students in another study read one assigned essay praising Castro and a second assigned essay condemning Castro. Both essays were purportedly by the same author one week apart. The students, however, assumed that the author changed his or her opinion rather than that the situational constraints changed (Allison, Mackie, Muller, & Worth, 1993).

The correspondence bias seems to be "built in" to the causal attribution process, at least in Western cultures (Fletcher & Ward, 1988). Social psychologists have spent a quarter of a century trying to find its limitations, without much success (Jones, 1979, 1990). Even in the face of massive evidence to the

If members of a debate team extol Cuban leader Fidel Castro's virtues after being ordered to take Castro's side in a debate, does that mean that they privately admire Castro?

contrary, people continue to assume that other people's words and deeds accurately reflect their underlying traits, attitudes, and intentions. In one study, for instance, two students sat facing each other across a table (Miller, Jones, & Hinkle, 1981). The experimenter had the students flip a coin to see which of them would write an essay on why "I Am the World's Biggest Introvert," and which would write the other essay on why "I Am the World's Biggest Extrovert." After they wrote on whichever topic they happened to draw, the two students read each other's essays. Each student then estimated the other student's true introversion versus extroversion. Even in these circumstances, where students had themselves experienced how easily a flip of the coin could get them to claim either of two opposing personality traits, they still insisted that the other student must have a personality that corresponded with whatever the other student's essay said.

Attributers display less correspondence bias when the other person claims to be following situational constraints reluctantly. They display less correspondence bias when they suspect that the other person has ulterior motives for following situational constraints. They also display less correspondence bias when they know they will have to justify their attributions to others. (Fein, Hilton, & Miller, 1990; Fleming & Darley, 1989; Tetlock, 1985). Nonetheless, the correspondence bias is a very robust phenomenon (Jones, 1990). It occurs even when attributers are themselves forcing the target person to behave as he or she does (Gilbert & Jones, 1986). It occurs even among students who say they are most aware of the situational constraints. It occurs even when the experimenter takes great pains to make the constraints obvious (Johnson, Jemmott, & Pettigrew, 1984). Finally, the correspondence bias occurs in the assigned essay setting even when the authors are deliberately trying to convey (through hyperbole, awkward wording, verbal hedges, and so on) that they do not actually mean what they are writing (Fleming, Darley, Hilton, & Kojetin, 1990).

The correspondence bias is "cost-effective." It often causes no "damage" and has considerable benefits (Gilbert & Malone, 1995). First, people have some control over the situations in which they find themselves. Students who know that a particular professor gives "killer exams" can usually avoid the professor's courses and thus avoid situations in which correspondence bias might cause them to doubt their own academic potential. Second, people may not care whether dispositional attributions are "accurate" in the sense of applying to other situations (Swann, 1984). Suppose they think that a coworker who works in another building is an obnoxious loudmouth because he acts that way when he gets drunk at the annual company party. They may not care that they are "wrong" and he is very pleasant in all other situations. They only see him at the annual party, where they are wise to avoid him. Third, people who have been raised in a Western culture may *value* the illusion that behaviors arise from internal, stable, controllable causes (Taylor & Brown, 1988). It may seem fair to them that people are held responsible for their own behaviors, even if they are held more responsible than an objective analysis of the situation might allow (Nisbett, 1987).

Nonetheless, we should not be complacent about the implications of correspondence bias. As a comprehensive review of the literature reminds us, "In the past year, a thousand people who thought they knew their acquaintances have been raped by them, ten thousand people who thought they knew their mates have divorced them, and a hundred thousand people who thought they knew their sovereigns have died as pawns in their wars" (Gilbert & Malone, 1995, p. 35).

The correspondence bias occurs for at least four reasons (Gilbert & Malone, 1995). First, attributers often overlook situational constraints. Second, attributers have unrealistic expectations for another person's behavior. Third, attributers overemphasize the link between the behavior and the person in their initial identification. Fourth, attributers do not make accurate "adjustments" after they initially identify and categorize the behavior. Table 4.3 provides summary descriptions of these four factors, which are also described in the following sections.

TABLE 4.3	Four Causes of the Correspondence Bias (Drawn from Gilbert & Malone, 1995)
CAUSE	**DESCRIPTION**
Overlooking Situational Constraints	Treating situational constraints as though they were invisible or useless for making causal attributions
Unrealistic Expectations	Assuming that people are unwilling or unable to follow situational constraints
Overemphasizing the Behavior-Person Link	Letting the behavior spontaneously define the person
Failing to Adjust Accurately	Being too cognitively busy to adjust appropriately the initial attribution that was based only on identification and categorization

■ OVERLOOKING SITUATIONAL CONSTRAINTS

The most fundamental cause of the correspondence bias is a pervasive tendency to overlook situational constraints. The **fundamental attribution error** is the tendency to underestimate the power of the situation (relative to dispositions) when making causal attributions (Ross, 1977). It is a tendency to treat the situation as though it were almost invisible (Gilbert & Malone, 1995).

In a compelling demonstration of the fundamental attribution error, pairs of college students played the roles of questioner and contestant in a quiz game (Ross, Amabile, & Steinmetz, 1977). The students drew cards to determine who would be the questioner and who would be the contestant. The questioner had 10–15 minutes to invent "general world knowledge" questions to which they happened to know the answers, but most people would not. The students who played the role of questioner invented such difficult questions as "What do the initials W. H. in W. H. Auden's name stand for?" Not surprisingly, the students who played the role of contestant could not answer very many of them. After the quiz, the researchers asked questioners, contestants, and observers to estimate each participant's general knowledge.

Figure 4.2 displays the results. On the left are ratings made by the questioner. As can be seen, questioners regarded themselves as slightly more knowledgeable than their contestants, but not significantly so. Either they took the situational constraints into appropriate account or they feigned modesty. The contestants, however, thought the questioners knew more than they did. They knew that the roles had been assigned by drawing cards, so that they might just as easily have been the questioner rather than the contestant. They also heard the experimenter instruct the other student to make up questions that were drawn from idiosyncratic areas of expertise so that the average person would be unlikely to know the answer. All participants knew about and experienced for themselves the powerful situational constraints, yet they virtually ignored those constraints. Instead, they were biased toward the dispositional attribution that the questioner knew more than they did.

Other students who observed the interaction were as easily led to ignore the situational constraints as were the contestants. As the right side of the figure shows, observers exaggerated the contestants' bias toward a dispositional

Are the people who make up the questions for quiz shows such as *Jeopardy!* extremely brilliant?

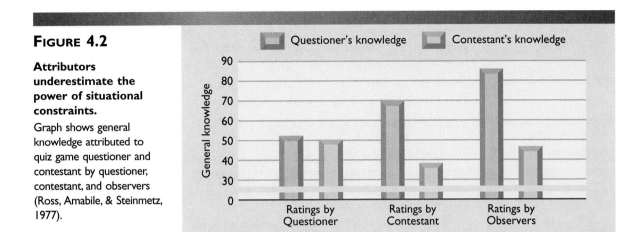

FIGURE 4.2

Attributors underestimate the power of situational constraints.

Graph shows general knowledge attributed to quiz game questioner and contestant by questioner, contestant, and observers (Ross, Amabile, & Steinmetz, 1977).

rather than a situational explanation of the questioner's behavior. Even though they saw the two students draw cards and overheard the experimenter's instructions, observers were extremely impressed by the questioner's general knowledge. They rated the questioner as more knowledgeable than 80 percent of students at their university. Observers failed to recognize the actual distinctiveness of the situation. They treated the one-sided quiz game setting as though it were an unbiased sample of the questioner's everyday behavior. They drew the correspondent inference that a student who acted smart must *be* smart, even though they should have discounted the performance because the quiz game format conferred an enormous advantage.

Interestingly, people sometimes fail to recognize the power of the situation even when they wield that power themselves. In a relevant study, college students "interviewed" another student, who was in a separate room from them (Gilbert & Jones, 1986). They read into a microphone a series of political questions that could be answered with either a conservative or a liberal statement. For each question, they had a typewritten list that showed the conservative answer and the liberal answer. By pressing one of two buttons they could force the person in the other room to read either the conservative answer or the liberal answer, word for word, exactly as it was typed on their list. Acting on instructions, half of the students forced the other person to read predominantly conservative answers; the other half forced the other person to read predominantly liberal answers. All students then estimated the other person's true political attitude. This was perhaps the most extreme test of correspondence bias ever staged. To display a correspondence bias the students had to ignore their own behavior, because they were the ones who made the other person do what he or she did. Even so, students who made the other person express conservative opinions thought the other person had a conservative political attitude. Likewise, students who made the other person express liberal opinions thought the other person had a liberal political attitude. In other words, the correspondence bias was found even when attributers should have been most aware of the situational constraints on the other person's behavior, because they produced those constraints.

The quiz game study and the forced answer study demonstrate that students in laboratory experiments have a pervasive tendency to overlook situational constraints. In everyday behavior outside the psychology laboratory, moreover, the fundamental attribution error might be even more pronounced than it is in the laboratory. Everyday observers might find bosses decisive, subordinates subservient, professors brilliant, students dumb, wealthy people industrious, and poor people lazy. They might easily overlook situational constraints that are far more ambiguous than the constraints in psychology experiments. The fundamental attribution error may be "fundamental" in its effect on individuals and on society.

■ UNREALISTIC EXPECTATIONS

The correspondence bias also occurs because attributers have unrealistic expectations for another person's behavior. They mistakenly assume that people will refuse to argue against their own attitudes and to misrepresent their own personality traits (Ross, 1977). They also mistakenly assume that people are *unable* to argue convincingly against their own attitudes and to misrepresent their own traits (Miller & Rorer, 1982).

In hundreds of psychology experiments, many of them described throughout this textbook, experimenters asked students to cooperate by performing very unusual behaviors. Because they were asked politely, students spent hours turning wooden pegs back and forth (Festinger & Carlsmith, 1959) and young men agreed to be locked in prison (Haney, Banks, & Zimbardo, 1973). Observers, however, are usually surprised that anyone would perform these behaviors without "a gun to the head." Most college students, for instance, falsely believe that people will not agree to write an essay contrary to their own personal opinions (Sherman, 1980). In one striking result (Bierbrauer, 1979), the experimenter told students about a study in which participants were asked to give severe electric shocks to a mild-mannered, middle-aged accountant who had a heart condition. (The electric shock study is described in greater detail in Chapter 14.) The experimenter then asked the students to estimate how many ordinary people would refuse to give electric shocks to another human being under such conditions. Overwhelmingly, the students said that they would never do such a thing and that no one else would do so either. In reality, many people gave the shocks. When they try to imagine situations that do not seem on the surface to involve powerful situational pressures, attributers harbor unrealistic expectations about what other people are willing to do.

Attributers also have unrealistic expectations about what behaviors people are *able* to perform (Reeder, Fletcher, & Furman, 1989). Participants in one study estimated that authors who themselves favored school busing could write a more convincing essay in favor of school busing than could authors who themselves opposed school busing (Miller & Rorer, 1982). Similarly, they estimated that antibusing advocates would write more convincing essays against busing than would authors who themselves favored busing. Perhaps because they thought that people would find it difficult to construct arguments on the "other side," the participants believed that a reader could see through the subterfuge.

In a subsequent study, college students were assigned to write essays either for or against legalization of abortion (Miller, Ashton, & Mishal, 1990). After they wrote the essays, the authors estimated how strong their essays were and how easy they were to write. They also imagined that other people read their essays, knowing that the particular side of the issue had been assigned rather than chosen, and tried to guess the authors' true attitude. The students were asked what attitude these readers would assume the authors had. As predicted, students regarded their essays as stronger and easier to write if they personally agreed with the position that they espoused than if they personally disagreed. They also thought that readers would be able to tell if the author was trying to create an impression opposite to the truth. They were wrong. When readers later read the essays, the readers could not detect any differences in essay strength, ease of writing, or the authors' true attitude. The expectation that it is impossible for people to "go against their grain" is an unrealistic one that contributes to the correspondence bias.

■ OVEREMPHASIZING THE BEHAVIOR-PERSON LINK

The attribution process, as described in the first section of this chapter, also overemphasizes the link between the behavior and the person. From the very start of the process, behaviors are easily tied to persons, both because behaviors imply trait inferences spontaneously and because behaviors help attributers to identify and classify the person.

In the model of causal attribution described earlier in the chapter, behavior occupies the central position. It influences the initial identification of both the situation and the person. The situation, in contrast, cannot influence the identification of the person, at least not directly. One consequence of this asymmetry is that the link between behavior and person becomes "automatic" (Carlston & Skowronski, 1994; Newman & Uleman, 1989). As with other automatic thought processes (described in Chapters 2 and 3), people are not aware that they draw spontaneous trait inferences from behavior, they do not intend to do it, and they cannot control it (Bargh, 1994). When we see someone failing a test, we automatically entertain the assumption that he or she might be stupid (Gilbert, 1991). Spontaneous trait inferences help us react to other people quickly and efficiently (Uleman & Moskowitz, 1994). They help us predict what other people might do. They are so useful that we do not notice how easily behaviors generate trait assumptions (Newman, 1993; Heider, 1958).

An unfamiliar person is likely to be defined by his or her behavior and not by the situation. If we see someone failing an exam and we know very little about the person, the behavior helps us to categorize the individual as "the type of person who fails an exam." Even if we know in advance that the exam will be a difficult one, the exam's difficulty only adds to how critically we view the behavior. As described earlier in this chapter, the situational constraint of exam difficulty "sets us up" to expect poor performance. We see the behavior as more lacking than we might have had we known nothing about the situation (Darley & Gross, 1983). When the behavior seems more extreme, the behavior doubly defines the test taker as "the type of person who fails."

In one study of how attributers let the behavior define the person, students watched a videotape of a young woman who was being interviewed (Snyder & Frankel, 1976). Because the sound was turned off, the experimenters could tell one group of students that the woman was being interviewed about politics. They told a second group of students that she was being interviewed about sex. As predicted, students who thought the woman was being interviewed about sex thought she seemed more nervous and anxious than did students who thought she was being interviewed about politics, even though both groups of students watched the same videotape. Students who thought she was being interviewed about sex also drew the correspondent inference that she was a dispositionally nervous, anxious person outside the interview situation. Knowing about the situation "helped" them to identify ambiguous behavior as nervous, anxious behavior, which in turn "helped" them to identify the person as "a nervous, anxious type."

As suggested by the two-stage model of attribution, the students took the situational constraints into account during the deliberative stage. They discounted by saying that "Anyone would act nervous and anxious if they were being interviewed about sex, so I guess she's not that much of a nervous wreck," but the damage had already been done. They saw the woman as more dispositionally anxious than did other students who saw the videotape first and only learned about the interview topic after watching the videotape. In other words, both groups of students adjusted their initial impressions to take the situational constraints into account. Students who knew about the constraints before watching the videotape, however, were starting from a more extreme interpretation of how anxiously the woman had behaved. Behavior inflates the way that the person who performs the behavior is initially identified and categorized (Gilbert & Malone, 1995).

■ FAILING TO ADJUST ACCURATELY

The correspondence bias also occurs because everything we see or hear is initially perceived as true or "face valid" (Gilbert, 1991). Subsequent adjustments to the initial "truth value" of behavior require a level of attributional complexity that attributers do not often use (Fletcher, Reeder, & Bull, 1990). Many causal attributions do not involve deliberative thinking. They depend entirely on initial identification and categorization, which (as we have seen) are heavily biased in favor of a behavior-person link. Anything that impairs the deliberative or "adjustment" stage of the process leaves us accepting the initial identification as true. The deliberative stage can be impaired by distracting events and by self-presentational concerns.

In one study of how distraction affects the attribution process, college students watched a silent videotape of a young woman who squirmed and fidgeted while she was talking (Gilbert, Pelham, & Krull, 1988). Some of the students were told that she was being interviewed about such anxiety-inducing topics as her most intimate sexual fantasies. Other students, who watched the same tape, were told that she was being interviewed about mundane topics such as her hobbies. Also, some students in each group were distracted and made "cognitively busy" by having to recite the interview topics mentally while they watched the videotape.

As you can see on the left side of Figure 4.3, when nondistracted students were asked how dispositionally nervous the woman was, those who thought she was being interviewed about mundane topics viewed her as having a more nervous personality than did those who thought she was being interviewed about anxiety-inducing topics. Presumably, the nondistracted students spontaneously "registered" the videotaped woman's squirms and fidgets as "the truth" about her underlying personality. They augmented this dispositional attribution when the topics were mundane and discounted it when the topics were likely to make anyone anxious (Newman & Uleman, 1989).

As you can see on the right side of Figure 4.3, students who were distracted by having to memorize the topics made very little adjustment for how anxiety-

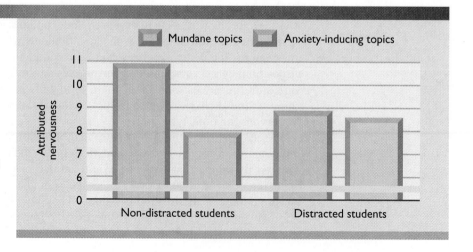

FIGURE 4.3

Cognitively busy attributors ignore salient situational constraints.

Graph shows nervousness that distracted and nondistracted students attributed to a woman being interviewed about mundane or anxiety-inducing topics (Gilbert et al., 1988).

inducing the topics were. They made almost equal attributions about the woman's dispositional nervousness regardless of whether they believed that she was being interviewed about mundane or anxiety-inducing topics. They did so even though they later remembered the situational constraints (the interview topics) *better,* not worse, than did the nondistracted students.

Distractions may occur more frequently during everyday attributions than they do in laboratory experiments (Osborne & Gilbert, 1992). In our everyday social encounters, we are frequently distracted from making appropriate "adjustments." If the behavior is at first difficult to comprehend, for instance, we might have to concentrate on categorizing the behavior rather than on the situational constraints (Gilbert, McNulty, Giuliano, & Benson, 1992). Similarly, we might be distracted by trying very hard to get the other person to like us. At such times, a behavior's surface meaning wins out over situational constraints, because the "behavior elicits corresponding trait" part of attribution occurs spontaneously and the deliberative stage is impaired. In one study, for instance, students watched a speech by a person who was supposedly assigned to espouse one or another side in a debate (Gilbert & Krull, 1988). Some of the students believed that the person who was making the speech could see them. They were asked to make the speaker laugh. The other students were given no such social interaction goal. The students who were trying to induce laughter made funny faces, bizarre gestures, and other weird behaviors, all to no avail because the speaker was actually on videotape. The "make him laugh" students were so busy trying to fulfill their social goal that, unlike "no goal" students, they failed to adjust for situational constraints and instead displayed a correspondence bias.

Distractions also interfere more with the deliberative thinking of people who are clinically depressed than with the "further thinking" of people who are not depressed. Because people who are very depressed feel a lack of control over their lives, they worry more than do their peers about the meaning of other people's words and deeds (Weary & Edwards, 1994). They worry that they do not understand their difficulties in dealing with others. They worry about other people's true intentions (Weary & Edwards, 1994, in press). Because of these interpersonal worries, depressed people do much deliberative

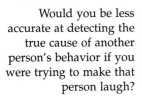

Would you be less accurate at detecting the true cause of another person's behavior if you were trying to make that person laugh?

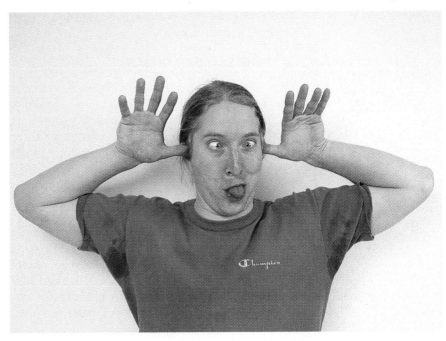

thinking. Thus they usually display less of a correspondence bias than do others (Yost & Weary, in press). The only time that depressed people display as much correspondence bias as anyone else is when they are distracted and thus unable to engage in deliberative thinking. In one study, for instance, people who were depressed read a pro-Castro speech that was assigned by a debate coach. Those who were not distracted while reading the speech displayed little or no correspondence bias. They did not think the author meant what he or she wrote. Those who were distracted, in contrast, displayed the same correspondence bias as anyone else (Yost & Weary, in press). The correspondence bias, then, occurs when attributers are either unwilling or unable to use the deliberative stage of the attribution process.

ACTOR-OBSERVER DIFFERENCES

To reiterate, according to the correspondence bias, people unnecessarily assign the causes of behavior to the person's corresponding disposition rather than to the situation. There are some differences, however, in how people explain their own behavior (as actors) as opposed to how they explain another person's behavior (as observers) (Jones & Nisbett, 1972). The **actor-observer difference** holds that the correspondence bias is much smaller, sometimes even nonexistent, when people explain their own behavior than when they explain another person's behavior. In one study, for instance, the investigators asked college men to explain why they or their roommate chose a specific major (Nisbett, Caputo, Legant, & Maracek, 1973). When they explained their own behavior (for which they were actors), they gave situational reasons such as "engineering pays well." The cause was something external to themselves. When they explained their roommate's behavior (for which they were observers), in contrast, they gave dispositional reasons such as "he's a greedy kind of guy." The cause was something internal to the roommate. People also view their own behavior as less stable and less predictable than the behavior of other people (Baxter & Goldberg, 1988; Sande, Goethals, & Radloff, 1988; White & Younger, 1988). Actor-observer differences occur because of differences between actors and observers in whether the person or the situation is more visually salient. Actor-observer differences also occur because people have a tendency, called "false consensus," to assume that the majority of other people share their own behavioral preferences.

■ VISUAL SALIENCE

One reason for actor-observer differences is that people can *see* the situational constraints better when they are the actor than when they are the observer. "Actors watch the environment (which includes the behavior of other people) more than they watch their own behavior. Observers watch the behavior of the actor more than they watch the actor's situation" (Storms, 1973, p. 166). When Tom Tippler is drinking at a bar, we observers see him and his behavior. We do not see the events of his hard day at work. Tom, in contrast, may be oblivious to how he looks. Instead, he may be reviewing in his mind's eye the stressful events (situational constraints) that happened at work.

In one experiment that tested the effect of visual salience on attributions, two previously unacquainted students held a getting-acquainted conversation (Storms, 1973). After the conversation, the experimenter showed each of them a videotape taken from a camera that was situated just behind one of the students. Some students saw the conversation on videotape from their own original perspective. Other students saw the conversation on videotape from the

FIGURE 4.4

Visual perspective affects actor-observer differences.

Graph shows how dispositional versus situational students viewed own and other's behavior from two perspectives (Storms, 1973).

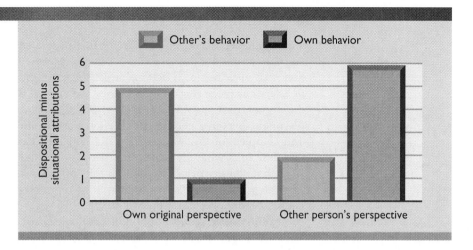

other person's original perspective. Both students were then asked how much they attributed their own and the other person's behavior to dispositional characteristics and how much they attributed it to characteristics of the situation. Figure 4.4 shows the results. On the left side of the figure are the situational and dispositional attributions made by students who watched a videotape that matched their own original perspective. When they were asked to explain the other person's behavior, they displayed a correspondence bias toward preferring dispositional over situational attributions. When they were asked to explain their own behavior, this bias almost disappeared. The actor-observer difference applied also to other students (whose data are not depicted in the figure), who made attributions based only on their experiences in the original conversation, without viewing any videotape.

The contribution of visual salience to actor-observer differences is shown on the right side of Figure 4.4. When students watched a videotape of the conversation as seen from the other person's perspective, they explained the other person's behavior slightly more through dispositional than through situational attributions. They did not, however, display as much correspondence bias as did the "original perspective" students. Also, as shown on the extreme right side of the figure, seeing the conversation from the other person's perspective *reversed* the usual actor-observer difference. These students explained their own behavior much more with dispositional than with situational attributions. It is as though the other-person's-perspective students were saying "I never realized until I saw myself as the center of attention how much I took control of the conversation and how little the surrounding circumstances mattered."

Other studies on visual salience have shown that observers remember more about and attribute a greater causal role to people who occupy the center of the field of vision and to people who sit under bright lights, wear distinctive clothing, and move rather than sit still (McArthur, 1981; McArthur & Post, 1977; Taylor & Fiske, 1975, 1978). People who "grab the eye" and capture attention are seen as more dynamic than their surroundings, so they are seen as making things happen rather than having things happen to them. Merely because of where our eyes are located on our bodies, we always view the situation (including other people) as dynamic and ourselves as static. We are less impressed, therefore, by the situational constraints that act on another person's behavior than we are by the situational constraints that act on our own behavior. This difference in visual perspective, therefore, produces actor-observer differences in making attributions about our own versus another person's behavior.

■ FALSE CONSENSUS

Visual salience is not the only factor that produces actor-observer differences. Another important determinant is false consensus. **False consensus** is the tendency to view our own actions and choices as more common than they are, or at least as more prevalent than they are viewed by other people who choose differently from us (Marks & Miller, 1987; Wetzel & Walton, 1985). Many people might perceive getting drunk after work as an unusual behavior, but the Tom Tipplers of this world might not. People estimate consensus from a limited sample of what they and other people do. They are most often right about what the majority of people do, but they are also sometimes wrong, especially when they base their estimates on their own preferences (Alicke & Largo, 1995; Dawes & Mulford, in press; Miller, 1993).

In the classic demonstration of false consensus, students volunteered for a study of "communication techniques" (Ross, Greene, & House, 1977). The experimenter showed each student a large sandwich board sign that said, in huge letters, "REPENT!" The experimenter asked the student to wear this sign around campus for 30 minutes and to keep track of the comments it elicited from other students. The experimenter added that "If you are not willing to do this we will still give you your experimental credit although you will miss the chance to have an interesting experience and to do us a big favor" (Ross, Greene, & House, 1977, p. 291). Exactly 50% of the students agreed to wear the sign and 50% refused. After each student had decided whether to wear the sign, the experimenter asked him or her to estimate the percentage of other students who would agree and the percentage who would refuse. Students who had themselves agreed to wear the sign estimated that 58.3% of other students would agree to do so (and 41.7% refuse). Students who had themselves refused to wear the sign estimated that only 23.3% of other students would agree (and 76.7% refuse). In other words, both students who agreed and students who refused to wear the sign overestimated the power of the situation to elicit from other students whichever choice they made themselves.

The sandwich board sign study suggests that people underestimate consensus for and situational constraints on other people's behavior. As we have seen in discussions of consistency, consensus, and distinctiveness (Kelley, 1967), estimates of high consensus lead to situational attributions and estimates of low consensus lead to dispositional attributions. After they made their estimates of what other students would do, students who participated in the sandwich board sign study were asked how confidently they could attribute various personality traits to other students who agreed and to other students who refused. Students who had themselves agreed to wear the sign felt that they had little basis for attributing personality characteristics to other students who agreed, but that they could confidently assign traits to "those oddballs" who refused. Students who had themselves refused to wear the sign were just as adamant that they could divine very little about the personality characteristics of people who, like themselves, refused, but that they could tell a lot about the personality of the "small minority" who would agree to engage in such outlandish behavior. False consensus, then, leads actors to make more dispositional and less situational attributions for other people's behaviors than they make for their own.

Students who agreed to wear the sandwich board sign may, as part of making a decision, have imagined a person (perhaps themselves) doing just that. "Seeing" the action in imagination may have made that action more salient and thus made it seem more common than it might have seemed had students not imagined someone doing it. Students who are asked to imagine engaging in a chosen behavior come to regard that behavior as more common. They es-

Are the people who wear sandwich-board signs in public really weird or are they ordinary folks just like you and me?

timate that a larger percentage of their peers would choose to behave that way (Kernis, 1984).

False consensus may also occur because people selectively associate with others who behave as they do (Mullen, Atkins, Champion, Edwards, Hardy, Story, & Vanderklok, 1985; Nisbett & Kunda, 1985). According to this "birds of a feather flock together" account, students who refused to wear the sign may have been correct when they estimated that 77% of their peers would refuse to do so. They were correct if they based their estimates only on their acquaintances. Because similarity is a reliable predictor of friendship, friends are more likely to respond in the same way to a situation than would two randomly chosen strangers (Byrne, 1971; Deutsch, 1988). Smokers, for instance, are more likely to overestimate the percentage of smokers in the population if they associate predominantly with other people who smoke cigarettes than if they associate with many nonsmokers (Sherman, Presson, Chassin, Corty, & Olshavsky, 1983). By selectively associating with people who agree with us on most issues, we may guarantee that our own behavioral choices have high consensus, which we may take to mean that these choices are highly constrained by the situation.

Finally, false consensus estimates may help us to feel good about ourselves. If other people agree with us, then our choices "must" be correct, or at least socially sanctioned. This may be why people perceive greater consensus for their own actions among members of groups they respect than among members of groups they dislike (Marks, Richardson, Lochner, McGuigan, & Levine, 1988). False consensus is also higher among people who are physically attractive rather than unattractive and among people who consider themselves "generally good" rather than "generally bad" (Marks & Miller, 1982; Sherman,

| TABLE 4.4 | The Three Dimensions on Which People Make Causal Attribution (Drawn from Weiner, 1985), with Examples Showing How We Might Attribute Mel's Receiving an A or an F on an Exam to Causes That Are Internal or External, Stable or Unstable, and Controllable or Uncontrollable |

MEL ACED THE EXAM

	INTERNAL CAUSES		EXTERNAL CAUSES	
	Stable	*Unstable*	*Stable*	*Unstable*
Controllable	**Typical Effort** Mel always studied hard	**Temporary Effort** Mel studied very hard for this exam	**Permanent Bias** Mel chose a gut course	**Temporary Bias** Mel chose to study the right questions for this exam
Uncontrollable	**Ability** Mel was brilliant	**Mood** Mel had just received good news and felt great	**Task Difficulty** The exams in a course Mel had to take were very easy	**Luck** The professor graded by throwing the exams downstairs and Mel's was on the top stair

MEL FAILED THE EXAM

	INTERNAL CAUSES		EXTERNAL CAUSES	
	Stable	*Unstable*	*Stable*	*Unstable*
Controllable	**Typical Effort** Mel always partied too much	**Temporary Effort** Mel spent his time studying for a different course's exam	**Permanent Bias** Mel chose a very difficult course	**Temporary Bias** Mel chose to study the wrong questions for this exam
Uncontrollable	**Ability** Mel had a learning disorder	**Mood** Mel had just received bad news and felt terrible	**Task Difficulty** The exams in a course Mel had to take were very difficult	**Luck** The professor graded by throwing the exams downstairs and Mel's was on the bottom stair

Chassin, Presson, & Agostinelli, 1984). High consensus for our own choices provides social support for our behavior and protects our self-esteem (Holtz & Miller, 1985). When we convince ourselves that we are "one of the good people," we may also convince ourselves that "any good, reasonable, intelligent person would behave the same way I would in this situation" (Marks & Miller, 1987). In this respect, false consensus estimates are similar to self-serving biases.

SELF-SERVING BIASES

When people make attributions for success and failure, they use three dimensions that are shown in Table 4.4. The three dimensions are the location of the cause (internal versus external), how stable the cause is, and how controllable it is (Weiner, 1985). The table illustrates how people might attribute the cause if a student named Mel received an A or an F on an exam. An internal-stable-controllable attribution, for instance, says that success or failure was due to the actor's typical effort. An external-unstable-uncontrollable attribution says that success or failure was due to luck. The three dimensions describe explanations for success and failure in athletic, academic, and business achievement, explanations for interpersonal acceptance and rejection, and explanations in many different cultures (Anderson, 1983; Feather & Davenport, 1981; Furnham, 1982; Schuster, Forsterling, & Weiner, 1989; Triandis, 1972).

Of the causes shown in Table 4.4, however, one is not necessarily "better" than another. As we know from the first section of the chapter, people make more extreme attributions when the event has emotional impact or affects them. In a relevant study, students thought they were participating in a quiz game against students at other colleges (Jones & DeCharms, 1957). The experimenter told some of the students that success depended entirely on intellectual *ability* (an internal-stable-uncontrollable cause in Table 4.4) and told other students that success depended entirely on how much *effort* they exerted (an internal-stable-controllable cause). Also, the experimenter told half of the students in each group that they would win a prize if they did well on the task as individuals. The experimenter told the other half that they would get the prize only if all members of their group did well. One of the "other students," however, was a confederate who deliberately failed. All students were then asked to evaluate the student who failed. As the left side of Figure 4.5 shows, when students

FIGURE 4.5

Emotional impact affects attributions for failure.

Graph shows how positively students viewed a partner who failed because of effort or ability, in two conditions (Jones & DeCharms, 1957).

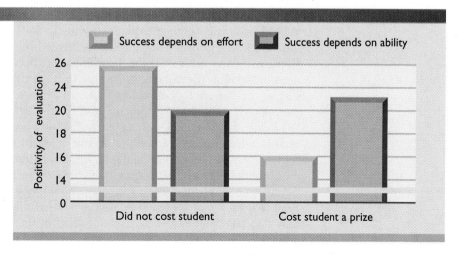

were not themselves negatively affected by the other person's poor performance, they evaluated him more negatively when success depended on intellectual ability than when it depended on effort. When students lost the prize themselves because the other person performed poorly, as shown on the right side of the figure, they evaluated him more negatively when success depended on effort than when it depended on ability. "I'll forgive a person who couldn't help it because he isn't very smart, but I will not forgive a person who was so lazy that he cost me the prize." Emotional impact and personal relevance reverse the usual favorableness with which attributers view failure that is due to controllable effort versus uncontrollable ability.

Attributions for success and failure also involve significant actor-observer differences. According to the **self-serving bias**, people tend to attribute their own successes more to internal-stable causes than they would when making attributions about other people and to attribute their own failures more to external-unstable causes than they would when making attributions about other people (Brown & Rogers, 1991; Carver, DeGregorio, & Gillis, 1980; Greenwald, 1980; Miller & Ross, 1975; Ross & Fletcher, 1985; Ross & Sicoly, 1979; Van Der Pligt & Eiser, 1983). Mel, for instance, is likely to attribute his getting an A on the exam to his excellent study habits or intellectual brilliance (internal-stable). He is also likely to attribute his getting an F to choosing (this once) to study the wrong questions or sheer bad luck. Mel might attribute his roommate's getting an A, in contrast, to choosing (this once) to study the right questions or good luck. He might also attribute his roommate's getting an F to the roommate's poor study habits or stupidity. Self-serving biases show up in self-enhancing attributions, egocentric attributions, and unrealistic optimism.

■ SELF-ENHANCING ATTRIBUTIONS

In several experiments, students who passed or failed exams have been asked to make causal attributions for their own success or failure. Almost invariably, students who did well on an exam attributed their success to their own effort or ability. Those who did poorly on the same exam attributed their failure to bad luck or to the type of questions that the professor happened to choose (Arkin & Maryuma, 1979; Davis & Stephan, 1980; DeJong, Koomen, & Mellenbergh, 1988; Whitley & Frieze, 1985). Similarly, when athletes and coaches win a game, they say they did so because they tried hard and had superior talent. When they lose, they say it was because the officials made poor decisions, the other team happened to be "on," or they got "bad breaks" (Grove et al., 1991; Lau, 1984; Lau & Russell, 1980). When gamblers win they think they are skillful, but when they lose they think they had bad luck (Gilovich, 1983). When business executives explain why the company is making a large profit, they think it is because they are such talented, hard-working administrators. When company profits decline, they think it is because of poor market conditions or inflation (Bettman & Weitz, 1983). It seems as though people attribute success and failure by consulting Table 4.4 to decide which attributions make them look good (Ickes & Layden, 1978; Snyder & Higgins, 1988).

When they make self-enhancing attributions, people are trying to look good both to others and to themselves. In one study of self-enhancing attributions, students thought they were taking an important test of their intellectual ability (Greenberg, Pyszczynski, & Solomon, 1982). The correct answers were sufficiently ambiguous that the investigators could lead half of the students to believe that they had scored very well. They led the other half to believe that they had failed miserably. In addition, half of the students who "succeeded" and half of the students who "failed" were allowed to compute their own test scores and to keep the scores confidential. The other half were required to

Calvin and Hobbes

by Bill Watterson

CALVIN AND HOBBES © Watterson. Dist. by UNIVERSAL PRESS SYNDICATE. Reprinted with permission. All rights reserved.

make their test scores public by affixing their names and handing in the forms. The investigators, of course, knew who had "succeeded" and who had "failed" whether the students thought that their scores were public or private.

All students were then asked which factors they thought were responsible for how they scored on the test. If students were merely seeking to create a good impression in the eyes of the experimenters, then only those in the "public" condition would have attributed their success to internal-stable factors and attributed their failure to external-unstable factors. Contrary to this prediction, students in both the "private" condition and the "public" condition attributed their scores more to ability than to luck if they did well on the test. Also, students who thought they had failed claimed that the test was defective, that the instructions were not clear, and that the test was measuring an ability of very little importance. They did so even in the "private" condition where they were convinced that no one else could possibly know their scores. Their self-serving biases, therefore, were not merely strategic self-presentations. Instead, they were a way of alleviating the aversive arousal that comes from having failed (Brown & Rogers, 1991). It is not as upsetting to think that you failed because of bad luck as it is to think that you failed because you did not try hard or lack ability.

■ EGOCENTRIC ATTRIBUTIONS

Self-serving biases are also evident in egocentric attributions, in which people see themselves as the "center of the universe" (Greenwald, 1980). They exaggerate the importance of their own role in life's events, especially their role in causing desirable outcomes. In one study of egocentric biases, the investigators asked married couples how often they performed a wide variety of household chores such as cleaning house, doing the dishes, caring for children, and taking out the garbage (Ross & Sicoly, 1979). In most couples, both the husband and the wife claimed that he or she performed the same chore more than half of the time, which is mathematically and logically impossible.

In another study, both of two siblings claimed that they did the majority of helping their elderly parents (Lerner et al., 1991). Similarly, married people blame their spouses more than themselves for not exerting enough effort to maintain a satisfactory sexual relationship, although men do this more than women (Maass & Volpato, 1989). Across many types of situations, from professional partnerships to marriages, people who are partners in a project that requires effort each claim that they exert most of the effort (Fiebert, 1990).

If a husband cooks 70% of the family's meals, how can his wife cook 75% of the family's meals?

Through their egocentric biases in attribution, people give themselves more credit than they deserve for life's desirable outcomes.

■ UNREALISTIC OPTIMISM

People also develop unrealistic optimism about their traits, abilities, and life chances. They become convinced that they are "better than average" in many ways (Campbell, 1986; Brown, 1986). In one study, for instance, automobile drivers estimated how safe and skillful they were compared to the average driver (Svenson, 1981). Even drivers who had been hospitalized because of serious automobile accidents insisted that they were "better than average" drivers (Manstead, Parker, Stradling, Reason, & Baxter, 1992). In another study, Australian workers estimated their own job performance. Almost all of them claimed that they were "better than average" at their work, which is another mathematical and logical impossibility. People also believe that they are more moral and less prejudiced than the average other person (Allison et al., 1989; Messick et al., 1985).

Finally, because people see their own successes as more controllable than the successes achieved by others, they develop unrealistically optimistic expectations. They come to believe that good things will happen to them and that the bad things that happen to others will not happen to them. Most people say they are much more likely than the average person to get good grades, land a great job, have a gifted child, and so on (Weinstein, 1980). Although they realize that many marriages in the United States end in divorce, U.S. college students are convinced that theirs will not. They overestimate the extent to which they can exert control over events and the extent to which they possess whatever traits are required for success (Lehman, Lempert, & Nisbett, 1988; Kunda, 1987).

Some types of unrealistic optimism, especially about the prospects of avoiding negative life events, can be potentially harmful. In one study, for instance, sexually active college women who did not use contraceptives claimed that they were *less* likely than their peers to have an unwanted pregnancy (Burger & Burns, 1988). In a study in The Netherlands, citizens whose behavior put them at greatest risk for contracting AIDS were most likely to display unrealistic optimism about their chances of doing so (van der Velde, van der Pligt, & Hooykaas, 1994). In another study in Scotland, adolescents said that they were less likely than their peers to become infected with the AIDS virus (Abrams, 1991). When people believe that they are less likely than the average person to develop drinking problems, heart attacks, AIDS, and other health risks, the danger is that they might not take reasonable precautions (van der Pligt, Otten, Richard, & van der Velde, 1993; Weinstein, 1980).

Gamblers in particular have the illusion that they can control their chances of winning. They believe that they have a better chance of winning a lottery, for example, if they are allowed to pick their own favorite ticket number than if they are merely assigned a ticket number at random (Langer, 1975). They also believe that they are more likely to win at dice games if they throw the dice themselves than if someone else does it for them (Fleming & Darley, 1989). Across a wide variety of situations, people are convinced that they can control events that are actually beyond their control (Crocker, 1982).

In most situations, however, unrealistic optimism serves useful functions. Without unrealistic optimism, people might consider themselves "worse than average" in effort and ability. They might not give themselves proper credit for their contributions. They might assume that terrible things are going to happen to them regardless of what they do (Greenberg, Pyszczynski, & Solomon, 1986). They might conclude that their lives are influenced by external, unstable forces that are beyond their control (Taylor & Brown, 1988). Such a pessimistic conclusion might make them give up on trying to accomplish their goals (Dweck, 1986; Deaux, 1984). It might also make them so anxious and depressed that they would never attempt to accomplish anything. They might also be more susceptible to illness (Cohen, Doyle, Skoner, Fireman, Gwaltney, & Newsom, 1995; Snyder & Higgins, 1988). In short, the benefits of self-serving bias probably outweigh its lack of realism.

SUMMARY OF ACCURACY IN CAUSAL ATTRIBUTION

The process of making causal attributions entails several "biases." First, attributers seem too ready to assume that another person's traits correspond with his or her words and deeds. This "correspondence bias" occurs because people overlook situational constraints, have unrealistic expectations for what other people are willing and able to do, overemphasize the link between the person and his or her behavior, and adjust their initial attributions inaccurately when they are "cognitively busy." Second, attributers draw less dispositional inferences about their own behavior than about another person's behavior, because their own behavior is less visually salient and because they believe that their own choices are more prevalent than they are, or at least more prevalent than they are viewed by other people who choose differently. False consensus occurs because our own behaviors are relatively easy to imagine, because we usually interact with "our own kind," and because it makes us feel good about ourselves. Self-serving biases include attributing our own (but not other people's) successes to internal-stable factors and our own (but not other people's) failures to external-unstable factors, taking more credit than is due for desirable outcomes, and unrealistic (but useful) optimism about our life prospects.

WHAT ARE SOME CONSEQUENCES OF CAUSAL ATTRIBUTION?

The first two sections of the chapter showed how causal attributions work and why they are not always accurate. This third section describes some important consequences of the attribution process. Although causal attributions have consequences for many types of events, space is limited. We discuss only the consequences of attributions for success and failure, and attributing responsibility.

ATTRIBUTIONS FOR SUCCESS AND FAILURE

Attributions for success and failure may occur either for another person's outcomes or for our own outcomes. The following discussion is organized according to three relationships that spring from the three dimensions of success and failure attributions that are depicted in Table 4.4 (Weiner, 1986). According to a comprehensive review of how people explain events (Anderson, Krull, & Weiner, in press), self-esteem is affected primarily by whether people view the cause of their own success or failure as internal versus external. Expectations for the future are affected primarily by whether people view the cause of their own success or failure as stable versus unstable. Emotional reactions are determined primarily by whether people view the causes of their own success or failure as controllable versus uncontrollable. Obviously, these are not airtight distinctions, but they are very useful.

■ INTERNALITY AND SELF-ESTEEM

The attributed location of the cause, whether it is perceived to be internal or external, affects self-esteem (Anderson et al., in press). If a professor praised Mel's academic performance, Mel might be happy, but he would also experience different emotions depending on whether he made an internal or an external attribution. An internal attribution, such as attributing the professor's praise to his own hard work, might elicit in Mel feelings of pride, self-worth, and positive self-esteem. An external attribution, for instance to the professor's weird grading system, might elicit emotions like gratitude or surprise, but it would not improve Mel's self-esteem (McFarland & Ross, 1982; Stipek & Weisz, 1981; Weiner, Russell, & Lerman, 1979).

The relationship between internality and self-esteem is obvious in many everyday contexts. In the previous section, for instance, we discussed self-enhancing attributions, in which people make internal attributions for their own successes and external attributions for their own failures. Self-enhancing attributions presumably occur because people want the perceived reasons for an event to "fit their wishes" (Heider, 1958). Attributing success to an internal cause makes success even more satisfying; attributing failure to an external cause relieves guilt and shame.

External attributions for failure also protect the self-esteem of people who believe that they are mistreated because of prejudice or discrimination (Crocker & Major, 1989). A job applicant, for instance, may be "better off" believing that she was rejected because of her membership in a stigmatized minority group than believing that she was rejected because she made a poor impression during the job interview. It may be infuriating to be discriminated against unfairly, but at least it allows a job applicant to approach the next interview with self-esteem and personal confidence intact. Similarly, people who avoid internal attributions for doing worse than a rival might avoid the painful emotion of jealousy (Mikulincer, Bizman, & Aizenberg, 1989).

Finally, people who consistently attribute success to external causes and failure to internal causes reduce their chances of becoming depressed (Abramson, Seligman, & Teasdale, 1978; Anderson & Riger, 1991; Brewin, 1985; Bruder-Mattson & Hovanitz, 1990). Because depression causes many problems in coping with everyday experience, people may be wise to avoid the self-esteem damaging cycle of attributing success externally and failure internally (Anderson & Riger, 1991; Weary & Edwards, 1994).

■ STABILITY AND EXPECTATIONS

The attributed stability of a cause affects expectations for the future. If Mel thought he did well on an exam because he was good at a subject (a stable cause), he would be more hopeful about future exams than if he believed that he did well only because he happened to be in a good mood (an unstable cause). Conversely, if Mel thought he flunked an exam because he was not very smart (stable), he would entertain less hope for the future than if he thought he flunked because he happened to be in a bad mood (unstable). A stable cause is one that is unlikely to change. An unstable cause might be absent in the future, so success or failure would not be repeated. The optimism associated with stable attributions for success and unstable attributions for failure leads to more persistence than the pessimism associated with unstable attributions for success and stable attributions for failure (Weiner, 1986).

The stability of attributions affects consequential decisions about both other people and the self. When deciding whether a prisoner should be paroled, for example, parole boards are more likely to grant parole to prisoners whose crimes the board attributes to unstable causes than to prisoners whose crimes the board attributes to stable causes (Carroll & Payne, 1976; Saulnier & Perlman, 1981). An otherwise law-abiding banker who embezzled money when faced with large one-time hospital bills (unstable cause) might be considered a better risk for parole than would a compulsive gambler who stole to avoid the retribution of a loan shark (stable cause). Similarly, victims of rape and other crimes can avoid hopelessness and depression by attributing the event to unstable causes rather than to stable causes (Abramson, Metalsky, & Alloy, 1989; Anderson, Miller, Riger, Dill, & Sedikides, 1994). The difference is between the hopeless "I'll never learn" and the more hopeful "I just happened to be in the wrong place at the wrong time."

Differences in perceived stability also affect self-attributions (Andersen, 1990). In self-attributions, for example, people who believe they failed to solicit donors for a blood drive because they used the wrong "sales technique" (an unstable cause because it can be altered by adopting a different strategy) expect to succeed in later efforts. People who believe they failed to solicit donors because they are not naturally persuasive (a stable cause) expect to fail again (Anderson, 1983). When people attribute their own failure to stable causes, they do not expect to succeed in the future. As a result, they do not adaptively renew their efforts. Instead, they become depressed (Andersen & Lyon, 1987; Andersen & Schwartz, 1992). Especially when they perceive the cause of failure as internal, stable, and uncontrollable, people develop learned helplessness, which means that they quit trying even in circumstances where they might succeed with very little effort (Seligman, 1975).

An important educational application of attribution theory lies in encouraging students who are initially having trouble in school to try harder instead of giving up (Dweck, 1986; Dweck & Repucci, 1973). Children and adults are unlikely to persist at any task for which they attribute initial failure to a stable, enduring "flaw" in their own character (Dweck, Hong, & Chiu, 1993). Some people, for instance, believe that intelligence is a fixed entity that does not change over a lifetime (Dweck & Leggett, 1988). They do not realize that children have sometimes raised their IQs from the bottom to the top 5 percent of the population when they were provided with better schooling (Heber, 1969). Both children and their parents might misinterpret an early deficit in intellectual tasks as a reason for giving up (Diener & Dweck, 1978; Dweck, Hong, & Chiu, 1993). They might naively assume that they will never have even average mental ability. They might quit school and never realize their potential.

Attributional retraining programs encourage participants to attribute their successes to stable causes and their failures to unstable causes rather than the other way around (Fosterling, 1985, 1986). In some attributional retraining programs, students are given tasks that are either difficult or ambiguous enough that the students will fail. The instructor induces the students to attribute their failure to unstable causes. The students are also given success experiences and taught how to attribute their successes to stable causes. When the instructor succeeds in changing a student's attribution process, the student typically develops renewed hope and persistence for doing well in school. Attributional retraining keeps students from dropping out of education (Van Overwalle, Segebart, & Goldstein, 1989).

■ CONTROLLABILITY AND EMOTIONS

The attributed controllability of a cause affects emotional reactions (Weiner, Russell, & Lerman, 1979; Weiner, 1986). It is easy to feel pity for someone who suffers from circumstances beyond his or her control, as might a person who got liver disease because it ran in his or her family. It is not as easy to pity someone who had control over his or her own fate. If Mel failed an exam because he came down with the flu, we might pity him and offer to bring him lecture notes if he had to miss class for a while. We would be unlikely to feel pity for him or offer to help him if he failed because he took a few days off to go skiing.

Many studies have shown that people give or withhold aid to victims based on whether they perceive that the victim did or did not have control (Schmidt & Weiner, 1988). They do so because people who suffer from an uncontrollable cause elicit a different emotion than do people who suffer from a controllable cause. Suffering from an uncontrollable cause elicits pity, whereas suffering from a controllable cause elicits anger (Betancourt, 1990; Miller & Eisenberg, 1988). Ambiguous actions by other people also elicit either aggression or nonaggression depending on whether we think that the other person had control (Dodge & Crick, 1990). If someone shoves us while we are standing in line, we are more likely to react with anger and possible aggression when we think they had control over their movements than when we think they "couldn't help it" (Dodge & Coie, 1987; Graham, Hudley, & Williams, 1992). When attributions change from controllable to uncontrollable, aggression is reduced (Hudley & Graham, 1993). Similarly, hyperactive children are rejected by their peers more often than are physically handicapped children, because people, whether they are correct or not, assume that hyperactive children have more control over their behavior than do physically handicapped children (Juvonen, 1991).

Emotional reactions to stigmatized people also differ depending on whether we think they had control over their problems. In one study, college students read about a department head who interviewed two candidates for the job of senior computer programmer at a major company (Rodin, Price, Sanchez, & McElligot, 1989). Both candidates had considerable experience and excellent letters of recommendation. The only difference in their credentials was that one candidate had a higher score on an aptitude test. In the interviews, both candidates seemed capable, easy to work with, and in excellent health, but the candidate with the higher aptitude test score was fat. The department head did not like to be around fat people, so he hired the other candidate. Half of the students learned that the fat candidate was fat for uncontrollable reasons, because he had a hormonal imbalance and not because he overate. The other half learned that the fat candidate was fat for controllable reasons, because he overate and not because he had a hormonal imbalance. Students perceived the department head's decision as more reasonable and less prejudiced when the candidate was fat for controllable rather than for uncontrollable reasons.

ATTRIBUTING RESPONSIBILITY

Attributions of responsibility illustrate how the strengths and weaknesses of the attribution process apply to consequential everyday events that occur outside the social psychology laboratory. At present, no one theoretical framework explains every possible attribution of responsibility. Some theories of responsibility emphasize one or another of the principles explained in the first two sections of this chapter (Heider, 1958). Other theories of responsibility emphasize such additional constructs as the actor's intentions, the actor's awareness of consequences, cultural prescriptions for the event, and whether the actor's identity requires abiding by those prescriptions (Fincham & Jaspars, 1980; Shaver, 1985; Shaver & Drown, 1986; Schlenker, Britt, Pennington, Murphy, & Doherty, in press). Any future theory that hopes to account for all attributions of responsibility needs to address attributions in a huge number of applied contexts, two of which are personal problems and social problems. As will become obvious, whether a problem qualifies as "personal" or "social" depends on the types of attributions that citizens of a culture make.

■ PERSONAL PROBLEMS

When we learn that someone had an accident or other personal disaster, we often wonder why it happened. Was it a random misfortune that might have happened to anyone or did the person's behavior contribute? As we might expect from the correspondence bias, attributers need very little evidence to cite "something about the person" as a prominent cause. They frequently blame the victim.

Flood victims, for instance, might seem to be free from possible blame. They could not possibly control the rain that made a river overrun its banks and destroy their possessions. Nonetheless, attributers have little sympathy for flood victims who "overreact" (Yates, 1992). Applying a peculiar form of "consensus information," they are more likely to credit external forces for a flood victim's anguish if other residents of the area were equally upset than if the specific citizen was the only one who got upset (Rubonis & Bickman, 1991).

Attributers also take an actor's intentions into account when assigning responsibility for automobile and other accidents. In one study, college students read about a driver named John who was driving 10 miles per hour over the speed limit (40 mph in a 30-mph zone) and hit another car at an intersection (Alicke, 1992). John hit the other car on the driver's side, causing the driver to receive multiple lacerations, a broken collar bone, and a fractured arm. John was not injured. Some students read that John was speeding because he wanted to get home in time to hide from his parents an anniversary present for them that he had inadvertently left out in the open. Other students read that John was speeding because he wanted to get home in time to hide from his parents a vial of cocaine that he had inadvertently left out in the open. The story about John also contained a situational cause that attributers could use if they wanted to. The cause was either that John had to navigate an oil spill, that John's vision was obscured by a fallen tree limb, or that the driver of the other car ran a stop sign.

How much sympathy should we have for flood victims who "go all to pieces" after their home is flooded?

As predicted, students who thought John wanted to hide an anniversary gift attributed the accident approximately equally to "something about John" and to "something about the situation." Students who thought John wanted to hide cocaine, in contrast, overwhelmingly attributed the accident to "something about John." From a logical application of attribution principles, the result is difficult to understand. If the students were trying to explain why John hit the other car, these differences are illogical. The "behavior" (speeding) was the same regardless of why John was doing it. The effects of his behavior were also the same regardless of why he was speeding. One way to make these attributions fit within the attribution model described earlier in the chapter, however, is to recognize that John's intentions provide additional information about the person who committed the act. When John was speeding to hide cocaine, he was a more "blameworthy" person than when he was speeding to hide an anniversary gift. Apparently, attributers alter their interpretations of a behavior's cause so that a more "blameworthy" person attracts more dispositional attributions for a behavior that turned out badly. The actor's reputation "instills an active desire to place a 'stain' on the source of the emotional response" (Alicke, 1992, p. 377).

Reactions to people with AIDS may also involve a "stain" on causal attributions. People make different attributions for an AIDS victim depending on how the person contracted the disease. Just as they seem to "want" to blame a person who was speeding to hide a vial of cocaine, attributers seem to "want" to blame AIDS victims who contracted the disease in a socially undesirable way. The **just world** hypothesis says that people "have a need to believe that they live in a world where people generally get what they deserve" (Lerner & Miller, 1978, p. 1030). Some people believe, for example, that AIDS is "God's punishment for homosexuals" (Herek & Glunt, 1988, p. 889). In one study of the just world hypothesis, college students read about a man named Mark who had a bachelor's degree in mathematics and worked for a large company (Anderson, 1992). As part of a routine medical exam, the doctor told Mark that he had the acquired immune deficiency syndrome (AIDS). Mark told the doctor that for the past five years he had been living with his lover. Half of the students learned that the lover was a man; the other half learned that the lover was a woman.

As predicted, students who thought Mark had been living with a male lover assigned him more blame for his own medical condition than did students who thought he had been living with a female lover. College women were as likely as college men to make attributions that were biased by whether they thought Mark was homosexual or heterosexual. Students who had taken a course in human sexuality were also as likely as students who had not taken such a course to make biased attributions of responsibility. The important difference, though, was between students who were very afraid of getting AIDS and students who were not. Students who agreed with such items as "If I found out a friend had AIDS, I would be afraid to hug him or her" were more likely than their less fearful peers to attribute greater blame to Mark when he was homosexual. The more afraid they were of catching the disease themselves, the more motivated students presumably were to claim that AIDS happens only to people who deserve it.

The students may also have believed that homosexuals are more responsible for catching AIDS because, unlike heterosexuals, they "brought it on themselves" through their previous behaviors (Graham, Weiner, Guiliano, & Williams, 1993). Both doctors and nurses, for instance, derogate patients who developed lung cancer, liver cirrhosis, heart attacks, breast lumps, and cervical cancer because they did not follow a doctor's orders (Marteau & Riordan, 1992). These health professionals presumably feel, as illustrated by the "liver disease" study at the very start of this chapter, that people have control over their own physical health and that those who do not take care of themselves are in part responsible for their own condition (Madey et al., 1993). Interestingly, these biases in attributing responsibility to people who became infected with AIDS in different ways are more pronounced in the United States than in other cultures (Murphy-Berman & Berman, 1993).

■ SOCIAL PROBLEMS

Although people make responsibility attributions for many types of social problems, in this section we review attributions for three: poverty, rape, and murder.

Many of the principles explained in earlier sections of this chapter apply when people attribute responsibility for poverty. Being poor can be attributed, for example, either to the poor person (a dispositional attribution) or to the circumstances (a situational attribution). One attribution is that people control their own financial destinies. If they are poor, they deserve it because they are inherently lazy, socially impaired, or otherwise lacking in the personal qualities required to earn a living. An alternative attribution is that poor people are victims of a society in which they were never given a chance. Perhaps because their parents were poor, they had no choice but to attend inferior schools where they were ill-prepared for meaningful work. They "got bad breaks" in life.

As described in the previous section, discrepant attributions for success and failure carry with them discrepant emotions. If people are poor because of causes that are internal, stable, and controllable, other citizens should be angry at them for not "pulling their load" and for being a "drain on society." If, instead, people are poor because of causes that are external, unstable, and uncontrollable, they deserve sympathy and help. In a study that tested whether these principles apply to attributions for poverty, students rated the importance of various causes for poverty, how controllable it is, how much poor people deserve blame for their own plight, whether they felt anger or pity toward poor people, how likely they would be to help poor people, and whether they thought that poor people deserve such forms of government assistance as welfare (Zucker & Weiner, 1993). The students were also asked whether they would describe themselves as political conservatives or as political liberals.

As predicted, conservatives were more likely than liberals to assign dispositional causes for poverty. They were also more likely to say that poor people could avoid poverty and less likely to express pity, offer personal help, or approve of government assistance. Because conservatives and liberals differ in how they assign blame for poverty and other social problems, they have different emotional reactions and endorse different social policies. Conservatives want to punish people who violate social norms and deter those who would "hitch a free ride" in the economy. Liberals, in contrast, want to avoid awkward trade-offs that put a monetary value on human life (Skitka & Tetlock, 1993). Thus liberals, who are loathe to assign dispositional causes, are willing to help anyone who needs help. Conservatives, who are more apt to assign dispositional causes, are willing to help only people that they believe are not responsible for their own problems. They discriminate, for example, between people who became poor from not working and people who were ruined financially by an unavoidable illness. They also discriminate between people who contracted AIDS from reckless behavior and those who contracted AIDS in an unavoidable accident such as a blood transfusion (Skitka & Tetlock, 1993).

Attributions matter also in how people assign responsibility for crime. Rape is an especially interesting crime for theories of attribution, because it is not clear what it is that attributers are trying to explain: the rapist's behavior or the victim's behavior. From the prosecution's perspective, it would be better to focus jurors' attention on the accused rapist. Let the jury try to explain "Why did he do it?" We have seen in earlier sections that dispositional attributions follow the focus of visual attention and that attributers unnecessarily and spontaneously assign to the actor a disposition that corresponds with the behavior. Especially if the prosecution can portray rape as a violent rather than an erotic act, jurors who concentrate on explaining the accused rapist's actions might be biased toward concluding that he is vicious and deserves to be punished. Conversely, the defense might do better to focus attention on the victim. Let the jury try to explain "Why did she get raped?" Especially if the defense can portray rape as an erotic rather than a violent act, jurors who concentrate on explaining the victim's actions might be biased toward concluding that "She asked for it."

Getting attributers to focus on the victim's actions rather than on the rapist's actions is not difficult. When mock jurors decide an accused male rapist's guilt and how severely he should be punished, their decisions are affected by three factors that relate to the woman who was his victim: her character, her behavior before the alleged rape, and whether she was "obliged" to consent (Pollard, 1992).

The woman's character would not matter if jurors concentrated only on her attacker's actions, but they do not. Both men and women blame a rapist more when he attacked a "respectable" woman than when he attacked a woman who was not so respectable. Participants in one study blamed a rapist less when his victim was divorced than when she was married (Jones & Aronson, 1973). Participants in another study blamed a rapist less when his victim was a topless dancer than when she was a nun (Luginbuhl & Mullin, 1981). Attributers also assign greater blame to rapists who attacked a virgin or a woman who had only one prior sexual experience than when they attacked a woman who was more experienced (Borgida & White, 1978; Pugh, 1983). Typically in such studies, the rapist's actions are equivalent in every respect. Only the victim's character differs from one condition to the other, so we know that jurors who have information about the woman's "respectability" take it into account.

The woman's behavior before the alleged rape also affects decisions about her attacker's guilt and how severely he should be punished. Jurors assign lower responsibility to a rapist when they conclude that "She asked for it." In some studies, the woman was merely careless, for instance by forgetting to lock her car (Damrosch, 1985; Howard, 1984). When she was subsequently attacked by a man who had hidden himself in the back seat, the rapist was held less responsible if his victim had been careless than if she had taken "sensible" precautions. In other studies, mock jurors found a rapist less guilty if his victim was provocatively dressed in "sexy," revealing clothing than if she dressed more demurely (Cahoon & Edmonds, 1989; Kanekar & Kolsawalla, 1980; Yarmey, 1985). In short, if the woman did anything that might be construed as inviting an attack, attributers believe that her attacker is less guilty. Also, prospective jurors are less likely to blame the rapist when the victim's past behavior gives them any reason to suspect that she might have "enjoyed it" (McCaul, Veltum, Boyechko, & Crawford, 1990).

Finally, jurors assign less guilt to a rapist if they conclude that the victim was in any way "obliged" to have sex with him. It may seem odd to say that a woman is ever "obliged" to have sex, but in several states a man cannot be charged with rape if the woman has either lived with him or had previous sexual relations with him. Also, even when the circumstances and the attack are otherwise identical, jurors typically assign less guilt for "date" or acquaintance rape than for rape by a stranger (Bridges & McGrail, 1989; Gerdes, Dammann, & Heilig, 1988; Quackenbush, 1989). In one study of "obligation" through previous consent, students read about Diane and Lee, two college students who had been seeing each other every weekend for the past two months (Shotland & Goodstein, 1992). After a movie, the couple returned to Lee's apartment to listen to music, drink some wine, and talk. Lee put his arm around

Diane, kissed her, and gently stroked her shoulder. After a while, Diane opened her mouth wider, allowing Lee's tongue to move inside her mouth. When Lee began fondling her breasts, Diane and Lee started removing each other's clothing, but when he touched her thighs, Diane said, "No, Lee, don't" and tried to push him away. Despite her continued protests and physical struggles, Lee removed the rest of Diane's clothing and got on top of her on the couch. Even though she punched him on the chin, bit him on the neck, and said, "Stop, Lee, I want to get up," Lee kept saying, "Relax, Diane, don't worry." He continued to kiss and fondle her and soon "penetrated her and intercourse occurred" (Shotland & Goldstein, p. 758).

All students read the same scenario, except for one sentence. Some students read that Diane and Lee had never previously had sexual intercourse. Some read that they had sexual intercourse once. Others read that they had sexual intercourse ten times. Compared to students who thought that Diane and Lee had sexual intercourse once or never, students who thought they had sexual intercourse ten times were less likely to view Lee's behavior as violent. They were also less likely to agree that "What Lee did was rape." The study's authors speculated that previous sexual experience sets a "precedent" that makes it less legitimate for the woman to refuse. According to the precedent interpretation, a woman who has sex with a man is somehow "obligated" to comply with his future sexual advances. Interestingly, the authors established in a second study that both men and women see *both* partners as "obligated through precedence." Perhaps because they believe in implicit social contracts, students in the second study said that as few as ten previous sexual experiences greatly affected either partner's right to stop when the other person wanted to continue. Not only was the woman obligated when the man wanted to continue, but the man was equally obligated when the woman wanted to continue (Shotland & Goldstein, 1992).

These examples make attributions of responsibility for rape seem complicated and difficult to understand. Attributions for murder can be equally curious. In one study, for instance, participants seemed to be saying that blame for killing another person depends on characteristics of the victim that were unknown to the killer (Alicke & Davis, 1989). Students read a description of an incident in which Peter Garmess shot and fatally wounded Lawrence Drake. When Garmess entered his house, he heard loud noises coming from upstairs and knew that it could not be his wife or daughter, because they were spending the week at the family's beach house. Taking a licensed gun with him, Garmess followed the noises to his daughter's bedroom. When he opened the

If people agree to have sex once, are they afterwards "obligated" to have sex whenever the other person wants to?

door to his daughter's bedroom, a stranger turned quickly and pointed his right hand, which contained a black object, toward Garmess. Although Garmess could not tell what the black object was, he shot the stranger through the heart and killed him instantly.

Some students learned that Drake was a criminal who had served three previous prison terms for burglary. When Garmess shot him, Drake was carrying a revolver in his right hand. Other students learned that Drake was a recent boyfriend of Garmess' daughter. The daughter had given Drake keys to the house so that he could retrieve some forgotten items and bring them to the beach house. In his right hand, he had a small black notebook that the daughter had asked for. Notice that Garmess could not possibly have known either set of facts at the time when he pulled the trigger. Nonetheless, students said that he was much less to blame and that he deserved a shorter jail sentence for killing a criminal than for killing his daughter's boyfriend. Their conclusion is curious because, although the outcome was less socially desirable in one condition than the other, Garmess could not have *intended* to cause different outcomes in the two different scenarios. This seems to be a case in which attributions of responsibility to the actor (Garmess) differed according to whether students attributed different dispositions to the target (Drake).

Also, attributions for murder differ from one culture to the next in a way that fits one of the major themes of the textbook. As described more at length in Chapter 1, people have both a personal identity and a social identity (Baumeister, 1987; Turner, 1991). The personal identity includes private thoughts about the self and the self's dispositions, whereas the social identity includes the roles that the person plays in society. As described in several other chapters, people who live in individualist cultures emphasize personal identity, whereas people who live in collectivist cultures emphasize social identity (Triandis, 1989; Triandis, McCusker, & Hui, 1990). The United States, for instance, has an individualist culture that emphasizes personal identity, whereas China has a collectivist culture that emphasizes social identity (Bond & Hwang, 1986). People who live in individualist cultures might be more likely than people who live in collectivist cultures to assume that behaviors are caused by "something about the person." People who live in collectivist cultures, in contrast, might be more likely to assume that behaviors are caused by "something about the situation." One example is that people in individualist cultures might blame a murderer's disposition for his or her actions, whereas people in collectivist cultures might blame the circumstances.

In a study of causal attribution across cultures, U.S. citizens and citizens of China (who were studying in the United States) read brief accounts of two murders that received international attention (Morris & Peng, 1994). In one case, a Chinese physics student who had failed to get an academic job shot his adviser and several other people at the University of Iowa before killing himself. In the other case, a recently fired postal worker shot his supervisor and several other people at a post office in Royal Oaks, Michigan, before killing himself. The citizens were asked how much they attributed the murders to dispositional factors and to situational factors. Dispositional factors included the murderer being mentally imbalanced, having chronic personality problems, being obsessed with getting his own way, and losing his grip on reality. Situational factors included "America's selfish, individualistic values," American movies and television that glorify violent revenge, unhelpful supervisors, daily violence in the surrounding community, and an economic recession.

Figure 4.6 shows the extent to which U.S. and Chinese citizens endorsed dispositional and situational attributions for the murders. As the figure shows, U.S. citizens preferred dispositional to situational attributions. Chinese citizens had the opposite preference. These preferences were reflected also in English-language and Chinese-language newspaper accounts of the two murders. The

FIGURE 4.6

FIGURE 4.6

Attributions for the same event differ across cultures.

Graph shows how much U.S. and Chinese citizens attributed two murders to situational and dispositional causes (Morris & Peng, 1994).

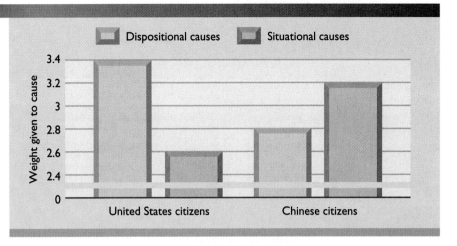

model of attribution described earlier in the chapter, as far as we can tell, applies to all cultures. People in all cultures take the same factors into account when they assign responsibility for murders and other less drastic actions. Nonetheless, attribution biases such as the correspondence bias may be culture-specific. In some cultures, the "bias" is not toward dispositional but rather toward situational attributions (Hess, Chang, & McDevitt, 1987; McGill, in press; Morris & Peng, 1994).

SUMMARY OF CAUSAL ATTRIBUTION'S CONSEQUENCES

The process and biases of causal attribution have important consequences for deciding what caused our own and other people's success and failure and for attributing responsibility or blame. When making attributions for success and failure, people who attribute their own success to internal causes and their own failure to external causes do more for their self-esteem than do people who make the opposite attributions. People who attribute their own success to stable causes and their own failure to unstable causes have more optimistic expectations for the future than do people who make the opposite attributions. Also, people who attribute another person's suffering to uncontrollable causes have more pity, less anger, and less urge to help than do people who attribute another person's suffering to controllable causes.

Attributions of responsibility influence how people react to personal and social problems. Dispositional attributions often elicit more punitive reactions than do situational attributions for disaster victims, quarreling spouses, drivers in automobile accidents, and for people with liver disease and other health problems. Political conservatives favor different remedies than do political liberals at least in part because conservatives make different attributions for poverty than do liberals. Prospective jurors also make different attributions and award different sentences for rape depending on characteristics of the victim. Finally, attributions for murder differ depending on characteristics of the victim that the killer did not know and depending on the culture. People from collectivist cultures are less biased toward dispositional attributions for murder than are people from individualist cultures.

The Self

Why are so many young women in Western Europe and North America on diets? In Western cultures, women are more likely than men to express dissatisfaction with their body shape. Women are also more likely than men to say they are self-conscious about their weight, to seek medical advice for reducing their weight, and to diet to lose weight (Fallon & Rozin, 1985; Polivy, Garner, & Garfinkel, 1986. More disturbingly, many young women carry their preoccupation with losing weight to the extreme of anorexia nervosa. Anorexia nervosa is an eating disorder that can eventually cause death from self-imposed starvation (Bruch, 1973; Garfinkel & Garner, 1982). Why do they do it?

Anorexia nervosa and pathological eating behavior have many causes (Polivy, Herman, Hackett, & Kuleshnyk, 1986; Rodin, Silberstein, & Striegel-Moore, 1985). One of the most interesting causes to social psychologists is the self-concept. Girls in modern Western cultures are raised to believe that they "ought" to be thin. They see strikingly thin women depicted in magazines. They are led to believe that a thin appearance is the key to popularity, professional status, and a desirable marriage. They compare themselves unfavorably to thinner women. To make themselves attractive, they try to match a thin self-image that can be attained only by constantly watching what they eat (Brown, Novick, Lord, & Richards, 1992; Deaux & Hannah, 1984; Guy, Rankin, & Norvell, 1980; Garner, Garfinkel, Schwartz, & Thompson, 1980; Jacobi & Cash, 1994; Silverstein, Perdue, Petersen, & Kelly, 1986; Strauman, Vookles, Berenstein, Chaiken, & Higgins, 1991).

Three social psychologists tested the idea that women eat lightly to make themselves attractive to desirable men. In their study, college men and women expected to get acquainted with a student of the opposite sex (Mori, Chaiken, & Pliner, 1987, Experiment 1). The experimenter told the students that before meeting their partners they would trade background information. The students

How might the pictures in fashion magazines make people ill?

read a description of their partners' hobbies, interests, and career goals. Although the student did not realize it, the partner was an experimental confederate who completed the questionnaire to look either desirable or undesirable. To look desirable, the partner wrote about being interested in travel, photography, athletics, reading, planning to attend law school, and being currently unattached. To look undesirable, the partner wrote about being currently attached, having no interests or hobbies other than watching television, parties, reading *National Lampoon,* and no career goals other than making money. The experimenter then left the student to hold a 20-minute conversation with the partner who had supposedly written the desirable or undesirable answers. On the way out of the room, seemingly as an afterthought, the experimenter paused in front of a cabinet, grabbed two bowls that contained a mixture of M&Ms and peanuts, and handed them to the students. The experimenter added that "these were left over from a lab party. Feel free to eat as much as you like."

As you may have guessed, the experimenters were interested not in what the student said during the conversation, but in how much the student ate. They weighed the M&Ms and peanuts before and after the conversation. Also, the confederate always ate the same amount. As Figure 5.1 shows, college men ate approximately the same amount whether the woman they were talking to was desirable or undesirable. If anything, they ate a little more when she was desirable. College women, in contrast, ate approximately one-quarter as much when the man was desirable than when he was undesirable. Because they were socialized to believe that eating lightly is attractive, they altered how much they ate depending on their male partner's desirability (Chaiken & Pliner, 1987).

In a follow-up study, college women held a getting-acquainted conversation with an attractive male confederate. Because of a staged mix-up of personality test results, the confederate saw the woman's scores (Mori et al., 1987, Experiment 2). The women thought the man had seen scores saying that they (the women) were very feminine or very unfeminine. During the conversation, women who thought the desirable man expected them to be unfeminine ate less than half the amount eaten by women who thought the desirable man expected them to be feminine. They seemed to say, "So, you think I'm not feminine, do you? I'll show you how feminine I can be. Even though I'm hungry, I wouldn't touch those M&Ms if it killed me!" Their self-concepts had been questioned. They responded by reaffirming their identity as "feminine" light eaters (Strauman et al., 1991). Preoccupation with protecting a thin self-image alters how much women in Western cultures eat.

FIGURE 5.1

Women think eating lightly is attractive.

Graph shows how much college men and women ate while getting acquainted with a desirable or undesirable person of the opposite sex (Mori, Chaiken, & Pliner, 1987).

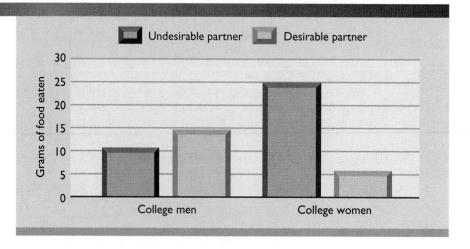

To summarize, many women develop an unrealistic image of how thin they ought to be if they want to be feminine and successful. They pursue this unrealistic self-image by constantly watching what they eat. When they interact with men they want to impress, these women eat lightly to present themselves as feminine. When their thin self-image is threatened, they protect the self by doing whatever it takes to establish that "I am the person I claim to be." This chapter is about these three aspects of the self. The first section describes how people arrive at self-knowledge, how they know who they are. The second section describes how people present themselves to others. The third section describes ways in which people protect their identities when the self is threatened.

HOW DO PEOPLE KNOW THE SELF?

People in Western cultures may have greater difficulty in knowing who they are today than they did in the past. Table 5.1 summarizes a comprehensive historical review of the self-concept (Baumeister, 1987, p. 164). The rows of the table represent six eras from Late Medieval to Late Twentieth Century in the literature of England, France, and the United States. The columns of the table refer, for each time period, to the ways in which people knew who they were, the accepted ways of achieving self-fulfillment, and the perceived relationship between the self and society.

In the "self-knowledge" column of the table, we see that knowing the self has become progressively more difficult. In earlier times, identity was fixed at birth by the family's recognized place in society. Today, people in many Western cultures have so much freedom and mobility that they have to "discover" who they are. People may no longer know which of many possible selves is "the real me" (Baumeister, 1987). In the "self-fulfillment" column, we see that ways of achieving self-fulfillment have changed along with ways of defining the self. In the Late Medieval period, for instance, Christians who observed the church's strictures were guaranteed fulfillment in heaven. Some psychologists believe that people in the modern era, in contrast, lead empty lives that they try to fill with meaningless consumption of material goods (Cushman, 1990). Modern people have a vague idea that they would like to achieve a goal called "self-actualization," but they are not certain what self-actualization is (Baumeister, 1987). In the "self and society" column, we see that the relationship between self and society has become progressively worse. People in the late medieval era derived both their identity and their fulfillment from their recognized place in what they regarded as a "great chain of being" in which all God's creatures had assigned places. By the early twentieth century, however, people came to believe that society was standing in the way of their personal fulfillment, so they became hostile and critical. In the late twentieth century, people know that society does little to help them in their voyage of self-discovery. They need to invent myths about how the world works and about the "leading role" that they play in the unfolding drama of life (Baumeister, 1987).

Table 5.1 also illustrates one of the major themes of the text. The theme is that people have both a personal identity and a "collective" or social identity (Brewer, 1991; Cousins, 1989; Crocker, Luhtanen, Blaine, & Broadnax, 1994; Deaux, 1993; Markus & Kitayama, 1994; Miller & Prentice, 1994; Oyserman, 1993; Trafimow, Triandis, & Goto, 1991; Turner, Oakes, Haslam, & McGarty, 1994). Personal identity is independent of other people; social identity consists of being identified with groups or categories. A high school girl who is anorexic, for instance, might view herself as an individual with unique characteristics, beliefs, and preferences (her personal identity). She might also

TABLE 5.1	The Different Views That People of Six Historical Time Periods Had of Self-Knowledge, Self-Fulfillment, and the Relationship of the Individual to Society (Summarized from a More Detailed Table in Baumeister, 1987, p. 164)		
TIME PERIOD	**WAYS OF ACHIEVING SELF-KNOWLEDGE**	**WAYS OF REACHING SELF-FULFILLMENT**	**RELATIONSHIP BETWEEN SELF AND SOCIETY**
Late Medieval (pre-16th century)	No problem. Self is fixed by society	Salvation will be in heaven	Individual is an integral part of "Great Chain of Being"
Early Modern (16th–18th century)	Self may change. Other people may have two selves	Primary salvation will be in heaven	Individual may move up or down the chain of being
Puritan (18th–19th century)	Self-conscious introspection. Self-deception is possible	Salvation pre-determined, but individual must struggle against inner sin and weakness	Society recognizes individual as saved if he/she is successful at work
Victorian (mid-19th century)	Repression, hypocrisy, concern with involuntary self-disclosure	Seek fulfillment alone and through private family life	Individual exists side by side with or may try to improve society
Early 20th century	Complete self-knowledge is recognized as impossible	Work is not fulfilling. Society prevents self-fulfillment	Individual is hostile to and critical of society
Late 20th century	Self is unique and must be explored	Seek celebrity and "self-actualization"	Individual accommodates to society and constructs myths about own role in society

view herself as a member of the in crowd of girls at school who have very thin waists (her social identity). A social identity is more than just a cognitive category. It is also a network of social relationships (Abrams, 1992; Ethier & Deaux, 1994).

People in modern Western cultures may emphasize the personal identity over the social identity. This emphasis, however, as shown in Table 5.1, may be a comparatively recent development (Baumeister, 1987). Even today, people in Western cultures sometimes rely on their social identities to help them define their personal identities (Brewer, 1993). Also, many contemporary non-Western cultures emphasize social identity over personal identity (Markus & Kitayama, 1991; Triandis, 1990). In Western cultures, where most research on "the self" has been conducted, however, the emphasis is on how people arrive at a personal identity. Table 5.2 lists two frequently used methods for arriving at a personal identity: reflecting on individual characteristics and using the social context. As the table indicates, people use four distinct processes when they reflect on their individual characteristics and two distinct processes when they use the social context to decide who they are. You may want to refer to Table 5.2 frequently as you read the rest of this section, because it provides a framework for understanding how this section of the chapter is organized.

REFLECTING ON INDIVIDUAL CHARACTERISTICS

The first four processes in Table 5.2 involve primarily private knowledge. They are ways of thinking about a personal identity that can occur without reference to other people. Even a hermit who has lived alone in the woods for many years could sit beneath a tree in solitude and reflect on his or her self-schemas, self-complexity, possible selves, and self-discrepancies.

■ SELF-SCHEMAS

A schema, as described in Chapter 2, is a set of beliefs that provides an organizing framework for understanding a topic, an event, or a person. A schema for physiques, for example, might help us to tell the difference between being fat and being muscular. To someone who does not have a schema for physiques, a fat person and a muscular person who weigh the same might both be classified as overweight. To someone who has a schema for physiques, for instance an aerobics instructor, the fat person and the muscular person belong to two entirely separate mental categories.

TABLE 5.2	Two Methods of Gaining Knowledge about the Self, with Some Processes that Contribute to Each Method, Aspects of the Self That Are Affected, and an Example Answer to the Question "Who Am I?"	
PROCESS	**ASPECT OF THE SELF**	**EXAMPLE ANSWER TO "WHO AM I?"**
Reflecting on Individual Characteristics		
Making a summary	Self-schemas	I'm independent!
Adding dimensions	Self-complexity	I'm independent, but I'm also gregarious, athletic, and thrifty.
Projecting into the future	Possible selves	I'm afraid of becoming dependent when I grow old.
Considering other perspectives	Self-discrepancies	My dad disagrees with me. He thinks I'm still dependent.
Using the Social Context		
Using other people as a yardstick	Social comparison	I'm more independent than Sally.
Standing out in a crowd	Self-distinctiveness	I'm the only person in my class who was independent enough to do the lab project without asking the teacher for help.

In the same way that we develop schemas to help us understand other people, we also develop schemas to help us organize what we know about ourselves. **Self-schemas,** then, are beliefs that provide an organizing framework to help us understand ourselves. Self-schemas summarize the personality traits, attitudes, values, interests, and other characteristics that we attribute to ourselves. They also include actions and interpersonal relationships. A "sacrificing to pay for the children's education" schema might allow a single mother to see the connection between working two jobs and buying only cheap clothes for herself. Another person might not think the two actions were related to each other. A "being independent" schema might allow a medical school student to see the connection between challenging her professor's opinions and insisting on paying her own way on dates. Self-schemas help us think efficiently about the relationships among our own actions. They help us justify claims about our own traits. They also help us ward off doubts about whether we truly have the characteristics that we attribute to ourselves.

In one study of self-schemas, the investigator asked college students how independent they were and whether being independent was important to them—in other words, whether they had a schema for being independent (Markus, 1977). Some students, "schematics," claimed that they were fiercely and consistently independent. Other students, "aschematics," claimed to be independent only part of the time and said that the trait did not matter to them. The aschematics had self-schemas for other characteristics, but not for being independent. The researcher subsequently asked schematics and aschematics whether they were individualistic, self-confident, assertive, and had other traits related to independence. Schematics answered faster, recalled more specific incidents when they had behaved independently, and were less likely than aschematics to believe the results of a bogus personality test that claimed they were conforming and dependent. Their self-schemas thus helped independent schematics to maintain an organized and coherent portrait of themselves. Other studies have shown that similar results apply to people who use self-schemas about being introverted versus outgoing, being masculine versus feminine, or being fat versus thin (Catrambone & Markus, 1987; Crane & Markus, 1982; Fong & Markus, 1982; Markus, Hamill, & Sentis, 1987).

Interestingly, people who have a self-schema for a trait get so good at "chunking" or lumping together instances of the trait as it applies to themselves that they also interpret other people's actions by using that trait. In one demonstration of how people apply their favorite self-schemas to others, the researchers asked 500 students how masculine they were and how much being masculine mattered to them (Markus, Smith, & Moreland, 1985). Of these 500 students, the researchers identified 26 men who had self-schemas for masculinity. The researchers also identified 24 aschematics, men who did not care very much whether they were masculine. The schematics and aschematics watched a videotape in which a male college student performed several routine actions in his dorm room. Some of the videotaped man's actions, like playing records, were irrelevant to masculinity. Others of his actions, like watching a baseball game and lifting weights, were traditionally masculine.

Student participants had to push a button whenever they saw one action end and a different action begin. The researchers explained that one might interpret walking across a room as ten separate steps or as one action. They explained that it was up to the students how much they separated versus lumped together the videotaped man's actions. Masculinity schematics and aschematics divided the irrelevant actions into approximately the same number of chunks. Masculinity schematics divided the masculinity-relevant actions, however, into fewer chunks than did aschematics. When they saw the videotaped man lifting weights, for instance, they did not interpret his actions at the detailed level of "grasping the weight, raising it, lowering it, raising it again," and so on. Instead, they saw the entire episode as one action of "working out." As masculinity experts, they knew working out when they saw it. They used their self-schemas to evaluate other people's actions.

Having a schema for a trait or characteristic help us to know who we are without having to think very hard about our identity (Markus, 1977). When we ask ourselves "Am I ambitious?" or "Am I fat?" for instance, we do not need to review mentally every act we have ever performed that might have been relevant to ambition or to weight control (Klein, Loftus, & Plog, 1992; Klein, Loftus, & Schell, 1994; Klein, Loftus, & Sherman, 1993). If the characteristic in question is one for which we have not developed a self-schema, we may mentally review specific relevant actions. If the characteristic is an important, meaningful dimension of self, though, we simply remember a trait summary that incorporates many relevant actions (Andersen, 1984; Andersen & Ross, 1984; Klein & Loftus, 1993; Klein, Loftus, Trafton, & Fuhrman, 1992).

We rely on trait summaries because our specific actions sometimes mislead us about what traits we have. We sometimes identify an action by its lower-level, specific components, such as "moving the weight up and down." At other times, we identify the same action by its higher-level goal, as in "building a better physique." One month before the wedding, prospective marriage partners describe "getting married" at a higher level, such as "expressing my love." One day before the wedding, they use lower-level labels such as "hiring the photographer," "picking up the outfit before the shop closes," and "coping with the caterers." One month after the wedding, many newlyweds describe "getting married" as "getting problems." This newly acquired higher-level label might foretell marital difficulties (Vallacher & Wegner, 1987; Wegner & Vallacher, 1986).

People who concentrate on the lower-level components can be misled about their own higher-level goals, with important implications for the self-concept (Wegner, Vallacher, Macomber, Wood, & Arps, 1984, p. 269). In one study of how actions acquire a new and sometimes far-fetched meaning, the researchers asked college students what they thought they were doing by going to college (Wegner et al., 1984). The students favored higher-level identifications such as "improving my chances at a good job" or "becoming independent of my parents." The researchers asked other college students to list the specific actions that they had to perform as part of going to college, such as "taking exams" and "buying books." Subsequently, both groups of students read an article supposedly taken from the *New York Times*. In the article, a researcher at the National Institute of Mental Health claimed to have discovered that college graduates have a richer and more satisfying sex life than do nongraduates.

After reading the article, the researchers asked all students a second time what they thought they were doing by going to college. Students who thought about the specific details of college life were more willing than students who remained at the higher level to claim that one of their reasons for attending college was "to improve my sex life." The new definition of college had not previously occurred to them, but it had obvious implications for the type of person they thought they were (Wegner, Vallacher, Kiersted, & Dizadji, 1986). Because the meaning of our actions changes so easily to fit the meaning suggested by the surrounding context, our actions are sometimes unreliable and misleading guides to our identity (Vallacher & Kaufman, in press). Such malleable and easily influenced self-concepts make it very difficult for people to discover a true identity.

SELF-COMPLEXITY

As Table 5.2 suggests, people differ not only in which characteristics they have self-schemas for, but also in how many dimensions their self-schemas have. Some people think of themselves along only one or two dimensions. Children may react extremely to failure because they have relatively simple self-schemas that include only a "good me" and a "bad me" (Dweck, Chiu, & Hong, 1995; Ruble & Dweck, in press). Anorexics may become so preoccupied with weighing themselves, examining their bodies in the mirror, and watching what they eat, that they think of themselves along only the one dimension of being fat versus thin. Good days are days when their weight goes down. Bad days are days when their weight goes up. As this example suggests, it may be dangerous to have too simple a self-schema. A college woman whose self-schema includes the traits necessary for success in athletics, courses, making female friends, and maintaining a satisfactory relationship with a man, for instance, may have a healthier self-schema than another woman whose self-schema centers on only body weight and grades. For the first woman, if she views each of her four selves as distinct from the others, a failed exam injures her self-esteem on only one of four dimensions. For the second woman, a failed exam may be more of a catastrophe because it injures her self-esteem on fully half of her dimensions (Kernis, Cornell, Sun, Bery, & Harlow, 1993; cf. Showers, 1992).

Students in one study of self-schema complexity received a deck of index cards. Each card contained a personality trait such as "imaginative," "humorous," "relaxed," "affectionate," or "mature" (Linville, 1985). The students had to form groups of traits that seemed related to each other when they thought about themselves, as in "When I'm with friends I am relaxed, softhearted, and affectionate." The students could use the same trait in more than one group. The idea was that people who had simple self-schemas would use only two or three groups of traits to describe themselves. People who had complex self-schemas would use many groups of traits. They would also place the same traits in several different groups. Then the researcher told some of the students that they had performed in the top 10% on a test of analytical ability. The researcher told other students that they had performed in the bottom 10%. As predicted, having a relatively complex self-schema protected students from becoming depressed about their performance. Figure 5.2 shows that students who had simple self-schemas had less positive moods after they learned that they failed than after they learned that they had succeeded. Students who had complex self-schemas were less influenced by whether they succeeded or failed. Self-schema

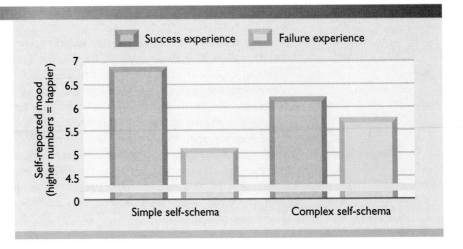

FIGURE 5.2

A complex self-schema minimizes the emotional impact of failure.

Graph shows mood reported by students with simple or complex self-schemas, after they experienced success or failure (Linville, 1985).

Calvin and Hobbes

by Bill Watterson

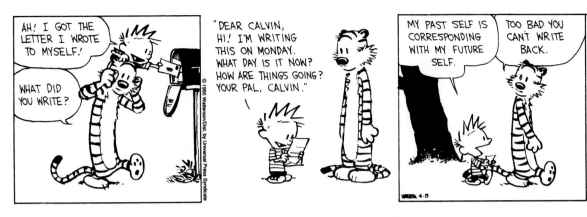

complexity (having more than one dimension to the self-schema) is an effective buffer against stress-related illness and depression (Linville, 1987).

■ POSSIBLE SELVES

Self-schemas are not confined to how people conceive of themselves in the present. As Table 5.2 shows, people who reflect on their individual characteristics also project their current selves into the future. They think ahead to the kind of person they would like to become or the kind of person they are afraid they might become (Markus & Nurius, 1986). **Possible selves** are projections of future possibilities for the expected, desired, and feared future self. Students may have a "graduate" possible self. Anorexics may have a "thin" possible self. Visitors to a doctor's office may have a "seriously ill" possible self. Possible selves are "the selves we could become, and the selves we are afraid of becoming" (Markus & Nurius, 1986, p. 954).

When male and female college students are asked to "tell us about what is possible for you," they mention possibilities that involve their future personality, lifestyle, physical condition, general abilities, occupation, and how others might feel toward them (Markus & Nurius, 1986). As Table 5.3 shows, students who are asked to describe both their present selves and their possible future selves tend to be optimistic. They *all,* even the minority who are not happy in the present, believe that they will be happy in the future. Considerable percentages of them reveal, however, that they fear becoming depressed, having a nervous breakdown, and becoming wrinkled or paralyzed, even if these unpleasant possibilities are not a part of their current self-schemas. The present or "now" self overlaps with but is not the same as the many possible future selves.

Possible selves can also affect the way people behave. People who desire a good possible self and fear a bad possible self, for instance, may be more motivated to take constructive actions than are people who fear a bad possible self but cannot imagine a good alternative. The researchers in one study asked youths between the ages of 13 and 16 to describe themselves as they expected to be in the future. They also asked the youths to describe themselves as they were afraid that they might become (Oyserman & Markus, 1990). Some of the youths were attending public school. According to police records, they were nondelinquents. Others were in a community placement plan (mild delinquents), in a group home (moderate delinquents), or in a training school

TABLE 5.3	Percentage of Respondents Who Used Each Item When Asked to Describe Themselves Now and When Asked about Their Possible Future Selves (Abstracted from Table 1 in Markus & Nurius, 1986, p. 959).	
ITEM	**DOES THIS DESCRIBE YOU NOW?**	**HAVE YOU EVER CONSIDERED THIS A POSSIBLE SELF?**
Personality		
Happy	85.0	100.0
Depressed	40.2	49.6
Lazy	36.2	45.3
Lifestyle		
Have lots of friends	74.6	91.2
Be destitute	4.5	19.6
Have nervous breakdown	11.1	42.7
Physical		
Sexy	51.7	73.5
Wrinkled	12.0	41.0
Paralyzed	2.6	44.8
General Ability		
Speak well publicly	59.0	80.3
Manipulate people	53.5	56.6
Cheat on taxes	9.4	17.9
Others' Feelings Toward You		
Powerful	33.3	75.2
Unimportant	12.8	24.8
Offensive	24.8	32.5
Occupation		
Media personality	2.2	56.1
Owner of a business	1.4	80.3
Prison guard	0.0	4.3

because they had committed serious vandalism, drug, theft, or violent crimes (severe delinquents). Nondelinquents and mild delinquents hoped to do well in school, to have friends, and to be happy. Severe delinquents also hoped to have friends and to be happy, but instead of hoping to do well in school, they hoped to drive a luxurious car and wear expensive clothing. Nondelinquents and mild delinquents feared most that they might fail in school, whereas the most feared possible self for severe delinquents, feared by 37% of them, was becoming a criminal, thief, or murderer.

The investigators also examined the youths' expected and feared selves for whether the good and bad imagined possibilities were in or out of balance. Possible selves are balanced when a feared possibility is offset by an expected or hoped-for possibility. For example, an individual might be afraid that he or she will flunk out of school but might also expect to graduate. Severe delinquents had possible selves that were out of balance when compared to the possible selves of nondelinquents. Severe delinquents had fears that were not offset by imagined positive possibilities. They feared being poor, but they had no expectations for getting a good job. They feared becoming criminals, but they had no expectations for attaining achievement through noncriminal activities. The imbalance between negative and positive possible selves better predicted criminal activities over the next few months after the study than did more traditional measures such as self-esteem. Severe delinquents continued to commit crimes, but not because they lacked self-esteem. They derived considerable self-esteem from intimidating their peers. They continued to commit crimes because they feared a life of crime and yet could not envision positive alternatives (Oyserman & Saltz, 1993).

In one study of how to change possible selves, the researchers instilled successful and unsuccessful possible selves in college students (Ruvolo & Markus, 1992). They instructed some of the students to imagine a future in which they worked hard and became very successful. One of the students in this "success through hard work" condition reported imagining that she had graduated with honors, gained an outstanding reputation as a design engineer in the automotive industry, married well, and enjoyed a rustic home and two wonderful children. The researchers instructed other students to imagine a dismal future in which they worked hard but "didn't get the breaks." Students in this "failure in spite of hard work" condition imagined themselves trapped in boring jobs and living in rat-infested slums.

After they imagined successful or unsuccessful future selves, all students participated in two tasks. One task required much persistence. The other required intense concentration. Students who imagined themselves succeeding persisted longer at the task that required sheer persistence and worked more accurately at the task that required concentration than did students who imagined themselves failing. Nondelinquents in the previously described study avoided criminal activities by imagining constructive future selves. Similarly, students in the persistence and concentration study found it useful to envision the constructive possibility of success through hard work. Our possible future selves are at least as important as are our present self-schemas, because they can motivate and guide us to success. Possible selves are thus related to mental simulation and counterfactual thinking (described in Chapter 2). Self-esteem and persistence at self-improvement are affected by imagined scenarios about

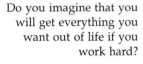

Do you imagine that you will get everything you want out of life if you work hard?

what might have been and what we might be (Andersen, Spielman, & Bargh, 1992; Boninger et al., 1995; Niedenthal, Tangney, & Gavanski, 1994; Roese & Olson, 1993).

Present self-schemas differ in complexity. So do future possible selves (Halberstadt, Niedenthal, & Setterlund, in press). The two "tenses" of the self, however, are not always identical, nor are their consequences. A person soon to enter prison might have many present selves and few future selves. A soon-to-be-divorced person might have just the opposite. In one study, college women described their present and future selves (Niedenthal, Setterlund, & Wherry, 1992). The experimenters gave the women bogus results of a questionnaire that purportedly assessed either adjustment to and success in dating relationships at present or adjustment to and success in marriage in the future. Some women got very positive assessments of their present or future prospects; other women got very negative assessments. After they read the bogus results, the women were asked about their moods. Negative assessments of their current dating prospects did not affect women with complex present selves as deeply as it did women with simple present selves. For women with complex present selves, self-esteem depended on many factors other than dating success. Similarly, negative assessments of their future marriage prospects did not affect women with complex future selves as deeply as they affected women with simple future selves. Complex present selves, however, did not protect women from negative assessments of their future marriage prospects, nor did complex future selves protect them from negative assessments of their current dating prospects.

■ SELF-DISCREPANCIES

Even within present selves, however, people can reflect on their individual characteristics from different perspectives. The self might be different when seen from different ones of these perspectives (Higgins, 1987). Present selves can be divided into three types: the actual self, the ideal self, and the ought self. As Table 5.4 shows, you can view each of these three types of self from two perspectives: the self as seen by the individual and as seen by important other people like a parent, a best friend, or a spouse. The actual self is what people often refer to as the self-concept. It consists of the attributes that the person believes he or she actually has (the actual own self) and the attributes that other people say he or she actually has (the actual other self). For an anorexic, for example, her actual own self might be fat and her actual other self (as her parents keep telling her) might be extremely thin.

The ideal self consists of the attributes that the person wishes he or she had (the ideal own self) and the attributes that the individual believes other people wish he or she had (the ideal other self). An anorexic's ideal own self might be thinner than she is. Her ideal other self (so her parents say) might not be as thin. The ought self consists of the attributes that the person thinks he or she is obligated to have (the ought own self) and the attributes that the individual believes other people think he or she is obligated to have (the ought other self). The anorexic's ought own self might have enough will power to stay on a diet and her ought other self might be the person that her parents blame her for not being. The ideal and ought selves derive from early interaction between the child and his or her caretaker (Higgins, 1989). By giving or withholding their affection, the parents convey the message "this is the type of person we wish you were," from which the children internalize an ideal self. When children actively violate norms of acceptable behavior, parents react with criticism or physical punishment. Punishment conveys the message "this is the way you ought to behave if you knew right from wrong," from which the children internalize an ought self.

TABLE 5.4	Self-Discrepancies Depend on the Fit Between Three Types of Self as Seen from Two Perspectives (Higgins, 1987).

TYPES OF SELF

	Actual	*Ideal*	*Ought*
Own Perspective	**Actual Own** Beliefs about our own attributes (I'm too fat)	**Ideal Own** Attributes we wish we had (I wish I looked thin)	**Ought Own** Attributes we think we are obligated to have (I feel obligated to weigh less)
Other's Perspective	**Actual Other** Another person's beliefs about us (My mom thinks I'm too thin)	**Ideal Other** Attributes another person wishes we had (My mom wishes I didn't look as thin as I do)	**Ought Other** Attributes another person thinks we are obligated to have (My mom thinks I am obligated to weigh more)

Problems arise when the individual perceives **self-discrepancies,** which are discrepancies between the actual self and either the ideal self or the ought self, whether from the individual's perspective or from other people's perspective. Both children and adults become depressed when other people withhold positive regard or when they are disappointed in themselves. When their actual self is discrepant from or fails to live up to their own ideal self they feel dejected. When their actual self is discrepant from an important other person's ideal for them they feel ashamed. In addition, both children and adults become anxious and irritable at the prospect of punishment when they realize that they are violating norms of correct or acceptable behavior. When their actual self is discrepant from what they think they are obligated to be, they feel guilt or self-contempt. When their actual self is discrepant from what an important other person thinks they are obligated to be, they feel afraid or anxious. The two major types of self-discrepancy thus elicit different types of emotional reaction. Discrepancies between the actual self and the ideal self make people feel sad; discrepancies between the actual self and the ought self make people feel anxious and agitated (Higgins, 1989).

Different types of self-discrepancies, then, elicit different emotional reactions. The researchers in one study asked college students to list attributes of their actual selves, their ideal selves, and their ought selves, as seen by themselves and as seen by the most important person in their lives (Higgins, Bond, Klein, & Strauman, 1986). The investigators examined these lists to identify students who listed opposite attributes for actual self and ideal self or for actual self and ought self. A student who listed "independent" for her actual self and "conforming" for her ideal self as seen by her mother, for instance, would get one actual-ideal discrepancy point. The investigators divided students who scored many discrepancy points for both actual-ideal and actual-ought into two groups. They reminded students in one group of their ideal selves by having them describe the hopes and goals that they and their parents had for them.

They reminded students in the other group of their ought selves by having them describe the duties and obligations that they and their parents expected of them.

Both before and after being reminded of either their ideal selves or their ought selves, all students completed a mood questionnaire. In the questionnaire, they indicated how much they felt dejection-related emotions such as sad, disappointed, and dissatisfied and how much they felt agitation-related emotions such as tense, anxious, and guilty. As Figure 5.3 shows, being reminded of their ideal selves increased the students' dejection-related emotions but not their agitation-related emotions. Being reminded of their ought selves increased the students' agitation-related emotions but not their dejection-related emotions. Being reminded of how little we have realized our goals makes us sad. Being reminded of how poorly we have met our obligations makes us anxious and agitated.

Other research suggests that large actual-ideal self-discrepancies can lead to behavioral and health-related symptoms. The symptoms include blaming yourself for minor errors, feeling helpless and apathetic, and losing interest in sex and other pleasures (Higgins, in press). Large actual-ought self-discrepancies, in contrast, can lead to panic attacks, heart palpitations, and losing weight (Higgins, Klein, & Strauman, 1985). Anorexics, who starve themselves, have large discrepancies between their actual selves and their ought selves. Bulimics, who gorge themselves during eating binges, have large discrepancies between their actual selves and their ideal selves (Higgins, Vookles, & Tykocinski, 1992). Different types of self-discrepancies predispose people toward different types of emotional and behavioral problems (Higgins, 1989, in press; Higgins, Roney, Crowe, & Hymes, 1994; Higgins, Tykocinski, & Vookles, 1990; Strauman & Higgins, 1987, 1988).

Self-discrepancies can also affect the immune system. In one study, people who were depressed and people who were anxious listed characteristics of their actual, ideal, and ought selves (Strauman, Lemieux, & Coe, 1993). Consistent with previous research, depressed people had more actual-ideal discrepancies and anxious people had more actual-ought discrepancies. Later, the experimenters reminded these two groups of their self-discrepancies. If a participant said that her ideal self got better grades than her actual self, for instance, the experimenters asked her to write an essay on "Would you say it was important for you to get better grades?" If a participant said that her ought self was thinner than her actual self, the experimenters asked her to write an essay on "Would you say it was important for you to be thinner?" As predicted,

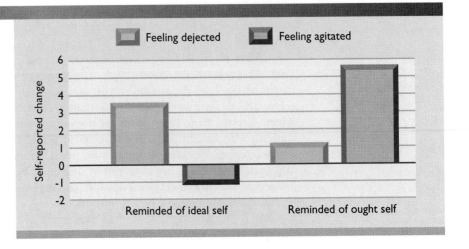

FIGURE 5.3

Different self-discrepancies elicit different emotions.

Graph shows change in feeling dejected and agitated when high self-discrepancy students were reminded of their ideal selves or their ought selves (Higgins, Bond, Klein, & Strauman, 1986).

people who wrote essays about their actual-ideal discrepancies conveyed considerable sadness, whereas people who wrote essays about their actual-ought discrepancies conveyed considerable anxiety. Finally, the experimenters analyzed each participant's blood for natural killer cell activity, which is an important immunological mechanism for fighting off tumors and other health problems. Being reminded of either self-ideal discrepancies or self-ought discrepancies temporarily reduced natural killer cell activity. Self-discrepancies made the study's participants more vulnerable to disease.

USING THE SOCIAL CONTEXT

Besides reflecting on their individual characteristics, as Table 5.2 shows, people arrive at a personal identity by using the social context. Hermits might arrive at simple or complex self-schemas, imagine possible future selves, and reflect on the self from different perspectives, but they would lack an important piece of information. They would not know how they compared to other people. They might *think* they were fat or independent, but how would they know for sure if they had not seen or interacted with another human being for many years? To arrive at a personal identity, then, people usually find it necessary to use the social context—to take into account the characteristics of others in their immediate surroundings. The last two rows in Table 5.2 show two processes (social comparison and self-distinctiveness) that use other people in the social context to decide "Who am I?"

■ SOCIAL COMPARISON

In the movie *Amadeus,* the composer Salieri, who might otherwise have regarded himself as a reasonably competent person, had the misfortune to find himself frequently in the company of one of the greatest musical geniuses who ever lived, namely Wolfgang Amadeus Mozart. According to some accounts, Salieri bitterly described Mozart as "a giggling child who can put on paper, without actually setting down his billiard cue, casual notes which turn my most considered ones into lifeless scratches." He complained that Mozart "ensured that I would know myself forever mediocre" (Shaffer, 1980, p. 61, quoted by Wood, 1989, p. 231). Similarly, a young woman of average height and weight might feel very depressed if she compared herself to one of the extraordinarily thin super-models in contemporary magazines. The self-concept depends importantly on the attributes of others who are either selected or available for comparison (Pelham, 1991; Rosenberg, 1993).

Social comparison occurs when people use others as standards of comparison against which to evaluate their own opinions, attributes, and abilities (Festinger, 1954). For some characteristics, no objective standard exists (Kruglanski & Mayseless, 1990). Am I thin enough to be attractive and successful? Do I have many friends? Such questions are difficult to answer in absolute terms. Estimates of what constitutes "many" friends are themselves subject to the self-serving attributional biases discussed in Chapter 4 (Agostinelli, Sherman, Presson, & Chassin, 1992). Lacking objective standards, people draw inferences by comparing themselves to others. But which others? Sometimes we get to choose from many possible others the specific people with whom we want to compare ourselves. At other times, we have no choice (Wood, 1989). Sometimes we assume our personal identity and compare the self with other individuals. At other times we assume our social identity and compare ourselves with members of our own or rival groups (Brewer & Weber, 1994). In either case, the result of social comparison has an important influence on who we think we are.

Do excellent musicians become depressed when they contemplate a child prodigy?

When people get to choose another person with whom to compare themselves, they sometimes prefer to learn about people who are similar to them on the dimension in question or on dimensions that are central to their self-schemas (Berscheid, 1966; Goethals & Darley, 1977; Miller, 1984). At other times, they prefer to learn about people who are a little better or a little worse. Comparing yourself with someone who is a little better is called *upward comparison.* Comparing yourself with someone who is a little worse is called *downward comparison.* Which makes people feel better about themselves? It depends. Upward comparison can lower people's self-esteem by suggesting that they are not performing as well as they might. It can also raise self-esteem by suggesting that improvement is possible (Testa & Major, 1990). Conversely, downward comparison can raise people's self-esteem by suggesting that they are doing very well. It can also lower self-esteem by reminding them that their performances and rewards might easily deteriorate (Aspinwall & Taylor, 1993; Stanton, 1992; Reis, Gerrard, & Gibbons, 1993; Taylor & Loebel, 1989).

When we are confident about where we stand on a dimension, we can afford to compare ourselves upward, but we cannot afford to do so when we are not completely confident (Pelham & Wachsmuth, 1995). In one study of marital satisfaction, for instance, people who were happily married and confident about their relationship were not affected by comparing themselves either "up" to couples who were more satisfied than themselves or "down" to couples who were having problems (Buunk, Collins, Taylor, Van Yperen, & Dakof, 1990). Couples who were dissatisfied with and uncertain about their marriage, in contrast, reported many negative emotions when they compared themselves down to marriages that were on the brink of divorce. The less confident we are about where we stand on a dimension, the more it hurts to compare ourselves to people who are worse off. Downward social comparison suggests the all-too-real possibility of personal deterioration, especially if we achieve downward comparison by derogating someone else (Gibbons & McCoy, 1991).

One dramatic example of downward comparison's negative impact involves cancer patients. When cancer patients talk about their illness, the vast majority of their spontaneous social comparisons are downward (Taylor, Falke, Shoptaw, & Lichtman, 1986). Women who have had minor surgery for breast

The ultimate threat to self is death. To avoid debilitating anxiety over their own eventual demise, people rely on reassuring "cultural worldviews" such as patriotism or religion. According to "terror management theory," cultures develop to help people overcome death anxiety by making them feel better about themselves, especially at times when they are depressed (Greenberg, Pyszczynski, & Solomon, 1995; Greenberg, Solomon, Pyszczynski, Rosenblatt, Burling, Lyon, Simon, & Pinel, 1992; Simon, Greenberg, Harmon-Jones, Solomon, & Pyszczynski, 1996; Solomon, Greenberg, & Pyszczynski, 1991). To reassure themselves, people who contemplate death endorse cultural leaders and symbols more strongly than they do when they have not been thinking about their own mortality (Greenberg, Pyszczynski, Solomon, Rosenblatt, Veeder, Kirkland, & Lyon, 1990; Rosenblatt, Greenberg, Solomon, Pyszczynski, & Lyon, 1989). The investigators in one study of mortality salience asked students to describe the emotions that the thought of their death aroused. They also asked the students to describe what they thought would happen to them when they died (Greenberg, Simon, Porteus, Pyszczynski, & Solomon, 1995). Under the guise of a creativity test, the students were also asked either to sift black dye out of sand or to affix a crucifix to the wall with a nail, but no hammer. The best solutions involved using a U.S. flag to sift the dye or using the crucifix to pound the nail. As predicted, students who had recently contemplated their death were more reluctant to violate these cherished icons than were students who had not recently contemplated their death.

■ SELF-DISTINCTIVENESS

The social environment can also conspire to make people feel that they are distinctive or stick out like a sore thumb. Sometimes people want to be unique (Snyder & Fromkin, 1980), but at other times they do not. Logically, people can only be aware of their own attributes by contrast with other people. Adults would not think of themselves as adult if people were born mature and were

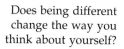

Does being different change the way you think about yourself?

never children. Men would not find it important to identify themselves as men if there were no women. To a large degree, then, the self-concept consists of ways in which we are distinctive or different from other people (Johnson & Boyd, 1995).

One way of finding out which of their characteristics people regard as salient is simply to ask them to "Tell us about yourself" (McGuire & McGuire, 1988). Researchers use responses to this question to test the hypothesis that people emphasize attributes that are different from the attributes of other people in their immediate social context. In one study of schoolchildren in grades 5, 7, 9, 11, and 12, for instance, all children were asked to "Tell us about yourself." As predicted, children who were very tall or very short for their age mentioned their height more often than did children of average height. Children who were very thin or very fat mentioned their weight more often than did children of normal weight. The few children with red hair mentioned their hair color more often than did others. Children who were born in a different state or a different country also mentioned their place of birth more often than did their classmates (McGuire & McGuire, 1981). For characteristic after characteristic, the children were more apt to mention attributes on which they stood out from the crowd. They did so even when the attribute was one like being obese that people would be unlikely to mention if they were only trying to make a good impression.

In other studies that used the "Tell us about yourself" question, children at a school that was 82% White mentioned their race more often if they were Black or Hispanic than White. Children who were the only child of their sex at home mentioned their sex more often. Boys from single-parent mother-only families mentioned being male more often (McGuire, McGuire, Child, & Fujioka, 1978; McGuire, McGuire, & Winton, 1979; McGuire & Padawer-Singer, 1976). People of all ages are more likely to include a characteristic as part of their self-schema if they are surrounded by other people who do not share the characteristic (McGuire & McGuire, 1988). College students of nontraditional age, for instance, are more likely than traditional age students to mention their age when they describe themselves (Kite, 1992). The spontaneous self-concept, then, depends importantly on ways in which we are different from the particular set of other people with whom we happen to have contact. A characteristic such as being male might normally go unnoticed. It becomes an important aspect of self-identity, though, for a boy who finds himself in a classroom that is two-thirds girls, especially if he then goes home to a mother and seven sisters.

Also, being distinctive in the social environment can sometimes be a handicap in life. Many businesses and academic units responded to early affirmative action policies by hiring or promoting one woman or minority member, a practice known as tokenism. Supervisors typically assigned tokens lower-status responsibilities in the organization. They also awarded tokens lower salaries and fewer pay raises, because they evaluated a token's performance unfairly (Brown & Ford, 1977; Hall & Hall, 1976; Moreland, 1985; Shaw, 1972). Tokens also complained that they did not perform as well as they could because they were self-conscious about being the only one of their kind (Kanter, 1977). Men who find themselves the only man in a group and women who find themselves the only woman in a group subsequently remember less of the information exchanged than do nontokens. Tokens also perform worse on intellectual tasks than do nontokens (Lord & Saenz, 1985; Lord, Saenz, & Godfrey, 1987; Saenz, 1994; Saenz & Lord, 1989). If standing out from the rest impairs performance, self-distinctiveness can easily alter a person's self-concept (Mead, 1934).

SUMMARY OF HOW PEOPLE KNOW THE SELF

People who lived in early European cultures did not have to worry about who they were. A person's self was defined and accepted by society from birth to death. In modern times, however, people have many choices about who they are and who they will become. As a result, they may find it hard to define a self-concept, to understand and fulfill their potential, and to relate to society.

Modern people define themselves in part by constructing a self-schema or set of beliefs about how they typically deal with life events. The self-schema can be relatively simple or complex. It includes beliefs about people's past and possible future actions. It also includes beliefs about what people wish they were, what they think they are obligated to be, what other people wish they would be, and what other people think they are obligated to be. Problems arise when people's beliefs about their actual selves are discrepant from what they or other people wish they were or from what they or other people think they are obligated to be.

People also define themselves by comparing themselves to others. We define self-esteem and personal fulfillment by how well we are doing compared to others. Comparing ourselves upward to others who are doing better can help plans for improvement, but it can also remind us of our shortcomings. Comparing ourselves downward to others who are doing worse can make us feel better, but it can also be discouraging. The modern sense of self is not fixed but is instead extremely malleable. Different aspects of the self become more important from one moment to the next, depending on whether the person is distinctive or stands out in the immediate social context.

HOW DO PEOPLE PRESENT THE SELF?

The first section of this chapter examined the question "How do people know themselves?" The answer might be summarized as "Many people in twentieth-century Western cultures do not know themselves confidently." They have so many present and future selves that it is difficult to keep all the possible selves in balance. They have large discrepancies between what they are, what they want to be, what they think they ought to be, and what other people think about them. They are subjected to changing social contexts that make a stable self-concept very difficult. The best they can do is to construct a tentatively held theory about a person called "myself." If the self is a theory that we have about the type of person we are and about the type of person we think we might become, then the theory is constantly evolving and being reinvented (Epstein, 1973; Gergen, 1982). The most important reason why a self-concept must be reinvented from day to day and from one social context to the next is that a self-concept must be validated by other people (Cooley, 1902; Mead,

1934; Schlenker, 1980; Swann, 1987). Individuals are free to believe that they are Napoleon or Jesus if they so desire. If they believe fervently enough in theories that everyone else rejects, however, we call them crazy and ignore their theories. A good self-concept is one that satisfies both the person who invents the theory and other people who are asked to agree.

This second section of the chapter describes ways in which people try to convince others that their beliefs about themselves are accurate. Under the heading of "self-presentation," we examine the intricate procedure of negotiating with other people to establish an agreed-upon identity. Under the heading of "self-verification" we examine a specific self-presentation technique that involves getting other people to tell us what we want to hear about ourselves. Finally, under the heading of "individual differences" we examine two ways in which people differ in presenting themselves to others.

SELF-PRESENTATION

Self-presentation involves playing a part or acting a role with an audience in mind. The most important function of self-presentation is not to deceive other people about who we are. It is to get help from them in refining or maintaining our self-concepts (Jones & Pittman, 1982; Leary & Kowalski, 1990; Schlenker, et al., in press; Schlenker & Wiegold, 1992). Self-presentation is a necessary part of a process known as identity negotiation. Also, effective self-presentation entails one of five different self-presentational strategies.

■ IDENTITY NEGOTIATION

Why might people who live in twentieth-century Western cultures find it more difficult to know who they are than did people who lived in the past? Earlier in this chapter, we speculated that people who lived in small European villages during the Late Medieval period were reinforced in their beliefs about themselves because everyone else agreed (Baumeister, 1987). In their day-to-day interactions, they met the same people every day, people who had known them all their lives and with whom they had come to an agreement about who they were. Their associations with other people granted them a social identity, from which they derived much of their personal identity. In a technologically sophisticated, highly mobile, densely urbanized twentieth-century society, in contrast, people do not often enjoy the reassurance of complete social agreement (Tedeschi, 1986). Citizens of a modern society interact with dozens of new people every day. Whether going away to college or taking a new job, they change locations frequently. The people they know today are an entirely different set of people than those with whom they interacted a few short years ago.

The self-concept is never known for certain (Gergen & Gergen, 1988). It is subject to constant modification that depends importantly on how other people respond to us. "Self-identification is the process . . . of showing oneself to be a particular type of person, thereby specifying one's identity" (Schlenker, 1986). We may claim to be well organized, socially adept, moral, or mathematically gifted, but these claims ring hollow if we cannot present the kind of evidence that would convince other people. When it comes to establishing an identity, other people are like a judge and jury who want proof (Schlenker, 1985). From childhood on, we realize that we will suffer scorn and worse if we make extravagant claims about ourselves and are unable to back up those claims. We moderate our claims about self, therefore, in ways that make the claims more acceptable (Goffman, 1959, 1961; Harre, 1987; Leary & Downs, 1995; Leary, Tambor, Terdal, & Downs, 1995).

The process of establishing an identity by reaching agreement with other people is called identity negotiation. Identity negotiation is a delicate, lifelong chore (Swann, 1987). In many subtle and not-so-subtle ways we offer for public criticism a particular story about who we are (Gergen, 1981, 1987; Gergen & Gergen, 1988). In many subtle and not-so-subtle ways other people let us know which parts of the story they are willing to believe and which parts they reject. We learn to omit the rejected parts of the story or to tell them in different, more convincing ways. We also realize that other people provide an important reality check on our self-concept (Baumeister & Cairns, 1992). If we make claims about ourselves that everyone else rejects, we are forced to acknowledge even to ourselves that we are not that type of person. Many business and diplomatic negotiations end in compromise. So do identity negotiations. In a relevant study, college roommates who had lived together for a semester adopted self-concepts that were a compromise between the self-concept that the individual initially tried to project and the roommate's initial expectations (McNulty & Swann, 1994). The bargaining tools that individuals bring to the process of identity negotiation include several effective self-presentational strategies.

■ SELF-PRESENTATIONAL STRATEGIES

Negotiating an identity is an important goal that we pursue throughout our lives. From childhood on, we develop increasingly effective strategies for presenting ourselves to others (Aloise-Young, 1993). Table 5.5 lists five important self-presentational strategies: ingratiation, self-promotion, intimidation, exemplification, and supplication (Jones & Pittman, 1982). Each of the five strategies pursues a different self-presentational goal. Each strategy attempts to arouse in the audience a different emotion, involves a different set of actions, and risks a different unwanted result.

TABLE 5.5	Five Frequently Used Self-Presentational Strategies (Suggested by Jones & Pittman, 1982).			
STRATEGY	**IDENTITY SOUGHT**	**DESIRED EMOTIONS**	**TYPICAL ACTIONS**	**RISKS SEEMING**
Ingratiation	likable	affection	subtle self-praise, favors, compliments	insincere
Self-promotion	competent	respect	performing well, or claiming to	fraud, conceited
Intimidation	dangerous	fear	threats, anger	wishy-washy, blusterer
Exemplification	morally worthy	guilt and imitation	self-denial, suffering	hypocrite
Supplication	helpless or unfortunate	nurturance	putting self down, cries for help	lazy, demanding

Ingratiation is the most frequently used of the five self-presentational strategies. The goal is to be liked. Almost everyone finds it rewarding to be liked by other people. As a result, people usually put their best foot forward (especially in job interviews and similar situations) by modestly showing their likable traits and by complimenting other people or doing favors for them. One of the unstated assumptions of the ingratiation strategy is that when we treat other people well, they reciprocate. They reassure us in our quest for self-identity that we play an accepted and valued role in the drama of life (Goffman, 1959). As shown in the "risks" column of Table 5.5, however, ingratiation must be pursued subtly. To be too obvious is to invite contempt and ridicule. The "ingratiator's dilemma" is that the more obviously we need another person's approval, the more likely the other person is to regard our flattery and favors as insincere (Jones & Pittman, 1982).

Self-promotion, the second most frequently used self-presentational strategy, also entails both rewards and risks. The goal is to be seen as competent. Most people would rather be regarded as competent than as incompetent. They command respect by performing competently in front of an audience and by claiming to be skilled at a variety of tasks. Talented athletes or artists display their awards. Physicians frame their medical degrees. Just as with the strategy of ingratiation, however, self-promotion entails risks. The "self-promoter's paradox" is that most of us have learned to distrust stories that people tell about their own competence. Without firsthand proof, we assume that the fish was not as large as the fisherman claimed and we assume that people who are genuinely wealthy or athletically gifted do not need to brag about it. As they say in Japan, "the talented falcon hides his claws." Self-promotion runs the risk of being perceived as fraudulent or conceited.

Intimidation is another frequently used self-presentational strategy. Intimidators want to be feared. To arouse fear, they make threats. The grade-school bully intimidates his classmates by threatening them with physical harm. Adult bosses intimidate their workers by threatening to fire them. Although these examples may suggest that successful intimidation requires physical or organizational power, the weakest among us can practice intimidation simply by threatening embarrassment. Those who have watched small children force their parents to buy candy in a supermarket by threatening to make a scene recognize immediately that this is intimidation. The risk intimidators take is that someone will call their bluff and their threats will be exposed as hollow.

The fourth commonly used self-presentational strategy is exemplification. As shown in Table 5.5, exemplifiers want to be seen as morally worthy. They try to make other people feel guilty by working harder and suffering more than anyone else. People who insist on telling everyone that they stayed at their desks until midnight are exemplifiers, as are people who brag about starving themselves to lose weight. Exemplifier parents deny themselves pleasures so that their children can enjoy luxuries. Exemplifier contributors give all their money to homes for stray cats. They want the rest of us to emulate them. When they are too obvious in their exemplification, however, they run the risk of being perceived as sanctimonious hypocrites.

The fifth self-presentational strategy is supplication, the self-presenter's last resort. Some people do not have the social skills to ingratiate. They are not talented enough to self-promote. They lack the power to intimidate. They do not have enough will power to exemplify. Even so, they can always use supplication, which is an effort to appear helpless. Supplicants want other people to take care of them. They try to arouse sympathy and nurturance by putting themselves down and by asking, directly or indirectly, for help. Wives who cannot imagine how to change a flat tire and husbands who have no clue about how to do laundry engage in mild forms of supplication. Supplicants, however, run the risk of carrying their self-presentational ploys to such an extreme that they are perceived as lazy and demanding.

These self-presentational strategies—ingratiation, self-promotion, intimidation, exemplification, and supplication—may be used in specific circumstances to deceive other people about an individual's true identity (Godfrey, Jones, & Lord, 1986). Even an introvert might deliberately pose as very outgoing when interviewing for a job selling used cars. In everyday social interactions, however, people use self-presentational strategies more to negotiate an identity than to deceive. They self-present more frequently to strangers than to close friends. They self-present more frequently to members of the opposite sex than to members of the same sex. They self-present to people they most want to impress and with whom they have not reached a satisfactory compromise. People who present themselves as very likable or competent gauge how likable or competent they are by how other people react to their presentations (Jones, 1990; Leary, Nezlak, Downs, Radford-Devenport, Martin, & McMullen, 1994; Rhodewalt, 1986).

In one study of self-presentation, the researchers asked students to present themselves in a very self-enhancing way for a job interview (Jones, Rhodewalt, Berglas, & Skelton, 1981). After making this self-presentation, the students adopted more positive self-concepts whether they thought that all other students had bragged about themselves or thought that all other students had been modest. From the students' perspective, they had portrayed themselves in a very positive way and had not been challenged, so "it must be true" even if appearing especially likable is what everybody does in the situation. Self-presentation, whether presenting yourself as likable, competent, dangerous, morally worthy, or helpless, can change how people view themselves (Jones, 1990).

As should be evident from Table 5.5 and from the discussion of self-presentational strategies, not everyone wants to establish an identity that is socially desirable. Everyone, however, needs an identity that other people support (Greenberg, Pyszczynski, & Solomon, 1986). Children are afraid of being abandoned or regarded as worthless by their parents. Adults are afraid of being abandoned or regarded as worthless by other members of their culture. One protection from such fears is to find a role in life that other people will allow us to play. Individuals seek security and reassurance by maintaining a sense of personal value within the "cultural drama" (Greenberg et al., 1986). Because there are many ways of achieving personal value, we negotiate with other people by letting them know the roles to which we aspire. The other people in turn let us know which of our claims to self-identity they are willing to support. When the negotiations have been completed and both sides have agreed upon their identities, other people help us to maintain our identity claims.

Finally, self-presentation may be hazardous to your health (Leary, Tchividjian, & Kraxberger, 1994). Many people do not use condoms to protect themselves from AIDS and other sexually transmitted diseases because they are concerned with how it will make them look to their partners (Abraham, Sheeran, Spears, & Abrams, 1992). Many people expose themselves to potential skin cancer to get a tan because they think it will impress others (Leary & Jones, 1993). Many anorexics starve themselves because they want to present themselves as attractive (Rezek & Leary, 1991). Many adolescents take up smoking to look independent and mature to their friends (Covington & Omelich, 1988). Clearly, self-presentation may be a necessary tool in identity negotiation, but it is also a tool that should be used with extreme caution.

Do some people risk
skin cancer just to look
"cool"?

SELF-VERIFICATION

Losing your identity is like being set adrift in the middle of the ocean in a leaky
boat (Rosenberg, 1993; Lecky, 1945). People spend a lifetime negotiating an
identity, so it is not surprising that they want to play their agreed-upon roles
(Schlenker, 1985). People who have established a likable identity would be very
uncomfortable in positions that require intimidation. People who have established a helpless identity would be very uncomfortable if asked to self-promote.
A self-concept is so susceptible to changes in the social context that people prefer to maintain their identities, established through years of difficult negotiations and self-presentational strategies, than to have those identities challenged.
People prefer to have their self-concepts verified rather than contradicted
(Swann, 1983). As a result, they engage in **self-verification,** which consists of
getting other people to verify what we believe to be true of ourselves.

The quest for self-verification sometimes conflicts with the quest for self-
enhancement (Swann & Schroeder, 1995). One of the major themes of the textbook (described more extensively in Chapter 1) is that people pursue two
major social interaction goals. People want to be likable; they also want to be
right (Jones & Thibaut, 1958; Sedikides, 1993; Snyder, 1992; Swann, 1990).
Even five-month-old children pay more attention to faces that smile at them
than to faces that do not smile. Later in childhood, they prefer positive to negative descriptions of themselves (Benenson & Dweck, 1986; Shapiro, Eppler,
Haith, & Reis, 1987). A big reason for developing effective self-presentational
strategies is to get others to like us (Baumeister & Leary, 1995). At the same
time, people want to be accurate in how they view the world. They prefer evidence that confirms rather than disconfirms their initial beliefs about themselves (Jones & Pittman, 1982; Kruglanski, 1990). Once they have established
a stable belief about themselves through identity negotiation, they do not want
to be told that they are wrong (Swann, Stein-Seroussi, & Giesler, 1992). The
two goals—being likable and being right about the self—may not be in conflict
for people who truly believe that they are wonderful human beings. What happens, though, when people believe that they are deficient? Would they rather
have their friends praise them or would they rather hear the truth?

The tendency to resist changes in self-concept occurs both in the majority of people who have negotiated positive identities and in the minority of people who have negotiated *negative* identities (Swann, 1987). People who are accustomed to seeing themselves (and being seen by others) as likable and competent do not appreciate being mistaken for nerds. Surprisingly, people who are accustomed to seeing themselves (and being seen by others) as bumbling oafs also do not appreciate being mistaken for geniuses. If people who are doing something wrong when they interact with others receive nothing but white lies in which others pretend to like them, they have little hope of improving themselves. Being made to feel good is not the same as getting the information necessary to adopt realistic goals and expectations (Jussim, Yen, & Aiello, 1995; Swann, Stein-Seroussi, & McNulty, 1992). Also, a twentieth-century sense of self is too fragile and easily disrupted to tolerate cases of mistaken identity. When they think about it, people who have negative self-concepts sometimes prefer to hear others put them down than to hear others praise them. They especially prefer to hear what they regard as "the truth" when they are relatively certain about who they are (Hixon & Swann, 1993; Pelham & Swann, 1994). The need to retain a consistent self-concept sometimes overrides people's usual preference for being told good things about themselves (Swann, 1987).

In one study of self-verification, male college students completed a questionnaire about whether they viewed themselves as likable and competent (Swann, Stein-Seroussi, & Giesler, 1992). Although the vast majority of students reported positive self-concepts, 20% reported that they were not well liked and that they had few social skills. Later in the semester, some of these students had an opportunity to interact for two to three hours with one of two strangers. The students had to decide which of the strangers they preferred as an interaction partner. To decide, the students used evaluations of them that the two strangers had written after reading the students' answers to the earlier questionnaire. One of the two strangers wrote: "He appears at ease with people he doesn't know very well. He seems to have little doubt about his social competence." This evaluation confirmed the self-concepts of positive identity students and disconfirmed the self-concepts of negative identity students. The other stranger wrote: "He appears to be ill at ease in social situations. There are probably times when he is around other people and just doesn't know what to do or say." This evaluation disconfirmed the self-concepts of positive identity students and confirmed the self-concepts of negative identity students. After reading these evaluations, students gave their reasons for preferring one rather than the other of the two strangers as their interaction partner.

Three-quarters of the students, whether they had positive or negative self-concepts, preferred to interact with whichever stranger agreed with them about themselves. "Just as 72% of participants who had positive self-concepts chose to interact with the favorable evaluator, 78% of participants with negative self-concepts chose to interact with the unfavorable evaluator" (Swann Stein-Seroussi, & Giesler, 1992, p. 395). Their reasons for preferring whichever partner agreed with them about themselves involved reassurance, harmony, and perceptiveness. Both positive identity students and negative identity students preferred to interact with whichever of the two strangers offered the most *reassurance* that the student knew himself accurately. They made comments such as "I'd feel more at ease with someone who can judge me for what I am." Both positive identity students and negative identity students also had practical reasons for preferring the self-verifying stranger. They believed that the interaction would flow more smoothly and that they would find themselves in greater *harmony* with someone who understood them than with someone who had misconceptions. They made comments such as "Seeing as he knows what he's dealing with, we might get along better." Finally, students (especially the negative identity students) also thought the self-verifying evaluator had more *perceptiveness* and intelligence, as in "He is more on target."

Individuals who want to have their identities confirmed have two ways to seek self-verification. One way is to structure their interactions so that other people will tell them what they want to hear about themselves. The other way is to select interaction partners who see them as they see themselves. Such partners can be counted on to provide social support when the self-concept is challenged.

■ STRUCTURING THE INTERACTION

In any technologically advanced society individuals move from place to place frequently. They meet many strangers who have no way of knowing what kind of identity the individual has previously negotiated with others. To avoid misunderstandings, people often send signals about who they are and how they expect to be treated (Swann, 1983). They wear conservative rather than flamboyant clothing. They drive sporty as opposed to more practical automobiles. They diet, lift weights, or have cosmetic surgery to project a youthful physical appearance. They fill their homes with modern versus traditional furniture. They adopt "no nonsense" instead of sexually provocative ways of holding their bodies and forceful rather than nonthreatening speech patterns.

What happens, though, when people meet a stranger who is not perceptive enough to read these signs and symbols of identity? Do they set the record straight during the ensuing interaction or are they content to let the stranger harbor a false impression? People who have either positive or negative self-concepts go out of their way to reestablish their identities when they find themselves interacting with strangers who do not realize how they want to be treated (Swann, 1987; Swann & Hill, 1982; Swann & Read, 1981). In one study, college women completed a questionnaire that asked how dominant or submissive they were (Swann & Hill, 1982). Later in the semester, students who considered themselves very dominant and students who considered themselves very submissive participated in a "problem-solving" study. The experimenter told the student and her partner to choose a leader and a follower for a set of problems. The partner suggested an arrangement that either verified or disconfirmed the student's self-concept. She said either "you should be the leader because you seem like a forceful, dominant person" or "you're probably happiest when someone else takes charge." Then the experimenter either interrupted or allowed the student to respond. Finally, the student completed the same dominance-submissiveness scale as earlier.

As shown on the left side of Figure 5.4, a stranger's disconfirming suggestions changed self-concepts significantly when the students were interrupted and not allowed to respond. As shown on the right side of the figure, disconfirming suggestions had far less impact when the students were allowed to respond. When they were not interrupted, students who saw themselves as dominant reacted to "you're happiest when someone else takes charge" by forcefully taking over the conversation. Students who saw themselves as submissive reacted to "you should be the leader" by saying, in effect, "What, me lead? You must be kidding!" In the process, they changed their self-concepts comparatively little in the direction suggested by the confederate.

■ CHOOSING INTERACTION PARTNERS

Besides structuring interactions to make self-concepts unmistakably clear, people protect their precarious identities by surrounding themselves with friends and significant others who agree with them. A high school girl who was thin

FIGURE 5.4

People who are allowed to respond reaffirm their self-concepts.

Graph shows change toward confederate's suggestion when students were or were not allowed to respond to a self-verifying or disconfirming suggestion (Swann & Hill, 1982).

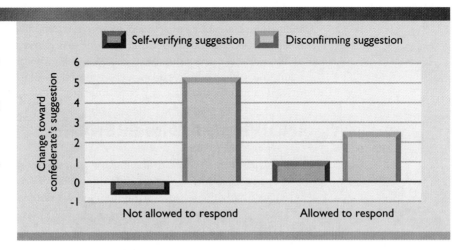

but still trying to lose weight, for instance, might choose as her best friend another anorexic. Such a best friend would likely confirm: "You still have a few pounds to lose if you want to be a model." Not only do friends and significant others offer reassurance about the self on a day-to-day basis, but they are invaluable sources of social and emotional support (Eisenberg, Fabes, & Murphy, 1995). In one study, the investigators asked college students how likable and socially competent they were (Swann & Predmore, 1985). Their significant others, with whom they had been intimate for at least two months, also described the student. Some significant others verified the student's self-concept; others disconfirmed it. Verifying significant others said that positive self-concept students were socially competent and that negative self-concept students were socially incompetent. Disconfirming significant others said that positive self-concept students were incompetent and that negative self-concept students were competent.

Later in the semester, an experimenter gave the student bogus results from a personality test that totally contradicted the student's self-concept. Those who thought they were socially competent were told that they were uncomfortable around people and did not handle social situations well. Those who thought they were socially incompetent were told that they were comfortable around people and handled social situations very well. The experimenter then left the student alone for five minutes with a stranger or with the student's significant other. After five minutes, the experimenter returned and took the student to another room, where he or she completed the social competence scale again. Students who had been left alone with a stranger changed their self-concepts considerably. If the personality test said they were competent (or incompetent), they believed it. So did students who had been left alone with a disconfirming significant other who said something like "these tests prove what I've been telling you all along." Students who had been left alone with a verifying significant other, in contrast, changed their self-concepts very little. The verifying significant other said something like "that test is all wet," so the student did not believe the personality test results.

As this study suggests, those who want to maintain their hard-won social identities should surround themselves with people who agree with them and avoid people who disagree with them. Perhaps that is why people who have positive self-concepts usually seek relationships with intimates who flatter and compliment them. The reverse side of this social support coin, unfortunately, is that people who have negative self-concepts gravitate toward relationships with intimates who are critical of them (Swann, Hixon, & De La Ronde, 1992).

In a world where the self is malleable and subject to all the sources of insta-bility that have been discussed in this chapter, it might be wise to maintain close relationships with people who endorse our view of self. Viewing the self as incompetent may not be the best of all possible worlds. For people who want to avoid ambiguity, however, it may be preferable to being set adrift with no self-concept at all (Roney & Sorrentino, 1995a & 1995b).

INDIVIDUAL DIFFERENCES

Not surprisingly, people differ in how much they depend on self-presentation and self-verification to define their identities. Two of the most important dif-ferences involve self-monitoring and self-awareness.

■ SELF-MONITORING

Some individuals are very sensitive to changes in the social context. These in-dividuals alter the way they present themselves to fit the demands of the spe-cific situation. When in Rome, they do what the Romans do. Because they con-stantly monitor their own behavior to decide whether it is appropriate for the occasion, these individuals are called high self-monitors. Other individuals are less sensitive to changes in the social context. They present themselves as the same type of person regardless of the situation. They try to be themselves al-ways, everywhere, with everybody. Because they do not often monitor whether their behavior fits the specific situation, they are called low self-monitors (Sny-der, 1979). **Self-monitoring,** then, consists of monitoring our own behavior for the impression it will make on others.

For research purposes, high self-monitors and low self-monitors are dis-tinguished by their answers to questions on the self-monitoring scale (Snyder, 1974). In answering scale items, high self-monitors say they would make good actors. They say they they act like very different people when they are in dif-ferent situations, they are not always the people they appear to be, and they look to the behavior of other people when they choose how to behave. They consider themselves very practical, flexible, and adaptive. Low self-monitors, in contrast, say that they cannot argue convincingly for ideas in which they do not believe. They say they do not alter their opinions or the way they do things to suit the situation or the audience. They say they have trouble changing their behavior to suit different people and different situations and that they try to make their actions express their self-concepts. They consider themselves very consistent and principled.

Low self-monitors try to maintain a comparatively fixed self-concept by structuring their social environments and by choosing their interaction part-ners selectively. High self-monitors welcome the opportunity to interact with many different people in many different situations so that they can display their role-playing versatility. Low self-monitors, in contrast, prefer to interact with the same people in the same situations repeatedly so that they can play the same social role from one occasion to the next (Snyder & Campbell, 1982). They do not feel comfortable, for instance, presenting themselves as other than what they are in job interviews (Larkin & Pines, 1994). In one study that tested willingness to play varying roles, college students completed the self-monitor-ing scale and another personality scale that measures whether people regard themselves as introverts or as extroverts (Snyder & Gangestad, 1982). Later in the semester, an experimenter asked the same students to act outgoing, talka-tive, self-assured, confident, and highly extroverted during a group discussion. High self-monitors said that they were willing to play the extrovert role whether they regarded themselves as extroverts or as introverts. Low self-monitors, in

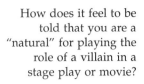

How does it feel to be told that you are a "natural" for playing the role of a villain in a stage play or movie?

contrast, were willing to play the extrovert role only if they considered themselves to be extroverts. Low self-monitors who regarded themselves as introverts were unwilling to play the extrovert role because they did not think they would be good at it and because they believed that it would make them uncomfortable. Low self-monitors are comfortable only when they are "type cast" or playing themselves.

One reason that low self-monitors feel uncomfortable pretending to be someone different is that they are afraid of what success might do to their self-concepts (Schlenker, Dlugolecki, & Doherty, 1994). How does it feel to be a movie actor who wins acclaim for his portrayal of a sadistic serial killer? Is it unnerving to be told that "You are very believable as a cannibal murderer?" Awards for such portrayals may not disturb professional actors, who score very high on the self-monitoring scale (Snyder 1974, 1979). Such awards, however, might disturb low self-monitors, who believe that their actions reflect their true selves. In a study that tested this possibility, college students were induced to play a role that would make many people feel uncomfortable (Jones, Brenner, & Knight, 1990). They were interviewed on tape about moral dilemmas, such as whether to make false insurance claims or return lost items of high value. The experimenter asked them to present themselves as cynical, selfish realists, "not some kind of head-in-the-clouds do-gooder, basking in self-righteousness" (Jones, 1990a & 1990b, p. 77).

One week later, the experimenter led some of the student participants to believe that they had succeeded brilliantly in playing the cynical, selfish role. These students listened to what they thought were taped evaluations of their performance by other students. The other students made remarks like "This guy wouldn't mind selling even his own mother down the river." The experimenter led other participants to believe that they had failed to be convincing. They heard remarks about their performance like "I get the feeling deep down that he wouldn't do any of the things he said he would." The researchers predicted that high self-monitors would feel better about themselves if they succeeded than if they failed. They also predicted that low self-monitors would feel better about themselves if they failed than if they succeeded. As shown in Figure 5.5, this is exactly what the researchers found when they measured self-esteem. High self-monitors are used to playing different roles. They are not

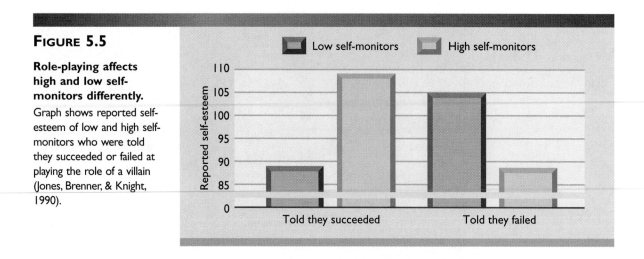

FIGURE 5.5

Role-playing affects high and low self-monitors differently. Graph shows reported self-esteem of low and high self-monitors who were told they succeeded or failed at playing the role of a villain (Jones, Brenner, & Knight, 1990).

likely to change their self-concepts because of a single self-presentational performance. Low self-monitors, in contrast, may avoid playing roles for which they believe they are not suited, because they fear that their performance might be all too convincing (Tice, 1992).

■ SELF-AWARENESS

Another important individual difference in self-presentation is self-awareness. **Self-awareness** involves being aware of ourselves as objects of attention. On the self-consciousness scale (Fenigstein, Scheier, & Buss, 1975), self-aware individuals say that they reflect about themselves a lot, are always trying to figure themselves out, are constantly examining their own motives, are alert to their own mood swings, and so on. Instead of focusing their attention outward to other people or their surroundings, they focus their attention inward to themselves. Self-aware individuals go through life scrutinizing themselves in the mirror of their own imagination.

Self-awareness exaggerates an individual's shortcomings (Duval & Wicklund, 1972; Wicklund, 1975). Everyone has at least some character flaws and everyone makes mistakes from time to time, but individuals differ in their reactions to their own flaws and mistakes. People who pay little attention to themselves may remain blissfully unaware that they are making fools of themselves. People who frequently scrutinize their motives and inner feelings are less fortunate, even if they are more realistic (Shepperd, Arkin, & Slaughter, 1995). When people are self-aware, they notice times when they do not live up to their own standards of acceptable behavior. In terms used earlier in this chapter, they are uncomfortably aware of discrepancies between the actual self and the ideal self, especially when they have simple rather than complex self-schemas (Dixon & Baumeister, 1991). To reduce the perceived discrepancies, anorexics may starve themselves and otherwise sensible people may expose themselves to unacceptable health risks (Leary, et al., 1994).

Awareness of our shortcomings is aversive (Duval & Wicklund, 1972; Ickes, Wicklund, & Ferris, 1973). Women who are self-conscious about their physique, for instance, do not go for cervical cancer screening as often as they should (Kowalski & Brown, 1994). When people become negatively aware of themselves as an object of attention, either because the circumstances conspired to make them self-aware or because they are dispositionally prone to self-consciousness, they want to reduce the aversiveness. They do so in one of two ways: They either change their behavior to fit ideal standards or they redirect their attention outward, away from themselves.

Two studies of aggression illustrate how self-awareness causes people to change their behavior to fit ideal standards. In the first study, male students were asked to shock a female "learner" whenever she made a mistake (Scheier, Fenigstein, & Buss, 1974). Their actions thus violated an ideal standard of correct or acceptable behavior. Some of the students were made self-aware by having to look at themselves in a mirror while they were shocking the woman. Other students did not have to see themselves while they were shocking the woman. Self-awareness makes people uncomfortably aware of their shortcomings and prompts them to bring their behavior more in line with ideal standards. The men who were made self-aware, therefore, chose to deliver less painful levels of shock than did the men who were not self-aware. Self-awareness decreased aggression.

In the other study, self-awareness increased aggression (Carver, 1974). Students were asked to shock a male learner and were told that the learner wanted to be shocked for mistakes so that he would learn the material faster. In such a situation, delivering painful shocks more closely approached ideal or correct behavior than did delivering shocks that were not as painful. As predicted, students who had to watch themselves in a mirror delivered *more* painful shocks than did students who were not made self-aware. Self-awareness prompts people to reduce perceived discrepancies between actual and ideal behavior, regardless of what the specific behavior might be.

The other way of coping with aversive self-awareness, a method available even in circumstances where the individual is unable to reduce an uncomfortable discrepancy, is to redirect attention away from the self. Unfortunately, redirecting attention away from the self is one effect of consuming alcohol, which is a major health problem in modern Western cultures. In a study that tested the effects of alcohol consumption on self-awareness, male college students who had not eaten for at least four hours were randomly assigned to one of four groups (Hull, Levenson, Young, & Sher, 1983). Some students were led to believe that they were drinking straight tonic, but half of them had tonic and half had tonic mixed with 80-proof vodka. Other students were led to believe that they were drinking vodka mixed with tonic, but only half had vodka and tonic; the others had straight tonic.

Forty-five minutes after consuming a generous portion of their assigned drinks, all students had to give an impromptu speech on the topic "What I like and dislike about my body and physical appearance." The researchers counted the percentage of first-person pronouns such as "I," "me," or "my." No matter what the students *thought* they were drinking, alcohol decreased the number of first-person pronouns that they used in their speeches. When speech content was analyzed more comprehensively by counting, not just pronouns, but any phrases that referred to the self as opposed to phrases that referred to other people, the results were the same. Drinking alcohol diverted attention away from the self, which is exactly what people who cannot resolve their self-discrepancies want to accomplish. In a related study, the investigators let students drink as much wine as they wanted after being told that they had either succeeded or failed on a task. As predicted, students who were high in dispositional self-awareness drank larger quantities of wine after being told that they had failed than after being told that they had succeeded. Students who were low in dispositional self-awareness did not (Hull & Young, 1983). Outside the psychology laboratory, problem drinkers often experience negative life events after they are discharged from rehabilitation programs. Problem drinkers who are high in dispositional self-awareness are almost twice as likely to relapse into drinking heavily as are problem drinkers who are low in dispositional self-awareness (Hull, Young, & Jouriles, 1986).

In the quest to establish a reliable self-concept through identity negotiation and self-presentation techniques, self-awareness can help or hinder the process. People do not mind being aware of themselves when they are doing well and living up to the highest standards of correct behavior. Self-awareness is a distinct handicap, however, when people perceive their actual selves as deficient. Being the center of attention might be beneficial for a golfer who leads the U.S. Open by an insurmountable seven strokes with one hole remaining. It can also be detrimental to the golfer who must sink a five-foot putt to avoid losing the championship (Vallacher, 1993). Considerable evidence suggests that self-awareness of the latter type can induce "choking under pressure." Choking occurs when skilled performances are disrupted by self-conscious attention to the details of our own actions and failure seems imminent (Baumeister, 1984; Baumeister & Showers, 1986; Schlenker, Phillips, Boniecki, & Schlenker, 1995). When the sports analogy is applied to the quest for a secure self-concept, negative self-awareness can undermine identity negotiations and produce an unsatisfactory self-concept. It can also induce alienation that might, in extreme cases, lead to suicide as the ultimate "escape from self" (Baumeister, 1990 a,b).

SUMMARY OF HOW PEOPLE PRESENT THE SELF

Because the modern self is so malleable and ill-defined, most people find it necessary to negotiate with others to establish an identity. People use different self-presentational techniques depending on the type of identity they are trying to establish. One of the most interesting self-presentational techniques is to structure interactions with other people in such a way that the other people are constrained to tell us what we want to hear about ourselves.

Some individuals are more likely than others to monitor the impression that they are making on other people and to adjust their behavior accordingly. In addition, some individuals scrutinize themselves and introspect about themselves more than do others. Self-aware individuals either alter their behavior to better match ideal standards of correct behavior or they take whatever action reduces their level of self-awareness. Alcohol consumption reduces self-awareness.

HOW DO PEOPLE PROTECT THE SELF?

Regardless of how carefully people try to craft their identities through negotiating with other people, there inevitably arise circumstances in which identities are called into question, either directly or indirectly. This section of the chapter concentrates on some mechanisms by which people protect positive identities when they feel that the self-concept is threatened. First, people are very skilled at repairing damage to a positive identity. Second, people use "self-handicapping" *before* a possible threat to the self-concept, so that their identity is protected no matter what the outcome may be.

REPAIRING DAMAGED IDENTITIES

What happens when the self-concept is damaged? For most people, all is not lost (Tesser, Martin, & Cornell, in press). At least two complicated but effective processes come to the rescue. These processes are called self-evaluation maintenance and symbolic self-completion.

■ SELF-EVALUATION MAINTENANCE

> I, who for the time have staked my all on being a psychologist, am mortified if others know much more psychology than I. But I am contented to wallow in the grossest ignorance of Greek. My deficiencies there give me no sense of personal humiliation at all. (William James, 1890/1950, p. 310)

People are eager to maintain their negotiated identities. Having reached an agreement with other people about how they want to be evaluated, people do not want their self-concepts disrupted. As a result, people who have positive self-concepts (which includes the vast majority of people) choose carefully when they compare themselves to others. A high school anorexic who does not care about grades, for instance, might not mind comparing herself to a fellow student who gets higher marks. She might, however, avoid comparing herself with a fellow student who is slimmer than she is.

Self-evaluation maintenance involves strategically managing performance, closeness to other performers, and relevance of the performance in ways that protect a positive self-concept (Tesser, 1988). Performance involves doing better or worse than another person. Closeness is how psychologically close versus distant the other person is, as in the difference between a close friend and a mere acquaintance. Relevance is what the famous psychologist William James was writing about in the quotation that opens this section. Some characteristics and abilities are more important and relevant to the integrity of the self-concept than are others. If other people were to outperform William James in knowledge of Greek he would not care, but if other people were to outperform him in knowledge of psychology, he would feel humiliated.

As the William James quotation implies, people do not always feel threatened when someone close to them outperforms them. Their reaction depends on whether the ability in question is one that matters to them. When the ability is one that is important to them and relevant to their self-concept, self-evaluation is threatened by unfavorable social comparison. When the ability is one that is not important to them, not relevant to their self-concept, their self-evaluation *increases* because they can "bask in reflected glory" (Cialdini, Borden, Thorne, Walker, Freeman, & Sloan, 1976). A musician who did not aspire to be regarded as a great composer, for instance, might be delighted to be in close contact with Mozart. A rival composer like Salieri, however, would find it a constant source of humiliation. Unless he had an alternative way to affirm his self-concept, a person with an ego as large as Salieri's might want to avoid being in the company of such a musical genius (Morf & Rhodewalt, 1993; Steele, 1988; Tesser & Cornell, 1991).

Self-evaluation maintenance prompts people to publicize and exaggerate how close they are to winners and to minimize or hide their association with losers. They either emphasize or minimize their social identities (Hirt, Zillmann, Erickson, & Kennedy, 1992). On the Monday morning after their team has won at football, for instance, college students are more likely to wear the school colors. They are also more likely to use the pronoun "we" when speaking of their college's football team after a victory than after a loss (Cialdini et al., 1976; Cialdini & Richardson, 1980). Similarly, individuals who have had their positive self-concepts called into question are quick to volunteer that they share characteristics as trivial as a birthday with a highly successful person. They are reluctant, though, to mention sharing a birthday with an unsuccessful person, even when they are questioned directly about what they have in common with him or her (Cialdini & DeNicholas, 1989).

In a study that showed how people try to manipulate closeness in the service of self-evaluation maintenance, the experimenter asked male college students how important various topics such as rock music, current events, and hunting were to their self-concepts (described by Tesser, 1988). The researchers tried to select for each student either a topic that would be as important to them as psychology was to William James or a topic that was as unimportant to them as Greek was to William James. The students then competed with another student (a confederate) at answering questions about the selected topic. The confederate either outperformed or lost to the student at a topic that was either relevant or irrelevant to the student's cherished identity. The experimenter then asked both students to take a seat in an adjoining room. The confederate always sat down first, so that the experimenter could measure "closeness" by seeing how far the student sat from the confederate.

As Figure 5.6 shows, when the topic was not important to students' self-concepts they sat nearer to a confederate who performed well than to a confederate who performed poorly. When the topic was important to their self-concepts, in contrast, they sat *farther* from a confederate who performed well than from a confederate who performed poorly. The students were willing to associate closely with a winner on an ability that they deemed irrelevant. They chose to distance themselves, however, from a winner who had called into question their own competence on an ability that played a central role in defining their self-concepts. In a related study, students were beaten by a close friend on a dimension central to their identities. Later, they tried to sabotage that friend's performance when the friend competed against a stranger (Tesser & Smith, 1980). We usually help people we like, but not when they start beating us at an activity so relevant to our identities that losing is a threat.

Interestingly, self-evaluation maintenance may operate differently in marriages and other close relationships than it does with friends and acquaintances (Beach & Tesser, 1995). It may be beneficial to compare yourself favorably with another person if the other person is a stranger, but not if the other person is someone you love (Beach & Tesser, 1993). In close relationships, making yourself feel good may simultaneously make the other person feel bad. Some spouses are in committed relationships where they take a communal orientation to each other's needs (Clark, Helgeson, Mickelson, & Pataki, 1994). Such spouses may

FIGURE 5.6

People use physical distance to maintain self-evaluation.

Graph shows how close students sat to confederate who did well or poorly on task that was or was not important to students' self-definition (Tesser, 1988).

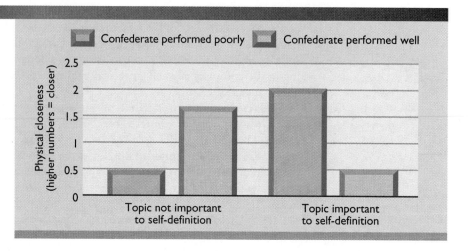

change the strategies of self-evaluation maintenance to reflect their communal orientation (Beach & Tesser, 1995). One of the most exciting developments in research on the self, then, lies in links with the principles of interpersonal attraction and close relationships that are discussed in Chapters 9 and 10.

■ SYMBOLIC SELF-COMPLETION

One way of looking at threats to identity is that they interrupt a lifelong pursuit of defining the self. We might have begun to imagine that we had our self-concepts under control. We might have begun to believe that our identity negotiations had been successful and that we could relax. Just then, we learn about new information that throws us off the track and threatens a secure sense of self. At such times, people feel incomplete. They are highly motivated to reinstate their self-concepts by whatever actions or symbols are available to set the record straight.

We discussed identity symbols earlier in this chapter. Identity symbols include blatant claims such as "I am thin." They also include self-defining actions such as eating lightly at an all-you-can-eat buffet, belonging to such organizations as weight-watching clubs, displaying the club's automobile bumper sticker, and so on. These and similar objects and actions "advertise" a person's identity. People routinely display such symbols, but **symbolic self-completion** involves exaggerating identity symbols when an important aspect of the self-concept has been threatened (Wicklund & Gollwitzer, 1982). In one study of symbolic self-completion, college women completed a preference scale. Some women said that becoming a good mother was far more important to them than being successful at a professional career (described in Wicklund & Gollwitzer, 1982). Later, an experimental confederate said that some of these women did not know much about being a mother. Other women did not have their identities challenged. Later, the women were all offered an opportunity to characterize themselves on a personality profile that supposedly depicted the ideal mother. Women whose identities had been challenged were more likely than the other women to depict themselves as very similar to the ideal mother profile. They acted as though they could set matters right by proving to the experimenter that they *were* suited to motherhood, no matter what anyone else said.

In an even more telling experiment, the researchers identified male college students who were deeply invested in activities like photography, swimming, or tennis (Gollwitzer & Wicklund, 1985). Later, they told some of these men that they had personalities that were very well suited to their most important, self-defining activity. They told other men that they had personalities

Calvin and Hobbes   by Bill Watterson

ill-suited to their most important, self-defining activity. Some of the men had their identities verified. Some of them had their identities challenged. In a later experimental session, the men expected to interact with an extremely attractive female student named Debbie. Some men were led to believe that Debbie, whom they very much wanted to meet and to impress favorably, liked only self-confident men. The others, who were equally attracted to Debbie, were led to believe that she liked only modest men.

The men were asked to describe themselves in writing so that Debbie could know a little about them before meeting them in person. Figure 5.7 shows that men who thought Debbie liked self-confidence bragged about themselves slightly more when their identities were called into question than when their identities were confirmed. The more interesting result, however, came when Debbie disliked self-confidence. Men who felt secure and complete in their identities were willing to be modest. Men who had their identities challenged, in contrast, had to brag about themselves even when they knew that bragging would hurt their chances with Debbie. They described themselves almost as glowingly as did men who thought Debbie liked self-confidence. It is difficult to escape the conclusion that these men, having been made to feel incomplete in a central part of their self-concepts, were driven to self-completion. They knew what Debbie liked, but when given a choice between impressing Debbie and repairing their damaged identities, they chose self-completion.

SELF-HANDICAPPING

The final topic to be discussed in this section on how people protect their sense of self is self-handicapping. Self-evaluation maintenance and symbolic self-completion both involve repairing the damage after an important identity has been challenged. **Self-handicapping,** in contrast, involves anticipating situations in which the self-concept might be challenged and trying to arrange matters in advance so that identity is secure no matter what happens (Rhodewalt, 1990). Self-handicapping takes two forms. One involves claiming to have disabilities or handicaps (Baumgardner, 1991). The other involves the paradoxical activity of erecting obstacles to our own success (Hirt, Deppe, & Gordon, 1991).

■ CLAIMING DISABILITIES

One way of self-handicapping is to claim a preexisting disability that would render poor performance unsurprising and good performance exceptional (Snyder & Smith, 1982; Snyder, Higgins, & Stucky, 1983). No one would expect a

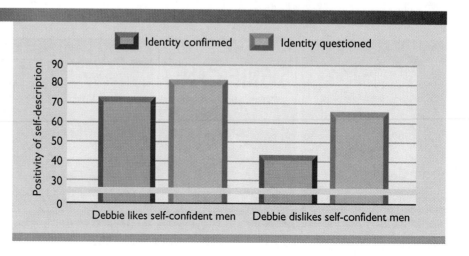

FIGURE 5.7

Self-completion can outweigh being liked.

Graph shows how positively men whose identities had been confirmed or questioned described themselves to an attractive woman who liked or disliked self-confident men (Gollwitzer & Wicklund, 1985).

runner with a pulled hamstring muscle to win a race. No one would expect a student who has test anxiety to score well on an important exam. By claiming to have a preexisting handicap, people can protect their positive self-concepts from being damaged by poor performance. They can do so passively without taking any overt action that might be seen as a deliberate self-presentational ploy.

In one study of how people claim disabilities as a self-handicapping strategy, hypochondriacs, who imagine they have serious health problems, believed that they were going to take a widely used test of social intelligence (Smith, Snyder, & Perkins, 1983). The researchers told some of the hypochondriacs that they were still developing the test, which was therefore not wholly reliable. They told other hypochondriacs that the test involved acting out a social situation in front of a group. The group would judge their performance. The test supposedly predicted interpersonal and job adjustment, satisfaction in intimate relationships, and social attractiveness. In other words, some of the hypochondriacs expected to be evaluated and others did not. A control group of nonhypochondriacs received the same instructions. Before taking the test, hypochondriacs and nonhypochondriacs were asked to indicate which ones of 138 health complaints and disorders were currently bothering them. Although nonhypochondriacs, who are not in the habit of telling people about a variety of imaginary illnesses, did not use health problems in a self-handicapping way, the hypochondriacs did. Hypochondriacs listed more health problems when they expected to be evaluated than when they did not.

Similar results have been obtained with other claims of disabilities that might excuse poor performance. Students who claim to be test anxious are more likely to describe themselves as test anxious when they think that poor performance on an imminent intelligence test might be excused by test anxiety than when they do not. Shy people describe greater feelings of shyness when they believe that shyness might excuse their poor performance in a role-playing situation than when shyness is said to be irrelevant. Students also report greater susceptibility to pain when they think that they might be unsuccessful on an analogies test during which they will be required to hold one hand immersed in freezing water (Mayerson & Rhodewalt, 1988; Smith, Snyder, & Handelsman, 1982; Snyder, Smith, Augelli, & Ingram, 1985).

When people claim to have a debilitating disability, they have a handy excuse, but they do not necessarily perform worse (Leary, 1986). If anything, they can relax because they do not have to worry as much about possible failure. Believable excuses protect positive self-concepts, prevent negative emotions, and facilitate such performances as sports, social presentation, selling products, and school achievement (Snyder & Higgins, 1988). When people have a handy excuse, they frequently perform better than usual.

■ ERECTING OBSTACLES TO SUCCESS

Claiming a disability is a relatively passive form of self-handicapping. The more active form involves erecting obstacles to our own success. In a classic study, male college students were told that they were participating in a study of two drugs that were thought to affect intellectual performance differently (Berglas & Jones, 1978). One drug supposedly facilitated performance by improving intellectual acuity. The other drug supposedly inhibited performance by interfering with concentration. Before they took either of the drugs, the men were given a practice test in which they were led to believe that they had solved a remarkable 16 out of 20 very difficult problems. The experimenter remarked that "Yours was one of the best scores seen to date!"

The only difficulty with the seemingly excellent practice test score was that some of the men had reason to suspect that their brilliant performance might have been a fluke that they could not repeat. Many of the problems were impossible to solve, but the answers were ambiguous enough that the experimenter could convincingly claim that they were correct. Other men had no such difficulty. Their problems were such that the correct answers were recognizable when revealed. These men had every reason to believe that they would be able to perform as well on the actual test as they had in practice. Put another way, some of the men had no reason to suspect that the results of the forthcoming test would threaten their positive self-concepts. The others were in the unfortunate position of new graduate students, most of whom suspect that "I'm not smart enough to be here. Any day now the faculty will discover that they made a mistake in admitting me."

Before the test, the experimenter explained that the student could choose to ingest either the performance-facilitating drug or the performance-inhibiting drug. Men who had done well in a way that led them to expect continued success tended to choose the performance-facilitating drug. Men who had done well on insoluble problems and thus could not be certain about their continued success, in contrast, preferred a drug that they thought would *impair* their performance! If their performance was worse than on the practice test, they could convince themselves and others that the deterioration was due to having taken a performance-inhibiting drug. If they unexpectedly did as well on the actual test as they had in practice, they could claim that they must have had extraordinary ability to overcome the debilitating effects of the drug.

Social psychologists have identified several reasons why people deliberately undermine their chances of success (Self, 1990). First, self-handicapping, like self-evaluation maintenance and symbolic self-completion, occurs only when an important part of the self-concept is placed in imminent jeopardy. Female students in the same ambiguous situation, for instance, do not choose the performance-inhibiting drug. The reason is that women, unlike men, do not attribute their initial success on ambiguous problems to their ability. Instead, they say "It was sheer luck that I did well." Unlike their male peers, women do not incorporate their initial success into their self-concepts. They do not feel threatened, therefore, by the possibility that they might not do as well on the actual test (Berglas & Jones, 1978). To induce women to self-handicap, for instance by deliberately listening to loud music while attempting a task that requires concentration, the experimenters have to take luck out of the picture. They have to emphasize that the task is a reliable and valid predictor of college and career success (Shepperd & Arkin, 1989).

Second, self-handicapping occurs only when people are uncertain about whether they will do well or poorly. People who feel confident that they will do well have no reason to self-handicap. People who fear possible failure, in contrast, need to arrange an excuse in advance, because they are threatened by possible regret over a poor decision (Josephs, Larrick, Steele, & Nisbett, 1992). Students who deliberately put little effort into their schoolwork and thus underachieve, students who stay out all night partying before big exams, athletes who practice less than usual before an important tournament, and men who stop at the local bar before a big date are all arranging excuses because they are uncertain about how well they will be able to perform (Higgins & Harris, 1988; Jones & Berglas, 1978; Rhodewalt, Saltzman, & Witner, 1984).

Third, the handicap must appear to be selected for a legitimate reason and not as a self-presentational ploy. When men who select the performance-inhibiting drug are asked why they did so, they do not answer "So that I would have an excuse in case I did poorly on the actual test." They offer instead such logical reasons as "I wanted to help the experimenter." Students who believe that they might fail an exam self-handicap by choosing a very difficult multiple-choice version over a less difficult essay version. They only make such a choice, however, when they can claim that they chose the more difficult exam because of the difference in format. They do not do it when the only difference between the two tests is that one is more difficult, because then the self-presentational ploy would be more obvious (Handelsman, Kraiger, & King, 1985). Similarly, people do not self-handicap when they already have an excuse for poor performance, like a distracting noise, because to do so would be regarded as an illegitimate "overkill" (Shepperd & Arkin, 1989). If self-handicapping is to be effective, the true motive must be disguised, even from ourselves.

Finally, self-handicapping may be a way for people with low self-esteem to avoid the negative implications of anticipated success. It is also, however, a way for people with high self-esteem to make success look truly outstanding (Rhodewalt, Morf, Hazlett, & Fairchild, 1991; Turner & Pratkanis, 1993). In a relevant study, college students had an opportunity to practice before taking a test that would "help us to identify people who are exceptional in this area" (Tice, 1991, p. 713). In these circumstances, people who had high self-esteem were more likely than people who had low self-esteem to curtail their practice. By practicing little, they increased the benefit to their self-concepts should they happen to be one of the few participants who qualified as exceptional.

SUMMARY OF HOW PEOPLE PROTECT THE SELF

The modern sense of self is so fragile that threats to the self-concept prompt people to protect their identities. When their identities are damaged, people repair the damage through self-evaluation maintenance and symbolic self-completion. Self-evaluation maintenance involves strategic social comparison. When people have no ambitions to competence at an activity, they emphasize their closeness and social identity with others who perform very well. When they have ambitions of their own, in contrast, they try to distance themselves from top performers. Symbolic self-completion involves strategic showing off, whether by bragging or by displaying identity symbols. People can usually afford to be modest, but not when their cherished identities have been challenged. When such damage occurs, they forget modesty. Instead, they use every means at their disposal to tell the world exactly who they think they are.

People also try to arrange events *in advance* so that their identities are never in danger and cannot be damaged, no matter what happens. They do so by claiming disabilities and by erecting obstacles to their own success. By claiming to have a disability or handicap before a performance, people try to insure that they cannot be evaluated negatively no matter how poorly they perform. They provide themselves with a convenient excuse. By erecting obstacles to their own success, people make it perfectly acceptable to fail and all the more remarkable if they happen to succeed.

People use these ways of protecting their identities only when an important aspect of the self is in danger, when they can do so without other people realizing that it is a self-presentational ploy, and when they lack confidence.

Evaluating Persons and Relationships

Attitudes

One pleasant summer evening in 1930, a car pulled into the parking lot of a moderately expensive restaurant on the Pacific coast. The driver was a middle-aged Caucasian male. He was on holiday with a younger Chinese couple who were his good friends. The threesome had been traveling all day, so they did not have reservations. Because the lot was almost full, the driver asked his friends to go in and get a table while he looked for a parking space. As the car drove away, the Chinese man and his wife hesitated at the front door and glanced at each other fearfully. The young couple had good reason to be afraid. Although they were suitably dressed for the restaurant, they were also Chinese. In the early 1930s, according to newspaper and radio reports, Californians intensely disliked anyone of Asian origin. Odd as it may seem to us today, Californians at the time had very negative attitudes about the recent influx of Asian immigrants, some legal and some illegal. Anti-Chinese sentiments were so strong that the Chinese couple suspected they would not only be unable to get a table, but they would be told to leave. Putting aside their fear, however, the couple dutifully entered the restaurant and requested a table for three.

To the Chinese couple's astonishment, they were shown to an excellent table by the window overlooking the ocean. The waiter was extremely courteous, both before and after they were joined by their friend. If anything, the

Did belonging to a negatively stigmatized group ever get anyone better-than-normal restaurant service?

Caucasian friend thought that they received more attentive service than he would have expected had he been alone or with other Caucasians. The scene was repeated after dinner when the threesome drove to a well-known area hotel. Again, the Caucasian driver parked while his Chinese friends went to reserve two rooms. Not only did they receive excellent rooms, but the receptionist, the bell captain, and all the hotel staff were extraordinarily polite and welcoming.

The threesome continued to take extensive motoring holidays together for the next two years. During that time, they visited 184 restaurants or cafés and 66 hotels, auto camps, and tourist homes. They were refused service only once, at a small autocamp. Some of the places the threesome visited were large and some were small; some were expensive and some were inexpensive. Sometimes the Caucasian driver accompanied the Chinese couple when they first asked for service and sometimes he did not. The Caucasian driver started keeping records of how many times they received a reception that he regarded as "normal," "better than normal," or "hesitant." As shown in Figure 6.1, their reception was usually normal or better than normal. If anything, the reception was more likely to be "better than normal" when the driver did not at first accompany his Chinese friends than when he did.

The Caucasian driver was a university professor who had mixed feelings about the reception that he and his Chinese friends received. He was pleased personally, but he was also worried professionally, because he studied attitudes. People's attitudes were supposed to predict how they would behave. If Californians had such negative attitudes toward Chinese as had been reported, then why was it so easy for his Chinese friends to be served? Were the newspaper and radio accounts wrong? Was it possible that Californians did not have negative attitudes toward Chinese people? To find out, the professor sent a questionnaire to restaurants and hotels throughout the region in which he and his Chinese friends had traveled. In the questionnaire, he asked the proprietors and managers of these establishments about their attitudes toward serving members of various races. The important question was "Will you accept members of the Chinese race as guests in your establishment?"

The professor received replies from 256 establishments. On the important question about serving Chinese individuals, 92% said "No," 7% said "Undecided; depend upon circumstances," and fewer than 1% said "Yes." Area ho-

FIGURE 6.1

Attitudes do not always predict behavior.
Graph shows how frequently a Chinese couple received three types of reception during a time of intense anti-Chinese attitudes, when accompanied or not accompanied by a Caucasian friend (LaPiere, 1934)

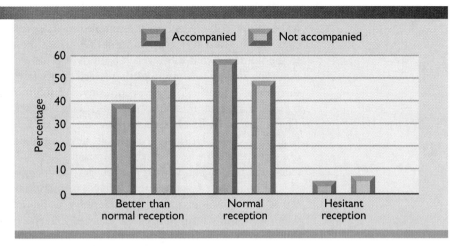

tels and restaurants overwhelmingly claimed that they would refuse service to Chinese people. Also, 128 of the respondents were the *same places* that the professor and his friends had visited. Their percentages were the same as for the larger sample. In other words, establishments claiming to have such negative attitudes that they would refuse service to Chinese people regardless of the circumstances, had provided a normal or better-than-normal reception to the professor's Chinese friends, whether he was with them or not.

You might at first be pleased that people who claimed to be racial bigots did not allow their negative attitudes to influence their behavior, but would you really want to live in a world where people did not follow through on their expressed attitudes? In such a world, would you want to marry someone who promised to "love, honor, and cherish" you forever? We *need* other people to "live up to" their expressed attitudes, so that we can predict what they might do. We also *need* to know our own attitudes, whether toward a particular professor, a job, a political party, or different types of food, so that we can plan our lives and make intelligent decisions (Pratkanis & Turner, 1994a). The world would be chaos if people did not have and behave according to positive or negative attitudes. Researchers have for many years regarded attitude as "the central concept in social psychology" (Allport, 1935). Without "attitudes," social psychologists would find it difficult or impossible to explain why two people respond entirely differently to the same circumstances, or to predict any individual's behavior (Eagly, 1992).

By serving the Chinese couple courteously, the restaurant and hotel proprietors and staffs violated the layperson's and psychologists' ideas about attitudes. To understand why the proprietors and staffs acted as they did, we need to know what attitudes are, how attitudes are formed, and the conditions under which attitudes do and do not predict behavior. The major sections of this chapter try to answer three questions: "What is an attitude?"; "How do people develop and maintain their attitudes?"; and "When do attitudes predict behavior?"

WHAT IS AN ATTITUDE?

The word "attitude" first entered the English language in approximately 1710. It was derived from a French term of the same spelling (Fleming, 1967). "Attitude" was originally a technical term used in statuary and painting to refer to a figure's posture, stance, physical leaning, or orientation in space. By 1725, the word had slipped into more general use to signify the way that a person's physical posture conveyed internal intentions and emotions. Stage actors, for instance, were said to "strike an attitude" when they cringed visibly to convey to the audience that they were afraid or when they leaned toward an actor of the opposite sex to show that they were "attracted" to that person. Vestiges of this original meaning occur even today. We might describe a person's attitude by saying, for example, that "she *leans* toward a conservative political position." The importance of physical orientation in attitudes is supported by modern laboratory research in which people developed different attitudes toward an object depending on whether their muscles were flexed or extended when they evaluated the object (Cacioppo, Priester, & Berntson, 1993).

Although the language that today's social psychologists use to define an attitude may sound technical, the "scientific" definition is roughly what we mean when we use the term in modern everyday conversation. One widely accepted definition is that an **attitude** is "a psychological tendency that is expressed by evaluating a particular entity with some degree of favor or disfavor" (Eagly & Chaiken, 1993, p. 1). The social psychologists who wrote the definition explained that a "psychological tendency" is a state that is internal to the person and that lasts for at least a short time. They also explained that "evaluating" can occur in any form, whether "overt or covert, cognitive, affective, or behavioral" and that an attitude is a "hypothetical construct" that psychologists invoke to explain an individual's evaluative orientation toward a particular target. A hypothetical construct is not tangible, but that does not stop people from using such hypothetical constructs as moods, traits, or attitudes in everyday conversation.

If you advised a Chinese friend, "Don't go to that college, because I know that the students have negative attitudes toward Chinese," you would mean roughly the same as the scientific definition. You would presumably be referring to something *internal* to the college's students, not anti-Chinese posters on the outside of dormitories. You would mean it as a *tendency,* not necessarily something the college's students would have forever, but something that would last at least long enough for your friend to enroll. You would mean that the college's students would tend to *evaluate* your friend negatively rather than positively. You would mean that the evaluation might occur either in open, *overt* ways or in hidden, *covert* ways. You would also mean that the negative evaluations might take three different forms. The college's students might show their disfavor in what they think *(cognitive),* in how they feel *(affective),* and in how they act *(behavioral).* Many social psychologists regard thoughts, feelings, and actions as the three components of an attitude.

THREE COMPONENTS

According to the **three-component theory of attitudes,** attitudes consist of people's tendencies toward positive or negative thoughts, feelings, and actions (Breckler, 1984; Insko & Schopler, 1967; Katz & Stotland, 1959; Krech & Crutchfield, 1948; Olson & Zanna, 1993; Ostrom, 1969; Rosenberg & Hovland, 1960; Smith, 1947; Triandis, 1991; Zanna & Rempel, 1988). One way of characterizing the differences among these three components is to say that thoughts are cold, calculating, emotionless beliefs, feelings are emotional gut responses, and actions are what we do. According to the three-component view, a person's attitude is a combination of what the person thinks, how the person feels, and how the person tends to act. The "tripartite distinction provides an important conceptual framework, one that allows psychologists to express the fact that evaluation can be manifested through responses of all three types"

(Eagly & Chaiken, 1993, p. 14). Not all theorists agree that we need three components to describe an attitude, but the three components are used in this book because they help to illustrate many of the ideas presented in this chapter and in Chapter 7, which treats of attitude change.

Table 6.1 illustrates the three-component theory of attitudes by showing how three different restaurant managers of the 1930s–Fred, Ted, and Ben– might have thought about, felt, and acted toward Chinese people. The examples of thoughts, feelings, and actions are necessarily simplistic, because reliable, valid ways of measuring the separate components are still being developed (Crites, Fabrigar, & Petty, 1994; Eagly, Mladinic, & Otto, 1994). As shown in the table, 100% of Ted's thoughts about Chinese people were negative, 50% of his feelings were negative, and 50% of his behaviors were negative. If Ted had

TABLE 6.1	Three Components of Attitudes, as Illustrated by the Percentages of Positive Thoughts, Feelings, and Actions That Each of Three Restaurant Managers in 1930 Might Have Had Toward Chinese People		
	THOUGHTS	**FEELINGS**	**ACTIONS**
Ted	thinks Chinese are stealing "American" jobs (*negative*)	angry that they sneak into the country (*negative*)	votes to cut off education for immigrants (*negative*)
	believes Chinese are genetically inferior (*negative*)	not repulsed by their physical appearance (*neutral*)	serves a Chinese couple (*neutral*)
	100% negative thoughts	50% negative feelings	50% negative actions
Fred	thinks Chinese are stealing "American" jobs (*negative*)	angry that they sneak into the country (*negative*)	votes to cut off education for immigrants (*negative*)
	does not believe Chinese are genetically inferior (*neutral*)	repulsed by their physical appearance (*negative*)	serves a Chinese couple (*neutral*)
	50% negative thoughts	100% negative feelings	50% negative actions
Ben	does not think Chinese are stealing "American" jobs (*neutral*)	angry that they sneak into the country (*negative*)	votes to cut off education for immigrants (*negative*)
	believes Chinese are genetically inferior (*negative*)	not repulsed by their physical appearance (*neutral*)	refuses to serve a Chinese couple (*negative*)
	50% negative thoughts	50% negative feelings	100% negative actions

only these six evaluative responses to Chinese people, then he evaluated them negatively two-thirds of the time. As the table shows, Fred and Ben also evaluated Chinese people negatively two-thirds of the time, but Fred's feelings were more negative than his thoughts or actions and Ben's actions were more negative than his thoughts or feelings. Fred, Ted, and Ben had equally negative attitudes toward Chinese people, but their negative attitudes differed in ways that the three-component perspective considers important. These individual differences in which of the three components predominates within an attitude will play a part in understanding ideas that will be stated later in this chapter.

As shown in Table 6.1, the three components need not always match (Edwards, 1990; Millar & Tesser, 1992; Zajonc, 1980, 1984). Although logic dictates at least a moderate degree of consistency among the components, researchers have no reason to expect complete consistency. Ted, for instance, might have had consistently negative thoughts about Chinese people, but he might not have had many negative gut feelings and he might not have taken many negative actions against them. Similarly, Fred might have had consistently negative gut feelings about Chinese people, but he might have had few negative thoughts about them and he might have taken few negative actions. Ben might have been the owner of the one auto camp that refused the Chinese couple. He might have consistently refused to serve Chinese individuals, but he might also have admitted that at least some of his thoughts and some of his feelings about Chinese people were not negative.

Although people's thoughts, feelings, and actions toward a target are likely to match moderately well, they do not have to do so. Instead of being merely negative versus neutral, as the components are in Table 6.1, attitudes can be ambivalent (Thompson, Zanna, & Griffin, 1995). Some parts of an attitude might be positive and some negative. At times when the positive part is salient, we have a positive attitude, but at times when the negative part is salient, we have a negative attitude (Schwarz & Strack, 1991; Tesser, 1978; Tourangeau & Rasinski, 1988; Wilson & Hodges, 1992; Zanna & Rempel, 1988). We can all remember times when we have let the "heart overrule the head" or vice versa, times when we thought it best not to act publicly on our feelings, and times when our actions contradicted our thoughts. Many cigarette smokers, for example, freely admit that smoking is bad for their health, but they keep smoking. When the restaurant and hotel proprietors said that they would not serve Chinese people, they might have been treating the question purely as an intellectual exercise, so their thoughts were salient. The thoughts might not have matched either their feelings or their subsequent actions.

ASSESSING ATTITUDES

The restaurant and hotel owners' attitudes also might not have been measured thoroughly. The attitude questionnaire did not ask about all three attitude components. It did not ask, for instance, how the proprietors *felt* about Chinese people. The questionnaire also assumed that the proprietors would tell the truth. Such an assumption might be more tenable for some types of attitudes than for others. If we wanted to predict the outcome of an election, for instance, we might use a "direct assessment" technique and simply ask potential voters to describe their attitudes. For other predictions, though, direct assessment techniques might be misleading. The two candidates, for instance, might be of different races. Because people might not want to look prejudiced, at least some citizens might disguise their true attitudes when we asked them directly and yet vote along racial lines once they were in the privacy of the polling place. When the attitude has a "politically correct" answer, we might find a more accurate measure of attitudes if we were to use "indirect assessment" rather than "direct assessment."

■ DIRECT ASSESSMENT

The direct method of assessing attitudes typically involves one of several different types of **attitude scales,** on which respondents indicate their attitudes by choosing a place along the scale that best represents how they think, feel, or tend to act toward the attitude target. Figure 6.2 illustrates three measurement techniques that involve attitude scales. One such technique involves summated rating scales, which are also called Likert scales (pronounced LICK-ert) (Likert, 1932; McNemar, 1946; Murphy & Likert, 1938). When attitude researchers use Likert scales, they typically ask people what they think of the attitude object on several scales that are all labeled in the same way, then sum

FIGURE 6.2

Three "direct assessment" scales for measuring attitudes.

I. LIKERT (SUMMATED RATING) SCALES
On each scale, circle the number that best represents your position

a. What is your opinion on allowing further immigration by Chinese people?

| -4 | -3 | -2 | -1 | 0 | +1 | +2 | +3 | +4 |

very much opposed   neither favor nor oppose   very much in favor

b. What are your "gut feelings" about Chinese people?

| -4 | -3 | -2 | -1 | 0 | +1 | +2 | +3 | +4 |

very negative   neither positive nor negative   very positive

c. How likely would you be to serve Chinese people in your establishment?

| -4 | -3 | -2 | -1 | 0 | +1 | +2 | +3 | +4 |

very unlikely   neither likely nor unlikely   very likely

2. SEMANTIC DIFFERENTIAL SCALES
Place an X on each line to indicate your position

Chinese people are: **bad** |_._|_._|_._|_._|_._|_._| **good**

Chinese people are: **unpleasant** |_._|_._|_._|_._|_._|_._| **pleasant**

Chinese people are: **undesirable** |_._|_._|_._|_._|_._|_._| **desirable**

3. LATITUDES OF ACCEPTANCE
Circle all attitude positions that you might be willing to accept. Leave uncircled any attitude positions that you would reject

My attitude toward Chinese people is

| -4 | -3 | -2 | -1 | 0 | +1 | +2 | +3 | +4 |

very negative   neither positive nor negative   very positive across the answers. As shown in the top panel of Figure 6.2, the professor might have used three Likert scales that asked about the restaurant and hotel proprietors' opinions on Chinese immigration, gut feelings toward Chinese people, and willingness to serve Chinese people. A proprietor who marked the three scales +3, +1, and +2 would have a summed attitude of +6 across the three scales. The summated rating method of measuring attitudes, as suggested by this example, can be used to measure whatever aspect of an attitude most interests the researcher. Although the assumption may be more valid in some circumstances than in others, the investigator assumes that more extreme scale positions represent more important or more strongly held attitudes (Boninger, Krosnick, Berent, & Fabrigar, 1995; Krosnick & Petty, 1995).

Closely related to Likert scales are semantic differential scales (Osgood, Suci, & Tannenbaum, 1957). According to semantic differential theory, words have two "meanings." One is the word's semantic or dictionary meaning; the other is the word's connotative meaning. The connotative meaning has three aspects: evaluation, potency, and activity, or how good, powerful, and active the thing or idea is that the word signifies. In measuring attitudes, investigators normally use only the evaluative dimension. To illustrate, the restaurant and hotel owners might have been asked to assess the word "Chinese" by placing a mark somewhere along each of three scales. The technique is called "differential" because each scale forces the respondent to differentiate between two opposite connotations. Typically, they ask respondents to evaluate the attitude object on such dimensions as Good-Bad, Pleasant-Unpleasant, and Desirable-Undesirable.

Whether they use Likert scales or semantic differential scales, investigators can ask respondents to indicate not just a single point along a dimension but rather a *range* of acceptable attitude positions—a "latitude of acceptance" (Sherif & Hovland, 1961). In Figure 6.3, for instance, a respondent might indicate a latitude of acceptance three scale positions wide by circling +1, +2, and +3. The "latitude of rejection" is the scale positions that are not circled. Two respondents might both have a +2 attitude, but differ in how "flexible" (as opposed to "rigid") their attitudes are. One respondent might accept only +2 (a latitude of acceptance one position wide), whereas the other might accept all attitudes except −4 (a latitude of acceptance eight positions wide). As discussed more extensively in Chapter 7, which treats of attitude change, the latitude of acceptance measure adds additional and often important information to "single-point" assessment techniques (Fazio, Zanna, & Cooper, 1977).

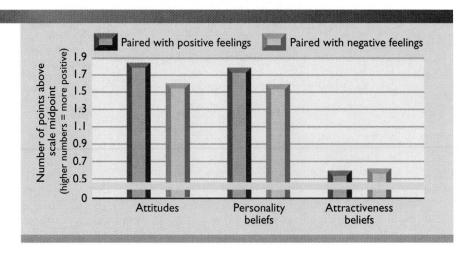

FIGURE 6.3

Attitudes can be classically conditioned without "information." Graph shows positivity of attitudes and beliefs by students who "saw" photos of a woman paired with pictures that aroused positive or negative feelings (Krosnick, et al., 1992)

Likert scales, semantic differential scales, and latitudes of acceptance are just three examples of many direct measurement techniques for attitudes (Dawes & Smith, 1985). Although most research, like the study of hotel and restaurant proprietors, uses just one or two questions to assess attitudes, more accurate assessments require several distinct measurement techniques. "Attitude strength" is not a simple construct. One attitude cannot be termed "stronger" than another just because it falls at $+3$ rather than $+2$ on a single scale or at $+6$ rather than $+5$ when summed across scales. Instead, attitude strength consists of extremity, certainty, importance, knowledge, intensity, interest, direct experience, accessibility, thought-feeling consistency, and latitudes of acceptance versus rejection (Krosnick, Boninger, Chuang, Berent, & Carnot, 1993). Attitude strength also involves both personal identity as an individual and social identity as a group member (Boninger, Krosnick, & Berent, 1995). These factors, many of which are discussed later in this chapter, are separate, conceptually independent aspects of having a "strong" versus "weak" attitude. Ideally, they should be measured separately.

■ INDIRECT ASSESSMENT

Even if we were to measure all these factors separately by using attitude scales and related forms of "direct" assessment, however, we might still find it difficult to detect truthful attitudes toward some issues and social groups. Researchers are often interested in attitudes that might be popular or unpopular, such as attitudes toward minority groups or persons with AIDS. In such cases, direct assessment techniques are often inadequate. Whenever there exists a "socially desirable" response, participants in attitude studies might give the socially desirable answer instead of their true attitudes (Orne, 1962). In a survey of 1930s attitudes, for instance, White students expressed very negative opinions of Black people (Katz & Braly, 1933). A 1969 study, 36 years later, *seemed* to find that these negative stereotypes had largely disappeared (Karlins, Coffman, & Walters, 1969). Had they really disappeared, or had it become less acceptable to admit publicly to harboring negative racial stereotypes? Were the 1969 subjects answering the "direct assessment" attitude scales honestly?

Social psychologists have developed several ingenious methods for getting at true attitudes on sensitive topics. Perhaps the best known is the **bogus pipeline technique,** which consists of convincing the respondent that the experimenter has a "pipeline" into the respondent's real attitudes, so that the respondent will provide honest answers to questions about attitudes that might be socially undesirable (Jones & Sigall, 1971). In one version of the bogus pipeline, the experimenter connects participants to an impressive-looking piece of electrical equipment that is supposed to be a "lie detection machine." The participant is asked to tell the truth on some practice questions and to tell deliberate lies on other practice questions, for instance, to tell the truth on questions 1, 3, and 5, and to tell lies on questions 2, 4, and 6. The experimenter shows the unsuspecting participant a prepared printout of his or her "emotional responses." The printout shows large discrepancies between the odd-numbered and the even-numbered questions. Once the participant is convinced that the machine "knows" the truth, the experimenter reads a list of attitude questions such as, "What is your attitude toward Blacks?" and asks the participant to guess what the machine has registered. In the bogus pipeline procedure, participants are likely to tell the truth about their attitudes because they think that the experimenter knows their true attitudes anyway. Researchers used the bogus pipeline technique to reassess White students' attitudes toward Blacks. They showed that White students *had* changed to having somewhat less negative attitudes toward Blacks in 1969 than they had in 1933, but that much of the negative stereotype remained (Sigall & Page, 1971). Bogus pipeline techniques are also effective in getting people to admit that they smoke too much, drink too much, and engage in other unhealthy, risky, or socially undesirable behaviors (Aguinis, Pierce, & Quigley, 1993).

The bogus pipeline technique increases truth-telling when people believe that the experimenter will "know" if they tell a lie (Roese & Jamieson, 1993). The technique is more useful, therefore, in getting truthful answers to questions of fact than in getting truthful answers to questions of opinion, such as questions about attitudes. The procedure is also difficult to implement, ethically questionable, and might itself alter attitudes that are not strongly held (Roese & Jamieson, 1993). For measuring attitudes, modern researchers have developed a less intrusive technique (Jamieson & Zanna, 1991). Instead of physically connecting participants to a "lie detector machine," the experimenter simply explains the machine's function and lets participants know that the machine might later be used to verify their responses. This less intrusive technique is at least as effective as the original procedure in reducing social desirability bias when participants are asked about their attitudes on "sensitive" issues (Roese & Jamieson, 1993).

Finally, recent advances in electrophysiology may remove the "bogus" from the bogus pipeline and make it possible to detect attitudes directly (Cacioppo & Petty, 1987; Cacioppo, Bush, & Tassinary, 1992). Certain muscle groups in the face respond differently when people see or imagine scenes they like than when they see or imagine scenes they dislike. Electromyographic recordings can detect minute changes in these muscles, accurately reflecting both the direction and the intensity of a person's feelings and thus directly tapping that person's attitudes. This technique is ideal for measuring attitudes on "sensitive" topics where people do not want to make themselves look bad by admitting to deeply held prejudices. The muscle changes are so minute that no outside observer, even one staring directly at the person's face, could detect them. Instead of trying to measure the "feelings" component of an attitude indirectly by marks on attitude scales, social psychologists of the future may take "direct" electrophysiological measures (Cacioppo, Crites, Gardner, & Berntson, 1994).

SUMMARY OF WHAT AN ATTITUDE IS

Both in scientific terms and in everyday language, the meaning of the word "attitude" has changed over the years from denoting an observable physical "stance" to denoting a psychological evaluation. Attitudes have three components: positive or negative thoughts, feelings, and actions.

A person's attitude can be measured directly by asking questions about thoughts, feelings, and likely actions toward the attitude object. In cases where the investigator suspects that respondents may be unwilling to disclose their true thoughts, feelings, or action tendencies, attitudes can be measured indirectly by pretending to know the true answers (bogus pipeline) or by physiological recordings of minute muscle movements.

HOW ARE ATTITUDES FORMED AND MAINTAINED?

One of the most interesting questions about attitudes is how people come to hold them. This section of the chapter describes four ways in which attitudes develop. A second interesting question, also addressed in this section of the chapter, is what people gain from holding attitudes, or what functions attitudes serve. Finally, we discuss "belief perseverance," or how attitudes maintain themselves, sometimes in the face of what might seem to be heavily disconfirming evidence.

DEVELOPING AN ATTITUDE

Human beings develop their attitudes in the same way that other animals learn to approach or avoid, to desire or fear various parts of their environment: through information gathered about the attitude object, classical conditioning, instrumental conditioning, and imitation or "modeling." Although each of these four attitude sources may contribute to each of the three attitude components, information might be most likely to shape the "thoughts" component of an attitude, classical conditioning to shape the "feelings" component, and instrumental conditioning and modeling to shape the "actions" component (Greenwald, 1968a).

■ INFORMATION

Attitudes are in part formed, maintained, and modified by information about the attitude object. One common way in which we gain information is through persuasive communications (Greenwald, 1968b; McGuire, 1968, 1969, 1985). A restaurant proprietor in 1930, for instance, might have developed a negative attitude toward Chinese individuals purely from hearing other people talk about how immigrants were demanding health care and education that the state could not afford. Through such information, the restaurant proprietor might have developed a negative attitude before ever meeting a Chinese person in the flesh. More disconcertingly, a child might overhear his or her parents' derogatory

Calvin and Hobbes — by Bill Watterson

remarks about a particular racial or ethnic minority group and develop a negative attitude before ever meeting a single group member. Secondhand information may be the primary source of attitudes toward new immigrant groups when people have not yet met a group member (Maio, Esses, & Bell, 1994).

Information from the communication media plays a powerful role in shaping positive or negative thoughts about an attitude object. The only Black people in early films, for instance, were "the plantation uncle, the broad-bosomed mammy . . . obsequious, affectionate, and faithful" (Leab, 1975, p. 10). Another common movie stereotype, even after World War II, in the United States was the Black man as ludicrous comic stooge or chicken-snatcher, most likely named Rastus, whom the "superior" White folks treated with condescension and derision (Leab, 1975). United States citizens in the 1930s who were raised with such negative and inaccurate media portrayals of Blacks, Chinese, and others might understandably have resisted letting their children attend school with children of other races. In case you think that modern media portrayals are less likely to create negative stereotypes and attitudes than in the past, many studies have shown that women continue to be portrayed in a less flattering light than men on television (Hall & Crum, 1994). Information from the news media also shapes public opinion by "setting the agenda" and focusing citizens' attention on some problems or political topics while ignoring others (Miller & Krosnick, in press). Although people often distort what is shown on television news, falsely believing that objective coverage is biased toward the other side's position, even distorted memories and beliefs may seem "real" to those whose attitudes are affected (Giner-Sorolla & Chaiken, 1994; Vallone, Ross, & Lepper, 1985).

■ CLASSICAL CONDITIONING

Classical conditioning of attitudes involves coming to like or dislike an attitude object because it has been previously associated with pleasurable or unpleasurable events. Although classical conditioning was first studied in dogs, it applies to every living organism. When two events reliably occur one after the other in rapid succession, the organism anticipates the second event whenever the first one occurs. If your hand is suddenly plunged into ice water, your blood vessels constrict—a natural bodily defense against the cold. Suppose that a buzzer always sounds immediately before your hand is plunged into the ice water. After several of these buzzer-then-cold pairings your body begins to anticipate the cold by constricting its blood vessels whenever the buzzer sounds. You have been classically conditioned to constrict your blood vessels at the sound of a buzzer (Menzies, 1937). Sights can be substituted for sounds as the first of the paired events. If an experimenter were to show slides of Chinese people immediately before plunging your hand into ice water, after several of these Chinese-then-cold pairings, your blood vessels would constrict at the mere sight of a Chinese person (Roessler & Brogden, 1943).

People can be conditioned through experience to associate pleasant or unpleasant feelings with words and ideas. In one study, a Soviet psychologist named Volkova (1953) whispered the word "good" in children's ears and then immediately squirted some cranberry juice into their mouths. After a while, the children salivated profusely at the mere mention of the word "good." To show that the children had learned to salivate for the abstract idea of goodness rather than merely for the sound of the word, Volkova whispered in their ears various phrases that the children were sure to regard as good or bad. When she whispered a "bad" idea such as "The fascists destroyed many cities," the children did not salivate. When she whispered a "good" idea such as "The young pioneer helps his comrade," they salivated profusely. In other words, they had been conditioned to salivate at the mention of any idea toward which they had a positive attitude.

How did these Soviet children get their positive attitudes toward young pioneers helping comrades in the first place? At least in part it was through classical conditioning. In one study, students memorized lists of words that contained both names of nationalities and various adjectives (Staats & Staats, 1958). One group of students got lists in which the word Dutch was always followed by a positive word like healthy, nice, or pretty, but the word Swedish was always followed by a negative word like nasty, ugly, or failure. A second group of students got lists in which Dutch was always followed by negative words and Swedish by positive words. The researcher presented the words separately and never said anything about connections between adjacent words. At the end of the "memory" experiment, all students were asked how they felt about various nationalities. As you may have guessed, the first group of students liked Dutch better than Swedish and the second group liked Swedish better than Dutch.

Classical conditioning of attitudes does not depend on information about the attitude object. In a relevant study, students saw nine photographs of a woman involved in everyday activities such as walking on a sidewalk, washing dishes, studying, and doing grocery shopping (Krosnick, Betz, Jussim, & Lynn, 1992, Study 2). Just before each photograph, another picture appeared so fast that the student was *unaware of its having been shown.* For some students, the picture was one that would arouse positive emotions, such as a bridal couple, a child with a large Mickey Mouse doll, or a group of smiling friends. For other students, the picture was one that would arouse negative emotions, such as a dead body, a bucket of snakes, or a face on fire.

All students were then asked about their attitudes toward the woman, whether they believed she had various positive and negative personality traits, and how attractive she was. As shown in Figure 6.3, students formed different attitudes toward the woman depending on whether she had been paired with positive or negative feelings, even though they were unaware of the pictures that aroused those feelings and thus had no different information about her. The figure also shows that the positive and negative attitudes created different beliefs about her probable personality traits. Because the photographs of everyday activities were ambiguous as to personality traits, liking or disliking the woman created a "halo effect," in which students assumed that the woman's unknown characteristics must also be positive (Thorndike, 1920). As the figure also shows, no such halo effect was possible for ratings of her attractiveness, for which students had objective evidence.

Could seeing Mickey Mouse make you like other people more?

One hour's worth of pairing the name of a race or ethnic group with negative traits can influence a person's attitude, as can nine brief pairings of unseen pictures with snapshots of a woman. It seems likely, then, that "An entire childhood spent hearing a certain group of people referred to with negative affect or seeing them, either in the media or in reality, associated with situations that arouse negative affect may generate a fairly strong negative attitude. This attitude may lead an individual to generate consonant beliefs about the group's characteristics" (Krosnick et al., 1992, p. 159). Classical conditioning is especially effective in shaping attitudes when people have very little information or direct experience with the attitude target (Cacioppo, Marshall-Goodell, Tassinary, & Petty, 1992), which is what most 1930s restaurant and hotel owners had about Chinese people.

Because classical conditioning works on the emotions, it might contribute most directly to shaping the "feelings" component of attitudes (Greenwald,

1968a). Negative feelings often go hand-in-hand with negative thoughts and actions, but negative emotional reactions are primarily acquired through classical conditioning—by having a previously neutral event paired consistently with a noxious experience (Cramer, Weiss, Steigleder, & Balling, 1985; Lott & Lott, 1968; Weiss, 1968; Staats, 1968).

■ INSTRUMENTAL CONDITIONING

A third way of acquiring attitudes is through **instrumental conditioning of attitudes,** which involves coming to behave positively or negatively toward an attitude object because doing so has previously been rewarded. The basic principle of instrumental conditioning is that all organisms do more of whatever they are rewarded for doing and less of whatever they are punished for doing. Suppose that a child is raised in an environment in which parents and peers smile whenever he or she puts down a particular minority group and frown whenever the child says anything good about that minority group. The child might develop a negative attitude toward the group and mature into an adult who tells cruel jokes about the minority group, because he or she expects peers to approve. Times and social attitudes, of course, might change. One day the bigoted adult might tell a cruel racist joke and notice that no one laughs. Then his or her attitude might change because bigotry is no longer socially rewarded. Participants in psychology experiments typically express more positive or negative attitudes toward various objects, persons, and events when an experimenter subtly reinforces them for doing so by smiling, nodding agreement, or saying "good" (Insko, 1965). Both attitude formation and attitude change can be explained by the principle of instrumental conditioning, which might affect action tendencies more than it affects the other two components (Greenwald, 1968a).

■ MODELING

People do not develop their attitudes only by being rewarded or punished themselves. They also learn their attitudes indirectly or vicariously, through imitation or modeling. **Modeling of attitudes** does not involve direct conditioning, either classical or instrumental. Instead, it involves adopting an attitude vicariously by watching others and imitating what they do when what they do seems successful (Bandura, 1986). We start by using our parents as role models. If they act positively toward a minority group or toward any other attitude object, we naturally assume that this is the correct stance to take, the "right" way to behave. If they act negatively toward a minority group, we are also likely to model our behavior after theirs. As we grow up, we develop other models of what behavior is considered "correct" and likely to lead to positive outcomes. Many of these vicarious learning experiences come from television and other media portrayals. Because cable television and video rentals are so widely available, observational learning or modeling may play a very important role in shaping the "actions" component of attitudes (McGuire, 1985).

■ ATTITUDE FUNCTIONS

Attitudes may develop through information, classical conditioning, instrumental conditioning, and modeling, but once we have our attitudes, they would not last long unless they served a useful purpose. Attitudes serve five important functions (Katz, 1960; Smith, Bruner, & White, 1956; Snyder, 1993). Attitudes help us to understand events, express deeply held values, protect self-esteem, maximize rewards, and match situations.

■ UNDERSTANDING EVENTS

The **knowledge function** of attitudes illustrates how attitudes help people to classify and interpret events. Attitudes help us to understand and to organize what can at times be a bewildering universe. They bring order to our lives by allowing us to categorize the people and objects around us. Attitudes make it possible to react quickly, without much cognitive effort. When the restaurant and hotel proprietors answered the professor's questionnaire, they no doubt believed that they understood Chinese people and how to treat them. They probably assumed (incorrectly, as it happened) that having a negative attitude toward Chinese individuals would tell them the appropriate way to respond to any Chinese person in any situation. They would not need to calculate all the pluses and minuses for each specific person and situation. As the study of restaurant and hotel owners illustrates, it is only genuine and not assumed knowledge that allows people to use their attitudes effectively (Wood, Rhodes, & Biek, 1995).

Table 6.2 lists ten types of evidence that attitudes serve a knowledge function. As the table shows, people who have opposite attitudes interpret the same events differently, have different expectations and inferences, slant their reasoning toward attitude-congruent conclusions, respond differently to persuasion, falsely believe that "everyone" shares their views, misremember facts to suit their attitudes, inflate or deflate statistics to buttress their attitudes, and make different predictions about future events (Pratkanis, 1989). Attitudes serve a knowledge function by directing what people pay attention to and how they perceive events (Fazio, Roskos-Ewoldsen, & Powell, 1994).

■ EXPRESSING VALUES

The **value expressive function** of attitudes indicates that attitudes help people to express their deeply held values and convictions (Abelson & Prentice, 1989; Katz, 1960; Kristiansen & Hotte, in press; Kristiansen & Zanna, 1994; Shavitt, 1989; Smith et al., 1956). In the 1930s, many critics of Chinese immigration genuinely felt that Chinese culture violated "American" moral standards and values. Their negative attitudes toward Chinese people expressed their anger and outrage at what they perceived as an erosion of public decency and morality by the "foreign menace." Such attitudes, ones that express firmly held values, are said to serve a value-expressive function. When people's attitudes express deeply held values, as is true for both sides of the abortion issue, suffering for their attitudes only makes people all the more committed to their attitudes (Murray, Haddock, & Zanna, in press).

Reprinted by permission: Tribune Media Services

TABLE 6.2	Ten Types of Evidence That Attitudes Serve a Knowledge Function (Adapted from Pratkanis, 1989)
COGNITIVE PROCESS AFFECTED	**EXAMPLE**
Interpretation and Explanation	Fans of both teams at football games interpret the play as evidence that the other side (but not their own) used "dirty tricks" (Hastorf & Cantril, 1954)
Expectations and Inferences	Physically attractive people are expected to be "better" than unattractive people (Hatfield & Sprecher, 1986)
Syllogistic Reasoning	Reasoning that leads to attitude-consistent conclusions is seen as more logical than equally valid reasoning that leads to attitude-inconsistent conclusions (Thistlethwaite, 1950)
Responses to Persuasion	Counter-attitudinal messages elicit a greater number of spontaneous counterarguments than proattitudinal messages (Petty, Ostrom, & Brock, 1981)
Interpersonal Attraction	We are more apt to like people who share our attitudes than people who disagree with us on important issues (Byrne, 1971)
False Consensus of Opinion	People believe that their own attitudes are more popular than they actually are (Wallen, 1943)
Fact Identification	People "remember" false facts ("Ronald Reagan had an A average in college") to fit their attitudes (Pratkanis, in press)
Biased Personal Memories	Past behavior is revised in memory to be consistent with current attitudes (Ross, McFarland, & Fletcher, 1981)
Information Estimation Errors	Of two equally incorrect answers ["murder rates are (2% or 8%) lower in death penalty states" when the actual answer is 5%] people think the one that supports their attitudes is more accurate (Weschler, 1950)
Predictions of Future Events	What people want to happen (for instance, a Democrat or Republican winning the next presidential election), they believe *will* happen (Cantril, 1940)

■ PROTECTING SELF-ESTEEM

The **ego defensive function** of attitudes shows that attitudes help people to protect their self-esteem. An unemployed Californian in the 1930s, for instance, might have put down Chinese immigrants as a way of protecting his own self-esteem. Instead of admitting that Chinese laborers were harder working than he was, which would injure his own ego, he might use the Chinese as a convenient scapegoat (Katz, 1960; Katz, McClintock, & Sarnoff, 1957).

In one study of ego-defensive attitude functions, the researchers asked students to write essays about why they had positive or negative attitudes toward lesbians and male homosexuals (Herek, 1987). The researchers scored the essays on how much they contained themes that exemplified each of the attitude functions. Ego-defensive themes involved being hostile toward and afraid of homosexuals, feeling anxious when lesbians or gays identified themselves publicly, being intolerant of cross-sex mannerisms, and being afraid that homosexuals might harm children. Approximately 22% of the student essays were exclusively ego-defensive. They contained no mention of the other functions. Students who wrote exclusively ego-defensive essays also portrayed themselves as similar to their own sex and different from the opposite sex. They said: "I am all man (or all woman), definitely *not* one of the other kind!" Both their attitudes toward gays or lesbians and their sex role claims were intended to defend their egos.

■ MAXIMIZING REWARDS

Attitudes can also serve a utilitarian function. The **utilitarian function** of attitudes illustrates how attitudes help people to maximize rewards and minimize punishments (Katz, 1960). For a restaurant or hotel owner in 1930s California to have negative attitudes toward Chinese would-be patrons might have served a utilitarian function if the owner honestly believed that recent immigrants were so threatening that people no longer wanted to travel, which would cut down on business. Even people who have positive attitudes toward volunteering to help the less fortunate members of society sometimes have attitudes that serve a utilitarian function if they think that volunteering will "look good on my résumé" (Clary, Snyder, Ridge, Miene, & Haugen, 1994).

■ MATCHING SOCIAL SITUATIONS

Finally, attitudes can also serve a social adjustive function. The **social adjustive function** of attitudes occurs when attitudes help people match the social situation by having attitudes that will impress others favorably. For a 1930s restaurant or hotel owner to have expressed positive attitudes toward Chinese guests at a cocktail party, for instance, might have invited scorn and contempt, because the attitude did not match the social situation. In those days, the "politically correct" attitude was to spurn the new immigrants. Expressing socially acceptable attitudes is an effective way to establish and maintain good interpersonal relations, thus matching the attitude to the social situation. Although the social adjustive function might be viewed as a way of maximizing social rewards, it also involves projecting a positive "social self" (Smith, Bruner, & White, 1956; Snyder & DeBono, 1987).

Several studies have shown that the social-adjustive function and the value-expressive function are used by different personality types (DeBono, 1987; Snyder & DeBono, 1985, 1987, 1989). High self-monitors, as described more in detail in Chapter 5, are people who pay much attention to the impression that they are creating (Snyder, 1974, 1979). They are good at making other people like them, they try to do and say things that others will like, they want to get along by "being" whatever kind of person other people will like, they sometimes pretend to be having a good time even when they are not, and they "put on a show" to impress or entertain other people. Low self-monitors, in contrast, are people who can only argue for ideas in which they already believe, who feel awkward in company, who make no attempt to do or say what others will like, who would not change their opinions to win favor, and who regard their behavior as an expression of their "true inner feelings."

High self-monitors use their attitudes to serve the social-adjustive function of getting rewards from other people. Low self-monitors, in contrast, use their attitudes to serve the value-expressive function of expressing their values and convictions (Snyder, 1974). One study compared how high self-monitors and low self-monitors reacted to product advertisements that were either about the product's image or about its quality. An "image" ad, for example, might show a brand of whiskey sitting on the blueprints for a fabulously expensive house. A "quality" ad might praise the whiskey's smooth taste (Snyder & DeBono,

1985). As predicted, high self-monitors (who had social adjustive attitudes) were more impressed by image than by quality ads, whereas low self-monitors (who had value-expressive attitudes) were more impressed by quality than by image ads. Especially for low self-monitors who are *quick* to say they can only argue for ideas in which they believe, attitudes express internal values (Mellema & Bassili, 1995).

■ DIFFERENCES AMONG FUNCTIONS

The five functions differ in several interesting ways. First, some of the functions have more to do with being right than with being likable. Others have more to do with being likable than with being right. One theme that runs through several chapters of this book, as explained in greater detail in Chapter 1, is that people have at least two fundamental goals: to be right, and to be likable (Baumeister & Leary, 1995; Snyder, 1993, 1994; Swann, 1987, 1990). When people are concerned about being right, they form impressions carefully and say what they really think rather than what might be "politically correct" (Snyder, 1993). When people are concerned about being likable, they form whatever impressions make them regard themselves as likable, do whatever they believe other people will praise them for doing, and pay particular attention to whether they are creating a likable impression on others (Deutsch & Lamberti, 1986; Snyder, 1993; Taylor & Brown, 1994). The knowledge function and the value-expressive functions of attitudes are ways in which people use their attitudes in the service of being right. The ego-defensive, utilitarian, and social-adjustive functions of attitudes are ways in which people use their attitudes in the service of being likable, either to themselves or to others.

Second, the different functions dictate different reasons for agreeing to engage in behaviors such as volunteering without pay to provide companionship to the lonely, health care to the sick, counsel to the troubled, tutoring to the poorly educated, food to the hungry, and shelter to the homeless (Clary, et al., 1994). Consider five women who have equally positive attitudes toward volunteering, but their attitudes serve five different functions. It might be most effective to remind one woman that volunteering would help her learn about human nature (knowledge function). We might remind the second woman that volunteering would let her show the caring, compassionate side of herself (value-expressive function). We might remind the third woman that volunteering would make her feel better about herself (ego-defensive function). We might remind the fourth woman that volunteering would strengthen her résumé (utilitarian function). Finally, we might remind the fifth woman that people she cares about would be very impressed (social-adjustive function). In a study that gave college students reasons for volunteering that either matched or mismatched each student's primary attitude function, matched reasons were more effective than mismatched reasons in soliciting help (Clary et al., 1994).

Third, as shown in Table 6.3, the four ways of developing attitudes might be related to the three attitude components and to the five attitude functions. Although most attitude theorists would agree that the methods of development, components, and functions do not line up as neatly as they are depicted in the table, the connections are similar to those in previously presented models (Greenwald, 1968a, p. 366). As can be seen in the table, information about a topic might affect primarily the thoughts component, whose function is to help us understand events (a knowledge function). Classical conditioning might affect primarily the feelings component, whose function is to express deeply held convictions (value expressive function) and to defend against threats to self-esteem (ego-defensive function). Finally, instrumental conditioning and modeling might affect primarily the actions component, whose function is to max-

TABLE 6.3	Possible Relationships among the Four Ways That Attitudes Are Formed, the Three Attitude Components, and the Four Attitude Functions (Adapted from Greenwald, 1968a)		
BASIS FOR ATTITUDE FORMATION	**ATTITUDE COMPONENT**	**ATTITUDE FUNCTIONS**
Information	Thoughts	Understanding events
Classical conditioning	Feelings	Expressing values & protecting self-esteem
Instrumental conditioning & modeling	Actions	Maximizing social & other rewards

imize rewards and minimize punishments (the utilitarian and social-adjustive functions).

BELIEF PERSEVERANCE

Once formed, attitudes and beliefs are notoriously resistant to change (McGuire, 1985). **Belief perseverance** occurs when attitudes and beliefs do more than passively resist disconfirmation, but instead actively maintain and sometimes strengthen themselves even in the face of disconfirming evidence (Nisbett & Ross, 1980; Ross & Lepper, 1980). People sometimes ignore evidence that totally contradicts the very assumptions on which their beliefs and attitudes were initially formed. They ignore such evidence by spontaneously inventing causal explanations or reasons why what they believe "must be so." They become so satisfied with their own ability to explain away disconfirming evidence that, in the process, their attitudes become more extreme.

■ IGNORING DISCONFIRMING EVIDENCE

One of the easiest ways for beliefs and attitudes to sustain themselves is for people to ignore new information whenever it is contradictory. Suppose, for instance, that we convinced a 1930s hotel owner that reports of the Chinese having poor personal hygiene were totally invalid. Would the hotel owner's negative attitude toward them change? To put the question more generally, suppose we could arrange a situation in which we knew the exact evidence on which an attitude or belief was originally formed and then proved beyond a shadow of doubt that the evidence in question was completely false. Might a belief or an attitude remain standing even if we removed its very foundation? This was the question addressed in a study that tested the outer limits of belief perseverance (Ross, Lepper, & Hubbard, 1975).

The researchers wanted to construct a new belief "from scratch" about a topic for which participants would not start with preexisting beliefs or attitudes. The topic was ability to discriminate fake from authentic suicide notes. The investigators showed students pairs of suicide notes and asked them to guess which was authentic and which was a fake written to look like a suicide note. After the student guessed, the experimenter gave the "correct" answer. Across

25 pairs of suicide notes, some students were led to believe that they were extraordinarily gifted at suicide note discrimination. They were told that the average person got about 16 correct, but, no matter which answers they gave, these students were told that they were correct on 24 of the 25 pairs. Other students were told that they got 17 correct. Yet other students were led to believe that they were correct on only 10 of the 25 pairs. The experimenters thus built a belief about ability to detect authentic suicide notes. The experimenters also knew the exact evidence on which the belief had been constructed, namely how many of 25 pairs students thought they had guessed correctly.

The researchers then completely discredited the initial evidence on which a student's belief had been based. The experimenter "explained" that, for extraneous reasons, it had been necessary to deceive the student. The sequence of "correct" and "incorrect" answers had been determined in advance and had absolutely nothing to do with the answers that the student gave. To be positive that the student could not possibly misunderstand that the initial answers had been totally false, the experimenter showed the student a typewritten answer sheet from which the experimenter had been reading when he said "correct" or "incorrect" after each of the student's guesses. The experimenter also insisted that the student explain the deception aloud and admit that the answers were totally irrelevant to the student's true ability at discriminating fake from authentic suicide notes.

Before releasing the student from the experiment, almost as an aside, the experimenter asked the question that assessed belief perseverance. The experimenter explained that the pairs of suicide notes actually contained one authentic note and one fake note. The experimenter then asked students to estimate how many pairs they had actually got correct. As shown in Figure 6.4, students who had initially been led to believe that they were good at the task estimated that they had really got about 17 of the pairs correct. Students who had initially been led to believe that they were poor at the task, in contrast, estimated that they had really got about 13 of the pairs correct. Students who had initially been led to believe that they were average continued to believe they were average. The students' beliefs survived even a total disconfirmation of the very evidence on which those beliefs had initially been established.

■ CAUSAL EXPLANATIONS

How is it possible for beliefs to survive total disconfirmation? One explanation of the suicide note study is that students might have spontaneously generated

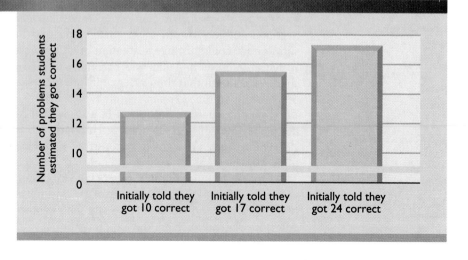

FIGURE 6.4

Beliefs survive total discrediting of the evidence on which they were based.

Graph shows how many problems students thought they got correct after learning that what they were initially told was fictitious (Ross, Lepper, & Hubbard, 1975).

"causal explanations" that were independent of the initial evidence (Anderson & Kellam, 1992; Ross et al., 1975). Consider the 1930s hotel owner who had been told that Chinese culture did not emphasize personal hygiene. Because of this false information, the owner might have imagined that he could smell body odor on a Chinese person who passed him in the street. Even though we might persuade him that Chinese culture actually *emphasized* personal hygiene, we could not remove the "body odor" that he thought he had detected. In the same way, students who thought they were performing extraordinarily well in the suicide note study might have been reminded of experiences that would help them to understand why they were doing so well. "I must be getting them all right because I read the complete works of that poet who committed suicide." When the experimenter later revealed that the answers were false and that the students' actual performance was unknown, these students might have said to themselves "I read the complete works of that poet, so I would probably be good at doing this." The students might not have realized that they only remembered reading the poet's works because they were trying to explain their unexpected success.

Do the best firefighters have risky or cautious personalities?

The "causal explanations" interpretation of belief perseverance was supported by an experiment in which researchers showed students data from one of two fictitious studies. Depending on which fictitious study the student read, good firefighters appeared to have either risky or cautious personalities (Anderson, Lepper, & Ross, 1980). Some of the students were asked to generate causal explanations for whichever relationship they had seen, such as "You have to be willing to take risks if you're going to rush into burning buildings and save lives" or "You have to be cautious, because rushing into burning buildings would lose more lives than it would save."

After the students had constructed their causal explanations, the experimenter revealed that the data were entirely fictitious. The students were asked what they thought the true relationship was. As predicted, students continued to believe whichever relationship they had explained. They did not realize that, had they been assigned to the other condition, they could just as easily have constructed causal explanations to justify an opposite belief. Instead, they "convinced themselves" so well with their self-generated reasons for why a risky or cautious person would make a better firefighter that, if anything, they were more confident than ever.

■ ATTITUDES BECOMING MORE EXTREME

As the firefighter study suggests, belief perseverance involves more than just maintaining beliefs and attitudes at their original intensities. It also involves "explaining away" disconfirming evidence so well that we become more convinced than ever that we were right. Beliefs and attitudes, if given suitably ambiguous new evidence on which to work their interpretive magic, can emerge from the encounter more extreme than they were before.

In one experiment on social policy attitudes, students who were very much for or against capital punishment read two fictitious studies, one of which showed the death penalty to deter homicides and the other of which showed no such deterrent effect (Lord, Ross, & Lepper, 1979). After reading both studies, the students were asked what changes had occurred in their attitudes toward capital punishment as a result of reading this new evidence, some of which confirmed and some of which disconfirmed their previous attitudes. Even though they read the same two studies, people who initially supported capital punishment reported that they *favored* it even more and people who initially opposed capital punishment reported that they *opposed* it even more. When asked about their reactions after the study, students whose attitudes had become more extreme claimed, "I knew that I might be biased and I was trying

Would protesters stop protesting if they read social science studies showing that they were wrong?

hard to be fair, but I never realized before how strong the evidence was on my side and how weak the evidence was on the other side." Although the tendency to evaluate mixed evidence as supporting initial attitudes is more pronounced among people whose thoughts and feelings are consistent rather than inconsistent, it contributes importantly to belief perseverance (Chaiken, Pomerantz, & Giner-Sorolla, 1995).

A follow-up study explored ways to keep attitudes from becoming more extreme in response to partially disconfirming evidence (Lord, Lepper, & Preston, 1985). One technique that did *not* work was to ask people to try harder to be fair and impartial. Students who received these instructions were slightly *more* likely than students who received no instructions to adopt more extreme attitudes after reading partially disconfirming evidence on capital punishment. When you try harder by using the same inappropriate strategy, you usually get the same results, only more so. The only effective remedy was to provide a different thinking strategy. Some students in the follow-up study were asked to consider how they would have evaluated each of the two death penalty studies if they had an initial attitude exactly opposite to their own. For these students, new evidence did not make attitudes more extreme. Belief perseverance might be less likely to lead to serious disagreements if people periodically reminded themselves to think about how new evidence might be evaluated by people who held opinions different from their own.

SUMMARY OF HOW ATTITUDES ARE FORMED AND MAINTAINED

Attitudes are formed through information, classical conditioning, instrumental conditioning, and modeling. Attitudes serve five functions: understanding events, expressing values, protecting self-esteem, maximizing rewards, and matching social situations. Attitudes that are formed through information may affect primarily the thoughts component and help us to understand events. Attitudes that are formed through classical conditioning may affect primarily the feelings component and help us to express values and protect self-esteem. Attitudes that are formed primarily through instrumental conditoning and modeling may affect primarily the actions component and help us to maximize rewards and match social situations.

Once formed, attitudes resist change by causing disconfirming evidence to be ignored, by generating causal explanations to support the underlying beliefs, and by "explaining away" disconfirming evidence so well that the attitude sometimes becomes more extreme.

WHEN DO ATTITUDES PREDICT BEHAVIOR?

It seems reasonable to expect all three components of an individual's attitude to lean toward the same side, whether positive or negative. Although we know that it is not impossible, it seems unlikely that the 1930s restaurant and hotel owners had 100 percent negative thoughts and feelings toward Chinese people, but took 100 percent positive actions. One attitude component might be stronger or more extremely held than the other two, as shown in Table 6.1, but the three components usually match each other fairly well. When people have positive or negative attitudes toward an attitude target, moreover, we expect these attitudes to predict whether they will behave positively or negatively toward the attitude target. Since the 1930s, however, social psychologists have discovered six factors that importantly affect whether attitudes predict behavior. The six factors, shown in Table 6.4, are thought-feeling consistency, subjective norms, specificity matching, direct experience, attitude accessibility, and introspection. You might want to use Table 6.4 as an organizing framework to follow the logic of the next six sections.

THOUGHT-FEELING CONSISTENCY

Attitudes are "stronger" and behaviors are more predictable when thoughts and feelings are consistent than when they are inconsistent with each other (Chaiken, et al., 1995). Suppose that Bob and Bill both had moderately negative attitudes toward Chinese people, but Bob's moderately negative attitude consisted of four moderately negative thoughts and feelings, whereas Bill's moderately negative attitude was an average of extremely negative thoughts and neutral or slightly positive feelings. We might more confidently predict that Bob would vote for a proposition that denied schooling to illegal immigrants than that Bill would vote for the proposition, even though they both had the same overall attitude, because Bob's thoughts and feelings were *more consistent with each other* than were Bill's thoughts and feelings.

Thought-feeling consistency (sometimes called "affective-cognitive consistency") occurs when thoughts and feelings about an attitude object are equally positive or equally negative. In two studies that tested the effects of thought-feeling consistency on behaviors, the researcher asked students about their *feelings* toward volunteering for psychology experiments, on a scale from very

| TABLE 6.4 | Six Factors That Affect Attitude-Behavior Consistency |

FACTORS THAT AFFECT HOW WELL ATTITUDES PREDICT BEHAVIOR	ATTITUDES PREDICT BEHAVIOR BETTER WHEN
Thought-feeling consistency	the person's thoughts and feelings are either both positive or both negative
Subjective norms	the person believes that important others will approve of the behavior
Specificity matching	the person's attitude and behavior are either both at a general level or both at a specific level
Direct experience	the person developed the attitude through direct personal experience with the attitude object
Attitude accessibility	the person has an attitude that comes easily to mind
Introspection	the person has recently introspected about feelings toward the attitude object and *not* about reasons for holding the attitude

favorable to very unfavorable (Norman, 1975). The researcher also asked students for their *thoughts* on volunteering to participate in psychology experiments, including how much volunteering would advance or block the student's goals. The students were then rank-ordered from most to least positive on feelings. They were also rank-ordered from most to least positive on thoughts. The researcher classified students who held roughly the same rank on both thoughts and feelings as high in thought-feeling consistency and classified students who held very different ranks (such as 3rd most positive on thoughts and 48th most positive on feelings) as low in thought-feeling consistency.

Three weeks later, for the measure of "behavior," a different investigator tried to recruit unpaid volunteers for a psychology experiment. In both studies it was relatively easy to predict the behavior of students who had high thought-feeling consistency. Those who had positive attitudes (combined thoughts and feelings) volunteered and showed up; those who had negative attitudes refused. For students who displayed low thought-feeling consistency, however, attitudes did not predict behavior. In this group, students who had negative attitudes toward volunteering were almost as likely to volunteer and to show up as were students who had positive attitudes toward volunteering. The effect of thought-feeling consistency on the predictability of behavior has been replicated several times (Chaiken & Baldwin, 1981). Interestingly, thought-feeling consistency is lower when a person responds to the actual object than when the person responds to a symbolic representation of the object, such as its name on an attitude scale. The difference between responding to an actual object and responding to a verbal label may partially explain why the hotel and restaurant proprietors reacted differently to the actual Chinese couple than to a question about "members of the Chinese race" on a questionnaire (Breckler, 1984; Breckler & Fried, 1993).

SUBJECTIVE NORMS

Many behaviors are performed in a social context. A person's attitude, whether positive or negative, may dictate one type of behavior and the perceived social norms may dictate an entirely different type of behavior. An attitude may predict what a person would *like* to do, without predicting what the person actually does in public.

The restaurant and hotel proprietors who greeted the professor's Chinese friends might have liked to turn them away, but they might have refrained from doing so because they feared that the Chinese couple would protest loudly and that a "scene" would upset the other patrons. The proprietors might have suspected that refusing service to a customer would violate **subjective norms,** which are an individual's subjective judgments about whether other people will approve of a behavior. Subjective norms matter, of course, only when we *care* what other people think (Ajzen & Fishbein, 1980). The auto camp proprietor who turned away the Chinese couple might not have cared in the least about subjective norms.

The **theory of reasoned action** shows how attitudes guide behavior through a reasoning process that takes into account both attitudes and subjective norms in deciding among alternative behaviors (Ajzen & Fishbein, 1980). As can be seen in the top panel of Figure 6.5, the theory of reasoned action holds that behavior is determined by the intention to behave in a given way. Behavioral intentions, in turn, are determined by both attitudes and subjective norms. This model of the attitude-behavior relationship is called "reasoned" because it assumes that people go through a conscious reasoning process to decide which of the possible behavioral alternatives they intend to enact in a specific situation.

In the theory of reasoned action, a person's attitude toward an action consists of the person's feelings about possible outcomes and the person's subjective norms consist of the person's assessments of whether important other people will approve. Subjective norms, of course, may differ from one culture to another, or even from one city to another (Fishbein, Chan, O'Reilly, Schnell, Wood, Beeker, & Cohn, 1992, 1993). In one demonstration of the theory, first-time mothers were asked, approximately two months before they gave birth, about the probable outcomes of breast-feeding versus bottle-feeding their babies and how important each outcome was to them (Manstead, Proffitt, & Smart, 1983). An expectant mother who had a positive attitude toward breast-feeding might say, for instance, that breast-feeding would establish a close bond between her and her baby and would protect the baby from infection, both of which were very important to her. The expectant mother might also say that, although breast-feeding would not allow the father to be as involved as would bottle-feeding, the father's involvement was relatively unimportant. An expectant mother who had a negative attitude toward breast-feeding might say that the important concerns were that breast-feeding would limit her social contacts, whereas bottle-feeding would be relatively trouble free and would allow the father to get involved. Attitudes were measured by multiplying the pros and cons by their respective importance weights and then summing.

The expectant mothers were also asked about their subjective norms for breast-feeding. "How much does your husband want you to breast-feed and

Figure 6.5

Top panel: The theory of reasoned action (Ajzen & Fishbein, 1980)
Bottom panel: The theory of planned behavior (Ajzen, 1985)

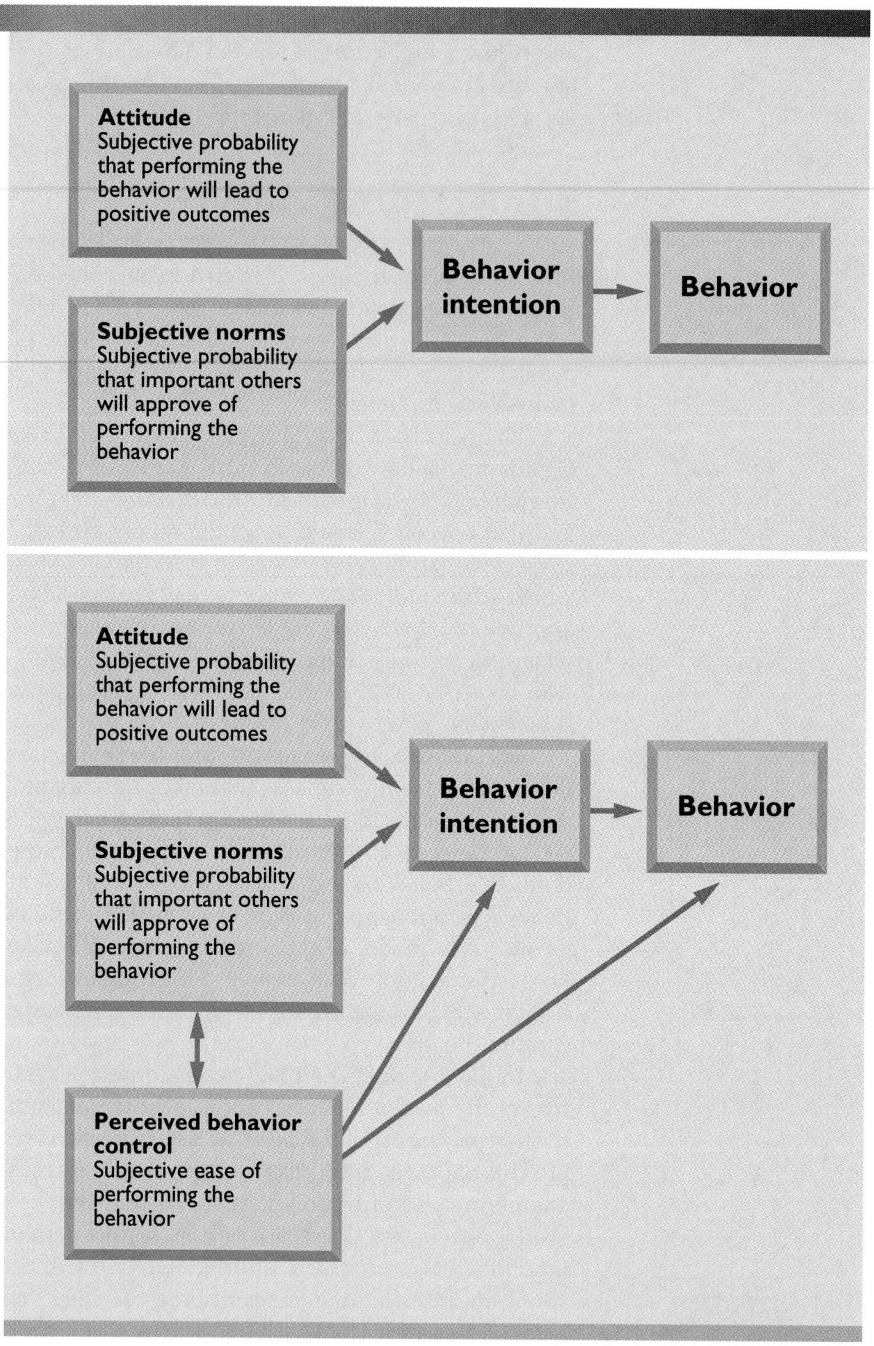

how much do you care what he wants?" "How much does your mother want you to breast-feed the baby and how much do you care what she wants?" "How about your closest female friend?" Subjective norms were measured by multiplying each person's desires by how important they were to the expectant mother and then summing.

As predicted by the theory of reasoned action, attitudes by themselves were good predictors of the women's intentions to breast-feed (a "behavioral intention"), and so were subjective norms. The best predictive power, however, came from combining attitudes with subjective norms. It took a combination of attitudes, subjective norms, and behavioral intentions to predict whether the mothers were still breast-feeding when their babies were six weeks old. The theory

How do new mothers decide whether to breast-feed or bottle-feed?

of reasoned action is useful for predicting a wide variety of important behaviors, including breast-feeding, getting exercise, recycling, dating, the use of contraceptives, and AIDS risk prevention (Bentler & Speckart, 1979; Cochran, Mays, Ciarletta, Caruso, & Mallon, 1992; Doll & Orth, 1993; Gallois, Kashima, Terry, McCamish, Timmins, & Chauvin, 1992; Pagel & Davidson, 1984; Vining & Ebreo, 1992; Winslow, Franzini, & Hwang, 1992).

The theory of reasoned action has a slightly more complicated version that is called the theory of planned behavior. The **theory of planned behavior,** as shown in the bottom panel of Figure 6.5, explicates how the effect of attitudes and subjective norms on behavior depends on the individual's subjective estimate of how much control he or she has over the behavior. As you can see in the figure, the theory of planned behavior differs from the theory of reasoned action in that it contains an additional factor of perceived behavior control (Ajzen, 1985). The theory of planned behavior recognizes that behavioral intentions differ in the extent to which the person believes that he or she has control over them. Perceived behavioral control might be limited by such factors as time, money, skills, and other resources. As people who make New Year's resolutions know, behavioral intentions do not always predict behavior, and goals are not always realized (Gollwitzer, 1993). Many overweight people have positive attitudes toward eating less to lose weight. They know that their families and best friends want them to eat less, they have sincere intentions to do so, and yet they continue to eat too much. Another example is getting an A in a college course. Many students have positive attitudes, subjective norms, and behavioral intentions and still do not get A's. A missing factor in both examples is perceived behavioral control. People often want to eat less and get better grades, but they do not feel capable of fulfilling their goals. They meet an obstacle that they cannot control and they redefine the goal or decide that they are "close enough" (Cochran & Tesser, in press).

The theory of reasoned action alone has difficulty in predicting actual behavior in such situations, but when perceived behavior control is added to the theory of reasoned action to make it into the theory of planned behavior, actions like eating less, getting better grades, and health-protective behaviors such as breast self-exams can be predicted very well (Ajzen & Madden, 1986; Madden, Ellen, & Ajzen, 1992; McCaul, Sandgren, O'Neill, & Hinsz, 1993; Schifter & Ajzen, 1985). People who believe they *can* turn their intentions into behaviors are likely to do so (Gollwitzer, 1990; Steffen, Sternberg, Teegarden, & Shepherd, 1994). When perceived behavioral control is complete (when the person perceives no uncontrollable interference), the theory of reasoned action and the theory of planned behavior are identical.

■ SPECIFICITY MATCHING

A second important factor that influences the link between attitudes and behavior is the match between how specific the attitude is and how specific the behavior is (Ajzen & Fishbein, 1977). General attitudes or behaviors are directed at an entire category of people, objects, or actions. Specific attitudes or behaviors are directed at specific people, objects, or actions. General attitudes are not precise enough to predict specific behaviors, because judgments about general cases differ in many ways from judgments about specific cases (Sherman, Beike, & Ryalls, in press; Wicker & August, 1995). Restaurant and hotel owners in 1930s California might have had negative attitudes toward Chinese people as a whole, but they might not have had negative attitudes toward serving a specific well-dressed Chinese couple at a specific time when they were too busy to argue with potential paying customers.

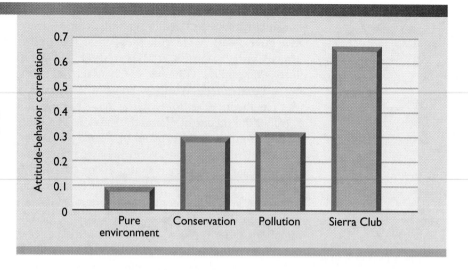

FIGURE 6.6

The more specific the attitude, the better it predicts behavior.

Graph shows correlation between four attitudes and the behavior of helping the Sierra Club (Weigel, Vernon, & Tognacci, 1974).

The **specificity matching hypothesis** illustrates how attitude-behavior consistency is greater when the attitude and the behavior match rather than mismatch in how general versus specific they are. In one study, 60 residents of a city in the western United States were asked about four of their attitudes: toward having a pure environment, controlling pollution, conserving natural resources, and helping the Sierra Club (Weigel, Vernon, & Tognacci, 1974). Five months later, a representative of the Sierra Club contacted the same residents. The club representative asked them to make a donation, to volunteer service on a club committee, and to join the club. As shown in Figure 6.6, general attitudes toward having a pure environment did little to predict which residents responded positively versus negatively. More specific attitudes (toward controlling pollution and conserving natural resources) predicted residents' reactions better. The *most* specific attitude, toward helping the Sierra Club, predicted very well who would help and who would not.

The Sierra Club study showed that attitudes toward specific activities predict "single act behaviors" better than do attitudes toward abstractions. Helping the Sierra Club is a single, well-defined act. Having a pure environment is a more abstract goal that might be realized in many different ways. Residents who had positive attitudes toward a pure environment might have demonstrated their attitudes in ways other than joining the Sierra Club. Similarly, the 1930s restaurant and hotel proprietors might have gone out of their way to treat Chinese people poorly when they were not at work. They might have treated Chinese people well only when the Chinese people were customers who had money to spend. The professor might have happened to observe the single act that was not dictated by the overall negative attitude.

A corollary of the specificity matching hypothesis is that general attitudes, which imply multiple acts, guide behavior when the behavior in question involves many activities rather than one activity. Several studies have shown that general attitudes may not predict single acts very well, but that when the single acts are combined into an overall "multiple-act behavior," general attitudes predict behavior very well (Ajzen, 1987).

An additional corollary of the specificity matching hypothesis is that general attitudes may predict behavior toward some specific targets but not others. The restaurant and hotel proprietors may have had negative attitudes to-

How would you predict
who will help to clean
the environment?

ward serving "members of the Chinese race" in general, but not the specific Chinese couple who accompanied the professor. Their general attitudes toward Chinese individuals may have been composed of more specific attitudes toward various types of Chinese, none of whom matched very well the couple who appeared in their establishments. In reporting the results, the professor wondered "Did the proprietors picture Chinese only as laborers in pigtails and coolie hats, and not ever recognize the couple before them as Chinese?" (LaPiere, 1934, pp. 201–202).

We should not expect general attitudes toward entire minority or other negatively stereotyped groups to guide behavior toward specific group members who are perceived as atypical. In a relevant study, male college students provided their attitudes toward male homosexuals (Lord, Lepper, & Mackie, 1984). The students also provided "profiles" of what they perceived to be the "typical" homosexual. Two months later, an experimenter gave these college men an opportunity to interact with or to avoid interacting with some "visiting students." One of the visitors, "John B.," was said to have on the wall of his dorm room a photograph of himself waving a placard during a recent Gay Rights rally in New York City.

John B. also had characteristics that either matched or mismatched the individual student's description of a "typical" homosexual. If a particular student described the typical homosexual as "creative, relaxed, and non-athletic," for instance, the experimenter told the student either that John B. had all of those traits or that John B. was not creative, was nervous, and was very athletic. Students who were led to believe that John B. matched their profile of the typical homosexual behaved in line with their attitudes toward homosexuals. Their positive or negative attitudes dictated whether they were willing to spend time with John, show him around campus, and introduce him to their friends. Students who were led to believe that John B. was "atypical" were less likely to behave in line with their attitudes. Attitude-behavior consistency is similarly affected even when match or mismatch to the "typical" member is on physical rather than personality characteristics and even when the characteristics are totally irrelevant to the reason for initially developing a positive or negative attitude (Lord, Desforges, Ramsey, Trezza, & Lepper, 1991).

DIRECT EXPERIENCE

Another limitation on attitudes predicting behavior occurs when the person has developed an attitude vicariously, without having much (or perhaps any) direct personal experience with the attitude object. Restaurant and hotel proprietors in the 1930s, for example, had very limited direct experience with people of Chinese origin. The only Chinese they were likely to see were poor immigrants working on farms. Their attitudes were presumably based on indirect rather than direct experience. In several studies, attitudes that were based on direct personal experience predicted behavior better than attitudes that were not based on direct personal experience (Fazio & Zanna, 1981). The experimenters in one study tried to predict from college students' attitudes toward volunteering in psychology experiments whether the students would agree to participate in a specific experiment. Attitudes predicted behavior more accurately for students who had previous experience as experimental subjects than for students who had never been in a psychology experiment (Fazio & Zanna, 1978).

There are several reasons why attitude-behavior consistency is higher when the attitude is based on direct rather than indirect experience. One reason is that people who have had previous direct experience with the attitude object know more about it and have more accurate information. In a representative study, the investigators tried to predict whether elderly veterans would follow doctor's orders and get a recommended flu shot. The veterans' attitudes toward flu shots were much more likely to predict getting the shot for veterans who had obtained flu shots before (and knew more about the experience) than for veterans who had no previous flu shots (Davidson, Yantis, Norwood, & Montano, 1985).

A second reason for the impact of direct experience on attitude-behavior consistency is derived from the theory of reasoned action. If you have done something before, you know for yourself whether you enjoyed it or not, so you place less weight on subjective norms about what other people want you to do than you might if you had never tried the action for yourself. Consistent with this reasoning, investigators tried to use attitudes of junior high and high school students to predict whether individual students would take up smoking cigarettes during the next three years. Previous direct experience of having tried a cigarette greatly increased the predictive power of attitudes but had no effect on the predictive power of subjective norms (Sherman, Presson, Chassin, Bensenberg, Corty, & Olshavsky, 1982).

ATTITUDE ACCESSIBILITY

The restaurant and hotel proprietors might also have served the Chinese couple because their attitudes toward Chinese people did not come easily to mind when the couple appeared at their establishments. One of the major themes of this book is the "two-stage process" idea that everyday social thinking involves a spontaneous initial reaction to new information, followed by a relatively deliberative adjustment. Some of people's reactions are relatively spontaneous and others are more deliberative (Beikke & Sherman, 1994; Brewer,

1988; Devine, 1989; Epstein et al., 1992; Fiske & Neuberg, 1990; Gilbert, 1991; Smith, 1994). For some attitude objects, people have such a strong spontaneous reaction that the attitude elicits a corresponding behavior "automatically" (Fazio, 1990). This spontaneous attitude-behavior link occurs especially when people are not motivated to devote careful consideration to the specific circumstances. For other attitude objects, the spontaneous reaction is not as strong and people are willing and able to "make adjustments" to their behavior (Schuette & Fazio, 1995). Thus we might expect different levels of attitude-behavior consistency depending on whether the attitude comes to mind spontaneously.

Attitude accessibility is the ease with which an attitude comes to mind (Fazio, 1986, 1989, 1990). The auto-camp proprietor who turned away the professor and his friends, for instance, might have had a negative attitude come to mind "automatically" at the mere mention or presence of a Chinese person (Bargh, Chaiken, Govender, & Pratto, 1992; Chaiken & Bargh, 1993; Fazio, 1993). Attitude accessibility may underlie the effects on attitude-behavior consistency of subjective norms, specificity matching, and direct experience (Fazio, 1986, 1989, 1990, 1995; Kallgren & Wood, 1986). If, as shown in Figure 6.5, behaviors and behavioral intentions are determined by a combination of attitudes and subjective norms about what is socially acceptable, then attitudes may predominate over subjective norms when the attitude comes easily to mind. Attitudes may be overwhelmed by subjective norms, however, when the attitude does not come easily to mind. Similarly, a typical instance of a category may be more likely to bring an attitude to mind than an atypical instance. In addition, attitudes that are formed on direct personal experience might come to mind more easily than attitudes that are formed only through indirect experience. When viewed from this perspective, attitude accessibility is a key mechanism that lies at the heart of the other previously discussed determinants of attitude-behavior consistency.

This reasoning about the effects of attitude accessibility suggested several interesting experiments (Fazio, Chen, McDonel, & Sherman, 1982; Fazio, Herr, & Olney, 1984; Fazio, Sanbonmatsu, Powell, & Kardes, 1986; Fazio & Williams, 1986; Powell & Fazio, 1984). One such experiment used a procedure almost identical to the study of belief perseverance that was described earlier in this chapter, in which students judged death penalty studies differently depending on the students' initial attitudes. In the follow-up experiment on attitude accessibility, students indicated their attitudes toward the death penalty by pressing one of five keys on a computer keyboard (Houston & Fazio, 1989). The keys were labeled on a 5-point scale from "strongly opposed" to "strongly in favor." The computer recorded not only each student's attitude position, but also how *quickly* that student answered the questions. Quick answers mean that the attitude comes easily to mind (Bassili, in press). At each point on the attitude scale, the students were divided into those who answered relatively quickly and those who answered relatively slowly. Even among students who held exactly the same attitude, students who had relatively accessible attitudes (answered quickly) were more likely than students who had relatively inaccessible attitudes (answered slowly) to let their attitudes bias their judgments about the two death penalty studies.

In a second experiment, the investigators *manipulated* attitude accessibility by having one group of students "rehearse" their attitudes more frequently than did another group (Houston & Fazio, 1989). Some students expressed their attitudes toward the death penalty six times on six semantic differential scales (for example, "approve/disapprove," "good/bad," "wise/foolish"). Other students expressed their attitudes toward the death penalty only once. The hypothesis was that students who had expressed their attitudes six times would,

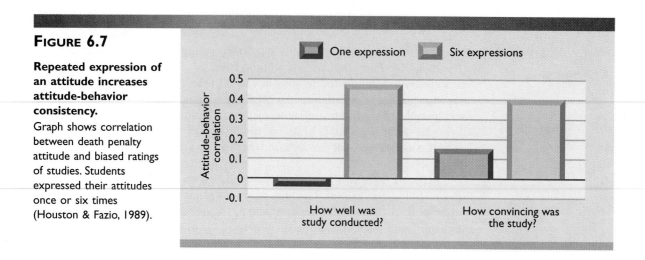

FIGURE 6.7

Repeated expression of an attitude increases attitude-behavior consistency.
Graph shows correlation between death penalty attitude and biased ratings of studies. Students expressed their attitudes once or six times (Houston & Fazio, 1989).

at least temporarily, have more accessible attitudes than would students who had expressed their attitudes only once.

As Figure 6.7 shows, the hypothesis was confirmed. Students who expressed their attitudes six times displayed greater attitude-behavior consistency in judging the death penalty studies than did students who expressed their attitudes once. Experiencing the connection between an attitude and its attitude object makes the connection easier to bring to mind, which in turn increases the probability that people's attitudes will predict their behavior (Fazio, 1995). Although repeated expression also increases attitude extremity, repeated expression affects attitude-behavior consistency primarily because people judge the importance of their attitudes by how quickly those attitudes come to mind (Downing, Judd, & Brauer, 1992; Roese & Olson, 1994). Low self-monitors, as discussed in this chapter and in Chapter 5, are especially likely to regard their internal values as important guides to behavior, so they are also more likely than high self-monitors to have their attitude-behavior consistency affected by repeatedly expressing the attitude (DeBono & Snyder, 1995).

Accessible attitudes are also very functional. In several studies, experimenters asked students who had either accessible or inaccessible attitudes to make attitude-relevant decisions (Blascovich, Ernst, Tomaka, Kelsey, Salomon, & Fazio, 1993). Students who had differentially accessible attitudes about paintings had to choose, for example, which of two abstract paintings they preferred (Fazio, Blascovich, & Driscoll, 1992). The investigators took physiological recordings while the students were making their decisions, because making difficult decisions increases blood pressure and other signs of physiological stress. As the investigators predicted, students who had relatively accessible attitudes made attitude-relevant discriminations faster, showed fewer signs of physiological stress while making their decisions, and made better decisions than did students who had relatively inaccessible attitudes. The more accessible the attitude, the better it is at helping people to approach or avoid attitude objects that might have positive or negative consequences for them (Roskos-Ewoldson & Fazio, 1992).

INTROSPECTION

Mentally rehearsing our attitudes, however, does not always increase attitude-behavior consistency (Tesser, Martin, & Mendolia, 1994). Certain ways of thinking about or introspecting on our attitudes disrupt attitude-behavior consistency. In one study of college students' dating relationships, some students who had been going steady were asked to introspect on the *reasons* why they liked their dating partners. Other students, who had also been going steady, were not asked to introspect (Wilson, Dunn, Bybee, Hyman, & Rotondo, 1984). All students then reported their current attitudes toward their dating relationship. Current attitudes were used to predict whether they would still be going out with their dating partner several months later. For students who did *not* engage in introspection, current attitudes predicted the future of the relationship very well. Those who had the most positive attitudes toward their current dating relationship were most likely to be still dating months later. Those who had the least positive attitudes toward their current dating relationship were most likely to have separated. For students who introspected about their reasons for liking their dating partners, however, there was almost no attitude-behavior consistency. It proved virtually impossible to predict from their current attitudes to the future of the relationship.

Many additional studies have provided strong convergent evidence that introspecting about our attitudes can disrupt attitude-behavior consistency for attitudes about dating partners, intellectual puzzles, political candidates, beverages, and other attitude objects (Wilson & Dunn, 1986; Wilson, Dunn, Kraft, & Lisle, 1989; Wilson & Kraft, 1993; Wilson, Kraft, & Dunn, 1989). Researchers have also discovered that introspection may affect attitudes, but it has no effect on behavior. In the study of dating couples, for instance, there was no difference between the students who engaged in introspection and the students who did not engage in introspection in how long their relationships lasted. Introspection did not uniformly cause students to say to themselves "Now that I

Would couples still be dating if they stopped to think about why they like each other?

think of it, I can't come up with many good reasons for going out with him (or her)." Instead, careful analysis revealed that in this and other similar studies, introspection altered attitudes without changing behaviors. Some of the students adopted more positive attitudes and some adopted more negative attitudes, but neither changed their behavior.

Introspecting about reasons might change attitudes by emphasizing the thoughts component. A person like Ted (in Table 6.1), whose thoughts about the Chinese were more negative than his feelings, might shift to an even more negative attitude if introspecting about his reasons focused his attention on his 100% negative thoughts and away from his 50% negative feelings. Similarly, a person like Fred (in Table 6.1), whose feelings about the Chinese were more negative than his thoughts, might shift to a *less* negative attitude if introspecting about his reasons focused his attention on his 50% negative thoughts and away from his 100% negative feelings. The components themselves would be unaffected. The only change would be in the weight given to each component in assessing the overall attitude.

This explanation of introspection implies that focusing on feelings might have an opposite effect on attitude-behavior consistency than focusing on reasons. This hypothesis was supported in two studies (Wilson & Dunn, 1986). In the first study, students who were waiting in line for dinner at a college cafeteria were asked to introspect on either their *reasons* for liking various beverages or their *feelings* about the beverages. Attitudes toward the different beverages were good predictors of which beverage a student chose to have with dinner when the students did not introspect. They were even better predictors when the students introspected about their *feelings* toward the beverages. The predictive power of attitudes was severely disrupted, however, when the students introspected about their *reasons* for liking or not liking each beverage. The second study found similar results for introspecting about reasons versus feelings toward various types of intellectual puzzles and the behavior of playing with the puzzles during free time. For behaviors like choosing a beverage or playing with a puzzle for fun, introspecting about the reasons for holding an attitude emphasizes the thoughts component and decreases attitude-behavior consistency, whereas introspecting about emotional reactions to the attitude object emphasizes the feelings component and increases attitude-behavior consistency (Tesser, Leone, & Clary, 1978).

Behaviors such as playing with puzzles for fun and drinking a particular type of beverage might be characterized as *consummatory* behaviors. In consummatory behaviors, we consume or use the attitude object for the pleasure that comes from enjoying the object for its own sake (Millar & Tesser, 1992). Other behaviors, however, are more *instrumental*. We use the attitude object as a tool or "instrument," as a means to an end (Millar & Tesser, 1992). Limiting an infant's sugar intake, using seat belts, and performing a testicular self-exam are all examples of instrumental rather than consummatory behaviors (Beale & Manstead, 1991; Brubaker & Fowler, 1990; Mittal, 1988; Steffen, 1990). Similarly, some dating relationships, some types of aggression, and some types of helping seem more consummatory and some seem more instrumental (Millar & Tesser, in press).

Consummatory behaviors might be driven primarily by feelings ("Does this beverage really taste great?"), whereas instrumental behaviors might be driven primarily by thoughts ("Does limiting sugar intake improve my baby's health?") (Millar & Tesser, 1992). If so, introspecting about *reasons* might increase the attitude-behavior consistency of instrumental behaviors (which are driven by thoughts) and might decrease the attitude-behavior consistency of consummatory behaviors (which are driven by feelings). Introspecting about *feelings,* in contrast, might increase the attitude-behavior consistency of consummatory behaviors and decrease the attitude-behavior consistency of instrumental behaviors.

In a study that tested these predictions, students gained direct experience by working on five types of intellectual puzzles at a computer terminal (Millar & Tesser, 1986). Some students were instructed to "go over in your mind what it is about each puzzle that makes you think it is likable or not" (introspecting about reasons). Other students were instructed to "go over in your mind how you are feeling while you perform each type of puzzle" (introspecting about feelings). Some students from each group were told that the puzzles were "useful in developing analytic ability" and that they would later be taking a test of analytic ability (instrumental behavior emphasized). Other students from each group were told that they would later be taking a test of social sensitivity (consummatory behavior emphasized, because the puzzles would not help scores on social sensitivity and would thus be played with only for personal enjoyment). After the students provided their attitudes toward the different puzzles, the experimenter unexpectedly left the room for 10 minutes, telling the students to stay at the computer terminals, where they could "occupy your time" by "working more puzzles if you like." The experimenter did not tell the students that the computer was recording how much time they spent on each type of puzzle, which was the primary measure of "behavior."

As shown in Figure 6.8, students who were led to construe working with the puzzles as an instrumental activity (a means to the end of preparing for the analytic ability test) displayed greater attitude-behavior consistency when they had been introspecting on their reasons than when they had been introspecting on their feelings. Introspecting about reasons brought out the thoughts component, which matched a logically based decision about the puzzles' instrumental value. Exactly the opposite result occurred for consummatory behavior, where introspecting about feelings produced greater attitude-behavior consistency than introspecting about reasons. Introspecting about feelings brought out the feelings component, which matched an emotionally based, consummatory decision about whether the puzzles were fun to do for their own sake.

The effects of introspection are limited to attitudes for which thoughts and feelings are inconsistent with each other before introspection (Millar & Tesser, 1989). Also, introspecting about reasons is more likely to disrupt newly formed

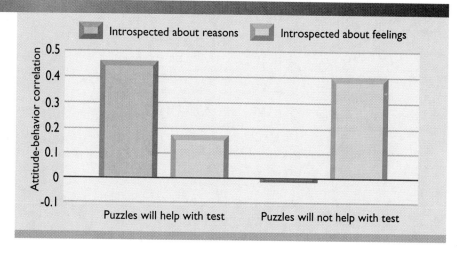

FIGURE 6.8

Introspecting about reasons differs from introspecting about feelings.

Graph shows attitude-behavior correlation when students introspected about thoughts or feelings and believed the behavior would or would not help them (Millar & Tesser, 1986).

attitudes, for which feelings still predominate, than to disrupt longer-held attitudes, for which we may have thought about the "pros" and "cons" many times. In the study of dating couples, for instance, introspecting about reasons disrupted attitude-behavior consistency for couples who had been dating only a short time, but had no effect on the attitude-behavior consistency of couples who had been dating for a long time (Wilson et al., 1989).

In conclusion, it is important in analyzing attitude-behavior consistency to match the type of behavior we are trying to predict with the attitude component that predominates. Attitudes that are based primarily on thoughts are likely to predict instrumental behaviors better than are attitudes that are based primarily on feelings. Attitudes that are based primarily on feelings are likely to predict consummatory behaviors better than are attitudes that are based primarily on thoughts (Greenwald, 1968a; Millar & Tesser, 1989). The restaurant and hotel owners in the 1930s study had little direct experience with Chinese patrons, so they may have answered the professor's attitude questionnaire with a "gut feeling" attitude, but their behavior was probably constrained by the instrumental considerations of accepting versus turning away paying customers during a time of economic depression.

SUMMARY OF WHEN ATTITUDES PREDICT BEHAVIOR

People's attitudes are more likely to predict their behavior (attitude-behavior consistency) when the thoughts and feelings components of an attitude match rather than mismatch. Attitude-behavior consistency is sometimes low because individuals choose their behaviors not only from their attitudes, but also from subjective norms about what is considered the socially approved way to behave. The way they actually behave is not necessarily the way they would like to behave. Attitude-behavior consistency is unlikely when the attitude involves feelings about an entire category of actions or people but the behavior in question is a specific action directed at a specific person. Attitude-behavior consistency is more likely when the attitude is based on previous direct personal experience than when it is not. Attitude-behavior consistency is also more likely when the attitude comes to mind easily than when it does not.

Introspecting about the feelings component of an attitude *increases* the predictability of consummatory behavior toward an attitude object. Introspecting about the thoughts component of an attitude *decreases* the predictability of consummatory behavior toward an attitude object. This effect of introspection is reversed when the behavior involves using the attitude object as an instrumental means to an end rather than as an end in itself. The reversal occurs because the feelings component of an attitude is more closely linked to consummatory or emotionally driven behavior, whereas the thoughts component of an attitude is more closely linked to instrumental or thought-driven behavior.

Attitude Change

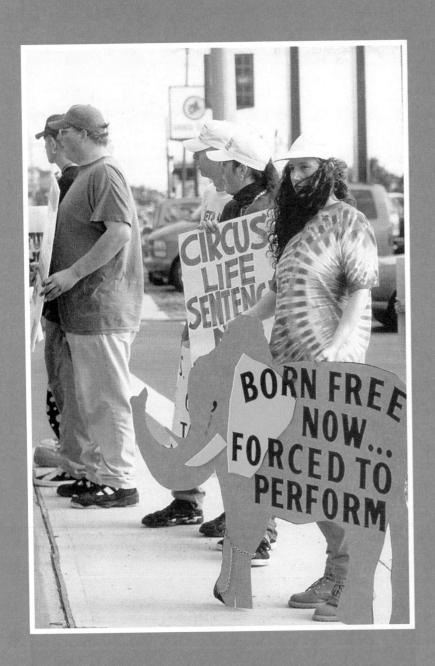

How much impact does "expert" testimony have on the verdict in jury trials? Imagine, for instance, that you were on the jury in the trial of a woman named Sally, who freely admitted that she shot and killed her husband. According to Sally, her husband had been beating her more and more severely for years. On the day in question, he started beating her in the morning. At one point, he shoved a loaded gun in her face and threatened to pull the trigger. After leaving the room for an hour, the husband returned and started beating Sally again. Fearing for her life, she picked up the gun and shot him. The prosecution argued that Sally intended to kill her husband. They presented evidence that Sally called her husband back after the first beating, chased her husband with the gun when he tried to get away, and gave the police no reason for her actions.

Sally's attorney suspected that jurors might bring to the trial certain biases and misperceptions. To find Sally not guilty of murder, jurors would have to conclude that she thought her life was in imminent danger and that the force she used to avert the danger was reasonable rather than excessive. Jurors, however, do not approach such cases with open minds. Many potential jurors erroneously believe that battered women provoke the abuse, that they feel free to leave the relationship if they really want to, and that they secretly enjoy being beaten (Dodge & Greene, 1991; Walker, Thyfault, & Browne, 1982). When jurors bring such preexisting beliefs and attitudes to the courtroom, they are likely to evaluate the evidence in a biased way (see Chapter 6). They might be biased in deciding ambiguous issues such as why, if the relationship was so abusive, the battered woman did not seek help earlier, whether she really believed her life was in danger, and whether deadly force was warranted, especially in cases where the woman killed her attacker after rather than during a beating.

To try to change jurors' preexisting attitudes, Sally's attorney asked the judge to allow an expert to testify on the "battered woman syndrome" (Kinsports, 1988; Walker, 1984). The expert would testify that male violence against women is an urgent social problem in the United States, Canada, and Western Europe and that each year millions of women are beaten, battered, and abused by their boyfriends, husbands, or ex-husbands (Mercy & Saltzman, 1987). Sometimes, the violence escalates until the woman kills her abusive partner (Schuller & Vidmar, 1992). Battering usually begins with a "minor abusive incident" stage, in which the woman tries to placate her attacker, followed by an "acute battering" stage, followed in turn by a "contrition stage" in which the male attacker expresses remorse and is extremely loving. The contrition stage encourages the woman to stay in the relationship, but then the three-stage cycle repeats itself, with a slightly higher level and frequency of violence (Walker, 1984). The woman is gradually drawn into a relationship so threatening that she fears for her own life, or her children's lives, if she tries to leave.

Some courts allow expert testimony about the battered woman syndrome in cases of women who are accused of killing their husbands, but others do not. Do you think that expert testimony might affect your verdict in the case described? To find out how expert testimony affects jury members, three social psychologists had students at a United States university listen to a 30-minute audiotaped summary of an actual court case that was essentially as described (Schuller, Smith, & Olson, 1994). As part of the case summary, some students (but not others) heard a psychologist testify about the battered woman syndrome. The psychologist discussed the syndrome, but did not refer to the specific case on trial. Figure 7.1 shows the impact of this expert testimony on verdicts rendered by male and female mock jurors. Expert testimony had no impact on the verdicts of male jurors. It had considerable impact, though, on the verdicts of female jurors. Persuasive communications sometimes have a dramatic impact on people's attitudes and decisions. At other times they have little or no impact. In this chapter, we discuss the conditions under which attempts at attitude change do and do not succeed. We also show that persuasive communications such as expert testimony represent just one of three major avenues to attitude change.

As Chapter 6 describes, attitudes have three components—thoughts, feelings, and actions (Breckler, 1984; Greenwald, 1968a; Insko & Schopler, 1967; Katz & Stotland, 1959; Krech & Crutchfield, 1948; Olson & Zanna, 1993; Ostrom, 1969; Rosenberg & Hovland, 1960; Smith, 1947; Triandis, 1971; Zanna & Rempel, 1988). Thoughts about an attitude object come primarily from what we know (information). Feelings come primarily from whether the attitude object has been paired with positive or negative events (classical conditioning). Actions come primarily from what we have been rewarded for doing (instrumental conditioning) or seen other people do (modeling). The three components tend to be consistent with each other, so changing one of the three components might cause changes in the other two (Eagly & Chaiken, 1993). One way of changing attitudes is to provide new information to alter the balance of "pro" and "con" thoughts that a person has about the attitude object—for instance, to have an expert testify in a court case. A second way of changing attitudes is to pair the attitude object consistently with positive or negative events to alter people's feelings. A third way of changing attitudes is to use selective rewards and modeling to change people's actions. The best procedure, where possible, is to use all three approaches. This chapter has three major divisions that correspond to the three approaches. As we shall see, changing attitudes is

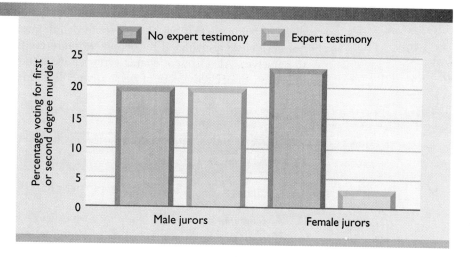

FIGURE 7.1

Expert testimony changes some attitudes but not others.

Graph shows percentage of men and women who found a woman guilty of murder, with and without expert testimony on the "battered woman syndrome" (Schuller, Smith, & Olson, 1994).

more difficult than one might expect from the simpleminded proposition that changing one of the three components alters the other two (Eagly & Chaiken, 1993). Social psychologists have gone far toward discovering how to change attitudes, but many conceptual problems remain to be solved.

CAN WE CHANGE ATTITUDES BY CHANGING PEOPLE'S THOUGHTS?

Persuasive communications try to change thoughts about a person, thing, or event by providing new information. People assume that when thoughts about a person, thing, or event change, feelings and actions are likely to follow. It is almost impossible to avoid persuasive communications on television, radio, in newspapers, magazines, junk mail, and telephone solicitation. These communications offer presumably persuasive information about commercial products, political candidates, AIDS, safe sex, getting exercise, breast self-examination, wearing seat belts, smoking, drug and alcohol abuse, international trade agreements, military intervention, and other topics. This section of the chapter examines three basic questions about persuasive communications. First, what qualities make a communication persuasive? Second, how does persuasion occur? Third, when do people resist persuasive communications?

WHAT QUALITIES MAKE A COMMUNICATION PERSUASIVE?

Three important factors determine the effectiveness of a persuasive communication: the source (who says it), the content (what they say), and the audience (to whom they say it) (Hovland, Lumsdaine, & Sheffield, 1949). These three factors are summarized in Table 7.1 and described in greater detail in the next three sections.

■ SOURCE

Why do television commercials for pain remedies so often have their message delivered by a medical doctor? Why do commercials for many products use stunningly attractive models? Why do the men and women who rave about laundry detergents always look like the "person next door"? The answer to these questions is that we believe some people more than others. We tend to be more easily persuaded by people who are credible, attractive, and similar to ourselves. Also, source characteristics have interesting delayed or "sleeper" effects on the effectiveness of persuasive communications.

TABLE 7.1	Source, Content, and Audience Factors That Make Communications Persuasive
SOURCE	
credibility	we believe communicators who are expert and trustworthy
attractiveness	we believe communicators who are physically attractive
similarity	we believe communicators who are similar to us
sleeper effect	we believe strong arguments from a noncredible source more after a delay than we do immediately, because we forget the source
CONTENT	
arguments	we believe communicators who use many supporting arguments, admit and rebut opposing arguments that would have occurred to us, and do not try to change our opinions drastically
appeals to emotion	we believe communicators who arouse fear and tell us what to do to reduce our fear
AUDIENCE	
intelligence	very intelligent audiences under-stand the arguments better, but they are also better able to shoot down arguments
gender	women are easier to persuade about "male" topics, and men are easier to persuade about "female" topics
age	18-25-year-olds change their attitudes more than do older adults, because they are typically experiencing greater life changes
culture	cultures differ in whether the more effective communications emphasize individual goals or group goals

CREDIBILITY   Communicator credibility affects the impact of persuasive communications even when the communication content does not vary. People are more persuaded by a high credibility source than a low credibility source. One way in which the person who delivers the communication enjoys high credibility is by being an expert on the topic. Jurors might regard a clinical psychologist, for instance, as an expert on the "battered woman syndrome," especially if the psychologist has strong credentials and uses language that conveys authority (Hurwitz, Miron, & Johnson, 1992). In one study of communicator expertise, students read powerful arguments that people need far fewer than eight hours' sleep per night to function effectively (Bochner & Insko, 1966). Some of the students were led to believe that the communication was written by an eminent physiologist. The others were led to believe that the communication was written by a YMCA director. Although the arguments were exactly the same in both cases, students who were led to believe that the source was an eminent physiologist were more persuaded than were students who thought the source was a YMCA director. The students accepted the arguments more when the communication was written by an expert than when it was written by a well-intentioned nonexpert.

A second way in which the person who delivers the communication might enjoy high credibility or suffer low credibility is by being perceived as either trustworthy or untrustworthy. People who argue for actions that would benefit them are not trusted and suffer from low credibility, whereas people who argue for actions that are contrary to their own vested interests enjoy very high trust and credibility. In one study of self-interest, a convicted criminal argued that the ability of police to maintain law and order is more important than the "rights" of criminals. The criminal was more persuasive than a judge who used the same arguments, because the criminal was arguing against self-interest and was thus perceived as especially trustworthy (Walster, Aronson, & Abrahams, 1966).

ATTRACTIVENESS   Another characteristic that influences the impact of persuasive communications is source attractiveness. Automobile advertisers, jeans makers, soft drink companies, and beer distributors know exactly what they are doing when they feature attractive members of both sexes in their television commercials. Persuasive arguments of all types (especially those that address emotional issues) have more impact when they come from a physically attractive source than from a relatively unattractive one (Dion & Stein, 1978; Pallak, Murroni, & Koch, 1983).

In one study of communicator attractiveness, for instance, physically attractive students were better able to persuade passersby on campus to complete a questionnaire and to sign a petition than were their less physically attractive peers (Chaiken, 1979). Source attractiveness may work on both thoughts and feelings, by pairing the persuasive arguments with a positive event such as the appearance of a beautiful person. People use the rule of thumb that "what is beautiful is good," so communications delivered by attractive sources benefit from the positive association (Dion, Berscheid, & Walster, 1972).

SIMILARITY   A third important determinant of attitude change is similarity. We are often more persuaded by people similar to ourselves than by glamorous experts. Television commercials for products such as laundry detergents deliberately feature actors who seem like "ordinary folks." People who buy such products do not see themselves as especially beautiful or talented. They have more in common with and are more likely to be persuaded by a communication from "one of their own" than from a celebrity who has probably never done his or her own laundry.

One study pitted source similarity against expertise and showed that similarity is, in some cases, more important than credibility (Brock, 1965). In the study, a paint store salesperson approached a customer who had just decided between two brands of paint and tried to get the customer to buy the other brand. The salesperson told the customer "I see you're deciding between those two brands. I've tried them both and I personally prefer the other brand." For half of the customers the salesperson continued, "I bought two gallons and painted a couple of rooms with it." For the other half, he continued, "I bought 40 gallons and painted some property that I own." Having bought 40 gallons made the salesperson seem like more of an expert, but it also made the salesperson dissimilar to the average customer who was looking for a gallon or two for a minor project. Customers were more swayed in their choice of paint by a salesperson who was perceived as similar to them than by a salesperson who was perceived as dissimilar. When we perceive people as similar rather than dissimilar to us, we like them more and we believe them more (Byrne, 1971; Roskos-Ewoldsen & Fazio, 1992).

Would you hire this man to sell jeans, or to sell laundry detergent?

"SLEEPER" EFFECT Highly credible, attractive, similar sources increase a communication's effectiveness; low credibility, unattractive, dissimilar sources decrease a communication's effectiveness. These factors, however, affect persuasion in different ways immediately after the message than later, after a delay. The **sleeper effect** occurs when strong arguments, initially unpersuasive because they came from a disreputable source, become more persuasive over time (Hovland, et al., 1949). Arguments that receive an extra "boost" because they come from a respected source lose their impact over time. Conversely, arguments that are negatively evaluated because they come from a suspect source can have greater effect after a delay, when the source has been forgotten but the arguments still carry weight.

In the classic sleeper effect study, students read a communication that contained very strong arguments (Hovland, & Weiss, 1952). The communication was attributed either to a highly credible expert or to a low credible source. As shown in Figure 7.2, immediately after they read the communication, students in the high credible source condition were far more persuaded than were students in the low credible source condition. Four weeks later, however, students in the low credible source condition were as persuaded as students in the high credible source condition. Low credible source students seemed to have awakened from a sleep and belatedly admitted that the arguments were compelling. The sleeper effect occurs when communication recipients initially

FIGURE 7.2

A "sleeper effect" occurs when a persuasive communication is initially ignored because of its source but has a delayed effect.

Graph shows attitude change immediately or four weeks after message from one of two sources (Hovland & Weiss, 1952).

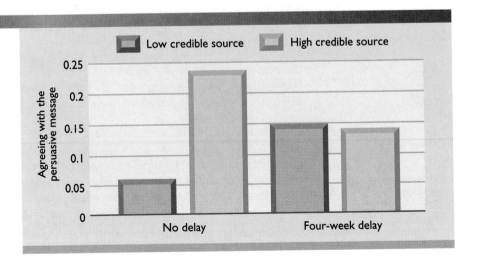

discount strong arguments because of the source, but later forget the source and remember only that the arguments were compelling. Also, the sleeper effect occurs only if the audience learns about the low credible source after (not before) reading the persuasive communication, because audience members do not pay attention to the arguments if they know in advance that the source is suspect (Greenwald, Pratkanis, Leippe, & Baumgardner, 1986; Gruder, Cook, Hennigan, Flay, Alessi, & Halamaj, 1978; Kelman & Hovland, 1953; Pratkanis, Greenwald, Leippe, & Baumgardner, 1988).

■ CONTENT

It helps to have persuasive communications delivered by sources who are credible and attractive. If you want to achieve maximum persuasion, however, you also need to build the best possible case. Even the most credible, attractive sources might have little effect if they failed to present compelling arguments. Social psychologists have examined two important factors that determine whether the communication itself is strong or weak: the communication arguments and whether the communication appeals to emotions such as fear.

■ COMMUNICATION ARGUMENTS

When they are trying to construct a persuasive communication, people need to make at least four important decisions: how many arguments to include, whether to mention arguments on the other side of the issue or not, whether to draw the logical conclusions for the audience or leave the conclusions unstated, and how discrepant the communication should be from what the audience initially believes.

The rule about how many arguments to include in a persuasive communication is that, at least within the bounds of audience patience, "more is better" (Calder, Insko, & Yandell, 1974). If an expert witness knows ten good reasons why battered women might feel trapped in an abusive relationship, it is usually better to mention them all than to mention only the two or three strongest. When sources offer many arguments instead of just a few, audiences assume that the sources are very knowledgeable. Handsome men and beautiful women tend to be believed whether they appear knowledgeable or not, but nonglamorous sources need all the arguments they can muster (Norman, 1976). If nonglamorous sources know of only a few good arguments, they can still appear to be knowledgeable about the topic by repeating and paraphrasing their few good arguments. Repeating the same arguments increases the effectiveness of a persuasive communication up to three repetitions, after which it either has

Calvin and Hobbes

by Bill Watterson

no additional impact or impairs persuasion (Cacioppo & Petty, 1979; Calder & Sternthal, 1980; Fehrenbach, Miller, & Thelan, 1979; Weiss, 1968).

A second important decision about constructing a persuasive communication is whether to include arguments on both sides of the issue or not. Should a defense witness simply describe why a battered woman was afraid to leave the abusive relationship (a "one-sided" communication), or admit also that the woman knew about shelters that would help her escape (a "two-sided" communication). The answer depends on the audience (Hovland, et al., 1949). For audience members who already agree with the message, it is better to use one-sided communications that do not raise arguments on the other side. For audience members who initially disagree, it is better to acknowledge the opposing arguments, but then to refute them. An expert witness might admit that the woman knew about shelters, for instance, but also explain why she was too afraid to use them. Persuasive communications that address both sides also help when audience members might later find out about counterarguments that were not addressed, for example when the prosecution is likely to bring them up during cross-examination (Lumsdaine & Janis, 1953; McGuire, 1964).

A third important decision in constructing a persuasive communication is whether to draw the conclusions explicitly or to let audience members draw the conclusions for themselves. At first thought this decision also seems to depend upon the audience. You might assume that it is best to give more knowledgeable audiences the facts ("her husband threatened her with a loaded gun") and leave them to draw the logical conclusions for themselves ("when he returned, the woman thought he was going to shoot her"). Less knowledgeable audiences might need to have the conclusions spelled out for them. This commonsense hypothesis has only limited research support (McGuire, 1969). A small percentage of audience members who are especially knowledgeable and highly motivated might exert the effort necessary to draw conclusions for themselves and thus be more persuaded or stay persuaded longer (Petty & Cacioppo, 1985). For all other audience members, however, it is better to draw the conclusions explicitly (Hovland & Mandell, 1952). To summarize years of research on this topic, "In communication, it appears, it is not sufficient to lead the horse to the water. One must also push his head underneath to get him to drink" (McGuire, 1969, p. 209).

A fourth important decision in constructing a persuasive message is how much difference there should be between what audience members believe and what the source would like them to believe. How much change can a communicator advocate and still remain credible? Student participants in one study ranked nine poems on artistic merit (Aronson, Turner, & Carlsmith, 1963). Then they read a communication supposedly written either by another student or the famous poet T. S. Eliot. The communication said that the poem the student had ranked as eighth out of nine was actually either fifth best, third best, or best. After reading the communication, students ranked the poems again. If the communication was from T. S. Eliot, the larger the discrepancy between his opinion and their own, the more students changed their attitudes. Even for a poem they initially ranked next-to-worst, if T. S. Eliot said it was best, then they agreed that the poem must be excellent. If the communication was only from another student, however, it lost its impact when the opinion expressed was too discrepant from the students' own initial attitude. If the other student said it was fifth best, they rated it only slightly higher than they had initially. If the other student said it was third best, they rated it moderately higher than they had initially. If the other student claimed it was the best poem, however, the students rated the poem no higher than if the other student had said it was fifth best. Except for very credible communicators, trying to change people's attitudes too much all at once is ineffective.

APPEALING TO EMOTIONS Emotional appeals *sometimes* make it easier to change attitudes by providing new information. At other times, persuasive communications are no more, or even less, persuasive when they arouse strong emotions. A case in point is constructing persuasive communications that arouse strong fear. Concerned scientists try to sway public opinion on the use of fluorocarbons by describing horrifying scenes of global warming. Groups concerned about drug use and the spread of disease show film clips that graphically depict the painful agony of dying from AIDS. On the surface, fear arousal seems like a good idea. It has proven effective in many experimental studies. In one study, for instance, the researchers urged college students to get tetanus shots (Dabbs & Leventhal, 1966). They gave some of the students facts in a straightforward manner. They gave other students vivid, unforgettably frightening information about the symptoms and consequences of getting tetanus. By consulting university health records, the investigators learned that the frightening communication had more impact. Approximately twice as many students who got the frightening communication later got tetanus shots as did students who got just the facts.

Fear arousal is not always so effective, however. Which do you think would be more effective in getting people to change their dental care habits, a movie that showed the facts about gum disease or a movie that showed stomach-turning photographs of festering gums and bloody mouths? When they were asked immediately after they viewed one of these movies in a psychology experiment, students who saw the frightening version reported being more impressed and more resolved to practice good dental care. One week later it was students who saw the *less* frightening movie on whom the persuasive communication had made a larger impact (Janis & Feshbach, 1953; Rogers, Deckner, & Mewborn, 1978). In some cases, fear arousal may even impair persuasion. Truly intense fear may distract the audience from what would otherwise be very strong arguments (Gleicher & Petty, 1992; Janis, 1967; Jepson & Chaiken, 1990). Fear arousal is effective only when the communication depicts extremely negative, fearful consequences of refusing to change (gum cancer, for instance), convinces the audience that these consequences are very likely without change, and offers strong reassurance that complying with the communication's recommendations will have positive results (Leventhal, Meyer, & Nerenz, 1980; Rogers, 1983). Fear may build an emotional tension that makes the audience more receptive to recommendations, but fear arousal does nothing to increase the effectiveness of a persuasive communication unless the communication conveys optimism that the fearful consequences can be avoided by following the recommendations (Beck & Frankel, 1981; Janis & Feshbach, 1953; Leventhal, 1970).

■ AUDIENCE

Even the most credible source, delivering a communication full of particularly compelling arguments, will have more success in persuading some audiences as opposed to others. Social psychologists have made important discoveries about the characteristics that render an audience member more receptive to persuasive communications. Four of the most interesting audience characteristics are intelligence, sex, age, and culture.

INTELLIGENCE Persuasive communications are more likely to influence audience members who have medium rather than either very high or very low intelligence (Hovland, et al., 1949). The reason is that successful persuasion involves both *understanding* the arguments and *accepting* them (McGuire, 1968). The greater the audience member's intelligence, the more likely he or she is to understand the arguments. An audience member who understands only two of a communication's ten arguments cannot possibly be persuaded by the other eight arguments, whereas an audience member who understands all ten arguments can potentially be persuaded by all ten. Acceptance, however, has the opposite relationship to intelligence. An intelligent audience member has the critical ability to generate *counterarguments* that question or invalidate the persuasive communication's main points. A person with very low intelligence may understand only two arguments but accept both arguments uncritically. A person with very high intelligence may understand all ten arguments but "shoot down" eight of them. Maximum persuasion occurs for medium intelligence audience members who are intelligent enough to understand most of the arguments but not intelligent enough to criticize their shortcomings.

Consistent with this reasoning, very complex persuasive communications, which depend on both understanding and acceptance to persuade, have no different effect on audience members at the three levels of intelligence. Extremely simple communications, which can be understood by everyone and thus involve only acceptance, are maximally effective for low intelligence audiences and minimally effective for high intelligence audiences (Eagly & Warren, 1976). In addition, related personality variables such as self-esteem bear the same relationship to how easy an audience is to persuade as does intelligence, although for different reasons (McGuire, 1968; Nisbett & Gordon, 1967; Rhodes & Wood, 1992). The higher an audience member's self-esteem, the more confidently the audience member holds his or her attitudes and the more confident he or she is about resisting influence.

■ **SEX** In the study of juror decisions about battered women, female jurors were more easily persuaded by expert testimony than were male jurors. Interestingly, women have been more easily persuaded than men in hundreds of psychology experiments (Cooper, 1979; Eagly, 1978; Maccoby & Jacklin, 1974; Sohn, 1980). The consistent sex difference has two explanations. First, women in Western cultures, where most of the studies were conducted, are socialized to be more cooperative than men in their social relationships (Eagly, 1978; Eagly & Carli, 1983). Women, not men, are expected to take the lead in maintaining social harmony, one aspect of which is to smooth over disagreements (Eagly & Carli, 1983). Women, not men, regard conforming with the opinions of others as a positive personality trait (Santee & Jackson, 1982). Because they are taught from an early age to value social harmony, the women who participate in studies of attitude change understand as many of the arguments as do the male audience members, but they may be more likely to accept the arguments uncritically. They are as *able* as men to "fight back" with counterarguments of their own, but they are less *willing* to do so.

Second, early attitude change studies were conducted primarily by male investigators who constructed all their persuasive communications around "male" topics for which women had little interest or knowledge (Eagly & Carli, 1983). Later studies compared persuasive communications about both male and female topics. In these studies, women were more easily persuaded by counterattitudinal arguments on male topics, but men were more easily persuaded by counterattitudinal arguments on female topics (Cacioppo & Petty, 1980; Sistrunk & McDavid, 1971). In one study, the researchers tried to change the opinions of both men and women about two topics: what constituted a good football tackle and what constituted a good fashion in women's attire (Cacioppo & Petty, 1980). The women were easier than men to persuade that a missed tackle was actually competent, but the men were easier than women to persuade that a dated or poorly coordinated outfit was actually chic.

■ **AGE** Another interesting difference in responding to persuasive communications is chronological age. Who is more easily persuaded, young peo-

Could anyone persuade you that these women are fashionably dressed?

ple or old people? One possibility is that adolescence and early adulthood are "impressionable years" during which attitudes, values, and worldviews are still being shaped (Sears, 1981, 1983). Once these impressionable years end, in approximately the mid-twenties, attitudes either remain relatively stable for the rest of the life span or become susceptible only when people get too old and mentally feeble to argue back (Glenn, 1980; Jennings & Niemi, 1981; Sears, 1981, 1986). Another possibility is that people remain open to change throughout their lives, whenever they have new experiences that might alter attitudes (Tyler & Schuller, 1991).

Some evidence suggests that people *are* especially prone to attitude change during the impressionable years. A relevant study examined the political attitudes of U.S. citizens in age groups 18–25, 26–33, 34–41, 42–49, 50–57, 58–65, and 66–83 during the years 1956–1976 (Krosnick & Alwin, 1989). People in the 18–25 age group had the least stable attitudes, but attitude stability neither increased nor decreased across the other six age groups. One reason for lower stability among the 18–25 age group might be that many change-inducing experiences, such as graduating from high school, going to college, being away from home for the first time, getting married, and becoming a parent, occur predominantly during those years. Momentous life events such as these are bound to have an unsettling and destabilizing influence on people's attitudes (Zaller, 1987). Other evidence supports the "open to new experience" hypothesis, by showing that older adults continue to be open to attitude change throughout their lives and that change occurs at whatever age an individual has change-inducing experiences (Tyler & Schuller, 1991).

CULTURE People from different cultures are persuaded by different types of communications. One of the major themes that recurs throughout this book is that people have both a personal identity and a "collective" or social identity (Brewer, 1991; Cousins, 1989; Crocker, Luhtanen, Blaine, & Broadnax, 1994; Deaux, 1993; Markus & Kitayama, 1994; Miller & Prentice, 1994; Oyserman, 1993; Trafimow, Triandis, & Goto, 1991; Turner, Oakes, Haslam, & McGarty, 1994). Personal identity is independent of other people; social identity involves being identified with groups or categories. The personal identity may be emphasized over the social identity in modern Western cultures, but many contemporary non-Western cultures emphasize social identity over personal identity (Markus & Kitayama, 1991; Triandis, 1990). These cultural differences suggest that it may be important to tailor the content of persuasive communications so that message arguments address either individualistic or collectivistic concerns, depending on the culture.

In one study of cultural differences in persuasion, the investigators examined advertisements for "personal" and "shared" products in two popular United States magazines and two popular Korean magazines (Han & Shavitt, 1994). Personal products are things you buy and use as an individual, such as chewing gum, cosmetics, and jewelry. Shared products are things you buy and use collectively with family members or friends, such as telephones, diapers, and television sets. The investigators rated each ad on how much it appealed to the personal, individualistic self and to the social, collectivistic self. Highly individualistic ads emphasized self-reliance, self-improvement, personal benefits, ambition, and personal goals. An individualistic ad might say "You, only better," "A leader among leaders," or "Make your way through the crowd." Highly collectivistic ads emphasized family integrity, group well-being, concern about others, interpersonal relationships, group goals, and harmony with others. A collectivistic ad might say "We have a way of bringing people together," "Sharing is beautiful," or "Mom's love–Baby's happiness."

Advertisements for personal products in both countries appealed more to individualistic than to collectivistic concerns. For shared products, however, the emphasis was different in the two different cultures. U.S. ads emphasized more individualistic concerns even when they were trying to sell shared products, for which Korean ads emphasized more collectivistic concerns. In a follow-up study, the investigators also showed that advertisers knew what they were doing. Ads for shared products that emphasized individualistic benefits were more effective in the United States, whereas ads that emphasized collectivistic benefits were more effective in Korea.

HOW DOES PERSUASION OCCUR?

At first glance, these discoveries about factors that determine the impact of persuasive communications might seem to have nothing in common with each other except that some of them are associated with the source, some with the communication content, and some with the audience. A closer look reveals, however, that the results discussed in the previous section make sense when you understand the two ways in which people get persuaded, or the two "routes to persuasion" (Cacioppo & Petty, 1987; Petty & Cacioppo, 1981, 1985; Cacioppo, Petty, & Crites, 1994; Chaiken, 1980, 1987; Chaiken & Eagly, 1983; Chaiken, Liberman, & Eagly, 1989).

One of the major themes that runs through this textbook is the "two-stage" idea that people have both spontaneous and deliberative reactions (Bargh, 1994; Beike & Sherman, 1994; Brewer, 1988; Epstein, et al., 1992; Gilbert, 1989; Martin, et al., 1990; Smith, 1994). Like the two-stage mechanisms discussed in Chapter 2 on social cognition, Chapter 3 on person perception, and Chapter 4 on attribution, attitude change through persuasive communication also involves both a relatively spontaneous stage and a relatively deliberative stage. The two stages, which constitute two routes to persuasion, are summarized in Figure 7.3 and described in the two sections below.

FIGURE 7.3

Two routes to attitude change through persuasive communications.

Abstracted from Cacioppo & Petty, 1987; Petty & Cacioppo, 1981, 1985; Cacioppo, Petty, & Crites, 1994; Chaiken, 1980; Chaiken & Eagly, 1983; Chaiken, Liberman, & Eagly, 1989.

PERIPHERAL ROUTE (relatively spontaneous)

Be swayed by cues peripheral to the message content, such as the source's expertise or attractiveness

Use heuristics or rules of thumb such as "People who speak rapidly must have many arguments" and "Speakers who draw applause must be making strong arguments"

Note: When attitudes are changed by persuasive communications, attitude change takes the peripheral route unless the audience is willing and able to deliberate on the message arguments. Attitude change that occurs through the peripheral route is relatively temporary, susceptible to further change, and unlikely to predict behavior.

CENTRAL ROUTE (relatively deliberative)

If you are willing and able to deliberate on the message arguments, then

Generate your own thoughts that are favorable or unfavorable to the message arguments

Use your self-generated reactions to arrive at an attitude that might be different from your initial attitude

Note: Attitude change that occurs through the central route is relatively permanent, resistant to further change, and likely to predict behavior.

■ PERIPHERAL ROUTE

The peripheral route to attitude change, as shown in Figure 7.3, involves cues that are peripheral to the communication's arguments. According to the **elaboration likelihood model** of how persuasive communications change attitudes, people take the peripheral route to persuasion when they rely on peripheral cues such as the source's expertise or physical attractiveness, whereas they take the central route to persuasion when they elaborate on the message arguments (Cacioppo & Petty, 1987; Priester & Petty, 1995; Wegener & Petty, 1995; Wegener, Petty, & Klein, 1994). Peripheral cues can affect attitudes even when the communication arguments are held constant. The same message can have greater impact when it comes from an expert than from a nonexpert, from an attractive rather than an unattractive source, and from someone who happens to be similar to rather than dissimilar from the message recipient.

The peripheral route to attitude change, as also shown in Figure 7.3, involves the use of heuristics or "rules of thumb," which are explained in greater detail in Chapter 2. According to the **heuristic-systematic model** of how persuasive communications change attitudes, people take the peripheral route to attitude change when they rely on heuristics or rules of thumb such as "many arguments are better than few" or "beautiful people don't lie," whereas they take the central route to persuasion when they think systematically about the topic.

A frequently used heuristic tells that attractive communicators are more truthful than unattractive communicators. Audiences follow this rule even when the attractive communicator merely states a position and advances no arguments (Norman, 1976). Another heuristic that requires no elaboration of the communication arguments suggests that people who speak rapidly are more knowledgeable than those who speak slowly. Audiences follow this "people who speak rapidly know more" rule even when the communicator is speaking in a foreign language and the communication arguments are incomprehensible (Miller, Maruyama, Beaber, & Valone, 1976). Yet another heuristic says that "more arguments are better." Some audience members follow this rule even when the communicator only *claims* to present ten arguments and actually presents six (Chaiken, 1987). Finally, some people are more easily persuaded when a speaker gets sustained applause from the rest of the audience than when the same speaker makes the same point without applause. They assume that "applauded arguments must be strong arguments" (Axsom, Yates, & Chaiken, 1987).

People who take the peripheral route to persuasion rely on peripheral cues and heuristics that involve source credibility, source attractiveness, communication length, number of arguments, and audience reaction. They often understand the communication arguments, but they do not use them (Axsom, et al., 1987; Chaiken, 1980; Chaiken & Eagly, 1983; Chaiken & Maheswaran, 1994; Pallak, 1983; Pallak, Muroni, & Koch, 1983; Petty & Cacioppo, 1984; Wood, Kallgren, & Priesler, 1985). They change their attitudes quickly and spontaneously because they are either unwilling or unable to go on to the more systematic, deliberative central route. As Figure 7.3 shows, however, their attitude change is relatively temporary, unstable, and unlikely to predict behavior (Cacioppo et al., 1994).

■ CENTRAL ROUTE

The central route to persuasion, as shown in Figure 7.3, involves deliberating on whatever relevant information is available. The relevant information might include the recipient's initial attitude, the strength of the arguments, and even cues that seem peripheral. If a woman with beautiful hair appears in a shampoo commercial, for instance, her attractiveness may be a peripheral cue if it merely enhances the product by association with a physically attractive image, but her lustrous hair may also constitute an argument for using the shampoo (Cacioppo et al., 1994). In the central route to persuasion, according to the elaboration likelihood model, the message generates thoughts that are favorable, unfavorable, or neutral toward the communication. These self-generated thoughts can elicit reactions consistent or inconsistent with the message. Weak arguments, for instance, might generate such unfavorable thoughts that the message recipient reacted in a way exactly *opposite* to what the source intended (Gruenfeld & Wyer, 1992). If the recipient's thoughts elicit reactions that are different from reactions the recipient used to have, as shown in the table, the result is "central attitude change." Central attitude change is relatively enduring, resists further change, and predicts behavior (Haugtvedt & Petty, 1992; Petty, Haugtvedt, & Smith, 1995).

With the distinction between the peripheral and central routes in mind, we can understand how factors such as source expertise, attractiveness, and sheer number of arguments might influence attitudes primarily through the peripheral route. Communications that arouse fear, for instance, might distract message recipients, making them less likely to rely on the central route and less likely to think about strong arguments. Very intelligent people might be hard to persuade because they generate thoughts that are predominantly unfavorable to all but the most compelling arguments. Men might be more motivated to take the central route for male topics and women might be more motivated to take the central route for female topics. Men and women might differ in the topics for which they are most able to generate unfavorable counterarguments. In short, the central and peripheral routes make sense of previous research on source, message, and audience characteristics in attitude change.

Taking the central rather than peripheral route depends on both ability and effort. In one study of *ability* as it affects elaboration likelihood, college students read either strong or weak arguments in favor of a 20% tuition increase at their school (Petty, Wells, & Brock, 1976). They read, for example, that "the extra money would allow the college to hire more and better quality faculty, thus improving teaching and lowering class sizes" (strong) or that "the extra money would allow the college to hire more gardeners to care for ornamental shrubs and flowers to impress campus visitors" (weak). Some students in each group listened to the persuasive communication without distraction. Others had to perform a complex computer task while they listened. Figure 7.4 shows that when students were not distracted, the strong arguments elicited considerable agreement with what was initially a disliked proposal for increasing their own college tuition, but the weak arguments had almost no effect. The same weak arguments had almost as much effect as did the strong arguments in the high distraction condition, where the simultaneous computer task kept students from generating counterarguments. Ability to process the information is also enhanced when sources repeat the message and audiences are relaxed, not too tense to deliberate (Cacioppo & Petty, 1985; DeBono & McDermott, 1994). Any factor that increases ability to process the message reduces reliance on peripheral cues.

The other major factor in determining elaboration likelihood is *motivation*. Some people are more willing than others to think deeply about ideas. The Need for Cognition scale (Cacioppo & Petty, 1982) measures this personality difference. People low in need for cognition say that "Thinking is not my idea of fun," "It is enough for me that something gets the job done; I don't care how or why it works" and "More often than not, more thinking just leads to more errors." People high in need for cognition say that "I really enjoy a task that involves coming up with new solutions to problems," "I tend to set goals that can be accomplished only by expending considerable mental effort," and

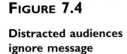

FIGURE 7.4

Distracted audiences ignore message content.

Graph shows attitude change by students who were or were not distracted from a persuasive message that had strong or weak arguments (Petty, Wells, & Brock, 1976).

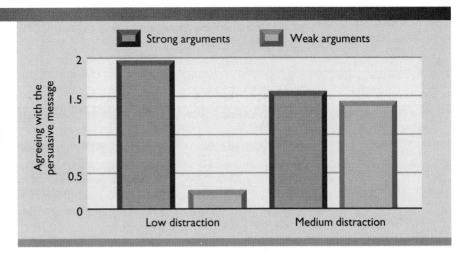

"I would prefer complex to simple problems." In one study, students who had low or high need for cognition received either weak or strong arguments for raising tuition at their university. Students who had low need for cognition agreed a little more with strong than with weak arguments, but they were impressed by both. Students who had high need for cognition were impressed only by strong arguments, because they generated their own compelling counterarguments that demolished weak arguments (Cacioppo, Petty, & Morris, 1983).

People who expect an issue to affect their own lives are also more involved and more motivated to generate supportive arguments or counterarguments than are people who expect the issue to affect someone else (Apsler & Sears, 1968; Johnson, 1994; Petty & Cacioppo, 1979; Petty, Cacioppo, & Haugtvedt, in press). The female jurors in the study of abused women at the start of this chapter, for instance, might have responded more to expert testimony than did male jurors because they found the topic more personally relevant. In one study of personal relevance, students read a communication about instituting a comprehensive examination at the student's university in ten years (low personal relevance) or immediately (high personal relevance). The communication was attributed either to a prestigious educational commission (high credibility) or to a local high school class (low credibility). Source credibility (the peripheral cue) mattered more for low personal relevance students (especially those who were given weak arguments), but argument strength mattered more for high personal relevance students (Petty, Cacioppo, & Goldman, 1981).

In summary, the elaboration likelihood and heuristic-systematic models specify circumstances in which audience members take the peripheral route and rely primarily on peripheral cues or heuristics, as well as circumstances in which audience members elaborate on the communication arguments. The models predict that both peripheral cues and central cues can affect a single decision. The models also predict that the same factor (physical attractiveness, for instance) can influence attitudes either primarily through the peripheral route (by mere positive association with the message) or primarily through the central route (as an argument in itself) (Petty, 1994; Petty, Priester, & Wegener, 1994; Shavitt, Swan, Lowrey, & Wänke, 1994). The models thus set the stage for future research on *why* peripheral factors have a reduced impact when elaboration likelihood is high. Peripheral factors might come less easily to mind, for example, when highly involved people integrate favorable and unfavorable thoughts. Peripheral cues might also be viewed less extremely in the context of additional thoughts or might seem less important in more involving contexts (Petty, 1994).

WHEN DO PEOPLE RESIST PERSUASIVE COMMUNICATIONS?

Discussions of attitude change may inadvertently suggest that it is easy to change people's attitudes by giving them new information. Exactly the opposite is true (McGuire, 1969, 1985). Television advertisements for commercial products, political campaigns, and public service announcements take full advantage of what is known about source, content, and audience factors. Considering the amount of money expended and the amount of time that citizens spend watching television, these advertisements have surprisingly little effect (McGuire, 1985). People have developed some very clever ways to avoid being influenced. They can resist influence when they are forewarned that a persuasive communication is coming, when they are "inoculated" by previous success in counterarguing persuasive communications, when they have high "need for cognitive closure" and have already formed an opinion, and when they employ one of four effective defensive strategies.

■ FOREWARNING

When people are forewarned that an attack is coming, they prepare their defenses. People who are warned about an imminent counterattitudinal communication are less persuaded than they might have been had they not been forewarned (Petty & Cacioppo, 1977; McGuire & Papageorgis, 1962). Forewarning, however, can take one of two forms: warning of the communication content, or warning of the intent to persuade. First, the audience may be forewarned of the communication content, as in "the next speaker will try to convince you that student tuition should be raised." Audience members who are warned of a communicator's position use the time that intervenes between the warning and the communication to develop their own arguments and counterarguments (McGuire & Papageorgis, 1962). The more time that intervenes between this kind of warning and the persuasive communication, the more able audience members are to resist being influenced (Freedman & Sears, 1965; Hass & Grady, 1975). If audience members are asked to list their thoughts during the interval between the warning and the communication, they list thoughts that anticipate the communicator's likely arguments and thoughts about their own likely counterarguments (Petty & Cacioppo, 1981).

The other kind of forewarning occurs when people know that someone will try to persuade them of something, but they do not know the topic. With this type of forewarning, the time between warning and communication makes no difference, because audience members have no way to prepare their defenses (Hass & Grady, 1975). Even so, audience members who are forewarned only of persuasive intent are less easily persuaded than are audience members who are not forewarned (Petty & Cacioppo, 1979). Forewarning of an imminent persuasive attempt arouses **psychological reactance,** which occurs when people deliberately ignore or act contrary to external pressure because they believe that their individual freedom is being threatened (Brehm, 1966). Psychological reactance elicits both the "you can't sway my opinion" heuristic behind some sex differences in persuasion and additional audience effort in identifying effective counterarguments during the communication (Eagly, 1983). In short, forewarning and perceived threats to freedom make audience members more likely to use the deliberative, central route to persuasion (Petty & Cacioppo, 1979).

■ INOCULATION

If developing counterarguments is an effective way to resist persuasion, then practice at doing so might be especially effective. One technique that involves practice at generating counterarguments is *inoculation,* so called because it is similar to the procedure used in immunizing people from physical diseases (McGuire & Papageorgis, 1962). In the medical form of inoculation against disease, people are exposed to a very mild form of the disease, to which the body's immune system develops resistance. A few days after the inoculation or immunization procedure, the body's resistance to the disease is heightened.

Inoculation against persuasive communications works the same way. It works especially well against persuasive communications that attack cultural truisms such as "you should brush your teeth after every meal." Cultural truisms are attitudes and beliefs that we learned from parents or other authorities without any supporting evidence. People have had no practice in defending such attitudes against persuasive attacks. In one study that tested the effectiveness of inoculation against persuasive communications, some students did not have their previously unquestioned beliefs attacked (McGuire & Papageorgis, 1962). Other students had their beliefs attacked two days after they received both weak persuasive arguments ("too much tooth brushing might harm the gums") and logical refutations ("gentle stimulation promotes healthy gums"). Yet other students had their beliefs attacked two days after they received only supportive arguments ("food trapped between the teeth can cause cavities"). Finally, some students had their beliefs attacked without any preparation. Continued belief in the cultural truisms varied across conditions. After the persuasive communication, students whose beliefs suffered "attack only" (with no preparation) had less continued belief than did students whose beliefs had not been attacked. Merely being exposed to supportive arguments conferred only slightly more resistance to persuasion than "attack only." Practice at refuting weak arguments (the inoculation procedure) conferred almost complete resistance to persuasion.

The inoculation technique is effective in reducing cigarette smoking and drug use among adolescents and preadolescents (McAlister, Perry, Killen, Slinkard, & Maccoby, 1980; McAlister, Perry, & Maccoby, 1979). Besides providing information about the dangers of nicotine and other drugs, inoculation-based programs give children practice in counterarguing peer arguments. When told that she's not a liberated woman unless she smokes, for instance, a teenager might respond "How liberated would I be if I got addicted?" When accused of being "chicken" for not trying cocaine, she might respond "I'd be a real chicken if I did it just to impress you." Medical inoculations have an "incubation period" during which the body builds resistance to a disease by fighting off a mild form of the disease. The inoculation procedure also works better when two or three days intervene between being exposed to refutations of weak arguments and the persuasive communication than when there is no delay (McGuire, 1962; Rogers & Thistlethwaite, 1969). This effect of delay may occur because people need time to anticipate the possible attack and to develop the best defensive strategies.

■ NEED FOR COGNITIVE CLOSURE

Some people have high need for cognitive closure (Kruglanski, in press). They prefer a definite answer on a topic–*any* answer–to confusion and ambiguity.

Cognitive closure gives them a sense that the world is stable and predictable. It also gives them a basis for confident action. Other people have low need for cognitive closure. Instead of reaching a conclusion, they prefer to leave their options open. By avoiding a final answer on a topic, they retain the flexibility to change their opinions based on new evidence. They cannot be criticized for their position on an issue if they have never completely committed themselves. Need for cognitive closure is measured by the Need for Cognitive Closure Scale (Webster & Kruglanski, 1994). On the scale, people who are high in need for cognitive closure say they like having clear rules, dislike uncertain situations, hate to change their plans at the last minute, and find it annoying to be with people who can't make up their minds. People who are low in need for cognitive closure say they are willing to consider different opinions even after they have made up their minds, have difficulty deciding what they want when they go shopping, can see how both sides in a conflict might be right, and like having friends who are unpredictable.

Need for cognitive closure affects resistance to persuasion. In a mock jury study, college students who had high or low need for cognitive closure read a court case in which a plane crashed, starting a brush fire (Kruglanski, Webster, & Klem, 1993). The fire spread, combined with a naturally caused fire, and burned a lumberyard. The lumberyard owners sued the airline company because the plane had a malfunction. Besides the description, some student jurors had complete evidence. They read a "legal analysis" that either blamed the airline for putting off a scheduled maintenance check or exonerated the airline by stating that the lumberyard would have been destroyed by the natural fire anyway. Other students had incomplete evidence. They did not read the legal analysis.

After reading this information, each student juror rendered a verdict that favored either the lumberyard or the airline. Then each juror discussed the case with "another juror" (a confederate). The confederate tried to get the juror to change his or her mind about the verdict. Figure 7.5 shows how much jurors changed their opinions. When the jurors had read the legal analysis and had made up their minds based on complete evidence before the other juror tried to persuade them, high need for cognitive closure students changed their opinions less than did low need for cognitive closure students. When the jurors had incomplete evidence and had *not* made up their minds before the other juror tried to persuade them, the results were exactly opposite. When they have made up their minds, people who have high need for cognitive closure resist new evidence, because they do not want to alter their conclusion.

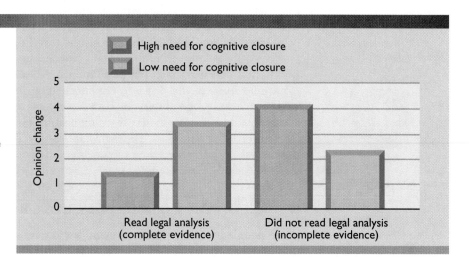

Figure 7.5

Resistance to persuasion depends on need for cognitive closure and basis of initial opinion.

Graph shows opinion change for two types of students when confederate tried to get them to change an opinion based on complete or incomplete evidence (Kruglanski, Webster, & Klem, 1993).

When they have not fully made up their minds, people who have high need for cognitive closure welcome new evidence, because it will help them to arrive at a definite answer.

■ DEFENSIVE STRATEGIES

Even when they are shown what appears to be undeniable evidence that their opinions are misguided, people have many ways to retain their original attitudes (Abelson, 1959; see the discussion of belief perseverance in Chapter 6). Some of the most frequently used techniques are denial, bolstering, differentiation, and transcendence. *Denial* is the simplest of these defense mechanisms. If a confirmed cigarette smoker is told of research that proves smoking causes lung cancer, for instance, denial would consist of saying something like "there's no such research." *Bolstering* is a little more complicated, because it requires generating new supportive arguments. If a confirmed cigarette smoker read an article in a prestigious medical journal and could no longer deny the existence of medical evidence that links smoking with lung cancer, he or she might admit that the evidence exists, but bolster a positive attitude toward smoking with additional reasons such as "Smoking relaxes me" or "Nicotine helps carry oxygen to the brain so that I think better."

Should bolstering fail, a resourceful or highly motivated smoker might use the *differentiation* strategy, in which undeniable evidence is separated into two parts, only one of which contradicts the established attitude. The smoker might, for instance, draw a distinction between "good" and "bad" cigarettes by saying that "The evidence applies only to nonfiltered tobacco. I smoke filtered cigarettes, so I'm safe." Finally, the most complicated defensive strategy of all is *transcendence,* in which people transcend the evidence by inventing a new theory that incorporates both the established attitude and the new evidence. "Cigarette smoke is an important tool of evolution that weeds out the weakest members of the human race and insures natural selection of the fittest. I smoke and I'm perfectly healthy, so by smoking I can prove that I'm one of the strong ones!"

SUMMARY OF CHANGING ATTITUDES BY CHANGING THOUGHTS

Persuasive communications attempt to change thoughts about a person, thing, or event by providing new information or arguments. The assumption is that when thoughts change, feelings and actions will follow. The impact of a persuasive communication depends not only on the quality of the persuasive arguments, but also on at least two factors that are extraneous to the communication content: the source and the audience. To predict whether a persuasive communication will change attitudes, we need to know *who* (the source) says *what* (the content) to *whom* (the audience).

Empirical discoveries about the impact of source, communication, and audience have been integrated by the elaboration likelihood and systematic-heuristic models of persuasion. A persuasive communication's impact depends in part on the thoughts and elaborations that audience members generate before, during, and after they receive a persuasive communication. If the audience members focus primarily on communication arguments, the persuasive attempt takes a central route to persuasion. If the audience members focus primarily on matters extraneous to communication arguments, such as a heuristic or "rule of thumb" about the source's credibility or attractiveness, the persuasive attempt takes a peripheral route to persuasion. Attitude change that relies on the central route endures longer than does attitude change that relies on the peripheral route.

Elaboration before, during, and after receiving the communication also explains resistance to persuasion, including the effects of forewarning, inoculation, and the recruitment of such defensive strategies as denial, bolstering, differentiation, and transcendence.

CAN WE CHANGE ATTITUDES BY CHANGING PEOPLE'S FEELINGS?

A different approach to changing people's attitudes is to change not their thoughts, but their feelings. If we wanted to deter spouse abuse, for instance, we might produce documentary films that show women who have received terrible injuries. We might not worry about conveying new information, but instead associate spouse abuse with other brutal practices that arouse negative feelings. When the famous and well-liked basketball player Magic Johnson announced that he had AIDS, people's attitudes became much less negative and people were much more willing to help AIDS victims for four months thereafter, not because they had learned anything new about the disease, but merely because a very positive person had become associated with AIDS (Penner & Fritzsche, 1993).

As discussed in Chapter 6, feelings toward attitude objects are "classically conditioned" by repeated association of the attitude object with positive or negative events. It might be effective, then, to arrange people's exposure to the attitude object so that it coincides with what we want them to feel. If we want people to develop positive attitudes toward a commercial product, a political candidate, or a social policy, we pair it repeatedly with positive events. If we want people to develop negative attitudes, we pair the object repeatedly with negative events. Unfortunately for this simpleminded idea, it is very difficult to be sure that we are changing feelings by themselves, without changing thoughts. Furthermore, changing feelings may be more effective for attitudes based on feelings than for attitudes based on thoughts. We may have to match the persuasion attempt with the attitude basis.

HOW ARE FEELINGS CHANGED?

Social psychologists know two ways to change people's feelings: classically condition the attitude or put people in a good mood.

■ CLASSICAL CONDITIONING OF ATTITUDES

One social psychologist derived part of his thinking about attitudes from an experiment that he conducted on his cat (Staats, 1983). Whenever he punished the cat for not using its litter box, he said the word "No" in a stern voice. We have no idea what the cat thought about this procedure, but the social psychologist was convinced that the word "No" developed unpleasant associations for the cat. Once words have developed pleasant or unpleasant associations, they might in turn be paired with previously neutral objects to create positive or negative attitudes. In subsequent experiments on human beings, the same social psychologist paired objects, persons, and minority group names with positive or negative words like good, bad, clean, and dirty. He and many other investigators found that by using procedures of this type they could instill in research participants either positive or negative attitudes toward objects as diverse as nonsense syllables, paintings, foods, and ballpoint pens (Allen & Madden, 1985; Byrne & Clore, 1970; Rozin & Zellner, 1985; Staats & Staats, 1957).

In one such study, the investigators repeatedly shocked or stopped shocking participants when a particular word such as "light" or "dark" occurred. The students later, in an unrelated context, said they had either positive or negative attitudes toward these words and toward synonyms such as "black" and "white," depending on whether "light" or "dark" had been paired with shock or the cessation of shock (Zanna, Kiesler, & Pilkonis, 1970). In another study, the experimenter repeatedly paired pleasant or unpleasant words with men's names like "George" and "Ed" (Berkowitz & Knurek, 1969). As part of a later "unrelated" experiment, the same participants met and evaluated a stranger whose first name "happened" to be either George or Ed. They rated the stranger more positively when his first name had previously been paired with pleasant rather than with unpleasant words. In yet another study, participants who received an unexpected prize reported more positive attitudes toward a stranger who "happened" to be present when they received the prize (Lott & Lott, 1985). In all these studies, attitudes toward previously neutral objects changed toward being either more positive or more negative after the object had been paired or associated with a pleasant or unpleasant event (Cacioppo, Marshall-Goodell, Tassinary, & Petty, 1992). In the language of the elaboration likelihood model, classical conditioning takes a "peripheral route" to attitude change (Petty, 1994).

■ MOOD EFFECTS

If pairing attitude objects with pleasant or unpleasant events affects attitudes, then it might also be possible to get people to like or dislike an attitude object because it was associated with their being in a good or a bad mood. When people are listening to pleasant music or enjoying food, they may be more easily persuaded to change their attitudes than at other times (Dabbs & Janis, 1965; Gorn, 1982). Such positive mood effects may, like classical conditioning, take the "peripheral" route to persuasion. People who do not find a coin in a public telephone return slot let another person cut in line only if they get a good reason, whereas people who unexpectedly find a coin let another person cut in without a reason (Schwarz, Bless, & Bohner, 1991). In other words, people who are in a good mood pay less attention to argument strength than do people who are in a neutral mood (Petty, Cacioppo, & Kasmer, 1988).

According to the elaboration likelihood and systematic-heuristic models of persuasion, people are not influenced by argument strength unless they are both willing and able to deliberate on the arguments (Petty & Cacioppo, 1986).

Motivation and ability also influence mood effects (Mackie & Worth, 1989b). In a relevant study, some German students described in vivid detail a particularly happy event in their lives (Bless, Bohner, Schwarz, & Strack, 1990). Other students described a particularly sad event. As you might imagine, describing the happy event put the students in a more positive mood than describing the sad event. Next, all students listened to a persuasive communication that contained either strong or weak arguments that student fees should be increased. Some of the students who were in each mood were asked to concentrate on aspects of the communication that were unrelated to the arguments. Others were asked to concentrate on the arguments. When the communication ended, all students indicated how much they agreed that fees should be raised.

Students who concentrated on unrelated aspects of the communication reacted differently depending on the mood they were in. If they were in a negative mood, they were more persuaded by strong than by weak arguments. If they were in a positive mood, argument strength did not matter. A positive mood, however, did not make them incapable of critically evaluating the arguments. Students who were asked to attend to communication arguments distinguished between strong and weak arguments regardless of their mood. Positive mood students who attended to unrelated aspects of the communication were *capable* of reacting differently to strong than to weak arguments (the "central" route), but they did not do so *spontaneously*. As predicted by the elaboration likelihood model, positive mood decreased the likelihood of spontaneously elaborating on persuasive communications. When people do not elaborate on message arguments, a positive mood affects attitude change directly, by associating the message with a positive event. When people *do* elaborate on message arguments, a positive mood increases attitude change indirectly, by eliciting self-generated arguments that support the message content (Petty, Schumann, Richman, & Strathman, 1993).

Finally, pleasant smells take the peripheral rather than the central route to persuasion. In a relevant study, some college students (but not others) got to sniff a card on which a new perfume had been sprayed (DeBono, 1992). Then, all students read advertisements for the perfume that contained either strong arguments ("You put it on in the morning and it lasts until late in the evening") or weak arguments ("Everyone is wearing it!") These arguments were attributed to an attractive or unattractive woman who was shown in an accompanying photograph (a peripheral cue). Because pleasant smells put people in good moods, students who smelled the perfume first were more affected by the woman's attractiveness (a peripheral cue), whereas students who did not smell the perfume first were more affected by argument strength (a central cue).

DO FEELINGS EVER CHANGE WITHOUT THOUGHT?

From studies of classical conditioning and mood effects, we know that we can change attitudes by manipulating people's feelings. We also know that these manipulations do not rely on the central route that involves differences between strengths and weaknesses of new information. The studies that have been described, however, do not allow us to say that positive and negative associations influence attitudes *entirely* through feelings, without prior thoughts. In some previous studies of classically conditioning attitudes, only participants who were aware of the manipulation changed their attitudes (Page, 1974; Page & Kahle, 1976). Many studies, however, have detected attitude change in situations where participants could not possibly know what was being measured, for example in the study in which students liked Ed more than George

(Berkowitz & Knurek, 1969). Classical conditioning effects on attitudes are caused by more than mere experimental demand (Eagly & Chaiken, 1993).

A more plausible explanation than experimental demand is that the positive or negative events that are paired with attitude objects constitute a form of "information" (Fishbein & Ajzen, 1975). Students who see positive or negative adjectives repeatedly paired with a certain nationality may believe that they are getting information about that nationality's characteristics (Kuykendall & Keating, 1990; Staats & Staats, 1958). When they later ascribe other positive or negative characteristics to the nationality or report positive or negative attitudes toward the nationality, it might be that the new information changed their thoughts, which in turn changed their feelings. It is impossible from such procedures to conclude that the investigators changed attitudes only by attacking feelings (Rosenberg, 1960). Did the new feelings cause thoughts to change or did the new thoughts cause feelings to change? Although we cannot be entirely sure, two lines of research, one on conditioning without awareness and the other on mere exposure, suggest that it is possible for feelings to change attitudes without the help of new information.

■ CONDITIONING WITHOUT AWARENESS

In one attempt to change attitudes entirely through feelings without prior thought, the experimenters took advantage of a little known fact: We have a more positive emotional reaction to people whose pupils are dilated than to people whose pupils are not dilated. The experimenters showed students photographs (Niedenthal & Cantor, 1986). Half of the people in the photographs had wide, dilated pupils; the other half had relatively small pupils. Although the students had no way to realize it on a conscious level, their feelings were being manipulated so that their emotional reactions were positive toward one set of photographed people and negative toward the other set. Then the experimenters asked the students to select from a list of thoughts the ones they had about each of the photographed people. As predicted, the students selected primarily positive thoughts ("She looks like a good mother") about the people with dilated pupils and selected primarily negative thoughts ("He looks paranoid") about the people with relatively small pupils. This clever study manipulated feelings without students being aware of the manipulation, yet the

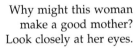

Why might this woman make a good mother? Look closely at her eyes.

manipulation caused participants to select different thoughts. The thoughts and feelings components of attitudes are so interrelated that a change in one component usually tugs the other component in the same direction.

Another technique for changing feelings without new information is to present the event that elicits positive or negative feelings *subliminally* (below the "perceptual threshold" at which human beings can tell what happened). Participants cannot draw inferences based on "information" that is not available to them. As described in greater detail in Chapter 6, experimenters in one study paired pictures of a person with positive or negative scenes that were shown so fast that the viewer could not possibly see them (Krosnick, Betz, Jussim, & Lynn, 1992). When they were later asked about their attitudes toward the person, students who had "seen" her paired with scenes that elicited positive feelings liked her more than did students who had "seen" her paired with scenes that elicited negative feelings. Attitudes were classically conditioned even when the students were unaware that any additional "information" had been presented, when different experimenters showed the slides and inquired about attitudes (eliminating demand characteristics), when the experimenters themselves did not know the hypothesis, and when students in the different conditions said they were not in different moods. Attitudes can be changed entirely through feelings.

■ MERE EXPOSURE

The other type of evidence for changing attitudes entirely through feelings comes from studies of mere exposure. In the **mere exposure** effect people like familiar objects more than ones that they have not seen before. When people see or hear a word, a person, a painting, a piece of music, or any other object several times, even with no information about the object, they develop more positive attitudes toward it (Bornstein, 1989; Zajonc, 1968). One explanation of this mere exposure effect was that the procedures "demanded" participants claim to like the frequently repeated objects. Another was that the procedures provided participants with enough "information" so that they could draw at least mildly positive inferences about the attitude object (Harrison, 1977; Stang, 1974). As in research on classical conditioning, researchers tested the "demand" explanation by separating the repeated exposure manipulation from the attitude measure so cleverly that it was impossible for participants to know what was being tested. Even with disguised attitude measures, mere exposure changed attitudes (Grush, 1976; Rajecki & Wolfson, 1973; Saegert, Swap, & Zajonc, 1973).

Researchers also tested the "information" explanation of mere exposure by presenting the attitude object repeatedly, but subliminally (Bonnano & Stillings, 1986; Kunst-Wilson & Zajonc, 1980; Moreland & Zajonc, 1977, 1979). Participants in one such study did not realize that, as part of an earlier "unrelated" task, they had "seen" a subliminally presented photograph of another student (Bornstein, Leone, & Galley, 1987). Later, they had to judge which one of two strangers was correct in his assessment of poetry selections. Although the participants could not possibly know that they had "seen" one of the strangers (but not the other) previously, they demonstrated a more positive attitude toward the one with whom they were "familiar" by agreeing with him more often.

Interestingly, mere exposure affects attitudes more when the positive or negative event is presented subliminally than when it is presented *supraliminally* (above threshold, so that all participants know it is there) (Bornstein, 1989). It may at first seem unusual that people would be more influenced by an event they know nothing about than by an event of which they are aware. The difference, however, makes sense if mere exposure, like classical conditioning, takes a peripheral route to attitude change. In the elaboration likelihood and systematic-heuristic models of attitude change, paying attention to peripheral cues reduces attention to communication arguments, and vice versa (Cacioppo et al., 1992; Eagly & Chaiken, 1993). If paying attention to information about an event decreases the event's impact on feelings, then people who have sufficient motivation and ability to gather information about an event may be less likely to experience a full range of feelings than are people who have less motivation and ability (Bornstein & D'Agostino, 1992). Deliberately scrutinizing an event may reduce the event's impact on feelings (Kihlstrom, 1987). Although classical conditioning and mere exposure in everyday settings most likely involve both thoughts and feelings, there may be circumstances in which changes in feelings precede changes in thoughts (Zajonc, 1980; Zajonc & Markus, 1984; Zajonc, Murphy, & Ingelhart, 1989; Zajonc, Pietromonaco, & Bargh, 1982).

■ MATCHING ATTITUDE CHANGE WITH ATTITUDE BASIS

Finally, attacks on feelings may be more effective in changing some types of attitudes than others (Edwards, 1990). Attacks on feelings may work well for changing attitudes that were initially based on feelings, but not work as well for attitudes that were initially based on information. In a relevant study, college men thought they were going to interview a woman for a public relations job (Edwards & von Hippel, 1995). The men got a photograph of the woman and her answers to a questionnaire. Because the photograph showed an extremely attractive, smiling woman and the questionnaire answers made her seem very outgoing and likable, the men formed a positive attitude toward her. Some of the men, however, got the photograph first and some got the questionnaire answers first. The experimenters reasoned that, although the men in the two conditions formed equally positive attitudes, ones who got the photograph first did so primarily because of positive *feelings*, whereas ones who got the questionnaire first did so primarily because of positive *thoughts*.

Then the experimenters tried to change the men's positive attitudes by attacking either their thoughts or their feelings. The woman interviewee (a confederate) gave poor answers during the interview, which should have changed the man's thoughts. She also snubbed him, which should have hurt his feelings. The woman either gave her poor answers (attacked thoughts) first or snubbed the man (attacked feelings) first. When she attacked thoughts first, she changed the attitudes of men whose attitudes were based on information from the questionnaire. When she attacked feelings first, she changed the attitudes of men whose attitudes were based on her attractiveness. When trying to change attitudes, it helps to know whether the attitude is based on thoughts or on feelings, and to tailor the communication to match the type of attitude that we want to change.

SUMMARY OF CHANGING ATTITUDES BY CHANGING FEELINGS

Social psychologists classically condition attitudes by pairing an attitude object repeatedly with either positive or negative events. Because classical conditioning takes a peripheral rather than a central route to persuasion, the technique is more effective for attitude objects with which a person has little previous experience. Another way to change feelings about an attitude object is to expose people to the object while they are in a good or a bad mood. Positive moods impair motivation and ability to take the central route that emphasizes communication arguments.

Attitudes can be classically conditioned by pairing a person, object, or event with events that elicit positive or negative feelings. Classical conditioning attacks primarily the feelings rather than the thoughts component of an attitude. Mere exposure, which involves liking familiar objects more than unfamiliar ones, also occurs without participants being aware that they have seen the objects previously. Mere exposure effects are more pronounced when participants are unaware than when they are aware, as though attention to central route factors decreases the effect of peripheral route factors. Finally, attacks on feelings are more effective in changing attitudes that were initially based on feelings than in changing attitudes that were initially based on thoughts.

CAN WE CHANGE ATTITUDES BY CHANGING PEOPLE'S ACTIONS?

The first two sections of the chapter examined attitude change techniques that change people's thoughts (through new information) and feelings (through positive or negative associations). The third and last section of the chapter examines attitude change techniques that change people's actions (through rewards and modeling). As in the other two attitude change techniques, the "change actions" technique assumes that when one of the three attitude components changes, so do the other two. If we could get people to act as though they liked or disliked an attitude object, their thoughts and actions might follow. If we could get people to volunteer at a shelter for abused women, try using seat belts, being the designated driver, or negotiating with their enemies rather than making war, they might develop positive thoughts and feelings toward these activities. The motto is "Try it, you'll like it."

The "change actions" technique, if handled properly, can change attitudes successfully. People who are induced to act as though they like (or dislike) an attitude object sometimes change the way they think and feel about the object. They do so for two reasons. First, people whose actions are inconsistent with their thoughts and feelings sometimes get so negatively aroused by the inconsistency that they "need" to restore consistency. Second, people who do not have strong attitudes sometimes infer their thoughts and feelings from their own actions.

DO PEOPLE "NEED" CONSISTENCY BETWEEN ATTITUDES AND ACTIONS?

According to **cognitive dissonance theory,** people change their attitudes to reduce the aversive arousal they experience when they have two cognitions (thoughts) that contradict each other, or are dissonant (Festinger, 1957). Specifically, people become upset when they realize that they have one kind of attitude or belief about a person, object, or event, and yet they have acted as though they had exactly the opposite attitude. People *need* consistency between their attitudes and their actions, because they get aversively aroused when their attitudes and their actions do not match. In cases where they cannot take back the way they acted, aversive arousal motivates people to change their attitudes to match their actions. One way to change people's attitudes, then, is to get them to act in a counterattitudinal way, as though their attitudes were different. Change actions, and thoughts and feelings may follow. The following sections explain cognitive dissonance, describe four circumstances when it occurs, and examine the process by which it occurs.

■ COGNITIVE DISSONANCE

To illustrate cognitive dissonance, imagine what happens to the attitudes and beliefs of people who belong to "doomsday groups" that predict the end of the world. What do they do when the world doesn't end? Do they admit that their attitudes and beliefs were wrong? Three social psychologists joined a doomsday group so they could observe firsthand how members reacted when the end of the world did not arrive (Festinger, Riecken, & Schachter, 1956). Members of this particular doomsday group had been receiving communications from extraterrestrial "Guardians" who were going to destroy the Earth. Members believed that they, and only they, would be picked up by a flying saucer and taken off the planet just before its destruction. They left their jobs and spouses, gave away their worldly possessions, and gathered at a Minnesota farmhouse in the dead of winter to await their salvation. Just before the appointed hour, they got a communication that they were not allowed to bring metal objects on board the flying saucer, so they threw away their wristwatches and cut the zippers out of their clothing. They even considered knocking the metal fillings out of their teeth, but decided to wait and ask the Guardians when they arrived.

When no flying saucer appeared and the world did not end, the group members at first became upset. They had taken very strong actions because of their beliefs. The two thoughts "I left my job and spouse" and "The world did not end" were extremely dissonant. Several hours after the time when the world should have ended, however, they received a communication from God, who was so impressed by the faith and fortitude of this one small band of human beings that he had intervened and saved the Earth from destruction. Formerly very secretive, the group members began phoning newspapers, trying to convince the rest of the world that they had performed a great service for

FRANK & ERNEST® by Bob Thaves

What do doomsday
groups do the day after
the world didn't end?

humanity. Although they were *punished* for acting on their beliefs, the group
members used transcendence to become all the more convinced that they were
right. By adopting new, transcendent beliefs that their actions saved the world,
they reduced the dissonance and made their attitudes again match their actions.

■ WHEN COGNITIVE DISSONANCE OCCURS

The theory of cognitive dissonance has been supported by hundreds of studies. By way of summarizing these studies, we may say that they have identified at least four meaningful circumstances in which attitudes change because
of cognitive dissonance. The four circumstances, as shown in Table 7.2, involve
postdecisional dissonance, effort justification, insufficient justification, and insufficient deterrence (Cooper & Fazio, 1984).

■ **POSTDECISIONAL DISSONANCE** **Postdecisional dissonance** occurs when people justify a choice by emphasizing its advantages over an almost equally attractive alternative. They make "I like A" match "I chose B" by
convincing themselves that B is far superior to A. In one study of postdecisional dissonance, college students rated the attractiveness of eight small appliances like an automatic toaster and a coffeemaker (Brehm, 1956). After the
ratings, the experimenter offered the student one of two appliances as a gift.
Students in one condition chose between two items that they had rated far
apart. Because they clearly preferred one to the other of these items, they experienced little aversive arousal after they made their choice. Students in the

other condition, in contrast, had to choose between two items that they had rated almost equally attractive. After they made their choice, they experienced aversive arousal over the "lost opportunity" offered by the unchosen item. They should have been motivated to find new positive features of the chosen item and to derogate the unchosen item (Gerard & White, 1983).

The experimenter, having gift wrapped the chosen item to emphasize the finality of the student's choice, asked the student to rate all items a second time. As predicted, students who made an easy choice repeated their earlier ratings, as did students who were merely given the preferred item as a gift without having to make a choice. Students who made a close decision, by contrast, rated the chosen item more positively and the unchosen item more negatively than they had before they committed themselves. In doing so, they made their attitudes more consistent with their actions (Gilovich, Medvec, & Chen, 1995).

▨ **EFFORT JUSTIFICATION Effort justification** occurs when people justify their effort to achieve a disappointing goal by emphasizing the goal's positive features. They make "I suffered to get A" match "A isn't so hot" by convincing themselves that A is actually attractive. In a classic study of effort justification, female college students had a chance to join a supposedly attractive group that met regularly to discuss sex (Aronson & Mills, 1959). The experimenter explained that the group accepted only students who were uninhibited enough to discuss sex openly. To prove that they were worthy of joining the group, therefore, these women had to read aloud some sexually explicit materials. In the "mild initiation" group, the women read aloud to a male experimenter words like "petting" and "prostitute." In the "severe initiation" group, the women read aloud to a male experimenter a list of words that cannot be printed in this book and the "dirtiest" passages in some X-rated novels.

TABLE 7.2	Four Types of Attitude Change through Cognitive Dissonance
Postdecisional dissonance	people are upset when they have to go without the alternative they did not choose, so they emphasize the attractive features of the chosen alternative
Effort justification	people are upset when they spend more effort on attaining a goal than it turns out to be worth, so they emphasize the attractive features of the goal
Insufficient justification	people are upset when they perform an undesirable action for a small inducement, so they emphasize the attractive features of the action
Insufficient deterrence	people are upset when they refrain from performing a desirable action because of a small deterrent, so they emphasize the unattractive features of the action

Because the experiment was conducted in a very conservative era, women in the severe initiation group had to "suffer" more to join the group.

After the women had read the sexually explicit materials aloud, the experimenter played an audiotape of a previous discussion by the group. The taped discussion concentrated, in the driest and most boring manner possible, on "secondary sex behavior in the lower animals." Students in a control group, who merely listened to the tape recording, regarded the discussion and the group members as boring and uninteresting. So did the women who had undergone only a mild initiation. Women who had undergone a severe initiation to join the group, however, said they liked the discussion and looked forward to joining with such interesting people. In other words, they changed their thoughts and feelings about the group to coincide with and *justify* the effort that they had put into joining the group. Similar results were obtained when the effort put into joining a group involved taking electric shocks rather than reading sexually explicit passages (Gerard & Mathewson, 1966).

The principle of effort justification has many applications to everyday experiences such as graduate school and marathon running. It applies also to psychotherapy. In one study, snake phobics who wound and rewound a yo-yo that had a 5-pound weight attached to it improved their ability to approach snakes by as much as did snake phobics who went through a legitimate form of psychotherapy (Cooper, 1980). Sometimes, people even convince themselves in advance that the consequences of a future action will justify the effort. In a relevant study, some students expected to hold their hands in ice water for 60 seconds so that they could watch a movie. These students liked the movie better than did students who expected to hold their hands in ice water for only 30 seconds (Seta, Hundt, & Seta, 1995).

INSUFFICIENT JUSTIFICATION **Insufficient justification** occurs when people justify an undesirable action, which they performed for a barely sufficient inducement, by emphasizing the action's positive features. They make "I did A for almost nothing" match "I despise doing A" by convincing themselves that doing A is actually attractive. In a classic demonstration of insufficient justification, the investigators had students turn wooden pegs back and forth for an hour (Festinger & Carlsmith, 1959). When the study was supposedly over, the experimenter discovered that he had no confederate to help him with the next subject. He told the student that the study had two conditions. In one condition, in which the student had just participated, subjects received no advance information about the peg-turning task. In the other condition, a confederate met subjects in the waiting room and claimed to have participated in and thoroughly enjoyed the experimental study. "Could you possibly help me," the experimenter asked, "by being my confederate and telling the next subject that she's going to *love* doing this task?" When placed under this type of social pressure to do the experimenter a favor, all students agreed, even though it is hard to imagine anyone enjoying the task.

The experimenter told some students they would get $20 "for helping me," whereas he told other students they would get $1. The $20 students had a perfectly good justification for saying they liked the peg-turning task. Twenty dollars in those days was equivalent to at least $50 today. They could justify their actions very easily. But what of the $1 students? Their actions were inconsistent with their true thoughts and feelings. They lied to a poor, unsuspecting next subject (an experimental confederate) by telling her that the peg-turning task was great fun. The inconsistency between their true attitude and their actions should have upset them deeply. The tiny $1 reward was an insufficient excuse or justification, especially when the experimenter kept insisting that they didn't "have to do me this favor. It's your choice, but you would be helping me a lot." Students in the $1 condition, therefore, should have been aversively aroused.

After deceiving the "fellow student," all student subjects were dismissed. They "happened," however, to be scheduled for a separate experiment during the next hour. In that experiment, they were asked how much they liked the most recent study in which they had participated. According to cognitive dissonance theory, the $20 students should have had no trouble with this question. As shown in Figure 7.6, they did not. They knew that they hated the task and they told the second experimenter just that. True, they had told someone else that it was fun, but they were induced to say this by the very large reward, which was justification enough to overcome their negative arousal. The $1 students had no such luck. The $1 reward was insufficient justification for lying to the other subject. They could not take back what they had done, so how could they possibly make their actions less negatively arousing? Of course! They need only convince themselves that they really liked turning those pegs. If that were true, then they did not lie to the other person at all. Just as cognitive dissonance theory predicted, students in the $1 condition claimed that they *liked* turning the pegs!

The insufficient justification effect occurs with any inducement that seems too small to justify a counterattitudinal action, not just money (Kelman, 1953). Performing a counterattitudinal action at the request of someone you like, for instance, seems like a greater justification than performing the same action at the request of someone you dislike. In one study, ROTC members were induced to eat fried grasshoppers (Zimbardo, Weisenberg, Firestone, & Levy, 1965). They did it to help an ROTC officer who was either a very nice guy (sufficient justification) or a jerk (insufficient justification). As cognitive dissonance theory predicted, students who did it to help the jerk adopted more positive attitudes toward grasshoppers as food than did students who did it to help the nice guy. The principle of insufficient justification holds even when the term "justification" is interpreted loosely.

INSUFFICIENT DETERRENCE Insufficient deterrence occurs when people justify refraining from a desirable action, which they avoided because of a barely sufficient deterrent, by emphasizing the action's negative features. They make "I avoided doing A for almost no reason" match "I love doing A" by convincing themselves that A is actually unattractive. In a classic study of insufficient deterrence, an adult experimenter led a five-year-old child into a room full of toys and then said "I have to leave for a few minutes. While

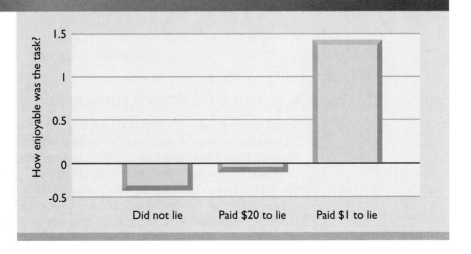

FIGURE 7.6

When people act counter to their attitudes for small reward, they change attitudes to correspond with their actions.

Graph shows how enjoyable students found a boring task after telling a fellow student about the task (Festinger & Carlsmith, 1959).

If this child can't have the toy, will she say it wouldn't have been much fun anyway?

I'm gone, feel free to play with any of these toys except that one" (pointing to a toy that most children found particularly attractive). In one condition he made a mild threat about being somewhat annoyed if the child played with the "forbidden toy." In the other condition he said that if the child played with that particular toy, he would be *very* angry and would take all the toys away. While the experimenter was gone from the room, no child played with the forbidden toy (Aronson & Carlsmith, 1963).

Later, a second experimenter questioned the children about how much they liked the various toys. The severe threat children had sufficient justification for not playing with the forbidden toy, so they did not need to reduce aversive arousal by changing their attitudes. They continued to like the forbidden toy. The mild threat children, in contrast, were very upset when they realized that they were not playing with the toy, even though doing so would have brought only mild punishment. Lacking sufficient justification for their actions, they could reduce the unpleasant arousal only by changing their attitudes after the fact. Interestingly, the children did not merely tell the second experimenter that they did not like the forbidden toy. When they were subsequently left alone with the previously attractive toy, they refused to play with it (Pepitone, McCauley, & Hammond, 1967). They were not merely convincing the experimenter. They were convincing themselves. Children's distaste for playing with a previously attractive but mildly forbidden toy continues for up to two months after an "insufficient deterrence" episode (Freedman, 1965; Lepper, 1973).

■ HOW COGNITIVE DISSONANCE OCCURS

Not all close decisions and not all counterattitudinal actions elicit dissonance. For people to become motivated to reduce negative arousal by bringing their thoughts and feelings into line with their actions, counterattitudinal actions must be more than merely inconsistent with an attitude. The action must cause aversive consequences, the person who performs the action must assume personal responsibility for causing those aversive consequences, and the person who performs the action must experience aversive arousal that is attributed to the action (Cooper & Fazio, 1984). Finally, the person must have no attractive way to reduce arousal other than through attitude change (Simon, Greenberg, & Brehm, 1995; Steele, 1988). The top part of Figure 7.7 summarizes these four criteria, without which attitudes cannot change through cognitive dissonance. You may find it useful to refer to the top part of Figure 7.7 and its examples as you read the following descriptions.

AVERSIVE CONSEQUENCES When students in the $1/$20 study of insufficient justification lied to the confederate and told her that she would love being in an experiment that they knew was tedious and boring, they did more than merely act in a counterattitudinal way (Festinger & Carlsmith, 1959). They also caused unwanted aversive consequences. They duped a fellow student. When they later decided that the task was fun, they also implied that they had done no harm. In one study that tested the impact of aversive consequences, college students who opposed the legalization of marijuana were induced, for a small reward (insufficient justification), to advocate legalization (Nel, Helmreich, & Aronson, 1969). Some students thought their arguments would be given to adults who were set in their opinions about legalization. Other students believed that their arguments would be given to schoolchildren who might be influenced to espouse a policy that the students considered repugnant. Even though the two groups of students took equally counterattitudinal actions, only students who thought their actions might cause aversive consequences later changed their attitudes.

Other studies have shown that students who lie to the confederate for $1 in the $1/$20 situation do not change their own attitudes toward turning the pegs if they have reason to believe that the "fellow student" did not believe them or if the "fellow student" was obnoxious toward them (Cooper & Worchel, 1970; Cooper, Zanna, & Goethals, 1974). Counterattitudinal behavior has no aversive consequences if it does not harm another person or if it harms someone who deserves to be harmed. Conversely, even proattitudinal behavior can

FIGURE 7.7

Two processes by which people change their attitudes after performing counterattitudinal actions.

Cognitive Dissonance (performing the counterattitudinal action makes people aversively aroused)
Attitude change occurs when:

People perceive their actions as causing aversive consequences

People feel personally responsible for the aversive consequences

People experience aversive arousal that they connect with the action

People have no other way to reduce the aversive arousal than to change their attitudes

Self-Perception (performing the counterattitudinal action does not make people aversively aroused)
Attitude change occurs when:

The action is one that logically implies a corresponding attitude

People do not spontaneously remember what their attitude used to be

People experience no physiological arousal that they need to explain

A previously attractive action becomes dictated by external controls induce attitude change if it has unwanted aversive consequences. Students in an ingenious study were induced to write *pro*attitudinal essays against raising tuition at their university (Scher & Cooper, 1989). Some students thought that their essays would be read by a university committee that tried to do what students wanted. Other students held the negatively arousing belief that the committee was likely to do the opposite of what students wanted. By writing against tuition increases, they were helping to *raise* tuition! As predicted, even a proattitudinal action caused the students' attitudes to become more favorable toward tuition increases, because the proattitudinal action was likely to cause aversive consequences.

Finally, cognitive dissonance can be aroused merely by *reminding* people that they might have caused aversive consequences in the past by not "living up" to their attitudes. In one study, members of the women's swim team at a California university, where people were trying to conserve water because of a drought, were interviewed as they left the pool for a shower (Dickerson, Thibodeau, Aronson, & Miller, 1992). The interviewer asked the women whether they *always* shut the water off while they were soaping or shampooing in the shower, whether they *always* made their showers as short as possible, and so on. Obviously, no one *always* conserves water, so the interview reminded the women that they had been acting negatively, but it did not remind them that they had positive attitudes. Other women were merely asked to sign their names on a poster urging people to conserve shower water. The poster read, "IF I CAN DO IT, SO CAN YOU!" Women who merely signed the poster were reminded of their positive attitudes, but they were not reminded about acting opposite to those attitudes. Finally, some women were both interviewed and signed the poster. They should have experienced cognitive dissonance, because they were reminded of *both* their positive attitudes toward water conservation and that they had been hypocritically wasting precious water. Subsequently, a different experimenter surreptitiously recorded how long a shower women in the three groups took. As predicted, women in the "hypocrisy" group took the shortest showers.

PERSONAL RESPONSIBILITY   Not only must an individual's actions cause aversive consequences for dissonance to be aroused and attitude change to occur, but the individual must also assume personal responsibility for having caused those consequences (Cooper & Fazio, 1984). In the $1/$20 study of insufficient justification, for instance, the experimenter exerted considerable social pressure to get the students to "do me a big favor" and lie to a fellow student about how interesting the peg-turning task was, but the experimenter also reminded students that they were *choosing* to do so. The so-called "choice" was an illusion, because the social pressure was sufficient to guarantee compliance, but the illusion of choice made students take personal responsibility for the aversive consequences.

Students in one study of personal responsibility were offered either a large or a small reward to urge a university committee to ban controversial speakers from campus—a counterattitudinal position (Linder, Cooper, & Jones, 1967). Students who were given no choice about writing the counterattitudinal essay displayed the opposite of a cognitive dissonance effect. They were more likely to change their attitudes in the direction of their essay when they were offered a large rather than a small reward for their action. If they had no choice, they felt no personal responsibility for the consequences. Students who were given the "illusion of choice," in contrast, were more likely to change their attitudes when they were offered a small rather than a large reward. Because they believed that they had a choice, they felt personally responsible for aversive consequences.

A sense of personal responsibility does not require that the aversive consequences of counterattitudinal behavior be *foreseen,* but only that they be *foreseeable.* In a relevant study, students were asked to record counterattitudinal communications for a university committee and were given an illusion of choice about doing so, to make them feel personally responsible for the consequences (Goethals, Cooper, & Naficy, 1979). Some of the students were later informed that, because of an equipment malfunction, the committee would never hear their arguments. As expected, students who thought that their communications would be used changed their attitudes to be more consistent with what they had done. For them, the aversive consequences were foreseen. Students who thought their communications would not be used, however, also changed their attitudes. Although they knew that they would not actually cause any aversive consequences, they also knew that they had acted in a way likely to do so. The equipment malfunction did not excuse their actions, because for them, the aversive consequences were foreseeable. Actions that cause foreseeable aversive consequences are negatively arousing, whether or not the aversive consequences occur.

AVERSIVE AROUSAL Cognitive dissonance theory assumes that when people feel personally responsible for causing (or intending to cause) aversive consequences, they experience aversive or unpleasant arousal. Aversive arousal makes people redefine their attitudes to match their actions, which in turn reduces the arousal (Croyle & Cooper, 1983). In one study of arousal and attitude change, students were told that they were taking either a tranquilizer that would make them feel relaxed, a stimulant that would make them feel aroused, or a placebo that would have no effect (Zanna & Cooper, 1974). In reality, all students took nothing but an inert placebo. The students were then either ordered or given a choice to write a counterattitudinal essay about banning controversial speakers from campus. Figure 7.8 shows that students who thought they took a placebo changed their attitudes more when they had the illusion of choice than when they had no choice. Students who thought they took a tranquilizer changed their attitudes even more with choice, most likely because they felt more aroused than they expected to feel. Students who thought they took a stimulant, however, did not change their attitudes, even with choice. They felt personally responsible for aversive consequences, but they could misattribute their arousal to the pill. Attitude change does not occur, even with aversive consequences and personal responsibility, when the aversive arousal associated with counterattitudinal actions can be misattributed

FIGURE 7.8

Misattribution of arousal eliminates cognitive dissonance.

Graph shows attitude change after counterattitudinal actions by students who all took a placebo but differed in what they were told (Zanna & Cooper, 1974).

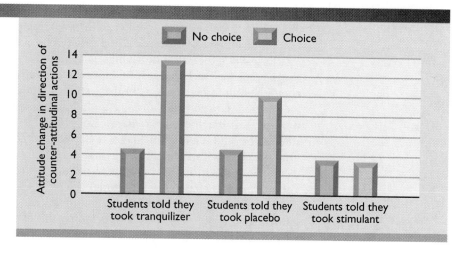

to another source (Brodt & Zimbardo, 1981; Fazio & Cooper, 1983; Worchel & Arnold, 1974).

■ **LACK OF ALTERNATIVES** People who perform counterattitudinal actions may be aversively aroused by doing so, but they do not always change their attitudes. Even when they feel aroused and responsible for creating aversive consequences, they may have available an alternative way of reducing aversive arousal. One such alternative is **self-affirmation,** which involves reducing aversive arousal by affirming a positive identity (Steele, 1988; Steele, Spencer, & Lynch, 1993). If people reduce aversive arousal by making themselves "look good," they do not need to change their attitudes to match their actions. In one study of self-affirmation, students chose between two record albums that they liked almost equally (Steele, 1988). Half of the students thought very highly of science, which to them was symbolized by the scientist's white lab coat. The other half were more interested in business. They had relatively little respect for science or lab coats. After they decided which album to keep, the students were asked to put on a scientist's lab coat in preparation for what was supposed to be a "second" study. Then they reevaluated the record albums. Students who cared little for science changed their attitudes to be consistent with their choices. Students who greatly respected science and lab coats did not. Wearing the lab coat reaffirmed for these students their positive identities, so they did not need to change their attitudes. They reduced aversive arousal in a different way (Steele & Lui, 1983).

Do medical doctors and scientists feel better about themselves when they put on their long white lab coats?

People also have alternatives other than self-affirmation to reduce aversive arousal without changing their attitudes. One such alternative is to trivialize the attitude. In a relevant study, students wrote a counterattitudinal essay, with the illusion of choice, that their school should adopt mandatory comprehensive examinations (Simon et al., 1995, Study 2). Some students got to rank the issue "in the grand scheme of things" before they restated their attitudes. Others did not. Students who ranked the issue before restating their attitudes said it was trivial, so they did not change their attitudes. The other students did. Another alternative is to give the injured party a gift, thus regaining self-respect without changing attitudes (Verhaege, 1976). Also, when payment for counterattitudinal actions is perceived as a "bribe," people change their attitudes more for a large than for a small reward (reversing the insufficient justification effect), because the larger payment injures the participant's self-respect more than does the smaller payment (Schlenker, Forsyth, Leary, & Miller, 1980). Such studies suggest that when a participant's positive identity is not called into question, there may be no need to claim attitude change (Riess & Schlenker, 1977). They also raise the interesting possibility that people who act contrary to their attitudes merely *say* they have changed their attitudes so that they will not look like fools, either to the experimenter or to themselves (Abelson, 1983; Tedeschi & Rosenfeld, 1981; Tedeschi, Schlenker, & Bonomoa, 1971).

To test whether attitude change is genuine, several studies have used the "bogus pipeline" technique (see Chapter 6) to get participants to "tell the truth" about their attitudes. In some of these studies, students did not "really" change their attitudes, even when all the conditions necessary for cognitive dissonance were present (Paulhus, 1982; Riess, Kalle, & Tedeschi, 1981). In other similar studies, they did (Guild, Strickland, & Barefoot, 1977; Jamieson & Zanna, 1982). One problem with such studies is that participants who are aroused by their own actions might misattribute their arousal to the "lie detection" equipment and not need to change their attitudes (Eagly & Chaiken, 1993). Related studies have tried to make the measurement of attitudes completely private, so that participants believe no one else (including the experimenter) will ever know what their true attitudes were. Some of these studies have detected attitude change when the attitude scales are "public," but no attitude change from the same procedures when the attitude scales are "private." Unfortunately, making the scales "private" reduces the negative arousal that is essential for the cognitive dissonance process (Gaes, Kalle, & Tedeschi, 1978; Malkis, Kalle, & Tedeschi, 1982). Also, it may be almost impossible to convince participants in psychology experiments that the experimenter has no way to know their answers (Leary & Kowalski, 1990; Tetlock & Manstead, 1985). What would be the point of conducting the study if the experimenter had no access to the data?

Ultimately, it may not matter whether participants are merely *claiming* changed attitudes to create a positive impression. In making such claims, people often convince themselves. Many studies have shown that people who know they are merely role-playing a particular attitude come to believe the "script" that they follow (Greenwald & Albert, 1968; Janis & King, 1954; Kelman, 1953). The effects of role-playing continue even after 18 months, when attitudes are assessed in a way that seems totally unrelated to the role-playing study (Mann & Janis, 1968). In a relevant study, ROTC students who had little likelihood of being drafted (and thus very little external justification for joining the ROTC) were more satisfied with ROTC one year later than were ROTC students who joined because they had a high probability of being drafted (Staw, 1974). Today's impression management can become tomorrow's genuine attitude change.

DO PEOPLE INFER THEIR ATTITUDES FROM THEIR ACTIONS?

Cognitive dissonance theory provides one process by which people sometimes change their attitudes to match their actions. Self-perception theory provides a second process (Bem, 1967). According to **self-perception theory,** people change weakly held attitudes because they draw the same inferences from perceiving their own actions that anyone else who perceived those actions would draw (Bem, 1972). If we get people to act as though they had positive or negative attitudes on an issue for which they have weakly held attitudes, they change their attitudes without realizing that they have done so, because they use their own actions to draw logical conclusions. The following sections explain self-perception and examine the process by which it occurs.

■ SELF-PERCEPTION

To understand the logic behind self-perception theory, it helps to know about a famous experiment on the "two-factor" theory of emotion (Schachter & Singer, 1962). Male college students got an injection that they believed might temporarily affect their performance on a vision test. In reality, the injection was a mild stimulant that causes a person's heart to race, hands to tremble, breathing to accelerate, and skin to feel flushed. Some of the students were told that the injection had these effects, so they expected to feel aroused. Other students were not told about any side effects, so they could not attribute their arousal to the injection. Yet other students were *misinformed* that the injection had effects like numb feet, that have nothing to do with arousal. Although all students got the same injection and thus experienced the same physiological arousal, half of the students in each of the three conditions were placed in a "happy" context and half were placed in an "angry" context while they waited with "another student" (a confederate) for the injection to take effect.

In the "happy" context, the confederate rolled up some scratch paper and started shooting baskets into a trash can. The confederate tried to get the student to join in the basketball game and other enjoyable activities such as making paper airplanes and shooting wads of paper with an elastic band—activities that the confederate said, with a big grin, made him "feel like a kid again." In the "angry" context, the student and the confederate completed a questionnaire while they waited. The confederate complained about the length of the questionnaire and became enraged about the questions. The questions became progressively more personal and insulting, from asking about the exact dates of childhood diseases through asking about family income. The last question was "With how many men (other than your father) has your mother had extramarital relationships?" The question had as the only possible answers "4 and under," "5–9," or "10 and over." When he saw this question, the confederate ripped up the questionnaire and stormed out of the room.

The experimenter then reentered the room and claimed that to assess the effects of the vitamin injection on vision, it was necessary to rule out artifacts such as the participants' feelings. Under this guise, all participants were asked how angry they felt and how happy they felt. Students in the uninformed and misinformed conditions, who felt their hearts racing, hands trembling, and skin being flushed for no reason known to them, said they were more happy (or angry, depending on which "context" the confederate had created) than did students who had been informed that these signs of arousal were the injection's expected side effects. In other words, when people experience emotions for which they have no ready explanation, they cannot tell the difference between two emotions that are as different from each other as happiness and anger. They know only that they are aroused, so they look to the context for a way to label their arousal. According to the two-factor theory of emotion (Schachter, 1964), all emotions involve the same generalized arousal (the first factor), but

Would you feel happy if you unknowingly ingested drugs and then spent some time with this person?

we label our emotions differently depending on the context (the second factor).

According to self-perception theory, the two-factor theory of emotions also applies to some attitudes (Bem, 1972). If people cannot tell the difference between their hearts beating fast because they are happy and their hearts beating fast because they are angry, then it must sometimes be difficult for them to tell the difference between positive and negative attitudes. This ambiguity would not occur for strongly held attitudes. The people who demonstrate outside abortion clinics or nuclear energy plants know their attitudes very well. Many everyday attitudes, however, including many of the attitudes investigated in psychology experiments, might be much weaker. Some experimental participants might care deeply about whether they get a toaster or a coffeemaker, how much they like a campus discussion group, and how much they like turning pegs in an experiment, but not everyone does. How do the other people—the ones with weakly held attitudes—know how they feel? They may operate like detectives investigating a crime: They may look for clues.

In thinking about what the "clues" might be, consider a study in which male college students were shown "centerfold" slides of beautiful naked or near-naked women in provocative poses (Valins, 1966). While viewing these centerfolds, the men were "wired up" with electrodes that relayed what was supposed to be their own heartbeat into earphones. The experimenter, however, controlled the sounds that the men heard, and could speed up or slow down the "heartbeat" at will. While a randomly selected one of the centerfold pictures was being shown (a different centerfold for each student), the experimenter increased the speed of the heartbeat. The men assumed that their heart was racing faster when they saw that particular woman than when they saw any of the others. When the experiment was presumably over, the experimenter told each student, "You might be able to have the original of one of these pictures to take home with you. Which one would you choose?" Overwhelmingly, the men chose whichever centerfold the experimenter had randomly selected to have their heart beat faster for. In other words, the men used a clue (how fast they thought their heart was beating) to determine how positively they viewed the centerfolds. They used what they thought were their own actions to infer what their feelings about the women must be.

According to self-perception theory, when people act in ways contrary to weakly held attitudes, they do not realize that they are acting "inconsistently." Instead, they infer what their attitudes must be from perceiving their own actions. People draw the same inferences from their own actions as might an uninvolved detective, using whatever "clues" are available. The most noticeable clue is usually their own actions (Olson & Roese, 1995). Weakly held attitudes change to match actions when the clues available after the action imply a different attitude than did the clues available before the action.

■ HOW SELF-PERCEPTION OCCURS

Look back at the bottom part of Figure 7.7. As the table shows, counterattitudinal actions can change attitudes even when the counterattitudinal actions do not elicit aversive arousal. Self-perception changes attitudes when the action implies a corresponding attitude, when people do not remember their previous attitudes, when there is no arousal to explain, and when a previously attractive action becomes perceived as dictated by external controls. You might refer to the bottom part of Figure 7.7 as you read the following sections.

▧ **ACTIONS IMPLY CORRESPONDING ATTITUDES** According to self-perception theory, *some* of the participants in cognitive dissonance studies might have changed their attitudes through self-perception rather than through cognitive dissonance. Participants who preferred a toaster only slightly to a coffeemaker, for example, might not have been aroused enough to experience postdecisional dissonance, but after they chose, they had as a clue in assessing their own attitudes their action of taking the toaster. Some college women who read embarrassing passages to a male experimenter might not have been so aroused that they had to "justify" the effort by claiming that the club was interesting, but any reasonable person would conclude that someone who expends much effort to join a club must like it more than someone who expends little effort. Some students who lied to "another student" about whether an experiment was "fun" might not have been very upset about doing it for insufficient justification, but any reasonable person would conclude that someone who is willing to rave about an activity for a mere $1 must like the activity more than someone who has to be paid $20 to give the same endorsement. Finally, who would you think likes a toy more–a child who refrains from playing with it just because the experimenter might be annoyed or a child who has to be threatened with severe punishment? In all these circumstances, even an uninvolved observer might have used the participants' actions to predict which group would have the more positive attitude after performing the action, simply by using the principles of attribution that are explained in Chapter 4. We attribute a person's actions to his or her attitudes when situational constraints are low and the actions unambiguously imply a corresponding attitude (Kelley, 1967; Jones & Davis, 1965).

This prediction was tested through an "interpersonal simulation" (Bem, 1967). Students listened to a tape recording in which a sophomore named Bob Downing described participating in the $1/$20 experiment. The students got a factual description of the peg-turning task and learned that Bob had accepted either $1 or $20 to tell the next subject that the task was "fun." They overheard Bob tell the "next subject" how much he had enjoyed the experiment. Then the students were asked to estimate, from everything they knew, Bob Downing's actual attitude toward the experimental task. As predicted, these uninvolved observers, who had caused no aversive consequences and had no reason to be aversively aroused, replicated the original results almost exactly. Students who thought Bob had agreed to say the experiment was fun for $1 estimated that he liked the task much more than did students who thought he had to be paid $20 to say it was fun. From these results, the experimenter concluded that even the nonaroused students in the original $1/$20 study had reason to adopt different attitudes depending on the amount of money they were paid. All they had to do was to use the clue of their own actions to draw the logical inference that someone who has to be paid only $1 to say an activity is fun must like it more than someone who has to be paid $20. One difference between "sufficient" and "insufficient" rewards, whether it is money or any other form of reward, is what the reward implies about the true attitude of the recipient, even when *you* are the recipient.

▓ **PEOPLE DO NOT REMEMBER PREVIOUS ATTITUDES** Self-perception also changes attitudes when people cannot remember what their initial attitudes were. Students who heard the Bob Downing tape did not have one clue that Bob had: that he initially disliked turning the pegs (Jones, Linder, Kiesler, Zanna, & Brehm, 1968). Bob became aroused because his action (saying the task was fun) conflicted with his initial negative attitude. He would not have been aroused (and cognitive dissonance could not have occurred) if he did not spontaneously recall his initial attitude. If observers did not know what Bob's initial attitude was, the "interpersonal simulations" might have replicated the difference between the $1 and $20 conditions of the original experiment, but the process for observers might have been entirely different from the process for participants. According to self-perception theory, however, one of the circumstances in which actions change attitudes is when the person who takes the action does not remember what his or her previous attitude was. People infer their attitudes today from the clues available today. People infer their attitudes next week from the clues available then (Wilson & Hodges, 1992). If people take a relevant action between assessing attitudes, that action is an important clue. They need not remember that the clues (and the inferences) were different last week. For the kinds of weakly held attitudes described by self-perception theory, people might easily forget what they said the last time someone asked about their attitude.

To test this hypothesis about memory for previous attitudes, students in one study were asked about their attitudes toward student control over the curriculum, which they all favored (Bem & McConnel, 1970). Later, the same students were induced, with either choice or no choice, to write counterattitudinal essays that argued for less student control. After the essay, attitudes were measured again. As usual, students in the "choice" condition changed their attitudes in the direction of less student control; students in the "no choice" condition did not. The experimenters then asked all students to recall, as accurately as possible, what their attitudes had been before they wrote the essay. As predicted by self-perception theory, students in both conditions "remembered" that their attitudes before they wrote the essay had been exactly what they were after they wrote the essay! Students in the no choice condition were correct, because they had not changed their attitudes. Students in the choice condition, however, were incorrect. They had changed their attitudes and yet, even when asked directly whether their attitudes had changed, they were unaware of having done so.

Several studies have since replicated this important finding–that people can change their attitudes without realizing that they have done so (Goethals & Reckman, 1973; Ross & Shulman, 1973; Shaffer, 1975). Interestingly, attitudes and actions seem to have reciprocal effects. When you change people's attitudes, they recall not only their previously held attitudes as having been consistent with their newly formed ones, but also their past actions as having been consistent with their newly formed attitudes (Ross, in press; Ross & Buehler, 1994). Not only that, but biased recall of relevant past actions (for example, misremembering how often you brushed your teeth in the past two weeks when you have recently decided that brushing your teeth is important) helps to solidify the newly formed attitude and protect it from subsequent change (Ross, McFarland, Conway, & Zanna, 1983; Lydon, Zanna, & Ross, 1988; Ross & Conway, 1986; Ross, McFarland, & Fletcher, 1981; Zanna, Fazio, & Ross, 1994). Attitudes sometimes "follow" actions because people cannot accurately remember their own previous attitudes, but instead creatively reconstruct them.

PEOPLE HAVE NO AVERSIVE AROUSAL TO EXPLAIN For cognitive dissonance to change attitudes, as Figure 7.7 shows, people must become aversively aroused. For self-perception to change attitudes, no arousal is necessary. It seems possible, then, that attitude change might occur through self-perception when the action is *not* discrepant enough from the initial attitude to be aversively arousing. It might occur through cognitive dissonance when the action *is* discrepant enough from the initial attitude to be aversively arousing. In a relevant study, students provided their attitudes on issues like legalizing marijuana, on scales that ranged from extremely liberal to extremely conservative (Fazio, Zanna, & Cooper, 1977). Besides indicating one position on the attitude scale, the students also indicated which of the other positions they could accept (their latitude of acceptance) and which of the other positions they totally rejected (their latitude of rejection). Latitudes of acceptance and rejection are explained in Chapter 6. People perceive attitude positions inside the latitude of acceptance as more similar to their own position than they really are. They perceive attitude positions in the latitude of rejection as more discrepant from their own position than they really are (Hovland et al., 1957; Insko, 1967; Sherif & Sherif, 1967). It should be very arousing, then, to argue for a position only slightly outside your latitude of acceptance, but not to argue for a position slightly inside your latitude of acceptance.

The experimenters induced some students to write essays expressing a political position different from their own, but within their latitude of acceptance. They induced other students to write essays expressing a political position that was equally different from their own, but within their latitude of rejection. (To see how this is possible, see Figure 7.3.) To introduce aversive consequences, the experimenters told all students that their essays would be shown to and might influence the political attitudes of schoolchildren. To introduce personal responsibility, students in two "choice" conditions were reminded that they were choosing to help the experimenter by writing the assigned essay, but that they did not have to do so. There was also a "no choice" condition in which students were simply told to write the assigned essay. The two "choice" conditions differed in whether the students had an opportunity to misattribute whatever arousal their actions elicited. According to cognitive dissonance theory, people who act in a counterattitudinal way do not "need" to change their attitudes if they can misattribute their negative arousal to something other than their own actions. To afford an opportunity for misattribution of arousal, the experimenters asked students in the "choice with misattribution" condition whether the "new booths" in which they were participating were too cramped, poorly ventilated, and poorly lighted. These students had an opportunity to blame whatever arousal they were feeling on the "claustrophobic" booths rather than on their own counterattitudinal actions. Students in the "choice no misattribution" condition were never asked about possible booth-related irritants, so they had no convenient way to misattribute their arousal. After they wrote the essays, all students reported their political attitudes again.

The results are shown in Figure 7.9. When students argued for a position in the latitude of rejection, the opportunity to misattribute arousal eliminated attitude change. Students who espoused a rejected position under "choice with misattribution" conditions changed their attitudes no more than did students in the "no choice" condition. They were presumably aroused about their counterattitudinal actions, which involved telling schoolchildren to adopt a position that the students found objectionable, but they misattributed their arousal to the booths, so changing their attitudes could not reduce the arousal. Students who espoused a rejected position under "choice no misattribution" conditions, in contrast, could *not* misattribute their arousal, so they reduced their arousal by adopting more liberal attitudes than did their "no choice" counterparts. Cognitive dissonance operated for counterattitudinal actions in the (arousing) latitude of rejection.

When students argued for a counterattitudinal position within their latitude of acceptance, in contrast, the opportunity to misattribute arousal made no difference. Attitudes changed more with than without choice regardless of whether students had an opportunity to misattribute arousal or not, presumably because they did not experience arousal. They did not change their attitudes to reduce negative arousal, but because they drew the same conclusions that any uninvolved observer would draw. When they saw a reasonable person (themselves) write a political essay when given a choice about influencing schoolchildren or not, they assumed that the person's attitude must correspond with the essay. The possibility that the person might have written the essay in a cramped, poorly ventilated, or poorly lighted booth did not change the fact that people who freely choose to espouse a position normally believe in it more

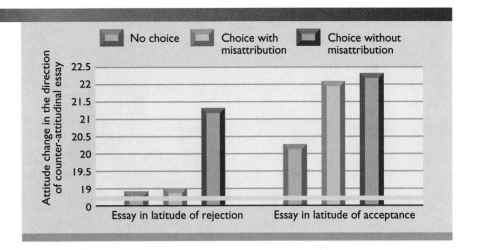

FIGURE 7.9

Cognitive dissonance and self-perception operate in different latitudes.

Graph shows attitude change by students who wrote counterattitudinal essays in different latitudes under three conditions (Fazio, Zanna, & Cooper, 1977).

than do people who are coerced into espousing the same position. Self-perception operates for counterattitudinal actions in the (nonarousing) latitude of rejection.

ACTIONS SEEM DICTATED BY EXTERNAL CONTROLS   An important educational application of self-perception theory holds that previously attractive activities lose their allure if they receive "overjustification." **Overjustification** occurs when people lose interest in a previously desirable activity because they had to perform it with too much justification, or under external control. According to self-perception theory, a person who has to have a large reward to engage in an activity probably *dislikes* doing it. People who see themselves engaging in an activity for a large reward might conclude that they enjoy the activity less than do people who see themselves engaging in the same activity for little or no reward. They might also infer that the activity must be unpleasant (Freedman, Cunningham, & Krismer, 1992). We do what we do either because of extrinsic motivation (external control) or because of intrinsic motivation (enjoying the activity "for its own sake") (Ryan, 1995; Ryan, Sheldon, Kasser, & Deci, in press). When people are offered an attractive reward or other external inducement to engage in an activity, the reward might be construed as a form of external control (Deci & Ryan, 1991). Because people do not like to be controlled by others, a reward might undermine intrinsic interest in the activity (Kipnis, 1993, 1994; O'Neal, Kipnis, & Craig, 1994).

The implications of overjustification are especially frightening when they are applied to educational practices. Teachers who reward their students by giving them candy or gold stars merely for working a set of math problems or for handing in assignments, for instance, might be telling students subtly that "doing math problems [or other schoolwork] is a task so onerous that people would not do it unless they were bribed." It is easy to see how subtle communications of this sort can undermine early education. In a study that tested this overjustification derivation of self-perception theory, nursery schoolchildren were observed through a one-way mirror as they moved from one to another of several attractive activities (such as drawing with magic markers) that their teachers had placed in a free play area (Lepper, Greene, & Nisbett, 1973). The observers recorded how much time each child spent on each activity. The activities were then removed from the play area.

Two weeks later, children who had spent considerable time playing with the magic markers were brought one at a time to a room in which an experimenter induced them to draw pictures with magic markers. Some of the children were in an "expected reward condition." They were offered what should

Would this child begin to detest drawing if you paid him to do it?

have seemed to them an excessive justification for doing something that they already enjoyed. The experimenter told them that if they would agree to draw pictures with the magic markers for six minutes, they would receive an attractive Good Player Award certificate with a big gold star and a red ribbon. Other children were in an "unexpected reward" condition. The experimenter simply asked if they would like to draw some pictures with the magic markers. No reward was mentioned. After they had drawn pictures for six minutes, however, they were unexpectedly given the attractive Good Player Award certificate, gold star and red ribbon. A third group of children in a "no reward" condition was neither offered nor received a reward for drawing with the magic markers.

From one to two weeks later, the teachers placed in the free play area the same set of attractive activities as during the initial observation period. The experimenters again recorded how much time each child spent drawing pictures with magic markers. As predicted by self-perception theory, children who had been offered a reward to play with magic markers played with the markers less than did children who had not been offered a reward. The reward itself did not decrease children's interest in drawing with magic markers, because children who received an unexpected reward spent as much time with the magic markers as did children who got no reward. The important difference between the expected and the unexpected reward conditions was the *contractual* nature of being hired to engage in an activity that the children used to do for fun. The contract implied the self-perception conclusion that "Anyone who has to be bribed with such an attractive reward to do this must not like doing it." Thus self-perception can undermine intrinsic motivation for previously interesting or creative activities by "turning play into work" (Amabile, Hennessey, & Grossman, 1986; Amabile, Hill, Hennessey, & Tighe, 1994; Boggiano, Harackiewicz, Bessette, & Main, 1985; Deci & Ryan, 1985; Pittman, Emery, & Boggiano, 1982).

Rewards do not always undermine intrinsic interest. Rewards have no overjustification effect on attitudes toward activities in which a person is not initially interested, because the self-perception conclusion "I wouldn't do that except for a reward" suggests exactly what the person's attitude was all along (Hitt, Marriott, & Esser, 1992). Also, there are two kinds of rewards. Some are given only for exceptional performance and send the message "I'm very competent at this activity." Rewards for exceptional performance increase rather than decrease intrinsic motivation for an activity (Sansone, 1989). Professional sports stars, for instance, do not lose their interest in playing their sport merely because they make millions for doing so (Frederick & Ryan, 1995; Pelletier, Fortier, Vallerand, Tuson, Briere, & Blais, 1995). Winning at an activity increases rather than decreases intrinsic motivation, because winning enhances perceived competence (Reeve & Deci, 1996; Reeve, Olson, & Cole, 1985, 1987). Just as self-perception theory predicts, only rewards that are provided merely for engaging in a previously attractive activity or for espousing a previously held position destroy positive attitudes toward the activity or position (Crano, Gorenflo, & Shackelford, 1988). When people are not motivated to achieve, setting high performance goals and standards might decrease intrinsic motivation, but when people are motivated to achieve, setting high performance goals and standards *increases* intrinsic motivation (Harackiewicz & Elliot, 1993; Elliot & Harackiewicz, 1994).

SUMMARY OF CHANGING ATTITUDES BY CHANGING ACTIONS

Cognitive dissonance theory suggests that we can change attitudes by changing people's actions. When actions change, attitudes follow, because people are negatively aroused by inconsistencies among their own thoughts, feelings, and actions and are motivated to resolve the inconsistency. The theory explains why people who choose one of two almost equally attractive alternatives adopt more positive attitudes toward the chosen alternative and less positive attitudes toward the unchosen alternative. It explains why people who suffer to achieve a goal have a more positive attitude toward that goal than do people for whom the goal came easily. It explains why people who are handsomely rewarded for espousing an opinion different from their own are less likely to adopt that opinion than are people who are given very little incentive to do so. It also explains why people who are threatened with severe punishment for performing an action are less likely to refrain from that action in the future than are people who are threatened with only mild punishment. Cognitive dissonance occurs when people believe that they are personally responsible for causing aversive consequences and so become negatively aroused. If their negative arousal can be misattributed to a source other than the counterattitudinal action, people do not change their attitudes to match their actions.

Self-perception theory, like cognitive dissonance theory, suggests that an effective way to change attitudes is to change actions. The theory describes how attitudes change when people have such weak attitudes that they are not negatively aroused by their own counterattitudinal actions. In such cases, people infer what their actions must be from the available clues, the most important of which is how they acted. People draw the same inferences from their own actions as would an uninvolved observer, because for weakly held attitudes they often do not spontaneously recall their previous attitudes. An important application of self-perception theory is that schoolchildren sometimes adopt negative attitudes toward otherwise interesting activities for which adults feel it necessary to reward them.

CHAPTER 8

Stereotyping, Prejudice, and Discrimination

Is justice color blind? When minority group members are accused of crimes, can they get a fair trial? Ideally, jurors ought to consider only legally relevant factors in determining a defendant's guilt or innocence. They should ignore such "extralegal" factors as the defendant's physical attractiveness, socioeconomic status, gender, and race (Mazzella & Feingold, 1994). Jurors, however, find it difficult to ignore extralegal factors (Bagby & Rector, 1992; Gerbasi, Zuckerman, & Reis, 1977; Kramer & Kerr, 1989; Pennington & Hastie, 1990; Ugwuegbu, 1979). Especially when the "facts" of the case are ambiguous, judges need to give jurors very carefully worded instructions if the jurors are to avoid reaching inappropriately biased verdicts (Gordon, 1993).

To investigate the effects of race on jury decisions, two social psychologists had White university students pretend to be jurors for a rape case (Pfeifer & Ogloff, 1991). The students read a nine-page transcript of a trial in which a man was accused of rape. The woman victim said she was sexually assaulted by a stranger. Because the attack occurred at night, she could describe the attacker's height and build, but she did not see his face clearly. As the stranger drove away from the scene of the attack, however, the woman saw his license plate number, which she reported to the police. When the police arrested the owner of the vehicle, who fit the description that the victim gave them, the man said that he had been home alone at the time of the incident. He also said

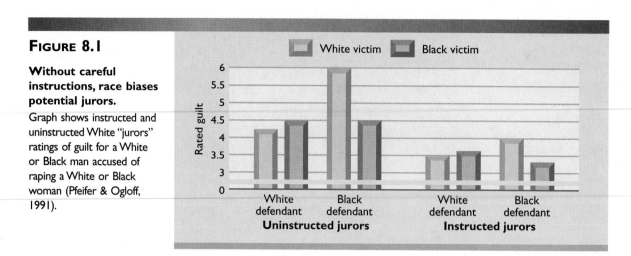

FIGURE 8.1

Without careful instructions, race biases potential jurors.

Graph shows instructed and uninstructed White "jurors" ratings of guilt for a White or Black man accused of raping a White or Black woman (Pfeifer & Ogloff, 1991).

that he had reported his car stolen earlier in the evening, which was corroborated by police reports. The prosecution maintained that the man had reported his car stolen so that he could use it later to commit a crime. In short, the facts of the case were ambiguous and most of the evidence against the defendant was circumstantial.

All student jurors read the same trial transcript, but they were divided into four groups. Some read that both the defendant and the victim were White. Some read that both the defendant and victim were Black. Some read that one was White and the other Black. Half of each group received judge's instructions that stressed the need to be free from "sympathy or prejudice." The other half of each group received no judge's instructions. Finally, all student jurors indicated how guilty they thought the defendant was, on a scale from 1 (not guilty) to 7 (extremely guilty). Figure 8.1 shows the results.

When the White student jurors received no "judge's instructions," as the left side of the figure shows, they found the Black man more guilty of rape than the White man, even though every other detail of the case was identical except the defendant's and the victim's race. Also, they found the Black man especially guilty when he was accused of raping a White woman. As shown on the right side of the figure, however, judge's instructions that stressed lack of prejudice or sympathy successfully reduced racial bias. Although the Black man accused of raping a White woman was still rated slightly more guilty than in any of the other three conditions, he was not rated significantly more guilty.

The mock jury results in Figure 8.1 raise important questions about stereotyping, prejudice, and discrimination not only in legal proceedings, but also in problems that women face in business, how the elderly are treated, biased media portrayals of minority groups, affirmative action practices, school integration, and many similar issues. One question is, *when* do and do not people display stereotyping, prejudice, and discrimination? A second question is, *why* do people engage in stereotyping, prejudice, and discrimination? A third question is, how might we try to *reduce* stereotyping, prejudice, and discrimination? These three questions represent the three major sections of the chapter.

WHEN DO PEOPLE DISPLAY STEREOTYPING, PREJUDICE, AND DISCRIMINATION?

The first important question about stereotyping, prejudice, and discrimination is when do they occur. The jury study at the start of this chapter showed that

White jurors sometimes let racial bias affect their estimates of a defendant's guilt, but they do not always do so. Bias against Black defendants was pronounced when the White jurors had no specific instructions, but it almost disappeared when the jurors were instructed to avoid sympathy or prejudice. In other words, people *can* display stereotyping, prejudice, and discrimination, but they can also *avoid* doing so. The first part of this section defines stereotyping, prejudice, and discrimination and provides everyday examples of when they occur. The second part of the section describes the process by which stereotyping, prejudice, and discrimination occur. The process suggests why stereotyping, prejudice, and discrimination occur in some circumstances but not in others.

EXAMPLES OF STEREOTYPING, PREJUDICE, AND DISCRIMINATION

As described in Chapter 6, attitudes have three components: thoughts, feelings, and actions (Breckler, 1984; Insko & Schopler, 1967; Katz & Stotland, 1959; Olson & Zanna, 1993; Ostrom, 1969; Rosenberg & Hovland, 1960; Smith, 1947; Triandis, 1971; Zanna & Rempel, 1988). Thoughts are beliefs; feelings are emotional responses; and actions are what we do (Eagly & Chaiken, 1993). Stereotypes, prejudice, and discrimination are the three components of negative attitudes toward social groups (Esses, Haddock, & Zanna, 1993; Zanna & Rempel, 1988). Stereotypes are biased *thoughts* or assumptions about a group. Prejudice entails biased *feelings* or emotional reactions to the group. Discrimination involves biased *actions* or unfair treatment.

■ BIASED ASSUMPTIONS (STEREOTYPING)

"**Stereotypes** are beliefs about the characteristics of members of a group" (Neuberg, 1994, p. 105). Stereotypical assumptions can occur in the thoughts of individuals or in the "consensus" of an entire society (Brewer, 1994; Gardner, 1994). In the jury study at the start of the chapter, for instance, individual White jurors may have assumed that Black men are more prone to violence than are White men. Individual jurors may also have lived in a society in which the White majority agreed on which traits and other characteristics the "typical" Black man has. The profile might be entirely erroneous, but even false assumptions are important when the individuals who harbor the assumptions live in a society where the majority of people share their beliefs (Batson & Burris, 1994).

Majority group members often assume the worst about groups other than their own (Fiske & Ruscher, 1993). In a relevant study, White college students watched a videotape of two students, one Black and one White, who were having an argument (Duncan, 1976; see also Allport & Postman, 1947; Sagar & Schofield, 1980). During the argument, one of the videotaped students shoved the other one. When it was the White student who shoved the Black student, very few of the White viewers regarded the shove as a violent act. Most of them thought the White student was merely making his point more emphatic or that he was "playing around." In contrast, when it was the Black student who shoved the White student, the majority of White viewers described the Black man's behavior as "violent." They assumed the worst about the Black man, presumably because they harbored stereotypes in which Black men are predisposed to violence.

In the early 1930s, White students at Princeton University were asked to list the five traits that they thought best described Black people (Katz & Braly, 1933). Negative traits such as superstitious, lazy, happy-go-lucky, and ignorant were most frequently nominated. Through the years, similar surveys revealed a progressively less negative stereotype for Black people (Brigham, 1993; Dovidio, Brigham, Johnson, & Gaertner, in press; Dovidio & Gaertner, 1986; Gilbert, 1951; Karlins, Coffman, & Walters, 1969). In 1993, for instance, the most frequently nominated traits were loyal to family, aggressive, straightforward, ambitious, and passionate. Aggressive, unfortunately, was still a part of the stereotype, as were quick-tempered and argumentative. Negative traits like stupid and physically dirty, however, which were among the most frequently nominated in 1933, have gradually disappeared from what White people in the United States say about Black people.

Survey questions, however, may not capture the full extent of negative assumptions and stereotyping (Biernat & Manis, 1994). When people are asked to rate how "financially successful" a man is and how "financially successful" a woman is, they might rate the man and the women as equally "successful," but on an objective yardstick such as "dollars earned per year" they might recognize that men earn more, which is an accurate stereotype (Biernat, Manis, & Nelson, 1991). When they call the woman "highly successful," they mean "compared to other women," which means they have shifted the criterion. Another problem with such surveys is that we do not know whether they accurately reflect current stereotypes. As described in Chapter 6, people who claim not to have negative attitudes when they respond to surveys sometimes unwittingly reveal very negative attitudes when the measures are disguised (Crosby, Bromley, & Saxe, 1980; Sears, 1988).

One clue to people's actual stereotypes is that they make different decisions based on whether a member of a negatively stigmatized group behaved in line with the stereotype. Potential jurors, for instance, say they would require higher bail for a Black man accused of assault than for a White man accused of committing exactly the same crime, presumably because "violent" is part of White people's stereotype for Black men (Gordon, 1993). Students in one study of stereotyping pretended they were on a parole board to consider the likelihood of a criminal committing further crimes if he were released from prison (Bodenhausen & Wyer, 1985). Some students read about criminals whose crime "fit" the stereotype of their race. They read that a man named Ashley Chamberlaine from Cambridge, Massachusetts, embezzled funds through forged signatures on company accounting books or that a man named Carlos Ramirez from Albuquerque, New Mexico, brutally attacked a man in a bar fight. These crimes "fit" the stereotype of the defendant's group. White males are assumed to be materialistic. Hispanic males are assumed to be violent. Other students read about criminals whose crime "misfit" the stereotype. Ramirez embezzled the company funds. Chamberlaine brutally attacked the fellow bar patron.

Students made different judgments of how likely the prisoner was to commit another crime depending on whether the prisoner's crime fit or didn't fit his group's stereotype. The students considered it more likely that Carlos Ramirez would attack another bar patron than that he would embezzle future company funds. They also considered it more likely that Ashley Chamberlaine would embezzle future company funds than that he would attack another bar patron. The students were also more likely to deny parole when their assumptions about the criminal's race fit the crime. Students denied Chamberlaine parole more often when he embezzled funds than attacked a bar patron and denied Ramirez parole more often when he attacked a bar patron than embezzled funds. Fit with a stereotype affects parole decisions because people pay greater attention to stereotype-consistent evidence than they do to stereotype-inconsistent evidence (Bodenhausen, 1988).

People assume the worst about many social groups. Throughout history, men wrote restrictive laws to keep women at home during times when there were fewer women than men, because they assumed that women would "play

Calvin and Hobbes

by Bill Watterson

the field." In the colonial United States, women who were unfaithful to their husbands were whipped in public, branded with the letter "A" on their foreheads and breasts, or put to death (Guttentag & Secord, 1983). In contrast, men wrote very permissive laws to allow promiscuity when there were fewer men than women (Guttentag & Secord, 1983). In texts written near 1900, women were described as a lower form of life than men. They were supposedly so passive that they were more similar to plants than to human beings (Degler, 1991). Women could not vote in U.S. elections because they were supposedly too influenced by emotions and incapable of rational thought (Degler, 1991). Similarly, otherwise respectable "scientists" as recently as the 1980s claimed that women cannot understand math and science as well as men because their brains do not get a "testosterone bath"–a story that was widely reported in the media but totally inaccurate (Fausto-Sterling, 1985; Hubbard, 1990; Tavris, 1992).

Old people are also the target of inaccurate stereotypes. Across the world, young adults believe that their 20s and 30s will be the most satisfying decades of their lives, with a gradual deterioration in the quality of life as they grow older (Williams, 1993). Many people in Western Europe and the United States believe that old age leads to inevitable decline in physical, mental, and personality characteristics (Achenbaum, 1978; Cole, 1992). Work performance supposedly deteriorates with age, so it "makes sense" to encourage early retirement and retain younger workers (Doering, Rhodes, & Schuster, 1983; Rosen & Jerdee, 1976). In reality, the average 70-year-old performs many job-related tasks *better* than does the average 25-year-old (Davies & Sparrow, 1985, Levine, 1988; Schaie, 1988; Waldman & Avolio, 1986; Walsh, 1983). Nonetheless, the negative stereotype of old people persists (Henwood, Giles, Coupland, & Coupland, 1993). Even six-year-old children believe that old people are inept, unlikable, and nasty. They do not sit as close to, talk as freely with, or make as much eye contact with 75-year-old adults as they do with 35-year-old adults (Isaacs & Bearison, 1986). When adults in the United States list the traits of elderly people, they say that old people are irritable, quarrelsome, stubborn, shallow, aimless, annoying, unproductive, hard to get along with, a nuisance, and "meddle in other people's affairs" (Butler, 1975; McTavish, 1971).

■ BIASED EMOTIONS (PREJUDICE)

"Prejudice is the feeling one has toward members of a group" (Neuberg, 1994, p. 105). People who are different from us arouse many negative feelings or emotions (Vanman & Miller, 1993). As described in Chapter 6, negative thoughts usually go hand in hand with negative feelings. It would be difficult to believe that a group's members are violent and physically dirty, for instance, without experiencing very negative emotions merely from thinking about them (Stephan, Ageyev, Coates-Shrider, Stephan, & Abalakina, 1994). People who have negative attitudes toward a group do not experience negative emotions only when they think about members of that group. They also experience negative emotional reactions to nonmembers who merely associate with the group. Prejudiced people have negative feelings, for instance, about nonhomosexuals who knowingly associate with homosexuals and about nonhomosexuals who support homosexuals by wearing such emblems as a "pro-gay" T-shirt (Neuberg, Smith, Hoffman, & Russell, 1994; Russell & Gray, 1992). Negative feelings are at least as important as negative thoughts in how people react to groups as diverse as homosexuals and rock music performers (Jussim, Nelson, Manis, & Soffin, 1995).

Negative emotions, however, are not all the same. The different negative emotions that we associate with different minority groups affect us in different ways. In a study of negative emotions in stereotyping, prejudice, and discrimination, the investigator sent anonymous questionnaires to residents of Amsterdam in The Netherlands (Dijker, 1987). The questionnaires asked what emotions the respondents experienced when they met, chatted with, did things with, or visited with immigrants from Surinam or immigrants from Turkey and Morocco. Immigrants from Surinam are more culturally similar to the Dutch majority than are immigrants from Turkey and Morocco. The questionnaires also asked how close the respondents lived to members of these groups, how many members of the group they knew, how well they knew them, and what their overall attitudes toward the groups were.

As expected, respondents who said they had positive attitudes reported being in a positive mood when they were around members of these ethnic minorities, whereas respondents who said they had negative attitudes reported being anxious, irritated, and concerned by their presence. Irritation and concern, however, played a larger part in Dutch respondents' attitudes toward Turks and Moroccans than in attitudes toward Surinamers. Simply meeting a member of either minority group elicited such negative feelings as anxiety and irritation. More personal forms of contact, though, had different effects depending on the group in question. Dutch people who exchanged visits with Surinamers, for instance, reported less anxiety, less concern, and a more positive attitude. Dutch people who visited Turks or Moroccans, in contrast, reported greater anxiety, irritation, and concern, as well as a more negative attitude. Dutch citizens who had ethnic minority members living next door had more negative attitudes toward them than did Dutch citizens who had minority members living in the neighborhood, but not immediately next to them. Finally, Dutch people who said they felt anxious about the presence of minority group members wanted to avoid meeting them; people who felt irritated also said they mentally addressed minority group members in an unfriendly way; and people who felt concern said they "wished they would move away." Negative emotions, then, play an important role in overall negative attitudes toward minority groups.

■ BIASED TREATMENT (DISCRIMINATION)

Discrimination is "inappropriate treatment to individuals due to their group membership—a selectively *unjustified* negative behavior toward members of a target group" (Dovidio, et al., in press, p. 4). Negative assumptions and emotions often go hand in hand with negative treatment. Women in the United States are too often treated as sex objects rather than as potentially successful individuals (McKenzie-Mohr & Zanna, 1990). We may think of today's society as more enlightened than in the past because women today are allowed to go out of the home and get a job. But what kind of job can they get? Perhaps the most important reason why the average woman makes less than the average man is that many of the best-paying jobs are traditionally "for men only," whereas many of the worst-paying "dead-end" jobs are traditionally reserved for women (Pratto, in press). Although we have laws against employers discriminating because of sex, women find it very difficult to break into the higher-paying jobs that are "supposed to be" for men.

In one of many studies that demonstrated sex discrimination, college students responded to job ads by telephone (Levinson, 1975). During the telephone conversation, they tried to get a personal interview. Some of the jobs were traditionally for men, such as auto salesperson, security guard, or management trainee. Other jobs were traditionally for women, such as receptionist, housekeeper, or clerk. When women called about the jobs that were traditionally for men (which were also higher-paying jobs with more opportunity for advancement) they were treated very politely, but they were often told that they lacked the necessary credentials. Women who called for management trainee jobs, for instance, were told that two years of college were not enough or that they should not apply without previous management experience. When a college man with two years of college and no management experience called about the same job, however, he was encouraged to "come in for a personal interview." Employers who treat men and women applicants differently do more than merely make biased assumptions or harbor biased emotions. They engage in outright discrimination.

Besides showing that minority group defendants are not fairly treated in criminal cases (Perez, Hosch, Ponder, & Trejo, 1993), many studies detected negative treatment for stigmatized groups by examining helping, aggression, and nonverbal behavior (reviewed by Crosby et al., 1980). In many studies of helping, for instance, a White person had an opportunity to help another person who was either Black or White. Sometimes the request for help came directly from the person who needed help. Either Black or White students, for instance, stopped White people and asked them for spare change. In other studies, either Black or White students stood by their cars with the hood raised or dropped loose items like coins or pencils. These "direct" requests for help were similar to survey questions, because refusing to help a Black person in public is as socially undesirable as calling Black people "lazy" on a survey. Not surprisingly, these "public" measures of helping detected only a slight favoritism for White people helping other White people more than they helped Black people.

Does the race of a stranded motorist change how likely other motorists are to stop and help?

An entirely different picture emerged, however, from studies where the person who needed help was not present and no one would know whether help was given (Crosby et al., 1980). In one such study, the experimenter left an envelope with a completed graduate school application in an airport phone booth to see whether the next White person who entered the phone booth would be a good Samaritan and mail it (Benson, Karabenick, & Lerner, 1976). A photograph with the application showed either a White student or a Black student. The average White adult who found a White student's application put it in a nearby mailbox. Many White adults who found a Black student's application, in contrast, left the application in the phone booth or threw it away. In another study, a student with a Black-sounding or White-sounding voice called a number selected at random from a White community's phone book and claimed to have reached a wrong number with his or her last coin while having automotive problems in a remote area (Clark, 1974). The caller asked the other person to "please call this number and tell them I'm stranded here."

White telephone subscribers relayed the call conscientiously for almost all White-sounding people who needed help, but less frequently when the voice on the other end of the line was obviously a Black person's voice.

In a study of aggression, White college students were assigned the role of "teacher" and could punish another student, who was either a Black or a White confederate, by delivering supposedly painful electric shocks whenever the "learner" gave a wrong answer (Donnerstein, Donnerstein, Simon, & Ditrichs, 1972). The White "teacher" chose the intensity and duration of shock. When the White students believed that the researchers were recording what shocks they gave, they shocked the Black and White learners the same. When they believed that no one would know how much or how long they shocked the other person, they administered more painful shocks to Black than to White learners who made the same mistakes. When they are face to face with the other person or believe that their actions can be observed and evaluated by others, Whites behave as though they are unbiased (Frey & Gaertner, 1986). When the other person is not physically present and they think that no one will know what they did, White people often discriminate against Black people (Crosby et al., 1980). Even Whites who normally hold their aggression toward Blacks in check often revert "to the old, historical pattern of racial discrimination" when they are angry (Rogers & Prentice-Dunn, 1981, p. 63).

It is more difficult to control our actions when we are angry. It is also more difficult to control nonverbal behaviors like tone of voice or how far we stand from another person than it is to watch what we say. Nonverbal behaviors often leak our true feelings even while we are saying whatever is socially desirable (Ekman, 1985). In one study of nonverbal behavior, White Princeton students interviewed either a Black or a White high school student who was actually a confederate (Word, Zanna, & Cooper, 1974). Although the Black and White confederates acted the same, the White interviewers unknowingly revealed their biases by sitting farther from a Black than from a White interviewee and by cutting the interview short when the interviewee was Black rather than White. In another study of nonverbal behavior, White women chose to sit farther from Black than from White conversation partners (Hendricks & Bootzin, 1976). Similarly, college women sat farther from an interviewee they thought had AIDS than from an interviewee they thought had cancer (Mooney, Cohn, & Swift, 1992). Finally, White students said all the "right things" to appear friendly and unprejudiced in a telephone conversation with a student they thought was Black, but they also conveyed an unfriendly nonverbal message through their tone of voice (Weitz, 1972). Even Whites who claim to be unbiased "give themselves away" through their nonverbal behavior.

THE PROCESS OF STEREOTYPING, PREJUDICE, AND DISCRIMINATION

Table 8.1 shows a model of when stereotypes, prejudice, and discrimination occur and when they might not occur (Macrae, Bodenhausen, Milne, & Jetten, 1994; Devine & Monteith, 1993; Fiske & Neuberg, 1990). The model is part of the "two-stage process" theme that occurs throughout this textbook (Bargh, 1994; Beike & Sherman, 1994; Brewer, 1988; Cacioppo, Petty, & Crites, 1994; Epstein et al., 1992; Fazio, 1990; Gilbert, 1989; Martin et al., 1990; Smith, 1994). The two-stage theme, which applies to such fundamental processes as social thinking (Chapter 2), person perception (Chapter 3), and attribution (Chapter 4), demonstrates that people have initial, relatively spontaneous reactions, followed by more deliberative "adjustments." When an individual meets a member of a negatively stigmatized group, the individual might have a negatively biased initial reaction (Devine, 1989). White jurors, for example, might believe that Black men are more likely than White men to commit rape and other violent crimes (a stereotype). They might also fear Black men (prejudice) and tend to vote against legislation that they believe benefits primarily Black people (discrimination). The overall negative attitude biases initial reactions, which might be why the "uninstructed" jurors found a Black defendant

TABLE 8.1	A Two-Stage Model of Stereotyping, Prejudice, and Discrimination (Adapted from Macrae, Bodenhausen, Milne, & Jetten, 1994; Devine & Monteith, 1993; and Fiske & Neuberg, 1990)
STEP	**DESCRIPTION**
Spontaneous Stage	
Categorization	"automatically" notice that the person is a member of a disliked sex, race, age group, or other social category
Biased assumptions	spontaneously assume the person has the negative characteristics "typical" of that group or category
Biased emotions	spontaneously experience negative emotional reactions to the person
Biased treatment	spontaneously lean toward acting negatively toward the person
Deliberative Stage	
Gather more information	add new information, preferably information that confirms the initial, negative reactions
Recategorize	if the new information disconfirms initial reactions, assign the person to a different, less negative category where possible
Avoid guilt	if the adjustment seems insufficient to avoid feeling guilty, deliberate more and/or monitor future initial reactions
Suppress reactions	deliberately avoid displaying initial negative reactions, but run the risk that such reactions will occur even more strongly in the future

Note: Stereotyping, prejudice, and discrimination proceed from the spontaneous stage unless we are both willing and able to enter the deliberative stage.

more guilty than a White defendant based on the same circumstantial evidence. These spontaneous negative reactions, however, can sometimes be overcome. When people are willing and able, for instance when a judge tells them to avoid sympathy or prejudice, they go beyond the spontaneous stage and enter the deliberative stage, in which they make adjustments to their initial reactions. These adjustments usually (but not always) reduce bias.

■ SPONTANEOUS REACTIONS

Table 8.1 presents a model similar to the model in Chapter 3 of how people form impressions. In this chapter, the emphasis is on *negative* reactions based on a person's group or category. In the spontaneous stage, we automatically notice that the person belongs to a race, sex, age group, or other category toward which we have a negative attitude. If all three attitude components are negative, we spontaneously assume that the person has the group's negative characteristics, experience negative emotions associated with the group, and lean toward negative actions. These spontaneous reactions occur very rapidly (Dovidio & Gaertner, 1993). In one study of negative thoughts and assumptions, students first thought about "White people" or "Black people" (Dovidio, Evans, & Tyler, 1986). Then they decided whether a trait could ever be true of Black or White people. The experimental hypothesis was that traits that are part of a category's stereotype come to mind quicker than traits that are not part of the stereotype. The average person, for instance, would respond faster when asked whether professors are absentminded than when asked whether professors are religious, because absentminded is part of the average person's stereotype for professors, but religious is not. Exactly the opposite results would apply if the question was whether nuns are religious.

Students in the study were faster (in milliseconds) to answer questions about traits that were part of their own race's stereotype than to answer questions about traits that were part of the other race's stereotype. Students answered faster for the positive trait "ambitious" than for the positive trait "musical" when they were asked about White people, but they also answered faster for "musical" than for "ambitious" when they were asked about Black people. Similarly, students answered faster for the negative trait "materialistic" than for the negative trait "lazy" when they were asked about White people, but they also answered faster for "lazy" than for "materialistic" when they were asked about Black people. Students were also faster to decide whether positive traits described White than Black people and faster to decide whether negative traits described Black than White people. The students reported unbiased opinions by endorsing as many positive traits for Blacks as for Whites, but their response times "gave them away" (Lalonde & Gardner, 1989).

Initial reactions can also be based entirely on a person's physical appearance (Zebrowitz, in press). Some of the first things we notice about other people are their race, sex, and age (Brewer & Lui, 1989; Stangor, Lynch, Duan, & Glass, 1992). It seems "natural" to categorize people along visually salient dimensions and to assume that people who look alike must also *be* alike in their traits, abilities, attitudes, and other attributes (Rothbart & Taylor, 1992). Women, for instance, have more childlike facial features than do men, a physical feature from which, as described in Chapter 3, perceivers spontaneously infer other childlike attributes such as warmth and dependence (Friedman & Zebrowitz, 1992). Judging a book by its cover is a pervasive consequence of our initial reactions to other people–reactions that encourage often inaccurate stereotypes about races and ethnic groups other than our own, women, old people, overweight people, and many other negatively stigmatized social groups (Pingitore, Dugoni, Tindale, & Spring, 1994; Zebrowitz, in press).

■ DELIBERATIVE ADJUSTMENTS

As Table 8.1 shows, the initial negative reaction often prevails. People sometimes stop at the spontaneous stage and never enter the deliberative stage. As described in other chapters throughout the book, people go beyond their spontaneous reactions only when they are both willing and able to do so (Fiske & Von Hendy, 1992). A racial bigot, for instance, might be satisfied with a negatively biased reaction and be unwilling to continue, whereas a person who takes pride in being unbiased or who has been instructed by a judge might be highly motivated to make deliberative adjustments (Devine & Monteith, 1993). No matter how motivated they are, however, people must also be *able* to engage in further processing. Stereotypes, prejudice, and discrimination flourish when people lack or are denied the cognitive capacity to make adjustments away from their initial negative reactions. In one study of *willingness* to engage in deliberative adjustment, described in greater detail in Chapter 2, student jurors who were in a happy mood relied on a stereotype for deciding a defendant's guilt, whereas student jurors who were in either a neutral or sad mood did not (Bodenhausen, Kramer, & Susser, 1994). People who are in a happy mood are typically unwilling to think deeply about topics (Esses, Haddock, & Zanna, 1994; Hamilton & Mackie, 1993). Instead, they rely on their initial, spontaneous reactions (Mackie, Queller, Stroessner, & Hamilton, in press).

A study of *inability* to engage in deliberative adjustment also used a mood manipulation. In the study, college students in one condition recalled and wrote about an episode that made them angry (Bodenhausen, Sheppard, & Kramer, 1994). Students in a second condition recalled and wrote about an episode that made them sad. Students in a third condition recalled and wrote about mundane events of the previous day. Then all students pretended to be on the college's peer judicial review board, which decided cases of alleged misconduct. In one case, a man was accused of assault. In the other, a man was accused of cheating on an exam. For half of the students in each mood condition, the defendant fit his group's stereotype. Because students at the school had a stereotype of male Hispanics as aggressive and student athletes as prone to cheating, the man accused of assault was Juan Garcia and the man accused of cheating was "a well-known track and field athlete." For the other half of the students in each mood, the defendant did not fit a stereotype. The man accused of assault was John Garner and the man accused of cheating was not an athlete. The investigators predicted that students who were angry would be so aroused that they would be unable to make adjustments and would rely on their stereotypes, whereas students who were in a neutral or sad mood would be able to make adjustments and would not rely on the stereotypes. As shown in Figure 8.2, their predictions were correct. Not all "bad moods" are the same in how they affect the use of stereotypes. People who are sad may engage in deliberative processing, but people who are angry are more likely to react impulsively and to find it difficult to concentrate (Bodenhausen, 1993; Hebb, 1946).

By relying on stereotypes, people gain the advantage of cognitive efficiency (Macrae, Hewstone, & Griffiths, 1993). Because they avoid the effort necessary to make adjustments, they are free to divide their attention and concentrate on whatever else seems important to them (Martell, 1991; Pendry & Macrae, 1994; Pratto & Bargh, 1991). In one study of cognitive efficiency, students tried to form impressions of a doctor, an artist, a real estate agent, and a skinhead (Macrae, Milne, & Bodenhausen, 1994). For some students, but not for others, the target persons had traits that fit the stereotype, which should have made thinking about them easier (Macrae, Stangor, & Milne, 1994). The skinhead, for instance, was said to be rebellious. While they were forming their impressions, the students also had to listen to a tape recording about the geography

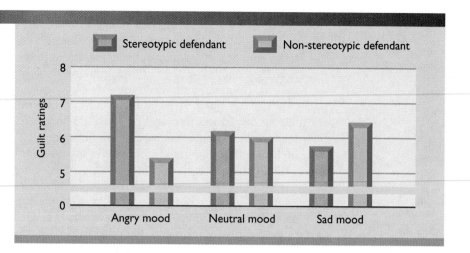

FIGURE 8.2

Angry people rely on stereotypes.

Graph shows guilt ratings by student "jurors" who were in three different moods, when defendant was stereotypic or nonstereotypic (Bodenhausen, Sheppard, & Kramer, 1994).

and economy of Indonesia. On a subsequent memory test, students who read descriptions with stereotypic traits remembered facts about Indonesia better than did students who did not read descriptions with stereotypic traits. The stereotypic traits made it easier for students to think about the target person, which left them with extra cognitive resources that they could "spend" on listening to the tape.

If they are willing and able, as shown in Table 8.1, people "adjust" their biased initial reactions and then decide whether the adjustment is sufficient. To justify making an adjustment, they need to believe that they have additional relevant information (Yzerbyt, Schadron, Leyens, & Rocher, 1994). When they do, they "think it over with themselves" in the same way that two people revise their impressions by talking to each other about whether their initial reaction to an event might have been mistaken (Ruscher & Hammer, 1994). Although (as described in Chapter 2) the adjustment can be too little or too much for the circumstances, perceivers who are satisfied with adjusting away from blatant stereotyping, prejudice, and discrimination usually make a less negatively biased response and feel good about doing so. The "instructed" White jurors presumably felt satisfied about their less biased ratings of guilt for a Black defendant. When the adjustment still seems insufficient, though, individuals might feel guilty, which might influence their initial reactions to the next member (Monteith, Devine, & Zuwerink, 1993). Because people do not like feeling guilty, guilt over an insufficient adjustment might cause them to have a less biased initial reaction the next time they meet a member of the group (Devine & Monteith, 1993; Devine, Monteith, Zuwerink, & Elliot, 1991).

In one study that showed how people can feel guilty about biased reactions, students were divided into two groups that did and did not have negatively biased attitudes toward homosexuals (Monteith, 1993, Experiment 2). Later in the semester, the students answered both explicit questions about homosexuality ("I avoid homosexuals whenever possible") and ambiguous questions. For some students, the ambiguous questions were about homosexuality ("Homosexuals are just like everyone else") and supposedly measured "subtle prejudice" that could not be detected directly. The ambiguous questions gave the researchers an excuse for telling students that "Your response was more prejudiced than your general attitude." For other students the ambiguous questions were about an unrelated topic. The researchers did not tell them that they were "subtly prejudiced." In a supposedly unrelated study, all students then rated the humorousness of several jokes, two of which were derogatory toward gay men. Students who admitted to negatively biased attitudes found the "gay-bashing" jokes moderately humorous regardless of whether the students had been told that they were subtly prejudiced or not. They presumably did not feel guilty about subtle prejudice and thus did not alter their subsequent responses. Students who did not admit to negatively biased attitudes toward homosexuals, in contrast, found the anti-gay jokes less humorous after they were told about their subtle prejudice than when they were not told. The results were consistent with the model in Table 8.1, because people who thought they had not adjusted their responses sufficiently to match their nonbiased self-concepts altered their subsequent responses to be less biased.

You might wonder, however, about the cognitive consequences for people who *are* satisfied because they have temporarily suppressed stereotypical thoughts. As described in Chapter 2 under "Ironic Effects of Thought Control," people who temporarily suppress unwanted thoughts sometimes incur a "rebound" of the unwanted thoughts later, when their temporary inhibitions have been relaxed (Wegner, 1994). In one study of stereotype rebound effects, the experimenters showed students a photograph of a male "skinhead" and asked them to write a description of a typical day in the skinhead's life (Macrae, et al., 1994, Experiment 1). Some students received no further instructions. Other students were warned to avoid using stereotypic preconceptions. After five minutes, the experimenter stopped the students, showed them a photograph of a different male skinhead, and asked them to spend five minutes describing him. This time, neither group got special instructions. They were free to let their imaginations soar.

Later, the experimenters rated the content of each student's descriptions on a 9-point scale from "not at all stereotypic" to "very stereotypic." As Figure 8.3 shows, students who were asked to suppress the stereotype in the first description did so. They were less likely than the "no instructions" group to include in their descriptions various rebellious, aggressive, dishonest, untrustworthy, and dangerous activities, which fit the prevailing stereotype of skinheads. When the suppression was "lifted" for describing the second skinhead, however, the "suppress stereotype" group wrote descriptions that were even more full of stereotypic activities than those of the "no instructions" group. Suppressing stereotypic thoughts in the first description may have filled a reservoir of stereotypes that were "let loose" in the second description. In a follow-up study, students who suppressed the stereotype of skinheads in their initial descriptions later chose to sit farther from the skinhead that they had described, as though "bottling up" stereotypic thoughts altered both subsequent stereotyping and discriminatory behavior (Macrae et al., 1994, Experiment 2).

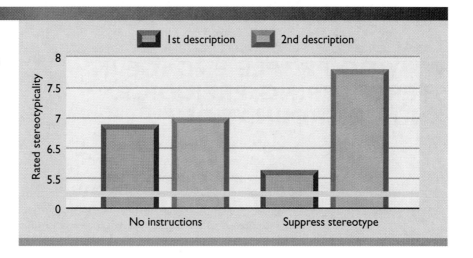

FIGURE 8.3

Suppressed stereotypes can "rebound."

Graph shows rated stereotypicality of students' descriptions of two skinheads when some students were told to suppress stereotypes in the first description (Macrae, Bodenhausen, Milne, & Jetten, 1994).

SUMMARY OF WHEN PEOPLE DISPLAY STEREOTYPING, PREJUDICE, AND DISCRIMINATION

People sometimes make biased assumptions about, have negative emotional reactions to, and treat poorly the members of negatively stigmatized groups. Biased assumptions lead people to "see" expectancy-confirming behaviors that minority group members do not commit. Although direct survey questions detect less stereotyping, prejudice, and discrimination of some social groups today than in the past, people reveal negative attitudes in subtle ways, for example by punishing criminals more when their crimes fit than don't fit their group's stereotype. People also have negative emotional reactions to stigmatized groups, including anxiety that leads to avoidance and irritation that leads to "wishing they would move away." Discrimination based on a person's race, sex, age, or other characteristics might be illegal today, but it nonetheless occurs in many ways, including less helping, greater aggression, and negative nonverbal behaviors.

People do not always engage in stereotyping, prejudice, and discrimination, however. When people meet or think about a member of a negatively stigmatized group, they have negatively biased initial reactions. These spontaneous initial reactions occur in milliseconds and are often based on such salient physical characteristics as race, sex, and age. If they are motivated to "adjust" their initial reactions, people sometimes arrive at less negative reactions to members of stigmatized groups. Emotions such as anger and competing demands such as cognitive efficiency, however, reduce people's ability to make adjustments, so they rely on the group's stereotype. When they rely on the stereotype, people who pride themselves on being unbiased sometimes feel guilty and monitor future reactions. When they suppress stereotypic thoughts, however, people sometimes "rebound" to thinking more stereotypically about the next group member they meet.

WHY DO PEOPLE ENGAGE IN STEREOTYPING, PREJUDICE, AND DISCRIMINATION?

In the study at the start of this chapter and in many other studies described in the first section of the chapter, people displayed stereotyping, prejudice, and discrimination against members of another race or ethnic group, another sex, another age group, people whose sexual preferences do not match their own, and numerous other negatively stigmatized groups or social categories. They did not *always* display stereotyping, prejudice, and discrimination, but they did so frequently enough that we might wonder why. We know from the model presented in Table 8.1 that people sometimes go beyond their spontaneous re-actions and make adjustments to their initial assumptions, emotional reactions, and action tendencies. We also know that when they make deliberative ad-justments, they are less likely to display stereotyping, prejudice, and discrimi-nation. If we want to know how to reduce stereotyping, prejudice, and dis-crimination, however, we need to understand their causes in greater detail than merely saying "people do less of it when they deliberate." We need to exam-ine the basic causes. This section of the chapter suggests that the causes of stereotyping, prejudice, and discrimination lie in people's minds, in their hearts, and in the social context that surrounds their actions. In this section of the chapter, therefore, we discuss the role of thought processes, personal relevance, and social functions in causing stereotyping, prejudice, and discrimination. The three basic causes are summarized in Table 8.2, to which you might refer as you read the rest of the section.

THOUGHT PROCESSES

The first, most "basic" cause of stereotyping, prejudice, and discrimination is the way people think about minority groups or categories. It is easy to "see" an illusory correlation between members of an infrequently encountered group and infrequent (usually bad) behaviors. It is also easy to think simply and ig-nore the proportion of a group's behaviors that fit our preconceptions. Finally, because people are often unaware of thought processes, they can unknowingly engage in implicit stereotyping.

■ ILLUSORY CORRELATION

Stereotypes and prejudice do not influence initial reactions because people *want* to be biased. Most White jurors do not *want* to consider Black defendants guiltier of rape than White defendants. Some of the bias occurs merely because some categories have more members than others. Sometimes the circumstances make it easier to associate a minority group than a majority group with nega-tive behaviors (Stangor & Lange, 1994). Illusory correlation involves overesti-mating the number of times that members of a large category are associated with frequent behaviors and the number of times that members of a small cat-egory are associated with infrequent behaviors. To use racism as an example, basic categorization processes, even without any negative feelings toward a racial group, might cause prospective jurors to believe that Black people en-gage in violent behaviors more often than do White people, simply because both Black people and violent behaviors occur relatively infrequently.

In a relevant study, students read a list of good and bad behaviors that had been performed by members of two hypothetical groups, X and Y (Hamilton & Gifford, 1976). They read, for instance, that an X returned a lost wallet, an-other X made decisions impulsively, a Y helped an elderly neighbor, and an-other Y bragged about accomplishments. Six Xs and 12 Ys were randomly dis-persed throughout the list. Overall, four (two-thirds) of the Xs performed good behaviors and two (one-third) performed bad behaviors. Similarly, eight (two-thirds) of the Ys performed good behaviors and four (one-third) performed bad behaviors. There were, therefore, 12 good behaviors and six bad behaviors. As in everyday life, good behaviors were relatively frequent and bad behaviors were relatively infrequent. When they had read all the individual behaviors, the students estimated from memory how many times members of each group did something good and how many times they did something bad. The stu-dents also reported how much they liked the members of each group.

The students falsely recalled that members of the majority group (Ys) per-formed more of the good behaviors than they did, and that members of the

TABLE 8.2	Three Causes of Stereotyping, Prejudice, and Discrimination

Thought Processes

illusory correlation	people easily connect infrequent behaviors with members of an infrequently encountered group
ignoring covariation	people analyze the relationship between groups and behaviors too simply
implicit stereotyping	people are not aware that their thought processes create erroneous stereotypes

Personal Relevance

social identity	people exaggerate perceived differences between their own group and other groups, including how similar members of each group are to each other
symbolic values	people connect outgroups with the violation of cherished values
ambivalence amplification	people who have conflicting emotions toward an outgroup react extremely toward members of that group

Social Functions

group goals	people resist letting an outgroup benefit if they believe that the outgroup will benefit at their own group's expense
media bias	people model their thoughts, feelings, and actions after those in media presentations
social roles	people justify long-standing divisions of labor, often at their own group's expense

minority group (Xs) performed more of the bad behaviors than they did. The students "saw" a correlation between the infrequent group and the infrequent behaviors that was illusory (Hamilton, Dugan, & Trollier, 1985; Spears, van der Plight, & Eiser, 1986). The correlation did not exist. The students also formed more positive impressions of the majority group than of the minority group. Even when the ratio of good-to-bad behaviors is identical for each group, students say that majority group members are superior to minority group members on intellectual dimensions like intelligence and on moral dimensions like honesty. Worse yet, students who learn only about good versus bad intellectual behaviors generalize from inferiority on intellectual behaviors to inferiority on moral behaviors (Acorn, Hamilton, & Sherman, 1988).

Illusory correlation is a basic phenomenon of human thinking that functions even without preexisting stereotypes, prejudice, and discrimination. Illusory correlation is more pronounced when people are emotionally aroused, as people often are when they are considering matters of race (Kim & Baron, 1988). Illusory correlation occurs because the combination of two infrequent events seems unusual enough to attract extra attention (Hamilton & Sherman, 1989, 1994) and because the 2–1 ratio of good to bad behaviors is based on more instances for the majority group than for the minority group and is thus perceived as more robust and memorable (Fiedler, 1991). Neither of these factors, distinctiveness or perceived robustness, depends on there being an actual difference in intelligence or morality between the two groups. Mere differences in category size and event frequency are sufficient to generate the effect. Illusory correlation thus explains how negative stereotypes might be formed even when they have no "kernel of truth" (Hamilton & Gifford, 1976).

Unlike many other biases, illusory correlation is *less,* not more, likely to occur when people are not willing and able to deliberate. In one study of mood effects on illusory correlation, students learned about two different groups' good and bad behaviors (Stroessner, Hamilton, & Mackie, 1992). First, however, the experimenters put some of the students in a good mood by having them watch a stand-up comic. They put other students in a bad mood by having them watch a film about child abuse. Students who were in a neutral mood displayed the usual illusory correlation. Students who were in either a good or a bad mood did not, because they did not do the deliberation necessary to pay greater attention to the minority groups' infrequent behaviors. Deliberation reduces stereotyping when people have an initial negative reaction from which they adjust. Deliberation, however, increases forming stereotypes from infrequent behaviors when people have no previous experience with the group (Hamilton, Stroessner, & Mackie, 1993). Unless people care so deeply that they pay strict attention to every behavior when they first learn about it, illusory correlation occurs after people learn about the group's behaviors and before they apply what they know to evaluate the group (McConnell, Sherman, & Hamilton, 1994; Sanbonmatsu, Shavitt, & Sherman, 1991).

Illusory correlation may play a fundamental role in stereotyping, prejudice, and discrimination even for groups that are not a statistical minority in the population. Although women are not a "minority" of the population, they have been consistently regarded as the "other sex" or the "opposite sex" in literature and in scientific research. Men have been taken as the "yardstick," reference point, or assumed normal state of affairs, so research in a wide range of scientific disciplines has been devoted to finding ways in which women differ from the "male standard" (Tavris, 1992). Stereotypes about women being less intelligent or less moral than men may arise from inappropriately pairing a "deviant" group with infrequent behaviors (Miller, Taylor, & Buck, 1991).

Illusory correlation might also serve different functions for men and women. Women might pay special attention to the health problems of the elderly because they fear getting old themselves. On the rare occasions when U.S. media show older women, the women are often severely incapacitated (Kubey, 1980). Men, in contrast, might not notice the health problems of old age, because they expect to become increasingly distinguished, powerful, and financially secure. If women knew that they might be inadvertently blaming old people because of their own fears, they might not be as prone to stereotype the elderly. Reminding *men* about old people's health problems, in contrast, might induce stereotyping, because it might arouse fears that the men did

FIGURE 8.4

Stereotypes of the elderly serve different functions for men and women.

Graph shows illusory correlation stereotyping by men and women who did or did not read a story that provided "insight" into using stereotypes because of one's own fears (Snyder & Miene, 1994).

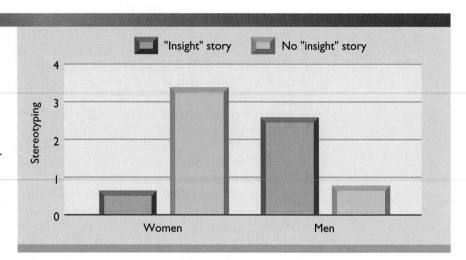

not previously have. In one study of stereotyping the elderly, the researchers had some college men and women but not others read about a character of their own sex who realized that he (or she) had been blaming the elderly for difficulties associated with old age and that stereotyping often occurs when people fear becoming severely incapacitated themselves (Snyder & Miene, 1994, Experiment 2). All students then read about young and old people who had traits, such as lonely and forgetful, that are part of the stereotype. Later, all students tried to recall how many times the stereotypic traits were paired with young people and with old people. Because stereotypic traits were paired equally often with old and young people, stereotyping consisted of overestimating the frequency of such traits for old people. As Figure 8.4 shows, women stereotyped less when they had recently gained insight into how people use the elderly as "scapegoats" for their own fears. Men stereotyped *more* when they read the same story, presumably because they did not have such fears until the story suggested them.

■ IGNORING COVARIATION

Another thought process that contributes to inappropriate stereotypes is seeing simple relationships while ignoring more complex relationships that covary with and might account for the simple ones. Here is a simple relationship, for example: Black children in the United States score lower on standardized achievement tests than do White children. The correlation is not illusory. In reality, a larger percentage of Black than White children score low. If we depended only on the simple relationship, we might draw the unwarranted conclusion that White children are smarter. Scientists who study such issues, however, realize that the simple relationship between race and scores is caused by other factors that *covary with* (go together with) both of the factors. A larger percentage of Black than White children come from poor families. Also, spending per pupil is greater in predominantly White schools than predominantly Black schools. Children who come from well-off homes and attend well-funded schools do better on achievement tests, regardless of whether they are White or Black, but more of them are White. Differences in family income and school budgets account for the simple relationship between and race and achievement test scores. When enough covarying factors are taken into account, the simple relationship disappears. Inaccurate stereotypes arise in part because people easily notice simple relationships and do not do the in-depth thinking necessary to discover covarying factors (Schaller, 1994).

To test whether people use simple relationships even when they have the information necessary to discover covariates, the investigators in one study presented college students with the results of anagram tests for 50 people, half from Group Y and half from Group X (Schaller & O'Brien, 1992). (Anagrams are words with the letters jumbled.) Had the results not been presented in random order, it would have been obvious that members of Group X outperformed members of Group Y on both very difficult and very easy anagrams. Xs attempted 20 very difficult anagrams, of which they got five right and 15 wrong (25%). They also attempted five very easy anagrams, of which they got all five right (100%). Ys attempted only five very difficult anagrams, of which they got none right (0%). They also attempted 20 easy anagrams, of which they got 15 right and five wrong (75%). After they read all 50 results, the students were asked which group would do better if other members of both groups were given the same anagrams and which group had the most verbal intelligence. As predicted, the average student thought that members of Group Y would do better and that Ys had greater verbal intelligence than Xs. They relied on the simple relationship that Ys got 15 of 25 anagrams right and Xs got only 10 of 25 anagrams right. They ignored the fact that, regardless of group, people got more of the very easy anagrams right and more of the very difficult anagrams wrong. Xs got fewer anagrams right only because they attempted more of the very difficult ones.

We often do not have the time or motivation to derive more complex relationships from individual instances. If we did, follow-up studies show, we would draw more accurate conclusions (Schaller, 1992). Also, a salient relationship often "blocks" us from noticing other relationships that might have been at least as informative (Sanbonmatsu, Akimoto, & Gibson, 1994). Finally, information often comes to us "summarized" by media sources that report only the simple relationship and ignore complex ones. When people know that they are going to have to communicate information to others, they usually simplify relationships in the retelling (Zajonc, 1960; Zukier, 1990). Even when the members of two groups are assigned to roles that give one group an advantage over the other, we often notice only the simple relationship that one group outperforms the other, from which we sometimes derive inaccurate stereotypes (Eagly, 1987; Schaller, 1994).

◼ IMPLICIT STEREOTYPING

The evidence on illusory correlation and ignoring covariation suggests that people can display stereotyping, prejudice, and discrimination without meaning to. People who believe that men are more successful than women, for example, might use a different criterion for judging a man's success than for judging a woman's success. They might do so without realizing that their thought processes are slanted. Because the word *implicit* means "implied or understood without being directly expressed," such effects are called implicit stereotyping. In studies of implicit stereotyping, college students read a list of 72 names silently and rated each name on how easy it was to pronounce (Banaji & Greenwald, 1995). Although they were not identified as such, half of the names were of famous people such as Hubert Humphrey, Peggy Fleming, Mark Spitz, and Gladys Knight. The other half were "invented" names of nonfamous people such as Joe Steiger, Anne Wyman, David Wharton, and Sandy Riggs. Also, half the people on the list had men's first names and half had women's first names. From one to three days later, the students returned for a second experiment in which they read a list that contained 144 names, 72 of which were the names used in the earlier experiment. For each of the 144 names, students were asked whether it was a person who was famous or nonfamous. Students more often mistook nonfamous names they had seen on the earlier list for famous people than they mistook nonfamous names that were *not* on the earlier list for famous people. The students also displayed a gender bias. They more frequently assigned mistaken fame to previously seen male than female names.

Women were as susceptible as men to implicit stereotyping. Women knew the stereotype about men being more famous as well as did men. In one study, students were asked whether they agreed with propositions such as "Women should change their names when they marry," "We do not need an Equal Rights Amendment," and "Maintaining gender roles makes a relationship better." Students who endorsed such propositions were no more likely to display implicit stereotyping than were students who rejected the propositions. Implicit stereotyping is not the same as conscious stereotyping (Greenwald & Banaji, in press). It involves both knowing the stereotype and having an opportunity to apply it *unintentionally,* so that the deliberate "adjustment" process shown in Table 8.1 has no chance to operate. Similarly, jurors who do not realize that they are influenced by implicit stereotyping would not realize that they needed to adjust their biased verdicts.

PERSONAL REASONS

Many of the causes in the previous section on thought processes are not the type that personally benefit the perceiver. Although the result is usually to benefit their own social group at the expense of other social groups, people do not intend to have prejudicial spontaneous reactions that occur in milliseconds, do not benefit from illusory correlations, and do not deliberately "use" implicit stereotyping to justify their own group's superiority. In this section, though, we discuss personal reasons for stereotyping, prejudice, and discrimination. Stereotypes, prejudice, and discrimination often help individuals to maintain a positive social identity, to express symbolic values about what is right and wrong, and to resolve conflicting emotions.

■ SOCIAL IDENTITY

One of the major themes of the textbook, discussed more in detail in Chapters 1 and 5, is that people have both a personal identity and a "collective" or social identity (Brewer, 1991; Cousins, 1989; Crocker, Luhtanen, Blaine, & Broadnax, 1994; Deaux, 1993; Markus & Kitayama, 1994; Miller & Prentice, 1994; Oyserman, 1993; Trafimow, Triandis, & Goto, 1991; Turner, Oakes, Haslam, & McGarty, 1994). An individual's personal identity involves unique, individual characteristics. An individual's social identity is the reputation that he or she gains merely by being a member of a particular social group. A member of a world champion sports team, for instance, enjoys a very positive social identity merely by being a member of the famous team, even if he or she is injured for most of the year and does not participate actively in team events. When our social groups succeed at the expense of negatively stereotyped social groups, we feel successful ourselves (Smith, 1993).

When two groups differ, the differences seem larger to group members than to outsiders, because exaggerating the differences between groups emphasizes each member's social identity (Turner, Hogg, Oakes, Reich, & Wetherell, 1987). The difference between Serbs and Croatians looks larger to the Serbs and Croatians themselves than it does to someone from the United States. These exaggerated differences "justify" treating one group better than the other (Turner, 1991). If a member of group Y believes that Ys work harder than Xs, then it makes sense for the Y who runs a business to hire members of Group Y before members of Group X. If the differences exaggerated by social identity are erroneously believed to be true, then stereotyping, prejudice, and discrimination "make sense." To test these hypotheses about social identity, investigators in several studies divided student participants into two *meaningless* groups (Tajfel, 1982; Tajfel & Turner, 1986; Turner et al., 1987). The researchers had students make trivial judgments about the numbers of dots shown on a screen or the quality of indistinguishable abstract paintings, or merely flipped a coin (Tajfel, Flament, Billig, & Bundy, 1971). Then they randomly told some students "You belong to Group X" and other students "You belong to Group Y" (Billig & Tajfel, 1973). After they told the students which group they "belonged to," the researchers let the students divide money between members of Group X and Group Y. A member of group X might have to decide, for instance, between Choice A (give a member of Group Y $10 and a member of Group X $10), and Choice B (give a member of Group Y $9 and a member of Group X $11).

Students in these social identity experiments were divided into categories only by a meaningless label, met no members of either "group" in person, and gained nothing for themselves. Nonetheless, they consistently favored members of "their own" group over members of "the other" group. The students discriminated even in situations where they had to give up money themselves (preferring Choice B to Choice A, for instance) if they wanted to favor their own group and penalize the other group (Turner, 1978). Also students who favored their own group felt better about themselves after doing so (Oakes & Turner, 1980). The social identity process depends on how highly people regard themselves, how much of their self-esteem they derive from their identification with a group, and how important it is to them that their own group be perceived as superior to other groups. Social identity exaggerates people's perceptions of differences between their own and even arbitrary other groups (Crocker & Luhtanen, 1990; Turner, et al., 1987; Wilder & Shapiro, 1991).

Part of exaggerating the differences between one's own group (the in-group) and other groups (outgroups) is believing that "they are all alike, but we are not." According to the **outgroup homogeneity effect** we view members of the outgroup as more "all alike" (homogeneous) than members of the in-group (Judd & Park, 1988). The unrealistic assumption that "they are all alike" underlies stereotyping, prejudice, and discrimination (Doyle & Aboud, 1995; Masson & Verkuyten, 1993; Vanbeselaere, 1991a). Treating all (or even most) members of a social group poorly makes no sense unless you think that they all think and act alike (Judd & Park, 1993). In a relevant study, Princeton and Rutgers students watched a videotape of a college-age man who had a choice about whether to wait alone or in the company of other students for a psychology experiment (Quattrone & Jones, 1980). Half of the students saw him choose to wait alone; half saw him choose to wait with others. Also, half of the Princeton and Rutgers students thought the man on the tape was from their own (in-group) university. The other half thought that he was from the other (outgroup) university. All students estimated what percentage of students from the same university as the videotaped man would make the same choice as he had. Because the results were similar regardless of whether the videotaped man chose to wait alone or to wait with others, Figure 8.5 contrasts the predictions of Princeton and Rutgers students when the man on the videotape decided to wait alone. As the figure shows, Princeton students believed that a larger percentage of Rutgers than Princeton students would choose the same as had the Princeton or Rutgers man on the videotape. Rutgers students believed the opposite. Students from both schools displayed the outgroup homogeneity effect by assuming that members of the outgroup are more similar to each other than members of the in-group.

The outgroup homogeneity effect occurs when fraternity and sorority members, students who have different college majors, Irish versus American students, White versus Black people, men versus women, and young versus old

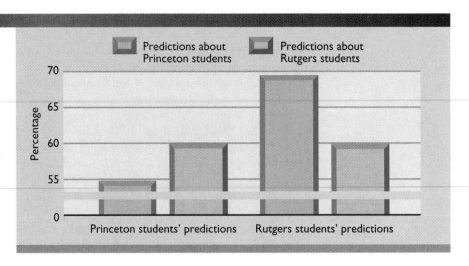

FIGURE 8.5

Outgroup members seem more "all alike" than in-group members.

Graph shows percentage of students that other students thought would make the same choices as had "one of their own" (Quattrone & Jones, 1980).

Who are more all alike—nurses or doctors?

people judge each other (Jones, Wood, & Quattrone, 1981; Judd, Ryan, & Park, 1991; Linville, Fischer, & Salovey, 1989; Linville & Jones, 1980; Park & Judd, 1990; Park & Rothbart, 1982). It even occurs when the groups are merely empty labels such as "Group X" or "Group Y" (Judd & Park, 1988; McGarty, Haslam, Turner, & Oakes, 1993). The effect is not related to liking the in-group more than the outgroup (Jones, Wood, & Quattrone, 1981; Park & Rothbart, 1982). It is related to drawing finer subcategory or subtype discriminations within the in-group than within the outgroup (Park, Ryan, & Judd, 1992). When male and female college students are introduced to other men and women who have a variety of college majors, for instance, the men are more apt to remember the other men's majors (or subtypes) than the women's majors. The reverse is true for women (Mackie & Worth, 1989a).

The outgroup homogeneity effect is more pronounced for naturally occurring groups such as students at rival universities than it is for an artificial Group X and Group Y (Ostrom & Sedikides, 1992). The effect is also reversed and becomes an "in-group homogeneity effect" when small groups that are very concerned about their social identity evaluate their own group versus the majority. Nursing students who study together for years to learn a common social identity, for instance, perceive themselves as more all alike than doctors on attributes that are central to being a nurse, but they perceive doctors as more all alike on attributes relevant to doctors (Brown & Wootton-Millward, 1993). People may judge the variability of outgroups by how closely the outgroup members match the stereotype, but they judge the variability of in-groups by resolving a tension between social identity and personal identity (Brewer, 1991, 1993; Ostrom, Carpenter, Sedikides, & Li, 1993). When the in-group is an embattled minority, social identity prompts its members to emphasize their similarities with each other. When the in-group is an established majority or the group that holds greater status and power, personal identity prompts its members to emphasize their distinctiveness from each other, which makes minority outgroups look all alike by comparison (Lorenzi-Cioldi, Eagly, & Stewart, 1995).

Finally, the outgroup homogeneity effect has important consequences for how individual members of the outgroup are treated (Park et al., 1991). People who assume that outgroup members are all alike may be more likely to vent their negative attitudes on individual outgroup members, such as Black defendants accused of raping White women, than are people who recognize the outgroup's diversity (Lambert & Wyer, 1990). Members of a noticeably different minority group might be discriminated against in jury trials, job interviews, and other important life decisions merely because of social identity processes that put the minority group at a disadvantage.

■ SYMBOLIC VALUES

Racism in modern times may be difficult to detect through straightforward survey questions, because modern negative racial attitudes in Western Europe and the United States are qualitatively different from negative racial attitudes 50 years ago (Pettigrew & Meertens, 1995). White people's racial stereotyping today might not represent a dislike of Black people. Instead, it might represent a dislike of policies that help Blacks at the expense of traditional values. White citizens might not express open hostility toward Blacks, but they often express intense animosity toward policies such as welfare and school busing, which they view as symbolizing the advancement of Black people's interests at the expense of the White majority. **Symbolic racism** (also called "modern racism") involves animosity toward policies that symbolize one race's advancement at another race's perceived expense (McConahay, 1982; Sears, 1988). In the United States, symbolic racism toward Blacks consists of antagonism toward Black people's demands ("Blacks are getting too demanding in their push for equal rights"), resentment of special favors for Black people (It is wrong to set up quotas to admit Black students to college who don't meet the usual standards"), and refusing to admit that racial discrimination still exists ("Blacks in my country are not denied jobs or promotions because of their race").

Symbolic racists believe that Black people today violate "such traditional American values as individualism and self-reliance, the work ethic, obedience, and discipline" (Kinder & Sears, 1981, p. 416). Many White people who would vehemently deny being racist are also unalterably opposed to school busing, welfare, and other social policies that they believe benefit primarily Blacks. These White people are genuinely committed to the Protestant work ethic and to the individualistic spirit of a capitalist economic system. They genuinely do not have negative attitudes toward Blacks. They would oppose nonindividualistic social policies even if they believed that the policy would help more Whites than Blacks. Similarly, many people have negative stereotypes, prejudice, and

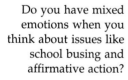

Do you have mixed emotions when you think about issues like school busing and affirmative action?

discrimination against those who are overweight because they believe that overweight people have low willpower, set a bad example, and violate other cherished ideological values about personal responsibility and restraint (Crandall, 1994).

In studies that tested the predictive power of old-fashioned racism propositions such as "I do not like Black people" against the predictive power of symbolic racism propositions, the old-fashioned racism propositions had little or no predictive power. Endorsement of symbolic racism propositions, in contrast, reliably predicts whether an individual will vote for or against a Black political candidate, oppose versus support school busing, and oppose versus support tax laws that benefit Whites at the expense of Blacks (Kinder & Sears, 1981; McConahay & Hough, 1976; Sears & Citrin, 1985). Modern or symbolic racism is such a good predictor of political actions that it often overwhelms even self-interest. It is easier to predict opposition to school busing from a parent's symbolic racism than from whether the parent's own child is affected by the policy (Kinder & Sears, 1981; Sears & Allen, 1984; Sears & Kinder, 1985).

Similarly, many modern attitudes toward homosexuals are not based entirely on negative stereotypes, but rather on beliefs that gay men and women are destroying traditional values (Esses, Haddock, & Zanna, 1993). Many people who have negative attitudes toward homosexuals sincerely believe that homosexuality reduces the importance of the traditional family and challenges religious precepts. Right-wing authoritarians, who strongly endorse conventional values and behave aggressively toward those who violate values and norms, say that values play a very important role in their lives (Altemeyer, 1994). They have a very positive attitude toward traditional housewives, for example, and a very negative attitude toward feminists (Haddock & Zanna, 1994). They also have attitudes toward homosexuals that are more laden with symbolic beliefs than are other people's attitudes (Haddock, Zanna, & Esses, 1993). When we firmly believe that a minority group threatens the values that we hold most dear, we readily accept inaccurate negative stereotypes about them, feel prejudice toward them, and discriminate against them without feeling guilty (Haddock et al., 1993).

■ CONFLICTING EMOTIONS

Many White United States citizens have conflicting emotions about Blacks and other racial and ethnic groups, because racial attitudes bring into conflict the two most important core values in the culture of the United States: equality and individualism (Keller, 1983). Equality means fairness, as in giving every citizen a fair chance in life, treating all defendants in rape trials alike, sympathizing with the underdog, and helping people who are trying to overcome unfair obstacles. Individualism means self-reliance, as in rewarding hard work, individual achievement, and other manifestations of the Protestant work ethic. Many White people want to help the oppressed through laws that emphasize fairness, for instance laws against racial discrimination in housing and education. Because they value individualism, however, many White people vehemently oppose laws that violate merit-based rewards and self-reliance, for instance laws that give preference to Black applicants for jobs or graduate schools (Lipset & Schneider, 1978). Many White people attribute high rates of Black unemployment and crime to personality flaws rather than to a previous history of oppression and a current lack of educational and job opportunities. As a result, they believe that preferential treatment for Blacks violates the principle of individualism, which they hold dear (Katz, Wackenhut, & Hass, 1986). These White people want to help the underdog, but not if it means giving Blacks more than they "deserve."

Because the core values of equality and individualism conflict, many White people have attitudes toward Black people that are characterized by ambivalence. Ambivalence means simultaneously liking and disliking the same person or group. People who experience ambivalence are like tightrope walkers delicately balanced on a narrow support. The greater the ambivalence, the "higher" is the tightrope and the harder they fall when they lose their balance. When people who are experiencing ambivalence toward a minority group lose their balance and "fall" to either the positive or the negative side in how they react to a minority group member, they do not react in a moderate way. Instead, they react extremely (Hass, Katz, Rizzo, Bailey, & Eisenstadt, 1991). Their conflict between positive and negative emotions builds an uncomfortable tension. Resolving the inner conflict releases pent-up energy that amplifies or exaggerates actions, whether the actions are positive or negative (Katz, 1981).

Ambivalence amplification occurs when people who both like and dislike a group react extremely toward one or more members of that group (Katz, 1981; Katz & Hass, 1988; Simon & Greenberg, in press). In several studies of ambivalence amplification, White college students were induced to deliver shocks or insults to either a Black or a White confederate (Katz, Glass, & Cohen, 1973; Katz, Glass, Lucido, & Farber, 1979). After they harmed the confederate, the White students had a chance to do the confederate a favor. White students who had a chance to help their "victim" did so more extremely if the victim was Black than if the victim was White. When they had a chance to justify their harmful actions by attributing negative characteristics to the victim, however, they treated a Black victim *worse* than a White victim.

White people differ in how much ambivalence they have toward Black people. Some individuals are not ambivalent, either because they value one of the two core values much more than the other or because they value neither very highly. Other individuals are very ambivalent because they believe fervently in both "A good society is one in which people feel responsible for one another" and "People who fail at a job have usually not tried hard enough" (Katz & Hass, 1988). In one study, relatively ambivalent and unambivalent White college students read graduate school applications by a White and a Black student. The ambivalent students amplified their evaluations of the Black applicant (Hass, et al., 1991; Linville & Jones, 1980). Given two excellent applications, the ambivalent students evaluated the Black applicant higher than the White applicant. Given two poor applications, they evaluated the Black applicant lower than the White applicant. Unambivalent students were more moderate in their evaluations, because they did not experience the conflicting emotions that heighten "normal" reactions.

Racial ambivalence also affects people's reactions to racial controversies. In one study of racial ambivalence, college students who were high and low on racial ambivalence heard an audiotape about a widely publicized incident in which White teenagers beat three young Black men in a predominantly White neighborhood of New York City (Hass, Katz, Rizzo, Bailey, & Moore, 1992). One of the Black men was struck by a car and killed when he tried to escape. On the audiotape, White people from the neighborhood made conflicting remarks such as "We don't need them coming here and bringing their welfare and crime and drugs" and "I am ashamed that this thing happened in my neighborhood." Other students did not hear the "racial controversy" audiotape. After listening to the tape, the students indicated their current mood as part of an "unrelated" study. Figure 8.6 shows that listening to the tape had a more detrimental effect on the moods of students who were high than low in racial ambivalence. Low ambivalence students "knew where they stood" on racial issues, whether pro or con, so they continued to have moderately positive moods even after listening to the inflammatory tape. High ambivalence

FIGURE 8.6

Racial controversy upsets racially ambivalent people.

Graph shows positivity of mood reported by low and high racial ambivalance students after listening or not listening to a racial controversy tape (Hass et al., 1992).

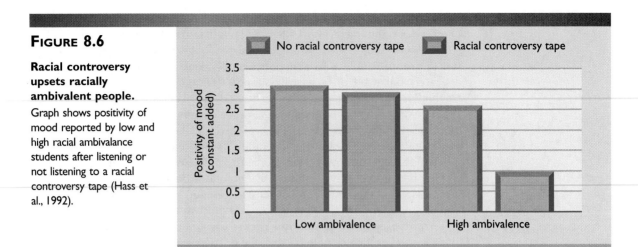

students, in contrast, were "torn" because they believed fervently in conflicting values relevant to the race issue. For them, listening to the "racial controversy" tape accentuated their dilemma and canceled their previously positive mood.

SOCIAL CONTEXT

Besides thought processes and personal relevance, stereotyping, prejudice, and discrimination also occur in a social context and serve important social functions. Majority groups also have their biased views "validated" daily by movies, television, and other media sources. Finally, people who are socialized into playing different social roles often continue to play their assigned roles, even when their assigned roles are not to their own personal benefit.

GROUP GOALS

Realistic conflict occurs when majority and minority groups compete for status, power, and other scarce resources. "Realistic conflict is like a note on an organ. It sets all prejudices that are attuned to it into simultaneous vibration. The listener can scarcely distinguish the pure note from the surrounding jangle" (Allport, 1954, p. 233). When there are not enough good schools or jobs to go around, one group's gain is another group's loss. Groups that hold political power benefit by depicting the members of powerless groups as unfit for education, unfit for employment, or in other ways flawed, because doing so lowers the likelihood that the powerful will lose ground to the powerless. When men have greater power than women, for instance, they are especially likely to treat women as sex objects and to discriminate against women (Bourhis, 1994; Rudman & Borgida, 1995). Erroneous stereotypes advance the dominant group's self-interests (Bobo, 1988). Majority group members frequently "blame the victim" by explaining Black people's poverty through "inherent laziness," women's low pay through "natural lack of assertiveness," and old people's mandatory retirement through "failing powers." In reality, Whites gain by keeping Black people poor, men gain by keeping women in low-status jobs, and younger people gain by forcing older people out of the job market.

Realistic group conflict develops because powerful groups have an investment in maintaining social inequality (Bobo, 1983; Tajfel & Turner, 1979). Attitudes toward minority groups and stereotypes of minority group members become especially negative whenever the majority group and the minority group have incompatible group interests and the minority group poses a threat to the majority group's interests (Bobo, 1988). Many White people support equality of education as an abstract principle but oppose school busing, because they believe that busing White children to schools in poor neighborhoods advances the interests of Black children *at the expense of* White children. Similarly, many White people support equality in employment but oppose affirmative action hiring practices because they believe that affirmative action practices advance the interests of Black job seekers *at the expense of* White job seekers (Murrell, Dietz-Uhler, Dovidio, Gaertner, & Drout, 1994). When majority group members perceive that their own interests are threatened, they welcome arguments that defend and justify the existing inequalities. The "dominant group seeks to articulate a set of beliefs that persuades themselves, as well as others, that their privileged status is for the general good" (Bobo, 1988, p. 99).

■ MEDIA BIAS

Majority groups also have their stereotypes "validated" by biased media presentations. Majority group members model their thoughts, feelings, and actions after movies, television, and other artistic portrayals. In early movies in the United States, for example, Black people were portrayed either as fools or as vicious enemies of Whites. Black men in early movies predictably danced, drank gin, rolled dice, cheated at cards, ate watermelons, and stole chickens (Leab, 1975). In *The Birth of a Nation,* the landmark 1915 film about the U.S. Civil War, southern Black men after the Civil War were seen pushing Whites off the sidewalk, grabbing their possessions, and trying to rape innocent White teenagers. Only the "heroic" intervention of the Ku Klux Klan saved the Whites in the movie from being enslaved by Blacks who wanted to found a degenerate barbarian empire. Even in modern films and modern television programs, Black actors often are not selected for serious dramatic roles. Instead, they are cast as caricatures who bring to the screen either comic relief or gratuitous violence (Leab, 1975). When a rare situation comedy like *The Cosby Show* tried to depict a Black family that had the same problems as any White middle-class family, many White people did not interpret the show's message as "Blacks and Whites are very similar to each other." Instead, they saw it as "Blacks are not discriminated against. They can make it if they try." Being reminded of a successful minority group member reduces stereotyping, prejudice, and discrimination only when the successful minority group member seems likable and typical. People do not change their overall negative attitudes merely because of one atypical minority group member (Bodenhausen, Schwarz, Bless, & Wänke, 1995).

The American Indian has fared no better than Black people in movies and on television. In reality, American Indian tribes such as Sioux and Arapahos differ from each other by at least as much as Europeans from different nations differ. Tribal differences, however, like individual differences within tribes, have been largely ignored by the media. Incredibly, modern history textbooks and novels continue to depict American Indians either as dirty, drunken, cruel, and treacherous savages or as noble but naive natives (Trimble, 1988). In most movies about the westward expansion in the United States, American Indians play the "bad guys" who viciously attacked innocent White settlers. They all wear feathers and warbonnets and they all speak in nonsense. Because most movie makers know no American Indian language, producers have sometimes recorded speeches in English and then played them backwards to simulate "What American Indians sound like." In one movie an actor supposed to be a Sioux spoke in Lakota and said the equivalent of "White man, you are nothing!" The subtitle read "I have been traveling a long time to talk with you!"

(Trimble, 1988, p. 190). The White audience had no way to know that the translation was inaccurate.

Stereotypes of women also flow easily from inaccurate and demeaning media portrayals. Women are typically depicted in paintings, even by women artists, as wives, mothers, housekeepers, or prostitutes. Men are typically shown as workers, leaders, and heroes (O'Kelly, 1980). Women have been depicted as relatively passive and accepting of a "lower status" than men in children's readers, movies, and television (Child, Potter, & Levine, 1946; McArthur & Resko, 1975). Women are also shown in biased ways on television commercials. The central character in most television commercials is either a product user or an authority. The product users tend to be women and the authorities tend to be men (McArthur & Resko, 1975). When the woman in a television commercial gives a reason for liking the product, it is usually a nonscientific reason. The scientific reasons are reserved for male actors. When women are included in commercials for such masculine products as razor blades, the women are obviously on screen for "decorative" purposes (Livingstone & Green, 1986). In addition, the disembodied narrator is a man's voice more than 90% of the time (Bretl & Cantor, 1988).

With role models such as these, it is difficult for viewers to conclude that women have as much status and are as competent as men (Saltzman, 1983). If anything, television commercials intended for children display even greater sex role stereotyping than do commercials intended for adults (Durkin, 1985). We know the effect of watching such commercials. In one study, some women watched "standard" commercials that had men in the active roles and women in the passive roles (Jennings, Geis, & Brown, 1980). Other women watched

specially prepared commercials in which the sex roles were reversed. Women who watched the standard commercials later displayed less self-confidence and greater conformity than did women who watched the commercials where sex roles were reversed. Even when well-informed parents, teachers, and textbooks educate people that there are no meaningful differences in what men and women can accomplish, television commercials tell a different story. That story has an important impact on stereotypes, prejudice, and discrimination.

Finally, television programs depict an equally inaccurate stereotype of old people. The corporations that sponsor commercial television programs appeal to the 18–55 age group of viewers, because 18–55-year-olds have the highest per capita spendable income (Davis & Davis, 1985). As a result, older people are seldom included in situation comedies, adventures, or soap operas (Cassata, Anderson, & Skill, 1980; Gerbner, Gross, Signorelli, & Morgan, 1980; Greenberg, Korzenny, & Atkin, 1979; Harris & Feinberg, 1977). Older women, especially, are almost never seen (Gerbner et al., 1980). When older people of either sex are seen on television, they are depicted at one of two extremes of physical health—either very ill and dying or in extraordinarily good health (Harris & Feinberg, 1977). People in the 55–75 age group, of course, are not all at one of these two extremes. In reality, they are as likely as any other age group to be in moderately good health (Davis & Davis, 1985). Older people, like minorities, are also underrepresented in children's programs. The few old people who appear almost never interact with children (Seefeldt, 1977). No wonder 90% of children say they have very negative attitudes toward old people (Seefeldt, 1977). Children who watch much television have every reason to assume from what they have witnessed that people beyond age 55 are relatively rare, isolated from "the rest of us," and unproductive (Davis & Davis, 1985).

■ SOCIAL ROLES

Groups are not always in conflict (Aboud, 1992). Sometimes the powerless cooperate with the powerful by implicitly agreeing to play their assigned social roles (Eagly, 1987). A social role is the role that a person is expected to play in a society, just as each actor in a play is expected to play an assigned role. Social roles are assigned subtly through media portrayals and other implicit messages about what is expected from different races, sexes, and age groups. As a result, many citizens accept uncritically their assigned roles. When they play those roles well, they convince the next generation of citizens that different types of social behavior come naturally to people of different social groups. Social roles cause stereotyping, prejudice, and discrimination because society subtly encourages people to learn their scripts and to perform as expected without causing any problems (Eagly, 1987).

The impact of social roles begins with a consensus about the appropriate division of labor, or how different tasks are to be divided between social groups. One example of an unequal division of labor is the tradition that women stay home and take care of the children, whereas men go out of the home to provide for the family. Although this division of labor between the sexes may rest on the biological fact that women and not men bear and nurse babies, the division is not inevitable. In some animal species the female gives birth and then leaves home to seek food. The male stays home with the young. In some human cultures as well, women deal with the world while the men stay at home and tend the garden. Every society has an *option* about whether to send the men, the women, or both out to wrest necessities from the world and about whether to have the men, the women, or both remain at home (Tavris, 1992). Nonetheless, modern stereotypes in Western Europe and the United States have reinforced an "ideal" division of labor between the sexes. The division of labor is so widely accepted that attempts to undo it through affirmative action encounter resistance from both sexes. Women who believe they are hired because of being women, for instance, evaluate their own ability and performance more negatively than do women who believe they are hired on merit (Turner, Pratkanis, & Hardaway, 1991; Turner & Pratkanis, 1994). Similarly, women in the workplace are almost as likely as men to dislike having a woman boss (O'Leary & Ickovics, 1990).

Although the evidence is not as clear-cut for race roles as it is for sex roles, an outdated division of labor may underlie racism and ageism as well. Black people were originally brought to the United States as slaves. Cotton and other crops had to be picked by hand. A viable economy required large numbers of people who had limited intelligence and were content to perform backbreaking physical labor. White southerners found (or more accurately "invented") such people by imprisoning them and by creating the myth that Black slaves *enjoyed* playing their assigned roles in the economy. The myth persisted in nineteenth- and twentieth-century movies that showed Blacks cheerfully singing while serving their White plantation masters (Leab, 1975). The myth persisted

Reprinted with special permission of King Features Syndicate.

also in the surviving stereotype of Black people as not very intelligent but very carefree and musical (Dovidio & Gaertner, 1986).

Another myth that "legitimizes" the existing social order is that old people have inferior traits and abilities. Old people in Canada falsely remember being better when they were young at traits that are supposed to deteriorate with age and falsely remember being worse at traits that are supposed to improve with age (McFarland, Ross, & Giltrow, 1992). Also, most citizens of the United States believe that memory inevitably declines in old age (Ryan, 1992). In China, by contrast, old people are honored as wise leaders (Ikels, 1991). When old and young people in the United States and China take memory tests, young people score the same in both countries, but old people in the United States score much lower than do old people in China, who score no lower than do young people in China (Levy & Langer, 1994). When people accept myths about social roles, the myths sometimes cause the types of self-fulfilling prophecies that are discussed in Chapter 11 (Neuberg, 1994).

Some individuals are more likely than others to cooperate in myths that "legitimize" unequal group status (Sidanius & Pratto, 1993). Some people want a world in which one group has greater power and status than others. On the Social Dominance Orientation Scale (Pratto, Sidanius, Stallworth, & Malle, 1994), they endorse such sentiments as "Some groups of people are simply inferior to others," "It is OK if some groups have more of a chance in life than others," and "Inferior groups should stay in their place." Typically, people who endorse such sentiments are themselves members of an advantaged group. Men, for instance, have significantly higher social dominance orientation than do women (Sidanius, Pratto, & Bobo, 1994). Regardless of which group they belong to, however, individuals who have higher social dominance orientation oppose women's rights and social programs such as welfare. They also endorse punitive police policies and military programs that keep "inferior" groups and nations in their place (Pratto et al., 1994). To people who are high in social dominance orientation, the myths that support unequal division of labor are not myths at all. They merely acknowledge that some groups are better than others in ways that count.

Also, minority group members might not complain about discrimination because they incorrectly assume that they are treated better than other members of their group (Taylor, Wright, Moghaddam, & Lalonde, 1990; Taylor, Wright, & Ruggiero, 1991). A woman, for instance, might deny being discriminated against as an individual, yet agree that women as a group are not treated fairly. This discrepancy between perceptions of being ill treated as an individual and perceptions of the group's treatment may occur because people think they deserve what happens to them as individuals, comparing themselves to other individuals is different from comparing their group to other groups, and individuals feel well off compared to the dramatic examples of discrimination that receive media attention (Taylor, Wright, & Porter, 1994). Thus women and other minority groups often accept their individual roles in society's division of labor while simultaneously acknowledging that their group is discriminated against.

Once society has decided on a division of labor, different groups are led to have different expectations about how they "ought" to behave and different groups are provided with skills suited to the tasks that they "ought" to pursue (Eagly, 1987). Parents and teachers communicate different expectations for how little boys and little girls "should" behave (Dweck, 1986; Deaux & Major, 1987; Hare-Musten & Maracek, 1988). Little boys are expected to be active, aggressive, fearless, nonnurturing, and inclined toward mathematics and science. Little girls are expected to be passive, nonaggressive, timid, nurturing, and uninterested in mathematics or science. Boys and girls know what is expected of them. By college age, for example, most men refuse to have their photographs

Would a genuinely feminine woman ever nail boards?

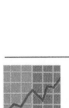

taken ironing napkins or cuddling babies and most women refuse to have their photographs taken nailing boards or oiling squeaky hinges (Bem, 1975, 1981; Bem, Martyna, & Watson, 1976). People in our society know that men and women are expected to behave differently and they usually follow their assigned scripts (Bem, 1985; Williams & Best, 1982). Similarly, many older people are persuaded that they would somehow be better off living on a fixed income while inflation and rising health costs erode their savings (Levine, 1988). Other old people worry about losing their memory or becoming less capable, merely because they are approaching the "deadly" age of 65.

Division of labor also requires that people have different skills, so the people who have been "chosen" to fulfill different social roles are taught different skills and beliefs about their own capabilities. Teenage girls baby-sit not only to earn money, but because society says that baby-sitting is a "sex-appropriate" activity that trains girls to be mothers. Playing a role changes people's beliefs about themselves and about the rewards and punishments that come from either following or ignoring the script (Jones, 1990b). Many men regard women very positively on dimensions such as warmth and nurturance that qualify women for low-status jobs (Eagly & Mladinic, 1994). Businessmen are rewarded for being assertive, whereas business*women* are punished for assertiveness by being called a "bitch on wheels." Blacks who take a subservient approach in dealing with White people are rewarded by being treated well; Blacks who demand concessions to make up for past injustices are called "uppity." Competent workers who reach age 65 and "gracefully bow out" are rewarded with a gold watch. Those who dare to question the system are treated as "troublemakers." With these kinds of rewards and punishments for either playing one's assigned social role or stepping out of line, it is small wonder that the traditional division of labor has such a profound impact on social behavior, even at a time in history when the original basis for dividing labor is no longer valid.

Ironically, members of disadvantaged groups sometimes *cooperate* by sharing negative stereotypes (Jost & Banaji, 1994). Hispanics and Blacks, for instance, have approximately the same stereotypes of one another that White people have of them (Triandis, 1989). Similarly, men and women subscribe to the same gender stereotypes (Ashmore & Del Boca, 1986; Banaji & Greenwald, 1994). Girls learn to be women by practicing a role in which they display different types and levels of emotion than do men (Shields, 1994). It seems possible, then, that even disadvantaged groups have a stake in preserving the status quo, which they do by endorsing negative stereotypes of themselves (Jost & Banaji, 1994). **System justification** involves explaining an "existing situation or arrangement with the result that the situation or arrangement is maintained" (Jost & Banaji, 1994, p. 10). If it is biologically possible for women, but not men, to bear and nurse children, for instance, then both men and women might view women as more nurturing and men as more independent. They might do so to justify what seems to them a biological "fact of life." If people in a society enjoy different levels of wealth, then members of both classes might view lower-class people as less intelligent and industrious. They might do so to rationalize the economic disparities. People might justify the existing social arrangement simply because it exists, even though they are themselves the "losers" in such an arrangement (Hoffman & Hurst, 1990).

By justifying the existing system, members of disadvantaged groups might reassure themselves that they live in a "just world" where people get what they deserve (Hafer & Olson, 1993; Lerner, 1980; Rudman, Borgida, & Robertson, 1995). They might also establish a plausible excuse for possible failure (Crocker & Major, 1994; Major & Crocker, 1993). A minority job applicant who is not hired for a high-status job, for instance, might benefit from "attributional ambiguity." It is better to tell yourself and your friends that "I was the victim of prejudice" rather than to say that "I was not good enough to get the job." It seems possible, given research on implicit stereotyping, that perceptions of a just world and conclusions drawn from attributional ambiguity might not occur consciously and deliberately (Jost & Banaji, 1994). Instead, members of groups that are disadvantaged by negative stereotypes might absorb implicit messages from the media and come to believe, without ever examining their reasons for believing, that the world "*has* to work this way."

SUMMARY OF WHY PEOPLE ENGAGE IN STEREOTYPING, PREJUDICE, AND DISCRIMINATION

Thought processes contribute importantly to stereotyping, prejudice, and discrimination. People spontaneously associate infrequently encountered members of minority groups with infrequently encountered violent and undesirable behaviors. People also favor simple relationships, such as that between children's race and achievement scores, over more accurate but complex relationships—for instance that low income correlates with both race and achievement scores. Stereotyping can be so implicit in people's thinking that they are unaware of its influence.

People also have personal reasons for stereotyping, prejudice, and discrimination. When people derive their primary identity from being part of a group, they exaggerate differences between their own and other groups and perceive members of other groups as "all alike." People also espouse such symbolic values as individualism and self-reliance. When helping negatively stigmatized groups violates traditional values, people experience conflict, which amplifies both positive and negative reactions to members of disadvantaged groups.

Finally, stereotyping, prejudice, and discrimination occur in a social context and serve important social functions. Groups that enjoy high status invent negative stereotypes of other groups in part to justify and preserve their advantages. The media often perpetuate inaccurate stereotypes. The inaccurate stereotypes sometimes become self-fulfilling prophecies. Members of both high and low status groups within a culture are socialized to play their assigned social roles. Members of lower status groups sometimes cooperate by justifying the very system that discriminates against them.

CAN WE REDUCE STEREOTYPING, PREJUDICE, AND DISCRIMINATION?

The first section of this chapter described evidence that stereotyping, prejudice, and discrimination are as widespread, even though not as blatant, in modern times as in the past. The second section described the causes of stereotyping, prejudice, and discrimination. This third section addresses ways to reduce stereotyping, prejudice, and discrimination. Finding new approaches and new answers to the problem of stereotyping, prejudice, and discrimination is one of the most challenging and potentially rewarding avenues for future research by social psychologists. Two promising lines of attack involve "contact" and "recategorization."

THE CONTACT HYPOTHESIS

You might think that we could reduce stereotyping, prejudice, and discrimination if groups knew each other better (Boaz, 1905). The **contact hypothesis** (Allport, 1954) holds that under certain conditions, contact with members of a negatively stereotyped minority group will ameliorate negative attitudes both toward the specific members with whom the contact occurred and toward group members as a whole. The necessary conditions for contact to reduce stereotyping, prejudice, and discrimination include mutual goals, equal status, and acquaintance potential.

■ MUTUAL GOALS

We have seen that realistic intergroup conflict is an important cause of stereotyping, prejudice, and discrimination. When groups meet each other only to decide how to divide limited resources, the inevitable result is competition and rivalry, not cooperation and mutual respect. Intergroup contact, however, can reduce prejudice and discrimination in circumstances where the two groups pursue mutual goals that neither group could reach by itself. The importance of a mutual goal was demonstrated in a field experiment that involved a summer camp for boys (Sherif, Harvey, White, Hood, & Sherif, 1961). The psychologists who ran the camp randomly divided the boys into two groups called the Rattlers and the Eagles. As expected, merely providing these category distinctions caused boys in the two groups, even those who had come to the camp as friends, to dislike each other. Subsequent team competitions used realistic conflict to turn the two groups' initial dislike into outright hostility. When the rivalry reached the point of violence, the psychologists tried to reduce intergroup prejudice in two ways. First, they tried forcing boys from the two groups

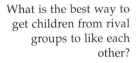

What is the best way to get children from rival groups to like each other?

to sit next to each other at movies, meals, and other enjoyable activities. Forced integration had no effect on intergroup hostility. If anything, it made matters worse.

Second, the psychologists arranged circumstances in which the two groups would have to cooperate with each other if they wanted to achieve a mutual goal. In one such incident, the boys were told that the truck that was bringing them lunch would not start, but that it could be started if all the boys from both groups would pull on ropes to get the truck to the top of an incline. After several such incidents in which the two groups of boys had to work together to achieve goals that both groups desired, intergroup hostility was greatly reduced. Several other studies have confirmed that mere contact between members of rival groups has no beneficial effect when the participants do not pursue mutual goals, but that contact does reduce stereotyping, prejudice, and discrimination when it involves active cooperation toward a mutual goal (Brown & Wade, 1987; Deschamps & Brown, 1983; Goldman, Stockbauer, & McAuliffe, 1977; Sherif, Harvey, White, Hood, & Sherif, 1961; Slavin, 1979; Weigel, Wiser, & Cook, 1975; Wilder & Shapiro, 1989; Worchell, Andreoli, & Folger, 1977).

■ EQUAL STATUS

A second important factor that increases the effectiveness of intergroup contact suggests that the participants have equal status. Equal status can overcome the detrimental effects of unequal social roles. In a mixed-race school classroom where the teacher obviously favors White children and awards them higher status, intergroup contact only exaggerates intergroup hostility. Imagine a teacher who divided students into an all-White "fast track" and an all-Black or all-Mexican-American "slow track." Such a division would do nothing to dispel prejudice and hostility. It would instead make members of the two groups despise each other all the more. To counteract such tendencies and promote equal status for participants in educational contact, social psychologists developed the "jigsaw" method of classroom learning (Aronson, 1984; Aronson & Gonzales, 1988; Aronson, Stephan, Sikes, Blaney, & Snapp, 1978; Blaney, Stephan, Rosenfield, Aronson, & Sikes, 1977).

In the jigsaw method, teachers divide students into "primary" groups of six that represent the classroom's racial and ethnic categories—for example, two White children, two Black children, and two Hispanic children. The teacher gives each child in each group one-sixth of the material that the group needs to study for an exam. If the exam were to be about the six innermost solar system planets other than Earth, for instance, one child in each primary group would get all the information about Mercury, one about Venus, one about Mars, and so on. Then the children from each primary group who had the information about one planet (such as Mars) would meet separately as a group of "experts" to discuss how to teach their planet's information to the other five members of their primary groups. Finally, the experts would go back to their primary groups to exchange information with the group members who knew about the other five planets, after which all children would be tested on their knowledge of the six planets.

Students' initial reaction to the jigsaw technique is predictable, because they have previously experienced the classroom as a competitive rather than a cooperative environment. When the experts go back to their primary groups, a boy named Carlos Ramirez who has trouble expressing himself in English, for instance, might stammer and hesitate when asked to tell the other five primary group members what they need to know about Mercury. Typically, a majority group member, let's say Ashley Chamberlaine, makes fun of Carlos by saying something like "You're stupid." The teacher might tell Ashley "Making

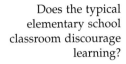

Does the typical elementary school classroom discourage learning?

fun of Carlos is not acceptable and it's not going to get you the information you need for the exam." Reminders like these are very effective in getting majority group members to pay attention to minority group members, who in the jigsaw arrangement enjoy equal status with majority group members.

The jigsaw technique has been used effectively in schools and classrooms that were previously disrupted by intergroup conflict. Majority group children learn as much from the jigsaw method as they do in the standard "frontal lecture" classroom setting. They have as high self-esteem as ever and continue to attend school regularly. Minority group children, however, benefit enormously. They increase their learning dramatically, develop much higher self-esteem, and improve their attendance. Minority group children, who had previously avoided being called on because they (and their classmates) thought they were dumb, discover through the jigsaw method that they can understand the material. They can teach the material as well as anyone else. Furthermore, they enjoy doing so. Majority group children come to realize that their minority group classmates are more competent and likable than they had ever imagined. They start playing with these children during their free time and make friends with them.

The jigsaw method works in part because majority and minority group members work together to achieve a mutual goal. Beyond affording mutual goals, however, the jigsaw technique succeeds because it provides majority and minority group members with equal status. Merely placing students in interracial groups and telling them to learn cooperatively has no beneficial effects on prejudice. Majority group students typically take control and tutor the "less gifted" minority students, thus emphasizing preexisting status differences (Cohen, 1984). Studies of the jigsaw technique and other studies that have manipulated status demonstrate that intergroup contact reduced stereotyping, prejudice, and discrimination when the participants have equal status during their interaction. It has little or no effect, though, when the participants are not explicitly given equal status (Cohen & Roper, 1972; Norvell & Worchell, 1981; Riordan & Ruggiero, 1980).

■ ACQUAINTANCE POTENTIAL

Finally, intergroup contact works best in eliminating intergroup hostility when the participants get to know each other as individuals rather than merely as representatives of their groups, when the contact situation has "acquaintance potential" (Cook, 1978). Acquaintance can overcome biased media portrayals. The jigsaw technique and other cooperative learning methods are usually supplemented with lunch break and other one-on-one conversations in which participants are encouraged to get acquainted with each other by exchanging personal information (Cook, 1978; Slavin, 1980; Schwarzwald & Amir, 1984). If Ashley thinks of Carlos only as "that Mexican-American kid," it is unlikely that any amount of forced contact with Carlos will ever get Ashley to play with Carlos during free time. If Ashley learns that Carlos has two older sisters, has a pet collie dog, is afraid of heights, and so on, then Ashley may start to think about Carlos as an individual, and a fairly competent and likable individual at that! Numerous studies have demonstrated that intergroup contact, even intergroup contact that includes mutual goals and equal status, reduces stereotyping, prejudice, and discrimination only when participants get to know each other as individuals (Amir & Ben-Ari, 1985; Hofman & Zak, 1969; Meer & Freedman, 1966; Wilner, Walkley, & Cook, 1952).

In summary, contact is meaningless or even counterproductive unless it affords mutual goals, equal status, and acquaintance potential. Educational settings that encourage the members of majority and minority groups to compete for academic recognition and other rewards do not satisfy the mutual goals requirement. Settings that merely force the members of different groups to study together virtually guarantee that preexisting status differences will increase (Riordan, 1978). Settings that require strict attention to the learning task and thus afford no opportunity for personal acquaintance do nothing to discourage participants from viewing each other as representatives of their rival groups rather than as unique individuals (Brewer & Miller, 1988). Because none of these three requirements was met when schools in the United States were desegregated, initial optimism about desegregated schools deteriorated into disappointment (Gerard, 1988). Social psychologists understood what was required, but school administrators did not implement desegregation in the way suggested by Allport's (1954) contact hypothesis.

■ GENERALIZATION

Unfortunately, the acquaintance potential requirement for successful intergroup contact has a paradoxical nature that makes it both helpful and harmful to the goal of reducing prejudice, discrimination, and stereotyping. Summer camps that emphasize mutual goals for rival groups, the jigsaw technique of classroom learning, and other contact manipulations that afford acquaintance potential have successfully reduced stereotyping, prejudice, and discrimination toward the *specific* minority group members with whom contact occurs, but not toward the minority group *as a whole* (Hewstone & Brown, 1986). To use a concrete example, a boy named Ashley might emerge from jigsaw learning with Carlos convinced that Carlos is a terrific person, but he might still retain his negative attitude and demeaning stereotype of Mexican-Americans. He might decide that Carlos is such a great guy because "He's an exception. He's different from most Mexican-Americans."

Most tests of the contact hypothesis in applied settings had as their only goal alleviating intergroup hostility within a specific setting such as a school or a neighborhood. These studies measured success through friendship choices, social distance, and other indicators of liking and respect for the other participants as individuals. Such studies have not included before-and-after measures of how contact affected overall attitudes toward the larger group, because the investigators were not concerned with *overall* attitudes. For social psychologists who are called in because Blacks and Whites have been physically attacking each other on the school ground, it is enough to know that their intervention restored racial harmony within the specific school, even if the changes in attitudes did not extend beyond that specific setting.

Other studies, however, measured changes in attitudes both toward the specific minority group members with whom contact occurred and toward minority group members as a whole. Except where the surrounding social context encouraged positive attitude change, these studies found no effect of contact, even contact that included mutual goals, equal status, and acquaintance potential, on broader racial and ethnic attitudes (Amir, 1969; Blaney, Stephan, Rosenfield, Aronson, & Sikes, 1977; Cook, 1978; Hewstone & Brown, 1986; Johnson & Johnson, 1981; Katz, 1970). Students who study cooperatively with students of other races increase the number of their crossracial friendships with those specific students, but they do not change their overall racial attitudes (Weigel, Wiser, & Cook, 1975). College students who cooperate with students from a rival college change their opinions about the specific students with whom they interacted, but not about the typical student at the rival college (Wilder & Thompson, 1980). Similarly, psychiatric nurses restrain equally Black and White patients who have been in their charge for a month or more, thus admitting that these specific Blacks are no more prone to violence than White patients. They continue to restrain new Black patients, however, four times as frequently as they do new White patients (Bond, DiCandia, & MacKinnon, 1988).

Although social psychologists are not certain why successful contact often does not generalize, one likely culprit is the requirement of acquaintance potential. If participants find out so much about each other that they come to view each other entirely as individuals and lose track of their group identities, then they have no reason to generalize (Rothbart & John, 1985). If the boy named Ashley stops noticing that Carlos is Mexican-American, then why should his increasing respect for Carlos generalize to a more positive attitude toward Mexican-Americans? Paradoxically, the secret to successful generalization of a contact experience is to do something that limits the success of the contact itself. The secret involves "making group affiliations *more* salient and not less, and ensuring that in some way the participants in the contact encounters see each other as representatives of their groups and not merely as 'exceptions to the rule'" (Hewstone & Brown, 1986, p. 18).

This prescription for successful generalization is backed by research evidence (Rothbart & Lewis, 1988). In a relevant study, students at two rival colleges had negative initial attitudes toward each other (Wilder, 1984). For each student, the investigator arranged a positive contact experience with a confederate who was said to be a student from the rival college. For half of the students, the confederate dressed and acted in ways that contradicted the rival college's stereotype. For the other half, the confederate dressed and acted exactly like the rival college's stereotype. Students who interacted with an atypical confederate liked that specific person, but they did not change their overall negative attitudes about the quality of students at the rival school. Students who interacted with a typical confederate changed their opinions both about the specific student with whom they interacted and the quality of students at the rival college. The "out-group member in the interaction must be perceived as representative of his or her social category if attitudes developed toward that individual are to be generalized to the group as a whole" (Brewer & Miller, 1988, p. 316). Acquaintance potential obviously makes it less likely that contact will induce generalization. Acquaintance potential instead increases the likelihood that the individual will be "recategorized" as an exception.

RECATEGORIZATION

It is difficult but not impossible to reduce stereotyping, prejudice, and discrimination toward negatively stigmatized social groups by increasing contact with them (Stephan & Stephan, 1984). Another possibility is to encourage recategorization, which takes one of two forms. First, separate groups might be *combined* into one larger group. If Blacks and Whites in the United States married each other and had children through several generations, for example, there would be no basis for stereotyping, prejudice, and discrimination based on skin color. Everyone would be coffee-colored. Second, we might try to break the existing categories into smaller *subtypes* or to further divide the subtypes into units so small that each individual was regarded as unique, as a "subtype of one."

■ COMBINATION

Forced contact between the races is unpopular with U.S. citizens. Interracial marriage is even more unpopular. Laws have been enacted to encourage interracial contact. No incentives have ever been advanced to promote interracial marriage, because most U.S. citizens are unalterably opposed. Marriage between Blacks and Whites is accepted in many countries of Western Europe, but citizens of the United States are far more opposed to interracial marriage than are the citizens of any other technologically advanced country (Pettigrew, 1988). Many U.S. citizens, for instance, believe that an unattractive White man marrying an attractive Black female is the only "fair" interracial arrangement, because his unattractiveness "compensates" for her skin color (Wade, 1991). The White majority in the United States may espouse a "melting pot" society in which all races and ethnic groups are "assimilated" with each other, but what they really mean is that minority groups should give up their own unique identities and adopt the ways and appearance of the majority (Pettigrew, 1988). They do not want each group to contribute equally. Instead, they want one side to give up its cultural heritage and the other side to give up nothing.

Black culture, American Indian culture, Mexican-American culture, and other cultures that differ from the dominant White culture in the United States have a lot to offer. With its African roots, Black culture offers attractive alternatives to White culture in at least five ways (Jones, 1986). First, White culture emphasizes a "future-oriented present" in which people take today's actions to ensure tomorrow's goals. Black culture, in contrast, is decidedly present-oriented. The Swahili language has no word for "future" and a popular saying in Trinidad is "Any time is Trinidad time!" White culture is remarkably uptight about time, to the point that time pressure may induce stress-related health problems. Second, White culture emphasizes a fixed rhythm, whereas Black culture emphasizes variation. White children perform better than Black children when test items are presented in blocks (all of one kind, then all of another, and so on), but Black children either equal or outperform White children when the same test items are presented in random order (Boykin, 1983). Third, White culture prefers planned activities, whereas Black culture prefers spontaneous activities that require improvisation. White basketball play-

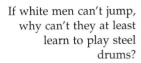

If white men can't jump, why can't they at least learn to play steel drums?

ers reliably outperform Black basketball players on free throws (from a standard distance with no interference), but Black basketball players reliably outperform White basketball players on shots from the field that must be improvised (Jones & Hochner, 1973). Fourth, White culture has a written tradition that is in sharp contrast to Black culture's oral tradition, where words accompany acts and give them meaning (Jahn, 1961). Black Africans, for example, appear to have poor memories for words when compared to White Americans on written tests, but they have every bit as good memories when the same words are embedded in folk stories (Cole, Gay, Glick, & Sharp, 1971). Fifth, White culture values personal control, in which people cause events. Black culture, in contrast, values a more environmentally friendly spirituality in which human beings are merely a part of a larger set of universal forces (Jones, 1986).

It would take more than racial intermarriage to combine Black people and White people into one superordinate social category. Recategorization would also require combining the two cultures. For White people to insist that Black people abandon their own cultural heritage and adopt instead the ways of White culture is shortsighted. If anything, the cultural differences suggest that White culture might benefit from adopting many of the precepts of Black culture. Instead of an educational approach that emphasizes an inflexible, time-obsessed preoccupation with exercising personal control over nature, it might be wiser for the future of the planet to adopt a more spontaneous, present-oriented perspective in which human beings are merely one part of an interdependent environment (Jones, 1986). One recategorization approach to eliminating stereotyping, prejudice, and discrimination, then, is to combine the best features of all cultures into one large category in which people do not differ. Some theorists believe that such a homogeneous culture would lack vitality. They believe it would be better to promote an "additive multiculturalism" in which White, Black, American Indian, Mexican-American, and other cultures retain their individual, equally valued identities (Triandis, 1988). A one-category society, however, would clearly be more harmonious than the current system in which one culture is the "standard" to which all other cultures are expected to adapt.

■ SUBTYPES AND INDIVIDUAL UNIQUENESS

The other recategorization approach, the mirror image of creating one social category to which everyone belongs, is to break existing categories into smaller and smaller subtypes. Eventually each individual would be seen as unique and larger category distinctions would lose their meaning. In a study that compared the two recategorization approaches, students were first divided into two three-person groups (Gaertner, Mann, Murrell, & Dovidio, 1989). As predicted from previous research, members of the two distinct groups displayed in-group favoritism and prejudice. They evaluated members of their own group more positively than members of the other group.

To reduce in-group favoritism, the investigators introduced two "recategorization" manipulations. In the "one big category" manipulation, they persuaded the students to regard themselves as belonging to one group of six rather than belonging to two separate groups of three. This manipulation had obvious relevance to the strategy used at the boys' summer camp of having the Rattlers and the Eagles pull together as one team to overcome obstacles. It was also relevant to the idea of combining different cultures into one "seamless" culture rather than requiring one culture to abandon its own perspective. The other manipulation emphasized individual uniqueness. The investigators persuaded the students to regard themselves as belonging to six groups of one rather than belonging to two groups of three. Both types of recategorization, having one big category and stressing individual uniqueness, significantly reduced in-group bias compared to a control condition in which students continued to view themselves as belonging to two groups of three. Interestingly, however, the individual uniqueness manipulation reduced in-group bias by causing students to think *less* highly of former in-group members. The one big category manipulation, in contrast, decreased prejudice by causing students to think *more* highly of former outgroup members.

The two different recategorization manipulations probably worked in these two different ways because of social identity processes. When students perceived themselves as belonging to two separate groups of three, they evaluated the two other members of the in-group positively because "they must be good if they are in the same group with me." When this connection with the self was broken by dividing students into six groups of one, evaluations of former in-group members suffered because the former in-group members no longer benefited from being associated with the self. Conversely, when students were combined into one big category, the former outgroup members benefited from their new association with the self. Making people feel unique causes them to evaluate people who belong to their own category more critically, whereas combining people into one big category causes them to award former outgroup members the benefit of "kinship." Subsequent research suggests that members

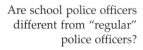

Are school police officers different from "regular" police officers?

of separate groups are more likely to recategorize themselves into one super-ordinate group when they are in a positive mood (Dovidio, Gaertner, Isen, & Lowrance, 1995).

Recategorization by forming smaller subtypes, unfortunately, is one way that bigoted people retain their bigotry (Allport, 1954; Weber & Crocker, 1983). White workers who believe that all Blacks are lazy, for instance, might have two Black coworkers who are very hard-working. Nonetheless, they might retain their negative stereotype by forming a subtype composed of the two Black coworkers, who presumably share a characteristic that separates them from other Blacks. In one study that tested this proposition, British students who had negative attitudes toward police found that a police officer had been assigned to their school (Hewstone, Hopkins, & Routh, 1992). After getting to know the specific police officer, the students did not change their general attitude toward police officers. Instead they decided that the subtype "school police officers" was composed of admirable people who constituted an exception to the larger (and still negatively regarded) "police officer" category. The students retained their negative attitudes through the same mechanism that hinders generalization in the contact hypothesis. When we know members of a despised category as individuals, we view them as a subcategory of one or as "the exception that proves the rule." The individual uniqueness approach to recategorization, then, will be successful only if people forget social categories created by differences in physical appearance or culture and instead view each person as a unique individual (Pratkanis & Turner, 1994). Paradoxically, combination may emphasize the uniqueness of each individual more than does making smaller and smaller subtypes. When everyone belongs to one large category, that category becomes meaningless and unique characteristics become the only way to separate individuals.

These studies on combination and recategorization offer hope that social psychologists will discover even more effective ways to reduce stereotyping, prejudice, and discrimination. Doing so is one of the most promising and exciting areas of research in modern social psychology.

SUMMARY OF REDUCING STEREOTYPING, PREJUDICE, AND DISCRIMINATION

According to the contact hypothesis, stereotyping, prejudice, and discrimination can be reduced or eliminated by bringing rival groups into contact. Contact by itself, however, has no such effect. To succeed in reducing stereotyping, prejudice, and discrimination, contact requires mutual goals, equal status, and an opportunity to get to know members of the rival group as individuals. Even when these requirements are met, contact often ameliorates attitudes toward the specific group members with whom contact occurred and not toward the group as a whole.

An approach different from contact is recategorization. One form of recategorization involves combining groups into one large category to which everyone belongs. A second form of recategorization involves breaking racial, ethnic, sex, and age group categories into smaller and smaller units, until eventually each individual is regarded as a unique "category of one."

CHAPTER 9

Interpersonal Attraction

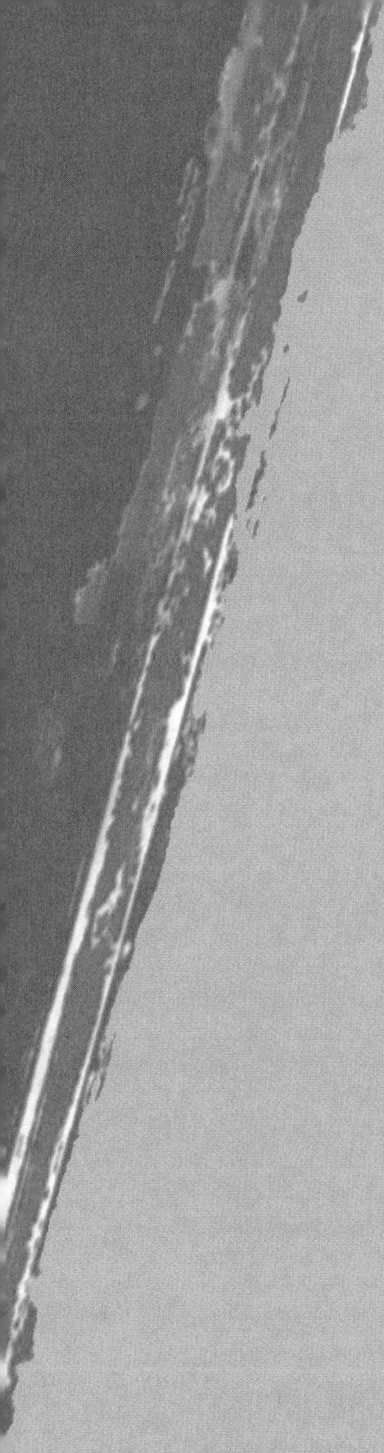

D id you ever wonder about the people who place personal ads in the newspaper? What do they want? Are they looking for love, sex, or companionship? If they had to choose, would they prefer that the person who answers their ad be physically attractive or wealthy? What do the people who place the ads think they need to say about themselves? If they give their ages, do younger advertisers get more replies? Do women get more replies than men? Do the people who respond live up to expectations? How often do the people who place and respond to personal ads meet each other? To answer these and other questions about interpersonal attraction, three social psychologists collected the personal ads from a large midwestern U.S. newspaper for a two-week period (Rajecki, Bledsoe, & Rasmussen, 1991). They scored each ad on whether it was written by a man or a woman, whether it offered physical attractiveness (looks) or resources, and whether it sought looks or resources. Ads that offered or sought looks, for instance, used terms such as "handsome," "pretty," "good-looking," "cute," "sexy," "stacked," and "well-proportioned." Ads that offered or sought resources used terms such as "affluent," "career person," "financially independent," "prosperous," "generous," "a good provider," and "sugar daddy."

Figure 9.1 shows the percentage of personal ads in which men and women offered and sought looks and resources. As the left side of the figure shows, women were more likely than men to offer looks by describing their physical assets, whereas men were more likely than women to offer resources by describing their material assets. As the right side of the figure shows, men were

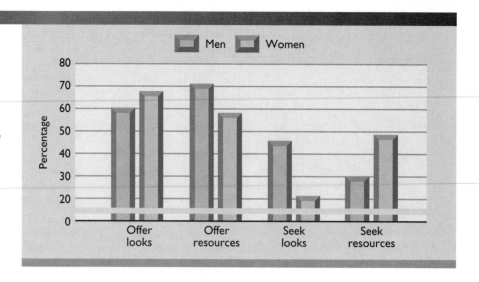

FIGURE 9.1

Men offer resources and seek good-looking women. Women offer good looks and seek men with resources.

Graph shows percentage of men and women who offered and sought looks and resources in personal ads (Rajecki, Bledsoe, & Rasmussen, 1991).

What do men and women look for in personal ads?

more likely than women to seek a good-looking partner, whereas women were more likely than men to seek a financially secure partner. These differences between what men and women offer and seek in a romantic partner are not confined to one region of the United States. Other studies reached the same conclusion by examining personal and "lonely hearts" newspaper ads in many geographical areas (Bolig, Stein, & McHenry, 1984; Deaux & Hanna, 1984; Harrison & Saeed, 1977; Hirschman, 1987; Kenrick & Keefe, 1992; Koestner & Wheeler, 1988; Lynn & Shurgot, 1984; Peres & Meivar, 1986; Sitton & Rippee, 1986). Across all these studies, men were more likely to seek looks and offer resources. Women, in contrast, were more likely to seek resources and offer looks.

In the study that produced the results shown in Figure 9.1, men who gave their age wanted to hear from women who were from nine years younger to two years older than themselves. Women who gave their age wanted to hear from men who were from two years younger to eight years older than themselves. Men received on average 12 replies, of which they considered four acceptable. Women received on average 22 replies, of which they considered ten acceptable. Both men and women eventually met an average of two respondents in person. In the most successful ads written by men, the writers gave their ages as 11 years *older* than in the least successful men's ads. In the most successful ads written by women, the writers gave their ages as 13 years *younger* than in the least successful women's ads. Older men tend to have greater resources, which is what most women sought; younger women tend to have greater physical attractiveness, which is what most men sought.

Are these differences peculiar to personal ads or do they tell us something about men, women, and interpersonal attraction? Are the men and women who place personal ads in newspapers typical? If they are, then why is the typical man in the United States more interested in a woman's looks than in her financial resources and why does the typical woman have an opposite perspective? Are men's and women's preferences in the United States unusual or do men and women across the world share their preferences? Are men's and women's preferences today different from what they were in previous centuries? These are but a few of the fascinating questions that concern social psychologists who study interpersonal attraction. Because we do not have space enough to examine *all* types of interpersonal attraction, this chapter concentrates on just one type: attraction between men and women. The first section of the chapter describes interpersonal attraction between men and women. The second section of the chapter explores reasons why men and women are attracted to each other. The third section of the chapter examines why some men or women are more attractive than others.

WHAT IS INTERPERSONAL ATTRACTION?

Can you define "love"? Poets, philosophers, and scientists have been trying to do so for thousands of years, without much success. Any one-sentence definition would be too simplistic. Many people would disagree, for instance, with author H. L. Mencken's definition that "Love is the triumph of imagination over intelligence." Even if we could use more than one sentence, "it is difficult, if not impossible, to answer the question 'What is love?' because any answer must reflect its time period and place" (Beall & Sternberg, 1995, p. 417). "Love" can take many different forms in many different times and places, from the fireworks of passionate sex to the contentment of lifelong companionship. The best we can do in this first section of the chapter is to provide an overview of love and interpersonal attraction. The first part of this section describes three factors that predispose men and women toward the types of interpersonal attraction detected in modern newspaper personal ads. The second part of this section describes how interpersonal attraction between men and women has differed and yet retained an underlying similarity across time and cultures. The third part of this section describes three ways of classifying types of interpersonal attraction.

EVOLUTION, NEED TO BELONG, AND CULTURE

Figure 9.2 shows how evolutionary pressures, a need to belong, and cultural standards might combine to produce the gender differences reflected in modern newspaper personal ads. The figure shows how one factor (need to belong) provides the basic motive for men and women to seek close attachments, which is why newspapers receive personal ads from both sexes. The figure also shows how two other factors (evolutionary pressures and cultural standards) might produce differences in the types of personal ads that men and women write.

■ EVOLUTIONARY PRESSURES

From an evolutionary perspective, the males of many species maximize their reproductive success by mating, whereas the females of many species maximize their reproductive success by parenting (Buss, 1991; Daly & Wilson, 1983; Kenrick, 1994; Trivers, 1972). The mating strategy is to have as many children as possible, hoping that some of them will live long enough to reproduce. Giant turtles, for instance, bury millions of eggs in the sand of a beach and leave their offspring to fend for themselves when they hatch. The turtles invest their energy in having sex rather than in protecting their offspring. Male human beings might also follow the mating strategy more than they follow the parenting strategy, because one man could conceivably make hundreds of women pregnant in a single year (Chisolm, 1993). Men's only biological investment in

FIGURE 9.2

How evolutionary pressures, an underlying need to belong, and traditional cultural standards may have combined to influence personal ads in modern newspapers.

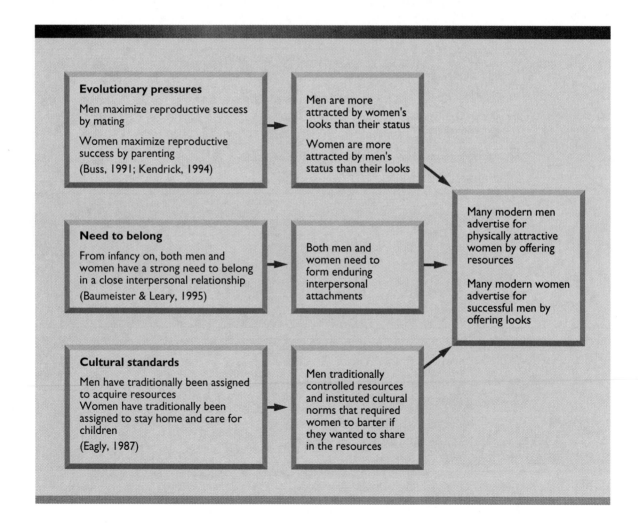

a child is the energy it takes to have sex (Daly & Wilson, 1983; Symons, 1979). It pays for men to mate with every female who is likely to produce healthy children (Hinde, 1984). The signs of being able to produce healthy children are a woman's youth, lustrous hair, rosy complexion, and well-rounded body (Hamilton & Zuk, 1982). If men follow a mating strategy, they should have been predisposed by millions of years of evolution to be attracted by women's looks and to have sex with any physically attractive woman who will let them (Buss & Schmitt, 1993).

The parenting strategy of maximizing reproductive success is more attractive to the females than to the males of many species (Epstein & Guttman, 1984; Fisher, 1992). The parenting strategy is to nurture and protect each child until it is old enough to fend for itself. In human beings, women invest far more energy than do men in each child. Before they give birth, women share their body's resources with the child inside them for nine months (Frisch, 1988). Then, at least in primitive societies, they must breast-feed the child and keep it safe from harm for many years. Also, women are typically capable of having only a few children in a lifetime. Their investment in each child is enormous compared to a man's. It has always been in women's reproductive interest to be selective about having sex (Townsend & Levy, 1990). In many animal species, the females choose to have sex only with males that establish their status and dominance over other males. Dominant males control material resources such as food and space—resources that the female and her children need to survive.

The ultimate parenting strategy is for a female to stand back while males butt heads to establish who is dominant, and then have sex with the male who wins (Clutton-Brock, 1991). That male will presumably protect his own offspring, because his children represent his genetic investment. If women follow a "parenting" strategy more than they follow a mating strategy, they should have been predisposed by millions of years of evolution to have relationships only with dominant men of high status (Buss & Schmitt, 1993; Feingold, 1992; Kenrick, Sadalla, Groth, & Trost, 1990; Sadalla, Kenrick, & Vershure, 1987). From an evolutionary perspective, females exercise more choice than do males. If only evolutionary pressures were operating, women would have almost complete power over men (Kenrick, 1995). Men would merely compete for a woman's attention, which she could bestow or withhold at her pleasure.

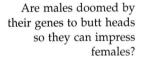

Are males doomed by their genes to butt heads so they can impress females?

■ NEED TO BELONG

One of the major themes of this book is that people have two goals: being right and being likable (Baumeister & Leary, 1995; Snyder, 1993, 1994; Swann, 1987, 1990). Although the goal of being likable is relevant to many other topics within social psychology, it is *central* to understanding interpersonal attraction. Evolutionary pressures by themselves do not fully explain why men and women are attracted to each other. After all, women might do some mating of their own. They maximize their chances of getting pregnant if they have sex with more than one man and if the men they choose are not only successful, but good-looking (and therefore healthy). Similarly, women know for sure when a child is their own, but a man cannot be sure that a woman's child is his own. The woman might have been impregnated by another man, so why should a man invest energy to protect a child that might not be his? One answer is that both men and women might actively *need* close and relatively enduring interpersonal attachments (Baumeister & Leary, 1995). They might *need* at least one other person in the world who regards them as likable.

The need to belong is very adaptive for human beings (Baumeister & Leary, 1995; Shaver, Hazan, & Bradshaw, 1988). "Each of us owes our very existence to the attraction that once existed between a man and a woman" (Berscheid, 1985, p. 413). In primitive times, children who wanted to be near their parents were more likely to survive than children who did not. Similarly, men and women who formed an enduring interpersonal bond were more likely to stay together long enough for their children to mature than were men and women who did not form close attachments. Without strong protective bonds between parents and their offspring, scientists estimate that the human species would have perished 500,000 years ago, when mortality rates were very high (Mellen, 1981). Close attachments between men and women increase the level of opioids in the body that make people feel good; breaking attachments decreases the level of these opioids (Panksepp, Siviy, & Normansell, 1985). Both men and women, then, *need* to form close interpersonal bonds. They need at least one other person with whom they can have frequent, pleasant interactions, within an ongoing relationship (Baumeister & Leary, 1995).

Considerable evidence suggests that human beings need to belong to each other and to form close attachments (Baumeister & Leary, 1995). People who have been through such aversive events as combat together often form close attachments. Such attachments are contrary to what we would expect if interpersonal attraction were merely a matter of associating another person with pleasant experiences (Elder & Clipp, 1988). People celebrate forming bonds, for instance, through engagement announcements and lavish weddings. They also resist breaking attachments, even when the consequences of maintaining a relationship are negative, as they are for battered women (Strube, 1988; Werner, Altman, Brown, & Ginat, 1993; Werner, Brown, Altman, & Staples, 1992). People think about a person to whom they are closely attached in the same way that they think about themselves, which is different from how they think about people to whom they are not attached (Aron, Aron, Tudor, & Nelson, 1991; Brown, 1986; Fincham, Beach, & Baucom, 1987).

People find it very unpleasant to be deprived of close attachments, which is why loneliness hurts so much (Baumeister & Tice, 1990; Leary, 1990; Leary & Downs, 1995; Russell, Cutrona, Rose, & Yurko, 1984; Tambor & Leary, 1993). People suffer both physical and psychological illness when they are deprived of close attachments (DeLongis, Folkman, & Lazarus, 1988; Goodwin, Hunt, Key, & Samet, 1987; Hamacheck, 1992; Kiecolt-Glaser, Garner, Speicher, Penn, Holliday, & Glaser, 1984). Finally, a close attachment is not satisfying without frequent interaction, as separated couples know, nor is mere contact satisfying without close attachment (Bunker, Zubeck, Vanderslice, & Rice, 1992; Gerstel & Gross, 1984). If we want to understand why men and women place personal ads at all, rather than why they place different types of personal ads, we need to recognize that something "draws them together." It seems reasonable to assume that human beings have a fundamental *need* to form close interpersonal attachments (Baumeister & Leary, 1995).

■ CULTURAL STANDARDS

Finally, interpersonal attraction is influenced importantly by cultural standards. As described in Chapter 8 under "Social Roles," primitive human beings had to choose the most effective division of labor (Eagly, 1987). If some group members had to go out and wrest valuable resources such as food from a hostile environment, it probably seemed sensible to have the men—who were physically stronger—do that job. If other group members had to keep the home fires burning and feed the children, it probably seemed sensible to have the women—who were physically smaller but had milk-secreting breasts—do that job. In the service of an adaptive division of labor, boys were socialized to be acquisitive, aggressive, and competitive, whereas girls were socialized to be nurturing and concerned with maintaining close personal attachments.

An important problem with such a division of labor is that *men got to control the resources*. If women wanted food and protection for themselves and their children, they had to depend on men. The men held power and could dictate cultural standards. A culture is "the shared way of life of a group of people" (Berry, Poortinga, Segall, & Dasen, 1992, p. 1). As described more at length in Chapter 10, people who share a culture usually emphasize one of four types of interpersonal relationships (Fiske, 1991). Some cultures emphasize "communal sharing," in which people share their resources without expecting specific reciprocation. Some cultures emphasize "equality matching," in which people take turns making equal contributions. Some cultures emphasize "authority ranking," in which people of lower status obey so that people of higher status will protect them. Finally, some cultures emphasize "market pricing," in which relationships involve an exchange of dissimilar commodities. When people are asked to characterize two-person relationships, they use these same four categories (Haslam, 1994).

The nations of Western Europe, North America, New Zealand, and Australia emphasize market pricing or "exchange" relationships (Fiske, 1991). As described in other chapters of this book, these Western nations also tend to have individualist cultures in which the rule is "every man (or woman) for himself (or herself)." If you want something in an individualist, market-pricing culture, you have to pay for it. You have to barter. For thousands of years, Western cultures have established and maintained a traditional division of labor in which men, not women, acquired and controlled material resources. From their positions of power, men made sure that women had only their physical bodies to barter for their share of material resources. An exchange culture is one way that men have of coercing women into sex (Hogben, Byrne, & Hamburger, in press).

The nations of Asia and the Pacific rim emphasize authority-ranking rather than market-pricing relationships. These Eastern nations also tend to have collectivistic cultures in which the rule is "promote the needs of your group before your personal needs" (Schwartz, 1994; Triandis, 1989a; Yamaguchi, 1994). In collectivistic cultures, family ties are more important than individual marriages. People in collectivistic cultures consider individualistic expectations for "love" very unrealistic (Hsu, 1985; Shaver, Wu, & Schwartz, 1991; Triandis, Bontempo, Villareal, Asai, & Lucca, 1988). In a collectivistic culture, you must cooperate with and obey the group's (often the family's) leaders (Chu, 1985; Hofstede, 1983). The leaders in Eastern authority-ranking cultures, however, are usually men, who often hold higher status merely because they happen to be male. The women in authority-ranking cultures have traditionally found themselves in as disadvantaged a position as have women in market-pricing cultures (Hatfield & Rapson, 1996). In either individualistic market pricing cultures or collectivistic authority-ranking cultures, the traditional division of labor favors men in interpersonal relationships. Men acquire and control the resources. If only traditional cultural standards were operating, men would have almost complete power over women. Women would be little more than possessions or followers that a man could buy, sell, or command at his pleasure.

■ COMBINING INFLUENCES

By combining these three influences—evolutionary pressures, need to belong, and cultural standards, we begin to understand why modern men might place personal ads that offer resources and seek good looks, whereas modern women might place personal ads that offer good looks and seek resources (Ickes, 1993b). Speculations about evolutionary pressures and prehistoric divisions of labor are only hypotheses. We cannot go back in time to conduct controlled experiments. Nonetheless, as the rest of this chapter shows, social psychologists have amassed considerable evidence suggesting that evolutionary pressures, need to belong, and cultural standards affect modern interpersonal attraction. Also, it is important to realize that neither evolutionary pressures nor cultural standards are "engraved in stone." As we shall see, different cultures in history and across the world have had very diverse standards for the "normal" relationship between men and women (Bem, 1993). Evolutionary pressures and traditional cultural standards may predispose the *majority* of human cultures toward some types of relationships more than others, but cultures have a wide leeway in what arrangements they adopt. Genetics should not and cannot be used to justify sexual oppression (Berscheid, 1993). Similarly, a culture may predispose a *majority* of individuals to prefer some types of interpersonal attraction to others, but neither evolution nor culture dictates what individuals or cultures of the future will do. Individuals might decide, for instance, to alter the current culture so that men and women have equal ability to acquire resources. In cultures of the future, interpersonal relationships might entail more communal sharing and equality matching than market pricing or authority ranking.

The individuals who are affected by evolutionary pressures and cultural standards are probably unaware of what motivates their behavior. As described in Chapter 2, which treats of social cognition, people are often unaware of the real reasons for their behavior (Nisbett & Wilson, 1977; Wilson & Brekke, 1994). Most modern men do not say to themselves when they spot an attractive woman in a bikini "I want to have sex with her because she will produce healthy children." Most modern women are not so coldly calculating that they prefer a medical doctor to an unemployed salesman as a lover because "The doctor would provide more resources for my children." As the research on "implicit stereotyping" in Chapter 8 suggests, evolutionary pressures and cultural traditions may be especially influential when people do not realize that they are being influenced. It is only by recognizing their influence that modern citizens who know social psychology can exercise intelligent choice about how they structure the culture of the future. Factors in the immediate context may often appear to explain interpersonal attraction without reference to evolutionary or cultural hypotheses. As we examine "immediate context" factors throughout this chapter, however, we might ask ourselves *why* modern men are aroused by attractive women and *why* modern women feel they have to bargain for resources. One possibility is that the immediate context reflects evolutionary pressures and cultural standards, even though those pressures and standards may no longer be adaptive.

The world today, especially in technologically advanced countries, is a far different environment than existed millions of years ago. In the past, it might have been adaptive for men to mate with every attractive woman and for women to prefer dominant men who controlled resources. It may not be as adaptive to do so today (Ickes, 1993b). In today's world, sex-typed men often have unsatisfactory personal relationships (Antill, 1983; Baucom & Aiken, 1984; Davidson & Sollie, 1987; Ickes & Barnes, 1978; Zamichieli, Golroy, & Sherman, 1988). It might have been effective in the past for men to acquire resources and women to stay home and feed babies. This division of labor may not be the most effective today (Eagly, 1987). Both men and women in technologically advanced cultures can learn how to do both—amass resources and feed babies. If human beings understand the evolutionary and cultural influences that led to the world we live in, they can change modern culture by changing socialization practices. They can produce equality of the sexes by socializing women to be as acquisitive, competitive, and power-hungry as men have traditionally been. Alternatively, they can socialize men to be as nurturing, caring, and closeness-oriented as women have traditionally been (Gilligan, 1982; Hatfield & Rapson, 1996).

ATTRACTION ACROSS TIME AND CULTURES

If the evolutionary, need to belong, and cultural hypotheses shown in Figure 9.2 are meaningful, we might be able to detect traces of their influence by examining what people in different historical eras regarded as "normal" relationships between men and women. We should also detect differences and similarities among modern cultures.

■ A HISTORY OF "LOVE"

One of the most instructive ways to define "interpersonal attraction" is to examine the feelings and activities that people have called "love" from early in recorded history to the modern era. As Table 9.1 shows, cultures of different historical eras differed in the types of attraction deemed "normal" or socially acceptable (Ackerman, 1994; Hunt, 1959). Men and women who lived in different eras also had different reasons for being attracted to each other and expressed their attraction in actions that to modern men and women may seem unusual. Table 9.1 is arranged in chronological order, from Athenian Greece to the modern era. It concentrates on Western Europe and North America because historical records from those regions are more available in English language sources than are records from other regions. The table is deliberately simplistic. Not all relationships in a historical era fit the "norm." The table is also admittedly sexist. It describes "love" from the perspective of the *men* who lived in each era. Women were kept illiterate and uneducated during much of recorded history, so accounts of interpersonal attraction in earlier centuries were almost all written by men (Ackerman, 1994; Hunt, 1959). From inspecting the table and the historical records, however, we may surmise how the women of each era responded when men were "attracted" to them.

In Athenian Greece, men of means were attracted to three types of women: wives, prostitutes, and "hetaerae." The Greek men of that era married because they needed someone to manage their homes and produce legitimate heirs. Although they may have fantasized about having a Greek goddess in their beds, they typically married a relatively uneducated teenage girl of their own social

TABLE 9.1	The History of "Love" in Western Civilization from the Man's Perspective (Abstracted from Ackerman, 1994; and Hunt, 1959).		
HISTORICAL ERA	**WOMEN TO WHOM MEN WERE ATTRACTED**	**REASONS FOR BEING ATTRACTED**	**ACTIONS THAT SHOWED ATTRACTION**
Athenian Greece	wives prostitutes hetaerae	home management physical pleasure stimulation	tutoring healthy sex learning
Ancient Rome	wives prostitutes married women	competence physical needs winning a "contest"	partnership degrading sex bragging; conquest
Early Christianity	wives	similar beliefs	celibacy in marriage
Early Middle Ages	wives slaves	ownership ownership	subjugation subjugation
11th-Century Europe	wives "heavenly angels"	home management "courtly love"	partnership feats of devotion
Renaissance Italy	wives mistresses	moral virtue & heirs physical pleasure	spiritual love sexual relations
Puritan Era	wives	similar beliefs	help resist "sin"
Age of Reason	wives mistresses	financial gain detached desire	partnership unemotional sex
Romantic Era	women of all types	exaggerated virtues	passionate praise
Modern Era	"life partners"	self-fulfillment	many different actions

and economic class (Townsend, 1992). They taught her how to hire and discipline slaves and servants, store and guard household goods, and manage the other mundane affairs of everyday home life. Ironically, these wives were prisoners in their own homes. They had to send servants on outside errands so that they would be available whenever their husbands returned. The husbands visited prostitutes for sex. Men of the era regarded the sexual appetite as similar to being hungry or thirsty. They thought no more of visiting a local prostitute for sex than they would of going to a restaurant for food or going to a barber for a haircut.

When the men of ancient Greece wanted more than sex, they also visited hetaerae—well-educated women who invited men into their homes (for an expensive fee) to have dinner, discuss politics or philosophy, and enjoy physical pleasure. Hetaerae maintained luxurious quarters, set splendid tables, conversed knowledgeably and wittily on topics of the day, wrote books on philosophy and etiquette, and exerted great influence on the leading men in Greek society. The hetaera Aspasia, who lived about 450 B.C. in Athens, gave lectures in her home on rhetoric and philosophy, taught rhetoric to the philosopher Socrates, and wrote many of the famous speeches delivered by Pericles and other male Athenian rulers (Hunt, 1959). Wealthy men of ancient Greece took full advantage of the evolutionary pressures and cultural standards shown in Figure 9.2. They had sex with many attractive women, enjoyed close attachments with hetaerae, and exchanged their resources for a healthy young woman at home, who would bear and nurture their children.

Table 9.1 shows that the men of Ancient Rome had interpersonal relationships similar, at least on the surface, to those of the Greeks. Romans had wives, visited prostitutes, and kept mistresses. The Romans treated these relationships differently, however, from the Greeks. Roman wives were well educated, self-sufficient, and as capable of divorcing their husbands as their husbands were of divorcing them. Roman prostitutes were regarded not as aids to good health, as they had been among the Greeks, but rather as a sordid temptation. To the Romans, the highest form of "love" was adultery. Sex with a married woman was like winning a contest. If the successful man had kept his conquest secret, modern evidence suggests that he might have become infatuated with the woman (Wegner, Lane, & Dimitri, 1994). Instead, Roman men let everyone know when they succeeded in seducing another man's wife. The Romans created a peculiar "exchange" culture in which the women were prizes in an elaborate contest by which men could demonstrate their dominance over other men.

The early years of Christianity introduced the notion that sexual relations, even with one's spouse, were sinful (Gay, 1984). Many religious couples of the day were attracted to each other because they shared ascetic beliefs about marriage and sex. The ideal marital relationship, which few accomplished, was for a man and woman to live together in celibacy, sleeping apart, half starving themselves, sometimes whipping their bodies to get rid of evil thoughts. The early Christians saw their lives as a never-ending battle between the pure spiritual self of the soul and the base, degrading animal instincts of the body (Hunt, 1959). Early Christian marriage was a peculiar combination of "equality matching" and "authority ranking." The man and woman contributed equal amounts of personal suffering to demonstrate their obedience to their religion's authority figures. Although attachment between men and women of similar religious beliefs might have been strong, abstaining from sex obviously did not serve either a mating or a parenting strategy.

In the Early Middle Ages, when savage Teutonic tribes conquered what was left of the Roman Empire, interpersonal "attraction" was brutal and barbaric. Women were regarded as men's property, to be used at the man's pleasure, sold to the highest bidder, and kept in conditions often worse than those of domesticated animals. Perhaps as a reaction to these savage customs, there arose in eleventh-century Europe the idea of courtly love, in which some women were regarded as heavenly creatures that a man of honor could not approach, but only worship from afar. One practitioner of courtly love, Ulrich von Lichtenstein, was so infatuated with a princess that he dressed himself in an ornate white gown, mounted a white stallion, and challenged every knight in Italy and Austria to a jousting contest. After besting knights across Europe for more than ten years in his lady's service and publicizing both his triumphs and his many poems to her beauty, Ulrich arrived at his lady's castle, cut off his finger, and had it sent to her in a green velvet case (Hunt, 1959). The princess, who was married but playing the role expected in her culture, let Ulrich climb a rope up the castle walls to her bedroom. When he was halfway up, the princess cut the rope, causing Ulrich to fall into the castle moat, which was used as the town's sewer. Undaunted, Ulrich continued to suffer humiliation in his lady's service for five more years, after which he recounts that she made him ecstatically happy, perhaps by letting him kneel and kiss her naked hand. Ulrich, by the way, was married during all these years to a woman who managed his estate. He and other wealthy men of the time "butted heads" like male rams, hoping against hope that a princess would reward them.

As you can see in the bottom half of Table 9.1, Renaissance Italy revived the Greek and Roman custom of men having a wife for producing legitimate heirs and a mistress for sexual pleasure. The Puritan era revived the Early Christian practice of taking a wife because of shared religious beliefs, as a "partner in purity" who would be helpful in resisting the temptations of the flesh. In the Age of Reason, both wives and mistresses were viewed as part of a dispassionate business arrangement. Men and women married because their spouses could bring them suitable dowries or financial gain. They stripped even sex of its pleasure and mystery, reducing flirtation to an *exchange* between two people who happened to have compatible needs. Although some legendary men like Don Juan seduced hundreds of women as a malicious, cold-blooded sport (the mating strategy), "courtship" in the Age of Reason was predominantly a time when the lawyers for each side haggled over details of the marriage contract. Not surprisingly, the Age of Reason was followed closely by its opposite, the Romantic Era. During the Romantic Era, men were expected once again to put women on pedestals, to worship them passionately, and swear undying oaths of obedience to their beloved's every wish, even if the "paragon of perfection" in question was an uneducated serving maid or farm girl. Women also expected to marry men who made them swoon and faint in delirious infatuation.

In the modern era, when "there is nothing most individuals desire more than a loving, intimate relationship that lasts for a lifetime" (Hatfield & Rapson, 1993, p. xv), all the trends of previous eras remain. Intimate relationships range from the adulation left over from the Romantic Era to the sadomasochistic subjugation of the Early Middle Ages, from the pleasant dalliance of the Ancient Greeks' relationships with hetaerae to the religious, spiritual marriages of the Puritan Era, from the frequent divorces and adultery of Ancient Rome to the business arrangements of the Age of Reason. Also, modern interpersonal attraction is more likely than in previous eras to emphasize self-fulfillment. As described in Chapter 5, which treats of the self, in previous eras boys and girls were raised in small, tightly knit communities among family and townspeople who had known them from birth and confirmed their identities. They had a well-established and constantly verified sense of self. They knew who they were and what place they occupied in society. In the modern era of anonymity in impersonal big-city crowds, many men and women feel lonely and incomplete (Baumeister, 1987). Many people seek close attachment with a life partner who will provide the security of an acknowledged identity. In various studies of modern attraction, from 40% to 70% of men and women across cultures say they are "in love right now" and from 80% to 95% say they have been "in love at least once" (Aron & Rodriguez, 1992; Sprecher, Aron, Hatfield, Cortese, Potapova, & Levitskaya, in press). One cross-cultural study found only one of 186 cultures across the world in which there was no evidence of passionate love (Janowiak & Fischer, 1992).

The recorded history of "love" in Western Europe and the United States fits well with hypotheses about evolutionary pressures, need to belong, and cultural standards. Because men usually controlled the material resources, they arranged exchange-oriented cultures in which women had to trade their bodies for resources and protection. In most of the cultures reviewed in the table, men enjoyed greater diversity in their sexual partners (the mating strategy) than did women. Similarly, men often kept women dependent on them for the resources women needed to support themselves and their children (the parenting strategy). Men had to do some parenting of their own. In many eras, though, they left the women home to keep house and nurture the children while they pursued more interesting activities, including sex with other women. Perhaps because men were in control, "love" sometimes had all the romance of the marketplace, in which one commodity (a woman's looks) was exchanged for another (a man's resources). This exchange orientation toward interpersonal attraction continues to characterize many modern relationships, especially in individualistic cultures such as the United States and Western Europe.

■ CULTURAL DIFFERENCES AND SIMILARITIES

At first glance, modern cultural standards for love and sex seem incredibly diverse (Frayser, 1985). Although some cultures keep the onset of menstruation relatively private, the Goajiro of Venezuela isolate girls for up to six months after their first menstruation and then have an elaborate ceremony that marks the transition from girlhood to womanhood (Santa Cruz, 1960). The Marquesans of Polynesia encourage boys and girls to be sexually experienced by the age of ten (Suggs, 1966), whereas Silwa Egyptians discourage sexual activity so extremely that they surgically alter young girls' genitals to prevent them from enjoying intercourse (Ammar, 1954). Men in the Tiwi tribe of Northern Australia are discouraged from marrying until they reach the age of 40, at which time they can have several young girls living with them as wives (Hart & Pillig, 1960). In many cultures around the world, marriages are arranged by families and neither the husband nor the wife has any choice (Hatfield & Rapson, 1996). In contrast, men and women among the Fon of Dahomey, West Africa, choose not only a marriage partner, but also which of 13 types of marriage arrangements they prefer (Herskovits, 1938). The marriage arrangements differ in who controls the couple's property and children, who can initiate a divorce, and even which sex is involved. In one of these arrangements, a wealthy woman can take a young girl as "wife" and "have children" by letting a man of her choice sleep with the "wife."

As diverse as these cultural customs may seem, however, some aspects of interpersonal attraction remain constant across cultures. In a study of more than 10,000 people from 37 cultures across six continents and five islands, males and females were asked what they wanted in a mate (Buss, 1989a). Although most of the characteristics that they mentioned differed more from one culture to the next than between men and women, two characteristics differed more between men and women than across cultures (Wallen, 1989). As evolutionary pressures and Western cultural traditions would predict, women in 34 of the 37 cultures were more concerned than men to find a partner who had good financial prospects. Women said they were attracted to men who had or who could reasonably expect to have the resources necessary to provide for their offspring (Buss & Barnes, 1986; Kenrick, Sadalla, Groth, & Trost, 1990). Typically, the "ideal" man was a few years older than the woman, presumably because the extra years would give him an additional opportunity to build a financial nest egg.

In this and other studies, men in all cultures were more concerned than were women to find a partner who was young and physically attractive (Buss, 1989a; Hatfield & Rapson, 1996; Kenrick & Trost, 1987). As discussed previously, features that are considered physically attractive, such as smooth skin, a physically fit body, lustrous hair and good complexion, usually signal health and fertility. Women are most likely to give birth to healthy children when they are young. Men continue to manufacture new sperm throughout most of their lives. Men in all cultures, therefore, maximize their reproductive success by preferring women who are younger than themselves (Wilson, 1991). Similarly, women in all cultures were interested in men who had gained status and demonstrated dominance over other men (Buss, 1989a; Kenrick & Trost, 1987). Consistent with women's preferences for older and more financially capable men and with men's preferences for younger and thus more fertile women, average marriage ages across cultures range from the man being older by 2.17 years in Ireland to the man being older by almost five years in Greece (Clare, 1986). Also, as men age, they prefer women who are progressively younger than themselves, whereas women of all childbearing ages tend to prefer men who are slightly older than themselves (Kenrick & Keefe, 1992). In cultures where men take several wives, each new wife tends to be as young as the last was, even while the man ages (van den Berghe, 1992).

These sex and age differences between men and women across cultures suggest that newspaper personal ads reflect tendencies that go beyond the midwestern United States (Kenrick, 1994). Even in modern China, men want beautiful, healthy mates who are good with children and women want strong, brave, men with status, who can provide for the family (Janowiak, 1993). Similarly, in a national survey of 13,017 people in the United States, men of all races were more likely to want youth and physical attractiveness in a mate, whereas women were more likely to want earning potential (Sprecher, Sullivan & Hatfield, 1994). The more financially secure men are, the more their personal ads insist that respondents be young and beautiful. The more attractive women think they are, the more their personal ads insist that a man be wealthy or he need not apply (Harrison & Saeed, 1977; Feingold, 1990). No wonder singles dating services have huge files of older women and younger men for whom they cannot find suitable partners (Wilson, 1983). We should not, however, overstate the case. Across cultures today, both men and women list *mutual attraction, dependable character, emotional stability,* and a *pleasing disposition* as their top four requirements for an ideal mate (Buss, 1989a). In the modern United States, Russia, and Japan, for instance, students want a mate who is kind, understanding, open, and has a good sense of humor (Hatfield & Rapson, 1996). Furthermore, the tendency for men to prefer women younger than themselves is weaker in technologically advanced than in less developed cultures (Glenn, 1989). In modern technologically advanced societies, women are almost as likely as men to acquire greater resources as they age.

Cultural standards can sometimes alter what would seem to be the demands of biology. Women always know that they are giving birth to a child that carries their own genes. Men can never be sure. Consequently, men in 62% of cultures are very concerned with a potential mate's previous chastity (Buss, 1989a). In some cultures, wives who commit adultery are branded, tortured, or killed. In the other 38% of cultures, however, customs differ markedly. The Aleut men of Alaska expect their wives to sleep with male overnight guests, a form of hospitality that renders their own paternity uncertain (Frayser, 1985). As should be obvious from this example and from the historical fluctuations shown in Table 9.1, different cultures approve different objects of interpersonal attraction and different ways of expressing interpersonal attraction. Nonetheless, these diverse objects and actions can be classified into different types of interpersonal attraction, as we shall see in the next section.

CLASSIFYING INTERPERSONAL ATTRACTION

Several schemes have been advanced for classifying types of interpersonal attraction (Davis & Laty-Mann, 1987; Berscheid & Walster, 1983; Hendrick & Hendrick, 1989; Lee, 1988; Sternberg, 1986). Some of the schemes differ in how many dimensions they use. One scheme uses only passionate as opposed to companionate love. A second scheme uses the three dimensions of passion, intimacy, and commitment. A third scheme postulates six basic love styles. All three classification schemes are "correct" and offer valuable insights into a concept that has no simple, easy definition.

■ PASSIONATE VERSUS COMPANIONATE LOVE

Imagine two couples at an amusement park. One couple buys tickets for the roller coaster. They hurtle up and down steep inclines, shrieking and clinging to each other as their hearts pound wildly. The second couple buys tickets for the tunnel of love. They float sedately through dark corridors, holding hands and gazing fondly into each other's eyes. The two couples might differ in whether they are experiencing passionate or companionate love. Passionate love also resembles what happens to infants when their mothers wander off for a second in a strange place. The child notices that the mother is missing, becomes frantic, and in turn becomes ecstatic when the mother returns. Companionate love resembles more those quiet times when a mother and infant simply hold each other, perfectly content in each other's embrace (Berscheid & Walster, 1983; Hatfield, 1988).

Figure 9.3 summarizes and contrasts passionate with companionate love. The figure also provides sample items from "love scales" that are designed to measure each type of love (Hatfield & Sprecher, 1986; Rubin, 1973). People

FIGURE 9.3

Two types of love, with illustrative statements.
Abstracted from Hatfield, 1988, and Rubin, 1970).

PASSIONATE LOVE
Intense arousal and longing for union with another
Ecstasy if reciprocated, misery if not

passionate thoughts	Sometimes I can't control my thoughts; they are obsessively on _____ .
	I yearn to know all about _____ .
passionate feelings	I would feel deep despair if _____ left me.
	Sometimes my body trembles with excitement at the sight of _____ .
passionate actions	I eagerly look for signs of _____'s desire for me.
	I take delight in studying the movements and angles of _____'s body.

COMPANIONATE LOVE
The affection we feel for those with whom our lives are deeply intertwined
Gentle feelings of affection, tenderness, concern, sharing, attachment, intimacy, and self-disclosure

self disclosure	I feel I can confide in _____ about virtually everything.
	I would greatly enjoy being confided in by _____ .
closeness	If I were lonely, my first thought would be to seek _____ out.
	It would be hard for me to get along without _____ .
concern	If _____ were feeling bad, my first duty would be to cheer him/her up.
	I would do almost anything for _____ .

who are in passionate love become physiologically aroused. They experience the same "rush" of excitement as produced by drugs such as amphetamine and cocaine (Liebowitz, 1983). They also experience the same intensely painful withdrawal symptoms when love is lost. Passionate love, then, is fueled by both ecstasy and misery. It can be a bittersweet experience. Companionate love, in contrast, is fueled by rewards and positive associations. People who are in companionate love enjoy intimacy and care about each other's well-being (Caspi & Herbener, 1990). They want to get close to each other, to explore similarities and differences in their personal histories, values, hopes, and fears. They reveal themselves to one another, feel responsible for each other, and quietly display their gentle, tender feelings for each other. Companionate love is a warm, comforting experience (Hatfield, 1988).

■ PASSION, INTIMACY, AND COMMITMENT

In another classification scheme, types of love are like three points of a triangle. According to the triangular theory of love, the three important dimensions are passion, intimacy, and decision or commitment (Sternberg, 1986). Figure 9.4 summarizes the three points, with sample items. Passion involves intense emotions and physiological arousal. When love has only passion (without in-

FIGURE 9.4

Three points in the triangular theory of love, with illustrative statements.

Abstracted from Acker & Davis, 1992, and Sternberg, 1988.

PASSION
the hot point of love
arousal and intense feelings
physical attraction, sexual consummation, and satisfying other drives and needs

> I cannot imagine being without my partner.
>
> I adore my partner.
>
> I find myself thinking about my partner frequently during the day.
>
> Just seeing my partner is exciting for me.
>
> I find my partner very attractive physically.

INTIMACY
the warm point of love
close, connected, bonded feelings in loving relationships
helping, being happy with, respecting, counting on, mutually understanding, sharing with, supporting, valuing

> I have a warm and comfortable relationship with my partner.
>
> I experience intimate communication with my partner.
>
> I feel emotionally close to my partner.
>
> I strongly desire to promote the well-being of my partner.
>
> I am willing to share myself and my possessions with my partner.

DECISION/COMMITMENT
the cool point of love
deliberate choice about loving someone and maintaining that love
short-term decisions about being in love and long-term commitment to a relationship

> I view my relationship with my partner as permanent.
>
> I would stay with my partner through the most difficult times.
>
> I view my relationship with my partner as, in part, a thought-out decision.
>
> I have great confidence in the stabililty of my relationship with my partner.
>
> I expect my love for my partner to last for the rest of my life.

timacy or commitment), it is often called "infatuation." We are infatuated with other people when we cannot stop thinking about them and become physiologically aroused by touching, seeing, or even thinking of them. When love has only intimacy (without passion or commitment), we might better call it "liking." We like other people when we enjoy just being with them, respect them, help them, and share with them. Finally, when love has only commitment, it is "empty love." We display empty love when we remain in a relationship from which all passion and intimacy have gone, as unhappy couples sometimes do "for the sake of the children."

If we drew passion, intimacy, and decision or commitment as the points of a triangle, the sides of the triangle would represent mixtures of two types. An equal mixture of passion and intimacy, for instance, is what many people mean when they use the term "romantic love." An equal mixture of intimacy and commitment seems very similar to what we described earlier as "companionate love." Finally, an equal mixture of passion and no commitment is fatuous love. Fatuous love is "the kind of love we sometimes associate with Hollywood or with whirlwind courtships; a couple meet one day, become engaged shortly thereafter, and marry soon after that" (Sternberg, 1988, p. 128).

Only equilateral triangles are completely balanced. Other triangles are unbalanced. Some sides are longer (and some points more pronounced) than others. It is possible, therefore, for people to have unequal mixtures of passion, intimacy, and commitment. Problems arise when a person is in passionate love with someone who wants only companionate love (and vice versa). Problems also arise when couples differ in which point of the triangle of love is longest (Sternberg, 1988). Someone long on commitment, for instance, might not welcome a relationship with someone long on passion and intimacy but short on commitment. Also, triangles of love can change their shape over time. Passion, for instance, declines in importance over time for women, but not for men. Although all three points of the triangle matter, commitment is the most powerful predictor of how satisfied people are in long-term relationships (Acker & Davis, 1992; Whitley, 1993).

■ SIX LOVE STYLES

A third scheme for classifying love uses six distinct types or "styles" (Hendrick & Hendrick, 1986; Lee, 1973, 1988). Both men and women enter into relationships characterized by each of these six types (and, in many instances, by more than one type simultaneously). A good way to remember the names that we will use to describe these six types is by the mnemonic "Love is a G-PLACE." The G . . . P . . . L . . . A . . . C . . . and E in this mnemonic device are the first letters of the six love styles shown in Table 9.2.

As the table shows, game players treat love like a contest or sport, as did the men of Ancient Rome. Game-playing lovers enjoy the passion and the intimacy, but they have little or no commitment (Dion & Dion, 1993). They "play the field." Game-players find casual sex perfectly acceptable and desirable, and they do not disclose their true feelings to partners (Hendrick & Hendrick, 1987, 1991). In the modern United States, men take the game-playing approach to relationships more often than do women (Hendrick & Hendrick, 1986). Game playing is reminiscent of the mating strategy in human reproduction.

Possessive lovers are like infants who despair when the mother leaves. They want complete union with the loved one. They are miserable and jealous if they do not get all of the lover's attention (Taraban & Hendrick, 1995). In the modern United States, more women than men endorse love scale items that reflect a possessive love style (Hendrick & Hendrick, 1986). Women's worries about being abandoned are realistic. Traditional cultural standards give them

TABLE 9.2	Six Love Styles, with Illustrative Statements (Abstracted from Hendrick & Hendrick, 1986; and Lee, 1988)

LOVE STYLE	ILLUSTRATIVE STATEMENTS
Game-playing (treating love like a game or sport)	I enjoy playing the 'game of love' with many different partners I try to keep my lover a little uncertain about my commitment to him/her
Possessive (wanting to bind the partner to an enduring relationship)	I cannot relax when I suspect that my partner is with someone else When he/she doesn't pay attention to me, I feel sick all over
Logical (treating love as a practical, down-to-earth decision)	An important factor in choosing a partner is whether he/she will make a good parent I try to plan my life carefully before choosing a partner
Altruistic (sacrificing for the sake of love; putting another person's happiness above your own)	I would rather suffer than let my partner suffer I am usually willing to sacrifice my own wishes to let my partner achieve his/hers
Companionate (loving affection, companionship, and friendship that develops over time)	Love is really a deep friendship, not some mysterious, mystical emotion The best kind of love grows out of a long friendship
Erotic (sheer physical excitement and sexual pleasure)	My partner and I have the right 'physical chemistry' between us Our lovemaking is very intense and satisfying

greater responsibility for child care than the father and put women at an economic disadvantage (Eagly, 1987).

Logical lovers treat love like a legally binding contract, as did the men of ancient Athens who took wives merely to manage their households. Logical love is very cool and detached, much like the "decision/commitment" point in the triangular model. More women than men in the modern United States endorse logical views of their current relationships (Hendrick & Hendrick, 1986). Fewer U.S. marriages are based on purely logical reasons today than in the past, however, because both men and women insist on "true romance" (Weiderman & Allgeier, 1992; Contreras, Hendrick, & Hendrick, in press; Gangestad, 1993; Simpson, Campbell, & Berscheid, 1986). In very poor, underdeveloped countries, by contrast, both men and women continue to say they would marry for logical reasons, even if they were not in love (Levine, Sato, Hashimoto & Verma, 1994).

Altruistic lovers are willing to sacrifice for the sake of the one they love. They are committed, caring, and giving (Taraban & Hendrick, 1995). They put the other person's happiness above their own. Approximately an equal number of modern men and women in the United States take an altruistic approach to their current relationships (Hendrick & Hendrick, 1986). The altruistic approach to interpersonal attraction was found in the lofty moral values of Renaissance Italy. Today, couples are more likely to use an altruistic style when they are first falling in love than later in the relationship (Hendrick & Hendrick, 1988).

Companionate love is almost indistinguishable from lasting friendship. When people in the modern United States are asked to list all the types of love they can think of, variations of companionate love are the first ones that come to mind (Fehr, 1988). Companionate lovers are seen as honest, loyal, and mature (Taraban & Hendrick, 1995). Most college students in the United States describe their romantic relationships as companionate and name their partner as their best friend (Hendrick & Hendrick, 1993). Women, however, emphasize companionate love slightly more than do men (Hendrick & Hendrick, 1986).

Finally, the "E" in G-PLACE stands for erotic attraction–sheer physical and sexual pleasure of the type that Athenian men enjoyed with prostitutes and hetaerae. During erotic love, which is most likely to occur at the start of a relationship, lovers experience strong physical excitement. In the modern United States, men and women are equally likely to emphasize the erotic style of love (Hendrick & Hendrick, 1986). Both men and women in some Eastern cultures, however, associate very erotic, passionate love with sadness and potential tragedy (Shaver et al., 1991). Interestingly, some studies suggest that erotic love declines in many marriages after four years. Four years is the time it takes for children in primitive cultures to mature enough that they will not necessarily die if left unattended (Fisher, 1992; Traupmann & Hatfield, 1981).

In the modern United States, women are most satisfied in relationships with men who are erotic and altruistic (Morrow, Clark, & Brock, 1995). They are least satisfied in relationships with men who are game playing and logical. Men are most satisfied in relationships with women who are erotic. They are least satisfied in relationships with women who are logical. Relationships are also more satisfactory for both men and women when their partner matches their own level of erotic, logical, and altruistic love (Morrow et al., 1995).

SUMMARY OF WHAT INTERPERSONAL ATTRACTION IS

It often seems as though modern men and women are attracted to each other only because of their unique characteristics and other aspects of the immediate context. Interpersonal attraction, however, may be subject to longer-term evolutionary pressures, an underlying need to belong, and cultural standards. Because males of many species have reproductive success by mating with any physically attractive female, men may be especially "tuned" to a woman's attractiveness. Because females of many species have reproductive success by mating selectively with dominant males, women may be especially "tuned" to a man's status and resources. Both men and women, however, *need* close interpersonal attachments. In the traditional division of labor, men acquired and controlled resources while women nurtured the children. The traditional division of labor encouraged cultural standards that forced women to trade their physical attractiveness for the material resources they needed to support themselves and their children. Interpersonal attraction has taken many different forms throughout history and across cultures. Ways of classifying love emphasize the difference between passion and companionship, the differences among passion, intimacy, and commitment, and six love styles: game playing, possessive, logical, altruistic, companionate, and erotic.

WHY ARE PEOPLE ATTRACTED TO EACH OTHER?

Strictly speaking, evolutionary pressures, the need to belong, and cultural standards do not *cause* interpersonal attraction. They are what scientists call distal (far away) causes, as opposed to proximal (nearby) causes. When bowling pins fall, the distal cause may be the law of gravity, but the proximal cause is most likely a bowling ball. To understand *why* the pins fall when they are struck by a bowling ball, we need to know about gravity and other laws of physics, but the bowling ball is what most of us would call the "cause." Similarly, when a physiologically aroused man "falls" for a woman who is physically attractive, we may need to know about evolutionary pressures, the need to belong, and cultural standards if we want to understand distal connections between his arousal and her attractiveness, but the proximal causes lie in the man, the woman, and the immediate context. This second section of the chapter is about proximal causes of interpersonal attraction. It describes three factors that make people "ready for love": physiological arousal, attachment, and loneliness.

PHYSIOLOGICAL AROUSAL

One of the most important factors that promotes interpersonal attraction is physiological arousal. The human species could not continue to exist if men and women did not become physiologically aroused in the presence of a physically attractive member of the opposite sex. Cultural standards also dictate what men and women are "supposed" to find arousing. Modern poets and romance novelists assume that men and women who are physiologically aroused, with their hearts racing and their blood pumping wildly, are especially likely to find members of the opposite sex attractive. Social psychologists have generated research evidence that modern poets and romance novelists are correct. Physiological arousal has important effects on interpersonal attraction. Social psychologists also understand at least part of the arousal-attraction relationship.

■ EFFECTS ON ATTRACTION

The investigators in one study of arousal and attraction escorted a male college student to a laboratory room full of intimidating electrical equipment (Dutton & Aron, 1974, Experiment 3). The other participant in the experiment "happened" to be a gorgeous female confederate. She sat between the man and the experimenter, so that when the man was listening to the experimenter's instructions, he could survey her physical charms. The experimenter explained that the two subjects would receive electric shocks that were either very painful or so mild as to be "an enjoyable tingle." Half of the men were led to believe that they would get the painful shocks (high arousal) and half were led to believe that they would get the mild shocks (low arousal). In addition, half of the men who expected painful shocks (and half of the men who expected mild shocks) thought that the woman would receive painful shocks. The other half thought that the woman would receive mild shocks. After delivering these instructions, the experimenter, claiming to need a few minutes to set up the equipment, asked the subjects to go to separate rooms to complete some questionnaires while waiting. The beautiful woman confederate then stepped directly in front of the man to search for a pencil in her coat pocket, so that he would *have* to notice her stunning good looks.

The questionnaires measured erotic attraction. One question asked the men how they felt about being shocked. As might be expected, men in the painful shock condition were dreading the experience more (and were thus presumably more physiologically aroused) than were men in the mild shock condition. On the important "attraction" questions, the men were asked how much they would like to ask the other subject out on a date and how much they would like to kiss her. As predicted, men who expected to receive painful electric shocks expressed greater interest in dating and kissing the confederate than did men who expected to receive only mild shocks. This effect of arousal occurred whether the men thought that the woman was going to get painful or mild shocks. The men were not motivated merely by the romantic idea of helping a "damsel in distress." The woman's potential distress did not affect wanting to date or kiss her. What mattered was whether the men were themselves internally aroused.

■ REASONS FOR THE RELATIONSHIP

Arousal heightens attraction in several ways. First, it is hard to tell one kind of physiological arousal from another. As described in Chapter 7, which treats of attitudes, people who have been given central nervous system stimulants (similar to amphetamine or cocaine) without their knowledge can be led to believe that their bodily symptoms (racing heart, faster breathing, and so on) stem from anger, joy, or several other seemingly incompatible emotions (Schachter & Singer, 1962). When a very attractive member of the opposite sex is present, any unexplained arousal, whether pleasant or unpleasant, might be confused with sexual excitement (Dutton & Aron, 1989). Women who have recently had an upsetting experience, for example, are subsequently more romantically attracted to a handsome man than they might have been without the upsetting experience. They would no doubt deny that they find the man appealing merely because they are upset (Jacobs, Berscheid, & Walster, 1971). Similarly, couples hold hands and hug each other more at arousing than nonarousing movies, even though they do not realize that anyone is watching (Cohen, Waugh, & Place, 1989).

Second, we like people who reward us by relieving the anxiety and unpleasant arousal of a frightening situation (Kenrick & Cialdini, 1977). Frightened monkeys cling to their mothers for protection (Harlow, 1958). Threatened chickens form attachments to their mother hens more readily than if they have not been threatened (Scott, 1962). Human beings who believe that they are about to receive painful electric shocks seek the company of other people who are about to be shocked (Schachter, 1959). Being with friends before undergoing an intrusive medical procedure reduces the level of free fatty acids in the blood (a physiological indicator of fear reduction) (Back & Bogdonoff, 1964). Hospital intensive care units have better recovery rates when the nurses are allowed to hug patients and to hold their hands (Holtzman, 1986).

Third, physiological arousal magnifies the usual response to many types of situations (Zajonc, 1965). In one study of arousal and attraction, male college students participated in a variety of unusual tasks. The last task was to run in place for either 15 seconds (low physiological arousal) or 120 seconds (high physiological arousal) (White, Fishbein, & Rutstein, 1981). Immediately after running in place, each man watched a videotape of a woman with whom he was to have an informal "date." Although the same woman appeared on both videotapes, half of the men saw her in form-fitting clothes and makeup that emphasized how beautiful she was. The beautiful woman claimed to have no current male friends and said that she was looking forward to the experiment as a way to meet someone special. The other half of the men saw the same woman in baggy clothes, dreadful makeup, and a dingy scarf over her head, which made her look very unattractive. She also had a bad cold, which made her an unappealing partner. After viewing the videotape, all men rated their potential date on how sexually warm, physically attractive, and exciting she seemed. They also rated how much they wanted to date her and how much they would like to kiss her.

The results, displayed in Figure 9.5, suggest that physiological arousal, even the "neutral," nonthreatening physiological arousal of running in place, heightens an individual's usual reaction to a person of the opposite sex. Men who watched a videotape of a very attractive woman found her more alluring than did men who watched a videotape of a physically unattractive woman. Also, physiological arousal made the woman seem even *more* attractive when she was attractive to begin with, and even *less* attractive when she was so unattractive that most men would not be interested. Similarly, the arousal of anticipating painful electric shock magnifies the appeal of an attractive woman. The effect occurs even when the men in question are reminded explicitly that the shocks are arousing, so they should know they are not aroused by the woman (Allen, Kenrick, Linder, & McCall, 1989). Also, people who are physiologically aroused exaggerate how much they have in common with each other, which may be why sometimes "love is blind" and people who are inherently incompatible enter dead-end relationships (McClanahan, Lenney, Ryckman, & Kulberg, 1990).

FIGURE 9.5

Arousal heightens "normal" reactions.

Graph shows aroused and non-aroused men's reported romantic attraction to attractive and unattractive women (White, Fishbein, & Rutstein, 1981).

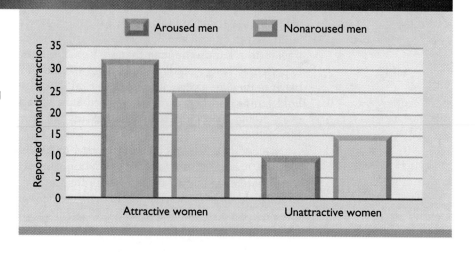

ATTACHMENT

Throughout most of recorded history, children born of their parents' momentary sexual arousal might have perished unless the parents were so attached to each other and to the child that they maintained a stable, protective, nurturing family unit after the child was born (Shaver, Hazan, & Bradshaw, 1988). The evolutionary function of affectional bonding in human beings is to protect infants from threats to their survival (Bowlby, 1979). Because attachment is so important to survival, children are born with instinctive reflexes that elicit a strong bond between themselves and their parents. Smiling is a good example. When babies smile, they encourage their parents to pick them up, feed them, cuddle them, hug them, and love them. Some evidence suggests that being cuddled and hugged increases the infant's neurological development and protects the infant from health threats such as sudden infant death syndrome (Lipsitt, 1979; Rice, 1977). Babies do not smile merely because they see their parents smile, because even blind babies smile when they are first born (Anastasiow, 1986). Although different cultures have different levels of intimacy between mothers and children, cultures that have a high level of physical affection between parents and their children also have a low level of violence (Hazan & Zeifman, 1994; Rohner, 1975).

■ ATTACHMENT STYLES

Some parent-child attachments, however, are stronger than others. In studies of infant attachment, investigators found three types of parent-child relationships: secure attachment, anxious/ambivalent attachment, and avoidant attachment (Ainsworth, Blehar, Waters, & Wall, 1978). When an infant has **secure attachment,** the child is easily reassured and loving when the mother returns from a brief absence. In *secure* attachment, infants do not get unduly upset by the mother's absence, because her previous interactions with them have been consistent. Through many types of interactions–feeding, cuddling, and responses to crying–the mother has always "been there when needed." Secure in the knowledge of parental protection, the infant explores his or her environment without constant reassurance and without being unduly distressed by the mother's brief absence.

When an infant has **anxious/ambivalent attachment,** the child gets very upset when the mother is absent and clings to the mother when she returns. In *anxious/ambivalent* attachment, infants become extremely upset when the mother is away for even a few moments, because their previous interactions with her have been inconsistent (Main & Solomon, 1990). They never know whether the mother is going to respond, so they cry a lot, cling to the mother, and lack the confidence to explore their surroundings on their own.

When an infant has **avoidant attachment,** the child acts as though he or she does not care when the mother returns from a brief absence and rejects her attention. In *avoidant* attachment, infants become extremely alarmed and upset when the mother is away for even a short time, but they reject close bodily contact when she returns. Because the mother has in the past rebuffed the infant's attempts to "get close" either physically or psychologically, infants in an avoidant relationship respond in kind. In research on early childhood attachment, approximately 62% of infant-mother relationships have been found to be secure, 15% anxious/ambivalent, and 23% avoidant (Campos, Barrett, Lamb, Goldsmith, & Stenberg, 1983).

Attachment is such a fundamental part of the "need to belong" that the pattern of a child's relationships with his or her caretaker in the formative years may persist into his or her adult relationships with members of the opposite

Do our adult romantic relationships imitate our childhood attachments?

sex (Hatfield & Rapson, 1996; Hazan & Shaver, 1987; Shaver et al., 1988). Table 9.3 shows some similarities between infant attachment and adult romantic love. The similarities are so striking that we might wonder whether the three types of infant-parent attachment (secure, anxious/ambivalent, and avoidant) occur as well in adult romantic relationships. They do. When asked which of the three descriptions in Table 9.4 best describes their current interpersonal relationships, 56% of adults choose the description closest to secure infant-parent attachment, 19% choose the description closest to anxious/ambivalent infant-parent attachment, and 25% chose the description closest to avoidant

TABLE 9.3	Parallels Between Infant Attachment and Adult Romantic Love (Abstracted from Shaver, Hazan, & Bradshaw, 1988)
INFANT ATTACHMENT	**ADULT ROMANTIC LOVE**
Quality of bond depends on parent's responsiveness	Quality of love depends on partner's interest and reciprocation
When parent provides a secure base, infant feels competent and safe to explore	When partner reciprocates affection, person feels confident, secure, and safe
When parent is present, infant is happier and less afraid of strangers	When partner reciprocates affection, person is happier, more optimistic, more outgoing, and kinder to others
When parent is absent, infant is anxious, preoccupied, and unable to explore freely	When partner is uninterested or rejecting, person becomes anxious, unable to concentrate, etc.
Infant seeks contact, holding, touching, caressing, kissing, rocking, smiling, etc.	Person wants to spend time with partner, holding, hugging, kissing, smiling, etc.

TABLE 9.3 (CONTINUED)	Parallels Between Infant Attachment and Adult Romantic Love (Abstracted from Shaver, Hazan, & Bradshaw, 1988)
When afraid, distressed, sick, or threatened, infant seeks physical contact with parent	When afraid, distressed, sick, or threatened, person wants to be held and comforted by partner
When separated from parent, infant cries out for parent, tries to find parent, and becomes sad and listless if reunion seems unlikely	When separated from partner, person cries, calls out for partner, tries to find partner, and becomes sad and listless if reunion seems unlikely
When reunited with parent, infant smiles, approaches, bounces and jiggles, reaches to be picked up	When reunited with partner or when reassured after relationship was in doubt, person feels ecstatic, hugs
Infant shares toys and discoveries with parent	Partners share experiences, give each other gifts, etc.
Infant maintains eye contact with parent, seems fascinated with parent, enjoys touching parent's nose, ears, hair, etc.	Partners maintain eye contact and seem fascinated with partner, touching partner's nose, ears, hair, etc.
Infant feels fused with parent and, with development, becomes ambivalent about fusion versus autonomy	Partners feel like a "unit," but in time worry also about maintaining separate interests, etc.
Although infant can become attached to more than one person at a time, there is usually one "central" person	Although adults can "love" more than one person, intense love usually occurs toward one person at a time
Separation, up to a point, increases intensity of attachment and need to be with parent	Separation and social disapproval, up to a point, increase intensity of partners' feelings and commitment
Infant coos, "sings," talks baby talk and much of infant-parent interaction is nonverbal	Lovers coo, sing, talk baby talk, use soft, maternal tones and communicate nonverbally
Responsive parent "reads the infant's mind" through powerful empathy	Person feels magically understood and empathized with
Infant regards parent as powerful, generous, all-knowing, a truly wonderful creature	Partners at first ignore each other's faults and see each other as special and miraculously good
When relationship is not going well, infant becomes anxious and hypervigilant to cues of parent's approval or disapproval	Before relationship becomes secure, lovers are hypersensitive to cues of the partner's reciprocation or nonreciprocation
Infant derives tremendous pleasure from parent's attention, applause, and approval	Early in a relationship, person's greatest happiness comes from the partner's attention and approval

TABLE 9.4	Adult Attachment Types and Their Frequencies (Percentages from Shaver et al., 1988)

ATTACHMENT TYPE	PERCENTAGE IN ADULT POPULATION
Secure	
I find it relatively easy to get close to others and am comfortable depending on them and having them depend on me. I don't often worry about being abandoned or about someone getting too close to me.	56%
Anxious/Ambivalent	
I find that others are reluctant to get as close as I would like. I often worry that my partner doesn't really love me or won't want to stay with me. I want to merge completely with another person, and this desire sometimes scares people away.	19%
Avoidant	
I am somewhat uncomfortable being close to others. I find it difficult to trust them completely, difficult to allow myself to depend on them. I am nervous when anyone gets too close, and often, love partners want me to be more intimate than I feel comfortable being.	25%

infant-parent attachment. The descriptions were constructed to match the way that infants in these three types of infant-parent relationships behave, according to extensive observational research. The percentages of endorsement among adults are remarkably similar to the percentages found for the three types of infant-parent attachment.

Adults who describe their romantic relationships in the three different ways also differ in how they describe their earlier relationships with their parents (Collins & Read, 1990; Davis, Kirkpatrick, Levy, & O'Hearn, 1994; Feeney & Noller, 1990; Hazan & Shaver, 1987; Simpson, 1990). Adults who describe their current romantic relationship as secure report that their parents were affectionate, caring, responsible, and sympathetic. Adults who describe their current romantic relationship as anxious/ambivalent or avoidant report that their parents were intrusive, demanding, cold, rejecting, uncaring, and unfair. Adult romantic relationships do not *have* to recreate an individual's infant attachment. People who were rejected by their parents sometimes compensate by lavishing attention on their children. Insecure children can learn to be loving adults. Nonetheless, an anxious/ambivalent or avoidant attachment experience early in life poses obstacles to a secure romantic relationship later in life (Mikulincer & Nachshon, 1991; Shaver & Brennan, 1992; Simpson et al., 1992).

■ ATTACHMENT AND LOVE STYLES

The three attachment styles also appear related to the six love styles that were described earlier (Mikulincer & Nachson, 1991; Shaver & Hazan, 1988). Secure individuals might enjoy attachment and feel free to express their affection openly, without fear of being neglected or abandoned. They may be unselfish and altruistic in romantic relationships (A) and capable of enjoying the physical, sexual rewards of a relationship (E). Anxious/ambivalent individuals may cling to a romantic partner and thus create a possessive (P) type of interpersonal attraction. Avoidant individuals may find it difficult to trust romantic partners, avoid commitment, be "off-again, on-again," and take a game-playing (G) orientation to interpersonal attraction.

Table 9.5 shows the results of two studies in which college students were asked about their adult romantic attachment styles and their preferred love styles. Game players scored high on avoidant attachment and low on secure attachment (Levy & Davis, 1988). Students who described their current romantic relationships as altruistic or erotic, by contrast, scored high on secure attachment and low on avoidant attachment. Those who described their current romantic relationships as possessive scored high on anxious/ambivalent attachment. As the investigators had predicted, attachment styles and love styles were related in a meaningful way (Shaver & Brennan, 1992).

LONELINESS

As described earlier in the chapter, people need to belong (Baumeister & Leary, 1995). Nearly everyone would rather have secure than anxious/ambivalent or avoidant attachments, but almost 50% of people admit that they do not (see Table 9.4). People who are anxious/ambivalent or avoidant, those who take a low commitment, game-playing approach or possessive orientation toward their relationships, also suffer for their maladaptive attachment styles. Possessive, anxious/ambivalent types, for example, desperately want to form a close attachment with another person, but their actions frequently produce the opposite effect. Because they cannot get close to people, anxious/ambivalent and avoidant children and adults often suffer the excruciating pangs of loneliness (Shaver & Rubenstein, 1980). In Daniel Defoe's novel *Robinson Crusoe,* which concerns a man who was stranded on a desert island, Crusoe suffered because "I have no soul to speak to, or to relieve me." In Charlotte Bronte's novel *Jane Eyre,* which explores the depths of interpersonal despair, Mr. Rochester told his love Jane that when she left him "I was desolate and abandoned—my life dark, lonely, hopeless—my soul athirst and forbidden to drink—my heart famished and never to be fed." In everyday modern life as well as in classic novels, people who describe their loneliness use such terms as "desperate," "panicked," "helpless," "afraid," vulnerable," and "abandoned" (Rubenstein & Shaver, 1982, p. 212).

TABLE 9.5	**Relationships Between the Six Love Styles and the Three Attachment Styles (Abstracted from Levy & Davis, 1988)**		
TYPE OF ATTRACTION	**ATTACHMENT STYLE**		
	SECURE	**ANXIOUS/AMBIVALENT**	**AVOIDANT**
Game playing	Low	–	High
Possessive	–	High	–
Logical	–	–	–
Altruistic	High	–	Low
Companionate	–	–	–
Erotic	High	–	Low

Can a blanket help ward
off loneliness?

■ COMPONENTS OF LONELINESS

The emotion that we commonly label "loneliness" has two components: feeling isolated from other people in general, and feeling isolated from a loved one. The latter component, feeling isolated from a loved one—whether because of death, divorce, separation, or never finding anyone who is willing to become attached to us—is similar to the "distress of a small child who fears that he has been abandoned by his parents" (Weiss, 1973, p. 20). One woman who was experiencing loneliness was asked to imagine a vivid scene in which her loneliness would be dispelled. She surprised herself by blurting out that she would no longer be lonely if she could snuggle against and "burrow under" an older man who, in her imagined scenario, was lying on the floor. The woman later recalled that when she was a little girl her father would come home from work, change his clothes, lie on the floor under an afghan to watch television, and "let me snuggle up to him" (Rubenstein & Shaver, 1982, p. 221). Lonely people experience emotions that are very similar to the separation anxiety and rejection that characterize the anxious/ambivalent and avoidant attachment styles (Shaver & Hazan, 1987). On a scale that is frequently used to measure loneliness, the UCLA Loneliness Scale (Russell, Peplau, & Cutrona, 1980), lonely people report that there is no one they can turn to. They also say that they feel close to no one and that no one really understands them.

Chronically lonely people suffer in more ways than merely being self-conscious and having low self-esteem (Peplau & Perlman, 1982). People who are extremely lonely have higher blood pressure than do their nonlonely peers; less effective immune systems; more sleep and eating disturbances, headaches, nausea, and other health problems (Goldstein, Edelberg, Meir, & Davis, 1991; Kiecolt-Glaser, Ricker, George, Messick, Speicher, Garner, & Glaser, 1984; Lynch, 1977; 1985). Very lonely people, especially women in the 18–20 age group, are more at risk of becoming alcoholics than the general population (Page & Cole, 1991). Another problem for the chronically lonely is that other people do not like them (Lau & Gruen, 1992). Even in grades kindergarten through four, very lonely children are less popular with their classmates than are nonlonely children (Cassidy & Asher, 1992; Quay, 1992). Also, when other people criticize them, lonely people are more likely than the nonlonely to remember disparaging remarks (Frankel & Prentice-Dunn, 1990).

PEANUTS reprinted by premission of United Feature Syndicate, Inc.

Chronically lonely people have two characteristics that contribute to their lack of popularity. First, they are often excessively critical. They often express negative views of family members, friends, neighbors, authority figures, and classmates (Hanley-Dunn, Maxwell, & Santos, 1985). They take a dim view of humanity (Jones, Freemon, & Goswick, 1981). They criticize themselves for having only superficial social relationships, but say they have little or no control over the situation (Anderson & Riger, 1991; Snodgrass, 1987; Williams & Solano, 1983). Second, chronically lonely people are socially inept (Berg & Peplau, 1982; Hill, 1989; Jones, 1982). They do not introduce themselves to other people, make very few telephone calls, and refuse to participate in group activities (Rook, 1984; Spitzberg & Hurt, 1987). They do not seem to know how to form a close attachment with another person or how to resolve the conflicts that inevitably arise in an ongoing relationship (Horowitz, French, & Anderson, 1982; Wittenburg & Reis, 1986). When you notice how chronically lonely people behave during social interactions, it is not surprising that they turn other people off (Jones, Hobbs, & Hockenbury, 1982; Jones, Sansone, & Helm, 1983; Jones, Carpenter, & Quintana, 1985). They often change the topic away from what the other person finds interesting and onto themselves and their troubles. When chronically lonely people watch videotapes of their previous interactions, they are extremely critical of their own interpersonal communication. They know they should have "done better," but they are not sure how to improve (Duck, Pond, & Leatham, 1994).

■ CURING LONELINESS

Although it is not *easy* for lonely people to improve their interpersonal relationships, it is nonetheless possible. One way in which people who are extremely lonely might improve is by choosing an appropriate level of "self-disclosure," which is how much we tell other people about ourselves. Non-lonely people, who tend to form secure rather than anxious/ambivalent or avoidant attachments, know almost intuitively how to manage self-disclosure within a relationship (Berndt & Hanna, in press). In any getting-acquainted process, self-disclosure is a matter of give-and-take. First one person discloses a little about himself or herself and then it is the other person's turn. Through this feeling-out process, two people mutually agree on whether they will have a superficial or an intimate relationship (Jourard, 1971). In addition, there are unwritten rules about how much you should disclose when you first meet a person of your own (versus the opposite) sex. Cultural standards often dictate what is an appropriate level of self-disclosure—for instance, for people who are romantically involved (Ting-Toomey, 1991).

In one study of self-disclosure to a same-sex as opposed to an opposite-sex stranger, very lonely and nonlonely male and female college students got a list of 72 possible conversation topics that they could talk about when they first met another student of either their own or the opposite sex (Solano, Batten, & Parish, 1982). The topics ranged from superficial ("The courses I'm taking this semester") to intimate ("The most embarrassing aspects of my personality"). As shown in Figure 9.6, nonlonely men and women started the conversation with a nonrevealing topic when they were talking to a member of their own sex, but they were more willing to offer initial self-disclosures to a member of the opposite sex. Very lonely men and women did exactly the opposite. They spilled their guts to a member of the same sex and clammed up when talking to a member of the opposite sex. This pattern of inappropriate disclosure continued throughout the conversation.

As we might expect, if loneliness stems from anxious/ambivalent or avoidant parental attachment early in life, however, loneliness is difficult to cure. Chronically lonely people, many of whose parents were divorced early in the lonely person's life, ensure by their self-focused interaction styles and inappropriate self-disclosures that they will have few close friends or romantic involvements (Berg & Peplau, 1982; Rubenstein & Shaver, 1982; Russell, Peplau, & Cutrona, 1980). When asked what they do when they feel lonely, they say that they cry, sleep, overeat, take tranquilizers, drink, "get stoned," watch television, or listen to music. Their musical tastes run to songs about broken hearts and lost loves (Rubenstein & Shaver, 1982). A better strategy for them would be to get out and meet people, join some groups, and practice a conversational style that focuses attention on the other person rather than on themselves (Jones, Hobbs, & Hockenbury, 1982). To overcome loneliness, chronically lonely people need to become more responsive to others and less self-absorbed (Jones, 1982). They also need to spend more time with women. People who spend more time with women, whether they are male or female themselves, are less likely to be lonely (Wheeler, Reis, & Nezlak, 1983). For both sexes, a satisfying adult relationship with a woman may parallel secure infant attachment to a mother (Shaver, Hazan, & Bradshaw, 1988). Women are more likely to avoid loneliness by having a close friend with whom they can share their feelings. Both men and women, however, benefit from establishing at least one close attachment with a desirable partner (Stokes & Levin, 1986).

SUMMARY OF WHY PEOPLE ARE ATTRACTED TO EACH OTHER

Three factors promote and enhance interpersonal attraction. First, when people become physiologically aroused, they are more likely to be romantically attracted, because arousal is easily confused with sexual excitement and magnifies our usual responses. Second, three types of infant-parent attachment predispose individuals to form secure, anxious/ambivalent, or avoidant adult relationships. Third, people who are chronically lonely tend to have anxious/ambivalent or avoidant relationships. They are unpopular because they are excessively critical of others and themselves. They also disclose personal information inappropriately. To reduce loneliness, they might study cultural standards for self-disclosure, get out and meet people, join groups, practice focusing attention on the other person rather than themselves, and spend more time with women.

FIGURE 9.6

Lonely people self-disclose inappropriately.

Graph shows rated intimacy of the first topic that lonely and nonlonely students chose to talk about with a stranger of either sex (Solano, Batten, & Parish, 1982).

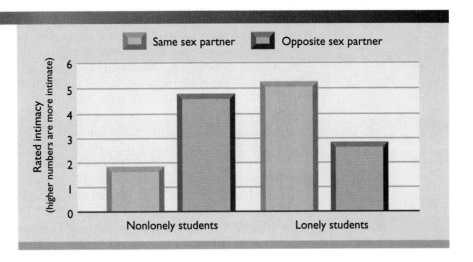

WHY DO WE FIND SOME PEOPLE MORE ATTRACTIVE THAN OTHERS?

Arousal, attachment, and loneliness are powerful forces that make us want to find someone to like or to love. But what characteristics do we seek in a desirable partner? What kind of person is likely to elicit attraction? In this section, we discuss three characteristics that make one partner more desirable than another: familiarity, physical attractiveness, and similarity to self.

FAMILIARITY

We tend to like familiar people better than unfamiliar people, and for good reason. Imagine that you are walking at night on a dark street and you see a large man approaching from the opposite direction. As the man draws near, you get a vague impression that you have "seen him around." You cannot remember his name or the exact context in which you have seen him previously, but you know he is a familiar face in the neighborhood. You feel relieved. You smile at the man and say "hello." He says "hello" and continues on his way. "I don't know his name," you think to yourself, "but he certainly seems like a nice man." Similarly, our distant ancestors who were initially wary of strange animals and unfamiliar human beings were more likely to live long enough to have children than were their peers who could not resist "getting closer to check it out." Animals are wary of unfamiliar things until they know that the object or person in question is not dangerous. Animals are thus more willing to approach a familiar object than one they have never seen before, and so are human beings. It is adaptive to be reassured by familiarity (Berlyne, 1970; Bornstein, 1989; Hill, 1978; Stang, 1975).

■ MERE EXPOSURE

The mere exposure effect, as explained in Chapter 7 ("Attitude Change"), is that we like objects and people better the more times we meet them (Zajonc, 1968). It is called a *mere* exposure effect because the object or person does not have to be intrinsically likable or encountered in pleasant circumstances to be liked a little more (or disliked a little less) each time it is encountered. Mere repeated exposure to an object or person in neutral circumstances is reassuring. The object or person takes on a warm glow of familiarity. Participants in dozens of experiments have reported liking foreign words that they saw many times more than foreign words that they saw only once (Zajonc, 1968). They like the letters in their name more than other letters of the alphabet (Hoorens, Nuttin, Herman, & Pavakanun, 1990; Nuttin, 1987). They like tunes they have heard several times more than tunes they have not heard before. They also like the faces in photographs they have seen many times more than those they have seen only once or twice (Kunst-Wilson & Zajonc, 1980).

A striking example of how familiarity can affect judgments without our being aware of its impact is that people even like *themselves* better when they are familiar than when they are unfamiliar (Mita, Dermer, & Knight, 1977). In one study, students evaluated several photographs of themselves. Although the students did not realize it, some of the photographs were mirror images, in which they saw themselves (as they were familiar with seeing themselves) in a mirror, which is reversed left-to-right from the way that other people see them. The other photographs were nonreversed "true-images" in which the students saw themselves as other people see them. The students liked the familiar mirror image photographs of themselves better than the unfamiliar true image ones. When asked to explain their preferences, the students said that some of the photographs looked "more natural," or "had a better facial angle." They were unaware of the actual difference between the two types of photographs. (The students' friends and lovers, by the way, preferred the true image photographs of the student, which was the perspective with which *they* were more familiar.)

The significance of mere exposure effects for interpersonal attraction is that human beings are more likely to like and love other people who are familiar, as opposed to unfamiliar. In a laboratory study of mere exposure, students moved from room to room, supposedly to taste different beverages that were located in the different rooms (Saegert, Swap, & Zajonc, 1973). Without the students realizing it, the experimenters arranged the rotation through rooms so that each student was in the same room with one of the other students once, with a different student twice, and so on, up to a student with whom they shared a room on ten occasions. Although the students did not know each other previously and were not allowed to speak, the students later reported liking each of the other participants better the more times they had shared a room. Interestingly, familiarity increased liking whether the students were tasting sweet or very bitter beverages, so the result did not depend on sharing a *positive* experience with the other person. Even a negative experience might increase attraction, as long as it increases familiarity.

■ LIVING ARRANGEMENTS

Familiarity increases liking both in the laboratory and in everyday life, where some people meet each other more frequently merely because of their living arrangements. Friendships in apartment complexes, for instance, are influenced by mere exposure and familiarity. If the physical arrangement is such that some residents are more likely than others to meet their neighbors frequently, the most "favorably placed" residents form the most friendships with other residents. In one study, residents lived either in two-story apartment buildings or in courtyards (Festinger, Schachter, & Back, 1950). In the apartment buildings, residents of the second floor had to get to their apartments by stairs located at either end of the building. On both floors, people were more likely to be friends with the next-door neighbor than with the neighbor two doors away, even less likely to be friends with the neighbor three doors away, and so on. These differences in liking for the other residents were surprisingly large given the short distances involved. The apartment doors were on average only 22 feet apart. Residents were more than four times as likely to make friends with someone who lived 22 feet away than with someone who lived 66 feet farther away.

The deciding factor was not sheer physical distance, but "functional distance." Residents who lived at the foot of the stairs, who were most likely to meet residents of the second floor apartments coming and going, had the most friends on the upper floor. Their popularity did not arise merely from having the end apartment, because residents who lived at the end of units in a nearby "courtyard" community were the *least* popular. Courtyard housing was arranged in a U-shape. All the apartments but the end two had doors that faced in toward the courtyard. Residents of the two end apartments usually came and went without seeing their neighbors. Functional isolation had a large impact on the number of other residents who liked the residents of the end apartments well enough to call them friends. Almost certainly the residents of the end apartments had no idea that the functional distance from their neighbors made them relatively unpopular.

Similar effects of functional distance on liking have been found for college students who live in dorms that have long corridors, police academy cadets who are assigned to rooms and classroom seats alphabetically, and elderly people who live in different units of an urban housing project (Nahemow & Lawton, 1975; Priest & Sawyer, 1967; Segal, 1974). In addition, surveys of marriage license applications invariably find that people are more likely to fall in love with and marry other people who live within a mile of them than they are to fall in love with and marry people who live two miles from them, even less with people who live several miles away, and so on (Bossard, 1932; Clarke, 1952; Katz & Hill, 1958; Ramsoy, 1966). Frequent exposure to an irritating person obviously does not increase liking for that person. Also, "too much of a good thing" might prove boring. Nonetheless, one of the most powerful influences on interpersonal attraction is mere exposure or familiarity (Bornstein, Kale, & Cornell, 1990; Swap, 1977).

PHYSICAL ATTRACTIVENESS

Familiarity aside, both men and women prefer physically attractive partners (Buss & Schmitt, 1993; Gangestad, 1993; Gangestad & Thornhill, 1994). Across cultures, the average man is attracted to young women who have childlike faces and firm young bodies (Alicke, Smith, & Klotz, 1986; Cunningham, 1986b; Franzoi & Herzog, 1987). The average woman is attracted to men who are taller than average, with broad shoulders, a slim waist, and tight buttocks (Buss, 1989a; Lavrakas, 1975; Lynn & Shurgot, 1984; Slowman, 1977). Also, as discussed earlier in the chapter, men in virtually all cultures and across all age groups value a partner's physical attractiveness more than do women (Buss & Barnes, 1986; Cooms & Kenkel, 1966; Feingold, 1990; Johnson & Pittenger, 1984; Stroebe, Insko, Thompson, & Layton, 1971). As a result, a woman's popularity with the opposite sex is much more influenced by her physical attractiveness than is true for men (Berscheid, Dion, Walster, & Walster, 1971). In addition, a spouse's physical attractiveness is more important to marital satisfaction for husbands than it is for wives (Peterson & Miller, 1980).

Men in different cultures across the world tend to agree on what makes a woman physically attractive (Buss & Schmitt, 1993). One important factor, as described in Chapter 3, which treats of person perception, is a face that has both childlike and sexually mature features (Cunningham, Roberts, Barbee, Druen, & Wu, 1995). Another important factor is a small waist-to-hip ratio at normal body weight (Singh, 1993). Perhaps because of both evolutionary pressures and traditional cultural standards in which women had to bargain for resources and did not have the luxury of choosing men by their looks, men seem to process information about a potential mate's physical attractiveness more "automatically" (see Chapter 2) than do women. Men, for instance, rate a woman's physical attractiveness the same regardless of what other men think. Women, in contrast, rate a man's physical attractiveness less positively if they know that other women think he is not good-looking (Graziano, Jensen-Campbell, Shebilske, & Lundgren, 1993).

■ EFFECTS ON ATTRACTION AND COMMITMENT

Also, seeing several extremely attractive members of the opposite sex may lower a man's commitment to a relationship, even if it does not lower a woman's commitment. In a relevant study, male and female college students rated photographs of extremely attractive or unattractive opposite-sex strangers (Kenrick, Neuberg, Zierk, & Krones, 1994). Then they rated their commitment to their current dating relationship. As Figure 9.7 shows, men said they were less committed to their current relationship after viewing photographs of physically attractive than unattractive women, whereas women were not affected by the photographed men's physical attractiveness. Interestingly, women were very much affected by how dominant the men in the photographs seemed. They reported being less committed to their current dating relationships when they had just viewed photographs of men who looked very dominant rather than like "wimps," regardless of how attractive the men were (Kenrick et al., 1994; Sadalla, Kenrick, & Vershure, 1987).

Many studies have established, however, that physical attractiveness has a large impact on initial attraction for both sexes (Cash & Kilcullen, 1985; Folkes, 1982; Hatfield & Sprecher, 1986). Investigators have arranged "coffee dates," organized college dances, and obtained the records of computer dating services (Green, Buchanan, & Heuer, 1984; Woll, 1986). In every instance, they found that men and women regard physically attractive partners as the most desirable. The prejudice toward physically attractive partners is even stronger than the participants themselves believe it to be. When men and women list the characteristics that they consider most important and desirable in a potential partner, both sexes give at least as much weight (and often more) to personality traits, values, and interests as to physical attractiveness. When asked to choose between a homely partner with a charming personality and a gor-

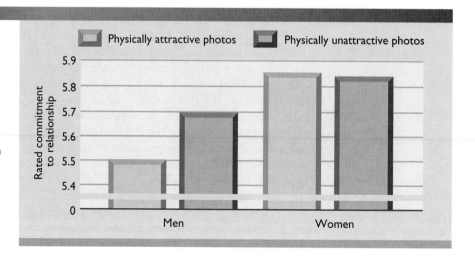

FIGURE 9.7

Physically attractive others affect men's more than women's commitment to a relationship.

Graph shows how committed men and women said they were to their current relationship after viewing opposite-sex photographs (Kenrick, Neuberg, Zierk, & Krones, 1994).

geous "airhead," however, both sexes find it very difficult to resist the allure of sheer physical magnetism (Buss & Barnes, 1986; Hudson & Hoyt, 1981).

One reason for the allure of a physically attractive face and body is that beautiful people are assumed to have many other desirable characteristics (Dion, Berscheid, & Walster, 1972). Both sexes believe that physically attractive people are more sociable, intelligent, well-adjusted, successful, and interesting than people who are not so attractive (Archer & Cash, 1985; Brigham, 1980; Hassebrauck, 1988; Moore, Graziano, & Millar, 1987). When a physically attractive person and a homely person perform identically, the physically attractive person's work is evaluated more positively (Landy & Sigall, 1974). When a physically attractive child and a relatively unattractive child misbehave, adults are more lenient in their treatment of the physically attractive child (Dion, 1972). When a physically attractive child and a physically unattractive child have identical grades in school, teachers think the physically attractive child is more intelligent (Clifford & Walster, 1973). When a physically attractive teacher and a physically unattractive teacher give equally informative lectures, students think that the better-looking lecturer is a better teacher (Chaikin, Gillen, Derlega, Heinen, & Wilson, 1978). Even judgments of morality and criminal intent favor the physically attractive (Dion et al., 1972). Judges and juries in court cases are notoriously loathe to find physically attractive defendants guilty or to give them harsh sentences (Deseran & Chung, 1979; Downs & Lyons, 1991; Efran, 1974; Mace, 1972). The only exception to preferential treatment occurs when defendants used physical attractiveness as a criminal tool, for example when a beautiful woman used her looks to swindle a lonely old bachelor (Sigall & Ostrove, 1975).

■ MATCHING HYPOTHESIS

If they had their way in a fantasy world, members of both sexes would mate only with the most physically attractive man or woman on the planet. Fortunately for the continuation of the human species, however, actual mate selection is moderated by a healthy dose of realism (Berscheid et al., 1971). In keeping with the **matching hypothesis,** both men and women tend to seek and find lovers who are roughly at their own level of physical attractiveness. Physically unattractive men and women may long for the embrace of someone who looks like a Greek god or goddess. When they get down to the serious business of finding a life partner, however, wishful thinking gives way to seeking a good match (Murstein, 1980). One reason for the matching hypothesis is that there are simply not enough beautiful people to go around. Another reason is that both men and women fear rejection, or at least realize that they have little chance of success with someone far more attractive than they are (Berscheid et al., 1971; Bernstein et al., 1983). Researchers at a college campus used a 5-point scale to rate the physical attractiveness of men and women who walked by (Berscheid & Walster, 1974). Of all the male-female couples that they observed, 85% were within one scale point of each other on the physical attractiveness scale. Handsome men tended to be walking with beautiful women, just as homely men tended to be walking with plain women.

SIMILARITY TO SELF

The third important characteristic of a desirable partner is similarity to self. In the study just described, where couples who were walking on a college campus tended to match each other in physical attractiveness, the researchers also observed that the better matched they were, the more likely the couples were to be touching each other as they walked. The 15% of couples who were more

Do opposites attract, or
do birds of a feather
flock together?

than a scale point apart in physical attractiveness tended to walk side by side without touching. Couples who matched each other, whether both were attractive or both were unattractive, tended to hold hands or have their arms around each other, as though they were on more intimate terms. One interpretation of these observations is that people are more attracted to others who are similar than to those who are dissimilar (Byrne, 1971).

■ DIMENSIONS OF SIMILARITY

It might at first seem obvious that similar people ought to like each other, but the relationship between similarity and attraction is stronger than you might think (Chapdelaine, Kenny, & LaFontana, 1994; Stephan, 1992). As compared to two people who are chosen at random, both friends and lovers tend to be very similar to each other in many characteristics other than physical attractiveness. People also prefer partners who are similar to them in age, race, religion, economic level, education, attitudes, academic and nonacademic skills, smoking and drinking habits, use of drugs like marijuana, preference for daytime versus nighttime activities, preferred tactics in strategic games and coping with everyday problems, height, weight, facial features, genetic makeup, and even *length of their ear lobes* (Buss, 1985; Eisenman, 1985; Gormly & Gormly, 1984; Griffin & Sparks, 1990; Hinsz, 1989; Kandel, 1978; Knight, 1980; Lykken & Tellegen, 1993; Ptacek & Dodge, 1995; Rodgers, Billy, & Udry, 1984; Rushton, 1989; Symons, 1992; Vandenberg, 1972; Watts et al., 1982). Couples are also more similar to each other than to other people on which of the six love types in "G-PLACE" they endorse and in which of the three attachment styles they have (Hendrick, Hendrick, & Adler, 1988; Kirkpatrick & Davis, 1994). The similarity-attraction relationship also applies to a person's typical moods (Locke & Horowitz, 1990; Rosenblatt & Greenberg, 1991; Wenzlaff & Prohaska, 1989). It might seem wise for people who frequently feel depressed to find happy partners to cheer them up. Nonetheless, happy people manage to find partners who are also happy, and sad people, either because they have to settle for what's left or because misery loves company, find partners who are every bit as down in the dumps (Hatfield, Traupmann, Sprecher, Utne, & Hay, 1985; Swann, De La Ronde, & Hixon, 1994; Utne, Hatfield, Traupmann, & Greenberger, 1984).

Spouses are more similar to each other than chance would allow on almost every conceivable characteristic, but not merely because they grow more similar to each other over time (Bochner, 1984; Byrne & Blaylock, 1963; Newcomb & Svehela, 1937; Schooley, 1936; Sunnafrank, 1986, 1991). By knowing two people's attitudes, beliefs, and values, researchers can predict *in advance* how well they will hit it off when they meet. In a classic study of predicting friendships, the researchers offered free housing to college students who were strangers to each other before they started to share living quarters (Newcomb, 1961). After the students got to know each other, they formed stable friendships that were predictable from their preexisting interests, attitudes, and values. Five men who each had politically liberal values and intellectual interests before they met, for instance, became close friends, as did three military veterans who had politically conservative views. Other researchers first identified attitudes and interests and then locked participants in a nuclear fallout shelter (Griffitt & Veitch, 1974). After living in close quarters for several days, the participants nominated the two other people they most wanted to keep in the study and the two other people they would most like to evict from the shelter. Almost invariably, participants wanted to keep people who had started with views similar to theirs. They also wanted to evict those who had started with dissimilar views.

For similarity to influence interpersonal attraction, the dimension on which two people are similar must be important (Wetzel & Insko, 1982). We are more impressed by finding a kindred soul who also likes to attend jazz concerts than by discovering that the other person also chews our favorite flavor of bubble gum. The most important topics have implications for future interaction and unusual preferences (Davis, 1989; Lea & Duck, 1982). When a Libertarian antique car collector meets "one of the same," a warm relationship is very likely. Similarity of preferred interests may generate greater liking (as opposed to mere respect) than does similarity of attitudes, but similarity on most dimensions predisposes people to like each other (Lydon, Jamieson, & Zanna, 1988).

■ WHY SIMILARITY IS IMPORTANT

Although men and women choose friends and lovers who are similar to themselves, they probably do not consciously calculate their reasons. Most women do not say to themselves "I love that man because he has the same size ear lobes as my father." Other reasons for the similarity-attraction relationship are almost as indirect and probably not a part of conscious deliberation. When people share our views, for example, they reassure us that our beliefs are valid (Goethals, 1986; Hummert, Crockett, & Kemper, 1990). Also, we intuitively assume—even before we have any dealings with them—that other people will evaluate us more positively if they share many characteristics with us than if they look and act like our exact opposites (Aronson & Worchel, 1966; Berscheid & Walster, 1983; Condon & Crano, 1988; Gonzales, Hope, Loney, Lukens, & Junghans, 1983). Most people have a high opinion of themselves. They implicitly assume that other people who share their traits, values, and interests must be very likable (Kaplan & Anderson, 1973; Wetzel & Insko, 1982). People may overestimate the actual level of similarity between themselves and other people who are popular, but perception counts more than reality (Gold, Ryckman, & Mosley, 1984; Judd, Kenny, & Krosnick, 1983; Levinger & Breedlove, 1966; Sillars & Scott, 1983).

The similarity-attraction relationship may also rest on another unconscious and implicit assumption: namely, that people who are dissimilar to us are unlikable. The **repulsion hypothesis** maintains that people are initially, spontaneously repulsed by strangers who are very dissimilar to themselves (Rosenbaum, 1986). Attitudes and values that contradict our own are physiologically arousing (Burdick & Burnes, 1958; Clore & Gormly, 1974; Dickson & McGinnies, 1966; Gormly, 1974; Steiner, 1966). Just as we implicitly assume that people who are similar to us will probably like us and treat us well, so we implicitly assume that people who are very different from us will probably dislike us and treat us poorly (Gonzales et al., 1983). Thus initial dissimilarities can cut a relationship short. Students whose roommates initially disagree with them on important topics, for instance, ask to change their accommodations as soon as they can (Nudd, 1965). At our first meeting, we probably eliminate dissimilar strangers as potential friends and lovers (Byrne, Clore, & Smeaton, 1986).

Finally, similarity to self is a good criterion for developing enduring relationships (Carli, Ganley, & Pierce-Otay, 1991; Deutsch, Sullivan, Sage, & Basile, 1991). Early childhood attachment to the opposite-sex parent, who is similar to the self but not too similar, predisposes people to remain in relationships with spouses who remind them of mom or dad (Thiessen & Gregg, 1980). One study in Italy, for instance, found that women who were born to older fathers tended to marry older men (Zei, Astoffi, & Jayakai, 1981). We are also more comfortable with people who behave in familiar, predictable ways than with people who behave in unfamiliar, unpredictable ways. When monkeys reared in isolation are mixed with more socialized monkeys, they segregate themselves into separate groups (Pratt & Sackett, 1969). In human couples, those who are most similar to each other in physical attractiveness and other important characteristics at the start of the relationship are most likely to have fallen deeply in love six to nine months later (Hill, Rubin, & Peplau, 1976; White, 1980). In one study, newly married couples who were similar to each other on 70% of their physical and cultural traits were more likely to stay together and less likely to get separated or divorced than were couples who were initially less similar (Bentler & Newcomb, 1978). The more similar a husband and wife are, the more satisfied they usually are with their marriage (Caspi & Herbener, 1990).

SUMMARY OF WHY WE FIND SOME PEOPLE MORE ATTRACTIVE THAN OTHERS

Three characteristics make one potential partner more desirable than another. First, people like familiar others better than unfamiliar others, even when they are unaware of having seen the other person before. Familiarity in everyday life may influence interpersonal attraction simply because we see people more often when we live or work near them. Second, men are more likely than women to value physical attractiveness in a potential partner. Both sexes, however, are more heavily influenced by physical attractiveness than they think they are. One reason is that we implicitly equate physical attractiveness with other admirable qualities. Most people, however, are realistic about interpersonal attraction. They expect to find a partner whose physical attractiveness is approximately equal to their own. Third, people like others who are similar to themselves because they expect similar others to evaluate them positively and because they are initially repulsed by dissimilar others. Couples who are similar on important and relevant dimensions are more attached to each other.

Close Relationships

I magine that you are walking across campus on your way to class. It is a beautiful spring day. The sun is shining. Many other students are outside, talking in groups, taking the sun, playing with a Frisbee, and walking in various directions. Because you are thinking about other things, you do not at first notice that another student, *an attractive member of the opposite sex*, is walking toward you and seems to want to say something. You vaguely remember seeing this other student on campus, but you know that you have never been introduced. You stop to find out what the other student wants. Smiling broadly, the other student says, "I've been noticing you around campus. I find you to be very attractive. Would you go to bed with me tonight?"

How would you react to this "opening line"? Would you be offended? Would you tell the other student to "get lost"? Would you call a campus security guard? Would you laugh and treat the approach as a joke? Can you imagine any circumstance in which you would accept this proposition from a good-looking, obviously sincere stranger? Would you react differently depending on whether you are a man or a woman?

To find our how men and women react to different types of opening lines, two social psychologists staged a scenario exactly like the one that was just described (Clark & Hatfield, 1989). When they spotted a male or female student walking alone across campus during the day, they had an attractive confederate of the other sex approach that student. The confederate said, "I've been noticing you around campus. I find you to be very attractive," and continued in one of three ways, which were randomly chosen. In some cases, the confederate continued, "Would you go out with me tonight?" In other cases, the

Will this woman agree to go out on a date with a complete stranger?

confederate continued, "Would you come over to my apartment tonight?" In yet other cases, the confederate continued, "Would you go to bed with me tonight?"

Figure 10.1 shows the percentage of men and women who accepted each of these propositions, in three separate studies that were reported in 1978, 1982, and 1990 (Clark, 1990). As the figure shows, approximately half of the men and half of the women agreed to go out on a date that evening with a complete stranger who merely walked up to them, said they were attractive, and asked them out. As discussed in Chapter 9, both men and women have a strong "need to belong" (Baumeister & Leary, 1995). They are better adjusted both physically and psychologically when they are in a close relationship than when they are not (Burman & Margolin, 1992). It is not surprising, then, that 50% of college students were ready to enter what might develop into a close relationship with an attractive member of the opposite sex. The two sexes, however, responded very differently to requests to "come over to my apartment" or "go to bed with me."

No woman in any of the three studies agreed to go to bed with a stranger who had spoken only three sentences to her. A few women in the first and third studies agreed to go to the man's apartment. Men, in contrast, were very open to an explicit sexual invitation. Across studies, approximately 70% of men readily accepted an invitation to go to bed with the woman, with no questions asked. Their attitude seemed to be "Why do we have to wait until tonight?" (Clark & Hatfield, 1989, p. 52). Women were shocked to be approached with a direct request for sex. They tended to reply "You've got to be kidding" or "What's wrong with you?" whereas even the minority of men who turned down a direct invitation for sex felt that they had to make an excuse to the woman, such as "I can't tonight, but how about tomorrow night?"

Men and women clearly have different criteria for acceptable offers of a close relationship. Do men and women also use different strategies when they want to initiate a close relationship? What types of close relationships do men and women want? Are some types of relationships better for long-term commitment than others? Why do some couples break up and others stay committed to each other for a lifetime? What types of problems arise in close relationships? Are there both constructive and destructive reactions to those

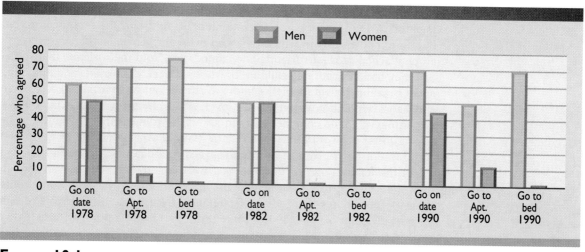

FIGURE 10.1 **Sex differences in responding to initiating strategies.**
Graph shows how college men and women at three times responded to "opening lines" from an opposite-sex stranger (Clark & Hatfield, 1989; Clark, 1990).

problems? These are a few of the important research questions that are described in this chapter, which is divided into three sections. The first section discusses research on how people initiate and deepen close relationships. The second describes the different types of close and not-so-close relationships that people have. The third describes how people cope with the inevitable problems that threaten relationships.

HOW DO PEOPLE INITIATE AND DEEPEN CLOSE RELATIONSHIPS?

Obviously, very few relationships begin with one person walking up to another and saying anything as explicit as "Would you go to bed with me tonight?" Nonetheless, all relationships have to start somewhere. Someone has to initiate a relationship before it has any chance of becoming closer and deeper. This first section of the chapter starts where relationships start. It first describes the mechanics of initiating a close relationship. Then it examines some factors that contribute to making a relationship closer and deeper.

INITIATING CLOSE RELATIONSHIPS

For a relationship to get off the ground, at least one person has to signal interest and the other person has to accept. Do men and women differ in the criteria they use for accepting offers of a close relationship? Also, what exactly do men and women do to signal their interest? Do men and women use different initiating strategies?

■ CRITERIA FOR ACCEPTANCE

When the experimenter in the 1990 study asked women why they did not agree to the man's request for a date, 37% of the refusers said they had a boyfriend, 34% said they did not know the man well enough, and 29% gave a variety of other reasons such as "I don't like being approached like that" or "I don't go out with aggressive people." Only one woman expressed any concern about sexually transmitted diseases. Was it merely that they were embarrassed to mention AIDS to a strange experimenter? To find out, the investigator conducted a fourth study in which he asked male and female confederates to call an unattached same-sex friend. The confederates told their friends that someone they had known since childhood, who had been depressed for a long time about breaking up with a high school sweetheart but was starting to date again and had a reputation as a fantastic lover, was coming to town (Clark, 1990, Experiment 2). The confederate then asked the friend either "Would you be willing to go out with him (or her)?" or "Would you be willing to go to bed with him (or her)?" Almost everyone agreed to a date: 50% of the males and 5% of the females agreed to go to bed with the stranger. Also, even though they were talking to a same-sex friend they had known for some time, only three of 44 women who refused gave sexually transmitted diseases as a reason for refusing. Fear of sexually transmitted diseases is not a primary reason why women refused direct offers for going to the man's apartment or going to bed with him.

A related question is why the men *didn't* refuse. As you read about the study, you might have wondered "What kind of woman would walk up to a strange man and ask him to go to bed? Wouldn't he think she must be very stupid?" The answer is that men and women use different characteristics to evaluate each other for different types of relationships (Williams, Munick, Saiz, & FormyDuval, 1995). The men in these studies might not have cared much about the woman's intellect, as long as they were only talking about a "one-night stand." In a relevant study, college students rated several characteristics on how important they were in an opposite-sex partner for different relationships such as a one-night stand or marriage (Kenrick, Groth, Trost, & Sadalla, 1993). As Figure 10.2 shows, women were more "choosy" than men for all types of relationships.

Especially striking, though, was how little importance men gave to a woman's intellect or agreeableness when the men were contemplating only a one-night stand. By far the most important characteristic that men required for a one-night stand was physical attractiveness, which is not shown in the figure because both men and women wanted a physically attractive partner for all relationships. For men who were considering a one-night stand, though, physical attractiveness was more than twice as important to them as the woman's intellect. When they were considering a woman for marriage, however, as the figure shows, men put just as much emphasis on intellect and agreeableness as

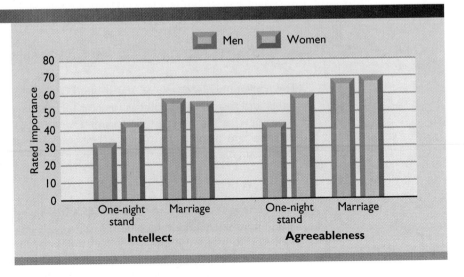

FIGURE 10.2

Men and women have different criteria for different types of relationships.

Graph shows men's and women's rated importance of characteristics in an opposite sex partner for two relationships (Kenrick, Groth, Trost, & Sadalla, 1993).

did women. Physical attractiveness may be an "early screening device" that men use for evaluating superficial relationships, but they apparently think twice when it comes to deeper commitment (Buss & Schmitt, 1993; Kenrick & Keefe, 1992).

■ SPECIFIC ACTIONS

We might also be interested, however, in exactly what men and women *do* to attract members of the opposite sex. What specific actions do they take to signal that they want a close relationship? The researchers in one study asked college men and women to answer these questions (Buss, 1988). Many of the specific actions that men and women listed were the same. Both sexes mentioned actions that were calculated to increase their exposure to members of the opposite sex (as though they had read the section on "mere exposure" in Chapter 9). Both men and women said they tell jokes and display humor. Both men and women said they display their sophistication in various ways and take whatever opportunity they get to touch the other person. Unfortunately, both men and women admitted that they do not always tell the truth.

Of greater interest were pronounced sex differences in the specific actions that men and women said they use to initiate relationships with members of the opposite sex. Figure 10.3 presents ten specific actions that men said they performed more than women and ten specific actions that women said they performed more than men. As you read these two lists, notice what they tell us about what specific actions men assume will favorably impress a woman and what specific actions women assume will favorably impress a man. The

FIGURE 10.3

Specific actions that men and women perform to make themselves attractive to members of the opposite sex (Buss, 1988).

10 Actions that men performed more frequently than women

He bragged about his accomplishments
He strutted in front of the group
He mentioned that he expected to earn a lot of money
He mentioned that he had a lot of status and prestige among his work colleagues
He talked about how good he was at sports
He showed off his driving skills
He looked at a woman repeatedly
He bought a woman dinner at a nice restaurant
He told her things she wanted to hear
He talked openly about having sex

10 Actions that women performed more frequently than men

She went on a diet to improve her figure
She wore stylish, fashionable clothes
She kept herself well-groomed
She got a new, interesting hairstyle
She used makeup that accentuated her looks
She spent more than one hour making her appearance pleasant
She lay out in the sun to get a tan
She wore perfume or cologne
She smiled a lot at a man
She was sympathetic to his troubles

men apparently thought that they had to brag, strut, and show off. They also thought that they had to pay considerable attention to the woman and make it plain that they were readily available for sex. The women, in contrast, apparently thought that they had to make themselves look as physically attractive as possible, smile, and be sympathetic.

The researchers asked a second group of male and female students to read the specific actions that the first group had mentioned and to rate each action on how effective they thought it would be in starting a relationship with the opposite sex. The second group of students agreed, for the most part, that the actions listed in Figure 10.3 work. They agreed that men have greater success in initiating relationships with women when the men brag about their accomplishments and pay close attention to a woman. They agreed that women have greater success in initiating relationships with men when they make themselves physically attractive and act sympathetic. Many people who read the list in Figure 10.3, however, wonder whether these strategies form the basis for a stable close relationship. As the years pass, what happens when the man's accomplishments are disappointing and he stops paying such close attention to the woman? What happens when the woman's physical attractiveness and patience wear thin? We leave these questions for later in the chapter. First, we need to examine how relatively superficial relationships develop into relationships that are closer and deeper.

DEEPENING COMMITMENT

Once a relationship has progressed beyond the initial initiating strategies, deeper commitment depends on at least three factors. Couples are more likely to develop a satisfactory, lasting relationship when they *rely* on each other, *support* each other, and *believe* in the relationship. Relying on each other involves interdependence. Support and belief are other important attributes of relationships that become deeper and closer.

■ INTERDEPENDENCE

When people rely on each other, social psychologists say that they have developed "interdependence" (Kelley, Berscheid, Christensen, Harvey, Huston, Levinger, McClintock, Peplau, & Peterson, 1983). **Interdependence** occurs when the couple agrees to be influenced by each other and to share their activities (Clark & Reis, 1988). Researchers often use a "Relationship Closeness Inventory" (RCI) to measure a couple's interdependence, whether the couple consists of friends or lovers (Berscheid, Snyder, & Omoto, 1989). The RCI asks the partners to estimate the amount of time they spend with each other, the number of activities that they do alone with the other person (such as preparing a meal, watching TV, eating a meal, exercising, going to a party, or having sexual relations), and the extent to which they are influenced by the other person in choosing how to spend money, their moods, where they live, their vacation plans, and so on. Whether measured by the RCI or by other assessment instruments, close relationships are marked by mutual influence and shared activities, whereas nonclose relationships are marked by independent decisions and not much time spent together.

In one study that used the RCI to predict the development of close relationships, people described the extent of mutual influence and shared activities for their closest interpersonal relationship (Berscheid et al., 1989). The researchers used these descriptions to categorize the relationships into those that exhibited low, medium, and high interdependence. Nine months later, almost

FRANK & ERNEST® by Bob Thaves

FRANK & ERNEST reprinted by permission of Newspaper Enterprise Association, Inc.

half of the relationships, all of which had been "my closest relationship" earlier, had dissolved. As predicted by the RCI scores, the low interdependence relationships were most likely to have broken up, the medium interdependence relationships were moderately likely to have broken up, and the high interdependence relationships were most likely to have endured.

In a related study, the researcher recruited couples whose marriage licenses had been published in a large daily newspaper (Kurdek, 1993). The husband and wife each completed a wide variety of questionnaires once a year for five years. One of the questions was whether the married couple pooled their finances. Did they maintain one bank account into which both contributed and from which both spent as needed, for instance, or did they each maintain separate bank accounts and each pay different bills? Obviously, couples who pooled their money were more financially interdependent than couples who did not. Other questions asked how much faith the husband and wife had in each other's continued support. One sample statement was "Though times may change and the future is uncertain, I have faith that my partner will always be ready and willing to offer me strength and support, come what may." Yet other questions asked how much the husband and wife derived intrinsic rewards from the relationship itself, for instance merely from "being close and together." The questions about pooled finances, faith in each other's support, and intrinsic rewards measured each couple's interdependence and reliance on each other at the start of the marriage.

During the five-year study, 64 couples dissolved their marriages and 222 remained together. As each of the 64 marriages dissolved, the researcher compared the couples' initial interdependence to the same measures in the 222 couples that remained together up to that time. Interdependence at the start of a newlywed couple's relationship predicted which couples were more likely to stay together. Stable marriages had greater initial interdependence in how likely they were to pool their resources, how much the husband and wife felt they could rely on each other for support, and how much merely being together gave the husband and wife intrinsic pleasure. The researcher also discovered that these and other measures of interdependence remained relatively stable across the five years for couples who stayed together. You could "see it coming" even before the relationship dissolved, however, when interdependence started to decrease from one year to the next. Marriages are more likely to last when couples maintain their initial interdependence and continue to rely on each other. Couples who stay married into their sixties, for instance, typically narrow their outside interests and become emotionally closer to their spouses (Levenson, Carstensen, & Gottman, 1994).

■ MUTUAL SUPPORT

Couples who stay together and deepen their commitment to the relationship do not merely have faith in each other's support. They also get it. Happily married couples who have developed a deep commitment compliment each other, try to bolster their partners' self-esteem, listen to their partners' problems, provide empathy, try to lift their partners' moods when he or she is "down," and help their partners to reinterpret situations in ways that are not damaging to the partners' self-esteem (Barbee & Cunningham, in press). Regardless of how the relationship goes, they believe that their relationship has more positive and fewer negative qualities than other people's relationships (Van Lange & Rusbult, 1995).

Couples who stay together also make up stories that turn their partners' faults into virtues. In a relevant study, the investigators asked college students who had an ongoing close relationship to choose between "my partner rarely initiates disagreements over the activities we may share" and "my partner is not particularly concerned with preserving harmony in our interactions . . . [and] . . . frequently initiates disagreements over the activities we may share" (Murray & Holmes, 1993, in press). As expected, almost all students indicated that their partners seldom initiated disagreements. Next, however, these students read a psychology journal article that described how mature intimacy depended on partners being willing to engage issues by initiating disagreements. The psychology journal article implied that the student's partner was hurting the relationship by avoiding conflict. After they read the article, students were given ten minutes to write narratives describing the development of intimacy in their relationship. The students wrote narratives that integrated their partner's negative attribute (avoiding conflict) into stories about being responsive and caring. They claimed that conflict was infrequent in the past but increasing, as in "I feel he is facilitating our growth by increasingly being able to tell me when he disagrees." They claimed that conflict might be infrequent, but also very meaningful, as in "We've only had three disagreements . . . we were able to get to the root of the problem, talk it out, and we managed to emerge from it closer than before." They also claimed that lack of conflict had positive aspects, as in "I could tell that a problem existed, but she refused to talk about it . . . on the other hand, she is very receptive to my needs, and willing to adapt if necessary. This is beneficial to our relationship." In other words, they imaginatively reinterpreted their relationship history to claim that their partners' supposed fault (avoiding conflict) was actually more of a virtue.

When inevitable conflicts arise, deeply committed spouses make "benign" rather than "nonbenign" attributions for their partner's behavior (Fincham & Bradbury, 1992). If a wife momentarily loses her temper and yells at her husband, for instance, a benign attribution might be that "She had a hard day at the office." A nonbenign attribution might be that "She's a short-tempered person." As described in Chapter 4, which deals with attribution, the benign attribution for a negative behavior is that the cause is external and unstable ("Something external to her made her do it this once"). The nonbenign attribution for a negative behavior is that the cause is internal and stable ("She did it because that's the kind of person she is, and it's not going to change").

As you might suspect from these examples, benign attributions help relationships to endure. In one study, couples who made benign attributions for each other's behavior were less likely to get angry when they worked on a problem together. They were also more likely to have stayed together one year later than couples who initially made nonbenign attributions (Fincham & Bradbury, 1993). Benign and nonbenign attributions can also be specific to a relationship. People who are depressed often blame themselves when things go wrong and some people have characteristic attributional styles in which they routinely try to blame someone else (Forgas, 1994a; see also Chapter 4). Even so, attributional style within a specific relationship affects both partners' commitment to that relationship beyond what we might expect from their attributional style in other situations (Karney, Bradbury, Fincham, & Sullivan, 1994; Sarason, Sarason, & Pierce, 1994). When a husband or wife says "You're yelling because you've had a hard day at the office," the relationship goes more smoothly than when a husband or wife says "You're yelling because you're a jerk!"

Some studies suggest that wives are more likely than husbands to monitor the tone and content of what they say to each other. Wives may be more concerned than husbands about the future of the relationship. Also, women are more skilled than men at interpersonal communications and detecting problems in relationships (Duck, Rutt, Hurst, & Strejc, 1991; Hill, Rubin, & Peplau, 1979). Perceptions of social support in marriage are more closely related to marital satisfaction for wives than for husbands, both in younger and in older couples (Acitelli & Antonucci, 1994; Julien & Markman, 1991). It is not surprising, then, that the wife's health often suffers more than the husband's when the marriage is in trouble (Levenson, Carstensen, & Gottman, 1993). The important factor is probably "psychological femininity," which means thinking more like a woman than like a man. Regardless of their biological sex, husbands and wives who display greater psychological femininity are less likely to snap at their mates when things go wrong. They are also more likely to initiate behaviors that are constructive than destructive for the relationship (Rusbult, Verette, Whitney, Slovik, & Lipkus, 1991). It is small wonder, as reported in Chapter 9, that both men and women are less likely to feel lonely when they spend much time with women (Wheeler et al., 1983).

■ BELIEF IN THE RELATIONSHIP

Finally, deep commitment and a lasting relationship depend on the beliefs, attitudes, and expectations that couples have, both about themselves and about the relationship (Fehr, 1993, 1994; Fincham, 1994; Fletcher & Fitness, 1990). When people enter romantic relationships, they have "mental models" of how they will act in the relationship and what their partner will be like (Fletcher & Thomas, in press; Rusbult, Onizuka, & Lipkus, 1993). They have expectations for the level of intimacy, passion, and individuality that will characterize the relationship (Fletcher & Kininmonth, 1992). Strongly held beliefs about relationships are more "automatic" than weakly held beliefs (see the discussion of automaticity in Chapter 2). They come to mind easily, even under "cognitive load" conditions that would disrupt more deliberative thinking (Fletcher, Rosanowski, & Fitness, 1994—see studies of attitude accessibility in Chapter 6). Newlyweds who lived together or dated for a long time before they were married probably begin their marriages with more realistic "mental models" of what the relationship will entail, so they stay together longer (Huston, McHale, & Crouter, 1986; Kurdek, 1993).

Realistic and securely held beliefs at the beginning of a marriage can insulate people from later problems. Spouses who are secure in their mental models are less likely to reject each other when problems arise. They also listen more to what the other person has to say (Kobak & Hazan, 1991). In one study of couples who had their first baby, partners who found themselves doing more of the extra work than they had anticipated became more dissatisfied with their relationships than did partners who had more realistic expectations (Hackel &

Ruble, 1992). The only exception to the rule was wives who had traditional sex-role attitudes. Traditional sex-role attitudes are, for example, that the man's career is more important than the woman's and that the woman has major responsibility for care of the children. When they found themselves doing more of the extra work than they anticipated before they had a baby, women with traditional sex-role attitudes became *more,* not less, committed to the marriage. This unusual discrepancy may help to explain why, in a 15-year study that tried to predict the success of college romances from college sex-role attitudes, many romances went sour before marriage and many ended in separation or divorce, but not one woman who had traditional sex-role attitudes while dating was ever divorced after marrying her childhood sweetheart (Peplau, Hill, & Rubin, 1993).

SUMMARY OF HOW PEOPLE INITIATE AND DEEPEN CLOSE RELATIONSHIPS

Both men and women enter close relationships readily. Men, however, have more lenient criteria for considering a "one-night stand" than do women. Men care just as much as do women about a prospective marriage partner's intellect and agreeableness. They care very little about a woman's intellect or agreeableness, however, when they are considering her merely for a one-night stand.

To signal their availability for a relationship, men brag about their accomplishments and pay close attention to a woman. Women enhance their physical appearance and lend a sympathetic ear. Once a relationship has begun, it becomes closer and deeper through growing interdependence, mutual support, and belief in the relationship. Interdependence occurs when people agree to be mutually influenced by each other and to share their activities. Marriages last longer, for instance, when couples have joint bank accounts than when they keep their money separate. Mutual support involves trying to bolster the partner's self-esteem, listening to the partner's problems, providing empathy, cheering the partner up, and making benign attributions that turn some of the partner's faults into virtues. Marriages last longer, for instance, when a husband or wife says "You're yelling because you had a hard day at the office" rather than "You're yelling because you're a jerk." Wives (and men who are psychologically "feminine") are usually better than husbands (and men who are psychologically "masculine") at offering mutual support. Finally, both men and women have relatively "automatic" beliefs about the characteristics of close relationships. Marriages last longer when those beliefs are realistic rather than unrealistic.

WHAT TYPES OF CLOSE RELATIONSHIPS DO PEOPLE HAVE?

One of the major themes that runs through several chapters of this book is that people have both a personal identity and a social identity (Abrams, 1992; Brewer, 1991; Cousins, 1989; Crocker, Luhtanen, Blaine, & Broadnax, 1994; Deaux, 1993; Ethier & Deaux, 1994; Markus & Kitayama, 1994; Miller & Prentice, 1994; Oyserman, 1993; Trafimow, Triandis, & Goto, 1991; Turner, Oakes, Haslam, & McGarty, 1994). Sometimes people think about themselves as individuals. They have a personal identity, in which they see themselves as a collection of unique, individual characteristics (Markus & Kitayama, 1994). At other times, people think about themselves as indistinguishable from a group. They have a "collective" or social identity (Tajfel, 1981; Turner, 1991). Cultures also differ in whether they emphasize the personal identity or the social identity. Individualistic cultures such as those of the United States, Canada, Great Britain, the Netherlands, Australia, and New Zealand emphasize the personal identity. Collectivistic cultures such as those of China, Japan, Korea, Pakistan, Jamaica, and countries in West Africa emphasize the social identity (Hofstede, 1983).

If a marriage or other close relationship between two people can be called a "group," then close relationships also differ in whether they emphasize the personal identity or the social identity. Some couples regard their relationship as a partnership, in which partners share equally in costs and benefits (Clark, Mills, & Powell, 1986). If the relationship is to continue, they want to know that they are getting as much out of it as they are putting in—that the relationship advances their personal identity. Other couples regard their relationship as one indivisible unit, not two separate individuals (Clark et al., 1986; Diener, 1980; Karau & Williams, 1993). They rejoice every bit as much when their partner is happy as when they are happy as individuals, because they experience a sense of "we-ness." The relationship advances their social identity as part of the couple.

This section of the chapter identifies close relationships as emphasizing either the personal identity or the social identity. First, we review evidence that social relationships of all types have one or more of four basic structures. These four basic "structures of social life" recur in cultures across the world and apply to close relationships as well as to work, play, or any other activity in which two or more people interact. Second, we examine a specific application of the four basic structures—namely, exchange versus communal orientations toward close relationships.

STRUCTURES OF SOCIAL LIFE

The top part of Table 10.1 shows four types of social relationships that people around the world have with each other. These four types of social relationships or structures of social life entail different motives and have different characteristics. The bottom part of Table 10.1 shows how the four basic structures help us to identify four types of close relationships. The table uses marriage to illustrate how close relationships differ, but the four basic structures of social life apply as well to close relationships within unmarried couples.

■ FOUR BASIC STRUCTURES

The first type of social relationship, **communal sharing**, involves sharing with others without expecting a specific favor in return. Communal sharing is prevalent in many collectivistic cultures around the world, where people share even scarce resources freely. In villages on the edge of the African desert where water is very scarce, for example, everyone feels free to use the public water as

TABLE 10.1	Four Types of Social Relationships and Four Types of Marriages (Abstracted from Fiske, 1991, 1992)

TYPES OF SOCIAL RELATIONSHIPS

Type	Motive	Characteristics	Examples
Communal Sharing	enhance group identity, sense of community, and solidarity	share resources with one's own kind without expecting specific reciprocation	people who share food, drinking water, or public space that all feel free to use
Authority Ranking	maintaining separate duties and responsibilities, civic stability	give tribute to higher-ranking people or protect subordinates simply because of their acknowledged position in hierarchy	military ranks in wartime; charismatic leaders and their disciples
Equality Matching	ensure equal status for participants	take turns, make equal contributions, find evenly matched relationships rewarding for their own sake	members of a car pool or baby-sitting co-op; voters in an election
Market Pricing	maximize the individual's gains relative to his/her costs	exchange according to a ratio principle that allows comparison of unlike commodities; make "rational" decisions	stock or commodity exchanges; anonymous employer-employee relationships

TYPES OF MARRIAGES

Type	Characteristics	First Spouse's View	Second Spouse's View
Communal Sharing	merging of selves; sharing of body, time, space, interests, values; selfless mutual caring	"We are one. What helps you helps us; what hurts you hurts us"	"We are one. What helps you helps us; what hurts you hurts us."
Authority Ranking	one spouse has control over and responsibility for the other; one spouse has higher status than the other	"I take responsibility for taking care of you, so I expect to have the last word"	"You have responsibility for taking care of me, so you can have the last word"
Equality Matching	spouses have equal rights and say, contribute equally, take turns at child care and housework; have distinct, coequal personalities	"You and I are separate people; each wants to contribute a fair and equal share to the marriage"	"You and I are separate people; each wants to contribute a fair and equal share to the marriage"
Market Pricing	spouses engage in "horse trading;" give as few concessions as possible and try to get the best possible terms	"I want the best of any exchange that involves sex, money, companionship, or entertainment"	"I want the best of any exchange that involves sex, money, companionship, or entertainment"

Why will this woman carry a heavy jug of water for many backbreaking miles and then share it freely with anyone who is thirsty?

needed (Fiske, 1990). When all the water is gone during a drought, villagers have to walk miles to get water and carry it back. When they do, the water is shared equally by all. The villagers do not share their food, water, grazing land, and other scarce commodities so freely because they "do not know any better." Many of them go away for a while to work for money in distant cities. They know that in other cultures time and work may be exchanged for money and goods. Nonetheless, they usually return to live in their home villages. They prefer living in a culture where a sense of community and group solidarity is enhanced by allowing all group members to take what they need. Communal sharing is evident in the "norm of loyalty" in which people are expected to help their own kind with no thought of reciprocation. Communal sharing emphasizes social identity. Group members feel satisfied when the group does well rather than when they do well as individuals.

The second type of social relationship, authority ranking, is prevalent in collectivistic cultures that maintain a strict hierarchy. In **authority ranking,** those "on top" make decisions and are responsible for those "on the bottom," who loyally follow orders (Fiske, 1991). When such an arrangement is voluntary rather than coercive, people at all ranks want to maintain a hierarchical division of duties and responsibilities, without trying to "beat the system" or gain personal advantage. In many traditional cultures, younger members of the community provide work, goods, and other tribute to their elders simply to show respect. The elders usually assume a responsibility to protect and provide for their subordinates, but they are under no obligation to do so. No one is counting. Authority ranking, like communal sharing, emphasizes social identity. Group members feel satisfied when the group does well rather than when they do well as individuals.

The third type of social relationship, **equality matching,** reflects a tendency of many human beings around the world to enjoy dealing with others on an equal footing, matching contributions equally (Fiske, 1991). When extra resources are available, people in both collectivistic and individualistic cultures often prefer to distribute those resources evenly. When it is time to harvest the crops or construct new public buildings, they take turns doing the work. They take pride in matching each other's contributions. They would be upset if they thought that someone else was contributing more time or resources, because doing so would spoil the pleasure of an equal relationship. An emphasis on equality matching may be seen in the "norm of reciprocity," wherein people are expected to return favors in kind, but not in excess (Gergen, Ellsworth, Maslach, & Seipel, 1975; Gouldner, 1960). Equality matching may emphasize the personal identity slightly more than the social identity. In equality matching, people keep strict count of what they are contributing to a social relationship, because they do not want to be outdone.

The fourth type of social relationship depicted in Table 10.1, market pricing, is perhaps the most familiar to residents of individualistic cultures such as those of the United States, Canada, New Zealand, Australia, and Western Europe. In **market pricing,** dissimilar commodities such as time, labor, skills, knowledge, objects, land, and even physical attractiveness are all assigned "values" and can be exchanged according to a universal standard such as money. People in market-pricing cultures relate to each other in a "rational" way by comparing alternatives and by bargaining until they have obtained a satisfactory ratio between costs and benefits. The more an individual can minimize his or her costs and maximize his or her gains, the more "rational" and satisfactory the exchange. Market pricing clearly emphasizes the personal identity. Individuals in market-pricing relationships keep track of both what they give and what they get, so that they can maximize the difference between their individual gains and their individual costs.

Interestingly, "in most societies throughout most of history, people have engaged in market pricing-transactions less frequently, and have valued them less, than they have any of the other three forms of interchange" (Fiske, 1991, p. 187). In many cultures around the world, market pricing is restricted to certain kinds of exchanges with strangers or is exhibited only toward enemies. In those cultures, people share freely with any other group member who is in need (communal sharing). They give and follow orders because they value a hierarchical system (authority ranking). They want to feel that they have contributed as much as anyone else (equality matching). People who have always lived in communal-sharing cultures, for instance, find it inconceivable that human beings would not freely share their food with each other (Fiske, 1995). They share with and mutually support each other primarily to sustain valued social relationships and not with any expectation of reciprocation or personal gain (Fiske, 1990, 1992).

■ APPLICABILITY TO CLOSE RELATIONSHIPS

As the bottom of Table 10.1 shows, the four basic structures of social life apply very well to describing and categorizing marriages and other close relationships (Fiske, 1992). Communal-sharing marriages entail a "merging of selves," in which two people become one. The two people function more as a couple than as individuals. They are interdependent, believe in the relationship as a single unit, and provide unfailing mutual support. They share bank accounts, do almost everything together, and care for each other selflessly.

Other marriages entail authority ranking. One spouse takes care of the other, but the arrangement is not mutual. One spouse makes the final decisions, which the other spouse accepts in return for being taken care of. Although logically either spouse might have the higher status, Chapter 9 described how men have traditionally controlled the resources in authority-ranking cultures. When two people who value traditional sex roles marry, they tend to favor an arrangement in which the man goes to work, handles the finances, and makes the ultimate decisions. The woman stays home, cares for the children, spends whatever money her husband provides, and acknowledges her husband's authority.

Many modern, less traditional marriages, however, entail equality matching. In "peer marriages," the husband and wife have equal rights and accord each other equal respect. They take turns caring for children and doing onerous chores around the house. They also develop their own distinct friends and interests (Schwartz, 1994). Neither spouse tries to take advantage of the other or "get the best of the deal." Instead, the spouses strive to match each other's contributions equally. Peer marriages might increasingly supplant authority-ranking marriages as women gain equal access to resources (Schwartz, 1994).

Finally, many modern marriages in individualistic cultures entail market pricing. A few years back, only Hollywood stars signed prenuptial legal contracts that described in detail how much each party expected to contribute to and take from a marriage. Today, the practice is increasingly common. A market-pricing approach to marriage is a form of barter or *exchange*. Each spouse retains a distinct personal identity and tries to advance that personal identity by giving few concessions and trying to get the best possible deal. In how much they emphasize the personal identity versus the social identity, market-pricing marriages and close relationships are very different from communal-sharing marriages and close relationships. It is not surprising, then, that researchers in social psychology have found it especially useful to compare close relationships that have an exchange versus communal orientation.

EXCHANGE VERSUS COMMUNAL ORIENTATIONS

One way of thinking about interdependence in a close relationship is that the partners influence each other in the same way that two negotiators influence each other. They barter and exchange contributions and rewards. They take an **exchange orientation,** in which each partner calculates his or her own costs and benefits of remaining in the relationship. People who live in market-pricing cultures often require equity, or an even exchange of benefits. They act like accountants or bank managers. If they believe that they are being cheated, that they are putting more into a relationship than they are getting out of it, then they start to withdraw from the relationship. They cast about for an alternative relationship that might entail a fairer exchange of costs and benefits (Kelley et al. 1983).

Chapter 9 surveyed evidence from "lonely hearts" advertisements, in which women who considered themselves beautiful were the most explicit about demanding that potential male partners be well off financially. Men who had considerable resources were just as explicit in specifying that they wanted to hear only from physically attractive women. From a market-pricing or "exchange" perspective, these men and women were simply insisting on a fair or equitable bargain. They knew that they had what the opposite sex wanted, so they insisted on getting what they wanted, which is exactly how market-pricing or "exchange" cultures work (Fiske, 1991). Equity theory operates in sharing activities as well. Partners often share many interests but have a few interests that are unique to one or the other of the partners. They usually arrive at an equitable arrangement where, to use the cultural stereotype, the wife agrees to go to the race track with her husband in the afternoon, as long as he agrees to attend the ballet with her that evening. Especially when people believe that they might be at a power disadvantage, they become very attuned to who is "getting the best" of any social arrangement (Bugental, Blue, Cortez, Fleck, Kopeikin, Lewis, & Lyon, 1993).

An alternative way of thinking about interdependence in a close relationship is that the partners share in a valued social identity. They take a **communal orientation,** in which partners do not keep track of their individual costs and benefits, because they regard themselves as having merged into a unit. Even people who live in market-pricing cultures and take an exchange perspective on their activities at work sometimes make an exception in the perspective they take toward their marriage or other close relationship. They share everything freely with their partner, because sharing with their partner is like sharing with themselves. They regard it as impossible that one partner should get more than the other out of the relationship, because when one benefits, so does the other (Clark & Mills, 1979).

One partner might share the other's preferred activities, for instance, because being together is what matters, not who "wins." Besides sharing their bank accounts, as previously discussed, people in some close relationships share everything, even remembering things for each other (Wegner, Erber, & Raymond, 1991). Lovers, and those who want to become lovers, often do things for the other person without expecting any compensation. If the races were held in the evening at the same time as the ballet, for instance, the wife might agree to an evening at the races just to make her husband happy. If the husband were to say "In exchange for your agreeing to go to the races with me, here's $100 to buy a new dress," the wife would probably be very upset. The point of making a sacrifice for a loved one is that you do not expect anything in return. Turning the arrangement into a crass "money-for-doing-what-I-want" affair would alter the nature of the relationship (Clark & Waddell, 1983; Hatfield, Traupmann, Sprecher, Utne, & Hay, 1985).

These examples suggest that partners can take either an exchange orientation or a communal orientation toward their relationship. In an exchange relationship, each partner expects to get as much as he or she gives. In a communal relationship, each partner cares more about the total pleasure that accrues to the partnership, considered as a unit, than about his or her own personal gain. As suggested by one of the major themes of this book (see Chapter 1), partners in exchange relationships each retain a personal identity, whereas partners in communal relationships develop a social identity in which "they are one."

KEEPING SCORE

One way to tell the difference between an exchange and a communal relationship is that people in exchange relationships keep track of how much they each contribute. A clever experiment showed that opposite-sex strangers send subtle signals to each other about whether they want an exchange relationship or a communal relationship (Clark, 1984, Study 1). In the experiment, male college students thought that they were participating in a study of "workers' performance and attitudes." The other participant was "Paula," a very beautiful woman of their own age who was actually a confederate. On a questionnaire that the man was allowed to read, Paula indicated either that her husband was picking her up immediately after the experiment or that she was single, had recently transferred to the university, and was eager to meet people. In other words, Paula's questionnaire responses were calculated to make the man think that she was or was not available for a possible close relationship. The experiment's hypothesis was that men who did not think Paula was available for a close relationship would send a signal that they wanted an exchange relationship with her. Men who thought Paula was available for a close relationship would send an equally strong signal that they wanted a communal relationship.

The experimenter explained that the male student and Paula were to take turns trying to find specific numbers that were embedded in a huge array of numbers. The male student and Paula would later split their team's reward, which depended on how many numbers the two of them (combined) could find. Paula, who always went first, circled some of the embedded numbers but left many of them for the man to find. To make her circles she used either a red pen or a black pen. When the man's turn came, he found on his desk two pens—one red and one black. If he used a different color pen from Paula's, it would be obvious how many numbers each of them contributed to the team's total score. If he used the same color pen as Paula had used, it would be impossible to keep track of their separate contributions. As predicted, 88.2 % of the men who thought that Paula was unavailable for romance chose the opposite color pen from Paula's. By doing so, they sent a clear signal that "We will have the kind of relationship where we keep track of our separate contributions." In sharp contrast, 88.5 % of the men who thought that Paula was "available" as a possible romantic partner chose the same color she had used. By doing so, they sent a signal that "We will have the kind of relationship where no one is counting contributions, because (I hope) we are going to merge our separate identities."

EXPECTING RECIPROCATION

People who have communal relationships share their emotions more readily than do people who have exchange relationships (Clark & Taraban, 1991). They are also more likely to watch for signs that the partner needs help. In a follow-up experiment that used a scenario similar to that of the "red pen" experiment, Paula and the male college student worked in separate rooms on making four-letter words out of letters that they had available to them (Clark, Mills, & Powell, 1986). The men learned that Paula's task was more difficult than theirs. Paula had only the letters A–L to work with, whereas the men had all the letters A–Z. Paula could put notes in a slot between the two rooms, asking the man to give her certain letters that she desperately needed. Because she placed her notes in a felt-lined box that made no noise, the man had to get up from his own task and walk across the room every time he wanted to see whether Paula needed help. Doing so cost him money, because in this experiment he and Paula were rewarded separately for the number of words they had each constructed. Also, half of the men in each condition learned that they would later switch places with Paula. When they switched places, the man would have the more difficult task and would need to send Paula notes asking her to give him letters. The other half of the men thought that they and Paula would keep their own tasks. Paula would never be able to reciprocate their help.

Men who thought that Paula was unavailable for romance presumably foresaw only an exchange relationship with her. They checked on Paula's possible needs almost twice as often when they thought that she could later reciprocate by giving them letters as when they thought that she would never be able to make it a fair or equitable exchange. If Paula was going to be able to help them in return, they were willing to take time out from their own tasks, lowering their own rewards, to keep track of her needs. If Paula would never be able to help them, they checked on her needs an average of just once in ten minutes and then said "She's out of luck." Men who saw Paula as a potential romantic partner, in contrast, did not care whether she would later be able to reciprocate their help or not. They were equally likely to leave their task to check on Paula's needs when she would have no opportunity to reciprocate as when she would. In communal relationships, the social identity prevails. Any benefits that come to one partner are benefits for both.

■ CONSEQUENCES OF ORIENTATION

Romantic relationships are more successful when the partners take a communal rather than an exchange orientation toward their relationship (Prins, Buunk, & Van Yperen, 1993). In one relevant study, married couples completed a questionnaire that measured how much of an exchange orientation each had (Buunk & Van Yperen, 1991). An exchange orientation consists of agreeing with such items as "I feel resentful if I believe I spent more on a friend's present than she spent on mine," "I resent being asked for help with someone else's responsibilities, because I don't ask anyone to help with my responsibilities," and "It is only with money which I earn that I feel I can spend it as I desire" (Murstein, Cerreto, & MacDonald, 1977). People who have a low exchange orientation presumably have a communal orientation (Clark & Mills, 1979). The married couples also indicated whether they thought that they got more out of their marriage than they contributed, got less than they contributed, or had an equal arrangement.

Finally, the spouses each indicated how satisfied he or she was with the marriage. As shown in Figure 10.4, spouses who had an exchange orientation were less satisfied with their marriages than were their more communally oriented peers, regardless of how much equity they perceived in the relationship.

FIGURE 10.4

Exchange orientations threaten marriages.

Graph shows (adjusted) marital satisfaction of people with two different orientations when they perceived different outcomes in a relationship (Buunk & Van Yperen 1991).

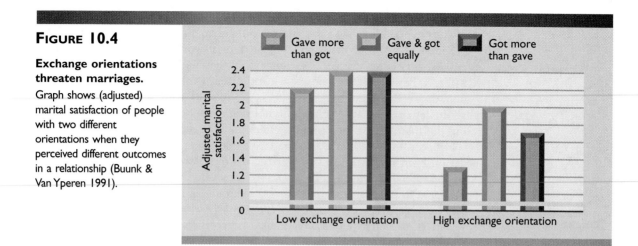

They were especially dissatisfied when they perceived the relationship as unequal, *even when the inequity was that they got more than they gave.* Perceived equity of the exchange did not matter for spouses low in exchange orientation, presumably because they saw themselves and their spouses as a communal unit. Anything that benefited one, benefited them both (Aron et al., 1991). Interestingly, women who were high in exchange orientation were even more dissatisfied than men when they perceived the marriage arrangements as inequitable (Buunk & Van Yperen, 1991).

Who stays married longer, couples who have separate bank accounts or couples who have joint bank accounts?

SUMMARY OF THE TYPES OF CLOSE RELATIONSHIPS

All social relationships fall into one or more of four basic types. These four basic types or "structures of social life" include communal sharing, authority ranking, equality matching, and market pricing. They characterize all types of relationships in diverse cultures across the world. Communal sharing, which involves a communal orientation, emphasizes the social identity. In communal-sharing relationships, people merge their separate identities into a single unit. They benefit when the group benefits. Market pricing, which involves an exchange orientation, emphasizes the personal identity. In market-pricing relationships, people retain and try to advance their separate, distinct identities. They benefit from a relationship when they minimize their costs and maximize their gains. These four basic structures of social life also characterize marriages and other close relationships.

Close relationships that have an exchange orientation differ from close relationships that have a communal orientation in several ways. Partners in exchange relationships keep track of their individual costs and benefits. Partners in communal relationships do not have to keep track of individual costs and benefits, because they view themselves as a unit. Furthermore, partners in exchange relationships support each other more when they know that the other person can reciprocate than when they know that the other person cannot reciprocate. Partners in communal relationships, in contrast, support each other without regard to whether the other person can reciprocate. The evidence suggests that communal relationships facilitate stable, long-lasting close relationships.

HOW DO PEOPLE COPE WITH PROBLEMS IN CLOSE RELATIONSHIPS?

As the study of marital satisfaction (Figure 10.4) suggests, not all close relationships have such a communal orientation that each partner is willing to sacrifice so that the other partner can benefit. Relationships in an individualistic "exchange" culture pose significant problems for men and women who value their autonomy and personal control over their lives (Dion & Dion, 1993). Even relationships that begin on a communal basis sometimes "turn sour." In this final part of the chapter, we discuss the reasons why relationships sometimes break up and the actions that men and women take that upset each other and threaten the relationship. We also discuss common reactions to the problems that inevitably arise, even within the closest of relationships.

PROBLEM BEHAVIORS

When married couples separate or get divorced, who or what do they blame? In a study conducted in New Zealand, men and women who had been separated from their spouses for less than 18 months were asked to explain, in their own words, why the marriage broke up (Fletcher, 1983). Their answers were tape recorded and later scored for the extent to which the primary cause fit into one of six categories. Almost one-third (31.5%) of the respondents blamed themselves. They said that the marriage did not work because "I'm such a jealous person" or because "I was too selfish." An additional 45.3% blamed their ex-spouse, as in "He did not help me around the house" or "She spent too much money." Almost 8% of them blamed an external influence to which they had been subjected, such as "Work pressure started to pile up on me" or "I was never the same after that car accident." Approximately 7% blamed an external influence to which their ex-spouse had been subjected, such as "Her mother put pressure on her to leave" or "His job kept him away from home most of the time." Another 6.5% blamed aspects of their own or the ex-spouse's background, such as "She was spoiled by her parents as a child" or "He could never get over being poor when he was growing up." Finally, 1.6% blamed having the wrong reasons for marriage, as in "I got married because I wanted security" or "I married him to get away from my family." People who broke off the relationship blamed themselves more than did people whose spouses took the initiative, and women were more likely than men to blame their ex-spouse. For both sexes, however, the most frequent cause was something that the ex-spouse had or had not done (see also Fletcher, Fincham, Cramer, & Heron, 1987).

■ UPSETTING ACTIONS

In an analysis of the specific actions that upset and anger close relationship partners in the United States, some interesting sex differences emerged (Buss, 1989b). In the relevant study, men and women who were either dating or had been married less than one year listed the specific actions their partners performed that irritated, annoyed, angered, or upset them. Many of the specific upsetting actions fell into four categories: being possessive, inconsiderate, abusive, and neglecting. Possessive actions included "demanded too much attention" and "demanded too much of my time." Inconsiderate actions included "left the toilet seat up (or down)," "did not help me clean up," and "yelled at me." Abusive actions included "slapped me," "verbally abused me," and "called me nasty names." Neglecting actions included "would not spend enough time with me," "did not tell me that he (or she) loved me," and "ignored my feelings."

The left panel of Figure 10.5 shows the proportion of men and women in dating couples who reported that their partner upset them by engaging in possessive, inconsiderate, abusive, or neglecting actions. As the figure shows, partners who were dating engaged in very few of these problem behaviors and sex differences were nonexistent or slight. The right panel of Figure 10.5 shows the proportion of newlywed men and women who reported that their partner upset them by engaging in the same four types of actions. Although the overall level of upsetting actions was not much different from the dating couples, large sex differences emerged within the first year of marriage. First, newly married women upset men more than newly married men upset women by possessive actions. Recall from the first section of this chapter that women who wanted to initiate close relationships with men lent a sympathetic ear and that men bragged about their accomplishments. Once they were married, however, women may have discovered that many of the man's boasts were unfounded. Sensing problems with the relationship, women may have demanded that the man pay at least as much attention as he did when they were dating. When women made these demands, the men got angry, irritated, and upset by such "possessive" behavior.

The right panel of Figure 10.5 also shows an enormous increase among newly married couples of men upsetting women by being inconsiderate. Ac-

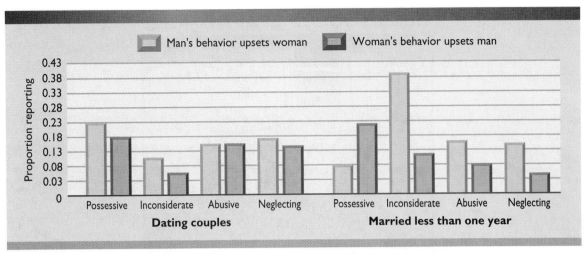

FIGURE 10.5 Men and women in dating vs. married couples are upset about different partner behaviors. Graph shows rates of being upset by the man or woman engaging in each behavior (Buss, 1989b).

cording to the women, their new husband's inconsiderate actions went well beyond merely leaving the toilet seat up. The women were angry about their husband not helping them clean up, belching or burping loudly, yelling at them, and teasing them about how long it took them to get dressed (the very action that they initially used to attract him). The other notable sex difference came in actions that newlyweds perceived as neglecting. Recall that men who wanted to attract women paid a great deal of attention to them. Among dating couples, men are not perceived as significantly more neglecting than women. Among newlyweds, however, women perceive men as being much more neglecting than men perceive women. The analysis of specific upsetting actions provides important clues to why so many marriages end in divorce.

Cultures differ widely in how willing people are to dissolve a marriage that is not working. In the United States, for instance, 35% agree that "If love has completely disappeared from a marriage, I think it is probably best for the couple to make a clean break and start new lives." An equal 35% disagree (Levine

Would marriages last longer if men thought more like women or if women thought more like men?

Ballard Street by Jerry Van Amerongen

... There followed a tense conversation, whereupon it was decided that Jerome felt there were too many pigs.

By permission of Jerry Van Amerongen and Creators Syndicate.

et al., 1994). (The rest are undecided.) In Brazil, in contrast, 78% agree with the statement and only 13% disagree. One of the most frequently cited reasons for breaking up a relationship, regardless of which culture we study, is that the husband and wife are no longer communicating effectively (Hortacsu & Karanci, 1987; Sprecher, in press). When men take a traditional sex role "macho" attitude and refuse to talk about the relationship, a marriage is in trouble, because wives become upset (Acitelli, 1992; Ickes, 1993b). When they do discuss their problems, negative statements (by either the husband or the wife) only make matters worse. Wives whose husbands make inconsiderate or abusive negative remarks early in a marriage make more negative remarks themselves as the relationship progresses (Huston & Vangelisti, 1991). In one study, the investigators rated the statements that husbands and wives made as they discussed a problem in their marriage. Compared to couples who made positive, constructive comments laced with humor, those who criticized, put the other person down, and complained were more likely four years later to be dissatisfied with their marriage. They were also more likely to have had health problems and be separated or divorced (Gottman & Levenson, 1992; Ickes, 1993b; Nadler & Dotan, 1992).

■ JEALOUSY

One of the biggest dangers to any relationship, of course, is jealousy. Jealousy is different from other negative emotions such as hate or anger (Fitness & Fletcher, 1993). Jealousy, however, is difficult to define because the incidents that provoke jealousy differ across cultures (Hatfield & Rapson, 1996). Spouses and dating couples are typically more jealous when their partners flirt, kiss, and have sex with another person than they are about dancing, hugging, or even sexual fantasies. Nonetheless, spouses in the old Soviet Union get more jealous over dancing than do spouses in other cultures. Spouses in the former Yugoslavia get very jealous over flirting and do not mind kissing or sexual fantasies. Spouses in the Netherlands get more jealous about sexual fantasies that involve an outsider than almost anything else (Buunk & Hupka, 1987).

In the United States, men get most jealous when they suspect that their wives may be having a sexual affair with another man (Buss & Schmitt, 1993). They sometimes become obsessed with mental images of their wife in someone else's arms, search her belongings, phone her unexpectedly, listen in to her phone calls, and even have her followed (Salovey & Rodin, 1985). Women, in turn, are more likely than men to get jealous over their partner spending considerable time with another woman with whom he has common interests (Buss & Schmitt, 1993). Although men sometimes deny their jealous feelings, women more freely acknowledge jealousy and worry about how much their man is emotionally, not just sexually, involved (Clanton & Smith, 1987). Finally, both men and women have either high or low levels of certainty orientation. An individual with high certainty orientation personifies the "wanting to be right" theme that runs through several chapters of this book. He or she is highly motivated to resolve uncertainty, wants clarity and predictability, and is uncomfortable with ambiguity (Sorrentino & Roney, 1990; Sorrentino, Roney, & Hanna, 1992). Interestingly, people who are high in certainty orientation would rather be in a relationship with someone they either know they can trust or know they *cannot* trust than with someone about whom they are not sure (Sorrentino, Holmes, Hanna, & Sharp, 1995).

■ THE FOUR HORSEMEN OF THE APOCALYPSE

One way to discover what men and women do that creates problems in close relationships is to ask them. Much of the research on upsetting actions and jealousy used direct questions. Another way is to put the partners in a conflict situation and observe how they handle it. In a comprehensive program of research, the researchers had married couples come to a psychology laboratory after not having spoken for at least eight hours (Gottman, 1994). Each partner wore physiological recording devices that monitored heart rate, sweating, blood pressure, and other signs of emotional arousal. Then the couple discussed first the events of the day, followed by a problem area of continuing disagreement in their marriage. During the latter discussion, the researchers carefully noted the wife's and the husband's behaviors.

After observing many such interactions, the researchers arrived at four behaviors that occurred very frequently, and in an orderly sequence, when married couples discussed issues of contention. Table 10.2 lists these four behaviors, which some have termed the "four horsemen of the apocalypse" for close relationships. First, one partner or the other complains and criticizes. He or she brings up the area of disagreement and calls attention to problems that threaten the relationship. The researchers discovered that the wife usually does more complaining and criticizing than the husband (Gottman, 1994).

Second, sometimes as a reaction to direct or implied criticism, one partner displays contempt for the other. Married couples often showed contempt by biting sarcasm or mockery. Third, one partner or the other (or both) becomes defensive. He or she denies blame and attributes to the other partner a variety of malicious intentions. Fourth, one partner or the other withdraws from the interaction by stonewalling. He or she acts like a stone wall, both verbally and nonverbally. A stonewalling partner says nothing—not even an "uh-huh" to indicate that he or she has heard. A stonewalling partner also looks away, as though refusing to acknowledge that the other person is communicating. If

TABLE 10.2	The "Four Horsemen of the Apocalypse." Four Behaviors That Corrode Marital Satisfaction and Can Lead to Marital Separation and Divorce (Gottman, 1994)

TYPES OF CORROSIVE BEHAVIOR	DESCRIPTION
Complaining and Criticizing	bring up areas of disagreement; call attention to perceived problems with partner and with the relationship
Contempt	put down partner; communicate verbally that partner is absurd or incompetent; show contempt with hostile humor, mockery, and sarcasm
Defensiveness	communicate blamelessness; deny responsibility, attribute negative motives, feelings, and actions to partner
Stonewalling	withdraw from an interaction; do not look at partner, nod, or in any other way acknowledge partner's communication

Note: The four behaviors often follow in order. Complaining and criticizing can elicit contempt. Contempt can elicit defensiveness. Defensiveness can elicit stonewalling.

they were not in a psychologist's office, of course, stonewalling might include walking out while the other person is speaking. Of all the partners who used stonewalling when discussing relationship problems, 85% were men (Gottman, 1994). Finally, the four horsemen of the apocalypse typically occur in order, as though one leads to the other. Complaining and criticizing may lead to contempt, which elicits defensiveness, which in turn elicits stonewalling and withdrawal.

You might look back at the gender differences for four newlywed couples' complaints in Figure 10.5 and think about how they relate to the four horsemen of the apocalypse. The fit is not perfect, but it is interesting that newlywed men accuse their wives of being too possessive and demanding, which seems similar to complaining and criticizing. Being inconsiderate and abusive might also be similar to showing contempt and defensiveness. Finally, newlywed women accuse their husbands of being neglecting, which seems very similar to stonewalling and withdrawal. In both ways of classifying problem behaviors, women are more likely to raise thorny issues and demand that something be done about them, whereas men are more likely to stonewall and withdraw.

The researchers in a relevant study examined this demand/withdrawal pattern of marital interaction by having parents, each with a son aged seven to 12, discuss two problem areas (Christensen & Heavey, 1990). One of the problem areas was something that the mother wanted the father to change about his behavior. The other problem area was something that the father wanted the mother to change about her behavior. These particular parents had some

FIGURE 10.6

Men and women have different ways of dealing with issues of conflict.

Graph shows likelihood of two different patterns of behavior when parents discussed mom's wanting dad to change or dad's wanting mom to change (Christiansen & Heavey, 1990).

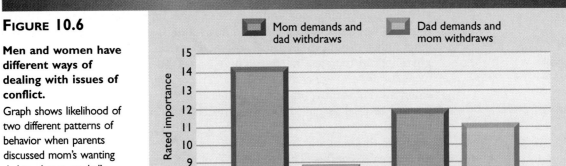

serious family problems to discuss, because more than half of them had sons who had been diagnosed with attention-deficit hyperactivity disorder.

The investigators scored the parents' communications on two possible patterns of behavior. In one pattern, the mother made demands and the father withdrew. In the other pattern, the father made demands and the mother withdrew. Figure 10.6 shows how likely it was that each pattern of behavior would occur when the parents were discussing how mom wanted dad to change or how dad wanted mom to change. The big difference, as you can see on the left side of the figure, occurred when mom brought up a behavior which she wanted dad to change. The "mom demands and dad withdraws" pattern was much more likely than its opposite. Even on issues where dad wanted mom to change, as the right side of the figure shows, mom still did more demanding and dad did more withdrawing. This particular pattern of the woman raising an area of conflict and the man changing the subject, ignoring her, or leaving is so prevalent that social psychologists believe it has a systematic cause.

REACTIONS TO PROBLEMS

The systematic cause behind sex differences in demanding and withdrawing from close relationship problems lies in men's and women's reactions to stressful events. One of the major themes that recurs through this book is that people have both spontaneous and deliberative reactions (Bargh, 1994; Beike & Sherman, 1994; Epstein, Lipson, Holstein, & Huh, 1992; Gilbert, 1989; Martin, Seta, & Crelia, 1990; Martin & Stoner, in press; Smith, 1994). Most of the time, people think in very simple ways. They go with their initial, spontaneous reactions (Smith, 1994). At other times, people react in a more deliberative, "controlled" way (Tesser, Martin, & Mendolia, 1994). Although it takes time and energy, people sometimes think things through instead of reacting off the top of the head. Two factors that determine whether people use predominantly spontaneous reactions or deliberative reactions are motivation and ability (Fiske & Neuberg, 1990; Fazio, 1990; Gilbert, 1991; Macrae, Hewstone, & Griffiths, 1993; Pendry & Macrae, 1994; Wegener & Petty, in press). When people are not motivated or when they are too aroused to think straight, they rely on spontaneous reactions. When they care enough and can think about an issue calmly, they rely more on deliberative reactions.

Recall that when researchers investigated the four horsemen of the apocalypse (complaining, contempt, defensiveness, and stonewalling), they had spouses "wired up." They recorded heart rate, sweating, blood pressure, and other indicators of physiological arousal (Gottman, 1994). By examining these physiological records, the researchers gained an important insight into *why* women raise areas of conflict within a close relationship and men stonewall or withdraw. Put simply, the answer is that men cannot shut down their aversive internal arousal as quickly as women do (Polferone & Manuck, 1987). Both men and women, for instance, secrete more epinephrine (a naturally occurring stimulant that prepares the body for fight or flight) when one of them brings up an area of conflict. The woman's level of epinephrine, however, returns to normal much faster than the man's (Gottman & Levenson, 1992). When relationship problems are raised, the man stays in a physiologically aroused state for a long time. He is still ready to fight someone or to run away long after the woman has calmed down.

When people become upset and aroused, they fall back on spontaneous reactions and do not go on to a second stage of more deliberative thinking about a problem (Gottman, 1994; Smith, 1994). The woman can raise an issue of conflict because she knows intuitively that she might be initially upset, but she will quickly calm down enough to discuss the matter logically and deliberatively. Her perspective is "let's get it out in the open, talk about it, and resolve the issue." The man, in contrast, would rather give in quickly ("OK, you win, let's do it your way") or flee from the interaction to avoid staying aversively aroused. If he cannot flee physically, he flees psychologically by turning into an unresponsive stone wall. He seems not to be listening or trying to resolve the issue, which often drives the woman to voice her complaints and criticism more insistently ("He's not getting it. This is a real problem in our relationship and he can't just ignore it. I must need to express myself more forcefully.").

Even so, men cannot completely ignore a dissatisfied spouse. Both men and women get very upset when their relationships break up (Stroebe & Stroebe, 1988). They fear that they will never find anyone else (Stephan, 1987). They construct stories about "what went wrong" to try to understand, learn from, and recover from the experience (Weber & Harvey, 1994). They sometimes blame themselves or seek constant reassurance that "it isn't so" (White & Mullen, 1989). To avoid a break-up, then, both men and women are highly motivated to deal with problems that arise. In doing so, however, some individuals and some couples take a more constructive approach than others. In the final section of the chapter, we describe four types of reaction to close relationship problems, when partners use each type, and some tentative prescriptions for a healthy marriage.

■ TYPES OF REACTIONS

When people reflect on times in their lives when they became dissatisfied with a romantic relationship and report on how they reacted to the situation, they typically mention reactions that fall into one or more of the four categories shown in Figure 10.7: exit, voice, neglect, and loyalty (Rusbult & Zembrodt, 1983).

An "exit" reaction to relationship problems is to terminate, or to consider terminating, the relationship. Specific exit reactions include talking about breaking up, doing things to drive the other person away, dating other people, agreeing to separate but remain "friends," moving out of a joint residence, and getting a divorce. A "voice" reaction is to seek solutions to the problem. Specific

FIGURE 10.7

Four reactions to problems that arise within close relationships.

Abstracted from Rusbult & Zembrodt, 1983, and Rusbult, 1987.

Active

EXIT

I ended it

I told him I wouldn't take it anymore

I slapped her around a bit

I divorced him

VOICE

We talked things over

I tried my hardest to make things work

I wrote him a letter to find out what was going on

We compromised

Destructive ———————————————— **Constructive**

NEGLECT

I just kind of quit. I didn't try to salvage it

I began to stay away from him as much as possible

We seemed to drift apart

I didn't care whether it ended or not

LOYALTY

I supported him even when my friends criticized him

I loved her so much that I ignored her faults

I just waited to see if things would get any better

I accepted that the husband is the head of the household

Passive

When do people exit a relationship?

voice reactions include asking the partner what is bothering him or her, compromising, changing one's own irritating behavior, and getting advice from friends, therapists, or members of the clergy. A "neglect" reaction is to ignore the problem and passively "let things fall apart." Specific neglect reactions include sulking rather than confronting the issue, refusing to talk about it, and spending less time with the partner. Finally, a "loyalty" reaction is to remain committed to the relationship in spite of its problems. Specific loyalty reactions include "graciously trying to live with it," "waiting patiently for it to pass," accepting the partner's faults and weaknesses, trusting the partner, and following the motto "forgive and forget."

As shown in Figure 10.7, two of these reactions to interpersonal problems – voice and loyalty–are constructive for maintaining the relationship. The other two–exit and neglect–are destructive to maintaining the relationship. To exit the relationship, for instance, might be a very constructive reaction for an individual who is being abused, but it is destructive from the perspective of its impact on the relationship itself. In addition, as also shown in the figure, two of the reactions (exit and voice) are relatively active. The individual engages in behavior that has an impact, either positive or negative, on the relationship. The other two reactions–neglect and loyalty–are relatively passive. In the case of neglect, the individual stands by and watches his or her relationship deteriorate. In the case of loyalty, the individual decides to "stand by my man (or woman)" without doing anything to resolve the irritating problems.

■ WHEN PARTNERS USE EACH TYPE OF REACTION

How can we predict whether an individual will react to relationship problems with exit, voice, neglect, or loyalty? One important factor is how satisfied versus dissatisfied the individual is with the relationship (Rusbult, 1987). Individuals who are satisfied with the relationship tend to respond in one of the two constructive ways, either with voice or with loyalty. Individuals who are dissatisfied with the relationship tend to respond in one of the two destructive ways, either with exit or with neglect.

Another important factor is how much the individual has invested in the relationship. Individuals who have a heavy emotional investment have devoted large amounts of their time or other resources to the relationship. They have such a large stake in continuing the relationship that they are likely to choose one of the constructive reactions (voice or loyalty) over either of the destructive reactions (exit or neglect). They use a strategy of "accommodation" (Rusbult, Verette, Whitney, Slovik, & Lipkus, 1991). Consistent with the "two-stage process" theme of spontaneous versus deliberative reactions that pervades this textbook, committed partners inhibit the initial, spontaneous impulses that prompt them to react in destructive ways. Instead, they stop and consider the other person's perspective and consider whether they are themselves entirely "free from sin." In one study, college students indicated how they would react if their dating partners took various actions that were either constructive or destructive (Yovetich & Rusbult, 1994). How would you react, for instance, if during an argument your dating partner shouted "I'd be better off without you"? An exit reaction might be "Fine. Let's try it." A voice reaction might be "Can we sit down and talk about why you're so upset with me?" A loyalty reaction might be "You're just in a bad mood, but I love you anyway." A neglect reaction might be "I haven't got time to talk about it." As the experimenter presented each scenario, some students were asked to respond quickly and answered within 3–10 seconds. Other students had plenty of time and typically took 10–30 seconds. As predicted, students who had plenty of time responded constructively to their partners' destructive behavior 64% of the time, whereas students who responded quickly used constructive alternatives less than half (48%) of the time. Taking the time to consider reactions, then, might save a relationship that would otherwise be headed for disaster.

When one or the other partner decides to end a relationship, each partner is likely to experience some guilt (Baumeister, Reis, & Delespaul, 1995). Participants in one study described a time when they either broke someone else's heart or had their heart broken (Baumeister, Wotman, & Stillwell, 1993). Contrary to what you might expect, partners who *initiated* the break-up felt worse about it than did partners who were themselves rejected. To assuage their guilt, the rejecters told stories in which they had been subjected to unreasonable demands. The stories of people who had been rejected, in contrast, seemed calculated to rebuild their damaged self-esteem. They were not as annoyed and did not feel as guilty, perhaps because they did not feel as responsible. People can also experience guilt, of course, over transgressions that occur while the relationship is still in progress. One partner or the other might feel guilty about perceived neglect, unfulfilled obligations, or selfish actions (Baumeister, Stillwell, & Heatherton, 1994). Especially in communal rather than exchange relationships, guilt is a natural reaction to a lapse of concern for the unit's welfare. The emotion of guilt may well have evolved in human beings as a way of keeping relationships together. Guilt often causes people to confess, apologize, recognize the other person's perspective, and treat the partner better (Baumeister et al., 1994).

Reactions to relationship problems depend on the availability and perceived attractiveness of alternative relationships (Jemmott, Ashby, & Lindenberg, 1989; Kelley et al., 1983). Individuals who have one or more attractive, romantically interested others available to them are motivated to choose one of the active reactions, either voice or exit. They can afford to tell their partners "either shape up or ship out," because they are secure in their knowledge that they will easily find another partner. Individuals who have no attractive alternative partners, by contrast, tend to settle for one of the passive reactions, either loyalty or neglect. If they are very satisfied with and heavily invested in the relationship, individuals who have no alternatives remain loyal. If they are dissatisfied and not heavily invested, they neglect the relationship and passively allow it to deteriorate. Individuals who are satisfied with and invested in a relationship, however, perceive other prospective partners as less attractive than do individuals who are dissatisfied and not heavily invested (Johnson & Rusbult, 1989). Men and women who are satisfied with their current relationships can meet physically attractive, obviously "interested" members of the opposite sex and view them as "not all that great." Had they been dissatisfied with their current relationships, they might well have found the same members of the opposite sex extremely attractive. Relationship satisfaction thus biases our perceptions of alternative romantic partners in ways that are likely to perpetuate a happy marriage or courtship.

Women are more apt than men to respond to relationship problems with one of the constructive rather than destructive reactions (Rusbult, Johnson, & Morrow, 1986). Women, as noted throughout the chapter, may have more at stake in maintaining a satisfactory relationship than do men. As a result, women who are satisfied with other aspects of the relationship tend to *voice* their complaints about the man's irritating habits. When men belch loudly, talk about how good-looking other women are, or leave the toilet seat up, women who are otherwise satisfied with the relationship choose an active, constructive reaction. They talk openly about their feelings. Although the men in question might regard the woman's "voice" as "nagging," they should consider how preferable "voice" is to more destructive or passive reactions like exit or neglect, which can easily evolve into a deadly cycle of reciprocal attacks (Margolin, John, & O'Brien, 1989). Unless they react constructively rather than destructively to the inevitable problems and conflicts, former husbands and wives might find themselves in the same situation as is predicted to be the fate of more than 50% of current marriages—the divorce courts.

■ PRESCRIPTIONS FOR A HEALTHY CLOSE RELATIONSHIP

To end on a positive note, social psychologists have discovered many principles that might be used to write a tentative prescription for having and maintaining healthy close relationships. The prescription is only tentative, though, because not all social psychologists would agree with every component of the list. Researchers differ, for instance, on whether there is only one or there are many stable types of marriage. In one classification system, shown in Table 10.3, stable marriages come in three basic types, whereas unstable marriages come in only two (Gottman, 1994; Fitzpatrick, 1984). In the three stable types, spouses are well matched in how much or how little they try to persuade each other. Some couples have perfectly stable marriages of the volatile type. To an outsider, they fight all the time. They have huge blowups in which each tries to change the other person's mind, with no holds barred. The next day (or sometimes even later the same day), they make up. They are again fully and

TABLE 10.3	Three Stable Types of Marriage and Two Unstable Types of Marriage (Gottman, 1994)	
STABLE MARRIAGES	**DESCRIPTION**	**RISKS**
Volatile	big fights and great times making up; intense emotions; partners very intent on persuading each other	no hurt is spared; can deteriorate into endless quarrels, bickering, even violence
Validating	calm, easy, good-natured conversations about issues on which partners disagree; hearing the partner out; understanding partner's view; only moderate attempts to persuade	romance dies away and is replaced by boredom; partners too sure of each other
Avoiding	avoid talking about areas of disagreement; very low emotional intensity	have to live with problems; afraid of negative emotions; lose skills to solve conflict problems
UNSTABLE MARRIAGES	**DESCRIPTION**	
Hostile	direct conflict; pay close attention to partner so as to detect any criticism; whine, complain, and attack; react defensively	
Hostile/Detached	act detached and uninvolved, but from time to time launch a hit-and-run attack; guerrilla warfare with intermittent periods of reciprocated attack and defensiveness	

ecstatically in love. Many such marriages last a lifetime, with the next-door neighbors listening to plates hit the wall and wondering when the divorce is coming. The primary risk to volatile marriages is that they deteriorate into an almost endless fight, with only brief rest periods.

Another stable type of marriage is one that is validating. In a validating marriage, the partners discuss areas of conflict in a calm, good-natured way. They hear each other out, insert humor to lighten the mood, and try to understand each other's perspective on relationship problems. Of all the personality traits essential for a good marriage, the most important seems to be the husband's ability to control his initial impulses (Kelly & Conley, 1987). It may be precisely such husbands, who have the temperament necessary to overcome their spontaneous "fight or flight" reactions, who are most likely to maintain validating marriages. They do not always agree with the wife when she raises thorny issues, but at least they give her the benefit of listening to her side and talking it out. If the partners in validating marriages have trouble validating, they usually "agree to disagree" and do not push too hard (Gottman, 1994).

The risk, of course, is that validating couples might become bored, because they have "worked it all out" and have nothing left to discuss.

Interestingly, as Table 10.3 shows, it may be possible to have a stable marriage in which both partners are avoiding (Gottman, 1994). They both know they have serious relationship problems, but they both go out of their way to avoid mentioning these areas of conflict. They never try to persuade each other. Perhaps because *both* the husband and the wife cannot tone down aversive arousal, they deliberately keep the emotional tone of their marriage at as low a level as possible. In the process, they may lose the skills necessary to deal with future problems.

Some marriages may be unstable merely because one spouse prefers a volatile, validating, or avoiding style, whereas the other prefers a different arrangement. We have already seen that women are more likely than men to confront issues that threaten a relationship, whereas men are more likely than women to avoid those issues. Mismatched preferences may lead to one or the other of the two types of unstable marriage: hostile and hostile/detached. In hostile marriages, the partners pay strict attention to each other. They are too sensitive to any statement, action, or facial expression that might be interpreted as critical, demanding, insulting, or abusive. They whine, complain, attack each other, and get very defensive. Like the hostile couple in the play *Who's Afraid of Virginia Woolf?*, they ride with the four horsemen of the apocalypse all the way to the divorce court. In hostile/detached marriages, by contrast, both partners appear on the surface to be avoiding. When each partner

FIGURE 10.8

Some tentative prescriptions for a healthy close relationship.

1. Value intellect and agreeableness over claimed accomplishments and physical attractiveness when initiating and accepting offers of a close relationship.

2. Create interdependence through mutual influence and shared activities.

3. Encourage mutual support by bolstering your partner's self-esteem, listening to your partner's problems, trusting your partner, making benign attributions for your partner's behavior, and constructing narratives that turn your partner's faults into virtues.

4. For men, practice being more psychologically feminine and taking a woman's perspective.

5. Foster a communal orientation toward the relationship. Do not keep score or worry about how much each partner gives and gets out of the relationship.

6. Be aware of and do not perform specific actions that are known to upset someone of your partner's sex.

7. When you see the "four horsemen of the apocalypse" sequence starting, take a break until you can discuss the issue without the usual slide toward disaster.

8. For women, practice soothing the man's physiological arousal and waiting until he has calmed down to continue discussing an issue that you have raised.

9. For men, practice controlling your initial impulses when aroused, which are usually to fight or flee.

10. Try to avoid becoming defensive when your partner raises a relationship issue.

11. If you cannot have a mutually validating relationship, at least choose a partner who matches you in preferring a volatile or avoiding relationship.

12. Whenever possible, react to relationship problems with voice and loyalty rather than exit and neglect.

least expects it, though, they launch a devastating sneak attack in which they are every bit as hostile as hostile couples. Suddenly, one attacks and the other reacts defensively. Then they withdraw from the fray to lick their wounds while waiting for another opportunity.

This classification scheme for stable and unstable marriages, coupled with information from other parts of the chapter, leads to the tentative prescriptions for a healthy relationship that are listed in Figure 10.8. Take these prescriptions with a grain of salt, because not all social psychologists would agree with all of them.

The figure speaks for itself, especially if you compare it to what you have read throughout the chapter. Be careful about the criteria that you use for initiating a relationship, because, as the section of Chapter 9 on familiarity describes, we often find ourselves married to people merely because we spend considerable time with them. Do everything you can to encourage interdependence, mutual support, trust, and a communal orientation. Try to think the way women do about relationships, even if you are male. Avoid specific actions that you know will upset your partner. Watch for signs that the "four horsemen of the apocalypse" sequence is starting and do something to break the sequence. If you are a woman, be aware that men stay aroused longer when conflict issues arise and try to soothe his aversive arousal before continuing (Gottman, 1994). If you are a man, practice makes perfect in controlling those unthinking impulses toward fight or flight. Try not to be defensive. Strive for a mutually validating relationship, or at least for one that is mutually volatile or mutually avoiding. Finally, practice using the constructive reactions voice and loyalty rather than the destructive reactions exit and neglect.

If you follow at least some of these prescriptions, then *your* close relationship may bring you great happiness.

SUMMARY OF HOW PEOPLE COPE WITH PROBLEMS IN CLOSE RELATIONSHIPS

In married couples, one spouse sometimes angers the other by being too possessive, inconsiderate, abusive, or neglecting. Men tend to think that women are too possessive. Women tend to think that men are too neglecting. One of the biggest dangers to a close relationship is jealousy, which typically occurs when one spouse is uncertain about the other's commitment. Many unhealthy marriages are characterized by four potentially corrosive behaviors: complaining and criticizing, contempt, defensiveness, and stonewalling or withdrawal. Women complain and criticize because they want to raise and work through issues that threaten the relationship. Men withdraw because they are not as able as women to turn off their aversive physiological arousal. Some reactions to relationship problems are more constructive than others. There are three types of stable marriages and two types of unstable marriages. An analysis of principles discussed in this chapter suggests some tentative prescriptions for a healthy close relationship.

Social Interaction

Social Influence Through Social Interaction

uman beings are raping the planet Earth. People are catching fish, killing wild animals, and cutting down forests faster than these living things can replenish themselves. In a world of increasingly scarce resources, it is no longer in each individual's self-interest to take as much as he or she can grab. If individuals continue to consume natural resources faster than the resources replenish themselves, human beings will overtax the planet's "carrying capacity," with disastrous consequences (Hardin, 1968).

To give you an idea of what might happen if human beings continue to rape the planet, imagine a rural lake that contains 60,000 fish. Around the edge of the lake live 20 poverty-stricken families. These families fish in the lake for food. They also derive extra income by selling the fish that they do not eat to tourists. Because of natural predators other than human beings, each "mom" and "dad" fish have only one child that grows to maturity per year. If each of the 20 families caught exactly 1,000 fish per year, the fish population of the lake would stay the same forever. If 20 families each caught 1,000 fish in a year, that is, the original fish population would decrease by 20,000 each year, from 60,000 to 40,000. The remaining 40,000 "parent fish," however, would produce 20,000 children, so the population would be back to 60,000.

What might happen if one family decided to increase its income by catching twice as many fish in the second year? Instead of 1,000 fish, that family caught 2,000 fish. The family members might have reasoned that an extra 1,000

Why might these people continue fishing until no more fish are left in the lake?

fish "wouldn't be missed" in a population of 60,000. As Figure 11.1 shows, however, that one family's decision might easily be the first step on the road to disaster for everyone. The figure shows that in the first year of our hypothetical scenario, each of the 20 families caught 1,000 fish, so the fish population stayed at 60,000. In the second year, when one family doubled its catch, 21,000 fish were removed from the lake. The 39,000 remaining fish produced 19,500 children. The fish population fell to 58,500.

In the third year, four other families said, "If they are going to make extra money by catching extra fish, so can we." Five families doubled their catches to 2,000 and 15 families stayed with their usual yearly total of 1,000. The total catch for year three was 25,000, which left 33,500 "moms" and "dads," which produced approximately 16,500 children, leaving the fish population at 50,000. In the fourth year, five more families decided "not to be left out." They expected the five greedy families to continue their greed and wanted to get their share "while the getting was good," so ten families took 2,000 fish each. The other ten families stayed with their normal catch of 1,000. Thirty thousand fish were removed from the lake. The 20,000 remaining fish produced 10,000 new fish, leaving 30,000. The fifth year was the same as the fourth. The same ten families caught 2,000 fish each. The other ten families caught 1,000

FIGURE 11.1

Self-interest destroys replenishable resources.

Graph shows number of fish remaining in a hypothetical self-sustaining lake when families decide to double their catches.

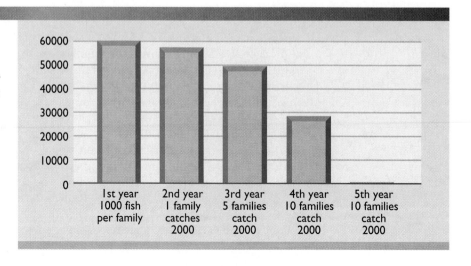

fish each. Together, they removed all 30,000 remaining fish. No "moms" and "dads" remained to have fish babies. The 20 poverty-stricken families at the edge of the lake never again had an extra income or fish to eat.

Admittedly, the tragedy of the lake is a hypothetical scenario. Fish do not produce exactly one child per year. Families might agree to limit their catches if they noticed that a valuable resource was being depleted. Nonetheless, dozens of laboratory simulations have shown that, given similar scenarios in which they can take as much as they want from a self-replenishing resource, ordinary citizens behave as did the hypothetical families. The laboratory results mirror with frightening accuracy what is happening to lakes, rivers, oceans, wildlife, the atmosphere, and the world's rain forests. In the Amazon rain forest, for example, thousands of poor families are clearing trees so that they can grow the food they need to keep from starving to death. By pursuing their separate interests, they may deplete the planet's oxygen supply and kill all life on Earth. One of the most important services that social psychologists can provide is to discover why self-interests are depleting the Earth's natural resources and what can be done about it.

Part of the answer lies in understanding social influence through social interaction—how people influence each other unintentionally, merely by interacting. All of social psychology, as Chapter 1 explains, is about social influence. Some types of social influence are deliberate and manipulative (Cialdini, 1993). The manipulative types of social influence are discussed in other chapters on persuasive communications (Chapter 7), requests for help (Chapter 12), minority influence (Chapter 14), and group decision making (Chapter 15). This chapter concentrates on subtle, nonmanipulative types of social influence such as those shown in Table 11.1. They are ways that people exert social influence *merely by interacting,* even when they are not deliberately trying to change each other's behavior. The five types of social influence in

TABLE 11.1	Five Types of Social Influence That Occur Merely Through Social Interaction, Even When People Are Not Deliberately Trying to Change Each Other's Behavior	
TYPE OF SOCIAL INFLUENCE	**DESCRIPTION**	**EXAMPLE**
Social Facilitation	People rely more on spontaneous, habitual reactions when others are present than when they are alone	Use resources faster when other people are also using resources
Social Loafing	People expend less effort when working with others than when working alone	Contribute little to collective efforts to conserve resources
Self-Fulfilling Prophecies	People act in a way that causes others to fulfill even erroneous expectations	Act as though you expect other people to use more than their share
Cooperation vs. Competition	People pursue their self-interests even in situations where the maximal strategy is mutual cooperation	Compete for shared resources instead of cooperating in their use
Social Dilemmas	People find it difficult to conserve dwindling resources instead of initiating a free-for-all	Grab what you can before others beat you to it

Table 11.1 are relevant to resource conservation and to many other practical, everyday social problems. The first two types, social facilitation and social loafing, help answer the question "How do people influence each other's behavior merely by interacting? The third type, self-fulfilling prophecies, helps answer the question "Why do people fulfill each other's expectations?" The last two types, dyadic competition and social dilemmas, help answer the question "What determines whether people cooperate with each other?"

HOW DO PEOPLE INFLUENCE EACH OTHER'S BEHAVIOR MERELY BY INTERACTING?

The central question in the first section of the chapter is how people influence each other's behavior indirectly, without any active, intentional interference. The family that first doubled its catch in the fishing story did not intend to influence anyone else's behavior. They were merely pursuing their own agenda, without realizing that anyone else would notice. Nonetheless, their behavior had such a profound influence on nine other lake families' behavior that all 20 families suffered. How did it happen? Was it merely that people imitate each other's behavior or were more general principles of social behavior at work? Social psychologists have long been interested in how one person influences another merely by being there and doing his or her own thing. The relevant research includes work on *social facilitation* and *social loafing,* which can both be described by *social impact theory.*

SOCIAL FACILITATION

The first social psychology experiment involved fishing lines. An early social psychologist named Norman Triplett was a bicycle-racing enthusiast. In studying the records of the Racing Board of the League of American Wheelmen, Triplett noticed that when bicycle racers were racing against each other their times were usually faster than when they raced by themselves against the clock. He reasoned that it was not just in bicycle racing but in a wide variety of activities that people perform better when someone else is doing the same thing.

To test his hypothesis, Triplett (1898) had 40 children wind fishing lines as fast as they could. The fishing lines were hooked to an elaborate apparatus that simulated a bicycle race. The faster the child wound the fishing reel, the faster a flag made a complete turn around a miniature track. The object was to get the flag around the track four times, as fast as possible. Each child took six turns at this task. On some of the turns, the child wound the reel alone and only one flag was on the track. On other turns, two children wound two separate reels and two flags were on the track. Triplett did not instruct the children to compete when another child was present. On the "two-person" turns, however, children could see whether their own flag was ahead or behind. They could try to catch up or to stay ahead. On the "alone" turns the children were merely racing against the clock.

When Triplett compared the two kinds of turns, he found that children wound their fishing reels faster when another child was winding a second reel than when they wound alone. Some children benefited more from having another "reeler" than did others. Girls, for instance, improved more in company versus alone than did boys. Also, a few children did not benefit from having another person "fishing." They got uptight when the two flags were very close.

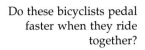

Do these bicyclists pedal faster when they ride together?

They lost all coordination, went to pieces, and performed worse than they had when alone. Triplett concluded that people put more energy into their actions when another person is present than when they are alone. Sometimes the extra energy facilitates performance. At other times it impairs performance.

■ FACILITATION AND IMPAIRMENT

Social facilitation illustrates how animals and human beings intensify their behavior when others of their species are present (Zajonc, 1965). Rats eat faster when another rat is in the cage with them than when they are alone, even though in both cases the supply of food is unlimited. Ants dig more dirt per hour when another ant is with them in a sandbox than when they are alone. Students who sit across a table from each other, separately putting slashes through every vowel in a text, work faster than do students who work on the same text in a room by themselves. Numerous results like these, as well as the original fishing reel study, indicate that animals and human beings sometimes do things better and faster when in the company of others than when working alone (Zajonc, 1965).

Other studies detected social facilitation effects in human beings outside as well as inside the experimental laboratory. In one such study, people kept diaries of everything they ate for one week (de Castro & Brewer, 1991). They also noted the circumstances at each meal or snack, including who else was present. When the investigators reviewed the diaries, they discovered that the participants had consumed larger and more fattening meals when other people were present than when they ate alone. In a related study, the experimenters unobtrusively observed shoppers in northern California supermarkets and discount stores (Sommer, Wynes, & Brinkley, 1992). Customers who shopped together with other people spent more time in the store and emerged with larger bundles than did customers who shopped alone. These are but two of many studies that have found facilitation of well-learned behaviors in real-world settings outside the social psychology laboratory.

Interestingly, though, the presence of others sometimes impairs rather than facilitates performance. Cockroaches take longer to escape from a lighted maze when other cockroaches are present (Zajonc, Heingartner, & Herman, 1969).

Even if the other cockroaches do not physically impede them, cockroaches that are trying to escape from a bright light start bumping off the walls in a disorganized way. They remind us of the children who "went all to pieces" in the fishing reel study. Human beings who are trying to solve difficult philosophy problems write more when working side by side with another student, but they write inferior arguments. Students also take longer to learn a list of meaningless words when they have an audience than when working alone. In these and other studies (reviewed by Zajonc, 1965), the presence of other people, whether as co-workers or as an audience, sometimes facilitates and sometimes impairs performance.

■ WHY FACILITATION AND IMPAIRMENT OCCUR

Although social facilitation and impairment may occur for different reasons in human beings than in insects and animals, social psychologists have identified five psychological states that contribute: arousal and increased drive, evaluation apprehension, distraction, self-presentation, and self-awareness. The five states, which are listed and described in Table 11.2, produce several predictable reactions, all of which have the same result. People perform easy tasks better and difficult tasks worse. The following paragraphs describe the relevant states and reactions.

▒ INCREASED "DRIVE" AND AROUSAL

First, the presence of others of our own species often increases arousal and "drive," which is another way of saying that people put greater energy into their responses (Geen & Bushman, 1989). People (and animals) who are aroused, like smokers who become nervous, fall back on old habits. If they are doing a simple task such as reeling a fishing line, the "easiest," most "automatic," best-learned response is to whip the fishing reel around. Whipping the reel around is a very easy task in which the most spontaneous reaction also increases a person's score. Increased drive and arousal makes people rely on spontaneous rather than deliberative reactions, which is one of the major themes discussed in this book (see Chapter 1). The presence of others thus enhances performance in simple tasks where the spontaneous reaction works best.

In one study of social facilitation, the investigators asked students to pronounce foreign-sounding words aloud (for example, afworbu, nigatso) (Zajonc & Sales, 1965). Students pronounced one of the words once, one of the words twice, one of them five times, one of them ten times, and one of them 25 times. The word that they had pronounced 25 times (a different one for each student) should have become almost second nature to them because they had said it so often. The investigators then flashed words on a screen so fast that no human being could see anything but a blur. They asked the students to guess which word was shown. (In reality, it *was* merely a blur and not one of the words.) The more times students had pronounced a word previously, the more likely they were to say it when asked what word was shown in the blur. This tendency to utter the easiest, best-learned response was greater when an audience watched the students than when they were alone. Audiences and coworkers facilitate simple tasks that involve instinctive or well-learned behavior, such as rats eating, ants digging, and human beings guessing words.

When people are doing complex tasks, however, the easiest, best-learned response is often wrong. The most "natural" thing for a cockroach to do when a bright light comes on is to run fast in a straight line directly away from the light. If the cockroach is in a maze that requires negotiating some turns to escape, the natural response is the wrong one, guaranteed to impair performance (Zajonc et al., 1969). The same analysis applies to students who have to write

TABLE 11.2	Five States in Which People Perform Easy Tasks Better and Difficult Tasks Worse with Others Present Than Alone
STATE	**REACTION**
Arousal and Increased Drive	Rely on spontaneous, habitual responses
Evaluation Apprehension	Rely on spontaneous, habitual responses
Distraction	Narrow attention and rely on spontaneous, habitual responses
Self-Presentation	Show off if confident; get flustered if lose confidence
Self-Awareness	Try harder if success seems likely; otherwise withdraw

answers to difficult logic problems. The "natural" response is to write fast, a strategy that results in putting many words on the page but also in very little deep reflection. Because the presence of another person is arousing, it intensifies the easiest, best-learned response and thus aids performance on simple or well-learned tasks and disrupts performance on complex tasks. Arousal may be like stepping on the accelerator in an automobile. It makes the car go faster and faster, until it is racing so fast that steering becomes too complex to handle. Then the driver loses control in the same way as did some of the children in Triplett's study. Consistent with this analysis, several studies have shown that people become more physiologically aroused when an audience watches them perform a difficult task than an easy task (Bond & Titus, 1983). In major league baseball statistics, for instance, batting performance is impaired in late-inning pressure situations and when the home team has two outs. Such situations are by definition very arousing, especially when thousands of spectators are watching (Davis & Harvey, 1992).

EVALUATION APPREHENSION A second cause of social facilitation and impairment, as shown in Table 11.2, involves evaluation apprehension, or fear of being evaluated negatively. A clever study replicated the one in which students first pronounced foreign-sounding words. Then they had to guess what word was presented in a blur (Cottrell, Wack, Sekerak, & Rittle, 1968). Just as in the original study, students who had an audience tended to guess the most-often pronounced word. The experimenters also included, however, a condition in which the "audience" members were blindfolded. The audience had no way to tell whether the students' answers were correct or not. In the blindfolded audience condition, social facilitation did not occur. When the audience could not see and evaluate them, the students performed exactly as they did when they were alone. Other people are threatening because they might criticize what we do.

Evaluation apprehension may contribute to decreases in workers' performance on complex tasks when they are monitored, either in person or electronically. Modern computer networks make it possible for supervisors to monitor individual workers' productivity without being physically present. The "psychological presence" of computer monitoring, however, might be as detrimental to performance on complex tasks as physical presence, because remote monitoring carries with it the threat of negative evaluation. In one study, college women solved anagrams (a complex task) at separate computers (Aiello & Svec, 1993). Some of the women thought that their work would be computer monitored. Others thought that, although the "master computer" was capable of monitoring their performance, it would not do so. A third group of women received no special instructions, but a female "observer" dressed like another student stood two feet behind them, facing the computer screen, the whole time they were working. Computer monitoring was at least as detrimental to productivity as having a supervisor look over the worker's shoulder.

Many studies have attempted to separate the mere presence of others from the possibility of negative evaluation. Even as children we learn to associate other people with possible negative consequences. They pose a threat and keep us on our toes merely by being there, even if they are not actively watching us (Bond & Titus, 1983; Guerin, 1993). In one study of mere presence, male college students had to change into unfamiliar clothing (oversized shoes and a lab coat that tied in the back) and later to change back into their own clothes (Markus, 1978). Some parts of the task, like tying and retying their own shoes, were easy and well practiced. Other parts, like tying a lab coat behind their backs, were relatively difficult. While the men were performing these tasks, they were either alone in the room, in the presence of an unexplained "other student" who sat watching them, or in the presence of a "workman" who was repairing a piece of apparatus, with his back to the student. Meanwhile, a hidden observer recorded how long it took the student to perform each part of changing clothes. As Figure 11.2 shows, students tied and retied their own shoes (the easy task) faster with a watching audience than when alone. They also took longer to put on the oversized shoes and lab coat (the difficult tasks). Interestingly, these social facilitation and impairment effects were almost as pronounced when the "audience" was a workman who had his back to the students. The workman was not watching, but the students could not be sure that he would not turn around and evaluate them negatively. Related studies have shown that people are aroused by the "mere presence" of others, but only when the other person's behavior is unpredictable (Guerin, 1986).

DISTRACTION A third cause of social facilitation and impairment, shown in Table 11.2, is distraction (Baron, 1986). Other people are distracting. Whether they are working on the same task that we are, or merely watching, we are never quite sure what they might do next. When other people are around, we tend to divide our attention between them and the task at hand. If the task is an easy one that does not require attention to many details, we can compensate. We can narrow the focus of our attention and concentrate on simple mechanics such as winding a fishing reel or making slashes on a piece of paper. For simple tasks, distraction has the paradoxical effect of facilitating performance. If the task is a difficult or complex one like solving logic problems or memorizing unfamiliar words, however, narrowing attention to one or two simple aspects is counterproductive. Complex tasks require integrating information from many different aspects of the problem, not just concentrating on one aspect. For complex tasks, distraction impairs performance.

Other human beings are not the only source of distraction that causes social facilitation and impairment effects. In one study, participants tried to memorize meaningless words either without distraction or with loud bells and buzzers going off intermittently (Pessin, 1933). Early on, when repeating the meaningless words was still a difficult task, distracting bells and buzzers *impaired* learning. Later, when the meaningless words were very well learned and practiced, the distracting bells and buzzers *facilitated* learning. In another study, students either copied letters and numbers as they appeared on a page or tried to copy the letters and numbers upside down and backwards (Sanders & Baron, 1975). While they were copying letters and numbers, some of the students were distracted by signals that told them to look up at a large letter "X" painted on

FIGURE 11.2

"Mere presence" of someone who is not watching facilitates performance on easy tasks and impairs performance on difficut tasks.

Graph shows how long students in three conditions took to complete easy and difficult tasks (Markus, 1978).

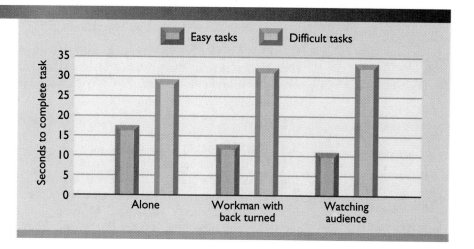

the wall. Again, nonsocial distraction facilitated the simple, easy copying task and impaired the more complex, difficult copying task.

Finally, even people who cannot possibly evaluate performance can produce social facilitation and impairment. Students in one experiment had to type their names in the normal way (simple task) and backwards, with ascending numbers between the letters (complex task) (Schmitt, Gilovich, Goore, & Joseph, 1986). While typing, they were either alone, with someone looking over their shoulder, or with a confederate who was wearing both a blindfold and headphones. The confederate was supposedly participating in a "sensory deprivation" experiment. As predicted, students did the easy typing faster and did the difficult typing slower when a confederate *who could not see or hear them* was present than when they were alone. No negative evaluation was even remotely possible. The social facilitation and impairment effects may have occured because a person wearing a blindfold and earphones is unusual and distracting.

■ **SELF-PRESENTATION** Table 11.2 shows that a fourth cause of social facilitation and impairment is that people want to make a good impression on others. In one study, students worked either on simple, easy-to-perform tasks or on complex, difficult-to-perform tasks (Bond, 1982). As expected, the students did better on the simple tasks and worse on the complex tasks when other students were watching than when they worked on the same tasks in a room by themselves. The experimenter also inserted one complex task in the set of simple tasks and inserted one simple task in the set of complex tasks. Students who were doing a set of simple tasks knew that they were making a positive impression. They did better on *all* the tasks, including the complex one. Students who were doing a set of complex tasks knew that the audience had much to criticize in their performance. They did no better on the simple item when watched than when they worked alone.

In a related study, students who first succeeded on a complex task later performed better on that task with than without an audience. Students who first failed on the task, in contrast, performed *worse* with than without an audience (Sanna & Shotland, 1990). The simplicity or complexity of the specific task is not as important as the impression that a person expects to make through his or her performance. People who are confident of doing well tend to perform especially well when other people are available to admire their prowess.

People who expect to fail or believe that the audience expects too much of them go all to pieces and suffer social impairment (Seta & Seta, 1995).

▓ **SELF-AWARENESS** Finally, social facilitation and impairment occur when performing in the presence of others makes people self-aware or self-conscious (Carver & Scheier, 1981; Wicklund, 1980). When people become self-conscious, they start evaluating themselves. They compare themselves to what they perceive as reasonable standards to see whether they are falling short. If they perceive a discrepancy between how well they are doing and how well they think they ought to be doing, they react in one of two ways. If they believe that they can correct the discrepancy by trying harder, as they might on simple tasks like winding a fishing reel, self-aware people exert greater effort. If they believe that simply exerting greater effort will not improve performance because the task is too complex, self-aware people quit trying. By withdrawing effort, they distance themselves from the task. They say, "This task has no bearing on whether I am a capable person." Thus self-awareness causes people to do better on simple tasks and to do worse on complex tasks.

In the five causes of social facilitation and impairment shown in Table 11.2, the presence of other people heightens both positive and negative consequences (Paulus, 1983). People become aroused, "energized," distracted, and made self-conscious by others because other people have treated them positively, negatively, or unpredictably in the past. If people perform well when they are alone, they are pleased. If they perform well with others, they are doubly pleased. Similarly, if people perform poorly when they are alone, they are unhappy. If they perform poorly with others, they are doubly unhappy. The presence of other people raises the stakes. By increasing the potential positive and negative consequences of behavior, other people (often merely by being present) exert a powerful social influence. They exert the same type of subtle, nonmanipulative social influence that makes it difficult to solve the fishing problem before all the fish are dead.

SOCIAL LOAFING

The opposite of social facilitation and impairment is social loafing. In the fishing story, families were tempted to catch *more* than their fair share of fish because doing so would get them more income. In other circumstances, people want *less* than their fair share. Suppose the families all realized that the lake had too many weeds. Removing the weeds, which was backbreaking work, would increase the fish population. Do you think that individual families would be tempted to contribute *more* than their fair share of weeding the lake, or *less?* If you said less, you believe in the possibility of social loafing. **Social loafing** involves expending less effort when working collectively with other people than when working alone (Karau & Williams, 1993). The phenomenon was first noticed in the 1800s when an agricultural engineer named Max Ringelmann had people try to pull a two-wheeled farm cart. Participants in Ringelmann's studies seemed to exert greater effort when they pulled the cart by themselves than when they pulled in groups of two or more (Kravitz & Martin, 1986).

In a modern study of social loafing, college students participated in groups of one, two, four, or six. The experimenter asked the students, who sat in a soundproof laboratory room, to clap their hands and to cheer as loudly as possible (Latané, Williams, & Harkins, 1979). According to readings from a sound meter, each student made the most noise when clapping and cheering alone, less noise when clapping and cheering with one other person, even less with two others, and so on. These effects occur for actual cheerleading squads as well as in the psychology laboratory (Hardy & Latané, 1988). Social loafing may constitute the "flip side" of social facilitation (Geen, 1991; Paulus, 1983;

Do these cheerleaders yell louder when they yell together?

Sanna, 1992). When other people watch us perform or when they are doing the same task that we are doing, they *raise* the stakes. They make the positive consequences of our behavior even more positive and the negative consequences of our behavior even more negative. Conversely, when other people work collectively with us as part of a team effort, they *lower* the stakes. They make the positive consequences of our behavior appear less positive and the negative consequences less negative (Shepperd, 1993). They reduce arousal and drive, reduce evaluation apprehension, and make our own efforts appear either "dispensable" or unwarranted.

■ DRIVE REDUCTION

Recall that when others are present, either as an audience or working separately on the same task, people put greater energy into their behaviors. They do better on easy tasks. They also do worse on complex tasks. To test whether other people might have the opposite effect on performance when they are part of a collective effort, college students in one study worked on computer mazes. The mazes were either easy, with wide paths and few blind alleys, or difficult, with narrow paths and many blind alleys (Jackson & Williams, 1985). In a "working separately" condition, two students sat at separate computer terminals and negotiated the mazes as individuals. As coworkers, they finished more of the easy mazes and fewer of the difficult mazes than had they been alone. In the "working collectively" condition, the students thought that the two computers were linked. They thought their score was how rapidly they got through each maze collectively *as a team*. No one would ever know how much each partner had contributed to the team outcome. As predicted, students who worked collectively finished no more of the easy mazes or fewer of the hard mazes than had they been alone. Being part of a collective effort reduced their arousal and drive to normal levels and extinguished social facilitation and impairment.

■ FREEDOM FROM NEGATIVE EVALUATION

Collective action also reduces the potential for negative evaluation. One of the themes that runs through this book suggests that people have both a personal identity and a social identity (Abrams, 1992; Brewer, 1991; Crocker et al., 1994;

Deaux, 1993; Ethier & Deaux, 1994; Markus & Kitayama, 1994; Miller & Prentice, 1994). Collective action increases social identity and decreases personal identity. It frees group members from individual responsibility (Trafimow et al., 1991; Turner et al., 1994). Participants in the computer maze study thought that no one could identify or criticize their individual contributions when they worked collectively. Participants in a study of cheering, in contrast, had individual microphones. The researchers could tell how loudly each team member shouted (Williams, Harkins, & Latané, 1981). When the participants thought that their individual contributions could be identified, they shouted as loudly in a team effort as they did when alone.

In a related study, the investigators examined intercollegiate swimmers' times in individual versus relay events (Williams, Nida, Baca, & Latané, 1989). The swimmers swam *faster* in relays than in individual events when their individual lap times were announced (social facilitation). They swam *slower* in relays than in individual events when only team times were announced (social loafing). Similarly, when participants have a standard to which they can compare their individual contributions, they do not loaf even though no one else would know whether they fell short of the standard (Harkins & Szymanski, 1989; Szymanski & Harkins, 1987). Whether the negative evaluation comes from other people or from themselves, people who think that their own contributions cannot be evaluated separately from the group's collective effort loaf. People who think that their own contributions might reflect negatively on them do not loaf (Kerr & Bruun, 1981).

■ "DISPENSABLE" CONTRIBUTIONS

Another consequence of collective action is that it often makes our individual contributions seem inconsequential or "dispensable." When paired with a competent and motivated partner, for instance, people might assume that the team will succeed even if they do not exert maximum effort. Such an assumption causes a "free rider effect." The **free rider effect** shows that individuals loaf because they can gain the rewards of group success while hitching a free ride on the effective efforts of others (Bornstein, 1992; Kerr, 1983). When the possibility of hitching a free ride occurs to team members, however, they often realize that other team members may be hitching a free ride on them (Kerr & Bruun, 1983). If they were to exert full effort, the other team members might "play them for a sucker" by loafing and letting them do all the work (van Dijk & Wilke, 1993). Both the free rider effect and the "sucker effect" induce social loafing, but for opposite reasons. In the free rider effect, individuals rely on other people's contributions. In the sucker effect, individuals worry that they are giving others a free ride. In both cases, collective performance suffers compared to what team members might have accomplished had they contributed as much as they could (Shepperd, 1993).

The free rider and sucker effects highlight the importance to social loafing of what people *expect* the other team members to do. If they expect their partners to perform well, they take a free ride. If they expect their partners to loaf, they decrease effort so as not to be taken for a sucker. In one study that showed how expectations affect social loafing, college women had to blow into a tube as hard as they could (Jackson & Williams, 1985). Then the women had to shout "Raaaah" as loudly as they could. Finally, the women put on headphones and blindfolds and tried to shout as loudly as they could, either alone or in a team with a partner. When they believed that their partners had tried very hard on the practice "Raaaah" and intended to do so again during the team test, the women shouted hard alone and with their partners. When they believed that their partners were bored by the task, had loafed earlier, and intended to loaf again, however, the women loafed alone or with their partners.

FIGURE 11.3

Expectations for partner induce either social loafing or social compensation, depending on the work arrangement (Williams & Karau, 1991).

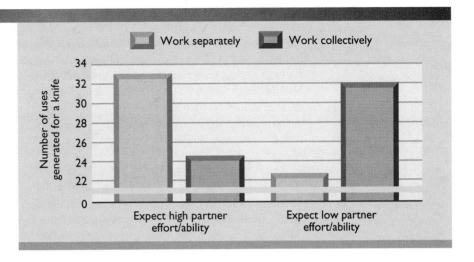

Expectations for their partners' likely effort influenced how much effort they were willing to exert.

■ IMPORTANCE OF OUTCOMES

When the team's outcome matters a great deal, however, people do not loaf, whether they expect their partners to do well or not. Students who are told that they must work in pairs and that both members of the pair will receive the same grade for a class project, for example, often exert *more,* not less, effort. They try to *compensate* for a partner's expected low effort or ability.

In two relevant studies, student participants had to invent as many uses for a knife as they could during a 12-minute "brainstorming" session that the experimenter described as an accurate measure of intelligence (Williams & Karau, 1991, Experiments 2 and 3). Everything about the instructions made the task seem important and relevant to the student's self-esteem. In the "working separately" condition, two students each wrote their ideas on slips of paper and inserted the slips of paper into separate boxes. The experimenter could identify individual contributions. In the "working collectively" condition, the students inserted their slips of paper into a common box. Neither the experimenter nor the students could identify individual contributions. Only the total team effort determined how they would both be evaluated. In one of the two studies, however, the other student, who was a confederate, revealed that he did or did not intend to try hard. In the other study, the confederate revealed that he had high or low ability at similar tasks. Figure 11.3 combines results from the two studies. Students who expected their partners to do well at the task generated fewer ideas of their own when working collectively than when working separately–the usual social loafing effect. Students who expected their partners to do poorly, in contrast, generated *more* ideas of their own when working collectively than when working separately. They compensated so that the team would not be negatively evaluated on a meaningful, important task.

SOCIAL IMPACT THEORY

One way of combining social facilitation and impairment effects with social loafing effects is through social impact theory (Latané, 1981). **Social impact theory** holds that the greater the number and status of people who are present, the more they influence our behavior. Conversely, the greater the number and status of others whom we try to influence, the less influence we exert on each of them. Social impact theory ascribes social facilitation and impairment to the number and status of influence *sources*. It ascribes social loafing to the number and status of influence *targets*. In social facilitation and impairment, influence sources exert greater influence when they are many and "strong." Five audience members or coworkers exert greater influence than do two. Higher-status audience members or coworkers (such as supervisors) exert greater influence than do those of lower status. In social loafing, influence targets are more likely to loaf when they are part of a large group and assume that their own contribution is insignificant.

■ NUMBER AND STRENGTH

To understand why number of sources or targets is important in social impact theory, look at Figure 11.4. The top part of the figure shows that two sources influence a target more than one source. In the "fishing at the lake" example, suppose that a "target" family saw one other "source" family catching more fish than usual. They might be slightly tempted to do so themselves. If they saw two other "source" families catching more fish than usual, they would be more tempted. If they saw all 19 other "source" families catching more fish than usual, they might feel compelled to do so themselves. The bottom part of the figure shows that social loafing is the mirror image of social facilitation and impairment. Suppose all families realized that more fish would live to maturity if the families removed weeds that were choking the lake, but removing the weeds was backbreaking work. One source family set a good example by working to remove the weeds. If only two families lived on the lake, the other

FIGURE 11.4

According to social impact theory, social facilitation and impairment increase with the number of sources that operate on one target. Conversely, social loafing by each target increases with the number of targets that "receive" one source's influence (Latané, 1981).

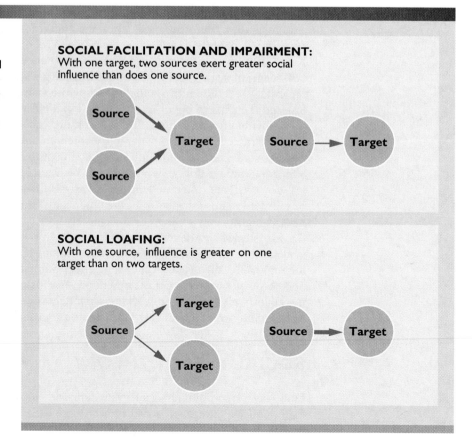

SOCIAL FACILITATION AND IMPAIRMENT:
With one target, two sources exert greater social influence than does one source.

Source → Target Source → Target

SOCIAL LOAFING:
With one source, influence is greater on one target than on two targets.

Source → Target Source → Target

family would be the only target and might feel compelled to help remove the weeds. If two other families were targets, each family would feel pressure to help, but not as much as if they were the only target. If one source family tried to set a good example for 19 other families, the impact on each of the 19 families would be so small that they might all loaf instead of working.

The "strength" or status of sources and targets is also important in social impact theory. A strong source exerts greater influence than a weak source. In the fishing at the lake example, suppose that 19 of the 20 families considered themselves social equals. They all looked up to the twentieth family, though, because the mother in that family was the town's mayor. Which do you think might have greater influence on everyone else's behavior—seeing one of the other families catching more fish than usual or seeing the *mayor's* family catching more fish? Similarly, if one source family tried to set a good example by removing weeds, a target family composed of a frail mother and three small children might feel pressure to help. According to social impact theory, they would feel less pressure to help if the family next door had two physically strong parents and three burly teenage sons. Thus social loafing is more likely when people think that their own efforts are dispensable.

■ RELATED PHENOMENA

Social impact theory describes many other phenomena in which people influence each other merely by being there and "doing what they do." These phenomena include conformity, imitation, crowding, arousal, stage fright, and tipping in restaurants (Latané, 1981; Sedikides & Jackson, 1990).

Conformity is discussed in greater detail in Chapter 14. Its relevance to social impact theory is that people ("targets") are more likely to agree with the group ("sources") when the group is larger rather than smaller. In the classic studies on conformity (Asch, 1956), participants had to answer perception problems after one or more confederates had given an obviously incorrect answer. When one confederate gave an incorrect answer, most participants ignored the incorrect answer and gave the correct answer. When two other people gave the same incorrect answer, approximately 20% of participants agreed with the group and gave the incorrect answer. When three other people all gave the same incorrect answer, conformity rose to 28%. When four other people did so, conformity was 35%. With each additional confederate that agreed on the incorrect answer, conformity rose, but each additional confederate mattered less. A majority of three exerts greater social influence than does a majority of two. Similarly, a majority of one hundred exerts greater social influence than does a majority of 99. The difference in social impact between a majority of three and a majority of two is greater, however, than the difference in social impact between a majority of one hundred and a majority of 99.

Many sources also have greater impact than few sources in studies of imitation. One study took advantage of the well-known phenomenon that if several people are all looking up at a tall building, other people also stop to gawk (Milgram, Bickman, & Berkowitz, 1969). The investigators had confederates stand on a busy sidewalk in New York City and stare up at the sixth floor of a building across the street. When one confederate did this, 40% of passersby imitated him. When three confederates did it, 60% of passersby imitated them. With ten confederates, imitation was at 75%. With 15 confederates, it was at 80%. Just as in laboratory experiments on conformity, social influence in "sidewalk studies" of imitation increased with the number of people exerting the influence. Each additional person added a little less to the total social impact.

Why do people look where someone else is looking, even if they can't see anything?

The importance of number is also evident in research on crowding in animals and human beings. When many animals are crowded into a small space, they behave abnormally. Rats, for instance, become either very aggressive or very apathetic (Calhoun, 1967). After living in crowded conditions for a long time, animals avoid others of their own species whenever they get the opportunity to do so (Latané, Cappell, & Joy, 1970). Similarly, college students who have crowded living quarters are more likely than their noncrowded peers to avoid social interaction when given an opportunity to do so in an experimental laboratory (Evans & Lepore, 1993). Crowding, whether in the household or in a large city, makes people (especially men) irritable and physiologically aroused (Evans & Carrere, 1991; Lepore, Evans, & Palsane, 1991; Paulus, 1980; Ruback & Riad, in press). Crowding is so distracting, perhaps because other people are unpredictable, that it brings on a "sensory overload" that can adversely affect health (Baum & Paulus, 1987; Milgram, 1970; Rodin, Solomon, & Metcalf, 1978). Crowding also increases both the positive and the negative consequences of behavior (Freedman, 1975). Enjoyable experiences are more enjoyable when we are surrounded by thousands of other people, for instance at a rock concert or football game. Unpleasant experiences are also especially unpleasant when we feel "hemmed in" by a crowd (Stokols, 1972). Interestingly, as the number of animals or people in a limited space increases, so do the behavioral effects, which partially explains why crowded prisons are dangerous places (Paulus, McCain, & Cox, 1981).

Social impact theory also describes stage fright. We all get a little self-conscious and embarrassed when we have to perform in front of a group (Miller, 1995). Several studies (reviewed by Latané, 1981) established that the size of the audience matters in "stage fright," and so does the status of audience members. In one such study, college students sat in a soundproof booth by themselves and imagined reciting a memorized poem in front of various size audiences. The more people in their imaginary audience, the more nervous, anxious, and tense the students said they felt. As in studies of conformity and imitation, each additional imaginary audience member added to the impact, but each one added a little less to the total. Also, as a way to examine the impact of "strength," the experimenter asked students to imagine an audience of teenagers or an audience of middle-aged males. Performing in front of middle-aged males made the students feel more nervous than did performing in front of teenagers. Stutterers also stutter more when they have to speak in front of a large audience than in front of a small audience (Latané, 1981). Finally, one study showed that binge eating in college women is especially contagious in college sororities, some of which exert strong peer pressure on members to be moderate (but not extreme) binge eaters (Crandall, 1988).

Number and strength have a complex relationship to social impact. In a relevant study, college students sat in front of a television camera and wore blood pressure cuffs (Seta & Seta, 1992). They tried to count the number of symbols of various types that appeared on each line of a printed page. Some of the students believed that their performance was being observed over closed circuit television. The "audience" was said to be one high school student, two high school students, one Ph.D. faculty member, or a "mixed" group of one high school student and one Ph.D. faculty member. Audience number mattered. The students had higher blood pressure when they thought they were being watched by two high school students than by one. Audience status also mattered. The college students also had higher blood pressure when they thought a Ph.D. faculty member was watching, rather than a high school student. The college students, however, had no higher blood pressure when working in front of a "mixed" audience (one high status and one low status) than when working alone. Audience number and status appear to be averaged rather than added.

One source also had less impact on multiple as opposed to single targets in studies conducted outside the laboratory (reviewed by Latané, 1981). In one such study, "clumsy" confederates dropped boxes of pencils or pennies in an elevator. They were more likely to get help when there was only one other person in the elevator than when there were several fellow riders. Another study showed that waiters in restaurants get smaller tips from each diner in a large party than they get from individual diners, which is why many restaurants automatically add a tip for large parties. Across a wide variety of behavioral measures, the number and "strength" of other people determine how much social influence they exert. If policymakers knew the principles of social impact theory, they might have a better grasp of which proposed solutions to environmental destruction are and are not feasible.

Are these people enjoying themselves more because they are in a crowd, or less?

Coworkers, audiences, and people who are merely present sometimes facilitate performance on easy tasks and impair performance on difficult tasks. Coworkers, audiences, and potential audiences intensify our reliance on easy, well-practiced responses. Other people might criticize what we do. Other people are distracting and make us self-conscious. We want to make a positive impression even on strangers. In short, other people raise the stakes of performing well or poorly.

Under certain circumstances, people put less effort into tasks when they work collectively rather than separately. Such social loafing is more likely when individual effort is submerged in a group outcome, when the group outcome is not important, and when individuals expect coworkers to take up the slack. In short, social loafing occurs when the expectations that go with collective action lower the stakes of performing well or poorly.

According to social impact theory, social influence depends on how many people are trying to influence the individual and, conversely, on how many people the individual is trying to influence. Each additional person increases (or decreases) the impact by a smaller amount. In addition, some people exert stronger social influence than do others. The relationship between number of other people, strength of the other people, and social impact holds for phenomena as diverse as conformity, imitation, crowding, arousal, stage fright, helping in emergencies, and tipping in restaurants.

WHY DO PEOPLE FULFILL OTHER PEOPLE'S EXPECTATIONS?

Research on social facilitation and impairment and on social loafing highlights the importance to social influence of expectations (Jussim & Eccles, in press). People alter their behavior to match or to compensate for the way that they expect other people to behave (Olson, Roese, & Zanna, in press). In the fishing story that began the chapter, for instance, four other families altered their usual yearly "catches" in the second year because they expected that the one greedy family would continue to be greedy. Suppose, however, that the four other families had not joined the "greedy" family in the second year. Instead, they might have acted as though "we expect you to come to your senses." Similarly, social loafing might not occur if we did not expect other people to take up the slack. At least part of how people influence each other merely by being there or doing what they do, therefore, depends on people having and fulfilling each other's expectations.

This section of the chapter examines two important aspects of people fulfilling each other's expectations. The first topic is how it happens that unrealistic expectations are fulfilled—why people act in a way that *behaviorally confirms* even inaccurate expectations. The second topic is how unrealistic, inaccurate expectations affect schooling—specifically, how *teacher expectations* determine students' educational experiences.

BEHAVIORAL CONFIRMATION

Sources of social influence sometimes create self-fulfilling prophecies (Merton, 1948). **Self-fulfilling prophecies** occur when people act toward others in ways that make their expectations for the other person come true. They believe something that is not true, act as though it were true, and in the process cause it to *be* true. Self-fulfilling prophecies, however, could not "come true" unless targets of social influence sometimes engaged in behavioral confirmation. **Behavioral confirmation** occurs when people who are treated differently because of another person's expectations behave in line with those expectations. Targets sometimes behave in such a way as to confirm the source's initially false belief about them (Darley & Fazio, 1980; Harris & Rosenthal, 1985; Jones, 1986; Jussim, 1986; Snyder, 1984, 1992). In the fishing story, four other families (the "sources") expected that the first family that had doubled its catch (the "targets") would continue to do so. Because of their expectations, the four other families doubled their catches. The first family might have intended to double its catch for just one year. When they saw that four other families were catching more fish in the second year, however, they concluded that doubling the catch was acceptable. The first family caught more fish again in the second year (behavioral confirmation). The other four families said, "See, I told you they would continue." Their prophecy had been fulfilled.

■ CONFIRMING STEREOTYPES

In a classic study of self-fulfilling prophecies and behavioral confirmation, the investigators tested whether inaccurate stereotypes about physical attractiveness might be confirmed during an ordinary getting-acquainted conversation (Snyder, Tanke, & Berscheid, 1977). Previously unacquainted college men and women sat in separate rooms and held getting-acquainted conversations through microphones and headphones. First, however, the experimenter asked each participant to provide some background information about academic major, high school attended, and so on. For the man only, the experimenter also took his photograph with a Polaroid camera. She explained the photograph by saying that some people "feel more comfortable when they have a mental picture of the person they're talking to." The experimenter then went to the room where the woman was waiting, collected her background information, and gave her the man's background information. She did not, however, give the woman the man's photograph, take the woman's photograph, or even mention photographs. When the experimenter returned to the man's room, she gave him background information on the woman and a photograph.

In this study, the men erroneously believed that the photograph was of the woman with whom they would be speaking. Half of the men got a photograph of an extremely attractive woman; the other half got a photograph of an extremely unattractive woman. The women did not know about the photograph. What expectations might these photographs have created? Before the conversation started, the men were asked, based only on the information that they had available to them, what they expected the woman to be like. Men who thought that the woman was physically attractive expected her to be more interesting, more sociable, more outgoing, and to have a better sense of humor than did men who thought that the woman was physically unattractive. Men who thought that they would be speaking to an unattractive woman expected her to be serious, unsociable, and socially inept. In other words, the men's expectations for the ensuing conversation were shaped by stereotypes before the conversation ever began.

Did the men behave differently when they thought they were talking to a beautiful woman than when they thought they were talking to a homely woman? Yes, they did. Unbeknownst to the participants, the experimenters recorded each side of the getting-acquainted conversation on a separate channel of an audiotape. Later, after the getting-acquainted conversations, the experimenters played each man's part of the conversation for other students who knew nothing about the photographs. These other students, who could hear only what the man was saying, rated the man's behavior on several dimensions. According to the raters, men who thought they were talking to an attractive woman were more animated, sociable, sexually warm, outgoing, and humorous than men who thought they were talking to an unattractive woman. They also seemed to be more comfortable, enjoying themselves more, and to like their partners more.

Did the women confirm the men's stereotype-based expectations? According to ratings by other students who listened to only the woman's part of the conversation, they did. Although the women knew nothing about the photographs, they were treated differently by the men. They responded in kind. Women who were supposed to be beautiful, regardless of their actual physical attractiveness, responded to the men's animated, interested, sociable approach by being more enthusiastic, interesting, outgoing, and socially adept than women who were supposed to be homely. The "beautiful" women seemed to

Are men more animated when they talk to attractive women?

be more comfortable, confident, self-assured, and enjoying themselves more than the "homely" women. Both women who were supposed to be attractive and women who were supposed to be unattractive behaviorally confirmed the men's erroneous expectations. The men's original false conceptions came true, which probably reinforced their beliefs in the physical attractiveness stereotype.

When we consider the process of behavioral confirmation and try to explain how it occurs, it is important to remember that if people did not confirm each other's expectations, cooperative social interaction might be impossible. Behavioral confirmation serves important functions, even if it sometimes leads to a "reign of error" in which inaccurate stereotypes are perpetuated. By examining the functions served by behavioral confirmation, we understand the process better (Snyder, 1992).

■ "GETTING TO KNOW" AND "GETTING ALONG"

First, why do perceivers (the men in the getting-acquainted study) act as though their expectations were true? Several studies suggest that perceivers who have preconceived beliefs act as they do because they are trying to acquire useful knowledge about the other person. Knowledge seems more useful when it confirms our expectations than when it disconfirms our expectations (Snyder, 1992). If men in the getting-acquainted study wanted to find out whether attractive women are really as sociable and outgoing as they are supposed to be, how would they go about testing their expectations during the conversation? Would they act as though their expectations were likely to be correct, in which case the world would be a stable, predictable, reassuring place? Would they instead act as though their expectations were likely to be false, in which case the world would be a chaotic, unpredictable, and possibly uncontrollable place?

In a relevant study, college women selected from a list of possible interview questions the ones that they thought would be most informative about another student's personality (Snyder & Swann, 1978a). Women who were trying to find out whether the other student was an extrovert selected questions like "What would you do if you wanted to liven things up at a party?" and "In what situations are you most talkative?" Women who were trying to find out whether the other student was an introvert selected questions like "What factors make it hard for you to really open up to people?" and "What things do you dislike about loud parties?" Given a choice between probing for information that might confirm or disconfirm their tentative hypotheses, as shown in Figure 11.5, the women chose to probe for confirming information. The average person could answer either the extrovert questions or the introvert questions with at least a few personal anecdotes. Target students who were asked the two types of leading questions, therefore, talked about themselves in ways that confirmed the women's tentative hypotheses.

Second, why do targets (the women in the getting-acquainted study) act as though the perceiver's expectations were true? Several studies suggest that targets who are treated in line with a perceiver's preconceived beliefs confirm those beliefs because they want the interaction to go smoothly (Snyder, 1992). If the women in the getting-acquainted study wanted to make the conversation go smoothly, how would they act? Would they "come on strong" with men who were acting very cool and reserved? Would they "hold back" with men who were acting animated and enthusiastic? These strategies seem much less likely than the "tit-for-tat" strategy of doing to others as they do unto you (Axelrod, 1984; Axelrod & Dion, 1988). Smooth social interaction requires coordination. Getting acquainted interactions are more harmonious when the people involved are on the same wavelength, disclosing facts about themselves

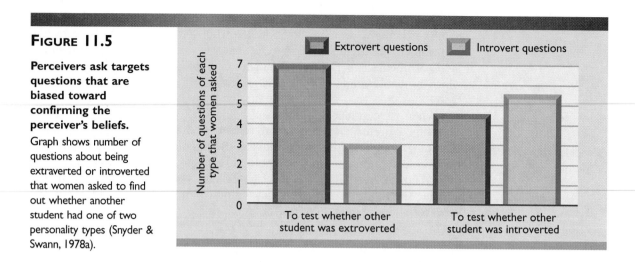

FIGURE 11.5

Perceivers ask targets questions that are biased toward confirming the perceiver's beliefs.

Graph shows number of questions about being extraverted or introverted that women asked to find out whether another student had one of two personality types (Snyder & Swann, 1978a).

equally, and matching each other's level of interpersonal involvement (Goffman, 1959; Jones, 1990b; Schlenker, 1980).

In a relevant study, college men got to use a "noise weapon" on each other. They chose how loud and irritating a noise to play in each other's earphones while the other man was trying to concentrate on a task (Snyder & Swann, 1978b). The investigators told some of the "target" men that the partner loved contact sports and described himself as relatively cruel, aggressive, and competitive. They told other "target" men that the partner enjoyed writing poetry and described himself as relatively sensitive, kind, and cooperative. When the task started, the target men chose to "give back" to the other man a level of noise that they thought would match the level he was most likely to give them. One target said, "If he's as mean and nasty as I think he is, then he will seize the first attempt to attack me with his noise weapon," so "better to get to him before he gets to me."

Consistent with the theme of "being right versus being likable" that is explained in Chapter 1 and recurs throughout this book, behavioral confirmation occurs when perceivers want to be right and targets want to be likable. Both perceivers and targets want to acquire knowledge about the other person and want the interaction to go smoothly. In many everyday social interactions, however, perceivers who hold the expectations are bosses, interviewers, teachers, therapists, and others who have high status. Because of their high status, they can use the interaction to test hypotheses about the target and find out whether they are right (Copeland & Snyder, 1995; Ross & Jackson, 1991). Targets of expectations are workers, interviewees, students, clients, and others of low status. Because of their low status, they are motivated to make the interaction go smoothly and to be likable. In the getting-acquainted study where the two participants supposedly had equal status, for instance, the men had the advantage. They had more information about the woman (the photograph) than she had about them. Thus they had more reason to think they knew how the conversation "should go." Also, many people expect the man to take the initiative in male-female interactions. In many circumstances, then, the perceiver who has the expectations may cause a self-fulfilling prophecy because of being in a position that seems to call for acquiring knowledge about the target. Targets, in contrast, may behave ambiguously or behave as expected because their lower status makes it more important for them than for the perceiver that the interaction go smoothly (Brown & Levinson, 1987).

If behavioral confirmation occurs because perceivers want to get to know and targets want to get along, then reversing the two motives might undo the effect. Two studies (described by Snyder, 1992) supported this reasoning. In a study similar to the getting-acquainted study, men saw a photograph that led them to believe they were talking to a woman who was either obese or of normal weight. The researchers asked some men to use the conversation as a way to get to know the woman—to get a stable, predictable sense of what she was like. These men treated the obese woman as though she were relatively unfriendly, reserved, boring, and sexually cold (the stereotype of fat people). The researchers asked other men to find ways to get along well with their partners. These men treated the "obese" woman no differently than they treated the "normal" woman. Because the women responded in kind, men who were trying to get to know their partners caused behavioral confirmation; men who were trying to get along with their partners did not.

In a second study, *targets* (who did not know that they were thought to be obese or of normal weight) were told either to make the conversation flow smoothly or to find out what their partners were like. The perceivers were given no instructions. As predicted, targets who were trying to get along confirmed expectations. They acted cold, unenthusiastic, and unresponsive when they were thought to be obese. They acted flirtatious, exciting, and energetic when they were thought to be of normal weight. Targets who were trying to get to know their partners, in contrast, behaved no differently whether the other person imagined them to be fat or "normal." The two studies—one on the motivation of perceivers and the other on the motivation of targets—suggest that behavioral confirmation occurs because perceivers want to get to know their partners, whereas targets want to get along with their partners (Snyder, 1992).

■ BEHAVIORAL *DISCONFIRMATION*

In certain circumstances, targets do more than fail to confirm their perceivers' expectations. Sometimes they engage in "behavioral *dis*confirmation," in which the target acts *opposite* to what was expected (Hilton & Darley, 1985, 1991; Miller & Turnbull, 1986; Snyder, 1992). One circumstance that causes behavioral disconfirmation is that in which targets know they have been inaccurately portrayed to the perceiver. When targets know the perceiver has been misled into having negative expectations about them, they go out of their way to show that "Regardless of what you may have been told, I'm not that type!" (Darley, Fleming, Hilton, & Swann, 1988).

A second circumstance that sometimes leads to behavioral disconfirmation is that in which targets are highly motivated to express their personal identities. Targets in one study (described by Snyder, 1992) were told to convey their true personalities to their partners. Although the targets did not realize that their partners had false information about their introversion or extroversion, they behaviorally *dis*confirmed their partners' expectations. The more their partners treated introverts as though they were extroverted, the more introverted they acted. Their actions seemed to say, "You don't seem to understand what type of person I am, so I'm going to make it perfectly clear to you" (Swann, 1983). The circumstances that elicit behavioral disconfirmation, however, are relatively rare. In most everyday situations, those who hold the expectations try to gather new information that shows how right they are. Targets of the expectations try to coordinate their own contributions with those of the other person so that they will get along. The result is a self-fulfilling prophecy.

TEACHER EXPECTATIONS

One of the most interesting and important applications of self-fulfilling prophecies and behavioral confirmation comes in the classroom (Rosenthal, in press). Teachers may have inaccurate expectations for their students because of secondhand information. The second-grade teacher, for instance, might tell the third-grade teacher that "You're going to love having Emily in your class, but Jeremy is a real terror." Teachers may also have inaccurate expectations for their students because of racial or ethnic stereotypes or because of a child's unusual performance during the first few days of a new school year (Jussim, 1991; Ross & Jackson, 1991). Teachers need to get to know their students to assign grades. Students need to get along with their teachers because teachers hold power. Especially in an elementary school setting, the conditions are ideal for students to confirm behaviorally both accurate and inaccurate teacher expectations (Rosenthal & Rubin, 1978).

In a classic study of teacher expectations, the investigators gave elementary school students a test that they called the "Harvard Test of Inflected Acquisition" (Rosenthal & Jacobson, 1968). The investigators told the school's teachers that the test reliably identified specific children who were due for "an unusual forward spurt of academic progress." In reality, the test was a standardized, nonverbal test of "IQ," or intelligence. At the end of the summer before the next academic year, the investigators distributed to each of the school's teachers a list of from one to nine children in the teacher's class. The children on the list had supposedly been identified by the Inflected Acquisition test as "late bloomers" who were on the verge of an unusual academic spurt. In reality, the researchers selected children's names *at random*. The only difference between children on the "late bloomer" list and their classmates was "in the mind of the teacher" (Rosenthal & Jacobson, 1968, p. 70).

Having given the teachers reason to believe that the children on the "late bloomer" list might spurt ahead of their peers, the investigators predicted that these teacher expectations, although based on false information, would be fulfilled. When the investigators readministered the IQ test at the end of the school year, the "late bloomers" had increased their IQ scores by significantly more than their classmates had. Interestingly, the school's administrators regarded these first- and second-grade teachers as outstanding educators, who cared a great deal about their pupils.

In the "late bloomer" study, children who were in each of three different academic "tracks" benefited equally from having their teachers expect them to spurt ahead. One student named José, for instance, was in a low ability track. José came from a relatively poor background. He was raised by an aunt who spoke only Spanish. He had struggled to keep up with the other children in kindergarten. Nonetheless, once his first-grade teacher got the idea that José was a "late bloomer," he developed great interest in reading and improved his IQ score during the first grade by *45 IQ points*. José's experience alerts us to the double-edged nature of teacher expectations and behavioral confirmation. When teachers inaccurately expect low ability, as they might if they believe in stereotypes, the teachers inadvertently keep low expectation children from reaching their full academic potential. When teachers inaccurately expect high ability, children can achieve far beyond what they or their parents might have dreamed possible. Expectations work both ways—negative and positive.

Would children be smarter if their teachers expected them to be bright?

Teacher expectations fit a three-stage model of how self-fulfilling prophecies and behavioral confirmation work (Brophy, 1983; Darley & Fazio, 1980; Harris & Rosenthal, 1985; Jussim, 1991; Miller & Turnbull, 1986; Neuberg,

TABLE 11.3	A Three-Stage Model of Self-Fulfilling Prophecies and Behavioral Confirmation (Abstracted from Brophy, 1983; Darley & Fazio, 1980; Harris & Rosenthal, 1985; Jussim, 1991; Miller & Turnbull, 1986; Neuberg, 1994; Rosenthal, 1981)	
STAGE	**DESCRIPTION**	**EXAMPLE**
Stage 1	Perceiver's initial expectations	A teacher is told that a student is due for an exceptional academic spurt
Stage 2	Differential treatment	The teacher pays more attention to the student and gives the student more challenging work to do
Stage 3	Target's reactions	The student gets more practice and starts believing that trying hard brings success

1994; Rosenthal, 1981). The three-stage model, shown in Table 11.3, describes expectations held by teachers, supervisors, interviewers, doctors, legislators, diplomatic ambassadors, law and enforcement officials. The model applies, for instance, to legal proceedings, in which juries routinely return whatever verdict the judge initially favored, despite carefully worded judges' instructions (Hart, 1995). First, a "perceiver" (in this case a teacher) holds inaccurate initial expectations for how a "target" (in this case a student) will behave. Second, the perceiver treats the target differently than might have been the case without the expectations. Third, the target reacts to the perceiver's actions in a way that confirms the perceiver's initial expectations.

■ INITIAL EXPECTATIONS

Before interacting with a student, a teacher can form expectations for that student's likely performance. Remarks by other teachers, the child's physical appearance, race, sex, social class, and other factors can predispose teachers to expect the best or the worst (Dusek & Joseph, 1985). Initial expectations also bias interpretation of subsequent evidence. Teachers might begin with positive or negative expectations for a child, observe the child's performance during the first few days of school, and have their expectations become *more,* not less, extreme.

In a study of initial expectations becoming more extreme after minimal exposure to a child, college students watched a videotape of a young girl named Hannah playing in "her neighborhood" (Darley & Gross, 1983). Some of the students saw Hannah playing in a stark, fenced-in urban schoolyard surrounded by run-down two-family homes. These "low expectation" students also learned that Hannah's parents were poorly educated. A second group of students saw Hannah playing in a tree-lined park amid a suburban neighborhood of five- and six-bedroom homes set on beautifully landscaped grounds. These "high expectation" students also learned that Hannah's father was an attorney and her mother a free-lance writer. The two groups of students had the same background information that a fourth-grade teacher might have about one of the new students at the start of the school year. They knew either that the little girl lived in an affluent neighborhood with wealthy, well-educated parents or that she lived in "the wrong part of town" with poor, uneducated parents.

Is this girl smart for her age, or dumb?

Some of the low expectation students and some of the high expectation students then watched a videotape of Hannah taking a 25-problem achievement test. They saw an adult tester read to Hannah problems on liberal arts, reading, and mathematics. The tester held up the possible solutions on cards, so that Hannah could answer orally. Hannah performed inconsistently, answering some of the hard problems correctly and some of the easy problems incorrectly. The adult tester did not comment on Hannah's performance. After they had watched the videotape, all students rated the grade level of Hannah's liberal arts, reading, and mathematics abilities. Across liberal arts, reading, and mathematics, students who watched only the "neighborhood" videotape estimated Hannah's academic ability slightly higher when they thought she lived in a wealthy neighborhood than when they thought she lived in a poor neighborhood. When students got additional information about the little girl by watching her take an achievement test, however, the difference between high and low expectations became more pronounced. The high expectation students and the low expectation students, both of whom watched the identical achievement test videotape, saw what they expected to see in Hannah's performance. They became all the more convinced that their initial expectations were correct. The Hannah study is a good example of the "spontaneous versus deliberative reaction" theme described in Chapter 1 of this book. The study illustrates that deliberative reactions can sometimes be more biased than spontaneous reactions (Wilson & Brekke, 1994).

Perceivers, whether they are teachers or not, interpret ambiguous evidence about a target person as supporting their initial expectations. They regard evidence that confirms their expectations as more diagnostic than evidence that disconfirms their expectations (Snyder, Campbell, & Preston, 1982). Perceivers also often remember evidence that confirms their expectations better than they remember evidence that disconfirms their expectations (Crocker, 1981). Finally, school systems that place children in "tracks" that supposedly have high, medium, and low academic ability lend such legitimacy to teacher expectations that the expectations become more confidently held. As a result, children seldom move from one track to another (Brophy & Good, 1974).

■ DIFFERENTIAL TREATMENT

Teachers' expectations could not be fulfilled unless the teachers treated high and low expectation students differently. Many studies have shown that teachers (and other perceivers) treat children (and other targets) differently in at least four ways (Harris & Rosenthal, 1985; Rosenthal, 1973). First, teachers create a warmer, more supportive emotional environment for children about whom they have high expectations. When they interact with high expectation students, teachers are more likely to smile, lean toward the child, make eye contact, and be encouraging (Chaiken, Sigler, & Derlega, 1974; Rubovitz & Maehr, 1973). Second, teachers provide more diagnostic comments to children for whom they have high expectations (Cooper, 1979a; Weinstein, 1976). Teachers are more likely to pay attention to what a high expectation child says, praise the child for good ideas, and explain the correct answers (Cooper & Good, 1983). Third, teachers provide more challenging tasks and learning materials to children for whom they have high expectations (Rist, 1970). Fourth, teachers wait longer for an answer when they ask questions of a high expectation student (Allington, 1980; Harris & Rosenthal, 1985). If low expectation students do not answer immediately, the teacher calls on a classmate. The teacher seems to say, "What's the point in waiting when José is very unlikely to know the answer?" Not all teachers provide such differential treatment (Jussim & Eccles, 1992), but teachers may do so without meaning to. Teachers are only human. Like everyone else, they enjoy interacting with students who are likely to be interested and to benefit. They do not enjoy interacting with students who are likely to be bored or unable to benefit.

Teachers provide differential treatment for several reasons (Jussim, 1986). First, teachers believe that high expectation children want to learn. They also believe that low expectation children would not do schoolwork unless they were closely watched (Cooper, 1979). In this respect, teachers are similar to supervisors, who attribute a closely watched worker's performance to their own supervision, which in turn makes the supervisor trust the worker less (Strickland, 1958). Second, teachers like students who are similar to them better than they like students who are dissimilar to them (Hamlish & Gaier, 1954). Because many teachers come from middle-class families that have positive attitudes toward education, the teachers favor children who have backgrounds and values similar to their own. Teachers who like high expectation children more than they like low expectation children can, without realizing they are doing so, treat high expectation children with greater emotional warmth. Third, teachers believe that high expectation children could do better with suitable encouragement, whereas low expectation children could not improve, no matter how hard they tried (Brophy & Good, 1974). It is all too easy to abandon teaching goals that appear impossible (Dweck & Elliott, 1984).

Differential treatment for high and low expectation children is not inevitable (Jussim, 1991; Snyder, 1992). The research on getting to know versus getting along goals suggests one way to overcome differential treatment: Have the perceiver try to get along instead of getting to know (Neuberg, in press). In a relevant study, college students played either the role of interviewer or the role of applicant in a "telephone job interview" (Neuberg, Judice, Virdin, & Carrillo, 1993). Because of their instructions, some students expected the applicant to be incompetent, whereas others had no expectations. To instill in interviewers a getting along rather than a getting to know goal, the researchers told some of the interviewers, but not others, that the most successful interviewers work hard at getting applicants to like them. They claimed that applicants who like an interviewer are more likely to reveal their true talents and liabilities.

The experimenters measured differential treatment by rating how warm the interviewer's opening statement seemed, how often the interviewer used the applicant's name, how many positive and negative questions the interviewer asked, how many questions the interviewer repeated, and how much time the interviewer spent listening to the applicant's reply. Figure 11.6 shows how positively interviewers behaved toward the applicants. As shown in the figure, interviewers who received no special instructions treated the low expectation applicant more negatively than the high expectation applicant. "Get the applicant to like you" interviewers, in contrast, treated the low expectation applicant more *positively* than they treated the applicant for whom they had no expectations. When they had low expectations, "get the applicant to like you" interviewers made a special effort to be pleasant. They asked fewer negative questions, for example, thus "avoiding potentially awkward or embarrassing exchanges" (Neuberg et al., 1993, p. 414). Teachers who want to avoid differential treatment of students might concentrate on getting their pupils to like them.

The applicants, according to other students who rated just the applicant's side of the conversation, responded in line with how they were treated. When the interviewer had no special instructions, applicants who supposedly had poor personalities made less favorable impressions than did applicants about whom the interviewer had no information. When the interviewer was trying to be likable, however, applicants who supposedly had poor personalities made

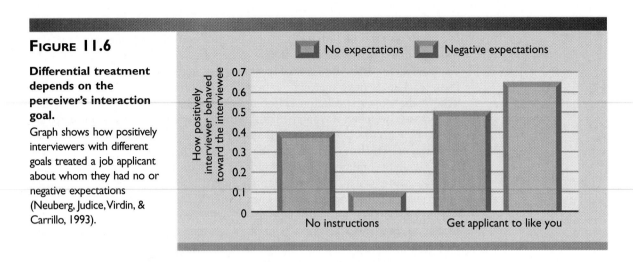

FIGURE 11.6

Differential treatment depends on the perceiver's interaction goal.

Graph shows how positively interviewers with different goals treated a job applicant about whom they had no or negative expectations (Neuberg, Judice, Virdin, & Carrillo, 1993).

more favorable impressions than did applicants about whom the interviewer had no information. Depending on the goal that the person with higher status pursues, differential treatment can sometimes elicit behavioral *dis*confirmation rather than behavioral confirmation.

■ **STUDENT REACTIONS**

The final stage of the three-stage model involves student reactions. Teachers may form inaccurate initial expectations and they may treat high expectation students differently from low expectation students, but how do high and low expectation students *react* to the differential treatment? When they are subjected to differential treatment, what do low expectation students do and think that makes the teacher's expectations into a self-fulfilling prophecy?

First, low expectation students get fewer opportunities to develop their academic skills. Teachers "pat them on the head" rather than give them the diagnostic information that they need to correct their mistakes. Teachers call on low expectation students less frequently and cut them off sooner when they stumble in answering questions. If practice makes perfect, then low expectation children have less opportunity to hone their skills, "less chance to think spontaneously, to attempt to articulate their ideas, to become aware of their own mistakes, and to make corrections" (Jussim, 1986, p. 439). Low expectation children are not given as much of a chance to advance as are high expectation children. Second, low expectation children come to believe they have little control over their academic success. Teachers praise high expectation children more than low expectation children (Cooper, 1979). Thus low expectation children are less likely to believe that trying hard brings success. To them, effort and persistence do not pay off, so why bother? (Dweck, 1975; Eccles & Wigfield, 1985) When motivation suffers, so does performance (Stipek & Weisz, 1981).

Third, low expectation children, because teachers treat them less warmly than their high expectation counterparts, may regard school as a punishing place where they are tightly controlled by the teachers, frequently criticized, and rarely praised (Nicholls, 1984). As a result, low expectation children may invent excuses for missing school days, opt out of classroom activities, and fail to develop intrinsic interest in learning for the sake of learning (Jussim, 1986). Worse yet, they may draw negative inferences about themselves and develop low self-esteem. Low self-esteem, in turn, may keep them from attempting schoolwork that is "too hard for me" (Harter, 1984; Parsons, Adler, Futterman,

Goff, Kaczala, Meece, & Midgley, 1983). Fulfilling other people's expectations may be a "gift" for high expectation children who care what the teacher thinks of them. For low expectation children, however, the "gift" may limit their likelihood of getting a good education.

SUMMARY OF WHY PEOPLE FULFILL OTHER PEOPLE'S EXPECTATIONS

People frequently behave in ways that confirm each other's expectations. When they perceive others, people want to acquire additional information, but they search preferentially for new evidence that is likely to confirm rather than to disconfirm their expectations. When they are the targets of perception, people want to make the social interaction go smoothly, so they behaviorally confirm the perceiver's expectations by behaving either ambiguously or in line with how they are being treated. The higher status person in an interaction usually wants to "get to know" the other person. The lower status person usually wants to "get along." Reversing these motivations can undo behavioral confirmation. In some circumstances, targets actively disconfirm what perceivers expect.

An interesting, important application of behavioral confirmation occurs in the classroom. Students often fulfill their teachers' academic expectations, even when those expectations are inaccurate. Teacher expectations and behavioral confirmation work in three stages. First, a perceiver has initial expectations about a target person. The initial expectations can become more extreme when the target person's behavior is ambiguous. Second, the perceiver treats high expectation targets differently from low expectation targets. Third, the target reacts to differential treatment by confirming initial expectations.

WHAT DETERMINES WHETHER PEOPLE COOPERATE WITH EACH OTHER?

In the fishing story that began this chapter, the tragedy was that the lake residents might have averted disaster if they had cooperated and coordinated their efforts. Had each family restricted its catch to 1,000 fish per year, the lake's fish population would never have changed. Had they cooperated, the families could have had fish to eat and sell for generation after generation. Similarly, if Earth's citizens could only cooperate in how they use the land, rivers, lakes, oceans, forests, and atmosphere, they might consume an amount of the planet's natural resources that other living things might replenish on their own. If we are to avert worldwide disaster, policymakers need to know not only how people influence each other merely through social interaction and why people fulfill each other's expectations. They also need to know what determines whether people cooperate with each other and coordinate their efforts, which is the topic discussed in this third section of the chapter. As we shall see, two people (a *dyad*) often engage in *dyadic competition* even when cooperation would be best for them both in the long run. The ability to cooperate with others is put to its sternest test in situations such as managing a dwindling resource—situations known as *social dilemmas*.

DYADIC COMPETITION

Psychologists, sociologists, anthropologists, historians, philosophers, and others have speculated that human beings spurted ahead of other animals when they developed the ability to cooperate. They gained, for instance, when they started to hunt in coordinated groups and combined their efforts to grow and store food (Alexander, 1987). Throughout the history of the species, however, individual human beings have been torn between cooperating on group goals and competing to satisfy their individual needs. We begin the discussion of cooperation and competition by describing situations in which the "group" is two people. To use a trivial example of cooperating on group goals versus satisfying individual needs, consider the situation depicted in the top panel of Figure 11.7.

■ THE "PRISONER'S DILEMMA"

Two men, "Mugsy" and "Fingers," were arrested and charged with breaking and entering a jewelry store. The police detective in charge of the case could easily get a conviction for breaking and entering, which carried a one-year prison term. He lacked the evidence necessary to convict Mugsy and Fingers

FIGURE 11.7

Three "games" used to simulate dilemmas in which participants must choose between cooperating and competing.

THE PRISONER'S DILEMMA

	Mugsy does not confess	Mugsy confesses
Fingers does not confess	Mugsy gets 1 year Fingers gets 1 year	Mugsy goes free Fingers gets 10 years
Fingers confesses	Mugsy gets 10 years Fingers goes free	Mugsy gets 5 years Fingers gets 5 years

A PRISONER'S DILEMMA GAME

	Mugsy cooperates	Mugsy competes
Fingers cooperates	Mugsy earns $5 Fingers earns $5	Mugsy earns $10 Fingers earns $0
Fingers competes	Mugsy earns $0 Fingers earns $10	Mugsy earns $1 Fingers earns $1

THREE PRISONER'S DILEMMA STRATEGIES

Mugsy maximizes joint payoff	Mugsy maximizes own payoff	Mugsy maximizes relative payoff
Mugsy earns $4 Fingers earns $4	Mugsy earns $5 Fingers earns $2	Mugsy earns $4 Fingers earns $0

on the more serious charge of grand theft. To do that, the detective needed a confession. He cleverly put Mugsy and Fingers in separate interrogation rooms and offered each man a choice: to confess or not. "I know the two of you committed grand theft," the detective told each man, "but I have only circumstantial evidence. If neither of you confesses I'll have to settle for the lesser offense, for which I have all the evidence I need to send each of you to jail for one year." (In the top panel, this outcome is shown in the top left corner formed by the intersection of Mugsy not confessing and Fingers not confessing.) "If you confess and turn state's evidence by testifying against your partner who refuses to confess," the detective continued, "you will go free while he serves ten years in jail. If you do not confess and your partner confesses and testifies against you, he'll go free and you'll go to jail for ten years." (In the top panel, these outcomes are shown in the top right and bottom left corners.) "Finally, if you both confess, you'll both go to jail for five years" (bottom right corner). "Also," the detective explained, "you have to decide whether to confess or not without knowing what your partner is doing in the other room."

What choice should Mugsy make? Should he confess or not? The clever police detective placed Mugsy on the horns of a dilemma. From Mugsy's perspective, he always obtained a better outcome by confessing. If Fingers did not confess, Mugsy either went to jail for one year by not confessing or he went free by confessing. If Fingers confessed, Mugsy either went to jail for ten years by not confessing or he went to jail for five years by confessing. Fingers also always did better by confessing. If each man looked at the situation only from the perspective of his own selfish interests, they would both confess and they would both serve five years in jail. If they were both sent to the same jail, Mugsy and Fingers would have five long years to remind each other that they could each have gotten away with one year had they only cooperated rather than followed their own selfish interests. The "Prisoner's Dilemma" is a model for many important everyday events—from management-labor disputes to international arms and trade negotiations. It has been studied extensively in laboratory simulations where two participants must choose, on each of several turns, whether to cooperate or to compete (Komorita & Parks, 1995; Luce & Raiffa, 1957; Pruitt & Kimmel, 1977). Laboratory Prisoner's Dilemma games usually involve points or money, not jail terms. Nonetheless, Mugsy and Fingers face the same dilemma in the middle panel of Figure 11.7 as in the top panel. On each turn of a Prisoner's Dilemma game for money, competing is clearly in each participant's interest, yet consistent cooperation would, in the long run, be more beneficial.

Calvin and Hobbes
by Bill Watterson

■ DILEMMA STRATEGIES

Several studies of the Prisoner's Dilemma Game have identified three strategies (shown in the bottom panel of Figure 11.7) that participants follow (Kuhlman & Marshello, 1975). Some participants play such games as though they care most about the *joint* payoff for themselves and the other person combined. The "joint" payoff in the figure, for instance, gets the highest total ($8) for the two criminals combined. Other participants seem to care most about their *own* outcome. Mugsy, for instance, gets the most money for himself ($5) by choosing "own" in the figure. Finally, some participants seem most concerned with maximizing their payoff *relative* to the other person. Mugsy beats Fingers by the most money ($4) if he chooses "relative" in the figure. People who consistently maximize *joint* payoffs in laboratory games are also described as idealistic by their college roommates. People who consistently maximize *own* payoffs are described by their roommates as predictable. People who consistently maximize *relative* payoffs are described by their roommates as manipulative and power-hungry. In other words, people behave in laboratory games that involve cooperation versus competition in much the same way as they behave in everyday life (Bem & Lord, 1979). Laboratory games may do exactly what they are intended to do: bring important real-world issues into the laboratory where we can study them under controlled conditions and find out what makes people cooperate and what makes them refuse to cooperate (Dawes, 1980).

"Competitors" play Prisoner's Dilemma Games differently than do "cooperators" because the two kinds of people have different expectations (Kelley & Stahelski, 1970). On the first round of a game, before either of the two players has chosen, the players are in the same situation as Mugsy and Fingers in their separate interrogation rooms. Neither knows for sure what the other will do, yet each must consider the other's probable choice in making his own. At that point, before play has begun, cooperators (those who prefer the *joint* choice in the bottom panel of Figure 11.7) expect some other players to cooperate and others to compete. They make the cooperative choice to "signal" to the other player, regardless of which way the other player chooses, that they want to cooperate. In contrast, competitors (those who prefer the *own* or *relative* choices in the bottom panel of Figure 11.7) expect *all* other players to compete. Confident that "it would be crazy for the other person to do anything but compete," they feel forced to defend themselves. As the middle panel of Figure 11.7 shows, if Mugsy is positive that Fingers will compete on the first round, then Mugsy has no choice but to compete himself.

Because of their expectations, competitors cause a self-fulfilling prophecy. If the other person competes on the first turn, competitors say "I knew it" and continue to compete. If the other person cooperates on the first turn, competitors suspect that "They're trying to lure me into cooperating so they can set me up for the kill. I'd better play it safe and compete on the next round." Meanwhile, cooperators see that their cooperative overture elicited competition. "I wondered whether I was playing against a cooperator or a competitor, but now I know" they say. "I'd better treat the other person on the next round as he or she treated me on the first round." They play the "tit-for-tat" strategy of "do unto others as they did unto you" (Axelrod, 1984; McClintock & Liebrand, 1988). Thus self-fulfilling prophecies and behavioral confirmation can turn Prisoner's Dilemma Games into bouts of mutual distrust and competition (Brickman, Becker, & Castle, 1979; Komorita, Sweeney, & Kravitz, 1980; Rosenbaum, 1980). Even when one player cooperates on every round and never competes, other players take advantage of the "weakness." They compete on every round, reaping huge payoffs. They tell themselves that "people who are so stupid as to cooperate on every turn deserve what they get" (Deutsch, Epstein, Canavan, & Gumpert, 1967; Reychler, 1979; Shure, Meeker, & Hansford, 1965).

■ SEX DIFFERENCES AND GROUP DIFFERENCES

When playing Prisoner's Dilemma Games, men compete more than do women (Knight & Dubro, 1984). Both men and women would rather play such games with women than with men. They expect that women, as a group, will make more cooperative and "trustworthy" choices than men (Orbell, Dawes, & Schwartz-Shea, 1994). One reason for this sex difference may be that men prefer equity, whereas women prefer equality (Mikula, 1974). Equity means that people get what they deserve, that people who work harder and play more skillfully win. Equality means that everyone gets a share and that no one is left out. Another reason for the sex difference is that males have traditionally been socialized differently from females. Men have been taught to care more about achievement, success, and prominence. Women have been taught to care more about interpersonal relationships, attachment, and intimacy (Watts, Messé, & Vallacher, 1982). More men want to "get ahead." More women want to "get along." As evidence that wanting to get along increases cooperation in Prisoner's Dilemma games, people who play against close friends often arrive at mutually cooperative choices in spite of the way the game is structured (Deutsch et al., 1967; McClintock & McNeil, 1967). So do people who think that they may have to meet and to interact with the other player after the game (Pruitt & Kimmel, 1977).

Finally, groups compete more than do individuals (Schopler, Insko, Graetz, Drigotas, Smith, & Dahl, 1993). Instead of having Mugsy play against Fingers, we might have Mugsy and several "teammates" play against Fingers and several "teammates." Instead of Mugsy making the cooperative or the competitive choice himself, Mugsy and his teammates would discuss the choice and reach a group decision. When a game like that shown in the middle panel of Figure 11.7 pits *groups* of players against each other, groups choose more competitively and less cooperatively than do individuals (Insko, Schopler, Hoyle, Dardis, & Graetz, 1990). When they have three choices like those shown in the bottom panel of Figure 11.7, groups are also more likely than individuals to maximize their payoff *relative* to the other group, even if it means sacrificing some of their own payoff (McCallum, Harring, Gilmore, Drenan, Chase, Insko, & Thibaut, 1985). In the heat of battle against an opposing group, group members may cooperate with *each other* more (Bornstein & Ben-Yossef, 1994). In dealing with a rival group, however, competitive, aggressive voices influence the group's decisions more than do the voices of moderation.

■ OPPORTUNITY TO NEGOTIATE

In the original Prisoner's Dilemma Game, Mugsy and Fingers had no opportunity to reach an agreement. The crafty police detective did not let them talk it over and agree on the best strategy. Even if he *had* let Mugsy and Fingers communicate, however, several lines of research suggest that the criminals might not have been able to reach an agreement through negotiation (Carnevale, 1994). First, it is all too easy for people who have incompatible interests to threaten each other. "You'd better agree with my plan, or else." When people threaten each other, they destroy the mutual trust necessary to reach a satisfactory agreement (Cole, Nail, & Pugh, 1995; Pruitt, 1981; Webb & Worchel, 1986).

Second, most ordinary people do not know about negotiation strategies that work. One such strategy is Graduated and Reciprocated Initiatives in Tension Reduction, or GRIT for short (Lindskold, 1978; Lindskold, Han, & Betz, 1986; Osgood, 1962). In GRIT, two people or groups are deadlocked, but one side makes a minor concession to "get the ball rolling." Union representatives, for instance, might reduce their demands for a minimum hourly wage, in hopes that the company would reduce one of its bargaining demands. If each side takes turns showing its good faith, individuals, business interests, and even nations can move gradually closer to a mutually acceptable solution to what had seemed an impasse (Lindskold, Walters, & Koutsourais, 1983). Another strategy is to seek the help of a neutral mediator, who is not emotionally involved. Both sides might agree in advance to accept the mediator's decision (Carnevale & Pruitt, 1992; Welton & Pruitt, 1987).

Third, people who are emotionally invested in a dispute often erroneously perceive that they have incompatible interests (Thompson, 1990; Thompson & Hastie, 1990; Thompson, 1993). If Mugsy and Fingers were splitting the loot after robbing a jewelry store, for instance, Mugsy might want the gemstone from a ring and Fingers might want the gold. Instead of fighting over who gets the ring, Mugsy and Fingers should take it apart and each take what he prefers. Such integrative solutions, however, are difficult to discover in the midst of conflict (Pruitt, 1986; Thompson, 1991).

Look at the preferences shown in Table 11.4. Mugsy and Fingers are trying to divide the proceeds from a museum heist where they made off with cash, metals, gems, and some valuable stamps and paintings. Mugsy, as shown in the figure, prefers old to new bank notes, gold to silver, diamonds to sapphires, U.S. to foreign stamps, and Renoir to Rembrandt paintings. Fingers prefers old bank notes, gold, sapphires, U.S. stamps, and Rembrandt paintings. To an impartial observer, it is easy to see that Mugsy and Fingers disagree about how to split the cash, metals, and stamps, but they *agree* on how to split the gems and paintings. Nonetheless, research shows that they might not realize that they agree on the gems and paintings. In discussing how to split the loot, each thief might assume that "He wants the opposite of what I want."

In one study that tested this prediction about perceived incompatibility, college students watched a videotaped negotiation between an employer and a prospective employee (Thompson, 1995). The two negotiators clearly stated different positions on salary, vacation time, annual raises, and medical coverage. They also clearly stated *identical* positions on which region of the country would be the employee's home base and the start date. The two negotiators agreed on these two issues, just as Mugsy and Fingers agreed on how to split the gems and paintings in Table 11.4. Some students watched the videotape from the perspective of either the employer or the prospective employee—to place themselves in that person's position and try to understand that person's point of view. Other students watched the same videotape with an objective,

TABLE 11.4	An Illustration of Compatible and Incompatible Interests in Negotiation (Modeled after Thompson, 1995)				
	BANK NOTES	**METALS**	**GEMS**	**STAMPS**	**PAINTINGS**
Mugsy Prefers	old notes	gold	diamonds	U.S.	Renoir
Fingers Prefers	old notes	gold	sapphires	U.S.	Rembrandt

PEANUTS reprinted by permission of United Feature Syndicate, Inc.

impartial perspective. Also, half of the students in each condition expected to participate in a similar negotiation themselves, whereas others did not. Those who expected to negotiate themselves felt much more involved in the issues.

After they watched the videotape, all students estimated the employer's and the prospective employee's preferred salary, vacation time, annual raise, start date, medical coverage, and region. As predicted, expecting to participate in a similar negotiation made people who "took sides" less accurate in detecting that the two sides agreed, even while it made objective observers *more* accurate. In another study, the investigator showed that participants in such negotiations are even more blind to agreement than are people who merely watch and take sides. Obviously, people who cannot detect areas of agreement are unlikely to use GRIT. They are unlikely to make concessions, give the other person favors and gifts, or find mutually compatible alternatives to conflict (Lawler & Yoon, in press). Instead, they blindly assume that "If the other person wants this, then it must be bad for me" and "If the other person is satisfied with the outcome, then I failed" (de Dreu, Carnevale, Emans, & van de Vliert, 1994). When they "lose" in such negotiations, they are disappointed. When they "win" the success is "bittersweet," because they suspect that they took advantage of the other person and acted less than honorably (Thompson, Valley, & Kramer, 1995).

SOCIAL DILEMMAS

The Prisoner's Dilemma Game represents one type of social dilemma (Komorita, Chan, & Parks, 1993; Liebrand, Messick, & Wilke, 1992; Rapoport, Budescu, Suleiman, & Weg, 1992). **Social dilemmas** are situations in which the immediate payoff to each participant favors competition over cooperation, but it would be better for all participants in the long run if they consistently cooperated. Social dilemmas typically involve more than two participants. They also involve uncertainty about how the other participants are behaving, little opportunity to "punish" a player who competes instead of cooperating, and a dwindling supply of replenishable resources (Dawes, 1980; Ostrom, 1990). In a hot summer drought, for example, individual householders might recognize that they need to use less water so that the reservoir does not run dry. Are they likely, though, to cooperate enough to avert the crisis? More than just two people are involved. The impending disaster might be attributed to "greedy" neighbors who insist on watering their dying lawns. It is counterproductive to play a "tit-for-tat" strategy. Using more water would affect a wasteful neighbor only indirectly. Similar reasoning applies to social dilemmas that involve community fuel shortages in winter; citizens walking, bicycling, or using car pools on "pollution alert" days in major cities; workers contemplating salary demands that might cause the company to go out of business; parents restricting their number of children in underdeveloped countries where children are the only form of "social security;" and cutting down the Amazon rain forests. In such social dilemmas, self-interest dictates individual actions that spell collective disaster (Knapp & Clark, 1991; Messick & Brewer, 1983).

One attempt to simulate replenishable resource dilemmas involved the "Nuts Game" (Edney, 1979). Several participants sat around a table, in the center of which was a bowl of metal nuts. The experimenter explained that every ten seconds he would double the number of nuts remaining in the bowl. If the bowl originally contained 60 nuts and 30 nuts were removed during the first ten seconds, for example, the experimenter would add 30 more, bringing the total back to 60. The researcher told participants that their goal was to get as many nuts as possible. They could reach into the bowl and take as many nuts as they wanted at any time. The nuts were similar to fish in the "fishing at the lake" scenario. If participants cooperated to manage their "nut pool," they would take only 30 nuts per ten seconds, the bowl would always stay full, and they could each reap a huge pile of nuts if the experiment continued. Unfortunately, the experiment was usually over almost before it began. Of all the groups that participated, 65% never got past the first ten seconds. When the experimenter said "Go," at least one participant reached for the bowl, which prompted others to grab for a handful of nuts. In several cases, the pushing and shoving knocked the bowl over, nuts scattered all over the floor, with the participants scrambling to pick them up, and the bowl was empty. Because two times zero is zero, the nuts were never replenished. Had the nuts been trees in the world's rain forests, the result would have been ecological calamity.

Do not be misled into thinking that the Nuts Game is not representative of real-world resource dilemmas because the participants did not care about "prizes" as trivial as metal nuts. Similar laboratory simulations used monetary prizes about which participants cared very much (Dawes, 1980). The games aroused such intense emotions that participants accused each other of cheating, threatened each other with physical harm, and insisted on leaving by separate doors (Bonacich, 1976; Dawes, McTavish, & Shaklee, 1977). Even when they are deeply and emotionally involved, participants in laboratory simulations often follow their own self-interests. They panic when the resource sup-

Why do people cut down rain forests?

ply starts decreasing, give up on social harmony, and grab as much as they can for themselves rather than find a way to cooperate (Mannix, 1991).

POTENTIAL FOR DICTATORSHIP

People who find themselves in social dilemmas have to invent their own rules for dealing with dwindling resources (Orbell, Dawes, & van de Kragt, 1995). Instead of agreeing to cooperate, people who face a rapidly diminishing common resource become ripe for handing power to a leader who exercises dictatorial power (Samuelson & Messick, 1995). In one study, college students played a resource dilemma game at separate computers that were supposedly connected. The students took as much as they wanted from the resource pool on each turn. Then they learned how much each of the other participants had taken and how much of the pool remained (Messick, Wilke, Brewer, Kramer, Zemke, & Lui, 1983). The experimenters could make it appear that some of the other students were taking more than the optimal amount that would keep the resource pool perpetually full, some were taking the optimal amount, and some were taking less than the optimal amount. They could also make it appear that the resource pool was either replenishing itself well or dwindling rapidly. At an intermission, the experimenters offered the students a choice. They could continue to play as individuals or they could elect a "leader." The leader would have dictatorial power to take whatever amount he or she wanted on each turn and then distribute whatever amount he or she chose to the other participants. When they could see that the resource pool was diminishing rapidly, a *majority* of the students chose dictatorship over continued freedom to take what they wanted as individuals.

Instead of vesting power in dictatorial leaders, many researchers would rather find ways for people to achieve voluntary cooperation (Cross & Guyer, 1980; Dawes, 1980; Hardin, 1968; Heilbroner, 1974; Ophuls, 1977; Orbell & Rutherford, 1973; Orbell, van de Kragt, & Dawes, 1988). By dividing resources into smaller pools that are managed by small rather than large groups, we increase prospects for achieving cooperation without coercion by a central authority (Edney, 1980; Gould, 1988). The smaller the group, the more likely group members are to cooperate on retaining a replenishable resource (Komorita & Lapworth, 1982). Individuals also keep replenishable resource pools going longer than do groups (Messick & McClelland, 1983). Small groups solve resource dilemmas and other conflicts without coercion because they have superior knowledge, morality, and trust (Arad & Carnevale, 1994; Dawes, 1980).

BENEFITS OF KNOWLEDGE

The more knowledge participants have about a social dilemma, the more likely they are to find a cooperative solution. Most people who are thrust into a scare resource dilemma, like participants in the Nuts Game, understand only the immediate payoff, which prompts them to satisfy their own self-interests (Dawes, 1980). Like people who smoke or overeat today because the consequences seem far in the future, they fall into a "social trap" (Platt, 1973). They do not realize that acting for the present only exacerbates the eventual dilemma. Participants who best understand the nature of social dilemmas are most likely to cooperate (Kelley & Grzelak, 1972). People who talk over the situation in advance also cooperate more in a replenishable resource dilemma, because they better understand how serious the problem is (Dawes et al., 1977; Edney & Harper, 1978; Jorgenson & Papciak, 1981). Also, people who know how the pool stands do not overestimate its size, as do people who have only partial knowledge. Participants who have precise knowledge are more likely to cooperate (Budescu, Rapoport, & Suleiman, 1990).

Knowledge also increases with experience. As previously described, individuals manage replenishable resource pools better than do groups. They may do so for at least four reasons (Messick & McClelland, 1983). First, the smaller the number of participants, the more responsible each is for the eventual outcome. Second, the smaller the number of participants, the less likely it is that each participant will consider the pool so large that "one little extra point to me won't matter." Third, individuals, unlike people in groups, do not have to worry about "looking dumb" if other people get more than they do. Fourth, individuals have a better idea of how their choices affect the size of the pool than can group members, the impact of whose own "harvests" may be lost in the total group "harvest." In a relevant study, students first managed a replenishable resource either by themselves or as part of a group (Allison & Messick, 1985). Then all students participated in a group dilemma. Groups whose members had previous individual experience fared better than did groups whose members had previous group experience. Previous individual experience also produced larger benefits when the final groups were larger.

■ MORALITY AND TRUST

A second important contributor to cooperation is morality (Dawes, 1980; Lynn & Oldenquist, 1986). People react differently to dilemmas caused by uncontrollable circumstances than to dilemmas that they believe were caused by other people's greed (Rutte, Wilke, & Messick, 1987). When people get to talk things over before the social dilemma begins, they remind each other about social norms against being greedy. They also remind each other that they are individually responsible for negative outcomes (Messick & Brewer, 1983; Stroebe & Frey, 1982). In one study of morality in social dilemmas, the experimenter delivered a sermon about moral values to participants (Dawes & Orbell, 1981). When people who listened to the sermon later faced a social dilemma, they were more likely to cooperate on the first turn than were people who had not been reminded of moral values. Finally, participants are less likely to surrender their individual freedom to a dictator when they believe that the resource pool is diminishing for reasons other than other people's greed (Samuelson, 1991). No one likes being taken for a sucker while others take a free ride (Coombs, 1973). In small as opposed to large groups, individuals who break the moral code are more noticeable and less anonymous, which reduces cheating.

Finally, if people are ever going to cooperate rather than surrender power to leaders when resources get scarce, they must trust each other (Parks, 1994; Yamagishi & Yamagishi, 1994). It may be easier to instill trust in a small number of neighborhood people who interact frequently than in citizens of a large city. To avert dictatorship, group members must expect each other to live up to their commitments (Bruins, Liebrand, & Wilke, 1989; Kerr & Kaufman-Gilliland, 1994; McCusker & Carnevale, 1995). Negative expectations produce self-fulfilling prophecies, behavioral confirmation, counterproductive strategies, and ultimate ruin (Deutsch, 1993, 1994). Communication improves trust (Messé & Sivacek, 1979). So does a sense of group identity, which is part of the "personal versus social identity" theme, described in Chapter 1 (Brewer, 1981; Edney, 1980). People regard members of their own group as more trustworthy, honest, and cooperative than outsiders (Brewer, 1979).

In one experiment, the researchers first identified students who had high versus low trust in others (Messick et al., 1983). Then they placed both high trust and low trust students in a typical laboratory social dilemma where, because the researchers controlled the resource pool, the remaining resources appeared to diminish rapidly. As shown in Figure 11.8, low trust students reacted to the scarcity by grabbing as much as they could for themselves, thus mak-

FIGURE 11.8

Trust affects reactions to social dilemmas.

Graph shows number of points harvested per round from a dwindling pool by students who had high or low trust in other people (Messick, Wilke, Brewer, Kramer, Zemke, & Lui, 1983).

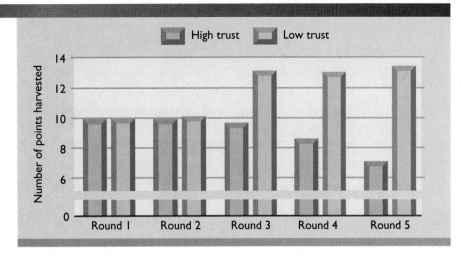

ing the dilemma worse. High trust students, in contrast, *decreased* what they took from the resource pool. Decreasing individual harvests can "save the day" when disaster threatens a replenishable resource. Even after the third year in the "fishing at the lake" example, when the resource pool was down to 50,000 and only two years from total extinction, the participants could have "got back on track" had they all trusted each other enough to take 500 fish apiece. After only one year of this kind of trust, they could have reverted to the original 1,000 fish apiece and been back to the original 60,000 fish, after which they could have kept the lake fully stocked with fish forever.

SUMMARY OF WHAT DETERMINES WHETHER PEOPLE CAN COOPERATE

Social psychologists use laboratory games to simulate real-world events in which people must choose whether to cooperate or to compete. The games are structured so that self-interests dictate competition, but the most beneficial long-term strategy is cooperation. Individuals behave in the laboratory games as they behave in their everyday social interactions. Competitors compete in part because they expect others to compete. Men compete more than do women. Groups compete more than do individuals.

Social psychologists also use laboratory games to simulate social dilemmas in which cooperation might save replenishable natural resources that might otherwise be depleted. When resources are decreasing rapidly, people are willing to sacrifice their individual freedom by electing leaders who have dictatorial control. An alternative to dictatorship is to divide the resource into smaller units that are controlled by small rather than large groups. Members of small groups may understand the risks of depletion better, feel more moral obligation to cooperate, and trust each other more.

Helping

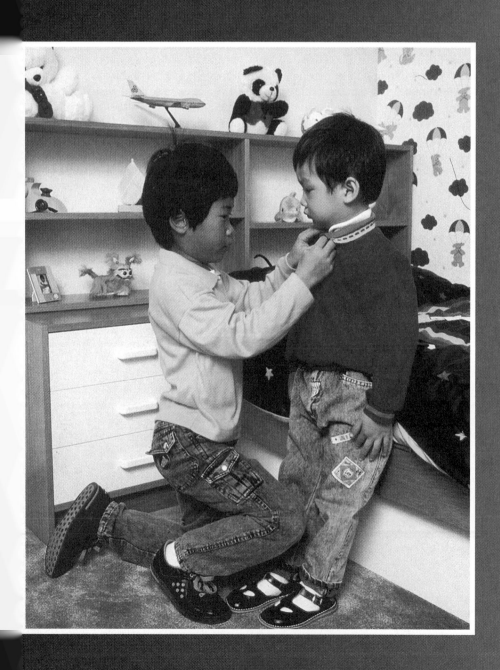

> A man was going down from Jerusalem to Jericho, and he fell among robbers, who stripped him and beat him, and departed, leaving him half dead. Now by chance a priest was going down the road; and when he saw him he passed by on the other side. So likewise a Levite, when he came to the place and saw him, passed by on the other side. But a Samaritan, as he journeyed, came to where he was; and when he saw him, he had compassion, and he went to him and bound his wounds, pouring on oil and wine; then he set him on his own beast and brought him to an inn, and took care of him. And the next day he took out two dennarii and gave them to the innkeeper, saying, "Take care of him; and whatever you spend, I will repay you when I come back."

One message we might draw from the well-known parable of the Good Samaritan is that people are capable of unselfish helping, as long as they have nothing better to do. The priest and Levite in the parable had important functions and religious activities to attend. They had places to go and people to see. "One can imagine the priest and Levite, prominent public figures, hurrying along with little black books full of meetings and appointments, glancing furtively at their sundials" (Darley & Batson, 1973, p. 101). The Samaritan, in contrast, was a religious outcast who had plenty of free time.

The parable of the Good Samaritan served as a model for one of the classic studies of social psychology (Darley & Batson, 1973). The researchers asked some students at the Princeton Theological Seminary to make a videotaped speech about the jobs or professions in which seminary students would be most effective. They asked others to make a videotaped speech about the parable of the Good Samaritan. After a few minutes for the students to make notes about what they were going to say, the experimenter explained that the videotaping facilities were located in the building next door, which was reached

PEANUTS reprinted by permission of United Feature Syndicate, Inc.

through an alley. For some of the students who were making each type of speech the experimenter said, "It'll be a few minutes before they're ready for you, but you might as well head on over. If you have to wait over there, it shouldn't be long." This statement was intended to make these students feel that they had plenty of time. For other students the experimenter said, "The assistant is ready for you, so please go right over." For the rest of the students the experimenter glanced at his watch and said, "Oh, you're late. They were expecting you a few minutes ago. We'd better get moving. The assistant should be waiting for you so you'd better hurry."

When the seminary students passed through the alley on the way to the other building, a respectably dressed male confederate "was sitting slumped in a doorway, head down, eyes closed, not moving" (Darley & Batson, 1973, p. 104). As the students went by, the man coughed twice and groaned, but did not move. The researchers rated seminary students on how much help they gave the "victim." Students got no "points" if they did not appear to notice him. They got 1 point if they thought he might need help but did not stop. They got 2 points if they did not stop but told the assistant in the next building about him. The maximum was 5 points if they refused to leave the victim and insisted on taking him someplace where he could be helped (in the same way that the Good Samaritan took the man to an inn). Figure 12.1 shows how much help the "victim" received from seminary students who thought they were early and might have to wait when they arrived at the other building, thought they were going to be exactly on time (in which case stopping to help would make them late), or thought they were already late. Time constraints had a large impact on helping, regardless of whether the seminary students were speaking about their job prospects or about the parable of the Good Samaritan. As the figure shows, participants who were late for an appointment scored on average either 1 point or one-half a point, which constituted virtually no helping.

The results of the Good Samaritan study are especially compelling because some of the seminary students were mentally rehearsing a story about the necessity for helping a man who was slumped on the side of the road! If being a few minutes late for an experimental appointment that had little relevance to their lives could deter the seminary students from helping a possible victim, then unselfish helping might be a rare occurrence. If unselfish helping is so rare, however, how do we explain the high incidence of modern volunteerism? Modern volunteerism involves difficult, time-consuming work in activities such as providing support to people with AIDS, companionship to the elderly, health care to the sick, tutoring for children at risk, counseling to victims of traumatic incidents, feeding the hungry, and giving shelter to the homeless (Clary & Snyder, 1991; Snyder & Omoto, 1992). In 1991 alone, 94.2 million people in the United States engaged in some form of volunteerism. Over 25 million of them

FIGURE 12.1

Time pressure decreases helping.

Graph shows amount of help seminary students gave to a man slumped in a doorway when they were early, on time, or late to deliver two different speeches (Darley & Batson, 1973)

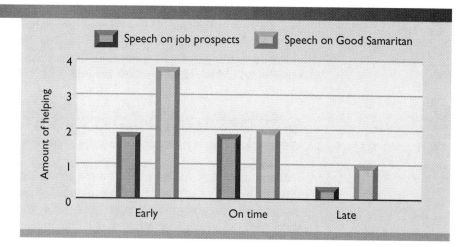

gave five or more hours per week to volunteer service (Omoto & Snyder, 1995). How also do we explain such seemingly unselfish acts as donating blood, a kidney, or other organs (Borgida, Conner, & Manteufel, 1992; Breckler, 1994)?

One explanation of volunteerism and other forms of helping, from the Good Samaritan through the present day, is that people only help others when they get something out of it. According to this "all helping is inherently selfish" perspective, the Good Samaritan, Mother Teresa, and modern volunteers probably helped for selfish reasons. They wanted to assuage their own guilt, to be praised by others, to have their favors reciprocated, to avoid a social revolution, or whatever (Batson, 1994). The logic is that "If they did not think that the benefits of helping outweighed the costs, they would not have done it." No one could quarrel with this logic, except in how we define "benefits."

In this chapter, we define "altruism" (unselfish helping) as helping in which the primary benefit sought is an improvement in the *other person's* condition (Batson, 1987). One could argue that seeking to improve another person's condition is "selfish" if seeing the other person's improvement would give the helper pleasure. To do so, however, would define the possibility of unselfish helping out of existence. Admittedly, most helping involves both selfish and unselfish motives. If we say that unselfish helping has as its primary goal an improvement in the *other person's* condition, though, we can ask whether any evidence suggests that unselfish helping exists, which is the topic discussed in the first section of the chapter. The second section of the chapter examines several reasons why people help. The third section describes reasons why people sometimes fail to help others in emergencies.

IS HELPING EVER UNSELFISH?

The "selfish" view of human nature is that people help each other only when it is in their own selfish interests to do so. According to the selfish view, individuals strive to maximize their own gains at minimal costs. People help each other *only* when the rewards that they expect to obtain by helping are greater than the personal sacrifices that they have to make in order to help. The "altruistic" view of human nature, in contrast, holds that people sometimes help each other to alleviate the other person's need, suffering, or distress (Batson, 1987, 1991). According to the altruistic view, individuals sometimes want to relieve the suffering of others, even when their only reward is a change in the other person's fortunes. The act of helping another human being can be rewarding for its own sake. This section of the chapter first describes factors that might create unselfish as well as selfish helping. Then we examine cross-cultural evidence suggesting that altruistic or unselfish helping might be as prevalent around the world as is selfish helping.

FACTORS THAT MIGHT CREATE UNSELFISH HELPING

This section of the chapter reviews three factors that might create unselfish or altruistic helping. One factor is the evolutionary principle of *inclusive fitness*. A second factor involves the tendency for people who live in groups to develop *spontaneous communication* of motives and emotions. A third factor involves practices that encourage the *socialization of empathy*.

■ INCLUSIVE FITNESS

The theory of evolution is based on "survival of the fittest." The individual members of a species who cope best with their environment have selfish, competitive characteristics. Such characteristics make them especially successful in securing food and shelter, surviving long enough to reach reproductive age, finding mates, and protecting their offspring (Darwin, 1872). As a result, they are more likely than their less "fit" peers to have children. Helping another member of the species without getting at least as much benefit in return, for example sharing scarce food or water, is a "non-fit" characteristic. A non-fit characteristic might reduce the individual's chances for survival. Over time, survival of the fittest increases the frequency within the species of individuals who have "fit" characteristics and decreases the frequency of individuals who have less fit characteristics.

Evolutionary fitness, however, consists of more than merely helping oneself and harming or ignoring everyone else. To survive long enough to pass on their genetic characteristics to succeeding generations, individuals must excel at two tasks: coping with the environment as individuals, and contributing to a group or community whose members help each other (Hoffman, 1981a). Early human beings did not live by themselves as individuals. From anthropological evidence, we know that our distant ancestors lived in small, nomadic *groups* that foraged for food and hunted other animals. Some of these early human beings had characteristics that allowed them to function well in groups. Others did not. Groups of individuals who were able to coordinate their efforts had a distinct evolutionary advantage over "loners" (Chency, Seyforth, & Smuts, 1986). Individuals who acted not just for their own best interests, but for the best interests of the group survived and flourished by working together (Alexander, 1972; Campbell, 1965).

Individuals who had "inclusive fitness" acted in ways that maximized the reproductive success of themselves and the members of their own groups, many of whom were close blood relatives (Hamilton, 1964, 1971). The closer the relative, the more likely the person was to share the individual's own genetic characteristics, so helping relatives was almost as good as helping oneself. Imagine an individual who died while successfully defending three brothers, two sisters, and four children from a saber-toothed tiger. That individual passed on more of his or her characteristics to the next generation than did an individual who ran away, leaving siblings and children to be slaughtered. Also, groups tend to be very protective of the surviving children of martyred heroes. The group may realize intuitively that the children of heroes are more likely than others to sacrifice their own interests for the group's interests in the future (Hoffman, 1981a).

In one modern study of inclusive fitness and helping, Japanese and U.S. college students were asked to imagine that they had time to save one, and only one, of three people who were sleeping in separate bedrooms when their home caught on fire (Burnstein, Crandall, & Kitayama, 1994). The three people differed in how closely related they were to the student. For instance, would a student save her grandmother, her cousin, or her sister? As the researchers predicted, students in both Japan and the United States were more willing to risk their lives trying to save a close genetic relative (a sister or a parent, for instance) than a distant genetic relative (a cousin).

These differences in helping close versus distant relatives occurred only when helping meant the difference between life and death, not merely doing a small favor. Also, students saved younger relatives, who might have future children, more often than they saved older relatives, who might not. The students were more likely to extend *everyday* helping to infants and the elderly. When it came to life or death, however, they preferred to help those who were near their child-bearing years. The principle of inclusive fitness makes it more adaptive to save a 12-year-old female cousin from a burning building than a 55-year-old female cousin. The 12-year-old cousin is very near to being able to have children. A 55-year-old cousin may have passed the age at which she can have children and pass on to succeeding generations some of *your* genetic characteristics (Burnstein et al., 1994).

The Carnegie Hero Commission, which has recognized close to 8,000 individuals for acts of heroism since 1904, almost never recognizes people who risked or sacrificed their lives to rescue a close relative (Burnstein et al., 1994). The commission members presumably realize that people look after their own in times of great peril, just as the principle of inclusive fitness says they should (Cunningham, 1986a; Dawkins, 1976, 1982). When a 60-year-old woman dies saving her 12-year-old granddaughter, she helps another person at great cost to herself. Her act seems less heroic, as the Carnegie Hero awards suggest, if we realize that her granddaughter's reproductive capacity is greater than her

Which of your close relatives would you rescue first from a burning building?

own. When it comes to a choice between her own life and her granddaughter's, the woman's life is less valuable for passing on her own genetic characteristics to succeeding generations. Inclusive fitness, then, might create the conditions necessary for acts of unselfish altruism.

■ SPONTANEOUS COMMUNICATION

Inclusive fitness is a form of altruism that benefits relatives and other group members when they need help. But how did early human beings, who for millions of years survived without benefit of language, communicate to each other that they needed help? One theory is that early human beings shared each other's emotions and motivations through "spontaneous communication" (Buck, 1984). **Spontaneous communication** is a nonintentional "leakage" of emotion from one person (the "sender") to another (the "receiver") through the sender's facial, body, and vocal cues (Buck, 1988; Buck & Ginsberg, 1991; Ginsberg, 1976).

In human beings, certain signals are necessary for individual and group survival. These signals are especially necessary for the coordination that gives the members of tight-knit groups an evolutionary advantage over loners. The signals include face, body, and vocal displays of the individual's emotions and motivations (Buck & Ginsberg, 1991). Some individuals are better than others at "sending" or displaying their spontaneous emotions and motivations. Similarly, some individuals are better than others at "receiving" emotional and motivational displays. Both sending and receiving abilities are essential for social coordination. The ability to be on the same wavelength as another human being, whether as sender or as receiver, is a necessary biological characteristic for inclusive fitness. Unlike spoken language, spontaneous communication is "direct." Senders do not send spontaneous communications deliberately, nor do receivers have to think about them in depth. The receiver *spontaneously* experiences emotions that are similar to the emotions being experienced by the sender (Eisenberg, 1986). When an infant sender cries and grimaces in pain, both child and adult receivers experience physiological arousal of their own (Bugental, Blue, Cortez, Fleck, & Rodriguez, 1992). Because the sender and the receiver both experience arousal, even though the arousal is caused by the sender's situation and not by the receiver's, both sender and receiver are motivated to end the arousal. The Good Samaritan might have helped because he could not stand to see another human being crying in anguish on the side of the road.

Spontaneous communication through facial, body, and vocal displays is a likely candidate for an evolutionarily adaptive, biological characteristic that might promote helping within social groups (Buck, 1984; Fabes, Eisenberg, & Miller, 1990; Hoffman, 1981a). According to the theory of spontaneous communication, people help each other in part because they become aroused by another group member's arousal. Even one- and two-day-old infants have enough spontaneous communication to experience another infant's arousal for themselves. When one infant cries in pain, nearby infants start crying, even though nothing about their own situation has changed (Sagi & Hoffman, 1976). Infants also cry more vehemently in response to another infant's cry than they do in response to equally loud nonhuman noises. It seems at least possible that the capacity for spontaneous communication exists at birth (Hoffman, 1981a). Very young infants mimic the facial expressions of adults (Field, Woodson, Greenberg, & Cohen, 1982). When an adult makes a happy face, the infant smiles. When an adult looks surprised, the infant widens his or her eyes and makes a circle with his or her mouth. When an adult grimaces in pain, the infant grimaces in turn and displays other signs of arousal, such as crying and fidgeting.

As they mature into adults, human beings display the reactions that we might expect if spontaneous communication creates empathic arousal, which in turn elicits helping. When they see another person in pain, adults betray their emotions not only in their facial expressions and body postures, but also by becoming physiologically aroused (Eisenberg & Fabes, 1991; Gaertner & Dovidio, 1977; Levine & Hoffman, 1975). Even when adults are asked to try *not* to experience the same emotions as a victim, they cannot help becoming physiologically aroused (Stotland, 1969). Empathic arousal is also greater when the person in pain is one of "my group" rather than an "outsider." Children display greater empathic arousal for other children of their own sex or race than for children of the opposite sex or a different race (Feshbach & Roe, 1968). In situations where perceived similarity is the only clue to who belongs in "my group," people display greater empathic arousal for and greater helping of other people whom they perceive as similar to rather than dissimilar from themselves (Krebs, 1983). Greater empathic arousal for a similar than for a dissimilar other is exactly what we would expect if empathic arousal evolved through inclusive fitness and through the spontaneous communication necessary for members of groups to coordinate their efforts (Buck & Ginsberg, 1991; Levenson & Ruef, 1992).

■ SOCIALIZATION OF EMPATHY

Empathic arousal may be spontaneous, but it is not guaranteed to happen. The development of empathy-related helping depends on socialization processes, during which practice, encouragement, and adult models are essential. "What appears to be a biologically based disposition to behave altruistically toward others in relation to their degree of apparent genetic similarity is reinforced by a variety of cultural prescriptions" (Krebs & Miller, 1985, p. 28). An infant's first opportunity to practice spontaneous communication is usually with his or her mother. Extensive research (described in Chapter 9) has shown that infants and their mothers develop three types of attachment: secure, anxious/ambivalent, or avoidant (Ainsworth, Blehar, Waters, & Wall, 1978; Bowlby, 1969). Secure attachment occurs when the infant is certain that the caretaker will respond when help is needed. Anxious/ambivalent attachment occurs when the caretaker sometimes responds and at other times does not. Avoidant attachment occurs when the caretaker behaves so negatively that the infant rebuffs attempts at physical or psychological closeness. Secure attachment, which is the norm among human beings, is the most likely of the three types of attachment to facilitate the development of empathy (Hendrick & Hendrick, 1986).

In a fascinating study with monkeys that were raised either by their mothers or in isolation, two monkeys learned that they would be shocked whenever a light came on, unless they could push a lever first (Miller, Caul, & Mirsky, 1967). Then one of the monkeys (the "sender") was placed in a room where the light was visible, but no lever was available. The second monkey (the "receiver"), that had the lever, could see the first monkey's face on a television monitor, but could not see the light. Normal "sender" monkeys made "distressed" faces whenever the light came on and normal "receiver" monkeys avoided shock for both of them by pressing the lever whenever the other monkey looked upset and anxious. Monkeys that had been raised in isolation, however, were unable to master the task, either as senders or as receivers. As senders, they looked terrified so frequently that even a normal monkey could not tell when to push the lever. As receivers, monkeys reared in isolation seemed to have no clue from facial expressions about the other monkey's internal arousal.

The monkey experiment suggests that spontaneous communication, empathic arousal, and empathic helping require certain kinds of experiences if they are to develop appropriately (Eisenberg & Fabes, 1991). The newborn infant's reactive cry must be nurtured by appropriate socialization processes if it is to develop into empathy-related helping among adults (Grusec, 1981; Hoffman, 1981b; Rushton, 1980; Staub, 1979). Parents frequently reward their child's helping behavior with thanks, smiles, hugs, and praise, all of which reliably increase the incidence of helping (Aronfreed, 1976; Gelfand & Hartmann, 1982; Rushton & Teachman, 1978). Parents also get their children to "internalize" helping by attributing helping behavior to positive personality characteristics. They make such statements as "That was very kind of you to let Johnny play with your truck when he was crying" (Grusec & Redler, 1980). Through such socialization practices, children gradually begin to associate helping with rewards and other positive, mood-elevating experiences (Cialdini & Kenrick, 1976). They learn to care about other people's welfare (Staub, 1992b).

Parents also teach their children by example (Bandura, 1973; Krebs, 1970; Rushton, 1975). Parents who display concern about the plight of others are likely to raise children who do the same. Parents who look the other way when other people need help are likely to produce children who are not as responsive to another person's suffering (Fabes, Eisenberg, & Miller, 1990). In one study of children in a day-care setting, most of the children reacted to another child's distress by becoming distressed themselves and by trying to help. Children who had been abused by their caretakers, in contrast, reacted to another child's distress with threats, anger, and actual physical attack (Main & George, 1985). To summarize, evolution favors individuals who are selfish when taking care of themselves, but also self-sacrificing when contributing to groups. People who live in groups get very good at detecting and responding to each other's motives and emotions. Parents also teach their children sympathy for other people who are suffering (Staub, 1993).

CROSS-CULTURAL COMPARISONS

If children who share a culture differ in how they are socialized to react when others are in distress, then it should come as no surprise that people who are raised in different cultures take different approaches to helping. These different approaches reflect four types of social relationships that occur across cultures: communal sharing, authority ranking, equality matching, and market pricing. Individuals differ in the relative strength of their motives to engage in each of the four types of relationships, which are described more extensively in Chapter 10. Cultural differences, however, are larger than individual differences (Fiske, 1991).

■ HELPING IN FOUR TYPES OF SOCIAL RELATIONSHIPS

The first type of social relationship, communal sharing, involves sharing resources and favors freely with others who need help. In cultures that practice communal sharing, people do not expect to have favors reciprocated (Fiske, 1990). The goal is to enhance a sense of community and solidarity. They share resources such as food, water, and land freely. They help each other primarily to sustain valued social relationships, not with any expectation of reciprocation or personal gain (Fiske, 1990, 1992). They cultivate a "norm of loyalty," in which community members help each other freely. In communal sharing, a genuine Good Samaritan expects nothing in return for his or her kindness.

The second type of social relationship, authority ranking, involves helping people of higher or lower status because you have a responsibility to do so. In cultures that practice authority ranking, people maintain separate duties and responsibilities (Fiske, 1991). They protect and help each other willingly, because they like the way the system operates. They do not try to "beat the system" or to gain personal advantage. Authority ranking imposes a "norm of social responsibility," in which people are expected to help those who depend on them (Berkowitz, 1972). In authority ranking, a priest might be expected to help a member of his own flock, but not people of other religions.

The third type of social relationship, equality matching, involves matching favors equally. In cultures that practice equality matching, people want to ensure equal status (Fiske, 1991). They take turns giving favors and resources to each other. They try to match each other's contributions. They would be upset if they thought that someone else was contributing more time or resources, because doing so would spoil the pleasure of an equal relationship. Equality matching imposes a "norm of reciprocity," in which people are expected to return favors in kind, but not in excess (Gergen, Ellsworth, Maslach, & Seibel, 1975; Gouldner, 1960). In equality matching, a Levite might help someone who had previously helped him, and precisely as much.

The fourth type of social relationship, market pricing, involves maximizing gains and minimizing costs. In cultures that practice market pricing, everything (including favors or help) has its price (Fiske, 1991). People exchange favors and try to get the best of the bargain. They carefully weigh both the costs and the benefits before they extend help. Market pricing imposes a "norm of equity," in which people help each other in proportion to their own costs and the other person's need (Greenberg & Cohen, 1982; Krebs, 1982). Market pricing might make it easy for priests, Levites, and other busy people to weigh the time it would cost against the benefits of stopping to help a victim.

The four types of social relationships differ in the motives for helping, but not necessarily in the likelihood that they will result in helping (Fiske, 1990, 1991). The goal of communal sharing, for instance, is to enhance a sense of community within your own group. This type of social relationship lends itself equally well to helping or to aggression. Our distant ancestors formed groups to protect themselves and their children against roving bands of strangers. Thus group solidarity often occurs at the expense of rival groups. A strong sense of group identity promotes both sharing of scarce resources within your own group and subjecting rival groups to genocide and "ethnic cleansing."

Similarly, authority ranking can be abused by those in power. Equality matching sometimes dictates eye-for-an-eye revenge. Market pricing includes slavery and crack dealing. The four types of social relationships are neither inherently "good" nor inherently "evil." Even in the United States, where socialization processes tend to promote market pricing, both children and adults frequently help others who are in need (Staub, 1970, 1971, 1974; Snyder & Omoto, 1992). The four types of social relationships differ primarily in whether helping, when it is offered, is more "collectivistic" or more "individualistic." Does helping serve the community or the individual?

■ COLLECTIVISTIC VERSUS INDIVIDUALISTIC ORIENTATIONS

Although specific social relationships usually involve a mixture of the four types, cultures differ in whether they have a collectivistic orientation or an individualistic orientation. **Collectivistic cultures** emphasize the group's goals and a group or social identity. **Individualistic cultures** emphasize the individual's goals and an individual or personal identity. In collectivistic cultures like those of southern Italy, traditional Greece, mid-Africa, Pakistan, and rural China, children learn to subordinate their individual goals to the goals of the group. In individualistic cultures like those of Northern and Western Europe, Canada, Australia, New Zealand, and the United States, children learn to pursue their individual goals even when those goals are at odds with those of a particular group (Hofstede, 1980; Triandis, 1989a). Approximately 70% of the world's population lives in predominantly collectivistic cultures and 30% in predominantly individualistic cultures (Bell, 1987).

Although all cultures contain elements of both collectivism and individualism, cultures differ dramatically in which of the orientations predominates in their socialization practices. They differ especially in how much help people expect and what types of social relationships operate within as opposed to between groups. One difference between individualistic and collectivistic cultures reminds us of a theme that is described in Chapter 1 and that permeates this book: People who live in individualistic cultures tend to emphasize their personal identity, whereas people who live in collectivistic cultures tend to emphasize their social identity (Abrams, 1992; Brewer, 1991; Cousins, 1989; Crocker, Luhtanen, Blaine, & Broadnax, 1994; Deaux, 1993; Ethier & Deaux, 1994; Markus & Kitayama, 1994; Miller & Prentice, 1994; Oyserman, 1993; Trafimow, Triandis, & Goto, 1991; Turner, Oakes, Haslam, & McGarty, 1994). The personal identity is the self as an individual. The social identity is the self as an indistinguishable part of a group. For people who have a strong social identity, helping another group member is the same as helping yourself.

As shown in Table 12.1, researchers have discovered many intriguing differences between cultures that have collectivistic versus individualistic orientations. Collectivistic orientations prevail in less wealthy countries where the culture is less complex, specifically in the number of groups to which an individual typically belongs. When individuals are relatively poor and belong to very few groups, they need the primary group's financial and emotional support. They have few attractive alternatives. In more affluent, complex cultures, individuals do not depend as much on one primary group for financial or emo-

Do people in Asian cultures help each other more than in Western cultures?

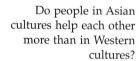

TABLE 12.1	Differences between Collectivistic and Individualistic Cultures (Abstracted from Triandis, 1989a; Triandis, Bontempo, Villareal, Asai, & Lucca, 1988; and Triandis, McCusker, & Hui, 1990)	
	COLLECTIVISTIC	**INDIVIDUALISTIC**
Local economy	poor	wealthy
Cultural complexity	low	high
Number of group memberships	low	high
Relationship with own group(s)	stable	unstable
Goals pursued	the group's	one's own
Valued accomplishments	group's	own
Perception of own group	homogeneous	heterogeneous
Perception of other groups	heterogeneous	homogeneous
Cooperation with group members	high	medium
Cooperation with nonmembers	low	medium
Exchanges within own group	equality and need	equity
Attention paid to	people	tasks
Skill at making friends	low	high
Commitment to friends	enduring	transient
Crime, divorce, child abuse	low	high
Suicide, emotional stress	low	high
Mental illness	low	high

tional support. Rejection by any one group is not as devastating. They are freer to pursue their own goals, even when their own goals conflict with a group's goal. Their pride comes from their own personal accomplishments rather than the group's accomplishments. Within their own groups, members of collectivistic cultures share resources equally according to need (Marin, 1985). In dealing with "outsiders" they insist on the market pricing or "equity" principle that they receive resources in direct proportion to their contributions.

People who live in collectivistic cultures find it very difficult to make new friends, but they also pay more attention to social relationships than to impersonal tasks. Once they have admitted another person to their "in group" the friendship is a lifelong, enduring commitment that involves mutual support in times of need. People who live in individualistic cultures, in contrast, tend to make friends more easily. They readily abandon friendships, however, when one of the "friends" needs help. The strong sense of group commitment in collectivistic cultures may contribute to their lower incidence of crime, divorce, child abuse, suicide, and emotional stress. People who live in collectivistic cultures, in contrast to those who live in individualistic cultures, enjoy a strong "social support network" that helps to overcome stressful life events (Triandis, 1989a).

Although the collectivistic orientation may lend itself more than the individualistic orientation to helping within the individual's own group, people in all cultures help each other for both collectivistic and individualistic reasons. Most of the research on helping has been conducted in individualistic cultures (Triandis, 1989a). The question "Why do people help?" has both collectivistic and individualistic answers, however, in every culture. People who live in individualistic cultures help their own group's members when they develop a strong social identity with the group (Branscombe & Wann, 1994). Unselfish helping is not as unusual as it may appear to people who live in individualistic, exchange-oriented cultures. Even in such cultures, it may be useful to encourage volunteerism by emphasizing concern over the plight of victims, as well as by reminding people of the personal benefits that they might reap from helping (Batson, 1994; Omoto & Snyder, 1995).

SUMMARY OF WHETHER HELPING IS EVER UNSELFISH

It is possible to define unselfish or altruistic helping out of existence by claiming that people never do anything unless they get something out of it. Some evidence suggests, however, that unselfish helping exists. People sometimes sacrifice their own interests to improve another person's condition. Evolution favors both the selfish, competitive characteristics necessary for individual survival and the cooperative, self-sacrificing characteristics necessary for group survival. Inclusive fitness involves aiding relatives and similar others who are included in your own genetic group, especially in matters of life and death. People who live in groups develop spontaneous communication, in which one group member's motives and emotions "leak" to other group members. Through spontaneous communication, people become empathically distressed and concerned when someone similar or close to them is in danger. Parents who develop secure relationships with their children encourage and model empathic distress and concern. Finally, many of the world's cultures emphasize sharing resources rather than the exchange orientation of Western Europe and the United States, in which people weigh personal costs against personal benefits before acting. In cultures that are predominantly collectivistic, people have a social identity, so helping other group members is the same as helping themselves. It may be only people who live in individualistic, exchange-oriented cultures who find the idea of unselfish helping difficult to imagine.

WHY DO PEOPLE HELP?

Having established that unselfish helping is theoretically and practically possible, it is time to discuss more specifically *why* people help each other. As we shall see, help springs from three sources: *self-interest, mood management,* and *empathic concern.* Each of these three sources can make helping either more or less

likely, depending on the circumstances. Self-interest and mood management, however, are selfish reasons for helping. Empathic concern is an unselfish reason.

SELF-INTEREST

Not surprisingly, both children and adults who are socialized in an individualistic, market pricing culture often base their decisions about helping or not helping on their own self-interests. They calculate how much helping will cost them and how much they have to gain (Dovidio, Piliavin, Gaertner, Schroeder, & Clark, 1991). When the costs are low and the possible gains are high, they help. When the costs are high and the possible gains are low, they look the other way. Studies of helping, most of which were conducted in predominantly individualistic cultures, have identified at least three potential costs of helping and three potential gains.

■ COSTS OF HELPING

Three frequently studied costs of helping are the risk of possible harm, aversion to the victim, and potential violation of social norms. Several studies have shown that helping is more frequent when the potential risk for the helper is low rather than high. In one such study, the student participant sat alone in a laboratory room completing questionnaires (Shotland & Straw, 1976). A few minutes later, a man and a woman confederate staged a "fight" in the corridor outside the student's room. As the man punched her, the woman several times yelled a phrase that was intended to give some of the students a different impression than others. For some of the onlooking students, she yelled, "I don't even know you." For others, she yelled, "I don't even know why I married you." Far fewer participants tried to help the woman when her attacker was apparently her husband than when her attacker was apparently a stranger. The students cited one primary reason for not helping in the "husband condition." They believed that a stranger might run away when they tried to intervene. A husband, in contrast, might attack them (perhaps with the wife's help!). One of the primary reasons for helping less in one situation than another, then, is the cost of potential injury to the helper.

Another cost of helping is having to overcome physical aversion in order to assist a victim who is repulsive or disgusting. Helping is more likely when we can help without being physically revulsed than when we have to do something that might turn our stomachs. The Good Samaritan, for instance, might have had to overcome initial repulsion to touching a man who was bleeding.

Could an ugly birthmark keep this man from getting help if he falls?

The effect of physical aversion on helping was tested in two studies that occurred *before* the public became aware of AIDS. In the first study, several college student confederates of the experimenter separately entered a Philadelphia subway car (Piliavin & Piliavin, 1972). As the train started, one of the confederates, a neatly dressed white male, started walking with a cane toward the end of the car. In full view of the unsuspecting subway passengers, he collapsed and lay still on the floor. To manipulate "repulsiveness" and to make helping the collapsed man seem costly and physically aversive, he sometimes "bled" profusely from his mouth (by biting an eye dropper full of red food coloring). At other times, he did not "bleed."

The other confederates, who made no move to help the fallen man, surreptitiously recorded how long it took for passengers to help. If no one had helped the victim by the time the next subway stop came, which was approximately three minutes, the other confederates helped the victim to his feet. Then they all left the train, to repeat their performance on the next train heading in the opposite direction. By the end of the day, the transit police wanted to talk to the experimenters because some of the unsuspecting passengers had pulled the train's emergency cord. After talking to the police, the confederates compared notes. As they had predicted, other passengers hesitated longer and helped less when the man was bleeding than when he was not bleeding.

In the second study of physical aversion as a cost of helping, the researchers wanted to eliminate the alternative explanation that subway passengers might have regarded touching a bleeding man as potentially harmful to the victim (Piliavin, Piliavin, & Rodin, 1975). To eliminate the "harmful to the victim" explanation, they restaged the subway collapse in New York City. The experimental scenario was the same as in Philadelphia, except that they did not use "blood." Instead, the victim sometimes had a large, ugly port wine stain birthmark (applied with theatrical makeup) on his left cheek. At other times, his face was unmarked. When he fell, the victim lay curled on his right side, so that the birthmark was plainly visible. Consistent with a "repulsiveness" explanation, the other subway passengers hesitated longer and helped less when the victim was facially disfigured than when he was not. It would be hard to argue that the ugly birthmark made the man seem more seriously injured. Instead, the researchers concluded that helping decreases as costs to the helper increase.

Finally, helping often involves a risky violation of implicit or explicit "rules of conduct," for which helpers may be reprimanded if it turns out that their help was not needed. In a compelling study with children as potential helpers, a seventh-grade (12-year-old) boy or girl sat in a laboratory room drawing pictures (Staub, 1971). The experimenter claimed to be interested in "what boys and girls of different ages like to draw best." She told the seventh grader that she had to go into an adjoining room to check on the progress of a seven-year-old girl who was also in the study. When she returned, the experimenter said that the little girl had finished her drawing and was playing by herself. Then the experimenter left by a different door. To some boys and girls, she said nothing more. To others, she said, "If you need more drawing pencils, you may go into the other room [pointing at the door to the adjoining room where the little girl was supposedly playing] where there are some pencils on the windowsill." In this way, the experimenter subtly gave some of the seventh graders "permission" to enter the adjoining room. By saying nothing, she left the other seventh graders with the implicit "rule of conduct" that they could not leave the experimental room.

The seventh grader did not realize that there was no little girl in the adjoining room, where the experimenter had started a tape recording. Ninety seconds after the experimenter left, a loud, very realistic crash came from the ad-

Will people break pencils (and rules) to help each other?

joining room. A young girl's voice could be heard clearly, first screaming when the crash occurred and then sobbing and crying, "Help, please help. . . . I fell off the ladder, my foot is caught, please help. . . . Please someone take the ladder off my foot," and so on for 70 seconds or until the seventh grader entered the adjoining room. If the seventh grader did not enter the adjoining room, the experimenter returned one minute after the recording had ended. She waited to see whether the seventh grader would report that the little girl next door was injured.

As predicted, more seventh graders went into the adjoining room to help the little girl if they thought that doing so fell within the "rules of conduct" than if they did not. Breaking the rules of conduct presumably risked adult disapproval. Perhaps the most dramatic evidence that the seventh graders felt they needed permission to enter the other room came when one of the students in the "permission" group listened intently to the little girl's cries. Then she very deliberately broke each of the points on her two drawing pencils. She knew that she could enter the adjoining room if she needed more drawing pencils. She first created such a need and then ran into the adjoining room to help. This seventh grader took no chances that she might have misinterpreted the little girl's cries. She made sure that the experimenter could not rebuke her for breaking an implicit rule of conduct.

■ GAINS FROM HELPING

Potential helpers calculate very carefully the possible costs of helping. They do so whether the costs are danger to themselves, physical aversion to the victim, violating rules of conduct, or other unwanted consequences. They also weigh the possible costs against the possible gains. One very attractive gain from helping is being praised or rewarded. As discussed in the earlier section on socialization of empathy, children who are praised for helping begin to help more often. Adults do the same. In a relevant study with college women who needed approval, the researcher thanked some of them profusely for being in an experiment (Deutsch & Lamberti, 1986). The experimenter dismissed others curtly. After the experiment, another student needed help to retrieve lost notebooks. Women who received profuse thanks helped more than did women who received curt dismissal. One of the most important gains to be had from helping is being praised or rewarded by others.

Another important gain from helping is avoiding guilt. The Good Samaritan, unlike the busy priest and Levite, might have felt unbearable guilt had he not stopped to help a man who had been robbed and beaten. Even when other people are not involved and social approval is unlikely, people have to live with themselves. People help in part because not offering assistance might elicit guilt and self-recrimination. People who feel guilty, then, might be more likely to help a victim than would people who do not feel guilty. In one study of the relationship between guilt and helping, visitors to the Portland Art Museum were the unwitting participants (Katsev, Edelsack, Steinmetz, Walker, & Wright, 1978). Signs at the entrance to the museum and next to each sculpture and Indian artifact warned visitors "Please Do Not Touch" the objects on display. The researchers noticed, however, that many visitors could not resist touching. On the day of the experiment, the experimenters had a confederate pose as a museum guard. For some of the visitors who touched one of the displayed objects, the "guard" firmly but politely reminded them about the sign. To make them feel guilty, he continued, "If everyone touched them, they will deteriorate." Other visitors who touched one of the displayed objects were not reprimanded. Another group of visitors never touched the objects.

Would museum visitors become more helpful if they inadvertently touched an art treasure?

Visitors from all three of these experimental groups had to pass through a hallway to reach the next part of the exhibit. When they did so, they passed an "art student" who was trying to draw one of the sculptures. "By accident," the student dropped a large number of art pencils that rolled all over the floor. The experimenters recorded the percentage of visitors from each of the three groups who stopped to help the art student pick up her pencils. As predicted, the most help (58%) came from visitors the guard had made feel guilty about touching museum displays. A medium amount of help (40%) came from visitors who had touched the objects but had not been admonished. (Some of them may have felt guilty on their own.) Least help (35%) came from visitors who had not touched the exhibits. Although these visitors might have been the most cooperative with museum authorities, they helped least. They had nothing to feel guilty about.

In another study of guilt and helping, a neatly dressed male experimenter approached women who were walking alone in a shopping center. The man asked the women to take his photograph with a very expensive-looking camera that he claimed to be using for "a project" (Regan, Williams, & Sparling, 1972). When a woman agreed, the experimenter mentioned that his camera was "sensitive" but that he had set it so that the woman need only turn the focus ring and snap the shutter. When she did so, the shutter did not release. For some women, the experimenter dismissed the problem by saying that his camera "acts up a lot." For others, he tried to make the woman feel guilty by saying that she must have turned the wrong dial and jammed the camera. He acted clearly upset about the damage to his expensive equipment, thanked the woman perfunctorily, and walked away. A few stores away, in the direction the woman had been walking, a female confederate was waiting. When she saw the woman who had "broken" the camera approaching, the confederate walked in front of her. The confederate carried a shopping bag in which the bottom corner had been torn. Loose candies leaked from the bag onto the floor behind her. The measure of helping was whether the woman notified the "fellow shopper" that she was losing candy from her torn bag. As predicted, 55 percent of the shoppers that the man made feel guilty about "breaking" his camera told the confederate that her bag was leaking. Only 15 percent of shoppers who did not feel guilty bothered to help her.

Other studies have demonstrated increased helping by people who only *witness* another person being harmed, even though they do not cause the harm themselves (Konecni, 1972; Rawlings, 1968; Regan, 1971). One explanation of the relationship between guilt and helping is that it is arousing either to cause or to witness another person's suffering. Merely witnessing another human being in anguish is sufficient to elicit spontaneous communication and empathic arousal. The sight of another person being harmed makes people feel upset, so they help because they seek relief from their own personal distress (Weiss, Boyer, Lombardo, & Stich, 1972). In a relevant study, college student participants met a female experimenter (Cialdini, Darby, & Vincent, 1973). The experimenter told the student that, for lack of space, the study would be conducted in the office of a fellow graduate student who was out of his office at the time. When the student and the experimenter arrived at the other graduate student's office, the experimenter staged a disaster. For some students, the experimenter pulled a chair out from the desk. For others, the experimenter pointed to the chair and asked the student to pull it out. In either case, the chair was rigged so that moving it dislodged three boxes of computer cards that spilled all over the floor. The experimenter exclaimed, "Oh, no! I think it's the data from Tom's master's thesis! And I know he doesn't have the time to put the cards back in order because he's studying for his qualifying exams." The procedure was designed to ensure that all participants felt distressed about Tom's thesis being ruined. They felt distressed whether they caused the disaster themselves or had merely been a part of the office-lending scheme that produced it.

Following the card-spilling accident, the experimenter tried to alleviate the distress experienced by some of the students. The experimenter had them work puzzles. The experimenter told some students that they had done amazingly well. The experimenter unexpectedly gave other students money for participating. If people help because they want to alleviate their distress on seeing another person harmed, then giving them "relief" from their distress should make them feel better and decrease their need to help. Other students, therefore, got no "relief." They received neither profuse praise nor extra money. They were presumably still distressed about Tom's thesis being ruined. The experimenter then left the office "to get the credit slip." Five minutes later, a woman confederate appeared in the office. She said that she had permission to request assistance on a telephone survey of undergraduate study habits. She could not offer experimental credit or any other reward to people who agreed to make telephone calls for her. She would, however, greatly appreciate their help. Regardless of whether they or the experimenter harmed Tom's thesis, students that the experimenter unexpectedly praised or paid were less likely to help than were students that the experimenter did not praise or pay. Receiving praise or pay relieved empathic distress and canceled the need to help.

MOOD MANAGEMENT

The study about Tom's computer cards suggests that people who experience a negative emotion feel better when they help someone. As this part of the section explains, other studies have shown that the potential helper's mood reliably increases helping. The effect occurs for both positive and negative moods. In addition, as also suggested by the computer card study, people who feel guilty or empathically distressed appear to realize intuitively that helping can improve their negative moods.

■ NEGATIVE AND POSITIVE MOODS INCREASE HELPING

Negative events like breaking cameras or spilling computer cards make people feel bad and increase helping. But what of positive events that make people feel good? Interestingly, many studies have shown that people who are in a positive mood, like people who are in a negative mood, increase their "normal" amount of helping. In one study of the effects of positive mood on helping, the experimenters surreptitiously placed a coin in the return slot of a shopping mall telephone that an unsuspecting shopper was about to use (Isen & Levin, 1972, Study 2). For other shoppers, the experimenters left no coin. As the shopper was walking away from the telephone (with or without a "gift" coin), a female confederate dropped a manila folder full of papers. The papers scattered on the floor in the shopper's path. Only 5% of shoppers who had not found a coin stopped to help. As predicted, however, 87% of shoppers who had found a coin helped the "victim."

In another study of positive mood and helping, the experimenters asked passersby on a college campus to help them by answering survey questions (Cunningham, 1979). Regardless of whether the experimenters requested help in summer or in winter, people helped more when there was bright sunshine than when the day was overcast and gloomy. Sunshine usually puts people in a good mood. Being in a positive mood, regardless of what caused the positive mood, makes people more helpful.

People who are in a good mood are not merely more cooperative. Their good mood makes them more willing to engage in specific behaviors that are helpful to other people, not merely in *any* cooperative behaviors. Experimenters in one study gave cookies to randomly selected college men who were studying at library carrels (Isen & Levin, 1972, Study 1). Other men did not get any cookies. A few minutes later, a different person tried to persuade each of the men to volunteer to assist in conducting a psychology experiment. Some of the men learned that they could assist by holding and turning various items while the study participants were trying to invent novel uses for the items. Having someone else display and manipulate the items was said to be very helpful to people's creativity. Others of the men learned that they could assist by making noises, rattling papers, and dropping books near people who were trying to study in the library. The experiment was supposedly about whether students became distracted more easily during finals week than at other times.

In summary, the experimenter asked some of the men who had either received or not received an unexpected gift of cookies to cooperate by being helpful. The experimenter asked other men to cooperate by being annoying. As Figure 12.2 shows, men who were merely studying and received no cookie "surprise" were as willing to annoy other people as to help them. Men who had recently received a cookie surprise to put them in a good mood, in contrast, were much more likely to volunteer to help others than to annoy others.

FIGURE 12.2

Good moods increase helping, not merely cooperation.

Graph shows percentage of men who agreed to help or annoy others after they were or were not put in a good mood by an unexpected gift (Isen & Levin, 1972)

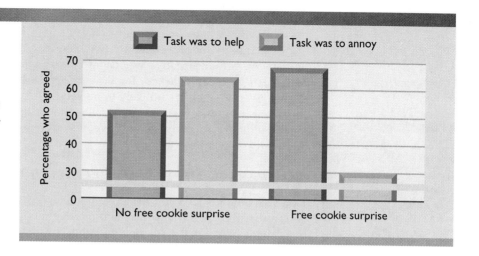

Positive mood so reliably increases helping that researchers use several labels to describe the phenomenon. They call it "the warm glow of success," "the glow of good will," and "feel good, do good" (Berkowitz & Connor, 1966; Isen, 1970; Rosenhan, Salovey, & Hargis, 1981). In addition, researchers have proposed several explanations, all of which contribute to the relationship between positive mood and helping (Carlson, Charlin, & Miller, 1988). First, people who are in an unusually good mood tend to see everything in a more positive light (Clark & Teasdale, 1985; Forgas, Bower, & Krantz, 1984). They exaggerate the likelihood and importance of potential gains from helping (Clark & Waddell, 1983). Second, people who are in a good mood are self-conscious about looking good to themselves and to others by adhering to "ideal" norms of socially acceptable behavior (Berkowitz, 1987; Gibbons & Wicklund, 1982). Third, people who are in a good mood perceive specific other people and the social community in a more positive way (Holloway, Tucker, & Hornstein, 1977). They take a more optimistic and positive view of human nature. They are thus more likely to believe that *they* would get help if they needed it. Fourth, people who are in a good mood are especially sensitive to the effect that different types of behavior might have on their mood (Wegener & Petty, 1994). They do not want to be "brought down" by refusing to help (Clark & Isen, 1982). Helping seems to them like an activity much more in keeping with and likely to sustain their current positive mood than not helping (Cialdini, Kenrick, & Baumann, 1982).

With all these factors contributing to the relationship between positive mood and helping, it is not surprising that positive moods have increased helping across many studies. Researchers have elicited and measured positive mood in many ways. They have given participants many different opportunities to help (Salovey, Mayer, & Rosenhan, 1991). The results have been very consistent. The lone exception to the rule is that people who are put in a positive mood by someone else's good fortune (not their own) are *less* rather than more likely to help. A relevant study demonstrated the difference between feeling good about one's own versus another person's situation. Students first imagined either themselves or their best friend on holiday in Hawaii (Rosenhan, Salovey, & Hargis, 1981). Both of these imaginary scenarios put the students in a very positive mood. The experimenter then gave students an opportunity to help with a different experimenter's project. Students who were in a positive mood because they imagined *themselves* in Hawaii helped more than did students who had no mood manipulation. Students who were in a positive

Would you help someone more if your best friend had just won a trip to Hawaii?

mood because they imagined *someone else* in Hawaii helped less. Their positive mood may have been tinged with jealousy.

In summary, negative and positive moods sometimes have similar effects on helping. Not all negative moods, of course, increase helping. People who have been viciously attacked, for instance, undoubtedly experience negative moods. Even so, they are unlikely to be very helpful to others. Nonetheless, at least some negative events create negative moods, which in turn increase helping. In addition, at least some positive events create positive moods, which in turn increase helping.

■ HELPING IMPROVES NEGATIVE MOODS

How can both positive and negative moods increase helping? Table 12.2 suggests an answer. Positive events elicit positive moods. People who are in positive moods help for the reasons described in the previous section. Negative events elicit negative moods. People who are in negative moods help because they believe that helping will alter their moods for the better. Positive moods and negative moods both increase helping, but for different reasons (Cunningham, Steinberg, & Grev, 1980).

As shown in the middle row of Table 12.2, the two processes sometimes cancel each other. Although a positive event and a negative event might both increase helping, they do so because of their effects on mood and the mood's subsequent effects on helping. When a negative event (such as harming another person or seeing another person harmed) deflates mood but a subsequent positive event (such as receiving a reward) inflates mood, the result is a neutral mood. The potential helper's mood is back to normal and helping does not change. The individual's attention shifts away from the mood, its cause, and its possible alleviation (Millar, Millar, & Tesser, 1988).

This argument about positive and negative moods depends on the assumption that people use helping strategically to alter their own negative moods. People who are in a negative mood are unlikely to help *unless* they think that helping will make them feel better. People who are in a positive mood help *regardless* of the anticipated mood effects. In a relevant experiment, students thought that they were participating in a memory study (Manucia, Baumann, & Cialdini, 1984). To put them in a negative mood, the researchers asked some of the students to remember their most personally distressing experiences. To leave their moods unchanged and presumably neutral, the researchers asked other students to remember the route they had taken to school. Students who remembered distressing experiences said that they were in a much worse mood than did students who remembered their route to school.

All students then drank a cup of a "memory drug" called Mnemoxine. (It was actually flat tonic water.) The researchers told some of the students in each mood condition that the drug had no mood-related side effects. They told other

TABLE 12.2	Relationships Between Events, Moods, Goals, and Their Effects on Helping		
EVENT	**MOOD**	**GOAL**	**EFFECT ON HELPING**
positive	positive	retain rosy view of world	increased helping
neutral or both negative and positive	neutral	none	normal helping
negative	negative	improve mood	increased helping

FIGURE 12.3

Negative moods do not increase helping when helping cannot improve mood.

Graph shows percentage of students in two moods who agreed to help a blood bank after drinking or not drinking a substance that "fixed" their moods (Manucia, Baumann, & Cialdini, 1984)

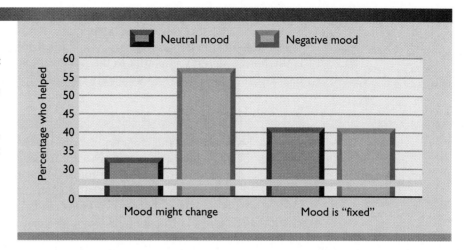

students that a standard side effect of the drug was to "preserve chemically whatever mood you are in when it takes effect" (Manucia et al., 1984, p. 360). For these students, mood was said to be "fixed" for at least 25 minutes. After the mood manipulation and the "memory drug," the experimenter pretended to run out of experimental forms and opened the door to leave. A confederate, wearing identification from a local nonprofit blood bank, appeared in the doorway and asked permission to speak to the students. When the experimenter had left, the confederate asked the students to make some phone calls to collect additional information from previous blood donors. Figure 12.3 shows the percentage of students who agreed to help in each condition.

Most important was the effect of "mood fixing" on helping. As shown in Figure 12.3, students who thought that their moods might change displayed the usual effect of negative moods on helping. A larger percentage of them helped if they were in a negative mood than if they were in a neutral mood. As also shown in Figure 12.3, students who thought that their moods could not change were *not* more likely to help if they were in a negative mood. Students who were in a negative mood helped only when they believed that helping might change their moods, and not when helping would not change their moods. In the same experiment, although it is not shown in Figure 12.3, the "mood-fixing" manipulation had no such effect on students who were in a positive mood, because people who are in a positive mood do not help as a way to change their mood. The results suggest, and other research corroborates, that people might sometimes willingly expose themselves to information about another person's suffering. They do so when they expect that the suffering will be quickly relieved, because it is sometimes more rewarding to have a negative mood relieved than never to have been distressed at all (Fultz & Nielsen, 1993; Mills, 1993; Schaller, 1993).

EMPATHIC CONCERN

The discussions of self-interest and mood management placed much emphasis on the "selfish," individualistic, market-pricing orientation of weighing costs against gains. According to this perspective, people help each other only when they believe that they will get more out of the exchange than they have to contribute. Even moods are part of the "exchange." People who are in a bad mood help only when they believe that helping might make them feel better. Besides selfish motives, however, researchers believe that people sometimes help for reasons that are genuinely altruistic (Batson, 1987, 1990, 1991, 1994). They help even when their only reward for helping is bettering another person's lot. Unselfish, altruistic helping, at least in individualistic cultures, depends importantly on the victim's similarity to the potential helper and on whether potential helpers experience predominantly empathic concern or empathic distress.

■ SIMILARITY TO SELF

As described earlier in the chapter, inclusive fitness involves helping relatives and members of your own group, who are usually very similar to you. Spontaneous communication is easier the more similar the sender and receiver are to each other. Altruistic types of social relationships such as communal sharing are usually limited to "your own kind." In collectivistic cultures, the individual's goals are subordinate to the group's goals. The group is usually composed of individuals who are very similar to you. When a person who needs help is a relative or similar to you, the costs of helping may seem small and the benefits of helping may seem large (McGuire, 1994).

People experience greater physiological arousal when they witness a person similar to themselves being harmed than when they witness the same harm to someone who is dissimilar (Krebs, 1975; Stotland, 1969). In addition, people are more likely to help their fellow citizens than to help foreigners (Feldman, 1968). They are also more likely to help people who dress the same way they do, share their political orientations, and have personalities and attitudes similar to theirs (Dovidio, 1984; Gray, Russell, & Blockley, 1991; Hansson & Slade, 1977; Hensley, 1981; Karylowski, 1976; Wagner, Hornstein, & Holloway, 1982). Perceived similarity reliably causes people to value another person's welfare when the other person is in need (Batson, Turk, Shaw, & Klein, 1995).

These facts suggest that if people are ever going to help for purely altruistic rather than selfish reasons, such helping should occur for victims who are similar to rather than dissimilar from themselves. But how can we distinguish an unselfish from a selfish motive for helping? One way might be to manipulate both victim similarity and how easy it is to *avoid* helping. In a relevant study, the experimenters told college women that they were investigating perceptions of workers (Batson, Duncan, Ackerman, Buckley, & Birch, 1981, Experiment 1). The student drew lots with "another student" named Elaine (a confederate) to see who would be the worker and who would be the observer. The drawing was rigged. The student was always the observer. Over closed-circuit television, the student watched Elaine being fitted with electrodes that supposedly delivered electric shock. Some of the students believed that they would have to watch only two of ten sets of shocks that Elaine had agreed to take. Others believed that they would have to watch all ten sets. The experimenter also manipulated similarity to self, by showing the student a copy of an "interests and values" questionnaire that Elaine had supposedly completed. According to the questionnaire, Elaine either shared most of the student's interests and values or had opposite interests and values.

The experimenter described the shocks, which came on and off intermittently for two minutes during each of the ten planned sets, as moderate and unlikely "to cause permanent damage." The shock level was said to be two or three times more uncomfortable than "if you scuff your feet walking across a carpet and touch something metal." On the first two sets of shocks, Elaine seemed to be suffering so intensely, grimacing and thrashing around, that the assistant interrupted to ask whether Elaine could continue. Elaine said that she could continue, but would like a glass of water. When the assistant returned with the water, she asked whether Elaine had ever had difficulty with electric shock in the past. Elaine answered that as a child a horse had thrown her onto an electric fence. After the incident, Elaine's doctor warned her that even mild electric shocks might be intensely painful. The assistant urged Elaine not to continue. Elaine said that she wanted to finish because she knew that the experiment was important. The assistant suggested that the other student (the actual participant, who was watching all of this on the television monitor in a nearby room) might be willing to trade places with Elaine. Elaine agreed that the experimenter could ask the other student about the possibility of trading places, but she said that she was willing to continue in either case.

Approximately 30 seconds later, the experimenter entered the student's room and explained the situation. The experimenter informed the student that she was under no obligation to trade places with Elaine. For students who expected to watch only two of the ten sets of shocks, she told them that if they decided not to trade places with Elaine, they could leave immediately. For students who expected to watch all ten sets, she reminded them that they would have to stay and watch Elaine receive the other eight sets of electric shock.

The results suggest that people decide "rationally" on whether to help someone who is dissimilar from themselves. They use a different criterion, though, when they decide whether to help someone who is very similar to them. As discussed previously, people who are negatively aroused help for the "selfish" reason of alleviating their own distress. This is exactly what students did when they thought that Elaine was very different from them. When they could leave and thus alleviate their distress by simply "walking away," very few of them volunteered to trade places with Elaine. Leaving the scene was a much more cost-effective way for them to get the gain that they wanted. When they had to stay and watch, they could not escape their own negative arousal, so they were more willing to help. By their different reactions to the two conditions, students who thought that Elaine was different from them revealed that they were "selfishly" calculating the costs (taking shocks themselves) against the gains (alleviating the distress caused by watching Elaine's pain).

Students who thought that Elaine was very similar to them, in contrast, did not seem to care whether they could leave or not. They helped in either case. Even when all they had to do was refuse to trade places and leave the experiment, Elaine was so similar to them that they could not merely walk away and know that she was still receiving painful electric shocks. Their goal, then, was not so much to alleviate their own distress. They could have alleviated their distress by following the maxim "out of sight, out of mind." Instead, they wanted to alleviate *Elaine's* distress. Sacrificing your own comfort to improve another person's lot, even though the action does nothing to improve your fortunes, is the definition of altruistic as opposed to selfish helping.

■ EMPATHIC DISTRESS VERSUS EMPATHIC CONCERN

Similarity to self may change the motive for helping from selfish to unselfish because it changes the nature of the empathic emotion that potential helpers experience. We may feel more concerned about people who are similar to us. In a follow-up study that used the scenario just described (except that similarity was not manipulated), both male and female students participated (Batson, O'Quin, Fultz, Vanderplas, & Isen, 1983, Study 1). The "other student" was of their own sex, named either Elaine or Charlie. While the assistant was out of the room getting water, the experimenter had participants complete a form that asked about their emotional reactions to seeing Elaine (or Charlie) shocked. Some of the students were experiencing empathic distress. **Empathic distress** entails aversive arousal (feeling upset and disturbed) that occurs spontaneously when witnessing another person who is in pain or suffering (Hoffman, 1981b).

Students who experienced empathic distress said that they felt alarmed, grieved, upset, worried, disturbed, distressed, troubled, and perturbed. Other students were experiencing empathic concern. **Empathic concern** entails concern (feeling compassionate and sympathetic) about the welfare of another person who is in pain or suffering (Hoffman, 1981b). Students who experienced empathic concern said that they felt sympathetic, moved, compassionate, warm, softhearted, and tender.

Figure 12.4 shows the percentage of empathically distressed and empathically concerned students who were willing to trade places with Elaine (or Charlie), depending on whether they could "walk away" or had to stay and watch. When students who reported empathic distress had an "easy way out," they took it. Their gain in doing so was to alleviate their own distress. Once they had walked away from the experiment, they were no longer bothered by being upset or disturbed. When students who reported empathic concern had the same "easy way out," they decided instead to take Elaine's (or Charlie's) place. Their gain came from knowing that the other person was no longer suffering. This type of "gain" seems unselfish and genuinely altruistic (Hoffman, 1981a). It occurs even when the victim will never know which decision the student made (Fultz, Batson, Fortenbach, McCarthy, & Varney, 1986).

Related research suggests that people experience empathic distress when they are unable to regulate their own emotional reactions to seeing someone else suffer (Eisenberg & Fabes, 1992). They get so "overaroused" that their primary reason for helping is to relieve their own aversive arousal rather than to improve the victim's condition (Eisenberg, Fabes, Murphy, Karbon, Maszk, Smith, Suh, & O'Boyle, 1994). People experience empathic concern, in contrast, when they *can* regulate and control their own emotional reactions to seeing someone else suffer. Their moderate arousal takes the form of sympathy and viewing the situation from the victim's perspective (Eisenberg, Fabes, Schaller, Miller, Carlo, Poulin, Shea, & Shell, 1991). Sympathy and perspective-taking motivate them to help for the "unselfish" reason of improving the other person's condition. These differences between empathic distress and empathic concerns emerge not only in one-time situations such as helping Elaine, but also in sustained helping. In one study, for instance, some elderly people reported empathic distress. They were more likely to volunteer at a hospital when they were unable to control their emotions on learning of other people's plight. Other elderly people reported empathic concern. They were more likely to volunteer when they were moderately aroused and could take the patient's perspective (Eisenberg & Okun, in press).

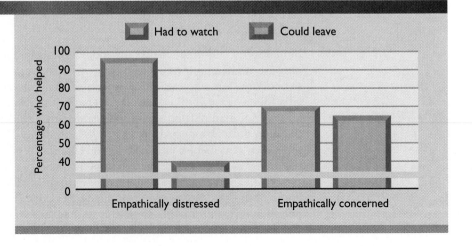

FIGURE 12.4

Empathic concern increases altruistic helping.

Graph shows percentage of empathically distressed and concerned students who volunteered to take shocks for a victim when they had to watch or could leave (Batson, O'Quin, Fultz, Vanderplas, & Isen, 1983)

Finally, people who experience predominantly empathic concern care more than do those who experience predominantly empathic distress about whether their intervention was successful. Their purpose in helping is to improve the other person's situation, so they help more if they will have an opportunity to witness a "happy ending." By knowing that the other person's situation has improved, their empathic concern turns into empathic joy. **Empathic** joy involves positive feelings that come merely from knowing that another person is no longer suffering. People who experience empathic distress, in contrast, are motivated only to improve their situation, not the other person's. Knowing the results of their possible help does not affect their cost-gains analysis.

To assess the influence of empathic joy on helping, student participants in one study watched a videotape on which a first-year student discussed her personal experiences in adjusting to life at a large university (Smith, Keating, & Stotland, 1989). The first-year student talked about several adjustment problems, including pressure from her parents, the difficulty of her courses, and feeling isolated and without friends. After they watched the videotape, the participating students reported their emotions, which reflected either empathic distress or empathic concern. The experimenter then offered the participating student two options for completing the experiment. One option was to watch and rate a different videotape. The other option was to write advice to the first-year student on "whether feeling isolated and under too much pressure is something everybody goes through." Some of the student participants learned that they would never know whether their advice helped the first-year student or not. Other participants learned that if they chose to help the first-year student, they would get to watch a second videotape of her the following week. On the second videotape, she would discuss her reactions to their advice and what difference it had made to her adjustment.

For students who reported predominantly empathic distress, knowing the effect of their advice did not matter. Their goal in helping was to improve their own situation, not the other person's. Only a few more of them helped when they would learn the effect of their advice than when they would not. For students who reported predominantly empathic concern, in contrast, the opportunity to know about possible changes in the other person's life mattered a great deal. Many more of them helped when they thought that they would learn the effect of their advice than when they thought that they would never know. To the empathically concerned (but not to the empathically distressed), empathic joy from improving the other person's situation was the goal, not improvement in their personal situation (Batson, Batson, Slingsby, Harrell, Peekna, & Todd, 1991). Empathic joy and alleviation of negative affect matter most when people get a chance to help someone with whom they desire a communal rather than an exchange relationship (Williamson & Clark, 1992).

SUMMARY OF WHY PEOPLE HELP

People help each other for at least three reasons: self-interest, mood management, and empathic concern. Self-interest and mood management are selfish reasons for helping; empathic concern appears to be genuinely unselfish or altruistic. When people help to further their self-interest, they must balance costs against gains. The possible costs include harm to themselves, aversion to the victim, and breaking rules of acceptable conduct. The possible gains include praise, rewards, avoiding guilt, and relieving empathic distress. When people help to manage their moods, they are either trying to maintain a good mood or trying to improve a bad mood. When people help because of empathic concern, they want to improve the condition of people who are similar to them or whose perspective they can adopt. Empathic concern, which involves feeling sympathy and compassion for another human being, is different from empathic distress, which involves feeling upset and disturbed by another person's plight. Empathic concern, unlike empathic distress, cannot be alleviated simply by "looking the other way." People who help from empathic concern want to experience the "empathic joy" of knowing that the other person is better off, even if they get no benefit for themselves except knowing that the other person's lot has improved.

WHY DO PEOPLE FAIL TO HELP IN EMERGENCIES?

If some people help to alleviate their own personal distress and other people help because they are empathically concerned, then why doesn't everyone help all the time? Why do so many victims of street violence, automobile and industrial accidents, and other emergencies go without assistance? Why do we read newspaper accounts and see television coverage of women who were beaten and even raped on city streets while hundreds of pedestrians and motorists passed without trying to intervene? Why are youths left to die on sidewalks after gang fights and no one stops to help? Why are bystanders so often apathetic in their reactions to victims of potentially debilitating or lethal emergencies? One answer to the question of why people fail to help in emergencies is that the costs of intervening outweigh the possible gains. Bystanders at an emergency are unlikely to feel similar to or psychologically close to the victim. Their feelings are more likely to involve empathic distress than empathic concern. As described earlier in the chapter, people who feel empathic distress, unlike those who feel empathic concern, find it more cost-effective to look the other way or to "walk on by" than to help. More specifically, though, researchers have tried to discover what goes on in people's heads when they unexpectedly come across an emergency and do not intervene. What factors influence the way bystanders think about an emergency and how they decide whether they are going to help?

One way of summarizing research on these issues is with the decision tree model of helping in emergencies (Latané & Darley, 1970), shown in Figure 12.5. A "decision tree" is a sequence of decisions. It is called a "tree" because, like the kind of tree that grows in the forest, it has a main artery and many possible branches that lead elsewhere (in the figure, to decisions not to help). According to the **decision tree model of helping,** bystanders help when they notice the event, interpret it as an emergency, assume personal responsibility, and believe themselves competent. The model portrays the sequence of deci-

FIGURE 12.5

The decision tree model of helping in emergencies.

Adapted from Latané & Darley, 1970.

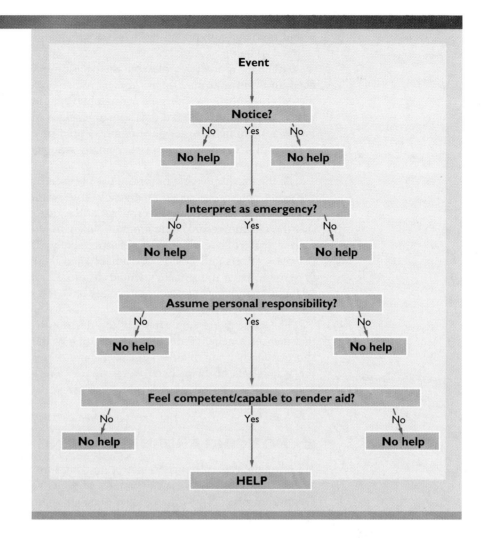

sions that a bystander must make affirmatively if he or she is to help the victim of an emergency. Even if a bystander answers "yes" at every "branch" of the tree, however, the decision to help does not guarantee action. The actual act of helping or not helping depends on being the right person in the right place.

DECISION TREE MODEL OF HELPING

At the first branch or decision point after an event occurs, as Figure 12.5 shows, the bystander must notice the event. In almost all studies described to this point in the chapter, the experimenters insured that participants could not help but notice. Just as the priest and the Levite in the parable of the Good Samaritan saw the man and crossed the street to avoid helping him, participants in the Elaine studies undeniably saw her plight. In everyday emergencies, in contrast, people who are passing might be so absorbed in other concerns that they pay no attention to an event that constitutes an "emergency" from the victim's perspective. If bystanders do not notice the event, they cannot help.

At the second possible branch in the decision tree, bystanders who have noticed an event have to interpret that event as an emergency. They have to conclude that another person is suffering or in danger. If the priest and the

Levite thought the man lying by the side of the road was intoxicated, they would not have interpreted the scene as an emergency. They would not have stopped to help.

At the third possible branch in the decision tree, bystanders who have noticed an event that they interpret as an emergency also have to assume that they are personally responsible for helping. The priest and the Levite, for instance, might have assumed that (as happened) someone else who was not late for an appointment (or a police officer) would surely stop to help the man. If they did not see themselves as personally responsible, they would not have helped.

At the fourth possible branch in the decision tree, bystanders might notice the event, interpret it as an emergency, and assume responsibility. They also have to ask themselves, however, whether they are capable of offering the help that the victim needs. People are more likely to attempt a task when they feel more capable of completing that task successfully (Brehm & Self, 1989; Wright, in press). Priests and Levites presumably had little or no medical training, so they might have thought they would do more harm than good by moving a victim. Bystanders who do not think they have the necessary expertise will not attempt to help.

The most depressing aspect of the decision tree shown in Figure 12.5 is that it takes a negative decision at only one of the four decision branches to short-circuit helping in an emergency. Three "yeses" and one "no" means that the victim gets no help. Even worse, four "yeses" signal merely a *decision* to help. Decisions do not always cause actions.

■ NOTICING AND INTERPRETING THE EVENT

We normally regard noticing, interpreting, and assuming as events that occur "inside the bystander's head." The most important influence on all of these decisions, however, is how many other people are present. (See the discussion of "social impact theory" in Chapter 11.) Even at the first two possible branches of the decision tree, people are more apt to notice an unusual event and interpret it as an emergency when they are alone than when other people are present. In a study of how quickly people notice a potential emergency, college students sat in a laboratory room either alone or with two "other students" who were confederates (Latané & Darley, 1970). The experimenter asked the students to complete some questionnaires and then left the room. Shortly thereafter, a few wisps of smoke started leaking under a locked closet door on the side of the room. The wisps of smoke quickly turned into a torrent of acrid smoke. Within four minutes, the room was filled with smoke so thick that it interfered with breathing and obscured vision. When the two confederates were present, they concentrated on their questionnaires and ignored the smoke no matter what the participating students did or said.

Meanwhile, the experimenter was waiting with a stopwatch, just outside the door to the corridor. One measure of noticing the event was the percentage of students in each condition (either alone or sitting with two strangers) who came out into the corridor to report a potentially dangerous emergency. As predicted, 75% of students who were alone left the room to report the smoke within six minutes. Only 10% of students who were in the company of two nonresponding strangers did so. Another measure of interest was how long it took the students to glance over at the smoke. Of those who were alone in the room, 63% looked over at the smoke within the first five seconds, whereas only 26% did so when there were other people present. Perhaps because of social norms against looking around and being caught "staring" at other people, students who were in the same room as two strangers took longer to notice and to report the unusual event.

Eventually, all students had to notice the smoke, whether they were alone or not. At the end of the study, the experimenters questioned them about how they had interpreted the event. Students who reported the smoke said that they considered it unusual and threatening enough to notify the experimenter. Those who failed to report the smoke came to entirely different conclusions. Even after the room had filled with smoke, they claimed that it seemed like "nothing to worry about." The nonreporters vehemently denied that the smoke might have been dangerous or might have constituted an "emergency." Some thought it was harmless steam or vapors from the building's heating or air conditioning system. Others thought it might be smog from outside the building. Two of the students independently concluded that the smoke was "a kind of truth gas that the experimenters were pumping under the door to make us answer the questionnaires truthfully."

■ ASSUMING RESPONSIBILITY

At the third branch of the decision tree, bystanders to an emergency have to assume responsibility if they are going to help. The primary determinant of people's thoughts about their responsibility appears to be the number of other potential helpers. The fewer the other potential helpers, the more responsible the individual bystander feels. The greater the number of other potential helpers, the more "diffuse" is the responsibility and the less likely is each bystander to perceive that he or she has the primary responsibility for intervening. According to the **diffusion of responsibility** principle, the greater the number of bystanders to an emergency, the less likely each bystander is to assume personal responsibility for helping.

In an elaborate study on diffusion of responsibility, college students entered one of several small rooms behind doors that opened off a long corridor (Darley & Latané, 1968). The students thought they would hold an intercom conversation with "other students," who presumably sat behind the other doors. Students in their separate rooms would take turns talking about the kinds of personal problems that they faced in adjusting to college life. Over the intercom, the experimenter explained that students were in separate rooms to maintain anonymity and avoid possible embarrassment while discussing potentially sensitive topics. Because the experimenter would not be listening, the experimenter continued, an automatic switching device would turn on the microphone in each participant's room for two minutes at a time. While one of the microphones was on, the others would be off. Only one of the students could be heard at any one time.

In reality, only one student participated. No one was in any of the other rooms. The "automatic switching device" started a tape-recorded message that was supposedly a fellow student speaking from room #1. After two minutes, it activated a different recorded message that was supposedly a different fellow student speaking from room #2, and so on, except when the student's turn came, which was last. The experimental manipulation consisted of how many other students were supposedly in the other rooms. Some students believed that only two people were participating–themselves and the student in room #1. Other students believed that three people were participating, including themselves. A third group of students believed that six people were participating, including themselves. During the first round of speaking, the student in room #1 mentioned that he had some adjustment difficulties and that he sometimes had seizures. When his second turn came, he began calmly, but then started speaking louder and said (in part):

"I-er-um-I think I-I need-er-if-if-could-er-er-somebody er-er-er-er-er-er-er give me a little er-give me a little help here because er-I-er-I'm-er-er-h-h-having a-a-a real problem. . . . I've got a-a one of the-er-sei——er-er-things coming on and-and-and I could really-er-use some help-uh-er-er-er-er-er-c-could somebody er-er-help-er-er-uh-uh-uh [choking sounds] I'm gonna die-er-er-I'm gonna die-er-help-er-seizure . . . "

After this plea for help, the man starting choking again. Then only silence came from the intercom speaker. Only the microphone in room #1 was supposed to be on at the time of the seizure. The student, therefore, had no way to get help for the "victim" except by leaving his or her room. The experimenter waited at the end of the corridor with a stopwatch, timing how long it took the student to leave the room to seek help. In that respect, the study was very similar to the "smoke-filled room" study. In other ways it was very different. Students in the "seizure" study, unlike students in the smoke-filled room study, had no way to know what the "other participants" were doing. They could not imitate the inaction of others, as students might have in the smoke-filled room study. Instead, they had to *assume* what others were doing. Also, the seizure study, unlike the smoke-filled room study, involved another person who was in grave danger.

Despite these differences between the two studies, the results told a similar story. People's thoughts about and actions in an emergency depend on the (assumed) number of other potential helpers. As predicted, 85% of students who thought they were the only potential helpers ran out of the room to get help. Their average time to go for help was 52 seconds from when the seizure began. Among students who thought that there was one other participant available, who shared responsibility two ways, 62% sought help by the end of the victim's turn. They took an average of 93 seconds to do so. Finally, among students who believed that four other participants heard the victim's seizure and shared the five-way responsibility for helping, only 31% of them sought help by the end of the victim's turn. They took an average of 166 seconds from the start of the seizure to do anything.

Most disturbingly for victims in everyday emergencies, no student who had not left the room within three minutes of the seizure's start ever did so. Students either acted quickly or waited in their rooms. If help had to occur within 45 seconds to save the victim, 50% of victims would have survived when there was one bystander. The victim would *never* have survived when there were five bystanders. Diffusion of responsibility acts against a victim receiving help when many people witness an emergency. Many apartment dwellers, for instance, have witnessed a robbery or assault from their separate windows and assumed that "someone else must have called the police." As discussed in Chapter 15 under "pluralistic ignorance," people often incorrectly assume that other people know what to do and are doing it. In situations where there is no recognized leader who is expected to act for the group, no one takes responsibility (Baumeister, Chesner, Senders, & Tice, 1988).

■ FEELING CAPABLE OF HELPING

One logical leader who is expected to take responsibility is the person who is most qualified to help. The fourth branch of the decision tree comes when potential helpers ask themselves "Do I know what to do?" Well-intentioned but incompetent help can sometimes be worse than no help at all. Even at this fourth branch in the decision tree, however, potential helpers are biased in decisions about their competence by the number and assumed expertise of other bystanders. Sometimes people assume they have greater expertise than any of the other bystanders. More often, people regard themselves as less competent when there are many rather than few other witnesses to an emergency.

In one study of perceived competence to help, the procedure was almost identical to that used in the previously described study of the man who had a seizure, except with six participants (Schwartz & Clausen, 1970). During his first turn, the man in room #6 either claimed or did not claim to be a premedical student. When he claimed to be premed, he said he worked nights in the emergency room of a local hospital. The "victim" was the person in room #1. Students delayed leaving their rooms to seek help for a much longer time if they thought that one of the other participants was a premedical student than if they did not. By comparison to someone who worked in an emergency room, they felt relatively incompetent to help and so did nothing.

People who are very competent are an exception to the usual rule about "less helping with more bystanders." The participants in one study were college women enrolled in either education courses or the Bachelor of Science in Nursing program (Cramer, McMaster, Bartell, & Dragna, 1988). The students from the nursing program were all registered nurses. They had an average 8.21 years of nursing experience. The women participated either as individuals or in the company of "another student," a confederate trained to do nothing when the "emergency" occurred. As they approached the experimental room, the student and the experimenter had to step around a ladder, on which a workman was repairing electrical light fixtures. Three minutes after the experimenter had left the room to go to a different part of the building, there came a resounding crash from just outside the door. It sounded as if the ladder had fallen, trapping the workman, who was moaning in pain.

As Figure 12.6 shows, the presence of a passive "other student" affected the percentage of education students who ran out to help the workman. Presence of another student did not affect the percentage of registered nurses who responded. In a subsequent questionnaire, the RNs said that they felt much more competent than did the education students to deal with the situation. The RNs were thus equally likely to help whether they were alone or with another person whose competence was unknown. Helpers also reported feeling more aroused than nonhelpers when the emergency occurred. The study suggested that the four decision points in the decision tree model of helping affect each other. People who feel especially competent to help may be especially likely to assume that they have a responsibility to help. They may be especially likely

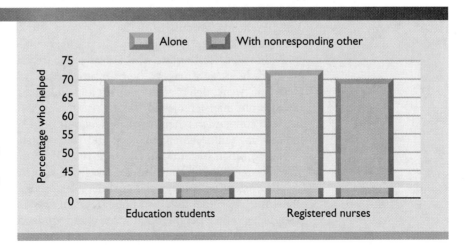

FIGURE 12.6

Very competent people help in emergencies regardless of who else is present.

Graph shows percentage of education students and R.N.s in two conditions who helped a fallen workman (Cramer, McMaster, Bartell, & Dragna, 1988)

to interpret the event as an emergency. They may also be especially likely to notice the event and to become aversively aroused.

THE "RIGHT" PERSON IN THE "RIGHT" PLACE

The best possible outcome of the decision tree is not helping, but a *decision* or intention to help. Good intentions, like New Year's resolutions, often fail to become actions. When it comes to helping, decisions do not become actions unless the potential helper is the "right person in the right place at the right time." Being the right person depends importantly on the potential helper's sex. Being in the right place depends on the potential helper's familiarity with his or her surroundings. The importance of the "right time" was evident in the Good Samaritan study.

■ SEX DIFFERENCES

In most of the studies on helping, bystanders had an opportunity to seize the initiative. They had a chance to take risks and defy implicit prohibitions by departing from an "expected" experimental scenario. In almost all of these studies, helping consisted of being a hero. With these experimental procedures, the male participants were overwhelmingly more likely to help than were female participants (Eagly & Crowley, 1986). Are men by nature more helpful than women? Of course not! It is *women,* not men, who have the reputation outside the psychology laboratory for being more helpful, caring, nurturing, and sympathetic. Women, for instance, helped Holocaust victims in World War II quietly by sheltering and feeding individual families for years, at great risk to their own lives. Many men (as shown in the movie *Schindler's List)* helped in more spectacular but not more commendable ways (Anderson, 1993; Oliner & Oliner, 1988). The research results are at odds with our everyday intuitions about gender differences in helping, but only because the experimental procedures have measured primarily a "male" kind of helping.

From an early age, many modern cultures teach girls a "female sex role" that calls for putting the needs of others, especially family members, before their own (Bernard, 1981). Parents and others teach girls (and women) to be empathically concerned and sympathetic (Eisenberg & Lennon, 1983; Feshbach, 1982). They reward females more than males for kindness and facilitating other people's goals (Ruble, 1983). As housewives, secretaries, and nurses (stereotypically feminine occupations), women become practiced at care giving and nurturing (Deaux, 1976; Eagly & Steffen, 1986; Piliavin & Unger, 1985; Walker & Woods, 1976).

From just as early an age, many modern cultures teach boys a "male sex role" that calls for heroism and chivalry (Hearnshaw, 1928). Parents and others teach boys (and men) to be calm in a crisis, willing to take risks, and protective of "weak, defenseless" women and children (Fraser, 1982). They reward males more than females for taking the initiative, being assertive, and breaking with convention when heroism demands bold action (Ruble, 1983). As firefighters, law enforcement officers, and soldiers (stereotypically masculine occupations), men become practiced at rushing to the aid of victims, especially children and "damsels in distress" (Eagly & Crowley, 1986).

Consistent with male and female roles, males helped more than did females in studies that involved potential danger to the helper. They also helped more when other people might notice and applaud their heroic act and when helping involved taking the initiative, not merely complying with a request.

Men help more than women when they regard themselves as more competent to help, they feel more comfortable helping, and their estimate of the potential risk is lower. Also, men (but not women) are more likely to help a female than a male "victim" (Eagly & Crowley, 1986).

It is no accident that almost all helping studies have incorporated characteristics that appeal to a "male" rather than to a "female" kind of helping. The "female" kind of helping typically involves long-term emotional support that is difficult to isolate in a psychology experiment, whether the experiment takes place in the laboratory or in a shopping mall. Also, social psychologists usually study the impact that the *immediate* context has on helping. They want to discover why victims do not receive help in emergencies, for instance, even when many potential helpers are present. To study the questions of greatest interest, investigators "staged" events that included a helpless victim. These events remind us of children's stories in which the valiant prince heroically rescues the damsel in distress.

■ FAMILIARITY WITH THE CONTEXT

Men help more because, at least in the emergencies staged by social psychologists, they feel "more comfortable" helping than do women (Eagly & Crowley, 1986). An important determinant of "feeling comfortable is whether the potential helper is familiar with his or her surroundings. People who feel right at home, either with their companions or with the physical setting, are more likely to help than those who feel out of place. Comfortable people are more likely to notice an unusual event, assume responsibility, and believe that they are competent to deal with it. As a result, they are more likely to help. Because they intuitively recognize their greater vulnerability, people who anticipate an appeal for help "on their home turf," for instance from a homeless person, sometimes go out of their way to avoid learning about the victim's plight (Shaw, Batson, & Todd, 1994).

Familiarity with our companions is an important aspect of feeling comfortable in the situation. Within limits, it is easy to feel at home even in distant lands, as long as we are surrounded by familiar relatives and friends. People who know each other well and are part of a tightly knit group should be especially likely to respond to an emergency in a collectivistic rather than in an individualistic way. They might even help *more,* not less, the greater the number of fellow group members who are present. It is difficult for an individual group member to say "someone else will respond" if group members feel equally responsible for coping with unexpected situations. In a study of familiarity and "solidarity" with companions at the time of an emergency, either two or four students participated in each experimental session (Rutkowski, Gruder, & Romer, 1983). For half of these groups, the experimenter asked them to spend 20 minutes getting well acquainted with each other. The experimenter asked them to share their feelings about college, extracurricular activities, student housing, social and family life, and what they had in common. Students in the other "groups" merely listened to a recording of a different group. They remained strangers to one another.

After this initiation, the experimenter led the students through a control room, where a workman, perched on top of a ladder, was supposedly doing maintenance work. The experimenter placed the students in separate rooms near the control room. The experimenter left the microphone in the control room on and instructed the students to work individually on some problems while he went to another part of the building for about 15 minutes. Approximately two minutes after the experimenter left, the students heard, over the intercom, a loud crash and a scream. The workman yelled "Oh, my God, my

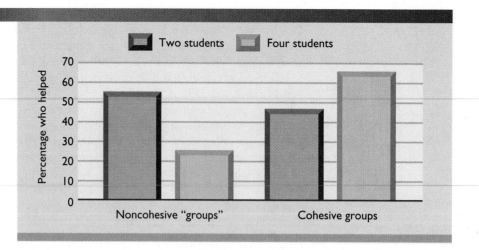

FIGURE 12.7

Presence of others has different effects on helping, depending on group cohesiveness.

Graph shows percentage of students in 2- or 4-person cohesive and noncohesive groups who helped a fallen workman (Rutkowski, Gruder, & Romer, 1983)

ankle . . . . I . . . . I can't move it. Oh . . . . my . . . . leg . . . . I . . . . can't get this . . . . off me." He continued moaning in pain for 60 seconds and then became quiet.

As Figure 12.7 shows, noncohesive "groups" of strangers displayed the usual diffusion of responsibility. A larger percentage of them helped within two minutes of the workman's fall when there were two potential helpers than when there were four. Groups of students who had become acquainted with one another and who had developed a sense of group cohesiveness by emphasizing their similarities, in contrast, displayed a "*reverse* diffusion of responsibility." A larger percentage of them helped when they were a group of four than when they were a group of two. Familiarity (and solidarity) with their companions seemed to increase rather than decrease their likelihood of helping, perhaps because of implicit group norms that dictate social responsibility (Berkowitz, 1972; Rutkowski, Gruder, & Romer, 1983). These results fit well with the theme of personal versus social identity that occurs in several chapters of this book (Abrams, 1992; Turner, Oakes, Haslam, & McGarty, 1994). Strangers who happen to be together are still thinking about themselves as individuals, each of whom has a personal identity. People who get to know each other and their similarities, in contrast, develop a social identity. They begin to think about the group as a unit. The larger the group, the more each member's collective or social identity has to gain from helping and the more each member's social identity would "look bad" by not helping (Branscombe & Wann, 1992).

Familiarity with the context applies not only to knowing the other bystanders, but also to knowing the place. Researchers in one study had a confederate on crutches fall to the ground in either a subway station or an airport. The victim received more help in the subway than in the airport (Latané & Darley, 1970). By questioning the helpers and nonhelpers in both places, the investigators learned that an important determinant of helping was the number of occasions on which the potential helper had previously been in the setting. Regardless of whether the "emergency" occurred in the subway station or in the airport, frequent commuters (or frequent flyers) helped more often than did travelers who had seldom visited the setting. People who were in a familiar setting presumably felt more at home and more comfortable with their surroundings.

Large cities contain a greater number and variety of physical settings, as well as a greater number and variety of strangers, than do small towns. You might suspect, then, that victims are more likely to be helped if their emergency occurs in a small town than in a large city. People who live in small towns, unlike people who live in large cities, confront emergencies in settings that they know very well, surrounded by familiar others with whom they feel a sense of solidarity. In one study of helping in rural versus urban areas, the researcher asked some passersby to help with a psychology study. The researchers also had a confederate give a "lost" person inaccurate directions that would have sent the person in exactly the wrong direction, staged a "fall" in which the victim clutched a bleeding leg, and solicited funds for research on multiple sclerosis (Amato, 1983). In every instance, people were more likely to help in smaller than in larger towns and cities. In another comprehensive study of helping in 36 cities across the United States, the investigators had a confederate drop a pen, feign a hurt leg, and request change (Levine, Martinez, Brase, & Sorenson, 1994). On all these measures, regardless of geographical region, the key factor was population density. The more densely people were packed into a city, regardless of its size, the less likely they were to help when given a variety of different opportunities.

Differences between helping in rural versus urban areas do not reflect personality differences between "small-town folk" and "city slickers." Instead, they reflect the sheer number and variety of strangers and other incidents that residents come across in a typical day (Steblay, 1987). City settings "overload" residents with congestion, loud noises, and other distractions that keep them from noticing events or from interpreting the events as emergencies (Milgram, 1970). Helping opportunities that occur in large cities also involve settings in which many other people are passing at the same time, which results in a diffusion of responsibility (Latané & Darley, 1970). In addition, people who might have felt capable of dealing with an emergency or a request for help when surrounded by friends do not feel as shielded from criticism and embarrassment when they are surrounded by dissimilar strangers (Fischer, 1976). For all we know, the priest and the Levite seldom walked the road from Jerusalem to Jericho, but the Good Samaritan passed that way every day and felt right at home.

SUMMARY OF WHY PEOPLE SOMETIMES FAIL TO HELP IN EMERGENCIES

Self-interest, mood management, and empathic concern are sometimes not enough to guarantee help for victims of emergency situations. According to the decision tree model of helping, victims do not receive help unless a bystander notices the event, deems it an emergency, assumes responsibility, and decides that he or she is competent to help. These criteria for providing assistance are surprisingly difficult to satisfy. They are also influenced in nonobvious ways by factors such as how many people are present when the emergency occurs. Women in Western cultures provide more quiet, long-term help than do men. They are also less likely to render assistance in emergency situations that resemble storybook events, in which heroic men typically rush to the aid of victims, including damsels in distress. Finally, both men and women help more when an emergency occurs in a familiar context than in a strange or chaotic environment.

Aggression

P olicymakers, police, and citizens in the late twentieth century are very concerned about high rates of violent crime—assaults, rapes, and murders. They want to know what makes people harm each other, so they can decide how to alleviate the problem. As this chapter explains, social psychologists can be of great help in understanding violence and aggression. Two social psychologists, for instance, wondered whether actual homicides might be merely the "tip of the iceberg." They wondered how many ordinary citizens of a modern, industrialized country have homicidal fantasies. How many people have not only wished another person dead, but also thought about doing it?

To investigate homicidal fantasies, the researchers asked 312 undergraduates in psychology courses at a large southwestern U.S. university whether they ever had thoughts of killing someone (Kenrick & Sheets, 1993). Overall, 68% of the students (73% of the males and 66% of the females) said they had fantasies about killing someone at least once in their lives. Many of the students (52% of the males and 37% of the females) reported that their most recent homicidal fantasies had lasted more than merely a few minutes. One student, for instance, said that throughout one week he had seriously contemplated how to kill his old girlfriend, who lived in a different city. He thought about the cost of airfare, how to set up an alibi, and how to make the death look like a robbery, but finally gave up on the idea because he could not be sure of getting away with it!

Of students who said they had at least one homicidal fantasy, 71% said their most recent thoughts of killing someone had occurred during the last year. Males and females differed on what triggered their most recent homicidal fantasy. As Figure 13.1 shows, men and women were equally likely to contemplate killing someone because of a personal threat or public humiliation.

FIGURE 13.1

Actual homicides may be merely the "tip of the iceberg" of aggression and violence.

Graph shows percentage of college men and women who reported having had recent homicidal fantasies over six types of incidents (Kenrick & Sheets, 1993).

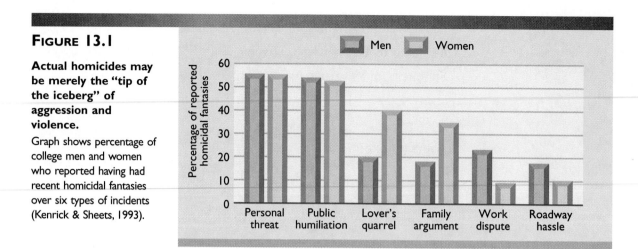

Although men had more homicidal fantasies overall, women who reported homicidal fantasies were more likely than men to have done so after a lover's quarrel or family argument. Men were more likely than women to have had homicidal fantasies over a work dispute or roadway hassle.

These results are not alone in showing that modern, industrialized countries have a serious problem with citizens thinking about and engaging in acts of aggression. Social psychologists define aggression as "any form of behavior that is intended to injure someone physically or psychologically" (Berkowitz, 1993a, p. 3). Although homicide rates are greater in the United States than in European countries, incidents of assault, rape, and murder are too high in many countries for citizens to feel secure. To deal with violence and aggression, policymakers need answers to several questions. First, policymakers need to know whether aggression is inevitable or amenable to change. Many people assume that human beings are inherently aggressive—that evolution predisposed human beings to fight and kill each other. According to this perspective, the "natural instinct" toward aggression might be held in check by tough penalties, but it can never be reduced or eliminated. Second, policymakers need to know what circumstances "trigger" aggression. If they could identify the circumstances that elicit or magnify aggression, policymakers and individual citizens might restructure their environments to avoid situations in which aggression typically occurs. Third, policymakers need to know whether aggressive actions such as assault, rape, and murder are related to specific factors that many citizens blame, such as media violence and pornography.

Social psychologists still have much to learn about aggression. Even so, they have solid evidence that provides at least preliminary answers to many of the policymakers' questions. The first section of this chapter examines whether aggression is "natural" or learned. The second section addresses specific factors that promote aggression. The third section discusses what social psychologists know about the relationship between media violence, pornography, and aggression.

IS AGGRESSION "NATURAL" OR LEARNED

One of the most pervasive myths of twentieth-century Western culture is that human beings, like other animals, are naturally aggressive. According to the **myth of the beast within** (Klama, 1988), people are "naturally" predisposed to fight and hurt each other, whether in individual conflicts or in wars. Evolution, so the myth goes, has promoted the survival of the most aggressive and ruthless among us. Violence is therefore genetically "programmed" into the human species. Aggression is a natural "instinct" against which society must constantly be on guard. Were it not for the threat of punishment and the provision of socially acceptable ways to rechannel their destructive drives, people would murder and rape at will, because aggression "builds up" inside them until it finds release. Many nonscientists and policymakers believe at least part of the myth. Scientists have been very concerned, therefore, to show that the myth of the beast within is false.

At a conference in 1986, 20 scientists from 12 countries around the world issued a joint statement on aggression and violence (Groebel & Hinde, 1989, pp. xiii–xvi). The scientists declared (in part) that human beings have *not* inherited a tendency to make war from our animal ancestors, war and other violent behaviors are *not* programmed into human nature, human evolution has *not* selected for aggressive behavior more than for any other kind of behavior, human beings do *not* have a "violent brain," and war is *not* caused by "instinct" or by any single motivation. The scientists' statement on aggression and violence was endorsed by 14 professional organizations, including the American Anthropological Association, the American Psychological Association, and the Society for Psychological Study of Social Issues. After examining all the available evidence, the scientists concluded that aggression is not a "built-in imperative" but rather just one of many ways that human beings cope with life's problems. The scientific evidence implies that *aggression in animals and human beings* is not "automatic." Socialization practices and developmental experiences importantly influence *learning to behave aggressively.*

AGGRESSION IN ANIMALS AND HUMAN BEINGS

The myth of the beast within is based on a misunderstanding of human and animal behavior. Contrary to the myth, animals in their natural habitats do not engage in constant "tooth and claw" struggles for survival and dominance. If animals have aggressive "instincts," then recent scientific discoveries suggest those instincts are less important than previously thought. Also, we do not fully understand the genetic and biochemical factors that might be inherited from successful ancestors.

■ AGGRESSIVE "INSTINCTS"

The theory of aggressive instincts holds that animals must compete for food, water, space, and mates if they are to survive. According to the theory, the more aggressive, dominant animals within a species get the resources that they need to survive and to produce offspring; less aggressive animals do not. Because parents pass on to their offspring many of their own biological characteristics, the proportion of animals that have aggressive characteristics has increased over time. These aggressive animals have evolved to the point where they "need" to fight in the same way that they need to eat. If they do not engage in aggressive behavior, they get more and more tense (Freud, 1933), until even a minor provocation causes them to explode in pent-up fury (Lorenz, 1966). Civilization's only hope, according to the theory of aggressive instincts, is to invent and encourage nonviolent ways of releasing aggressive urges, for example through competitive sports.

At one time, many scientists accepted the theory of aggressive instincts (Baron, 1977; Klama, 1988). Today, most scientists agree that animals and human beings have only the *potential* for aggression (as well as the potential for cooperation), but that "such tendencies are strongly affected by experience and learning, even in animals" (Staub, 1989, p. 53). Because of biases in media reporting of research on aggression, however, the general public may not be aware of several serious flaws in the idea that aggression is instinctive in either animals or human beings (J. Goldstein, 1989). First, "survival of the fittest" does not necessarily reward aggression. Animals survive sometimes by fighting, sometimes by fleeing, and sometimes by cooperating (Bateson, 1989). The fittest animals survive not only by "looking out for number one," but also by helping and protecting close relatives and others that are likely to reciprocate (Hamilton, 1971; Trivers, 1971). Animals most likely to survive long enough to have children are those that strike the best balance between competition and cooperation, using each strategy when it is most effective (Axelrod & Hamilton, 1981).

Second, genetic differences in aggressiveness can be easily undone (Manning, 1989). Through selective breeding, scientists can create genetic differences in the tendency of mice to attack each other (Lagerspetz & Lagerspetz, 1971). Genetically aggressive male rats have heavier testicles and produce more testosterone (the male sex hormone) at puberty, regardless of whether they are raised by aggressive or nonaggressive rat parents. Selective breeding of genetic and biological differences is obviously many times more powerful than anything that human beings might accomplish for themselves. The resulting differences in aggression, however, are surprisingly shortlived. All it takes is for the experimenter to "rig" a few initial fights so that a genetically docile rat defeats a genetically aggressive rat, and the two rats' tendencies to initiate aggression are reversed! The successful rats from the supposedly "docile" strain become more likely to initiate attacks than the unsuccessful rats from the supposedly "aggressive" strain (Lagerspetz & Lagerspetz, 1971).

Third, being dominant within a group of animals is not the same as being the most aggressive animal in that group, at least not when aggressiveness is defined as trying to injure other animals (Huntingford, 1989). The dominant animal in a group is not the one that fights most often. It is the one that is most likely to control scarce resources. The dominant animal seldom has to fight, because other animals in the group know they will lose, so they simply defer. In addition, animals that are dominant in one setting are not necessarily dominant when the group moves to a different setting. The dominant animal seems to be the one that copes best with a particular environment, whether "coping" involves aggression, escape, or cooperation (Benton, 1982; Bernstein, 1981).

Experimental evidence from observation of rats, pigs, monkeys, birds, and many other species shows that animals weigh the risks of injury against the possible gains from attacking another animal (Huntingford, 1989). As a result, aggression among animals is surprisingly infrequent (Karli, 1991). Animals do not attack other animals when a more dominant animal is present or when they find themselves in an unfamiliar setting (Marler, 1976). In addition, they often choose a reaction other than aggression when other ways of coping with the situation are available (Blanchard, 1984). Far from being driven by instinctive needs to aggress, animals resort to physical aggression only in situations where aggression is the survival strategy most likely to succeed and in situations where aggression has proven effective in the past (Karli, 1991). If the evidence from animal aggression carries any message for understanding human aggression, it is that aggression is *not* an "instinct."

■ "GENETIC" AND BIOCHEMICAL FACTORS

Even if "human nature" is not aggressive, however, it is still possible that certain unfortunate individuals may be genetically or biologically predisposed to violence. Like children who are born with Down's syndrome and thus have learning difficulties, some individuals may be born with genetic or biochemical abnormalities that make them more likely than the average citizen to fly into a rage when criticized, get into fights in bars, and assault both men and women.

In one study that attracted much media attention, the investigators reported that three out of every one hundred male prison inmates had an extra Y chromosome, a genetic abnormality that occurs in only 1 out of every 1000 nonimprisoned men (Jacobs, Brunton, Melville, Brittain, & McClemont, 1965). Men have a Y chromosome that they get from their fathers and an X chromosome that they get from their mothers; women have two X chromosomes, one from each parent. Consequently, the Y chromosome is regarded as the "male" chromosome. Across many species of animals (including human beings), the male commits more acts of physical aggression than does the female (Maccoby & Jacklin, 1974, 1980; Eagly & Steffen, 1986), so reporters erroneously labeled men who had the three chromosomes, X, Y, and an extra Y, "supermales." Reporters also claimed that the men's extra Y chromosome made them behave more aggressively, which is why they committed violent crimes. These XYY men, so the story went, were "driven" to murder and to rape because they were unfortunate enough to have been born with an XYY configuration of chromosomes rather than with the usual XY configuration.

Fortunately for those of us who do not want to see rapists and murderers exonerated because they were "driven" by too much "maleness," the story told by the media was misleading on several counts (Baron, 1977). First, 97% of XYYs have never committed a crime of any sort, so they must not have been "driven" to violence by their genetic constitution (Manning, 1989). Second, XYY prison inmates are no more likely than XY prison inmates to have been imprisoned for acts of *violence* (Price & Whatmore, 1967). Most of them are in prison for burglaries, auto thefts, selling or possessing drugs, and other nonviolent crimes. Third, XYYs in the nonprison population have less education, greater unemployment, and lower scores on standardized intelligence tests than XYs. When XYYs commit nonviolent crimes such as burglaries, they are more likely to be caught and put in jail than are XYs because they are often less intelligent than XYs (Witkin, Mednick, Schulsinger, Bakkestrom, Christiansen, Goodenough, Hirschhorn, Lundsteen, Owen, Philip, Rubin, & Stocking, 1976). Men who have an extra female (X) chromosome, XXYs, also score low on intelligence tests and are as overrepresented in the prison population as are XYYs (Bartlett, Hurley, Brand, & Poole, 1968). The scientists who reported the initial XYY results emphasized learning deficits of XYYs and were cautious in not interpreting their results as evidence of an "instinct to aggress." Media sources, though, slanted their reporting to encourage nonscientists to believe the "myth of the beast within."

Another interesting hypothesis about genetic and biochemical influences on aggression concerns the "male sex hormone" testosterone. Both males and females of many species have the sex hormones testosterone and estrogen. Males typically have more testosterone relative to estrogen than do females. Males of many species, including human beings, increase their level of testosterone when they reach puberty, at which time they also increase their aggressive actions (Barfield, 1984; Benton, 1981; Gandelman, 1981). Finally, young male rats that are castrated decrease both their testosterone levels and their aggressive actions. When these castrated rats receive injections of testosterone, they increase their acts of aggression (Wagner, Beuving, & Hutchinson, 1980).

Among male human beings, some studies found that prison inmates who committed violent crimes have higher testosterone levels than prison inmates who committed nonviolent crimes (Dabbs, Frady, Carr, & Besch, 1987; Dabbs, Carr, Frady, & Riad, in press). Other studies found that male military veterans who have high testosterone levels are more likely than their counterparts to report criminal activities and substance abuse (Dabbs & Morris, 1990). In addition, men who work in very competitive occupations, such as actors, have higher testosterone levels than do men who work in less competitive, more nurturing occupations such as ministers (Dabbs, de La Rue, & Williams, 1990). From such evidence, it would be easy to believe that men who are unfortunate enough to have high levels of testosterone are "driven" to violence by the hormonal "beast within."

The research evidence on testosterone in animals and human beings, however, is complicated. The effect of sex hormones on aggression varies with the species involved, the animal's age, the type of aggressive behavior studied, the animal's previous experiences, and the immediate context (Benton, Brain, & Haug, 1986; Brain, 1981; Herbert, 1989; van de Poll, Swanson, & van Oyen, 1981; Zillmann, 1984). Testosterone level has no connection with aggression in some species of monkeys (Eaton & Resko, 1974). In addition, in rat, pig, and monkey species for which the testosterone-aggression connection normally occurs, testosterone levels fluctuate with the circumstances. Testosterone levels typically increase following frustration and decrease when the animal loses a fight (Dixson, 1980). An animal's subsequent reluctance to fight depends more on how much the animal's testosterone level decreased following the most recent defeat than on the animal's current testosterone level (Leshner, 1981). An injection of testosterone can even *decrease* a male rat's level of aggression toward another rat, if the other rat is a pregnant or lactating female (Haug, Mandel, & Brain, 1981). An injection of testosterone also decreases rather than increases a female rat's tendency to fight intruders when she has small offspring to protect (Barfield, 1984). The only reasonable conclusion that can be drawn from such mixed evidence is that in animals, depending "on the type of aggression studied, testosterone might activate, inhibit, or have no effect on aggression" (Karli, 1991, p. 146).

In human beings, testosterone levels may have more of an indirect than a direct influence on aggression (Zillmann, 1984). Testosterone levels and aggressive acts may both increase when males reach puberty, but there may be no causal connection. Aggressive acts may not increase because of higher testosterone levels. Instead, they may increase because adolescent males are just beginning to compete with each other for a resource (access to females) that was previously unimportant to them (Zillmann, 1984). Prison inmates who committed violent crimes may have high testosterone levels once they are in prison, but were their testosterone levels high at the time they committed their violent crimes? Male infants and children who have high levels of testosterone develop larger and more muscular physiques, win more fights, and are thus more likely to be rewarded for acting aggressively (Scott, 1958). They may also be treated differently while they are in prison or they may stay in the violent prison environment longer, which raises their testosterone levels (Zillmann, 1979).

Finally, high levels of testosterone occur in individuals who are high in "emotional reactivity," which is defined as sensitivity to frustration, threat, provocation, and other irritations (Olweus, Mattson, Schalling, & Loow, 1980). As we shall see in the second major section of this chapter, frustration and provocation reliably increase the probability of aggression. Emotionality and irritability may cause elevated testosterone and aggressive behaviors, but elevated testosterone and aggressive behaviors may have no causal relationship with each other (Viken & Knutson, 1983; Knutson & Viken, 1984; Caprara, Renzi, Alcini, D'Imperio, & Travaglia, 1983; Karli, 1991). Even if men who have high testosterone levels are predisposed toward aggression, the vast majority of men who have high testosterone levels cope with life in ways other than lashing out at their neighbors. Testosterone levels do not in any sense *compel* or *drive* men to attack other men or to rape women.

LEARNING TO BEHAVE AGGRESSIVELY

Learning and cultural experiences can significantly alter any genetic or biological tendencies human beings might have toward aggression. Residents of modern Sweden, for instance, are known for being nonaggressive. Many are direct descendants of Vikings who were ferocious warriors just a few hundred years ago—too short a time for genetic changes to occur. The environment in which they are raised turns children into aggressive or nonaggressive adults. *Socialization practices* can produce aggressive or nonaggressive individuals, as well as aggressive or nonaggressive cultures. In addition, different socialization practices produce important *sex differences* in aggression.

■ SOCIALIZATION PRACTICES

Children learn how to cope with aversive experiences from their parents, other adults, and peers. They may find certain types of experiences, such as violent scenes, distressing, but whether they react to distress with aggression or with more constructive activities depends on what has "worked" for them and for familiar other people in the past (Staub, 1992a; Weiss, Dodge, Bates, & Pettit, 1992). When parents argue and attack each other, whether verbally or physically, young children become very upset. Laboratory simulations of aggression and in-home observations of parental arguments have shown that one- and two-year-old children display signs of personal distress when their parents and other adults behave aggressively toward each other (Cummings, Zahn-Waxler, & Radke-Yarrow, 1981). While the adults are fighting, the children yell angrily, cry, cover their ears, cover their heads with blankets, and get pained expressions on their faces. When the adults finish fighting, the children shove and hit each other, snatch toys away from each other, and display such intense aggression toward each other that adults sometimes have to intervene to prevent serious physical harm. In addition, being a witness to aggression has a cumulative effect. In the experimental laboratory, children who observe adults fighting for a second time display more intense post-fight aggression than do children who witness the fight for the first time (Cummings, Iannotti, & Zahn-Waxler, 1983).

Children who witness or suffer from parental violence often grow into violent adults. In studies of habitually violent adult offenders, between 60% and 80% had as children witnessed extreme violence between their parents (Bachy-Rita & Veno, 1974; Lewis, Shanok, Pincus, & Glaser, 1979). Other studies found that 66% of juveniles who were incarcerated for such violent crimes as assault with a weapon, unprovoked assault, murder, and rape had been beaten by one or both of their parents with a belt or an extension cord, 29% had been beaten so severely that they bled, and 8% had been beaten so severely that they had to be hospitalized (Widom, 1989). In addition, abused children often grow into abusive parents (Herrenkohl, Herrenkohl, & Toedter, 1983). According to a comprehensive review, 70% of mothers who abused their children remembered their own parents throwing them against a wall, hitting them with a variety of objects, and even burning them for minor infractions (Widom, 1989). Another study found that mothers of premature and ill newborns were subsequently more likely to be reported for child abuse if they had themselves been beaten severely when they were children (Hunter & Kihlstrom, 1979).

Parents and other role models can inadvertently encourage aggression in their children by suggesting, through their remarks or their actions, that aggression is an effective, acceptable way to behave (Krebs, 1970; Krebs & Miller, 1985). Children learn to be aggressive by observing and imitating aggression in their families and in society (Bandura, 1973; Widom, 1989). They develop a repertoire of aggressive behaviors by observing and enacting "aggressive scripts" (Huesmann & Miller, 1994). In addition, when the children (especially boys) try aggression for themselves, they are often complimented by their parents for "standing up for themselves" or they find that aggression gets what they want (Patterson, Littman, & Bricker, 1967; Slaby, 1974).

Modeling of aggression occurs when people imitate an aggressive role model, especially someone similar to themselves, who appears to be rewarded for aggression. In a classic study of children imitating aggressive adults, nursery school children (ages 35–69 months) were brought one at a time to a "playroom." The playroom contained a chair, a table, some coloring paper, and some multicolored stickers that could be used to create a picture (Bandura, Ross, & Ross, 1963). An adult (sometimes a man and sometimes a woman) "happened" to walk by. The experimenter invited the adult to join the game by playing with some Tinker toys in a different corner of the room from where the child sat. The experimenter then left the child alone in the room with the adult. Approximately one minute after the experimenter had left the playroom, the adult "model" stopped playing with the Tinker toys and turned his or her attention instead to a 5-foot-high inflated plastic "punching doll" of the kind that bounces back up when you hit it. As the child watched, the adult threw the doll to the floor, sat on it, and punched it repeatedly in the nose, saying,

When do children imitate adult aggression?

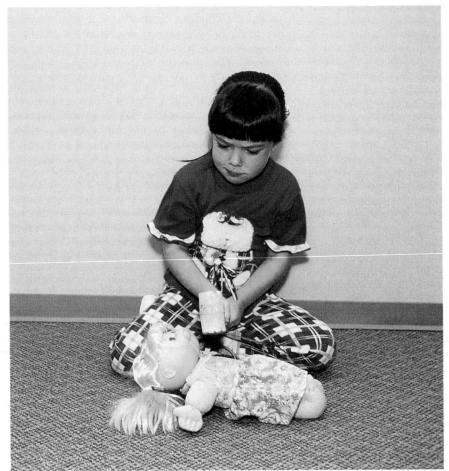

"Sock him in the nose." The adult then stood the doll up and started smashing it on top of the head repeatedly with a wooden mallet, saying, "Hit him down." Finally, the adult tossed the doll into the air and kicked it aggressively from one side of the room to the other, all the while saying, "Kick him, kick him!"

When the adult model had finished this extraordinary display of aggressive behavior, the experimenter returned, acted as though unaware that anything unusual had happened, and escorted the child (but not the adult) to a different playroom that contained extremely attractive toys. When the child began to play with the toys, the experimenter said, "You know, these are my very best toys and I don't let just anyone play with them. I think I'll save these for some other children." The experimenter then led the child to yet another playroom that contained less attractive toys, some of which were nonaggressive toys like a tea set, crayons, and plastic farm animals. Also in the room, however, were toys that might lend themselves to aggressive behavior, including a mallet, two dart guns, a tether ball with a face painted on it, and a 3-foot-high inflated punching doll much like the one that the child had recently seen an adult attack.

Compared to a control group of children who did not see an adult behaving aggressively, the nursery school children who had witnessed adult aggression (and then been angered by being denied attractive toys) played in an extremely aggressive way. They punched, smashed, and kicked the inflated doll in exactly the same way that they had seen the adult do (complete with the same verbal statements like "Punch him" and "Kick him"). They also invented new aggressive behaviors that the adult had not performed, such as kicking other objects in the room and firing the dart gun. Boys and girls differed slightly in the specific aggressive acts that they performed and in whether they were more likely to imitate the male or the female adult. Both sexes, however, behaved more aggressively when they had seen an adult punching, smashing, and kicking than when they had not.

The study also tested whether aggression has to be performed *in person* in order for children to imitate it. In two other conditions that are relevant to the issue of television and movie violence, some children watched a movie of the man or woman adult attacking the inflated doll. Others watched a cartoon in which "Herman the Cat" attacked the doll. The type of witnessed aggression made little difference in how aggressively the nursery school children behaved. They were just as violent in their actions whether they had seen aggression in person, in a movie, or in a cartoon.

These results suggest that parents who beat their children or their spouses may be "training" aggression in their children. They provide an aversive, distressing environment. They also show the child that physical violence is a normal, acceptable way to deal with life's inevitable problems (Straus, 1980; Strauss, Gelles, & Steinmetz, 1980). The results suggest that children might be raised to become nonviolent adults by parents and teachers who model constructive rather than destructive ways to deal with frustration and aversive arousal (Eron, 1980).

When children witness alternatives to aggression, they frequently prefer behaviors other than violent ones, even in response to provocation (Christy, Gelfand, & Hartmann, 1971). In one study of alternatives to aggression, 40 boys and girls (ages 7–9) at a summer camp were trained to behave either aggressively or constructively (Davitz, 1952). One activity that trained aggression was "cover the spot," in which the children were encouraged to cover an X on the floor with their bodies while knocking everyone else away. Another was "break the ball," in which the children tried to break everyone else's Ping Pong balls while protecting their own. The constructive training consisted of being encouraged and rewarded for cooperating with other children in painting murals,

What would this child do if you snatched away his candy?

completing jigsaw puzzles, and performing other nonaggressive activities. After the children had been taught either aggressive or constructive behaviors, the experimenter sat all the children in a projection room and gave them candy bars that they thought they were going to be able to eat while watching movies. Shortly after the first movie began, the experimenter suddenly, without explanation, snatched the candy bars out of the children's hands and made them leave the projection room. The children were confined to a playroom, which was equipped with modeling clay, dolls, building logs, dump trucks, plastic punching dolls, hammers, and other toys. The children could see through a window that the movies were still being shown in the projection room, but they could not see the movie screen.

Figure 13.2 shows the number of children in each group who behaved either more aggressively or less aggressively immediately after having their movies and candy taken away from them. As the figure shows, children who had been trained in aggressiveness reacted by playing more aggressively than they had before being deprived of the candy and movies. They were more likely after than before the aversive experience to hit, kick, and throw the playroom toys, sometimes at the other children. Children who had been trained constructively, in contrast, reacted to the same distressing experience by behaving more constructively (and less aggressively). Both groups responded to the aversive experience by doing more of whatever they had been rewarded for doing in the past. Depending on the socialization practices to which they are exposed early in life, people can learn how to cope with unpleasant experiences in ways other than aggression (Bandura, 1986).

Differences in the way children are socialized and educated produce marked differences in the climate of violence or nonviolence within different

FIGURE 13.2

Previous training alters reactions to frustration.

Graph shows number of children who reacted to frustration by playing more aggressively or less aggressively, after being previously taught constructive or aggressive behaviors (Davitz, 1952)

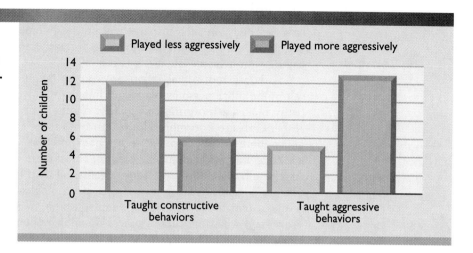

cultures around the world. Among the Yanomamo Indians of the Amazon region, for example, almost half of the men 25 and older have killed at least one person and approximately 30% of adult deaths are due to violence (Chagnon, 1988). From a very early age, elders teach Yanomamo children that violence and brutal revenge are necessary to maintain respect for established institutions (Boehm, 1984). In direct contrast to the violence of Yanomamo culture, certain rural communities in Tahiti consistently teach their children that physical violence is "unthinkable" and will not be tolerated under any circumstances (Karli, 1991). Not surprisingly, acts of aggression are virtually nonexistent in such cultures.

The Utku Eskimos of northwest Canada have no words in their language for anger and aggression (Briggs, 1970). Their children sometimes act in ways that outside observers might label "aggression." The Utku dismiss such actions as signs of immaturity. Adults simply do not behave that way. In addition, not all cultures have the tradition that people settle conflicts and disputes by trying to hurt each other. Some Eskimos settle disagreements by a public contest in which two opponents see who can sing the more abusive songs about the other. Similarly, quarreling Indians of Santa Marta, Colombia, strike a rock or a tree with sticks. The first one who breaks the stick is considered the braver person and is declared the winner (Boring, Langfeld, & Weld, 1939). "From a cross-cultural perspective, aggressive behavior is learned from others, primarily through socialization and enculturation, involving both teaching and learning by observation" (Segall, 1989, p. 173).

■ SEX DIFFERENCES IN AGGRESSION

Perhaps nowhere are the effects of socialization practices more evident than in the frequently noted fact that men in the United States and other Western cultures are more aggressive than women. Psychologists differ in whether they believe that boys and girls have different temperaments at birth. Any differences, however, are soon overwhelmed by different "sex roles" into which boys and girls are socialized (Eagly & Steffen, 1986; Maccoby & Jacklin, 1974, 1980; Tieger, 1980). When adults believe that an infant is a girl, they regard the infant as more delicate and fragile than if they believe that the same infant is a boy (Seavey, Katz, & Zalk, 1975). Parents and other adults pick boy infants up and handle them physically, whereas they talk to girl infants and cuddle them softly (Moss, 1967). These two ways of handling predict how physically active and independent the infants will be shortly after their first birthdays (Goldberg & Lewis, 1969). By the time they enter middle school, boys have learned to use direct, often physically aggressive means of solving their problems. Girls have learned that such displays will not be tolerated (Connor, Serbin, & Ender, 1978). As a result, girls have had to learn more subtle, indirect ways of coping with aversive situations (Eron, 1980).

Girls are more likely than boys to be taught empathy, or putting oneself in the other person's place and imagining how he or she might feel. Empathy makes it more difficult to hurt another person (Feshbach & Feshbach, 1969). Girls are also more likely than boys to be taught that they should feel guilty about causing another person pain and that it is dangerous to take physical risks (Eagly & Steffen, 1986; Eron, Huesmann, Lefkowitz, & Walder, 1972). As a result, male adults are more aggressive than female adults about hurting another person physically rather than psychologically, when aggression might result in dangerous retaliation, when there is no audience that might disapprove, and when the circumstances maximize potential guilt (Eagly & Steffen, 1986).

Parents and teachers show girls more than boys how to solve their problems through prosocial behaviors such as asking for help, getting other people to cooperate, and apologizing for inadvertent transgressions (Eron & Huesmann, 1984). As a result, boys have a comparatively limited repertoire of behaviors (many of them aggressive) that they can bring to bear on life's inevitable problems and frustrations (Eron, 1987). When they have aversive experiences, boys and girls both become aroused. Emotional arousal, however, "can facilitate a variety of behaviors, depending on the type of responses the person has learned for coping with stress and their relative effectiveness" (Bandura, 1973, p. 53). Boys are more apt to choose aggressive responses because "If a child is to avoid aggressive behaviors and thus not develop the trait of aggression, he or she must learn nonaggressive behaviors to solve those problems he or she might otherwise try to solve with aggressive behaviors" (Eron, 1987, p. 440). In addition, studies show that across many world cultures, males and females do not differ in their overall amount of aggression. Instead, they differ in the ways in which they express aggression and the targets that they choose (Rosenblatt, Jackson, & Walsh, 1972; Whiting & Edwards, 1973).

Sex differences in aggression may be narrowing in the United States, but in a possibly undesirable direction (Eron, 1987; Eron & Huesmann, 1984). Girls may not have imitated the aggressive adult as much as did boys in previous studies such as the "punching doll" study described earlier in the chapter, but females who are encouraged can be every bit as aggressive as males (Bandura et al., 1963; Frodi, Macaulay, & Thome, 1977; Shope, Hedrick, & Geen, 1978). Aggression includes not only physical abuse, but also verbal abuse and psychological "torture," at which females are as adept as males (Hyde, 1986; Macaulay, 1985). By every indication, young girls today are starting to watch and to enjoy almost as much violent television as do young boys. Girls are also increasingly socialized to be as assertive and physically direct as are young boys (Eron & Huesmann, 1984). The result may be a future society in which both sexes are equally violent and aggressive.

An alternative approach might be to socialize boys so that they learn as many nonaggressive ways to solve their problems as do girls (Eron, 1987). It is possible to train boys to have as much empathy for other people as do girls (Feshbach, Feshbach, Fauvre, & Ballard-Campbell, 1983). It is possible to teach boys how to start a conversation, how to give and receive compliments, how to make sincere apologies, how to ask for help, how to deal with embarrassment, how to cope with failure, how to set realistic goals, and how to cope with other problems as nonaggressively as do girls (A. Goldstein, 1983). These socialization practices, all of which might bring the level of male aggression down to the level of female aggression (rather than the reverse), have been developed in extensive and carefully validated research programs (Patterson, 1982). If the intervention begins at an early age, children who are taught social and emotional skills in managing anger, negotiating, and adopting another child's perspective display a reduced level of aggression throughout their lives. The study of sex differences and their causes, therefore, has led researchers to an understanding of how to alter socialization practices to reduce the level of violence in society. Whether society will pay any attention to these discoveries is an open question (Eron & Huesmann, 1984).

SUMMARY OF WHETHER AGGRESSION IS "NATURAL" OR LEARNED

The "myth of the beast within" holds that animals and human beings are inherently and instinctively aggressive. According to the myth, genetic and biological factors predispose human beings toward violent and destructive behavior. In reality, aggression is just one of several "natural" ways in which human beings cope with their environment.

Whether and how people display aggression is determined importantly by their developmental learning experiences. As a result of different socialization and education practices, cultures differ dramatically in the level of aggression that they tolerate and in how they settle disputes. Because of differences in how they are socialized, men and women differ in how often and in which circumstances they display aggression. Considerable research suggests that if male children were taught as many nonaggressive ways to cope with life's problems as female children are, the level of violence in society might be reduced.

WHY DO PEOPLE HURT EACH OTHER?

The question of why people hurt each other has many possible answers. Some of the answers apply to "instrumental aggression," or aggressive behavior that is used as a means to an end (Baron, 1977; Berkowitz, 1989). When a robber kills a store owner who blocks the cash drawer, for instance, the aggression might be instrumental if it was used as a means to get the money. Other answers to the question "Why do people hurt each other?" apply to "hostile aggression," the kind of aggression where people lash out at each other in anger, for no other purpose than to injure and punish (Feshbach, 1964). When a robber kills a cooperative store owner out of sheer frustration at how little cash was on hand, the aggression is not instrumental but hostile. Hostile aggression is an end in itself.

It is impossible to draw a clear dividing line between instrumental and hostile aggression. Is rape, for instance, instrumental or hostile? Nonetheless, the previous section of the chapter emphasized more of the reasons behind instrumental aggression, whereas the current section emphasizes more of the reasons behind hostile aggression. The first answer to "Why do people hurt each other?", as explained in the previous section, is that they "get something out of it" or have seen other people use aggression effectively. The second answer, hinted at near the end of the first section, is that "aggression is all they know." Because they have learned no other way to react, people behave aggressively when they have *aversive experiences,* experience negative *arousal,* or experience a state of *disinhibition* that temporarily removes constraints of social disapproval and personal responsibility. They act in ways that might be rewarding to them and thus in some sense "instrumental," but that to observers seem very "hostile."

AVERSIVE EXPERIENCES

Many types of aversive experiences increase the likelihood that people will try to harm each other (Berkowitz, 1989). Aggression becomes more likely when people are verbally or physically *attacked,* because they often retaliate. Aggression also becomes more likely when people are *frustrated* in their attempts to reach goals that are important to them. Finally, aggression becomes more likely when the *environmental conditions* are especially irritating. Table 13.1 presents a model of how aversive experiences produce either aggression or alternative, nonaggressive actions (Anderson, Deuser, & DeNeve, 1995). According to the model, these three types of aversive experiences elicit immediate reactions such as hostile thoughts, anger, and physiological arousal (Berkowitz, 1993b; Huesmann, 1988; Zillmann, 1971).

These immediate reactions influence people's interpretations of the other person's intent and their own feelings. People who are aroused, for instance, might be biased toward labeling an accidental injury as intentional or labeling their own feelings as "enraged" rather than merely "upset." Interpretations, in turn, bias the coping strategies that people consider, as well as evaluations of each strategy's likely consequences. From the coping strategies that come to mind, the person who has an aversive experience chooses either an aggressive or a nonaggressive action (Anderson et al., 1995). The model of aggression in Table 13.1 fits well with the theme of spontaneous versus deliberative reactions that pervades this book. As discussed in the earlier section on learning to behave aggressively, some people never learned any other way to cope with aversive experiences but to lash out in anger. Lashing out in anger, however, is not the only way to react. Aggression often represents a failure to regulate spontaneous reactions with more deliberative and constructive coping strategies (Baumeister & Heatherton, 1996). The next sections of the chapter describe the thoughts, emotions, arousal, intrpretations, and coping strategies that people use when they react to attack, frustration, and irritating environmental conditions.

TABLE 13.1	Components of Aggressive and Nonaggressive Reactions to Aversive Experiences Such as Attack, Frustration, and Irritating Environmental Conditions (Abstracted from Anderson, Deuser, & DeNeve, 1995).				
	THOUGHTS	**EMOTIONS**	**AROUSAL**	**INTERPRETATIONS**	**COPING STRATEGIES**
Aggressive Reactions	hostile	anger	increased	hostile	aggressive
Nonaggresive Reactions	nonhostile	nonanger	no change	nonhostile	nonaggressive

Calvin and Hobbes

by Bill Watterson

■ ATTACK

When animals are attacked, they often (but not always) fight back (Blanchard & Blanchard, 1984; Hutchinson, 1973). Whether animals fight back because they are angry or because they are afraid and trying to protect themselves is an open question. Given sufficient provocation and no opportunity to escape from the situation, however, one likely response to physical attack is retaliation. Human beings have similar tendencies. In a study of responses to provocation, male college students wrote a brief essay on controlling crime rates (Baron, 1974). A male "other student," (a confederate) evaluated the student's essay positively or negatively by making favorable or unfavorable comments and by delivering either light flashes or electric shocks to the student. In the nonattack condition, the other student commented favorably on the essay and delivered only one light flash. In the attack condition, the other student commented unfavorably and delivered *nine electric shocks!*

In the second phase of the study, the experimenter claimed to be studying the effects of electric shocks on physiological reactions. The experimenter chose the confederate to receive the shocks and the student to administer the shocks. Shocks were administered through an "aggression machine," an apparatus designed to measure the amount of physical pain that research participants are willing to give other people (Buss, 1961). The machine had ten buttons that the student could press to administer ten levels of electric shock that ranged from mild to very painful. Pushing buttons on a machine may not be the type of aggression that people use outside the psychology laboratory, but the procedure involves "real" aggression, because students believe that they are injuring another person (Berkowitz & Donnerstein, 1982). (See the discussion of experimental realism in Chapter 1.)

When the controls on the aggression machine had been explained to the student (who received a sample 4–5 level shock that was very painful), the experimenter explained that whenever a light came on, the student was to press one of the shock buttons. The confederate, whom the student had seen being fitted with wrist and arm electrodes in a nearby room, would receive whatever shocks the student selected, and would keep being shocked for as long as the student held the button down. Thus student participants had a chance to injure "another student" who had either treated them well or attacked and angered them. The experimenter also explained that any of the ten shock levels would provide equally useful data about physiological responses. We might interpret using anything more than the lowest setting, then, as a form of retaliation or counterattack.

The confederate was in a separate room from the student, so the student could not see directly the effect that the shocks were having. (For ethical reasons, although the students did not realize it, in this as in all the "aggression machine" studies described in this chapter, no shocks were actually delivered, regardless of which buttons they pressed.) Some of the attacked and some of the nonattacked students, however, saw a "pain meter," which displayed after each shock how subjectively painful the other student supposedly found it to be. In reality, the meter simply reflected the level of shock that the student had selected. As might be expected, students who had not been attacked were greatly influenced by whether they knew or did not know how much pain the other student was experiencing. Students who had no "pain meter," and thus had no way to tell how much pain the other student might be in, administered significantly higher levels of shock than did students who could see for themselves how much pain they were causing. The nonattacked students followed what would seem to be a reasonable rule of "If you've knocked the other person down and he is writhing in pain, then it's time to stop the aggression." Students who had been attacked, however, did not follow the rule. If anything, *they shocked their attacker more when they could see that he was in pain than when they could not.* Similar results occurred in a related study, in which students who had been attacked, unlike those who had not been attacked, used high levels of shock regardless of whether their attacker would or would not have an opportunity to shock them back (Baron, 1973).

Attack, then, has a large impact on the likelihood of aggression, even to the point of rendering inhibiting influences like the victim's pain cues or the risk of retaliation unimportant. Whether the attack takes the form of physical harm or verbal insults, human beings and animals frequently retaliate and "teach the attacker a lesson" (Knutson, Fordyce, & Anderson, 1980; O'Leary & Dengerink, 1973; Leshner & Nook, 1976; Potegal, 1979). In human beings, the level of retaliation is sometimes lowered by whether the attack was intentional or not, whether the attacker apologized or not, and whether the attacker was perceived as having malicious intent (Dodge, Murphy, & Buchsbaum, 1984; Johnson & Rule, 1986; Ohbuchi & Kambara, 1985; Ohbuchi, Kameda, & Agarie, 1989; Zillmann & Cantor, 1976). Perceived malicious intent to attack can prompt aggressive retaliation even if the attack itself does not occur (Epstein & Taylor, 1967). In addition, human beings who are experiencing pain, even when there is no specific "attacker," respond to situations where aggression is a likely response by aggressing more than they would if they were not in pain (Berkowitz, 1983; Berkowitz, Cochran, & Embree, 1981).

The most obvious reason why people aggress when they have been attacked is that the attack makes them angry. Aggression, however, is not the only possible response to anger (Averill, 1983). People who are asked what they do when they become angry report that they often have an initial impulse to hurt another person directly or indirectly, either physically or verbally, but that they seldom do so. More frequently, they aggress "symbolically," do something that they know will help them to calm down, or talk the incident over with the person who injured them or with a third party.

In one study, students described incidents in which another person made them angry and incidents in which they made another person angry. Perpetrators and victims had entirely different interpretations of what happened (Baumeister, Stillwell, & Wotman, 1991). The "perpetrator" and the "victim" differed dramatically in their attributions about the perpetrator's intentions, the perceived morality of and justification for the injury, and the perceived consequences. When they described incidents in which another person made them angry, students saw the incident as incomprehensible and as having long-term negative consequences. "For no reason at all, he threw a fit. Things will never be the same between us." When they described incidents in which they angered someone else, by contrast, students saw the incident as justified given the mitigating circumstances and as having "cleared the air" and strengthened the relationship. "She had been getting on my nerves for a long time, so I told her just what I thought of her. It's all over and forgotten." Perpetrators in anger-arousing incidents find their own actions much more consistent, moral, unavoidable, and justified than do victims. For victims, the attack often appears arbitrary, senseless, and incomprehensible. Unfortunately for social harmony, people are unaware of these large discrepancies in how they interpret and react to provocation by themselves as opposed to provocation by other people.

■ FRUSTRATION

One of the most aversive aspects of interpersonal attacks is that they are frustrating. Most people want to get along with and be treated well by others, so an attack frustrates the important goal of social harmony. Researchers have found that other types of frustration also increase the likelihood of aggression (Berkowitz, 1978). According to the **frustration-aggression hypothesis,** frustration occurs when people are unexpectedly blocked from achieving a goal that they thought was within their grasp (Dollard, Doob, Miller, Mowrer, & Sears, 1939; Berkowitz, 1989). In the "punching doll" study described in the first section of the chapter, for instance, the children were deliberately frustrated by being shown very attractive toys and then being told that "These are my very best toys and I don't let just anyone play with them. I think I'll save these for some other children." To make the children angry and "set the stage" for them to imitate the adult's aggressive behaviors, the experimenters deliberately raised the possibility of playing with very attractive toys and then prevented the children from achieving that goal. Children are more likely to imitate aggressive models when the children have first been frustrated than when they have not been frustrated (Hanratty, O'Neal, & Sulzer, 1972).

Animals also behave aggressively when they are frustrated (Looney & Cohen, 1982). In a well-known study, a monkey learned a "shell game" in which the experimenter hid a piece of banana under a cup (Tinklepaugh, 1928). After the monkey had become expert at finding the banana, the experimenter surreptitiously substituted a piece of lettuce. When the monkey picked up the cup and saw the lettuce instead of the expected (and much preferred) banana, the monkey did a "double-take," looked around for the banana, and (finding no banana) became very agitated. The monkey threw the cup and the lettuce on the floor, stomped on the lettuce, and screeched at the experimenter.

Adult human beings sometimes react as negatively to frustration as animals do, especially when they are frustrated by another person's action that seems arbitrary rather than justifiable (Berkowitz, 1993a). People who lose their money in telephones or soft drink dispensers frequently kick and punch the offending machine (Moser & Levy-Leboyer, 1985). Drivers frequently blast their horns when the car at the front of the line does not move soon after a traffic light has changed (Turner, Layton, & Simons, 1975). The more attractive the expected prize and the nearer they are to achieving the goal when they are interrupted, the more upset people become. In one study of frustration, students pulled a knob on a machine that dispensed free coins (Kelly & Hake, 1970). The only "catch" was that at random intervals a loud, irritating noise blasted into their ears. The students could shut off the noise, however, either by pushing a button or by punching a cushion. Because pushing the button

Do people punch drink machines merely to dislodge coins that might be stuck, or is there another reason?

was easier than punching the cushion, most of the students used the button to turn off the noise. Unexpectedly, the machine stopped dispensing money. The aversive noise kept blasting into the students' ears, but they were frustrated by no longer receiving their expected rewards. Many of the students reacted to this frustration by choosing to turn off the noise with a vigorous punch rather than with a simple button push, even though both actions turned off the noise.

In another study of frustration, an experimental confederate cut into long lines of people waiting at restaurants, stores, banks, and ticket counters (Harris, 1974). The next person in line often reacted aggressively, by yelling at or threatening the confederate. Reactions were much more aggressive when the person cut in front of was near the front of the line (and near the anticipated goal) than when the person was near the rear of the line (and far from the anticipated goal). Frustration is especially aversive when the individual is so close to the goal that he or she can easily imagine getting and enjoying it (Folger, 1986).

One of the myths about frustration is that it creates pent-up anger that must be released (remember the "myth of the beast within"). In the same way that heat builds steam pressure inside a boiler, so the myth goes, frustration builds potentially lethal emotions inside human beings (Berkowitz, 1969; Geen & Quanty, 1977). Just as releasing some steam reduces the pressure inside a boiler, so releasing a little aggression lowers the emotional pressure on frustrated people and prevents an "explosion." **Catharsis** supposedly occurs when behaving aggressively releases pent-up anger and prevents an "explosion" of aggression later. Catharsis, however, is a myth. If anything, aggression breeds *increased* aggression, rather than the other way around.

In one study of catharsis, some laid-off workers got a chance to talk about their hostility and resentment toward their former employers (Ebbesen, Duncan, & Konecni, 1975). They were later *more,* not less, critical in describing those employers than were other workers who had not had the earlier opportunity to criticize. In a more direct test of catharsis and physical aggression, two male college students first exchanged opinions on controversial issues (Geen, Stonner, & Shope, 1975). The "other participant," an experimental confederate, got to evaluate the student's opinions by giving the student electric shocks for each "ill-conceived" opinion. The confederate gave some of the students two mild shocks, which constituted a positive evaluation. The confederate gave other students eight painful shocks, which constituted a negative evaluation. Students who received eight strong shocks had higher blood pressure after this negative "evaluation" than did students who received two mild shocks. Being shocked and negatively evaluated made them angry.

Next, the tables were turned. The student got to play the role of "teacher" in a maze-learning task where the "learner" was the confederate who had previously shocked them. For one-third of the students, a red light came on every time the learner made a mistake. Nothing else happened. For a different third of the students, when the red light came on, the experimenter pushed a button that supposedly gave the learner a painful electric shock. For the last third of the students, when the red light came on, they got to push the button and deliver the shocks themselves. To test the catharsis hypothesis, the experimenter then announced a third task (deciphering coded messages), in which the student would again play teacher and the confederate would play learner. For each of ten mistakes that the confederate made, the student got to shock him by choosing from ten levels of electric shock on an aggression machine. Getting to shock the confederate personally was the only experimental manipulation that reduced students' blood pressure. Even so, previously attacked students who got to shock the confederate personally during the maze-learning task subsequently gave the confederate more painful shocks for mistakes on the decoding task. Contrary to the catharsis hypothesis, a little aggression now breeds *more,* not less, aggression later.

The consensus from years of research on frustration is that people who are frustrated find the experience very aversive, but that aggression is just one of several ways in which they react to frustration (Berkowitz, 1989). Aggression is *less* likely to follow frustration when the frustration is interpreted as somehow justified, unintentional, or unavoidable and when people have alternative, nonaggressive ways to deal with the situation (Dodge, 1986; Ferguson & Rule, 1983; Moser & Levy-Leboyer, 1985; Weiner, 1985). Aggression is *more* likely to follow from frustration (or from attack, or from any other aversive experience) when the frustrated person has never learned alternative, nonaggressive ways to cope with frustration, when the frustrated person has been rewarded for aggression in the past, and when cues in the environment suggest or call to mind aggressive actions (Carlson, Marcus-Newhall, & Miller, 1989).

In the **aggressive cues hypothesis** anger is more likely to result in overt aggression when some characteristic of the surrounding context reminds people of aggression (Berkowitz, 1974, 1982, 1983). Weapons, for example, might trigger thoughts related to aggression. In a classic study of aggressive cues, male college students received either seven shocks or one shock from "another student" (a confederate) who was evaluating the student's ideas (Berkowitz & LePage, 1967). As in other studies of aggression, the student next got an opportunity to use an aggression machine to deliver electric shocks to the confederate. For some of the students, there was an empty table next to the aggression machine. For other students, lying on the table were a 12-gauge shotgun and a .38-caliber revolver! The experimenter dismissed the presence of these weapons by saying that they must "belong to someone else" who "must have been doing an experiment in here." Nonetheless, during the entire time that students in the "weapons" condition were pressing buttons to deliver electric shocks that supposedly ranged from mild to very painful, they saw, lying on a table next to the aggression machine, items that were likely to remind them of aggression.

Figure 13.3 shows the average number of shocks delivered by students who had been evaluated positively (received one shock from the confederate) or evaluated negatively (received seven shocks from the confederate), and who saw either weapons or no weapons on the table. As the figure shows, students who had been evaluated negatively (attacked, frustrated, and presumably angered) shocked the confederate more often when they got the chance than did students who had been evaluated positively. The effect of negative evaluation

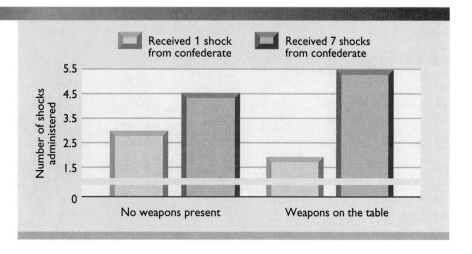

FIGURE 13.3

Aggressive cues magnify aggressive reactions.

Graph shows number of shocks students gave a confederate who had shocked them, when weapons were or were not present (Berkowitz & LePage, 1967)

Received 1 shock from confederate   Received 7 shocks from confederate

Number of shocks administered

No weapons present   Weapons on the table

on aggression was enhanced when there were weapons present. People who are not angered do not try to hurt other people whether weapons are in sight or not. People who are angry are more likely to turn their anger into physical violence when they are reminded of aggression by the presence of weapons. Similar intensification of aggression occurs when people are reminded of aggression by recently having seen a very violent movie (Geen & Berkowitz, 1967). *Anything* that reminds people of aggression can increase their likelihood of turning anger into physical harm toward others. In a relevant study, participants first learned to associate the color green with aggressive thoughts. Later, they got a chance to punish "another student" by shocking him at aggression machines that had been painted in different colors. The participants shocked the confederate more when they were using a *green* machine (Fraczek, 1974).

■ ENVIRONMENTAL CONDITIONS

Another type of aversive experience that increases the likelihood of aggression comes from the environment. A pleasant environment may encourage cooperation, but an unpleasant environment can set the stage for such aggressive actions as child sexual abuse (Holman & Stokols, 1994; Stokols, 1990, 1992). When people are uncomfortable because of a "long, hot summer," when they get "hot under the collar," when they "get steamed" or they "do a slow burn," their "tempers flare." These common idioms and cultural wisdom remind us that high temperatures are similar to pain, attack, frustration, and other aversive experiences in that they can lead to aggression. In William Shakespeare's play *Romeo and Juliet,* for example, Benvolio says:

> I pray thee, good Mercutio, let's retire;
> The day is hot, the Capulets abroad,
> And, if we meet, we shall not 'scape a brawl,
> For now, these hot days, is the mad blood stirring.

Scientists have collected many different kinds of evidence to support Benvolio's intuition that summer heat can intensify aggression. According to police records in many different cities and countries around the world, violent crimes (but not most nonviolent crimes) are more likely to occur during the hot summer months than during the rest of the year (Anderson, 1987). Figure 13.4 displays the quarterly incidence of homicides, rapes, and assaults as a percentage of the yearly total, collapsing across many different studies (Anderson,

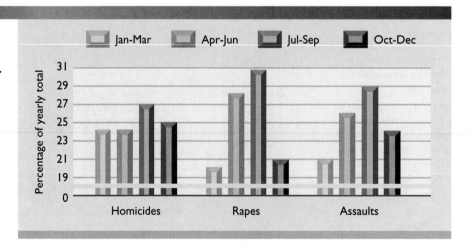

FIGURE 13.4

Aggressive crimes increase in hot summer months.

Graph shows percentage of yearly homicides, rapes, and assaults in each quarter of the year (Anderson, 1989)

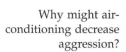

Why might air-conditioning decrease aggression?

1989). It is clear from the figure that violent aggression reaches its peak in the hot summer months.

If we divide days of the year according to how hot they were, as researchers did in a study of violent crimes in Dallas, Texas, during an 18-month time span that included a summer of 63 100-degree-plus days, we find a similar and very striking relationship between aversive temperatures and aggression (Harries & Stadler, 1988). Violent crimes, but not nonviolent crimes, are more prevalent on hotter days, especially in poor neighborhoods where the homes and apartments are less likely to have air conditioning (Cotton, 1986; Harries & Stadler, 1988). People who have air conditioning in their homes or cars can escape from aversive heat. In one study of heat and aggression, a confederate driver stopped at a traffic light in front of an unsuspecting motorist. The hotter the outdoor temperature was, the more likely the motorist was to blast the horn in irritation when the light turned green and the confederate driver did not move. The connection between outdoor temperature and horn honking occurred, however, only for drivers who had their windows down rather than up, presumably because they did not have air conditioning in their cars (Kenrick & MacFarlane, 1986).

Even in organized sports, high temperatures may create a "climate of aggression." One reason that professional football players play rougher and get more penalties when the team is wearing black rather than white uniforms may be that the color black is an "aggressive cue" (Frank & Gilovich, 1988). Another reason may be that black uniforms are more likely to absorb heat and to make the players uncomfortable. In a study of batters being hit by pitched balls in professional baseball games, the researchers noted that pitchers who are frustrated (for example, when the opposing team starts getting home runs) deliberately throw fastballs at or very near the batter to reestablish control of the game (Reifman, Larrick, & Fein, 1991). If heat makes aggression more likely, the researchers reasoned, then the number of batters hit (which is not related to the pitcher losing control and throwing wild pitches) should be greater as the outdoor temperature increases. The relationship was as predicted. The hotter the day, the more likely pitchers were to hit batters, in some cases causing severe injuries.

When it gets "too hot to move," of course, aggression may decrease rather than increase. In several laboratory experiments, students were angered and then confined to either comfortable, hot, or very hot rooms where they had an opportunity to aggress against a confederate. Students who were in hot rooms punished the confederate more than did students who were in either comfortable or *very* hot rooms (Baron & Bell, 1975; Bell & Baron, 1977). Similarly, students who have an opportunity to aggress in a room that has either no odor, an unpleasant odor, or an extremely obnoxious stench are more aggressive with an unpleasant odor than with no odor or with an unbearable stench (Rotton, Frey, Barry, Milligan, & Fitzpatrick, 1979). When the experience is too aversive, participants are probably thinking more about escaping from the situation ("No, I don't want to give him any shocks. Now let me out of here") than about punishing anyone. Under such extreme conditions, they are unlikely to think the kinds of aggressive thoughts that are elicited by moderately high temperatures.

Outside the psychology laboratory, however, intense heat may trigger violent thoughts. At least one study has shown that students who are confined to hot as opposed to comfortable experimental booths are more likely to complete ambiguous story beginnings about car accidents and poor service at restaurants by mentioning frustration, anger, pounding, shouting, insulting, hitting, and slapping (Rule, Taylor, & Dobbs, 1987). With such thoughts coming readily to people's minds in hot weather (as well as with high air pollution and atmospheric electricity), it is small wonder that their tempers flare and they sometimes hurt each other (Baron, Russell, & Arms, 1985; Rotton & Frey, 1985).

AROUSAL

As Table 13.1 suggests, arousal plays an important role in how people react to aversive experiences. Heat, attack, frustration, and other aversive experiences make people physiologically aroused. Their hearts race, they perspire, their adrenaline levels increase, and their blood pressure rises (Anderson, 1989; Hokanson, Burgess, & Cohen, 1963). Physiological arousal, in turn, may facilitate aggression (Rule & Nesdale, 1976; Zillmann, 1979). *Excitation-transfer* theory explains the conditions under which physiological arousal of any kind, whether it is produced by aversive experiences or not, facilitates aggression. More specifically, there may be an unfortunate link between *sexual arousal and aggression* (Malamuth & Donnerstein, 1983; Zillmann, 1984).

■ EXCITATION TRANSFER

When people are physiologically aroused, they sometimes react more intensely to annoyance, provocation, and frustration than they might have in other circumstances. People who have recently engaged in strenuous physical exercise, for example, might be more likely than they would at other times to strike out against someone who insulted them. According to **excitation transfer theory,** physiological excitement or arousal can, under specific conditions, be transferred from its actual cause to a different object (Zillmann, 1971, 1978, 1983a, 1983b, 1984).

To use a concrete example of excitation transfer, suppose that a businessman who was trying to catch a flight had to run from his car to the airport terminal, carrying a heavy suitcase. When he got to the gate, he stood in line for a while to get a boarding pass, during which time he *thought* he had recovered from his physical exertion. People sometimes *think* they have recovered from physical exercise, even though their heart rates, blood pressure, adrenaline levels, and other signs of physiological arousal are still elevated. When the businessman entered the airplane, another man was standing in the aisle with his right foot on the businessman's seat, tying his shoe lace. Instead of asking the man to take his shoe off the seat, the businessman roughly slapped the man's leg away, which led to a fistfight. According to excitation transfer theory, the businessman was still physiologically excited from his run but did not realize it. His physiological excitation from running transferred to (and was added to) the excitation from being provoked. His normal reaction to the other man's callous behavior was magnified. Had the businessman not been provoked or had he not been physiologically excited without realizing why, no excitation transfer would have occurred.

In a study of physiological arousal with and without provocation, college men were first provoked or not by an experimental confederate (Zillmann, Katcher, & Milavsky, 1972). Then they either pedaled an exercise bike for 2.5 minutes or sat in a chair to thread disks onto a string. After waiting quietly for a few more minutes (time enough for the men who rode the bike to *think* that they had recovered, even though physiological recordings showed that their heart rates and blood pressure were still elevated), the students chose shock levels to punish the confederate's mistakes on a decoding task. Exercise-induced arousal had little effect on aggression by men who had not themselves been shocked by the confederate. Across four blocks of three mistakes each, unprovoked men gave the confederate very mild shocks, regardless of whether they had pedaled the exercise bike or not. Shock level increased slightly across blocks, perhaps because the men's initial inhibitions about causing another person pain were gradually overcome by doing so in a socially sanctioned context. Exercise-induced arousal, however, increased aggression by men who had been provoked, and did so increasingly as the elapsed time between pedaling and punishing increased. Provoked men who had ridden the bicycle were only slightly more aggressive than were men who had not ridden the bicycle for the first two blocks of mistakes, but as time went on, the difference grew wider. Once people had overcome their initial inhibitions, the combination of arousal from being attacked and additional arousal from exercise combined to elicit very high levels of aggression. Athletes who recover from exercise rapidly, of course, do not display excitation transfer, nor do out-of-shape people who *know* why their hearts are racing (Zillmann, Johnson, & Day, 1974).

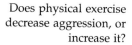

Does physical exercise decrease aggression, or increase it?

The additional arousal need not come only from physical exercise. Physiological arousal has virtually identical effects on aggression whether it comes from physical exercise, competitive games, listening to some types of music, or any other activity that gets the blood pumping and the heart racing (Christy, Gelfand, & Hartmann, 1971; Geen, 1975; Rogers & Ketchen, 1979; Zillmann, 1984). The sympathetic nervous system produces the same bodily symptoms whether the arousal is from positive events like winning the lottery, negative events like being insulted, or neutral events like running a half mile (Averill, 1969; Levi, 1965, Patkai, 1971). It is difficult for people to tell how much of their physiological arousal comes from each of two or three possible sources. People do not usually say to themselves "one-half of my arousal is from running and one-half from being insulted." Instead, they experience an overall level of physiological excitement that they blame on whatever cause is most noticeable at the moment (Zillmann, 1978). When people have become physiologically aroused from another source but do not attribute their arousal to that source, they blame an insult or injury received from another person for the accumulated arousal (Zillmann, 1979).

■ SEXUAL AROUSAL AND AGGRESSION

One particularly interesting source of a racing heart and pounding pulse is sexual arousal. Many different species of male animals display sexual arousal both when they are mating and when they are fighting (Zillmann, 1984). From relevant animal studies, psychologists suspect that sex and aggression have close connections. They suspect that excitation transfer might be at least as likely to occur when the "extra" source of arousal comes from sexually related thoughts as when it comes from other sources such as physical exercise.

To test the excitation transfer properties of sexual arousal, an experimental confederate in one study gave male college students a "negative evaluation" of nine electric shocks (Zillmann, 1971). The students then watched either a nonarousing documentary film called *Marco Polo's Travels,* the violent, physiologically arousing prizefight film *Body and Soul,* or an erotic, sexually exciting film called *The Couch.* After watching one of the films, the men got an opportunity to retaliate for the earlier negative evaluation by giving the confederate electric shocks. Watching a violent movie increased aggression compared to watching a documentary, even though the violent movie produced physiological arousal without physical exercise. Watching the erotic movie also increased aggression even more than did watching the violent movie, even though the violent movie was full of "aggressive cues." In addition, the discrepancy between aggression from the violent movie and aggression from the erotic movie widened over time. Sexually induced arousal may last longer than arousal from other sources (Zillmann, Hoyt, & Day, 1974).

Other studies investigated the effects of sexually induced arousal on women's aggression and on women as the target of men's aggression. They found that women may be as susceptible to excitation transfer from sexual arousal as are men. Like men, women who are provoked and then watch an erotic film aggress more, either against a person whose sex is not known or against another woman, than do women who are provoked and watch either no film or a nonarousing film (Baron, 1979; Cantor, Zillmann, & Einsiedel, 1978). In addition, men who are provoked by either male or female confederates and then watch an erotic film aggress at least as much against a female provoker as against a male provoker (Donnerstein & Barrett, 1978). In two separate studies, sexually aroused men aggressed more against a woman who had provoked them than against a man who had provoked them, and did so more over time (Donnerstein & Hallam, 1978). Recall, however, that excitation transfer occurs only under limited circumstances, during a small "window in time" when people who have been provoked are still aroused without realizing it (Zillmann, 1979, 1984). As we shall see, men who *know* that they are sexually excited by pictures of naked women do *not* transfer their sexual excitement to aggression against women (Linz, Donnerstein, & Penrod, 1988).

DISINHIBITION

Disinhibition involves a weakening or removal of inhibitions that normally restrain people from acting on their impulses. For aggressive behavior, inhibitions include the risk that other people might disapprove, the risk that the person aggressed against might retaliate, the possibility that the other person might have a legitimate excuse for an earlier provocation, and a sense of personal responsibility for any harm that the aggression might cause. Throughout the preceding sections of this chapter, we have seen that aggression increases when inhibitions are lowered. Studies of "modeling" showed that both children and adults aggress more when they have seen another person aggress, in part because the other person's actions make aggression seem more legitimate (Bandura et al., 1963). Studies of attack and provocation showed that enraged participants ignore their victim's pain, which inhibits aggression in nonenraged participants (Baron, 1973). Studies of catharsis showed that a moderate amount of initial aggression elicits *more,* not less, subsequent aggression against the same target, in part because getting away with aggression increases confidence that aggression is acceptable (Geen & Quanty, 1977). Studies of excitation transfer showed that aggression increases over time, as long as the aggression occurs in a laboratory context where the experimenter seems to find aggression acceptable (Zillmann et al., 1972). Studies of the connection between sexual arousal and aggression showed that over time, as they find that they are getting away with punishing a woman for her mistakes, men increase their aggression against women at a more accelerated pace than they increase their aggression against other men (Donnerstein & Hallam, 1978).

These results fit the pattern of behaviors that have both an "instigating component" and an "inhibiting component" (Steele & Southwick, 1985). In studies of aggression, the instigating component is usually an attack, insult, or frustration that increases the likelihood of aggression. The inhibiting component involves social disapproval, mitigating circumstances, a sense of personal responsibility, and any other consideration that argues against direct physical aggression. This section of the chapter describes two factors that lower inhibitions that normally constrain people from open aggression: alcohol and deindividuation.

■ ALCOHOL

Alcohol impairs people's ability to "think straight." When people have been drinking, they are less able than when they are sober to pay attention to important details, remember the lessons of previous experience, deal with abstractions, draw accurate conclusions, and integrate pieces of evidence that come from more than one source (Hull & Bond, 1986; Steele & Southwick, 1985). Under the influence of alcohol, therefore, people who have aversive experiences are less likely to notice mitigating circumstances that explain or excuse a provocation, remember and be guided by abstract moral principles that dictate nonaggression, and worry about the risks of possible retaliation or social censure. They are also less aware of their personal responsibility for unpleasant consequences and less likely to inhibit their aggressive tendencies (Pernanen, 1976; Zeichner & Phil, 1979, 1980). In situations that involve conflict between the instigating component and the inhibiting component of aggression, therefore, people who have been drinking alcohol, except for those who are very experienced in acting under the influence of alcohol, have the inhibiting component weakened. As a result, they are more likely to try to engage in behaviors that they might normally have inhibited (Laplace, Chermack, & Taylor, 1994). Alcohol facilitates aggression not so much "by 'stepping on the gas' but rather by paralyzing the brakes" (Muehberger, 1956, p. 40).

In a review of studies that involved both provocation to aggress and inhibition against aggressing (for example, where public censure for aggression was likely versus unlikely), the reviewers found that alcohol was much more likely to increase aggression when the inhibiting component and the instigating component were in conflict than when they were not (Steele & Southwick, 1985). In the studies that they reviewed, some participants actually drank alcohol, whereas other participants were merely tricked by an artificial taste and smell into thinking that they were drinking alcohol. Although part of alcohol's disinhibiting effect may involve giving drinkers an excuse for aggression, participants who merely thought they were drinking alcohol did not ignore the inhibiting factors. Only participants who had actually consumed alcohol ignored the inhibiting factors and displayed more of the normally inhibited behavior in high conflict than in low conflict situations. When the instigating factors are clearly more powerful than the inhibiting factors (for instance, when physical exercise and provocation are so extreme that possible excuses seem insignificant), alcohol has little effect (Zillmann, Bryant, Cantor, & Day, 1975). When the instigating factors are almost equally balanced against inhibiting factors (for instance, when men are provoked by a woman and get the chance to punish her physically while an experimenter is watching), alcohol dampens inhibitions and facilitates aggression (Steele & Southwick, 1985).

According to some crime statistics, approximately 50% of murderers had been drinking before they killed (Holcomb & Anderson, 1983; MacDonald, 1961). Alcohol consumption has also been linked with other violent behaviors, including assault, spouse abuse, and rape (Gayford, 1975; Johnson, Gibson, & Linden, 1978; Myers, 1982). Across many studies of the relationship between alcohol and aggression, alcohol clearly increases aggression. It only does so, however, in situations where the intoxicated person has been provoked and where both instigating and inhibiting considerations come into play (Bushman & Cooper, 1990; Taylor & Leonard, 1983).

In one study that involved the inhibiting influence of possible social censure, male students traded shocks in a "game" with a confederate who kept increasing the intensity of shock that he gave the student (Taylor & Gammon, 1976). While the student and confederate were exchanging shocks, a second confederate was with the student, putting social pressure on him to restrain his aggression. The social pressure kept sober students from punishing the offender with intense electric shocks, but it had little restraining influence on intoxicated students. Alcohol reduced the inhibition that would otherwise come from a well-meaning stranger's nonaggressive advice.

In a related study that involved the inhibiting influence of an opponent's altered intentions, sober and intoxicated students "overheard" their opponent in a shock-trading game tell the experimenter either that he intended to use the lowest level of shock on every round or that he intended to use the highest level (Leonard, 1989). On the first round, however, the opponent gave the student the lowest level of shock. Students who had consumed alcohol set a higher level of shock for their opponent on the first round than did students who had not consumed alcohol. In addition, students who thought that their opponent was going to shock them with the highest level set a higher level for

FIGURE 13.5

Alcohol removes inhibitions against aggression.

Graph shows intensity of shock sober and intoxicated students gave a confederate after he said he was going to give them high or low shock, but in both cases gave them low shock (Leonard, 1989)

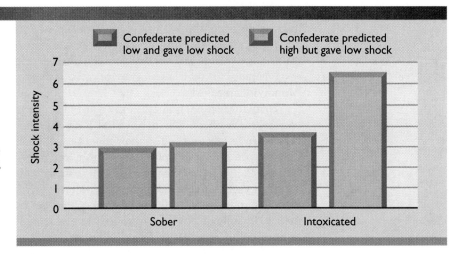

him to receive than did students who thought that their opponent was going to shock them with the lowest level. On the second round, however, as Figure 13.5 shows, when all students discovered that their opponent had used the lowest level of shock, sober students acted more in line with the opponent's actions than with his stated intentions. Intoxicated students, in contrast, shocked the opponent even more in line with his stated intentions, despite that he had obviously changed his mind. Even a threatening opponent's "change of heart," which might inhibit sober people from aggression, had no inhibiting effect on an intoxicated person's aggression.

Alcohol also "takes people out of themselves." When intoxicated, they do not feel as self-conscious and are thus willing to perform behaviors that would otherwise burden them with social responsibility. In one study of alcohol's effects on self-awareness, students consumed either alcohol or a drink that smelled and tasted like alcohol (Hull, Levenson, Young, & Sher, 1983, Experiment 2). Half of the students in each group were told that they were drinking alcohol; the other half were told that the drink contained no alcohol. Subsequently, all students delivered a speech on "What I like and dislike about my body and physical appearance." Students who consumed alcohol used fewer first-person pronouns (I, me, my, mine) in their speeches than did students who consumed no alcohol, regardless of what the students thought they were drinking. Although other studies have shown that people sometimes behave abnormally merely because they *think* they drank alcohol, even though they did not, many studies suggest that alcohol keeps people from thinking about themselves (Hull & Bond, 1986). Not thinking about themselves may be one of alcohol's most attractive characteristics for people who are feeling defeated, anxious, or guilty (Baumeister, 1990a).

■ DEINDIVIDUATION

Deindividuation involves losing track of personal identity, often as part of a crowd, so that personal responsibility for the consequences of actions is lessened (Festinger, Pepitone, & Newcomb, 1952; Zimbardo, 1970). Deindividuation thus exemplifies one of the major themes that recur throughout this book—that people have both a personal identity and a social identity (Abrams, 1992; Brewer, 1991; Turner, Oakes, Haslam, & McGarty, 1994). Sometimes they think of themselves as individuals. At other times, they think of themselves more as part of a group than as an individual. People who are intoxicated with alcohol, for instance, think more about "we did it" than about "I did it" (Hull et al., 1983). They think more about "our responsibility" than about "my responsibility." They are less self-conscious and less aware of accountability and responsibility for their own behavior *as individuals*. They are thus described as "*de*individuated."

Drinking alcohol is not the only way to become deindividuated. Anonymity has the same effect. When Ku Klux Klan members terrorized Black people, they wore hoods to disguise their identities. When violent mobs loot and kill, they rely on the "safety of numbers" to avoid personal responsibility (Staub & Rosenthal, 1994). When soldiers form a firing squad to execute a war criminal, their commanders tell them that some of the rifles have blank bullets, thus ensuring anonymity for the soldier who fired the fatal shot. Being anonymous means "escaping from a sense of self" and personal responsibility just as much as does being intoxicated. Deindividuation, therefore, is another way to overcome the inhibiting factors that would otherwise restrain aggressive behavior (Zimbardo, 1970). Deindividuation contributes importantly to such aggressive behaviors as youth violence and genocide (Staub, in press).

When people act as part of a cohesive group rather than as individuals, when they are psychologically absorbed in or focused on the group rather than on themselves, when they believe that they cannot be identified or held responsible for their actions, they are less likely than under normal conditions to remember their own standards of appropriate behavior. They are less likely to care what other people think of them. They concentrate on the immediate situation rather than on unwanted future consequences of their actions. As a result, they easily overcome their normal inhibitions. They are more likely than otherwise to behave in ways that in different circumstances might be inhibited, especially when their group's identity is threatened (Branscombe & Wann, 1992; Diener, 1980; Prentice-Dunn & Rogers, 1983, 1989; Rogers & Prentice-Dunn, 1981; Zimbardo, 1970). Sometimes relaxed inhibitions and lowered self-consciousness facilitate positive behaviors like kissing a friend in public, "losing yourself" in an enthusiastic concert crowd, or helping another person (Diener, 1980; Wegner & Schaeffer, 1978; Zimbardo, 1970). At other times, deindividuation facilitates antisocial behaviors like aggression. Police officers who patrol in groups, for instance, sometimes concentrate on their identity as a group and react very aggressively toward suspected criminals (Wilson & Brewer, 1993).

In one study of deindividuation, college women in one condition were "deindividuated" (Zimbardo, 1970). They wore bulky clothing and hoods that concealed their identity, were never called by name, and participated in a dimly lit room. Women in another condition were "individuated." They wore large name tags, were frequently called by name, and participated in a brightly lit room. When they delivered electric shocks to women confederates, one of whom had previously been pleasant to them and the other of whom had previously been obnoxious to them, women in the deindividuated condition delivered more intense shocks, especially to the obnoxious confederate. In a study that used a similar manipulation, women "helped" some protesters who wanted to experience in advance what it might be like to march in a picket line on campus. Women who were wearing hoods and could not otherwise be identified cursed, shoved, knocked down, and kicked the passive demonstrators. The experiment had to be stopped before participants caused serious physical harm (Zimbardo, 1970). Across many different ways of manipulating deindividuation and many ways of measuring aggression, deindividuation reliably increases aggression in situations where aggression is the most likely behavior (Diener, Diener, Endresen, Beaman, & Fraser, 1975; Diener, 1980; Prentice-Dunn & Rogers, 1983, 1989).

SUMMARY OF WHY PEOPLE HURT EACH OTHER

Aggression is more likely when people have aversive experiences, when they are physiologically aroused, and when their normal inhibitions against aggression are lowered. Some aversive experiences that increase aggression are attack, frustration, and irritating environmental conditions. Being attacked makes people angry and frustrated, because they have been prevented from reaching desirable, expected goals such as social harmony. Contrary to the catharsis hypothesis, frustration does not build internal pressure that must be vented to avoid a subsequent "explosion of aggression." Instead, aggression breeds further aggression. Frustration is especially likely to elicit aggression when aggressive cues such as weapons or violent movies are present. Aggression is also facilitated by such aversive environmental conditions as excessive summer temperatures. Physiological arousal or "excitation" from sources not related to aggression, such as physical exercise and erotic movies, can "transfer" to increased aggression. Excitation transfer occurs in circumstances where people do not realize that two sources of excitation are combining to intensify arousal.

Finally, aggression is facilitated by circumstances that remove or reduce concerns such as the risk of social censure or personal responsibility that might otherwise inhibit aggression. Alcohol reduces inhibitions against aggression by reducing people's ability to notice or take into account extenuating circumstances, moral standards, and personal responsibility. Alcohol reduces self-awareness and takes people "out of themselves." Deindividuation, which consists of losing your identity and being submerged in a group, has effects similar to those of alcohol. Deindividuation removes or reduces people's normal inhibitions against both prosocial and antisocial behaviors.

DO MEDIA VIOLENCE AND PORNOGRAPHY PROMOTE AGGRESSION?

The first two sections of this chapter addressed the basic questions of whether aggression is "natural" for human beings and, if aggression is not natural, then why do people hurt each other? As described in the two earlier sections, aggression is no more "natural" for human beings than are generosity, cooperativeness, or any other of the diverse ways in which people cope with their worlds. People *can* try to hurt each other, but they do not *have* to try to hurt each other. Depending on how they have been socialized, however, some people use physical or verbal aggression because it is the only way they have learned to cope with frustrating or difficult circumstances. The likelihood of using aggression in such circumstances is increased by seeing other people use aggression successfully, by "cues" that bring to mind aggressive thoughts, and by "disinhibiting" suggestions that aggression is a normal, acceptable way to behave. As we shall see in this third section of the chapter, *television and movie violence,* as well as violent *pornography,* provide many aggressive models, aggressive ideas, and disinhibiting suggestions that set the stage for aggression (Bushman & Geen, 1990; Friedrich-Cofer & Hustron, 1986; Geen, 1990; Geen & Thomas, 1986; Parke, Berkowitz, Leyens, West, & Sebastian, 1977; Phillips, 1986).

TELEVISION AND MOVIE VIOLENCE

Numerous studies conducted over several decades in both laboratory and "real world" settings provide solid evidence that a relationship exists between media violence and aggression (Wood, Wong, & Chachere, 1991). In addition, scientists have proposed several very convincing reasons to explain the relationship.

■ RELATIONSHIP BETWEEN MEDIA VIOLENCE AND AGGRESSION

Television programs and movies present a distorted view of reality, especially regarding acts of aggression. The average one-hour television program in the United States and Canada contains eight acts of verbal aggression and nine acts of physical aggression (Signiorelli, Gross, & Morgan, 1982; Williams, Zabrack, & Joy, 1982). Television characters are three times as likely to work in law enforcement as in all blue-collar and service professions combined. Crime is ten times as rampant on television as it is in the real world (Gerbner, Gross, Morgan, & Signiorelli, 1982). Only very rarely do the characters use means other than aggression to settle disputes or to resolve conflicts (Williams et al., 1982).

Besides being unrealistically frequent, television and movie violence are also unrealistically lacking in negative consequences (Gerbner et al., 1982; Williams et al., 1982). When television characters cut each other up with vicious, hostile, obscene, degrading remarks, a laugh track often lets the audience know that the verbal aggression is not problematic but rather clever and commendable. When television and movie characters punch, stab, or shoot each other, the target of the attack usually submits, withdraws, retaliates in kind, or simply dies. Targets of television or movie aggression almost never display pain or suffering, try to be conciliatory, try to deflect the attacker's anger, ask a third party to arbitrate the dispute, or call for help. Also, the actors who play

"witnesses" to television and movie violence seldom intervene. If anything, they assist or encourage the attacker!

People who watch violent television and movies react to this bloody and successful mayhem in predictable ways (Rubenstein, 1984). When television was first introduced into rural Canadian towns that previously had few problems with assault and homicide, violent crimes increased (Joy, Kimball, & Zabrack, 1986). When heavyweight title boxing matches have been widely publicized in the United States, homicide rates have increased after the fight (Phillips, 1983). When the evening news showed vivid footage of brutal murders and assassinations, crimes against property did not increase, but violent crimes against persons did (Berkowitz & Macaulay, 1971). Whether from coverage of sporting events, soap opera suicides, or sensational news stories, television violence reliably precedes viewer aggression (Geen, 1990; Huesmann, 1986; Parke et al., 1977).

In addition, children who watch much violent television early in life have a tendency to use aggression later in life. One longitudinal study found that three-year-old boys who watched many hours of violent television were more likely than were three-year-old boys who watched few hours of violent television to behave aggressively seven years later, when they were ten years old (Lefkowitz, Eron, Walder, & Huesmann, 1977). Another longitudinal study found that the sheer amount of television, whether violent or nonviolent, that a boy watched at age ten predicts the seriousness of his crimes as an adult at age 30 (Huesmann, Lagerspetz, & Eron, 1984; see also Milavsky, Kessler, Stipp, & Rubins, 1982). The "serious" adult crimes predicted by early television viewing include firing a gun at someone, attacking someone with a knife or broken bottle, and setting fire to buildings (Belson, 1978; Cook, Kendzierski, & Thomas, 1983; Singer & Singer, 1981).

When do children imitate media violence?

The reverse relationship–that aggressive behavior at an early age predicts watching violent television programs later in life–does not occur reliably for boys. It does occur for girls, whose traditional adult sex roles may allow them to express their feelings only by watching rather than by participating in violent events (Eron & Huesmann, 1980). Nonetheless, laboratory studies show that participating in aggressive behavior whets the appetite for viewing violent films and programs (Fenigstein, 1979). The relationship between media violence and aggression is both well established and circular. Watching violent episodes or playing violent video games promotes aggression, but behaving aggressively also promotes watching violent episodes and playing violent video games (Anderson & Morrow, 1995; Schutte, Malouff, Post-Gordon, & Rodasta, 1988).

■ REASONS FOR THE RELATIONSHIP

Why is media violence related to viewer aggression? How does viewing television violence increase the likelihood that people will use aggression as a way to cope with difficult situations? The answers to these questions can be found in the earlier sections of this chapter, in discussions of modeling, aggressive cues, disinhibition, and arousal. Briefly, media violence creates an atmosphere of suspicion and mistrust, shows admirable people using and being rewarded for aggression, lends legitimacy to aggression, brings hostile thoughts and associations to mind, and gets people so used to violence that it no longer bothers them (Berkowitz, 1984; Geen, 1990; Geen & Thomas, 1986).

People who watch much television have different "worldviews" than do people who watch very little television. People who watch much television, who witness an unrealistically high level of violent incidents, believe that the world is a sinister, brutal, and threatening place, in which no one can be trusted

(Gerbner et al., 1982). They are convinced that "most people would take advantage of you if they got the chance" (Gerbner, Gross, Eleey, Jackson-Beeck, Jeffries-Fox, & Signiorelli, 1977). They believe that they are vulnerable to an "epidemic" of increasingly violent crime and that the government should do more to protect them, even if it means restricting the freedom of its citizens (Bryant, Carveth, & Brown, 1981; Cantor, 1982; Gerbner et al., 1982; Groebel & Krebs, 1983; Williams et al., 1982). Such negative worldviews may lead to excessive reactive aggression, in which people misconstrue ambiguous actions as threatening and strike out in "self-defense" (Dodge & Coie, 1987). Thus, a homeowner might shoot a masked teenager who came to the door to ask directions to a Halloween party because the homeowner's worldview led him or her to expect strangers to be dangerous.

The story lines of violent movies and television programs convey the message that the world is a dangerous place. They also imply that "good" people use aggression successfully. Like the adult who attacked the punching doll in the study of modeling, television and movie characters not only get away with extremely violent behavior, but they are also applauded for doing so. A typical television or movie script demonstrates that "bad person provokes good person unmercifully, but good person eventually gets violent revenge" (Huesmann, 1986). Program writers and directors go out of their way to make the "good person" in such scripts someone similar to the average viewer, so that viewers find it easy to imagine themselves behaving as the hero behaves. We know from numerous studies of aggression that both children and adults are more influenced by witnessing aggression when they are similar to the aggressor than when they are not (Huesmann, Eron, Klein, Brice, & Fischer, 1983; Leyens & Picus, 1973; Perry & Perry, 1976; Turner & Berkowitz, 1972; Turner & Goldsmith, 1976). Violent television and movie heroes make very effective role models.

By emphasizing justifiable revenge, television and movie scripts also make aggression seem more legitimate. Modern television violence includes shows in which the viewer "rides along" with the police and experiences the vicarious excitement of violence in the service of law and order. In a study about the impact of watching justifiable violence on viewer aggression, juvenile delinquent boys had their answers to questions evaluated by a confederate "partner" who either made neutral remarks or insulted them (Parke et al., 1977). Next, some of the boys saw a movie in which one prizefighter beat another into a bloody pulp. Before watching the brutal beating, some of the boys received background information that the losing fighter was a likable character. Other boys learned that he was a scoundrel who had sadistically exploited other people in the past. Finally, all boys had an opportunity to give electric shocks of varying intensity to their "partners." The film and background information had little effect on the level of shock administered by boys who had not been insulted. The film and background information, however, had a large impact on the level of shock administered by boys who *had* been insulted. Perhaps because the movie violence made it seem legitimate to exact revenge on scoundrels, boys who had been angered subsequently used a higher level of shock when they had recently watched a film clip that showed justifiable aggression.

In a related study, students watched a male confederate make an obscene gesture at an aggravating female experimenter who had momentarily turned her back (Hansen & Hansen, 1990). Students who had recently watched *neutral* MTV rock music videos evaluated the man more negatively when he made the obscene gesture at her than when he did not. Students who had instead watched MTV music videos that contained scenes of trashing homes, stealing cars, and defying authority evaluated the confederate more *positively* when he made the obscene gesture! Many rock music videos are difficult to distinguish from violent pornography, which increases men's acceptance of violence toward women (St. Lawrence & Joyner, 1991). Whatever inhibitions might normally restrain people from committing or condoning aggression, movie and television scenes that legitimize violence remove those restraints, at least for people who have been angered (Berkowitz & Geen, 1967; Comstock, 1980; Geen & Stonner, 1973; Hoyt, 1970; Turner & Goldsmith, 1976).

Television and movie violence also bring to mind violent ideas and associations (Bushman & Geen, 1990). Angered students were more aggressive when they saw shotguns on the table in the "aggressive cues" study. Television and movie viewers are more likely to express their aggressive feelings toward other people when something about the situation reminds them of the violence that they saw on the screen. In one study of the aggressive cues provided by media violence, students who watched a violent film starring the actor Kirk Douglas also shocked an insulting confederate more if the confederate gave his name as "Kirk" than if he called himself "Bob" (Berkowitz & Geen, 1967).

In another study of aggressive cues in media presentations, second- and third-grade boys were frustrated when a promised "neat" cartoon videotape turned into unwatchable static on their television screens (Josephson, 1987). Next, some of the boys watched a film about police officers forming a SWAT team to revenge sniper killings of other police officers. During the extremely violent climax in which the police officers "blew away" the snipers, members of the SWAT team used walkie-talkies to communicate. After watching either the SWAT team episode or a nonviolent film, all the boys played floor hockey. Just before the hockey game started, an adult referee interviewed each boy, using either a tape recorder or a walkie-talkie like the one used by the movie SWAT team. During the game, observers recorded such violent acts as hitting or kicking another player, knocking another player down, and hitting him with the hockey stick. For children who had initially been rated as interpersonally aggressive, watching the SWAT team episode increased floor hockey aggression more when the referee wore a walkie-talkie than when he did not. Recalling and using movie or television violence depends on the extent to which the television or movie episode resembles a subsequent real-life situation (Huesmann, 1982, 1986). When the circumstances or the potential target of aggression are closely associated with previously witnessed violent images, aggression becomes more likely (Bushman & Geen, 1990; Donnerstein & Berkowitz, 1981).

Another aspect of television and movie violence that affects subsequent real-world aggression is physiological arousal (Zillmann, 1971). As explained in the earlier description of excitation transfer theory, people who are already physiologically aroused can become more than normally angered by an aversive experience (Bryant & Zillmann, 1979). As a result, they react extremely to even slight or unintended provocations (Doob & Kirshenbaum, 1973; Thomas & Drabman, 1975, 1978). Spectators at exciting sporting events, for example, sometimes become very hostile toward each other, perhaps because "real" violence is more physiologically arousing than staged violence (Arms, Russell, & Sandilands, 1979; Goldstein & Arms, 1971).

In one study of media violence and arousal, students received either mild or strong shocks from a confederate. Then they watched a filmed fight between two men in a parking lot (Geen, 1975). Some of the students believed that the fight was staged as part of a television photography class; others believed that the fight was real. It had been filmed by a passing television photographer. Even though all students watched the same film clip, those who thought the fight was real remained more aroused after the film had ended than did students who thought the fight was staged. Next, when they had a chance to shock the confederate who had attacked them, witnesses to a fight they thought was real aggressed more than did witnesses to a fight they thought was staged. Similar increases in aggression occur when viewers think that a film prizefighter intends to punish his opponent rather than merely do his job as a professional (Berkowitz & Alioto, 1973). Because real violence is especially arousing, it makes a person's usual responses more extreme (Geen & O'Neal, 1969).

Paradoxically, people who get aroused repeatedly by television and movie violence become "desensitized" (Cline, Croft, & Courrier, 1973; Geen, 1990). Boys who watch 25 or more hours of television per week, for instance, become accustomed to seeing people stabbed, shot, and "splattered." They can watch brutal fight scenes with very little increase in their physiological arousal (Cline et al., 1973). Adults who watch two violent films in a row become less aroused during the second film than do adults who watch a nonviolent film first (Thomas, Horton, Lippincott, & Drabman, 1977). Desensitization lowers inhibitions (such as guilty feelings) that might otherwise restrain frequent viewers from acts of aggression (Geen, 1981; Thomas, 1982). Once people become accustomed to seeing physical aggression, they lose some of their capacity to become upset or disturbed by violent actions, whether those actions are performed by someone else or by themselves (Thomas et al., 1977).

For all these reasons—creating an atmosphere of suspicion, providing aggressive role models and aggressive cues, making aggression seem justified, getting people aroused, and over time rendering them "desensitized"—television and movie violence increase the likelihood that people otherwise predisposed to aggression will behave violently themselves. Television and movie violence, however, do not *cause* real-world aggression. No sane person is ever "compelled" to aggress by having witnessed media violence (Freedman, 1984).

Thinking back on the studies described in this chapter, both children and adults can witness incredibly violent episodes without behaving aggressively themselves unless they have also been frustrated or provoked. Females, who are socialized differently from males in the United States and Canada, are *not* more likely to pursue an adult life of crime if they were heavy as opposed to light television viewers when they were girls (Eron & Huesmann, 1980). Young girls are also slightly *less,* not more, likely to hurt other people after watching "real" than "staged" film violence (Geen, 1983). When watching a film that contains both violent and nonviolent role models, both boys and girls tend to imitate the behaviors that they liked best, but for girls the best-liked behaviors are nonviolent (Slife & Rychlak, 1982). Japanese viewers also watch as much television violence as do citizens of the United States, but without a noticeable increase in the level of national violence. Japanese television programs are more likely than U.S. programs to show the victim suffering. Japanese audiences also view the violent action as part of a romantic mythology in which warriors use weapons in ancient rites (Iwao, de Sola Pool, & Hagiwara, 1981; Slife, 1984).

Viewers who focus on the artistic quality of film violence display very little subsequent aggression of their own (Leyens, Cisneros, & Hossay, 1976). In addition, children can be taught to view film violence in ways that reduce the likelihood of their own personal aggression (Huesmann et al., 1983). Once they learn that aggressive behaviors are not normal, that television and film "violence" is an artistic illusion, and that there are many nonviolent ways to solve the dilemmas faced by screen actors, children are *not* negatively influenced by media violence. The children in one study of "inoculation" against the ill effects of media violence produced videotapes of their own, in which they taught other children to take television and movie violence with a grain of salt (Huesmann et al., 1983). After doing so, the child producers no longer reacted to media violence with aggression. The world might be a safer place if adult audience members could imitate these children.

PORNOGRAPHY

The level of violence in television and movies is very high. So is the level of implicit and explicit sex. From beer commercials to "adult" movies, people today are surrounded by images that are intended to be sexually arousing. Not surprisingly, scientists and the general public worry about the possible effects of sexually oriented material. Is it dangerous to arouse men's lust? Do "girlie" pictures drive men to assault women? Should adult bookstores and topless bars be banned because they contribute to real-world violence against women? These and similar questions about pornography are debated vigorously in scientific conferences and public forums (Koop, 1987).

In discussing the scientific evidence about pornography's effects, it is important to recognize a distinction between two types of pornography: erotic pornography and violent pornography. Erotic pornography includes pictures of nudes and of consenting adults who freely engage in sex acts of all kinds. The individuals and couples in images of erotic pornography usually appear to be enjoying themselves immensely. No violence or aggression is involved, either explicitly or implicitly. Violent pornography, in contrast, contains images of physical aggression, usually in scenes that depict men raping women and forcing them to participate in humiliating and degrading sex acts. Erotic pornography and violent pornography have entirely different effects on aggression, whether the aggression is directed against men or against women (Linz, Donnerstein, & Penrod, 1987). The two types of pornography may also create different attitudes toward women.

■ AGGRESSION AGAINST MEN AND WOMEN

This woman is crossing a busy street at a traffic light. What do you think will happen if the first vehicle in line hesitates when the light changes?

In several studies, erotic pornography has either failed to increase aggression or *reduced* aggression. In one such study, men were physically and verbally attacked by a male confederate (Baron, 1974). Next, some of the men viewed nonerotic pictures of scenery, furniture, and abstract paintings. The other men viewed erotic pictures of nude and seminude women in sexually alluring poses. Then all the men got a chance to shock their attacker. Men who had viewed the erotic pictures shocked the confederate *less* than did men who had viewed the nonerotic pictures.

In another study of erotic pornography and aggression, men were verbally attacked by a male confederate (Baron, 1978). The men then viewed either the nonerotic pictures just described, sexual cartoons in which men exploited women, or sexual cartoons in which men did not exploit women. An exploitative cartoon showed a fully dressed male business executive looking up from a telephone conversation to speak to an attractive young woman who was putting on her underwear. The executive was saying, "Don't get dressed yet, Miss Collins . . . I'm not through hiring you." A nonexploitative cartoon showed a smiling couple posing for a photographer. The photographer was saying to the woman, who had her hand inside the man's pants, "That's not what I meant when I said 'hold it.'" Both types of sexual "humor," but especially the exploitative cartoons, *decreased* the intensity of shocks that the men gave to their male attacker.

Erotic images do not always reduce men's aggression against other men. In some circumstances, sexual arousal exaggerates anger from being attacked, through the excitation-transfer process that was discussed earlier in the chapter (Donnerstein, Donnerstein, & Evans, 1975; Zillmann, 1971). Scenes that are both sexually arousing and unpleasant to the viewer do not reduce, and in some circumstances increase, men's aggression against other men (White, 1979; Zillmann, Bryant, Comisky, & Medoff, 1981). When mildly erotic scenes reduce aggression, however, they may do so both because they distract men from thoughts of having been attacked and because they remind most men of "love-making," a tender, caring activity that is incompatible with aggression (Baron, 1983). In a study of responses that are incompatible with aggression, male motorists were blocked at a traffic light by a male confederate who did not move his car when the light changed. Before this provocation occurred, during the time when the light was red, a female confederate walked across the street in front of the motorist. She was either wearing conservative attire, hobbling on crutches, dressed in a clown suit, or wearing "next to nothing." Although the woman was out of sight by the time the red light changed to green, her unusual attire decreased aggressive horn honking. Ninety percent of motorists blasted their horns at the unmoving confederate driver when the woman had not appeared or when she dressed conservatively. This percentage was dramatically reduced when she was on crutches, dressed in a clown suit, or almost naked. Men are unlikely to aggress against other men when they are experiencing sympathy for a person on crutches, when they are laughing at an outlandish clown, or when they have just seen a scantily clad woman.

The pornography studies discussed so far, however, examined the effects of pornography on men's aggression toward men. What are the effects of pornography on men's aggression toward *women?* To summarize the evidence, *erotic* pornography does not increase men's aggression against women; *violent* pornography does. In a representative study, men were verbally and physically attacked by either a male or a female confederate (Donnerstein & Barrett, 1978). Then the men watched either a wildlife documentary or sexually explicit movies that depicted a variety of common and uncommon sex acts. Finally, the men got to deliver electric shocks to their attacker. Although blood pressure recordings showed that the men were more aroused when they were attacked by a woman than by another man, they were less likely (regardless of which film they watched) to take their anger out on the female confederate than on the male confederate.

In a related study, men were verbally attacked by either a male confederate or a female confederate. Then they watched one of four films: a documentary, an erotic pornography movie with plenty of consenting sex but no aggression, a violent movie in which a man ties and beats a woman but both are fully clothed and there are no sexual connotations, or a rape movie in which a man forces a woman into sex acts at the point of a gun (Donnerstein, 1983, pp. 144–145). Figure 13.6 shows the intensity of shocks that the men gave to a male attacker and to a female attacker after watching each of the four

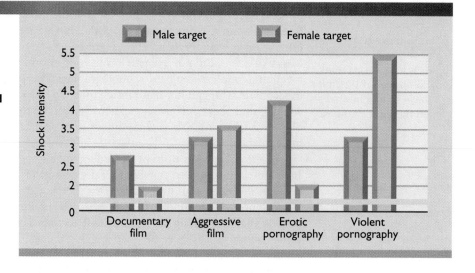

FIGURE 13.6

Violent and erotic pornography have different effects on male aggression toward women.

Graph shows intensity of shock that men who watched four different films gave to a male or female confederate who attacked them (Donnerstein, 1983)

movies. The most informative part of the results is that men shocked a woman *less* than they shocked another man after watching erotic pornography, but they shocked a woman *more* than they shocked another man after watching violent pornography. Men also shocked women *who did not attack them* more intensely after watching violent pornography than after watching erotic pornography (Donnerstein, 1980).

■ ATTITUDES TOWARD WOMEN

Violent pornography increases men's aggression against women for the same reasons that media violence increases aggression. Violent pornography provides male "role models" who hurt women. Violent pornography also provides aggressive cues that associate women with "victims of violence." In addition, most violent pornography contains elements that subtly alter male viewers' attitudes toward women, most notably regarding the "rape myth" (Burt, 1980). The **rape myth** is the erroneous belief that women may at first resist being raped, but their bodies involuntarily become sexually aroused, after which they participate willingly. This myth has been around for a long time. In his famous book *The Art of Love,* the ancient Roman poet Ovid advised men:

> Perhaps she will struggle at first . . . yet she will wish to be beaten in the struggle. . . . You may use force; women like you to use it; they often wish to give unwillingly what they like to give. (quoted in Zillmann, 1984, p. 2).

Nothing, of course, could be further from the truth. Normal people do not enjoy pain. Yet the rape myth is a story that has been told and retold so many times, especially in violent pornography, that some men (and even some women) believe it (Ellis, O'Sullivan, & Sowards, 1992; Malamuth & Check, 1983; Malamuth & Donnerstein, 1983). Even news stories about rapes use the passive voice more to report violence against women than other crimes, which encourages readers to believe that women accept being violated (Henley, Miller, & Beazley, 1995).

In a study of violent pornography that either included or did not include the rape myth, men were verbally and physically attacked by a male confederate or by a female confederate (Donnerstein & Berkowitz, 1981, Experiment 1), after which the men watched one of four films. The neutral film was a talk show interview that contained no hint of sex or aggression. The erotic film showed a man and woman having sexual intercourse. The rape film showed a young woman who came to study with two men. The men started shoving her, forced her to drink alcohol, tied her up, stripped her, slapped her around, and attacked her sexually, during all of which the woman struggled and obviously detested the experience. The *rape myth* movie showed the same scene, except that gradually the woman ceased resisting, started smiling, and became a willing participant in the sexual activities. After watching one of these four films, the men got to shock the male or female confederate who had attacked them. As in previous research, they shocked a female attacker *less* than they shocked a male attacker after watching erotic pornography. They also shocked a female attacker *more* than they shocked a male attacker after watching violent pornography, especially when the violent pornography contained the rape myth that women are sexually aroused by rape. In a follow-up study, men who watched the "resisting rape" film gave very mild shocks to a woman who had not attacked them, but men who watched the rape myth film gave high intensity shocks even to a woman who had *not* attacked them (Donnerstein & Berkowitz, 1981, Experiment 2).

The experience of watching rape myth movies also alters men's attitudes toward women. In relevant studies, men who watched several rape myth movies revised their opinions about whether women who get raped "deserve it" and about the jail sentences that convicted rapists should receive (Linz, Donnerstein, & Penrod, 1984; Linz et al., 1988; Zillmann & Bryant, 1984). A sizable minority of men use and enjoy violent pornography. In one survey of male college students, 35% said they had used violent pornography, depicting bondage, spankings, beatings, torture, and forced sex, during the previous year (Demare, Briere, & Lips, 1988). Twenty-seven percent of all the college men in this study said that they might rape women if they thought they could do so without being caught or punished. Men who frequently view violent pornography also have attitudes that accept violence toward women (Malamuth & Check, 1981). When men develop attitudes accepting of violence toward women, their normal inhibitions against rape are reduced or eliminated (Scully & Marolla, 1984; Walker, Rowe, & Quinsey, 1993). Their victim's pain cues may encourage rather than inhibit further aggression, just as pain cues do for men who are intensely angered (Baron, 1974; Malamuth, 1986). Convicted rapists cite hostility toward women and the urge to dominate women, not mere sexual arousal, as their primary motivation for rape (Groth, 1979). Also, college men who admit having used physical force to make a woman participate in sex express attitudes that reflect underlying anger toward women (Lisak & Roth, 1988). These men feel that they have been teased, hurt, and ridiculed by women in the past and that women "deserve what they get" (Zillmann & Bryant, 1984).

Rape is not so much a sex act as an act of revenge and aggression against victims who, according to the rape myth, enjoy being brutalized. Men who use violent pornography come to accept violence against women as a legitimate and successful way to behave. In a study of college men, for instance, those who watched the feature films *Swept Away* and *The Getaway* (which have been shown in movie theaters all over the world) adopted more callous attitudes toward men hurting women (Malamuth & Check, 1981). Although the two movies contain no explicit sex scenes, the plot of *Swept Away* portrays a rich arrogant woman taunting a poor deckhand, who is then shipwrecked with her on a deserted island, where he slaps her around and eventually rapes her, after which she falls in love with him. The plot of *The Getaway* tells how the hero kidnaps a woman and her husband. He rapes the woman, she falls in love with him, and they taunt her husband until the husband commits suicide. Such plots seem far more dangerous than erotic movies that involve explicit sex but no violence.

The authors of one review urged readers to "Consider a woman shown in a reclining position with genitals displayed, wearing only red feathers and high-heeled shoes, holding a gun and accompanied by a caption offering a direct invitation to sexual activity" (Linz et al., 1987, p. 952). After reviewing the available evidence about the effects of pornography on aggression, the authors concluded that they were more concerned about the *weapon* than about any of the other elements of the scene. Aggressive cues that become associated with women are far more likely to elicit rape and other physical assaults than are images that are merely sexually arousing.

A last but very important point about research on pornography and aggression is that men who watch rape myth movies in laboratory experiments *do not* come to accept violence toward women. Watching a rape myth movie as part of a social psychology experiment is different from watching such movies outside the social psychology laboratory, because experiments end with a thorough debriefing. The experimenter explains carefully that women do not get "turned on" by being attacked and why it is both foolish and dangerous to think that they do. In a representative study, men who watched violent pornography and were then carefully debriefed were *less*, not more, likely after the debriefing to think that rape victims are promiscuous, that rape victims tease and then get what they deserve, that women have an unconscious wish to be raped, and that "being roughed up is sexually stimulating to many women" (Donnerstein & Berkowitz, 1981, Experiment 2). Experiments on violent pornography thus have two benefits. First, the experiments help us to understand why violence against women occurs. Second, the experiments make the men who participate less likely to accept violence against women (Check & Malamuth, 1984; Malamuth & Check, 1984).

SUMMARY OF WHETHER MEDIA VIOLENCE AND PORNOGRAPHY PROMOTE AGGRESSION

Violence on television and in movies is more frequent and has fewer negative consequences than in real life. Both in the experimental laboratory and in the real world, media violence is often followed by increased aggression. Television and movies teach people that the world is a sinister place, that "good" people aggress successfully, and that aggression is legitimate. Media violence brings to mind aggressive ideas and desensitizes people so that they are not as easily upset by aggression. Nonetheless, media violence merely increases the *likelihood* of aggressive responses. It does not *make* people behave aggressively. If they take a critical perspective, both children and adults can watch television and movie violence without behaving aggressively themselves.

In assessing the relationship between pornography and aggression, it is important to distinguish between erotic pornography and violent pornography. Erotic pornography, which includes nudes and sex acts between consenting adults, is more apt to *reduce* than to increase men's aggression against either men or women. Violent pornography, which includes beatings and forced sex, *increases* men's aggression against women, especially when the pornographic scenes foster the "rape myth" that women enjoy being raped. Any materials that show women as willing victims of violence can promote men's acceptance of aggression against women. Such materials can also promote men's willingness to rape if they think they can get away with it. Because experiments on violent pornography end with careful debriefings that expose the fallacies of the rape myth, men who participate in such experiments are *less*, not more, likely to accept violence against women.

CHAPTER 14

Interpersonal Power

World War II was arguably the most cataclysmic event of the twentieth century. Historians have been trying to explain it for 50 years, as have social psychologists. The events that led to U.S. involvement in the war, for instance, raise several questions about how and why people acquire, use, and abuse interpersonal power.

When the Nazis assumed power in Germany, majority opinion in England and the United States held that Adolph Hitler was "just another foreign leader." Even when Hitler's forces began to take over other European countries, both legislators and the general public insisted on retaining the majority opinion that Germany posed no threat to peace (Gold & Raven, 1992). British Prime Minister Neville Chamberlain was widely congratulated on signing a peace pact that gave Hitler the territory he had annexed by force. Winston Churchill and a small minority in the British parliament kept insisting that Hitler was a menace who must be stopped before he subjugated all of Europe. Churchill was roundly criticized for his "war-mongering" speeches against Hitler. As Hitler continued to extend his empire, however, Churchill's minority opinion prevailed. Eventually, Winston Churchill was elected prime minister and took charge of the war against Nazi Germany.

Churchill knew that his best hope of stopping Nazi aggression was to enlist the aid of the United States. He used all his leadership skills to persuade President Franklin D. Roosevelt that the United States should enter the war on Britain's side. More than 50 years later, two social psychologists examined Churchill's letters to Roosevelt, to discover the "social power strategies" that Churchill used (Gold & Raven, 1992). In his letters, Churchill emphasized that he knew more about war developments than did Roosevelt, that the United States and Britain had common interests, that the United States was in danger if Britain failed to stop Hitler's advance, that Britain was making a painful sacrifice from which the United States would benefit, that Churchill could grant the United States military bases on Caribbean islands owned by Britain, and that without tangible U.S. aid the appeasers might take power in Britain and surrender to Hitler the entire British fleet and all Britain's overseas bases. These social power strategies worked, because President Roosevelt acted against the wishes of an isolationist congress and citizenry. Roosevelt gave Britain 50 destroyers in exchange for 99-year leases on military bases at several British island territories. Churchill rejoiced, not merely because of the bases-for-destroyers deal, but also because the arrangement was a first step that would almost inevitably lead to U.S. military intervention against Hitler.

While Churchill was wielding social power to enlist U.S. aid, Hitler and the other Nazi leaders were wielding power in a far different way. They ordered German soldiers to arrest Jewish men, women, and children, incarcerate these people in concentration camps, and then systematically exterminate them. As shown in the movie *Schindler's List,* some German citizens resisted these destructive orders at great personal peril. Nonetheless, thousands of German soldiers obeyed.

World War II has been a fruitful source of social psychology questions for the past 50 years. First, how do majorities and minorities exert power? Why, for instance, did so many legislators and citizens in England and the United States initially conform to the majority opinion that Hitler was a statesman rather than a menace? Conversely, how did Winston Churchill exert enough power against the majority that his minority viewpoint eventually prevailed? Second, how do leaders wield power? What types of social power, for instance, did Churchill exert on President Roosevelt and the United States in trying to persuade them to help Britain? Third, when and how do leaders abuse their power? Why did so many German soldiers, for instance, obey Nazi orders that were obviously destructive and evil? The three sections of this chapter address these three basic questions about interpersonal power.

HOW DO MAJORITIES AND MINORITIES EXERT POWER?

When we ask how majorities exert power and why people conform or "go along with the majority," we address a fundamental tension that exists whenever individuals try to function as a group (Moscovici, 1985; Turner, 1991). Some tasks, like defeating Nazi Germany, cleaning the environment, and exploring the solar system, are better performed by groups than by individuals. Such tasks require a concerted group effort, which would obviously be impeded were individual members of the group to find themselves in conflict. Nonetheless, groups whose members all think alike are unlikely to develop new, innovative ideas and strategies. When people perform group tasks, therefore, there is often a tension between pressure for all group members to agree and the need for some disagreement with established thoughts and practices. When the normal, expected behavior involves appeasing a dictator or committing genocide, we hope that at least some group members will object. For civilization to advance, both the majority and the minority must exert social power.

Table 14.1 may help you to understand how majorities and minorities exert power. As the table shows, majorities and minorities exert power by threat-

TABLE 14.1	How the Majority and the Minority Exert Interpersonal Power When the Majority and the Minority Initially Disagree		
	THREAT	**GOAL**	**COMPLIANCE OR ACCEPTANCE**
Majority Exerts Normative Influence on the Minority	Large, similar majority threatens the minority's being likable	Minority wants to avoid rejection and restore social harmony	Minority complies publicly, but does not accept majority position privately
Majority Exerts Informational Influence on the Minority	Disagreeing majority threatens minority's being right	Minority assumes majority position likely to be correct, and reinterprets the issue and its position	Minority complies publicly, and also accepts majority position privately
Minority Exerts Informational Influence on the Majority	Small, salient group minority that takes its position consistently threatens majority's being right	Majority wants to avoid losing face, wonders what minority sees, checks validity of own side's arguments, and broadens thinking	Majority publicly rejects and does not immediately accept minority position in private, but begins to think more flexibly about the issue

ening two important goals. One of the major themes that recurs throughout the text is that people want to be right and they also want to be likable (Baumeister & Leary, 1995; Snyder, 1993, 1994; Swann, 1987, 1990). People are very concerned about being right. They want to have a correct, objectively valid view of themselves, other people, and relationships (Kenny, 1991; Mischel & Shoda, 1995). People are also very concerned about being likable. They want to feel good about themselves and make a good impression on others (Swann, Hixon, & de La Ronde, 1992). Because people value being right and being likable, threats to either goal, as shown in Table 14.1, can elicit compliance, acceptance, or both.

The top two rows in the table show two routes by which the majority exerts power over the minority: by normative influence or by informational influence. In the first row, a large majority, especially one that is similar to the minority, threatens the minority's being likable. To avoid rejection and restore social harmony, the minority complies with the majority publicly, but does not accept the majority position privately. The first row of the table represents *normative influences on conformity*. In the second row, a majority of any size, especially one that is dissimilar from the minority, threatens the minority's being right. Minority members assume that the majority position "must" be correct. As a result, minority members reinterpret the issue and positions. They comply with the majority position both publicly and privately. The second row of the table represents *informational influences on conformity*. Finally, the bottom row in the table shows a route by which the minority exerts power over the majority. A minority, especially when it is a small group with a salient identity, sometimes takes its position consistently and threatens the majority's goal of being right. To avoid losing face, the majority publicly rejects the minority position. They do not accept it even in private. Nonetheless, they wonder what the minority sees. Majority group members check the validity of minority arguments and broaden their thinking. They think more flexibly about the issue and about related issues. The bottom row of Table 14.1 represents a time *when minority influence prevails*. The following three sections examine the rows of Table 14.1 in greater detail.

NORMATIVE INFLUENCES ON CONFORMITY

A **normative influence on conformity** occurs when, because people want to be liked and to maintain social harmony, they sometimes *comply* with the majority's "norms" or standards for acceptable behavior. Compliance is not the same as acceptance. Compliance involves merely agreeing with the majority in public. Acceptance, in contrast, involves a genuine change of opinion. According to Table 14.1, the normative route to conformity can bring compliance without acceptance. Imagine, for instance, that you were a member of the British parliament when Hitler first started taking over other European countries. Your colleagues and party leaders said that Adolph Hitler was a statesman who had a legitimate claim on the land he had annexed and that he wanted peace in the future. If you privately suspected that Hitler was a menace, what would you do? Would you give a speech in which you disagreed with the majority opinion or would you "go along with the crowd"? It seems easy to say in hindsight (as explained in Chapter 2) that you would have resisted peer pressure to conform, but how easy is it to resist in public when all your peers say you are wrong?

■ THE ASCH LINE-JUDGING STUDY

Participants in a classic study of conformity were placed in just such a situation. Social psychologist Solomon Asch had groups of seven to nine participants view a series of slides that depicted one target line and three comparison lines. The experimenter called on each participant in turn to say which of the three comparison lines was the same length as the target line (Asch, 1951, 1956). In Figure 14.1, for example, which of the three lines on the right do *you* think is the same length as the target line on the left? It is obvious that B is correct and that A and C are incorrect. The correct answer is not ambiguous, the task is not difficult, and the participants are all peers, none of whom can claim to be any more "expert" than the others.

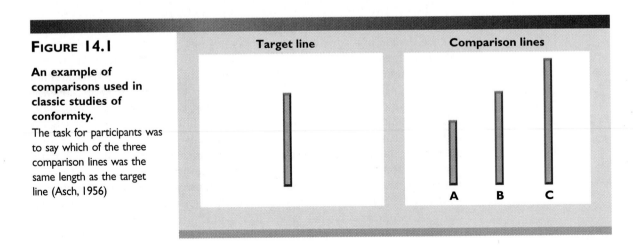

FIGURE 14.1

An example of comparisons used in classic studies of conformity.

The task for participants was to say which of the three comparison lines was the same length as the target line (Asch, 1956)

FIGURE 14.2

People sometimes go along with a mistaken majority.

Graph shows percentage of participants who gave each number of incorrect answers when 6-8 confederates gave obviously incorrect answers on 12 line-length comparisons (Asch, 1956)

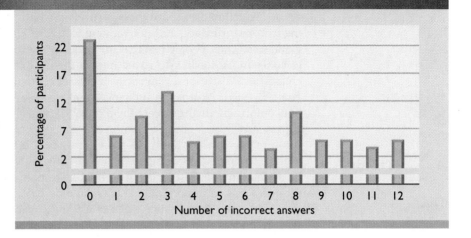

In each experimental session, only one of the people present was an actual participant. All the others (6–8) were confederates of the experimenter. The confederates had agreed in advance that they would all give the same obviously incorrect answer on certain critical slides. The seats were arranged so that the one real participant had to answer last, after hearing all the others give the same incorrect answer. What would you do if you answered last and eight other seemingly normal, rational people of approximately your own age and background had all answered "C" to the problem presented in Figure 14.1?

Of 18 such comparisons, the six to eight confederates all gave the same correct answer on six slides and all gave the same *incorrect* answer on 12 slides. It was possible, therefore, for each participant to "go along with the crowd" by giving an obviously incorrect answer to anywhere from 0 to 12 slides. The term "obviously incorrect" seems appropriate, because only one of 37 people who judged the slides by themselves made a mistake on one of the 12 slides and one made a mistake on two of the 12. Figure 14.2 shows how many of 123 participants gave 0, 1, 2, 3, 4, 5, 6, 7, 8, 9, 10, 11, or 12 obviously incorrect answers when they had to respond after six to eight confederates agreed on an incorrect answer. Although 23.6% of the participants demonstrated their independence by never going along with the group, the other 76.4% of them gave at least one incorrect answer. Also, 61.8% of them gave three or more incorrect answers, which no one in the "judging by themselves" group ever did (Asch, 1956). Finally, 31.9% of the participants gave the majority's obviously incorrect answer on more than half of the critical slides.

■ FACTORS THAT INCREASE NORMATIVE CONFORMITY

Did the participants who gave the same incorrect answer as the confederates believe in what they were saying? No, they did not. When they were interviewed after the study, participants typically admitted that they knew some of their answers were incorrect, but that they decided to agree with the group for the sake of social harmony (Asch, 1956). The participants in subsequent line-length studies were allowed to write their answers privately instead of announcing the answers out loud so that the other group members could hear. Under such "private" circumstances, they did not agree with a mistaken majority (Asch, 1956). Thus Figure 14.2 shows that normative influence produces public compliance but not private acceptance.

The factors that increase normative conformity, as suggested by the topmost row of Table 14.1, are those associated with a fear of rejection, not wanting to appear deviant, and not wanting to "make waves." Normative influence works best when people feel that the majority exerts "social pressure" on them to conform. According to social impact theory (Chapter 11), the pressure increases as the size of the majority increases (Latané & Wolf, 1981; Tanford & Penrod, 1984). Normative influence also increases when people believe that not conforming might subject them to social punishments. People who deviate consistently from a group's opinion are subjected to increasingly intense social pressure. If a deviant holds out too long without making any concessions, majority group members cease communicating with the deviant and act as though he or she did not exist (Schachter, 1951). Normative influence increases when the group has an important goal that can only be achieved by having all group members agree, for instance when a jury must reach a unanimous decision or remain sequestered (Kiesler & Kiesler, 1969). Normative influence is also more likely to occur in groups that are "cohesive," which means that group members are similar to each other, respect each other, and depend on each other (Back, 1951; Forsyth, 1992; Hogg, 1987; Lott & Lott, 1961). When even one other person breaks the group cohesiveness and unanimity by giving the correct answer, very few people conform in the Asch line-judging procedure, because "the pressure is off" when even one other person speaks the truth (Asch, 1956).

INFORMATIONAL INFLUENCES ON CONFORMITY

The second row of Table 14.1 shows how the majority exerts informational influence. An **informational influence on conformity** occurs when, because people want to understand and perceive reality correctly, they sometimes comply with and *accept* the majority's "norms" or standards for acceptable behavior. Imagine, for instance, that you were a member of the British parliament when Hitler first started taking over other European countries. Although you thought that Adolph Hitler was a menace, your party leaders said that Hitler was a peace-loving statesman. You might begin to suspect that the party leaders had access to secret intelligence information—that the prime minister, for instance, might have held secret negotiations in which Hitler bent over backwards to cooperate. You might wonder whether Hitler was the most moderate civilian leader who could be elected in Germany in a time of economic collapse and that it was in your government's best interests to support him and avoid a military coup. It seems easy to say in hindsight that you would never have harbored doubts about Hitler, but at the time events are occurring, their interpretation often seems less like a matter of fact (as was the Asch line-judging task) and more like a matter of subjective opinion. It is always tempting, and sometimes more rational, to trust an opinion on which many people agree than to trust your own unique and possibly incorrect interpretation.

■ THE AUTOKINETIC EFFECT STUDIES

One way to test whether people conform because of informational influence is to arrange a situation in which objective reality is very ambiguous. Just such a situation occurs in the autokinetic effect. *Autokinetic* means "self-moving." If you sit in a completely dark room and a stationary pinpoint of light is shown on a screen, after a few seconds the light appears to move. The illusion of movement is so strong that it occurs even for people who are aware that the light is stationary. People who do not know that the light is stationary differ in how far they think the light is moving. Some individuals estimate that it moves in a circle, a spiral, or back and forth by an inch or two from left to right. Others, perhaps because they assume that the screen is large and far away, estimate that the light moves by as much as one or two feet. People think they "know," but they are not positive that they are right. These perceptual ambiguities make the autokinetic effect an ideal vehicle for testing whether individuals conform with majority opinion because of informational influence (Sherif, 1936).

In a classic study of conformity, the investigator got three individuals, each alone in an experimental room, to estimate how far an "autokinetic effect" light moved (Sherif, 1935). One individual might estimate 1 inch, for example, a second individual might estimate 2 inches, and a third individual might estimate 10 inches. After obtaining their individual estimates, the investigator put the three participants together, turned on the pinpoint of light for a short time, and then asked the participants to state their estimates of how much it moved. The first participant to answer might say "I think it moved about 1 inch." The second might say "I'd estimate 2 inches." The third might say "7 inches." After a brief interval, the investigator turned the light on again and asked for new estimates. The three "second round" estimates might be 2, 3, and 6. The three "third round" estimates might be 3, 3, and 3. The group would have reached a consensus that was different from any of the three participants' initial estimates. In the study, each group of three participants arrived at a consensus after a few trials and then stuck to that consensus round after round. Some groups came to agree on a short distance like 2 inches, some on 4 or 5 inches, and some on as much as 8 or 10 inches. The groups differed, but the individuals in each group tended to agree with each other, even though they had made three very different estimates when they were alone.

Subsequent studies of the autokinetic effect showed that participants do not merely go along with the group in public. People who initially estimated 10 inches, for example, not only changed to the same 3-inch estimate as everyone else when they were answering in a group that arrived at a 3-inch consensus. They also continued to provide estimates around 3 inches when they returned to an individual setting and answered in private (Sherif, 1936). Even when they were retested as much as one year later, participants gave estimates that were much closer to the consensus of the group in which they had participated than to their initial individual estimates (Rohrer, Baron, Hoffman, & Swandler, 1954). The group established "norms" or standards that the individual group members "internalized" and adopted as their own. If members of the prewar British parliament assumed that the majority party and its leaders had expert, "insider" knowledge, they might have thought that the majority "must" be right and begun to doubt their own interpretations of the situation. The result, suggested by Table 14.1, would be *both* public compliance and private acceptance.

Other studies showed that the "norms" of autokinetic effect groups continue for generations, even after the initial group members who established those norms have left the group. In one study, for instance, the initial group had three confederates and one real participant (Jacobs & Campbell, 1961). The three confederates consistently gave either very large or very small estimates of how much the light moved. Almost invariably, the real participant accepted their estimate and gave it as his or her own. Then, one by one, the experimenters substituted new real participants for the initial confederates. As each new participant entered the group, he or she adopted the inflated or deflated estimates that had become the group "norm." Eventually, none of the initial confederates remained, yet four real participants continued to agree on the unusually large or small estimates that the initial confederates had established as the "norm." It is easy to see from such studies how political parties in parliaments and legislatures retain agreed-upon opinions on subjective matters even when old members are defeated or retire.

■ FACTORS THAT INCREASE INFORMATIONAL CONFORMITY

Informational influence, unlike normative influence, does not depend on minority members perceiving themselves as similar to the majority. It might be at least as disconcerting to discover that dissimilar others have a different opinion as that similar others have a different opinion, because dissimilar others are difficult to ignore (Wood et al., 1994). Informational influence is also most likely to occur when the topic is ambiguous or the task is difficult, when the majority are supposed to be experts, and when the majority are unanimous in their endorsement of the correct or "normal" response (Harkins & Petty, 1987; Nemeth & Chiles, 1988). Sheer number in the majority, however, is less important to acceptance of a majority opinion than to compliance. In one study, college women participated in a "color discrimination test" (Insko, Smith, Alicke, Wade, & Taylor, 1985). The women had to judge which of two comparison colors (for instance, one blue and one green) was more similar to a target color (for instance, a blue-green mix). On the 12 critical comparisons, some of the women answered after hearing one "other participant" (a confederate) give the answer that approximately 80% of people think is incorrect. Other women answered after hearing four "other participants" give the wrong answer. Also, some of the women had to announce their answers out loud, whereas others got to write their answers in private and put them in a large box where the answers would supposedly be anonymous. The experimenter made the task seem ambiguous by telling the women that there were no correct answers.

Figure 14.3 shows how many times (out of a possible 12) a real participant conformed, either in public or in private, with the incorrect answer given by either one or four confederates. As the figure shows, number of confederates influenced public compliance, but it did not influence private acceptance, which was as high with one as with four confederates. We might suspect, therefore, that public compliance, even on this deliberately subjective judgment, took more of a normative route to conformity, whereas private acceptance took more of an informational route to conformity.

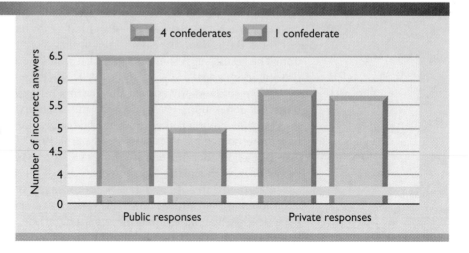

FIGURE 14.3

For subjective opinions, majority group size affects public but not private conformity.

Graph shows number of answers on which women in two conditions agreed with 4 or 1 incorrect confederates (Insko, Smith, Alicke, Wade, & Taylor, 1985)

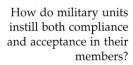

How do military units instill both compliance and acceptance in their members?

Most instances of conformity involve both normative influence and informational influence (Turner, 1991). Normative influence and informational influence can sometimes complement each other. In the autokinetic effect studies, most of the conformity may have been due to informational influence and may have generated private acceptance. Some of the initial conformity, however, may have occurred merely because participants did not want to "look different" by giving an answer very much discrepant from the answer endorsed by their peers. In the line-judging studies, most of the conformity may have been due to normative influence and generated only public compliance rather than private acceptance. Nonetheless, when people start to identify themselves with a group and are attracted to group members, their initial identification can change compliance into acceptance (Kelman, 1958). People who are initially drafted into the armed services against their will, for example, sometimes become so attached to their military units that they cease "going through the motions" of doing what their peers are doing and begin believing in their own actions (Bem, 1972; Turner, Hogg, Oakes, Reicher, & Wetherell, 1987). Once a majority of citizens comply with or accept the evil dictates of a leader like Adolph Hitler, it is difficult for others to resist.

WHEN MINORITY INFLUENCE PREVAILS

British admirers of Adolph Hitler did not remain in the majority, nor did Winston Churchill remain in the minority. Many current majority groups were at one time in the minority, yet their beliefs eventually gained widespread support. Rather than try to censor the minority opinion, which often has a "rebound effect" of gaining sympathy for the minority cause, majorities sometimes conform with the opinions of the minority (Clark, 1994). It is beneficial at some times for deviants and minorities to "go along" so that the group can have the cohesiveness and unity necessary to accomplish its goals. It is also beneficial at other times for majorities to change to accommodate the innovations suggested by a minority (Moscovici, 1985). Progress in social groups requires both conformity to the majority and influence by the minority (Wood, Lundgren,

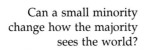

Can a small minority change how the majority sees the world?

Ouellette, Busceme, & Blackstone, 1994). The route to minority influence is shown in the bottom row of Table 14.1.

■ THE BLUE-GREEN STUDY

In a pioneering study of **minority influence,** a group composed of four actual participants and two confederates viewed slides that were either blue or green and that differed also in brightness (Moscovici, Lage, & Naffrechoux, 1969). Each time a slide was shown, the six group members had to say whether the color was blue or green and how bright it was. All 36 slides were clearly blue in their physical wavelength. Of 22 people who answered alone rather than in a group, only one ever answered "green" (on 2 of 36 slides). In the six-person groups, however, the two confederates answered "green" all 36 times. The test of minority influence was how often the four actual participants "gave in" by saying "green" themselves. Minority influence was also measured both by public responses and by subsequent private responses. After the group session, the four actual participants took part in a second "unrelated" study, in which a different experimenter had them rate how blue or green some color disks appeared to them. Because the disks were a mixture of blue and green, private acceptance involved shading their answers toward the green end of the spectrum.

Several interesting results emerged from the "blue-green" study. First, the minority exerted some influence. Thirty-two percent of the actual participants, even though they were clearly in the majority, changed their answers by saying "green" four or more times. Second, the minority exerted influence only when they disagreed consistently. In a separate condition in which the two minority members answered "green" only two-thirds of the time, the four actual participants virtually ignored them. Third, minority influence was stronger on the measure of private acceptance than on the measure of public compliance. When they subsequently rated the blue-green disks in private, the four actual participants shaded their answers more to the green end of the spectrum than did participants who had not been subjected to a consistently disagreeing minority. Fourth, the less influenced participants were in their public answers, the more likely they were to be influenced in their private answers. It was especially participants who publicly ignored the minority and continued to say "blue" who later shifted their private color judgments toward the green end of the spectrum.

One interpretation of these results is that minority influence takes the informational route (Moscovici, 1985). When the majority opinion prevails, it is sometimes because minority group members are concerned about the negative social consequences of continuing to disagree. Their decision to comply is based on an analysis of potential social costs and gains. They give no further thought to the target that they are supposed to judge. When the minority opinion gains converts, in contrast, it is because majority group members are concerned about being in touch with reality. They assume that minority members are wrong, but they wonder why minority members appear so confident (Maass, Clark, & Haberkorn, 1982; Maass, West, & Cialdini, 1987; Moscovici et al., 1969). Also, because majority group members are in no danger of social rejection, they feel relatively secure about making an effort to consider alternative perspectives. "What is it about this slide that might look green to a normal person?" they ask themselves (Wood et al., 1994). In the process of entertaining alternative perspectives, majority group members are influenced without realizing it. They continue to side with the majority in public and often even in private, but they devote greater attention to the issues involved. They are also more open to divergent, creative thinking than they were before they met with a disagreeing minority opinion (Nemeth, 1987; Nemeth & Kwan, 1985). In other words, minority influence has a latent or "hidden" effect on private acceptance (Maass & Clark, 1984).

It is difficult, of course, to conclude from reported shifts in the color spectrum that majority members had begun to think differently about the topic. Regardless of how hard an experimenter tries to convince participants that responses are private, some participants remain suspicious. They reason that "the experimenter must have a way to discover my answers, or else why conduct the study" (Tetlock & Manstead, 1985). In an attempt to show that minority influence "really" alters the way reality is perceived, investigators in several studies used the little-known fact that blue and green have different "after-images" (Doms & Van Avermaet, 1980; Moscovici & Doms, 1982; Moscovici & Personnaz, 1980, 1986, 1991). An *after-image* is the image that people see when, after concentrating on an object, the object is removed and they stare at a blank white screen. The after-image of blue is yellow-orange, whereas the after-image of green is red-purple.

In the relevant studies, majority group members not only biased their subsequent judgments of blue-green disks toward the green end of the spectrum following exposure to a consistent green-responding minority, they also reported after-images that were more red-purple than yellow-orange. Because participants in such studies typically do not know what the "appropriate" after-image for each color is, they could not be falsifying their responses merely to please the experimenter. Unexpected disagreement may make them examine the target slides more carefully, which in turn changes the after-image that they perceive (Sorrentino, King, & Leo, 1980). Greater examination of the target or issue may occur as well for minority group members who meet with an *unexpected* majority opinion, as in the line-judging procedure, so both majorities and minorities may experience some latent influence (Baker & Petty, 1994). The evidence is clearer that minorities experience latent influence than that majorities do not (Levine, 1989).

■ MECHANISMS OF MINORITY INFLUENCE

Minority influence, as suggested by the bottom row of Table 14.1, occurs because the majority does not want to lose face by agreeing with the minority, but has nagging doubts about whether the minority "sees something that I missed." Across studies, minority influence (like the "sleeper effect" in attitude change discussed in Chapter 7) is more likely to have a delayed than an immediate effect and to occur on "indirect" measures like an after-image or thinking about a related but different topic than to have a "direct" effect on the topic on which the minority initially disagrees (Wood et al., 1994). Furthermore, minority influence on indirect measures is more likely to occur when the minority is *small rather than large,* because a small, clearly defined minority has a distinct identity that is not easy to ignore and that "sets the majority thinking" (Wood et al., 1994).

A consistently disagreeing minority gets majority group members to consider new perspectives and to engage in divergent, creative thinking (Nemeth, 1986). Even when it is wrong, a consistently disagreeing minority alters what majority group members pay attention to, as well as whether majority group members entertain novel ideas (Nemeth, 1987; Nemeth & Kwan, 1987). In one study of minority influence on creativity, students heard three word lists (Nemeth, Mayseless, Sherman, & Brown, 1990). Each 14-word list contained two types of birds (for example, robin and eagle), two types of furniture (couch, chair), two types of tools (hammer, saw), and so on. Although the words were otherwise presented at random, the first and last two words in each list were always from the category–fruits (for example, orange, apple). The experimenter asked the students to name the first category of words that they noticed. Because of the way the list was arranged, almost all students noticed the category of fruits first in each list. Some of the students got no information about the categories that other people noticed first. Other students were told that a *majority* of people noticed the category of birds first in all three lists. Yet others were told that a *minority* of people noticed the category of birds first in all three lists. Subsequently, all students heard a list of the 42 words that had been included in the three lists, but in a different order than when initially presented. After that, the students tried to recall as many items as they could from the three lists and from a list of 30 *new* words from six *new* categories such as gems (ruby, diamond) and professions (lawyer, professor).

Previous research had shown that imaginative "clustering" and categorizing helps people to recall words that fall into categories (Bower, Clark, Lesgold, & Winzenz, 1969). If students who were exposed to majority influence simply adopted the majority's favorite category (birds), it would not help them (and might even hinder them) in recalling subsequent lists, because they would be thinking about only the one, most obvious category. If students who were exposed to minority influence took to heart the message that "You can think about these words in creative new ways that are not immediately apparent," it would help them to discover additional, nonobvious categories, which would help them to remember more of the words. Consistent with this interpretation of the results, students who were exposed to minority influence were marginally more likely to recall the words in "clusters" according to category (for example, recalling the two tools one after the other and the two gems one after the other) than were students who were exposed to majority influence. In summary, "exposure to a consistent minority position stimulates a reassessment that is broader than just a consideration of the dissenting position itself" (Nemeth et al., 1990, p. 436), which may be why juries that have to contend with minority opinions to reach a unanimous verdict consider cases more carefully than do juries that need less than unanimous agreement (Nemeth, 1977).

In a study of how minority influence works in jury settings, student jurors read a summary of the case portrayed in the movie *Twelve Angry Men* that starred Henry Fonda (Clark, 1994). In the movie, a 21-year-old man was accused of stabbing his father to death in a large city apartment. The prosecution presented three main pieces of evidence. First, the murder weapon was a pocket knife that had a unique design. A store clerk testified that he had only one such knife in stock, which he sold to the son. Second, an old man, who had suffered two strokes and walked with the aid of two canes, testified that he heard a loud argument in the murdered man's apartment, which was directly above his own bedroom. When he heard a crash, he ran to the door of his own apartment, arrived 15 seconds later, opened his door, and saw the son on the stairs. Third, a woman who lived in an apartment across some train tracks testified that she had been trying to sleep, but looked out her window and clearly saw the son commit the murder through the windows as a train was passing between the two apartments. On the first ballot, 11 members voted guilty and only Henry Fonda voted not guilty. Although the majority exerted enormous social pressure on him, Henry Fonda persisted. In the movie, he refuted each piece of evidence in turn. First, he walked to a nearby junk shop and bought a knife identical to the supposedly unique one sold to the defendant. Second, he reenacted the old man's trip from his bedroom to the door and showed that it could not be done in less than 39 seconds. Third, he suggested that the woman could not have seen the defendant clearly, because she was nearsighted and people do not wear glasses when they are in bed trying to go to sleep.

In the movie, Henry Fonda gradually won over the other members of the jury and got a unanimous verdict of not guilty, which proved to be correct. In

Would you believe a witness who saw the commitment of a crime through the windows of a passing train?

the study based on the movie, some students read a summary of the original script, some students did not receive information about Henry Fonda's arguments, and some students did not receive information about other jury members changing their opinions. The study showed that both types of information affected student jurors' verdicts. Although they were at first convinced by the prosecution's evidence, students who saw one juror dissent were willing at least to consider his minority arguments. They were more apt to change their own opinions when he presented valid arguments than when he did not. Similarly, they were more apt to change their own opinions when they learned that other jurors were changing theirs than when they did not have such information available. It took both convincing arguments and a shift by other majority group members for the minority to exert maximum social power.

These insights about majority and minority influence help us to understand the constant tension that exists between majorities and minorities within cultures (Moscovici, 1985; Nemeth & Staw, 1989). Members of the majority normally hold positions of power—positions from which they can dictate to ordinary citizens the norms and rules of acceptable ideas and conduct (Mugny, 1982; Mugny & Pérez, 1991). Members of dissenting minorities challenge the accepted norms and rules. In the battle between those who hold power and minority groups, those who hold power try to portray dissidents as "strange" and misguided. To get other citizens to consider their ideas seriously, members of minority groups must be consistent in stating their position. They must be unwilling to compromise with those who hold power, but they must also appear open-minded and very willing to negotiate with ordinary citizens (Papastamou & Mugny, 1985). Majority influence can be beneficial because it focuses group members on the central task and the "accepted" way to approach that task, but minority influence can also be beneficial because it gets people thinking about the task more creatively and flexibly (Peterson & Nemeth, 1996).

SUMMARY OF HOW MAJORITIES AND MINORITIES WIELD POWER

Even when reality is unambiguous, people sometimes comply with a mistaken majority's "norms" or standards of acceptable conduct. Normative influence occurs because people want to be liked, avoid social rejection, and restore social harmony. Normative influence usually involves public compliance, but not private acceptance. Informational influence, in contrast, often involves private acceptance of the majority position. Especially when "reality" is ambiguous, people sometimes agree with a mistaken majority because they assume that the majority is likely to have better information. The informational influence of a mistaken majority can establish arbitrary beliefs that endure for many generations.

Consistently disagreeing minorities sometimes influence the majority. Minority influence, in contrast to majority influence, has more of an indirect effect than a direct effect. Majority group members often comply with the minority very little in public and do not immediately accept the minority's view even in private. A small, socially distinct, consistently disagreeing minority, however, gets the majority to think about the issue more creatively and in greater depth.

HOW DO LEADERS WIELD POWER?

Winston Churchill was never in a minority of one. He was never the only member of parliament who recognized the danger posed by Adolph Hitler. Churchill, however, was the acknowledged leader of the minority, and later of the majority. When he became Prime Minister, he was also the acknowledged leader of nations allied against Nazi Germany. In his role as leader, he had to exert interpersonal power on U.S. President Franklin Roosevelt and other world leaders to enlist their aid in stopping Hitler. How did he do it? What strategies did he use? Why did the British people and other nations acknowledge his leadership? Was it something unique about Churchill or could anyone else have done as well in the same situation? Could a woman prime minister, for instance, have done as well? The second section of the chapter examines how leaders wield power. The discussion includes the different types of power that leaders use, several influential theories of leadership, and the question of sex differences in leadership.

TYPES OF POWER

As described at the start of the chapter, Winston Churchill exerted considerable interpersonal power in his letters to Franklin D. Roosevelt, in which Churchill tried to bring the United States into the war on Britain's side (Gold & Raven, 1992). The letters contained six types of interpersonal or social power that Churchill and other leaders use: expert power, referent power, informational power, legitimate power, reward power, and coercive power (French & Raven, 1959; Hinken & Schriesheim, 1989; Raven, 1965, 1983, 1992, 1993).

■ THE SIX TYPES

Table 14.2 shows the six types of social power and provides examples drawn from Churchill's letters to Roosevelt and from how supervisors use power in the modern workplace. These six types of social power are not, of course, used only by national leaders trying to persuade each other to join a war effort and by supervisors in the modern workplace. They occur in many types of social situations (Carson, Carson, & Roe, 1993; Schminke, 1993). As you read the table, imagine how easy it is for some types of workplace power, particularly reward power and coercive power, to be abused—for example in the service of sexual harassment (Tata, 1993).

Expert power comes from having superior knowledge or ability. Britain was already in the war, so Churchill knew many secrets that Roosevelt did not know. If Churchill said that Britain was on the verge of defeat, Roosevelt did not have enough knowledge of the military situation to contradict him. Similarly, modern subordinates in the workplace often do not have access to the organization's plans and problems. Supervisors wield expert power because they know details of the organization that subordinates do not know.

Referent power involves emphasizing a common identity. Churchill always signed his letters to Roosevelt "Former Naval Person." Although such a signature may seem odd for the leader of the British Empire, it emphasized that Churchill and Roosevelt had both served their countries' navies. Before becoming president, Franklin Roosevelt had served as U.S. Secretary of the Navy. Similarly, modern workplace supervisors wield referent power over subordinates by making them feel like part of a team. Referent power depends on building a *social identity,* which is explained in Chapter 1 and recurs as part of a major theme throughout this book.

Informational power consists of using arguments that are logically compelling. When Churchill emphasized the danger to the United States should Britain be defeated, Roosevelt found the argument very convincing. After each new country that Hitler conquered, world leaders had hoped he would be satisfied, only to discover that they were wrong. It was logical to assume that Hitler would not be content merely with defeating Britain. He would then use Britain's bases

TABLE 14.2	Six Types of Interpersonal Power, with Examples from Churchill's Wartime Letters to Roosevelt and How Supervisors Use Each Type of Power in the Workplace (Abstracted from French & Raven, 1959; Frost & Stahelski, 1988; Gold & Raven, 1992)		
TYPE OF POWER	**DESCRIPTION**	**CHURCHILL'S LETTERS**	**WORKPLACE ACTIONS**
Expert	having superior knowledge or ability	knew military secrets unknown to Roosevelt	impress subordinates with knowledge and ability; advise and assist them; make on-the-spot corrections; make effective assignments
Referent	emphasizing a common identity	signed letters to Roosevelt "Former Naval Person"	use good relations with subordinates; rely on their not wanting to let the organization down; make them feel part of the team
Informational	using logically compelling arguments	emphasized danger to U.S. if Britain were defeated	persuade subordinates that the job is worth doing, that it is worth doing right, and that the leader's way is the most effective strategy
Legitimate	invoking social norms and obligations	shared military secrets to put U.S. in his debt; emphasized Britain's sacrifices	let subordinates know leader deserves unquestioned obedience; expect subordinates to assume that leader knows best
Reward	using ability to grant or withhold rewards	offered long-term leases on Caribbean bases vital to U.S. national security	demonstrate ability to promote subordinates, recommend them for awards or bonuses, rate their performance high, give them extra time off
Coercive	using or threatening punishment	warned Roosevelt that appeasers might surrender British warships to Germany	demonstrate ability to demote subordinates, recommend them for disciplinary action, "chew them out," give them extra work

around the world to launch attacks on the United States. Modern workplace supervisors also wield informational power by giving subordinates reason to believe that their orders represent the most effective strategy for getting the job done.

Legitimate power is based on social norms and obligations, especially reciprocating when someone else has done you a favor. Churchill first put Roosevelt in his debt by sharing military secrets that were vital to U.S. interests. Then he emphasized that Britain was sacrificing to defend the United States and other countries from subjugation. In the modern workplace, supervisors take advantage of legitimate power when they make subordinates go through the "chain of command" and obey the orders of "superiors" without question.

Reward power comes from ability to grant rewards. Churchill knew that the United States wanted military bases in the Caribbean, where Britain owned many islands. By raising the possibility of long-term leases on these islands, Churchill was offering a reward for cooperation—a reward that would be very important to U.S. security in the Western Hemisphere. Modern workplace supervisors also use reward power selectively to accomplish their goals. The person who controls your promotions and pay raises is in a good position to demand obedience.

Coercive power involves a threat of punishment. If Britain were defeated, the United States would have preferred that they destroy all their own warships rather than surrender them to Germany. Instead of using coercive power directly, Churchill told Roosevelt that appeasers in his own country might take power if the war continued to go badly. "I would never give Germany the warships it needs to attack the United States," he was saying, "but I can't answer for my successor if you do not help us." Modern workplace supervisors also wield coercive power indirectly. Most supervisors do not come right out and say "Do it my way or else," but the coercive threat often lurks just below the surface of interactions between a supervisor and a subordinate.

■ WHEN THE TYPES ARE USED

Different leaders use different ones of these six types of power. To use coercive power effectively, for instance, a leader must be perceived as willing and able to administer punishment (Nesler, Aguinis, Quigley, & Tedeschi, 1993). In one study of using different types of power in business organizations, men who supervised five to seven workers were asked how often they performed each of the workplace actions given as examples in Table 14.2 (Frost & Stahelski, 1988). Second-level managers, who supervised the supervisors, were also asked about their actions. As predicted, supervisors and managers had individual styles of leadership. Those who used one of the actions associated with referent power, for example, tended to use others.

Also, as Figure 14.4 shows, second-level managers used coercive, reward, and legitimate power significantly more than did first-level supervisors, who had to rely on their expert and referent power. The higher in the organization a leader was and the more people the leader supervised directly or indirectly, the more the leader used threats of punishment, promises of rewards, and appeals to company loyalty to get followers to obey (Stahelski, Frost, & Patch, 1989). Power affects a leader's choice of influence tactics in settings as diverse as industry and psychotherapy (Kipnis, 1984). Hitler and his Nazis came to rely almost exclusively on coercive power. People who use coercive power detract from their own expert, referent, and legitimate power, but absolute dictators like Adolph Hitler often do not need to use types of power other than brutal coercion (Gaski, 1986; Raven, 1992).

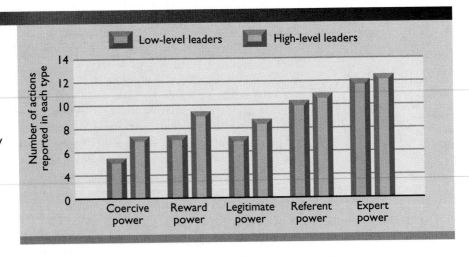

FIGURE 14.4

High- and low-level leaders differ primarily in their use of coercive, reward, and legitimate power.

Graph shows how frequently leaders at different levels of a large service organization used each type of power (Frost & Stahelski, 1988)

THEORIES OF LEADERSHIP

Whenever a group needs one of its members to coordinate group efforts, a leader emerges, just as Winston Churchill emerged to lead Britain's fight against Nazi Germany. What factors determine who will lead? Different theories of leadership emphasize three different factors that determine leadership: the characteristics that make a successful leader (the "great person" perspective), the type of situation that calls for leadership (the "situational" perspective), and the match between the person and the situation (the "contingency" theory of leadership).

■ THE "GREAT PERSON" PERSPECTIVE

One perspective on leadership is that some people are born to lead and others are born to follow. According to this "trait" or "great person" perspective, some people are more clever or dominant than others, so they rise to the top. Early anthropological studies suggested that groups of animals arrange themselves in a pecking order or "dominance hierarchy." The leader gets greater access to resources like food or attractive mates (Mitchell & Maple, 1985). It seemed possible, based on these anthropological studies, that certain human beings also have traits that make them "natural leaders." One such trait is intelligence. In some groups, the leader is more intelligent than his or her followers (Bass & Avolio, 1993; Stogdill, 1948).

Intellectually gifted individuals often make very successful leaders. Among presidents of the United States, for instance, those who are regarded as "great" by political historians (George Washington, Abraham Lincoln, Franklin Roosevelt) may have been the most intelligent (Simonton, 1986; McCann, 1992). Another trait associated with leadership is talkativeness. In some studies of small groups, the person who talked most became the group leader (Riecken, 1958; McGrath & Julian, 1963). Two other important traits are a need for achievement and being perceptive about other people's needs (Ellis, 1988; Sorrentino & Field, 1986). The best leaders seem to be people who are both strongly driven to succeed and skillful at maintaining good relationships with their followers.

■ THE SITUATIONAL PERSPECTIVE

A second perspective on leadership holds that the situation creates the leader. According to this "situational" perspective, the person who becomes a group's

Calvin and Hobbes   by Bill Watterson

leader is the one who happened to be in the right place at the right time (Cooper & McGaugh, 1969). Adolph Hitler rose to power in pre-World War II Germany because citizens who had suffered military and economic collapse wanted the most forceful leader they could find. Groups frequently respond to crisis by choosing a leader who in other circumstances might be perceived as too authoritarian (Helmreich & Collins, 1967; Worchel, Andreoli, & Folger, 1977). Situational factors as trivial as who sits at the head of the table can also affect who emerges as the group leader (Howells & Becker, 1962).

Finally, situational factors affect who talks the most in a group, which in turn affects who emerges as leader. In one study of talkativeness and leadership, four college men held a group discussion (Bavelas, Hastorf, Gross, & Kite, 1965). The men sat at a table that had four lights arranged so that each man could see only his own light and not the other three. To facilitate the discussion, the experimenter explained, he would flash a green light at a participant who made a contribution that might lead to a constructive, intelligent conclusion. He would flash a red light at a participant who made a contribution that, according to previous studies, might eventually hamper group progress. The experimenter also explained that he might flash a green or a red light at a participant who was silent, because silence at certain points in a discussion might be either facilitative or dysfunctional. When the discussion began, however, the experimenter used the green and red lights to encourage one of the quieter group members to talk more often. By flashing a red light when the target man was silent and a green light whenever he spoke, the experimenter successfully changed the nature of the discussion. Over time, the randomly selected man "took over" the conversation. The other three men, who saw green lights every time they let the target man speak or agreed with his opinion, spoke less. After the discussion had ended, the four men rated each other on traits like leadership. The more the target man talked, the higher he was rated on leadership. In other words, a purely situational factor, having nothing to do with the man's own personality, cast him in the role of group leader.

■ THE CONTINGENCY THEORY OF LEADERSHIP

Both the trait perspective and the situational perspective on leadership, however, have problems explaining who emerges as the leader in groups of animals or human beings. In animals, for instance, anthropological evidence shows that groups of apes and other animals have different leaders as they move from one situation to another (Mitchell & Maple, 1985; Shively, 1985). One situation may call for a leader who is very forceful and who keeps the group focused on the task at hand. Another situation may call for a leader who maintains group harmony. Groups function best when they adopt as leader whichever animal or human being has the specific skills called for by the task, switching from one "specialist" to another as the task and the situation change. According to the **contingency theory of leadership,** the group member who acts as leader is *contingent,* or dependent, on what the group needs to accomplish (Fiedler, 1964, 1967, 1971, 1993).

According to the contingency theory of leadership, potential leaders differ in whether they are task-oriented or relationship-oriented. Task-oriented leaders concentrate the group's energies on the task at hand. They are impatient with and intolerant of group members who do not contribute to the group effort. Relationship-oriented leaders, in contrast, concentrate the group's energies on maintaining cohesion, harmony, and cooperation. They tend to get along well with subordinates, even those who may not be contributing as much as they might to a particular group effort.

To measure individual differences in task-orientation versus relationship-orientation, psychologists who take a contingency theory perspective on leadership developed the Least Preferred Co-Worker (LPC) scale. On the LPC scale, each group member is asked to describe the *one* person, among all the people he or she has ever worked with, who is or was the most difficult to work with. The group member rates his or her least preferred coworker on scales like pleasant-unpleasant, friendly-unfriendly, warm-cold, loyal-backbiting, sincere-insincere, and nice-nasty. The assumption behind the scale is that individuals who give very negative ratings to their least preferred coworker are so concerned with getting the task done that they get frustrated with and angry at coworkers who get in the way of group success. They are relatively task-oriented. In contrast, individuals who give less negative (or even positive) ratings to the "most difficult to work with" coworker take the attitude that "Getting the job done isn't everything. Even though I can't work with a person, that person might still be a worthwhile human being." Such individuals are relatively relationship-oriented.

Who makes the best leader—someone who is task-oriented or someone who is relationship-oriented? According to the contingency theory of leadership, "it all depends" (Fiedler & Garcia, 1987). In some situations a task-oriented leader is more effective. In other situations, a relationship-oriented leader is more effective. The determining factor is how much control the leader has. The leader's control depends on three factors: the leader's relationship with the group; the degree to which the group's task is structured or well defined; and the leader's power to bestow rewards or punishments. In "favorable" situations where the leader has good relations with subordinates, the task is well defined, and the leader's power is unquestioned, a task-oriented leader is best for both group effectiveness and group members' satisfaction. Interestingly, a task-oriented leader is also best for "unfavorable" situations, where the leader has very poor relations with subordinates, the task is very unstructured, and the leader has little real power. A relationship-oriented leader functions best, however, in the "mid-range" situations where leader-follower relations are moderately good, the task is neither structured nor unstructured, and the leader's "legitimate" power is moderate.

In one test of contingency theory, university administrators were identified as either task-oriented or relationship-oriented (Chemers, Hays, Rhodewalt, & Wysocki, 1985). Their jobs were classified as either low, moderate, or high in situational control. Low situational control jobs, for example, were jobs in which there were few clear guidelines and the administrator had very little power to reward or to punish subordinates. High situational control jobs were

FIGURE 14.5

Task-oriented and relationship-oriented leaders differ in the situations they find stressful.

Graph shows how stressful the two types of leaders said they found situations that differed in how much control the leader had (Chemers, Hays, Rhodewalt, & Wysocki, 1985)

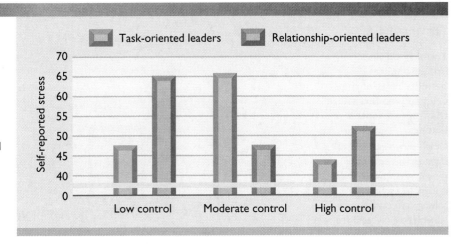

those in which the procedures to be followed were clear, the task demands very predictable, and the administrator held great power over subordinates. The administrators were asked how much stress they experienced in trying to do their jobs. As predicted by contingency theory, and as shown in Figure 14.5, task-oriented leaders felt under the most stress when their leadership situation was uncertain—when they held neither high nor low situational control. Relationship-oriented leaders, in contrast, felt under the greatest stress when they had low rather than moderate control over the situation. Task-oriented leaders also reported far more stress-related physical illnesses (such as angina pectoris, colitis, and eczema) than did relationship-oriented leaders in moderate situational control jobs, whereas relationship-oriented leaders reported more stress-related illnesses in low situational control jobs. In several related studies, both subordinate satisfaction and job performance also suffered when the leader's orientation did not match the degree of situational control afforded by the leader's position (Chemers, 1993; Fiedler, 1993; Hollander, 1985, 1993; Strube & Garcia, 1981).

The match between a leader's orientation and the leader's situational control is important because of the two different ways that task-oriented and relationship-oriented leaders function. Task-oriented leaders "tell people what to do, are punitive, and are not too concerned about others' feelings" (Fiedler, 1993, p. 6), which may be just what is needed to keep subordinates "on track" in relatively unstructured situations. A task-oriented leader specializes in providing structure by "taking charge." Relationship-oriented leaders, in contrast, "are considerate, provide rewards, are nondirective, and invite subordinate participation" (Fiedler, 1993, p. 7). A relationship-oriented leader specializes in providing the interpersonal support that motivates subordinates who already have a structured work environment. Thus training in task performance may benefit relationship-oriented leaders, by showing them a procedure for getting the job done, whereas training in task performance may sometimes hinder task-oriented leaders.

In a study that addressed the effects of training on task-oriented versus relationship-oriented leaders, three-person teams of college students tried to decode letter substitution—coded messages like the following (Chemers, Rice, Sundstrom, & Butler, 1975):

```
GKKW    GK    MW   WQK   CWMWRFT   WDKCOMZ   GFVTRTJ
- - - -  - -   - -  - - -    S - - - - - -   - - - S - - -   - - R - - - -


R BRSS   NK    OVKCCKO   RT   M   NSMLH   FXKVLFMW
- - -LL  - -   - R - S S - -   - -  -   - L - - -   - - - R - - - -
```

FIGURE 14.6

Training on an impersonal task benefits relationship-oriented leaders more than task-oriented leaders.

Graph shows number of cryptograms solved by groups when two types of leaders had trained or not in solving cryptograms (Chemers, Rice, Sundstrom, & Butler, 1975)

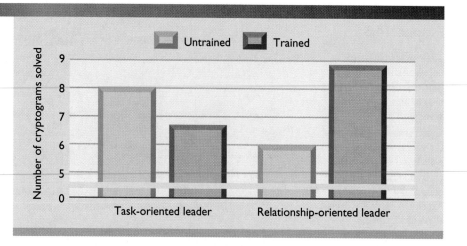

In this particular message, each C is always decoded as an S, each V is always decoded as an R, and each S is always decoded as an L. Each other letter also has a corresponding decoded value.

Each three-person team had either a task-oriented or a relationship-oriented ROTC cadet as its designated leader and two "followers," another ROTC cadet and a psychology major. The leader had no power to reward or to punish subordinates, the psychology majors resented being "led" by an ROTC cadet, and most people have little idea how to solve such problems. The leader had very low situational control. In some teams, but not others, the leader gained additional control over the situation by first learning useful strategies for decoding messages. One such strategy is to realize that E is the most frequent letter in many English sentences. The K in the coded message might be an E. Another such strategy is to look for word positions likely to be occupied by vowels. Each M in the coded message might be an A. Yet another strategy is to look for common endings. The RTJ at the end of the first line might be an ING, which would make the first word in the second line I.

As Figure 14.6 shows, in groups where the leader had no previous training (so the task remained unstructured and the "correct" procedures ill-defined), task-oriented leaders got their groups to solve more codes than did relationship-oriented leaders. As predicted by contingency theory, however, previous training, by providing more clearly defined procedures, helped groups led by relationship-oriented leaders and hurt the performance of groups led by task-oriented leaders. Once they know the correct procedures, followers no longer respond well to task-oriented leaders who take the heavyhanded "Do it my way" approach (Fiedler, 1978; 1993). (The correct answer to the sample message, by the way, is "Meet me at the station Tuesday Morning. I will be dressed in a black overcoat.") Effective leadership, therefore, depends as much on what followers do (for example, how they react to different leadership styles in different types of circumstances) as it does on what leaders do (Hollander, 1985, 1993).

SEX DIFFERENCES IN LEADERSHIP

Do men or women make better leaders? Many of history's worst tyrants, like Adolph Hitler, were men, but the Byzantine Empress Theodora was no less an abuser of power than her male counterparts. On the positive side, modern male leaders like Franklin Roosevelt and Winston Churchill were matched by equally great women leaders like Indira Ghandi and Golda Meir. The available evidence suggests that women are as capable of leading as are men, but that women leaders may be expected to lead in a different way than men (Eagly, Karau, & Makhijani, 1995).

■ DIFFERENT SEX FOR DIFFERENT TASKS?

Across many studies of emergent leadership in mixed-sex groups, women are chosen as leaders by groups that are pursuing "feminine" tasks, whereas men are chosen as leaders by groups that are pursuing "masculine" tasks (Eagly & Karau, 1991; Eagly et al., 1994). According to the traditional stereotype, "feminine" tasks include deciding how to spend wedding money, sewing buttons on a panel, and getting to know other group members by sharing feelings. "Masculine" tasks include ranking the desirability of auto accessories, repairing a machine, and discussing how to survive in a disaster. In other words, groups chose as leader a person who is expected to have expert power.

Unfortunately for qualified women, most business tasks seem "masculine." When businessmen and businesswomen in the United States describe the ideal leader or the ideal manager, they typically describe someone who acts like the male sex role stereotype and not someone who acts like the female sex role stereotype (Fagenson, 1990; Heilman, Block, Martell, & Simon, 1989; Lord, DeVader, & Alliger, 1986). Subordinates perceive women business executives, for instance, as having more of all six types of power (see Table 14.2) when the women wear a jacket and "look like a man" than when they do not (Temple & Loewen, 1993). According to traditional sex role stereotypes, acting like a man involves being independent, masterful, competent, and assertive, whereas acting like a woman involves being friendly, unselfish, and concerned about other people's feelings (Bakan, 1966; Eagly, 1987). It is unclear whether these sex-role stereotypes are the same as being task-oriented versus relationship-oriented, but both men and women in the workplace prefer male bosses (Cann & Siegfried, 1990; Chapman, 1975; Ferber, Huber, & Spitze, 1979; Lord, Phillips, & Rush, 1980).

Members of organizations have implicit and explicit expectations about what a leader is supposed to do (Kenney, Blascovich, & Shaver, 1994; Maurer, Maher, Ashe, Mitchell, Hein, & Van Hein, 1993; Wit, Wilke, & Van Dijk,

Do women have to be twice as good as a man to get the job done?

1989). When men lead, subordinates expect them to provide information and
direct the group task. When women lead, subordinates expect them to provide
interpersonal support and let everyone have a say (Eagly, Makhijani, & Klonsky, 1992). As a result, men have an easier time directing subordinates in traditional business and other male-dominated settings than do women (Nieva
& Gutek, 1980). If the group's task requires a task-oriented rather than a
relationship-oriented approach, women almost have to be "twice as good as a
man" to get the job done (Eagly et al., 1992). If women leaders do not provide
assertive direction, they are criticized for failing to fulfill the leadership role. If
they provide assertive direction, they are criticized for violating what is considered appropriate feminine behavior (Dobbins, Cardy, & Truxillo, 1988; Ragins & Sundstrom, 1989). Women in business careers are constantly frustrated
because the traditional "feminine" stereotype prevents them from using interpersonal power the same way men do (Tepper, Brown, & Hunt, 1993).

■ REACTIONS TO WOMEN AS LEADERS

Especially when they try to lead in traditionally masculine domains such as
business, manufacturing, or athletic coaching, women are likely to be evaluated negatively (Eagly et al., 1995; Landy & Farr, 1980; Ragins & Sundstrom,
1989). Women are so rare in such leadership roles that they attract much attention and much criticism (Johnson & Schulman, 1989; Ott, 1989; Swim,
Borgida, Marayuma, & Myers, 1989). Men, who are free from the sex role expectations that bind women leaders, can get away with being much more assertive, authoritarian, and directive without losing the respect and obedience
of their subordinates (Eagly et al., 1992).

In one study of how subordinates react to male versus female leaders,
groups of four college students held a discussion (Butler & Geis, 1990). The
group's goal was to rank how important various items (for example, food, a
first-aid kit, water, a compass, rope, a star map) would be for surviving a spaceship crash on the moon. Only two of the four group members (one man and
one woman) were actual participants. The other two group members were confederates who had studied all possible arguments for and against each survival
item. In some of the group discussions, either the male or the female confederate "took over" and started leading the group. The "solo leader," whether
male or female, directed the discussion and provided the final rationale for
each group decision. The other confederate, although he or she offered good
suggestions, adopted the role of "follower." In other group discussions, the male
and female confederates both "took over." With their greater preparation, the
confederates were easily able to direct and to dominate the discussion and the
group's decisions.

When the discussion ended, the experimenters asked participants to rate
each other's competence. The participants did *not* display sex bias by rating
female leaders as less competent than male leaders. They rated the woman
confederate as competent as the man, whether she took charge by herself as a
solo leader or took charge with the man as a coleader. The experimenters also
asked participants whether they thought that women in general were less able
to lead and whether they disliked women who talked too much or who dom-
inated a group discussion. Again, the participants claimed to have no sex bias.
The experimenters suspected, though, that participants might be biased without being aware of it. During the discussion, the experimenters placed observers behind one-way mirrors to record the facial expressions of participants.
According to these observers, whose ratings agreed with each other, participants betrayed their true feelings by smiling and nodding agreement whenever
the male confederate "took charge" and by frowning and tightening their fa-

FIGURE 14.7

Women who begin to dominate a group discussion elicit different facial expressions than do men.

Graph shows pleased and displeased expressions by other participants when a male or female emerged as the group's solo leader (Butler & Geis, 1990)

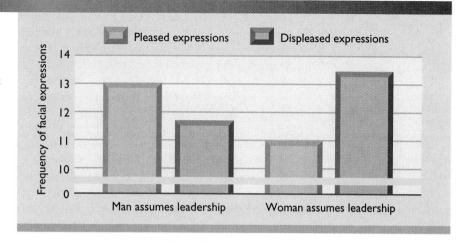

cial muscles whenever the female confederate "took charge." As shown in Figure 14.7, the sex difference in pleased and displeased facial expressions occurred when a confederate "took charge" as a solo leader. Also, when participants were later asked to describe each other's personality traits, both men and women described the female solo leader as bossy and excessively dominating. When she talked more than everyone else and forced the group to be task-oriented, which she *had* to do to become a solo leader, the female solo leader violated sex role expectations and "earned" the condemnation of other group members (Eagly, 1987).

Although both men and women prefer a male boss, the few women who have risen to the top in politics or business, such as big-city mayors, state governors, and company presidents, function as effectively as do men (Ayman, 1993). One reason may be that women are not allowed to live down their stereotypes unless they hold the highest power in an organization, because being at any lower level forces them to behave differently than they would like. Another reason may be that the few women who have managed to achieve top leadership positions actually *are* "twice as good as a man."

SUMMARY OF HOW LEADERS WIELD POWER

Leaders use six types of power to control their subordinates: expert power, referent power, informational power, legitimate power, reward power, and coercive power. Expert power is knowing how to get the job done. Referent power involves making people feel accepted. Informational power depends on logical arguments. Legitimate power involves obligations to obey authority figures. Reward power is the ability to provide benefits. Coercive power is the ability to impose punishments. The higher in a hierarchy a leader is and the larger the number of subordinates the leader has, the more likely the leader is to use coercive power, reward power, and legitimate power. People who use coercive power detract from their own expert, referent, and legitimate power.

Although leaders are sometimes more intelligent, more talkative, and more favored by external circumstances than their subordinates, different types of leaders function best for different group tasks. According to the contingency theory of leadership, leaders who denigrate their least preferred coworker are task-oriented, whereas leaders who accept their least preferred coworker are relationship-oriented. Task-oriented leaders function best when they have either much or little control over the situation. Relationship-oriented leaders function best when they have moderate control over the situation. Leader control depends on the leader's relations with subordinates, the degree to which the group task is structured or well defined, and the power vested in the leader. Task-oriented leaders have more stress-related illnesses when they have moderate situational control, whereas relationship-oriented leaders have more stress-related illnesses when they have little situational control. The most important determinant of leader stress, group effectiveness, and follower satisfaction is the "match" between the leader's orientation and the specific circumstances.

Women make neither better nor worse leaders than men. Women are more likely to emerge as leaders in mixed-sex groups that are trying to solve interpersonal problems, whereas men are more likely to emerge as leaders in mixed-sex groups that are trying to solve impersonal problems. The most important difference between male and female leaders lies in what subordinates expect. Both men and women expect male leaders to be masterful and assertive. In contrast, they expect female leaders to be democratic and concerned about group solidarity. When women unexpectedly "take charge" in mixed-sex groups that are trying to solve impersonal problems, both male and female followers, even those who claim not to be biased against women, reveal through their facial expressions and through their trait attributions that they are displeased.

WHEN IS POWER ABUSED?

As described in the first section of the chapter, people sometimes "go along" with completely arbitrary beliefs, norms, and traditions, just so long as "everyone else does it." The beliefs, norms, and traditions discussed in the first section, however, do not address the full extent of interpersonal power. Studies of conformity help us to understand why legislators and ordinary citizens might have been blind to Hitler's ambitions, but these instances of conformity do not involve causing other people direct physical harm. Mere conformity or "going along with the crowd" does not seem like a sufficient reason for German soldiers to follow Hitler's immoral, monstrous orders to incarcerate and exterminate millions of their fellow human beings.

The most obvious explanation for blind obedience to evil commands is that people who have little power fear for their own safety. When Hitler ordered his soldiers to commit atrocities, what choice did they have? Suppose that one among them had said "I refuse to herd people into cattle cars, put them in prison, and then gas them to death." Can anyone doubt that the disobedient soldier would have been tortured and killed, most likely accompanied by his entire family? In many situations, people obey depraved orders because they have no choice. It is literally either "kill or be killed." In this section of the chapter, however, we address the disturbing possibility that people who have nothing to fear and nothing to gain from obedience might hurt other people on command. First, we review a study in which people who had nothing to gain abused their power merely because they had it. Second, we review classic studies on destructive obedience. Third, we discuss the reasons why people who have nothing to gain obey orders to hurt others.

POWER OF THE SITUATION

What happens when otherwise ordinary people discover that, because of the situation, they can give orders and be obeyed? Was Lord Acton correct when he said that power corrupts and absolute power corrupts absolutely?

■ THE STANFORD PRISON EXPERIMENT

In a study that tried to answer these questions about how the situation can create abuse of power, a Stanford University professor advertised in a Palo Alto, California, newspaper for college-age men to participate in a study (Haney, Banks, & Zimbardo, 1973). When the men appeared, the experimenter gave them an extensive battery of tests and interviews to select only the most stable, both physically and psychologically. The experimenter then randomly assigned half of the most stable men to be "prisoners" and the other half to be "guards" in a "psychological study of prison life." The guards were told that they could make whatever prison rules they desired, but that they could not inflict physical punishment. The prisoners were told to be at home on a given Sunday, when the experiment would begin.

On the appointed Sunday, a squad car from the Palo Alto police department pulled up in front of each prisoner's home. In full view of the neighbors, the man was arrested, handcuffed, and taken to the police station to be fingerprinted and placed in a detention cell. From there, each prisoner was blindfolded and taken to a mock prison, part of the Stanford University psychology department building that had been blocked off and prepared with barred prison cell doors on what had formerly been laboratory rooms. When each prisoner arrived, the guards decided that they should force him to strip, be sprayed with a delousing agent, and stand naked for a while in the cell yard. From then on, the prisoners had to spend 24 hours per day in their cells, while the guards rotated three eight-hour shifts "on duty."

In examining what happened during the study, it is important to remember that both guards and prisoners were well-adjusted young men who had merely been assigned labels of "guard" and "prisoner" in a laboratory experiment. They were randomly selected for these roles. According to the psychological tests, the guards were neither bigger nor physically tougher than the prisoners. They were merely ordinary people who were playing whatever roles they thought were required of them in a setting that was as much like an actual prison as possible.

How did the guards react to their suddenly assumed position of power? They *abused* that power. At first, they taunted the prisoners in little ways. The guards decided that the prisoners should wear loosely fitting muslin smocks with no underwear, so that the prisoners would feel like women who were wearing dresses. The guards made the prisoners wear nylon stocking caps on their heads. The guards made the prisoners wear chains on their ankles, so that they would be reminded of their captivity even in their sleep, when they rolled over and the chain raked their legs. The guards routinely got the prisoners up in the middle of the night to line up in the cell yard and "count off" their prisoner numbers. These countdowns, at first lasting only a few minutes, became longer and more humiliating to the prisoners as the experiment continued. The guards also tortured the prisoners verbally, by calling them a wide variety of demeaning names. After the prison routine had been in place for a few days, the guards abused their power even more. Because the cells were only converted laboratory rooms, they contained no toilets. The guards made prisoners beg for the privilege of visiting the men's room. The guards punished rebellious statements or attitudes by denying food, blankets, and toilet privileges. One guard locked a prisoner in a 2-foot by 2-foot closet all night, concealing this information from the experimenters, who he thought were too soft on the prisoners. The guards' brutality increased so rapidly that the experiment, originally scheduled for two weeks, had to be called off after a mere six days, before a prisoner got seriously injured.

How did the prisoners react to their sudden loss of power? They *obeyed*. Typical prisoners became helpless and apathetic. They shuffled back and forth from their cells in a "zombie-like" trance. They followed even the most humiliating orders given to them by the guards. In the privacy of their cells, the prisoners, who were strangers to each other at the start of the experiment, did not spend their time getting to know each other's history and background. Instead, when they were not lying on their bunks staring at the ceiling, they talked only of prison conditions, food, privileges, and guard harassment. When one of their fellow prisoners got in trouble and was punished by the guards, the prisoners tended to agree that he had been a "bad prisoner," a "troublemaker" who deserved to be punished. Several of the prisoners became so emotionally disturbed that they had to be released from the experiment early. In short, the prisoners accepted the authority of guards, even though they knew that "guard" was, like "prisoner," a mere label that had been arbitrarily assigned. In accepting the label, they were also willing to cooperate in their own degradation.

When the experiment ended, the Stanford professor provided professional counseling for all participants, so that they could gain greater insight into the power that situations have to induce harmful behavior. The participants eventually realized how easy it is to get caught up in an unhealthy situation and that they were not in any way unusual. Absolute power corrupts absolutely.

■ TRAINING TORTURERS

Perhaps the most disturbing aspect of the prison study was that both guards and prisoners were normal, well-adjusted young men, yet the situation and an

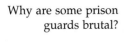

Why are some prison guards brutal?

THE FAR SIDE   By GARY LARSON

"And I say we go outside and we *play with this ball*!"

arbitrarily assigned label made them behave in deplorable ways. Similarly, the 1967–1974 Greek military regime had great success in taking ordinary civilians and making them into official torturers (Haritos-Fatouros, 1988). The military junta selected stable, well-adjusted fishermen, farmers, carpenters, civil servants, shoemakers, cooks, lorry drivers, and small businessmen for "special training." During their training, the men were gradually introduced to brutality. They were often kept from eating, urinating, and defecating for days at a time. They were ordered to eat lighted cigarettes. They were "forced to run while beaten until there were drops of sweat hanging from the ceiling" (Haritos-Fatouros, 1988, p. 1116).

At the end of the training, the apprentice torturers had to swear on their knees their undying allegiance and obedience to the military rulers. After enduring torture themselves, they first watched more experienced torturers and then gradually joined in unbelievably sadistic torture of citizens who were suspected of being disloyal to the ruling junta. Through these carefully orchestrated indoctrination procedures, ordinary citizens were turned into blind instruments of paranoiac, evil dictators.

DESTRUCTIVE OBEDIENCE

During World War II, thousands of ordinary German soldiers obeyed the Nazis' depraved orders to incarcerate, torture, and kill millions of Jews. For a long time after the war had ended, people wondered how Hitler's systematic extermination plan could possibly have been implemented. Why didn't the guards at the concentration camps refuse orders to herd their prisoners into the gas chambers? Did they obey merely because they feared the personal consequences of disobedience, or did they respect authority so much that they closed their hearts to the immorality of their actions and did what they were told? To investigate scientifically situations in which people are asked to obey immoral orders but have nothing to lose by disobeying, Stanley Milgram invented what may be the most disturbing social psychology experiment ever conducted (Milgram, 1963, 1965a, 1974; Miller, 1986).

■ THE MILGRAM OBEDIENCE STUDIES

Milgram advertised for men to participate in a psychology experiment at Yale University. The 40 men who participated came from many occupations. They were postal clerks, high school teachers, salesmen, engineers, and laborers. Their education ranged from not finishing elementary school to attaining a doctorate or other professional degree. When the men appeared at the experimental laboratory, they were told that they had earned their participation fee merely by showing up. They were free to leave with the money at any time, no matter what happened after they arrived.

The experimenter introduced each man to "another participant," a 47-year-old, mild-mannered, likable accountant who was actually a confederate. The experimenter then explained that the experiment was about whether punishment improves learning and that one of the men would be the teacher and the other man would be the learner. The teacher would give the learner tests and deliver electric shock after each mistake. After a rigged drawing in which the actual participant was always selected as the teacher, the experimenter led both men to an adjacent room that contained what looked like an "electric chair." The actual participant then watched as the accountant "learner" was strapped into the chair. Although the experimenter explained the straps as necessary to prevent "excessive movement," it was obvious that the accountant could not free himself from the chair once he had been strapped in. The experimenter also applied electrode paste to the learner's wrist before firmly securing an electrode that would supposedly deliver shock. The experimenter explained that the electrode paste was necessary "to avoid blisters and burns," but that the shocks would "cause no permanent tissue damage."

Next, the experimenter took the actual participant "teacher" back to the control room, which contained an impressive "Shock Generator." The shock generator had 30 lever switches arranged in a horizontal line. The 30 switches were labeled from "15 volts" on the left to "450 volts" on the right. Each set of four switches was also labeled. The labels, from left to right, read: Slight Shock, Moderate Shock, Strong Shock, Very Strong Shock, Intense Shock, Extreme Intensity Shock, and Danger: Severe Shock. The last two switches to the right were labeled XXX. To demonstrate the Shock Generator, the experimenter gave the teacher a sample 45-volt shock. When the 45-volt lever was pulled, a bright red light came on next to the switch, a buzzing sound was heard, a blue light on a "voltage energizer" flashed, a voltage meter dial swung to the right, relay clicks were heard, and the teacher got a mild electric shock. Because of all these authentic details, participants fully believed that the Shock Generator would deliver electric shock to the learner in the next room.

The experimenter explained that the electric shocks must be given in order, starting with the lowest 15-volt setting and moving to the next highest setting for each mistake. The experimenter then told the teacher to read a practice list of ten word pairs (for example, boat-tranquil, loyalty-secure, cabbage-attractive) to the learner and then to quiz the learner by asking him to choose the correct one from four alternatives for each word (for example, What was paired with loyalty—attractive, watchful, secure, or tranquil?). These practice trials were presented as a way to get used to asking the questions and pulling the switches. The confederate, who indicated his answers by pressing one of four buttons, made seven mistakes. The teacher pulled the 15-volt switch for the first mistake, the 30-volt switch for the second mistake, and so on up to the 105-volt switch (Moderate Shock) for the seventh mistake. After these practice trials, the experimenter handed the teacher a longer list and said to start at the beginning (15 volts) and to keep going over the list until the learner got them all correct.

Although several different versions of the experimental procedure were used (in some of which the accountant mentioned as he was being strapped into the chair that he had a heart condition), a typical session went as follows. As the learner kept making mistakes, the teacher pulled switches from 15-volts through 135 volts. Each time a switch was pulled, the learner in the other room would say something like "Ugh" or "Ow." At 120-volts, he said, "This really hurts." At the 150-volt level, however, the learner yelled more loudly and said, "Experimenter! That's all. Get me out of here. I told you I had heart trouble. I refuse to go on." The teacher typically turned to the experimenter and said, "You want me to go on?" The experimenter stayed very calm and answered, "Please continue."

The teacher read another question, which the learner also got wrong. The teacher pulled the 165-volt switch. The learner in the other room yelled loudly and started banging on the wall, saying "Let me out." The teacher typically turned to the experimenter again for guidance. One teacher said, "That guy is hollering in there. He's got a heart condition. You want me to go on?" The experimenter replied, "Please go on." If the teacher hesitated, the experimenter said, "It is absolutely essential that you continue." After the 180-volt shock, the learner yelled, "I can't stand the pain." After the 195-volt shock, the learner started screaming, "Let me out of here. Let me out of here. My heart's bothering me. You have no right to keep me here." At this point, many teachers said something like, "I'm not going to kill that man in there. He can't stand it. What if something happens to him? I refuse to take responsibility. Who's going to take responsibility if anything happens to him?" Each time the teacher protested, the experimenter first ordered him to continue, then said it was essential that he continue, then said, "You have no other choice. You *must* go on until he has learned all the word pairs correctly."

Each time the teacher pulled a new, higher voltage lever, the learner screamed more loudly. At 300 volts (Intense Shock), the learner was almost in hysterics. He yelled that he was not going to answer any more questions. When the learner did not answer the next question, the teacher looked to the experimenter for guidance. The experimenter told the teacher that lack of an answer was the same as an incorrect answer and that he should continue with the experiment. Teachers who got to this point typically became very nervous and agitated. They began to sweat, to tremble, to stutter, to bite their lips, and to dig their fingernails into their palms. Several teachers erupted into uncontrollable, hysteric laughter as they pleaded with the experimenter to let them stop.

After an extremely agonizing scream at 315 volts, the learner neither responded to the questions nor yelled after the next shock was administered. All the way through the shocks from 375 through 420 volts (labeled Danger: Severe Shock) and through the 435-volt and 450-volt shocks (labeled **XXX**), teachers who went that far heard nothing from the other room but dead silence.

How many ordinary postal clerks, high school teachers, salesmen, engineers, and laborers do you think would carry their obedience to authority so far that they would keep on giving electric shocks to a mild-mannered accountant right through the maximum 450-volt level, even though for all they knew he had probably been unconscious or dead during the last seven shocks?

When people have the experiment described to them, they usually estimate that no more than 3% (presumably sadists) would continue to obey through the maximum 450-volt level. The men who participated had nothing to lose by refusing to obey. They could at any time have taken their payment (or refused to take it), walked out the door, and never seen the experimenter again. The experimenter had no power over them other than the "legitimate power" authority vested in his position as a researcher at a prestigious university.

Disturbingly, 65% of the men went all the way through the 450-volt level. They perspired and they became extremely agitated about what they were doing, but they continued to obey. In the initial study, no participant disobeyed the experimenter before the 300-volt level at which the learner screamed loudly and refused to answer any more questions. In one study, 12% quit at 300 volts (intense shock), 20% quit between 315 volts and 360 volts (when the learner presumably passed out or died), and 3% quit during the Danger: Severe Shock phase. All the rest pulled every switch that the experimenter requested, including the XXX switch.

The men who participated in these studies were, of course, intensely relieved when the "learner" later walked into the room smiling and shook their hands. When the experimenter explained that the study provided important insights into the dangers of blind obedience and the need to question the orders of malevolent governments, many participants volunteered that they were glad they had been a part of the project and that they would willingly participate in other studies that might be conducted by the same experimenters at the same laboratory. Like the experimenter, they thought it important for the world to learn that "With numbing regularity good people were seen to knuckle under [to] the demands of authority and perform actions that were callous and severe" (Milgram, 1965a, p. 74).

In a series of follow-up studies, Milgram (1974) explored factors that increased or reduced destructive obedience. One such factor was physical proximity of the victim. When the confederate was in a separate room where the "teacher" could not see or hear him, teachers administered particularly intense levels of shock. They were less willing to follow orders when they could see or hear the victim, and least willing to follow orders when they had to force the victim's hand down onto the electrodes. Being close to the victim's pain, as explained in Chapters 12 and 13, which dealt with Helping and Aggression, was probably distressing for participants. A second important factor was the immediate environment. When the experimenter did not wear a scientist's white lab coat or the setting was a dingy office building rather than a scientific laboratory at a major university, participants were far less likely to follow destructive orders, presumably because the orders seemed less legitimate. A third factor was how close the experimenter stood to the teacher. When the experimenter stood next to the teacher, obedience and levels of shock were high. When the experimenter "called in" his instructions from another room over a telephone, destructive obedience was low. The experimenter was a less powerful source of "social impact" (see Chapter 11) when he was not physically present. Finally, two experimenters exerted greater power and elicited greater destructive obedience than did one experimenter, whereas two teachers more successfully resisted the experimenter's power than did one, as long as one of the teachers was reluctant to obey.

■ OBEDIENCE IN EVERYDAY SETTINGS

Many studies have established the generality of these results, both by varying the conditions of the original procedure and by testing obedience in entirely different settings. In one study that used the original procedure on ordinary citizens of Germany, 85% of participants administered shocks all the way through the highest level (Mantell, 1971). In another study conducted in Australia, a country where citizens are more prone to question and defy established authority, 40% of participants obediently administered the maximum shock (Kilham & Mann, 1974). In yet another study, a female experimenter got considerable obedience from children in Jordan. Regardless of their own sex or age, 73% of children from ages six through 16 obediently administered the maximum level of shock to a same-sex peer (Shanab & Yahya, 1977).

Experimenters have also found disturbingly high levels of destructive obedience in business settings and in hospitals. In one application of Milgram's procedure to a different setting, experimenters in the Netherlands asked participants to interview applicants for a job (Meeus & Raaijmakers, 1986). At the time of the experiment, unemployment was so high in the Netherlands that people who failed an interview were unlikely to find work. Unlike the Milgram setting where participants might have fooled themselves into thinking that there would be no "permanent damage," all participants in the job interview study realized that disrupting an applicant's performance would do serious harm to the applicant. After they reviewed the applicant's qualifications (which were outstanding), the experimenter told the interviewer to make "stress remarks" (for example, "This job is too difficult for you") at 15 points during the interview and to continue making these psychologically devastating remarks regardless of whether the applicant complained. The experimenter said that he wanted to see how applicants handled stress and that he would not hire an applicant who could not perform well under stress. Just as the 15 shocks in the Milgram procedure became progressively more punishing, so did the 15 stress remarks.

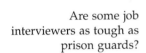

The applicant, who was a confederate, seemed self-confident and assured at the beginning of the interview. As the stress remarks became more demeaning, however, he became more and more visibly upset and his performance deteriorated badly. After repeatedly saying that the remarks were ruining his chances at a job that he needed desperately and begging the interviewer to stop interrupting, the applicant refused to answer any more questions. In every way, the job interview procedure was modeled closely after Milgram's procedure.

Are some job interviewers as tough as prison guards?

How many normal citizens would ruin people's lives by subjecting deserving applicants to psychological torture, merely because an experimenter said that they had to do so? Twenty-two of 24 interviewers ignored the applicant's pleas and continued to the end, making all 15 of the increasingly humiliating "stress remarks." Destructive obedience in the psychological laboratory has potentially devastating parallels in the business world (Meeus & Raaijmakers, 1987).

In another application of Milgram's results, nurses in an Ohio hospital were working the "late shift," at a time when few other nurses were present (Hofling, Brotzman, Dalrymple, Graves, & Pierce, 1966). The unsuspecting nurse received a telephone call from a Dr. Hanford, who said that he had seen a patient earlier in the day and would like the patient to have some medication before "seeing him again this evening." Although Dr. Hanford was listed as a psychiatrist in the hospital directory, the nurse had never met him. Also, official hospital policy dictated that nurses must have a *written* order from a doctor before administering medication. Dr. Hanford said, "Will you please check the medicine cabinet and see if you have some Astroten?" The nurse had never heard of Astroten (because there was no such drug), but in the cabinet the nurse found a prominently placed pillbox labeled "ASTROTEN, 5 mg. capsules. Usual dose: 5 mg. Maximum daily dose: 10 mg." When the nurse returned to the telephone, Dr. Hanford told the nurse to "please give Mr. Carson (an actual patient) a stat [immediate] dose of 20 milligrams—that's four capsules—of Astroten. I'll be up within ten minutes, and I'll sign the order then, but I'd like the drug to have started taking effect."

Would nurses give patients dangerous doses of medication if a doctor ordered them to?

How many nurses would obey the doctor's orders when the hospital regulations required a written (not telephone) prescription and the label on the pillbox indicated that the nurse would be giving some helpless patient twice the maximum daily dose, all at once? When the experimenters asked other experienced nurses, 10 of 12 said they would refuse to do so. They were also sure that other nurses would refuse to follow the doctor's order. When the experimenters asked nursing students, 21 of 21 said they would disobey the doctor. Unfortunately, as we saw in the Milgram obedience studies, hearing about a situation is different from being in it. Of the 22 nurses who received a call from Dr. Hanford, 21 of them obeyed. They took the four capsules of Astroten and headed for the patient's room. (They were, of course, intercepted on the way by one of the experimenters, who explained what had happened and why the study was important.) In other words, otherwise competent, professional nurses were willing to take the chance of seriously injuring a patient under their care, merely because they had been ordered to do so (illegitimately) by an authority figure—a doctor.

REASONS FOR DESTRUCTIVE OBEDIENCE

We know from these studies of destructive obedience that people may protest orders to harm others, but they also obey. Why do they obey? By examining Milgram's and related studies, social psychologists have learned that four important factors are belief in legitimate authority, gradual commitment, lack of personal responsibility, and lack of dissent.

■ LEGITIMATE AUTHORITY

Participants in Milgram's initial studies were impressed by the legitimate authority of a researcher at prestigious Yale University. As long as they remained convinced that the experiment was a legitimate scientific enterprise, which it *must* have been if it was being conducted in such impressive surroundings, the participants might have felt almost as much duty to obey as would a military private to obey a general. When Milgram subsequently replicated his study in a run-down office building located in a seedy section of Bridgeport, Connecticut, "only" 48% of participants (as compared to the initial study's 65%) administered the maximum 450 volts (Milgram, 1965a). Recall also that participants in Australia, where it is traditional to question authority, obeyed less than did citizens of Connecticut.

Finally, personality correlates of obedience show that people who do not trust authority figures and people who insist on controlling their own actions are less obedient in the Milgram situation than are more trusting peers (Blass, 1991). Many crimes of obedience might be avoided if ordinary citizens were more willing to challenge governments and authority figures (Kelman & Hamilton, 1988).

■ GRADUAL COMMITMENT

Another important aspect of Milgram's procedure tells us that participants became committed gradually. It seems likely that very few people would agree to deliver the XXX 450 volts right at the start, but the "practice session" was the start of a gradual commitment. Once they had pulled the 15-volt switch (a seemingly innocuous act), then why not deliver 30 volts? It was only 15 extra volts. Social psychologists call the principle of gradual commitment a foot-in-the-door effect (Freedman & Fraser, 1966). According to the **foot-in-the-door effect,** if you can get people to comply with a small, seemingly harmless request (getting your foot in the door), they sometimes feel committed to go along with subsequent increasingly important requests. When Milgram's participants agreed to give the learner 15 volts, they did not realize how quickly this small concession would escalate into physically torturing a helpless middle-aged accountant (Milgram, 1974). Through gradual commitment, small requests pave the way for obeying later, more disturbing requests.

■ LACK OF PERSONAL RESPONSIBILITY

Milgram's initial results also reflected a perception by participants that they were not personally responsible. Many participants asked the experimenter whether he would absolve them of personal responsibility should anything happen to the learner (Milgram, 1965a). Destructive obedience was much higher when the experimenter said that he would take responsibility than when he did not (Milgram, 1974). Even without an explicit acknowledgment of responsibility, however, juries assign greater responsibility to the military officer who orders soldiers to massacre innocent civilians than to the soldiers who pull the triggers (Hamilton, 1978), so it is possible that at least some of Milgram's participants felt little personal responsibility for their actions.

To increase their sense of personal responsibility, Milgram varied the procedure so that, instead of having an electrode strapped to his wrist, the learner had his hand resting on an electrode and could avoid the shock by raising his hand. In these conditions, the experimenter ordered the teacher to force the screaming accountant's hand down onto the electrode. Obedience was greatly reduced by this method of increasing personal responsibility, but it was far from eliminated (Milgram, 1974).

■ LACK OF DISOBEDIENT ROLE MODELS

Finally, obedience may have been high in the Milgram situation because the teacher had no role models—no other people who refused to obey. Recall that in the Asch line-judging procedure conformity was reduced almost to zero when even one other person in the group gave the correct answer. Similarly, when the study of nurse's obedience was changed so that other nurses were present when the doctor gave the illegitimate telephone medication order, only 11% obeyed (Rank & Jacobson, 1977). When Milgram (1965b) varied his procedure so that the actual participant first saw two "other teachers" (confederates) challenge the experimenter's orders, only 10% of them continued to the 450-volt level. When they challenged the experimenter's orders, the two other teachers got the experimenter to reveal that he was not a professor, but only a student doing unsupervised research.

It might seem that the reduction in obedience occurred primarily because the experimenter had been made to seem illegitimate and not merely because the participants had seen a role model disobey. A subsequent study, however, included four conditions (Rosenhan, 1969). The first (no model) condition was simply a replication of the standard Milgram procedure. In the second (obedient model) condition, the actual participant first saw "another teacher" protest but deliver the maximum shock. In the third (delegitimizing model) condition, the actual participant first watched "another teacher" stomp out of the room after discovering that the experimenter was only an unsupervised freshman. In the fourth (humane model) condition, the actual participant first watched "another teacher" courteously inform the experimenter that he could not continue because the learner was in great pain. The humane model reduced the actual participant's subsequent obedience by as much as did the delegitimizing model, so the mere act of disobedience, rather than the nature of that disobedience, may be the primary factor in resisting the influence of a malevolent authority such as Adolph Hitler.

SUMMARY OF WHEN POWER IS ABUSED

Those who find themselves in a position of power sometimes abuse that power. Because people seldom challenge "legitimate" authority, even ordinary citizens can be trained to become professional torturers in the service of sadistic tyrants.

People are surprisingly willing to obey orders to hurt others. In classic studies of destructive obedience, 65% of ordinary men administered increasingly severe electric shocks to a mild-mannered accountant, even past the point where the accountant had presumably gone unconscious or died. Similar destructive obedience has been found in studies conducted across cultures and across age groups. People obey authority figures by administering electric shock, by psychologically torturing needy job applicants, and by preparing potentially lethal doses of medication for hospital patients.

High levels of obedience occur in people who are predisposed to trust legitimate authority, when the commitment to harm others is gradual, when people do not feel personally responsible, and when no one else disobeys.

Groups

Did you ever wonder why people who are accused of serious crimes such as murder are *entitled* to be tried by a jury rather than by a judge? The word "entitled" implies that a group decision might be more advantageous for the defendant than a decision made by one individual, even if that individual happens to be a judge who is an expert on the law. Jury members are ordinary citizens who might have more in common with the defendant than would a judge. Beyond mere similarity to the defendant, however, citizens of the United States and other Western countries have an almost mystical faith in collective wisdom. Hundreds of movies such as *Twelve Angry Men* depict jury deliberation as essential to "getting at the truth" and arriving at a just verdict. Popular movies and novels imply that something magical happens when jurors form themselves into a group. In such fictitious accounts, people who are ignorant and prejudiced are somehow transformed into paragons of wisdom and virtue merely by being part of a group that is charged with a momentous decision. In other words, being part of a group somehow changes individuals so that they become "better than themselves."

Does being part of a group change individuals? Do groups render wiser or more moderate decisions than do individuals? Much of what we know about the way groups render decisions comes from research on jury deliberations (Davis, 1992). Juries might be instructed to reach consensus, but the procedure that they use to do so can influence the eventual decision. When a jury considers three charges that vary in seriousness such as reckless homicide, aggravated battery, and property damage against the same defendant, juries that consider reckless homicide first are more likely to convict on the aggravated battery charge than are juries that consider the property damage first (Davis, Tindale, Nagao, Hinsz, & Robertson, 1984). Similarly, a jury with five members for conviction and five members for acquittal can enlist the two undecided jurors on whichever side's jurors get to vote first in a straw poll (Davis, Stasson, Ono, & Zimmerman, 1988). Jury decisions depend as much on group processes as on individual preferences.

Juries also reach decisions that are different from what the individual members might have reached by themselves (Davis, 1992). In one study, the researchers first identified people who had authoritarian or nonauthoritarian political philosophies (Bray & Noble, 1987). Authoritarians typically believe in a "get-tough" approach to crime prevention. They believe that we could reduce the number of murders, rapes, assaults, and other violent crimes if we made the punishments severe enough. Nonauthoritarians are less impressed with severe punishment as a way to deter violent crime. The investigators suspected that authoritarian jurors would, as individuals, recommend harsher sentences for convicted criminals than would nonauthoritarian jurors. The investigators wondered, however, what effect deliberating *as a group* might have on the jurors' individual opinions if all the jurors happened to be authoritarians or if all the jurors happened to be nonauthoritarians. Would group deliberation work to the defendant's advantage? Would both types of juries moderate their initial tendencies, or would they become more extreme?

To examine the effect of group deliberation on sentencing, the investigators had mock juries, each jury composed either entirely of authoritarians or entirely of nonauthoritarians, listen to a recording of a murder trial (Bray & Noble, 1987). In the trial, two men were accused of killing a Chicago woman who had earlier rebuffed their advances at a nightclub. Besides deciding the defendants' guilt or innocence, the jurors were asked—should the verdict be guilty—how many years in prison the defendants should receive. Figure 15.1 shows the sentencing recommendations of authoritarian and nonauthoritarian jurors before and after the jury deliberation. As shown in the figure, nonauthoritarian jurors initially favored a relatively lenient sentence of 38 years. After deliberating with others of their own kind, they changed to an even more lenient sentence of approximately 28 years. Authoritarian jurors, by contrast, initially favored a relatively harsh sentence of 56 years. After deliberating with others of *their* own kind, they changed to an even more harsh sentence of approximately 68 years.

Jury deliberation, then, is not always advantageous to a criminal defendant. Groups are not always more lenient than the group members might have been as individuals. Nonauthoritarians advocated more lenient sentences when they were in groups, but authoritarians did just the opposite. The safest conclusion to be drawn from the jury study is that being part of a group sometimes changes the individual group members. When you think about how much in our society depends on group actions, from jury deliberations to legislative decisions and work teams, you soon realize how important it is to know what groups do to the individuals who belong and how well groups function. This chapter addresses these two basic questions about groups. The first section of the chapter concentrates on ways in which groups change the individuals who belong to them. The second section of the chapter concentrates on how well groups perform.

FIGURE 15.1

Group discussion increases differences of opinion between groups.

Graph shows number of years in prison recommended for a convicted murderer before and after deliberation by groups of authoritarians and nonauthoritarians (Bray & Noble, 1987)

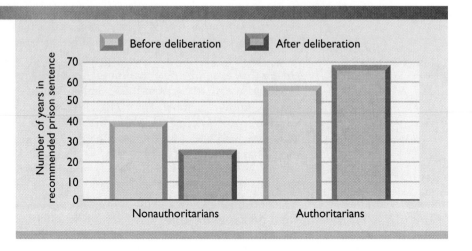

Calvin and Hobbes   by Bill Watterson

HOW DO GROUPS CHANGE INDIVIDUALS?

Groups are "social aggregates that involve mutual awareness and potential mutual interaction" (McGrath, 1984, p. 7). Groups are not mere categories like "people who have ever served on jury duty" or "people who have been convicted of murder," nor are they unorganized aggregates like "a crowd," "an audience," or "a culture." People who belong to categories and unorganized aggregates are not "mutually aware" of any special relationship with each other, nor do they usually plan to interact (Shaw, 1981; Paulus, 1989). The jurors who serve together on a specific case, in contrast, are a group, as are the nuns at a particular convent, members of a local labor union, astronauts on a specific mission, or members of a work or academic committee.

Natural groups differ in the scope of their activities and in how long they interact (McGrath, 1984). Some groups engage in a limited set of activities, whereas others engage in a broad range of activities. Similarly, some groups dissolve as soon as they have accomplished the group goal, whereas other groups stay together indefinitely, because their goals are never completely accomplished. Table 15.1 shows four different types of natural groups, with examples. A jury, for instance, is a "task force"–a group that forms for a limited purpose and that typically disbands as soon as the group accomplishes its task. A sports team like the Dallas Cowboys football team is a "standing crew." It

TABLE 15.1	Natural Groups May Be Divided into Four Types, Depending on Whether They Engage in Limited or Broad Activities and Whether They Operate for a Limited Time or Long-Term (Abstracted from McGrath, 1984)		
ACTIVITIES	**TIME**	**TYPE OF GROUP**	**EXAMPLES**
limited	limited	task forces	juries, study commissions
limited	long-term	standing crews	sports teams, work teams
broad	limited	expeditions	space crews, college students
broad	long-term	embedded systems	families

also has a very limited purpose (to win football games), but the group expects to pursue that goal throughout many football seasons. The crew of a spaceship, in contrast to juries and sports teams, is an "expedition" that pursues a broad range of activities, from landing on the moon to conducting scientific experiments and repairing orbiting telescopes. Nonetheless, a space mission–like a mountain-climbing expedition–has a definite, limited duration. The group usually disbands as soon as the mission has been accomplished. A family, in contrast, is an "embedded system." It engages in a broad range of activities that often endure for a lifetime.

Regardless of which type of group is involved, however, considerable evidence suggests that being part of a group changes the individuals who belong. This section of the chapter examines two ways in which groups change individuals. First, people who belong to groups assume a social or group identity. Second, people who belong to groups display ingroup favoritism.

GROUP IDENTITY

One of the major themes of this book, explained in Chapter 1 and elsewhere throughout, is that people have both a personal identity and a social identity (Abrams, 1992; Brewer, 1991; Cousins, 1989; Crocker, Luhtanen, Blaine, & Broadnax, 1994; Deaux, 1993; Ethier & Deaux, 1994; Markus & Kitayama, 1994; Miller & Prentice, 1994; Oyserman, 1993; Trafimow, Triandis, & Goto, 1991; Turner, Oakes, Haslam, & McGarty, 1994). The personal identity is about the self as an individual. The social identity is about the self as a member of a group or category. Belonging to a group often increases an individual's social identity. Instead of saying "I live in the United States," many people say "I am an American." Instead of saying "I attend Texas A&M University, many students say "I am an Aggie." A social or group identity is the part of an individual's self-concept that derives from knowing that he or she belongs to a "social group (or groups) together with the value and emotional significance attached to that membership" (Tajfel, 1981, p. 255). People who take seriously their group identity may bask in the reflected glory of their in-group's accomplishments. They may also enjoy heightened collective self-esteem that can, in some instances, compensate for a lack of personal self-esteem.

■ BASKING IN REFLECTED GLORY

People who take pride in their group identity can "announce" their affiliation either directly or indirectly. One frequently used indirect method of announcing a prestigious group identity is by "association" (Cialdini & De Nicholas, 1989). If people can suffer "guilt by association," they can also take "pride by association." **Basking in reflected glory** involves sharing the glory of a successful other with whom you are in some way associated. People from Indiana, for example, can bask in the warm glow of pride when a fellow Hoosier wins a gold medal at the Olympic Games. Members of a college class can claim for themselves a part of the glory when one of their own later becomes famous. By mentioning casually that "San Francisco 49ers quarterback Steve Young and I were in the same class in college," they can use his fame to present themselves in a more favorable light (Cialdini & Richardson, 1980).

In one study of basking in reflected glory, professors at seven large universities observed how their introductory psychology students dressed to attend Monday classes throughout the fall semester (Cialdini, Borden, Thorne, Walker, Freeman, & Sloan, 1976, Experiment 1). On every Monday, the investigators recorded the percentage of students who wore buttons, jackets, sweaters, T-shirts, and other items of apparel that displayed the school name, team nickname, mascot, or university insignia. They did not count nonapparel items such as notebooks or book covers, nor did they count merely wearing the school colors. Later, the investigators divided the fall semester Mondays into those that had followed a win by the school's football team and those that had followed a loss. As predicted, students were much more likely to wear apparel that advertised their school affiliation on a Monday after their football team had won than on a Monday after their football team had lost. No such difference occurred for wearing names and insignia of universities other than their own, so the difference did not occur merely because the students were more aware of university affiliations. Instead, the students were emphasizing a *favorable* group identity.

During the following year's football season, the same investigators conducted a telephone "survey," during which they convinced individual students that they had scored either very well or very poorly on a test of how much they knew about their university (Cialdini et al., 1976, Experiment 2). The investigators then asked the students to describe the outcome of a recent football game in which the school team had either won or lost. The investigators asked "Can you tell me the outcome of that game?" Figure 15.2 shows the percentage of students who used the pronoun "We" to describe the team's outcome. Overall, students were more likely to say "We won" when their school's football team had triumphed and "They lost" or "The score was 14–6" when their school's football team had been defeated. This result is simply pride by association or "basking in reflected glory."

When do college students wear the school's colors?

Figure 15.2

When self-esteem is threatened, people associate themselves with a successful in-group and dissociate themselves from an unsuccessful in-group.

Graph shows percentage of students who used "We" to describe their school's football team, in two conditions (Cialdini, Borden, Thorne, Walker, Freeman, & Sloan, 1976)

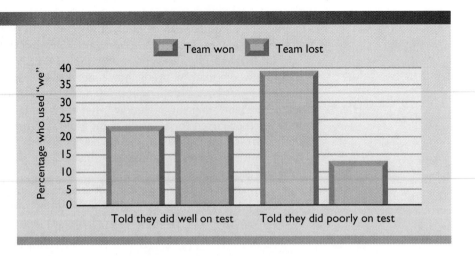

As the figure also shows, however, students used pride by association selectively, depending on whether they had themselves done well or poorly. When students learned that they did well on a test as individuals, they did not need to bolster their egos by calling the school's football team "We." They used "We" no more frequently whether the school team had won or lost. When students learned that they did very poorly on a test, in contrast, they were much more likely to use "We" for a win and less likely to use "We" for a loss. When the team did well and the students' individual identities had been threatened, they took a share of the credit by saying "We won" and "We're number one!" When the team did poorly and the students' individual identities had been threatened, they "disconnected" their association by saying "*They* lost." Dissociating oneself from a failed social identity is a way of protecting self-esteem (Snyder, Higgins, & Stucky, 1983; Snyder, Lassegard, & Ford, 1986).

Basking in reflected glory and suffering from a failed social identity have effects that extend beyond merely feeling "up" or "down." People who are strongly invested in a social identity, such as avid sports fans who identify with a specific team, let the team's success or failure affect their own perceived competence. For one study, the investigators recruited male undergraduates at Indiana University who were devoted fans of IU's men's basketball team (Hirt, Zillmann, Erickson, & Kennedy, 1992, Study 2). Some of the men watched Indiana win an away game on television. Others watched Indiana lose an away game on television. A third group of men did not watch a basketball game. The experimenter then asked all men to estimate how well they would perform on three tasks that they expected to perform as part of an "unrelated" experiment: scoring points in a Velcro dart game, solving anagrams, and asking an attractive woman for a date.

Their team's success or failure influenced how well the men thought *they* would do on all three tasks. Men who had just watched their school's basketball team win were confident that they would do well at darts, anagrams, and getting a date. Men who had just watched their school's basketball team lose, in contrast, were pessimistic about their own skills, whether those skills involved a motor, mental, or social task. Furthermore, this decrease in expected performance occurred above and beyond merely being in a good or bad mood. The effect seemed to occur primarily because of a boost or injury to the men's self-esteem. The men derived part of their self-esteem from what happened to the team, which is exactly what should have happened if they genuinely identified with the group.

■ COLLECTIVE SELF-ESTEEM

Research on basking in reflected glory suggests that people benefit from having a positive group identity and that the social or group identity is sometimes different from a person's individual identity. Some cultures emphasize collective pride in the group's accomplishments and discourage individualistic pride; other cultures emphasize individualism more than collectivism (Triandis, 1989a; Triandis, McCusker, & Hui, 1990). Even in highly individualistic cultures like that of the United States, however, people display both individualistic and collectivistic tendencies. They take comfort from a positive group identity and feel better about themselves when their group does well.

Collective self-esteem is the self-esteem that derives from a positive group identity (Crocker & Luhtanen, 1990). Table 15.2 shows four aspects of collective self-esteem, with example items from the Collective Self-Esteem Scale that is used to identify research participants who have high versus low collective self-esteem (Luhtanen & Crocker, 1992). People who are high in collective self-esteem pride themselves on being worthy members, privately congratulate themselves on belonging, believe that their groups are widely respected, and view their group membership as an important part of who they are. Collective self-esteem is different from individual self-esteem (Luhtanen & Crocker, 1992).

Some people report feeling good (or bad) about themselves both as individuals and as group members. Other people report no such connection. They can acknowledge being poor students, for example, and yet take pride in their school's lofty academic reputation. They can also regard themselves as the star of a group that is "lucky to have them." In one study of the connection between collective self-esteem and biased inferences, students who had either high or low collective self-esteem (measured by private pride in group membership) were told that, because of a random drawing, they belonged to either "Group A" or "Group B" (Crocker & Luhtanen, 1990). To threaten group identity, the experimenter told each student that his or her *group* (not the student himself or herself) had done either very well or very poorly on a test of social sensitivity and intellectual maturity. Students then had an opportunity to draw biased or unbiased inferences. They could praise or criticize the test by attributing positive or negative traits to people who scored high versus low on the test.

As shown in Figure 15.3, students who had low collective self-esteem drew no different inferences about the test's validity whether their own group was said to have scored high or low. Either way, if the experimenter claimed that it was a test of social sensitivity and intellectual maturity, then they thought that high scorers would be more likely than low scorers to have positive personality traits like being motivated, ambitious, creative, and considerate. Students who were high in collective self-esteem, in contrast, praised high scorers

TABLE 15.2	Four Aspects of Collective Self-Esteem, with Example Items from the Collective Self-Esteem Scale (Luhtanen & Crocker, 1992)
ASPECT	**EXAMPLE ITEM**
Worthy Membership	"I am a worthy member of the social groups I belong to"
Private Pride	"In general, I'm glad to be a member of the social groups I belong to"
Public Respect	"In general, others respect the social groups that I am a member of"
Identity	"The social groups I belong to are an important reflection of who I am"

FIGURE 15.3

Collective self-esteem increases biased inferences about groups.

Graph shows how positively students described high and low scorers after being told that their own group scored high or low on a test (Crocker & Luhtanen, 1990)

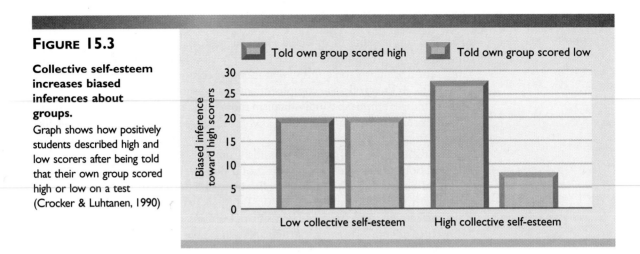

more if their own group did well than if their own group did poorly. For people who take great pride in their group identities, tasks on which their own group does well are valid, but tasks on which their own group does poorly are suspect.

As discussed in Chapter 8, group identity and collective self-esteem contribute importantly to in-group favoritism, prejudice, and discrimination. New group members are often insecure in their in-group status and may not feel fully accepted. They display greater in-group bias toward the in-group and against the outgroup than do long-standing group members (Moreland & Levine, 1989). Also, people who are induced to think of both their own group and an outgroup as part of a larger group greatly reduce their prejudice and discrimination against the former outgroup (Gaertner, Mann, Dovidio, Murrell, & Pomare, 1990; Gaertner, Mann, Murrell, & Dovidio, 1989). A strong sense of social identity and pride in one's own group benefits the individual, but it is also dangerous for intergroup relations (Turner, 1991).

IN-GROUP FAVORITISM

As suggested by the study of collective self-esteem, one way in which groups might change the individuals who belong is that people who belong to groups might treat each other better than they treat others. Once people have joined a group, the other group members typically give them preferential treatment. They give members of their own group a larger share of rewards and other resources than they give to nonmembers. They also give fellow in-group members the benefit of doubt over outgroup members when drawing inferences about traits and actions.

■ ALLOCATING REWARDS

You might expect group members to treat "their own kind" (the in-group) better than they treat members of groups to which they do not belong (the outgroup). As discussed in Chapter 12, reciprocal altruism is the norm within groups. Group members know that if they do favors for one of their own, the favors are likely to be returned, so both sides benefit. Jury members may treat each other very politely early in the deliberations, because they expect reciprocal consideration later in the deliberations when disagreements may emerge. Members of space crews and sports teams obviously find it in their own individual interests to help teammates, either because their teammates have helped them in the past or because they may later need help themselves. Family members are expected to stick together because "blood is thicker than water." As we shall see, however, people also display favoritism toward members of the in-group in situations where the "in-group" is determined by a trivial distinction that carries with it no previous history or future promise of reciprocal rewards.

In a classic study of in-group bias in allocating rewards, high school boys guessed the number of dots in a cluster of dots that were projected on a screen for less than one-half second (Tajfel, Billig, Bundy, & Flament, 1971, Experiment 1). Because the exposure time was so brief, the investigators could easily convince a specific student either that his estimates were consistently too high or that his estimates were consistently too low. A randomly selected half of the boys were told that "you are an overestimator." The other half were told that "you are an underestimator." The boys belonged to two **minimal groups,** that is, groups formed on the basis of an empty category label that denotes a trivial distinction. Minimal groups qualify as "groups" because the members are mutually aware of their group identity and because they might potentially interact.

Next, the experimenter asked each boy to assign rewards and penalties to some of the other boys who had participated in the study, by choosing the number of points that two other participants would receive. The boys never got to assign points (which they knew were worth money) to themselves, but only to other participants. The other participants were identified only by code number and by one of the terms "of your group" or "of the other group." As predicted, the boys assigned greater rewards to anonymous members of their "own group" than to anonymous members of the "other group," even though they did not know who the other participants were, they had no history of interacting with members of "their own group," and they had not been led to expect future interaction in which members of "their own group" might return the favor. In other words, the mere group label, by itself, was sufficient to induce favoritism toward "my own kind."

In subsequent studies, in-group favoritism in assigning rewards occurred regardless of how the minimal groups were established. Having participants rate abstract paintings and telling them that "you are one of the people who prefer paintings by the artist Klee, whereas other people prefer paintings by the artist Kandinski," for instance, elicits as much in-group favoritism as does the overestimator-underestimator label (Tajfel et al., 1971, Experiment 2). Also, the minimal groups manipulation is enough to make members avoid rewards that are either optimal for their own group or equitable to both groups, in favor of rewards in which members of their in-group *beat* members of the outgroup (Tajfel et al., 1971, Experiment 3). Finally, in-group favoritism occurs not just for rewards, but for evaluating other people's performances, inferring other people's traits and motives, and other ways of discriminating for the in-group and against the outgroup (Messick & Mackie, 1989; Thompson, 1993; Vanbeselaere, 1991b, 1993). In-group favoritism is surprisingly pervasive in minimal group situations, given that in-group and outgroup labels in such studies are usually based on trivial, meaningless distinctions (Messick & Mackie, 1989).

One of the reasons for in-group favoritism may be that discriminating against the outgroup in favor of the in-group makes people feel good about themselves (Chin & McClintock, 1993). "If there are two kinds of people in this world," they seem to be saying, "then my kind is the better kind, and I'll prove it by drawing a sharp distinction between the rewards that members of each kind deserve." In one study of in-group favoritism and self-esteem, male and female college students drew slips of paper to learn their secret code number and which of two groups they had been assigned to (Lemyre & Smith, 1985). Some of the students learned that they belonged to Group Red; others learned that they belonged to Group Blue. Then the students allocated rewards to anonymous other students, about each of whom they knew nothing more than a meaningless code number and whether the person belonged to Group Red or to Group Blue.

Some Red and Blue students choose rewards for one member of the in-group and one member of the outgroup before reporting their current level of self-esteem. Students in this "discriminate before" condition, who discriminated by allocating greater rewards to in-group members than to outgroup members, reported relatively high self-esteem. Discriminating against an outgroup made them feel better about themselves. Other students completed the self-esteem scales before they discriminated against outgroup members. These "discriminate after" students reported moderate levels of self-esteem. Students in a third condition were *forced* to be fair, because all reward choices were equal for the in-group and outgroup. They reported low self-esteem. Finally, some students were *forced* to discriminate, because all reward choices favored their in-group. Even forced discrimination increased self-esteem. Although other analyses from the study suggested that being categorized may temporarily lower self-esteem, which the act of discriminating then restores, these results and others like them suggest that people in minimal groups, especially those who feel threatened, feel better about themselves when they practice in-group favoritism (Branscombe & Wann, 1994; Chin & McClintock, 1993; Hogg & Sunderland, 1991).

When people first join groups, they may not feel entirely accepted (Cini, Moreland, & Levine, 1993; Moreland, 1985; Moreland & Beach, 1992). They may feel that they are still "on the periphery" of the group and that they need to prove themselves to the "core" group members (Moreland & Levine, 1982, 1989). As a result, new group members may be especially likely to derogate and punish outgroups. New pledge members of fraternities and sororities, for instance, may believe that they can prove they "really belong" by putting down rival fraternities or sororities, at least when they get the opportunity to impress "core" members by doing so. In one study of how peripheral membership affects new group members, the investigators asked both pledge members and active members of a fraternity or sorority to participate in each experimental session (Noel, Wann, & Branscombe, 1995). The participants rated "conciliatory" and "coercive" persuasion techniques on how effective they would be for members of their own fraternity or sorority and for members of other fraternities or sororities on campus. A sorority member, for instance, rated how effective it would be to get a member of her own or a different sorority to donate money to the American Red Cross by praising the member's generosity if she donated (a conciliatory strategy) and by questioning her morals and threatening social disapproval if she refused (a coercive strategy). Half of the participants believed that their answers would be public (known to the other members of their own fraternity or sorority) and half believed that their answers would be entirely private.

Figure 15.4 shows how much pledge and active members in the "public" and "private" conditions endorsed coercive strategies for members of their own as opposed to other fraternities or sororities. The left side of the figure shows that active, core members endorsed more coercive strategies for members of other fraternities or sororities than for members of their own fraternity or sorority, regardless of whether they answered in public or in private. The right side of the figure, by contrast, shows that pledge members were much more coercive toward members of other fraternities or sororities than toward members of their own, but only when other members of their own group would know what they said. In public, they said that members of rival groups should be put down and threatened. In private, they did not. Publicly derogating mem-

FIGURE 15.4

Peripheral group members publicly derogate outgroups.

Graph shows how much active and pledge fraternity/sorority members publicly and privately endorsed coercive measures against their own and other groups (Noel, Wann, & Branscombe, 1995)

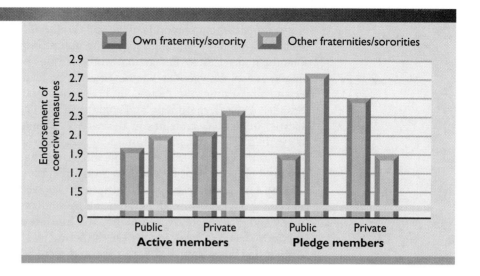

bers of other groups was a way for new pledge members to reaffirm their identity as a "good" group member. Jury members are typically strangers who *all* feel insecure in their social identity. Thus authoritarian juries may be more willing to endorse coercive measures against outgroup "criminals" than they would be as individuals.

■ DRAWING INFERENCES

Another important aspect of in-group bias is that in-group members give each other the benefit of doubt when drawing inferences, and infer the worst about members of an outgroup. In-group bias affects many types of inference, two of which are inferences about traits and inferences about actions. In one study of biased inferences of positive traits, college men and women were asked to pretend that they were president of an aerospace company that had recently given 40 employees a test of leadership ability (Schaller, 1992, Experiment 1). The students examined lists of test results in which a much larger proportion of executives than office workers scored high on leadership ability. There were also more good leaders among the men on the list than among the women, but only because male executives outnumbered female executives. Within the executives and within the office workers, females had as much leadership ability (or lack of leadership ability) as males. The advantage that men had over women was solely a function of their situational advantage in holding more leadership positions, an advantage that could easily have come from sex discrimination in hiring or promotion policies.

After they examined the lists, the men and women judged whether leadership ability was related to one's sex and whether, all else being equal, it would be better to hire a new executive who was male rather than female. As predicted, men used the simplistic inference that "there are more good leaders who are male than good leaders who are female, so being male is related to being a good leader and I would rather hire a male than a female executive." Women, in contrast, used the more complicated inference that "the same proportion of men and women executives are good leaders, so mere numerical superiority does not provide evidence for a gender difference in leadership."

Men do not always think more simplistically than women, however. A second experiment used the same materials, except that the male and female workers' names were switched (Schaller, 1992, Experiment 2). When sheer number of female executives favored women and proportions favored men, inference strategies were reversed. Women used the simplistic reasoning that "there's more women who are good leaders, so I'd rather hire a woman." Men, in contrast, used the more complex reasoning about proportions to claim that, "despite the numerical advantage that women in this particular company enjoyed among executives, gender has no bearing on leadership." A third study detected similar in-group biases in inferential strategies by minimal groups (Schaller, 1992, Experiment 3). People readily switch from simplistic to complicated inferential strategies in the service of making their own group look better than an outgroup.

In-group bias appears also in the inferences that people draw about the intentions behind actions taken by in-group members versus outgroup members (Thompson, 1993; Weber, 1994). In a study that examined in-group bias among religious groups, Muslim and Hindu college students in Bangladesh were asked to imagine that an otherwise unidentified Muslim or Hindu treated them well or poorly (Islam & Hewstone, 1993, Experiment 1). A person who was either Muslim or Hindu helped them or ignored them when they fell off a bicycle, for example, or the person either agreed or refused to afford them temporary shelter from a heavy rain. The students were asked to draw inferences about what caused the Muslim or the Hindu person to act as he or she did.

Although Muslims were more likely than Hindus to derogate members of the other religion, both groups displayed considerable bias in the inferences that they drew about other people's motives and intentions. According to the students, members of their in-group helped them because they were dispositionally "good," helped of their own free choice, and were likely to help at different times and in different situations. Members of the other religious group helped only because of external constraints, had little choice, and were likely to help in only the one instance. When they did not help, in-group members were externally constrained, had little choice, and would be unlikely to repeat their inhospitality. Outgroup members were dispositionally unhelpful, could have chosen to do otherwise, and were likely to repeat their lack of hospitality at other times and in other situations. Also, biased inferences became more pronounced when Muslims and Hindus were reminded of their religious affiliation before they made attributions (Islam & Hewstone, 1993, Experiment 3). When group identity is salient, the in-group, it seems, can do nothing wrong and the outgroup can do nothing right.

Group membership also alters the way individuals describe actions that are performed by members of their own versus other groups. A specific action can be described at several levels of abstraction. Suppose, for instance, that you saw Tony offer a spare bedroom in his home to a friend "until you locate a place of your own." You might describe the action by saying that Tony offered a room to a friend, that he helped a friend, or that he was a helpful person. Offering a room to a friend is very specific and does not imply that Tony would engage in other desirable actions. Helping a friend is more abstract, but the guest might be a special friend. Being a helpful person is the most abstract description. It attributes to Tony a generally helpful personality. Conversely, you might describe an undesirable action by saying that Sal punched Tony, that Sal was hurting Tony, or that Sal is an aggressive person. Each increase in abstraction indicates that you see the action as more indicative of the other person's general disposition.

Group members describe each other's actions at a higher or lower level of abstraction than they use to describe the actions of nonmembers who belong to other groups, depending on whether the action is desirable or undesirable. The experimenters in one study contacted the members of rival *contrada* in Ferrara, Italy (Maass, Salvi, Arcuri, & Semin, 1989). The *contrada* are rival groups from different sections of the city who have been competing with each

Will the losing jockey's friends throw water balloons at the winning jockey and try to drug his horse?

other in a yearly public horse race that has been held every year since 1279, with only a brief interruption during the Black Plague. During the week leading up to the yearly festival, members of the rival contrada steal flags from each other's clubhouses, have water balloon fights, and secretly try to drug the other team's horses. In each contrada's clubhouse, the experimenters showed members cartoons in which a person from their own group or from the rival group engaged in a desirable or undesirable action such as offering a guest a room or punching someone. Each club member chose the best description of the scene from a list of four descriptions that varied in how abstract they were.

Figure 15.5 shows how abstractly members described desirable and undesirable actions performed by a member of their own or a rival group. As the figure shows, contrada members described desirable actions more abstractly when performed by a member of their own group and described undesirable actions more abstractly when performed by a member of a rival group. They were saying that "When one of us does something good it's because we are good people, but when one of them does something good it's just an isolated action. When one of us does something bad it's an isolated action, but when

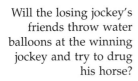

FIGURE 15.5

Group membership affects abstract thinking.

Graph shows how abstractly members described desirable and undesirable actions by members of their own versus rival groups (Maass, Salvi, Arcuri, & Semin, 1989)

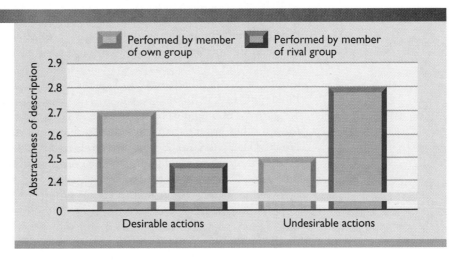

one of them does something bad it's because that's they way they are." People expect members of their own group to behave positively and expect members of other groups to behave negatively, so they view such actions as part of a more general, abstract idea (Burnstein, Abboushi, & Kitayama, 1993). People do not expect members of their own group to behave negatively or members of rival groups to behave positively, so they view those actions as specific, isolated incidents (Maass, Milesi, Zabbini, & Stahlberg, 1995). Group membership alters the specific versus abstract nature of how we think about actions that we witness. Authoritarians who participated in the jury study at the start of this chapter, for instance, might have assigned more severe sentences after deliberating as a group because their group identity made them think about the defendant more abstractly as "an evil person" rather than less abstractly as "a person who committed an evil act."

■ COMPETING RUTHLESSLY

Biased inferences also affect cooperating or competing with other people. Especially when group membership is salient, groups compete more fiercely and ruthlessly than do individuals (Bettencourt, Brewer, Croak, & Miller, 1992; Schopler & Insko, 1992). In the prisoner's dilemma game, which is explained in greater detail in Chapter 11, two individuals or two groups decide, simultaneously and without knowing what the other intends to do, whether to cooperate or to compete (Messick & Liebrand, 1995). The possible outcomes, as in real-world scenarios that the prisoner's dilemma game emulates, are that both parties to the conflict gain moderately if they both cooperate, they both gain a little if they compete, and if one competes and the other cooperates, the one that competes gains at the expense of the one who cooperates. In the prisoner's dilemma game and in similar conflicts of interest, groups are more likely to compete (and less likely to cooperate) with other groups than individuals are to compete with other individuals (Schopler & Insko, 1992).

Groups are more likely to compete with each other than are individuals because groups are more motivated than are individuals by fear and greed. In one study that examined the role of fear in competition and cooperation, the investigators had either groups or individuals play one trial of a prisoner's dilemma game (Schopler, Insko, Graetz, Drigotas, Smith, & Dahl, 1993, Experiment 1). Along with the usual options of cooperating or competing, however, the investigators offered participants a third action that they termed "withdrawal." Instead of cooperating (and possibly being taken advantage of) or competing, the groups or individuals could accept a medium payoff that was guaranteed regardless of what the other group or individual did. As predicted, groups who were dealing with other groups took far fewer cooperative actions than did individuals who were dealing with other individuals. Instead, groups accepted the medium payoff that ensured them against a mean-spirited opponent. In other words, groups were more likely to fear the worst from other groups than individuals were to fear the worst from other individuals (Hoyle, Pinkley, & Insko, 1989).

Groups also tend to be more aggressive, competitive, barbaric, and greedy toward other groups than individuals are toward each other (Insko, Schopler, Hoyle, Dardis, & Graetz, 1990). In a relevant study, each group of participants in a ten-trial prisoner's dilemma game consisted of two actual participants and one trained confederate (Schopler et al., 1993, Experiment 2). Group members were led to believe either that the other group cooperated with them at every opportunity, the other group competed with them at every opportunity, or the other group sometimes cooperated and sometimes competed. Within each of these conditions, the confederate suggested that the participants' group cooperate or suggested that the participants' group compete. The confederate's suggestions influenced the group's competitiveness in all three conditions, but did so most when the other group was supposedly being completely cooperative and laying itself open to exploitation. When the confederate suggested competing to take advantage of the other group's vulnerable cooperation, one of the participants in this condition replied, "Oh, you animal, you. Yeah, let's get 'em" (Schopler et al., 1993, p. 429). In a follow-up study, college women in groups consistently took advantage of cooperative actions by other groups of women, with or without a confederate who suggested that they do so (Schopler et al., 1993, Experiment 3). "In the context of intergroup relations, 'turning the other cheek' is a prescription for being slapped on both cheeks" (Schopler et al., 1993, p. 430).

SUMMARY OF HOW GROUPS CHANGE INDIVIDUALS

A group is a social aggregate that involves mutual awareness and potential mutual interaction. Being part of a group changes the individual in several ways. First, people who become part of a group often assume a social or group identity. They feel good about themselves when their group does well and feel depressed or embarrassed when their group does poorly. As a result, the individual's social identity is stronger when the group succeeds than when it fails. The self-esteem that derives from a positive group identity is called collective self-esteem.

Second, people who are part of a group display in-group favoritism. They treat members of their own group better than members of other groups, even when what makes them a "group" is nothing more than a meaningless label. People assign greater rewards to in-group than to out-group members because doing so increases their collective self-esteem. New or peripheral group members use in-group favoritism as a way to show that they "belong."

Third, people draw flattering inferences about actions performed by members of their in-group and draw unflattering inferences about actions performed by members of outgroups. These biased inferences extend to thinking about other people's actions in specific versus abstract terms, depending on whether the actions fit the positive or negative expectations that derive from group membership.

Fourth, groups compete more with other groups than individuals compete with other individuals. When they become members of groups that can compete or cooperate, individuals become more motivated by negative emotions such as fear and greed. With very little encouragement, they exploit cooperative overtures from outgroup members.

HOW WELL DO GROUPS PERFORM?

As described in the first section of the chapter, people change when they become members of a group. They draw part of their self-esteem from the group and engage in in-group favoritism, both of which might explain why juries who all think alike at the start of a trial might render extreme verdicts. It is often impossible to tell, however, whether extreme verdicts are "right" or "wrong." The first section of the chapter did not address the important question of whether, regardless of what being a member of a group does to self-concepts and to biased inferences or actions toward others, groups perform better or worse than individuals. This second section of the chapter, in contrast, examines the evidence on group performance.

Many tasks might be difficult to perform without groups. Groups, for instance, can function well in additive tasks, disjunctive tasks, and conjunctive tasks. In an **additive task** group members' separate performances are added to produce a combined effect. Group members who perform an additive task try to combine their skills, talents, and activities into a coordinated performance (McGrath, 1984; Shaw, 1981). Examples of additive tasks include tugs-of-war, in which a group of people combine their separate rope-pulling efforts, and constructing a space shuttle, in which a group of scientists and engineers combine their separate talents. Theoretically, the greater the number of individuals who combine their efforts on an additive task, the greater the group product (Littlepage, 1991). In reality, the group product in additive tasks is usually less than the total of what individuals can produce on their own. When "social loafing" (discussed in Chapter 11 and later in this chapter) occurs, individuals do not exert maximal effort (Karau & Williams, 1993). In other situations, groups contain too few or too many individuals to get the job done effectively. In groups that have too many members, individuals get in each other's way, with inevitable loss of coordination (Steiner, 1972).

In a **disjunctive task** the group's accomplishment is measured by the most effective group member's performance. A one hundred-person group composed of 99 nonswimmers can rescue a drowning person as long as one member of the group is a trained lifeguard. Similarly, a group playing Trivial Pursuit would know the answer to "Who starred in *Twelve Angry Men?*" as long as one member of the group happened to have been an old movie buff. In a disjunctive task, it is an advantage for group members to have diverse areas of expertise. It is also an advantage in disjunctive tasks to have a large group, because the more members the group has, the more likely it is that at least one member will have the skills necessary to get the job done (Bray, Kerr, & Atkin, 1978; Laughlin & Hollinshead, in press; Laughlin, Kerr, Davis, Halff, & Marciniak, 1975).

In a **conjunctive task,** by contrast, the group's accomplishment is limited to the least effective group member's performance. It takes only one lax prison guard for the group of guards to let a convicted mass murderer escape. Similarly, it takes only one unreasonable juror to hang a 12-person jury and prevent justice from being done (Valenti & Downing, 1975). In conjunctive tasks, unlike additive and disjunctive tasks, having more members is a distinct disadvantage. A chain is only as strong as its weakest link, so groups that engage in conjunctive tasks are only as strong as their weakest member. For some additive, disjunctive, and conjunctive tasks, as explained in this section of the chapter, group performance falls short of what we might expect. Three such shortcomings—brainstorming, group polarization, and groupthink—have been extensively investigated because of the insight that they provide into how groups function.

BRAINSTORMING

Many modern business firms believe in the efficacy of a technique that seems, at first glance, like an additive task. To invent creative ideas for developing a new product line, marketing an existing product, or expanding the company, for instance, business leaders often advocate "brainstorming" (Paulus, Brown, & Ortega, in press). **Brainstorming** is a technique by which group members try to generate as many novel ideas as possible by building on and never criticizing each other's ideas. In a brainstorming session, group members add to each other's ideas (Osborn, 1975). When groups in business, for example, want to generate as many new and creative ideas as possible, they follow four guidelines: "toss off" as many ideas as possible; the wilder the ideas the better; build on the ideas advanced by other group members; and never criticize an idea, no matter how weird or impractical it may at first seem. By following these four guidelines, professional and other groups believe that they can generate a much larger number of creative ideas than they might if they worked on the same problem as individuals (Paulus, Dzindolet, Poletes, & Camacho, 1993; Stroebe, Diehl, & Abakoumkin, 1992). The effectiveness of brainstorming as a way to approach creative tasks, however, is more an illusion than a reality.

Although groups perform very well in other tasks such as inducing rules from evidence, people who generate ideas in groups produce *fewer,* not more, nonredundant ideas than they would have had they spent the same time trying to invent novel, creative ideas on their own (Bond & Van Leeuwen, 1991; Diehl & Stroebe, 1987; McGlynn, Tubbs, & Holzhausen, 1995; Mullen, Johnson, & Salas, 1991). A typical finding is that four people who work on a problem as individuals generate approximately 25 nonredundant ideas each in 25 minutes, for a total of one hundred novel ideas. The same four people brainstorming as a group for 25 minutes produce only 50 novel ideas (Paulus & Dzindolet, 1993). Also, the results for quality are similar to the results for quantity. The more ideas a group produces, the more *good* ideas it is likely to produce (Mullen et al., 1991; Paulus & Dzindolet, 1993). If we define being creative as producing high quality ideas that no one else thought of, then four-person brainstorming groups generate approximately half as many good ideas as they might have had they worked as individuals. The larger the group, the more group productivity suffers compared to individual productivity (Bond & Van Leeuwen, 1991; Bouchard & Hare, 1970). Table 15.3 lists three phenomena (and five reasons) that explain why brainstorming is counterproductive: production blocking, evaluation apprehension, and social loafing.

■ PRODUCTION BLOCKING

Production blocking, as shown in Table 15.3, occurs because group members cannot all speak at the same time. They need to wait their turns (Stasser & Taylor, 1991). The larger the group, the longer they have to wait between turns.

Calvin and Hobbes   by Bill Watterson

TABLE 15.3	Three Phenomena That Lead to Five Reasons for Productivity Loss (Accomplishing Less Than They Might Have as Individuals) in Brainstorming Groups
PHENOMENON	**REASON FOR LOSS**
production blocking	forget ideas while waiting to speak
production blocking	distracted by other ideas and considerations
evaluation apprehension	suppress unusual ideas
social loafing	think own ideas are dispensable and unidentifiable
social loafing	misperceive "normal" level of productivity

While they are waiting, group members get distracted by what other people are saying or by looking for a polite way to "jump in." As a result, they sometimes get off on a different track, forget what they were going to say, or discover that someone else beat them to it. Production blocking is not merely a matter of speaking time (Diehl & Stroebe, 1987). Although it is true that each member of a four-person group can speak for only five minutes in a 20-minute session, whereas individuals who are alone can each spend the full 20 minutes speaking into tape recorders, it is also true that individuals usually run out of ideas fairly quickly. In one study, individuals who were given 20 minutes to speak their previously invented ideas into tape recorders generated approximately the same number of nonredundant ideas as did individuals who were given the same time to generate ideas but were given only five minutes to speak those ideas. Also, the advantage of individuals over groups remains constant throughout a typical brainstorming session (Diehl & Stroebe, 1991). Mere speaking time is not the problem (Stroebe & Diehl, 1994).

The primary production-blocking problem is that group members have to wait their turns before voicing their ideas (Diehl & Stroebe, 1991). While they are waiting, they can be distracted by trying to retain their own ideas or by looking for a way to "break in" to the conversation. In one study of production blocking, four college students sat in separate rooms that were connected by microphones so that they could hear each other's ideas during a 15-minute brainstorming session on "how handicapped people could be better integrated into society" (Diehl & Stroebe, 1991, Experiment 3). For one group of participants, the brainstorming session was "unorganized." Group members could "jump in" whenever they had an idea and no one else was speaking. In a second experimental condition, group members had to take turns. They had to remember what they wanted to say and wait until next turn to voice their ideas. In a third experimental condition, group members not only had to remember what they wanted to say until their turns came, but they also had to push a button that would place their name on a "waiting list" to speak.

The researchers compared these three production-blocking groups of students to a *nominal group* (a group in name only), in which group members sat in separate rooms and spoke into tape recorders. When the four sets of ideas generated by the nominal group were combined into one list, that list contained an average of 99 nonredundant ideas for helping the handicapped. In the *unorganized* condition where members jumped in whenever an idea occurred to them and someone else paused, the group average was 68 nonredundant ideas. When the strain on group members' memories was increased by making them wait their turns, the group average fell to 49 nonredundant ideas. Finally, when group members had to worry about both speaking in turn and making appointments to speak, group productivity fell to a mere 29 nonredundant ideas. The more participants had to worry about during the inevitable waiting time, the worse the group performed.

If remembering one's own ideas during the waiting time is a major factor in production blocking, then taking notes might help. Some students in another production-blocking experiment were encouraged to write down their ideas so that they would not forget them while other group members were suggesting ideas about "How can the costs of the health system be reduced?" Other students were not allowed to take notes (Diehl & Stroebe, 1991, Experiment 4). Even though they were physically located in separate rooms, the students in each group could hear each other, just as participants in face-to-face brainstorming groups can. Also, just as in real brainstorming groups, the relevant students believed that their separate ideas would be merged into a common "group product." As predicted, it helped to take notes. Students generated an average of 39 nonredundant ideas per group when they took notes, but fewer than 30 nonredundant ideas when they did not take notes.

With the increasing availability of computer networks like the Internet, production blocking might also be attenuated through computer software that allows group members to learn about each other's ideas and simultaneously take notes on their own ideas. Groups that interact through computer networks perform differently than do face-to-face groups on several types of intellectual tasks (Laughlin, Chandler, Shupe, Magley, & Hulbert, 1995). In *electronic brainstorming,* group members, who can be located in separate parts of the world while they work together, type their ideas onto a computer screen as the ideas occur to them, without waiting. The computer screen displays other group members' previously generated ideas. Participants can feed off each other's creativity (which was the original purpose of brainstorming) without having to worry about remembering their ideas during the waiting time that inevitably occurs in face-to-face interacting groups. When they have an idea, they can type it into the computer immediately, without having to wait and without fear of interruption (Gallupe, Cooper, Grisé, & Bastianutti, 1994; Nagasundaram & Dennis, 1993; Valacich, Dennis, & Connolly, 1994).

In one study that compared electronic brainstorming to traditional brainstorming, students tried to generate ideas about the "thumbs problem," which concerns "the practical benefits or difficulties that would arise if everyone had an extra thumb on each hand after next year" (Gallupe, Bastianutti, & Cooper, 1991). As predicted, groups that used computers for electronic brainstorming outperformed groups that used traditional brainstorming. Electronic brainstorming, though, helped nominal groups (in which students could not see other people's ideas) as much as it helped interacting groups. In another study, electronic brainstorming increased creativity (over nominal groups) for 12-member groups, but not for six-member groups (Dennis & Valacich, 1993). Although production blocking is a major reason for productivity loss in idea-generating groups, it is not the only reason.

■ EVALUATION APPREHENSION

A second important factor in productivity loss, as Table 15.3 shows, is evaluation apprehension, or fear of being evaluated negatively. Despite traditional brainstorming instructions that "the wilder the ideas, the better," people may be afraid of making a bad impression by voicing ideas that are bizarre or controversial. When discussing ways to improve the health care system, for example, most group members would be afraid to speak aloud ideas about letting poor people die if they cannot afford health insurance. Because they fear negative evaluation, people in a group setting might hold back ideas that they would be willing to voice when sitting alone in front of a tape recorder.

If evaluation apprehension induces group members to inhibit or suppress ideas, then production blocking might be more pronounced in larger than in smaller groups. Larger groups contain a larger number of other people who pose a potential threat. As described previously, productivity loss does increase with group size (Mullen et al., 1991; Bond & Van Leeuwen, 1991). Also, several studies have shown that people generate fewer ideas in "nominal" groups where the participants are all in the same room (but working individually) than in "nominal" groups where the participants are alone in separate rooms (Mullen et al., 1991; Bond & Van Leeuwen, 1991). Again, the potential for negative evaluation is greater when other people are present, who might overhear an inane, "weird," or unpopular idea.

Evaluation apprehension also implies that the number of ideas produced by people who know they are being watched and evaluated should be less than the number of ideas produced by people who are not aware of being observed. In one study of evaluation apprehension as it applies to productivity losses in brainstorming (Diehl & Stroebe, 1987, Experiment 2), the investigators asked German university students to brainstorm as individuals about topics that were either uncontroversial ("How can entertainment programs on television be improved?") or controversial ("How can economic growth be increased in Germany?"). The investigators told some of the students that their ideas would be rated for quality and originality, either by judges who were sitting behind a one-way mirror or by other students who would later watch them on videotape as part of a social psychology class. They told other students nothing about one-way mirrors or videotaping equipment.

As predicted, students who thought they were being watched and evaluated voiced far fewer ideas than did students who were unaware of being observed. The inhibiting effect of evaluation apprehension occurred regardless of whether the topic was controversial or uncontroversial and regardless of whether students thought they were being watched by anonymous "judges" or by other students. In a related study, audience expertise increased productivity losses (Collaros & Anderson, 1969). When the investigators led members of a brainstorming group to believe that one or more other members were experts on the topic under discussion, they "clammed up" and volunteered very few ideas of their own. They presumably feared that experts would find their ideas laughable.

■ SOCIAL LOAFING

The study in which other group members were portrayed as experts need not, however, have produced idea suppression merely because of evaluation apprehension. Another major factor in productivity losses, as shown in Table 15.3, is social loafing. As described in Chapter 11, social loafing occurs when group members believe that their own contributions will be "lost in the crowd" (Shepperd, in press). Participants in the "audience expertise" study might have imagined that their own ideas were dispensable, because the expert or experts in the group would be sure to know all the telling arguments in advance. As long as no one would notice that they were not contributing much, they might have felt that they could go through the motions of brainstorming and get a "free ride" (Harkins & Petty, 1982; Kerr & Bruun, 1983). According to this interpretation of productivity losses, social loafing occurs in brainstorming groups when individuals believe that their contributions will be pooled with the contributions of others, so that their own ideas will be unidentifiable and dispensable.

To test the "unidentifiable and dispensable" interpretation of productivity losses, the investigators in one study asked German students to brainstorm about how to improve relations between the German population and foreign immigrant workers (Diehl & Stroebe, 1987, Experiment 1). Some students brainstormed in four-person groups; others brainstormed as individuals. All students were told that the ideas were being recorded, but some of the students thought that their own ideas would later be compared to the ideas of one other person (personal identifiability). Other students thought that the total group ideas would later be compared with the total ideas produced by a different group (no personal identifiability). Real groups produced fewer ideas than did nominal groups and students whose ideas were to be personally identified produced more ideas than did students whose ideas were to be "lost" in the collective group effort rather than personally identified. These results implicate social loafing as a factor in brainstorming productivity losses, because they show that group members are capable of doing more if they know that their own contributions to the group effort are being identified and counted. The results do not, however, show that social loafing is unique to real groups, because students in the nominal group conditions also performed better when their own ideas were to be personally identified (Diehl & Stroebe, 1987, 1991).

Another way in which social loafing might contribute to productivity losses is that members of brainstorming groups overestimate what they accomplish. If they were sitting alone in a room speaking into a tape recorder, they might be embarrassed to leave long gaps on the tape between ideas. In a four-person group, in contrast, they can speak only occasionally, have the gaps "filled in" by the other group members, and still feel that "we are all doing a great job." If they realized that they would be voicing more opinions per minute if they were alone, they might want to avoid "loafing" by coming up with more ideas themselves. They are unlikely, though, to realize what would happen in a "nominal group" condition that they never experience firsthand. Instead, they simply match "what everyone else is doing" (Paulus & Dzindolet, 1993).

To test this "misperceiving the normal effort level" aspect of social loafing, the experimenters in one study told brainstorming students the number of ideas that are typically produced in a 25-minute brainstorming session on the "thumbs problem" (Paulus & Dzindolet, 1993, Experiment 5). The investigators told students who brainstormed in real four-person groups that the average individual produces one idea per minute, so that to match the nominal groups they would have to produce one hundred ideas as a group. They told students who brainstormed as individuals that the average individual produces 65 ideas in 25 minutes, which is much higher than the actual average. Real groups produced many more ideas when they were given the "100 ideas" standard than when they were not. Although nominal groups also improved when they were given a higher standard, it is evident from the results that real groups could do better than they usually do if they thought that they were *expected* to do better. The most impressive aspect of the results is that, when they were merely made aware of what nominal groups usually accomplish, real interacting groups produced approximately the same number of ideas as did uninstructed nominal groups. The irony of the results is that, although brainstorming was originally conceived as an additive task, it may appear to participants like a conjunctive task, in which they try to match the weakest rather than the strongest group member.

■ ILLUSION OF EFFECTIVENESS

One of the most intriguing aspects of productivity losses is that people who brainstorm in groups are very satisfied with themselves and with the group product (Paulus et al., 1993). Brainstorming "is still widely used in business organizations and advertising agencies, in spite of consistent empirical evidence that people produce many more ideas when they work individually rather than in groups" (Stroebe et al., 1992, p. 643). In study after study, people who brainstorm as individuals say they would have produced *more,* not fewer, ideas had they worked in groups. People who work in groups are also more satisfied with what they accomplish than are people who work as individuals. Finally, people who work in groups say they enjoyed it more and felt stimulated by other people's contributions, even though the evidence shows conclusively that they were not. What accounts for this "illusion of group effectiveness"?

One possibility, already alluded to, is that people who work in groups do not realize how much they might have produced had they worked alone (Paulus et al., 1993). Another possibility is that, in the process of developing and expanding on other group members' ideas (which is what the brainstorming instructions tell them to do), participants appropriate the ideas as their own. Without realizing it, they overestimate how much of each idea that they "worked on" was their own (Wicklund, 1989). To test this possibility, the investigators in one study had high school girls brainstorm about how to improve traffic safety (Stroebe et al., 1992). As usual, girls who brainstormed as individuals produced more ideas per person than did girls who brainstormed in groups, but they falsely believed that they would have done better in groups.

Two weeks later, the girls were given a deck of cards, each card of which contained one of the ideas that had been presented in their own real or nominal group. The girls tried to identify the ideas that they had presented, the ideas that had occurred to them but that someone else had presented, and the ideas that had never occurred to them. Although girls who participated in the real groups did not claim to have presented more than the expected 25% of ideas in a four-person group, they were much more likely than girls who participated in nominal groups to claim that an idea someone else presented had also occurred to them. Girls from the real groups claimed that 61% of the total ideas presented during the group session had occurred to them, even though someone else presented most of the ideas while they were waiting to speak. Girls from nominal groups took credit for having thought of only 47% of the ideas presented by themselves and the three other individuals.

Although we cannot know whether these claims of having ideas "stolen" by others were true or exaggerated, overlapping ideas might be more likely in a group than individual setting. The "conversation" might take a particular direction (for example, hidden monitoring devices on roadways to improve traffic safety) that lends itself to the same types of ideas (cameras, computers, embedded grids, and so on) occurring to several group members simultaneously. Members of brainstorming groups might have many related ideas that someone else announces first. They might also engage in the types of self-serving biases described in Chapter 5, in which they falsely remember having made more of a contribution than they did, or in the social or group identity processes described in Chapter 1 and elsewhere in the text, in which they draw positive conclusions about a group to which they (and their good ideas) belong.

GROUP POLARIZATION

Do groups make different decisions than do the individual group members? When jury members are discussing how long to keep a convicted murder in prison, for instance, they must decide whether to take a cautious approach and keep the person in jail for a long time or to take a more risky approach and recommend a sentence that might allow early release of a potentially dangerous person. Groups that discuss such issues arrive at different conclusions than do individuals. Specifically, as suggested by the results for authoritarians and nonauthoritarians in the jury study at the start of this chapter, group discussion often elicits more extreme or polarized decisions. As the jury example illustrates, more extreme decisions are neither "good" nor "bad." They do, however, show one way in which groups operate differently than do individuals.

In an early attempt to discover whether groups make different decisions than do individuals, the experimenters asked college students to consider hypothetical scenarios in which a protagonist had to choose between risky and conservative courses of action (Wallach, Kogan, & Bem, 1962). In one such scenario, a prisoner of war had to choose between attempting escape, with the risk of execution if caught, versus remaining in the prison camp under very harsh conditions. In another scenario, the captain of a college football team, in the last seconds of the "big game," had to choose between a risky play that would lead to sure victory or defeat, versus a more cautious play that would almost certainly tie the game. For each scenario, the students were asked to indicate the lowest chance of success for which they would recommend the risky alternative. Should the risky football play, for example, have one chance in ten of succeeding, three chances in ten, five chances in ten, seven chances in ten, or nine chances in ten before the student would give it a try?

After the students had made their individual recommendations, the experimenter surprised them by saying that he wanted them to discuss each scenario as a group and to arrive at a group recommendation. On most of the scenarios, the students as individuals had recommended relatively risky courses of action. They might have required only four chances of success in ten, for instance, to recommend the risky football play. After they discussed such scenarios as a group, however, they arrived at a more extreme recommendation that the risky play be attempted even if the chances of success were only three in ten (Stoner, 1961). On other scenarios where students initially favored caution, however, group discussion produced an even more cautious decision. According to the **group polarization** phenomenon, groups reach more polarized decisions (more extreme on the side of the issue that the majority of group members initially favor) than the average group member would have reached as an individual. Group polarization involves more than merely "going along with the group." People who adopt more polarized opinions as a result of group discussion retain those more polarized opinions after the discussion has ended. Students who participated in groups that made more extreme recommendations than their own initial recommendations for the prisoner-of-war escape or the football play, for instance, reported individual opinions similar to the group's (and different from their own initial opinions) two to six weeks after the experiment (Wallach et al., 1962).

Following group discussion, group members who fall predominantly on one side or the other of an issue adopt more extreme jury recommendations, more positive or negative attitudes on a variety of issues, more extreme opinions of whether a behavior is ethical, and more extreme judgments of both other people and consumer products (Baron, Roper, & Baron, 1974; Johnson & Andrews, 1971; Moscovici & Zavalloni, 1969; Myers & Bishop, 1970; Myers & Lamm, 1976; Turner, 1991). Group decisions also produce more extreme gambling at the racetrack and at the blackjack table, more extreme estimates of how far a light is moving in a dark room, and more extreme estimates of how wide categories are (Baron & Roper, 1976; Blascovich, Ginsberg, & Howe, 1975; Blascovich, Ginsberg, & Veach, 1975; Knox & Safford, 1976; Vidmar, 1974). For instance, when students are told the average number of lynchings per year in the United States between 1900 and 1940 and are asked to estimate the largest and smallest number of lynchings in any one year, they arrive at more extreme estimates of both the largest and the smallest value when they discuss the issue in groups than when they make the same estimates as individuals (Vidmar, 1974). Finally, groups are more likely than individual decision makers to throw good money after bad by committing additional resources to a failing business enterprise in which they have "too much invested to quit" (Whyte, 1993). In short, group polarization is a general phenomenon, not a phenomenon restricted to risky versus cautious decisions.

Group polarization goes beyond mere conformity. If the six individual members of a group initially want 3, 3, 4, 4, 5, and 5 chances of success to recommend a risky course of action such as early parole for a convict, mere conformity would dictate that the individuals would all converge, during discussion, on the individual average or "consensus" of 4. The more likely result, however, confirmed in hundreds of group polarization studies, is that the group decision will be more extreme than the individual average (Cartwright, 1971; Dion, Baron, & Miller, 1970; Isenberg, 1986; Myers & Lamm, 1976; Pruitt, 1971a,b). It seems as though the two individuals who were initially at 3 "won" and somehow persuaded the others to join them (Laughlin & Earley, 1982).

Do groups have "a mind of their own"? Is group polarization related to other inexplicable events like lynchings, where no one member of the group would act so extremely if he or she had to act as an individual? Because group polarization seems to be an instance of the group being "more than the sum

Are people more likely to throw good money after bad when they gamble in groups?

TABLE 15.4	Three Types of Influence That Lead to Group Polarization		
TYPE OF INFLUENCE	**GOAL**	**THOUGHTS**	**ACTIONS**
informational influence	to be right	attend to persuasive arguments	shift opinion in direction indicated by novel, valid arguments
normative influence	to be likable	discover other members' opinions	adopt an opinion that is more socially desirable than the average opinion
social identity	draw self-esteem from the group	misperceive the group's average opinion	match or conform to the misperceived in-group norm

of its parts," social psychologists have devoted considerable effort to understanding how the phenomenon works. The best available evidence implicates three processes: the informational influence of persuasive arguments, the normative influence of social comparison, and the biasing influence of social identity. The three processes are outlined in Table 15.4. Informational influence and normative influence, as explained in other chapters, represent one of the major themes that recurs throughout this book: that people want to be right, but they also want to be likable (Baumeister & Leary, 1995; Snyder, 1993, 1994; Swann, 1987, 1990). People are swayed by information because they want to make correct decisions. People are also swayed by prevailing norms of acceptable behavior because they want to appear likable—both to themselves and to others.

■ INFORMATIONAL INFLUENCE

Informational influence occurs because people want to be right. In trying to arrive at the correct answer, they are sometimes swayed by the additional information or persuasive arguments that other people impart or are expected to impart (Trafimow & Davis, 1993). When people get together in a group to discuss an issue on which a majority of group members agree, they are likely to advance arguments that lie predominantly on one rather than the other side of the issue. If twelve jurors were individually leaning toward a guilty verdict, for example, some of them might mention arguments for acquittal, but most of the arguments expressed in the jury deliberations would be on the side of the question that the individual jurors initially favored.

Because people want to be right, as shown in Table 15.4, they pay attention to and later remember the persuasive arguments that are presented during the group discussion. They are more likely to remember arguments that seem new and valid than arguments that they already know or arguments that seem questionable (Vinokur & Burnstein, 1978). If 10/12ths of the arguments are on the same side of the issue as an individual group member initially favored, then it is likely that 10/12ths of the arguments that the group member perceives as novel and valid will also be on that side. When they discuss the issue with other like-minded individuals, that is, group members are likely to learn about additional compelling reasons for favoring the side that they already favored. When they do, they become all the more convinced that the initially favored side of the issue is "correct," so they adopt more extreme positions.

As a concrete example of informational influence in group polarization, the experimenters in one study asked a local police department to introduce them to active burglars (Cromwell, Marks, Olson, & Avary, 1991). By offering $50 and a guarantee of anonymity, the experimenters induced 27 male and three female burglars to describe burglaries that they had committed. The burglars showed the experimenters sites that they had recently "hit" and other sites that they considered too risky, and tried to explain the differences. Later, the burglars rated their own and other burglars' sites on how attractive and vulnerable the sites were for burglary. The burglars were interviewed alone. They were also interviewed in groups, in the company of their usual co-offenders.

Do burglars take more or fewer risks when they work as a team rather than alone?

The burglars' group decisions were more cautious than their individual decisions. Although the burglars claimed that they took greater risks when they had accomplices, group discussion more often resulted in eliminating potential sites that individual burglars had deemed attractive. For one site that was rated by a group, for example, the first burglar rated it attractive, but a second burglar said, "Don't you see that dude inside that house [across the street] watching through the curtains?", after which both burglars agreed that the site was much too risky. For another site, two male burglars thought it was attractive, but a woman accomplice noted that the time of day (3 P.M.) made it likely that children would be getting out of school and playing nearby. When she offered this additional information, the other burglars immediately agreed that the location was too risky for an immediate "hit." The burglars tended to be cautious as individuals, but even more cautious in groups, because it took only one burglar to notice a danger sign for a site to be dismissed as unattractive. Group decisions were strongly influenced by new information that seemed valid.

Persuasive arguments also affect group polarization in laboratory studies. Merely reading an unbalanced set of arguments that contains more arguments on one side than the other is enough to produce polarization without any group discussion (Vinokur & Burnstein, 1974). The number and the rated persuasiveness of arguments are also more important to group polarization than is the number of people who take one or the other position (Burnstein, Vinokur, & Trope, 1973; Madsen, 1978). Even in groups where members merely state their initial positions without advancing any arguments, polarization occurs when the individuals are encouraged to think about the arguments that *might* have been advanced. It does not occur when the individuals are distracted by another task so that they cannot generate likely arguments for themselves (Burnstein & Vinokur, 1975). Finally, group polarization follows the preponderance of arguments even in groups where individuals are not sure that the arguments presented represent the other group members' true opinions (Burnstein & Vinokur, 1973). An imbalance of persuasive arguments obviously predisposes groups to reach more extreme positions than would the average group member (Hinsz & Davis, 1984).

■ NORMATIVE INFLUENCE

Persuasive arguments, however, do not explain every instance of group polarization. Another important determinant of group polarization, as shown in the middle row of Table 15.4, is normative influence. One of the major themes of this book is that people may want to be right, but they also want to be likable. They want to get along with other members of their own group and they fear being rejected (Kruglanski & Webster, 1991). In the interests of social harmony, they sometimes go along with what they perceive as the group consensus or "norm." They agree with opinions that the majority consider socially desirable.

A group discussion lets individuals discover other people's opinions—lets them find out what the group norm or socially desirable position is (Kaplan, Schaefer, & Zinkiewicz, 1994). Juries, for instance, discuss information when they first begin to deliberate, but switch to discussing group norms as they near the end of deliberation (Hansen, Schaefer, & Lawless, 1993). Once they have discovered the opinions of other group members, they are not content merely to adopt the consensus. Instead, in a process known as "social comparison," they want to compare favorably to the other group members. To do so, they adopt an opinion that is even more on the socially desirable side than is the average opinion (Sanders & Baron, 1977).

With everyone trying to look "just a little better" than average, group polarization is inevitable. If group members discover, for example, that their initial individual opinions are predominantly on the risky side at 3, 3, 4, 4, 5, and 5 chances in 10 of success for an early parole recommendation or any other important decision, the average position might be at 4, but the only way to look a little better than average would be to advocate 3. During the discussion, therefore, the 4s and 5s shift toward portraying themselves as more on the socially desirable side than average and the group arrives at a consensus of 3. In other words, normative influence produces group polarization because people want to be positively different from others.

Normative influence occurs in interesting ways. First, people suffer from **pluralistic ignorance,** which occurs when each individual in a group falsely assumes that other group members know more than he or she does. One example of pluralistic ignorance occurs when each student in a class is afraid to ask the teacher a question for fear of "looking dumb," because everyone else *must* have understood or else someone would be asking a question. Another example occurs when students are asked to estimate their fellow students' initial opinions on risky-versus-cautious decisions like the POW escape and the football play. For decisions that normally produce group polarization toward risk, students falsely believe that other students have a more moderate opinion than their own. They also admire most a position more extreme than their own (Levinger & Schneider, 1969). For other types of decisions as well, decisions that have nothing to do with risk versus caution, people falsely believe that others espouse a more neutral stance than their own (Myers & Bishop, 1971).

False beliefs lay the groundwork for two discoveries during subsequent group discussion. The first discovery is that the average other group member holds an opinion as extreme as their own. The second discovery is that (for most group members) at least one other person holds an opinion more extreme than their own. These two discoveries, in turn, lead to two consequences that produce group polarization. First, people who discover that they hold an average opinion on the desirable side of an issue are not content to be merely average. According to social comparison theory (discussed in greater detail in Chapter 5), people want to compare themselves favorably with others of their own kind. Thus they try to outdo the average other group member and be "holier than thou." Second, people who discover that at least one other member holds a more extreme opinion are "released from inhibition" to adopt a position more like their initial "ideal." They initially stated a less-than-ideal position because they did not want to appear immoderate, but once they know that another person is willing to stick his or her neck out they feel free to become more extreme themselves.

One study tested both social comparison and release from inhibition in group polarization (Myers, 1978). The experimenter asked some students their individual opinions on four decisions that normally produce group polarization toward risk and on four other decisions that normally produce group polarization toward caution. Subsequently, one group of other students did or did not receive information about how the average student viewed the issue (social comparison information). A second group did or did not receive information about the percentage of their peers who held an extreme position (a basis for release from inhibition). Although there was no group and no discussion, students' opinions polarized (became more risky on the "risky" decisions and more cautious on the "cautious" decisions). When they discovered that the average student's position was as extreme as their own, students took the "social comparison" route to normative influence. They adopted positions more extreme than the average student's. When they discovered that some of their peers had positions more extreme than their own, students took the "release from inhibition" route to normative influence. They adopted positions more similar to those held by their most extreme peers, whom they most admired. The study thus showed that both social comparison and release from inhibition exert normative influence on group polarization.

Several other studies have shown the importance of normative influence in producing group polarization. First, polarization occurs even for decisions on which there appear to be no rational persuasive arguments, such as category widths and how far a light is moving (Baron & Roper, 1976; Vidmar, 1974). Second, polarization occurs when group members can only announce their positions, but not add any additional information (Teger & Pruitt, 1969). Third, people polarize their initial positions merely because they are told that people who hold more extreme positions are more intelligent or have greater ability (Goethals & Zanna, 1979; Jellison & Riskind, 1970). Fourth, people shift even toward a "fake" norm that does *not* represent the average peer's opinion (Baron, Monson, & Baron, 1973). Fifth, the more discrepant the "most admired" position is from an individual's own initial opinion, the more that individual shifts his or her opinion during the group discussion (Singleton, 1979). Finally, group polarization occurs even when group members already know all the possible persuasive arguments and additional information in advance (Zuber, Crott, & Werner, 1992). These studies combine to suggest that, although much of group polarization might occur merely because of informational influence, an additional impetus comes from normative influence.

■ SOCIAL IDENTITY

Finally, as the bottom row of Table 15.4 shows, group polarization also occurs because people want a positive social identity (Turner, 1991). As described in an earlier section of this chapter, people exaggerate distinctions between their own group and other groups and perceive their own group as "better." During group discussion for which it is explicit or implicit that other groups might reach a different conclusion, therefore, members misperceive the in-group consensus as more extreme than it is (McGarty, Turner, Hogg, David, & Wetherell, 1992). They shift their own opinions to adopt or conform to the misperceived or "extremitized" in-group norm. The social identity route to group polarization, then, is very similar to the normative influence route. The major difference between the two routes is that the normative influence process occurs because people initially underestimate the extremity of other people's opinions. The social identity process, in contrast, occurs because, during the group discussion, people *overestimate* the extremity of their fellow in-group members' opinions.

In one study of social identity's contribution to group polarization, students gave their opinions on the issue of whether standardized tests such as the SAT and GRE should be retained or abolished as criteria for admission to institutes of higher education (Mackie & Cooper, 1984). Students who moderately favored retention subsequently participated in a study in which, they were told, two groups of three people were going to discuss to consensus the issue of standardized tests. According to the experimenter, the group that deliberated best, regardless of what decision they reached, would receive a monetary prize. The experimenter also told some of the students that the group had already held one discussion and had two more sessions scheduled, but that one of the members had had to drop out of the study. They would be taking that person's place in the last two discussions, after listening to a tape recording of the first session to "get the idea of what a typical session is like." Other students were told that they were listening to the *other* group's first session. In reality, although some students thought it was their own group and other students thought it was the other group, all students listened to exactly the same tape recording, which was either of a group that seemed to favor retention or of a group that seemed to favor abolition.

When the tape had ended, the experimenter asked each student to estimate "where the group on the tape would have formed their consensus on the issue." The experimenter also asked each student to estimate his or her own position. Students perceived the group's consensus as more extreme when they thought it was their own group than when they thought it was a group to which they did not belong. Students also estimated their own group's position as more extreme than did other students who merely listened to the tape, without thinking that they would be a member of either the same or a different group. When asked for their own opinions, students matched rather than tried to surpass their group's opinions. The students' post-discussion opinions were *not* more extreme (that is, they were *not* more on the retention side for the retention discussion or more on the abolition side for the abolition discussion) than the misestimated group norm. Similar results occurred in other studies, which showed that the social identity route to group polarization is more likely to occur when participants focus on their role as group members than when they focus on themselves as individuals, when participants are reminded of the differences between contrasting groups, when the in-group is competing with a rival out-group, and when the in-group is composed of friends rather than strangers (Doise, 1969; Hogg, Turner, & Davidson, 1990; Mackie, 1986; Runyan, 1974; Turner, Wetherell, & Hogg, 1989; van Knippenberg & Wilkie, 1988). These factors may have in common that they increase participants' involvement in the decision.

■ DECISION TYPES AND DECISION RULES

The three routes to group polarization–informational influence, normative influence, and social identity–depend on the type of decision the group is making and the decision rule the group is using (Rugs & Kaplan, 1993). Some group decisions are more "intellective" and some are more "judgmental." Intellective issues have demonstrably correct answers. When a jury awards compensatory damages (for instance, lost wages and medical bills) for a defendant's negligence, jury members are making an intellective decision. If all the facts were available, jury members could sum the defendant's actual costs and arrive at a demonstrably correct answer. Judgmental issues, in contrast, have no demonstrably correct answer. They depend instead on preferences or moral values. When a jury awards exemplary or punitive damages, the decision is judgmental because it depends on subjective judgments about what constitutes the proper, just, or "correct" amount to set an example and to deter others. Because intellective decisions have a demonstrably correct answer, the best persuasive arguments should "win." The route to group polarization for intellective decisions is more likely to be through informational influence than through normative influence. Because judgmental decisions depend on people's preferences and values, group norms (correctly or incorrectly perceived) should prevail. The route to group polarization for judgmental decisions is more likely to be through normative considerations and through social identity.

The impact of task type, however, may depend on the decision rule that the group is using. Some studies of group polarization required group members to discuss the issue until they arrived at a single decision with which all members agreed. When a group must reach a unanimous decision, as might be the case for a jury deliberating an accused murderer's guilt or innocence, normative influences can be brought to bear. If 11 members of a jury have one opinion and one jury member disagrees, members who are in the majority can apply considerable social pressure for conformity, which they are likely to do when the decision rule requires unanimity. The dynamics of a group discussion are far different when majority group members realize that they can simply outvote the minority rather than having to persuade them to change their opinions.

Instructions to reach a unanimous decision presumably elicit such *normative* concerns as people's desire to be likable, their desire to support the ingroup, their personal involvement in the decision, their desire to look better than or to conform with their colleagues, and their admiration for people who voice more extreme arguments. Instructions merely to indicate individual opinions before and after sharing arguments emphasize *informational* concerns and make it unlikely that individual participants will experience a sense of group or social identity. They are likely to change their opinions only if they hear new, valid persuasive arguments. In other words, a unanimous decision rule offers the most opportunity for group polarization to occur through normative influence or through social identity, whereas a majority decision rule offers more opportunity for group polarization to occur through informational influence (Kaplan & Miller, 1987).

In one study that compared intellective and judgmental decisions under unanimous versus majority decision rules, college women read a legal case in which the defendant (a furnace manufacturer) was clearly negligent (Kaplan & Miller, 1987). The plaintiff, who was injured when a poorly constructed furnace exploded, asked for compensatory damages higher than the furnace manufacturer was willing to pay. The women first expressed their individual opinions about awards for both compensatory damages (an intellective decision) and exemplary damages (a judgmental decision). Then they deliberated on both compensatory and exemplary damages in six-member "juries." Some of the juries had to reach a unanimous decision; others needed only a majority.

Figure 15.6 shows the average dollar amount that the women awarded to the defendant before and after discussion. The most important aspect of the figure is that group polarization occurred only when the women had to reach a unanimous decision about a judgmental issue (exemplary damages). Women in the other three experimental conditions did not change their opinions from before to after the group discussion. Presumably, the issue of compensatory damages had such an obviously correct answer that only the relevant information mattered and group normative pressures were rendered ineffective. The issue of exemplary damages, in contrast, posed a judgmental dilemma for which people might, if the decision rule were favorable, look to the opinions of others for guidance. With a majority decision rule, the women could stick to their initial positions and ignore normative and social identity pressures. With a unanimous decision rule, they could not.

The experimenters also tape-recorded and later analyzed what the women said during their "jury" deliberations. Some of the women's statements were clearly informational. They referred to facts, to details of the testimony, or to

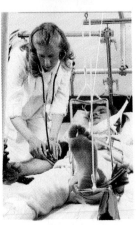

Would a jury award larger or smaller damages to this injured worker if they had to reach a unanimous decision?

FIGURE 15.6

Unanimous decisions encourage group polarization on judgmental issues.

Graph shows compensatory and exemplary damages "juries" with two decision rules awarded to an injured worker before and after group deliberation (Kaplan & Miller, 1987)

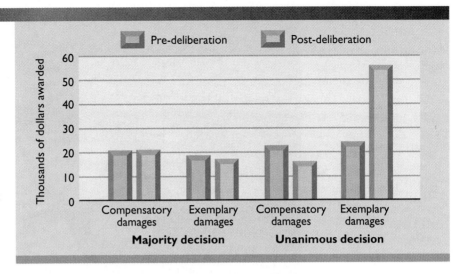

dollar amounts of expenses that the defendant had incurred. Other of the women's statements were clearly normative. They reflected values, norms, preferences, and social pressure. One example of a normative statement was "do what the majority thinks is right." As expected, the women used more informational than normative statements when discussing compensatory damages. They also used more normative than informational statements when discussing exemplary damages. Use of normative statements reached its peak in unanimous decision juries that were discussing exemplary damages.

Group polarization, then, is most likely for issues that have no correct answer—such as whether to attempt an escape or to try a risky football play—and in situations where group members are motivated to achieve a unanimous consensus. It is small wonder that revolutionary groups in many countries, when they adopted courses of action more daring than anyone might attempt as an individual, had as their implicit or explicit motto "United we stand. Divided we fall."

GROUPTHINK

Groups, like individuals, make decisions that are at times successful and at other times spectacularly unsuccessful (Janis, 1972, 1982, 1989; Tetlock, Peterson, McGuire, Chang, & Feld, 1992). Consider these seven decisions made at the highest levels of the U.S. government.

1. In 1941, Admiral Kimmel, commander-in-chief of the U.S. Pacific Fleet, met with high-level staff members at his headquarters in Hawaii to discuss whether they should prepare for possible attack by Japan or continue with normal training exercises. The admiral and his advisers, all of whom shared similar backgrounds and perspectives, discounted many warnings of imminent attack and decided to continue with business as usual. As a result, U.S. forces were completely unprepared for the devastating Japanese attack on Pearl Harbor (Prange, 1986).

2. In 1947, U.S. Secretary of State Marshall asked George Kennan to produce a plan for rebuilding a European economy shattered by World War II. Kennan assembled a group of thinkers from very diverse backgrounds, who engaged in wide open debate, encouraging and then mercilessly criticizing alternative plans. As leader of the group, Kennan participated actively, but he

Why do brillant military leaders sometimes make dumb decisions?

encouraged the others to attack his ideas as relentlessly as any others. The result was the Marshall Plan, a strikingly successful strategic decision. The United States invested huge sums of money in rebuilding the economies of all European nations who wanted to participate, including vanquished Germany. Most historians believe that the Marshall Plan kept Western Europe from embracing communism and forged trading partnerships that helped the United States to prosper (Mee, 1984).

3. In 1950, the United States had repulsed a North Korean attack on South Korea and had to decide whether to call a halt at the original demarcation line or to invade North Korea. President Harry S Truman met in secret with his cabinet, all of whom agreed with the president's opinion that North Korea had to be punished. Not one of the president's advisers anticipated that when U.S. troops reached the border between North Korea and the Chinese province of Manchuria, China would become concerned enough to send hundreds of thousands of soldiers into the fray, dragging the war on for three more bloody years before both sides agreed on a stalemate (Kaufman, 1986).

4. In 1961, Cuban President Fidel Castro was ranting against the United States in bellicose speeches and was confiscating U.S. property without compensation. Thousands of Cubans, who had fled to the United States when Castro instituted a communist government in Cuba, wanted U.S. backing for an invasion that would re-take the island. President John F. Kennedy, who had made supporting the anti-Castro exiles a campaign promise, held secret meetings with his cabinet and advisers to decide whether to back an invasion. Kennedy made his own support known, cut off debate, and had his brother, Robert Kennedy, urge doubters to support the invasion plan. When the invasion at the Bay of Pigs failed, Cuba turned away from the United States and became a "client state" of the Soviet Union (Vandenbrouke, 1984).

5. In 1962, a spy plane spotted the construction of installations on Cuba for nuclear missiles aimed at the United States. President Kennedy assembled essentially the same team that had made the disastrous Bay of Pigs invasion decision, but this time he deliberately stayed away from early meetings, solicited advice from experts in different fields, and told his brother to play devil's

advocate, trying to shoot down all proposals. Instead of the unanimous backing for the Bay of Pigs decision, Kennedy had only a simple majority for the eventual decision, which was to blockade Cuba, stopping especially any ships that appeared to be carrying nuclear missiles from the Soviet Union. After a tense stand-off at sea, the Soviet Union agreed to withdraw not only the 20 missiles on the ships, but also the 20 nuclear missiles that were already in Cuba, which Castro had asked them to launch at the United States. A possible nuclear holocaust was narrowly averted (Blight & Welch, 1989).

6. From 1965 through 1968, President Lyndon B. Johnson and his advisers met frequently. At each meeting, they decided to escalate U.S. involvement in the war in Vietnam. During their meetings, Johnson let it be known that disagreeing with him was the same as being disloyal to the country and that those who did not want to widen the war were "losing their effectiveness." Johnson and his advisers continued to pursue a goal of military victory despite mounting evidence that the goal was unattainable. In 1965, the war cost U.S. taxpayers $25 billion and resulted in the deaths of 26 U.S. military personnel per day. By 1968, the figures were $70 million and 280 deaths a day! Eventually, the United States had to admit defeat and withdraw ignominiously (Donovan, 1984).

7. In 1972, burglars were caught in the Democratic Party's national headquarters at the Watergate apartment complex in Washington, D.C. Three of the burglars were on the payroll of the Committee to Re-Elect the President (CREEP). When President Richard M. Nixon and his closest advisers met in secret to decide how to handle the affair, they concluded that it was best to pay "hush money" to the three burglars, so that the burglary could not be connected with the administration. Nixon let his advisers know that he favored a continuing coverup, which they supported despite mounting evidence that it could not work, because too many people knew. Eventually, when Nixon's part in the coverup was revealed, he was forced to resign in disgrace (Kutler, 1990).

When we examine these seven momentous group decisions, what separates the two good decisions (the Marshall Plan and the Cuban Missile Crisis) from the five bad decisions? Is it merely that some group decisions happened to have successful outcomes and others did not? No. Good group decisions are arrived at in a different way from bad group decisions, which emerge from a process that has been disparagingly called "groupthink" (Janis, 1972, 1982, 1989). **Groupthink** occurs when group members seek concurrence, consensus, and unanimity more than they seek the best possible alternative (Janis, 1972, 1982). Table 15.5 shows three important contributors to groupthink—three factors that separate the two good group decisions from the five bad ones. First, cohesive groups sometimes make poorer quality decisions than do incohesive groups. "Cohesive" in this context means more than merely members being similar to one another or liking each other (Longley & Pruitt, 1980). Cohesiveness means wanting to be identified with the group and drawing social identity or collective self-esteem from the group, so that group members are not secure enough to voice disagreement. (Berenthal & Insko, 1993; Turner, 1991) Admiral Kimmel's naval officers were all from similar backgrounds and greatly valued the prestige of being part of the commander's inner group, as did President Nixon's advisers. They cared too much about being part of the inner circle to "make waves" by disagreeing with the consensus.

Second, groups that are under stress sometimes seek consensus prematurely and make poorer quality decisions than do groups that are not under stress—especially the stress caused by external threats to the group's positive identity (Janis, 1982). All seven decisions were arrived at under tremendous stress, because the consequences of failure were so catastrophic. No one wants

TABLE 15.5	Three Factors That Contribute to a Group's Concern with Consensus (Discouraging Disagreement, Overlooking Shared Information, and Reaching Premature Conclusion) and Generate Poor Quality Group Decisions (No Contingency Plans, Illusion of Vulnerability, and Possible Entrapment)
FACTOR	**UNDERLYING MECHANISMS**
Cohesiveness and Social Identity	group members are similar to and like each other
	group members draw collective self-esteem from the group
	group members fear the group's rejection
Stressful Threat to Group Identity	group members fear the group's performance will be evaluated negatively
	group has experienced previous failures
	group is faced with moral dilemmas
Restrictive Decision Procedures	group leader is directive
	group is isolated from outside influence
	group requires unanimous agreement

to be identified as one of the "inner circle" that made a wrong decision when the fate of the country (or the world) was at stake. Stressful threat occurs when the group may be evaluated negatively, when the group has had previous failures, and when the group faces a moral dilemma such as that faced by the Nixon White House on whether to help cover up immoral actions. Stressful threat, as we shall see, interacts with group cohesiveness in an interesting way.

Third, groups are more likely to engage in groupthink when they follow restrictive decision procedures. When the leader is too directive, as was President Truman on invading North Korea, President Kennedy on the Bay of Pigs, President Johnson on escalating the Vietnam War, and President Nixon on covering up the Watergate scandal, group members are afraid to voice disagreement (Flowers, 1977; Leana, 1985). Also, when the group's deliberations are conducted in secret, isolated from outside opinions and information, as were many of the five disastrous decisions, new perspectives are not introduced and groupthink is a likely outcome (McCauley, 1989). Finally, as we shall see, requiring unanimity rather than a simple majority can have important consequences for group deliberation and for the eventual decision.

When groupthink sets in, as shown in Table 15.5, the deliberation process becomes more concerned with seeking consensus than with seeking a correct answer. Competing ideas are not encouraged, group members are pressured into conformity, and criticism and open debate are discouraged or cut short. The discussion is simplistic, with frequent references to positive in-group symbols like "the honor of the nation" or "the credibility of the Presidential office" (Tetlock, 1979). In their haste to reach consensus and to maintain group harmony, members focus their discussion on facts and opinions that they all know and share, at the expense of unshared information that individual members might otherwise have shared with the rest of the group (Gigone & Hastie, 1993; Larson, Foster-Fishman, & Keys, 1994; Tindale, Smith, Thomas, Filkins, & Sheffey, in press). The group also reaches a conclusion prematurely. The initial consensus is given the benefit of doubt, other alternatives are ignored, and possible drawbacks of the preferred solution are not examined (Stasser, 1992; Stasser & Stewart, 1992).

Consensus-seeking deliberations produce poor quality decisions. No one thinks to develop contingency plans, because the group develops the "illusion of invulnerability" that their plan cannot possibly fail (Janis, 1982). In the service of the illusion, group members rationalize their decision and negatively evaluate unchosen alternatives. When subsequent problems arise, the group is so convinced that it made a wise decision that group members cannot escape from the trap of committing more and more resources to a failing enterprise. Groupthink creates and exacerbates poor quality decisions. Content analysis of historical documents shows that the three factors—an insecure need for group cohesiveness, stressful threats to a positive group identity, and restrictive decision procedures—all contribute to seek concurrence rather than the best possible alternative, but restrictive decision procedures may be the biggest culprit (Tetlock et al., 1992). Beyond content analysis of historical documents, however, social psychologists have tried to bring the groupthink phenomenon into the experimental laboratory, where it can be examined more precisely.

■ GROUP COHESIVENESS AND STRESSFUL THREAT

In one study of groupthink, the investigators manipulated both group cohesiveness and stressful threat (Turner, Pratkanis, Probasco, & Leve, 1992, Experiment 1). To manipulate group cohesiveness, the investigators gave names to each of the "high cohesiveness" groups and had group members wear tags that prominently displayed the group's name. Manipulations such as this had successfully induced social identity in other studies discussed previously in this chapter. "Low cohesiveness" groups, in contrast, received neither name tags nor group identities. To manipulate threat, the investigators told "high threat" groups that their group's session would be videotaped and used in subsequent training classes. Experts would use their group's performance to evaluate "dysfunctional group processes." The investigators made no such threatening claims to "low threat" groups.

After these manipulations of cohesiveness and threats, the investigators asked all groups to recommend a solution for an automobile production problem. The problem was that some assembly workers who produced automobile instrument panels had decreased their productivity. An older worker named Joe was letting his work pile up, with the result that the entire assembly line was suffering. Company procedures and environmental conditions rendered some solutions, like hiring additional workers, difficult or impossible. The problem had been used in previous research that rank-ordered the quality of possible solutions (Maier, 1952; Steiner, 1982). Promoting Joe, for instance, is a poor quality solution, removing Joe from his station is a medium quality solution, and rotating workers on an hourly basis (so that pileups do not occur) is a high quality solution.

Figure 15.7 displays the average solution quality for high and low cohesiveness groups when threat was low or high. As the figure shows, cohesiveness and threat interacted in an interesting way. According to previous research, when no threat is present, it is usually an advantage to have a highly cohesive group with a strong sense of group identity (Evans & Dion, 1991). Thus high cohesive groups arrived at better quality decisions than did low cohesive groups in the low threat condition. When threat is high, however, the danger is that cohesiveness will lead to concurrence seeking and to groupthink (Janis, 1972). As can be seen in the figure, high cohesive groups reached poorer quality decisions than did low cohesive groups in the high threat condition. Groupthink,

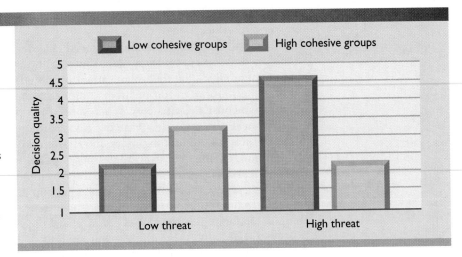

FIGURE 15.7

Group cohesiveness affects decision quality differently depending on whether the group feels threatened.

Graph shows quality of decisions made by two types of groups that were under high or low threat while trying to solve an assembly production problem (Turner, Pratkanis, Probasco, & Leve, 1992)

then, may be viewed as an attempt to avert stressful threats to group identity or collective self-esteem through intragroup agreement (Turner & Pratkanis, in press; Turner et al., 1992).

To support the "stressful threat to collective self-esteem" interpretation of groupthink, two studies showed that when group members do not fear a negative social identity, decision making is not impaired. In the first study, groups tried to solve a "lost at sea" problem that involved ranking the usefulness of various items to survivors of a shipboard fire (Callaway, Marriott, & Esser, 1985). Decision quality was determined by comparing each group's answers to those of experts. The groups were composed either entirely of people who scored high on the personality trait of dominance or entirely of people who scored low on dominance. As predicted, groups with dominant members reported lower levels of anxiety, made more disagreeing statements during their deliberations, and arrived at higher quality decisions. Dominant people have sufficient self-esteem that they voice their own opinions in spite of social pressure. They care very little what other group members think of them when they disagree with the consensus (Edwards, 1954). Dominant people care so little for collective self-esteem that they are unlikely to fall prey to the consensus-seeking of groupthink.

The second study tested whether groupthink can be averted by decreasing threats to collective self-esteem. Groups of college students worked on the previously described automobile production problem with high cohesiveness instructions that maximized group identity and collective self-esteem (Turner et al., 1992, Experiment 3). Some of the groups worked under low threat. The investigators never mentioned possible criticisms. Other groups worked under high threat. The investigators claimed that experts would later critique them for "dysfunctional decision processes." Half of the high threat groups, however, had a good excuse for possible failure. The investigators claimed that the background music being played during the experiment might be very distracting and detrimental to their performance. In reality, the background music was not at all distracting, but the cover story gave group members a good excuse for poor performance, which should have alleviated any perceived threat. Consistent with this prediction, groups in the high threat condition felt more stress and made poorer quality decisions than did groups in the low threat condition, but only when they had no "background music" excuse. When they had a good excuse, they felt no more stress than did the low threat groups and they made decisions just as good as those of the low threat groups.

■ RESTRICTIVE GROUP PROCEDURES

Finally, as shown in Table 15.5, restrictive group decision procedures contribute importantly to groupthink. When the leader is too directive, when the group is isolated from outside perspectives, and when unanimity is required, the likelihood of groupthink increases (Flowers, 1977; Janis, 1982; Leana, 1985). In the seven momentous decisions described previously, in many of which group members merely complied publicly rather than agreed privately, restrictive group procedures undoubtedly contributed to poor quality decisions (McCauley, 1989).

One important procedural flaw in group decision making involves overlooking unshared information. Different members of Admiral Kimmel's staff had different pieces of information that, when combined, would have alerted even the most complacent group members to the impending Japanese attack on Pearl Harbor (Prange, 1986). Unfortunately, high-level staff discussions at Pacific Fleet headquarters were so harmonious that these separate pieces of information remained unshared. Group members concentrated on the reassuring information that they all knew about, at the expense of sharing alarming bits of evidence that were available only to one or two members. Subsequent evidence suggests that Admiral Kimmel and his staff might have followed a more effective procedure and made a better group decision had they regarded the question of a Japanese attack as having a demonstrably correct answer, rather than as merely a judgment call (Stasser, 1991).

In a study that tested the effects of problem-solving perspective on sharing previously unshared information, groups of college students read interviews from a homicide investigation (Stasser & Stewart, 1992). The interviews contained 24 clues that were either incriminating or exonerating for each of three suspects. For convenience, think of the suspects as Mike, Bert, and Ernie. Although each suspect had six incriminating clues, Bert and Ernie also each had three exonerating clues. By combining the six incriminating clues for Mike with the six clues that exonerated Bert and Ernie, it was possible to detect that Mike had both motive and opportunity to commit the murder and that he had attempted to frame Bert. The problem was that all group members knew about the clues that made Bert look like the murderer, whereas only individual group members knew about the separate clues that revealed Mike's guilt and the attempted frame. Only by sharing information and revealing this "hidden profile" of clues could groups arrive at a correct decision.

The investigators told some of the groups that their decision was strictly a judgment. They claimed that detectives had insufficient evidence to charge anyone with the crime and that the group members were to rate the three suspects on how likely each was to have done it. In contrast, the investigators told other groups that there was a demonstrably correct answer—that only one of the suspects could have committed the crime and that it was their task to discover which suspect had done it. As the investigators predicted, groups that perceived the problem as having a correct answer were more likely to discuss and to focus on the unshared information than were groups that perceived the problem as a mere judgment. As a result, "correct answer" groups easily outperformed "judgment" groups in reaching a correct conclusion. When people assume that there is no correct answer, they do not share with each other information that might avert premature consensus on an incorrect decision.

Another important procedural flaw in group decision making involves using an inappropriate decision rule. During the disastrous Bay of Pigs deliberations, President Kennedy and his brother Robert exerted considerable pressure on cabinet members to agree, so that the group's actions would have unanimous consent (Vandenbrouke, 1984). During the successful Cuban Missile Crisis deliberations, in contrast, President Kennedy required only a majority rather than a unanimous decision (Blight & Welch, 1989). Although unanimous decisions may have much to recommend them, evidence from laboratory research suggests that requiring a unanimous rather than a majority decision may be detrimental to some types of decisions, especially those that involve "psychological entrapment." Psychological entrapment occurs when people "escalate their commitment to a previously chosen, though failing, course of action to justify or 'make good on' prior investments" (Brockner & Rubin, 1985, p. 5). It is like throwing good money (or lives) after bad, just as President Johnson and his advisers did during their escalation of the Vietnam War (Donovan, 1984). A unanimous decision rule, by emphasizing group consensus and discouraging dissenting opinions, may be more likely than a majority decision rule to invite groupthink and psychological entrapment.

In a relevant study, groups of Japanese college women who wanted to teach nursery school had to decide which of two expensive trampolines to buy for a school playground (Kameda & Sugimori, 1993). Some groups decided by a coin flip, whereas others decided either by a majority decision rule or by a unanimous decision rule. After receiving each month's report on how many children were using the trampoline, the women had to decide whether to keep paying on the purchase contract or not. If they decided to cancel the contract, the nursery school would lose all the money that they had spent up to that point, because the manufacturer would take back the trampoline.

Would you and your friends continue to pay for this expensive school equipment even if the children stopped using it?

Although 80% of the children used the trampoline during the first month, the percentage dropped to 38% in the second month, followed by 12, 6, 4, 2%, and so on. With each passing month, the benefits to the children decreased, but the cumulative loss of canceling the purchase contract increased. Groups that were responsible for choosing the trampoline in the first place, whether by majority or by unanimous decision, continued to "throw good money after bad" longer than did groups that merely followed the course indicated by a coin flip. Also, groups that used a unanimous decision rule became especially entrapped. They kept paying on the purchase contract for eight months, long after it had become apparent that they were wasting the nursery school's valuable funds.

When they were given an opportunity to reevaluate canceling the contract, unanimous decision rule groups continued to justify their initial decision by rating cancellation much more negatively than did either the coin flip groups or the majority decision groups. Rather than revising their course of action, the unanimous decision rule groups followed the groupthink procedure of seeking consensus. They concentrated on developing "rationalizations in line with shared illusions about the invulnerability of the group's current policies" (Kameda & Sugimori, 1993, p. 291). In other words, they became psychologically entrapped, which is why it is advisable in capital murder cases to have one jury decide guilt and a separate jury decide the punishment.

SUMMARY OF HOW WELL GROUPS PERFORM

Although groups accomplish many tasks that could not be accomplished by individuals working alone, groups can also fall prey to three widely investigated shortcomings: production losses in brainstorming, group polarization, and groupthink.

Production losses in brainstorming occur when group members produce fewer, not more, novel ideas than they would have had they spent an equivalent time trying to generate ideas on their own. Brainstorming fails in part because of production blocking. Group members cannot all speak at the same time, so they must wait their turns. While waiting, they get distracted or hear someone else voice ideas that they had been trying to remember. Brainstorming also fails because, despite instructions to the contrary, group members are afraid to voice ideas that are too bizarre or controversial, lest they be negatively evaluated. Finally, brainstorming fails because, when they perceive their own ideas as unidentifiable and dispensable and when they underestimate what they might have accomplished alone, people loaf. Although they may loaf, people have the illusion that they are more productive in brainstorming groups than as individuals, because they give themselves credit for developing ideas that are voiced by others.

The group polarization phenomenon holds that groups sometimes make more extreme decisions than the average group member would have made as an individual. Group polarization occurs in part because, during discussion, the majority of group members learn about additional persuasive arguments favoring the side that they already prefer. Group polarization also occurs because people who want to be likable try to equal or surpass what they perceive as the group consensus or "norm." Finally, group polarization occurs because people misperceive their own group's consensus as more extreme than it actually is. They conform to the misperceived or "extremitized" norm. Group polarization is most likely to occur when the group must reach a unanimous decision about an issue that has no demonstrably correct answer.

Many historically significant and disastrous group decisions may have suffered from groupthink, a decision-making process in which group members seek concurrence, consensus, and unanimity more than they seek the best possible alternative. Groupthink occurs when cohesive groups, in which members value their social identities, must make decisions under the stress of possible negative evaluation. Groupthink also occurs when the group leader is very directive, when the group is isolated from outside opinion and advice, and when the group requires unanimity on an issue that has no demonstrably correct answer. Groups that require unanimity can easily become "psychologically entrapped" into escalating commitment to a previously chosen, though failing, course of action.

actor-observer difference the correspondence bias is much smaller, sometimes even nonexistent, when people explain their own behavior than when they explain another person's behavior

additive task group members' separate performances are added to produce a combined effect

aggressive cues hypothesis anger is more likely to result in overt aggression when some characteristic of the surrounding context reminds people of aggression

ambivalence amplification people who both like and dislike a group react extremely toward one or more members of that group

anchoring and adjustment heuristic when making a judgment, people start from an initial "anchor point" and make mental adjustments

anxious/ambivalent attachment the child gets very upset when the mother is absent and clings to the mother when she returns

attitude a psychological tendency that is expressed by evaluating a particular entity with some degree of favor or disfavor

attitude accessibility the ease with which an attitude comes to mind

attitude scales respondents indicate their attitudes by choosing a place along the scale that best represents how they think, feel, or tend to act toward the attitude object

augmentation making a stronger dispositional attribution when the behavior was performed in spite of powerful constraints

authority ranking those "on top" make decisions and are responsible for those "on the bottom," who loyally follow orders

availability heuristic people judge the frequency of an event by how easy it is to bring to mind

avoidant attachment the child acts as though he or she does not care when the mother returns from a brief absence and rejects her attention

basking in reflected glory sharing the glory of a successful other with whom you are in some way associated

behavioral confirmation people who are treated differently because of another person's expectations behave in line with those expectations

belief perseverance attitudes and beliefs do more than passively resist disconfirmation, but instead actively maintain and sometimes strengthen themselves even in the face of disconfirming evidence

bogus pipeline technique convincing the respondent that the experimenter has a "pipeline" into the respondent's real attitudes, so that the respondent will provide honest answers to questions about attitudes that might be socially undesirable

brainstorming a technique by which group members try to generate as many novel ideas as possible by building on and never criticizing each other's ideas

catharsis the erroneous belief that behaving aggressively releases pent-up anger and prevents an "explosion" of aggression later

central traits traits that carry an unusually wide range of inferences about other traits and behaviors

change of meaning initial information about a target person changes the meaning of subsequent information

classical conditioning of attitudes coming to like or dislike an attitude object because it has been previously associated with pleasurable or unpleasurable events

cognitive dissonance theory people change their attitudes to reduce the aversive arousal they experience when they have two cognitions (thoughts) that contradict each other, or are dissonant

collective self-esteem self-esteem that derives from a positive group identity

collectivistic cultures emphasize the group's goals and a group or social identity

communal orientation partners do not keep track of their individual costs and benefits, because they regard themselves as having merged into a unit

communal sharing sharing with others without expecting a specific favor in return

conjunctive task the group's accomplishment is limited to the least effective group member's performance

consensus whether other people behave the same as the person when they are faced with the identical situation

consistency whether the person always behaves the same way when faced with the same situation

contact hypothesis under certain conditions, contact with members of a negatively stereotyped minority group will ameliorate negative attitudes both toward the specific members with whom the contact occurred and toward group members as a whole

contingency theory of leadership the group member who acts as leader is contingent, or dependent, on what the group needs to accomplish

correlation degree of relationship between two variables

correspondence bias a tendency to assume that a person's words and deeds correspond with that person's underlying traits, attitudes, and intentions, even when the words or deeds were facilitated by situational constraints

counterfactual thinking imagining ways in which events might have occurred differently

debriefing explaining to participants both the actual hypothesis and the reason, if scientifically necessary, for withholding or misstating the purpose of the procedure

decision tree model of helping bystanders help when they notice the event, interpret it as an emergency, assume personal responsibility, and believe themselves competent

deindividuation losing track of personal identity, often as part of a crowd, so that personal responsibility for the consequences of actions is lessened

dependent variables aspects of the participant's behavior that the experimenter measures

diffusion of responsibility for helping the greater the number of bystanders to an emergency, the less likely each bystander is to assume personal responsibility for helping

discounting making a weaker dispositional attribution when situational constraints might have facilitated the behavior

discrimination inappropriate treatment of individuals due to their group membership—a selectively unjustified negative behavior toward members of a target group

disinhibition a weakening or removal of inhibitions that normally restrain people from acting on their impulses

disjunctive task the group's accomplishment is measured by the most effective group member's performance

dispositional attribution inferring that an event was caused by a person's temperament, tendency, or inclination—by something internal to the person

distinctiveness whether the person behaves this way only in this specific situation and not in other seemingly similar situations

effort justification people justify their effort to achieve a disappointing goal by emphasizing the goal's positive features

ego defensive function of attitudes attitudes help people to protect their self-esteem

elaboration likelihood model people take the peripheral route to persuasion when they rely on peripheral cues such as the source's expertise or physical attractiveness, whereas they take the central route to persuasion when they elaborate on the message arguments

empathic concern concern (feeling compassionate and sympathetic) about the welfare of another person who is in pain or suffering

empathic distress aversive arousal (feeling upset and disturbed) that occurs spontaneously when witnessing another person who is in pain or suffering

empathic joy positive feelings that come merely from knowing that another person is no longer suffering

equality matching a tendency of many human beings around the world to enjoy dealing with others on an equal footing, matching contributions equally

exchange orientation each partner calculates his or her own costs and benefits of remaining in the relationship

excitation transfer theory physiological excitement or arousal can, under specific conditions, be transferred from its actual cause to a different object

experiment a procedure used to test whether one event (which is manipulated) causes a second event (which is not manipulated, but merely measured)

experimental demand the experiment or study is constructed in such a way that the experimenter or the procedure virtually demands that participants behave in the predicted way

experimental realism participants become so caught up in the experimental scenario that they react as they would to important, involving events outside the laboratory

extraneous variables aspects of the experimental situation that might vary of their own accord, if the experimenter did not control them

face-in-the-crowd effect one angry face in a crowd of neutral or happy faces is easier to "spot" than one happy face in a crowd of neutral or angry faces

false consensus a tendency to view our own actions and choices as more common than they are, or at least as more prevalent than they are viewed by other people who choose differently from us

foot-in-the-door effect if you can get people to comply with a small, seemingly harmless request (getting your foot in the door), they sometimes feel committed to go along with subsequent increasingly important requests

free rider effect individuals loaf because they can gain the rewards of group success while hitching a free ride on the effective efforts of others

frustration-aggression hypothesis frustration occurs when people are unexpectedly blocked from achieving a goal that they thought was within their grasp

fundamental attribution error a tendency to underestimate the power of the situation (relative to dispositions) when making causal attributions

group polarization groups reach more polarized decisions (more extreme on the side of the issue that the majority of group members initially favor) than the average group member would have reached as an individual

groupthink group members seek concurrence, consensus, and unanimity more than they seek the best possible alternative

heuristic-systematic model people take the peripheral route to attitude change when they rely on heuristics or rules of thumb such as "many arguments are better than few" or "beautiful people don't lie," whereas they take the central route to persuasion when they think systematically about the topic

hindsight bias people who know an outcome erroneously believe that they knew the outcome or would have known the outcome in advance

implicit personality theories people believe that some trait pairs are more likely than others to belong to the same person and that knowing one piece of information about a person allows confident inferences about other traits of the person

independent variable the aspect of the participant's experience that the investigator (or someone else) manipulates

individualistic cultures emphasize the individual's goals and an individual or personal identity

informational influence on conformity because people want to understand and perceive reality correctly, they sometimes comply with and accept the majority's "norms" or standards for acceptable behavior

informed consent research participants must be told in advance as much as possible of what will happen to them

instrumental conditioning of attitudes coming to behave positively or negatively toward an attitude object because doing so has previously been rewarded

insufficient deterrence people justify refraining from a desirable action, which they avoided because of a barely sufficient deterrent, by emphasizing the action's negative features

insufficient justification people justify an undesirable action, which they performed for a barely sufficient inducement, by emphasizing the action's positive features

interdependence a couple agrees to be influenced by each other and to share their activities

just world hypothesis people need to believe that they live in a world where people generally get what they deserve

knowledge function of attitudes attitudes help people to classify and interpret events

manipulation check a test of whether the experimental manipulation had the intended effect

market pricing dissimilar commodities such as time, labor, skills, knowledge, objects, land, and even physical attractiveness are all assigned "values" and can be exchanged according to a universal standard such as money

matching hypothesis both men and women tend to seek and find lovers who are roughly at their own level of physical attractiveness

mere exposure effect people like familiar objects more than ones that they have not seen before

microexpressions fleeting facial expressions that last only a brief fraction of a second and that might give away a person's actual emotion before he or she can rearrange facial muscles to disguise it

minimal groups groups formed on the basis of an empty category label that denotes a trivial distinction

modeling of aggression people imitate an aggressive role model, especially someone similar to themselves, who appears to be rewarded for aggression

modeling of attitudes adopting an attitude vicariously by watching others and imitating what they do when what they do seems successful

motivational impairment effect the more motivated a liar is to avoid detection, the more emotional the liar becomes and the easier it is for perceivers to detect deception by paying attention to nonverbal cues

mundane realism extent to which the laboratory setting is superficially—as opposed to psychologically—similar to the real world

myth of the beast within the erroneous belief that people are "naturally" predisposed to fight and hurt each other, whether in individual conflicts or in wars

normative influence on conformity because people want to be liked and to maintain social harmony, they sometimes comply with the majority's "norms" or standards for acceptable behavior

Othello error misinterpreting a truthful person's emotional response to being accused of lying as evidence that the person is lying

outgroup homogeneity effect viewing members of the outgroup as more "all alike" (homogeneous) than members of the in-group

overjustification people lose interest in a previously desirable activity because they had to perform it with too much justification, or under external control

pluralistic ignorance each individual in a group falsely assumes that the other group members know more than he or she does

possible selves projections of future possibilities for the expected, desired, and feared future self

post-decisional dissonance people justify a choice by emphasizing its advantages over an almost equally attractive alternative

prejudice the feeling one has toward members of a group

primacy effects perceivers place greater weight on initial information than on later information in forming an impression

prototype the category member that a person imagines to best represent a category

psychological reactance people deliberately ignore or act contrary to external pressure because they believe that their individual freedom is being threatened

random assignment assigning participants to conditions randomly rather than systematically, so that possible extraneous variables occur equally across conditions

rape myth the erroneous belief that women may at first resist being raped, but their bodies involuntarily become sexually aroused, after which they participate willingly

realistic conflict majority and minority groups compete for status, power, and other scarce resources

recapitulation hypothesis we remember people by their social categories before we remember them by their personality traits

representativeness heuristic people judge a person, object, or event by how similar it is to what they imagine as the typical representative of its category

repulsion hypothesis people are initially, spontaneously repulsed by strangers who are very dissimilar to themselves

schemas mental maps or blueprints for how familiar people, objects, and events usually function

script stereotyped sequence of actions that defines a well-known situation

secure attachment the child is easily reassured and loving when the mother returns from a brief absence

self-affirmation reducing aversive arousal by affirming a positive identity

self-awareness being aware of ourselves as objects of attention

self-discrepancies discrepancies between the actual self and either the ideal self or the ought self, whether from the individual's perspective or from other people's perspective

self-evaluation maintenance strategically managing performance, closeness to other performers, and relevance of the performance in ways that protect a positive self-concept

self-fulfilling prophecies people act toward others in ways that make their expectations for the other person come true

self-handicapping anticipating situations in which the self-concept might be challenged and trying to arrange matters in advance so that identity is secure no matter what happens

self-monitoring monitoring our own behavior for the impression it will make on others

self-perception theory people change weakly held attitudes because they draw the same inferences from perceiving their own actions that anyone else who perceived those actions would draw

self-schemas beliefs that provide an organizing framework to help us understand ourselves

self-serving bias people tend to attribute their own successes more to internal-stable causes and their own failures more to external-unstable causes than they would when making attributions about other people

self-verification getting other people to verify what we believe to be true of ourselves

set-reset hypothesis exposure to a trait construct sets an anchor point from which social thinkers adjust by resetting the "anchor"

simulation heuristic people invent "mental simulations" or scenarios of past, future, and alternative "realities" against which to judge the information that they receive

situational attribution inferring that an event was caused by some pressure exerted by the situation or circumstances—by something external to the person

sleeper effect strong arguments, initially unpersuasive because they came from a disreputable source, become more persuasive over time

social adjustive function of attitudes attitudes help people match the social situation by having attitudes that will impress others favorably

social comparison people use others as standards of comparison against which to evaluate their own opinions, attributes, and abilities

social dilemmas situations in which the immediate payoff to each participant favors competition over cooperation, but it would be better for all participants in the long run if they consistently cooperated

social facilitation animals and human beings intensify their behavior when others of their species are present

social impact theory the greater the number and status of people who are present, the more they influence our behavior. Conversely, the greater the number and status of others whom we try to influence, the less influence we exert on each of them

social loafing expending less effort when working collectively with other people than when working alone

specificity matching hypothesis attitude-behavior consistency is greater when the attitude and the behavior match rather than mismatch in how general versus specific they are

spontaneous communication nonintentional "leakage" of emotion from one person (the "sender") to another (the "receiver") through the sender's facial, body, and vocal cues

spontaneous trait inferences relatively "automatic" inferences from another person's behavior to that person's likely personality traits

stereotypes beliefs about the characteristics of members of a group

story model of juror decision making jurors impose a narrative story organization on trial information, in which causal and intentional relations between events are central

subjective norms an individual's subjective judgments about whether other people will approve of a behavior

symbolic racism animosity toward policies that symbolize one race's advancement at another race's perceived expense

symbolic self-completion exaggerating identity symbols when an important aspect of the self-concept has been threatened

system justification explaining an "existing situation" or arrangement with the result that the situation or arrangement is maintained

theory of planned behavior the effect of attitudes and subjective norms on behavior depends on the individual's subjective estimate of how much control he or she has over the behavior

theory of reasoned action attitudes guide behavior through a reasoning process that takes into account both attitudes and subjective norms in deciding among alternative behaviors

thought-feeling consistency thoughts and feelings about an attitude object are equally positive or equally negative

three-component theory of attitudes attitudes consist of people's tendencies toward positive or negative thoughts, feelings, and actions

utilitarian function of attitudes attitudes help people to maximize rewards and minimize punishments

value expressive function of attitudes attitudes help people to express their deeply held values and convictions

REFERENCES

Abelson, R. P. (1959). Modes of resolution of belief dilemmas. *Journal of Conflict Resolution, 3,* 343–352.

Abelson, R. P. (1976). Script processing in attitude formation and decision making. In J. S. Carroll & J. W. Payne (Eds.), *Cognition and social behavior.* Hillsdale, NJ: Erlbaum.

Abelson, R. P. (1981). The psychological status of the script concept. *American Psychologist, 36,* 715–729.

Abelson, R. P. (1983). Whatever became of consistency theory? *Personality and Social Psychology Bulletin, 9,* 37–54.

Abelson, R. P., & Prentice, D. A. (1989). Beliefs as possessions: A functional perspective. In A. R. Pratkanis, S. J. Breckler, & A. G. Greenwald (Eds.), *Attitude structure and function.* Hillsdale, NJ: Erlbaum.

Aboud, F. E. (1992). Conflict and group relations. In C. V. Schantz & W. H. Hartup (Eds.), *Conflict in child and adolescent development.* New York: Cambridge University Press.

Abraham, C., Sheeran, P., Abrams, D., Spears, R., & Marks, D. (1992). Young people learning about AIDS: A study of beliefs and information sources. *Health Education Research, 6,* 19–29.

Abraham, C., Sheeran, P., Spears, R., & Abrams, D. (1992). Health beliefs and promotion of HIV-preventive intentions among teenagers: A Scottish perspective. *Health Psychology, 11,* 363–370.

Abrams, D. (1992). Processes of social identification. In G. Breakwell (Ed.), *Social psychology of identity and the self concept.* New York: Surrey University Press.

Abramson, L. Y., Metalsky, G. I., & Alloy, L. B. (1989). Helplessness depression: A theory-based subtype of depression. *Psychological Review, 96,* 358–372.

Abramson, L. Y., Seligman, M. E. P., & Teasdale, J. D. (1978). Learned helplessness in humans: Critique and reformulation. *Journal of Applied Psychology, 87,* 49–74.

Achenbaum, W. A. (1978). *Old age in the new land.* Baltimore: Johns Hopkins University Press.

Acitelli, L. K. (1992). Gender differences in relationship awareness and marital satisfaction among young married couples. *Personality and Social Psychology Bulletin, 18,* 102–110.

Acitelli, L. K., & Antonucci, T. C. (1994). Gender differences in the link between marital support and satisfaction in older couples. *Journal of Personality and Social Psychology, 67,* 688–698.

Acker, M. & Davis, M. H. (1992). Intimacy, passion and commitment in adult romantic relationships: A test of the triangular theory of love. *Journal of Social and Personal Relationships, 9,* 21–50.

Ackerman, D. (1994). *A natural history of love.* New York: Random House.

Acorn, D. A., Hamilton, D. L., & Sherman, S. J. (1988). Generalization of biased perceptions of groups based on illusory correlations. *Social Cognition, 6,* 345–372.

Affleck, G., Tennen, H., Pfeiffer, C., Fifield, J., & Rowe, J. (1987). Downward comparison and coping with serious medical problems. *American Journal of Orthopsychiatry, 57,* 570–578.

Agostinelli, G., Sherman, S. J., Presson, C. C., & Chassin, L. (1992). Self-protection and self-enhancement biases in estimates of population prevalence. *Personality and Social Psychology Bulletin, 18,* 631–642.

Aguinis, H., Pierce, C. A., & Quigley, B. M. (1993). Conditions under which a bogus pipeline procedure enhances the validity of self-reported cigarette smoking: A meta-analytic review. *Journal of Applied Social Psychology, 23,* 352–373.

Aiello, J. R., & Svec, C. M. (1993). Computer monitoring of work performance: Extending the social facilitation framework to electronic presence. *Journal of Applied Social Psychology, 23,* 537–548.

Ainsworth, M. D. S., Blehar, M. C., Waters, E., & Wall, S. (1978). *Patterns of attachment: A psychological study of the strange situation.* Hillsdale, NJ: Erlbaum.

Ajzen, I. (1985). From intentions to actions: A theory of planned behavior. In J. Kuhl & J. Beckman (Eds.), *Action-control: From cognition to behavior.* Heidelberg: Springer.

Ajzen, I. (1987). Attitudes, traits, and actions: Dispositional prediction of behavior in personality and social psychology. In L. Berkowitz (Ed.), *Advances in experimental social psychology* (Vol. 20). San Diego, CA: Academic Press.

Ajzen, I., & Fishbein, M. (1977). Attitude-behavior relations: A theoretical analysis and review of empirical research. *Psychological Bulletin, 84,* 888–918.

Ajzen, I., & Fishbein, M. (1980). *Understanding attitudes and predicting social behavior.* Englewood Cliffs, NJ: Prentice-Hall.

Ajzen, I., & Madden, T. J. (1986). Prediction of goal-directed behavior: Attitudes, intentions, and perceived behavioral control. *Journal of Experimental Social Psychology, 22,* 453–474.

Albright, L., Kenny, D. A., & Malloy, T. E. (1988). Consensus in personality judgments at zero acquaintance. *Journal of Personality and Social Psychology, 55,* 387–395.

Alexander, R. D. (1972). The evolution of social behavior. *Annual Review of Ecology and Systematics, 5,* 325–383.

Alexander, R. D. (1987). *The biology of moral systems.* Harthorne, NY: Aldine de Gruter.

Alicke, M. D. (1992). Culpable causation. *Journal of Personality and Social Psychology, 63,* 368–378.

Alicke, M. D., & Davis, T. L. (1989). The role of a posteriori victim information in judgments of blame and sanction. *Journal of Applied Social Psychology, 25,* 362–377.

Alicke, M. D., Klotz, M. L., Breitenbecher, D. L., Yurak, T. J., & Vredenburg, D. S. (1995). Personal contact, individuations and the better than average affect. *Journal of Personality and Social Psychology, 68,* 804–825.

Alicke, M. D., & Largo, E. (1995). The role of the self in the false consensus effect. *Journal of Experimental Social Psychology, 31,* 28–47.

Alicke, M. D., Smith, R. H., & Klotz, M. L. (1986). Judgments of physical attractiveness: The role of faces and bodies. *Personality and Social Psychology Bulletin, 12,* 381–389.

Allen, C. T., & Madden, T. J. (1985). A closer look at classical conditioning. *Journal of Consumer Research, 12,* 301–315.

Allen, J. B., Kenrick, D. T., Linder, D. E., & McCall, M. A. (1989). Arousal and attraction: A response-facilitation alternative to misattribution and negative-reinforcement models. *Journal of Personality and Social Psychology, 57,* 261–270.

Allington, R. (1980). Teacher interruption behaviors during primary grade oral reading. *Journal of Educational Psychology, 72,* 371–377.

Allison, S. T., Mackie, D. M., Muller, M. M., & Worth, L. T. (1993). Sequential correspondence biases and perceptions of change: The Castro studies revisited. *Personality and Social Psychology Bulletin, 19,* 151–157.

Allison, S. T., & Messick, D. M. (1985). Effects of experience on performance in a replenishable resource trap. *Journal of Personality and Social Psychology, 49,* 943–948.

Allison, S. T., Messick, D. M., & Goethals, G. R. (1989). On being better but not smarter than others: The Muhammad Ali effect. *Social Cognition, 7,* 275–295.

Allport, G. W. (1935). Attitudes. In C. Murchison (Ed.), *A handbook of social psychology.* Worcester, MA: Clark University Press.

Allport, G. W. (1954). *The nature of prejudice.* Reading, MA: Addison-Wesley.

Allport, G. W. (1961). *Pattern and growth in personality.* New York: Henry Holt.

Allport, G. W. (1985). The historical background of social psychology. In G. Lindzey & E. Aronson (Eds.), *The handbook of social psychology* (3rd edition, Vol. I). New York: Random House.

Allport, G. W., & Postman, L. (1947). *The psychology of rumor.* New York: Holt, Rinehart & Winston.

Aloise-Young, P., A. (1993). The development of self-presentation: Self-promotion in 6- to 10-year-old children. *Social Cognition, 11,* 201–222.

Altemeyer, B. (1994). Reducing prejudice in right-wing authoritarians. In M. P. Zanna & J. M. Olson (Eds.), *The psychology of prejudice: The Ontario symposium* (Vol. 7). Hillsdale, NJ: Erlbaum.

Amabile, T. M., Hennessey, B. A., & Grossman, B. S. (1986). Social influences on creativity: The effects of contracted-for reward. *Journal of Personality and Social Psychology, 50,* 14–23.

Amabile, T. M., Hill, K. G., Hennessey, B. A., & Tighe, E. M. (1994). The work preference inventory: Assessing intrinsic and extrinsic motivational orientations. *Journal of Personality and Social Psychology, 66,* 950–967.

Amato, P. R. (1983). Helping behavior in rural and urban environments: Field studies based on a taxonomic organization of helping episodes. *Journal of Personality and Social Psychology, 45,* 571–586.

Amir, Y. (1969). Contact hypothesis in ethnic relations. *Psychological Bulletin, 71,* 319–341.

Amir, Y., & Ben-Ari, R. (1985). International tourism, ethnic contact and attitude change. *Journal of Social Issues, 41,* 105–115.

Ammar, H. (1954). *Growing up in an Egyptian village: Silwa, province of Aswan.* London: Routledge & Paul.

Anastasiow, N. (1986). *Development and disability.* Baltimore, MD: Paul H. Brooks.

Andersen, J. F., Andersen, P. A., & Lustig, M. W. (1987). Opposite sex touch avoidance: A national replication and extension. *Journal of Nonverbal Behavior, 11,* 89–109.

Andersen, S. M. (1984). Self-knowledge and social inference: II. The diagnosticity of cognitive/affective and behavioral data. *Journal of Personality and Social Psychology, 46,* 294–307.

Andersen, S. M. (1990). The inevitability of future suffering: The role of depressive predictive certainty in depression. *Social Cognition, 8,* 203–228.

Andersen, S. M., & Cole, S. W. (1990). "Do I know you?": The role of significant others in general social perception. *Journal of Personality and Social Psychology, 59,* 384–399.

Andersen, S. M., & Glassman, N. S. (in press). Responding to significant others when they are not there: Effects on interpersonal inference, motivation, and affect. In R. M. Sorrentino & E. T. Higgins (Eds.), *Handbook of motivation and cognition* (Vol. 3).

Andersen, S. M., Klatzky, R. L., & Murray, J. (1990). Traits and social stereotypes: Efficiency differences in social information processing. *Journal of Personality and Social Psychology, 59,* 192–201.

Andersen, S. M., & Lyon, J. E. (1987). Anticipating undesired outcomes: The role of outcome certainty in the onset of depressive affect. *Journal of Experimental Social Psychology, 23,* 428–443.

Andersen, S. M., & Ross, L. (1984). Self-knowledge and social inference: I. The impact of cognitive/affective and behavioral data. *Journal of Personality and Social Psychology, 46,* 280–293.

Andersen, S. M., & Schwartz, A. H. (1992). Intolerance of ambiguity and depression: A cognitive vulnerability factor linked to hopelessness. *Social Cognition, 10,* 271–298.

Andersen, S. M., Spielman, L. A., & Bargh, J. A. (1992). Future-event schemas and certainty about the future: Automaticity in depressives' future-event predictions. *Journal of Personality and Social Psychology, 63,* 711–723.

Anderson, C. A. (1983a). Abstract and concrete data in the perseverance of social theories: When weak data lead to unshakeable beliefs. *Journal of Experimental Social Psychology, 19,* 93–108.

Anderson, C. A. (1983b). Imagination and expectation: The effect of imagining behavioral scripts on personal intentions. *Journal of Personality and Social Psychology, 45,* 293–305.

Anderson, C. A. (1987). Temperature and aggression: Effects of quarterly, yearly, and city rates of violent and non-violent crime. *Journal of Personality and Social Psychology, 52,* 1161–1173.

Anderson, C. A. (1989). Temperature and aggression: The ubiquitous effects of heat on the occurrence of human violence. *Psychological Bulletin, 106,* 74–96.

Anderson, C. A., Deuser, W. E., & DeNeve, K. M. (1995). Hot temperatures, hostile affect, hostile cognition, and arousal: Tests of a general model of affective aggression. *Personality and Social Psychology Bulletin, 21,* 434–448.

Anderson, C. A., & Godfrey, S. S. (1987). Thoughts about actions: The effects of specificity and availability of imagined behavioral scripts on expectations about oneself and others. *Social Cognition, 5,* 238–258.

Anderson, C. A., & Kellam, K. L. (1992). Belief perseverance, biased assimilation, and covariation detection: The effects of hypothetical social theories and new data. *Personality and Social Psychology Bulletin, 18,* 555–565.

Anderson, C. A., Krull, D. S., & Weiner, B. (in press). Explanations:

Processes and consequences. In E. T. Higgins & A. W. Kruglanski (Eds.), *Social psychology: Handbook of basic principles.*

Anderson, C. A., Lepper, M. R., & Ross, L. (1980). Perseverance of social theories: The role of explanation in the persistence of discredited information. *Journal of Personality and Social Psychology, 39,* 1037–1049.

Anderson, C. A., Miller, R. S., Riger, A. L., Dill, J. C., & Sedikides, C. (1994). Behavioral and characterological attributional styles as predictors of depression and loneliness: Review, refinement, and test. *Journal of Personality and Social Psychology, 66,* 549–558.

Anderson, C. A., & Morrow, M. (1995). Competitive aggression without interaction: Effects of competitive versus cooperative instructions on aggressive behavior in video games. *Personality and Social Psychology Bulletin, 21,* 1020–1030.

Anderson, C. A., & Riger, A. L. (1991). A controllability attributional model of problems in living: Dimensional and situational interactions in the prediction of depression and loneliness. *Social Cognition, 9,* 149–181.

Anderson, N. H. (1974). Information integration: A brief survey. In D. H. Krantz, R. C. Atkinson, R. D. Luce, & P. Suppes (Eds.), *Contemporary developments in mathematical psychology.* San Francisco, CA: Freeman.

Anderson, N. H. (1981). *Foundations of information integration theory.* New York: Academic Press.

Anderson, R. C., & Pichert, J. W. (1978). Recall of previously unrecallable information following a shift in perspective. *Journal of Verbal Learning and Verbal Behavior, 17,* 1–12.

Anderson, V. L. (1993). Gender differences in altruism among Holocaust rescuers. *Journal of Social Behavior and Personality, 8,* 43–58.

Anderson, V. N. (1992). For whom is this world just?: Sexual orientation and AIDS. *Journal of Applied Social Psychology, 22,* 248–259.

Antill, J. K. (1983). Sex role complementarity versus similarity in married couples. *Journal of Personality and Social Psychology, 45,* 145–155.

Apsler, R., & Sears, D. O. (1968). Warning, personal involvement, and attitude change. *Journal of Personality and Social Psychology, 9,* 162–166.

Arad, S., & Carnevale, P. J. (1994). Partisanship effects in judgments of fairness and trust in third parties in the Palestinian-Israeli conflict. *Journal of Conflict Resolution, 38,* 423–451.

Archer, D., Iritani, B., Kimes, D. D., & Barrios, M. (1983). Face-ism: Five studies of sex differences in facial prominence. *Journal of Personality and Social Psychology, 45,* 725–735.

Archer, R. P., & Cash, T. F. (1985). Physical attractiveness and maladjustment among psychiatric inpatients. *Journal of Social and Clinical Psychology, 3,* 170–180.

Arcuri, L. (1982). Three patterns of social categorization in attribution memory. *European Journal of Social Psychology, 12,* 271–282.

Arkin, R. M., & Baumgardner, A. H. (1985). Self-handicapping. In J. H. Harvey & G. Weary (Eds.), *Attribution: Basic issues and applications.* New York: Academic Press.

Arkin, R. M., & Maryuma, G. M. (1979). Attribution, affect, and college exam performance. *Journal of Educational Psychology, 71,* 85–93.

Arms, R. L., Russell, G. W., & Sandilands, M. L. (1979). Effects on the hostility of spectators of viewing aggressive sports. *Social Psychology Quarterly, 42,* 275–279.

Aron, A., Aron, E. N., Tudor, M., & Nelson, G. (1991). Close relationships as including other in self. *Journal of Personality and Social Psychology, 60,* 241–253.

Aron, A., & Rodriguez, G. (1992). *Scenarios of falling in love among Mexican-, Chinese-, and Anglo-Americans.* Sixth International Conference on Personal Relationships. Orono, ME.

Aronfreed, S. (1976). Moral development from the standpoint of general psychological theory. In T. Lickman (Ed.), *Moral development and behavior.* New York: Holt, Rinehart & Winston.

Aronoff, J., Woike, B. A., & Hyman, L. M. (1992). Which are the stimuli in facial displays of anger and happiness? Configurational bases of emotion recognition. *Journal of Personality and Social Psychology, 62,* 1050–1066.

Aronson, E. (1968). Dissonance theory: Progress and problems. In R. Abelson, E. Aronson, W. McGuire, T. Necomb, M. Rosenberg, & P. Tannenbaum (Eds.), *The cognitive consistency theories: A source book.* Chicago: McNally.

Aronson, E. (1984). Modifying the environment of the desegregated classroom. In A. J. Stewart (Ed.), *Motivation and society.* San Francisco: Jossey-Bass.

Aronson, E., Brewer, M., & Carlsmith, J. M. (1985). Experimentation in social psychology. In G. Lindzey & E. Aronson (Eds.), *Handbook of social psychology* (Vol. 1). Hillsdale, NJ: Erlbaum.

Aronson, E., & Carlsmith, J. M. (1963). The effect of the severity of threat on the devaluation of forbidden behavior. *Journal of Abnormal and Social Psychology, 66,* 584–588.

Aronson, E., & Gonzales, A. (1988). Desegregation, jigsaw, and the Mexican-American experience. In P. A. Katz & D. A. Taylor (Eds.), *Eliminating racism: Profiles in controversy.* New York: Plenum. Pp. 301–314.

Aronson, E., & Mills, J. (1959). The effects of severity of initiation on liking for a group. *Journal of Abnormal and Social Psychology, 59,* 177–181.

Aronson, E., & Pratkanis, A. R. (1993). Introduction: What is social psychology? In E. Aronson & A. R. Pratkanis (Eds.), *Social Psychology* (Vol. 1). Cheltenham, Gloucestershire: Edward Elgar.

Aronson, E., Stephan, C., Sikes, J., Blaney, N., & Snapp, M. (1978). *The jigsaw classroom.* Beverly Hills, CA: Sage.

Aronson, E., Turner, J. A., & Carlsmith, J. M. (1963). Communicator credibility and communication discrepancy as determinants of opinion change. *Journal of Abnormal and Social Psychology, 67,* 31–36.

Aronson, E., & Worchel, P. (1966). Similarity versus liking as determinants of interpersonal attractiveness. *Psychonomic Science, 5,* 157–158.

Asch, S. E. (1946). Forming impressions of personality. *Journal of Abnormal and Social Psychology, 41,* 258–290.

Asch, S. E. (1951). Effects of group pressure upon the modification and distortion of judgments. In H. Guetzkow (Ed.), *Groups, leadership and men.* Pittsburgh: Carnegie Press.

Asch, S. E. (1956). Studies of independence and conformity: I. A minority of one against a unanimous majority. *Psychological Monographs, 70* (Whole No. 416).

Asch, S. E., & Zukier, H. (1984). Thinking about persons. *Journal of Personality and Social Psychology, 46,* 1230–1240.

Ashmore, R. D., & del Boca, F. K. (1986). Sex stereotypes and implicit personality theory: Toward a cognitive-social psychological conceptualization. *Sex Roles, 5,* 219–248.

Aspinwall, L. G., & Taylor, S. E. (1993). Effects of social comparison direction, threat, and self-esteem on affect, self-evaluation, and expected success. *Journal of Personality and Social Psychology, 64,* 708–722.

Averill, J. R. (1969). Autonomic response patterns during sadness and mirth. *Psychophysiology, 5,* 399–414.

Averill, J. R. (1983). Studies on anger and aggression: Implications for theories of emotion. *American Psychologist, 38,* 1145–1160.

Axelrod, R. (1984). *The evolution of cooperation.* New York: Basic Books.

Axelrod, R., & Dion, D. (1988). The further evolution of cooperation. *Science, 242,* 1385–1390.

Axelrod, R., & Hamilton, W. D. (1981). The evolution of cooperation. *Science, 211,* 1390–1396.

Axsom, D., Yates, S., & Chaiken, S. (1987). Audience response as a heuristic cue in persuasion. *Journal of Personality and Social Psychology, 53,* 30–40.

Ayman, R. (1993). Leadership perception: The role of gender and culture. In M. M. Chemers & R. Ayman (Eds.), *Leadership theory and research: Perspectives and directions.* San Diego, CA: Academic Press.

Bach-y-Rita, G., & Veno, A. (1974). Habitual violence: A profile of 62 men. *American Journal of Psychiatry, 131,* 1015–1017.

Bachman, J. G., & O'Malley, P. M. (1984). Black-White differences in self-esteem: Are they affected by response styles? *American Journal of Sociology, 90,* 624–639.

Bachman, J. G., & O'Malley, P. M. (1986). Self-concepts, self-esteem, and educational experiences: The frog pond revisited (again). *Journal of Personality and Social Psychology, 50,* 35–46.

Back, K., & Bogdonoff, M. (1964). Plasma lipid responses to leadership, conformity, and deviation. In P. Leiderman & D. Shapiro (Eds.), *Psychobiological approaches to social behavior.* Stanford, CA: Stanford University Press.

Back, K. W. (1951). Influence through social communication. *Journal of Abnormal and Social Psychology, 46,* 9–23.

Bagby, R. M., & Rector, N. A. (1992). Prejudice in a simulated legal context: A further application of social identity theory. *European Journal of Social Psychology, 22,* 397–406.

Bakan, D. (1966). *The duality of human existence: An essay on psychology and religion.* Chicago: Rand McNally.

Baker, S. M., & Petty, R. E. (1994). Majority and minority influence: Source-position imbalance as a determinant of message scrutiny. *Journal of Personality and Social Psychology, 67,* 5–19.

Baldwin, M. W. (1992). Relational schemas and the processing of social information. *Psychological Bulletin, 112,* 461–484.

Baldwin, M. W., Carrell, S. E., & Lopez, D. F. (1990). Priming relationship schemas: My advisor and the Pope are watching me from the back of my mind. *Journal of Experimental Social Psychology, 26,* 435–454.

Banaji, M. R., & Greenwald, A. G. (1994). Implicit stereotyping and unconscious prejudice. In M. P. Zanna & J. M. Olson (Eds.), *The psychology of prejudice: The Ontario symposium* (Vol. 7). Hillsdale, NJ: Erlbaum.

Banaji, M. R., & Greenwald, A. G. (1995). Implicit gender stereotyping in judgments of fame. *Journal of Personality and Social Psychology, 68,* 181–198.

Banaji, M. R., & Prentice, D. A. (1994). The self in social contexts. *Annual Review of Psychology, 45,* 297–332.

Bandura, A. (1973). *Aggression: A social learning analysis.* Englewood Cliffs, NJ: Prentice-Hall.

Bandura, A. (1986). *Social foundations of thought and action. A social cognitive theory*. Englewood Cliffs, NJ: Prentice-Hall.

Bandura, A., Ross, D., & Ross, S. A. (1963). Imitation of film-mediated aggressive models. *Journal of Abnormal and Social Psychology, 66,* 3–11.

Barbee, A. P., & Cunningham, M. R. (in press). An experimental approach to social support communications: Interactive coping in close relationships. *Communication Yearbook.*

Barfield, R. J. (1984). Reproductive hormones and aggressive behavior. In K. J. Flannelly, R. J. Blanchard, & D. C. Blanchard (Eds.), *Biological perspectives on aggression* (pp. 105–134). New York: Alan Liss.

Bargh, J. A. (1994). The four horsemen of automaticity: Awareness, intention, efficiency, and control in social cognition. In R. S. Wyer, Jr. & T. K. Srull (Eds.), *Handbook of social cognition* (Vol. 1). Hillsdale, NJ: Erlbaum.

Bargh, J. A., Bond, R. N., Lombardi, W. J., & Higgins, E. T. (1988). Automaticity of chronically accessible constructs in person X situation effects on person perception: It's just a matter of time. *Journal of Personality and Social Psychology, 50,* 869–879.

Bargh, J. A., Chaiken, S., Govender, R., & Pratto, F. (1992). The generality of the automatic attitude activation effect. *Journal of Personality and Social Psychology, 62,* 893–912.

Bargh, J. A., Litt, J., Pratto, F., & Spielman, L. A. (1989). On the preconscious evaluation of social stimuli. In A. F. Bennett & K. M. McConkey (Eds.), *Cognition in individual and social contexts.* Amsterdam: Elsevier/North-Holland.

Bargh, J. A., & Pietromonaco, P. (1982). Automatic information processing and social perception: The influence of trait information presented outside of conscious awareness on impression formation. *Journal of Personality and Social Psychology, 43,* 437–449.

Bargh, J. A., & Thien, R. D. (1985). Individual construct accessibility, person memory, and the recall-judgment link: The case of information overload. *Journal of Personality and Social Psychology, 49,* 1129–1146.

Baron, R. A. (1973). Threatened retaliation from the victim as an inhibitor of physical aggression. *Journal of Research in Personality, 7,* 103–115.

Baron, R. A. (1974). The aggression-inhibiting influence of heightened sexual arousal. *Journal of Personality and Social Psychology, 30,* 318–332.

Baron, R. A. (1977). *Human aggression.* New York: Plenum.

Baron, R. A. (1978). Aggression-inhibiting influence of sexual humor. *Journal of Personality and Social Psychology, 36,* 189–197.

Baron, R. A. (1979). Heightened sexual arousal and physical aggression: An extension to females. *Journal of Research in Personality, 13,* 91–102.

Baron, R. A. (1983). The control of human aggression: A strategy based on incompatible responses. In R. G. Geen & E. Donnerstein (Eds.), *Aggression: Empirical and theoretical reviews, Vol. 2, Issues in research* (pp. 173–190). New York: Academic Press.

Baron, R. A., & Bell, P. A. (1975). Aggression and heat: Mediating effects of prior provocation and exposure to an aggressive model. *Journal of Personality and Social Psychology, 31,* 825–832.

Baron, R. A., Russell, G. W., & Arms, R. L. (1985). Negative ions and behavior: Impact on mood, memory, and aggression among type A and type B persons. *Journal of Personality and Social Psychology, 48,* 746–754.

Baron, R. M., & Misovich, S. J. (1993). Dispositional knowing from an ecological perspective. *Personality and Social Psychology Bulletin, 19,* 541–552.

Baron, R. S. (1986). Distraction-conflict theory: progress and problems. In L. Berkowitz (Ed.), *Advances in experimental social psychology* (Vol. 19). New York: Academic Press.

Baron, R. S., Monson, T. C., & Baron, P. H. (1973). Conformity pressure as a determinant of risk taking: Replication and extension. *Journal of Personality and Social Psychology, 28,* 406–413.

Baron, R. S., & Roper, G. (1976). Reaffirmation of social comparison views of choice shifts: Averaging and extremity effects in an autokinetic situation. *Journal of Personality and Social Psychology, 33,* 521–530.

Baron, R. S., Roper, G., & Baron, P. H. (1974). Group discussion and the stingy shift. *Journal of Personality and Social Psychology, 30,* 538–545.

Barr, C. L., & Kleck, R. E. (1995). Self/other perception of the intensity of facial expressions of emotion: Do we know what we show? *Journal of Personality and Social Psychology, 68,* 608–618.

Bartlett, D. J., Hurley, W. P., Brand, C. R., & Poole, E. W. (1968). Chromosomes of male patients in a security prison. *Nature, 219,* 351–354.

Bass, B. M., & Avolio, B. J. (1993). Transformational leadership: A response to critiques. In M. M. Chemers & R. Ayman (Eds.), *Leadership theory and research: Perspectives and directions.* San Diego, CA: Academic Press.

Bassili, J. N. (1989). Trait encoding in behavior identification and dispositional inference. *Personality and Social Psychology Bulletin, 15,* 285–296.

Bassili, J. N. (1993). Procedural efficiency and the spontaneity of trait inference. *Personality and Social Psychology Bulletin, 19,* 200–205.

Bassili, J. N. (in press). The "how" and "why" of response latency measurement in telephone surveys. In N. Schwarz & S. Sudman (Eds.), *Cognitive processes in surveys.* New York: Springer-Verlag.

Bateson, P. (1989). Is aggression instinctive? In J. Groebel & R. A. Hinde (Eds.), *Aggression and war: Their biological and social bases* (pp. 35–47). New York: Cambridge University Press.

Batson, C. D. (1987). Prosocial motivation: Is it ever truly altruistic? In L. Berkowitz (Ed.), *Advances in experimental social psychology* (Vol. 20, pp. 65–122). New York: Academic Press.

Batson, C. D. (1990). How social an animal? *American Psychologist, 45,* 336–346.

Batson, C. D. (1991). *The altruism question: Toward a social-psychological answer.* Hillsdale, NJ: Erlbaum.

Batson, C. D. (1994). Why act for the public good? Four answers. *Personality and Social Psychology Bulletin, 20,* 603–610.

Batson, C. D., Batson, J. G., Slingsby, J. K., Harrell, K. L., Peekna, H. M., & Todd, R. M. (1991). Empathic joy and the empathy-altruism hypothesis. *Journal of Personality and Social Psychology, 61,* 413–426.

Batson, C. D., & Burris, C. T. (1994). Personal religion: Depressant or stimulant of prejudice and discrimination? In M. P. Zanna & J. M. Olson (Eds.), *The psychology of prejudice: The Ontario symposium* (Vol. 7). Hillsdale, NJ: Erlbaum.

Batson, C. D., Duncan, B., Ackerman, P., Buckley, T., & Birch, K. (1981). Is empathic emotion a source of altruistic motivation? *Journal of Personality and Social Psychology, 40,* 290–302.

Batson, C. D., Dyck, J. L., Brandt, J. R., Batson, J. G., Powell, A. L., McMaster, M. R., & Griffitt, C. (1988). Five studies testing two new egoistic alternatives to the empathy-altruism hypothesis. *Journal of Personality and Social Psychology, 55,* 52–77.

Batson, C. D., O'Quin, K., Fultz, J., Vanderplas, M., & Isen, A. (1983). Self-reported distress and empathy and egoistic versus altruistic motivation for helping. *Journal of Personality and Social Psychology, 45,* 706–718.

Batson, C. D., Turk, C. L., Shaw, L. L., & Klein, T. R. (1995). Information function of empathic emotion: Learning that we value the other's welfare. *Journal of Personality and Social Psychology, 68,* 300–313.

Batson, C. D., & Weeks, J. L. (1996). Mood effects of unsuccessful helping: Another test of the empathy-altruism hypothesis. *Personality and Social Psychology Bulletin, 22,* 148–157.

Baucom, D. H., & Aiken, P. A. (1984). Sex role identity, marital satisfaction, and response to behavioral marital therapy. *Journal of Consulting and Clinical Psychology, 52,* 438–444.

Baum, A., & Paulus, P. (1987). Crowding. In D. Stokols & I. Altman (Eds.),

Handbook of environmental psychology (Vol. 1). New York: Wiley.

Baumeister, R. F. (1984). Choking under pressure: Self-consciousness and paradoxical effects of incentives on skillful performance. *Journal of Personality and Social Psychology, 46,* 610–620.

Baumeister, R. F. (1987). How the self became a problem: A psychological review of historical research. *Journal of Personality and Social Psychology, 52,* 163–176.

Baumeister, R. F. (1990a). Suicide as escape from self. *Psychological Review, 97,* 90–113.

Baumeister, R. F. (1990b). The optimal margin of illusion. *Journal of Social and Clinical Psychology, 8,* 176–189.

Baumeister, R. F., & Cairns, K. J. (1992). Repression and self-presentation: When audiences interfere with self-deceptive strategies. *Journal of Personality and Social Psychology, 65,* 851–862.

Baumeister, R. F., Chesner, S. P., Senders, P. S., & Tice, D. M (1988). Who's in charge here: Group leaders do lend help in emergencies. *Personality and Social Psychology Bulletin, 14,* 17–22.

Baumeister, R. F., & Heatherton, T. F. (1996). Self-regulation failure: An overview. *Psychological Inquiry,* I,1–15.

Baumeister, R. F., & Leary, M. R. (1995). The need to belong: Desire for interpersonal attachments as a fundamental human motivation. *Psychological Bulletin, 117,* 491–529.

Baumeister, R. F., Reis, H. T., & Delespaul, A. E. G. (1995). Subjective and experiental correlates of guilt in daily life. *Personality and Social Psychology Bulletin, 21,* 1256–1268.

Baumeister, R. F., & Scher, S. J. (1988). Self-defeating behavior patterns among normal individuals: Review and analysis of common self-destructive tendencies. *Psychological Bulletin, 104,* 3–22.

Baumeister, R. F., & Showers, C. J. (1986). A review of paradoxical performance effects: Choking under pressure in sports and mental tests. *European Journal of Social Psychology, 16,* 361–383.

Baumeister, R. F., Stillwell, A. M., & Heatherton, T. F. (1994). Guilt: An interpersonal approach. *Psychological Bulletin, 115,* 243–267.

Baumeister, R. F., Stillwell, A., & Wotman, S. R. (1991). Victim and perpetrator accounts of interpersonal conflict: Autobiographical narratives about anger. *Journal of Personality and Social Psychology, 59,* 994–1005.

Baumeister, R. F., & Tice, D. M. (1990). Anxiety and social exclusion. *Journal of Social and Clinical Psychology, 9,* 165–195.

Baumeister, R. F., Wotman, S. R., & Stillwell, A. M. (1993). Unrequited love: On heartbreak, anger, guilt,

scriptlessness, and humiliation. *Journal of Personality and Social Psychology, 64,* 377–394.

Baumgardner, A. H. (1991). Claiming depressive symptoms as a self-handicap: A protective self-presentation strategy. *Basic and Applied Social Psychology, 12,* 97–113.

Baumgardner, A. H., Heppner, P. P., & Arkin, R. M. (1986). Role of causal attribution in personal problem solving. *Journal of Personality and Social Psychology, 50,* 636–643.

Bavelas, A., Hastorf, A. H., Gross, A. E., & Kite, W. R. (1965). Experiments on the alteration of group structure. *Journal of Experimental Social Psychology, 1,* 55–70.

Baxter, T. L., & Goldberg, L. R. (1988). Perceived behavioral consistency underlying trait attributions to oneself and another: An extension of the actor-observer effect. *Personality and Social Psychology Bulletin, 13,* 437–447.

Beach, S. R. H., & Tesser, A. (1993). Decision making power and marital satisfaction: A self-evaluation maintenance perspective. *Journal of Social and Clinical Psychology, 12,* 471–494.

Beach, S. R. H., & Tesser, A. (1995). Self-esteem and the extended self-evaluation maintenance model: The self in social context. In M. Kernis (Ed.), *Efficacy, agency, and self-esteem.* New York: Plenum.

Beale, D. A. & Manstead, A. S. (1991). Predicting mothers' intentions to limit frequency of infants' sugar intake: Testing the theory of planned behavior. *Journal of Applied Social Psychology, 21,* 409–431.

Beall, A. E., & Sternberg, R. J. (1995). *The psychology of gender.* New York: Guilford Press.

Beauvais, C., & Spence, J. (1987). Gender, prejudice, and categorization. *Sex Roles, 16,* 89–99.

Beck, K. H., & Frankel, A. (1981). A conceptualization of threat communications and protective health behavior. *Social Psychology Quarterly, 44,* 204–217.

Beike, D. R., & Sherman, S. J. (1994). Social inference: Inductions, deductions, and analogies. In R. S. Wyer, Jr. & T. K. Srull (Eds.), *Handbook of social cognition* (Vol. 1). Hillsdale, NJ: Erlbaum.

Bell, B. E., & Loftus, E. F. (1989). Trivial persuasion in the courtroom: The power of (a few) minor details. *Journal of Personality and Social Psychology, 56,* 669–679.

Bell, D. (1987). The world and the United States in 2013. *Daedalus, 116,* 1–31.

Bell, P. A., & Baron, R. A. (1977). Aggression and ambient temperature: The inhibiting and facilitating effects of hot and cold environments. *Bulletin of the Psychonomic Society, 9,* 443–445.

Belson, W. (1978). *Television violence and the adolescent boy.* Hampshire, England: Saxon.

Bem, D. J. (1965). An experimental analysis of self-persuasion. *Journal of Experimental Social Psychology, 1,* 199–218.

Bem, D. J. (1967). Self-perception: An alternative explanation of cognitive dissonance phenomena. *Psychological Review, 74,* 183–200.

Bem, D. J. (1972). Self-perception theory. In L. Berkowitz (Ed.), *Advances in experimental social psychology* (Vol. 6). New York: Academic Press.

Bem, D. J., & Lord, C. G. (1979). Template matching: A proposal for probing the ecological validity of experimental settings in social psychology. *Journal of Personality and Social Psychology, 37,* 833–846.

Bem, D. J., & McConnell, H. K. (1970). Testing the self-perception explanation of dissonance phenomena: On the salience of premanipulation attitudes. *Journal of Personality and Social Psychology, 14,* 23–31.

Bem, S. L. (1975). Sex-role adaptability: One consequence of psychological androgyny. *Journal of Personality and Social Psychology, 31,* 634–643.

Bem, S. L. (1981). Gender schema theory: A cognitive account of sex differences. *Psychological Review, 88,* 354–364.

Bem, S. L. (1985). Androgyny and gender schema theory: A conceptual and empirical integration. In T. B. Sonderegger (Ed.), *Nebraska symposium on motivation: psychology and gender.* Lincoln: University of Nebraska Press.

Bem, S. L. (1993). *The lenses of gender.* New Haven, CT: Yale University Press.

Bem, S. L., Martyna, W., & Watson, C. (1976). Sex typing and androgyny: Further explorations of the expressive domain. *Journal of Personality and Social Psychology, 34,* 1016–1023.

Benenson, J. F., & Dweck, C. S. (1986). The development of trait explanations and self-evaluation in the academic and social domains. *Child Development, 57,* 1179–1187.

Benson, P. L., Karabenick, S. A., & Lerner, R. M. (1976). Pretty pleases: The effects of physical attractiveness, race, and sex on receiving help. *Journal of Experimental Social Psychology, 12,* 409–415.

Bentler, P. M. & Speckart, G. (1979). Models of attitude-behavior relations. *Psychological Bulletin, 86,* 452–464.

Bentler, P. M., & Newcomb, M. D. (1978). Longitudinal study of marital success and failure. *Journal of Consulting and Clinical Psychology, 46,* 1053–1070.

Benton, D. (1981). The extrapolation from animals to man: the example of testosterone and aggression. In P. F. Brain & D. Benton (Eds.), *Multidisci-*

plinary approaches to aggression research (pp. 401–418). Amsterdam: Elsevier.

Benton, D. (1982). Is the concept of dominance useful in understanding rodent behavior? *Aggressive Behavior, 8,* 104–107.

Benton, D., Brain, P. F., & Haug, M. (1986) *The aggressive female.* Montreal: Eden.

Berenthal, P. R., & Insko, C. A. (1993). Cohesiveness without groupthink: The interactive effects of social and task cohesion. *Group & Organizational Management, 18,* 66–87.

Berg, J. H., & Peplau, L. A. (1982). Loneliness: The relationship of self-disclosure and androgyny. *Personality and Social Psychology Bulletin, 8,* 624–630.

Berglas, S., & Jones, E. E. (1978). Drug choice as a self-handicapping strategy in response to noncommittal success. *Journal of Personality and Social Psychology, 36,* 405–417.

Berkowitz, L. (1969). The frustration-aggression hypothesis. In L. Berkowitz (Ed.), *Roots of aggression: A re-examination of the frustration-aggression hypothesis* (pp. 1–28). New York: Atherton.

Berkowitz, L. (1972). Social punishments, feelings, and other factors affecting helping and altruism. In L. Berkowitz (Ed.), *Advances in experimental social psychology* (Vol. 6, pp. 63–108). New York: Academic Press.

Berkowitz, L. (1974). External determinants of impulsive aggression. In J. de Wit & W. W. Hartup (Eds.), *Determinants and origins of aggressive behavior* (pp. 147–165). The Hague: Mouton.

Berkowitz, L. (1978). Whatever happened to the frustration-aggression hypothesis? *American Behavioral Scientist, 32,* 691–708.

Berkowitz, L. (1982). Aversive conditions as stimuli to aggression. In L. Berkowitz (Ed.), *Advances in experimental social psychology* (Vol. 15, pp. 249–288). New York: Academic Press.

Berkowitz, L. (1983). The experience of anger as a parallel process in the display of impulsive, "angry" aggression. In R. G. Geen & E. I. Donnerstein (Eds.), *Aggression: Theoretical and empirical reviews* (pp. 103–134). New York: Academic Press.

Berkowitz, L. (1984). Some effects of thoughts on anti- and prosocial influences of media events: A cognitive neoassociation analysis. *Psychological Bulletin, 95,* 410–427.

Berkowitz, L. (1987). Mood, self-awareness, and willingness to help. *Journal of Personality and Social Psychology, 52,* 721–729.

Berkowitz, L. (1989). Frustration-aggression hypothesis: Examination and reformulation *Psychological Bulletin, 106,* 59–73.

Berkowitz, L. (1993a). *Aggression: Its causes, consequences, and control.* New York: McGraw-Hill.

Berkowitz, L. (1993b). Towards a general theory of anger and emotional aggression: Implications of the cognitive-neoassociationistic perspective for the analysis of anger and other emotions. In R. S. Wyer, Jr., & T. K. Srull (Eds.), *Advances in social cognition: Vol. 6. Perspectives on anger and emotion.* Hillsdale, NJ: Erlbaum.

Berkowitz, L., & Alioto, J. T. (1973). The meaning of an observed event as a determinant of its aggressive consequences. *Journal of Personality and Social Psychology, 28,* 206–217.

Berkowitz, L., Cochran, S., & Embree, M. (1981). Physical pain and the goal of aversively stimulated aggression. *Journal of Personality and Social Psychology, 40,* 687–700.

Berkowitz, L., & Connor, W. H. (1966). Success, failure, and social responsibility. *Journal of Personality and Social Psychology, 4,* 664–669.

Berkowitz, L., & Devine, P. G. (1995). Has social psychology always been cognitive? And what is "cognitive" anyhow? *Personality and Social Psychology Bulletin, 21,* 696–703.

Berkowitz, L., & Donnerstein, E. (1982). External validity is more than skin deep: Some answers to the criticisms of laboratory experiments. *American Psychologist, 37,* 245–257.

Berkowitz, L., & Geen, R. B. (1967). Stimulus qualities of the target of aggression. *Journal of Personality and Social Psychology, 5,* 364–368.

Berkowitz, L., & Knurek, D. (1969). Label-mediated hostility generalization. *Journal of Personality and Social Psychology, 13,* 200–206.

Berkowitz, L., & LePage, A. (1967). Weapons as aggression-eliciting stimuli. *Journal of Personality and Social Psychology, 7,* 202–207.

Berkowitz, L., & Macauley, J. (1971). The contagion of criminal violence. *Sociometry, 34,* 238–260.

Berlyne, D. E. (1970). Novelty, complexity, and hedonic value. *Perception and Psychophysics, 8,* 279–286.

Bernard, J. (1981). *The female world.* New York: Macmillan.

Berndt, T. J., & Hanna, N. A. (in press). Intimacy and self-disclosure in friendships. In K. J. Rotenberg (Ed.), *Disclosure processes in children and adolescents.* New York: Springer-Verlag.

Bernieri, F. J., Reznik, J. S., & Rosenthal, R. (1988). Synchrony, pseudosynchrony, and dissynchrony: Measuring the entrainment process in mother-infant interactions. *Journal of Personality and Social Psychology, 54,* 243–253.

Bernieri, F. J., Zuckerman, M., Koestner, R., & Rosenthal, R. (1994). Measuring person perception accuracy: Another look at self-other agreement. *Personality and Social Psychology Bulletin, 20,* 367–378.

Bernstein, I. S. (1981). Dominance: The baby and the bathwater. *Behavioral and Brain Sciences, 4,* 419–457.

Bernstein, W. M., Stephenson, B. O., Snyder, M. L., & Wicklund, R. A. (1983). Causal ambiguity and heterosexual affiliation. *Journal of Experimental Social Psychology, 19,* 78–92.

Berry, D. S. (1990). Taking people at face value: Evidence for the kernel of truth hypothesis. *Social Cognition, 8,* 343–361.

Berry, D. S. (1991a). Accuracy in social perception: Contributions of facial and vocal information. *Journal of Personality and Social Psychology, 61,* 298–307.

Berry, D. S. (1991b). Attractive faces are not all created equal: Joint effects of facial babyishness and attractiveness on social perception. *Personality and Social Psychology Bulletin, 17,* 523–531.

Berry, D. S. (1992). Vocal types and stereotypes: Joint effects of vocal attractiveness and vocal maturity on person perception. *Journal of Nonverbal Behavior, 16,* 41–54.

Berry, D. S., & Brownlow, S. (1989). Were the physionomists right? Personality correlates of facial babyishness. *Personality and Social Psychology Bulletin, 15,* 266–279.

Berry, D. S., & McArthur, L. Z. (1986). Perceiving character in faces: The impact of age-related craniofacial changes on social perception. *Psychological Bulletin, 100,* 3–18.

Berry, D. S., & Zebrowitz-McArthur, L. (1988). What's in a face: Facial maturity and the attribution of legal responsibility. *Personality and Social Psychology Bulletin, 14,* 23–33.

Berry, J. W., Poortinga, Y. H., Segall, M. H., & Dasen, P. R. (1992). *Cross-cultural psychology: Research and applications.* Cambridge: Cambridge University Press.

Berscheid, E. (1966). Opinion change and communicator-communicatee similarity and dissimilarity. *Journal of Personality and Social Psychology, 4,* 670–680.

Berscheid, E. (1985). Interpersonal attraction. In G. Lindzey & E. Aronson (Eds.), *Handbook of social psychology* (3rd edition, Vol. 2). Hillsdale, NJ: Erlbaum.

Berscheid, E. (1993). Foreword. In A. E. Beale & R. J. Sternberg (Eds.), *The psychology of gender.* New York: Guilford Press.

Berscheid, E., Dion, K., Walster, E., & Walster, G. W. (1971). Physical attractiveness and dating choice: A test of the matching hypothesis. *Journal of Experimental Social Psychology, 7,* 173–189.

Berscheid, E., Snyder, M., & Omoto, A. M. (1989). The Relationship Closeness Inventory: Assessing the closeness of interpersonal relationships. *Journal of Personality and Social*

Psychology, 57, 792–807.

Berscheid, E., & Walster, E. (1974). Physical attractiveness. In L. Berkowitz (Ed.), *Advances in Experimental Social Psychology.* New York: Academic Press. Pp. 157–215.

Berscheid, E., & Walster, E. (1983). *Interpersonal attraction.* Reading, MA: Addison-Wesley.

Betancourt, H. (1990). An attribution-empathy model of helping behavior: Behavioral intentions and judgments of help-giving. *Personality and Social Psychology Bulletin, 16,* 573–591.

Bettencourt, B. A., Brewer, M. B., Croak, M. R., & Miller, N. (1992). Cooperation and the reduction of intergroup bias: The role of reward structure and social orientation. *Journal of Experimental Social Psychology, 28,* 301–319.

Bettman, J. R., & Weitz, B. A. (1983). Attributions in the board room: Causal reasoning in corporate annual reports. *Administrative Science Quarterly, 28,* 165–183.

Bickman, L. (1971). The effects of another bystander's ability to help on bystander intervention in an emergency. *Journal of Experimental Social Psychology, 7,* 367–379.

Bierbrauer, G. (1979). Why did he do it? Attribution of obedience and the phenomenon of dispositional bias. *European Journal of Social Psychology, 9,* 67–84.

Biernat, M., & Manis, M. (1994). Shifting standards and stereotype-based judgments. *Journal of Personality and Social Psychology, 66,* 5–20.

Biernat, M., Manis, M., & Nelson, T. E. (1991). Stereotypes and standards of judgment. *Journal of Personality and Social Psychology, 60,* 485–499.

Billig, M., & Tajfel, H. (1973). Social categorization and similarity in intergroup behavior. *European Journal of Social Psychology, 3,* 27–52.

Black, J. B., Galambos, J. A., & Read, S. J. (1984). Comprehending stories and social situations. In R. S. Wyer, Jr., & T. K. Srull (Eds.), *Handbook of social cognition* (Vol. 3). Hillsdale, NJ: Erlbaum.

Blanchard, D. C., & Blanchard, R. J. (1984). Affect and aggression: An animal model applied to human behavior. In R. J. Blanchard & D. C. Blanchard (Eds.), *Advances in the study of aggression* (Vol. 1, pp. 1–62). Orlando, FL: Academic Press.

Blanchard, R. J. (1984). Pain and aggression reconsidered. In K. J. Flannelly, R. J. Blanchard, & D. C. Blanchard (Eds.), *Biological perspectives on aggression.* New York: Alan Liss.

Blanck, P. D., Bellack, A. S., Rosnow, R. L., Rotheram-Borus, M. J., & Schooler, N. R. (1992). Scientific rewards and conflicts of ethical choices in human subjects research. *American Psychologist, 47,* 959–965.

Blaney, N. T., Stephan, S., Rosenfield, D., Aronson, E., & Sikes, J. (1977). Interdependence in the classroom: A field study. *Journal of Educational Psychology, 69,* 121–128.

Blascovich, J., Ernst, J. M., Tomaka, J., Kelsey, R. M., Salomon, K. L., & Fazio, R. H. (1993). Attitude accessibility as a moderator of autonomic reactivity during decision making. *Journal of Personality and Social Psychology, 64,* 165–176.

Blascovich, J., Ginsberg, G. P., & Howe, R. C. (1975). Blackjack and the risky shift, II: Monetary stakes. *Journal of Experimental Social Psychology, 11,* 224–232.

Blascovich, J., Ginsberg, G. P., & Veach, T. L. (1975). A pluralistic explanation of choice shifts on the risk dimension. *Journal of Personality and Social Psychology, 31,* 422–429.

Blass, T. (1991). Understanding behavior in the Milgram obedience experiment: The role of personality, situations, and their interactions. *Journal of Personality and Social Psychology, 60,* 398–413.

Bless, H., Bohner, G., Schwarz, N., & Strack, F. (1990). Mood and persuasion: A cognitive response analysis. *Personality and Social Psychology Bulletin, 16,* 331–345.

Blight, J. G., & Welch, D. A. (1989). *On the brink: Americans and Soviets reexamine the Cuban Missile Crisis.* New York: Hill & Wang.

Boaz, F. (1905). The Negro and the demands of modern life: Ethnic and anatomical considerations. *Charities, 15,* 85.

Bobo, L. (1983). Whites' opposition to busing: Symbolic racism or realistic group conflict? *Journal of Personality and Social Psychology, 45,* 1196–1210.

Bobo, L. (1988). Group conflict, prejudice, and the paradox of contemporary racial attitudes. In P. A. Katz & D. A. Taylor (Eds.), *Eliminating racism: Profiles in controversy.* New York: Plenum. Pp. 85–114.

Bochner, A. P. (1984). The functions of communication in interpersonal bonding. In C. C. Arnold & J. W. Bowers (Eds.), *Handbook of rhetorical and communication theory.* Boston: Allyn & Bacon. Pp. 544–621.

Bochner, S., & Insko, C. A. (1966). Communicator discrepancy, source credibility, and opinion change. *Journal of Personality and Social Psychology, 4,* 614–621.

Bodenhausen, G. V. (1988). Stereotypic biases in social decision making and memory: Testing process models for stereotype use. *Journal of Personality and Social Psychology, 55,* 726–737.

Bodenhausen, G. V. (1993). Emotion, arousal, and stereotypic judgment: A heuristic model of affect and stereotyping. In D. Mackie & D. Hamilton (Eds.), *Affect, cognition, and stereotyping: Interactive processes in intergroup perception.* San Diego, CA: Academic Press.

Bodenhausen, G. V., Kramer, G. P., & Süsser K. (1994). Happiness and stereotypic thinking in social judgment. *Journal of Personality and Social Psychology, 66,* 621–632.

Bodenhausen, G. V., Schwarz, N., Bless, H., & Wänke, M. (1995). Effects of atypical exemplars on racial beliefs: Enlightened racism or generalized appraisals? *Journal of Experimental Social Psychology, 31,* 48–63.

Bodenhausen, G. V., Sheppard, L. A., & Kramer, G. P. (1994). Negative affect and social judgment: The differential impact of anger and sadness. *European Journal of Social Psychology, 24,* 45–62.

Bodenhausen, G. V., & Wyer, R. S., Jr. (1985). Effects of stereotypes on decision making and information-processing strategies: *Journal of Personality and Social Psychology, 48,* 267–282.

Boehm, C. (1984). *Blood revenge: The anthropology of feuding in Montenegro and other tribal societies.* Lawrence, KS: University Press of Kansas.

Boggiano, A. K., Harackiewicz, J. M., Bessette, J. M., & Main, D. S. (1985). Increasing children's interest through performance-contingent reward. *Social Cognition, 3,* 400–411.

Bolig, R., Stein, P. J., & McHenry, P. C. (1984). The self-advertisement approach to dating: Male-female differences. *Family Relations, 33,* 587–592.

Bonacich, P. (1976). Secrecy and solidarity. *Sociometry, 39,* 200–208.

Bond, C. F., Jr. (1982). Social facilitation: A self-presentational view. *Journal of Personality and Social Psychology, 42,* 1042–1050.

Bond, C. F., Jr., Berry, D. S., & Omar, A. (1994). The kernel of truth in judgments of deceptiveness. *Basic and Applied Social Psychology, 15,* 523–534.

Bond, C. F., Jr., & Brockett, D. R. (1987). A social context-personality index theory of memory for acquaintances. *Journal of Personality and Social Psychology, 52,* 1110–1121.

Bond, C. F., Jr., DiCandia, C. G., & MacKinnon, J. R. (1988). Responses to violence in a psychiatric setting: The role of the patient's race. *Personality and Social Psychology Bulletin, 14,* 448–458.

Bond, C. F., Jr., Kahler, K. N., & Paolicelli, L. M. (1985). The miscommunication of deception: An adaptive perspective. *Journal of Experimental Social Psychology, 21,* 331–345.

Bond, C. F., Jr., Omar, A., Mahmoud, A., & Bonser, R. N. (1990). Lie detection across cultures. *Journal of Nonverbal Behavior, 14,* 189–204.

Bond, C. F., Jr., Omar, A., Pitre, U., Lashley, B. R., Skaggs, L. M., & Kirk, C. T. (1992). Fishy-looking liars: Deception judgment from expectancy violation. *Journal of Personality and Social Psychology, 63,* 969–977.

Bond, C. F., Jr., & Robinson, M. (1988). The evolution of deception. *Journal of Nonverbal Behavior, 12,* 295–307.

Bond, C. F., Jr., & Sedikides, C. (1988). The recapitulation hypothesis in person retrieval. *Journal of Experimental Social Psychology, 24,* 195–221.

Bond, C. F., Jr., & Titus, L. J. (1983). Social facilitation: A meta-analysis of 241 studies. *Psychological Bulletin, 94,* 265–292.

Bond, C. F., Jr., & Van Leeuwen, M. D. (1991). Can a part be greater than the whole? On the relationship between primary and meta-analytic evidence. *Basic and Applied Social Psychology, 12,* 33–40.

Bond, M. H. (1993). Emotions and their expression in Chinese culture. *Journal of Nonverbal Behavior, 17,* 245–262.

Bond, M. H., & Hwang, K. K. (1986). The social psychology of Chinese people. In M. H. Bond (Ed.), *The psychology of Chinese people.* Hong Kong: Oxford University Press.

Boninger, D. S., Krosnick, J. A., & Berent, M. K. (1995). Origins of attitude importance: Self-interest, social identification, and value relevance. *Journal of Personality and Social Psychology, 68,* 61–80.

Boninger, D. S., Krosnick, J. A., Berent, M. K., & Fabrigar, L. R. (1995). In R. E. Petty & J. A. Krosnick (Eds.), *Attitude strength: Antecedents and consequences.* Hillsdale, NJ: Erlbaum.

Bonnano, G. A., & Stillings, N. A. (1986). Preference, familiarity and recognition after repeated brief exposures to random geometric shapes. *American Journal of Psychology, 99,* 403–415.

Borelli, M., & Heidt, P. (1981). *Therapeutic touch: A book of readings.* New York: Springer.

Borgida, E., Conner, C., & Manteufel, L. (1992). Understanding living kidney donation: A behavioral decision-making perspective. In S. Spacapan & S. Oskamp (Eds.), *Helping and being helped: Naturalistic studies.* London, New Delhi: Sage Publications.

Borgida, E., & White, P. (1978). Social perception of rape victims: The impact of legal reform. *Law and Human Behavior, 2,* 339–350.

Boring, E. G., Langfeld, H. S., & Weld, H. P. (1939). *Introduction to psychology.* New York: Wiley.

Bornstein, G. (1992). The free-rider problem in intergroup conflicts over step-level and continuous public goods. *Journal of Personality and Social Psychology, 62,* 597–606.

Bornstein, G., & Ben-Yossef, M. (1994). Cooperation in intergroup and single-group social dilemmas. *Journal of Experimental Social Psychology, 30,* 52–67.

Bornstein, R. F. (1989). Exposure and affect: Overview and meta-analysis of research, 1968–1987. *Psychological Bulletin, 106,* 265–289.

Bornstein, R. F., & D'Agostino, P. R. (1992). Stimulus recognition and the mere exposure effect. *Journal of Personality and Social Psychology, 63,* 545–552.

Bornstein, R. F., Kale, A. R., & Cornell, K. R. (1990). Boredom as a limiting condition on the mere exposure effect. *Journal of Personality and Social Psychology, 58,* 791–800.

Bornstein, R. F., Leone, D. R., & Galley, D. J. (1987). The generalizability of subliminal mere exposure effects: Influence of stimuli perceived without awareness on social behavior. *Journal of Personality and Social Psychology, 53,* 1070–1079.

Bossard, J. H. S. (1932). Residential propinquity as a factor in marriage selection. *American Journal of Sociology, 38,* 219–224.

Bouchard, T. J., & Hare, M. (1970). Size, performance, and potential in brainstorming groups. *Journal of Applied Psychology, 54,* 51–55.

Bourhis, R. Y. (1994). Power, gender, and intergroup discrimination: Some minimal group experiments. In M. P. Zanna & J. M. Olson (Eds.), *The psychology of prejudice: The Ontario symposium* (Vol. 7). Hillsdale, NJ: Erlbaum.

Bower, G. H., Clark, M. D., Lesgold, A. J., & Winzenz, D. (1969). Hierarchical retrieval schemas in recall of categorized word lists. *Journal of Verbal Learning and Verbal Behavior, 8,* 323–343.

Bowlby, J. (1969). *Attachment and loss: Vol. 1. Attachment.* New York: Basic Books.

Bowlby, J. (1979). *The making and breaking of affectional bonds.* London: Tavistock.

Boykin, A. W. (1983). The academic performance of Afro-American children. In J. Spence (Ed.), *Achievement and achievement motives.* San Francisco: W. H. Freeman.

Bradbury, T. N., & Fincham, F. D. (1990). Attributions in marriage: Review and critique. *Psychological Bulletin, 107,* 3–33.

Bradbury, T. N., & Fincham, F. D. (1992). Attributions and behavior in marital interaction. *Journal of Personality and Social Psychology, 63,* 613–628.

Brain, P. F. (1981). Biological explanations of human aggression and the resulting therapies offered by such approaches: A critical evaluation. In R. J. Blanchard & D. C. Blanchard (Eds.), *Advances in the study of aggression* (Vol. 1, pp. 63–102). Orlando, FL: Academic Press.

Branco, K. J., & Williamson, J. B. (1982). Stereotyping and the life cycle: Views of aging and the aged. In A. G. Miller (Ed.), *In the eye of the beholder: Contemporary issues in stereotyping.* New York: Praeger.

Brandt, D., Miller, G., & Hocking, J. (1980). The truth-deception attribution: Effects of familiarity on the ability of observers to detect deception. *Human Communication Research, 6,* 99–110.

Branscombe, N. R., & Wann, D. L. (1992). Physiological arousal and reactions to outgroup members during competitions that implicate an important social identity. *Aggressive Behavior, 18,* 85–93.

Branscombe, N. R., & Wann, D. L. (1994). Collective self-esteem consequences of outgroup derogation when a valued social identity is on trial. *European Journal of Social Psychology, 24,* 641–657.

Branscombe, N. R., & Weir, J. A. (1992). Resistance as stereotype-inconsistency: Consequences for judgments of rape victims. *Journal of Social and Clinical Psychology, 11,* 80–102.

Bransford, J. D., & Franks, J. J. (1971). The abstraction of linguistic ideas. *Cognitive Psychology, 2,* 331–350.

Bray, R. M., Kerr, N. L., & Atkin, R. S. (1978). Effects of group size, problem difficulty, and sex on group performance and member reactions. *Journal of Personality and Social Psychology, 36,* 1224–1240.

Bray, R. M., & Noble, A. M. (1987). Authoritarianism and decisions of mock juries: Evidence of jury bias and group polarization. In L. S. Wrightsman, S. M. Kassin, & C. E. Willis (Eds.), *In the jury box: Controversies in the courtroom.* Newbury Park, CA: Sage.

Breckler, S. J. (1984). Empirical validation of affect, behavior, and cognition as distinct components of attitude. *Journal of Personality and Social Psychology, 47,* 1191–1205.

Breckler, S. J. (1994). Memory for the experience of donating blood: Just how bad was it? *Basic and Applied Social Psychology, 15,* 467–488.

Breckler, S. J., & Fried, H. S. (1993). On knowing what you like and liking what you smell: Attitudes depend on the form in which the object is represented. *Personality and Social Psychology Bulletin, 19,* 228–240.

Brehm, J. W. (1956). Post-decision changes in desirability of alternatives. *Journal of Abnormal and Social Psychology, 52,* 384–389.

Brehm, J. W. (1966). *A theory of psychological reactance.* New York: Academic Press.

Brehm, J. W., & Self, E. (1989). The intensity of motivation. In M. R. Rosenzweig & L. W. Porter (Eds.), *Annual review of psychology.* Palo Alto: Annual Reviews, Inc.

Bretl, D. J., & Cantor, J. (1988). The portrayal of men and women in U. S. television commercials: A recent content analysis and trends over 15 years. *Sex Roles, 18,* 595–609.

Cacioppo, J. T., & Petty, R. E. (1985). Central and peripheral routes to persuasion: The role of message repetition. In A. Mitchell & L. Alwitt (Eds.), *Psychological processes and advertising effects*. Hillsdale, NJ: Erlbaum.

Cacioppo, J. T., & Petty, R. E. (1987). Stalking rudimentary processes of social influence: A psychophysiological approach. In M. P. Zanna, J. M. Olson, & C. P. Herman (Eds.), *Social influence: The Ontario Symposium* (Vol. 5). Hillsdale, NJ: Erlbaum.

Cacioppo, J. T., Petty, R. E., & Crites, S. L., Jr. (1994). Attitude change. *Encyclopedia of Human Behavior, 1,* 261–270.

Cacioppo, J. T., Petty, R. E., Losch, M. E., & Kim, H. S. (1986). Electromyographic specificity during simple physical and attitudinal tasks: Location and topographical features of integrated EMG responses. *Biological Psychology, 18,* 85–121.

Cacioppo, J. T., Petty, R. E., & Morris, K. (1983). Effects of need for cognition on message evaluation, recall, and persuasion. *Journal of Personality and Social Psychology, 45,* 805–818.

Cacioppo, J. T., Priester, J. R., & Berntson, G. G. (1993). Rudimentary determinants of attitudes: II. Arm flexion and extension have differential effects on attitudes. *Journal of Personality and Social Psychology, 65,* 5–17.

Cahoon, D. D., & Edmonds, E. M. (1989). Male-female estimates of opposite-sex first impressions concerning females' clothing styles. *Bulletin of the Psychonomic Society, 27,* 280–281.

Cain, K. M., & Dweck, C. S. (1989). The development of children's conceptions of intelligence: A theoretical framework. In R. J. Sternberg (Ed.), *Advances in the psychology of human intelligence* (Vol. 5). Hillsdale, NJ: Erlbaum.

Calder, B. J., Insko, C., & Yandell, B. (1974). The relation of cognitive and memorial processes to persuasion in a simulated jury trial. *Journal of Applied Social Psychology, 4,* 62–93.

Calder, B. J., & Sternthal, B. (1980). Television commercial wearout: An information processing view. *Journal of Marketing Research, 17,* 173–186.

Calhoun, J. B. (1967). Ecological factors in the development of behavioral anomalies. In E. Zubin (Ed.), *Comparative psychopathology.* New York: Grune & Stratton.

Callaway, M. R., Marriott, R. G., & Esser, J. K. (1985). Effects of dominance on group decision making: Toward a stress-reduction explanation of groupthink. *Journal of Personality and Social Psychology, 49,* 949–952.

Campbell, D. T. (1965). Ethnocentric and other altruistic motives. In D. Levine (Ed.), *Nebraska symposium on motivation* (Vol. 13). Lincoln: University of Nebraska Press.

Campbell, J. D. (1986). Similarity and uniqueness: The effects of attribute type, relevance, and individual differences in self-esteem and depression. *Journal of Personality and Social Psychology, 50,* 281–294.

Campos, J. J., Barrett, K. C., Lamb, M. E., Goldsmith, H. H., & Stenberg, C. (1983). Socioemotional development. In M. M. Haith & J. J. Campos (Eds.), *Handbook of child psychology: Vol. 2. Infancy and psychobiology.* New York: Wiley.

Cann, A., & Siegfried, W. D. (1990). Gender stereotypes and dimensions of effective leader behavior. *Sex Roles, 23,* 413–419.

Cantor, J. R. (1982). Adolescent fright reactions from TV programming. *Journal of Communication, 32,* 87–99.

Cantor, J. R., Zillmann, D., & Einsiedel, E. F. (1978). Female responses to provocation after exposure to aggressive and erotic films. *Communication Research, 5,* 395–411.

Cantril, H. (1940). America faces the war: A study in public opinion. *Public Opinion Quarterly, 4,* 387–407.

Caprara, G. V., Renzi, P., Alcini, P., D'Imperio, G., & Travaglia, G. (1983). Instigation to aggress and escalation of aggression examined from a personological perspective: The role of irritability and emotional susceptibility. *Aggressive Behavior, 9,* 345–351.

Carli, L. L., Ganley, R., & Pierce-Otay, A. (1991). Similarity and satisfaction in roommate relationships. *Personality and Social Psychology Bulletin, 17,* 419–426.

Carlsmith, J. M., Ellsworth, P. C., & Aronson, E. (1976). *Methods of research in social psychology.* New York: Random House.

Carlson, M., Charlin, V., & Miller, N. (1988). Positive mood and helping behavior: A test of six hypotheses. *Journal of Personality and Social Psychology, 55,* 211–229.

Carlson, M., Marcus-Newhall, A., & Miller, N. (1989). Evidence for a general construct of aggression. *Personality and Social Psychology Bulletin, 15,* 377–389.

Carlston, D. E. (1980). Events, inferences, and impression formation. In R. Hastie, T. Ostrom, E. Ebbesen, R. Wyer, D. Hamilton, & D. Carlston (Eds.), *Person memory: The cognitive basis of social perception.* Hillsdale, NJ: Erlbaum.

Carlston, D. E., & Skowronski, J. J. (1994). Savings in the relearning of trait information as evidence for spontaneous inference generation. *Journal of Personality and Social Psychology, 66,* 840–856.

Carnevale, P. J. (1994). Negotiation. *Encyclopedia of Human Behavior, 3,* 271–281.

Carnevale, P. J., & Pruitt, D. G. (1992). Negotiation and mediation. *Annual Review of Psychology, 43,* 531–582.

Caron, A. J., Caron, R. F., & MacLean, D. J. (1988). Infant discrimination of naturalistic emotional expressions: The role of face and voice. *Child Development, 39,* 604–616.

Carroll, J. S., & Payne, J. W. (1976). *Cognition and social behavior.* Hillsdale, NJ: Erlbaum.

Carson, P. P., Carson, K. D., & Roe, C. W. (1993). Social power bases: A meta-analytic examination of interrelationships and outcomes. *Journal of Applied Psychology, 23,* 1150–1169.

Cartwright, D. (1971). Risk taking by individuals and groups: An assessment of research employing choice dilemmas. *Journal of Personality and Social Psychology, 20,* 361–378.

Carver, C. S. (1974). Facilitation of physical aggression through objective self-awareness. *Journal of Experimental Social Psychology, 10,* 365–370.

Carver, C. S., DeGregorio, E., & Gillis, R. (1980). Ego-defensive attribution among two categories of observers. *Personality and Social Psychology Bulletin, 6,* 44–50.

Carver, C. S., & Scheier, M. F. (1981). The self-attention-induced feedback loop and social facilitation. *Journal of Experimental Social Psychology, 17,* 545–568.

Cash, T. F., & Kilcullen, R. N. (1985). The aye of the beholder: Susceptibility to sexism and beautyism in the evaluation of managerial applicants. *Journal of Applied Social Psychology, 15,* 591–605.

Casper, J. D., Benedict, K., & Kelly, J. R. (1988). Cognitions, attitudes, and decision-making in search and seizure cases. *Journal of Applied Social Psychology, 18,* 93–113.

Casper, J. D., Benedict, K., & Perry, J. L. (1989). Juror decision making, attitudes, and the hindsight bias. *Law and Human Behavior, 13,* 291–310.

Caspi, A., & Herbener, E. S. (1990). Continuity and change: Assortative marriage and the consistency of personality in adulthood. *Journal of Personality and Social Psychology, 58,* 250–258.

Cassata, B., Anderson, P., & Skill, T. (1980). The older adult in daytime serial drama. *Journal of Communication, 30,* 48–49.

Cassidy, J., & Asher, S. R. (1992). Loneliness and peer relations in young children. *Child Development, 63,* 350–365.

Catrambone, R., & Markus, H. R. (1987). The role of self-schemas in going beyond the information given. *Social Cognition, 5,* 349–368.

Cervone, D., Kopp, D. A., Schaumann, L., & Scott, W. D. (1994). Mood, self-efficacy, and performance standards: Lower moods induce higher standards for performance. *Journal of Personality and Social Psychology, 67,* 499–512.

Cervone, D., & Peake, P. (1986). Anchoring, efficacy, and action: The influence of judgmental heuristics on self-efficacy judgments and behavior. *Journal of Personality and Social Psychology, 50,* 492–501.

Cervone, D., & Scott, W. D. (in press). Self-efficacy theory of behavioral change: Foundations, conceptual issues, and therapeutic implications. In W. O'Donohue & L. Krasner (Eds.), *Theories in behavior therapy.* Washington, DC: American Psychological Association.

Chagnon, N. A. (1988). Life histories, blood revenge, and warfare in a tribal population. *Science, 239,* 985–991.

Chaiken, A. L., Gillen, H. B., Derlega, V., Heinen, J., & Wilson, M. (1978). Students' reactions to teachers' physical attractiveness and non-verbal behavior: Two exploratory studies. *Psychology in the Schools, 15,* 588–595.

Chaiken, A. L., Sigler, E., & Derlega, V. J. (1974). Nonverbal mediators of teacher expectancy effects. *Journal of Personality and Social Psychology, 30,* 144–149.

Chaiken, S. (1979). Communicator physical attractiveness and persuasion. *Journal of Personality and Social Psychology, 3,* 1387–1397.

Chaiken, S. (1980). Heuristic versus systematic information processing and the use of source versus message cues in persuasion. *Journal of Personality and Social Psychology, 45,* 805–818.

Chaiken, S. (1987). The heuristic model of persuasion. In M. P. Zanna, J. M. Olson, & C. P. Herman (Eds.), *Social influence: The Ontario Symposium* (Vol. 5). Hillsdale, NJ: Erlbaum.

Chaiken, S., & Baldwin, M. W. (1981). Affective-cognitive consistency and the effect of salient behavioral information on the self-perception of attitudes. *Journal of Personality and Social Psychology, 34,* 605–614.

Chaiken, S., & Bargh, J. A. (1993). Occurrence versus moderation of the automatic attitude activation effect: Reply to Fazio. *Journal of Personality and Social Psychology, 64,* 759–765.

Chaiken, S., & Eagly, A. H. (1983). Communication modality as a determinant of persuasion: The role of communicator salience. *Journal of Personality and Social Psychology, 45,* 241–256.

Chaiken, S., Giner-Sorolla, R., & Chen, S. (in press). Beyond accuracy: Defense and impression motives in heuristic and systematic information processing. In P. M. Gollwitzer & J. A. Bargh (Eds.), *The psychology of action: Linking motivation and cognition to behavior.* New York: Guilford.

Chaiken, S., Liberman, A., & Eagly, A. H. (1989). Heuristic and systematic information processing within and beyond the persuasion context. In J. S. Uleman & J. A. Bargh (Eds.), *Unintended thought.* New York: Guilford.

Chaiken, S., & Maheswaran, D. (1994). Heuristic processing can bias systematic processing: Effects of source credibility, argument ambiguity, and task importance on attitude judgment. *Journal of Personality and Social Psychology, 66,* 460–473.

Chaiken, S., & Pliner, P. (1987). Women, but not men, are what they eat: The effect of meal size and gender on perceived femininity and masculinity. *Personality and Social Psychology Bulletin, 13,* 166–176.

Chaiken, S., Pomerantz, E. M., & Giner-Sorolla, R. (1995). Structural consistency and attitude strength. In R. E. Petty & J. A. Krosnick (Eds.), *Attitude strength: Antecedents and consequences.* Hillsdale, NJ: Erlbaum.

Chapdelaine, A., Kenny, D. A., & LaFontana, K. M. (1994). Matchmaker, matchmaker, can you make me a match? Predicting liking between two unacquainted persons. *Journal of Personality and Social Psychology, 67,* 83–91.

Chapman, J. B. (1975). Comparisons of male and female leadership styles. *Academy of Management Journal, 18,* 645–650.

Chapman, L. J., & Chapman, J. P. (1969). Illusory correlation as an obstacle to the use of valid psychodiagnostic signs. *Journal of Abnormal Psychology, 14,* 271–280.

Check, J. V. P., & Malamuth, N. M. (1984). Can participation in pornography experiments have positive effects? *The Journal of Sex Research, 20,* 14–31.

Chemers, M. M. (1993). An integrative theory of leadership. In M. M. Chemers & R. Ayman (Eds.), *Leadership theory and research: Perspectives and directions.* San Diego, CA: Academic Press.

Chemers, M. M., Hays, R. B., Rhodewalt, F., & Wysocki, J. (1985). A person-environment analysis of job stress: A contingency model explanation. *Journal of Personality and Social Psychology, 49,* 628–635.

Chemers, M. M., Rice, R. W., Sundstrom, E., & Butler, W. M. (1975). Leader esteem for the least preferred co-worker scale, training, and effectiveness: An experimental examination. *Journal of Personality and Social Psychology, 31,* 401–409.

Chency, D., Seyforth, R., & Smuts, B. (1986). Social relationships and social cognition in nonhuman primates. *Science, 234,* 1361–1366.

Child, I. L., Potter, E. H., & Levine, E. M. (1946). Children's textbooks and personality development: An exploration in the social psychology of education. *Psychological Monographs, 60* (3, Whole No. 279).

Chin, M. G., & McClintock, C. G. (1993). The effects of intergroup discrimination and social values on level of self-esteem in the minimal group paradigm. *European Journal of Social Psychology, 23,* 63–75.

Chisolm, J. S. (1993). Death, hope, and sex: Life-history theory and the development of reproductive strategies. *Current Anthropology, 34,* 1–12.

Christiansen, A., & Heavey, C. L. (1990). Gender and social structure in the demand/withdraw pattern of marital conflict. *Journal of Personality and Social Psychology, 59,* 73–81.

Christy, P. R., Gelfand, D. M., & Hartmann, D. P. (1971). Effects of competition-induced frustration on two classes of modeled behavior. *Developmental Psychology, 5,* 104–111.

Chu, G. C. (1985). The changing concept of self in contemporary China. In A. J. Marsella, G. DeVos, & F. L. K. Hus (Eds.), *Culture and self: Asian and Western perspectives.* London, England: Tavistock.

Cialdini, R. B. (1993). *Influence: Science and practice.* New York: HarperCollins.

Cialdini, R. B., Borden, R. J., Thorne, A., Walker, M. R., Freeman, S., & Sloan, L. R. (1976). Basking in reflected glory: Three (football) field studies. *Journal of Personality and Social Psychology, 34,* 366–375.

Cialdini, R. B., Darby, B. L., & Vincent, J. E. (1973). Transgression and altruism: A case for hedonism. *Journal of Experimental Social Psychology, 9,* 502–516.

Cialdini, R. B., & De Nicholas, M. E. (1989). Self-presentation by association. *Journal of Personality and Social Psychology, 57,* 626–631.

Cialdini, R. B., & Kenrick, D. T. (1976). Altruism as hedonism: A social development perspective on the relationship of negative mood state and helping. *Journal of Personality and Social Psychology, 34,* 907–914.

Cialdini, R. B., Kenrick, D. T., & Baumann, D. J. (1982). Effects of mood on prosocial behavior in children and adults. In N. Eisenberg (Ed.), *The development of prosocial behavior* (pp. 339–359). New York: Academic Press.

Cialdini, R. B., & Richardson, K. D. (1980). Two indirect tactics of impression management: Basking and blasting. *Journal of Personality and Social Psychology, 39,* 406–415.

Cicone, M. V., & Ruble, D. N. (1978). Beliefs about males. *Journal of Social Issues, 34(1),* 5–16.

Cini, M. A., Moreland, R. L., & Levine, J. M. (1993). Group staffing levels and responses to prospective and new group members. *Journal of Personality and Social Psychology, 65,* 723–734.

Clanton, G., & Smith, L. G. (Eds.) (1987). *Jealousy.* Lantham, MA: University Press of America.

Clare, A. (1986). *Lovelaw: Love, sex, and marriage around the world.* London: BBC Publications.

Clark, D. M., & Teasdale, J. D. (1985). Constraints on the effects of mood on memory. *Journal of Personality and Social Psychology, 52,* 749–758.

Clark, L. F. (1994). Social cognition and health psychology. In R. S. Wyer, Jr., & T. K. Srull (Eds.), *Handbook of social cognition* (Vol. 2). Hillsdale, NJ: Erlbaum.

Clark, M. S. (1984). Record keeping in two types of relationships. *Journal of Personality and Social Psychology, 47,* 549–557.

Clark, M. S., Helgeson, V. S., Mickelson, K., & Pataki, S. P. (1994). Some cognitive structures and processes relevant to relationship functioning. In R. S. Wyer, Jr., & T. K. Srull (Eds.), *Handbook of social cognition* (Vol. 2). Hillsdale, NJ: Erlbaum.

Clark, M. S., & Isen, A. M. (1982). Toward understanding the relationship between feeling states and social behavior. In A. Hastorf & A. Isen (Eds.), *Cognitive social psychology.* New York: Elsevier North-Holland.

Clark, M. S., & Mills, J. (1979). Interpersonal attraction in exchange and communal relationships. *Journal of Personality and Social Psychology, 37,* 12–24.

Clark, M. S., Mills, J., & Powell, M. (1986). Keeping track of needs in communal and exchange relationships. *Journal of Personality and Social Psychology, 51,* 333–338.

Clark, M. S., & Reis, H. T. (1988). Interpersonal processes in close relationships. *Annual Review of Psychology, 39,* 609–672.

Clark, M. S., & Taraban, C. (1991). Reactions to and willingness to express emotions in communal and exchange relationships. *Journal of Experimental Social Psychology, 27,* 324–336.

Clark, M. S., & Waddell, B. A. (1983). Effects of moods on thoughts about helping, attraction and information acquisition. *Social Psychology Quarterly, 46,* 31–35.

Clark, R. D. III, & Hatfield, E. (1989). Gender differences in receptivity to sexual offers. *Journal of Psychology and Human Sexuality, 2,* 39–55.

Clark, R. D. III. (1974). Effects of sex and race on helping behavior in a non-reactive setting. *Representative Research in Social Psychology, 5,* 1–6.

Clark, R. D., III (1990). The impact of AIDS on gender differences in willingness to engage in casual sex. *Journal of Applied Social Psychology, 20,* 771–782.

Clark, R. D. III. (1994). A few parallels between group polarization and minority influence. In S. Moscovici, A. Mucchi-Faina, & A. Maass (Eds.), *Minority influence.* Chicago, IL: Nelson Hall.

Clark, R. D., III. (1994). The role of censorship in minority influence. *European Journal of Social Psychology, 24,* 331–338.

Clarke, A. C. (1952). An examination of the operation of residential propinquity as a factor in mate selection. *American Sociological Review, 27,* 17–22.

Clary, E. G., & Snyder, M. (1991). A functional analysis of altruism and prosocial behavior. In M. Clark (Ed.), *Prosocial behavior, Review of Personality and Social Psychology* (Vol. 12). London Sage Publications.

Clary, E. G., Snyder, M., Ridge, R. D., Miene, P. K., & Haugen, J. A. (1994). Matching messages to motives in persuasion: A functional approach to promoting volunteerism. *Journal of Applied Social Psychology, 24,* 1129–1149.

Clifford, M. M., & Walster, E. H. (1973). The effect of physical attractiveness on teacher expectation. *Sociology of Education, 46,* 248–258.

Cline, V. B., Croft, R. G., & Courrier, S. (1973). Desensitization of children to television violence. *Journal of Personality and Social Psychology, 27,* 360–365.

Clore, G. L., & Gormly, J. B. (1974). Knowing, feeling, and liking: A psychophysiological study of attraction. *Journal of Research in Personality, 8,* 218–230.

Clore, G. L., Ortony, A., & Foss, M. A. (1987). The psychological foundations of the affective lexicon. *Journal of Personality and Social Psychology, 53,* 751–766.

Clutton-Brock, T. H. (1991, October). Lords of the lek. *Natural History,* pp. 34–41.

Cochran, S. D., Mays, V. M., Ciarletta, J., Caruso, C., & Mallon, D. (1992). Efficacy of the theory of reasoned action in predicting AIDS-related sexual risk reduction among gay men. *Journal of Applied Social Psychology, 22,* 1481–1501.

Cochran, W., & Tesser, A. (in press). The "What the hell effect": Some effects of goal proximity and goal framing on performance. In L. Martin & A. Tesser (Eds.), *Goals and affect.*

Cohen, B., Waugh, G., & Place, K. (1989). At the movies: An unobtrusive study of arousal attraction. *Journal of Social Psychology, 129,* 691–693.

Cohen, C. E. (1981). Person categories and social perception: Testing some boundaries of the processing effects of prior knowledge. *Journal of Personality and Social Psychology, 40,* 441–452.

Cohen, C. E. (1983). Inferring the characteristics of other people: Categories and attribute accessibility. *Journal of Personality and Social Psychology, 44,* 34–44.

Cohen, E. G. (1984). The desegregated school: Problems in status power and interethnic climate. In N. Miller & M. B. Brewer (Eds.), *Groups in contact: The psychology of desegregation.*

Orlando, FL: Academic Press. Pp. 77–96.

Cohen, E., & Roper, S. (1972). Modification of interracial interaction disability: An application of status characteristics theory. *American Sociological Review, 6,* 643–657.

Cohen, S., Doyle, W. J., Skoner, D. P., Fireman, P., Gwaltney, J. M., Jr., & Newsom, J. T. (1995). State and trait negative affect as predictors of objective and subjective symptoms of respiratory viral infections. *Journal of Personality and Social Psychology, 68,* 159–169.

Cole, M., Gay, J., Glick, J., & Sharp, D. (1971). *The cultural context of learning and thinking.* New York: Basic Books.

Cole, S. G., Nail, P. R., & Pugh, M. (1995). Coalition preferences as a function of expected values in a tetradic weighted-majority game. *Basic and Applied Social Psychology, 16,* 109–120.

Cole, T. R. (1992). *The journey of life: A cultural history of aging in America.* New York: Cambridge University Press.

Collaros, P. A., & Anderson, L. R. (1969). Effect of perceived expertness upon creativity of members of brainstorming groups. *Journal of Applied Psychology, 53,* 159–163.

Collins, N. L., & Read, S. J. (1990). Adult attachment, working models, and relationship quality in dating couples. *Journal of Personality and Social Psychology, 58,* 644–663.

Collins, R. L., Taylor, S. E., & Skokan, L. A. (1990). A better world or a shattered vision? Changes in life perspectives following victimization. *Social Cognition, 8,* 263–285.

Colvin, C. R., & Block, J. (1994). Do positive illusions foster mental health? An examination of the Taylor and Brown formulation. *Psychological Bulletin, 116,* 3–20.

Comstock, G. (1980). New emphases in research on the effects of television and film violence. In E. Palmer & A. Dorr (Eds.), *Children and the faces of television* (pp. 129–148). New York: Academic Press.

Condon, J. W., & Crano, W. D. (1988). Inferred evaluation and the relation between attitude similarity and interpersonal attraction. *Journal of Personality and Social Psychology, 54,* 789–797.

Connor, J., Serbin, L., & Ender, R. (1978). Responses of boys and girls to aggressive, assertive, and passive behaviors of male and female characters. *Journal of Genetic Psychology, 133,* 56–69.

Contreras, R., Hendrick, S. S., & Hendrick, C. (in press). Perspectives on marital love and satisfaction in Mexican American and Anglo couples. *Journal of Counseling and Development.*

Cook, S. W. (1978). Interpersonal and attitudinal outcomes in cooperating interracial groups. *Journal of Research and Development in Education, 12,* 97–113.

Cook, T. D., Kendzierski, D. A., & Thomas, S. V. (1983). The implicit assumptions of television: An analysis of the 1982 NIMH Report on Television and Behavior. *Public Opinion Quarterly, 47,* 161–201.

Cooley, C. H. (1902). *Human nature and the social order.* New York: Scribner.

Coombs, C. A. (1973). A reparameterization of the prisoner's dilemma game. *Behavioral Science, 18,* 424–428.

Cooms, R. H., & Kenkel, W. F. (1966). Sex differences in dating aspirations and satisfaction with computer-selected partners. *Journal of Marriage and the Family, 28,* 62–66.

Cooper, H. M. (1979a). Pygmalion grows up: A model for teacher expectation communication and performance influence. *Review of Educational Research, 49,* 389–410.

Cooper, H. M. (1979b). Statistically combining independent studies: Meta-analysis of sex differences in conformity research. *Journal of Personality and Social Psychology, 37,* 131–146.

Cooper, H., & Good, T. (1983). *Pygmalion grows up: Studies in the expectation communication process.* New York: Longman.

Cooper, J. (1980). Reducing fears and increasing assertiveness: The role of dissonance reduction. *Journal of Experimental Social Psychology, 16,* 199–213.

Cooper, J., & Fazio, R. H. (1984). A new look at dissonance theory. In L. Berkowitz (Ed.), *Advances in experimental social psychology* (Vol. 17). New York: Academic Press.

Cooper, J., & Worchel, S. (1970). Role of undesired consequences in arousing cognitive dissonance. *Journal of Personality and Social Psychology, 16,* 199–206.

Cooper, J., Zanna, M. P., & Goethals, G. R. (1974). Mistreatment of an esteemed other as a consequence affecting dissonance reduction. *Journal of Experimental Social Psychology, 10,* 224–233.

Cooper, J., Zanna, M. P., & Taves, P. A. (1978). Arousal as a necessary condition for attitude change following induced compliance. *Journal of Personality and Social Psychology, 36,* 1101–1106.

Cooper, J. E., & McGaugh, J. L. (1969). Leadership: Integrating principles of social psychology. In C. A. Gibb (Ed.), *Leadership.* Baltimore: Penguin.

Coovert , M. D., & Reeder, G. D. (1990). Negativity effects in impression formation: The role of unit formation and schematic expectations. *Journal of Experimental Social Psychology, 26,* 49–62.

Copeland, G. A. (1989). Face-ism and prime-time television. *Journal of Broadcasting and Electronic Media, 33,* 209–214.

Copeland, J., & Snyder, M. (1995). When counselors confirm: A functional analysis. *Personality and Social Psychology Bulletin, 21,* 1210–1220.

Costin, F. (1985). Beliefs about rape and a woman's social roles. *Archives of Sexual behavior, 14,* 319–325.

Cotton, J. L. (1986). Ambient temperature and violent crime. *Journal of Applied Social Psychology, 16,* 786–801.

Cottrell, N. B., Wack, D. L., Sekerak, G. J., & Rittle, R. H. (1968). Social facilitation of dominant responses by the presence of an audience and the mere presence of others. *Journal of Personality and Social Psychology, 9,* 245–250.

Cousins, S. D. (1989). Culture and self-perception in Japan and the United States. *Journal of Personality and Social Psychology, 56,* 124–131.

Covington, M. V., & Omelich, C. L. (1988). I can resist anything but temptation: Adolescent expectations for smoking cigarettes. *Journal of Applied Social Psychology, 18,* 203–227.

Cramer, R. E., McMaster, M. R., Bartell, P. A., & Dragna, M. (1988). Subject competence and minimization of the bystander effect. *Journal of Applied Social Psychology, 18,* 1133–1148.

Cramer, R. E., Weiss, R. F., Steigleder, M. K., & Balling, S. S. (1985). Attraction in context: Acquisition and blocking of person-directed action. *Journal of Personality and Social Psychology, 49,* 1221–1230.

Crandall, C. S. (1988). Social contagion of binge eating. *Journal of Personality and Social Psychology, 55,* 588–598.

Crandall, C. S. (1994). Prejudice against fat people: Ideology and self-interest. *Journal of Personality and Social Psychology, 66,* 882–894.

Crane, M. & Markus, H. R. (1982). Gender identity: The benefits of a self-schema approach. *Journal of Personality and Social Psychology, 43,* 1195–1197.

Crano, W. D., Gorenflo, D. W., & Shackelford, S. L. (1988). Overjustification, assumed consensus, and attitude change: Further investigation of the incentive-aroused ambivalence hypothesis. *Journal of Personality and Social Psychology, 55,* 12–22.

Crites, S. L., Jr., Fabrigar, L. R., & Petty, R. E. (1994). Measuring the affective and cognitive properties of attitudes: Conceptual and methodological issues. *Personality and Social Psychology Bulletin, 20,* 619–634.

Crocker, J. (1981). Judgment of covariation by social perceivers. *Psychological Bulletin, 90,* 272–292.

Crocker, J. (1982). Biased questions in judgment of covariation studies. *Personality and Social Psychology Bulletin, 8,* 214–220.

Crocker, J., & Luhtanen, R. (1990). Collective self-esteem and ingroup bias. *Journal of Personality and Social Psychology, 58,* 60–67.

Crocker, J., Luhtanen, R., Blaine, B., & Broadnax, S. (1994). Collective self-esteem and psychological well-being among White, Black, and Asian college students. *Personality and Social Psychology Bulletin, 20,* 503–513.

Crocker, J., & Major, B. (1989). Social stigma and self-esteem: The self-protective properties of stigma. *Psychological Review, 96,* 608–630.

Crocker, J., & Major, B. (1994). Reactions to stigma: The moderating role of justification. In M. P. Zanna & J. M. Olson (Eds.), *The psychology of prejudice: The Ontario symposium* (Vol. 7). Hillsdale, NJ: Erlbaum.

Cromwell, P. F., Marks, A., Olson, J. N., & Avary, D. W. (1991). Group effects on decision-making by burglars. *Psychological Reports, 69,* 577–588.

Crosby, F. (1976). A model of egotistical relative deprivation. *Psychological Review, 83,* 85–113.

Crosby, F., Bromley, S., & Saxe, L. (1980). Recent unobtrusive studies of black and white discrimination and prejudice: A literature review. *Psychological Bulletin, 52,* 177–193.

Cross, J. G., & Guyer, M. J. (1980). *Social traps.* Ann Arbor: University of Michigan Press.

Crowne, D. P., & Marlowe, D. (1964). *The approval motive: Studies in evaluation dependence.* New York: Wiley.

Croyle, R., & Cooper, J. (1983). Dissonance arousal: Physiological evidence. *Journal of Personality and Social Psychology, 44,* 55–66.

Crusco, A. H., & Wetzel, C. G. (1984). The Midas touch: The effects of interpersonal touch on restaurant tipping. *Personality and Social Psychology Bulletin, 10,* 512–517.

Cummings, E. M., Iannotti, R. J., & Zahn-Waxler, C. (1983). Influence of conflict between adults on the emotions and aggression of young children. *Developmental Psychology, 21,* 495–507.

Cummings, E. M., Zahn-Waxler, C., & Radke-Yarrow, M. (1981). Young children's responses to expressions of anger and affection by others in the family. *Child Development, 52,* 1274–1282.

Cunningham, M. R. (1979). Weather, mood, and helping behavior: Quasi experiments with the sunshine samaritan. *Journal of Personality and Social Psychology, 37,* 1947–1956.

Cunningham, M. R. (1986a). Levites and brother's keepers: A sociobiological perspective on prosocial behavior. *Humboldt Journal of Social Relations, 13,* 35–67.

Cunningham, M. R. (1986b). Measuring the physical in physical attractiveness: Quasi-experiments on the sociobiology of female facial beauty. *Journal of Personality and Social Psychology, 50,* 925–935.

Cunningham, M. R., Barbee, A. P., & Pike, C. L. (1990). What do women want? Facialmetric assessment of multiple motives in the perception of male facial physical attractiveness. *Journal of Personality and Social Psychology, 59,* 61–72.

Cunningham, M. R., Roberts, A. R., Barbee, A. P., Druen, P. B., & Wu, C. (1995). "Their ideas of beauty are, on the whole, the same as ours": Consistency and variability in the cross-cultural perception of female physical attractiveness. *Journal of Personality and Social Psychology, 68,* 261–279.

Cunningham, M. R., Steinberg, J., & Grev, R. (1980). Wanting to and having to help: Separate motivations for positive mood and guilt-induced helping. *Journal of Personality and Social Psychology, 38,* 181–192.

Cushman, P. (1990). Why the self is empty: Toward a historically situated psychology. *American Psychologist, 45,* 599–611.

Dabbs, J. M., Jr., Carr, T. S., Frady, R. L., & Riad, J. K. (in press). Testosterone, crime, and misbehavior among 692 male prison inmates. *Personality and Individual Differences.*

Dabbs, J. M. Jr., de La Rue, D., & Williams, P. M. (1990). Testosterone and occupational choice: Actors, ministers, and other men. *Journal of Personality and Social Psychology, 59,* 1261–1265.

Dabbs, J. M., Jr., Frady, R. L., Carr, T. S., & Besch, N. F. (1987). Saliva testosterone and criminal violence in young adult prison inmates. *Psychosomatic Medicine, 49,* 174–182.

Dabbs, J. M., Jr., & Leventhal, H. (1966). Effects of varying the recommendations in a fear-arousing communication. *Journal of Personality and Social Psychology, 4,* 525–531.

Dabbs, J. M., Jr., & Morris, R. (1990). Testosterone, social class, and antisocial behavior in a sample of 4,462. *Psychological Science, 1,* 209–211.

Dabbs, M. J., Jr., & Janis, I. L. (1965). Why does eating while reading facilitate opinion change?–An experimental inquiry. *Journal of Experimental Social Psychology, 1,* 133–144.

Daly, M., & Wilson, M. (1983). *Sex, evolution, and behavior.* Boston: Willard Grant Press.

Damrosch, S. P. (1985). How perceived carelessness and time of attack affect nursing students' attributions about rape victims. *Psychological Reports, 56,* 531–536.

Darley, J. M., & Batson, C. D. (1973). "From Jerusalem to Jericho": A study of situational and dispositional variables in helping behavior. *Journal of Personality and Social Psychology, 27,* 100–108.

Darley, J. M., & Fazio, R. H. (1980). Expectancy confirmation processes arising in the social interaction se-quence. *American Psychologist, 35,* 867–881.

Darley, J. M., Fleming, J. H., Hilton, J. L., & Swann, W. B., Jr. (1988). Dispelling negative expectancies: The impact of interaction goals and target characteristics on the expectancy confirmation hypothesis. *Journal of Experimental Social Psychology, 24,* 19–36.

Darley, J. M., & Gross, P. H. (1983). A hypothesis-confirming bias in labelling effects. *Journal of Personality and Social Psychology, 44,* 20–33.

Darley, J. M., & Latané, B. (1968). Bystander intervention in emergencies: Diffusion of responsibility. *Journal of Personality and Social Psychology, 8,* 377–383.

Darwin, C. (1872). *The expression of the emotions in man and animals.* London: J. Murray.

Davidson, A. R., Yantis, S., Norwood, M., & Montano, D. E. (1985). Amount of information about the attitude object and attitude-behavior consistency. *Journal of Personality and Social Psychology, 49,* 1184–1198.

Davidson, B., & Sollie, D. L. (1987). Sex-role orientation and marital adjustment. *Social Behavior and Personality, 15,* 59–69.

Davies, D. R., & Sparrow, P. R. (1985). Age and work behavior. In N. Charness (Ed.), *Aging and human performance.* New York: Wiley.

Davis, J. A. (1966). The campus as a frog pond: An application of the theory of relative deprivation to career decisions of college men. *American Journal of Sociology, 72,* 17–31.

Davis, J. H. (1989). Psychology and the law: The last 15 years. *Journal of Applied Social Psychology, 19,* 119–230.

Davis, J. H. (1992). Some compelling intuitions about group consensus decision, theoretical and empirical research, And interpersonal aggregation phenomena: Selected examples, 1950–1990. *Organizational Behavior and Human Decision Processes, 52,* 3–38.

Davis, J. H., Stasson, M., Ono, K., & Zimmerman, S. (1988). Effects of straw polls on group decision making: Sequential voting pattern, timing, and local majorities. *Journal of Personality and Social Psychology, 55,* 918–926.

Davis, J. H., Tindale, R. S., Nagao, D. H., Hinsz, V. B., & Robertson, B. (1984). Order effects in multiple decision by groups: A demonstration with mock juries and trial procedures. *Journal of Personality and Social Psychology, 47,* 1003–1012.

Davis, K. E., Kirkpatrick, L. A., Levy, M. B., & O'Hearn, R. E. (1994). Stalking the elusive love style: Attachment styles, love styles, and relationship development. In R. Erber & R. Gilmour (Eds.), *Theoretical frameworks for personal relationships.* Hillsdale, NJ: LEA.

Davis, K. E., & Latty-Mann, H. (1987). Love styles and relationship quality: A contribution to validation. *Journal of Social and Personal Relationships, 4,* 409–428.

Davis, M. H., & Harvey, J. C. (1992). Declines in major league batting performance as a function of game pressure: A drive theory analysis. *Journal of Applied Social Psychology, 22,* 714–735.

Davis, M. H., & Stephan, W. G. (1980). Attributions for exam performance. *Journal of Applied Social Psychology, 10,* 235–248.

Davis, R. H., & Davis, J. A. (1985). *TV's image of the elderly: A practical guide for change.* Lexington, MA: D. C. Heath.

Davitz, J. R. (1952). The effects of previous training on postfrustration behavior. *Journal of Abnormal and Social Psychology, 47,* 309–315.

Dawes, R. M. (1980). Social dilemmas. *Annual Review of Psychology, 31,* 169–193.

Dawes, R. M., McTavish, J., & Shaklee, H. (1977). Behavior, communication, and assumptions about other people's behavior in a commons dilemma situation. *Journal of Personality and Social Psychology, 35,* 1–11.

Dawes, R. M., & Mulford, M. (1993). Diagnoses of alien kidnappings that result from conjuction effects in memory. *Skeptical Inquirer, 18,* 50–51.

Dawes, R. M., & Mulford, M. (in press). The false consensus effect and overconfidence: Flaws in judgment, or flaws in how we study judgment? *Organizational Behavior and Human Performance.*

Dawes, R. M., & Orbell, J. (1981). Social dilemmas. In G. Stephenson & J. Davis (Eds.), *Progress in applied social psychology* (Vol. 1). Chichester: John Wiley Ltd.

Dawes, R. M., & Smith, T. L. (1985). Attitude and opinion measurement. In G. Lindsey & E. Aronson (Eds.), *Handbook of social psychology* (Vol. I). New York: Random House.

Dawkins, R. (1976). *The selfish gene.* Oxford: Oxford University Press.

Dawkins, R. (1982). *The extended phenotype: The gene as a unit of selection.* New York: Oxford University Press.

Deaux, K. (1976). *The behavior of men and women.* Monterey, CA: Brooks/Cole.

Deaux, K. (1984). From individual differences to social categories: Analysis of a decade's research on gender. *American Psychologist, 39,* 105–116.

Deaux, K. (1993). Reconstructing a social identity. *Personality and Social Psychology Bulletin, 19,* 4–12.

Deaux, K., & Hanna, R. (1984). Courtship in the personals column: The influence of gender and sexual orientation. *Sex Roles, 11,* 363–375.

Deaux, K., & Major, B. (1987). Putting gender into context: An inreactive model of gender-related behavior. *Psychological Review, 94,* 369–389.

DeBono, K. G. (1987). Investigating the social-adjustive and value-expressive functions of attitudes: Implications for persuasion processes. *Journal of Personality and Social Psychology, 52,* 279–287.

DeBono, K. G. (1992). Pleasant scents and persuasion: An information processing approach. *Journal of Applied Social Psychology, 22,* 910–919.

DeBono, K. G., & McDermott, J. B. (1994). Trait anxiety and persuasion: Individual differences in information processing strategies. *Journal of Research in Personality, 28,* 395–407.

DeBono, K. G., & Snyder, M. (1995). Acting on one's attitudes: The role of a history of choosing situations. *Personality and Social Psychology Bulletin, 21,* 629–636.

de Castro, J. M., & Brewer, E. M. (1991). The amount eaten in meals by humans is a power function of the number of people present. *Physiology & Behavior, 51,* 121–125.

Deci, E. L., & Ryan, R. M. (1985). *Intrinsic motivation and self-determination in human behavior.* New York: Plenum.

Deci , E. L., & Ryan, R. M. (1991). A motivational approach to self: Integration in personality. In R. Dienstbier (Ed.), *Nebraska symposium on motivation: Vol. 38. Perspectives on motivation.* Lincoln, NE: University of Nebraska Press.

Deci, E. L., & Ryan, R. M. (1995). Human autonomy: The basis for true self-esteem. In M. Kernis (Ed.), *Agency, efficacy, and self-esteem.* New York: Plenum.

de Dreu, C. K. W., Carnevale, P. J. D., Emans, B. J. M., & van de Vliert, E. (1994). Effects of Gain-loss frames in negotiation: Loss aversion, mismatching, and frame adoption. *Organizational Behavior and Human Decision Processes, 60,* 90–107.

Degler, C. N. (1991). *In search of human nature: The decline and revival of Darwinism in American social thought.* New York: Oxford University Press.

de Jong, P. F. Koomen, W., & Mellenbergh, G. J. (1988). Structure of causes for success and failure: A multidimensional scaling analysis of preference judgments. *Journal of Personality and Social Psychology, 55,* 718–725.

DeLongis, A., Folkman, S., & Lazarus, R. S. (1988). The impact of daily stress on health and mood: Psychological and social resources as mediators. *Journal of Personality and Social Psychology, 54,* 486–495.

Demare, D., Briere, J., & Lips, H. M. (1988). Violent pornography and self-reported likelihood of sexual aggression. *Journal of Research in Personality, 22,* 140–153.

Dennett, D. C. (1978). *Brainstorms: Philosophical essays on mind and psychology.* Montgomery, VT: Bradford Books.

Dennis, A. R., & Valacich, J. S. (1993). Computer brainstorms: More heads are better than one. *Journal of Applied Psychology, 78,* 531–537.

DePaulo, B. M. (1992). Nonverbal behavior and self-presentation. *Psychological Bulletin, 111,* 203–243.

DePaulo, B. M., & Coleman, L. M. (1986). Verbal and nonverbal communication of warmth to children, foreigners, and retarded adults. *Journal of Nonverbal Behavior, 11,* 75–88.

DePaulo, B. M., Kirkendol, S. E., Tang, J., & O'Brien, T. P. (1988). The motivational impairment effect in the communication of deception: Replication and extensions. *Journal of Nonverbal Behavior, 12,* 177–203.

DePaulo, B. M., Lanier, K., & Davis, T. (1983). Detecting the deceit of the motivated liar. *Journal of Personality and Social Psychology, 45,* 1096–1103.

DePaulo, B. M., Lassiter, G. D., & Stone, J. I. (1982). Attentional determinants of success at detecting deception and truth. *Personality and Social Psychology Bulletin, 8,* 273–279.

DePaulo, B. M., LeMay, C. S., & Epstein, J. A. (1991). Effects of importance of success and expectations for success on effectiveness at deceiving. *Personality and Social Psychology Bulletin, 17,* 14–24.

DePaulo, B. M., & Pfeifer, R. L. (1986). On-the-job experience and skill at detecting deception. *Journal of Applied Social Psychology, 16,* 249–267.

DePaulo, B. M., & Rosenthal, R. (1982). Measuring the development of sensitivity to non-verbal communication. In C. E. Izard (Ed.), *Measuring emotions in infants and children.* Cambridge: Cambridge University Press.

DePaulo, B. M., Rosenthal, R., Eisenstat, R. A., Rogers, P. L., & Finkelstein, S. (1978). Decoding discrepant nonverbal cues. *Journal of Personality and Social Psychology, 36,* 313–323.

DePaulo, B. M., Stone, J. I., & Lassiter, G. D. (1985a). Deceiving and detecting deceit. In B. R. Schlenker (Ed.), *The self and social life.* New York: McGraw-Hill.

DePaulo, B. M., Stone, J. I., & Lassiter, G. D. (1985b). Telling ingratiating lies: Effects of target sex and target attractiveness on verbal and nonverbal deceptive success. *Journal of Personality and Social Psychology, 48,* 1191–1203.

DePaulo, B. M., Zuckerman, M., & Rosenthal, R. (1980). Detecting deception: Modality effects. In L. Wheeler (Ed.), *The review of personality and social psychology* (Vol. 1). Beverly Hills, CA: Sage.

Deschamps, J. C., & Brown, R. (1983). Superordinate goals and intergroup conflict. *British Journal of Social Psychology, 22,* 189–195.

Deseran, F. A., & Chung, C. S. (1979). Appearance, role-taking and reactions to deviance: Some experimental findings. *Social Psychology Quarterly, 42,* 426–430.

Desforges, D. M., Lord, C. G., Ramsey, S. L., Mason, J. A., Van Leeuwen, M. D., West, S. C., & Lepper, M. R. (1991). Effects of structured cooperative contact on changing negative attitudes toward stigmatized social groups. *Journal of Personality and Social Psychology, 60,* 531–544.

Deutsch, F. M. (1988). When friends lead us astray: Evidence for the selective exposure hypothesis. *Journal of Social Psychology, 128,* 271–273.

Deutsch, F. M., & Lamberti, D. M. (1986). Does social approval increase helping? *Personality and Social Psychology Bulletin, 12,* 149–158.

Deutsch, F. M., Sullivan, L., Sage, C., & Basile, N. (1991). The relations among talking, liking, and similarity between friends. *Personality and Social Psychology Bulletin, 17,* 406–411.

Deutsch, M. (1993). Educating for a peaceful world. *American Psychologist, 48,* 510–517.

Deutsch, M. (1994). Constructive conflict resolution: Principles, training, & research. *Journal of Social Issues, 50,* 13–32.

Deutsch, M., Epstein, Y., Canavan, P., & Gumpert, P. (1967). Strategies of inducing cooperation. *Journal of Conflict Resolution, 11,* 345–360.

Devine, P. G. (1989). Stereotypes and prejudice: Their automatic and controlled components. *Journal of Personality and Social Psychology, 56,* 5–18.

Devine, P. G., & Monteith, M. J. (1993). The role of discrepancy-associated affect in prejudice reduction. In D. M. Mackie & D. L. Hamilton (Eds.), *Affect, cognition, and stereotyping: Interactive processes in intergroup perception.* San Diego, CA: Academic Press.

Devine, P. G., Monteith, M. J., Zuwerink, J. R., & Elliot, A. J. (1991). Prejudice with and without compunction. *Journal of Personality and Social Psychology, 60,* 817–830.

Devine, P. G., Sedikides, C., & Fuhrman, R. W. (1989). Goals in social information processing: The case of anticipated interaction. *Journal of Personality and Social Psychology, 56,* 680–690.

DeWall, F. (1986). Deception in the natural communication of chimpanzees. In R. W. Mitchell & N. S. Thompson (Eds.), *Deception: Perspectives on human and nonhuman deceit.* Albany: State University of New York Press.

Dickerson, C. A., Thibodeau, R., Aronson, E., & Miller, D. (1992). Using cognitive dissonance to encourage water conservation. *Journal of Applied Social Psychology, 22,* 841–854.

Dickson, H. W., & McGinnies, E. (1966). Affectivity in the arousal of attitudes as measured by galvanic skin response. *American Journal of Psychology, 79,* 584–589.

Diehl, M., & Stroebe, W. (1987). Productivity loss in brainstorming groups: Toward the solution of a riddle. *Journal of Personality and Social Psychology, 53,* 497–509.

Diehl, M., & Stroebe, W. (1991). Productivity loss in idea-generating groups: Tracking down the blocking effect. *Journal of Personality and Social Psychology, 61,* 392–403.

Diener, C. I., & Dweck, C. S. (1978). An analysis of learned helplessness: Continuous changes in performance, strategy, and achievement cognitions following failure. *Journal of Personality and Social Psychology, 36,* 451–462.

Diener, E. (1980). Deindividuation: The absence of self-awareness and self-regulation in group members. In P. Paulhus (Ed.), *Psychology of group influence* (pp. 209–242). Hillsdale, NJ: Erlbaum.

Diener, E. (1984). Subjective wellbeing. *Psychological Bulletin, 95,* 542–575.

Diener, E., Dineen, J., Endresen, K., Beaman, A. L., & Fraser, S. C. (1975). Effects of altered responsibility, cognitive set, and modeling on physical aggression and deindividuation. *Journal of Personality and Social Psychology, 31,* 328–337.

Dijker, A. J. M. (1987). Emotional reactions to ethnic minorities. *European Journal of Social Psychology, 17,* 305–325.

Dion, K. K. (1972). Physical attractiveness and evaluations of children's transgressions. *Journal of Personality and Social Psychology, 24,* 285–290.

Dion, K. K., Berscheid, E., & Walster, E. (1972). What is beautiful is good. *Journal of Personality and Social Psychology, 24,* 285–290.

Dion, K. K., & Dion, K. L. (1993). Individualistic and collectivistic perspectives on gender and the cultural context of love and intimacy. *Journal of Social Issues, 49,* 53–69.

Dion, K. K., & Stein, S. (1978). Physical attractiveness and its interpersonal influence. *Journal of Experimental Social Psychology, 14,* 97–108.

Dion, K. L., Baron, R. S., & Miller, N. (1970). Why do groups make riskier decisions than individuals? In L. Berkowitz (Ed.), *Advances in experimental social psychology* (Vol. 5). New York: Academic Press.

Dixon, T. M., & Baumeister, R. F. (1991). Escaping the self: The moderating effect of self-complexity. *Personality and Social Psychology Bulletin, 17,* 363–368.

Dixson, A. F. (1980). Androgens and aggressive behavior in primates: A review. *Aggressive Behavior, 6,* 37–67.

Dobbins, G. H., Cardy, R. L., & Truxillo, D. M. (1988). The effects of purpose of appraisal and individual differences in stereotypes of women on sex differences in performance ratings: A laboratory and field study. *Journal of Applied Psychology, 73,* 551–558.

Dodge, K. A. (1986). Social information-processing variables in the development of aggression and altruism in children. In C. Zahn-Waxler, E. M. Cummings, & R. Iannotti (Eds.), *Altruism and aggression: Biological and social origins.* Cambridge, England: Cambridge University Press.

Dodge, K. A., & Coie, J. D. (1987). Social information processing factors in reactive and proactive aggression in children's peer groups. *Journal of Personality and Social Psychology, 53,* 1146–1158.

Dodge, K. A., & Crick, N. R. (1990). Social information-processing bases of aggressive behavior in children. *Personality and Social Psychology Bulletin, 16,* 8–22.

Dodge, K. A., Murphy, R. R., & Buchsbaum, K. (1984). The assessment of intention-cue detection skills in children: Implications for developmental psychopathology. *Child Development, 55,* 163–173.

Dodge, M., & Greene, E. (1991). Juror and expert conceptions of battered women. *Violence and Victims, 6,* 271–282.

Doering, M., Rhodes, S. R., & Schuster, M. (1983). *The aging worker: research and recommendations.* Beverly Hills, CA: Sage.

Doise, W. (1969). Intergroup relations and polarization of individual and collective judgments. *Journal of Personality and Social Psychology, 12,* 136–143.

Doll, J., & Orth, B. (1993). The Fishbein and Ajzen theory of reasoned action applied to contraceptive behavior: Model variants and meaningfulness. *Journal of Applied Social Psychology, 23,* 395–415.

Dollard, J., Doob, L. W., Miller, N. E., Mowrer, O. H., & Sears, R. R. (1939). *Frustration and aggression.* New Haven: Yale University Press.

Doms, M., & Van Avermaet, E. (1980). Majority influence, minority influence and conversion behavior: A replication. *Journal of Experimental Social Psychology, 16,* 283–292.

Donnerstein, E. (1980). Aggressive erotica and violence against women. *Journal of Personality and Social Psychology, 39,* 269–277 .

Donnerstein, E. (1983). Erotica and human aggression. In R. Geen & E. Donnerstein (Eds.), *Aggression: Theoretical and empirical reviews, Vol. 2: Issues in research* (pp. 127–154). New York: Academic Press.

Donnerstein, E., & Barrett, G. (1978). Effects of erotic stimuli on male aggression toward females. *Journal of Personality and Social Psychology, 36,* 180–188.

Donnerstein, E., & Berkowitz, L. (1981). Victim reactions in aggressive erotic films as a factor in violence against women. *Journal of Personality and Social Psychology, 41,* 710–724.

Donnerstein, E., Donnerstein, M., & Evans, R. (1975). Erotic stimuli and aggression: Facilitation of inhibition. *Journal of Personality and Social Psychology, 32,* 237–244.

Donnerstein, E., Donnerstein, M., Simon, S., & Ditrichs, R. (1972). Variables in interracial aggression: Anonymity, expected retaliation, and a riot. *Journal of Personality and Social Psychology, 22,* 236–245.

Donnerstein, E., & Hallam, J. (1978). Facilitating effects of erotica on aggression against women. *Journal of Personality and Social Psychology, 36,* 1270–1277.

Donovan, R. J. (1984). *Nemesis: Truman and Johnson in the coils of war in Asia.* New York: St. Martin's-Marek.

Doob, A. N., & Krishenbaum, H. M. (1973). The effects on arousal of frustration and agressive films. *Journal of Experimental Social Psychology, 9,* 57–64.

Dovidio, J. F. (1984). Helping behavior and altruism: An empirical and conceptual overview. In L. Berkowitz (Ed.), *Advances in experimental social psychology* (Vol. 17, pp. 361–427). New York: Academic Press.

Dovidio, J. F., Brigham, J. C., Johnson, B. T., & Gertner, S. L. (in press). Stereotyping, prejucice, and discrimination: Another Look. In N. Macrae, M. Hewstone, & C. Stangor (Eds.), *Foundations of Stereotypes and Stereotyping.* New York: Guilford.

Dovidio, J. F., Evans, N., & Tyler, R. B. (1986). Racial stereotypes: The contents of their cognitive representation. *Journal of Experimental Social Psychology, 22,* 22–37.

Dovidio, J. F., & Gaertner, S. L. (1986). Prejudice, discrimination, and racism: Historical trends and contemporary approaches. In J. F. Dovidio & S. L. Gartner (Eds.), *Prejudice, discrimination, and racism.* Orlando, FL: Academic Press.

Dovidio, J. F., & Gaertner, S. L. (1993). Stereotypes and evaluative intergroup bias. In D. Mackie & D. Hamilton (Eds.), *Affect, cognition, and stereotyping: Interactive processes in intergroup perception.* San Diego, CA: Academic Press.

Dovidio, J. F., Gaertner, S. L., Isen, A. M., & Lowrance, R. (1995). Group representations and intergroup bias: Positive affect, similarity, and group size. *Personality and Social Psychology Bulletin, 21,* 856–865.

Dovidio, J. F., Piliavin, J. A., Gaertner, S. L., Schroeder, D. A., & Clark, R. D. (1991). The arousal: cost-reward model and the process of intervention: A review of the evidence. In M. S. Clark (Ed.), *Prosocial behav-*

ior (pp. 86–118). Newbury Park, CA: Sage.

Downing, J. W., Judd, C. M., & Brauer, M. (1992). Effects of repeated expressions on attitude extremity. *Journal of Personality and Social Psychology, 63,* 17–29.

Downs, A. C., & Lyons, P. M. (1991). Natural observations of the links between attractiveness and initial legal judgments. *Personality and Social Psychology Bulletin, 17,* 541–547.

Doyle, A. B., & Aboud, F. E. (1995). A longitudinal study of White children's racial prejudice as a social cognitive development. *Merrill-Palmer Quarterly, 41,* 209–228.

Driscoll, D. M., Hamilton, D. L., & Sorrentino, R. M. (1991). Uncertainty orientation and recall of person-descriptive information. *Personality and Social Psychology Bulletin, 17,* 494–500.

Duck, S. (1994). Strategems, spoils, and a serpent's tooth: On the delights and dilemmas of personal relationships. In W. R. Cupach & B. H. Spitzberg (Eds.), *The dark side of interpersonal communication.* Hillsdale, NJ: LEA.

Duck, S., Pond, K., & Leatham, G. (1994). Loneliness and the evaluation of relational events. *Journal of Social and Personal Relationships, 11,* 253–276.

Duck, S., Rutt, D. J., Hurst, M. H., & Strejc, H. (1991). Some evident truths about conversations in everyday relationships: All communications are not created equal. *Human Communication Research, 18,* 228–267.

Duncan, D. L. (1976). Differential social perception and attribution of intergroup violence: Testing the lower limits of stereotyping of blacks. *Journal of Personality and Social Psychology, 34,* 590–598.

Dunning, D., Griffin, D. W., Milojkovic, J., & Ross, L. (1990). The overconfidence effect in social prediction. *Journal of Personality and Social Psychology, 58,* 568–581.

Dunning, D., & Madey, S. F. (in press). Comparison processes in counterfactual thought. In N. J. Roese & J. M. Olson (Eds.), *What might have been: The social psychology of counterfactual thinking.* Hillsdale, NJ: Erlbaum.

Dunning, D., & Story, A. L. (1991). Depression, realism, and the overconfidence effect: Are the sadder wiser when predicting future actions and events? *Journal of Personality and Social Psychology, 61,* 521–532.

Durkin, K. (1985). Television and sex-role acquisition 1: Content. *British Journal of Social Psychology, 24,* 101–113.

Dusek, J., & Joseph, G. (1985). The bases of teacher expectancies. In J. Dusek (Ed.), *Teacher expectancies.* Hillsdale, NJ: Erlbaum.

Dutton, D. G., & Aron, A. (1989). Romantic attraction and generalized liking for others who are sources of

conflict-based arousal. *Canadian Journal of Behavioral Science, 21,* 246–257.

Dutton, D. G., & Aron, A. P. (1974). Some evidence for heightened sexual attraction under conditions of high anxiety. *Journal of Personality and Social Psychology, 30,* 510–517.

Duval, S., & Wicklund, R. A. (1972). *A theory of objective self-awareness.* New York: Academic Press.

Dweck, C. S. (1975). The role of expectations and attributions in the alleviation of learned helplessness. *Journal of Personality and Social Psychology, 31,* 674–685.

Dweck, C. S. (1986). Motivational processes affecting learning. *American Psychologist, 41,* 1040–1048.

Dweck, C. S., Chiu, C., & Hong, Y. (1995). Implicit theories and their role in judgments and reactions: A world from two perspectives. *Psychological Inquiry, 6,* 322–333.

Dweck, C. S., & Elliott, E. S. (1984). Achievement motivation. In P. H. Mussen (Ed.), *Handbook of Child Psychology* (Vol. 4). New York: Wiley.

Dweck, C. S., Hong, Y., & Chiu, C. (1993). Implicit theories: Individual differences in the likelihood and meaning of dispositional inference. *Personality and Social Psychology Bulletin, 19,* 644–656.

Dweck, C. S., & Leggett, E. L. (1988). A social-cognitive approach to motivation and personality. *Psychological Review, 95,* 256–273.

Dweck, C. S., & Repucci, N. D. (1973). Learned helplessness and reinforcement responsibility in children. *Journal of Personality and Social Psychology, 25,* 109–116.

Eagly, A. H. (1978). Sex differences in influenceability. *Psychological Bulletin, 85,* 86–116.

Eagly, A. H. (1983). Gender and social influence: A social psychological analysis. *American Psychologist, 38,* 971–981.

Eagly, A. H. (1987). *Sex differences in social behavior: A social-role interpretation.* Hillsdale, NJ: Erlbaum.

Eagly, A. H. (1992). Uneven progress: Social psychology and the study of attitudes. *Journal of Personality and Social Psychology, 63,* 693–710.

Eagly, A. H., Ashmore, R. D., Makhijani, M. G., & Longo, L. C. (1991). What is beautiful is good, but. . . .: A meta-analytic review of research on the physical attractiveness stereotype. *Psychological Bulletin, 110,* 109–128.

Eagly, A. H., & Carli, L. L. (1983). Sex of researchers and sex-typed communications as determinants of sex differences in influenceability: A meta-analysis of social influence studies. *Psychological Bulletin, 90,* 1–20.

Eagly, A. H., & Chaiken, S. (1993). *The psychology of attitudes.* New York: Harcourt, Brace, Jovanovich.

Eagly, A. H., & Crowley, M. (1986). Gender and helping behavior: A meta-analytic review of the social-psychological literature. *Psychological Bulletin, 100,* 283–308.

Eagly, A. H., & Karau, S. J. (1991). Gender and the emergence of leaders: A meta-analysis. *Journal of Personality and Social Psychology, 60,* 685–710.

Eagly, A. H., Karau, S. J., & Makhijani, M. G. (1995). Gender and the effectiveness of leaders: A meta-analysis. *Psychological Bulletin, 117,* 125–145.

Eagly, A. H., Makhijani, M. G., & Klonsky, B. G. (1992). Gender and the evaluation of leaders: A meta-analysis. *Psychological Bulletin, 111,* 3–22.

Eagly, A. H., & Mladinic, A. (1994). Are people prejudiced against women? Some answers from research on attitudes, gender stereotypes, and judgments of competence. In E. Stroebe & M. Hewstone (Eds.), *European review of social psychology* (Vol. 5).

Eagly, A. H., Mladinic, A., & Otto, S. (1994). Cognitive and affective bases of attitudes toward social groups and social policies. *Journal of Experimental Social Psychology, 30,* 113–137.

Eagly, A. H., & Steffen, V. J. (1986). Gender and aggressive behavior: A meta-analytic review of the social-psychological literature. *Psychological Bulletin, 100,* 309–330.

Eagly, A. H., & Warren, R. (1976). Intelligence, comprehension, and opinion change. *Journal of Personality, 44,* 226–242.

Eaton, G. G., & Resko, J. A. (1974). Plasma testosterone and male dominance in a Japanese macaque (Macca fuscata) troop compared with repeated measures of testosterone in laboratory males. *Hormones and Behavior, 5,* 251–259.

Ebbesen, E. G., Duncan, B., & Konecni, V. J. (1975). Effects of content of verbal aggression on future verbal aggression: A field experiment. *Journal of Experimental Social Psychology, 11,* 192–204.

Eccles, J., & Wigfield, A. (1985). Teacher expectations and student motivation. In J. Dusek (Ed.), *Teacher expectancies.* Hillsdale, NJ: Erlbaum.

Edney, J. J. (1979). The nuts game: A concise commons dilemma analog. *Environmental Psychology and Nonverbal Behavior, 3,* 252–254.

Edney, J. J. (1980). The commons problem: Alternative perspectives. *American Psychologist, 35,* 131–150.

Edney, J. J., & Harper, C. S. (1978). The commons dilemma: A review of contributions from psychology. *Environmental Management, 2,* 491–507.

Edwards, A. L. (1954). *Edwards Personal Preference Schedule.* New York: The Psychological Corporation.

Edwards, J. A., & Weary, G. (1993). Depression and the impression-formation continuum: Piecemeal processing despite the availability of category information. *Journal of Personality and Social Psychology, 64,* 636–645.

Edwards, K. (1990). The interplay of affect and cognition in attitude formation and change. *Journal of Personality and Social Psychology, 59,* 202–216.

Edwards, K., & von Hippel, W. (1995). Hearts and minds: The priority of affective versus cognitive factors in persona perception. *Personality and Social Psychology Bulletin, 21,* 996–1011.

Efran, M. G. (1974). The effect of physical appearance on the judgment of guilt, interpersonal attraction, and severity of recommended punishment in a simulated jury task. *Journal of Experimental Research in Personality, 8,* 45–54.

Einhorn, H. J., & Hogarth, R. M. (1981). Behavioral decision theory: Processes of judgment and choice. *Annual Review of Psychology, 32,* 52–88.

Eisenberg, N. (1986). *Altruistic emotion, cognition and behavior.* Hillsdale, NJ: Erlbaum.

Eisenberg, N., & Fabes, R. A. (1991). Prosocial behavior and empathy: A multimethod developmental perspective. In M. S. Clark (Ed.), *Prosocial behavior* (pp. 34–61). Newbury Park, CA: Sage.

Eisenberg, N., & Fabes, R. A. (1992). Emotion, regulation, and the development of social competence. In M. S. Clark (Ed.), *Review of personality and social psychology, Vol. 14. Emotion and social behavior.* Newbury Park, CA: Sage.

Eisenberg, N., Fabes, R. A., & Murphy, B. (1995). The relations of shyness and low sociability to regulation and emotionality. *Journal of Personality and Social Psychology, 68,* 505–517.

Eisenberg, N., Fabes, R. A., Murphy, B., Karbon, M., Maszk, P., Smith, M., Suh, K., & O'Boyle, C. (1994). The relations of emotionality and regulation to dispositional and situational empathy-related responding. *Journal of Personality and Social Psychology, 66,* 776–797.

Eisenberg, N., Fabes, R. A., Schaller, M., Miller, P. A., Carlo, G., Poulin, R., Shea, C., & Shell, R. (1991). Personality and socialization correlates of vicarious emotional responding. *Journal of Personality and Social Psychology, 61,* 459–471.

Eisenberg, N., & Lennon, R. (1983). Sex differences in empathy and related capacities. *Psychological Bulletin, 94,* 100–131.

Eisenberg, N., & Okun, M. A. (in press). The relations of dispositional regulation and emotionality to elders' empathy-related responding and affect while volunteering. *Journal of Personality.*

Eisenman, R. (1985). Marijuana use and attraction: Support for Byrne's similarity-attraction concept. *Perceptual and Motor Skills, 61,* 582.

Eisenman, R. (1993). Belief that drug usage in the United States is increasing when it is really decreasing: An example of the availability heuristic. *Bulletin of the Psychonomic Society, 31,* 249–252.

Ekman, P. (1972). Universals and cultural differences in facial expressions of emotion. In J. Cole (Ed.), *Nebraska Symposium on Motivation* (Vol. 19). Lincoln: University of Nebraska Press.

Ekman, P. (1982). *Emotion in the human face* (2nd ed.). Cambridge: Cambridge University Press.

Ekman, P. (1985). *Telling lies: Clues to deceit in the marketplace, politics, and marriage.* New York: Norton.

Ekman, P., & Friesen, W. V. (1969). Non-verbal leakage and cues to deception. *Psychiatry, 32,* 88–106.

Ekman, P., & Friesen, W. V. (1971). Constants across cultures in the face and emotion. *Journal of Personality and Social Psychology, 17,* 124–129.

Ekman, P., Friesen, W. V., & Ellsworth, P. (1982). What are the similarities and differences in facial behavior across cultures? In P. Ekman (Ed.), *Emotion in the human face* (2nd ed.). Cambridge: Cambridge University Press.

Ekman, P., Friesen, W. V., & O'Sullivan, M. (1988). Smiles when lying. *Journal of Personality and Social Psychology, 54,* 414–420.

Ekman, P., Friesen, W. V., O'Sullivan, M., Chan, A., Diacoyanni-Tarlatzis, I., Heider, K., Krause, R., LeCompte, W. A., Pitcairn, T., Ricci-Bitti, P. E., Scherer, K., Tomita, M., & Tzavaras, A. (1987). Universals and cultural differences in the judgments of facial expressions of emotion. *Journal of Personality and Social Psychology, 53,* 712–717.

Ekman, P., Friesen, W. V., & Tomkins, S. S. (1971). Facial affect scoring technique (FAST): A first validity study. *Semiotica, 3,* 37–58.

Ekman, P., & O'Sullivan, M. (1991). Who can catch a liar? American Psychologist, 46, 913–920.

Elder, G. H., & Clipp, E. C. (1988). Wartime losses and social bonding: Influences across 40 years in men's lives. *Psychiatry, 51,* 177–198.

Elkin, R. A., & Leippe, M. R. (1986). Physiological arousal, dissonance and attitude change: Evidence for a dissonance-arousal link and a "don't remind me" effect. *Journal of Personality and Social Psychology, 51,* 55–66.

Elliot, A. J., & Harackiewicz, J. M. (1994). Goal setting, achievement orientation, and intrinsic motivation: A mediational analysis. *Journal of Personality and Social Psychology, 66,* 968–980.

Ellis, N. L., O'Sullivan, C., & Sowards, B. A. (1992). *Journal of Applied Social Psychology, 22,* 889–895.

Ellis, R. J. (1988). Self-monitoring and leadership emergence in groups. *Personality and Social Psychology Bulletin, 14,* 681–693.

Enzle, M. E., Harvey, M. D., & Wright, E. F. (1980). Personalism and distinctiveness. *Journal of Personality and Social Psychology, 39,* 542–552.

Epstein, E., & Guttman, R. (1984). Mate selection in man: Evidence, theory, and outcome. *Social Biology, 31,* 243–278.

Epstein, S. (1973). The self-concept revisited, or a theory of a theory. *American Psychologist, 28,* 404–416.

Epstein, S., Lipson, A., Holstein, C., & Huh, E. (1992). Irrational reactions to negative outcomes: Evidence for two conceptual systems. *Journal of Personality and Social Psychology, 62,* 328–339.

Epstein, S., & Taylor, S. P. (1967). Instigation to aggression as a function of degree of defeat and perceived aggressive intent of the opponent. *Journal of Personality, 35,* 265–289.

Erber, R., & Fiske, S. T. (1984). Outcome dependency and attention to inconsistent information. *Journal of Personality and Social Psychology, 47,* 709–726.

Eron, L. D. (1980). Prescription for the reduction of aggression. *American Psychologist, 35,* 244–252.

Eron, L. D. (1987). The development of aggressive behavior from the perspective of a developing behaviorism. *American Psychologist, 42,* 435–442.

Eron, L. D., & Huesmann, L. R. (1980). Adolescent aggression and television. *Annals of the New York Academy of Science, 347,* 319–331.

Eron, L. D., & Huesmann, L. R. (1984). The control of aggressive behavior by changes in attitudes, values, and the conditions of learning. In R. J. Blanchard & D. C. Blanchard (Eds.), *Advances in the study of aggression* (Vol. 1, pp. 139–171). Orlando, FL: Academic Press.

Eron, L. D., Huesmann, L. R., Lefkowitz, M. M., & Walder, L. D. (1972). Does television violence cause aggression? *American Psychologist, 27,* 253–262.

Esses, V. M., Haddock, G., & Zanna, M. P. (1994). Values, stereotypes, and emotions as determinants of intergroup attitudes. In D. Mackie & D. Hamilton (Eds.), *Affect, cognition, and stereotyping: Interactive processes in intergroup perception.* San Diego, CA: Academic Press.

Esses, V. M., Haddock, G., & Zanna, M. P. (1994). The role of mood in the expression of intergroup stereotypes. In M. P. Zanna & J. M. Olson (Eds.), *The psychology of prejudice: The Ontario symposium* (Vol. 7). Hillsdale, NJ: Erlbaum.

Ethier, K. A., & Deaux, K. (1994). Negotiating social identity when contexts change: Maintaining identification and responding to threat. *Journal of Personality and Social Psychology, 67,* 243–251.

Evans, C. R., & Dion, K. L. (1991). Group cohesion and performance. *Small Group Research, 22,* 175–186.

Evans, G. W., & Carrere, S. (1991). Traffic congestion, perceived control, and psychophysiological stress among urban bus drivers. *Journal of Applied Psychology, 76,* 658–663.

Evans, G. W., & Lepore, S. J. (1993). Household crowding and social support: A quasiexperimental analysis. *Journal of Personality and Social Psychology, 65,* 308–316.

Eysenck, H. J. (1973). *Eysenck on extraversion.* New York: John Wiley & Sons.

Fabes, R. A., Eisenberg, N., & Miller, P. (1990). Maternal correlates of children's vicarious emotional responsiveness. *Developmental Psychology, 26,* 639–648.

Fagenson, E. A. (1990). Perceived masculine and feminine attributes examined as a function of individual's sex and level in the organizational power hierarchy: A test of four theoretical perspectives. *Journal of Applied Psychology, 75,* 204–211.

Fallon, A. E., & Rozin, P. (1985). Sex differences in perceptions of desirable body shape. *Journal of Abnormal Psychology, 94,* 102–105.

Fausto-Sterling, A. (1985). *Myths of gender: Biological theories about women and men.* New York: Basic Books.

Fazio, R. H. (1986). How do attitudes guide behavior? In R. M. Sorrentino & E. T. Higgins (Eds.), *Handbook of motivation and cognition: Foundations of social behavior.* New York: Guilford Press.

Fazio, R. H. (1989). On the power and functionality of attitudes: The role of attitude accessibility. In A. R. Pratkanis, S. J. Breckler, & A. G. Greenwald (Eds.), *Attitude structure and function.* Hillsdale, NJ: Erlbaum.

Fazio, R. H. (1990). Multiple processes by which attitudes guide behavior: The MODE model as an integrative framework. In M. P. Zanna (Ed.), *Advances in experimental social psychology* (Vol. 23). New York: Academic Press.

Fazio, R. H. (1993). Variability in the likelihood of automatic attitude activation: Data reanalysis and commentary on Bargh, Chaiken, Govender, & Pratto (1992). *Journal of Personality and Social Psychology, 64,* 753–758.

Fazio, R. H. (1995). Attitudes as object-evaluation associations: Determinants, consequences, & correlates of attitude accessibility. In R. E. Petty & J. A. Krosnick (Eds.), *Attitude strength: Antecedents and consequences.* Hillsdale, NJ: Erlbaum.

Fazio, R. H., Blascovich, J., & Driscoll, D. (1992). On the functional value of attitudes: The influence of accessible attitudes upon the ease and quality of decision making. *Personality and Social Psychology Bulletin, 18,* 388–401.

Fazio, R. H., Chen, J. M., McDonel, E. C., & Sherman, S. J. (1982). Attitude accessibility, attitude-behavior consistency, and the strength of the object-evaluation association. *Journal of Experimental Social Psychology, 18,* 339–357.

Fazio, R. H., & Cooper, J. (1983). Arousal in the dissonance process. In J. T. Cacioppo & R. E. Petty (Eds.), *Social psychophysiology.* New York: Guilford.

Fazio, R. H., Herr, P. M., & Olney, T. J. (1984). Attitude accessibility following a self-perception process. *Journal of Personality and Social Psychology, 47,* 277–286.

Fazio, R. H., Roskos-Ewoldsen, D. R., & Powell, M. C. (1994). Attitudes, perception, and attention. In P. M. Niedenthal & S. Kitayama (Eds.), *The heart's eye: Emotional influences in perception and attention.* New York: Academic Press.

Fazio, R. H., Sanbonmatsu, D. M., Powell, M. C., & Kardes, F. R. (1986). On the automatic activation of attitudes. *Journal of Personality and Social Psychology, 50,* 229–238.

Fazio, R. H., & Williams, C. J. (1986). Attitude accessibility as a moderator of the attitude-perception and attitude-behavior relations: An investigation of the 1984 presidential election. *Journal of Personality and Social Psychology, 51,* 505–514.

Fazio, R. H., & Zanna, M. P. (1978). Attitudinal qualities relating to the strength of the attitude-behavior relationship. *Journal of Experimental Social Psychology, 14,* 398–408.

Fazio, R. H., & Zanna, M. P. (1981). Direct experience and attitude-behavior consistency. In L. Berkowitz (Ed.), *Advances in experimental social psychology* (Vol. 14). New York: Academic Press.

Fazio, R. H., Zanna, M. P., & Cooper, J. (1977). Dissonance and self-perception: An integrative view of each theory's proper domain of application. *Journal of Experimental Social Psychology, 13,* 464–479.

Feather, N. T., & Davenport, P. R. (1981). Unemployment and depressive affect: A motivational and attributional analysis. *Journal of Personality and Social Psychology, 41,* 422–436.

Feeney, J. A., & Noller, P. (1990). Attachment style as a predictor of adult romantic relationships. *Journal of Personality and Social Psychology, 58,* 281–291.

Fehr, B. (1988). Prototype analysis of the concepts of love and commitment. *Journal of Personality and Social Psychology, 55,* 557–579.

Fehr, B. (1993). How do I love thee …? Let me consult my prototype. In S. Duck (Ed.), *Individuals in relationships* (Vol. 1). Newbury Park, CA: Sage.

Fehr, B. (1994). Prototype-based assessment of laypeople's views of love. *Personal Relationships, 1,* 309–331.

Fehrenbach, P. A., Miller, D. J., & Thelan, M. H. (1979). The importance of consistency of modeling behavior upon imitation: A comparison of single and multiple models. *Journal of Personality and Social Psychology, 37,* 1412–1417.

Fein, S., Hilton, J. L., & Miller, D. T. (1990). Suspicion of ulterior motivation and the correspondence bias. *Journal of Personality and Social Psychology, 58,* 753–764.

Feingold, A. (1990). Gender differences in effects of physical attractiveness on romantic attraction: A comparison across five research paradigms. *Journal of Personality and Social Psychology, 59,* 981–993.

Feingold, A. (1992). Gender differences in mate selection preferences: A test of the parental investment model. *Psychological Bulletin, 112,* 125–139.

Feldman, J. M. (1994). On the synergy between theory and application: Social cognition and performance appraisal. In R. S. Wyer, Jr., & T. K. Srull (Eds.), *Handbook of social cognition* (Vol. 2). Hillsdale, NJ: Erlbaum.

Feldman, R. L. (1968). Response to compatriots and foreigners who seek assistance. *Journal of Personality and Social Psychology, 10,* 202–214.

Fenigstein, A. (1979) Does aggression cause a preference for viewing media violence? *Journal of Personality and Social Psychology, 37,* 2307–2317.

Fenigstein, A., Scheier, M. F., & Buss, A. H. (1975). Public and private self-consciousness: Assessment and theory. *Journal of Consulting and Clinical Psychology, 43,* 522–527.

Fenster, C. A., Blake, L. K., & Goldstein, A. M. (1977). Accuracy of vocal emotional communication among children and adults and the power of negative emotions. *Journal of Communication Disorders, 10,* 301–314.

Ferber, M. J., Huber, J., & Spitze, G. (1979). Preference for men as bosses and professionals. *Social Forces, 58,* 466–476.

Ferguson, T. J., & Rule, B. G. (1983). An attributional perspective on anger and aggression. In R. G. Geen & E. I. Donnerstein (Eds.), *Aggression: Theoretical and methodological issues* (pp. 41–74). New York: Academic Press.

Feshbach, N. D. (1982). Sex differences in empathy and social behavior in children. In N. Eisenberg (Ed.), *The development of prosocial behavior* (pp. 315–338). New York: Academic Press.

Feshbach, N. D., & Feshbach, S. (1969). The relationship between empathy and aggression in two age groups. *Developmental Psychology, 1,* 102–107.

Feshbach, N. D., Feshbach, S., Fauvre, M., & Ballard-Campbell, M. (1983). *Learning to care: Classroom activities for social and affective development.* Glenview, IL: Scott, Foresman.

Feshbach, N. D., & Roe, K. (1968). Empathy in six- and seven-year-olds. *Child Development, 39,* 133–145.

Feshbach, S. (1964). The function of aggression and the regulation of aggressive drive. *Psychological Review, 71,* 257–262.

Festinger, L. (1954). A theory of social comparison processes. *Human Relations, 7,* 117–140.

Festinger, L. (1957). *A theory of cognitive dissonance.* Stanford, CA: Stanford University Press.

Festinger, L. (1964). *Conflict, decision, and dissonance.* Stanford, CA: Stanford University Press.

Festinger, L., & Carlsmith, J. M. (1959). Cognitive consequences of forced compliance. *Journal of Abnormal and Social Psychology, 58,* 203–210.

Festinger, L., Pepitone, A., & Newcomb, T. M. (1952). Some consequences of deindividuation in a group. *Journal of Abnormal and Social Psychology, 47,* 790–797.

Festinger, L., Riecken, H. W., & Schachter, S. (1956). *When prophecy fails.* Minneapolis: University of Minneapolis Press.

Festinger, L., Schachter, S., & Back, K. (1950). *Social pressures in informal groups: A study of human factors in housing.* New York: Harper Bros.

Fiebert, M. S. (1990). Dimensions of the female role. *Psychological Reports, 67,* 633–634.

Fiedler, F. E. (1964). A contingency model of leadership effectiveness. In L. Berkowitz (Ed.), *Advances in experimental social psychology* (Vol. 1). New York: Academic Press.

Fiedler, F. E. (1967). *A theory of leadership effectiveness.* New York: McGraw-Hill.

Fiedler, F. E. (1971). Validation an extension of the contingency model of leadership effectiveness: A review of empirical findings. *Psychological Bulletin, 76,* 128–148.

Fiedler, F. E. (1978). Recent developments in research on the contingency model. In L. Berkowitz (Ed.), *Group processes.* New York: Academic Press.

Fiedler, F. E. (1993). The leadership situation and the black box in contingency theories. In M. M. Chemers & R. Ayman (Eds.), *Leadership theory and research: Perspectives and directions.* San Diego, CA: Academic Press.

Fiedler, F. E., & Garcia, J. E. (1987). *Improving leadership effectiveness: Cognitive resources and organizational performance.* New York: Wiley.

Fiedler, K. (1991). The tricky nature of skewed frequency tables: An information loss account of distinctiveness-based illusory correlation. *Journal of Personality and Social Psychology, 60,* 24–36.

Field, T. M., Woodson, R., Greenberg, R., & Cohen, D. (1982). Discrimination and imitation of facial expressions in neonates. *Science, 218,* 179–181.

Fincham, F. D. (1994). Cognition in marriage: Current status and future challenges. *Applied & Preventive Psychology, 3,* 185–198.

Fincham, F. D., Beach, S. R., & Baucom, D. H. (1987). Attribution processes in distressed and nondistressed couples: 4. Self-partner attribution differences. *Journal of Personality and Social Psychology, 52,* 739–748.

Fincham, F. D., & Bradbury, T. N. (1992). Assessing attributions in marriage: The Relationship Attribution Measure. *Journal of Personality and Social Psychology, 62,* 457–468.

Fincham, F. D., & Bradbury, T. N. (1993). Marital satisfaction, depression, and attributions: A longitudinal analysis. *Journal of Personality and Social Psychology, 64,* 442–452.

Fincham, F. D., & Jaspars, J. M. (1980). Attribution of responsibility: From man the scientist to man as lawyer. In L. Berkowitz (Ed.), *Advances in experimental social psychology* (Vol. 13, pp. 82–139). New York: Academic Press.

Fischer, C. S. (1976). *The urban experience.* New York: Harcourt, Brace, & Jovanovich.

Fischer, D. H. (1977) *Growing old in America.* New York: Oxford University Press.

Fischhoff, B. (1975). Hindsight ≠ foresight: The effects of outcome knowledge on judgment under uncertainty. *Journal of Experimental Psychology: Human Perception and Performance, 1,* 288–299.

Fischhoff, B. (1980). For those condemned to study the past: Reflections on historical judgment. In R. A. Shweder (Ed.), *New directions for methodology of social and behavioral science* (Vol. 4). San Francisco: Jossey-Bass.

Fischhoff, B. (1982). For those condemned to study the past: Heuristics and biases in hindsight. In D. Kahneman, P. Slovic, & A. Tversky (Eds.), *Judgment under uncertainty: Heuristics and biases.* New York: Cambridge University Press.

Fishbein, M., & Ajzen, A. (1974). Attitudes toward objects as predictive of single and multiple behavioral criteria. *Psychological Review, 81,* 59–74.

Fishbein, M., & Ajzen, I. (1975). *Belief, attitude, intention, and behavior: An introduction to theory and research.* Reading, MA: Addison-Wesley.

Fishbein, M., Chan, D., O'Reilly, K., Schnell, D., Wood, R., Beeker, C., & Cohn, D. (1992). Attitudinal and normative factors as determinants of gay men's intentions to perform AIDS-related sexual behaviors: A multisite analysis. *Journal of Applied Social Psychology, 22,* 999–1011.

Fishbein, M., Chan, D., O'Reilly, K., Schnell, D., Wood, R., Beeker, C., & Cohn, D. (1993). Factors influencing gay men's attitudes, subjective norms, and intentions with respect to performing sexual behaviors. *Journal of Applied Social Psychology, 23,* 417–438.

Fisher, M. E. (1992). *The anatomy of love: The natural history of monogamy, adultery, and divorce.* New York: W. W. Norton.

Fiske, A. P. (1990). *Structures of social life: The four elementary forms of human relationships.* New York: Free Press.

Fiske, A. P. (1991). The cultural relativity of selfish individualism: Anthropological evidence that humans are inherently social. In M. S. Clark (Ed.), *Prosocial behavior* (pp. 176–214.). Newbury Park, CA: Sage.

Fiske, A. P. (1992). The four elementary forms of sociality: Framework for a unified theory of social relations. *Psychological Review, 99,* 689–723.

Fiske, A. P. (1995). The cultural dimensions of psychological research: Method effects imply cultural mediation. In P. Shrout & S. Fiske (Eds.), *Personality research, methods and theory: Festschrift for Donald Fiske.* Hillsdale, NJ: Erlbaum.

Fiske, A. P., Haslam, N., & Fiske, S. T. (1991). Confusing one person with another: What errors reveal about the elementary forms of social relations. *Journal of Personality and Social Psychology, 60,* 656–674.

Fiske, S. T., & Linville, P. W. (1980). What does the schema concept buy us? *Personality and Social Psychology Bulletin, 6,* 543–557.

Fiske, S. T., & Neuberg, S. L. (1990). A continuum of impression-formation, from category-based to individuating processes: Influences of information and motivation on attention and interpretation. In M. P. Zanna (Ed.), *Advances in experimental social psychology* (Vol. 23). New York: Academic Press.

Fiske, S. T., Neuberg, S. L., Beattie, A. E., & Millberg, S. J. (1987). Category-based and attribute-based reactions to others: Some informational conditions of stereotyping and individuating processes. *Journal of Experimental Social Psychology, 23,* 399–427.

Fiske, S. T., & Ruscher, J. B. (1993). Negative interdependence and prejudice: Whence the affect? In D. Mackie & D. Hamilton (Eds.), *Affect, cognition, and stereotyping: Interactive processes in intergroup perception.* San Diego, CA: Academic Press.

Fiske, S. T., & Taylor, S. E. (1984). *Social cognition.* Reading, MA: Addison-Wesley.

Fiske, S. T., & Taylor, S. E. (1991). *Social cognition.* New York: McGraw-Hill.

Fiske, S. T., & Von Hendy, H. M. (1992). Personality feedback and situational norms can control stereotyping processes. *Journal of Personality and Social Psychology, 62,* 577–596.

Fitness, J., & Fletcher, G. J. O. (1993). Love, hate, anger, and jealousy in close relationships: A prototype and cognitive appraisal analysis. *Journal of Personality and Social Psychology, 65,* 942–958.

Fitzpatrick, M. A. (1984). A typological approach to marital interaction: Recent theory and research. In L. Berkowitz (Ed.), *Advances in experimental social psychology* (Vol. 18). Orlando, FL: Academic Press.

Fleming, D. (1967). Attitude: The history of a concept. In D. Fleming & B. Bailyn (Eds.), *Perspectives in American history* (Vol. 1). Cambridge, MA: Charles Warren Center for Studies in American History.

Fleming, J. H., & Darley, J. M. (1989). Perceiving choice and constraint: The effects of contextual and behavioral cues on attitude attribution. *Journal of Personality and Social Psychology, 56,* 27–40.

Fleming, J. H., Darley, J. M., Hilton, J. L., & Kojetin, B. A. (1990). Multiple audience problem: A strategic communication perspective on social perception. *Journal of Personality and Social Psychology, 58,* 593–609.

Fletcher, G. J. O. (1983). The analysis of verbal explanations for marital separation: Implications for attribution theory. *Journal of Applied Social Psychology, 13,* 245–258.

Fletcher, G. J. O., & Kininmonth, L. (1992). Measuring relationship beliefs: An individual differences measure. *Journal of Research in Personality, 26,* 371–397.

Fletcher, G. J. O., Fincham, F. D., Cramer, L., & Heron, N. (1987). The role of attributions in the development of dating relationships. *Journal of Personality and Social Psychology, 53,* 481–489.

Fletcher, G. J. O., & Fitness, J. (1990). Occurrent social cognition in close relationship interaction: The role of proximal and distal variables. *Journal of Personality and Social Psychology, 59,* 464–474.

Fletcher, G. J. O., Rosanowski, J., & Fitness, J. (1994). Automatic processing in intimate contexts: The role of relationship beliefs. *Journal of Personality and Social Psychology, 67,* 888–897.

Fletcher, G. J. O., & Thomas, G. (in press). Close relationship lay theories: Their structure and function. In G. Fletcher & J. Fitness (Eds.), *Knowledge structures in close relationships: A social psychological approach.* Hillsdale, NJ: Erlbaum.

Fletcher, G. J. O., & Ward, C. (1988). Attribution theory and processes: A cross-cultural perspective. In M. H. Bond (Ed.), *The cross-cultural challenge to social psychology.* Newbury Park, CA: Sage Publications.

Fletcher, G. J.. O., Reeder, G. D., & Bull, V. (1990). Bias and accuracy in attitude attribution: The role of attributional complexity. *Journal of Experimental Social Psychology, 26,* 275–288.

Flowers, M. (1977). A laboratory test of some implications of Janis' groupthink hypothesis. *Journal of Personality and Social Psychology, 35,* 888–896.

Folger, R. (1986). A referent cognitions theory of relative deprivation. In J. M. Olson, C. P. Herman, & M. P. Zanna (Eds.), *Relative deprivation and social comparison* (pp. 33–55). Hillsdale, NJ: Erlbaum.

Folkes, V. S. (1982). Forming relationships and the matching hypothesis. *Journal of Personality and Social Psychology, 8,* 631–636.

Fong, G. T., & Markus, H. R. (1982). Self-schema and judgments about others. *Social Cognition, 1,* 171–204.

Forgas, J. P. (1992). Mood and the perception of unusual people: Affective asymmetry in memory and social judgments. *European Journal of Social Psychology, 22,* 531–547.

Forgas, J. P. (1994a). Sad and guilty? Affective influences on the explanation of conflict in close relationships. *Journal of Personality and Social Psychology, 66,* 56–68.

Forgas, J. P. (1994b). The effects of mood on judgments and memory about prototypical and atypical targets. *Personality and Social Psychology Bulletin.*

Forgas, J. P. (1995). The affect infusion model (AIM): Review and an integrative theory of mood effects on judgments. *Psychological Bulletin, 117,* 39–66.

Forgas, J. P., Bower, G. H., & Krantz, S. E. (1984). The influence of mood on perceptions of social interactions. *Journal of Experimental Social Psychology, 20,* 497–513.

Forsterling, F. (1985). Attributional retraining: A review. *Psychological Bulletin, 98,* 495–512.

Forsterling, F. (1986). Attributional conceptions in clinical psychology. *American Psychologist, 41,* 275–285.

Forsyth, D. R. (1992). *An introduction to group dynamics* (2nd ed.). Monterey, CA: Brooks/Cole.

Frable, D. E., & Bem, S. L. (1985). If you are gender schematic, all members of the opposite sex look alike. *Journal of Personality and Social Psychology, 49,* 459–468.

Fraczek, A. (1974). Informational role of situation as a determinant of aggressive behavior. In J. de Wit & W. W. Hartup (Eds.), *Determinants and origins of aggressive behavior.* The Hague: Mouton Press.

Frank, M. G., & Gilovich, T. (1988). The dark side of the self and social perception: Black uniforms and aggression in professional sports. *Journal of Personality and Social Psychology, 54,* 74–85.

Frank, R. E., & Greenberg, M. G. (1980). *The public's use of television: Who watches and why.* Beverly Hills, CA: Sage.

Frankel, A., & Prentice-Dunn, S. (1990). Loneliness and the processing of self-relevant information. *Journal of Social and Clinical Psychology, 9,* 303–315.

Franzoi, S. L., & Herzog, M. E. (1987). Judging physical attractiveness: What body aspects do we use? *Personality and Social Psychology Bulletin, 13,* 19–33.

Fraser, J. (1982). *America and the patterns of chivalry.* New York: Cambridge University Press.

Frayser, S. G. (1985). *Varieties of sexual experience: An anthropological perspective on human sexuality.* New Haven, CT: HRAF Press.

Frederick, C. M., & Ryan, R. M. (1995). Self-determination in sport: A review using cognitive evaluation theory. *International Journal of Sport Psychology, 26,* 5–23.

Freedman, J. L. (1965). Confidence, utility, and selective exposure: A partial replication. *Journal of Personality and Social Psychology, 2,* 778–780.

Freedman, J. L. (1975). *Crowding and behavior.* San Francisco: Freeman.

Freedman, J. L. (1984). Effects of television violence on aggressiveness. *Psychological Bulletin, 96,* 227–246.

Freedman, J. L., Cunningham, J. A., & Krismer, K. (1992). Inferred values and the reverse-incentive effect in induced compliance. *Journal of Personality and Social Psychology, 62,* 357–368.

Freedman, J. L., & Fraser, S. (1966). Compliance without pressure: The FITD effect. *Journal of Personality and Social Psychology, 4,* 195–202.

Freedman, J. L., & Sears, D. O. (1965). Warning, distraction, and resistance to persuasion. *Journal of Personality and Social Psychology, 1,* 262–266.

French, J. R. P., & Raven, B. H. (1959). The bases of social power. In D. Cartwright (Ed.), *Studies in social power.* Ann Arbor, MI: Institute for Social Research.

Freud, S. (1933). *New introductory lectures on psycho-analysis.* New York: Norton.

Frey, D. L., & Gaertner, S. L. (1986). Helping and the avoidance of inappropriate interracial behavior: A strategy that perpetuates a nonprejudiced self-image. *Journal of Personality and Social Psychology, 50,* 1083–1090.

Frey, K. P., & Smith, E. R. (1993). Beyond the actor's traits: Forming impressions of actors, targets, and relationships from social behavior. *Journal of Personality and Social Psychology, 65,* 486–493.

Frick, R. W. (1985). Communicating emotion: The role of prosodic features. *Psychological Bulletin, 97,* 412–429.

Fridlund, A. J. (1990). Evolution and facial action in reflex emotion, and paralanguage. In P. K. Accles, J. R.

Jennings, & M. G. H. Coles (Eds.), *Advances in psychophysiology.* Greenwich, CT: JAI Press.

Fried, L. S., & Holyoak, K. J. (1984). Induction of category distributions: A framework for classification learning. *Journal of Experimental Psychology: Learning, Memory, and Cognition, 10,* 234–257.

Friedman, H., & Zebrowitz, L. A. (1992). The contribution of typical sex differences in facial maturity to sex role stereotypes. *Personality and Social Psychology Bulletin, 18,* 430–438.

Friedrich-Cofer, L., & Huston, A. C. (1986). Television violence and aggression: The debate continues. *Psychological Bulletin, 100,* 364–371.

Frisch, R. E. (1988, March). Fatness and fertility. *Scientific American,* pp. 88–95.

Frodi, A., Macaulay, J., & Thome, P. R. (1977). Are women always less aggressive than men? A review of the experimental literature. *Psychological Bulletin, 84,* 634–660.

Frost, D. E., and Stahelski, A. J. (1988). The systematic measurement of French and Raven's bases of social power in workgroups. *Journal of Applied Social Psychology, 18,* 375–389.

Fultz, J., Batson, C. D., Fortenbach, V. A., McCarthy, P. M., & Varney, L. L. (1986). Social evaluation and the empathy-altruism hypothesis. *Journal of Personality and Social Psychology, 50,* 761–769.

Fultz, J., & Nielsen, M. E. (1993). Anticipated vicarious affect and willingness to be exposed to another's suffering. *Basic and Applied Social Psychology, 14,* 273–283.

Funder, D. C. (1991). Global traits: A neo-Allportian approach to personality. *Psychological Science, 2,* 31–39.

Funder, D. C., & Colvin, C. R. (1988). Friends and strangers: Acquaintanceship, agreement, and the accuracy of personality judgment. *Journal of Personality and Social Psychology, 55,* 149–158.

Funder, D. C., & Dobroth, K. M. (1987). Differences between traits: Properties associated with interjudge agreement. *Journal of Personality and Social Psychology, 52,* 409–418.

Furnham, A. (1982). Explanations for unemployment in Britain. *European Journal of Social Psychology, 12,* 335–352.

Gaertner, S. L., & Dovidio, J. F. (1977). The subtlety of white racism, arousal, and helping behavior. *Journal of Personality and Social Psychology, 35,* 691–708.

Gaertner, S. L., Mann, J. A., Dovidio, J. F., Murrell, A. J., & Pomare, M. (1990). How does cooperation reduce intergroup bias? *Journal of Personality and Social Psychology, 59,* 692–704.

Gaertner, S. L., Mann, J. A., Murrell, A. J., & Dovidio, J. F. (1989). Reduc-ing ingroup bias: The benefits of positive and negative characteristics. *Journal of Personality and Social Psychology, 57,* 239–249.

Gaertner, S. L., & McLaughlin, J. P. (1983). Racial stereotypes: Associations and ascriptions of positive and negative characteristics. *Social Psychology Quarterly, 46,* 23–30.

Gaes, G. G., Kalle, R. J., & Tedeschi, J. T. (1978). Impression management in the forced compliance situations. *Journal of Experimental Social Psychology, 14,* 493–510.

Gallois, C., Kashima, Y., Terry, D., McCamish, M., Timmins, P., & Chauvin, A. (1992). Safe and unsafe sexual intentions and behavior: The effects of norms and attitudes. *Journal of Applied Social Psychology, 19,* 1521–1545.

Gallupe, R. B., Bastianutti, L. M., & Cooper, W. H. (1991). Unblocking brainstorms. *Journal of Applied Psychology, 76,* 137–142.

Gallupe, R. B., Cooper, W. H., Grisé, M., & Bastianutti, L. M. (1994). Blocking electronic brainstorms. *Journal of Applied Psychology, 79,* 77–86.

Gandelman, R. (1981). Androgen and fighting behavior. In P. F. Brain & D. Benton (Eds.), *The biology of aggression* (pp. 215–230). Alphen aan den Rijn: Sijthoff & Noordhoff.

Gangestad, S. W. (1993). Sexual selection and physical attractiveness: Implications for mating dynamics. *Human Nature, 4,* 205–235.

Gangestad, S. W., Simpson, J. A., DiGeronimo, K., & Biek, M. (1992). Differential accuracy in person perception across traits: Examination of a functional hypothesis. *Journal of Personality and Social Psychology, 62,* 688–698.

Gangestad, S. W., Thornhill, R., & Yeo (1994). Facial attractiveness, developmental stability, and fluctuating asymmetry. *Ethnology and Sociobiology, 15,* 73–85.

Gardner, R. C. (1994). Stereotypes as consensual beliefs. In M. P. Zanna & J. M. Olson (Eds.), *The psychology of prejudice: The Ontario symposium* (Vol. 7). Hillsdale, NJ: Erlbaum.

Garfinkel, P. E., & Garner, D. M. (1982). *Anorexia nervosa: A multidirectional perspective.* New York: Brunner/Mazel.

Garner, D. M., Garfinkel, P. E., Schwartz, D., & Thompson, M. (1980). Cultural expectations of thinness in women. *Psychological Reports, 47,* 483–491.

Gaski, J. F. (1986). Interrelations among a channel entity's power sources: Impact of the exercise of reward and coercion on expert, referent, and legitimate power sources. *Journal of Marketing Research, 23,* 62–77.

Gavanski, I., & Wells, G. L. (1989). Counterfactual processing of normal and exceptional events. *Journal of Experimental Social Psychology, 25,* 314–325.

Gay, P. (1984). *The bourgeois experience: Victoria to Freud. Education of the senses* (Vol. 1). New York: Oxford University Press.

Gayford, J. J. (1975). Wife battering: A preliminary survey of 100 cases. *British Medical Journal, 1,* 194–197.

Gayley, C. M. (1965). *The classic myths in English literature and in art.* New York: Blaisdell Publishing Company.

Geen, R. G. (1975). The meaning of observed violence: Real vs. fictional violence and consequent effects on aggression and emotional arousal. *Journal of Research in Personality, 9,* 270–281.

Geen, R. G. (1981). Behavioral and physiological reactions to observed violence: Effects of prior exposure to aggressive stimuli. *Journal of Personality and Social Psychology, 40,* 868–875.

Geen, R. G. (1983). Aggression and television violence. In R. G. Geen & E. I. Donnerstein (eds.), *Aggression: Theoretical and empirical reviews, Vol. 2: Issues in research* (pp. 103–125). New York: Academic Press.

Geen, R. G. (1990). *Human aggression.* Pacific Grove, CA: Brooks/Cole.

Geen, R. G. (1991). Social motivation. *Annual Review of Psychology, 42,* 377–399.

Geen, R. G., & Berkowitz, L. (1967). Some conditions facilitating the occurrence of aggression after the observation of violence. *Journal of Personality, 35,* 666–676.

Geen, R. G., & Bushman, B. J. (1989). The arousing effects of social presence. In H. Wagner & A. Manstead (Eds.), *Handbook of social psychophysiology.* New York: Wiley.

Geen, R. G., & O'Neal, E. C. (1969). Activation of cue-elicited aggression by general arousal. *Journal of Personality and Social Psychology, 11,* 289–292.

Geen, R. G., & Quanty, M. B. (1977). The catharsis of aggression: An evaluation of a hypothesis. In L. Berkowitz (Ed.), *Advances in Experimental Social Psychology* (Vol. 10). New York: Academic Press.

Geen, R. G., & Stonner, D. (1973). Context effects in observed violence. *Journal of Personality and Social Psychology, 25,* 145–150.

Geen, R. G., Stonner, D., & Shope, G. L. (1975). The facilitation of aggression by aggression: Evidence against the catharsis hypothesis. *Journal of Personality and Social Psychology, 31,* 721–726.

Geen, R. G., & Thomas, S. L. (1986). The immediate effects of media violence on behavior. *Journal of Social Issues, 42,* 7–27.

Gelfand, D. M., & Hartmann, D. P. (1982). Response consequences and attributions: Two contributors to prosocial behavior. In N. Eisenberg

(Ed.), *The development of prosocial behavior*. New York: Academic Press.

Gerard, H. B. (1988). School desegregation: The social science role. In P. A. Katz & D. A. Taylor (Eds.), *Eliminating racism: Profiles in controversy.* New York: Plenum. Pp. 225–236.

Gerard, H. B., & Mathewson, G. (1966). The effects of severity of initiation on liking for a group: A replication. *Journal of Experimental Social Psychology, 2,* 278–287.

Gerard, H. B., & White, G. L. (1983). Post-decisional dissonance reevaluation of choice alternatives. *Personality and Social Psychology Bulletin, 9,* 365–369.

Gerbasi, K. C., Zuckerman, M., & Reis, H. T. (1977). Justice needs a new blindfold: A review of mock jury research. *Psychological Bulletin, 84,* 323–345.

Gerbner, G., Gross, L., Eleey, M. F., Jackson-Beeck, M., Jeffries-Fox, S., & Signiorelli, N. (1977). TV violence profile no. 8: The highlights. *Journal of Communication, 27,* 171–180.

Gerbner, G., Gross, L., Morgan, M., & Signiorelli, N. (1982). Charting the mainstream: Television's contributions to political orientations. *Journal of Communication, 32* (Spring), 100–127.

Gerbner, G., Gross, L., Signorelli, N., & Morgan, M. (1980). Aging with television: Images on television drama and concepts of social reality. *Journal of Communication, 30,* 37–47.

Gerdes, E. P., Dammann, E. J., & Heilig, K. E. (1988). Perceptions of rape victims and assailants: Effects of physical attractiveness, acquaintance, and subject gender. *Sex Roles, 19,* 141–153.

Gergen, K. J. (1981). The functions and foibles of negotiating self-conception. In M. D. Lynch, A. A. Norem-Hebeisen, & K. J. Gergen (Eds.), *Self-concept: Advances in theory and research* (pp. 59–74). Cambridge, MA: Ballinger.

Gergen, K. J. (1982). From self to science: What is there to know? In J. Suls (Ed.), *Psychological perspectives on the self* (Vol. 1). Hillsdale, N. J.: Erlbaum.

Gergen, K. J. (1987). Toward self as a relationship. In K. Yardley & T. Honess (Eds.), *Self and identity: Psychosocial perspectives* (pp. 53–63). New York: Wiley.

Gergen, K. J., Ellsworth, P., Maslach, C., & Seipel, M. (1975). Obligation, donor resources, and reactions to aid in three nations. *Journal of Personality and Social Psychology, 3,* 390–400.

Gergen, K. J., & Gergen, M. M. (1988). Narrative and the self as relationship. In L. Berkowitz (Ed.), *Advances in experimental social psychology* (Vol. 21). New York: Academic Press.

Gerstel, N., & Gross, H. (1984). Commuter marriage: A study of work and family. New York: Guilford.

Gibbons, F. X. (1985). Social stigma perception: Social comparison among mentally retarded persons. *American Journal of Mental Deficiency, 90,* 98–106.

Gibbons, F. X., Gerrard, M., Lando, H. A., & McGovern, P. G. (1991). Social comparison and smoking cessation: The role of the "typical smoker." *Journal of Experimental Social Psychology, 27,* 239–258.

Gibbons, F. X., & McCoy, S. B. (1991). Self-esteem, similarity, and reactions to active versus passive downward comparison. *Journal of Personality and Social Psychology, 60,* 414–424.

Gibbons, F. X., & Wicklund, R. A. (1982). Self-focused attention and helping behavior. *Journal of Personality and Social Psychology, 43,* 462–474.

Gigone, D., & Hastie, R. (1993). The common knowledge effect: Information sharing and group judgment. *Journal of Personality and Social Psychology, 65,* 959–974.

Gilbert, D. T. (1989). Thinking lightly about others: Automatic components of the social inference process. In J. S. Uleman & J. A. Bargh (Eds.), *Unintended thought.* New York, NY: Guilford Press.

Gilbert, D. T. (1991). How mental systems believe. *American Psychologist, 46,* 107–119.

Gilbert, D. T., & Hixon, J. G. (1991). The trouble of thinking: Activation and application of stereotypic beliefs. *Journal of Personality and Social Psychology, 60,* 509–517.

Gilbert, D. T., & Jones, E. E. (1986). Perceiver-induced constraint: Interpretations of self-generated reality. *Journal of Personality and Social Psychology, 50,* 269–280.

Gilbert, D. T., & Krull, D. S. (1988). Seeing less and knowing more: The benefits of perceptual ignorance. *Journal of Personality and Social Psychology, 54,* 193–202.

Gilbert, D. T., & Malone, P. S. (1995). The correspondence bias. *Psychological Bulletin, 117,* 21–38.

Gilbert, D. T., McNulty, S. E., Giuliano, T. A., & Benson, J. E. (1992). Blurry words and fuzzy deeds: The attribution of obscure behavior. *Journal of Personality and Social Psychology, 62,* 18–25.

Gilbert, D. T., Pelham, B. W., & Krull, D. S. (1988). On cognitive busyness: When person perceivers meet persons perceived. *Journal of Personality and Social Psychology, 54,* 733–739.

Gilbert, D. T., Tafarodi, R. W., & Malone, P. S. (1993). You can't not believe everything you read. *Journal of Personality and Social Psychology, 65,* 221–233.

Gilbert, G. M. (1951). Stereotype persistence and change among college students. *Journal of Abnormal and Social Psychology, 46,* 245–254.

Gilligan, C. (1982). New maps of development: New visions of maturity. *American Journal of Orthopsychiatry, 52,* 199–212.

Gilovich, T. (1981). Seeing the past in the present: The effect of associations to familiar events on judgments and decisions. *Journal of Personality and Social Psychology, 40,* 797–808.

Gilovich, T. (1983). Biased evaluation and persistence in gambling. *Journal of Personality and Social Psychology, 44,* 1110–1126.

Gilovich, T., & Medvec, V. H. (1994). The temporal pattern to the experience of regret. *Journal of Personality and Social Psychology, 67,* 357–365.

Gilovich, T., Medvec, V. H., & Chen, S. (1995). Commission, omission, and dissonance reduction: Coping with regret in the "Monty Hall" problem. *Personality and Social Psychology Bulletin, 21,* 182–190.

Giner-Sorolla, R., & Chaiken, S. (1994). The causes of hostile media judgments. *Journal of Experimental Social Psychology, 30,* 165–180.

Ginsberg, B. E. (1976). Evolution of communication patterns in animals. In M. E. Hahn & E. C. Simmel (Eds.), *Communicative behavior and evolution* (pp. 59–79). New York: Academic Press.

Gitter, A. G., Black, H., & Mostofsky, D. (1972). Race and sex in the perception of emotion. *Journal of Social Issues, 28,* 63–78.

Gleicher, F., Kost, K. A., Baker, S. M., Strathman, A. J., Richman, S. A., & Sherman, S. J. (1990). The role of counterfactual thinking in judgments of affect. *Personality and Social Psychology Bulletin, 16,* 284–295.

Gleicher, F., & Petty, R. E. (1992). Expectations of reassurance influence the nature of fear-stimulated attitude change. *Journal of Experimental Social Psychology, 28,* 86–100.

Glenn, N. D. (1980). Values, attitudes, and beliefs. In O. G. Brim & J. Kagan (Eds.), *Constancy and change in human development.* Cambridge, MA: Harvard University Press.

Glenn, N. D. (1989). Intersocietal variation in the mate selection preferences of males and females. *Behavioral and Brain Sciences, 12,* 21–23.

Godfrey, D. K., Jones, E. E., & Lord, C. G. (1986). Self-promotion is not ingratiating. *Journal of Personality and Social Psychology, 50,* 106–115.

Goethals, G. R. (1986). Social comparison theory: Psychology from the lost and found. *Personality and Social Psychology Bulletin, 12,* 261–278.

Goethals, G. R., Cooper, J., & Naficy, A. (1979). Role of foreseen, foreseeable, and unforseen behavioral consequences in the arousal of cognitive dissonance. *Journal of Personality and Social Psychology, 37,* 1179–1185.

Goethals, G. R., & Darley, J. M. (1977). Social comparison theory: An attributional approach. In J. Suls & R. L.

Miller (Eds.), *Social comparison processes: Theoretical and empirical perspectives* (pp. 259–278). Washington, DC: Hemisphere.

Goethals, G. R., & Reckman, R. F. (1973). The perception of consistency in attitudes. *Journal of Experimental Social Psychology, 9,* 491–501.

Goethals, G. R., & Zanna, M. P. (1979). The role of social comparison in choice shifts. *Journal of Personality and Social Psychology, 37,* 1469–1476.

Goffman, E. (1959). *The presentation of self in everyday life.* Garden City, NY: Doubleday.

Goffman, E. (1961). *Encounters.* Indianapolis: Bobbs-Merrill.

Gold, G. J., & Raven, B. H. (1992). Interpersonal influence strategies in the Churchill-Roosevelt bases-for-destroyers exchange. *Journal of Social Behavior and Personality, 7,* 245–272.

Gold, J. A., Ryckman, R. M., & Mosley, N. R. (1984). Romantic mood induction and attraction to a dissimilar other: Is love blind? *Personality and Social Psychology Bulletin, 10,* 358–368.

Goldberg, S., & Lewis, M. (1969). Play behavior in the year-old infant. *Child Development, 40,* 21–31.

Goldman, M., Stockbauer, J. W., & McAuliffe, T. G. (1977). Intergroup and intragroup competition and cooperation. *Journal of Experimental Social Psychology, 13,* 81–88.

Goldstein, A. P. (1983). *Prevention and control of aggression.* Pergamon Press.

Goldstein, H. S., Edelberg, R., Meier, C. F., & Davis, L. (1991). Suppressor effects in the relations of psychological variables to resting blood pressure. *Psychological Reports, 69,* 283–288.

Goldstein, J. H. (1989). Beliefs about human aggression. In J. Groebel & R. A. Hinde (Eds.), *Aggression and war: Their biological bases.* Cambridge, England: Cambridge University Press.

Goldstein, J. H., & Arms, R. L. (1971). Effects of observing athletic contests on hostility. *Sociometry, 34,* 83–90.

Gollwitzer, P. M. (1990). Action phases and mind-sets. In E. T. Higgins & R. M. Sorrentino (Eds.), *Handbook of motivation and cognition: Foundations of social behavior* (Vol. 2). New York: Guilford Press.

Gollwitzer, P. M. (1993). Goal achievement: The role of intentions. In W. Stroebe & M. Hewstone (Eds.), *European review of social psychology* (Vol. 4). Chichester, England: Wiley.

Gollwitzer, P. M., & Wicklund, R.A. (1985). Self-symbolizing and the neglect of others' perspectives. *Journal of Personality and Social Psychology, 48,* 702–715.

Gonzales M., Hope, D. J. M., Loney, G. L., Lukens, C. K., & Junghans, C. M. (1983). Interactional approach to interpersonal attraction. *Journal of Personality and Social Psychology, 44,* 1192–1197.

Goodwin, J. S., Hunt, W. C., Key, C. R., & Samet, J. M. (1987). The effect of marital status on stange, treatment, and survival of cancer patients. *Journal of the American Medical Association, 258,* 3125–3130.

Gordon, R. A. (1993). The effect of strong versus weak evidence on the assessment of race stereotypic and race nonstereotypic crimes. *Journal of Applied Social Psychology, 23,* 734–749.

Gormly, A. V., & Gormly, J. B. (1984). The impact of discussion on interpersonal attraction. *Bulletin of the Psychonomic Society, 22,* 45–48.

Gormly, J. (1974). A comparison of predictions from consistency and affect theories for arousal during interpersonal disagreement. *Journal of Personality and Social Psychology, 30,* 658–663.

Gorn, G. J. (1982). The effects of music in advertising on choice behavior: A classical conditioning approach. *Journal of Marketing, 46,* 94–101.

Gottman, J. M. (1994). *What predicts divorce? The relationship between marital processes and marital outcomes.* Hillsdale, NJ: Erlbaum.

Gottman, J. M., & Levenson, R. W. (1992). Marital processes predictive of later dissolution: Behavior, physiology, and health. *Journal of Personality and Social Psychology, 63,* 221–233.

Gould, S. J. (1981). *The mismeasure of man.* New York: W. W. Horton & Co.

Gould, S. J. (1988, July). Kropotkin was no crackpot. *Natural History,* pp. 12–21.

Gouldner, A. W. (1960). The norm of reciprocity: A preliminary statement. *American Sociological Review, 25,* 161–179.

Graham, S., Hudley, C., & Williams, E. (1992). Attributional and emotional determinants of aggression among African-American and Latino young adolescents. *Developmental Psychology, 28,* 731–740.

Graham, S., Weiner, B., Giuliano, T., & Williams, E. (1993). An attributional analysis of reactions to Magic Johnson. *Journal of Applied Social Psychology, 23,* 996–1010.

Gray, C., Russell, P., & Blockley, S. (1991). The effects upon helping behaviour of wearing pro-gay identification. *British Journal of Social Psychology, 30,* 171–178.

Graziano, W. G., Jensen-Campbell, L. A., Shebilske, L. J., & Lundgren, S. R. (1993). Social influence, sex differences, and judgments of beauty: Putting the *interpersonal* back in interpersonal attraction. *Journal of Personality and Social Psychology, 65,* 522–531.

Green, S. K., Buchanan, D. R., & Heuer, S. K. (1984). Winners, losers, and choosers: A field investigation of dating initiation. *Personality and Social Psychology Bulletin, 10,* 502–511.

Greenberg, B. S., Korzenny, F., & Atkin, C. (1979). The portrayal of the aging: Trends on commercial television. *Research on Aging, 1,* 319–334.

Greenberg, J., & Cohen, R. L. (1982). *Equity and justice in social behavior.* New York: Academic Press.

Greenberg, J., Pyszczynski, T. A., & Solomon, S. (1982). The self-serving attributional bias: Beyond self-presentation. *Journal of Experimental Social Psychology, 18,* 56–67.

Greenberg, J., Pyszczynski, T. A., & Solomon, S. (1986). The causes and consequences of the need for self-esteem: A terror management theory. In R. F. Baumeister (Ed.), *Public self and private self.* New York: Springer-Verlag.

Greenberg, J., Pyszczynski, T. A., & Solomon, S. (1995). Toward a dual motive depth psychology of self and social behavior. In M. Kernis (Ed.), *Agency, efficacy, and self-esteem.* New York: Plenum.

Greenberg, J., Pyszczynski, T., Solomon, S., Rosenblatt, A., Veeder, M., Kirkland, S., & Lyon, D. (1990). Evidence for terror management theory II: The effects of mortality salience reactions to those who threaten or bolster the cultural worldview. *Journal of Personality and Social Psychology, 58,* 308–318.

Greenberg, J., Simon, L., Porteus, J., Pyszczynski, T., & Solomon, S. (1995). Evidence of a terror management function of cultural icons: The effects of mortality salience on the inappropriate use of cherished cultural symbols. *Personality and Social Psychology Bulletin, 21,* 1221–1228.

Greenberg, J., Solomon, S., Pyszczynski, T., Rosenblatt, A., Burling, J., Lyon, D., Simon, L., & Pinel, E. (1992). Why do people need self-esteem? Converging evidence that self-esteem serves an anxiety-buffering function. *Journal of Personality and Social Psychology, 63,* 913–922.

Greenwald, A. G. (1968a). On defining attitudes and attitude theory. In A. G. Greenwald, T. C. Brock, & T. M. Ostrom (Eds.), *Psychological foundations of attitudes.* New York: Academic Press.

Greenwald, A. G. (1968b). Cognitive learning, cognitive response to persuasion, and attitude change. In A. G. Greenwald, T. C. Brock, & T. M. Ostrom (Eds.), *Psychological foundations of attitudes.* New York: Academic Press.

Greenwald, A. G. (1980). The totalitarian ego: Fabrication and revision of personal history. *American Psychologist, 35,* 603–618.

Greenwald, A. G., & Albert, R. D. (1968). Acceptance and recall of improvised arguments. *Journal of Personality and Social Psychology, 8,* 31–34.

Greenwald, A. G., & Banaji, M. R. (1995). Implicit social cognition: Attitudes, self-esteem, and stereotypes. *Psychological Review, 102,* 4–27.

Greenwald, A. G., Pratkanis, A. R., Leippe, M. R., & Baumgardner, M. H. (1986). Under what conditions does theory construct research progress? *Psychological Review, 93,* 216–229.

Gregory, W. L., Cialdini, R. B., & Carpenter, K. M. (1982). Self-relevant scenarios as mediators of likelihood estimates and compliance: Does imagining make it so? *Journal of Personality and Social Psychology, 43,* 89–99.

Griffin, D., Dunning, D., & Ross, L. (1990). The role of construal processes in overconfident predictions about the self and others. *Journal of Personality and Social Psychology, 59,* 1128–1139.

Griffin, E., & Sparks, G. C. (1990). Friends forever: A longitudinal exploration of intimacy in same-sex friends and platonic pairs. *Journal of Social and Personal Relationships, 7,* 29–46.

Griffit, W., & Veitch, R. (1974). Preacquaintance attitude similarity and attraction revisited: Ten days in a fallout shelter. *Sociometry, 37,* 163–173.

Groebel, J., & Hinde, R. A. (1989). A multi-level approach to the problems of aggression and war. In J. Groebel & R. A. Hinde (Eds.), *Aggression and war: Their biological and social bases* (pp. 223–229). New York: Cambridge University Press.

Groebel, J., & Krebs, D. (1983). A study of the effects of television on anxiety. In C. D. Spielberger & R. Diaz-Guerrero (Eds.), *Cross-cultural anxiety* (vol. 2, pp. 89–98). Washington, DC: Hemisphere.

Groth, A. N. (1979). *Men who rape: The psychology of the offender.* New York: Plenum.

Grove, J. R., Hanrahan, S. J., & McInman, A. (1991). Success/failure bias in attributions across involvement categories in sport. *Personality and Social Psychology Bulletin, 17,* 93–97.

Gruder, C. L., Cook, T. D., Hennigan, K. M., Flay, B. R., Alessi, C., & Halamaj, J. (1978). Empirical tests of the absolute sleeper effect predicted from the discounting cue hypothesis. *Journal of Personality and Social Psychology, 36,* 1061–1074.

Gruenfeld, D. H., & Wyer, W. S., Jr. (1992). Semantics and pragmatics of social influence: How affirmations and denials affect beliefs in referent propositions. *Journal of Personality and Social Psychology, 62,* 38–49.

Grusec, J. E. (1981). Socialization processes in the development of altruism. In J. P. Rushton & R. M. Sorrentino (Eds.), *Altruism and helping behavior* (pp. 65–90). Hillsdale, NJ: Erlbaum.

Grusec, J. E. (1991). The socialization of altruism. *Review of Personality and Social Psychology, 12,* 9–33.

Grusec, J. E., & Redler, E. (1980). Attribution, reinforcement, and altruism: A developmental analysis. *Developmental Psychology, 16,* 525–534.

Grush, J. E. (1976). Attitude formation and mere exposure phenomena: A nonartificial explanation of empirical findings. *Journal of Personality and Social Psychology, 33,* 281–290.

Guerin, B. (1986). Mere presence effects in humans: A review. *Journal of Experimental Social Psychology, 22,* 38–77.

Guerin, B. (1993). *Social facilitation.* Cambridge: Cambridge University Press.

Guerrero, L. K., & Andersen, P. A. (1994). Patterns of matching and initiation: Touch behavior and touch avoidance across romantic relationship stages. *Journal of Nonverbal Behavior, 18,* 137–153

Guild, P. D., Strickland, L. H., & Barefoot, J. C. (1977). Dissonance theory, self-perception, and the bogus pipeline. *European Journal of Social Psychology, 7,* 465–476.

Guttentag, M., & Secord, P. F. (1983). *Too many women? The sex ratio question.* Beverly Hills, CA: Sage.

Guy, R. F., Rankin, B. A., & Norvell, M. J. (1980). The relation of sex role stereotyping to body image. *Journal of Psychology, 105,* 167–173.

Hackel, L. S., & Ruble, D. N. (1992). Changes in the marital relationship after the first baby is born: Predicting the impact of expectancy disconfirmation. *Journal of Personality and Social Psychology, 62,* 944–957.

Haddock, G., & Zanna, M. P. (1994). Preferring "housewives" to "feminists": Categorization and the favorability of attitudes toward women. *Psychology of Women Quarterly, 18,* 25–52.

Haddock, G., Zanna, M. P., & Esses, V. M. (1993). Assessing the structure of prejudicial attitudes: The case of attitudes toward homosexuals. *Journal of Personality and Social Psychology, 65,* 1105–1118.

Hafer, C. L., & Olson, J. M. (1993). Beliefs in a just world, discontent, and assertive actions by working women. *Personality and Social Psychology Bulletin, 19,* 30–38.

Halberstadt, J. B., Niedenthal, P., & Setterlund, M. B. (in press). Cognitive organization of different "tenses" of the self mediates affect and decision making. In L. Martin & A. Tesser (Eds.), *Striving and feeling: Interactions between goals and affect.* Hillsdale, NJ: Erlbaum.

Hall, C. C. I., & Crum, M. J. (1994). Women and "body-isms" in television beer commercials. *Sex Roles, 31,* 329–337.

Hall, J. A. (1984). *Nonverbal sex differences: Communication accuracy and expressive style.* Baltimore, MD: Johns Hopkins University Press.

Hall, J. A., & Braunwald, K. G. (1981). Gender cues in conversations. *Journal of Personality and Social Psychology, 40,* 99–110.

Hall, J. A., Roter, D. L., & Rand, C. S. (1981). Communication of affect between patient and physician. *Journal of Health and Social Behavior, 22,* 18–30.

Hall, J. A., & Veccia, E. M. (1990). More "touching" observations: New insights on men, women, and interpersonal touch. *Journal of Personality and Social Psychology, 59,* 1155–1162.

Hall, S. F., & Hall, D. T. (1976). Effects of job incumbents' race and sex on evaluation of managerial performance. *Academy of Management Journal, 19,* 476–481.

Hamacheck, D. (1992). *Encounters with the self* (4th edition). Fort Worth, TX: Harcourt Brace Jovanovich.

Hamilton, D. L., Dugan, P. M., & Trolier, T. K. (1985). The formation of stereotypic beliefs: Further evidence for distinctiveness-based illusory correlations. *Journal of Personality and Social Psychology, 48,* 5–17.

Hamilton, D. L., & Gifford, R. K. (1976). Illusory correlation in interpersonal perception: A cognitive basis of stereotypic judgments. *Journal of Experimental Social Psychology, 12,* 392–407.

Hamilton, D. L., Grubb, P. D., Acorn, D. A., Trolier, T. K., & Carpenter, S. (1990). Attributional difficulty and memory for attribution-relevant information. *Journal of Personality and Social Psychology, 59,* 891–898.

Hamilton, D. L., Katz, L. B., & Leirer, V. O. (1980). Cognitive representation of personality impressions: Organizational processes in first impression formation. *Journal of Personality and Social Psychology, 39,* 1050–1063.

Hamilton, D. L., & Mackie, D. M. (1993). Cognitive and affective processes in intergroup perception: The developing interface. In D. Mackie & D. Hamilton (Eds.), *Affect, cognition, and stereotyping: Interactive processes in intergroup perception.* San Diego, CA: Academic Press.

Hamilton, D. L., & Sherman, J. W. (1994). Stereotypes. In R. S. Wyer, Jr., & T. K. Srull (Eds.), *Handbook of social cognition* (Vol. 2). Hillsdale, NJ: Erlbaum.

Hamilton, D. L., & Sherman, S. J. (1989). Illusory correlations: Implications for stereotype theory and research. In D. Bar-Tal, C. F. Graumann, A. W. Kruglanski, & W. Strobe (Eds.), *Stereotypes and prejudice: Changing conceptions.* New York: Springer-Verlag.

Hamilton, D. L., Stroessner, S. J., & Mackie, D. M. (1993). The influence of affect on stereotyping: The case of illusory correlations. In D. Mackie & D. Hamilton (Eds.), *Affect, cognition, and stereotyping: Interactive processes in intergroup perception.* San Diego, CA: Academic Press.

Hamilton, V. L. (1978). Obedience and responsibility: A jury simulation. *Journal of Personality and Social Psychology, 36,* 126–146.

Hamilton, W. D. (1964). The genetic evolution of social behavior. *Journal of Theoretical Biology, 7,* 1–51.

Hamilton, W. D. (1971). Selection of selfish and altruistic behavior in some extreme models. In J. F. Eisenberg & W. S. Dillon (Eds.), *Man and beast: Comparative social behavior.* Washington, DC: Smithsonian Institution Press.

Hamilton, W. D., & Zuk, M. (1982). Heritable true fitness and bright birds: A role for parasites? *Science, 218,* 384–387.

Hamlish, E., & Gaier, E. L. (1954). Teacher-student similarities and marks. *School Review, 62,* 265–273.

Han, S., & Shavitt, S. (1994). Persuasion and culture: Advertising appeals in individualistic and collectivistic societies. *Journal of Experimental Social Psychology, 30,* 326–350.

Handelsman, M. M., Kraiger, K., & King, C. S. (1985, April). Self-handicapping by task choice: An attribute ambiguity analysis. Paper presented at the meeting of the Rocky Mountain Psychological Association, Tucson, AZ.

Haney, C., Banks, C., & Zimbardo, P. (1973). Interpersonal dynamics in a simulated prison. *International Journal of Criminology and Penology, 1,* 69–97.

Hanley-Dunn, P., Maxwell, S. E., & Santos, J. F. (1985). *Personality and Social Psychology Bulletin, 11,* 445–456.

Hanratty, M. A., O'Neal, E., & Sulzer, J. L. (1972). Effect of frustration upon imitation of aggression. *Journal of Personality and Social Psychology, 21,* 30–34.

Hansen, C. H., & Hansen, R. D. (1988a). Finding the face in the crowd: An anger superiority effect. *Journal of Personality and Social Psychology, 54,* 917–924.

Hansen, C. H., & Hansen, R. D. (1988b). How rock music videos can change what is seen when boy meets girl: Priming stereotypic appraisal of social interaction. *Sex Roles, 19,* 287–316.

Hansen, C. H., & Hansen, R. D. (1990). Rock music videos and antisocial behavior. *Basic and Applied Social Psychology, 11,* 357–369.

Hansen, C. H., & Hansen, R. D. (1991). Schematic information processing of heavy metal lyrics. *Communication Research, 18,* 373–411.

Hansen, K. L., Schaefer, E. G., & Lawless, J. J. (1993). Temporal patterns of normative, informational, and procedural-legal discussion in jury deliberations. *Basic and Applied Social Psychology, 14,* 33–46.

Hansson, R. O., & Slade, K. M. (1977). Altruism toward a deviant in city and small town. *Journal of Applied Social Psychology, 7,* 272–279.

Harackiewicz, J. M., & Elliot, A. J. (1993). Achievement goals and intrinsic motivation. *Journal of Personality and Social Psychology, 65,* 904–915.

Hardin, C., & Banaji, M. R. (1993). The influence of language on thought. *Social Cognition, 11,* 277–308.

Hardin, G. (1968). The tragedy of the commons. *Science, 162,* 1243–1248.

Hardy, C. J., & Latané, B. (1988). Social loafing in cheerleaders: Effects of team membership and competition. *Journal of Sport and Exercise Psychology, 10,* 109–114.

Hare-Musten, R. T., & Maracek, J. (1988). The meaning of difference: Gender theory, post-modernism, and psychology. *American Psychologist, 43,* 455–464.

Haritos-Fatouros, M. (1988). The official torturer: A learning model for obedience to the authority of violence. *Journal Applied Social Psychology, 18,* 1107–1120.

Harkins, S. G., & Petty, R. E. (1982). Effects of task difficulty and task uniqueness on social loafing. *Journal of Personality and Social Psychology, 43,* 1214–1229.

Harkins, S. G., & Petty, R. E. (1987). Information utility and the multiple source effect. *Journal of Personality and Social Psychology, 52,* 260–268.

Harkins, S. G., & Szymanski, K. (1989). Social loafing and group evaluation. *Journal of Personality and Social Psychology, 56,* 934–941.

Harlow, H. (1958). The nature of love. *American Psychologist, 12,* 673–685.

Harre, R. (1987). The social construction of self. In K. Yardley and T. Honess (Eds.), *Self and identity: Psychosocial perspectives* (pp. 41–52). New York: Wiley.

Harries, K. D., & Stadler, S. J. (1988). Heat and violence: New findings from Dallas field data, 1980–1981. *Journal of Applied Social Psychology, 18,* 129–138.

Harris, A., & Feinberg, J. (1977). Television and aging: Is what you see what you get? *Gerontologist, 17,* 464–468.

Harris, M. B. (1974). Mediators between frustration and aggression in a field experiment. *Journal of Experimental Social Psychology, 10,* 561–571.

Harris, M. J., & Rosenthal, R. (1985). Mediation of interpersonal expectancy effects: 31 meta-analyses. *Psychological Bulletin, 97,* 363–386.

Harrison, A. A. (1977). Mere exposure. In L. Berkowitz (Ed.), *Advances in experimental social psychology* (Vol. 10). San Diego, CA: Academic Press.

Harrison, A. A., & Saeed, L. (1977). Let's make a deal: An analysis of revelations and stipulations in lonely hearts advertisements. *Journal of Personality and Social Psychology, 35,* 257–264.

Hart, A. J. (1995). Naturally occurring expectation effects. *Journal of Personality and Social Psychology, 68,* 109–115.

Hart, C. W. M., & Pillig, A. R. (1960). *The Tiwi of North Australia.* New York: Holt, Rinehart and Winston.

Harter, S. (1984). Developmental perspectives on the self-system. In P. H. Mussen (Ed.), *Handbook of Child Psychology* (Vol. 4). New York: Wiley.

Harter, S. (1985). Competence as a dimension of self-evaluation. In R. L. Leahy, (Ed.), *The development of the self* (pp. 55–121). San Diego: Academic Press.

Harvey, J. H., & Barnes, M. K. (1994). Interpersonal perception and communication. *Encyclopedia of Human Behavior, 2,* 701–707.

Harvey, J. H., & Martin, R. (1995). Celebrating the story in social perception, communication, and behavior. In R. S. Wyer & T. K. Srull (Eds.), *Knowledge and Memory: Advances in social cognition* (Vol. 8). Hillsdale, NJ: Erlbaum.

Haslam, N. (1994). The mental representation of social relationships: Dimensions, laws or categories? *Journal of Personality and Social Psychology, 67,* 575–584.

Hass, R. G., & Grady, K. (1975). Temporal delay, type of forewarning, and resistance to influence. *Journal of Experimental Social Psychology, 11,* 459–469.

Hass, R. G., Katz, I., Rizzo, N., Bailey, J., & Einstadt, D. (1991). Cross-racial appraisal as related to attitude ambivalence and cognitive complexity. *Personality and Social Psychology Bulletin, 17,* 83–92.

Hass, R. G., Katz, I., Rizzo, N., Bailey, J., & Moore, L. (1992). When racial ambivalence evokes negative affect, using a disguised measure of mood. *Personality and Social Psychology Bulletin, 18,* 786–797.

Hassebrauck, M. (1988). Beauty is more than "name" deep: The effect of women's first names on ratings of physical attractiveness and personality attributes. *Journal of Applied Social Psychology, 18,* 721–726.

Hastie, R. (1981). Schematic principles in human memory. In E. T. Higgins, C. P. Herman, & M. P. Zanna (Eds.), *Social cognition: The Ontario Symposium* (Vol. 1). Hillsdale, NJ: Erlbaum.

Hastie, R., Ostrom, T. M., Ebbesen, E. B., Wyer, R. S., Hamilton, D. L., & Carlston, D. E. (1980). *Person memory: The cognitive basis of social perception.* Hillsdale, NJ: Erlbaum.

Hastie, R., & Park, B. (1986). The relationship between memory and judgment depends on whether the judgment task is memory-based or on-line. *Psychological Review, 93,* 258–268.

Hastorf, A. H., & Cantril, H. (1954). They saw a game. *Journal of Abnormal and Social Psychology, 49,* 129–134.

Hatfield, E. (1988). Passionate and companionate love. In R. Sternberg & M. L. Barnes (Eds.), *The psychology of love.* New Haven: Yale University Press.

Hatfield, E., & Rapson, R. L. (1993). *Love, sex, and intimacy.* New York: HarperCollins.

Hatfield, E., & Rapson, R. L. (1996). *Love and sex: A cross-cultural perspective.* Boston: Allyn & Bacon.

Hatfield, E., & Sprecher, S. (1986). *Mirror, mirror. . . .: The importance of looks in everyday life.* Albany: State University of New York Press.

Hatfield, E., Traupmann, J., Sprecher, S., Utne, M., & Hay, J. (1985). Equity and intimate relations: Recent research. In W. Ickes (ed.), *Compatible and incompatible relationships* (pp. 91–117). New York: Springer-Verlag.

Hatfield, E., Walster, G. W., & Traupmann, J. (1978). Equity and premarital sex. *Journal of Personality and Social Psychology, 37,* 82–92.

Haug, M., Mandell, P., & Brain, P. F. (1981). Studies on the biological correlates of attack by group-housed mice on lactating intruders. In P. F. Brain & D. Benton (Eds.), *The biology of aggression* (pp. 509–517). Alphen aan den Rijn: Sijthoff & Noordhoff.

Haugtvedt, C. P., & Petty, R. E. (1992). Personality and persuasion: Need for cognition moderates the persistence and resistance of attitude changes. *Journal of Personality and Social Psychology, 63,* 308–319.

Hawkins, S. A., & Hastie, R. (1990). Hindsight: Biased judgments of past events after the outcomes are known. *Psychological Bulletin, 107,* 311–327.

Hazan, C., & Shaver, P. (1987). Romantic love conceptualized as an attachment process. *Journal of Personality and Social Psychology, 52,* 511–524.

Hazan, C., & Zeifman, D. (1994). Sex and the psychological tether. In K. Bartholomew & D. Perlman (Eds.), *Attainment processes in adulthood: Advances in personal relationships* (Vol. 5). London, England: Jessica Kingsley Publishers, Ltd.

Hearnshaw, F. J. C. (1928). Chivalry and its place in history. In E. Prestage (Ed.), *Chivalry: A series of studies to illustrate its significance and civilizing influence* (pp. 1–35). New York: Knopf.

Heath, L., Acklin, M., & Wiley, K. (1991). Cognitive heuristics and AIDS risk assessment among physicians. *Journal of Applied Social Psychology, 21,* 1859–1867.

Hebb, D. O. (1946). On the nature of fear. *Psychological Review, 53,* 259–276.

Heber, R. (1969). Rehabilitation of families at risk for mental retardation (Regional Rehabilitation Center, University of Wisconsin). Described in S. P. Strickland (1971), *American Education,* 7,3.

Heider, F. (1958). *The psychology of interpersonal relations.* New York: Wiley.

Heilbroner, R. (1974). *An inquiry into the human prospect.* New York: Norton.

Heilman, M. E., Block, C. J., Martell, R. F., & Simon, M. C. (1989). Has anything changed? Current characterizations of men, women, and managers. *Journal of Applied Psychology, 74,* 935–942.

Helgeson, V. S., & Taylor, S. E. (1993). Social comparisons and adjustment among cardiac patients. *Journal of Applied Social Psychology, 23,* 1171–1195.

Helmreich, R. L., & Collins, B. E. (1967). Situational determinants of affiliative preference under stress. *Journal of Personality and Social Psychology, 6,* 79–85.

Hendrick, C., & Hendrick, S. (1986). A theory and method of love. *Journal of Personality and Social Psychology, 50,* 392–402.

Hendrick, C., & Hendrick, S. S. (1988). Lovers wear rose colored glasses. *Journal of Social and Personal Relationships, 5,* 161–183.

Hendrick, C., & Hendrick, S. S. (1989). Research on love: Does it measure up? *Journal of Personality and Social Psychology, 56,* 784–794.

Hendrick, C., & Hendrick, S. S. (1991). Dimensions of love: A sociobiological interpretation. *Journal of Social and Clinical Psychology, 10,* 206–230.

Hendrick, S. S., & Hendrick, C. (1987). Love and sexual attitudes, self-disclosure and sensation seeking. *Journal of Social and Personal Relationships, 4,* 281–297.

Hendrick, S. S., & Hendrick, C. (1993). Lovers as friends. *Journal of Social and Personal Relationships, 10,* 459–466.

Hendrick, S. S., Hendrick, C., & Adler, N. L. (1988). Romantic relationships: Love, satisfaction, and staying together. *Journal of Personality and Social Psychology, 54,* 980–988.

Hendricks, M., & Bootzin, R. (1976). Race and sex as stimuli for negative affect and physical avoidance. *Journal of Social Psychology, 98,* 111–120.

Henley, N. M., Miller, M., & Beazley, J. A. (1995). Syntax, semantics, and sexual violence: Agency and the passive voice. *Journal of Language and Social Psychology, 14,* 60–84.

Hensley, W. E. (1981). The effects of attire, location, and sex on aiding behavior: A similarity explanation. *Journal of Nonverbal Behavior, 6,* 3–11.

Henwood, K., Giles, H., Coupland, J., & Coupland, N. (1993). Stereotyping and affect in discourse: Interpreting the meaning of elderly, painful self-disclosure. In D. Mackie & D. Hamilton (Eds.), *Affect, cognition, and stereotyping: Interactive processes in intergroup perception.* San Diego, CA: Academic Press.

Hepworth, J. T., & West, S. G. (1988). Lynchings and the economy: A time-series reanalysis of Hovland and Sears (1940). *Journal of Personality and Social Psychology, 55,* 239–247.

Herbert, J. (1989). The physiology of aggression. In J. Groebel & R. A. Hinde (Eds.), *Aggression and war: Their biological and social bases* (pp. 58–71). New York: Cambridge University Press.

Herek, G. M. (1987). Can function be measured? A new perspective on the functional approach to attitudes. *Social Psychology Quarterly, 50,* 285–303.

Herek, G. M., & Glunt, E. K. (1988). An epidemic of stigma: Public reactions to AIDS. *American Psychologist, 43,* 886–891.

Herr, P. M. (1986). Consequences of priming: Judgment and behavior. *Journal of Personality and Social Psychology, 51,* 1106–1115.

Herrenkohl, E. C., Herrenkohl, R. C., & Toedter, L. J. (1983). Perspectives on the intergenerational transmission of abuse. In D. Finkelhor, R. Gelles, G. T. Hotaling, & M. A. Straus (Eds.), *The dark side of families* (pp. 305–316). Beverly Hills, CA: Sage.

Herskovits, M. J. (1938). *Dahomey, an ancient West African kingdom.* New York: J. J. Augustin.

Heslin, R., & Alper, T. (1983). Touch: A bonding gesture. In J. M. Wiegmann & R. P. Harrison (Eds.), *Nonverbal interaction.* Beverly Hills, CA: Sage.

Hess, R. D., Chang, C., & McDevitt, T. M. (1987). Cultural variations in family beliefs about children's performance in mathematics: Comparisons among People's Republic of China, Chinese-American, and Caucasian-American families. *Journal of Educational Psychology, 79,* 179–188.

Hewstone, M., & Brown, R. (1986). Contact is not enough: An intergroup perspective on the 'contact hypothesis.' In M. Hewstone & R. Brown (Eds.), *Contact and conflict in intergroup encounters.* New York: Basil Blackwell Ltd.

Hewstone, M., Hopkins, N., & Routh, D.A. (in press). Cognitive models of stereotype change: (3) Generalization and subtyping in young people's views of the police. *European Journal of Social Psychology.*

Higgins, E. T. (1987). Self-discrepancy: A theory relating self and affect. *Psychological Review, 94,* 319–340.

Higgins, E. T. (1989). Self-discrepancy theory: What patterns of self-beliefs cause people to suffer? In L. Berkowitz (Ed.), *Advances in experimental social psychology* (Vol. 22). New York: Academic Press.

Higgins, E. T. (in press). Continuities and discontinuities in self-regulatory and self-evaluative processes: A developmental theory relating self and affect. *Journal of Personality.*

Higgins, E. T., & Bargh, J. A. (1992). Unconscious sources of subjectivity and suffering: Is consciousness the solution? In L. L. Martin & A Tesser (Eds.), *The construction of social judgments.* Hillsdale, NJ: Erlbaum

Higgins, E. T., Bond, R. N., Klein, R., & Strauman, T. (1986). Self-discrepancies and emotional vulnerability: How magnitude, accessibility, and type of discrepancy influence affect. *Journal of Personality and Social Psychology, 51,* 5–15.

Higgins, E. T., Klein, R., & Strauman, T. (1985). Self-concept discrepancy theory: A psychological model for distinguishing among different aspects of depression and anxiety. *Social Cognition, 3,* 51–76.

Higgins, E. T., Rholes, W. S., & Jones, C. R. (1977). Category accessibility and impression formation. *Journal of Experimental Social Psychology, 13,* 141–154.

Higgins, E. T., Roney, C. J., Crowe, E., & Hymes, C. (1994). Ideal versus ought predilections for approach and avoidance distinct self-regulatory systems. *Journal of Personality and Social Psychology, 66,* 276–286.

Higgins, E. T., Tykocinski, O., & Vookles, J. (1990). Patterns of self-beliefs: The psychological significance of relations among the actual, ideal, ought, can, and future selves. In J. M. Olson & M. P. Zanna (Eds.), *Self-inference processes: The Ontario symposium.* Hillsdale, NJ: Erlbaum.

Higgins, E. T., Vookles, J., & Tykocinski, O. (1992). Self and health: How "patterns" of self-beliefs predict types of emotional and physical problems. *Social Cognition, 10,* 125–150.

Higgins, R. L., & Harris, R. N. (1988). Strategic "alcohol" use: Drinking to self-handicap. *Journal of Social and Clinical Psychology, 6,* 191–202.

Hill, C. T., Rubin, Z., & Peplau, L. A. (1976). Breakups before marriage: The end of 103 affairs. *Journal of Social Issues, 32,* 147–168.

Hill, C. T., Rubin, Z., & Peplau, L. A. (1979). The volunteer couple: Sex differences, couple commitment and participation in research on interpersonal relationships. *Social Psychology Quarterly, 42,* 415–420.

Hill, G. J. (1989). An unwillingness to act: Behavioral appropriateness, situational constraint, and self-efficacy in shyness. *Journal of Personality, 57,* 871–890.

Hill, W. F. (1978). Effects of mere exposure on preferences in non-human animals. *Psychological Bulletin, 85,* 1177–1198.

Hilton, D. J., & Slugoski, B. R. (1986). Knowledge-based causal attribution: The abnormal condition focus model. *Psychological Review, 93,* 75–88.

Hilton, J. L., & Darley, J. M. (1985). Constructing other persons: A limit to the effect. *Journal of Experimental Social Psychology, 21,* 1–18.

Hilton, J. L., & Darley, J. M. (1991). The effects of interaction goals on person perception. In M. P. Zanna (Ed.), *Advances in experimental social psychology* (Vol. 24). San Diego, CA: Academic Press.

Hilton, J. L., & Fein, S. (1989). The role of typical diagnosticity in stereotype-based judgments. *Journal of Personality and Social Psychology, 57,* 201–211.

Hinde, R. A. (1984). Why do the sexes behave differently in close relationships? *Journal of Social and Personal Relationships, 1,* 471–501.

Hinken, T. R., & Schriesheim, C. A. (1989). Relations between subordinate perceptions of supervisor influence tactics and attributed bases of supervisory power. *Human Relations, 43,* 221–237.

Hinsz, V. B. (1989). Facial resemblance in engaged and married couples. *Journal of Social and Personal Relationships, 6,* 223–229.

Hinsz, V. B., & Davis, J. H. (1984). Persuasive arguments theory, group polarization, and choice shifts. *Personality and Social Psychology Bulletin, 10,* 260–268.

Hirschman, E. C. (1987). People as products: Analysis of a complex marketing exchange. *Journal of Marketing, 51,* 98–108.

Hirt, E. R., Deppe, R. K., & Gordon, L. J. (1991). Self-reported versus behavioral self-handicapping: Empirical evidence for a theoretical distinction. *Journal of Personality and Social Psychology, 61,* 981–991.

Hirt, E. R., McDonald, H. E., & Melton, J. (in press). In L. L. Martin & A. Tesser (Eds.), *Striving and feeling: Interactions between goals and affect.* Hillsdale, NJ: Erlbaum.

Hirt, E. R., Zillmann, D., Erickson, G. A., & Kennedy, C. (1992). Costs and benefits of allegiance: Changes in fans' self-ascribed competencies after team victory versus defeat. *Journal of Personality and Social Psychology, 63,* 724–738.

Hitt, D. D., Marriott, R. G., & Esser, J. K. (1992). Effects of delayed rewards and task interest on intrinsic motivation. *Basic and Applied Social Psychology, 13,* 405–414.

Hixon, J. G., & Swann, W. B., Jr. (1993). When does introspection bear fruit? Self-reflection, self-insight, and interpersonal choices. *Journal of Personality and Social Psychology, 64,* 35–43.

Hoffman, C., & Hurst, N. (1990). Gender stereotypes: Perception or rationalization? *Journal of Personality and Social Psychology, 58,* 197–208.

Hoffman, C., Mischel, W., & Mazze, K. (1981). The role of purpose in the organization of information about behavior: Trait-based versus goal-based categories in person cognition. *Journal of Personality and Social Psychology, 40,* 211–225.

Hoffman, M. L. (1981a). Is altruism part of human nature? *Journal of Personality and Social Psychology, 40,* 121–137.

Hoffman, M. L. (1981b). The development of empathy. In J. P. Rushton &

R. M. Sorrentino (Eds.), *Altruism and helping behavior: Social, personality, and developmental perspectives* (pp. 41–63). Hillsdale, NJ: Erlbaum.

Hofling, C. K., Brotzman, E., Dalrymple, S., Graves, N., & Pierce, C. M. (1966). An experimental study in nurse-physician relationships. *Journal of Nervous and Mental Disease, 143,* 171–180.

Hofman, J. E., & Zak, I. (1969). Interpersonal contact and attitude change in a cross-cultural situation. *Journal of Social Psychology, 78,* 165–171.

Hofstede, G. (1980). *Culture's consequences.* Beverly Hills, CA: Sage.

Hofstede, G. (1983). National culture revisited. *Behavior Science Research, 18,* 285–305.

Hogben, M., Byrne, D., & Hamburger, M. E. (in press). Coercive heterosexual sexuality in dating relationships of college students: Similar or dissimilar male-female experiences? *Journal of Psychology and Human Sexuality.*

Hogg, M. A. (1987). Social identity and group cohesiveness. In J. C. Turner, M. A. Hogg, P. J. Oakes, S. D. Reicher, & M. S. Wetherell (Eds.), *Rediscovering the social group: A self-categorization theory.* Oxford: Basil Blackwell.

Hogg, M. A., & Sunderland, J. (1991). Self-esteem and intergroup discrimination in the minimal group paradigm. *British Journal of Social Psychology, 30,* 51–62.

Hogg, M. A., Turner, J. C., & Davidson, B. (1990). Polarized norms and social frames of reference: A test of the self-categorization theory of group polarization. *Basic and Applied Social Psychology, 11,* 77–100.

Hokanson, J. E., Burgess, M., & Cohen, M. F. (1963). Effects of displaced aggression on systolic blood pressure. *Journal of Abnormal and Social Psychology, 67,* 214–218.

Holcomb, W. R., & Anderson, W. P. (1983). Alcohol and drug abuse in accused murderers. *Psychological Reports, 52,* 159–164.

Hollander, E. P. (1985). Leadership and power. In G. Lindzey & E. Aronson (Eds.), *Handbook of social psychology* (Vol. II). New York: Random House.

Hollander, E. P. (1993). Legitimacy, power, and influence: A perspective on relational features of leadership. In M. M. Chemers & R. Ayman (Eds.), *Leadership theory and research: Perspectives and directions.* San Diego, CA: Academic Press.

Holloway, S., Tucker, L., & Hornstein, H. (1977). The effect of social and nonsocial information in interpersonal behavior of males: The news makes news. *Journal of Personality and Social Psychology, 35,* 514–522.

Holman, E. A., & Stokols, D. (1994). The environmental psychology of child sexual abuse. *Journal of Environmental Psychology, 14,* 1–16.

Holtgraves, T., & Grayer, A. R. (1994). I am not a crook: Effects of denials on perceptions of a defendant's guilt, personality and motives. *Journal of Applied Social Psychology, 24,* 2132–2150.

Holtz, R., & Miller, N. (1985). Assumed similarity and opinion certainty. *Journal of Personality and Social Psychology, 48,* 890–898.

Holtzman, D. (1986). Intensive care nurses: A vital sign. *Insight, 1,* 56.

Hoorens, V., & Buunk, B. P. (1993). Social comparison of health risks: Locus of control, the person-positivity bias, and unrealistic optimism. *Journal of Applied Social Psychology, 23,* 291–302.

Hoorens, V., Nuttin, J. M., Herman, I. E., & Pavakanun, U. (1990). Mastery pleasure versus mere ownership: A quasi-experimental cross-cultural and cross-alphabetical test of the name letter effect. *European Journal of Social Psychology, 20,* 181–205.

Horowitz, L. M., French, R. de S., & Anderson, C. A. (1982). The prototype of a lonely person. In L. A. Peplau & D. Perlman (Eds.), *Loneliness: A sourcebook of current theory, research and therapy.* New York: Wiley.

Hortacsu, N., & Karanci, A. N. (1987). Premarital breakups in a Turkish sample: Perceived reasons, attributional dimensions and affective reactions. *International Journal of Psychology, 22,* 57–74.

Houston, D. A., & Fazio, R. H. (1989). Biased processing as a function of attitude accessibility: Making objective judgments subjectively. *Social Cognition, 7,* 51–56.

Hovland, C. I., Harvey, O. J., & Sherif, M. (1957). Assimilation and contrast effects in reactions to communications and attitude change. *Journal of Abnormal and Social Psychology, 55,* 244–252.

Hovland, C. I., Lumsdaine, A. A., & Sheffield, F. D. (1949). Experiments on mass communication. Princeton, NJ: Princeton University Press.

Hovland, C. I., & Mandell, W. (1952). An experimental comparison of conclusion-drawing by the communicator and by the audience. *Journal of Abnormal and Social Psychology, 47,* 581–588.

Hovland, C. I., & Sears, R. R. (1940). Minor studies of aggression: Correlations of lynchings with economic indices. *Journal of Psychology, 9,* 301–310.

Hovland, C. I., & Weiss, W. (1952). The influence of source credibility on communication effectiveness. *Public Opinion Quarterly, 15,* 635–650.

Howard, J. A. (1984). Societal influences on attribution: Blaming some victims more than others. *Journal of Personality and Social Psychology, 47,* 494–505.

Howells, L. T., & Becker, S. W. (1962). Seating arrangement and leadership emergence. *Journal of Abnormal and Social Psychology, 64,* 148–150.

Hoyle, R. H., Pinkley, R. L., & Insko, C. A. (1989). Perceptions of social behavior: Evidence of differing expectations for interpersonal and intergroup interaction. *Personality and Social Psychology Bulletin, 15,* 365–376.

Hoyt, J. L. (1970). Effect of media violence "justification" on aggression. *Journal of Broadcasting, 14,* 455–464.

Hsu, F. L. K. (1985). The self in cross-cultural perspective. In A. J. Marsella, G. DeVos, & F. L. K. Hsu (Eds.), *Culture and self: Asian and Western perspectives.* London, England: Tavistock.

Hubbard, R. (1990). *The politics of women's biology.* New Brunswick, NJ: Rutgers University Press.

Hudley, C., & Graham, S. (1993). An attributional intervention to reduce peer-directed aggression among African-American boys. *Child Development, 64,* 124–138.

Hudson, J. W., & Hoyt, L. L. (1981). Personal characteristics important in mate preference among college students. *Social Behavior and Personality, 9,* 93–96.

Huesmann, L. R. (1982). Television violence and aggressive behavior. In D. Pearl, L. Bouthilet, & J. Lazar (Eds.), *Television and behavior: Ten years of scientific progress and implications for the eighties* (Vol. 2). Washington, DC: U.S. Government Printing Office.

Huesmann, L. R. (1986). Psychological processes promoting the relation between exposure to media violence and aggressive behavior by the viewer. *Journal of Social Issues, 42,* 125–139.

Huesmann, L. R. (1988). An information processing model for the development of aggression. *Aggressive Behavior, 14,* 13–24.

Huesmann, L. R., Eron, L. D., Klein, R., Brice, P., & Fischer, P. (1983). Mitigating the imitation of aggressive behaviors by changing children's attitudes about media violence. *Journal of Personality and Social Psychology, 44,* 899–910.

Huesmann, L. R., Lagerspetz, K., & Eron, L. D. (1984). Intervening variables in the TV violence-aggression relation: Evidence from two countries. *Developmental Psychology, 20,* 1120–1134.

Huesmann, L. R., & Miller, L. S. (1994). Long-term effects of repeated exposure to media violence in childhood. In L. R. Huesmann (Ed.), *Aggressive behavior: Current perspectives.* New York: Plenum.

Hull, J. G., & Bond, C. F. (1986). Social and behavioral consequences of alcohol consumption and expec-

tancy: A meta-analysis. *Psychological Bulletin, 99,* 347–160.

Hull, J. G., Levenson, R. W., Young, R. D., & Sher, K. J. (1983). Self-awareness reducing effects of alcohol consumption. *Journal of Personality and Social Psychology, 44,* 461–473.

Hull, J. G., & Young, R. D. (1983). Self-consciousness, self-esteem, and success-failure as determinants of alcohol consumption in male social drinkers. *Journal of Personality and Social Psychology, 44,* 1097–1109.

Hull, J. G., Young, R. D., Jouriles, E. (1986). Applications of the self-awareness model alcohol consumption: Predicting patterns of use and abuse. *Journal of Personality and Social Psychology, 51,* 790–796.

Hummert, M. L., Crockett, W. H., & Kemper, S. (1990). Processing mechanisms underlying the use of the balance schema. *Journal of Personality and Social Psychology, 58,* 5–21.

Hunt, M. M. (1959). *The natural history of love.* New York: Alfred A. Knopf.

Hunter, R. S., & Kihlstrom, N. (1979). Breaking the cycle in abusive families. *American Journal of Orthopsychiatry, 56,* 142–146.

Huntingford, F. A. (1989). Animals fight but do not make war. In J. Groebel & R. A. Hinde (Eds.), *Aggression and war: Their biological and social bases* (pp. 25–34). New York: Cambridge University Press.

Hupka, R. B., & Ryan, J. M. (1990). The cultural contribution to jealousy: Cross-cultural aggression in secular jealousy situations. *Behavior Science Research, 24,* 51–71.

Hurwitz, S. D., Miron, M. S., & Johnson, B. T. (1992). Source credibility and the language of expert testimony. *Journal of Applied Social Psychology, 22,* 1909–1939.

Huston, T. L., McHale, S. M., & Crouter, A. C. (1986). When the honeymoon's over: Changes in the marriage relationship over the first year. In R. Gilmour & S. Duck (Eds.), *The emerging field of personal relationships.* New York: Erlbaum.

Huston, T. L., & Vangelisti, A. L. (1991). Socioemotional behavior and satisfaction in marital relationships: A longitudinal study. *Journal of Personality and Social Psychology, 61,* 721–733.

Hutchinson, R. R. (1973). The environmental cues of aggression. In J. K. Cole & D. D. Jensen (Eds.), *Nebraska symposium on motivation.* Lincoln, NE: University of Nebraska Press.

Hyde, J. S. (1986). Gender differences in aggression. In J. S. Hyde & M. C. Linn (Eds.), *The psychology of gender: Advances through meta-analysis.* Baltimore, MD: Johns Hopkins University Press.

Hyman, R. (1989). The psychology of deception. *Annual Review of Psychology, 40,* 133–154.

Ickes, W. (1993a). Empathic accuracy. *Journal of Personality, 61,* 587–609.

Ickes, W. (1993b). Traditional gender roles: Do they make, and then break, our relationships? *Journal of Social Issues, 49,* 71–85.

Ickes, W., & Barnes, R. D. (1978). Boys and girls together–and alienated: On enacting stereotyped sex roles in mixed-sex dyads. *Journal of Personality and Social Psychology, 36,* 669–683.

Ickes, W., & Gonzalez, R. (1994). "Social" cognition and social cognition: From the subjective to the intersubjective. *Small Groups Research, 25,* 294–315.

Ickes, W., & Layden, M. A. (1978). Attributional style. In J. H. Harvey, W. Ickes, & R. F. Kidd (Eds.), *New directions in attribution research* (Vol. 2). Hillsdale, NJ: Erlbaum.

Ickes, W., Wicklund, R. A., & Ferris, C. B. (1973). Objective self-awareness and self-esteem. *Journal of Experimental Social Psychology, 9,* 202–219.

Ikegami, T. (1993). Positive-negative asymmetry of priming effects on impression formation. *European Journal of Social Psychology, 23,* 1–16.

Ikels, C. (1991). Aging and disability in China: Cultural issues in measurement and interpretation. *Social Science and Medicine, 32,* 649–665.

Insko, C. A. (1965). Verbal reinforcement of attitude. *Journal of Personality and Social Psychology, 21,* 621–623.

Insko, C. A. (1967). *Theories of attitude change.* New York: Appleton-Century-Crofts.

Insko, C. A., & Schopler, J. (1967). Triadic consistency: A statement of affective-cognitive-conative consistency. *Psychological Review, 74,* 361–376.

Insko, C. A., Schopler, J., Hoyle, R. H., Dardis, G. J., & Graetz, K. A. (1990). Individual-group discontinuity as a function of fear and greed. *Journal of Personality and Social Psychology, 58,* 68–79.

Insko, C. A., Smith, R. H., Alicke, M. D., Wade, J., & Taylor, S. (1985). Conformity and group size: The concern with being right and the concern with being right. *Personality and Social Psychology Bulletin, 11,* 41–50.

Isaacs, L. W., & Bearison, D. J. (1986). The development of children's prejudice against the aged. *International Journal of Aging and Human Development, 23,* 175–194.

Isen, A. M. (1970). Success, failure, and reaction to others: The warm glow of success. *Journal of Personality and Social Psychology, 15,* 294–301.

Isen, A. M. (1993). Positive affect and decision making. In M. Lewis & J. M. Haviland (Eds.), *Handbook of emotions.* New York: Guilford.

Isen, A. M., & Levin, P. F. (1972). Effect of feeling good on helping: Cookies and kindness. *Journal of Personality and Social Psychology, 21,* 344–348.

Isenberg, D. J. (1986). Group polarization: A critical review and meta-analysis. *Journal of Personality and Social Psychology, 50,* 1141–1151.

Islam, M. R., & Hewstone, M. (1993). Intergroup attributions and affective consequences in majority and minority groups. *Journal of Personality and Social Psychology, 64,* 936–950.

Iwao, S., de Sola Pool, I., & Hagiwara, S. (1981). Japanese and U.S. media: Some cross-cultural insights in TV violence. *Journal of Communication, 31,* 28–36.

Iyengar, S., & Ottati, V. (1994). Cognitive perspective in political psychology. In R. S. Wyer, Jr., & T. K. Srull (Eds.), *Handbook of social cognition* (Vol. 2). Hillsdale, NJ: Erlbaum.

Izard, C. E. (1969). The emotions and emotion constructs in personality and culture research. In R. B. Cattell (Ed.), *Handbook of modern personality theory.* Chicago: Aldine.

Izard, C. E. (1977). *Human emotions.* New York: Plenum Press.

Jackson, J. M., & Williams, K. D. (1985). Social loafing on difficult tasks: Working collectively can improve performance. *Journal of Personality and Social Psychology, 49,* 937–942.

Jackson, L. A., & Hymes, R. W. (1985). Gender and social categorization: Familiarity and ingroup polarization in recall and evaluation. *Journal of Social Psychology, 125,* 81–88.

Jacobi , L., & Cash, T. F. (1994). In pursuit of the perfect appearance: Discrepancies among self-ideal percepts of multiple physical attributes. *Journal of Applied Social Psychology, 24,* 379–396.

Jacobs, L., Berscheid, E., & Walster, E. (1971). Self-esteem and attraction. *Journal of Personality and Social Psychology, 17,* 84–91.

Jacobs, P., Brunton, M., Melville, M., Brittain, R., & McClemont, W. (1965). Aggressive behavior, mental subnormality and the XYY male. *Nature, 208,* 1351–1353.

Jacobs, R., & Campbell, D. T. (1961). The perpetuation of an arbitrary tradition through several generations of a laboratory micro-culture. *Journal of Abnormal and Social Psychology, 62,* 649–658.

Jacobs, S. L., Kulik, C. T., & Fichman, M. (1993). Category-based and feature-based cognitive processes in job impressions. *Journal of Applied Social Psychology, 23,* 1226–1248.

Jahn, J. (1961). *Muntu: An outline of the new African culture.* New York: Grove Press.

James, W. (1890/1950). *The principles of psychology* (Vols. 1 and 2). New York: Dover.

Jamieson, D. W., & Zanna, M. P. (1982). *Attitude change under threat of lie detection: A dissonance or impression management phenomenon?* Paper presented at the meeting of the American Psychological Association, Washington, DC.

Jamieson, D. W., & Zanna, M. P. (1991). The lie detection expectation procedure: Ensuring veracious self-reports of attitude. Unpublished manuscript.

Janis, I. L. (1967). Effects of fear arousal on attitude change: Recent developments in theory and experimental research. In L. Berkowitz (Ed.), *Advances in experimental social psychology* (Vol. 3). New York: Academic Press.

Janis, I. L. (1972). *Victims of groupthink.* Boston: Houghton Mifflin.

Janis, I. L. (1982). *Groupthink: Psychological studies of policy decisions and fiascos.* Boston: Houghton Mifflin.

Janis, I. L. (1989). *Crucial decisions: Leadership in policymaking and crisis management.* New York: Free Press.

Janis, I. L., & Feshbach, S. (1953). Effects of fear-arousing communications. *Journal of Abnormal and Social Psychology, 48,* 78–92.

Janis, I. L., & King, B. T. (1954). The influence of role playing on opinion change. *Journal of Abnormal and Social Psychology, 49,* 211–218.

Janowiak, W. R. (1993). *Sex, death, and hierarchy in a Chinese city: An anthropological account.* New York: Columbia University Press.

Janowiak, W. R., & Fischer, E. F. (1992). A cross-cultural perspective on romantic love. *Ethology, 31,* 149–155.

Jaspars, J., Hewstone, M., & Fincham, F. D. (1983). Attribution theory and research: The state of the art. In J. Jaspars, F. D. Fincham, & M. Hewstone (Eds.), *Attribution theory and research: Conceptual, developmental and social dimensions.* London: Academic Press.

Jellison, J. M., & Riskind, J. (1970). A social comparison of abilities interpretation of risk-taking behavior. *Journal of Personality and Social Psychology, 15,* 375–390.

Jemmott, J. B. III, Ashby, K. L., & Lindenfeld, K. (1989). Romantic commitment and the perceived availability of opposite sex persons: On loving the one you're with. *Journal of Applied Social Psychology, 19,* 1198–1211.

Jennings, J., Geis, F., & Brown, V. (1980). Influence of television commercials on women's self-confidence and independent judgment. *Journal of Personality and Social Psychology, 38,* 203–210.

Jennings, M. K., & Niemi, R. G. (1981). *Generations and politics.* Princeton, NJ: Princeton University Press.

Jepson, C., & Chaiken, S. (1990). Chronic issue-specific fear inhibits systematic processing of persuasive communications. *Journal of Social Behavior and Personality, 5,* 61–84.

Johannson, G. (1973). Visual perception of biological motion and a model for its analysis. *Perception and Psychophysics, 14,* 201–211.

Johnson, B. T. (1994). Effects of outcome-relevant involvement and prior information on persuasion. *Journal of Experimental Social Psychology, 30,* 556–579.

Johnson, D. F., & Pittenger, J. B. (1984). Attribution, the attractiveness stereotype, and the elderly. *Developmental Psychology, 20,* 1168–1172.

Johnson, D. J., & Rusbult, C. E. (1989). Resisting temptation: Devaluation of alternative partners as a means of maintaining committment in close relationships. *Journal of Personality and Social Psychology, 57,* 967–980.

Johnson, D. L., & Andrews, I. R. (1971). The risky shift hypothesis tested with consumer products as stimuli. *Journal of Personality and Social Psychology, 20,* 382–385.

Johnson, D. W., & Johnson, R. T. (1981). Effects of cooperative and individualistic learning experiences on interethnic interaction. *Journal of Educational Psychology, 73,* 444–449.

Johnson, J. T., & Boyd, K. R. (1995). Dispositional traits vs. the context of experience: Actor-observer differences in judgments of the "authentic self." *Personality and Social Psychology Bulletin, 21,* 375–383.

Johnson, J. T., Boyd, K. R., & Magnani, P. S. (1994). Causal reasoning in the attribution of rare and common events. *Journal of Personality and Social Psychology, 66,* 229–242.

Johnson, J. T., Jemmott, J. B., & Pettigrew, T. F. (1984). Causal attribution and dispositional inference: Evidence of inconsistent judgments. *Journal of Experimental Social Psychology, 20,* 567–585.

Johnson, M. K., Hashtroudi, S., & Lindsay, D. S. (1993). Source monitoring. *Psychological Bulletin, 114,* 3–28.

Johnson, R. A., & Schulman, G. I. (1989). Gender-role composition and role entrapment in decision-making groups. *Gender & Society, 3,* 355–372.

Johnson, S. D., Gibson, L., & Linden, R. (1978). Alcohol and rape in Winnipeg, 1966–1975. *Journal of Studies on Alcohol, 39,* 1887–1894.

Johnson, T. E., & Rule, B. G. (1986). Mitigating circumstance information, censure, and aggression. *Journal of Personality and Social Psychology, 50,* 537–542.

Jones, C., & Aronson, E. (1973). Attributions of fault to a rape victim as a function of the respectability of the victim. *Journal of Personality and Social Psychology, 26,* 415–419.

Jones, E. E. (1979). The rocky road from acts to dispositions. *American Psychologist, 34,* 107–117.

Jones, E. E. (1986). Interpreting interpersonal behavior. *Science, 234,* 41–46.

Jones, E. E. (1990a). Constrained behavior and self-concept change. In J. M. Olson and M. P. Zanna (Eds.). *Self-inference processes: The Ontario Symposium* (Vol. 6), pp. 69–86. Hillsdale, NJ: Erlbaum.

Jones, E. E. (1990b). *Interpersonal perception.* New York: W. H. Freeman.

Jones, E. E., & Berglas, S. (1978). Control of attributions about the self through self-handicapping strategies: The appeal of alcohol and the role of underachievement. *Personality and Social Psychology Bulletin, 4,* 200–206.

Jones, E. E., Brenner, K., & Knight, J. G. (1990). When failure elevates self-esteem. *Personality and Social Psychology Bulletin,* 200–209.

Jones, E. E., & Davis, K. E. (1965). From acts to dispositions. The attribution process in person perception. In L. Berkowitz (Ed.), *Advances in experimental social psychology* (Vol. 2). New York: Academic Press.

Jones, E. E., Davis, K. E., & Gergen, K. J. (1961). Role playing variations and their information value for person perception. *Journal of Abnormal and Social Psychology, 63,* 302–310.

Jones, E. E., & DeCharms, R. (1957). Changes in social perception as a function of the personal relevance of behavior. *Sociometry, 20,* 75–85.

Jones, E. E., & Harris, V. A. (1967). The attribution of attitudes. *Journal of Experimental Social Psychology, 3,* 1–24.

Jones, E. E., & McGillis, D. (1976). Correspondent inferences and the attribution cube: A comparative reappraisal. In J. H. Harvey, W. J. Ickes, and R. F. Kidd (Eds.), *New directions in attribution research* (Vol. 1). Hillsdale, N. J.: Erlbaum.

Jones, E. E., & Nisbett, R. E. (1972). The actor and the observer: Divergent perceptions of the causes of behavior. In E. E. Jones, D. E. Kanouse, H. H. Kelley, R. E. Nisbett, S. Valins, & B. Weiner (Eds.), *Attribution: Perceiving the causes of behavior.* Morristown, NJ: General Learning Press.

Jones, E. E., & Pittman, T. S. (1982). Toward a general theory of strategic self-presentation. In J. Suls (Ed.), *Psychological perspectives on the self* (Vol. 1). Hillsdale, NJ: Erlbaum.

Jones, E. E., Rhodewalt, F. T., Berglas, S., & Skelton, J. A. (1981). Effects of strategic self-presentation on subsequent self-esteem. *Journal of Personality and Social Psychology, 41,* 407–421.

Jones, E. E., Rock, L., Shaver, K. G., Goethals, G. R., & Ward, L. M. (1968). Pattern of performance and ability attribution: An unexpected primacy effect. *Journal of Personality and Social Psychology, 10,* 317–340.

Jones, E. E., & Sigall, H. (1971). The bogus pipeline: A new paradigm for measuring affect and attitude. *Psychological Bulletin, 76,* 349–364.

Jones, E. E., & Thibaut, J. W. (1958). Interaction goals as bases of inference in interpersonal perception. In R. Tagiuri & L. Petrullo (Eds.), *Person perception and interpersonal behavior.* Stanford, CA: Stanford University Press.

Jones, E. E., Wood, G. C., & Quattrone, G. A. (1981). Perceiving variability of personal characteristics in in-groups and out-groups: The role of knowledge and evaluation. *Personality and Social Psychology Bulletin, 7,* 523–528.

Jones, J. M. (1986). Racism: A cultural analysis of the problem. In J. F. Dovidio & S. L. Gaertner (Eds.), *Prejudice, discrimination, and racism.* Orlando, FL: Academic Press. Pp. 279–314.

Jones, J. M., & Hochner, A. (1973). Racial differences in sports activities: A look at the self-paced versus reactive hypothesis. *Journal of Personality and Social Psychology, 27,* 86–95.

Jones, R. A., Linder, D. E., Kiesler, C. A., Zanna, M. P., & Brehm, J. W. (1968). Internal states or external stimuli: Observers' attitude judgments and the dissonance-theory–self-persuasion controversy. *Journal of Experimental Social Psychology, 4,* 247–269.

Jones, W. H. (1982). Loneliness and social behavior. In L. A. Peplau & D. Perlman (Eds.), *Loneliness: A sourcebook of current theory, research and therapy.* New York: Wiley.

Jones, W. H., Carpenter, B. N., & Quintana, D. (1985). Personality and interpersonal predictors of loneliness in two cultures. *Journal of Personality and Social Psychology, 48,* 1503–1511.

Jones, W. H., Freemon, J. E., & Goswick, R. A. (1981). The persistence of loneliness: Self and other determinants. *Journal of Personality, 49,* 27–48.

Jones, W. H., Hobbs, S. A., & Hockenbury, D. (1982). Loneliness and social skill deficits. *Journal of Personality and Social Psychology, 42,* 682–689.

Jones, W. H., Sansone, C., & Helm, B. (1983). Loneliness and interpersonal judgments. *Personality and Social Psychology Bulletin, 9,* 437–441.

Jorgenson, D. O., & Papciak, A. S. (1981). The effects of communication, resource feedback, and identifiability on behavior in a simulated commons. *Journal of Experimental Social Psychology, 17,* 373–385.

Josephs, R. A., Larrick, R. P., Steele, C. M., & Nisbett, R. E. (1992). Protecting the self from the negative consequences of risky decisions. *Journal of Personality and Social Psychology, 62,* 26–37.

Josephson, W. J. (1987). Television violence and children's aggression: Testing the priming, social script, and disinhibition predictions. *Journal of Personality and Social Psychology, 53,* 882–890.

Jost, J. T., & Banaji, M. R. (1994). The role of stereotyping in system-justification and the production of false consciousness. *British Journal of Social Psychology, 33,* 1–27.

Jourard, S. M. (1971). *The transparent self.* New York: Van Nostrand.

Joy, L. A., Kimball, M. M., & Zabrack, M. L. (1986). Television and aggressive behavior. In T. M. Williams (Ed.), *The impact of television: A natural experiment involving three towns* (pp. 303–360). New York: Academic Press.

Judd, C. M., Kenny, D. A., & Krosnick, J. A. (1983). Judging the positions of political candidates: Models of assimilation and contrast. *Journal of Personality and Social Psychology, 44,* 952–963.

Judd, C. M., & Park, B. (1988). Outgroup homogeneity: Judgments of variability at the individual and group levels. *Journal of Personality and Social Psychology, 54,* 778–788.

Judd, C. M., & Park, B. (1993). Definition and assessment of accuracy in social stereotypes. *Psychological Review, 100,* 109–128.

Judd, C. M., Ryan, C. S., & Park, B. (1991). Accuracy in the judgment of in-group and out-group variability. *Journal of Personality and Social Psychology, 61,* 366–379.

Julien, D., & Markman, H. J. (1991). Social support and social networks as determinants of individual and marital outcomes. *Journal of Social and Personal Relationships, 8,* 549–568.

Jussim, L. (1986). Self-fulfilling prophecies: A theoretical and integrative review. *Psychological Review, 93,* 429–445.

Jussim, L. (1991). Social perception and social reality: A reflection-construction model. *Psychological Review, 98,* 54–73.

Jussim, L., & Eccles, J. (in press). Naturally occurring interpersonal expectancies. *Review of Personality and Social Psychology.*

Jussim, L., & Eccles, J. S. (1992). Teacher expectations II: Construction and reflection of student achievement. *Journal of Personality and Social Psychology, 63,* 947–961.

Jussim, L., Nelson, T. E., Manis, M., & Soffin, S. (1995). Prejudice, stereotypes, and labeling effects: Sources of bias in person perception. *Journal of Personality and Social Psychology, 68,* 228–246.

Jussim, L., Yen, H. & Aiello, J. R. (1995). Self-consistency, self-enhancement, and accuracy in reactions to feedback. *Journal of Experimental Social Psychology, 31,* 322–356.

Juvonen, J., (1991). Deviance, perceived responsibility, and negative peer reactions. *Developmental Psychology, 27,* 672–681.

Kahneman, D., & Miller, D. T. (1986). Norm theory: Comparing reality to its alternatives. *Psychological Review, 93,* 136–153.

Kahneman, D., & Tversky, A. (1973). On the psychology of prediction. *Psychological Review, 80,* 237–251.

Kahneman, D., & Tversky, A. (1982). The simulation heuristic. In D. Kahneman, P. Slovic, & A. Tversky (Eds.), *Judgment under uncertainty: Heuristics and biases.* New York: Cambridge University Press.

Kallgren, C. A., & Wood, W. (1986). Access to attitude-relevant information in memory as a determinant of attitude-behavior consistency. *Journal of Experimental Social Psychology, 22,* 328–338.

Kameda, T., & Sugimori, S. (1993). Psychological entrapment in group decision making: An assigned decision rule and a groupthink phenomenon. *Journal of Personality and Social Psychology, 65,* 282–292.

Kandel, D. B. (1978). Similarity in real-life adolescent friendship pairs. *Journal of Personality and Social Psychology, 36,* 306–312.

Kanekar, S., & Kolsawalla, M. B. (1980). Responsibility of a rape victim in relation to her respectability, attractiveness, and provocativeness. *Journal of Social Psychology, 112,* 153–154.

Kanter, R. M. (1977). *Men and women of the corporation.* New York: Basic Books.

Kaplan, M. F., & Anderson, N. H. (1973). Information integration theory and reinforcement theory as approaches to interpersonal attraction. *Journal of Personality and Social Psychology, 28,* 301–312.

Kaplan, M. F., & Miller, C. E. (1987). Group decision making and normative versus informational influence: Effects of type of issue and assigned decision rule. *Journal of Personality and Social Psychology, 53,* 306–313.

Kaplan, M. F., Schaefer, E. G., & Zinkiewicz, L. (1994). Member preferences for discussion content in anticipated group decisions: Effects of type of issue and group interactive goal. *Basic and Applied Social Psychology, 15,* 489–508.

Karau, S. J., & Williams, K. D. (1993). Social loafing: A meta-analytic review and theoretical integration. *Journal of Personality and Social Psychology, 65,* 681–706.

Kardes, F. R. (1994). Consumer judgment and decision processes. In R. S. Wyer, Jr., & T. K. Srull (Eds.), *Handbook of social cognition* (Vol. 2). Hillsdale, NJ: Erlbaum.

Karli, P. (1956). The Norway rat's killing-response to the white mouse. An experimental analysis. *Behaviour, 10,* 81–103.

Karli, P. (1991). *Animal and human aggression.* New York: Oxford University Press.

Karlins, M., Coffman, T. L., & Walters, G. (1969). On the fading of social stereotypes: Studies in three generations of college students. *Journal of Personality and Social Psychology, 13,* 1–16.

Karney, B. R., Bradbury, T. N., Fincham, F. D., & Sullivan, K. T. (1994). The role of negative affectivity in the association between attributions and marital satisfaction. *Journal of Personality and Social Psychology, 66,* 413–424.

Karylowski, J. (1976). Self-esteem, similarity, liking, and helping. *Personality and Social Psychology Bulletin, 2,* 71–74.

Katsev, R., Edelsack, L., Steinmetz, G., Walker, T., & Wright, R. (1978). The effect of reprimanding transgression on subsequent helping behavior: Two field experiments. *Personality and Social Psychology Bulletin, 4,* 326–329.

Katz, A. M., & Hill, R. (1958). Residential propinquity and marital selection: A review of theory, method, and fact. *Marriage and Family Living, 20,* 237–335.

Katz, D. (1960). The functional approach to the study of attitudes. *Public Opinion Quarterly, 24,* 163–204.

Katz, D., & Braly, K. W. (1933). Racial stereotypes of 100 college students. *Journal of Abnormal and Social Psychology, 28,* 280–290.

Katz, D., McClintock, C., & Sarnoff, D. (1957). The measurement of ego-defense as related to attitude change. *Journal of Personality, 25,* 465–474.

Katz, D., & Stotland, E. (1959). A preliminary statement to a theory of attitude structure and change. In S. Koch (Ed.), *Psychology: A study of a science* (Vol. 3). New York: McGraw-Hill.

Katz, I. (1970). Experimental studies of Negro-white relationships. In L. Berkowitz (Ed.), *Advances in experimental social psychology* (Vol. 5). New York: Academic Press.

Katz, I. (1981). *Stigma: A social psychological analysis.* Hillsdale, NJ: Erlbaum.

Katz, I., Glass, D. C., & Cohen, S. (1973). Ambivalence, guilt, and the scapegoating of minority group victims. *Journal of Experimental Social Psychology, 9,* 423–436.

Katz, I., Glass, D. C., Lucido, D. J., & Farber, J. (1979). Harm-doing and victim's racial or orthopedic stigma as determinants of helping behavior. *Journal of Personality, 47,* 340–364.

Katz, I., & Hass, R. G. (1988). Racial ambivalence and American value conflict: Correlational and prime studies of dual cognitive structures. *Journal of Personality and Social Psychology, 55,* 893–905.

Katz, I., Wackenhut, J., & Hass, R. G.

(1986). Racial ambivalence, value duality, and behavior. In J. F. Dovidio & S. L. Gaertner (Eds.), *Prejudice, discrimination, and racism.* Orlando, FL: Academic Press. Pp. 35–60.

Kaufman, B. (1986).*The Korean war: Challenges in crisis, credibility, and command.* Philadelphia: Temple University Press.

Kaye, L. W., & Applegate, J. S. (1990). Men as elder caregivers: A response to changing families. *American Journal of Orthopsychiatry, 60,* 86–95.

Keller, E. B. (1983). A changing climate for civil rights. *Perspectives, 15,* 10–15.

Kelley, H. H. (1950). The warm-cold variable in first impressions of persons. *Journal of Personality, 18,* 431–439.

Kelley, H. H. (1967). Attribution theory in social psychology. *Nebraska symposium on motivation, 14,* 192–241.

Kelley, H. H. (1972). Attribution in social interaction. In E. E. Jones, D. E. Kanouse, H. H. Kelley, R. E. Nisbett, S. Valins, & B. Weiner (Eds.), *Attribution: Perceiving the causes of behavior.* Morristown, NJ: General Learning Press.

Kelley, H. H., Berscheid, E., Christensen, A., Harvey, J. H., Huston, T. L., Levinger, G., McClintock, E., Peplau, L. A., & Peterson, D. R. (1983). *Close relationships.* New York: W. H. Freeman & Co.

Kelley, H. H., & Grzelak, J. (1972). Conflict between individual and common interest in an N-person relationship. *Journal of Personality and Social Psychology, 21,* 190–197.

Kelley, H. H., & Stahelski, A. J. (1970). Social interaction basis of cooperators' and competitors' beliefs about others. *Journal of Personality and Social Psychology, 16,* 66–91.

Kelly, E. L., & Conley, J. J. (1987). Personality and compatibility: A prospective analysis of marital stability and marital satisfaction. *Journal of Personality and Social Psychology, 52,* 27–40.

Kelly, J. F., & Hake, D. F. (1970). An extinction-induced increase in an aggressive response with humans. *Journal of the Experimental Analysis of Behavior, 14,* 153–164.

Kelman, H. C. (1953). Attitude change as a function of response restriction. *Human Relations, 6,* 185–214.

Kelman, H. C. (1958). Compliance, identification, and internalization: Three processes of attitude change. *Journal of Conflict Resolution, 2,* 51–60.

Kelman, H. C., & Hamilton, V. L. (1988). *Crimes of obedience: Toward a social psychology of authority and responsibility.* New Haven, CT: Yale University Press.

Kelman, H. C., & Hovland, C. I. (1953). "Reinstatement" of the communicator in delayed measurement of opinion change. *Journal of Abnormal and Social Psychology, 48,* 327–335.

Keltner, D., Ellsworth, P. C., & Edwards, K. (1993). Beyond simple pessimism: Effects of sadness and anger on social perception. *Journal of Personality and Social Psychology, 64,* 740–752.

Kendon, A. (1989). How gestures can become like words. In F. Poyatos (Ed.), *Cross-cultural perspectives in nonverbal communication.* Toronto: Hogrefe.

Kenney, R. A., Blascovich, J., & Shaver, P. R. (1994). Implicit leadership theories: Prototypes for new leaders. *Basic and Applied Social Psychology, 15,* 409–437.

Kenny, D. A. (1991). A general model of consensus and accuracy in interpersonal perception. *Psychological Review, 98,* 155–163.

Kenny, D. A., & Albright, L. (1987). Accuracy in interpersonal perception: A social relations analysis. *Psychological Bulletin, 102,* 390–402.

Kenny, D. A., Albright, L., Malloy, T. E., & Kashy, D. A. (1994). Consensus in interpersonal perception: Acquaintance and the big five. *Psychological Bulletin, 116,* 245–258.

Kenny, D. A., Horner, C., Kashy, D. A., & Chu, L. (1992). Consensus at zero acquaintance: Replication, behavioral cues, and stability. *Journal of Personality and Social Psychology, 62,* 88–97.

Kenny, D. A., & Kashy, D. A. (1994). Enhanced coorientation in the perception of friends: A social relations analysis. *Journal of Personality and Social Psychology, 67,* 1024–1033.

Kenny, D. A., & La Voie, L. (1984). The social relations model. In L. Berkowitz (Ed.), *Advances in experimental social psychology* (Vol. 18). Orlando, FL: Academic Press.

Kenrick, D. T. (1994). Evolutionary social psychology: From sexual selection to social cognition. In M. P. Zanna (Ed.), *Advances in Experimental Social Psychology* (Vol. 26). San Diego: Academic Press.

Kenrick, D. T. (1995). Evolutionary theory versus the confederacy of dunces. *Psychological Inquiry, 6,* 56–62.

Kenrick, D. T., & Cialdini, R. B. (1977). Romantic attraction: Misattribution versus reinforcement explanations. *Journal of Personality and Social Psychology, 35,* 381–391.

Kenrick, D. T., Groth, G., Trost, M. R., & Sadalla, E. K. (1993). Integrating evolutionary and social exchange perspectives on relationships: Effects of gender, self-appraisal, and involvement level on mate selection. *Journal of Personality and Social Psychology, 64,* 951–969.

Kenrick, D. T., & Keefe, R. C. (1992). Age preferences in mates reflect sex differences in human reproductive strategies. *Behavioral and Brain Sciences, 15,* 75–133.

Kenrick, D. T., & MacFarlane, S. W. (1986). Ambient temperature and horn honking: A field study of the heat/aggression relationship. *Environment and Behavior, 18,* 179–191.

Kenrick, D. T., Neuberg, S. L., Zierk, K., & Krones, J. (1994). Evolution and social cognition: Contrast effects as a function of sex, dominance, and physical attractiveness. *Personality and Social Psychology Bulletin, 20,* 210–217.

Kenrick, D. T., Sadalla, E. K., Groth, G., & Trost, M. R. (1990). Evolution, traits, and the stages of human courtship: Qualifying the parental investment model. *Journal of Personality, 58,* 7–116.

Kenrick, D. T., & Sheets, V. (1993). Homicidal fantasies. *Ethology and Sociobiology, 14,* 231–246.

Kenrick, D. T., & Trost, M. R. (1987). A biosocial theory of heterosexual relationships. In K. Kelly (Ed.), *Females, males, and sexuality.* Albany: State University of New York Press.

Kephart, W. M. (1967). Some correlates of romantic love. *Journal of Marriage and the Family, 29,* 470–479.

Kernis, M. H. (1984). Need for uniqueness, self-schemas, and thoughts as moderators of the false-consensus effect. *Journal of Experimental Social Psychology, 20,* 350–362.

Kernis, M. H., Cornell, D. P., Sun, C., Berry, A., & Harlow, T. (1993). There's more to self-esteem than whether it is high or low: The importance of stability of self-esteem. *Journal of Personality and Social Psychology, 65,* 1190–1204.

Kerr, N. L. (1983). Motivation losses in small groups: A social dilemma analysis. *Journal of Personality and Social Psychology, 45,* 819–828.

Kerr, N. L., & Bruun, S. (1981). Ringelmann revisited: Alternative explanations for the social loafing effect. *Personality and Social Psychology Bulletin, 7,* 224–231.

Kerr, N. L., & Bruun, S. (1983). The dispensability of member effort and group motivation losses: Free rider effects. *Journal of Personality and Social Psychology, 44,* 78–94.

Kerr, N. L., & Kaufman-Gilliland, C. M. (1994). Communication, commitment, and cooperation in social dilemmas. *Journal of Personality and Social Psychology, 66,* 513–529.

Kettlewell, H. (1973). *The evolution of melanism.* Oxford: Oxford University Press.

Kiecolt-Glaser, J. K., Garner, W., Speicher, C., Penn, G. M., Holliday, J., & Glaser, R. (1984). Psychosocial modifiers of immunocompetence in medical students. *Psychosomatic Medicine, 46,* 7–14.

Kiecolt-Glaser, J. K., Ricker, D., George, J., Messick, G., Speicher, C., Garner, W., & Glaser, R. (1984). Urinary cortisol levels, cellular immuno-competency, and loneliness in psychiatric patients. *Psychosomatic Medicine, 46,* 15–23.

Kiesler, C. A., & Kiesler, S. B. (1969). *Conformity.* Reading, MA: Addison-Wesley.

Kihlstrom, J. F. (1987). The cognitive unconscious. *Science, 237,* 1445–1452.

Kilham, W., & Mann, L. (1974). Level of destructive obedience as a function of transmitter and executant roles in the Milgram obedience paradigm. *Journal of Personality and Social Psychology, 29,* 696–702.

Kim, H. S., & Baron, R. S. (1988). Exercise and the illusory correlation: Does arousal heighten stereotypic processing? *Journal of Experimental Social Psychology, 24,* 366–380.

Kinder, D. R., & Sears, D. O. (1981). Prejudice and politics: Symbolic racism versus racial threats to the good life. *Journal of Personality and Social Psychology, 40,* 414–431.

Kinsports, K. (1988). Defending battered women's self-defense claims. *Oregon Law Review, 67,* 393–465.

Kipnis, D. (1984). The use of power in organizations and in interpersonal settings. In S. Oskamp (Ed.), *Applied social psychology annual #5.* Beverly Hills, CA: Sage.

Kipnis, D. (1993). Unanticipated consequences of using behavior technology. *Leadership Quarterly, 4,* 149–171.

Kipnis, D. (1994). Accounting for the use of behavior technologies in social psychology. *American Psychologist, 49,* 165–172.

Kirkpatrick, L. A., & Davis, K. E. (1994). Attachment style, gender, and relationship stability: A longitudinal analysis. *Journal of Personality and Social Psychology, 66,* 502–512.

Kite, M. E. (1992). Age and the spontaneous self-concept. *Journal of Applied Social Psychology, 22,* 1828–1837.

Klama, J. (1988). *Aggression: The myth of the beast within.* New York: Wiley.

Klatzky, R. L., Martin, G. L., & Kane, R. A. (1982). Influence of social-category activation on processing of visual information. *Social Cognition, 1,* 95–109.

Kleck, R. E., & Mendolia, M. (1990). Decoding of profile versus full-face expression of affect. *Journal of Nonverbal Behavior, 14,* 35–50.

Klein, S. B., & Kihlstrom, J. F. (1986). Elaboration, organization, and the self-reference effect in memory. *Journal of Experimental Psychology: General, 115,* 26–38.

Klein, W. M., & Kunda, Z. (1993). Maintaining self-serving comparisons: Biased reconstruction of one's past behaviors. *Personality and Social Psychology Bulletin, 19,* 732–739.

Klein, S. B., & Loftus, J. (1993). Behavioral experience and trait judgments about the self. *Personality and Social Psychology Bulletin, 19,* 740–745.

Klein, S. B., Loftus, J., & Plog, A. E. (1992). Trait judgments about the self: Evidence from the encoding specificity paradigm. *Personality and Social Psychology Bulletin, 18,* 730–735.

Klein, S. B., Loftus, J., & Schell, T. (1994). Repeated testing: A technique for assessing the roles of elaborative and organizational processing in the representation of social knowledge. *Journal of Personality and Social Psychology, 66, 830–839.*

Klein, S. B., Loftus, J., & Sherman, J. W. (1993). The role of summary and specific behavioral memories in trait judgments about the self. *Personality and Social Psychology Bulletin, 19,* 305–311.

Klein, S. B., Loftus, J., Trafton, J. G., & Fuhrman, R. W. (1992). Use of exemplars and abstractions in trait judgments: A model of trait knowledge about the self and others. *Journal of Personality and Social Psychology, 63, 739–753.*

Knapp, A., & Clark, M. S. (1991). Some detrimental effects of negative mood on individuals' ability to solve resource dilemmas. *Personality and Social Psychology Bulletin, 17,* 678–688.

Knight, G. P. (1980). Behavioral similarity, confederate strategy, and sex composition of dyads as determinants of interpersonal judgments and behavior in the prisoner's dilemma game. *Journal of Research in Personality, 14,* 91–103.

Knight, G. P., & Dubro, A. F. (1984). Cooperative, competitive, and individualistic social values: An individualized regression and clustering approach. *Journal of Personality and Social Psychology, 46,* 98–105.

Knox, R. E., & Safford, R. K. (1976). Group caution at the race track. *Journal of Experimental Social Psychology, 12,* 317–324.

Knutson, J. F., Fordyce, D. J., & Anderson, D. J. (1980). Escalation of irritable aggression: Control by consequences and antecedents. *Aggressive Behavior, 6,* 347–359.

Knutson, J. F., & Viken, R. J. (1984). Animal analogues of human aggression: Studies of social experience and escalation. In K. J. Flannelly, R. J. Blanchard, & D. C. Blanchard (Eds.), *Biological perspectives on aggression* (pp. 75–94). New York: Alan Liss.

Kobak, R. R., & Hazan, C. (1991). Attachment in marriage: Effects of security and accuracy of working models. *Journal of Personality and Social Psychology, 60,* 861–869.

Koehler, D. J. (1991). Explanation, imagination, and confidence in judgment. *Psychological Bulletin, 110,* 499–519.

Koestner, R., & Wheeler, L. (1988). Self-presentation in personal advertisements: The influence of implicit notions of attraction and role expectations. *Journal of Social and Personal Relationships, 5,* 149–160.

Kolditz, T. A., & Arkin, R. M. (1982). An impression management interpretation of the self-handicapping strategy. *Journal of Personality and Social Psychology, 43,* 492–502.

Komorita, S. S., Chan, D. K. S., & Parks, C. D. (1993). The effects of reward structure and reciprocity in social dilemmas. *Journal of Experimental Social Psychology, 29,* 252–267.

Komorita, S. S., & Lapworth, C. W. (1982). Cooperative choice among individuals versus groups in an N-person dilemma situation. *Journal of Personality and Social Psychology, 42,* 487–496.

Komorita, S. S., & Parks, C. D. (1995). Interpersonal relations: Mixed-motive interaction. *Annual Review of Psychology, 46.*

Komorita, S. S., Sweeney, J., & Kravitz, D. A. (1980). Cooperative choice in the N-person dilemma situation. *Journal of Personality and Social Psychology, 38,* 504–516.

Konecni, V. J. (1972). Some effects of guilt on compliance. *Journal of Personality and Social Psychology, 23,* 30–32.

Konner, M., Dovore, I., & Konner, M. (1974). Infancy in hunter-gatherer life: An ethological perspective. In N. White (Ed.), *Ethology and psychiatry.* Toronto: University of Toronto Press.

Koop, C. E. (1987). Report of the surgeon general's workshop on pornography and public health. *American Psychologist, 42,* 944–945.

Koper, G., van Knippenberg, D., Bouhuijs, F., Vermunt, R., & Wilke, H. (1993). Procedural fairness and self-esteem. *European Journal of Social Psychology, 23,* 313–325.

Kowalski, R. M. (1992). Nonverbal behaviors and perceptions of sexual intentions: Effects of sexual connotativeness, verbal response, and rape outcome. *Basic and Applied Social Psychology, 13,* 427–445.

Kowalski , R. M., & Brown, K. J. (1994). Psychosocial barriers to cervical cancer screening: Concerns with self-presentation and social evaluation. *Journal of Applied Social Psychology, 24,* 941–958.

Kramer, G. P., & Kerr, N. L. (1989). Laboratory simulation and bias in the study of juror behavior: A methodological note. *Law and Human Behavior, 13,* 89–99.

Krauss, R. M., Morrel-Samuels, P., & Colasante, C. (1991). Do conversational hand gestures communicate? *Journal of Personality and Social Psychology, 61,* 743–754

Kraut, R. E. (1980). Humans as lie-detectors: Some second thoughts. *Journal of Communication, 30,* 209–216.

Kraut, R. E., & Poe, D. (1980). Behavioral roots of person perception: The deception judgments of customs inspectors and laymen. *Journal of Per-*

sonality and Social Psychology, 39, 784–798.

Kravitz, D. A., & Martin, B. (1986). Ringelmann rediscovered: The original article. *Journal of Personality and Social Psychology, 50,* 936–941.

Krebs, D. L. (1970). Altruism—an examination of the concept and a review of the literature. *Psychological Bulletin, 73,* 258–302.

Krebs, D. L. (1975). Empathy and altruism. *Journal of Personality and Social Psychology, 32,* 1134–1146.

Krebs, D. L. (1982). Altruism—a rational approach. In N. Eisenberg (Ed.), *The development of prosocial behavior* (pp. 53–76). New York: Academic Press.

Krebs, D. L. (1983). Commentaries and critiques. In D. Bridgeman (Ed.), *The nature of prosocial development: Interdisciplinary theories and strategies.* New York: Academic Press.

Krebs, D. L., & Miller, D. T. (1985). Altruism and aggression. In G. Lindzey & E. Aronson (Eds.), *Handbook of social psychology* (Vol. 2). New York: Random House.

Krech, D., & Crutchfield, R. S. (1948). *Theory and problems of social psychology.* New York: McGraw-Hill.

Kristiansen, C. M., & Hotte, A. M. (in press). Morality and the self: Implications for the when and how of value-attitude-behavior relations. In C. Seligman, J. Olson, & M. P. Zanna (Eds.), *The Ontario symposium: The psychology of values* (Vol. 8).

Kristiansen, C. M., & Zanna, M. P. (1994). The rhetorical use of values to justify social and intergroup attitudes. *Journal of Social Issues, 50,* 47–65.

Krosnick, J. A., & Alwin, D. F. (1989). Aging and susceptibility to attitude change. *Journal of Personality and Social Psychology, 57,* 416–425.

Krosnick, J. A., Betz, A. L., Jussim, L. J., & Lynn, A. (1992). Subliminal conditioning of attitudes. *Personality and Social Psychology Bulletin, 18,* 152–162.

Krosnick, J. A., Boninger, D. S., Chuang, Y. C., Berent, M. K., & Carnot, C. G. (1993). Attitude strength: One construct or many related constructs? *Journal of Personality and Social Psychology, 65,* 1132–1151.

Krosnick, J. A., & Petty, R. E. (1995). Attitude strength: An overview. In R. E. Petty & J. A. Krosnick (Eds.), *Attitude strength: Antecedents and consequences.* Hillsdale, NJ: Erlbaum.

Krueger, J., & Rothbart, M. (1988). Use of categorical and individuating information in making inferences about personality. *Journal of Personality and Social Psychology, 55,* 187–195.

Kruglanski, A. W. (1989). The psychology of being "right": The problem of accuracy in social perception and cognition. *Psychological Bulletin, 108,* 195–208.

Kruglanski, A. W. (1990). Lay epistemic theory in social-cognitive psychology. *Psychological Inquiry, 1,* 181–197.

Kruglanski, A. W. (in press). A motivated gatekeeper of our minds: Need for closure effects on social cognition and interaction. In R. M. Sorrentino & E. T. Higgins (Eds.), *Handbook of motivation and cognition: Foundations of social behavior* (Vol. 3).

Kruglanski, A. W., & Freund, T. (1983). The freezing and unfreezing of lay-inferences: Effects of interpersonal primacy, ethnic stereotyping, and numerical anchoring. *Journal of Experimental Social Psychology, 19,* 448–468.

Kruglanski, A. W., & Mayseless, O. (1987). Motivational effects in the social comparison of opinions. *Journal of Personality and Social Psychology, 53,* 834–853.

Kruglanski, A. W., & Mayseless, O. (1988). Contextual effects in hypothesis testing: The role of competing alternatives and epistemic motivations. *Social Cognition, 6,* 1–20.

Kruglanski, A. W., & Mayseless, O. (1990). Classic and current social comparison research: Expanding the perspective. *Psychological Bulletin, 108,* 195–208.

Kruglanski, A. W., & Webster, D. M. (1991). Group members' reactions to opinion deviates and conformists under varying degrees of proximity to decision deadline and environmental noise. *Journal of Personality and Social Psychology, 61,* 212–225.

Kruglanski, A., Webster, D. M., & Klem, A. (1993). Motivated resistance and openness to persuasion in the presence or absence of prior information. *Journal of Personality and Social Psychology, 65,* 861–876.

Krull, D. S. (1993). Does the grist change the mill? The effect of the perceiver's inferential goal on the process of social inference. *Personality and Social Psychology Bulletin, 19,* 340–348.

Kubey, R. W. (1980). Television and aging: Past, present, and future. *Gerontologist, 20,* 16–35.

Kuhlman, D. M., & Marshello, A. F. J. (1975). Individual differences in game motivation as moderators of preprogrammed strategy effects in Prisoner's Dilemma. *Journal of Personality and Social Psychology, 32,* 922–931.

Kunda, Z. (1987). Motivated inference: Self-serving generation and evaluation of causal theories. *Journal of Personality and Social Psychology, 53,* 636–647.

Kunst-Wilson, W. R., & Zajonc, R. B. (1980). Affective discrimination of stimuli that cannot be recognized. *Science, 207,* 557–558.

Kurdek, L. A. (1993). Predicting marital dissolution: A 5-year prospective longitudinal study of newlywed cou-

ples. *Journal of Personality and Social Psychology, 64,* 221–242.

Kutler, S. I. (1990). *The wars of Watergate: The last crisis of Nixon.* New York: Knopf-Random House.

Kuykendall, D., & Keating, J. P. (1990). Altering thoughts and judgements through repeated association. *British Journal of Social Psychology, 29,* 79–86.

Lagerspetz, K. M., & Lagerspetz, K. Y. H. (1971). Changes in the aggressiveness of mice resulting from selective breeding, learning, and social isolation. *Scandinavian Journal of Psychology, 12,* 241–248.

Lalonde, R. N. & Gardner, R. C. (1989). An intergroup perspective on stereotype organization and processing. *British Journal of Social Psychology, 28,* 289–303.

Lambert, A. J., & Wyer, R. S. (1990). Stereotypes and social judgment: The effects of typicality and group homogeneity. *Journal of Personality and Social Psychology, 59,* 676–691.

Landman, J. (1988). Regret and elation following action and inaction. *Personality and Social Psychology Bulletin, 13,* 524–536.

Landman, J., & Manis, J. O. (1992). What might have been: Counterfactual thoughts concerning personal decisions. *British Journal of Psychology, 83,* 473–477.

Landy, D., & Sigall, H. (1974). Beauty is talent: Task evaluation as a function of the performer's physical attractiveness. *Journal of Personality and Social Psychology, 29,* 299–304.

Landy, F. J., & Farr, J. L. (1980). Performance rating. *Psychological Bulletin, 87,* 70–107.

Langer, E. (1975). The illusion of control. *Journal of Personality and Social Psychology, 32,* 311–328.

LaPiere, R. T. (1934). Attitudes versus actions. *Social Forces, 13,* 230–237.

Laplace, A. C., Chermack, S. T., & Taylor, S. P. (1994). Effects of alcohol and drinking experience on human physical aggression. *Personality and Social Psychology Bulletin, 20,* 439–444.

Larkin, J. E., & Pines, H. A. (1994). Affective consequences of self-monitoring style in a job interview setting. *Basic and Applied Social Psychology, 15,* 297–310.

Larson, J. R., Jr., Foster-Fishman, P. G., & Keys, C. B. (1994). Discussion of shared and unshared information in decision-making groups. *Journal of Personality and Social Psychology, 67,* 446–461.

Lassiter, G. D., Slaw, R. D., Briggs, M. A., & Scanlan, C. R. (1992). The potential for bias in videotaped confessions. *Journal of Applied Social Psychology, 22,* 1838–1851.

Latané, B. (1981). The psychology of social impact. *American Psychologist, 36,* 343–356.

Latané, B., Cappell, H., & Joy, V. (1970). Social deprivation, housing density, and gregariousness in rats. *Journal of Comparative and Physiological Psychology, 70,* 221–227.

Latané, B., & Darley, J. M. (1970). *The unresponsive bystander: Why doesn't he help?* New York: Appleton-Century-Crofts.

Latané, B., Williams, K., & Harkins, S. (1979). Many hands make light the work: The causes and consequences of social loafing. *Journal of Personality and Social Psychology, 37,* 822–832.

Latané, B. & Wolf, S. (1981). The social impact of majorities and minorities. *Psychological Review, 88,* 438–453.

Lau, R. R. (1984). Dynamics of the attribution process. *Journal of Personality and Social Psychology, 46,* 1017–1028.

Lau, R. R., & Russell, D. (1980). Attributions in the sports pages. *Journal of Personality and Social Psychology, 39,* 29–38.

Lau, S., & Gruen, G. E. (1992). The social stigma of loneliness: Effect of target person's and perceiver's sex. *Personality and Social Psychology Bulletin, 18,* 182–189.

Laughlin, P. R., Chandler, J. S., Shupe, E. I., Magley, V. J., & Hulbert, L. G. (1995). Generality of a theory of collective induction: Face-to-face and computer-mediated interaction, amount of potential information, and group versus member choice of evidence. *Organizational Behavior and Human Decision Processes, 63,* 98–111.

Laughlin, P. R., & Earley, P. C. (1982). Social combination models, persuasive arguments theory, social comparison theory, and choice shift. *Journal of Personality and Social Psychology, 42,* 273–280.

Laughlin, P. R., & Hollinshead, A. B. (in press). A theory of collective induction. *Organizational Behavior and Human Decision Processes.*

Laughlin, P. R., Kerr, N. L., Davis, J. H., Halff, H. M., & Marciniak, K. A. (1975). Group size, member ability, and social decision schemes on an intellective task. *Journal of Personality and Social Psychology, 31,* 522–535.

Lavine, H., Borgida, E., & Rudman, L. A. (1994). Social cognition. *Encyclopedia of Human Behavior, 4,* 213–223.

Lavrakas, P. J. (1975). Female preferences for male physiques. *Journal of Research in Personality, 9,* 324–334.

Lawler, E. J., & Yoon, J. (in press). Power and emotional processes in negotiations: A social exchange approach. In R. Kramer & D. Messick (Eds.), *The social contexts of negotiation.*

Lazarus, R. S., & Folkman, S. (1984). *Stress, appraisal, and coping.* New York: Springer.

Lea, M., & Duck, S. (1982). A model for the role of similarity of values in friendship development. *British Journal of Social Psychology, 21,* 301–310.

Leab, D. J. (1975). *From Sambo to Superspade: The black experience in motion pictures.* Boston, MA: Houghton Mifflin.

Leana, C. R. (1985). A partial test of Janis' groupthink model: Effects of group cohesiveness and leader behavior on defective decision making. *Journal of Management, 11,* 5–17.

Leary, M. R. (1986). The impact of interactional impediments on social anxiety and self-presentation. *Journal of Experimental Social Psychology, 22,* 22–135.

Leary, M. R. (1990). Responses to social exclusion: Social anxiety, jealousy, loneliness, depression, and low self-esteem. *Journal of Social and Clinical Psychology, 9,* 221–229.

Leary, M. R., & Downs, D. L. (1995). Interpersonal functions of the self-esteem motive: The self-esteem system as a sociometer. In M. Kernis (Ed.), *Efficacy, agency, and self-esteem.* New York: Plenum.

Leary, M. R., & Jones, J. L. (1993). The social psychology of tanning and sunscreen use: Self-presentational motives as a predictor of health risk. *Journal of Applied Social Psychology, 23,* 1390–1406.

Leary, M. R., & Kowalski, R. M. (1990). Impression management: A literature review and two-component model. *Psychological Bulletin, 107,* 34–47.

Leary, M. R., Nezlak, J. B., Downs, D., Radford-Devenport, J., Martin, J., & McMullen, A. (1994). Self-presentation in everyday interactions: Effects of target familiarity and gender composition. *Journal of Personality and Social Psychology, 67,* 664–673.

Leary, M. R., Tambor, E. S., Terdal, S. K., & Downs, D. L. (1995). Self-esteem as an interpersonal monitor: The sociometer hypothesis. *Journal of Personality and Social Psychology, 68,* 518–530.

Leary, M. R., Tchividjian, L. R., & Kraxberger, B. E. (1994). Self-presentation can be hazardous to your health: Impression management and health risk. *Health Psychology, 13,* 461–470.

Lecky, P (1945). *Self-consistency: A theory of personality.* New York: Island Press.

Lee, J. A. (1973). *The colors of love: An exploration of the ways of loving.* Don Mills, Ontario: New Press.

Lee, J. A. (1988). Love-styles. In R. J. Sternberg & M. L. Barnes (Eds.), *The psychology of love.* New Haven, CT: Yale University Press.

Lefkowitz, M. M., Eron, L. D., Walder, L. O., & Huesmann, L. R. (1977). *Growing up to be violent: A longitudinal study of the development of aggression.* New York: Pergamon.

Lehman, D. R., Lempert, R. O., & Nisbett, R. E. (1988). The effects of graduate training on reasoning. *American Psychologist, 43,* 431–442.

Lemyre, L., & Smith, P. M. (1985). Intergroup discrimination and self-esteem in the minimal group paradigm. *Journal of Personality and Social Psychology, 49,* 660–670.

Leonard, K. E. (1989). The impact of explicit aggressive and implicit nonaggressive cues on aggression in intoxicated and sober males. *Personality and Social Psychology Bulletin, 15,* 390–400.

Lepore, S. J., Evans, G. W., & Palsane, M. N. (1991). Social hassles and psychological health in the context of chronic crowding. *Journal of Health and Social Behavior, 32,* 357–367.

Lepper, M. R. (1973). Dissonance, self-perception, and honesty in children. *Journal of Personality and Social Psychology, 25,* 65–74.

Lepper, M. R., Greene, D., & Nisbett, R. E. (1973). Undermining children's intrinsic interest with extrinsic rewards: A test of the "overjustification" hypothesis. *Journal of Personality and Social Psychology, 28,* 129–137.

Lerner, M. J. (1980). *The belief in a just world: A fundamental delusion.* New York: Plenum.

Lerner, M. J., & Miller, D. T. (1978). Just world research and the attribution process: Looking back and ahead. *Psychological Bulletin, 85,* 1030–1051.

Lerner, M. J., Somers, D. G., Reid, D., Chiriboga, D., & Tierney, M. (1991). Adult children as caregivers: Egocentric biases in judgments of sibling contributions. *Gerontologist, 31,* 746–755.

Leshner, A. I. (1981). The role of hormones in the control of submissiveness. In P. F. Brain & D. Benton (Eds.), *Multidisciplinary approaches to aggression research* (pp. 309–322). Amsterdam: Elsevier.

Leshner, A. I., & Nook, B. L. (1976). The effects of experience on agonistic responding: An expectancy theory interpretation. *Behavioral Biology, 17,* 561–566.

Levenson, R. W., Carstensen, L. L., & Gottman, J. M. (1993). Long-term marriage: Age, gender, and satisfaction. *Psychology and Aging, 8,* 301–313.

Levenson, R. W., Carstensen, L. L., & Gottman, J. M. (1994). The influence of age and gender on affect, physiology, and their interrelations: A study of long-term marriages. *Journal of Personality and Social Psychology, 67,* 56–68.

Levenson, R. W., & Reuf, A. M. (1992). Empathy: A physiological substrate. *Journal of Personality and Social Psychology, 63,* 234–246.

Leventhal, H. (1970). Findings and theory in the study of fear communications. In L. Berkowitz (Ed.), *Advances in experimental social psychology* (Vol. 5). New York: Academic Press.

Leventhal, H., Diefenbach, M., & Leventhal, E. A. (1992). Illness cognition: Using common sense to understand treatment adherence and affect cognition interactions. *Cognitive Therapy & Research, 16,* 143–163.

Leventhal, H., Meyer, D., & Nerenz, D. (1980). *The common sense representation of illness danger.* In S. Rachman (Ed.), *Medical psychology (Vol. 2).* New York: Pergamon.

Leventhal, H., & Patrick-Miller, L. (1993). Emotion and illness: The mind is in the body. In M. S. Lewis & J. Haviland (Eds.), *Handbook of emotions.* New York: Guilford.

Levesque, M. J., & Kenny, D. A. (1993). Accuracy of behavioral predictions at zero acquaintance: A social relations analysis. *Journal of Personality and Social Psychology, 65,* 1178–1187.

Levi, L. (1965). The urinary output of adrenalin and noradrenalin during pleasant and unpleasant emotional states: A preliminary report. *Psychosomatic Medicine, 27,* 80–85.

Levine, J. M. (1989). Reaction to opinion deviance in small groups. In P. B. Paulus (Ed.), *The psychology of group influence* (2nd ed.). Hillsdale, NJ: Erlbaum.

Levine, L., & Hoffman, M. L. (1975). Empathy and cooperation in 4-year-olds. *Developmental Psychology, 11,* 533–534.

Levine, M. L. (1988). *Age discrimination and the mandatory retirement controversy.* Baltimore, MD: Johns Hopkins Press.

Levine, R. V., Martinez, T. S., Brase, G., & Sorenson, K. (1994). Helping in 36 U.S. cities. *Journal of Personality and Social Psychology, 67,* 69–82.

Levine, R., Sato, S., Hashimoto, T., & Verma, J. (1994). *Love and marriage in eleven cultures.* Unpublished manuscript. California State University, Fresno, CA.

Levinger, G., & Breedlove, J. (1966). Interpersonal attraction and agreement: A study of marriage partners. *Journal of Personality and Social Psychology, 3,* 367–372.

Levinger, G., & Schneider, D. J. (1969). Test of the "risk is a value" hypothesis. *Journal of Personality and Social Psychology, 11,* 165–169.

Levinson, R. M. (1975). Sex discrimination and employment practices: An experiment with unconventional job inquiries. *Social Problems, 22,* 553–543.

Levy, B., & Langer, E. (1994). Aging free from negative stereotypes: Successful memory in China and among the American deaf. *Journal of Personality and Social Psychology, 66,* 989–997.

Levy, M. B., & Davis, K. E. (1988). Lovestyles and attachment styles compared: Their relations to each other and to various relationship characteristics. *Journal of Social and Personal Relationships, 5,* 439–471.

Levy, R. I. (1983). The emotions in comparative perspective. In K. R. Scherer & P. Ekman (Eds.), *Approaches to emotion.* Hillsdale, NJ: Erlbaum.

Lewin, K. (1943). Defining the "field at a given time." *Psychological Review, 50,* 292–310.

Lewis, D. O., Shanok, S. S., Pincus, J. H., & Glaser, G. H. (1979). Violent juvenile delinquents: Psychiatric, neurological, psychological and abuse factors. *Journal of the American Academy of Child Psychiatry, 18,* 307–319.

Lewontin, R. C., Rose, S., & Kamin, L. J. (1984). *Biology, ideology, and human nature: Not in our genes.* New York: Pantheon.

Leyens, J.-P., Cisneros, T., & Hossay, J. (1976). Decentration as a means for reducing aggression after exposure to violent stimuli. *European Journal of Social Psychology, 5,* 229–236.

Leyens, J.-P., & Picus, S. (1973). Identification with the winner of a fight and name mediation: Their differential effects upon subsequent aggressive behaviour. *British Journal of Social and Clinical Psychology, 12,* 374–377.

Liebowitz, M. (1983). *The chemistry of love.* New York: Berkley Books.

Liebrand, W. B. G., Messick, D. M., & Wilke, H. A. M. (1992). *Social dilemmas.* Tarrytown, NY: Pergamon.

Likert, R. (1932). A technique for the measurement of attitudes. *Archives of Psychology,* No. 140.

Linder, D. E., Cooper, J., & Jones, E. E. (1967). Decision freedom as a determinant of the role of incentive magnitude in attitude change. *Journal of Personality and Social Psychology, 6,* 245–254.

Lindskold, S. (1978). Trust development, the GRIT proposal, and the effect of conciliatory acts on conflict and cooperation. *Psychological Bulletin, 85,* 772–793.

Lindskold, S., Han, G., & Betz, B. (1986). Repeated persuasion in interpersonal conflict. *Journal of Personality and Social Psychology, 51,* 1183–1188.

Lindskold, S., Walters, P. S., & Koutsourais, H. (1983). Cooperators, competitors, and response to *GRIT. Journal of Conflict Resolution, 27,* 521–532.

Linville, P. W. (1985). Self-complexity and affective extremity: Don't put all your eggs in one cognitive basket. *Social Cognition, 3,* 94–120.

Linville, P. W. (1987). Self-complexity as a cognitive buffer against stress-related depression and illness. *Journal of Personality and Social Psychology, 52,* 663–676.

Linville, P. W., Fischer, G. W., & Salovey, P. (1989). Perceived distributions of the characteristics of ingroup and out-group members: Empirical evidence and a computer simulation. *Journal of Personality and Social Psychology, 57,* 165–188.

Linville, P. W., & Jones, E. E. (1980). Polarized appraisals of outgroup members. *Journal of Personality and Social Psychology, 38,* 689–703.

Linz, D. G., Donnerstein, E., & Penrod, S. (1984). The effects of multiple exposures to filmed violence against women. *Journal of Communication, 34,* 130–147.

Linz, D. G., Donnerstein, E., & Penrod, S. (1987). The findings and recommendations of the attorney general's commission on pornography: Do the psychological "facts" fit the political fury? *American Psychologist, 42,* 946–953.

Linz, D. G., Donnerstein, E., & Penrod, S. (1988). Effects of long-term exposure to violent and sexually degrading depictions of women. *Journal of Personality and Social Psychology, 55,* 758–768.

Lipe, M. G. (1991). Counterfactual reasoning as a framework for attribution theories. *Psychological Bulletin, 109,* 456–471.

Lipset, S. M., & Schneider, W. (1978). The Bakke case: How would it be decided at the bar of public opinion? *Public Opinion, 1,* 38–44.

Lipsitt, L. (1979). Critical conditions in infancy: A psychological perspective. *American Psychologist, 34,* 973–980.

Lisak, D., & Roth, S. (1988). Motivational factors in nonincarcerated sexually aggressive men. *Journal of Personality and Social Psychology, 55,* 795–802.

Littlepage, G. E. (1991). Effects of group size and task characteristics on group performance: A test of Steiner's model. *Personality and Social Psychology Bulletin, 17,* 449–456.

Livingstone, S., & Green, G. (1986). Television advertisement and the portrayal of gender. *Journal of Social Psychology, 25,* 149–154.

Lloyd, J. E. (1986). Firefly communication and deception: "Oh, what a tangled web." In R. W. Mitchell & N. S. Thompson (Eds.), *Deception: Perspectives on human and nonhuman deceit.* Albany: State University of New York Press.

Locke, K. D., & Horowitz, L. M. (1990). Satisfaction in interpersonal interactions as a function of similarity in level of dysphoria. *Journal of Personality and Social Psychology, 58,* 823–831.

Locurto, C. (1991). *Sense and nonsense about IQ: The case for uniqueness.* New York: Praeger.

Longley, J., & Pruitt, D. G. (1980). Groupthink: A critique of Janis' theory. In L. Wheeler (Ed.), *Review of personality and social psychology* (Vol. 1). Beverly Hills, CA: Sage.

Looney, T. A., & Cohen, P. S. (1982). Aggression induced by intermittent positive reinforcement. *Neurosci. Biobehav. Review, 6,* 15–37.

Lord, C. G., Desforges, D. M., Ramsey, S. L., Trezza, G. R., & Lepper,

M. R. (1991). Typicality effects in attitude-behavior consistency: Effects of category discrimination and category knowledge. *Journal of Experimental Social Psychology, 27,* 550–575.

Lord, C. G., Lepper, M. R., & Mackie, D. (1984). Attitude prototypes as determinants of attitude-behavior consistency. *Journal of Personality and Social Psychology, 46,* 1254–1266.

Lord, C. G., Lepper, M. R., & Preston, E. (1985). Considering the opposite: A corrective strategy for social judgment. *Journal of Personality and Social Psychology, 47,* 1231–1243.

Lord, C. G., Ross, L., & Lepper, M. R. (1979). Biased assimilation and attitude polarization: The effects of prior theories on subsequently considered evidence. *Journal of Personality and Social Psychology, 37,* 2098–2109.

Lord, C. G., & Saenz, D. S. (1985). Memory deficits and memory surfeits: Differential cognitive consequences of tokenism for tokens and observers. *Journal of Personality and Social Psychology, 49,* 918–926.

Lord, C. G., Saenz, D. S., & Godfrey, D. K. (1987). Effects of perceived scrutiny on participant memory for social interactions. *Journal of Experimental Social Psychology, 23,* 498–517.

Lord, R. G., De Vader, C. L., & Alliger, G. M. (1986). A meta-analysis of the relation between personality traits and leadership perceptions: An application of validity generalization procedures. *Journal of Applied Psychology, 71,* 402–410.

Lord, R. G., Phillips, J. S., & Rush, M. C. (1980). Effects of sex and personality on perceptions of emergent leadership, influence, and social power. *Journal of Applied Psychology, 65,* 176–182.

Lorenz, K. (1966). *On aggression.* New York: Harcourt, Brace & World.

Lorenzi-Cioldi, F., Eagly, A. H., & Stewart, T. L. (1995). Homogeneity of gender groups in memory. *Journal of Experimental Social Psychology, 31,* 193–217.

Lott, A. J., & Lott, B. E. (1961). Group cohesiveness, communication level and conformity. *Journal of Abnormal and Social Psychology, 62,* 408–412.

Lott, A. J., & Lott, B. E. (1968). A learning theory approach to interpersonal attitudes. In A. G. Greenwald, T. C. Brock, & T. M. Ostrom (Eds.), *Psychological foundations of attitudes.* New York: Academic Press.

Lott, B. E., & Lott, A. J. (1985). Learning theory in contemporary social psychology. In G. Lindzey & E. Aronson (Eds.), *Handbook of social psychology* (3rd edition, Vol. 1). New York: Random House.

Luce, R. D., & Raiffa, H. (1957). *Games and decisions.* New York: Wiley.

Luchins, A. S. (1957). Primacy-recency in impression formation. In C. Hovland (Ed.), *The order of presentation in persuasion.* New Haven, CT: Yale University Press.

Luginbuhl, J., & Mullin, C. (1981). Rape and responsibility: How and how much is the victim blamed? *Sex Roles, 7,* 547–559.

Luhtanen, R., & Crocker, J. (1992). A collective self-esteem scale: Self-evaluation of one's social identity. *Personality and Social Psychology Bulletin, 18,* 302–318.

Lumsdaine, A. A., & Janis, I. L. (1953). Resistance to "counterpropaganda" produced by one-sided and two-sided "propaganda" presentation. *Public Opinion Quarterly, 17,* 311–318.

Lutz, C. (1982). The domain of emotion words on Ifaluk. *American Ethnologist, 9,* 113–128.

Lydon, J. E., Jamieson, D. W., & Zanna, M. P. (1988). Interpersonal similarity and the social and intellectual dimensions of first impressions. *Social Cognition, 6,* 269–286.

Lydon, J. E., Zanna, M. P., & Ross, M. (1988). Bolstering attitudes by autobiographical recall: Attitude persistence and selective memory. *Personality and Social Psychology Bulletin, 14,* 78–86.

Lykken, D. T. (1974). Psychology and the lie detector industry. *American Psychologist, 29,* 725–739.

Lykken, D. T., & Tellegen, A. (1993). Is human mating adventitious or the result of lawful choice? A twin study of mate selection. *Journal of Personality and Social Psychology, 65,* 56–68.

Lynch, J. J. (1977). *The broken heart: The medical consequences of loneliness.* New York: Basic Books.

Lynch, J. J. (1985). *The language of the heart: The body's response to human dialogue.* New York: Basic Books.

Lynn, M., & Mynier, K. (1993). Effect of server posture on restaurant tipping. *Journal of Applied Social Psychology, 23,* 678–685.

Lynn, M., & Oldenquist, A. (1986). Egoistic and nonegoistic motives in social dilemmas. *American Psychologist, 41,* 529–534.

Lynn, M., & Shurgot, B. A. (1984). Responses to lonely hearts advertisements: Effects of reported physical attractiveness, physique, and coloration. *Personality and Social Psychology Bulletin, 10,* 349–357.

Maass, A., & Clark, R. D. III (1984). Hidden impact of minorities: Fifteen years of minority influence research. *Psychological Bulletin, 95,* 428–450.

Maass, A., Clark, R. D. III, & Haberkorn, G. (1982). The effects of differential ascribed category membership and norms on minority influence. *European Journal of Social Psychology, 12,* 89–104.

Maass, A., Milesi, A., Zabbini, S., & Stahlberg, D. (1995). Linguistic intergroup bias: Differential expectancies or in-group protection? *Journal of Personality and Social Psychology, 68,* 116–126.

Maass, A., Salvi, D., Arcuri, L., & Semin, G. (1989). Language use in intergroup contexts: The linguistic intergroup bias. *Journal of Personality and Social Psychology, 57,* 981–993.

Maass, A., & Volpato, C. (1989). Gender differences in self-serving attributions about sexual experiences. *Journal of Applied Social Psychology, 19,* 517–542.

Maass, A., West, S. G., & Cialdini, R. B. (1987). Minority influence and conversion. In C. Hendrick (Ed.), *Group processes: Review of personality and social psychology* (Vol. 8). Newbury Park, CA: Sage.

Macauley, J. (1985). Adding gender to aggression research: Incremental or revolutionary change? In V. E. O'Leary, R. K. Unger, & B. S. Wallston (Eds.), *Women, gender, and social psychology* (pp. 191–224). Hillsdale, NJ: Erlbaum.

Maccoby, E. E., & Jacklin, C. N. (1974). *The psychology of sex differences.* Stanford: Stanford University Press.

Maccoby, E. E., & Jacklin, C. N. (1980). Sex differences in aggression: A rejoinder and reprise. *Child Development, 51,* 954–980.

MacDonald, J. M. (1961). *The murderer and his victim.* Springfield, IL: Charles C. Thomas.

Mace, K. C. (1972). The "over-bluff" shoplifter: Who gets caught? *Journal of Forensic Psychology, 4,* 26–30.

Mackie, D. (1986). Social identification effects in group polarization. *Journal of Personality and Social Psychology, 50,* 720–728.

Mackie, D. M., & Cooper, J. (1984). Attitude polarization: Effects of group membership. *Journal of Personality and Social Psychology, 46,* 575–585.

Mackie, D. M., Queller, S., Stroessner, S. J., & Hamilton, D. L. (in press). Making stereotypes better or worse: Multiple roles for positive affect in group impressions. In R. M. Sorrentino & E. T. Higgins (Eds.), *Handbook of motivation and cognition* (Vol. 3). New York: Guilford.

Mackie, D. M., & Worth, L. T. (1989a). Differential recall of subcategory information about in-group and out-group members. *Personality and Social Psychology Bulletin, 15,* 401–413.

Mackie, D. M., & Worth, L. T. (1989b). Processing deficits and the mediation of positive affect in persuasion. *Journal of Personality and Social Psychology, 57,* 27–40.

Mackie, D. M., & Worth, L. T. (1991). "Feeling good but not thinking straight": Positive mood and persuasion. In J. P. Forgas (Ed.), *Emotion and social judgments.* Oxford: Pergamon.

Macrae, C. N. (1992). A tale of two curries: Counterfactual thinking and accident-related judgments. *Personality and Social Psychology Bulletin, 18,* 84–87.

Macrae, C. N., Bodenhausen, G. V., Milne, A. B., & Jetten, J. (1994). Out of mind but back in sight: Stereotypes on the rebound. *Journal of Personality and Social Psychology, 67,* 808–817.

Macrae, C. N., Hewstone, M., & Griffiths, R. J. (1993). Processing load and memory for stereotype-based information. *European Journal of Social Psychology, 23,* 77–87.

Macrae, C. N., Milne, A. B., & Bodenhausen, G. V. (1994). Stereotypes as energy-saving devices: A peek inside the cognitive toolbox. *Journal of Personality and Social Psychology, 66,* 37–47.

Macrae, C. N., Milne, A. B., & Griffiths, R. J. (1993). Counterfactual thinking and the perception of criminal behavior. *British Journal of Psychology, 84,* 221–236.

Macrae, C. N., Shepard, J. W., & Milne, A. B. (1992). The effects of source credibility on the dilution of stereotype-based judgments. *Personality and Social Psychology Bulletin, 18,* 765–775.

Macrae, C. N., Stangor, C., & Milne, A. B. (1994). Activating social stereotypes: A functional analysis. *Journal of Experimental Social Psychology, 30,* 370–389.

Madden, T. J., Ellen, P. S., & Ajzen, I. (1992). A comparison of the theory of planned behavior and the theory of reasoned action. *Personality and Social Psychology Bulletin, 18,* 3–9.

Madey, S. F., DePalma, M. T., Bahrt, A. E., & Beirne, J. (1993). The effect of perceived patient responsibility on characterological, behavioral, and quality-of-care assessments. *Basic and Applied Social Psychology, 14,* 193–213.

Madsen, D. B. (1978). Issue importance and group choice shifts: A persuasive arguments approach. *Journal of Personality and Social Psychology, 36,* 1118–1127.

Maier, N. R. F. (1952). *Principles of human relations.* New York: Wiley.

Mail, P. D., & McDonald, D. R. (Eds.). (1980). *Tulapai to Tokay.* New Haven, CT: HRAF Press.

Main, M., & George, C. (1985). Responses of abused and disadvantaged toddlers to distress in agemates: A study in the day care setting. *Developmental Psychology, 21,* 407–412.

Main, M., & Solomon, J. (1990). Procedures for identifying infants as disorganized/disoriented during the Ainsworth strange situation. In M. T. Greenberg, D. Cicchetti, & E. M. Cummings (Eds.), *Attachment in the preschool years.* Chicago: University of Chicago Press.

Maio, G. R., Esses, V. M., & Bell, D. W. (1994). The formation of attitudes toward new immigrant groups. *Journal*

of Applied Social Psychology, 24, 1762–1776.

Major, B., & Crocker, J. (1993). Social stigma: The consequences of attributional ambiguity. In D. Mackie & D. Hamilton (Eds.), *Affect, cognition, and stereotyping: Interactive processes in intergroup perception.* San Diego, CA: Academic Press.

Malamuth, N. M. (1986). Predictors of naturalistic sexual aggression. *Journal of Personality and Social Psychology, 50,* 953–962.

Malamuth, N. M., & Check, J. V. P. (1981). The effects of mass media exposure on acceptance of violence against women. *Journal of Research in Personality, 15,* 436–446.

Malamuth, N. M., & Check, J. V. P. (1983). Sexual arousal to rape depictions: Individual differences. *Journal of Abnormal Psychology, 92,* 55–67.

Malamuth, N. M., & Check, J. V. P. (1984). Debriefing effectiveness following exposure to pornographic rape depictions. *Journal of Sex Research, 20,* 1–13.

Malamuth, N. M., & Donnerstein, E. (1983). The effects of aggressive-erotic stimuli. In L. Berkowitz (Ed.), *Advances in experimental social psychology* (Vol. 15). New York: Academic Press.

Malatesta, C. Z., Fiore, M. J., & Messina, J. J. (1987). Affect, personality, and facial expression characteristics of older people. *Psychology and Aging, 2,* 64–69.

Malatesta, C. Z., Izard, C. E., Culver, C., & Nicolich, M. (1987). Emotion communication skills in young, middle-aged, and older women. *Psychology and Aging, 2,* 193–203.

Malkis, F., Kalle, R., & Tedeschi, J. T. (1982). Attitudinal politics in the forced compliance situation. *Journal of Social Psychology, 117,* 79–91.

Malloy, T. E., Sugarman, D. B., Montvilo, R. K., & Ben-Zeev, T. (1995). Children's interpersonal perceptions: A social relations analysis of perceiver and target effects. *Journal of Personality and Social Psychology, 68,* 418–426.

Mann, L., & Janis, I. L. (1968). A follow-up study on the long-term effects of emotional role playing. *Journal of Personality and Social Psychology, 8,* 339–342.

Manning, A. (1989). The genetic bases of aggression. In J. Groebel & R. A. Hinde (Eds.), *Aggression and war: Their biological and social bases* (pp. 48–57). New York: Cambridge University Press.

Mannix, E. A. (1991). Resource dilemmas and discount rates in decision making groups. *Journal of Experimental Social Psychology, 27,* 379–391.

Manstead, A. S. R., Parker, D., Stradling, S. G., Reason, J. T., & Baxter, J. S. (1992). Perceived consensus in estimates of the prevalence

of driving errors and violations. *Journal of Applied Social Psychology, 22,* 509–530.

Manstead, A. S. R., Proffitt, C., & Smart, J. L. (1983). Predicting and understanding mothers' infant-feeding intentions and behavior: Testing the theory of reasoned action. *Journal of Personality and Social Psychology, 44,* 657–671.

Mantell, D. M. (1971). The potential for violence in Germany. *Journal of Social Issues, 27,* 101–112.

Manucia, G. K., Baumann, D. J., & Cialdini, R. B. (1984). Mood influences on helping: Direct effects or side effects? *Journal of Personality and Social Psychology, 46,* 357–364.

Margolin, G., John, R. S., & O'Brien, N. (1989). Sequential affective patterns as a function of marital conflict style. *Journal of Social and Clinical Psychology, 8,* 45–61.

Marin, G. (1985). The preference for equity when judging the attractiveness and fairness of an allocator: The role of familiarity and culture. *Journal of Social Psychology, 125,* 543–549.

Mark, M. M., & Mellor, S. (1991). Effect of self-relevance of an event on hindsight bias: The foreseeability of a layoff. *Journal of Applied Psychology, 76,* 569–577.

Markman, K. D., Gavanski, I., Sherman, S. J., & McMullen, M. N. (1993). The mental simulation of better and worse possible worlds. *Journal of Experimental Social Psychology, 29,* 87–109.

Markman, K. D., Gavanski, I., Sherman, S. J., & McMullen, M. N. (1995). The impact of perceived control on the imagination of better and worse possible worlds. *Personality and Social Psychology Bulletin, 21,* 588–595.

Marks, G., & Miller, N. (1982). Target attractiveness as a mediator of assumed attitude similarity. *Personality and Social Psychology Bulletin, 8,* 728–735.

Marks, G., & Miller, N. (1987). Ten years of research on the false-consensus effect: An empirical and theoretical review. *Psychological Bulletin, 102,* 72–90.

Marks, G., Richardson, J. L., Lochner, L. T., McGuigan, K. A., & Levine, A., (1988). Assumed similarity of attitudes about AIDS among gay and heterosexual physicians. *Journal of Applied Social Psychology, 18,* 774–786.

Markus, H. R. (1977). Self-schemata and processing information about the self. *Journal of Personality and Social Psychology, 35,* 63–78.

Markus, H. R. (1978). The effect of mere presence on social facilitation: An unobtrusive test. *Journal of Experimental Social Psychology, 14,* 389–397.

Markus, H. R., Hamill, R., & Sentis, K. P. (1987). Thinking fat: Self schemas for body weight and the processing of weight relevant information. *Journal of Applied Social Psychology, 17,* 50–71.

Markus, H. R., & Kitayama, S. (1991). Culture and the self: Implications for cognition, emotion, and motivation. *Psychological Review, 98,* 224–253.

Markus, H. R., & Kitayama, S. (1994). A collective fear of the collective: Implications for selves and theories of selves. *Personality and Social Psychology Bulletin, 20,* 568–579.

Markus, H. R., & Kunda, Z. (1986). Stability and malleability of the self-concept. *Journal of Personality and Social Psychology, 51,* 858–866.

Markus, H. R., & Nurius, P. (1986). Possible selves. *American Psychologist, 41,* 954–969.

Markus, H. R., Smith, J., & Moreland, R. L. (1985). Role of the self-concept in the perception of others. *Journal of Personality and Social Psychology, 49,* 1494–1512.

Marler, P. (1976). On animal aggression: The roles of strangeness and familiarity. *American Psychologist, 31,* 239–246.

Marteau, T. M., & Riordan, D. C. (1992). Staff attitudes towards patients: The influence of causal attributions for illness. *British Journal of Clinical Psychology, 31,* 107–110.

Martell, R. F. (1991). Sex bias at work: The effects of attentional and memory demands on performance ratings of men and women. *Journal of Applied Social Psychology, 21,* 1939–1960.

Martin, L. L. (1986). Set/reset: Use and misuse of concepts in impression formation. *Journal of Personality and Social Psychology, 51,* 493–504.

Martin, L. L., Seta, J. J., & Crelia, R. A. (1990). Assimilation and contrast as a function of people's willingness and ability to expend effort in forming an impression. *Journal of Personality and Social Psychology, 59,* 27–37.

Martin, L. L., & Stoner, P. (in press). Mood as input: What we think about how we feel determines how we think. In L. L. Martin & A. Tesser (Eds.), *Striving and feeling: Interactions between goals and affect.* Hillsdale, NJ: Erlbaum.

Martin, L. L., & Tesser, A. (in press). Some ruminative thoughts. In R. S. Wyer & T. K. Srull (Eds.), *Advances in social cognition.* Hillsdale, NJ: Erlbaum.

Martin, L. L., Tesser, A., & McIntosh, W. D. (1993). Wanting but not having: The effects of unattained goals on thoughts and feelings. In D. M. Wegner & J. W. Pennebaker (Eds.), *The handbook of mental control.* New York: Prentice-Hall.

Masson, C. N., & Verkuyten, M. (1993). Prejudice, ethnic identity, contact and ethnic group preferences among Dutch young adolescents. *Journal of Applied Social Psychology, 23,* 156–168.

Matsumoto, D., & Kudoh, T. (1993). American-Japanese cultural differences in attributions of personality based on smiles. *Journal of Nonverbal Behavior, 17,* 231–244.

Maurer, D., & Maurer, C. (1988). *The world of the newborn.* New York: Basic Books.

Maurer, T. J., Maher, K. J., Ashe, D. K., Mitchell, D. R. D., Hein, M. B., & Van Hein, J. (1993). Leadership perceptions in relation to a presidential vote. *Journal of Applied Psychology, 23,* 959–979.

Mayer, J. D., & Hanson, E. (1995). Mood-congruent judgment over time. *Personality and Social Psychology Bulletin, 21,* 237–244.

Mayer, J. D., McCormick, L. J., Resnick, A., & Strong, S. E. (1995). Mood-congruent memory and natural mood: New evidence. *Personality and Social Psychology Bulletin, 21,* 736–746.

Mayerson, N. H., & Rhodewalt, F. (1988). The role of self-protective attributions in the experience of pain. *Journal of Social and Clinical Psychology, 6,* 203–218.

Mayr, E. (1972). Sexual selection and natural selection. In B. Campbell (Ed.), *Sexual selection and the descent of man 1871–1971.* London: Heineman.

Mazzella, R., & Feingold, A. (1994). The effects of physical attractiveness, race, socioeconomic status, and gender of defendants and victims on judgments of mock jurors: A meta-analysis. *Journal of Applied Social Psychology, 24,* 1315–1344.

McAlister, A., Perry, C., Killen, J., Slinkard, L. A., & Maccoby, N. (1980). Pilot study of smoking, alcohol, and drug abuse prevention. *American Journal of Public Health, 70,* 719–721.

McAlister, A., Perry, C., & Maccoby, N. (1979). Adolescent smoking: Onset and prevention. *Pediatrics, 63,* 650–658.

McArthur, L. A. (1972). The how and what of why: Some determinants and consequences of causal attributions. *Journal of Personality and Social Psychology, 22,* 171–193.

McArthur, L. Z. (1981). What grabs you? The role of attention in impression formation and causal attribution. In E. T. Higgins, C. P. Herman, & M. P. Zanna (Eds.), *Social cognition: The Ontario Symposium* (Vol. 1, pp. 201–246). Hillsdale, NJ: Erlbaum.

McArthur, L. Z. (1982). Judging a book by its cover: A cognitive analysis of the relationship between physical appearance and stereotyping. In A. Hastorf & A. Isen (Eds.), *Cognitive social psychology.* New York: Elsevier/North-Holland.

McArthur, L. Z., & Berry, D. S. (1987). Cross-cultural agreement in perceptions of babyfaced adults. *Journal of Cross-Cultural Psychology, 18,* 165–192.

McArthur, L. Z., & Post, D. L. (1977). Figural emphasis and person perception. *Journal of Experimental Social Psychology, 13,* 520–535.

McArthur, L., & Resko, B. (1975). The portrayal of men and women in American television commercials. *Journal of Social Psychology, 97,* 209–220.

McCallum, D. M., Harring, K., Gilmore, R., Drenan, S., Chase, J. P., Insko, C. A., & Thibaut, J. (1985). Competition and cooperation between groups and between individuals. *Journal of Experimental Social Psychology, 21,* 301–320.

McCann, S. J. H. (1992). Alternative formulas to predict the greatness of U. S. Presidents: Personological, situational, and zeitgeist factors. *Journal of Personality and Social Psychology, 62,* 469–479.

McCaul, K. D., Sandgren, A. K., O'Neill, H., & Hinsz, V. B. (1993). The value of the theory of planned behavior, perceived control, and self-efficacy for predicting health-protective behaviors. *Basic and Applied Social Psychology, 14,* 231–252.

McCaul, K. D., Veltum, L. G., Boyechko, V., & Crawford, J. J. (1990). Understanding attributions of victim blame for rape: Sex, violence, and forseeability. *Journal of Applied Social Psychology, 20,* 1–26.

McCauley, C. (1989). The nature of social influence in groupthink: Compliance and internalization. *Journal of Personality and Social Psychology, 57,* 250–260.

McClanahan, K. K., Gold, J. A., Lenney, E., Ryckman, R. M., & Kulberg, G. E. (1990). Infatuation and attraction to a dissimilar other: Why is love blind? *Journal of Social Psychology, 130,* 433–445.

McClintock, C. G., & Liebrand, W. B. (1988). Role of interdependence structure, individual value orientation, and another's strategy in social decision making. *Journal of Personality and Social Psychology, 55,* 396–409.

McClintock, C. G., & McNeil, S. P. (1967). Prior dyadic experience and monetary reward as determinants of cooperative and competitive game behavior. *Journal of Personality and Social Psychology, 5,* 282–294.

McConahay, J. B. (1982). Self-interest versus racial attitudes as correlates of anti-busing attitudes in Louisville: Is it the buses or the blacks? *Journal of Politics, 44,* 692–720.

McConahay, J. B., & Hough, J. C., Jr. (1976). Symbolic racism. *Journal of Social Issues, 32,* 23–45.

McConnell, A. R., Sherman, S. J., & Hamilton, D. L. (1994). Illusory correlation in the perception of groups: An extension of the distinctiveness-based account. *Journal of Personality and Social Psychology, 67,* 414–429.

McCusker, C., & Carnevale, P. J. (1995). Framing in resource dilemmas: Loss aversion and the moderating effects of sanctions. *Organizational Behavior and Human Decision Processes, 61,* 190–201.

McFarland, C., & Ross, M. (1982). Impact of causal attributions on affective reactions to success and failure. *Journal of Personality and Social Psychology, 43,* 937–946.

McFarland, C., Ross, M., & Giltrow, M. (1992). Biased recollections in older adults: The role of implicit theories of aging. *Journal of Personality and Social Psychology, 62,* 837–850.

McGarty, C., Haslam, S. A., Turner, J. C., & Oakes, P. J. (1993). Illusory correlation as accentuation of actual intercategory difference: Evidence for the effect with minimal stimulus information. *European Journal of Social Psychology, 23,* 391–410.

McGarty, C., Turner, J. C., Hogg, M. A., David, B., & Wetherell, M. S. (1992). *British Journal of Social Psychology, 31,* 1–20.

McGill, A. L. (in press). American and Thai managers' explanations for poor company performance: Role of perspective and culture in causal selection. *Organizational Behavior and Human Decision Processes.*

McGlynn, R. P., Tubbs, D. D., & Holzhausen, K. G. (1995). Hypothesis generation in groups constrained by evidence. *Journal of Experimental Social Psychology, 31,* 64–81.

McGrath, J. E. (1984). *Groups: Interaction and performance.* Englewood Cliffs, NJ: Prentice-Hall.

McGrath, J. E., & Julian, J. W. (1963). Interaction process and task outcome in experimentally created negotiation groups. *Journal of Psychological Studies, 14,* 117–138.

McGuire, A. M. (1994). Helping behaviors in the natural environment: Dimensions and correlates of helping. *Personality and Social Psychology Bulletin, 20,* 45–56.

McGuire, W. J. (1962). Persistence of the resistance to persuasion induced by various types of prior belief defenses. *Journal of Abnormal and Social Psychology, 64,* 241–248.

McGuire, W. J. (1964). Inducing resistance to persuasion: Some contemporary approaches. In L. Berkowitz (Ed.), *Advances in experimental social psychology* (Vol. 1). New York: Academic Press.

McGuire, W. J. (1968). Personality and attitude change: An information processing theory. In A. G. Greenwald, T. C. Brock, & T. M. Ostrom (Eds.), *Psychological foundations of attitudes.* New York: Academic Press.

McGuire, W. J. (1969). Attitudes and attitude change. In G. Lindzey & E. Aronson (Eds.), *Handbook of social psychology* (Vol. 3). Reading, MA: Addison-Wesley.

McGuire, W. J. (1985). Attitudes and attitude change. In G. Lindzey & E. Aronson (Eds.), *Handbook of social psychology* (Vol. 2). New York: Random House.

McGuire, W. J., & McGuire, C. V. (1981). The spontaneous self-concept as affected by personal distinctiveness. In M. D. Lynch, A. A. Norem-Hebeisen, & K. Gergen (Eds.), *Self-concept: Advances in theory and research.* Cambridge, MA: Ballinger.

McGuire, W. J., & McGuire, C. V. (1988). Context and process in the experience of self. In L. Berkowitz (Ed.), *Advances in experimental social psychology* (Vol. 21). New York: Academic Press.

McGuire, W. J., McGuire, C. V., Child, P., & Fujioka, T. (1978). Salience of ethnicity in the spontaneous self-concept as a function of one's ethnic distinctiveness in the social environment. *Journal of Personality and Social Psychology, 36,* 511–520.

McGuire, W. J., McGuire, C. V., & Winton, W. (1979). Effects of household sex composition on the salience of one's gender in the spontaneous self-concept. *Journal of Experimental Social Psychology, 15,* 77–90.

McGuire, W. J., & Padawer-Singer, A. (1976). Trait-salience in the spontaneous self-concept. *Journal of Personality and Social Psychology, 33,* 743–754.

McGuire, W. J., & Papageorgis, D. (1962). Effectiveness of forewarning in developing resistance to persuasion. *Public Opinion Quarterly, 26,* 24–34.

McKenzie-Mohr, D., & Zanna, M. P. (1990). Treating women as sexual objects: Look to the (gender schematic) male who has viewed pornography. *Personality and Social Psychology Bulletin, 16,* 296–308.

McNemar, Q. (1946). Opinion-attitude methodology. *Psychological Bulletin, 43,* 289–374.

McNulty, S., & Swann, W. B., Jr. (1994). Identity negotiation in roommate relationships: The self as architect and consequence of social reality. *Journal of Personality and Social Psychology, 67,* 1012–1023.

McTavish, D. G. (1971). Perceptions of old people: A review of research methodologies and findings. *Gerontologist, 11,* 90–101.

Mead, G. H. (1934). *Mind, self, and society.* Chicago: University of Chicago Press.

Medcof, J. W. (1990). PEAT: An integrative model of attribution processes. In M. P. Zanna (Ed.), *Advances in experimental social psychology* (Vol. 23). San Diego: Academic Press.

Medin, D. L. (1989). Concepts and conceptual structure. *American Psychologist, 44,* 1469–1481.

Mee, C. L. (1984). *The Marshall Plan: The launching of Pax Americana.* New York: Simon & Schuster.

Meer, B., & Freedman, E. (1966). The impact of Negro neighbors on white homeowners. *Social Forces, 45,* 11–19.

Meeus, W. H. J., & Raaijmakers, Q. A. W. (1986). Administrative obedience: Carrying out orders to use psychological-administrative violence. *European Journal of Social Psychology, 16,* 311–324.

Meeus, W. H. J., & Raaijmakers, Q. A. W. (1987). Administrative obedience as a social phenomenon. In W. Doise & S. Moscovici (Eds.), *Current issues in European social psychology* (Vol. 2). Cambridge, England: Cambridge University Press.

Mehrabian, A. (1972). *Nonverbal communication.* Chicago: Aldine.

Mehrabian, A., & Wiener, M. (1967). Decoding of inconsistent communication. *Journal of Personality and Social Psychology, 6,* 108–114.

Mellema, A., & Bassili, J. N. (1995). On the relationship between attitudes and values: Exploring the moderating effects of self-monitoring and self-monitoring schematicity. *Personality and Social Psychology Bulletin, 21,* 885–892.

Mellen, S. (1981). *The evolution of love.* San Francisco: W. H. Freeman.

Menzies, R. (1937). Conditioned vasomotor responses in human subjects. *Journal of Psychology, 4,* 75–120.

Mercy, J. A., & Saltzman, L. E. (1987). Fatal violence among spouses in the United States, 1976–1985. *American Journal of Public health, 79,* 595–599.

Merton, R. K. (1948). The self-fulfilling prophecy. *Antioch Review, 8,* 193–210.

Messé, L. A., & Sivacek, J. M. (1979). Predictions of others' responses in a mixed-motive game: Self-justification or false consensus? *Journal of Personality and Social Psychology, 37,* 602–607.

Messé, L. A., & Watts, B. L. (1983). Complex nature of the sense of fairness: Internal standards and social comparison as bases for reward evaluations. *Journal of Personality and Social Psychology, 41,* 684–693.

Messick, D. M., Bloom, S., Boldizar, J. P., & Samuelson, C. D. (1985). Why we are fairer than others. *Journal of Experimental Social Psychology, 21,* 480–500.

Messick, D. M., & Brewer, M. B. (1983). Solving social dilemmas. In L. Wheeler & P. Shaver (Eds.), *Review of Personality and Social Psychology* (Vol. 4). Beverly Hills: Sage.

Messick, D. M., & Liebrand, W. B. G. (1995). Individual heuristics and the dynamics of cooperation in large groups. *Psychological Review, 102,* 131–145.

Messick, D. M., & Mackie, D. M. (1989). Intergroup relations. *Annual Review of Psychology, 40,* 45–81.

Messick, D. M., & McClelland, C. L. (1983). Social traps and temporal traps. *Personality and Social Psychology Bulletin, 9*, 105–110.

Messick, D. M., Wilke, H., Brewer, M. B., Kramer, R. M., Zemke, P. E., & Lui, L. (1983). Individual adaptations and structural change as solutions to social dilemmas. *Journal of Personality and Social Psychology, 44*, 294–309.

Mikula, G. (1974). Nationality, performance, and sex as determinants of reward allocation. *Journal of Personality and Social Psychology, 29*, 435–445.

Mikulincer, M. (1988). Reactance and helplessness following exposure to unsolvable problems: The effects of attributional style. *Journal of Personality and Social Psychology, 54*, 679–686.

Mikulincer, M., Bizman, A., & Aizenberg, R. (1989). An attributional analysis of social comparison jealousy. *Motivation and Emotion, 13*, 235–258.

Mikulincer, M., & Nachshon, O. (1991). Attachment styles and patterns of self-disclosure. *Journal of Personality and Social Psychology, 61*, 321–331.

Milavsky, J. R., Kessler, R. C., Stipp, H. H., & Rubens, W. S. (1982). *Television and aggression: A panel study.* New York: Academic Press.

Milgram, S. (1963). Behavioral study of obedience. *Journal of Abnormal and Social Psychology, 67*, 371–378.

Milgram, S. (1965a). Some conditions of obedience and disobedience to authority. *Human Relations, 18*, 57–76.

Milgram, S. (1965b). Liberating effects of group pressure. *Journal of Personality and Social Psychology, 1*, 127–134.

Milgram, S. (1970). The experience of living in cities. *Science, 167*, 1461–1468.

Milgram, S. (1974). *Obedience to authority: An experimental view.* New York: Harper & Row.

Milgram, S., Bickman, L., & Berkowitz, L. (1969). Note on the drawing power of crowds of different size. *Journal of Personality and Social Psychology, 13*, 79–82.

Millar, M. G., Millar, K. U., & Tesser, A. (1988). The effects of helping and focus of attention on mood states. *Personality and Social Psychology Bulletin, 14*, 536–543.

Millar, M. G., & Tesser, A. (1986). Effects of affective and cognitive focus on the attitude-behavior relation. *Journal of Personality and Social Psychology, 51*, 270–276.

Millar, M. G., & Tesser, A. (1989). The effects of affective-cognitive consistency and thought on the attitude-behavior relation. *Journal of Experimental Social Psychology, 25*, 189–202.

Millar, M. G., & Tesser, A. (1992). The role of beliefs and feelings in guiding behavior: The mismatch model. In L. L. Martin & A. Tesser (Eds.), *The construction of social judgments.* Hillsdale, NJ: Erlbaum.

Miller, A. G. (1986). *The obedience experiments: A case study of a controversy in social science.* New York: Praeger.

Miller, A. G., Ashton, W. A., & Mishal, M. (1990). Beliefs concerning the features of constrained behavior: A basis for the fundamental attribution error. *Journal of Personality and Social Psychology, 59*, 635–650.

Miller, A. G., Jones, E. E., & Hinkle, S. (1981). A robust attribution error in the personality domain. *Journal of Experimental Social Psychology, 17*, 587–600.

Miller, A. G., & Rorer, L. G. (1982). Toward an understanding of the fundamental attribution error: Essay diagnosticity in the attitude attribution paradigm. *Journal of research in Personality, 16*, 41–59.

Miller, C. T. (1984). Self-schemas, gender, and social comparison: A clarification of the related attributes hypothesis. *Journal of Personality and Social Psychology, 46*, 1222–1229.

Miller, C. T. (1986). Categorization and stereotypes about men and women. *Personality and Social Psychology Bulletin, 12*, 502–512.

Miller, C. T. (1993). Majority and minority perceptions of consensus and recommendations for resolving conflict about land use regulation. *Personality and Social Psychology Bulletin, 19*, 389–398.

Miller, D. T., & Gunasegaram, S. (1990). Temporal order and the perceived mutability of events: Implications for blame assignment. *Journal of Personality and Social Psychology, 59*, 1111–1118.

Miller, D. T., & Prentice, D. A. (1994). The self and the collective. *Personality and Social Psychology Bulletin, 20*, 451–453.

Miller, D. T., & Ross, M. (1975). Self-serving biases in the attribution of causality: Fact or fiction? *Psychological Bulletin, 82*, 213–225.

Miller, D. T., & Taylor, B. R. (in press). Counterfactual thought, regret, and superstition: How to avoid kicking yourself. In N. J. Roese & J. M. Olson (Eds.), *What might have been: The social psychology of counterfactual thinking.* Hillsdale, NJ: Erlbaum.

Miller, D. T., Taylor, B., & Buck, M. L. (1991). Gender gaps: Who needs to be explained? *Journal of Personality and Social Psychology, 61*, 5–12.

Miller, D. T., & Turnbull, W. (1986). Expectancies and interpersonal processes. *Annual Review of Psychology, 37*, 233–256.

Miller, D. T., Turnbull, W., & McFarland, C. (1990). Counterfactual thinking and social perception: Thinking about what might have been. In M. P. Zanna (Ed.), *Advances in experimental social psychology* (Vol. 23). San Diego: Academic Press.

Miller, J. M., & Krosnick, J. A. (in press). News media impact on the ingredients of presidential evaluations: A program of research on the priming hypothesis. In D. C. Mutz & P. M. Sniderman (Eds.), *Political persuasion and attitude change.* Ann Arbor, MI: University of Michigan Press.

Miller, N., Maruyama, G., Beaber, R., & Valone, K. (1976). Speed of speech and persuasion. *Journal of Personality and Social Psychology, 34*, 615–625.

Miller, P. A., & Eisenberg, N. (1988). The relation of empathy to aggressive and externalizing/antisocial behavior. *Psychological Bulletin, 103*, 324–344.

Miller, R. E., Caul, W. F., & Mirsky, I. A. (1967). Communication of affects between feral and socially isolated monkeys. *Journal of Personality and Social Psychology, 7*, 231–239.

Miller, R. S. (1995). On the nature of embarrassability: Shyness, social-evaluation, and social skill. *Journal of Personality, 63*, 315–359.

Mills, J. (1993). The appeal of tragedy: An attitude interpretation. *Basic and Applied Social Psychology, 14*, 255–271.

Mills, J., & Ford, T. E. (1995). Effects of importance of a prospective choice upon private and public evaluations of the alternatives. *Personality and Social Psychology Bulletin, 21*, 256–266.

Mischel, W., & Shoda, Y. (1995). A cognitive-affective system theory of personality: Reconceptualizing the invariances in personality and the role of situations. *Psychological Review, 102*, 246–268.

Mita, T. H., Dermer, M., & Knight, J. (1977). Reversed facial images and the mere-exposure hypothesis. *Journal of Personality and Social Psychology, 35*, 597–601.

Mitchell, G., & Maple, T. L. (1985). Dominance in nonhuman primates. In S. L. Ellyson & J. Dovidio (Eds.), *Power, dominance, and nonverbal behavior.* New York: Springer-Verlag.

Mittal, B. (1988). Achieving higher seat belt usage: The role of habit in bridging the attitude-behavior gap. *Journal of Applied Social Psychology, 18*, 993–1016.

Monteith, M. J. (1993). Self-regulation of prejudiced responses: Implications for progress in prejudice-reduction efforts. *Journal of Personality and Social Psychology, 65*, 469–485.

Monteith, M. J., Devine, P. G., & Zuwerink, J. R. (1993). Self-directed versus other-directed affect as a consequence of prejudice-related discrepancies. *Journal of Personality and Social Psychology, 64*, 198–210.

Montepare, J. M., Goldstein, S. B., & Clausen, A. (1987). The identification of emotions from gait information. *Journal of Nonverbal Behavior, 11*, 33–42.

Montepare, J. M., & Vega, C. (1988). Women's vocal reactions to intimate and casual friends. *Personality and Social Psychology Bulletin, 14,* 103–113.

Montepare, J. M., & Zebrowitz, L. A. (1993). A cross-cultural comparison of impressions created by age-related variations in gait. *Journal of Nonverbal Behavior, 17,* 55–68.

Montepare, J. M., & Zebrowitz-McArthur, L. (1988). Impressions of people created by age-related qualities of their gaits. *Journal of Personality and Social Psychology, 55,* 547–556.

Mooney, K. M., Cohn, E. S., & Swift, M. B. (1992). Physical distance and AIDS: Too close for comfort? *Journal of Applied Social Psychology, 22,* 1442–1452.

Moore, J. S., Graziano, W. G., & Millar, M. G. (1987). Physical attractiveness, sex role orientation, and the evaluation of adults and children. *Personality and Social Psychology Bulletin, 13,* 95–102.

Moreland, R. L. (1985). Social categorization and the assimilation of "new" group members. *Journal of Personality and Social Psychology, 48,* 1173–1190.

Moreland, R. L., & Beach, S. (1992). Exposure effects in the classroom: The development of affinity among students. *Journal of Experimental Social Psychology, 28,* 255–276.

Moreland, R. L., & Levine, J. M. (1982). Socialization in small groups: Temporal changes in individual-group relations. In L. Berkowitz (Ed.), *Advances in experimental social psychology* (Vol. 15). New York: Academic Press.

Moreland, R. L., & Levine, J. M. (1989). Newcomers and oldtimers in small groups. In P. B. Paulus (Ed.), *Psychology of group influence.* Hillsdale, NJ: Erlbaum.

Moreland, R. L., & Zajonc, R. B. (1977). Is stimulus recognition a necessary condition for the occurrence of exposure effects? *Journal of Personality and Social Psychology, 35,* 191–199.

Moreland, R. L., & Zajonc, R. B. (1979). Exposure effects may not depend on stimulus recognition. *Journal of Personality and Social Psychology, 37,* 1085–1089.

Morency, N. L., & Krauss, R. M. (1982). Children's nonverbal encoding and decoding of affect. In R. S. Feldman (Ed.), *Development of nonverbal behavior in children.* New York: Springer-Verlag.

Morf, C. C., & Rhodewalt, F. (1993). Narcissism and self-evaluation maintenance: Explorations in object relations. *Personality and Social Psychology Bulletin, 19,* 668–676.

Mori, D., Chaiken, S., & Pliner, P. (1987). "Eating lightly" and the self-presentation of femininity. *Journal of Personality and Social Psychology, 53,* 693–702.

Morland, J. K. (1965). Token desegregation and beyond. In A. M. Rose & C. B. Rose (Eds.), *Minority problems.* New York: Harper & Row.

Morris, M. W., & Peng, K. (1994). Culture and cause: American and Chinese attributions for social and physical events. *Journal of Personality and Social Psychology, 67,* 949–971.

Morrow, G. D., Clark, E. M., & Brock, K. F. (1995). Individual and partner love styles: Implications for the quality of romantic involvements. *Journal of Social and Personal Relationships, 12,* 363–387.

Morse, S. J., & Gergen, K. J. (1970). Social comparison, self-consistency, and the presentation of self. *Journal of Personality and Social Psychology, 16,* 148–159.

Moscovici, S. (1985). Social influence and conformity. In G. Lindzey & E. Aronson (Eds.), *The handbook of social psychology* (Vol. 2, 3rd ed.). New York: Random House.

Moscovici, S., & Doms, M. (1982). Compliance and conversion in a situation of sensory deprivation. *Basic and Applied Social Psychology, 3,* 81–94.

Moscovici, S., Lage, E., & Naffrechoux, M. (1969). Influence of a consistent minority on the responses of a majority in a color perception task. *Sociometry, 32,* 365–380.

Moscovici, S., & Personnaz, B. (1980). Studies in social influence: V. Minority influence and conversion behavior in a perceptual task. *Journal of Experimental Social Psychology, 16,* 270–282.

Moscovici, S., & Personnaz, B. (1986). Studies on latent influence by the spectrometer method I: The impact of psychologization in the case of conversion by a minority or a majority. *European Journal of Social Psychology, 16,* 345–360.

Moscovici, S., & Personnaz, B. (1991). Studies in social influence VI: Is Lenin orange or red? Imagery and social influence. *European Journal of Social Psychology, 21,* 101–118.

Moscovici, S., & Zavalloni, M. (1969). The group as a polarizer of attitudes. *Journal of Personality and Social Psychology, 12,* 125–135.

Moser, G., & Levy-Leboyer, C. (1985). Inadequate environment and situation control: Is a malfunctioning phone always an occasion for aggression? *Environment and Behavior, 17,* 520–533.

Moskowitz, G. B. (1993). Individual differences in social categorization: The influence of personal need for structure on spontaneous trait inferences. *Journal of Personality and Social Psychology, 65,* 132–142.

Moss, H. A. (1967). Sex, age, and state as determinants of mother-child interaction. *Merrill-Palmer Quarterly, 13,* 19–36.

Muehberger, C. W. (1956). Medicolegal aspects of alcohol intoxication. *Michigan State Bar Journal, 35,* 38–42.

Mugny, G. (1982). *The power of minorities.* New York: Academic Press.

Mugny, G., & Pérez, J. A. (1991). *The social psychology of minority influence.* Cambridge, England: Cambridge University Press.

Mullen, B., Atkins, J. L., Champion, D. S., Edwards, E., Hardy, D., Story, J. E., & Vanderklok, M. (1985). The false consensus effect: A meta-analysis of 115 hypothesis tests. *Journal of Experimental Social Psychology, 21,* 262–283.

Mullen, B., Johnson, C., & Salas, E. (1991). Productivity loss in brainstorming groups: A meta-analytic integration. *Basic and Applied Social Psychology, 12,* 3–23.

Murphy, G., & Likert, R. (1938). *Public opinion and the individual: A psychological study of student attitudes on public questions, with a retest five years later.* New York: Harper.

Murphy, S. T., & Zajonc, R. B. (1993). Affect, cognition, and awareness: Affective priming with optimal and suboptimal stimulus exposures. *Journal of Personality and Social Psychology, 64,* 723–739.

Murphy-Berman, V. A., & Berman, J. J. (1993). Effects of responsibility for illness and social acceptability on reactions to people with AIDS: A cross-cultural comparison. *Basic and Applied Social Psychology, 14,* 215–229.

Murray, S. L., Haddock, G., & Zanna, M. P. (in press). On creating value-expressive attitudes: An experimental approach. In C. Seligman, J. M. Olson, & M. P. Zanna (Eds.), *The Ontario symposium: The psychology of values* (Vol. 8). Hillsdale, NJ: Erlbaum.

Murray, S. L., & Holmes, J. G. (1993). Seeing virtues in faults: Negativity and the transformation of interpersonal narratives in close relationships. *Journal of Personality and Social Psychology, 65,* 707–722.

Murray, S. L., & Holmes, J. G. (in press). The construction of relationship realities. In G. Fletcher & J. Fitness (Eds.), *Knowledge structures and interaction in close relationships: A social psychological approach.* Hillsdale, NJ: Erlbaum.

Murrell, A. J., Dietz-Uhler, B. L., Dovidio, J. F., Gaertner, S. L., & Drout, C. (1994). Aversive racism and resistance to affirmative action: Perceptions of justice are not necessarily color blind. *Basic and Applied Social Psychology, 15,* 71–86.

Murstein, B. I. (1980). Love at first sight: A myth. *Medical Aspects of Human Sexuality, 14,* 39–41.

Murstein, B. I., Cerreto, M., & MacDonald, M. G. (1977). A theory and investigation of the effect of exchange-orientation on marriage and friendship. *Journal of Marriage and the Family, 39,* 543–548.

Myers, D. G. (1978). Polarizing effects of social comparison. *Journal of Experimental Social Psychology, 14,* 554–563.

Myers, D. G., & Bishop, G. D. (1970). Discussion effects on racial attitudes. *Science, 169,* 778–789.

Myers, D. G., & Bishop, G. D. (1971). Enhancement of dominant attitudes in group discussion. *Journal of Personality and Social Psychology, 20,* 386–391.

Myers, D. G., & Diener, E. (1995). Who is happy? *Psychological Science, 6,* 10–19.

Myers, D. G., & Lamm, H. (1976). The group polarization phenomenon. *Psychological Bulletin, 83,* 602–627.

Myers, T. (1982). Alcohol and crime re-examined: Self-reports from two subgroups of Scottish male prisoners. *British Journal of Addiction, 77,* 399–413.

Nadler, A., & Dotan, I. (1992). Commitment and rival attractiveness: Their effects on male and female reactions to jealousy and arousing situations. *Sex Roles, 26,* 293–310.

Naftolin, F. (1981). Understanding the bases of sex differences. *Science, 211,* 1263–1264.

Nagasundaram, M., & Dennis, A. R. (1993). When a group is not a group. *Small Group Research, 24,* 463–489.

Nahemow, L., & Lawton, M. P. (1975). Similarity and propinquity in friendship formation. *Journal of Personality and Social Psychology, 32,* 205–213.

Nel, E., Helmreich, R., & Aronson, E. (1969). Opinion change in the advocate as a function of the persuasibility of his audience: A clarification of the meaning of dissonance. *Journal of Personality and Social Psychology, 12,* 117–124.

Nelson, C. A. (1987). The recognition of facial expressions in the first two years of life: Mechanisms of development. *Child Development, 58,* 889–909.

Nemeth, C. J. (1977). Interactions between jurors as a function of majority vs unanimity decision rules. *Journal of Applied Social Psychology, 7,* 38–56.

Nemeth, C. J. (1986). Differential contributions of majority and minority influence. *Psychological Review, 93,* 23–32.

Nemeth, C. J. (1987). Influence processes, problem solving and creativity. In M. P. Zanna, J. M. Olson, & C. P. Herman (Eds.), *Social influence: The Ontario Symposium* (Vol. 5). Hillsdale, NJ: Erlbaum.

Nemeth, C. J. (in press). Dissent as driving cognition, attitudes and judgments. *Social Cognition.*

Nemeth, C. J., & Chiles, C. (1988). Modelling courage: The role of dissent in fostering independence. *European Journal of Social Psychology, 18,* 275–280.

Nemeth, C. J., & Kwan, J. (1985). Originality of work associations as a function of majority vs. minority influence processes. *Social Psychology Quarterly, 48,* 277–282.

Nemeth, C. J., & Kwan, J. (1987). Minority influence, divergent thinking and detection of correct solutions. *Journal of Abnormal and Social Psychology, 17,* 788–799.

Nemeth, C. J., Mayseless, O., Sherman, J., & Brown, Y. (1990). Exposure to dissent and recall of information. *Journal of Personality and Social Psychology, 58,* 429–437.

Nemeth, C. J., & Staw, B. M. (1989). The tradeoffs of social control and innovation in groups and organizations. In L. Berkowitz (Ed.), *Advances in experimental social psychology* (Vol. 22). San Diego, CA: Academic Press.

Nesler, M. S., Aguinis, H., Quigley, B. M., & Tedeschi, J. T. (1993). The effect of credibility on perceived power. *Journal of Applied Psychology, 23,* 1407–1425.

Neuberg, S. L. (1989). The goal of forming accurate impressions during social interactions: Attenuating the impact of negative expectancies. *Journal of Personality and Social Psychology, 56,* 374–386.

Neuberg, S. L. (1994). Expectancy-confirmation processes in stereotype-tinged social encounters: The moderating role of social goals. In M. P. Zanna & J. M. Olson (Eds.), *The psychology of prejudice: The Ontario Symposium* (Vol. 7). Hillsdale, NJ: Erlbaum.

Neuberg, S. L. (in press). Expectancy influences in social interaction: The moderating role of social goals. In P. M. Gollwitzer & J. A. Bargh (Eds.), *The psychology of action: Linking motivation and cognition to behavior.*

Neuberg, S. L., & Fiske, S. T. (1987). Motivational influences on impression formation: Outcome dependency, acuracy-driven attention, and individuating processes. *Journal of Personality and Social Psychology, 53,* 431–444.

Neuberg, S. L., Judice, T. N., Virdin, L. M., & Carrillo, M. (1993). Perceiver self-presentational goals as moderators of expectancy influences: Ingratiation and the disconfirmation of negative expectancies. *Journal of Personality and Social Psychology, 64,* 409–420.

Neuberg, S. L., Smith, D. M., Hoffman, J. C., & Russell, F. J. (1994). When we observe stigmatized and "normal" individuals interacting: Stigma by association. *Personality and Social Psychology Bulletin, 20,* 196–209.

Newcomb, T. M. (1961). *The acquaintance process.* New York: Holt, Rinehart, & Winston.

Newcomb, T. M., & Svehla, G. (1937). Intra-family relationships in attitudes. *Sociometry, 1,* 180–205.

Newman, L. S. (1991). Why are traits inferred spontaneously? A developmental approach. *Social Cognition, 9,* 221–253.

Newman, L. S. (1993). How individualists interpret behavior: Idiocentrism and spontaneous trait inference. *Social Cognition, 11,* 243–269.

Newman, L. S., & Uleman, J. S. (1989). Spontaneous trait inference. In J. S. Uleman & J. A. Bargh (Eds.), *Unintended thought.* New York: Guilford.

Newman, L. S., & Uleman, J. S. (1993). When are you what you did? Behavior identification and dispositional inference in person memory, attribution, and social judgment. *Personality and Social Psychology Bulletin, 19,* 513–525.

Nicholls, J. G. (1984). Achievement motivation: Conceptions of ability, subjective experience, task choice, and performance. *Psychological Review, 91,* 328–346.

Niedenthal, P. M., & Cantor, N. (1986). Affective responses as guides to category-based influences. *Motivation & Emotion, 10,* 217–231.

Niedenthal, P. M., Setterlund, M. B., & Wherry, M. B. (1992). Possible self-complexity and affective reactions to goal-relevant evaluation. *Journal of Personality and Social Psychology, 63,* 5–16.

Niedenthal, P. M., Tangney, J. P., & Gavanski, I. (1994). "If only I weren't" V. "If only I hadn't:" Distinguishing shame and guilt in counterfactual thinking. *Journal of Personality and Social Psychology, 67,* 585–595.

Nieva, V. F., & Gutek, B. A. (1980). *Women and work: A psychological perspective.* New York: Praeger.

Nisbett, R. E. (1987). Lay personality theory: Its nature, origin, and utility. In N. E. Grunberg, R. E. Nisbett, J. Rodin, & J. E. Singer (Eds.), *A distinctive approach to psychological research: The influence of Stanley Schachter.* Hillsdale, NJ: Erlbaum.

Nisbett, R. E., Caputo, C., Legant, P., & Maracek, J. (1973). Behavior as seen by the actor and as seen by the observer. *Journal of Personality and Social Psychology, 27,* 154–164.

Nisbett, R. E., & Gordon, A. (1967). Self-esteem and susceptibility to social influence. *Journal of Personality and Social Psychology, 5,* 268–276.

Nisbett, R. E., & Kunda, Z. (1985). Perception of social distributions. *Journal of Personality and Social Psychology, 48,* 297–311.

Nisbett, R. E., & Ross, L. (1980). *Human inference: Strategies and shortcoming in social judgment.* Englewood Cliffs, NJ: Prentice-Hall.

Nisbett, R. E., & Wilson, T. D. (1977). Telling more than we can know: Verbal reports on mental processes. *Psychological Review, 84,* 231–259.

Noel, J. G., Wann, D. L., & Branscombe, N. R. (1995). Peripheral ingroup membership status and public negativity toward outgroups. *Journal of Personality and Social Psychology, 68,* 127–137.

Norem, J. K., & Illingworth, K. S. S. (1993). Strategy-dependent effects of reflecting on self and tasks: Some implications of optimism and defensive pessimism. *Journal of Personality and Social Psychology, 65,* 822–835.

Norman, R. (1975). Affective-cognitive consistency, attitudes, conformity, and behavior. *Journal of Personality and Social Psychology, 32,* 83–91.

Norman, R. (1976). When what is said is important: A comparison of expert and attractive sources. *Journal of Experimental Social Psychology, 12,* 294–300.

Norris, A. E., & Devine, P. G. (1992). Linking pregnancy concerns to pregnancy risk avoidant action: The role of construct accessibility. *Personality and Social Psychology Bulletin, 18,* 118–127.

Norvell, N., & Worchell, S. A. (1981). A reexamination of the relation between equal status contact and intergroup attraction. *Journal of Personality and Social Psychology, 41,* 902–908.

Nudd, T. R. (1965). Satisfied and dissatisfied college roommates. *Journal of College Student Personnel, 6,* 161–164.

Nuttin, J. M. (1987). Affective consequences of mere ownership: The name letter effect in 12 European languages. *European Journal of Social Psychology, 17,* 381–402.

O'Kelly, C. (1980). Sex-role imagery in modern art: An empirical examination. *Sex Roles, 6,* 99–112.

O'Leary, M. R., & Dengerink, H. A. (1973). Aggression as a function of the intensity and patterns of attack. *Journal of Research in Personality, 7,* 482–492.

O'Leary, V. E., & Ickovics, J. R. (1990). Women supporting women: Secretaries and their bosses. In H. Grossman & N. Chester (Eds.), *The experience and meaning of work for women.* Hillsdale, NJ: Erlbaum.

O'Neal, E. C., Kipnis, D., & Craig, K. M. (1994). Effects on the persuader of employing a coercive influence technique. *Basic and Applied Social Psychology, 15,* 225–238.

Oakes, P., & Turner, J. C. (1980). Social categorization and intergroup behavior: Does minimal intergroup discrimination make social identity more positive? *European Journal of Social Psychology, 10,* 295–301.

Ohbuchi, K., & Kambara, T. (1985). Attacker's intent and awareness of outcome, impression management, and retaliation. *Journal of Experimental Social Psychology, 21,* 321–330.

Ohbuchi, K., Kameda, M., & Agarie, N. (1989). Apology as aggression control: Its role in mediating appraisal of and response to harm.

Journal of Personality and Social Psychology, 56, 219–227.

Oliner, S. P., & Oliner, J. M. (1988). *The altruistic personality: Rescuers of Jews in Nazi Europe.* New York: Free Press.

Olson, J. M., & Hafer, C. L. (in press). Affect, motivation, and cognition in relative deprivation research. In R. M. Sorrentino & E. T. Higgins (Eds.), *Handbook of motivation and cognition: The interpersonal context* (Vol. 3). New York: Guilford.

Olson, J. M., Herman, C. P., & Zanna, M. P. (Eds.). (1986). *Relative deprivation and social comparison: The Ontario symposium* (Vol. 4). Hillsdale, NJ: Erlbaum.

Olson, J. M., & Roese, N. J. (1995). The perceived funniness of humorous stimuli. *Personality and Social Psychology Bulletin, 21,* 908–913.

Olson, J. M., Roese, N. J., & Zanna, M. P. (in press). Expectancies. In E. T. Higgins & A. W. Kruglanski (Eds.), *Social psychology: Handbook of basic principles.* New York: Guilford.

Olson, J. M., & Zanna, M. P. (1993). Attitudes and attitude change. *Annual Review of Psychology, 44,* 117–154.

Olweus, D., Mattson, A., Schalling, D., & Loow, H. (1980). Testosterone, aggression, physical and personality dimensions in normal adolescents. *Psychosomatic Medicine, 42,* 253–269.

Omoto, A. M., & Snyder, M. (1995). Sustained helping without obligation: Motivation, longevity of service, and perceived attitude change among AIDS volunteers. *Journal of Personality and Social Psychology, 68,* 671–688.

Ophuls, W. (1977). *Ecology and the politics of scarcity.* San Francisco: Freeman.

Orbell, J. M., & Rutherford, B. (1973). Can Leviathan make the life of man less solitary, poor, nasty, brutish, and short? *British Journal of Political Science, 3,* 383–407.

Orbell, J., Dawes, R., & Schwartz-Shea, P. (1994). Trust, social categories, and individuals: The case of gender. *Motivation and Emotion, 18,* 109–128.

Orbell, J., Dawes, R., & van de Kragt, A. (1995). Cooperation under laissez-faire and majority decision rules in group-level social dilemmas. In D. Schroeder (Ed.), *Social dilemmas.* Westport, CT: Praeger.

Orbell, J., van de Kragt, A., & Dawes, R. (1988). Explaining discussion-induced cooperation. *Journal of Personality and Social Psychology, 54,* 811–819.

Orbuch, T. L., Harvey, J. H., Davis, S. H., & Merbach, N. J. (1994). Account-making and confiding as acts of meaning in response to sexual assault. *Journal of Family Violence, 9,* 249–264.

Orne, M. T. (1962). On the social psychology of the psychological experiment: With particular reference to

demand characteristics and their implications. *American Psychologist, 17,* 776–783.

Osborn, A. F. (1975). *Applied imagination.* New York: Scribner.

Osborne, R. E., & Gilbert, D. T. (1992). The preoccupational hazards of social life. *Journal of Personality and Social Psychology, 62,* 219–228.

Osgood, C. E. (1962). *An alternative to war or surrender.* Urbana, IL: University of Illinois Press.

Osgood, C. E., Suci, G. J., & Tannenbaum, P. H. (1957). *The measurement of meaning.* Urbana: University of Illinois Press.

Osgood, C. E., & Tannenbaum, P. H. (1955). The principle of congruity in the prediction of attitude change. *Psychological Review, 62,* 42–55.

Ostrom, E. (1990). *Governing the commons.* New York: Cambridge University Press.

Ostrom, T. M. (1969). The relationship between the affective, behavioral and cognitive components of attitude. *Journal of Experimental Social Psychology, 5,* 12–30.

Ostrom, T. M. (1994). Foreword. In R. S. Wyer, Jr., & T. K. Srull (Eds.), *Handbook of social cognition* (Vol. 1). Hillsdale, NJ: Erlbaum.

Ostrom, T. M., Carpenter, S. L., Sedikides, C., & Li, F. (1993). Differential processing of in-group and out-group information. *Journal of Personality and Social Psychology, 64,* 21–34.

Ostrom, T. M., & Sedikides, C. (1992). Out-group homogeneity effects in natural and minimal groups. *Psychological Bulletin, 112,* 536–552.

Ott, E. M. (1989). Effects of the male-female ratio at work: Policewomen and male nurses. *Psychology of Women Quarterly, 13,* 41–57.

Oyserman, D. (1993). The lens of personhood: Viewing the self and others in a multicultural society. *Journal of Personality and Social Psychology, 65,* 993–1009.

Oyserman, D., & Markus, H. R. (1990). Possible selves and delinquency. *Journal of Personality and Social Psychology, 59,* 112–125.

Oyserman, D., & Saltz, E. (1993). Competence, delinquency, and attempts to attain possible selves. *Journal of Personality and Social Psychology, 65,* 360–374.

Page, M. M. (1974). Demand characteristics and the classical conditioning of attitudes experiment. *Journal of Personality and Social Psychology, 30,* 468–476.

Page, M. M., & Kahle, L. R. (1976). Demand characteristics in the satiation-deprivation effect on attitude conditioning. *Journal of Personality and Social Psychology, 33,* 553–562.

Page, R. M., & Cole, G. E. (1991). Loneliness and alcoholism risk in late adolescence: A comparative study of adults and adolescents. *Adolescence, 26,* 925–930.

Pagel, M. D., & Davidson, A. R. (1984). A comparison of three social-psychological models of attitude and behavior plan: Prediction of contraceptive behavior. *Journal of Personality and Social Psychology, 47,* 517–533.

Pallak, S. R. (1983). Salience of a communicator's physical attractiveness and persuasion: A heuristic versus systematic processing interpretation. *Social Cognition, 2,* 156–168.

Pallak, S. R., Murroni, E., & Koch, J. (1983). Communicator attractiveness and expertise, emotional versus rational appeals, and persuasion: A heuristic versus systematic processing interpretation. *Social Cognition, 2,* 120–139.

Panksepp, J., Siviy, S., & Normansell, L. (1985). The psychobiology of play: Theoretical and methodological perspectives. *Neuroscience and Biobehavioral Reviews, 8,* 465–492.

Papastamou, S., & Mugny, G. (1990). Synchronic consistency and psychologization in minority influence. *European Journal of Social Psychology, 20,* 85–98.

Park, B., DeKay, M. L., & Kraus, S. (1994). Aggregating social behavior into person models: Perceiver-induced consistency. *Journal of Personality and Social Psychology, 66,* 437–459.

Park, B., & Judd, C. M. (1989). Agreement on initial impressions: differences due to perceivers, trait dimensions, and target behaviors. *Journal of Personality and Social Psychology, 56,* 493–505.

Park, B., & Judd, C. M. (1990). Measures and models of perceived group variability. *Journal of Personality and Social Psychology, 59,* 173–191.

Park, B., Judd, C. M., & Ryan, C. S. (1991). Social categorization and the representation of variability information. *European review of social psychology* (Vol. 2). New York: Wiley.

Park, B., & Rothbart, M. (1982). Perception of out-group homogeneity and levels of social categorization: Memory for the subordinate attributes of in-group and out-group members. *Journal of Personality and Social Psychology, 42,* 1051–1068.

Park, B., Ryan, C. S., & Judd, C. M. (1992). Role of meaningful subgroups in explaining differences in perceived variability for in-groups and out-groups. *Journal of Personality and Social Psychology, 63,* 553–567.

Parke, R. D., Berkowitz, L., Leyens, J. P., West, S. G., & Sebastian, R. J. (1977). Some effects of violent and nonviolent movies on the behavior of juvenile delinquents. In L. Berkowitz (Ed.), *Advances in experimental social psychology* (Vol. 10, pp.136–172). New York: Academic Press.

Parks, C. D. (1994). The predictive ability of social values in resource dilemmas and public goods games. *Personality and Social Psychology Bulletin, 20,* 431–438.

Parsons, J. E., Adler, T. F., Futterman, R., Goff, S. B., Kaczala, C. M., Meece, J. L., & Midgley, C. (1983). Expectancies, values, and academic behaviors. In J. Spence (Ed.), *Achievement and achievement motivation.* San Francisco: W. H. Freeman.

Patkai, P. (1971). Catecholamine excretion in pleasant and unpleasant situations. *Acta Psychologia, 35,* 352–363.

Patterson, F. G., & Linden, E. (1981). *The education of Koko.* New York: Holt, Rinehart, & Winston.

Patterson, G. R. (1982). Developmental changes in antisocial behavior. In R. D. Peters, R. J. McMahon, & V. L. Quinsey (Eds.), *Aggression and violence throughout the life span.* Newbury Park, CA: Sage.

Patterson, G. R. (1984). Siblings: Fellow travelers in coercive family processes. In R. J. Blanchard & D. C. Blanchard (Eds.), *Advances in the study of aggression* (Vol. 1, pp 173–215). Orlando, FL: Academic Press.

Patterson, G. R., Littman, R. A., & Bricker, W. (1967). Assertive behavior in children: A step toward a theory of aggression. *Monographs of the Society for Research in Child Development, 32* (5).

Patterson, M. L. (1994a). Interaction behavior and person perception: An integrative approach. *Small Groups Research, 25,* 172–188.

Patterson, M. L. (1994b). Strategic functions of nonverbal exchange. In J. A. Daly & J. M. Wiemann (Eds.), *Strategic interpersonal communication.* Hillsdale, NJ: Erlbaum.

Paulhus, D. (1982). Individual differences, self-presentation, and cognitive dissonance: Their concurrent operation in forced compliance. *Journal of Personality and Social Psychology, 43,* 838–852.

Paulhus, D. L., & Bruce, M. N. (1992). The effect of acquaintanceship on the validity of personality impressions: A longitudinal study. *Journal of Personality and Social Psychology, 63,* 816–824.

Paulus, P. B. (1980). Crowding. In P. B. Paulus (Ed.), *Psychology of group processes.* Hillsdale, NJ: Erlbaum.

Paulus, P. B. (1983). Group influences on individual task performance. In P. B. Paulus (Ed.), *Basic group processes.* New York: Springer-Verlag.

Paulus, P. B. (1989). *Psychology of group influence* (2nd ed.). Hillsdale, NJ: Erlbaum.

Paulus, P. B., Brown, V., & Ortega, A. H. (in press). Group creativity. In R. E. Purser & A. Montuori (Eds.), *Social creativity in organizations.* Cresskill, NJ: Hampton Press.

Paulus, P. B., & Dzindolet, M. T. (1993). Social influence processes in group brainstorming. *Journal of Personality and Social Psychology, 64,* 575–586.

Paulus, P. B., Dzindolet, M. T., Poletes, G., & Camacho, L. M. (1993). Perception of performance in group brainstorming: The illusion of group productivity. *Personality and Social Psychology Bulletin, 19,* 78–89.

Paulus, P. B., McCain, G., & Cox, V. C. (1981). Prison standards: Some pertinent data on crowding. *Federal Probation, 15,* 48–54.

Pavelchak, M. (1989). Piecemeal and category-based evaluation: An idiographic analysis. *Journal of Personality and Social Psychology, 56,* 354–363.

Pelham, B. W. (1991). On the benefits of misery: Self-serving biases in the depressive self-concept. *Journal of Personality and Social Psychology, 61,* 670–681.

Pelham, B. W., & Swann, W. B. (1994). The juncture of intrapersonal and interpersonal knowledge: Self-certainty and interpersonal congruence. *Personal and Social Psychology Bulletin, 20,* 349–357.

Pelham, B. W., & Wachsmuth, J. O. (1995). The waxing and waning of the social self: Contrast and assimilation in social comparison. *Journal of Personality and Social Psychology, 69,* 825–838.

Pelletier, L. G., Fortier, M. S., Vallerand, R. J., Tuson, K. M., Briere, N. M., & Blais, M. R. (1995). Toward a new measure of intrinsic motivation, extrinsic motivation, and amotivation in sports: The Sport Motivation Scale (SMS). *Journal of Sport & Exercise Psychology, 17,* 35–53.

Pendry, L. F., & Macrae, C. N. (1994). Stereotypes and mental life: The case of the motivated but thwarted tactician. *Journal of Experimental Social Psychology, 30,* 303–325.

Pennebaker, J. W. (1989). Confession, inhibition, and disease. In L. Berkowitz (Ed.), *Advances in experimental social psychology* (Vol. 22). New York: Academic Press.

Pennebaker, J. W., & Beall, S. K. (1986). Confronting a traumatic event: Toward an understanding of inhibition and disease. *Journal of Abnormal Psychology, 95,* 274–281.

Pennebaker, J. W., Colder, M., & Sharp, L. K. (1990). Accelerating the coping process. *Journal of Personality and Social Psychology, 58,* 528–537

Pennebaker, J. W., Hughes, C. F., & O'Heeron, R. C. (1987). The psychophysiology of confession: Linking inhibitory and psychosomatic processes. *Journal of Personality and Social Psychology, 52,* 781–793.

Pennebaker, J. W., & O'Heeron, R. C. (1984). Confiding in others and illness rate among spouses of suicide and accidental death victims. *Journal of Abnormal Psychology, 93,* 473–476.

Pennebaker, J. W., & Susman, J. R. (1988). Disclosure of traumas and psychosomatic processes. *Social Science and Medicine, 26,* 327–332.

Penner, L. A., & Fritzsche, B. A. (1993). Magic Johnson and reaction to people with AIDS: A natural experiment. *Journal of Applied Social Psychology, 23,* 1035–1050.

Pennington, N., & Hastie, R. (1986). Evidence evaluation in complex decision making. *Journal of Personality and Social Psychology, 51,* 242–258.

Pennington, N., & Hastie, R. (1990). Practical implications of psychological research on juror and jury decision making. *Personality and Social Psychology Bulletin, 16,* 90–105.

Pennington, N., & Hastie, R. (1992). Explaining the evidence: Tests of the story model for juror decision making. *Journal of Personality and Social Psychology, 62,* 189–206.

Pepitone, A., McCauley, C., & Hammond, P. (1967). Change in attractiveness of forbidden toys as a function of severity of threat. *Journal of Experimental Social Psychology, 3,* 221–229.

Peplau, L. A., Hill, C. T., & Rubin, Z. (1993). Sex role attitudes in dating and marriage: A 15-year follow-up of the Boston couples study. *Journal of Social Issues, 49,* 31–52.

Peplau, L. A., & Perlman, D. (1982). Perspectives on loneliness. In L. A. Peplau & D. Perlman (Eds.), *Loneliness: A sourcebook of current theory, research and therapy.* New York: Wiley.

Peres, Y., & Meivar, H. (1986). Self-presentation during courtship: A content analysis of classified advertisements in Israel. *Journal of Comparative Family Studies, 17,* 19–32.

Perez, D. A., Hosch, H. M., Ponder, B., & Trejo, G. C. (1993). Ethnicity of defendants and jurors as influences on jury decisions. *Journal of Applied Social Psychology, 23,* 1249–1262.

Pernanen, K. (1976). Alcohol and crimes of violence. In B. Kissin & H. Bergleiter (Eds.), *Biology of alcoholism* (Vol. 4, pp. 351–443). New York: Plenum.

Perry, D. G., & Perry, L. C. (1976). Identification with film characters, covert aggressive verbalization, and reactions to film violence. *Journal of Research in Personality, 10,* 399–409.

Pessin, J. (1933). The comparative effects of social and mechanical stimulation on memorizing. *American Journal of Psychology, 45,* 263–270.

Peterson, J., & Miller, C. (1980). Psychological attractiveness and marriage adjustment in older American couples. *Journal of Psychology, 105,* 247–252.

Peterson, R. S., & Nemeth, C. J. (1996). Focus versus flexibility: Majority and minority influence can both improve performance. *Personality and Social Psychology Bulletin, 22,* 14–23.

Pettigrew, T. F. (1988). Integration and pluralism. In P. A. Katz & D. A. Taylor (Eds.), *Eliminating racism: Profiles in controversy.* New York: Plenum. Pp. 19–30.

Pettigrew, T. F., & Meertens, R. W. (1995). Subtle and blatant prejudice in Western Europe. *European Journal of Social Psychology, 25,* 57–75.

Petty, R. E. (1994). Two routes to persuasion: State of the art. In G. d'Ydewalle, P. Eeelen, & P. Bertelson (Eds.), *International perspectives on psychological science* (Vol. 2). Hillsdale, NJ: Erlbaum.

Petty, R. E., & Cacioppo, J. T. (1977). Forewarning, cognitive responding, and resistance to persuasion. *Journal of Personality and Social Psychology, 35,* 645–655.

Petty, R. E., & Cacioppo, J. T. (1979). Issue involvement can increase or decrease persuasion by enhancing message-relevant cognitive responses. *Journal of Personality and Social Psychology, 37,* 1915–1926.

Petty, R. E., & Cacioppo, J. T. (1981). *Attitudes and persuasion: Classic and contemporary approaches.* Dubuque, IA: Brown.

Petty, R. E., & Cacioppo, J. T. (1984). *Attitude change: Central and peripheral routes to persuasion.* New York: Springer-Verlag.

Petty, R. E., & Cacioppo, J. T. (1985). The elaboration likelihood model of persuasion. In L. Berkowitz (Ed.), *Advances in experimental social psychology* (Vol. 19). New York: Academic Press.

Petty, R. E., & Cacioppo, J. T. (1986). *Communication and persuasion: Central and peripheral routes to attitude change.* New York: Springer-Verlag.

Petty, R. E., Cacioppo, J. T., & Goldman, R. (1981). Personal involvement as a determinant of argument-based persuasion. *Journal of Personality and Social Psychology, 40,* 432–440.

Petty, R. E., Cacioppo, J. T., & Haugtvedt, C. P. (in press). Ego-involvement and persuasion: An appreciative look at the Sherif's contribution to the study of self-relevance and attitude change. In D. Granberg & G. Sarup (Eds.), *Social judgment and intergroup relations: Essays in honor of Muzafer Sherif.* New York: Springer-Verlag.

Petty, R. E., Cacioppo, J. T., & Kasmer, J. A. (1988). The role of affect in the elaboration likelihood model of persuasion. In L. Donohew, H. E. Sypher, & E. T. Higgins (Eds.), *Communication, social cognition and affect.* Hillsdale, NJ: Erlbaum.

Petty, R. E., Haugtvedt, C. P., & Smith, S. M. (1995). Elaboration as a determinant of attitude strength: Creating attitudes that are persistent, resistant, and predictive of behavior. In R. E. Petty & J. A. Krosnick (Eds.), *Attitude strength: Antecedents and consequences.* Hillsdale, NJ: Erlbaum.

Petty, R. E., Ostrom, T. M., & Brock, T. C. (1981). *Cognitive responses in persuasion.* Hillsdale, NJ: Erlbaum.

Petty, R. E., Priester, J. R., & Wegener, D. T. (1994). Cognitive processes in attitude change. In R. S. Wyer & T. K. Srull (Eds.), *Handbook of social cognition* (Vol. 2). Hillsdale, NJ: Erlbaum.

Petty, R. E., Schumann, D. W., Richman, S. A., & Strathman, A. J. (1993). Positive mood and persuasion: Different roles for affect under high- and low-elaboration conditions. *Journal of Personality and Social Psychology, 64,* 5–20.

Petty, R. E., Wells, G. L., & Brock, T. C. (1976). Distraction can enhance or reduce yielding to propaganda: Thought disruption versus effort justification. *Journal of Personality and Social Psychology, 34,* 874–884.

Pfeifer, J. E., & Ogloff, J. R. P. (1991). Ambiguity and guilt determinations: A modern racism perspective. *Journal of Applied Social Psychology, 21,* 1713–1725.

Pfungst, O. (1911). *Clever Hans (the horse of Mr. von Osten): A contribution to experimental, animal, and human psychology.* (Translated by C. L. Rahn.) New York: Holt.

Phillips, D. P. (1983). The impact of mass media violence on U.S. homicides. *American Sociological Review, 48,* 560–568.

Phillips, D. P. (1986). Natural experiments on the effects of mass media violence on fatal aggression: Strengths and weaknesses of a new approach. In L. Berkowitz (Ed.), *Advances in experimental social psychology* (Vol. 19, pp.207–250). New York: Academic Press.

Piliavin, I. M., Piliavin, J. A., & Rodin, J. (1975). Costs, diffusion and the stigmatized victim. *Journal of Personality and Social Psychology, 32,* 429–438.

Piliavin, J. A., & Piliavin, I. M. (1972). Effect of blood on reactions to a victim. *Journal of Personality and Social Psychology, 23,* 353–361.

Piliavin, J. A., & Unger, R. K. (1985). The helpful but helpless female: Myth or reality? In V. E. O'Leary, R. Unger, & B. S. Wallston (Eds.), *Women, gender, and social psychology* (pp. 149–189). Hillsdale, NJ: Erlbaum.

Pingitore, R., Dugoni, B. L., Tindale, R. S., & Spring, B. (1994). Bias against overweight job applicants in a simulated employment interview. *Journal of Applied Social Psychology, 79,* 909–917.

Pittman, T. S., & D'Agostino, P. R. (1985). Motivation and attribution: The effects of control deprivation on subsequent information processing. In J. H. Harvey & G. Weary (Eds.), *Attribution: Basic issues and applications.* New York: Academic Press.

Pittman, T. S., & D'Agostino, P. R. (1989). Motivation and cognition: Control deprivation and the nature of subsequent information processing. *Journal of Experimental Social Psychology, 25,* 456–480.

Pittman, T. S., Emery, J., & Boggiano, A. K. (1982). Intrinsic and extrinsic motivational orientations: Reward-induced changes in preference for complexity. *Journal of Personality and Social Psychology, 42,* 789–797.

Platt, G. (1973). Social traps. *American Psychologist, 28,* 641–651.

Plous, S. (1989). Thinking the unthinkable: The effects of anchoring on likelihood estimates of nuclear war. *Journal of Applied Social Psychology, 19,* 67–91.

Polferone, J. M., & Manuck, S. B. (1987). Gender differences in cardiovascular and neuroendocrine response to stressors. In R. C. Barnett, L. Biener, & G. K. Baruch (Eds.), *Gender and stress.* New York: Free Press.

Polivy, J., Garner, D. M., & Garfinkel, P. E. (1986). Causes and consequences of the current preference for thin female physiques. In C. P. Herman, M. P. Zanna, & E. T. Higgins (Eds.), *Physical appearance, a stigma and social behavior: The Ontario symposium* (Vol. 3). Hillsdale, NJ: Erlbaum.

Polivy, J., Herman, C. P., Hackett, R., & Kuleshnyk, I. (1986). The effects of self-attention and public attention on eating in restrained and unrestrained subjects. *Journal of Personality and Social Psychology, 50,* 1253–1260.

Pollard, P. (1992). Judgements about victims and attackers in depicted rapes: A review. *British Journal of Social Psychology, 31,* 307–326.

Posner, M. I., & Keele, S. W. (1968). On the genesis of abstract ideas. *Journal of Experimental Psychology, 77,* 353–363.

Potegal, M. (1979). The reinforcing value of several types of aggressive behavior: A review. *Aggressive Behavior, 5,* 353–373.

Powell, J. L. (1988). A test of the knew-it-all-along effect in the 1984 Presidential and statewide elections. *Journal of Applied Social Psychology, 18,* 760–773.

Powell, M. C., & Fazio, R. H. (1984). Attitude accessibility as a function of repeated attitudinal expression. *Personality and Social Psychology Bulletin, 10,* 139–148.

Prange, G. W. (1986). *Pearl Harbor: The verdict of history.* New York: McGraw-Hill.

Prasad, J. A. (1950). A comparative study of rumours and reports in earthquakes. *British Journal of Psychology, 41,* 129–144.

Pratkanis, A. R. (1989). The cognitive representation of attitudes. In A. R. Pratkanis, S. J. Breckler, & A. G. Greenwald (Eds.), *Attitude structure and function.* Hillsdale, NJ: Erlbaum.

Pratkanis, A. R. (in press). The attitude heuristic and selective fact identification. *British Journal of Social Psychology.*

Pratkanis, A. R., Greenwald, A. G., Leippe, M. R., & Baumgardner, M. H. (1988). In search of reliable persuasion effects: III. The sleeper effect is dead. Long live the sleeper effect. *Journal of Personality and Social Psychology, 54,* 203–218.

Pratkanis, A. R., & Turner, M. E. (1994a). Of what value is a job attitude? A socio-cognitive analysis. *Human Relations, 47,* 1545–1576.

Pratkanis, A. R., & Turner, M. E. (1994b). The year Cool Papa Bell lost the batting title: Mr. Branch Rickey and Mr. Jackie Robinson's plea for affirmative action. *NINE: A Journal of Baseball History and Social Policy Perspectives, 2,* 260–276.

Pratt, C. L., & Sackett, G. P. (1969). Selection of social partners as a function of peer contact during rearing. In R. B. Zajonc (Ed.), *Animal Social Psychology.* New York: Wiley. Pp. 137–140.

Pratto, F. (in press). Sexual politics: The gender gap in the bedroom and the cabinet. In D. M. Buss & N. Malamuth (Eds.), *Sex, power, and conflict: Evolutionary and feminist perspectives.* Oxford University Press.

Pratto, F., & Bargh, J. A. (1991). Stereotyping based on apparently individuating information: trait and global components of sex stereotypes under attention overload. *Journal of Experimental Social Psychology, 27,* 26–47.

Pratto, F., & John, O. P. (1991). Automatic vigilance: The attention-grabbing power of negative social information. *Journal of Personality and Social Psychology, 61,* 380–391.

Pratto, F., Sidanius, J., Stallworth, L. M., & Malle, B. F. (1994). Social dominance orientation: A personality variable predicting social and political attitudes. *Journal of Personality and Social Psychology, 67,* 741–763.

Prentice-Dunn, S., & Rogers, R. W. (1983). Deindividuation in aggression. In R. G. Geen & E. Donnerstein (Eds.), *Aggression: Theoretical and empirical reviews: Vol. 2. Issues in research* (pp. 155–177). New York: Academic Press.

Prentice-Dunn, S., & Rogers, R. W. (1989). Deindividuation and the self-regulation of behavior. In P. Paulhus (Ed.), *Psychology of group influence* (2nd ed., pp. 87–109). Hillsdale, NJ: Erlbaum.

Price, W. H., & Whatmore, P. B. (1967). Behaviour disorders and pattern of crime among XYY males identified at a maximum security hospital. *British Medical Journal, 1,* 533–536.

Priest, R. F., & Sawyer, J. (1967). Proximity and peership: Bases of balance in interpersonal attraction. *American Journal of Sociology, 72,* 633–649.

Priester, J. R., & Petty, R. E. (1995). Source attributions and persuasion: Perceived honesty as a determinant of message scrutiny. *Personality and Social Psychology Bulletin, 21,* 637–654.

Prins, K. S., Buunk, B. P., & VanYperen, N. W. (1993). Equity, normative disapproval and extramarital relationships. *Journal of Social and Personal Relationships, 10,* 39–53.

Pruitt, D. G. (1971a). Choice shifts in group discussion: An introductory review. *Journal of Personality and Social Psychology, 20,* 339–360.

Pruitt, D. G. (1971b). Conclusions: Toward an understanding of choice shifts in group discussion. *Journal of Personality and Social Psychology, 20,* 495–510.

Pruitt, D. G. (1981). *Negotiation behavior.* New York: Academic Press.

Pruitt, D. G. (1986). Achieving integrative agreements in negotiation. In R. K. White (Ed.), *Psychology and the prevention of nuclear war.* New York: New York University Press.

Pruitt, D. G., & Kimmel, M. J. (1977). Twenty years of experimental gaming: Critique, synthesis, and suggestions for the future. *Annual Review of Psychology, 28,* 363–392.

Ptacek, J. T., & Dodge, K. L. (1995). Coping strategies and relationship satisfaction in couples. *Personality and Social Psychology Bulletin, 21,* 76–84.

Pugh, M. D. (1983). Contributory fault and rape convictions: Loglinear models for blaming the victim. *Social Psychology Quarterly, 46,* 233–242.

Quackenbush, R. L. (1989). A comparison of androgynous, masculine sex-typed, and undifferentiated males on dimensions of attitudes toward rape. *Journal of Research in Personality, 23,* 318–342.

Quattrone, G. A. (1982). Overattribution and unit formation: When behavior engulfs the person. *Journal of Personality and Social Psychology, 42,* 593–607.

Quattrone, G. A., & Jones, E. E. (1980). The perception of variability within ingroups and outgroups: Implications for the law of small numbers. *Journal of Personality and Social Psychology, 38,* 141–152.

Quay, L. C. (1992). Personal and family effects of loneliness. *Journal of Applied Developmental Psychology, 13,* 97–110.

Ragins, B. R., & Sundstrom, E. (1989). Gender and power in organizations: A longitudinal perspective. *Psychological Bulletin, 105,* 51–88.

Rajecki, D. W., Bledsoe, S. B., & Rasmussen, J. L. (1991). Successful personal ads: Gender differences and similarities in offers, stipulations, and outcomes. *Basic and Applied Social Psychology, 12,* 457–469.

Rajecki, D. W., & Wolfson, C. (1973). The rating of materials found in the mailbox. Effects of frequency of receipt. *Public Opinion Quarterly, 37,* 110–114.

Ramsoy, N. R. (1966). Assortative mating and the structure of cities. *American Journal of Sociology, 31,* 773–786.

Rank, S. G., & Jacobson, C. K. (1977). Hospital nurses' compliance with medication overdose orders: A failure to replicate. *Journal of Health and Social Behavior, 18,* 188–193.

Rapoport, A., Budescu, D. V., Suleiman, R., & Weg, E. (1992). Social dilemmas with uniformly distributed resources. In W. B. G. Liebrand, D. M. Messick, & H. A. M. Wilke (Eds.), *Social dilemmas.* Oxford: Pergamon.

Rasinski, K. A., Crocker, J., & Hastie, R. (1985). Another look at sex stereotypes and social judgments: An analysis of the social perceiver's use of subjective probabilities. *Journal of Personality and Social Psychology, 49,* 317–326.

Raven, B. H. (1965). Social influence and power. In I. D. Steiner & M. Fishbein (Eds.), *Current studies in social psychology.* New York: Holt, Rinehart, & Winston.

Raven, B. H. (1983). Interpersonal influence and social power. In B. H. Raven & J. Z. Rubin (Eds.), *Social psychology.* New York: Wiley.

Raven, B. H. (1992). A power/interaction model of interpersonal influence: French and Raven thirty years later. *Journal of Social Behavior and Personality, 7,* 217–244.

Raven, B. H. (1993). The bases of power: Origins and recent developments. *Journal of Social Issues, 49,* 227–251.

Rawlings, E. I. (1968). Reactive guilt and anticipatory guilt in altruistic behavior. In J. R. Macaulay & L. Berkowitz (Eds.), *Altruism and helping behavior* (pp. 163–177). New York: Academic Press.

Read, S. J., & Miller, L. C. (1993). Rapist or "regular guy": Explanatory coherence in the construction of mental models of others. *Personality and Social Psychology Bulletin, 19,* 526–540.

Reed, G. M., Taylor, S. E., & Kemeny, M. E. (1993). Perceived control and psychological adjustment in gay men with AIDS. *Journal of Applied Social Psychology, 23,* 791–824.

Reeder, G. D. (1993). Trait-behavior relations and dispositional inference. *Personality and Social Psychology Bulletin, 19,* 586–593.

Reeder, G. D., & Brewer, M. B. (1979). A schematic model of dispositional attribution in interpersonal perception. *Psychological Review, 86,* 61–79.

Reeder, G. D., & Coovert, M. D. (1986). Revising an impression of morality. *Social Cognition, 4,* 1–17.

Reeder, G. D., Fletcher, G. J., & Furman, K. (1989). The role of observers' expectations in attitude attribution. *Journal of Experimental Social Psychology, 25,* 168–188.

Reeder, G. D., & Fulks, J. L. (1980). When actions speak louder than words: Implicational schemata and the attribution of ability. *Journal of Experimental Social Psychology, 16,* 33–46.

Reeder, G. D., Pryor, J. B., & Wojciszke, B. (1992). Trait-behavior relations in social information processing. In G. R. Semin & K. Fiedler, Eds.), *Language, interaction, and social cognition.* London: Sage.

Reeve, J., & Deci, E. L. (1996). Elements of the competitive situation that affect intrinsic motivation. *Personality and Social Psychology Bulletin, 22,* 24–33.

Reeve, J., Olson, B. C., & Cole, S. G. (1985). Motivation and performance: Two consequences of winning and losing in competition. *Motivation and Emotion, 9,* 291–298.

Reeve, J., Olson, B. C., & Cole, S. G. (1987). Intrinsic motivation in competition: The intervening role of four individual differences following objective competence information. *Journal of Research in Personality, 21,* 148–170.

Regan, D. T., Williams, M., & Sparling, S. (1972). Voluntary expiation of guilt: A field replication. *Journal of Personality and Social Psychology, 24,* 42–45.

Regan, J. W. (1971). Guilt, perceived injustice, and altruistic behavior. *Journal of Personality and Social Psychology, 18,* 124–132.

Reifman, A. S., Larrick, R. P., & Fein, S. (1991). Temper and temperature on the diamond: The heat-aggression relationship in major league baseball. *Personality and Social Psychology Bulletin, 17,* 580–585.

Reis, T. J., Gerrard, M., & Gibbons, F. X. (1993). Social comparison and the pill: Reactions to upward and downward comparison of contraceptive behavior. *Personality and Social Psychology Bulletin, 19,* 13–20.

Reychler, L. (1979). The effectiveness of a pacifist strategy in conflict resolution. *Journal of Conflict Resolution, 23,* 228–260.

Rezek, P. J., & Leary, M. R. (1991). Perceived control, drive for thinness, and food consumption: Anorexic tendencies as displaced reactance. *Journal of Personality, 59,* 129–142.

Rhodes, N., & Wood, W. (1992). Self-esteem and intelligence affect influenceability: The mediating role of message reception. *Psychological Bulletin, 111,* 156–171.

Rhodewalt, F. (1986). Self-presentation and the phenomenal self: On the stability and malleability of self-conceptions. In R. F. Baumeister (Ed.), *Public self and private self* (pp. 117–142). New York: Springer-Verlag.

Rhodewalt, F. (1990). Self-handicappers: Individual differences in the preference for anticipatory self-protective acts. In R. Higgins, C. R. Snyder, & S. Berglas (Eds.), *Self-handicapping: The paradox that isn't.* New York: Plenum Press.

Rhodewalt, F., Morf, C., Hazlett, S., & Fairfield, M. (1991). Self-handicapping: The role of discounting and augmentation in the preservation of self-esteem. *Journal of Personality and Social Psychology, 61,* 122–131.

Rhodewalt, F., Saltzman, A. T., & Wittmer, J. (1984). Self-handicapping among competitive athletes: The role of practice in self-esteem protection. *Basic and Applied Social Psychology, 5,* 197–210.

Rice, R. (1977). Neural development in premature infants following stimulation. *Developmental Psychology, 13,* 69–76.

Riecken, H. W. (1958). The effect of talkativeness on ability to influence group solutions to problems. *Sociometry, 21,* 309–321.

Rieder, C., & Rosenthal, R. (1994). Speaking of women: Men and women talking, listening, and being talked about. *Journal of Social Behavior and Personality, 9,* 443–454.

Riess, M., Kalle, R. J., & Tedeschi, J. T. (1981). Bogus pipeline attitude assessment, impression management, and misattribution in induced compliance settings. *Journal of Social Psychology, 115,* 247–258.

Riess, M., & Schlenker, B. R. (1977). Attitude change and responsibility avoidance as modes of dilemma resolution in forced compliance settings. *Journal of Personality and Social Psychology, 35,* 21–30.

Riordan, C. (1978). Equal-status interracial contact: A review and revision of the concept. *International Journal of Intercultural Relations, 2,* 161–185.

Riordan, C., & Ruggerio, J. (1980). Equal status interracial interaction: A replication. *Social Psychology Quarterly, 43,* 131–136.

Rist, R. (1970). Student social class and teacher expectations: The self-fulfilling prophecy in ghetto education. *Harvard Educational Review, 40,* 411–451.

Rodgers, J. L., Billy, J. O. B., & Udry, J. R. (1984). A model of friendship similarity in mildly deviant behaviors. *Journal of Applied Social Psychology, 14,* 413–425.

Rodin, J., Silberstein, L., & Striegel-Moore, R. (1985). Women and weight: A normative discontent. In T. B. Sonderegger (Ed.), *Nebraska symposium on motivation. Vol. 32. Psychology and gender.* Lincoln, NE: University of Nebraska Press.

Rodin, J., Solomon, S., & Metcalf, J. (1978). The role of control in mediating perceptions of density. *Journal of Personality and Social Psychology, 36,* 988–999.

Rodin, M., Price, J., Sanchez, F., & McElligot, S. (1989). Derogation, exclusion, and unfair treatment of persons with social flaws: Controllability of stigma and the attribution of prejudice. *Personality and Social Psychology Bulletin, 15,* 439–451.

Roese, N. J. (1994). The functional basis of counterfactual thinking. *Journal of Personality and Social Psychology, 66,* 805–818.

Roese, N. J., & Jamieson, D. W. (1993). Twenty years of bogus pipeline research: A critical review and meta-analysis. *Psychological Bulletin, 114,* 363–375.

Roese, N. J., & Olson, J. M. (1993). The structure of counterfactual thought. *Personality and Social Psychology Bulletin, 19,* 312–319.

Roese, N. J., & Olson, J. M. (1994). Attitude importance as a function of repeated attitude expression. *Journal of Experimental Social Psychology, 30,* 39–51.

Roessler, R. L., & Brogden, W. J. (1943). Conditioned differentiation of vasoconstriction to subvocal stimuli. *American Journal of Psychology, 56,* 78–86.

Rogers, R. W. (1983). Cognitive and physiological processes in fear appeals and attitude change: A revised theory of protection motivation. In J. T. Cacioppo & R. E. Petty (Eds.), *Social psychophysiology: A sourcebook.* New York: Guilford.

Rogers, R. W., Deckner, C. W., & Mewborn, C. R. (1978). An expectancy-value theory approach to the long-term modification of smoking behavior. *Journal of Clinical Psychology, 34,* 562–566.

Rogers, R. W., & Ketchen, C. M. (1979). Effects of anonymity and arousal on aggression. *Journal of Psychology, 102,* 13–19.

Rogers, R. W., & Prentice-Dunn, S. (1981). Deindividuation and anger-mediated interracial aggression: Unmasking regressive racism. *Journal of Personality and Social Psychology, 41,* 63–73.

Rogers, R. W., & Thistlethwaite, D. L. (1969). An analysis of active and passive defenses in inducing resistance to persuasion. *Journal of Personality and Social Psychology, 11,* 301–308.

Rohner, R. (1975). *They love me, they love me not: A worldwide study of the effects of parental acceptance and rejection.* New York: HRAF Press.

Rohrer, J. H., Baron, S. H., Hoffman, E. L., & Swander, D. V. (1954). The stability of autokinetic judgment. *Journal of Abnormal and Social Psychology, 49,* 595–597.

Rojahn, K., & Pettigrew, T. F. (1992). Memory for schema-relevant information: A meta-analytic resolution. *British Journal of Social Psychology, 31,* 81–109.

Roney, C. J. R., & Sorrentino, R. M. (1995a). Reducing self-discrepancies or maintaining self congruence? Uncertainty orientation, self-regulation, and performance. *Journal of Personality and Social Psychology, 68,* 485–497.

Roney, C. J. R., & Sorrentino, R. M. (1995b). Self-evaluation motives and uncertainty orientation: Asking the "who" question. *Personality and Social Psychology Bulletin, 21,* 1319–1329.

Rook, K. S. (1984). Promoting social bonding: Strategies for helping the lonely and socially isolated. *American Psychologist, 39,* 1389–1407.

Rose, S., & Frieze, I. H. (1993). Young singles' contemporary dating scripts. *Sex Roles, 28,* 499–509.

Rosen, B., & Jerdee, T. H. (1976). The influence of age stereotypes on managerial decisions. *Journal of Applied Psychology, 61,* 428.

Rosenbaum, M. E. (1980). Cooperation and competition. In P. B. Paulus (Ed.), *The psychology of group influence.* Hillsdale, NJ: Erlbaum.

Rosenbaum, M. E. (1986). The repulsion hypothesis: On the nondevelopment of relationships. *Journal of Personality and Social Psychology, 51,* 1156–1166.

Rosenberg, E. L., & Ekman, P. (1994). Coherence between expressive and experiential systems in emotion. *Cognition and Emotion, 8,* 201–229.

Rosenberg, M. J. (1960). Cognitive reorganization in response to the hypnotic reversal of attitudinal affect. *Journal of Personality, 28,* 39–63.

Rosenberg, M. J., & Hovland, C. I. (1960). Cognitive, affective, and behavioral components of attitudes. In C. I. Hovland & M. J. Rosenberg (Eds.), *Attitude organization and change* (pp. 1–14). New Haven, CT: Yale University Press.

Rosenberg, S. (1993). Social self and the schizophrenic process: Theory and research. In R. L. Crowell & C. R. Snyder (Eds.), *Schizophrenia: origins, processes, treatment, and outcome.* New York: Oxford University Press.

Rosenblatt, A., & Greenberg, J. (1991). Depression and interpersonal attraction: The role of perceived similarity. *Journal of Personality and Social Psychology, 55,* 112–119.

Rosenblatt, A., Greenberg, J., Solomon, S., Pyszczynski, T., & Lyon, D. (1989). Evidence for terror management theory: I. The effects of mortality salience on reactions to those who violate or uphold cultural values. *Journal of Personality and Social Psychology, 57,* 681–690.

Rosenblatt, P. C., Jackson, D. A., & Walsh, R. P. (1972). Coping with anger and aggression in mourning. *Omega Journal of Death and Dying, 3,* 271–284.

Rosenhan, D. (1969). Some origins of concern for others. In P. Mussen, J. Langer, & M. Covington (Eds.), *Trends and issues in developmental psychology.* New York: Holt, Rinehart, & Winston.

Rosenhan, D. L., Salovey, P., & Hargis, K. (1981). The joys of helping: Focus of attention mediates the impact of positive affect on altruism. *Journal of Personality and Social Psychology, 40,* 899–905.

Rosenthal, R. (1966). *Experimenter effects in behavioral research.* New York: Appleton-Century-Crofts.

Rosenthal, R. (1973). The mediation of Pygmalion effects: A four-factor "theory." *Papua New Guinea Journal of Education, 9,* 1–12.

Rosenthal, R. (1981). Pavlov's mice, Pfungst's horse, and Pygmalion's PONS: Some models for the study of interpersonal expectancy effects. In T. A. Sebeok & R. Rosenthal (Eds.), *The Clever Hans phenomenon: Communication with horses, whales, apes, and people.* Annals of the New York Academy of Sciences (No. 364). New York: New York Academy of Sciences.

Rosenthal, R. (in press). Interpersonal expectancy effects: A thirty-year perspective. *Current Directions in Psychological Science.*

Rosenthal, R., & Fode, K. L. (1963). The effect of experimenter bias on the performance of the albino rat. *Behavioral Science, 8,* 183–189.

Rosenthal, R., Hall, J. A., DiMatteo, M. R., Rogers, P. L., & Archer, D. (1979). *Sensitivity to nonverbal communication.* Baltimore, MD: Johns Hopkins University Press.

Rosenthal, R., & Jacobson, L. (1968). *Pygmalion in the classroom: Teacher expectation and pupils' intellectual development.* New York: Holt, Rinehart & Winston.

Rosenthal, R., & Rubin, D. B. (1978). Interpersonal expectancy effects: The first 345 studies. *Behavioral and Brain Sciences, 3,* 377–386.

Roskos-Ewoldsen, D. R., & Fazio, R. H. (1992). On the orienting value of attitudes: Attitude accessibility as a determinant of an object's attraction of visual attention. *Journal of Personality and Social Psychology, 63,* 198–211.

Rosnow, R. L. (1991). Inside rumor. *American Psychologist, 46,* 486–496.

Rosnow, R. L., Rotheram-Borus, M. J., Ceci, S. J., Blanck, P. D., & Koocher, G. P. (1993). The institutional review board as a mirror of scientific and ethical standards. *American Psychologist, 48,* 821–826.

Ross, L. (1977). The intuitive psychologist and his shortcomings: Distortions in the attribution process. In L. Berkowitz (Ed.), *Advances in experimental social psychology* (Vol. 10). New York: Academic Press.

Ross, L. (1987). The problem of construal in social inference and social psychology. In N. E. Grunberg, R. E. Nisbett, J. Rodin, & J. E. Singer (Eds.), *A distinctive approach to psychological research: The influence of Stanley Schachter.* Hillsdale, NJ: Erlbaum.

Ross, L. (1989). Recognizing construal processes. In I. Rock (Ed.), *The legacy of Solomon Asch: Essays in cognition and social psychology*. Hillsdale, NJ: Erlbaum.

Ross, L., Amabile, T. M., & Steinmetz, J. L. (1977). Social roles, social control, and biases in social-perception processes. *Journal of Personality and Social Psychology, 35,* 485–494.

Ross, L., Greene, D., & House, P. (1977). The "false consensus effect": An egocentric bias in social perception and attribution processes. *Journal of Experimental Social Psychology, 13,* 279–301.

Ross, L., & Lepper, M. R. (1980). The perseverance of beliefs: Empirical and normative considerations. In R. A. Shweder & D. Fiske (Eds.), *New directions for methodology of behavioral science: Fallible judgment in behavioral research*. San Francisco: Jossey-Bass.

Ross, L., Lepper, M. R., & Hubbard, M. (1975). Perseverance in self-perception and social perception: Biased attribution processes in the debriefing paradigm. *Journal of Personality and Social Psychology, 32,* 880–892.

Ross, L., Lepper, M. R., Strack, F., & Steinmetz, J. (1977). Social explanation and social expectation: Effects of real and hypothetical explanations on subjective likelihood. *Journal of Personality and Social Psychology, 35,* 817–829.

Ross, L., & Nisbett, R. E. (1991). *The person and the situation: Perspectives of social psychology*. New York: McGraw-Hill.

Ross, M. (in press). Validating memories. In N. L. Stein, P. A. Ornstein, B. Tversky, & C. Brainerd (Eds.), *Memory for everyday and emotional events*. Hillsdale, NJ: Erlbaum.

Ross, M., & Buehler, R. (1994). Creative remembering. In U. Neisser & R. Fivush (Eds.), *The remembering self.* New York: Cambridge University Press.

Ross, M., & Conway, M. (1986). Remembering one's own past: The construction of personal histories. In R. M. Sorrentino & E. T. Higgins (Eds.), *Handbook of motivation and cognition: Foundations of social behavior*. New York: Guilford Press.

Ross, M., & Fletcher, G. J. O. (1985). Attribution and social perception. In G. Lindzey & A. Aronson (Eds.), *The handbook of social psychology* (3rd ed., Vol. 2). Reading, MA: Addison-Wesley.

Ross, M., McFarland, C., Conway, M., & Zanna, M. P. (1983). Reciprocal relation between attitudes and behavior recall: Committing people to newly formed attitudes. *Journal of Personality and Social Psychology, 45,* 257–267.

Ross, M., McFarland, C., & Fletcher, G. J. O. (1981). The effect of attitude on the recall of personal history.

Journal of Personality and Social Psychology, 40, 627–634.

Ross, M., & Shulman, R. F. (1973). Increasing the salience of initial attitudes: Dissonance versus self-perception theory. *Journal of Personality and Social Psychology, 28,* 138–144.

Ross, M., & Sicoly, F. (1979). Egocentric biases in availability and attribution. *Journal of Personality and Social Psychology, 37,* 322–336.

Ross, S. I., & Jackson, J. M. (1991). Teachers' expectations for Black males' and Black females' academic achievement. *Personality and Social Psychology Bulletin, 17,* 78–82.

Rotenberg, K. J., Simourd, L., & Moore, D. (1989). Children's use of a verbal-nonverbal consistency principle to infer truth and lying. *Child Development, 60,* 309–322.

Rothbart, M., Evans, M., & Fulero, S. (1979). Recall for confirming events: Memory processes and the maintenance of social stereotypes. *Journal of Experimental Social Psychology, 15,* 343–355.

Rothbart, M., & John, O. (1985). Social categorization and behavioral episodes: A cognitive analysis of the effects of intergroup contact. *Journal of Social Issues, 41,* 81–104.

Rothbart, M., & Lewis, S. (1988). Inferring category attributes from exemplar attributes: geometric shapes and social categories. *Journal of Personality and Social Psychology, 55,* 861–872.

Rothbart, M., & Taylor, M. (1992). Category labels and social reality: Do we view social categories as natural kinds? In G. R. Semin & K. Fiedler (Eds.), *Language, interaction and social cognition*. London, England: Sage.

Rotton, J., & Frey, J. (1985). Air pollution, weather, and violent crimes: Concomitant time-series analysis of archival data. *Journal of Personality and Social Psychology, 49,* 1207–1220.

Rotton, J., Frey, J., Barry, T., Milligan, M., & Fitzpatrick, M. (1979). The air pollution experience and physical aggression. *Journal of Applied Social Psychology, 9,* 397–412.

Rozin, P., & Zellner, D. (1985). The role of Pavlovian conditioning in the acquisition of food likes and dislikes. *Annals of the New York Academy of Sciences, 443,* 189–202.

Ruback, R. B., & Riad, J. K. (in press). The more (men), the less merry: Social density, social burden, and social support. *Sex Roles.*

Rubenstein, C. M., & Shaver, P. (1982). The experience of loneliness. In L. A. Peplau & D. Perlman (Eds.), *Loneliness: A sourcebook of current theory, research and therapy*. New York: Wiley.

Rubenstein, E. A. (1984). Television and the young viewer. In J. Rubinstein & B. Slife (Eds.), *Taking sides: Clashing views on controversial psychological issues* (pp. 248–263). Guilford, CT: Dushkin.

Rubin, Z. (1970). Measurement of romantic love. *Journal of Personality and Social Psychology, 16,* 265–273.

Rubin, Z. (1973). *Liking and loving: An invitation to social psychology*. New York: Holt, Rinehart, & Winston.

Ruble, D. N., & Dweck, C. S. (in press). Self-conceptions, person conceptions, and their development. In N. Eisenberg (Ed.), *Review of personality and social psychology. Development and social psychology: The interface* (Vol. 15). Thousand Oaks, CA: Sage.

Ruble, T. L. (1983). Sex stereotypes: Issues of change in the 1970s. *Sex Roles, 9,* 397–402.

Rubonis, A. V., & Bickman, L. (1991). A test of the consensus and distinctiveness attribution principles in victims of disaster. *Journal of Applied Social Psychology, 21,* 791–809.

Rubovitz, R., & Maehr, M. (1973). Pygmalion black and white. *Journal of Personality and Social Psychology, 25,* 210–218.

Rudman, L. A., & Borgida, E. (1995). The afterglow of construct accessibility: The behavioral consequences of priming men to view women as sexual objects. *Journal of Experimental Social Psychology, 31,* 493–517.

Rudman, L. A., Borgida, E., & Robertson, B. (1995). Suffering in silence: Procedural justice versus gender socialization issues in university sexual harassment grievance procedures. *Basic and Applied Social Psychology, 17,* 519–541.

Rugs, D., & Kaplan, M. F. (1993). Effectiveness of informational and normative influences in group decision making depends on the group interactive goal. *British Journal of Social Psychology, 32,* 147–158.

Rule, B. G., & Nesdale, A. R. (1976). Emotional arousal and aggressive behavior. *Psychological Bulletin, 83,* 851–863.

Rule, B. G., Taylor, B. R., & Dobbs, A. R. (1987). Priming effects of heat on aggressive thoughts. *Social Cognition, 5,* 131–143.

Runyan, D. L. (1974). The group risky-shift effect as a function of emotional bonds, actual consequences, and extent of responsibility. *Journal of Personality and Social Psychology, 29,* 670–676.

Rusbult, C. E. (1987). Responses to dissatisfaction in close relationships: The exit-voice-loyalty-neglect model. In D. Perlman and S. Duck (Eds.), *Intimate relationships: Development, dynamics, and deterioration* (pp. 209–237). Newbury Park, CA: Sage.

Rusbult, C. E., Johnson, D. J., & Morrow, G. D. (1986). Predicting satisfaction and commitment in adult romantic involvements: An assessment of the generalizability of the investment model. *Social Psychology Quarterly, 49,* 81–89.

Rusbult, C. E., Onizuka, R. K., & Lipkus, I. (1993). What do we really want? Mental models of ideal romantic involvement explored through multidimensional scaling. *Journal of Experimental Social Psychology, 29,* 493–527.

Rusbult, C. E., Verette, J., Whitney, G. A., Slovik, L. F., & Lipkus, I. (1991). Accommodation processes in close relationships: Theory and preliminary empirical evidence. *Journal of Personality and Social Psychology, 60,* 53–78.

Rusbult, C. E., & Zembrodt, I. M. (1983). Responses to dissatisfaction in romantic involvements: A multidimensional scaling analysis. *Journal of Experimental Social Psychology, 19,* 274–293.

Ruscher, J. B., Fiske, S. T., Miki, H., & Van Manen, S. (1991). Individuating processes in competition: Interpersonal versus intergroup. *Personality and Social Psychology Bulletin, 17,* 595–605.

Ruscher, J. B., & Hammer, E. D. (1994). Revising disrupted impressions through conversation. *Journal of Personality and Social Psychology, 66,* 530–541.

Rushton, J. P. (1975). Generosity in children: Immediate and long-term effects of modeling, preaching, and moral judgment. *Journal of Personality and Social Psychology, 31,* 459–466.

Rushton, J. P. (1980). *Altruism, socialization, and society.* Englewood Cliffs, NJ: Prentice-Hall.

Rushton, J. P. (1989). Genetic similarity, human altruism, and group selection. *Behavioral and Brain Sciences, 12,* 503–559.

Rushton, J. P., & Teachman, G. (1978). The effects of positive reinforcement, attributions, and punishment on model induced altruism in children. *Personality and Social Psychology Bulletin, 4,* 322–325.

Russell, D., Cutrona, C. E., Rose, J., & Yurko, K. (1984). *Journal of Personality and Social Psychology, 46,* 1313–1321.

Russell, D., Peplau, L. A., & Cutrona, C. E. (1980). The revised UCLA Loneliness Scale: Concurrent and discriminant validity evidence. *Journal of Personality and Social Psychology, 39,* 472–480.

Russell, J. A. (1980). A circumplex model of affect. *Journal of Personality and Social Psychology, 39,* 1161–1178.

Russell, J. A., Lewicka, M., & Niit, T. (1989). A cross-cultural study of a circumplex model of affect. *Journal of Personality and Social Psychology, 57,* 848–856.

Russell, P. A., & Gray, C. D. (1992). Prejudice against a progay man in an everyday situation: A scenario study. *Journal of Applied Social Psychology, 22,* 1676–1687.

Rutkowski, G. K., Gruder, C. L., & Romer, D. (1983). Group cohesiveness, social norms, and bystander intervention. *Journal of Personality and Social Psychology, 44,* 545–552.

Rutte, C. G., Wilke, H. A. M., & Messick, D. M. (1987). Scarcity or abundance caused by people or the environment as determinants of behavior in the resource dilemma. *Journal of Experimental Social Psychology, 23,* 208–216.

Ruvolo, A. P., & Markus, H. R. (1992). Possible selves and performance: The power of self-referent imagery. *Social Cognition, 10,* 95–124.

Ryan, E. B. (1992). Beliefs about memory across the life span. *Journal of Gerontology: Psychological Sciences, 47,* 41–47.

Ryan, E. D. (1970). The cathartic effect of vigorous motor activity on aggressive behavior. *Research Quarterly, 41,* 542–551.

Ryan, R. M. (1995). The integration of behavioral regulation within life domains. *Journal of Personality, 63,* 397–427.

Ryan, R. M., Sheldon, K. M., Kasser, T., & Deci, E. L. (in press). All goals were not created equal: An organismic perspective on the nature of goals and their regulation. In P. M. Gollwitzer & J. A. Bargh (Eds.), *Action science: Linking cognition to motivation and action.* New York: Guilford.

Sabatelli, R., Buck, R., & Dreyer, A. (1980). Communication via facial cues in intimate dyads. *Personality and Social Psychology Bulletin, 6,* 242–247.

Sabatelli, R., Buck, R., & Dreyer, A. (1982). Nonverbal communication accuracy in married couples: Relationships with marital complaints. *Journal of Personality and Social Psychology, 43,* 1088–1097.

Sadalla, E. K., Kenrick, D. T., & Vershure, B. (1987). Dominance and heterosexual attraction. *Journal of Personality and Social Psychology, 52,* 730–738.

Saegert, S., Swap, W., & Zajonc, R. B. (1973). Exposure, context, and interpersonal attraction. *Journal of Personality and Social Psychology, 25,* 234–242.

Saenz, D. S. (1994). Token status and problem-solving deficits: Detrimental effects of distinctiveness and performance monitoring. *Social Cognition, 12,* 61–74.

Saenz, D. S., & Lord, C. G. (1989). Reversing roles: A cognitive strategy for undoing memory deficits associated with token status. *Journal of Personality and Social Psychology, 56,* 698–708.

Sagar, H. A., & Schofield, J. W. (1980). Racial behavioral cues in black and white children's perceptions of ambiguously aggressive acts. *Journal of Personality and Social Psychology, 39,* 590–598.

Sagi, A., & Hoffman, M. L. (1976). Empathic distress in newborns. *Developmental Psychology, 12,* 175–176.

St. Lawrence, J. S., & Joyner, D. J. (1991). The effects of sexually violent rock music on males' acceptance of violence against women. *Psychology of Women Quarterly, 15,* 49–63.

Salovey, P., Mayer, J. D., & Rosenhan, D. L. (1991). Mood and helping: Mood as a motivator of helping and helping as a regulator of mood. In M. S. Clark (Ed.), *Prosocial behavior* (pp. 215–237). Newbury Park, CA: Sage.

Salovey, P., & Rodin, J. (1985, September). The heart of jealousy. *Psychology Today, 19,* 22–29.

Saltzman, J. (1983). Fact vs. fiction. *Emmy, 4,* 118–119.

Samuelson, C. D. (1991). Perceived task difficulty, causal attributions, and preferences for structural change in resource dilemmas. *Personality and Social Psychology Bulletin, 17,* 181–187.

Samuelson, C. D., & Messick, D. M. (1995). When do people want to change the rules for allocating shared resources? In D. A. Schroeder (Ed.), *Social dilemmas.* Westport, CT: Praeger.

Sanbonmatsu, D. M., Akimoto, S. A., & Gibson, B. D. (1994). Stereotype-based blocking in social explanation. *Personality and Social Psychology Bulletin, 20,* 71–81.

Sanbonmatsu, D. M., Shavitt, S. & Sherman, S. J. (1991). The role of personal relevance in the formation of distinctiveness-based illusory correlation. *Personality and Social Psychology Bulletin, 17,* 124–132.

Sande, G. N., Goethals, G. R., & Radloff, C. E. (1988). Perceiving one's own traits and others': The multifaceted self. *Journal of Personality and Social Psychology, 54,* 13–20.

Sanders, G. S., & Baron, R. S. (1975). The motivating effects of distraction on task performance. *Journal of Personality and Social Psychology, 32,* 956–963.

Sanders, G. S., & Baron, R. S. (1977). Is social comparison irrelevant for producing choice shifts? *Journal of Experimental Social Psychology, 13,* 303–314.

Sanna, L. J. (1992). Self-efficacy theory: Implications for social facilitation and social loafing. *Journal of Personality and Social Psychology, 62,* 774–786.

Sanna, L. J., & Shotland, R. L. (1990). Valence of anticipated evaluation and social facilitation. *Journal of Experimental Social Psychology, 26,* 82–92.

Sansone, C. (1989). Competence feedback, task feedback, and intrinsic interest: An examination of process and context. *Journal of Experimental Social Psychology, 25,* 343–361.

Santa Cruz, A. (1960). Acquiring status in Goajiro society. *Anthropological Quarterly, 33,* 115–127.

Santee, R. T., & Jackson, S. E. (1982). Identity implications of conformity: Sex differences in normative and attributional judgments. *Social Psychology Quarterly, 45,* 121–125.

Sarason, I. G., Sarason, B. R., & Pierce, G. R. (1994). Social support: Global and relationship-based levels of analysis. *Journal of Social and Personal Relationships, 11,* 295–312.

Saulnier, K., & Perlman, D. (1981). The actor-observer bias is alive and well in prison: A sequel to Wells. *Personality and Social Psychology Bulletin, 7,* 559–564.

Schachter, S. (1951). Deviation, rejection and communication. *Journal of Abnormal and Social Psychology, 46,* 190–207.

Schachter, S. (1964). The interaction of cognitive and physiological determinants of emotional state. In L. Berkowitz (Ed.), *Advances in experimental social psychology* (Vol. 1). New York: Academic Press.

Schachter, S., & Singer, J. E. (1962). Cognitive, social, and physiological determinants of emotional state. *Psychological Review, 69,* 379–399.

Schachter, S. (1959). *The psychology of affiliation.* Stanford, CA: Stanford University Press.

Schaie, K. W. (1988). Ageism in psychological research. *American Psychologist, 43,* 179–183.

Schaller, M. (1992a). In-group favoritism and statistical reasoning in social inference: Implications for formation and maintenance of group stereotypes. *Journal of Personality and Social Psychology, 63,* 61–74.

Schaller, M. (1992b). Sample size, aggregation, and statistical reasoning in social inference. *Journal of Experimental Social Psychology, 28,* 65–85.

Schaller, M. (1993). Feeling bad to feel good: Comments and observations. *Basic and Applied Social Psychology, 14,* 285–294.

Schaller, M. (1994). The role of statistical reasoning in the formation, preservation and prevention of group stereotypes. *British Journal of Social Psychology, 33,* 47–61.

Schaller, M., & Maass, A. (1989). Illusory correlation and social categorization: Toward an integration of motivational and cognitive factors in stereotype formation. *Journal of Personality and Social Psychology, 56,* 709–721.

Schaller, M., & O'Brien, M. (1992). "Intuitive analysis of covariance" and group stereotype formation. *Personality and Social Psychology Bulletin, 18,* 776–785.

Schank, R. C., & Abelson, R. P. (1977). *Scripts, plans, goals, and understanding: An inquiry into human knowledge structures.* Hillsdale, NJ: Erlbaum.

Scheier, M. F., Fenigstein, A., & Buss, A. H. (1974). Self-awareness and physical aggression. *Journal of Experimental Social Psychology, 10,* 264–273.

Scher, S., & Cooper, J. (1989). Motivational basis of dissonance: The singular role of behavioral consequences. *Journal of Personality and Social Psychology, 56,* 899–906.

Scherer, K. R. (1986). Vocal affect expression: A review and a model for future research. *Psychological Bulletin, 99,* 143–165.

Scherer, K. R., & Wallbott, H. G. (1994). Evidence for universality and cultural variation of differential emotion response patterning. *Journal of Personality and Social Psychology, 66,* 310–328.

Schifter, D. B., & Ajzen, I. (1985). Intention, perceived control, and weight loss: An application of the theory of planned behavior. *Journal of Personality and Social Psychology, 49,* 843–851.

Schlenker, B. R. (1980). *Impression management: The self-concept, social identity, and interpersonal relations.* Belmont, CA: Brooks/Cole.

Schlenker, B. R. (1986). Self-identification: Toward an integration of the private and public self. In R. F. Baumeister (Ed.), *Public self and private self* (pp. 21–62). New York: Springer-Verlag.

Schlenker, B. R., Britt, T. W., & Pennington, J. (in press). Impression regulation and management: Highlights of a theory of self-identification. In R. M. Sorrentino & E. T. Higgins (Eds.), *Handbook of motivation and cognition: The interpersonal context* (Vol. 3). New York: Guilford.

Schlenker, B. R., Britt, T. W., Pennington, J., Murphy, R., & Doherty, K. (1994). The triangle model of responsibility. *Psychological Review, 101,* 632–652.

Schlenker, B. R., Dlugolecki, D. W., & Doherty, K. J. (1994). The impact of self-presentations on self-appraisals and behaviors: The power of public commitment. *Personality and Social Psychology Bulletin, 20,* 20–33.

Schlenker, B. R., Forsyth, D. R., Leary, M. R., & Miller, R. S. (1980). Self-presentational analysis of the effects of incentives on attitude change following counterattitudinal behavior. *Journal of Personality and Social Psychology, 39,* 553–577.

Schlenker, B. R., & Leary, M. R. (1982). Audiences' reactions to self-enhancing, self-denigrating, and accurate self-presentations. *Journal of Experimental Social Psychology, 18,* 89–104.

Schlenker, B. R., Phillips, S. T., Boniecki, K. A., & Schlenker, D. R. (1995). Championship pressures: Choking or triumphing in one's own terriitory? *Journal of Personality and Social Psychology, 68,* 632–652.

Schlenker, B. R., & Weigold, M. F. (1992). Interpersonal processes involving impression regulation and management. *Annual Review of Psychology, 43,* 133–168.

Schlenker, B. R. (Ed.) (1985). *The self and social life.* New York: McGraw-Hill.

Schmidt, G., & Weiner, B. (1988). An attribution-affect-action theory of behavior: Replications of judgments of help-giving. *Personality and Social Psychology Bulletin, 14,* 610–621.

Schminke, M. (1993). Consequences of power in a simulated job: Understanding the turnover decision. *Journal of Applied Psychology, 23,* 52–78.

Schmitt, B. H., Gilovich, T., Goore, N., & Joseph, L. (1986). Mere presence and social facilitation: One more time. *Journal of Experimental Social Psychology, 22,* 242–248.

Schneider, D. J. (1973). Implicit personality theory: A review. *Psychological Bulletin, 79,* 294–309.

Schneider, D. J., & Blankmeyer, B. L. (1983). Prototype salience and implicit personality theories. *Journal of Personality and Social Psychology, 44,* 712–722.

Schooley, M. (1936). Personality resemblances among married couples. *Journal of Abnormal and Social Psychology, 31,* 340–347.

Schopler, J., & Insko, C. A. (1992). The discontinuity effect in interpersonal and intergroup relations: Generality and mediation. In W. Stroebe & M. Hewstone (Eds.), *European review of social psychology* (Vol. 5). Chichester, England: Wiley.

Schopler, J., Insko, C. A., Graetz, K. A., Drigotas, S., Smith, V. A., & Dahl, K. (1993). Individual-group discontinuity: Further evidence for mediation by fear and greed. *Personality and Social Psychology Bulletin, 19,* 419–431.

Schuette, R. A., & Fazio, R. H. (1995). Attitude accessibility and motivation as determinants of biased processing: A test of the MODE model. *Personality and Social Psychology Bulletin, 21,* 704–710.

Schuller, R. A. (1992). The impact of battered woman syndrome evidence in the courtroom: A review of the literature. *Law and Human Behavior, 16,* 597–620.

Schuller, R. A., Smith, V. L., & Olson, J. M. (1994). Jurors' decisions in trials of battered women who kill: The role of prior beliefs and expert testimony. *Journal of Applied Social Psychology, 24,* 316–337.

Schuller, R. A., & Vidmar, N. (1992). Battered woman syndrome evidence in the courtroom: A review of the literature. *Law and Human Behavior, 16,* 273–291.

Schulz, R., & Decker, S. (1985). Long-term adjustment to physical disability: The role of social support, perceived control, and self-blame. *Journal of Personality and Social Psychology, 48,* 1162–1172.

Schuster, B., Forsterling, F., & Weiner, B. (1989). Perceiving the causes of success and failure: A cross-cultural examination of attributional concepts. *Journal of Cross-Cultural Psychology, 20,* 191–213.

Schutte, N. S., Malouff, J. M., Post-Gorden, J. C. & Rodasta, A. L. (1988). Effects of playing video games on children's aggressive and other behaviors. *Journal of Applied Social Psychology, 18,* 454–460.

Schwartz, G. M., Izard, C. E., & Ansul, S. E. (1985). The 5-month-old's ability to discriminate facial expressions of emotion. *Infant Behavior and Development, 8,* 65–77.

Schwartz, G. M., & Shaver, P. (1987). Emotions and emotion knowledge in interpersonal relations. In W. Jones & D. Perlman (Eds.), *Advances in personal relationships* (Vol. 1). Greenwich, CT: JAI Press.

Schwartz, P. (1994). *Peer marriage: How love between equals really works.* New York: Free Press.

Schwartz, S. H. (1994). Beyond individualism-collectivism: New cultural dimensions of values. In U. Kim, H. C. Triandis, C. Kagitcibasi, S. Choi, & G. Yoon (Eds.), *Individualism and collectivism: Theory, method, and applications. Cross cultural research and methodology, 18.*

Schwartz, S. H., & Claussen, G. T. (1970). Responsibility, norms, and helping in an emergency. *Journal of Personality and Social Psychology, 16,* 299–310.

Schwartzwald, J. & Amir, Y. (1984). Interethnic relations and education: An Israeli perspective. In N. Miller & M. B. Brewer (Eds.), *Groups in contact: The psychology of desegregation.* Orlando, FL: Academic Press. Pp. 53–76.

Schwarz, N. (1990). Feelings as information: Informational and motivational functions of affective states. In E. T. Higgins & R. M. Sorrentino (Eds.), *Handbook of motivation and cognition* (Vol. 2). New York: Guilford.

Schwarz, N., & Bless, H. (1992). Scandals and the public's trust in politicians: Assimilation and contrast effects. *Personality and Social Psychology Bulletin, 18,* 574–579.

Schwarz, N., Bless, H., & Bohner, G. (1991). Mood and persuasion: Affective states influence the processing of persuasive communications. In M. Zanna (Ed.) *Advances in experimental social psychology* (Vol. 24). San Diego, CA: Academic Press.

Schwarz, N., Bless, H., Strack, F., Klumpp, G., Rittenauer-Schatka, H., & Simons, A. (1991). Ease of retrieval as information: Another look at the availability heuristic. *Journal of Personality and Social Psychology, 61* 195–202.

Schwarz, N., & Clore, G. L. (1983). Mood, misattribution, and judgments of well-being: Informative and directive functions of affective states. *Journal of Personality and Social Psychology, 45,* 513–523.

Schwarz, N., & Strack, F. (1991). Context effects in attitude surveys: Applying cognitive theory to social research. In W. Stroebe & M. Hewstone (Eds.), *European review of social psychology* (Vol. 2). Chichester, England: Wiley.

Schwarz, N., & Wyer, R. S., Jr. (1985). Effects of rank ordering stimuli on magnitude ratings of these and other stimuli. *Journal of Experimental Social Psychology, 21,* 30–46.

Scott, J. (1962). Critical periods in behavioral development. *Science, 138,* 949–958.

Scott, J. P. (1958). *Aggression.* Chicago: University of Chicago Press.

Scully, D., & Marolla, J. (1984). Convicted rapists: Vocabulary of motives, excuses, and justifications. *Social Problems, 31,* 530–544.

Sears, D. O. (1981). Life stage effects on attitude change, especially among the elderly. In S. B. Kiesler, J. N. Morgan, & V. K. Oppenheimer (Eds.), *Aging: Social change.* New York: Academic Press.

Sears, D. O. (1983). The persistence of early political dispositions: The roles of attitude object and life stage. In L. Wheeler (Ed.), *Review of personality and social psychology* (Vol. 4). Beverly Hills, CA: Sage.

Sears, D. O. (1986). College sophomores in the laboratory: Influences of a narrow data base on social psychology's view of human nature. *Journal of Personality and Social Psychology, 51,* 515–530.

Sears, D. O. (1988). Symbolic racism. In P. A. Katz & D. A. Taylor (Eds.), *Eliminating racism: Profiles in controversy.* New York: Plenum.

Sears, D. O., & Allen, H. M., Jr. (1984). The trajectory of local desegregation controversies and whites' opposition to busing. In N. Miller & M. Brewer (Eds.), *Groups in contact: The psychology of desegregation* New York: Academic Press.

Sears, D. O., & Citrin, J. (1985). *Tax revolt: Something for nothing in California* (enlarged ed.). Cambridge: Harvard University Press.

Sears, D. O., & Kinder, D. R. (1985). Whites' opposition to busing: On conceptualizing and operationalizing group conflict. *Journal of Personality and Social Psychology, 48,* 1141–1147.

Seavey, C. A., Katz, P. A., & Zalk, S. R. (1975). Baby X: The effect of gender labels on adult responses to infants. *Sex Roles, 1,* 103–109.

Sedikides, C. (1990). Effects of fortuitously activated constructs versus activated communication goals on person impressions. *Journal of Personality and Social Psychology, 58,* 397–408.

Sedikides, C. (1993). Assessment, enhancement, and verification determinants of the self-evaluation process. *Journal of Personality and Social Psychology, 65,* 317–338.

Sedikides, C., & Jackson, J. M. (1990). Social impact theory: A field test of source strength, source immediacy and number of targets. *Basic and Applied Social Psychology, 11,* 273–281.

Seefeldt, C. (1977). Young and old together. *Children Today, 6,* 22.

Segal, M. W. (1974). Alphabet and attraction: An unobtrusive measure of the effect of propinquity in a field study. *Journal of Personality and Social Psychology, 30,* 654–657.

Segall, M. H. (1989). Cultural factors, biology and human aggression. In J. Groebel & R. A. Hinde (Eds.), *Aggression and war: Their biological and social bases* (pp. 173–185). New York: Cambridge University Press.

Seidlitz, L., & Diener, E. (1993). Memory for positive versus negative life events: Theories for the differences between happy and unhappy persons. *Journal of Personality and Social Psychology, 64,* 654–663.

Self, E. A. (1990). Situational influences on self-handicapping. In R. L. Higgins, C. R. Snyder, & S. Berglas (Eds.), *Self-handicapping: The paradox that isn't.* New York: Plenum.

Seligman, M. E. P. (1975). *Helplessness: On depression, development, and death.* San Francisco: Freeman.

Selye, H. (1976). *The stress of life.* New York: McGraw-Hill.

Semin, G. R., & Rubini, M. (1990). Unfolding the concept of person by verbal abuse. *European Journal of Social Psychology, 20,* 463–474.

Seta, C. E., & Seta, J. J. (1992). Increments and decrements in mean arterial pressure as a function of audience composition: An averaging and summation analysis. *Personality and Social Psychology Bulletin, 18,* 173–181.

Seta, C. E., & Seta, J. J. (1995). When audience presence is enjoyable: The influences of audience awareness of prior success on performance and task interest. *Basic and Applied Social Psychology, 16,* 95–108.

Seta, J. J., Hundt, G. M., & Seta, C. E. (1995). Cost's influence on value. *Basic and Applied Social Psychology, 17,* 267–283.

Shaffer, D. R. (1975). Another look at the phenomenological equivalence of pre- and post-manipulation attitudes in the forced compliance experiment. *Personality and Social Psychology Bulletin, 1,* 497–500.

Shaffer, P. (1980). *Amadeus.* New York: Samuel French.

Shanab, M. E., & Yahya, K. A. (1977). A behavioral study of obedience in children. *Journal of Personality and Social Psychology, 35,* 530–536.

Shapiro, B., Eppler, M., Haith, M., & Reis, H. (1987). An event analysis of facial attractiveness and expressiveness. Paper presented at the Society for Research in Child Development, Baltimore, MD.

Shapiro, M. A., & McDonald, D. G. (1992). I'm not a real doctor but I play one in virtual reality: Implications of virtual reality for judgments about reality. *Journal of Communication, 42,* 94–114.

Shaver, K. G. (1985). *The attribution of blame: Causality, responsibility, and blame-worthiness.* New York: Springer-Verlag.

Shaver, K. G., & Drown, D. (1986). On causality, responsibility, and self-blame: A theoretical note. *Journal of Personality and Social Psychology, 50,* 697–702.

Shaver, P., & Hazan, C. (1987). Being lonely, falling in love: Perspectives from attachment theory. *Journal of Social Behavior and Personality, 2,* 105–124.

Shaver, P., & Hazan, C. (1988). A biased overview of the study of love. *Journal of Social and Personal Relationships, 5,* 473–501.

Shaver, P., Hazan, C., & Bradshaw, D. (1988). Love as attachment: The integration of three behavioral systems. In R. J. Sternberg & M. L. Barnes (Eds.), *The psychology of love.* New Haven, CT: Yale University Press.

Shaver, P., & Rubenstein, C. (1980). Childhood attachment experience and adult loneliness. In L. Wheeler (Ed.), *Review of personality and social psychology* (Vol. 1). Beverly Hills, CA: Sage.

Shaver, P. R., & Hazan, C. (1988). A biased overview of the study of love. *Journal of Social and Personal Relationships, 5,* 474–501.

Shaver, P. R., & Brennan, K. A. (1992). Attachment styles and the "big five" personality traits: Their connections with each other and with romantic relationship outcomes. *Personality and Social Psychology Bulletin, 18,* 536–545.

Shaver, P. R., Wu, S., & Schwartz, J. C. (1991). Cross-cultural similarities and differences in emotion and its representation: A prototype approach. In M. S. Clark (Ed.), *Review of personality and social psychology* (Vol. 13). Beverly Hills, CA: Sage Publications.

Shavitt, S. (1989). Operationalizing functional theories of attitude. In A. R. Pratkanis, S. J. Breckler, & A. G. Greenwald (Eds.), *Attitude structure and function.* Hillsdale, NJ: Erlbaum.

Shavitt, S., Swan, S., Lowrey, T. M., & Wänke, M. (1994). The interaction of endorser attractiveness and involvement in persuasion depends on the goal that guides message processing. *Journal of Consumer Psychology.*

Shaw, E. A. (1972). Differential impact of negative stereotypes in employee selection. *Personnel Psychology, 25,* 333–338.

Shaw, L. L., Batson, C. D., & Todd, R. M. (1994). Empathy avoidance: Forestalling feeling for another in order to escape the motivational consequences. *Journal of Personality and Social Psychology, 67,* 879–887.

Shaw, M. E. (1981). *Group dynamics: The psychology of small group behavior* (3rd ed.). New York: McGraw-Hill.

Shepperd, J. A. (1993). Productivity loss in performance groups: A motivation analysis. *Psychological Bulletin, 113,* 67–81.

Shepperd, J. A. (in press). Remedying motivation and productivity loss in collective settings. *Current Directions in Psychological Science.*

Shepperd, J. A., Arkin, R. M. (1989). Self-handicapping: The moderating roles of public self-consciousness and task importance. *Personality and Social Psychology Bulletin, 15,* 252–265.

Shepperd, J. A., Arkin, R. M., & Slaughter, J. (1995). Constraints on excuse making: The deterring effects of shyness and anticipated retest. *Personality and Social Psychology Bulletin, 21,* 1061–1072.

Sherif, M. (1935). A study of some social factors in perception. *Archives of Psychology, 27,* No. 187.

Sherif, M. (1936). *The psychology of social norms.* New York: Harper & Row.

Sherif, M., Harvey, O. J., White, B. J., Hood, W. R., & Sherif, C. W. (1961). *Intergroup conflict and cooperation: The Robber's Cave experiment.* Norman, OK: University of Oklahoma Press.

Sherif, M., & Hovland, C. I. (1961). *Social judgment: Assimilation and contrast effects in communication and attitude change.* New Haven: Yale University Press.

Sherif, M., & Sherif, C. W. (1967). Attitude as the individual's own categories: The social judgment-involvement approach to attitude and attitude change. In C. W. Sherif & M. Sherif (Eds.), *Attitude, ego involvement and change.* New York: Wiley.

Sherman, J. W., & Hamilton, D. L. (1994). On the formation of interitem associative links in person memory. *Journal of Experimental Social Psychology, 30,* 203–217.

Sherman, R. C., Lim, K. M., Seidel, S. D., Sinai, K. A., & Newman, K. M. (1995). Processing causally relevant information. *Journal of Personality and Social Psychology, 68,* 365–376.

Sherman, S. J. (1980). On the self-erasing nature of errors of prediction. *Journal of Personality and Social Psychology, 39,* 211–221.

Sherman, S. J., Beike, D. R., & Ryalls, K. R. (in press). Inconsistencies in judgments of general versus specific cases. *Organizational Behavior and Human Decision Processes.*

Sherman, S. J., Chassin, L., Presson, C. C., & Agostinelli, G. (1984). The role of evaluation and similarity principles in the false consensus effect. *Journal of Personality and Social Psychology, 47,* 1244–1262.

Sherman, S. J., & McConnell, A. R. (in press). Dysfunctional implications of counterfactual thinking: When alternatives to reality fail us. In N. J. Roese & J. M. Olson (Eds.), *What might have been: The social psychology of counterfactual thinking.* Hillsdale, NJ: Erlbaum.

Sherman, S. J., Presson, C. C., Chassin, L., Bensenberg, M., Corty, E., & Olshavsky, R. W. (1982). Smoking intentions in adolescents: Direct experience and predictability. *Personality and Social Psychology Bulletin, 8,* 376–383.

Sherman, S. J., Presson, C. C., Chassin, L., Corty, E., & Olshavsky, R. (1983). The false consensus effect in estimates of smoking prevalence: Underlying mechanisms. *Personality and Social Psychology Bulletin, 9,* 197–207.

Shields, S. A. (1994). The role of emotion beliefs and values in gender development. In N. Eisenberg (Ed.), *Social development. Review of personality and social psychology* (Vol. 15).

Shimoda, K., Argyle, M., & Ricci Bitti, P. (1978). The intercultural recognition of emotional expressions by three national racial groups: English, Italian, and Japanese. *European Journal of Social Psychology, 8,* 169–179.

Shively, C. (1985). The evolution of dominance hierarchies in nonhuman primate society. In S. L. Ellyson & J. Dovidio (Eds.), *Power, dominance, and nonverbal behavior.* New York: Springer-Verlag.

Shoda, Y., & Mischel, W. (1993). Cognitive social approach to dispositional inferences: What if the perceiver is a cognitive social theorist? *Personality and Social Psychology Bulletin, 19,* 574–585.

Shope, G. L., Hedrick, T. E., & Geen, R. G. (1978). Physical/verbal aggression: Sex differences in style. *Journal of Personality, 46,* 23–42.

Shotland, R. L., & Goodstein, L. (1992). Sexual precedence reduces the perceived legitimacy of sexual refusal: An examination of attributions concerning date rape and consensual sex. *Personality and Social Psychology Bulletin, 18,* 756–764.

Shotland, R. L., & Straw, M. K. (1976). Bystander response to an assault: When a man attacks a woman. *Journal of Personality and Social Psychology, 34,* 990–999.

Showers, C. (1992). Evaluatively integrative thinking about characteristics of the self. *Personality and Social Psychology Bulletin, 18,* 719–729.

Shrum, L. J., & O'Guinn, T. C. (1993). Processes and effects in the construction of social reality: Construct accessibility as an explanatory variable. *Communication Research, 20,* 436–471.

Shure, G. H., Meeker, R. J., & Hansford, E. A. (1965). The effectiveness of pacifist strategies in bargaining games. *Journal of Conflict Resolution, 9,* 106–117.

Sidanius, J., & Pratto, F. (1993). The inevitability of oppression and the dynamics of social dominance. In P. Sniderman & P. Tetlock (Eds.), *Prejudice, politics, and the American dilemma.* Stanford, CA: Stanford University Press.

Sidanius, J., Pratto, F., & Bobo, L. (1994). Social dominance orientation and the political psychology of gender: A case of invariance? *Journal of Personality and Social Psychology, 67,* 998–1011.

Sigall, H. E., Aronson, E., & Van Hoose, T. (1970). The cooperative subject: Myth or reality? *Journal of Experimental Social Psychology, 6,* 1–10.

Sigall, H., & Ostrove, N. (1975). Beautiful but dangerous: Effects of offender attractiveness and nature of the crime on juridic judgments. *Journal of Personality and Social Psychology, 31,* 410–414.

Sigall, H., & Page, R. (1971). Current stereotypes: A little fading, a little faking. *Journal of Personality and Social Psychology, 18,* 247–255.

Signiorelli, N., Gross, L., & Morgan, M. (1982). Violence in television programs: Ten years later. In D. Pearl, L. Bouthilet, & J. Lazar (Eds.), *Television and behavior: Ten years of scientific progress and implications for the eighties: Vol. 2. Technical reviews* (pp. 158–173). Washington, DC: U.S. Government Printing Office.

Sillars, A. L., & Scott, M. D. (1983). Interpersonal perception between intimates: An integrative review. *Human Communication Research, 10,* 153–176.

Silver, R. L., & Wortman, C. B. (1980). Coping with undesirable life events. In J. Garber & M. E. P. Seligman (Eds.), *Human helplessness: Theory and applications.* New York: Academic Press.

Silverstein, B., Perdue, L., Petersen, B., & Kelly, E. (1986). The role of the mass media in promoting a thin standard of bodily attractiveness for women. *Sex Roles, 14,* 519–532.

Simon, L., & Greenberg, J. (in press). The role of pre-existing racial attitudes in reactions to derogatory ethnic labels: Evidence of compensation when ambivalence is high. *Personality and Social Psychology Bulletin.*

Simon, L., Greenberg, J., & Brehm, J. (1995). Trivialization: The forgotten mode of dissonance reduction. *Journal of Personality and Social Psychology, 68,* 247–260.

Simon, L., Greenberg, J., Harmon-Jones, E., Solomon, S., & Pyszczynski, T. (1996). Mild depression, mortality salience, and the defense of the worldview: Evidence of intensified terror management in the mildly depressed. *Personality and Social Psychology Bulletin. 22,* 81-90.

Simonton, D. K. (1986). Presidential personality: Biographical use of the Gough Adjective Check List. *Journal of Personality and Social Psychology, 51,* 149–160.

Simpson, J. A. (1990). Influence of attachment styles on romantic relationships. *Journal of Personality and Social Psychology, 59,* 971–980.

Simpson, J. A., Campbell, B., & Berscheid, E. (1986). The association between romantic love and marriage: Kephart (1967) twice revisited.

Personality and Social Psychology Bulletin, 12, 363–372.

Simpson, J. A., & Gangestad, S. W. (1991). Individual differences in sociosexuality: Evidence for convergent and discriminant validity. *Journal of Personality and Social Psychology, 60,* 870–883.

Simpson, J. A., Rholes, W. S., & Nelligan, J. S. (1992). Support seeking and support giving within couples in an anxiety-provoking situation: The role of attachment styles. *Journal of Personality and Social Psychology, 62,* 434–446.

Singer, J. L., & Singer, D. G. (1981). *Television, imagination, and aggression: A study of preschoolers.* Hillsdale, NJ: Erlbaum.

Singh, D. (1993). Adaptive significance of female physical attractiveness: Role of waist-to-hip ratio. *Journal of Personality and Social Psychology, 65,* 293–307.

Singleton, R., Jr. (1979). Another look at the conformity explanation of group-induced shifts in choice. *Human Relations, 32,* 37–56.

Sistrunk, F., & McDavid, J. W. (1971). Sex variables in conforming behavior. *Journal of Personality and Social Psychology, 17,* 200–217.

Sitton, S., & Rippee, E. T. (1986). Women still want marriage: Sex differences in lonely hearts advertisements. *Psychological Reports, 58,* 257–258.

Skitka, L. J., & Tetlock, P. E. (1993). Providing public assistance: Cognitive and motivational processes underlying liberal and conservative policy preferences. *Journal of Personality and Social Psychology, 65,* 1205–1223.

Skowronski, J. J., Betz, A. L., Thompson, C. P., & Shannon, L. (1991). Social memory in everyday life: Recall of self-events and other-events. *Journal of Personality and Social Psychology, 60,* 831–843.

Skowronski, J. J., & Carlston, D. E. (1987). Social judgment and social memory: The role of cue diagnosticity in negativity, positivity, and extremity biases. *Journal of Personality and Social Psychology, 52,* 689–699

Slaby, R. (1974). Verbal regulation of aggression and altruism. In J. De Wit & W. Hartup (Eds.), *Determinants and origins of aggressive behavior.* The Hague: Mouton Press.

Slavin, R. E. (1979). Effects of biracial learning teams on cross-racial friendships. *Journal of Educational Psychology, 71,* 381–387.

Slavin, R. E. (1980). Cooperative learning. *Review of Educational Research, 50,* 315–342.

Slife, B. (1984). A theoretical critique of the research on televised violence. In J. Rubinstein & B. Slife (Eds.), *Taking sides: Clashing views on controversial psychological issues* (pp. 264–275). Guilford, CT: Dushkin.

Slife, B., & Rychlak, J. F. (1982). Role of affective assessment in modeling aggressive behavior. *Journal of Personality and Social Psychology, 43,* 861–868.

Slovic, P., Fischhoff, B., & Lichtenstein, S. (1976). Cognitive processes and societal risk taking. In J. S. Carroll & J. W. Payne (Eds.), *Cognition and social behavior.* Hillsdale, NJ: Erlbaum.

Slowman, L. (1977). The role of attractiveness and mate selection in phylogenetics. *Biological Psychiatry, 12,* 487–493.

Smith, C. A., Wallston, K. A., & Dwyer, K. A. (1995). On babies and bathwater: Disease impact and negative affectivity in the self-reports of persons with rheumatoid arthritis. *Health Psychology, 14,* 64–73.

Smith, E. E., Adams, N., & Schorr, D. (1978). Fact retrieval and the paradox of inference. *Cognitive Psychology, 10,* 438–464.

Smith, E. R. (1988). Category accessibility effects in a simulated exemplar-based memory. *Journal of Experimental Social Psychology, 24,* 448–463.

Smith, E. R. (1993). Social identity and social emotions: Toward a new conceptualization of prejudice. In D. Mackie & D. Hamilton (Eds.), *Affect, cognition, and stereotyping: Interactive processes in intergroup perception.* San Diego, CA: Academic Press.

Smith, E. R. (1994). Procedural knowledge and processing strategies in social cognition. In R. S. Wyer, Jr., & T. K. Srull (Eds.), *Handbook of social cognition* (Vol. 1). Hillsdale, NJ: Erlbaum.

Smith, E. R., Stewart, T. L., & Buttram, R. T. (1992). Inferring a trait from a behavior has long-term, highly specific effects. *Journal of Personality and Social Psychology, 62,* 753–759.

Smith, E. R., & Zarate, M. A. (1990). Exemplar and prototype use in social categorization. *Social Cognition, 8,* 243–262.

Smith, K. D., Keating, J. P., & Stotland, E. (1989). Altruism revisited: The effect of denying feedback on a victim's status to empathic witnesses. *Journal of Personality and Social Psychology, 57,* 641–650.

Smith, M. B. (1947). The personal setting of public opinions: A study of attitudes toward Russia. *Public Opinion Quarterly, 11,* 507–523.

Smith, M. B., Bruner, J. S., & White, R. W. (1956). *Opinions and personality.* New York: Wiley.

Smith, T. W., Snyder, C. R., & Handelsman, M. M. (1982). On the self-serving function of an academic wooden leg: Test anxiety as a self-handicapping strategy. *Journal of Personality and Social Psychology, 42,* 314–321.

Smith, T. W., Snyder, C. R., Perkins, S. C. (1983). The self-serving function of hypochondriacal complaints: Physical symptoms as self-handicapping strategies. *Journal of Personality and Social Psychology, 44,* 787–797.

Smith, V. L. (1991). Prototypes in the courtroom: Lay representations of legal concepts. *Journal of Personality and Social Psychology, 61,* 857–872.

Snodgrass, M. A. (1987). The relationships of differential loneliness, intimacy, and characterological attributional style to duration of loneliness. *Journal of Social Behavior and Personality, 2,* 173–186.

Snyder, C. R. (1994). Hope and optimism. *Encyclopedia of Human Behavior, 2,* 535–542.

Snyder, C. R., & Fromkin, H. L. (1980). Abnormality as a positive characteristic: The development and validation of a scale measuring need for uniqueness. *Journal of Abnormal Psychology, 86,* 518–527.

Snyder, C. R., Harris, C., Anderson, J. R., Holleran, S. A., Irving, L. M., Sigmon, S. T., Yoshinobu, L., Gibb, J., Langelle, C., & Harney, P. (1991). The will and the ways: Development and validation of an individual-differences measure of hope. *Journal of Personality and Social Psychology, 60,* 570–585.

Snyder, C. R., Higgins, E. T., & Stucky, R. J. (1983). *Excuses: Masquerades in search of grace.* New York: Wiley Interscience.

Snyder, C. R., & Higgins, R. L. (1988). Excuses: Their effective role in the negotiation of reality. *Psychological Bulletin, 104,* 23–35.

Snyder, C. R., Lassegard, M., & Ford, C. E. (1986). Distancing after group success and failure: Basking in reflected glory and cutting off reflected failure. *Journal of Personality and Social Psychology, 51,* 382–388.

Snyder, C. R., & Smith, T. W. (1982). Symptoms as self-handicapping strategies: The virtues of old wine in a new bottle. In G. Weary & H. L. Mirels (Eds.), *Integrations of clinical and social psychology.* New York: Oxford University Press.

Snyder, C. R., Smith, T. W., Augelli, R. W., Ingram, R. E. (1985). On the self-serving function of social anxiety: Shyness as a self-handicapping strategy. *Journal of Personality and Social Psychology, 48,* 970–980.

Snyder, M. (1974). The self-monitoring of expressive behavior. *Journal of Personality and Social Psychology, 30,* 526–537.

Snyder, M. (1979). Self-monitoring processes. In L. Berkowitz (Ed.), *Advances in experimental social psychology* (Vol. 12). New York: Academic Press.

Snyder, M. (1984). When belief creates reality. In L. Berkowitz (Ed.), *Advances in experimental social psychology* (Vol. 18). Orlando, FL: Academic Press.

Snyder, M. (1992). Motivational foundations of behavioral confirmation. In M. P. Zanna (Ed.), *Advances in ex-*

perimental social psychology (Vol. 25). San Diego, CA: Academic Press.

Snyder, M. (1993). Basic research and practical problems: The promise of a "functional" personality and social psychology. *Personality and Social Psychology Bulletin, 19,* 251–264.

Snyder, M. (1994). Traits and motives in the psychology of personality. *Psychological Inquiry, 5,* 162–166.

Snyder, M., & Campbell, B. H. (1982). Self-monitoring: The self in action. In J. Suls (Ed.), *Psychological perspectives on the self* (Vol. 1). Hillsdale, NJ: Erlbaum.

Snyder, M., Campbell, B., & Preston, E. (1982). Testing hypotheses about human nature: Assessing the accuracy of social stereotypes. *Social Cognition, 1,* 256–272.

Snyder, M., & DeBono, K. G. (1985). Appeals to images and claims about quality: Understanding the psychology of advertising. *Journal of Personality and Social Psychology, 49,* 586–597.

Snyder, M., & DeBono, K. G. (1987). A functional approach to attitudes and persuasion. In M. P. Zanna, J. M. Olson, & C. P. Herman (Eds.), *Social influence: The Ontario symposium* (Vol. 5). Hillsdale, NJ: Erlbaum.

Snyder, M., & DeBono, K. G. (1989). Understanding the functions of attitudes: Lessons from personality and social behavior. In A. R. Pratkanis, S. J. Breckler, & A. G. Greenwald (Eds.), *Attitude structure and function.* Hillsdale, NJ: Erlbaum.

Snyder, M., & Gangestad, S. (1982). Choosing social situations: Two investigations of self-monitoring processes. *Journal of Personality and Social Psychology, 43,* 123–135.

Snyder, M., & Miene, P. K. (1994). Stereotyping of the elderly: A functional approach. *British Journal of Social Psychology, 33,* 63–82.

Snyder, M., & Omoto, A. M. (1992). Who helps and why? The psychology of AIDS volunteerism. In S. Spacapan & S. Oskapmp (Eds.), *Helping and being helped: Naturalistic studies.* London, New Delhi: Sage Publications.

Snyder, M., & Swann, W. B., Jr. (1978a). Hypothesis-testing in social interaction. *Journal of Personality and Social Psychology, 36,* 1202–1212.

Snyder, M., & Swann, W. B., Jr. (1978b). Behavioral confirmation in social interaction: From person perception to social reality. *Journal of Experimental Social Psychology, 14,* 148–162.

Snyder, M., Tanke, E. D., & Berscheid, E. (1977). Social perception and interpersonal behavior: On the self-fulfilling nature of social stereotypes. *Journal of Personality and Social Psychology, 35,* 656–666.

Snyder, M. L., & Frankel, A. (1976). Observer bias: A stringent test of behavior engulfing the field. *Journal of*

Personality and Social Psychology, 34, 857–864.

Sogon, S., & Izard, C. E. (1987). Sex differences in emotion recognition by observing body movements: A case of American students. *Japanese Psychological Research, 29,* 89–93.

Sohn, D. (1980). Critique of Cooper's meta-analytic assessment of the findings on sex differences in conformity behavior. *Journal of Personality and Social Psychology, 39,* 1215–1221.

Solano, C. H., Batten, P. G., & Parish, E. A. (1982). Loneliness and patterns of self-disclosure. *Journal of Personality and Social Psychology, 43,* 524–531.

Solomon, S., Greenberg, J., & Pyszczynski, T. (1991). A terror management theory of social behavior: The psychological functions of self-esteem and cultural worldviews. In M. P. Zanna (Ed.), *Advances in experimental social psychology* (Vol. 24). New York: Academic Press.

Sommer, R., Wynes, M., & Brinkley, G. (1992). Social facilitation effects in shopping behavior. *Environment and Behavior, 24,* 285–297.

Sorrentino, R. M., & Field, N. (1986). Emergent leadership over time: The functional value of positive motivation. *Journal of Personality and Social Psychology, 50,* 1091–1099.

Sorrentino, R. M., Holmes, J. G., Hanna, S. E., & Sharp, A. (1995). Uncertainty orientation and trust in close relationships: Individual differences in cognitive styles. *Journal of Personality and Social Psychology, 68,* 314–327.

Sorrentino, R. M., King, G., & Leo, G. (1980). The influence of the minority on perception: A note on a possible alternative explanation. *Journal of Experimental Social Psychology, 16,* 293–301.

Sorrentino, R. M., & Roney, C. J. R. (1990). Uncertainty orientation: Individual differences in the self-inference process. In J. M. Olson & M. P. Zanna (Eds.), *Self-inference processes: The Ontario symposium* (Vol. 6). Hillsdale, NJ: Erlbaum.

Sorrentino, R. M., Roney, C. J. R., & Hanna, S. E. (1992). Uncertainty orientation. In C. P. Smith (Ed.), *Motivation and personality: Handbook of thematic analysis.* Cambridge: Cambridge University Press.

Spears, R., van der Plight, J., & Eiser, J. R. (1986). Generalizing the illusory correlation effect. *Journal of Personality and Social Psychology, 51,* 1127–1134.

Spitzberg, B. H., & Hurt, H. T. (1987). The relationship of interpersonal competence and skills to reported loneliness across time. *Journal of Social Behavior and Personality, 2,* 157–172.

Sprecher, S. (in press). Two sides to the breakup of dating relationships. *Personal Relationships.*

Sprecher, S., Aron, A., Hatfield, E., Cortese, A., Potapova, E., & Levitskaya, A. (in press). Love: American style, Russian style, and Japanese style. *Personal Relationships*.

Sprecher, S., Sullivan, Q., & Hatfield, E. (1994). Mate selection preferences: Gender differences examined in a national sample. *Journal of Personality and Social Psychology, 66*, 1074–1080.

Srull, T. K., & Brand, J. F. (1983). Memory for information about persons: The effect of encoding operations upon subsequent retrieval. *Journal of Verbal Learning and Verbal Behavior, 22*, 219–230.

Srull, T. K., & Wyer, R. S., Jr. (1979). The role of category accessibility in the interpretation of information about persons: Some determinants and implications. *Journal of Personality and Social Psychology, 37*, 1660–1672.

Staats, A. W. (1968). Social behaviorism and human motivation: Principles of the attitude-reinforcer discriminative system. In A. G. Greenwald, T. C. Brock, & T. M. Ostrom (Eds.), *Psychological foundations of attitudes*. New York: Academic Press.

Staats, A. W. (1983). Paradigmatic behaviorism: Unified theory for social-personality psychology. In L. Berkowitz (Ed.), *Advances in experimental social psychology* (Vol. 16). San Diego, CA: Academic Press.

Staats, A. W., & Staats, C. K. (1958). Attitudes established by classical conditioning. *Journal of Abnormal and Social Psychology, 57*, 37–40.

Staats, C. K., & Staats, A. W. (1957). Meaning established by classical conditioning. *Journal of Experimental Psychology, 54*, 74–80.

Stahelski, A. J., Frost, D. E., & Patch, M. E. (1989). Use of socially dependent bases of power: French and Raven's theory applied to workgroup leadership. *Journal of Applied Social Psychology, 19*, 283–297.

Stalans, L. J. (1993). Citizens' crime stereotypes, biased recall, and punishment preferences in abstract cases: The educative role of interpersonal sources. *Law and Human Behavior, 17*, 451–470.

Stang, D. J. (1974). Methodological factors in mere exposure research. *Psychological Bulletin, 81*, 1014–1025.

Stang, D. J. (1975). Effects of mere exposure on learning and affect. *Journal of Personality and Social Psychology, 31*, 7–12.

Stangor, C., & Lange, J. E. (1994). Mental representations of social groups: Advances in understanding stereotypes and stereotyping. In M. P. Zanna (Ed.), *Advances in experimental social psychology* (Vol. 26). San Diego, CA: Academic Press.

Stangor, C., Lynch, L., Duan, C., & Glass, B. (1992). Categorization of individuals on the basis of multiple social features. *Journal of Personality and Social Psychology, 62*, 207–218.

Stangor, C., & McMillan, D. (1992). Memory for expectancy-congruent and expectancy-incongruent information: A review of the social and social developmental literatures. *Psychological Bulletin, 111*, 42–61.

Stangor, C., & Ruble, D. N. (1989). Differential influences of gender schemata and gender constancy on children's information processing and behavior. *Social Cognition, 7*, 353–372.

Stanton, A. L. (1992). Downward comparison in infertile couples. *Basic and Applied Social Psychology, 13*, 389–403.

Stasser, G. (1992). Information salience and the discovery of hidden profiles by decision-making groups: A "thought experiment." *Organizational Behavior and Human Decision Processes, 52*, 156–181.

Stasser, G. (1991). In S. Worchel, W. Wood, & J. A. Simpson (Eds.), *Group process and productivity*. Beverly Hills, CA: Sage.

Stasser, G., & Stewart, D. (1992). Discovery of hidden profiles by decision-making groups: Solving a problem versus making a judgment. *Journal of Personality and Social Psychology, 63*, 426–434.

Stasser, G., & Taylor, L. A. (1991). Speaking turns in face-to-face discussions. *Journal of Personality and Social Psychology, 60*, 675–684.

Staub, E. (1970). A child in distress: The influence of age and number of witnesses on children's attempts to help. *Journal of Personality and Social Psychology, 14*, 130–140.

Staub, E. (1971). Helping a person in distress: The influence of implicit and explicit "rules" of conduct on children and adults. *Journal of Personality and Social Psychology, 17*, 137–145.

Staub, E. (1974). Helping a distressed person: Social, personality, and stimulus determinants. In L. Berkowitz (Ed.), *Advances in experimental social psychology* (Vol. 7, pp. 293–341). New York: Academic Press.

Staub, E. (1979). *Positive social behavior and morality: Socialization and development* (Vol. 2). New York: Academic Press.

Staub, E. (1989). *The roots of evil: the origins of genocide and other group violence*. New York: Cambridge University Press.

Staub, E. (1992a). The origins of aggression and the creation of positive relations among groups. In S. Staub & P. Green (Eds.), *Psychology and social responsibility: Facing global challenges*. New York: New York University Press.

Staub, E. (1992b). Transforming the bystanders: Altruism, caring, and social responsibility. In H. Fein (Ed.), *Genocide watch*. New Haven: Yale University Press.

Staub, E. (1993). The psychology of bystanders, perpetrators, and heroic helpers. *International Journal of Intercultural relations, 17*, 315–341.

Staub, E. (in press). The cultural-societal roots of violence: The examples of genocide, and of contemporary youth violence in the U.S. In R. Feldman (Ed.), *The psychology of adversity*. Amherst: University of Massachusetts Press.

Staub, E., & Rosenthal, L. H. (1994). Mob violence: Cultural-societal sources, group processes and participants. In L. Eron, J. Gentry, & P. Schlessel (Eds.), *Reason to hope: A psychosocial perspective on violence and youth*. Washington, DC: American Psychological Association.

Staw, B. M. (1974). Attitudinal and behavioral consequences of changing a major organizational reward: A natural field experiment. *Journal of Personality and Social Psychology, 29*, 742–752.

Steblay, N. M. (1987). Helping behavior in rural and urban environments: A meta-analysis. *Psychological Bulletin, 102*, 346–356.

Steele, C. M. (1988). The psychology of self-affirmation: Sustaining the integrity of the self. In L. Berkowitz (Ed.), *Advances in experimental social psychology* (Vol. 21). San Diego, CA: Academic Press.

Steele, C. M., & Lui, T. J. (1983). Dissonance processes in self-affirmation. *Journal of Personality and Social Psychology, 45*, 5–19.

Steele, C. M., & Southwick, L. (1985). Alcohol and social behavior I: The psychology of drunken excess. *Journal of Personality and Social Psychology, 48*, 18–34.

Steele, C. M., Spencer, S. J., & Lynch, M. (1993). Self-image resilience and dissonance: The role of affirmational resources. *Journal of Personality and Social Psychology, 64*, 885–896.

Steffen, V. J. (1990). Men's motivation to perform the testicle self-exam: Effects of prior knowledge and an educational brochure. *Journal of Applied Social Psychology, 20*, 681–702.

Steffen, V. J., Sternberg, L., Teegarden, L. A., & Sheperd, K. (1994). Practice and persuasive frame: Effects of beliefs, intention, and performance of a cancer self-examination. *Journal of Applied Social Psychology, 24*, 897–925.

Steiner, I. D. (1966). The resolution of interpersonal disagreements. *Progress in Experimental Personality Research, 3*, 195–240.

Steiner, I. D. (1972). *Group process and productivity*. New York: Academic Press.

Steiner, I. D. (1982). Heuristic models of groupthink. In H. Brandstatter, J. H. Davis, & G. Stocker-Kreichgauer (Eds.), *Group decision making*. San Diego, CA: Academic Press.

Stephan, W. G. (1992). Sexual motivation, patriarchy and compatibility. *Behavioral and Brain Sciences, 15*, 111–112.

Stephan, W. G., Ageyev, V., Coates-Shrider, L., Stephan, C. W., & Abalakina, M. (1994). On the relationship between stereotypes and prejudice: An international study. *Personality and Social Psychology Bulletin, 20,* 277–284.

Stephan, W. G., & Stephan, C. W. (1984). The role of ignorance in intergroup relations. In N. Miller & M. B. Brewer (Eds.), *Groups in contact: The psychology of desegregation.* Orlando, FL: Academic Press. Pp. 229–255.

Stephen, T. (1987). Attribution and adjustment to relationship termination. *Journal of Social and Personal Relationships, 4,* 47–61.

Sternberg, R. J. (1986). A triangular theory of love. *Psychological Review, 93,* 119–135.

Sternberg, R. J. (1988). Triangulating love. In R. Sternberg & M. L. Barnes (Eds.), *The psychology of love.* New Haven: Yale University Press.

Stiff, J. B., Miller, G. R., Sleight, C., Mongeau, P. L., Garlick, R., & Rogon, R. (1989). Explanations for visual cue primacy in judgments of honesty and deceit. *Journal of Personality and Social Psychology, 56,* 555–564.

Stipek, D. J., & Weisz, J. R. (1981). Perceived pesonal control and academic achievement. *Review of Educational Research, 51,* 101–137.

Stogdill, R. M. (1948). Personal factors associated with leadership: A survey of the literature. *Journal of Psychology, 25,* 35–71.

Stokes, J. P., & Levin, I. (1986). Gender differences in predicting loneliness from social network characteristics. *Journal of Personality and Social Psychology, 51,* 1069–1074.

Stokols, D. (1972). A social-psychological model of human crowding phenomena. *Journal of the American Institute of Planners, 38,* 72–83.

Stokols, D. (1990). Instrumental and spiritual views of people-environment relations. *American Psychologist, 45,* 641–646.

Stokols, D. (1992). Establishing and maintaining healthy environments. *American Psychologist, 47,* 6–22.

Stoner, J. A. F. (1961). A comparison of individual and group decisions involving risk. Unpublished master's thesis, Massachusetts Institute of Technology, Cambridge, MA.

Storms, M. D. (1973). Videotape and the attribution process: Reversing actors' and observers' points of view. *Journal of Personality and Social Psychology, 27,* 165–175.

Storms, M. D., & Nisbett, R. E. (1970). Insomnia and the attribution process. *Journal of Personality and Social Psychology, 16,* 319–328.

Stotland, E. (1969). Exploratory investigations of empathy. In L. Berkowitz (Ed.), *Advances in experimental social psychology* (Vol. 4). New York: Academic Press.

Strack, F. (1992). The different routes to social judgments: Experiential versus informational strategies. In L. L. Martin & A. Tesser (Eds.), *The construction of social judgments.* Hillsdale, NJ: Erlbaum.

Strack, F., Schwarz, N., Bless, H., Kübler, A., & Wänke, M. (1993). Awareness of the influence as a determinant of assimilation versus contrast. *European Journal of Social Psychology, 23,* 53–62.

Strauman, T. J., & Higgins, E. T. (1987). Automatic activation of self-discrepancies and emotional syndromes: When cognitive structures influence affect. *Journal of Personality and Social Psychology, 53,* 1004–1014.

Strauman, T. J., & Higgins, E. T. (1988). Self-discrepancies as predictors of vulnerability to distinct syndromes of chronic emotional distress. *Journal of Personality, 56,* 685–707.

Strauman, T. J., Lemieux, A. M., & Coe, C. L. (1993). Self-discrepancy and natural killer cell activity: Immunological consequences of negative self-evaluation. *Journal of Personality and Social Psychology, 64,* 1042–1052.

Strauman, T. J., Vookles, J., Berenstein, V., Chaiken, S., & Higgins, E. T. (1991). Self-discrepancies and vulnerability to body dissatisfaction and disordered eating. *Journal of Personality and Social Psychology, 61,* 946–956.

Strauss, M. A. (1980). A sociological perspective on the causes of family violence. In M. R. Green (Ed.), *Violence and the family.* Washington, DC: American Association for the Advancement of Science.

Strauss, M. A., Gelles, R. J., & Steinmetz, S. K. (1980). *Behind closed doors: Violence in the American family.* Garden City, NY: Anchor Books.

Strickland, L. (1958). Surveillance and trust. *Journal of Personality, 26,* 200–215.

Stroebe, M. S., & Stroebe, W. (1988). Who suffers more? Sex differences in health risks of the widowed. *Psychological Bulletin, 93,* 279–301.

Stroebe, W., & Diehl, M. (1994). Why groups are less effective than their members: On productivity losses in idea-generating groups. In W. Stroebe & M. Hewstone (Eds.), *European Review of Social Psychology* (Vol. 5). New York: Wiley.

Stroebe, W., Diehl, M., & Abakoumkin, G. (1992). The illusion of group effectivity. *Personality and Social Psychology Bulletin, 18,* 645–650.

Stroebe, W., & Frey, B. S. (1982). Self-interest and collective action: The economics and psychology of public goods. *British Journal of Social Psychology, 21,* 121–137.

Stroebe, W., Insko, C. A., Thompson, V. D., & Layton, B. D. (1971). Effects of physical attractiveness, attitude similarity, and sex on various aspects of interpersonal attraction. *Journal of*

Personality and Social Psychology, 18, 79–91.

Stroessner, S. J., Hamilton, D. L., & Mackie, D. M. (1992). Affect and stereotyping: The effect of induced mood on distinctiveness-based illusory correlations. *Journal of Personality and Social Psychology, 62,* 564–576.

Strube, M. J. (1988). The decision to leave an abusive relationship: Empirical evidence and theoretical issues. *Psychological Bulletin, 104,* 236–250.

Strube, M., & Garcia, J. (1981). A meta-analysis investigation of Fiedler's contingency model of leadership effectiveness. *Psychological Bulletin, 90,* 307–321.

Suggs, R. C. (1966). *Marquesan sexual behavior.* New York: Harcourt, Brace & World.

Sunnafrank, M. (1986). Communicative influences on perceived similarity and attraction: An expansion of the interpersonal goals perspective. *Western Journal of Speech Communication, 50,* 158–170.

Sunnafrank, M. (1991). Interpersonal attraction and similarity: A communication-based assessment. *Communication Yearbook, 14,* 451–483.

Svenson, O. (1981). Are we all less risky and more skillful than our fellow drivers? *Acta Psychologica, 47,* 143–148.

Swann, W. B., Jr. (1983). Self-verification: Bringing social reality into harmony with the self. In J. Suls (Ed.), *Psychological perspectives on the self* (Vol. 2). Hillsdale, NJ: Erlbaum.

Swann, W. B., Jr. (1984). Quest for accuracy in person perception: A matter of pragmatics. *Psychological Review, 91,* 457–477.

Swann, W. B., Jr. (1987). Identity negotiation: Where two roads meet. *Journal of Personality and Social Psychology, 53,* 1038–1051.

Swann, W. B., Jr. (1990). To be adored or to be known: The interplay of self-enhancement and self-verification. In E. T. Higgins & R. M. Sorrentino (Eds.), *Handbook of motivation and cognition: Foundations of social behavior* (Vol. 2). New York: Guilford.

Swann, W. B., Jr., & Hill, C. A. (1982). When our identities are mistaken: Reaffirming self-conceptions through social interaction. *Journal of Personality and Social Psychology, 43,* 59–66.

Swann, W. B., Jr., Hixon, J. G., & De La Ronde, C. (1992). Embracing the bitter "truth": Negative self-concepts and marital commitment. *Psychological Science, 3,* 118–121.

Swann, W. B., Jr., & Predmore, S. C. (1985). Intimates as agents of social support: Sources of consolation or despair? *Journal of Personality and Social Psychology, 49,* 1609–1617.

Swann, W. B., Jr., & Read, S. J. (1981). Self-verification processes: How we sustain our self-conceptions. *Journal of Experimental Social Psychology, 17,* 351–372.

Swann, W. B., Jr., & Schroeder, D. G. (1995). The search for beauty and truth: A framework for understanding reactions to evaluations. *Personality and Social Psychology Bulletin, 21,* 1307–1318.

Swann, W. B., Jr., Stein-Seroussi, A., & Geisler, R. B. (1992). Why people self-verify. *Journal of Personality and Social Psychology, 62,* 392–401.

Swann, W. B., Jr., Stein-Seroussi, A., & McNulty, S. E. (1992). Outcasts in a white-lie society: The enigmatic worlds of people with negative self-conceptions. *Journal of Personality and Social Psychology, 62,* 618–624.

Swap, W. C. (1977). Interpersonal attraction and repeated exposure to rewarders and punishers. *Personality and Social Psychology Bulletin, 3,* 248–251.

Swim, J., Borgida, E., Marayuma, G., & Myers, D. G. (1989). Joan McKay versus John McKay: Do gender stereotypes bias evaluations? *Psychological Bulletin, 105,* 409–425.

Symons, D. (1979). *The evolution of human sexuality.* New York: Oxford University Press.

Symons, D. (1992). What do men want? *Behavioral and Brain Sciences, 15,* 113–114.

Szymanski, K., & Harkins, S. G. (1987). Social loafing and self-evaluation with a social standard. *Journal of Personality and Social Psychology, 53,* 891–897.

Tajfel, H. (1981). *Human groups and social categories: Studies in social psychology.* Cambridge, England: Cambridge University Press.

Tajfel, H. (1982). *Social identity and intergroup relations.* Cambridge, MA: Cambridge University Press.

Tajfel, H., Billig, M. G., Bundy, R. P., & Flament, C. (1971). Social categorization and intergroup behavior. *European Journal of Social Psychology, 1,* 149–178.

Tajfel, H., Flament, C., Billig, M., & Bundy, R. P. (1971). Social categorization and intergroup behavior. *European Journal of Social Psychology, 1,* 149–177.

Tajfel, H., Sheikh, A. A., & Gardner, R. C. (1964). Content of stereotypes and the inferences of similarity between members of stereotyped groups. *Acta Psychologia, 22,* 191–201.

Tajfel, H., & Turner, J. C. (1979). An integrative theory of intergroup conflict. In W. Austin & S. Worchel (Eds.), *The social psychology of intergroup relations.* Monterey, CA: Brooks/Cole. Pp. 33–47.

Tajfel, H., & Turner, J. C. (1986). The social identity theory of intergroup behavior. In S. Worchel & W. G. Austin (Eds.), *Psychology of intergroup relations.* Chicago: Nelson-Hall.

Tambor , E. S., & Leary, M. R. (1993). Perceived exclusion as a common factor in social anxiety, loneliness, jealousy, depression, and low self-esteem. Unpublished manuscript. Wake Forest University.

Tanford, S., & Penrod, S. (1984). Social influence model: A formal integration of research on majority and minority influence processes. *Psychological Bulletin, 95,* 189–225.

Taradan, C. B., & Hendrick, C. (1995). Personality stereotypes associated with six styles of love. *Journal of Social and Personal Relationships, 12,* 453–461.

Tata, J. (1993). The structure and phenomenon of sexual harassment: Impact of category of sexually harassing behavior, gender, and hierarchical level. *Journal of Applied Psychology, 23,* 199–211.

Tavris, C. (1992). *The mismeasure of woman.* New York: Simon & Schuster.

Taylor, D. M., Wright, S. C., Moghaddam, F. M., & Lalonde, R. N. (1990). The personal/group discrimination discrepancy: Perceiving my group, but not myself, to be a target for discrimination. *Personality and Social Psychology Bulletin, 16,* 254–262.

Taylor, D. M., Wright, S. C., & Porter, L. E. (1994). Dimensions of perceived discrimination: The personal/group discrimination discrepancy. In M. P. Zanna & J. M. Olson (Eds.), *The psychology of prejudice: The Ontario symposium* (Vol. 7). Hillsdale, NJ: Erlbaum.

Taylor, D. M., Wright, S. C., & Ruggiero, K. (1991). The personal/group discrimination discrepancy: Responses to experimentally induced personal and group discrimination. *Journal of Social Psychology, 131,* 847–858.

Taylor, S. E., Aspinwall, L. G., Giuliano, T. A., Dakof, G. A., & Reardon, K. K. (1993). Storytelling and coping with stressful events. *Journal of Applied Social Psychology, 23,* 703–733.

Taylor, S. E., & Brown, J. D. (1988). Illusion and well-being: A social psychological perspective on mental health. *Psychological Bulletin, 103,* 193–210.

Taylor, S. E., & Brown, J. D. (1994). Illusion and well-being revisited: Separating fact from fiction. *Psychological Bulletin, 116,* 21–27.

Taylor, S. E., & Crocker, J. (1981). Schematic bases of social information processing. In E. T. Higgins, C. P. Herman, & M. P. Zanna (Eds.), *Social cognition: The Ontario Symposium* (Vol. 1). Hillsdale, NJ: Erlbaum.

Taylor, S. E., & Falcone, H. (1982). Cognitive bases of stereotyping: The relationship between categorization and prejudice. *Personality and Social Psychology Bulletin, 8,* 426–432.

Taylor, S. E., Falke, R. L., Shoptaw, S. J., & Lichtman, R. R. (1986). Social support, support groups, and the cancer patient. *Journal of Clinical and Consulting Psychology, 54,* 608–615.

Taylor, S. E., & Fiske, S. T. (1975). Point-of-view and perceptions of causality. *Journal of Personality and Social Psychology, 32,* 439–445.

Taylor, S. E., & Fiske, S. T. (1978). Salience, attention, and attribution: Top of the head phenomena. In L. Berkowitz (Ed.), *Advances in experimental social psychology* (Vol. 11, pp. 249–288). New York: Academic Press.

Taylor, S. E., Fiske, S. T., Etcoff, N. L., & Ruderman, A. J. (1978). Categorical biases in person memory and stereotyping. *Journal of Personality and Social Psychology, 36,* 778–793.

Taylor, S. E., & Loebel, M. (1989). Social comparison activity under threat: Downward evaluations and upward contacts. *Psychological Review, 96,* 569–575.

Taylor, S. P., & Gammon, C. B. (1976). Aggressive behavior of intoxicated subjects: The effect of third party intervention. *Journal of Studies on Alcohol, 37,* 917–930.

Taylor, S. P., & Leonard, K. E. (1983). Alcohol and human physical aggression. In R. G. Geen & E. I. Donnerstein (Eds.), *Aggression: Theoretical and empirical reviews* (Vol. 2). New York: Academic Press.

Tedeschi, J. T. (1986). Private and public experiences of the self. In R. F. Baumeister (Ed.), *Public self and private self* (pp. 1–20). New York: Springer-Verlag.

Tedeschi, J. T., & Rosenfeld, P. (1981). Impression management theory and the forced compliance situation. In J. T. Tedeschi (Ed.), *Impression management theory and social psychological research.* New York: Academic Press.

Tedeschi, J. T., Schlenker, B. R., & Bonomoa, T. V. (1971). Cognitive dissonance: Private ratiocination or public spectacle? *American Psychologist, 26,* 685–695.

Teger, A. I., & Pruitt, D. G. (1969). Components of group risk taking. *Journal of Experimental Social Psychology, 3,* 189–205.

Temple, L. E., & Loewen, K. R. (1993). Perceptions of power: First impressions of a woman wearing a jacket. *Perceptual and Motor Skills, 76,* 339–348.

Tepper, B. J., Brown, S. J., & Hunt, M. D. (1993). Strength of subordinates' upward influence tactics and gender congruency effects. *Journal of Applied Psychology, 23,* 1903–1919.

Tesser, A. (1978). Self-generated attitude change. In L. Berkowitz (Ed.), *Advances in experimental social psychology* (Vol. 11). New York: Academic Press.

Tesser, A. (1988). Toward a self-evaluation maintenance model of social behavior. In L. Berkowitz (Ed.), *Ad-*

vances in experimental social psychology (Vol. 21). New York: Academic Press.

Tesser, A., & Cornell, D. P. (1991). On the confluence of self processes. *Journal of Experimental Social Psychology, 27,* 501–526.

Tesser, A., Leone, C., & Clary, E. (1978). Affect control: Process constraints versus catharsis. *Cognitive Therapy and Research, 2,* 265–274.

Tesser, A., Martin, L., & Cornell, D. (in press). On the substitutability of self-protective mechanisms. In P. M. Gollwitzer & J. A. Bargh (Eds.), *The psychology of action: Linking motivation and cognition to behavior.* New York: Guilford.

Tesser, A., Martin, L., & Mendolia, M. (1994). The impact of thought on attitude extremity and attitude-behavior consistency. In R. E. Pety & J. A. Krosnick (Eds.), *Attitude strength: Antecedents and consequences.* Hillsdale, NJ: Erlbaum.

Tesser, A., & Smith, J. (1980). Some effects of task relevance and friendship on helping: You don't always help the one you like. *Journal of Experimental Social Psychology, 16,* 582–590.

Testa, M., & Major, B. (1990). The impact of social comparisons after failure: The moderating effects of perceived control. *Basic and Applied Social Psychology, 11,* 205–218.

Tetlock, P. E. (1979). Identifying victims of groupthink from public statements of decision makers. *Journal of Personality and Social Psychology, 37,* 1314–1324.

Tetlock, P. E. (1985). A social check on the fundamental attribution error. *Social Psychological Quarterly, 48,* 227–236.

Tetlock, P. E., & Kim, J. I. (1987). Accountability and judgment processes in a personality prediction task. *Journal of Personality and Social Psychology, 52,* 700–709.

Tetlock, P. E., & Manstead, A. S. R. (1985). Impression management versus intrapsychic explanations in social psychology: A useful dichotomy? *Psychological Review, 92,* 59–77.

Tetlock, P. E., Peterson, R. S., McGuire, C., Chang, S., & Feld, P. (1992). Assessing political group dynamics: A test of the groupthink model. *Journal of Personality and Social Psychology, 63,* 403–425.

Thiessen, D., & Gregg, B. (1980). Human assortative mating and genetic equilibrium: An evolutionary perspective. *Ethology and Sociobiology, 1,* 111–140.

Thistlethwaite, D. (1950). Attitude and structure as factors in the distortion of reasoning. *Journal of Abnormal and Social Psychology, 45,* 442–458.

Thomas, M. (1982). Physiological arousal, exposure to a relatively lengthy aggressive film, and aggressive behavior. *Journal of Research in Personality, 16,* 72–81.

Thomas, M. H., & Drabman, R. S. (1975). Toleration of real-life aggression as a function of exposure to televised violence and age of subject. *Merrill-Palmer Quarterly, 21,* 227–232.

Thomas, M. H., & Drabman, R. S. (1978). Effects of television violence on expectations of others' aggression. *Personality and Social Psychology Bulletin, 4,* 73–76.

Thomas, M. H., Horton, R. W., Lippincott, E. C., & Drabman, R. S. (1977). Desensitization to portrayals of real-life aggression as a function of exposure to television violence. *Journal of Personality and Social Psychology, 7,* 419–434.

Thompson, E. P., Roman, R. J., Moskowitz, G. B., Chaiken, S., & Bargh, J. A. (1994). Accuracy motivation attenuates covert priming: The systematic reprocessing of social information. *Journal of Personality and Social Psychology, 66,* 474–489.

Thompson, L. (1990). Negotiation behavior and outcomes: Empirical evidence and theoretical issues. *Psychological Bulletin, 108,* 515–532.

Thompson, L. (1991). Information exchange in negotiation. *Journal of Experimental Social Psychology, 27,* 161–179.

Thompson, L. (1993). The impact of negotiation on intergroup relations. *Journal of Experimental Social Psychology, 29,* 304–325.

Thompson, L. (1995). They saw a negotiation: Partisanship and involvement. *Journal of Personality and Social Psychology, 68,* 839–853.

Thompson, L., & Hastie, R. (1990). Social perception in negotiation. *Organizational Behavior and Human Decision Processes, 47,* 98–123.

Thompson, L., Valley, K. L., & Kramer, R. M. (1995). The bittersweet feeling of success: An examination of social perception in negotiation. *Journal of Experimental Social Psychology, 31,* 467–492.

Thompson, M. M., Zanna, M. P., & Griffin, D. W. (1995). Let's not be indifferent about (attitudinal) ambivalence. In R. E. Petty & J. A. Krosnick (Eds.), *Attitude strength: Antecedents and consequences.* Hillsdale, NJ: Erlbaum.

Thorndike, E. L. (1920). A constant error in psychological ratings. *Journal of Applied Psychology, 4,* 25–29.

Tice, D. (1991). Esteem protection or enhancement? Self-handicapping motives and attributions differ by trait self-esteem. *Journal of Personality and Social Psychology, 60,* 711–725.

Tice, D. (1992). Self-concept change and self-presentation: The looking glass self is also a magnifying glass. *Journal of Personality and Social Psychology, 63,* 435–451.

Tickle-Degnan, L., Hall, J. A., & Rosenthal, R. (1994). Nonverbal behavior. *Encyclopedia of Human Behavior, 3,* 293–302.

Tieger, T. (1980). On the biological basis of sex differences in aggression. *Child Development, 51,* 943–963.

Tindale, R. S., Smith, C. M., Thomas, L. S., Filkins, J., & Sheffey, S. (in press). Shared representations and asymmetric social influence. In J. Davis & E. Witte (Eds.), *Understanding group behavior: Consensual action by small groups* (Vol. 1).

Ting-Toomey, S. (1991). Intimacy expressions in three cultures: France, Japan, and the United States. *International Journal of Intercultural Relations, 15,* 29–46.

Tinklepaugh, O. L. (1928). An experimental study of representative factors in monkeys. *Journal of Comparative Psychology, 8,* 197–236.

Tomaka, J., & Blascovich, J. (1994). Effects of justice beliefs on cognitive appraisal of and subjective physiological, and behavioral responses to potential stress. *Journal of Personality and Social Psychology, 67,* 732–740.

Tomaka, J., Blascovich, J., Kelsey, R. M., & Leitten, C. L. (1993). Subjective, physiological, and behavioral effects of threat and challenge appraisal. *Journal of Personality and Social Psychology, 65,* 248–260.

Tomkins, S. S. (1962). *Affect, imagery, and consciousness.* New York: Springer.

Toner, H. L., & Gates, G. R. (1985). Emotional traits and recognition of facial expression of emotion. *Journal of Nonverbal Behavior, 9,* 48–66.

Toris, C., & DePaulo, B. M. (1984). Effects of actual deception and suspiciousness of deception on interpersonal perceptions. *Journal of Personality and Social Psychology, 47,* 1063–1073.

Tourangeau, R., & Rasinski, K. A. (1988). Cognitive processes underlying context effects in attitude measurement. *Psychological Bulletin, 103,* 299–314.

Townsend, J. M. (1992). Measuring the magnitude of sex differences. *Behavioral and Brain Sciences, 15,* 115–116.

Townsend, J. M., & Levy, G. D. (1990). Effects of potential partners' costume and physical attractiveness on sexuality and partner selection. *Journal of Psychology, 124,* 371–389.

Trafimow, D., & Davis, J. H. (1993). The effects of anticipated informational and normative influence on perceptions of hypothetical opinion change. *Basic and Applied Social Psychology, 14,* 487–496.

Trafimow, D., & Schneider, D. J. (1994). The effects of behavioral, situational, and person information on different attribution judgments. *Journal of Experimental Social Psychology, 30,* 351–369.

Trafimow, D., Triandis, H. C., & Goto, S. G. (1991). Some tests of the distinction between the private self and the collective self. *Journal of Personality and Social Psychology, 60,* 649–655.

Trapp, F. A. (1971). *The attainment of Delacroix.* Baltimore, MD: The Johns Hopkins Press.

Traupmann, J., & Hatfield, E. (1981). Love and its effect on mental and physical health. In R. Fogel, E. Hatfield, S. Kiesler, & E. Shanas (Eds.), *Aging: Stability and change in the family.* New York: Academic Press.

Triandis, H. C. (1971). *Attitude and attitude change.* New York: Wiley.

Triandis, H. C. (1972). *The analysis of subjective culture.* New York: Wiley.

Triandis, H. C. (1976). *Variations in black and white perceptions of the social environment.* Urbana: University of Illinois Press.

Triandis, H. C. (1988). The future of pluralism revisited. In P. A. Katz & D. A. Taylor (Eds.), *Eliminating racism: Profiles in controversy.* New York: Plenum. Pp. 31–50.

Triandis, H. C. (1989a). Cross-cultural studies of individualism and collectivism. In G. Jahoda, H. C. Triandis, C. Kagitsibasi, J. Berry, J. G. Draguns, & M. Cole (Eds.), *Cross-cultural perspectives: Nebraska symposium on motivation* (Vol. 37, pp.41–133). Lincoln: University of Nebraska Press.

Triandis, H. C. (1989b). The self and social behavior in differing cultural contexts. *Psychological Review, 96,* 506–520.

Triandis, H. C. (1990). Cross-cultural studies of individualism and collectivism. In J. J. Berman (Ed.), *Nebraska symposium on motivation, 1989* (Vol. 37). Lincoln, NE: University of Nebraska Press.

Triandis, H. C. (1991). Attitude and attitude change. *Encyclopedia of Human Biology, 1,* 485–496.

Triandis, H. C. (1994). *Culture and social behavior.* New York: McGraw-Hill.

Triandis, H. C., Bontempo, R., Villareal, M. J., Asai, M., & Lucca, N. (1988). Individualism and collectivism: Cross-cultural perspectives on self-ingroup relationships. *Journal of Personality and Social Psychology, 54,* 323–338.

Triandis, H. C., McCusker, C., & Hui, C. H. (1990). Multimethod probes of individualism and collectivism. *Journal of Personality and Social Psychology, 59,* 1006–1020.

Trimble, J. E. (1988). Stereotypical images, American Indians, and prejudice. In P. A. Katz & D. A. Taylor (Eds.), *Eliminating racism: Profiles in controversy.* New York: Plenum Press.

Triplet, R. G. (1992). Discriminatory biases in the perception of illness: The application of availability and representativeness heuristics to the AIDS crisis. *Basic and Applied Social Psychology, 13,* 303–322.

Triplett, N. (1898). The dynamogenic factors in pacemaking and competition. *American Journal of Psychology, 9,* 507–533.

Trivers, R. (1971). The evolution of reciprocal altruism. *Quarterly Review of Biology, 46,* 35–57.

Trivers, R. (1972). Parental investment and sexual selection. In B. Campbell (Ed.), *Sexual selection and the descent of man: 1871–1971* (pp. 136–179). Chicago: Aldine.

Trivers, R. (1985). *Social evolution.* Menlo Park, CA: Benjamin/Cummings Publishers.

Trope, Y. (1986). Identification and inferential processes in dispositional attribution. *Psychological Review, 93,* 239–257.

Trope, Y., & Cohen, O. (1989). Perceptual and inferential determinants of behavior-correspondent attributions. *Journal of Experimental Social Psychology, 25,* 142–158.

Trope, Y., & Liberman, A. (1993). The use of trait conceptions to identify other people's behavior and to draw inferences about their personalities. *Personality and Social Psychology Bulletin, 19,* 553–562.

Trope, Y., & Neter, E. (1994). Reconciling competing motives in self-evaluation: The role of self-control in feedback seeking. *Journal of Personality and Social Psychology, 66,* 646–657.

Turnbull, W. (1981). Naive conceptions of free will and the deterministic paradox. *Canadian Journal of Behavioural Science, 13,* 1–13.

Turner, C. W., & Berkowitz, L. (1972). Identification with film aggressor (covert role taking) and reactions to film violence. *Journal of Personality and Social Psychology, 21,* 256–264.

Turner, C. W., & Goldsmith, D. (1976). Effects of toy guns on children's antisocial free play behavior. *Journal of Experimental Child Psychology, 21,* 303–315.

Turner, C. W., Layton, J. F., & Simons, L. S. (1975). Naturalisitic studies of aggressive behavior: Aggressive stimuli, victim visibility, and horn honking. *Journal of Personality and Social Psychology, 31,* 1098–1107.

Turner, J. C. (1978). Social categorization and social discrimination in the minimal group paradigm. In H. Tajfel, *Differentiation between social groups.* New York: Academic Press.

Turner, J. C. (1991). *Social influence.* Pacific Grove, CA: Brooks/Cole.

Turner, J. C., Hogg, M. A., Oakes, P. J., Reicher, S. D., & Wetherell, M. S. (Eds.), (1987). *Rediscovering the social group: A self-categorization theory.* Oxford: Basil Blackwell.

Turner, J. C., Oakes, P. J., Haslam, S. A., & McGarty, C. (1994). Self and collective: Cognition and social context. *Personality and Social Psychology Bulletin, 20,* 454–463.

Turner, J. C., Wetherell, M. S., & Hogg, M. A. (1989). Referent informational influence and group polarization. *British Journal of Social Psychology, 28,* 135–147.

Turner, M. E., & Pratkanis, A. R. (1993). Effects of preferential and meritorious selection on performance: An examination of intuitive and self-handicapping perspectives. *Personality and Social Psychology Bulletin, 19,* 47–58.

Turner, M. E., & Pratkanis, A. R. (1994). Affirmative action: Insights from social psychological and organizational research. *Basic and Applied Social Psychology, 15,* 1–11.

Turner, M. E., & Pratkanis, A. R. (in press). Social identity maintenance prescriptions for preventing groupthink: Reducing identity protection and enhancing intellectual conflict. *International Journal of Conflict Management.*

Turner, M. E., Pratkanis, A. R., & Hardaway, T. J. (1991). Sex differences in reactions to preferential selection: Towards a model of preferential selection as help. *Journal of Social Behavior and Personality, 6,* 797–814.

Turner, M. E., Pratkanis, A. R., Probasco, P., & Leve, C. (1992). Threat, cohesion, and group effectiveness: Testing a social identity maintenance perspective on groupthink. *Journal of Personality and Social Psychology, 63,* 781–796.

Tversky, A., & Kahneman, D. (1973). Availability: A heuristic for judging frequency and probability. *Cognitive Psychology, 5,* 207–232.

Tversky, A., & Kahneman, D. (1974). Judgment under uncertainty: Heuristics and biases. *Science, 185,* 1124–1131.

Tversky, A., & Kahneman, D. (1982). Judgments of and by representativeness. In D. Kahneman, P. Slovic, & A. Tversky (Eds.), *Judgment under uncertainty: Heuristics and biases.* New York: Cambridge University Press.

Tversky, A., & Kahneman, D. (1983). Extensional versus intuitive reasoning: The conjunction fallacy in probability judgments. *Psychological Review, 90,* 293–315.

Tyler, T. R., & Schuller, R. A. (1991). Aging and attitude change. *Journal of Personality and Social Psychology, 61,* 689–697.

Ugwuegbu, D. C. (1979). Racial and evidential factors in juror attribution of legal responsibility. *Journal of Experimental Social Psychology, 15,* 133–146.

Uleman, J. S., & Moskowitz, G. B. (1994). Unintended effects of goals on unintended inferences. *Journal of Personality and Social Psychology, 66,* 490–501.

Utne, M. K., Hatfield, E., Traupmann, J., & Greenberger, D. (1984). Equity, marital satisfaction, and stability. *Journal of Social and Personal Relations, 1,* 323–332.

Valacich, J. S., Dennis, A. R., & Connolly, T. (1994). Idea generation in computer-based groups: A new ending to an old story. *Organizational Behavior and Human Decision Processes, 57,* 448–467.

Valenti, A. C., & Downing, L. L. (1975). Differential effects of jury size on verdicts following deliberation as a function of the apparent guilt of a defendant. *Journal of Personality and Social Psychology, 32,* 653–655.

Valins, S. (1966). Cognitive effects of false heart-rate feedback. *Journal of Personality and Social Psychology, 4,* 400–408.

Vallacher, R. R. (1993). Mental calibration: Forging a working relationship between mind and action. In D. M. Wegner & J. W. Pennebaker (Eds.), *Handbook of mental control.* Englewood Cliffs, NJ: Prentice-Hall.

Vallacher, R. R., & Kaufman, J. (in press). Time in action: Dynamics and the mental control of behavior. In P. M. Gollwitzer & J. A. Bargh (Ed.), *The psychology of action: Linking motivation and cognition to behavior.* New York: Guilford.

Vallacher, R. R., & Nowak, A. (1994). The chaos in social psychology. In *Dynamical systems in social psychology.* New York: Academic Press.

Vallacher, R. R., & Wegner, D. M. (1987). What do people think they're doing? Action identification and human behavior. *Psychological Review, 94,* 3–15.

Vallone, R. P., Griffin, D. W., Lin, S., & Ross, L. (1990). The overconfident prediction of self and others. *Journal of Personality and Social Psychology, 58,* 582–592.

Vallone, R. P., Ross, L., & Lepper, M. R. (1985). The hostile media phenomenon: Biased perception and perceptions of media bias in coverage of the Beirut massacre. *Journal of Personality and Social Psychology, 49,* 577–585.

Van Bezooijen, R., Otto, S. A., & Heenan, T. A. (1983). Recognition of vocal expressions of emotion. *Journal of Cross-Cultural Psychology, 14,* 387–406.

van de Poll, N. E., Swanson, H. H., & van Oyen, H. G. (1981). Gonadal hormones and sex differences in aggression in rats. In P. F. Brain & D. Benton (Eds.), *The biology of aggression* (pp. 243–252). Alphen aan den Rijn: Sijthoff & Noordhoff.

Van den Berghe, P. L. (1992). Wanting and getting ain't the same. *Behavioral and Brain Sciences, 15,* 116–117.

van der Pligt, J., & Eiser, J. R. (1983). Actors' and observers' attributions, self-serving bias and positivity bias. *European Journal of Social Psychology, 13,* 95–104.

van der Pligt, J., Otten, W., Richard, R., & van der Velde, F. (1993). Perceived risk of AIDS: Unrealistic optimism and self-protective action. In J. B. Pryor & G. D. Reeder (Eds.), *The social psychology of HIV infection.* Hillsdale, NJ: Erlbaum.

van der Velde, F. W., van der Pligt, J., & Hooykaas, C. (1994). Perceiving AIDS-related risk: Accuracy as a function of differences in actual risk. *Health Psychology, 13,* 25–33.

van Dijk, E., & Wilke, H. (1993). Differential interests, equity, and public good provision. *Journal of Experimental Social Psychology, 29,* 1–16.

van Knippenberg, A., & Wilkie, H. (1988). Social categorization and attitude change. *European Journal of Social Psychology, 18,* 395–406.

Van Lange, P. A. M., & Rusbult, C. E. (1995). My relationship is better than–and not as bad as–yours is: The perception of superiority in close relationships. *Personality and Social Psychology Bulletin, 21,* 32–44.

Van Overwalle, F., Segebarth, K., & Goldchstein, M. (1989). Improving performance of freshmen through attributional testimonies from fellow students. *British Journal of Educational Psychology, 59,* 75–85.

Vanbeselaere, N. (1991a). The different effects of simple and crossed categorizations: A result of the category differentiation process or of differential category salience? In W. Stroebe & M. Hewstone (Eds.), *European review of social psychology* (Vol. 2). New York: Wiley.

Vanbeselaere, N. (1991b). The impact of in-group and out-group homogeneity/heterogeneity upon intergroup relations. *Basic and Applied Social Psychology, 12,* 291–301.

Vanbeselaere, N. (1993). Ingroup bias in the minimal group situation: An experimental test of the inequity prevention hypothesis. *Basic and Applied Social Psychology, 14,* 385–400.

Vandenberg, S. G. (1972). Assortative mating, or who marries whom? *Behavior Genetics, 2,* 127–157.

Vandenbrouke, L. (1984). Anatomy of a failure: The decision to land at the Bay of Pigs. *Political Science Quarterly, 99,* 471–491.

Vanman, E. J., & Miller, N. (1993). Applications of emotion theory and research to stereotyping and intergroup relations. In D. Mackie & D. Hamilton (Eds.), *Affect, cognition, and stereotyping: Interactive processes in intergroup perception.* San Diego, CA: Academic Press.

Verhaeghe, H. (1976). Mistreating other persons through simple discrepant role playing: Dissonance arousal or response contagion. *Journal of Personality and Social Psychology, 34,* 125–137.

Vidmar, N. (1974). Effects of group discussion on category width judgments. *Journal of Personality and Social Psychology, 29,* 187–195.

Viken, R. J., & Knutson, J. F. (1983). Effects of reactivity to dorsal stimulation and the social role on aggressive behavior in laboratory rats. *Aggressive Behavior, 9,* 287–301.

Vining, J., & Ebreo, A. (1992). Predicting recycling behavior from global and specific environmental attitudes and changes in recycling opportunities. *Journal of Applied Social Psychology, 22,* 1580–1607.

Vinokur, A., & Burnstein, E. (1974). Effects of partially shared persuasive arguments on group-induced shifts. *Journal of Personality and Social Psychology, 29,* 305–315.

Vinokur, A., & Burnstein, E. (1978). Depolarization of attitudes in groups. *Journal of Personality and Social Psychology, 36,* 872–885.

Volkova, V. D. (1953). On certain characteristics of conditioned reflexes to speech stimuli in children. *Fiziologicheskii Zhurnal SSSR, 39,* 540–548.

Vrij, A. (1994). The impact of information and setting on detection of deception by police detectives. *Journal of Nonverbal Behavior, 18,* 117–136.

Vrij, A., & Winkel, F. W. (1992). Cross-cultural police-citizen interactions: The influence of race, beliefs, and nonverbal communication on impression formation. *Journal of Applied Social Psychology, 22,* 1546–1559.

Wade, T. J. (1991). Marketplace economy: The evaluation of interracial couples. *Basic and Applied Social Psychology, 12,* 405–422.

Wagner, G. C., Beuving, L. J., & Hutchinson, R. R. (1980). The effects of gonadal hormone manipulations on aggressive target-biting in mice. *Aggressive Behavior, 6,* 1–7.

Wagner, M. L., MacDonald, J., & Manstead, A. S. R. (1986). Communication of individual emotions by spontaneous facial expressions. *Journal of Personality and Social Psychology, 50,* 737–743.

Wagner, S., Hornstein, H. A., & Holloway, S. (1982). Willingness to help a stranger: The effects of social context and opinion similarity. *Journal of Applied Social Psychology, 12,* 429–443.

Waldman, D., & Avolio, B. (1986). A meta-analysis of age differences in job performance. *Journal of Applied Psychology, 71,* 33–38.

Walker, K., & Woods, M. (1976). *Time use: A measure of household production of family goods and services.* Washington, DC: American Home Economics Association.

Walker, L. (1984). *The battered woman syndrome.* New York: Springer.

Walker, L. E., Thyfault, R. K., & Browne, A. (1982). Beyond the juror's ken: Battered women. *Vermont Law Review, 7,* 1–14.

Walker, W. D., Rowe, R. C., & Quinsey, V. L. (1993). Authoritarianism and sexual aggression. *Journal of Personality and Social Psychology, 65,* 1036–1045.

Wallach, M. A., Kogan, N., & Bem, D. J. (1962). Group influence on individual risk taking. *Journal of Abnormal and Social Psychology, 65,* 75–86.

Wallbott, H. G. (1988). In and out of context: Influences of facial expression and context information in determining emotion attributions. *British Journal of Social Psychology, 27,* 357–369.

Wallen, K. (1989). Mate selection: Economics and affection. *Behavior and Brain Sciences, 12,* 37–38.

Wallen, R. (1943). Individuals' estimates of group opinion. *Journal of Social Psychology, 17,* 269–274.

Walsh, D. A. (1983). Age differences in learning and memory. In D. S. Woodruff & J. E. Birren (Eds.), *Aging: Scientific perspectives and social issues* (2nd ed.), Monterey, CA: Brooks/Cole.

Walster, E. (1966). Assignment of responsibility for an accident. *Journal of Personality and Social Psychology, 3,* 73–79.

Walster, E., Aronson, E., & Abrahams, D. (1966). On increasing the persuasiveness of a low-prestige communicator. *Journal of Experimental Social Psychology, 2,* 325–343.

Wasserman, D., Lempert, R. O., & Hastie, R. (1991). Hindsight and causality. *Personality and Social Psychology Bulletin, 17,* 30–35.

Watts, B. L., Messé, L. A., & Vallacher, R. R. (1982). Toward understanding sex differences in pay allocation: Agency, communion, and reward distribution behavior. *Sex Roles, 8,* 1175–1187.

Weary, G., & Edwards, J. A. (1994a). Individual differences in causal uncertainty. *Journal of Personality and Social Psychology, 67,* 308–318.

Weary, G., & Edwards, J. A. (1994b). Social cognition and clinical psychology: Anxiety, depression, and the processing of social information. In R. S. Wyer, Jr., & T. K. Srull (Eds.), *Handbook of social cognition* (Vol. 2). Hillsdale, NJ: Erlbaum.

Weary, G., & Edwards, J. A. (in press). Causal uncertainty beliefs and related goal structures. In R. Sorrentino & E. T. Higgins (Eds.), *Handbook of motivation and cognition, Vol. 3: The interpersonal context.*

Webb, W., & Worchel, P. (1986). Trust and distrust. In S. Worchel & W. G. Austin (Eds.), *The psychology of intergroup relations.* Chicago: Nelson-Hall.

Weber, A. L., & Harvey, J. H. (1994). Accounts in coping with relationship loss. In A. L. Weber & J. H. Harvey (Eds.), *Perspectives on close relationships.* Boston, MA: Allyn & Bacon.

Weber, J. G. (1994). The nature of ethnocentric attribution bias: Ingroup protection or enhancement? *Journal of Experimental Social Psychology, 30,* 482–504.

Weber, R., & Crocker, J. (1983). Cognitive processes in the revision of stereotypic beliefs. *Journal of Personality and Social Psychology, 45,* 961–977.

Webster, D. M., & Kruglanski, A. W. (1994). Individual-differences in need for cognitive closure. *Journal of Personality and Social Psychology, 67,* 1049–1062.

Wegener, D. T., & Petty, R. E. (1994). Mood management across affective states: The hedonic contingency hypothess. *Journal of Personality and Social Psychology, 66,* 1034–1048.

Wegener, D. T., & Petty, R. E. (in press). Effects of mood on persuasion processes: Enhancing, reducing, and biasing scrutiny of attitude-relevant information. In L. L. Martin & A. Tesser (Eds.), *Striving and feeling: Interactions between goals and affect.* Hillsdale, NJ: Erlbaum.

Wegener, D. T., & Petty, R. E. (1995). Flexible correction processes in social judgment: The role of naive theories in corrections for perceived bias. *Journal of Personality and Social Psychology, 68,* 36–51.

Wegener, D. T., Petty, R. E., & Klein, D. J. (1994). Effects of mood on high elaboration attitude change: The mediating role of likelihood judgments. *European Journal of Social Psychology, 24,* 25–43.

Wegner, D. M. (1989). *White bears and other unwanted thoughts.* New York: Viking.

Wegner, D. M. (1994). Ironic processes of mental control. *Psychological Review, 101,* 34–52.

Wegner, D. M., Erber, R., & Raymond, P. (1991). Transactive memory in close relationships. *Journal of Personality and Social Psychology, 61,* 923–929.

Wegner, D. M., Erber, R., & Zanatos, S. (1993). Ironic processes in the mental control of mood and mood-related thought. *Journal of Personality and Social Psychology, 65,* 1093–1104.

Wegner, D. M., Lane, J. D., & Dimitri, S. (1994). The allure of secret relationships. *Journal of Personality and Social Psychology, 66,* 287–300.

Wegner, D. M., & Schaeffer, D. (1978). The concentration of responsibility: An objective self-awareness analysis of group size effects in helping situations. *Journal of Personality and Social Psychology, 36,* 147–155.

Wegner, D. M., Schneider, D. J., Carter, S. III, & White, L. (1987). Paradoxical effects of thought suppression. *Journal of Personality and Social Psychology, 53,* 5–13.

Wegner, D. M., Shortt, J. W., Blake, A. W., & Page, M. S. (1990). The suppression of exciting thoughts. *Journal of Personality and Social Psychology, 58,* 409–418.

Wegner, D. M., & Vallacher, R. R. (1986). Action identification. In R. M. Sorrentino & E. T. Higgins (Eds.), *Handbook of motivation and cognition: Foundations of social behavior* (pp. 550–582). New York: Guilford.

Wegner, D, M., Vallacher, R. R., Kiersted, G. W., & Dizadji, D. (1986). Action identification in the emergence of social behavior. *Social Cognition, 4,* 18–38.

Wegner, D. M., Vallacher, R. R., Macomber, G., Wood, R., Arps, K. (1984). The emergence of action. *Journal of Personality and Social Psychology, 46,* 269–279.

Wegner, D. M., & Wenzlaff, R. M. (in press). Mental control. In E. T. Higgins & A. W. Kruglanski (Eds.), *Social psychology: Handbook of basic principles.* New York: Guilford.

Weiderman, M. W., & Allgeier, E. R. (1992). Gender differences in mate selection criteria: Sociobiological or socioeconomic explanation? *Ethology and Sociobiology, 13,* 115–124.

Weigel, R. H., Vernon, D. T. A., & Tognacci, L. N. (1974). Specificity of the attitude as a determinant of attitude-behavior congruence. *Journal of Personality and Social Psychology, 30,* 724–728.

Weigel, R. H., Wiser, P. I., & Cook, S. W. (1975). The impact of cooperative learning experiences on cross-ethnic relations and attitudes. *Journal of Social Issues, 31,* 219–244.

Weiner, B. (1985). An attributional theory of achievement motivation and emotion. *Psychological Review, 92,* 548–573.

Weiner, B. (1986). *An attributional theory of achievement and motivation.* New York: Springer-Verlag.

Weiner, B., Perry, R. P., & Magnusson, J. (1988). An attributional analysis of reactions to stigmas. *Journal of Personality and Social Psychology, 55,* 738–748.

Weiner, B., Russell, D., & Lerman, D. (1979). The cognition-emotion process in achievement-related contexts. *Journal of Personality and Social Psychology, 37,* 1211–1220.

Weinstein, N. D. (1980). Unrealistic optimism about future life events. *Journal of Personality and Social Psychology, 39,* 806–820.

Weinstein, R. S. (1976). Reading group membership in first grade: Teacher behaviors and pupil experience over time. *Journal of Educational Psychology, 68,* 103–116.

Weiss, B., Dodge, K. A., Bates, J. E., & Pettit, G. S. (1992). Some consequences of early harsh discipline: Child aggression and a maladaptive social information processing style. *Child Development, 63,* 1321–1335.

Weiss, R. F. (1968). An extension of Hullian learning theory to persuasive communication. In A. G. Greenwald, T. C. Brock, & T. M. Ostrom (Eds.), *Psychological foundations of attitudes.* New York: Academic Press.

Weiss, R. F., Boyer, J. L., Lombardo, J. P., & Stich, M. H. (1972). Altruistic drive and altruistic reinforcement. *Journal of Personality and Social Psychology, 25,* 390–400.

Weiss, R. S. (1973). *Loneliness: The experience of emotional and social isolation.* Cambridge, MA: MIT Press.

Weisz, C., & Jones, E. E. (1993). Expectancy disconfirmation and dispositional inference: Latent strength of target-based and category-based expectancies. *Personality and Social Psychology Bulletin, 19,* 563–573.

Weitz, S. (1972). Attitude, voice and behavior: A repressed affect model of interracial interaction. *Journal of Personality and Social Psychology, 24,* 14–21.

Wells, G. L., & Gavanski, I. (1989). Mental simulation of causality. *Journal of Personality and Social Psychology, 56,* 161–169.

Welton, G. L., & Pruitt, D. G. (1987). The mediation process: The effects of mediator bias and disputant power. *Personality and Social Psychology Bulletin, 14,* 123–133.

Wenzlaff, R. M., & Prohaska, M. L. (1989). When misery prefers company: Depression, attributions, and responses to others' moods. *Journal of Experimental Social Psychology, 25,* 220–233.

Wenzlaff, R. M., Wegner, D. M., & Roper, D. W. (1988). Depression and mental control: The resurgence of unwanted negative thoughts. *Journal of Personality and Social Psychology, 55,* 882–892.

Werner, C. M., Altman, I., Brown, B. B., & Ginat, J. (1993). Celebrations in personal relationships: A transactional/dialectical perspective. In S. Duck (Ed.), *Social context and relationships: Understanding relationship processes* (Vol. 3). Newbury Park, CA: Sage.

Werner, C. M., Brown, B. B., Altman, I., & Staples, B. (1992). Close relationships in their physical and social contexts: A transactional perspective. *Journal of Social and Personal Relationships, 9,* 411–431.

Weschler, I. R. (1950). An investigation of attitudes toward labor and management by means of the error-choice method: I. *Journal of Social Psychology, 32,* 51–62.

Westmeyer, J. J. (1974). The drunken Indian—myths and realities. *Psychiatric Annual, 4,* 29–36.

Wetzel, C. G., & Insko, C. A. (1982). The similarity-attraction relationship: Is there an ideal one? *Journal of Experimental Social Psychology, 18,* 253–276.

Wetzel, C. G., & Walton, M. D. (1985). Developing biased judgments: The false consensus effect. *Journal of Personality and Social Psychology, 49,* 1352–1359.

Wheeler, L., Reis, H., & Nezlak, J. (1983). Loneliness, social interaction, and sex roles. *Journal of Personality and Social Psychology, 45,* 943–953.

White, G. L. (1980). Physical attractiveness and courtship progress. *Journal of Personality and Social Psychology, 39,* 660–668.

White, G. L., Fishbein, S., & Rutstein, J. (1981). Passionate love and the misattribution of arousal. *Journal of Personality and Social Psychology, 41,* 56–62.

White, G. L., & Mullen, P. E. (1989). *Jealousy: Theory, research, and clinical strategies.* New York: Guilford.

White, L. A. (1979). Erotica and aggression: The influence of sexual arousal, positive affect, and negative affect on aggressive behavior. *Journal of Personality and Social Psychology, 37,* 591–601.

White, P. A., & Younger, D. P. (1988). Differences in the ascription of transient internal states to self and other. *Journal of Experimental Social Psychology, 24,* 292–309.

Whiting, B., & Edwards, C. P. (1973). A cross-cultural analysis of the behavior of children aged 3–11. *Journal of Social Psychology, 91,* 171–188.

Whitley, B. E. (1993). Reliability and aspects of the construct validity of Sternberg's triangluar love scale. *Journal of Social and Personal Relationships, 10,* 475–480.

Whitley, B. E., & Frieze, I. H. (1985). Children's causal attributions for success and failure in achievement settings: A meta-analysis. *Journal of Educational Psychology, 77,* 608–616.

Whyte, G. (1993). Escalating commitment in individual and group decision making: A prospect theory approach. *Organizational Behavior and Human Decision Making, 54,* 430–455.

Wicker, A. W., & August, R. A. (1995). How far should we generalize? The case of a workload model. *Psychological Science, 6,* 39–44.

Wicklund, R. A. (1975). Objective self-awareness. In L. Berkowitz (Ed.), *Advances in experimental social psychology* (Vol. 8). New York: Academic Press.

Wicklund, R. A. (1980). Group contact and self-focused attention. In P. B. Paulus (Ed.), *Psychology of group influence.* Hillsdale, NJ: Erlbaum.

Wicklund, R. A. (1989). The appropriation of ideas. In P. Paulus (Ed.), *The psychology of group influence.* Hillsdale, NJ: Erlbaum.

Wicklund, R. A., & Brehm, J. W. (1976). *Perspective on cognitive dissonance.* Hillsdale, NJ: Erlbaum.

Wicklund, R. A., & Gollwitzer, P. M. (1982). *Symbolic self-completion.* Hillsdale, NJ: Erlbaum.

Widmeyer, W. N., & Loy, J. W. (1988). When you're hot, you're hot! Warm-cold effects in first impressions of persons and teaching effectiveness. *Journal of Educational Psychology, 80,* 118–121.

Widom, C. S. (1989). Does violence beget violence? A critical examination of the literature. *Psychological Bulletin, 106,* 3–28.

Wilder, D. A. (1984). Intergroup contact: The typical member and the exception to the rule. *Journal of Experimental Social Psychology, 20,* 177–194.

Wilder, D. A., & Shapiro, P. (1989). Role of competition-induced anxiety in limiting the beneficial impact of positive behavior of an out-group member. *Journal of Personality and Social Psychology, 56,* 60–69.

Wilder, D. A., & Shapiro, P. (1991). Facilitation of outgroup stereotypes by enhanced ingroup identity. *Journal of Experimental Social Psychology, 27,* 431–452.

Wilder, D. A., & Thompson, J. G. (1980). Intergroup contact with independent manipulations of ingroup and outgroup interaction. *Journal of Personality and Social Psychology, 38,* 589–603.

Williams, J. E. (1993). Young adults' views of aging: A 19-nation study. In M. I. Winkler (Ed.), *Documentos conferencias del XXIV Congreso Interamericano de Psicología.* Santiago, Chile: Sociedad Interamericano de Psicología.

Williams, J. E., & Best, D. L. (1982). *Measuring sex stereotypes: A thirty-nation study.* Beverly Hills, CA: Sage.

Williams, J. E., Munick, M. L., Saiz, J. L., & FormyDuval, D. L. (1995). Psychological importance of the "big five": Impression formation and context effects. *Personality and Social Psychology Bulletin, 21,* 818–826.

Williams, J. G., & Solano, C. H. (1983). The social reality of feeling lonely: Friendship and reciprocation. *Personality and Social Psychology Bulletin, 9,* 237–242.

Williams, K. D., Harkins, S., & Latané, B. (1981). Identifiability as a deterrent to social loafing: Two cheering experiments. *Journal of Personality and Social Psychology, 40,* 303–311.

Williams, K. D., & Karau, S. J. (1991). Social loafing and social compensation: The effects of expectations of co-worker performance. *Journal of Personality and Social Psychology, 61,* 570–581.

Williams, K. D., Nida, S. A., Baca, L. D., & Latané, B. (1989). Social loafing and swimming: Effects of identifiability on individual and relay performance in intercollegiate swimmers. *Basic and Applied Social Psychology, 10,* 73–81.

Williams, S. S., Kimble, D. L., Covell, N. H., Weiss, L. H., Newton, K. J., Fisher, J. D., & Fisher, W. A. (1992). College students use implicit personality theory instead of safe sex. *Journal of Applied Social Psychology, 22,* 921–933.

Williams, T. M., Zabrack, M. L., & Joy, L. A. (1982). The portrayal of aggression on North American television. *Journal of Applied Social Psychology, 12,* 360–380.

Williamson, G. M., & Clark, M. S. (1992). Impact of desired relationship type on affective reactions to choosing and being required to help. *Personality and Social Psychology Bulletin, 18,* 10–18.

Wills, T. A. (1981). Downward comparison principles in social psychology. *Psychological Bulletin, 90,* 245–271.

Wilner, D. M., Walkey, R. P., & Cook, S. W. (1952). *Human relations in interracial housing.* Minneapolis: University of Minnesota Press.

Wilson, C., & Brewer, N. (1993). Individuals and groups dealing with conflict: Findings from police on patrol. *Basic and Applied Social Psychology, 14,* 55–67.

Wilson, G. (1983). *Love and instinct.* New York: Quill.

Wilson, G. (1991). *The science of love: Understanding love and its effects on mind and body.* Buffalo, NY: Prometheus Books.

Wilson, T. D., & Brekke, N. (1994). Mental contamination and mental correction: Unwanted influences on judgments and evaluations. *Psychological Bulletin, 116,* 117–142.

Wilson, T. D., & Dunn, D. S. (1986). Effects of introspection on attitude-behavior consistency: Analyzing reasons versus focusing on feelings. *Journal of Experimental Social Psychology, 22,* 249–263.

Wilson, T. D., Dunn, D. S., Bybee, J. A., Hyman, D. B., & Rotondo, J. A. (1984). Effects of analyzing reasons on attitude-behavior consistency. *Journal of Personality and Social Psychology, 47,* 5–16.

Wilson, T. D., Dunn, D. S., Kraft, D., & Lisle, D. J. (1989). Introspection, attitude change, and attitude-behavior consistency: The disruptive effects of explaining why we feel the way we do. In L. Berkowitz (Ed.), *Advances in experimental social psychology* (Vol. 22). New York: Academic Press.

Wilson, T. D., & Hodges, S. D. (1992). Attitudes as temporary constructions. In L. L. Martin & A. Tesser (Eds.), *The construction of social judgments.* Hillsdale, NJ: Erlbaum.

Wilson, T. D., & Kraft, D. (1993). "Why do I love thee? Effects of repeated introspections about a dating relationship on attitudes toward the relationship. *Personality and Social Psychology Bulletin, 19,* 409–418.

Wilson, T. D., Kraft, D., & Dunn, D. S. (1989). The disruptive effects of explaining attitudes: The moderating effect of knowledge about the attitude object. *Journal of Experimental Social Psychology, 25,* 379–400.

Wilson, T. D., Lisle, D. J., Schooler, J. W., Hodges, S. D., Klaaren, K. J., & LaFleur, S. J. (1993). Introspecting about reasons can reduce post-choice satisfaction. *Personality and Social Psychology Bulletin, 19,* 331–339.

Wilson, T. D., & Schooler, J. (1991). Thinking too much: Introspection can reduce the quality of preferences and decision. *Journal of Personality and Social Psychology, 60,* 181–192.

Winslow, R. W., Franzini, L. R., & Hwang, J. (1992). Perceived peer norms, casual sex, and AIDS risk reduction. *Journal of Applied Social Psychology, 22,* 1809–1827.

Winter, L., & Uleman, J. S. (1984). When are social judgments made? Evidence for the spontaneousness of trait inferences. *Journal of Personality and Social Psychology, 47,* 237–252.

Winter, L., Uleman, J. S., & Cunniff, C. (1985). How automatic are social judgments? *Journal of Personality and Social Psychology, 49,* 904–917.

Wit, A. P., Wilke, H. A. M., & Van Dijk, E. (1989). Attribution of leadership in a resource management situation. *European Journal of Social Psychology, 19,* 327–338.

Witkin, H. A., Mednick, S. A., Schulsinger, F., Bakkestrom, E., Christiansen, K. O., Goodenough, D. R., Hirschhorn, K., Lundsteen, C., Owen, D. R., Phillip, J., Rubin, D. B., & Stocking, M. (1976). Criminality in XYY and XXY men. *Science, 193,* 547–555.

Wittenburg, M. T., & Reis, H. T. (1986). Loneliness, social skills, and social perception. *Personality and Social Psychology Bulletin, 12,* 121–130.

Wojciszke, B., Brycz, H., & Borkenau, P. (1993). Effects of information content and evaluative extremity on positivity and negativity biases. *Journal of Personality and Social Psychology, 64,* 327–355.

Woll, S. (1986). So many to choose from: Decision strategies in video dating. *Journal of Social and Personal Relationships, 3,* 43–52.

Wood, J. V. (1989). Theory and research concerning social comparisons of personal attributes. *Psychological Bulletin, 106,* 231–248.

Wood, W., Kallgren, C. A., & Priesler, R. M. (1985). Access to attitude-relevant information in memory as a determinant of persuasion: The role of message attributes. *Journal of Experimental Social Psychology, 21,* 73–85.

Wood, W., Lundgren, S., Ouellette, J. A., Busceme, S., & Blackstone, T. (1994). Minority influence: A meta-analytic review of social influence processes. *Psychological Bulletin, 115,* 323–345.

Wood, W., Rhodes, N., & Biek, M. (1995). Working knowledge and attitude strength: An information-processing analysis. In R. E. Petty & J. A. Krosnick (Eds.), *Attitude strength: Antecedents and consequences.* Hillsdale, NJ: Erlbaum.

Wood, W., Wong, F. Y., & Chachere, J. G. (1991). Effects of media violence on viewers' aggression in unconstrained social interaction. *Psychological Bulletin, 109,* 371–383.

Woodworth, R. S. (1938). *Experimental psychology.* New York: Holt.

Worchel, S., Andreoli, V., & Folger, R. (1977). Intergroup cooperation and intergroup attraction: The effect of previous interaction and outcome of combined effort. *Journal of Experimental Social Psychology, 13,* 131–140.

Worchel, S., & Arnold, S. E. (1974). The effect of combined arousal states on attitude change. *Journal of Experimental Social Psychology, 10,* 549–560.

Word, C. H., Zanna, M. P., & Cooper, J. (1974). The non-verbal mediation of self-fulfilling prophecies in interracial interaction. *Journal of Experimental Social Psychology, 10,* 109–120.

Wright, R. A. (in press). Brehm's theory of motivation as a model of effort and cardiovascular response. In P. Gollwitzer & J. A. Bargh (Eds.), *The psychology of action: Linking cognition and motivation to behavior.* New York: Guilford.

Wyer, R. S., & Martin, L. L. (1986). Person memory: The role of traits, group stereotypes and specific behaviors in the cognitive representation of persons. *Journal of Personality and Social Psychology, 50,* 661–675.

Wyer, R. S., & Srull, T. K. (1986). Human cognition in its social context. *Psychological Review, 93,* 322–359.

Wyer, R. S., Jr., Budesheim, T. L., Shavitt, S., Riggle, E., Melton, R. J., & Kuklinski, J. H. (1991). Image, issues, and ideology: The processing of information about political candidates. *Journal of Personality and Social Psychology, 61,* 533–545.

Wyer, R. S., Jr., & Srull, T. K. (1980). The processing of social stimulus information: A conceptual integration. In R. Hastie, T. M. Ostrom, E. B. Ebbesen, R. S. Wyer, D. L. Hamilton, & D. E. Carlston (Eds.), *Person memory: The cognitive basis of social perception.* Hillsdale, NJ: Erlbaum.

Wyer, R. S., Jr., & Srull, T. K. (1981). Category accessibility: Some theoretical and empirical issues concerning the processing of social stimulus information. In E. T. Higgins, C. P. Herman, & M. P. Zanna (Eds.), *Social cognition: The Ontario Symposium* (Vol. 1). Hillsdale, NJ: Erlbaum.

Yamagishi, T., & Yamagishi, M. (1994). Trust and commitment in the United States and Japan. *Motivation and Emotion, 18,* 129–166.

Yamaguchi, S. (1994). Collectivism among the Japanese: A perspective from the self. In U. Kim, H. C. Triandis, C. Kagitcibasi, S. Choi, & G. Yoon (Eds.), *Individualism and collectivism: Theory, method, and applications. Cross cultural research and methodology, 18.*

Yarmey, A. D. (1985). Older and younger adults' attributions of responsibility toward rape victims and rapists. *Canadian Journal of Behavioural Science, 17,* 327–338.

Yates, S. (1992). Lay attributions about distress after a natural disaster. *Personality and Social Psychology Bulletin, 18,* 217–222.

Yost, J. H., & Weary, G. (1996). Depression and the correspondent inference bias: Evidence for more effortful cognitive processing. *Personality and Social Psychology Bulletin, 22,* 192–200.

Yovetich, N. A., & Rusbult, C. E. (1994). Accommodative behavior in close relationships: Exploring transformation of motivation. *Journal of Experimental Social Psychology, 30,* 138–164.

Yzerbyt, V. Y., Schadron, G., Leyens, J., & Rocher, S. (1994). Social judgeability: The impact of meta-informational cues on the use of stereotypes. *Journal of Personality and Social Psychology, 66,* 48–55.

Zadny, J., & Gerard, H. B. (1974). Attributed intentions and informational selectivity. *Journal of Experimental Social Psychology, 10,* 34–52.

Zajonc, R. B. (1960). The process of cognitive tuning in communication. *Journal of Abnormal and Social Psychology, 61,* 159–167.

Zajonc, R. B. (1965). Social facilitation. *Science, 149,* 269–274.

Zajonc, R. B. (1968). Attitudinal effects of mere exposure. *Journal of Personality and Social Psychology Monographs, 9*(2, Pt. 2), 1–27.

Zajonc, R. B. (1980). Feeling and thinking: Preferences need no inferences. *American Psychologist, 35,* 151–175.

Zajonc, R. B. (1984). On the primacy of affect. *American Psychologist, 39,* 117–123.

Zajonc, R. B., Heingartner, A., & Herman, E. M. (1969). Social enhancement and impairment of performance in the cockroach. *Journal of Personality and Social Psychology, 13,* 83–92.

Zajonc, R. B., & Markus, H. (1984). Affect and cognition: The hard interface. In C. E. Izard, J. Kagan, & R. B. Zajonc (Eds.), *Emotions, cognition, and behavior.* New York: Cambridge University Press.

Zajonc, R. B., Murphy, S. T., & Ingelhart, M. (1989). Feeling and facial efference: Implications of the vascular theory of emotion. *Psychological Review, 96,* 395–416.

Zajonc, R. B., Pietromonaco, P., & Bargh, J. A. (1982). Independence and interaction of affect and cognition. In M. S. Clark & S. T. Fiske (Eds.), *Affect and cognition: The 17th annual Carnegie symposium on cognition.* Hillsdale, NJ: Erlbaum.

Zajonc, R. B., & Sales, S. M. (1966). Social facilitation of dominant and subordinate responses. *Journal of Experimental Social Psychology, 2,* 160–168.

Zaller, J. R. (1987). Diffusion of political attitudes. *Journal of Personality and Social Psychology, 53,* 821–833.

Zammichieli, M. E., Gilroy, F. D., & Sherman, M. F. (1988). Relation between sex-role orientation and marital satisfaction. *Personality and Social Psychology Bulletin, 14,* 747–754.

Zanna, M. P., & Cooper, J. (1974). Dissonance and the pill: An attribution approach to studying the arousal properties of dissonance. *Journal of Personality and Social Psychology, 29,* 703–709.

Zanna, M. P., Fazio, R. H., & Ross, M. (1994). The persistence of persuasion. In R. C. Schank & E. Langer (Eds.), *Beliefs, reasoning, and decision making: Psychologic in honor of Bob Abelson.* Hillsdale, NJ: Erlbaum.

Zanna, M. P., & Hamilton, D. L. (1977). Further evidence for meaning change in impression formation. *Journal of Experimental Social Psychology, 13,* 224–238.

Zanna, M. P., Kiesler, C. A., & Pilkonis, P. A. (1970). Positive and negative attitudinal affect established by classical conditioning. *Journal of Personality and Social Psychology, 14,* 321–328.

Zanna, M. P., & Rempel, J. K. (1988). Attitudes: A new look at an old concept. In D. Bar-Tal & A. W. Kruglanski (Eds.), *The social psychology of knowledge.* Cambridge, England: Cambridge University Press.

Zebrowitz, L. A. (1990). *Social perception.* Pacific Grove, CA: Brooks/Cole.

Zebrowitz, L. A. (in press). Physical appearance as a basis of stereotyping. In N. Macrae, M. Hewstone, & C. Stangor (Eds.), *Foundations of stereotypes and stereotyping.* New York: Guilford Press.

Zebrowitz, L. A., Brownlow, S., & Olson, K. (1992). Baby talk to the babyfaced. *Journal of Nonverbal Behavior, 16,* 143–158.

Zebrowitz, L. A., & McDonald, S. M. (1991). The impact of litigants' babyfacedness and attractiveness on adjudications in small claims court. *Law and Human Behavior, 15,* 603–623.

Zebrowitz, L. A., & Montepare, J. M. (1992). Impressions of babyfaced individuals across the life span. *Developmental Psychology, 28,* 1143–1152.

Zebrowitz, L. A., Montepare, J. M., & Lee, H. K. (1993). They don't all look alike: Individuated impressions of other racial groups. *Journal of Personality and Social Psychology, 65,* 85–101.

Zebrowitz, L. A., Olson, K., & Hoffman, K. (1993). Stability of babyfacedness and attractiveness across the life span. *Journal of Personality and Social Psychology, 64,* 453–456.

Zebrowitz, L. A., Tenenbaum, D. R., & Goldstein, L. H. (1991). The impact of job applicants' facial maturity, gender, and academic achievement on hiring recommendations. *Journal of Applied Social Psychology, 21,* 525–548.

Zebrowitz-McArthur, L., & Montepare, J. M. (1989). Contributions of a babyface and a childlike voice to impressions of moving and talking faces. *Journal of Nonverbal Behavior, 13,* 189–203.

Zei, G., Astoffi, P., & Jayakai, S. D. (1981). Correlation between father's age and husband's age: A case of imprinting? *Journal of Biosocial Science, 13,* 409–418.

Zeichner, A., & Pihl, R. O. (1979). Effects of alcohol and behavioral contingencies on human aggression. *Journal of Abnormal Psychology, 88,* 153–160.

Zeichner, A., & Pihl, R. O. (1980). Effects of alcohol and instigator intent on human aggression. *Journal of Studies on Alcohol, 43,* 714–724.

Zillmann, D. (1971). Excitation transfer in communication-mediated aggressive behavior. *Journal of Experimental Social Psychology, 7,* 419–434.

Zillmann, D. (1978). Attribution and misattribution of excitatory reactions. In J. H. Harvey, W. J. Ickes, & R. F. Kidd (Eds.), *New directions in attribution research* (Vol. 2). Hillsdale, NJ: Erlbaum.

Zillmann, D. (1979). *Hostility and aggression.* Hillsdale, NJ: Erlbaum.

Zillmann, D. (1983a). Arousal and aggression. In R. G. Geen & E. Donnerstein (Eds.), *Aggression: Theoretical and empirical reviews.* New York: Academic Press.

Zillmann, D. (1983b). Transfer of excitation in emotional behavior. In J. T. Cacioppo & R. Petty (Eds.), *Social psychophysiology.* New York: Guilford Press.

Zillmann, D. (1984). *Connections between sex and aggression.* Hillsdale, NJ: Erlbaum.

Zillmann, D., & Bryant, J. (1984). Effects of massive exposure to pornography. In N. M. Malamuth & E. Donnerstein (Eds.), *Pornography and sexual aggression.* New York: Academic Press.

Zillmann, D., Bryant, J., Cantor, J. R., & Day, K. D. (1975). Irrelevance of mitigating circumstances in retaliatory behavior at high levels of excitation. *Journal of Research in Personality, 9,* 282–293.

Zillmann, D., Bryant, J., Comisky, P. W., & Medoff, N. J. (1981). Excitation and hedonic valence in the effects of erotica on motivated intermale aggression. *European Journal of Social Psychology, 11,* 233–252.

Zillmann, D., & Cantor, J. R. (1976). Effect of timing of information about mitigating circumstances on emotional responses to provocation and retaliatory behavior. *Journal of Experimental Social Psychology, 12,* 38–55.

Zillmann, D., Hoyt, J. L., & Day, K. D. (1974). Strength and duration of the effect of aggressive, violent, and erotic communications on subsequent aggressive behavior. *Communication Research, 1,* 286–306.

Zillmann, D., Johnson, R. C., & Day, K. D. (1974). Attribution of apparent arousal and proficiency of recovery from sympathetic activation affecting excitation transfer to aggressive behavior. *Journal of Experimental Social Psychology, 10,* 503–515.

Zillmann, D., Katcher, A. H., & Milavsky, B. (1972). Excitation transfer from physical exercise to subsequent aggressive behavior. *Journal of Experimental Social Psychology, 8,* 247–259.

Zimbardo, P. G. (1970). The human choice: Individuation, reason, and order versus deindividuation, impulse, and chaos. In W. J. Arnold, D. Levine (Eds.), *Nebraska symposium on motivation* (pp. 237–307). Lincoln, NE: University of Nebraska Press.

Zimbardo, P. G., Andersen, S. M., & Kabat, L. G. (1981). Induced hearing deficit generates experimental paranoia. *Science, 212,* 1529–1531.

Zimbardo, P. G., Cohen, A., Weisenberg, M., Dworkin, L., & Firestone, I. (1969). The control of experimental pain. In P. G. Zimbardo (Ed.), *The cognitive control of motivation.* Glenview, IL: Scott, Foresman.

Zimbardo, P. G., Weisenberg, M., Firestone, I., & Levy, B. (1965). Communicator effectiveness in producing public conformity and private attitude change. *Journal of Personality, 33,* 233–256.

Zuber, J. A., Crott, H. W., & Werner, J. (1992). Choice shift and group polarization: An analysis of the status of arguments and social decision schemes. *Journal of Personality and Social Psychology, 62,* 50–61.

Zucker, G. S., & Weiner, B. (1993). Conservatism and perceptions of poverty: An attributional analysis. *Journal of Applied Social Psychology, 23,* 925–943.

Zuckerman, M. (1986). On the meaning and implications of facial prominence. *Journal of Nonverbal Behavior, 10,* 215–229.

Zuckerman, M., DeFrank, R. S., Hall, J. A., Larrance, D. T., & Rosenthal, R. (1979). Facial and vocal cues of honesty and deception. *Journal of Experimental Social Psychology, 15,* 378–396.

Zuckerman, M., DePaulo, B. M., & Rosenthal, R. (1981). Verbal and nonverbal communication of deception. In L. Berkowitz (Ed.), *Advances in experimental social psychology* (Vol. 14). New York: Academic Press.

Zuckerman, M., & Kieffer, S. C. (1994). Race differences in face-ism: Does facial prominence imply dominance? *Journal of Personality and Social Psychology, 66,* 86–92.

Zuckerman, M., & Miyake, K. (1993). The attractive voice: What makes it so? *Journal of Nonverbal Behavior, 17,* 119–135.

Zuckerman, M., & Przewuzman, S. J. (1979). Decoding and encoding facial expressions in preschool-age children. *Environmental Psychology and Nonverbal Psycholosy, 3,* 147–163.

Zukier, H. (1990). Aspects of narrative thinking. In I. Rock (Ed.), *The legacy of Solomon Asch: Essays in cognition and social psychology.* Hillsdale, NJ: Erlbaum.

CREDITS

Chapter Opener 1 © Will & Deni McIntyre / Photo Researchers; p. 2, © Vlado Matisic / Image Finders / Tony Stone Images; p. 7, © Comstock; p. 9, © Steven Peters / Tony Stone Images; p. 13, © Esbin Anderson / The Image Works; p. 17, © Comstock; p. 29, © David H. Wells / The Image Works; p. 30, © Jon Randolph / Tony Stone Images; p. 31, © The Granger Collection, New York.

Chapter Opener 2 © Dorothy Littell Greco / Stock Boston; p. 42, © Patrick Ward / Stock Boston; p. 58, © Brad Mangin / Duomo; p. 61, © Tim Davis / Photo Researchers; p. 64, © Marc DeVille / Gamma-Liaison; p. 71, © Ed Lallo / Gamma-Liaison; p. 74, © Comstock; p. 78, © Johnny Johnson / Alaska Stock.

Chapter Opener 3 © Ilene Perlman Haines / Stock Boston; p. 86, © Nancy Sheehan / Picture Cube; p. 93, © Bara-King Photographic, Inc. / King Visual Technology, License granted by Intellectual Properties Management, Atlanta, Georgia, as exclusive licensor of the King Estate; p. 95, © Marc Grimberg / The Image Bank; p. 105, © Brian Smith / Stock Boston; p. 110, © W. Hill, Jr. / The Image Works; p. 113, © Benn Mitchell / The Image Bank; p. 119, © Ken Tannenbaum / The Image Bank; p. 122, Sandra Lord / Harcourt Brace.

Chapter Opener 4 © Comstock/ Christina Rose Mufson; p. 136, © George Munday / Leo de Wys; p. 140, © Les Stone / Sygma; p. 142, Photofest; p. 147, Sandra Lord / Harcourt Brace; p. 151, © David H. Wells / The Image Works; p. 156, © Bob Daemmrich / Stock Boston; p. 161, © Bob Daemmrich / Stock Boston; p. 165, © John Riley / Tony Stone Images.

Chapter Opener 5 © Rosanne Olson / Tony Stone Images; p. 170, © Chris Harvey / Tony Stone Images; p. 179, © Comstock; p. 184, © G & M David de Lossy / The Image Bank; p. 187, © Bob Daemmrich / The Image Works; p. 194, © Bob Krist / Leo de Wys; p. 199, © Cosimo Scianna / The Image Bank.

Chapter Opener 6 © Barros & Barros / The Image Bank; p. 214, © Gary Faber / The Image Bank; p. 225, © Rick Berkowitz / The Picture Cube; p. 233, © Comstock / Gary Benson; p. 234, © J. Jacobson / The Image Works; p. 239, Sandra Lord / Harcourt Brace; p. 241, © B. Daemmrich / Stock Boston; p. 245, © Comstock.

Chapter Opener 7 © Beringer-Dratch / The Picture Cube; p. 256, © R. Michael Stuckey / Comstock; p. 261, © Capital Features / The Image Works; p. 273, © C. Seghers / Photo Researchers; p. 278, © Tom Hurl / Stock Boston; p. 282, © Lawrence Migdale / Tony Stone Images; p. 286, Sandra Lord / Harcourt Brace; p. 288, Sandra Lord / Harcourt Brace; p. 294, Sandra Lord / Harcourt Brace.

Chapter Opener 8 © Bob Daemmrich / Stock Boston; p. 303, © Daniel Grogan / Uniphoto; p. 318, © Custom Medical Stock Photo; p. 319, © Jeff Cadge / The Image Bank; p. 327, Sandra Lord / Harcourt Brace; p. 329, © Bob Daemmrich / The Image Works; p. 331, © Frank Siteman / The Picture Cube; p. 335, © Ann F. Purcell / Photo Researchers; p. 336, © Thomas J. Edwards / Third Coast Stock Source.

Chapter Opener 9 © Elan Sun Star / Tony Stone Images; p. 340, Sandra Lord / Harcourt Brace; p. 343, © Robert Lankinen / The Wildlife Collection; p. 362, © Comstock; p. 362, © Comstock; p. 366, © Denise Marcotte / Stock Boston; p. 374, © Bokelberg / The Image Bank.

Chapter Opener 10 © Dan Bosler / Tony Stone Images; p. 380, Sandra Lord / Harcourt Brace; p. 391, © Marcel Isy-Schwart / The Image Bank; p. 396, Sandra Lord / Harcourt Brace; p. 399, © Infocus International / The Image Bank; p. 405, Sandra Lord / Harcourt Brace.

Chapter Opener 11 © John Coletti / Stock Boston; p. 416, © John Neubauer / PhotoEdit; p. 419, © Steve Satushek / The Image Bank; p. 425, © Bob Daemmrich / The Image Works; p. 430, © Robert Fox /

Impact Visuals; p. 431, © Reinstein / The Image Works; p. 434, © A. Boccaccio / The Image Bank; p. 438, © Chip Henderson / Tony Stone Images; p. 440, © Grant V. Faint / The Image Bank; p. 450, © James H. Carmichael / The Image Bank.

Chapter Opener 12 © Lawrence Migdale / Tony Stone Images; p. 459, © Grant Haller / Leo de Wys; p. 464, © Wayne Eastep / Tony Stone Images; p. 468, © Comstock / Sven Marsten; p. 469, Sandra Lord / Harcourt Brace; p. 470, © Ira Wyman / Monkmeyer; p. 474, © Rick Rusing / Leo de Wys.

Chapter Opener 13 © Bob Daemmrich / Stock Boston; p. 498, Sandra Lord / Harcourt Brace; p. 500, Sandra Lord / Harcourt Brace; p. 507, © Dion Ogust / The Image Works; p. 511, © Frieda Leinwand / Monkmeyer; p. 513, © Comstock; p. 521, © Keith Philpott / The Image Bank; p. 525, © Bokelberg / The Image Bank.

Chapter Opener 14 © Terry Vine / Tony Stone Images; p. 539, © Art Stein / Photo Researchers; p. 540, © Arthur Tress / Photo Researchers; p. 543, © Eric Carle / Superstock; p. 553, © Howard Grey / Tony Stone Images; p. 558, © John Eastcott & Yva Momatiuk / Photo Researchers; p. 563, © Bruce Ayres / Tony Stone Images; p. 564, © Blair Seitz / Photo Researchers.

Chapter Opener 15 © John Maher / Stock Boston; p. 573, © Bob Daemmrich / Stock Boston; p. 581, © Romilly Lockyer / The Image Bank; p. 592, © David J. Sams / Stock Boston; p. 594, © Bruce Ayres / Tony Stone Images; p. 598, © Arthur Tilley / Tony Stone Images; p. 600, © Randy G. Jolly / Arms Communications USA; p. 606, © John Eastcott & Yva Momatiuk / The Image Works.